THE OXFORD ENCYCLOPEDIA OF
FOOD AND DRINK IN AMERICA

EDITORIAL BOARD

THE OXFORD ENCYCLOPEDIA

OF

FOOD AND DRINK

IN

AMERICA

Andrew F. Smith

Editor in Chief

VOLUME 2

K–Z
Appendixes
Topical Outline of Articles
Directory of Contributors
Index

OXFORD
UNIVERSITY PRESS
2004

OXFORD
UNIVERSITY PRESS

Oxford   New York

Auckland   Bangkok   Buenos Aires   Cape Town   Chennai
Dar es Salaam   Delhi   Hong Kong   Istanbul   Karachi   Kolkata
Kuala Lumpur   Madrid   Melbourne   Mexico City   Mumbai   Nairobi
São Paulo   Shanghai   Taipei   Tokyo   Toronto

Copyright © 2004 by Oxford University Press, Inc.

Published by Oxford University Press, Inc.
198 Madison Avenue, New York, New York, 10016
http://www.oup.com

Oxford is a registered trademark of Oxford University Press

Library of Congress Cataloging-in-Publication Data

Encyclopedia of food and drink in America / Andrew F. Smith, editor in chief.
p. cm.
ISBN 0-19-515437-1 (Set) – ISBN 0-19-517551-4 (Volume 1: alk. paper)
– ISBN 0-19-517552-2 (Volume 2: alk. paper)
1. Food–Dictionaries. 2. Cookery, American–Dictionaries.
3. Beverages–Dictionaries. I. Smith, Andrew F., 1946-
TX349.E45 2004
641.3'003–dc22

2003024873

9 8 7 6 5 4 3 2 1

Printed in the United States of America
on acid-free paper

COMMON ABBREVIATIONS USED IN THIS WORK

AI, adequate intake

AID, Agency for International Development

AVA, American Viticultural Area

BATF, Bureau of Alcohol, Tobacco, and Firearms

B.C.E, before the Common Era (= B.C.)

BLT, bacon, lettuce, and tomato sandwich

CARE, Cooperative for American Relief Everywhere

C.E., Common Era (= A.D.)

DRI, dietary reference intake

EAR, estimated average requirement

FDA, Food and Drug Administration

GM, genetically modified

GMO, genetically modified organism

NAFTA, North American Free Trade Agreement

PL, Public Law

RDA, recommended dietary allowance

UNICEF, United Nations International Children's Emergency Fund

USFA, United States Food Administration

USDA, United States Department of Agriculture

WHO, World Health Organization

WTO, World Trade Organization

THE OXFORD ENCYCLOPEDIA OF
FOOD AND DRINK IN AMERICA

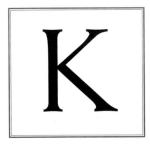

Kale

Kale is a member of the *Brassica oleracea* species, *acephala* group, also known as Old World cabbages. This headless vegetable originated in the Mediterranean countries and was the main greenstuff of the poor in Europe until the Middle Ages, when headed cabbages were cultivated. The name is derived from the Scottish term for the plant, which is *kail*. In the United States, collard greens, a form of kale, are a staple in southern cooking, but otherwise kale is underused by most American cooks. It is eaten primarily by Americans from northern Europe and Iberia, where kale is most often encountered.

[*See also* Cabbage; Southern Regional Cookery.]

BIBLIOGRAPHY

Schneider, Elizabeth. *Vegetables from Amaranth to Zucchini: The Essential Reference.* New York: William Morrow, 2002.

DAVID LEITE

Karo Syrup

Southern cuisine owes much to the Corn Products Refining Company of New York and Chicago, inventor of Karo Corn Syrup, a liquid sugar produced from cornstarch. The bottled flavoring, not as sweet as cane sugar, with the consistency of honey, is essential to numerous down-home recipes. Pecan pie cannot be made without it. Before its introduction in 1902, housewives carried jugs to the grocery store for refilling from barrels. These barrels contained various regional brands of corn syrup, but not the crystal-clear Karo we know today. The origins of the name are shrouded in mystery. Some company historians believe the chemist who invented it named it after his wife, Caroline. Others trace the name back to an earlier brand name, Kairomel.

Karo is a prime example of successful advertising. Within a year of its first appearance, the company was running full-page ads in *Ladies' Home Journal* touting the purported wholesomeness of the syrup, though its value as a source of nutrition differs little from cane sugar. A massive quarter-million-dollar publicity blitz in 1910 (unprecedented in scale at the time), including distribution of a free cookbook of Karo recipes, made Karo a household word even before many people had tried it. In the early 1930s the wife of a corporate sales executive devised a recipe of corn syrup, sugar, eggs, vanilla, and pecans baked in a pie shell, which became the now-famous pecan pie. A variant of that recipe, without pecans, became another southern favorite known as chess pie. In 1934 in still another marketing coup, the company enlisted the Dionne quintuplets, born in Callander, Ontario, for what became a decade-long endorsement by the internationally famous girls.

Capitalizing on the popularity of syrups as toppings for breakfast foods, the company launched "waffle syrup" to compete with much more expensive genuine maple syrup. The company's original light and dark corn syrups continued to gather a following for their usefulness in the manufacture of homemade hard candies, baked goods, and desserts. The light syrup is clarified and decolorized and contains vanilla for flavor. The dark syrup has the flavor and color of caramel and a stronger taste.

In the latter part of the twentieth century, corn and corn products began to replace other staple foodstuffs in the United States, especially in increasingly-popular processed foods. Starches, meal, and alcohol derived from corn were substituted for more expensive products as modern farming technology made corn production more efficient. In 2001 a trade dispute erupted between the United States and Mexico over Mexico's assertion that American manufacturers were illegally dumping corn syrups onto the Mexican market, depressing that country's cane sugar industry. It was an early test of the terms of the North American Free Trade Agreement (NAFTA) and was settled by a World Trade Organization (WTO) panel decision in favor of the United States. Eventually, corn syrup eclipsed cane sugar as the prevalent sweetening agent in soft drinks and processed foods (replacing cane sugar in Coca-Cola in 1985, for example).

While the commercial use of corn syrup has increased dramatically, fewer people than ever are manufacturing candies in the home. Karo is widely distributed for commercial use and, though regional brands exist, it remains the only brand available in grocery stores nationwide.

[*See also* Advertising; Advertising Cookbooklets and Recipes; Breakfast Foods; Clarifying; Coca-Cola; Corn Syrup; Pies and Tarts; Southern Regional Cookery; Sugar.]

BIBLIOGRAPHY

U.S. Department of State International Information Programs. "US Wins WTO Case on High Fructose Corn Syrup." http://usinfo. state.gov/topical/econ/wto/pp0622b.htm.
The Nut Factory, http://www.thenutfactory.com/kitchen/facts/facts-candy.html

JAY WEINSTEIN

Kashruth, *see Jewish Dietary Laws*

Kellogg, John Harvey

No single individual influenced American eating habits during the early twentieth century more than Dr. John Harvey Kellogg (1852–1943). Born in Tyrone, Michigan, one of sixteen children, Kellogg studied medicine at Bellevue Hospital College in New York and in 1876 was asked to manage the Western Reform Institute in Battle Creek, Michigan. The Institute was a small health clinic specializing in hydrotherapy; it was sponsored by the Seventh Day Adventists, who encouraged a vegetarian diet.

Kellogg changed the Institute's name to the Sanitarium (though it was occasionally referred to as the Sanatorium), and under his guidance it thrived. America's rich and famous flocked to the Sanitarium. Over the years its patients included Henry Ford, J. C. Penney, Thomas Edison, and President William Howard Taft.

At the Sanitarium Kellogg enforced a vegetarian regimen and sought to develop new vegetarian products. He was also a strong believer in the importance of thorough mastication of food. Patients with sore teeth, missing teeth, or no teeth had difficulty chewing hard substances,

John Harvey Kellogg. Illustration by Glory Brightfield from *Famous Vegetarians and Their Favorite Recipes,* by Rynn Berry (New York and Los Angeles, 2003), p. 151. *Collection of Rynn Berry*

such as zwieback, then a common food in hospitals. To make such substances easier to chew, Kellogg ground them up into small pieces or granules.

Subsequent experiments with pressing grains and nuts between rollers led to successes with flattened kernels of wheat and maize that were baked in the oven and emerged as flakes. Kellogg also developed substitutes for meat and dairy products. In an attempt to find an alternative to dairy butter, he invented nut butters which were quickly adopted by vegetarians and then became known to the broader public. Peanuts were inexpensive, so peanut butter soon became an American fad food.

To promote and advance his medical theories, John Harvey Kellogg wrote more than fifty books and thousands of articles and lectured to hundreds of thousands of Americans throughout the nation in over five thousand public presentations. He was not averse to making money on his discoveries and he created a number of businesses to sell his products, but he had little personal interest in running the companies. He selected his younger brother, Will K. Kellogg, to manage several of them, including the Toasted Corn Flake Company. John Harvey

Kellogg was unwilling to conduct the marketing necessary to compete with the imitators that had sprung up, so a split developed between the brothers.

John Harvey Kellogg was originally the majority stockholder, but he had distributed stock to the sanitarium physicians. Will Kellogg bought up the stock, took control of the company, and renamed it the Kellogg Company. Will then put his signature on the product boxes and later, to enhance sales, added sugar and other nutrients to the cereal. The estranged brothers did not speak to each other for years, and battled in court, but in the end Will won.

The Sanitarium began to lose money in the Depression, and it closed in 1942. John Harvey Kellogg died the following year, aged ninety-one. His influence on America's breakfast table endures.

[See also Breakfast Foods; Food and Nutrition Systems; Health Food; Kellogg Company; Nutrition; Peanut Butter; Vegetarianism.]

BIBLIOGRAPHY

Carson, Gerald. *Cornflake Crusade*. New York: Rinehart, 1957.
Powell, Horace B. *The Original Has This Signature—W. K. Kellogg*. Englewood Cliffs, NJ: Prentice-Hall, 1956.
Smith, Andrew F. *Peanuts: The Illustrious History of the Goober Pea*. Urbana: University of Illinois Press, 2002.

ANDREW F. SMITH

Kellogg Company

Founded in 1906 by Will Keith Kellogg (1860–1951) as the Battle Creek Toasted Cornflake Company, the Kellogg Company develops, manufactures, and promotes high-fiber, low-fat, ready-to-eat breakfast cereals such as Kellogg's Corn Flakes, All-Bran, and Rice Krispies. These cereals are primarily whole grains that have been cooked, flaked, and then toasted. They reflect a longstanding corporate tenet that convenient, low-cost, nutritious breakfast cereals can improve health.

Although the Kellogg corporate doctrine has a scientific basis, the company has historical roots in the religious principles of the Seventh-Day Adventist Church, which established the Western Health Reform Institute at Battle Creek, Michigan, in 1866. Later renamed the Battle Creek Sanitarium, this facility functioned as a retreat, hospital, and spa, focusing on a vegetarian menu and dietary counseling. The vegetarian diet represented a form of abstinence, a religious response to the high-fat, low-fiber American diet prevalent in the late nineteenth century.

Dr. John Harvey Kellogg (1852–1943), a prominent Seventh-Day Adventist, was chief physician at the Battle Creek Sanitarium; his brother Will was business manager. One goal of the Kellogg brothers was to develop a ready-to-eat breakfast cereal for their patients. In 1894, after experimenting unsuccessfully for several years, the brothers accidentally discovered a way to make a ready-to-eat whole-grain cereal. Wheat grains were first boiled, then soaked in water for several days to hydrate. Prolonged soaking allowed the moisture within each kernel of wheat to equalize. When the cooked, soaked grains were passed through rollers they formed large thin flakes, which the brothers named "Granose" partly because the rollers were the same ones they used to make their "Gran-ola." Granose was not only very popular at the Battle Creek Sanitarium but also sold by mail order.

In 1902 the brothers created a ready-to-eat, malt-flavored corn flake. Called Toasted Corn Flakes, this cereal was crisper and tastier than the wheat flakes. In 1906, after breaking with his brother and the sanitarium, Will Kellogg founded his own company to manufacture and promote Toasted Corn Flakes. The product was a huge financial success but Will Kellogg was less concerned with money than with providing Americans with healthful breakfast food. Recognizing the importance of fiber to a good diet, Will Kellogg in 1916 introduced All-Bran, the gold standard of high-fiber cereals. Other Kellogg bran cereals followed: Bran-Flakes (1923), Raisin Bran (1942), Bran Buds (1961), and Cracklin' Bran (1976).

In 1941 the Kellogg Company started adding extra nutrients to its breakfast cereals. Special K, a fat-free

All-Bran Advertisement. From the back cover of *The Housewife's Almanac: A Book for Homemakers 1938*, published by Kellogg (Battle Creek, Michigan, 1938). *Collection of Andrew F. Smith*

flaked-rice cereal introduced in 1955, was "fortified" with seven vitamins and minerals. Launched in 1966, Product 19, so-named because it was the nineteenth Kellogg cereal product, is enhanced with thirteen added vitamins and minerals. In 1998 the company went even further with Smart Start: of the fourteen vitamins and minerals added to it, ten supply 100 percent of the recommended daily requirement. The company introduced Smart Start Soy Protein in 2004, adding cinnamon-flavored soy granola clusters to Smart Start. This makes the cereal heart-healthy because soy protein is known to lower blood cholesterol.

In 1923 Will Kellogg created a Home Economics Services Department within the company. This department developed free educational materials so that home economics teachers could provide school children with information about the benefits of low-fat, high-fiber breakfast cereals. To interest children in its cereals, the Kellogg Company created cartoon characters as advertising symbols for some of its products: Tony the Tiger for Frosted Flakes; Snap! Crackle! Pop! for Rice Krispies; and Toucan Sam for Fruit Loops. Somewhat controversially, the company adds artificial sweeteners to some of its products. In 2004, in response to consumer demand, Kellogg introduced reduced-sugar versions of two of its popular children's cereals: One-third Less Sugar Frosted Flakes and One-third Less Sugar Fruit Loops.

As a result of diversification in the 1990s and with the acquisition of Keebler Foods in 2001, the company's products include a wide variety of snack and convenience foods. The complete product line generated sales of nearly $9 billion in 2003, with sales in more than 180 countries. Kellogg employs 25,000 people, with manufacturing facilities in 17 countries. Kellogg's net income for 2003 was $787 million.

To promote "the health, happiness and well-being of children," Will Kellogg established the W. K. Kellogg Child Welfare Foundation in 1930. Later renamed the W. K. Kellogg Foundation, it is primarily funded by a trust that holds Kellogg Company shares of stock donated by Will Kellogg in 1934. The foundation holds about 30 percent of the company stock; as a result, every purchase of a Kellogg product generates money for the foundation, making it one of the world's largest private philanthropic foundations.

[See also Advertising; Advertising Cookbooklets and Recipes; Breakfast Foods; Cereal, Cold; Food and Nutrition Systems; Health Food; Home Economics; Kellogg, John Harvey; Nutrition; Vegetarianism.]

BIBLIOGRAPHY

Cooper, Lenna Frances. *The New Cookery.* 4th ed., rev. and enlarged. Battle Creek, MI: Good Health Publishing, 1916.
Kellogg Company. *A Citizen's Petition: The Relationship between Diet and Health.* Battle Creek, MI: Kellogg Company, 1985.
Kellogg Company. http://www.kelloggs.com
W. K. Kellogg Foundation. http://www.wkkf.org

ROBERT W. BROWER

Kentucky Fried Chicken

Kentucky Fried Chicken, a franchised restaurant chain founded by Colonel Harland Sanders, introduced chicken to the fast food marketplace, thereby starting a diversification of fast food content and challenging the singular dominance of the hamburger. The success of Sanders's brand also increased the overall popularity of chicken as a mainstream American food, causing a surge in domestic chicken production and consumption. Not to be overshadowed by his company's achievements, Harland Sanders himself became a legendary figure in American advertising and, in a broader sense, in American cultural history.

Born in Indiana in 1890, Harland Sanders worked at several jobs growing up, including as a streetcar conductor, as a soldier in Cuba, as a railroad fireman, and on a farm. As a young man he studied law, sold insurance, worked on a steamboat, and held court as a justice of the peace in Little Rock, Arkansas. Finally Sanders settled on selling tires and operating an automobile service station on the busy U.S. Route 25 in Corbin, Kentucky.

In 1930 Sanders began serving meals to hungry travelers stopping at his station, and he quickly discovered that his food—especially his seasoned fried chicken, which he made in a pressure cooker—was more popular and profitable than gasoline or tires. He expanded the business to a restaurant and motel across the street from his service station, and the growing fame of his chicken eventually attracted the acclaim of the celebrity food critic Duncan Hines. As a result of this national exposure, Kentucky governor Ruby Laffoon bestowed on Sanders the title of Kentucky Colonel.

Sanders's initial success proved short-lived, however. In 1955 Interstate 75 opened up three miles to the west of Corbin and diverted the heavy traffic from his restaurant. Forced to auction off his property, and reduced to living on a Social Security retirement check of $105 each month, Sanders set out to franchise his popular chicken recipe and cooking technique. In black formal attire and sporting a gold-tipped cane, Sanders drove a white Cadillac from state to state, pitching his franchise offer to restaurant owners and other potential investors. His secret recipe, he claimed, was "a blend of eleven herbs and spices." He cooked his fried chicken for investors, and, thanks to his smooth salesmanship, usually left with a handshake agreement for a new franchise. Under his standard franchising arrangement, restaurateurs agreed to pay him five cents for each Kentucky Fried chicken sold.

His nickels soon began to add up; he had more than six hundred franchisees under contract by 1963. The following year, already seventy-four years old, Sanders sold his company for $2 million to investors led by John Y. Brown and Jack Massey. Colonel Sanders remained as the company's "good will advisor," and, changing to a white suit, became a popular, familiar figure in print and television advertisements. The company boomed under Massey and Brown's direction, selling shares publicly on the New York Stock Exchange in 1966, and growing in size to 3,500 company-owned or franchised outlets by 1970.

In 1971 Brown sold out to Heublein Inc. for $285 million. A distiller and food manufacturer, Heublein proved ill-prepared to operate fast-food restaurants. Profits fell and fewer new franchisees signed up. Fortunes rebounded, however, when R. J. Reynolds acquired Heublein in 1982. Four years later, in 1986, RJR Nabisco sold KFC to PepsiCo Inc. for $840 million. In addition to its beverage business, PepsiCo understood the fast food industry, having owned the Taco Bell and Pizza Hut chains since the 1970s. Eventually PepsiCo combined those two chains, KFC, A&W All-American Restaurants, and Long John Silver's into an independent subsidiary called Tricon Global Restaurants Inc. In 2002 PepsiCo changed the name Tricon Global to Yum! Brands Inc. At that point it was the world's largest restaurant company, with a combined total of 32,500 units worldwide.

Despite this succession of corporate owners, KFC maintained its identity and Harland Sanders continued as spokesman, still travelling a quarter million miles each year to promote the company, until his death in 1980. At the beginning of the twenty-first century, KFC had more than ten thousand outlets and was growing most rapidly outside the United States. In 2002, the company opened its seven hundredth restaurant in China, only fifteen years after starting business there. The "Colonel's Chicken" is standard fare around the globe, but his recipe's "eleven herbs and spices" remain a closely guarded secret.

[See also Advertising; Chicken; Fast Food; Hamburger; Hines, Duncan; Roadhouses; Sanders, Colonel.]

BIBLIOGRAPHY

Jakle, John A. *Fast Food: Roadside Restaurants in the Automobile Age.* Baltimore: John Hopkins University Press, 1999.
Thomas, R. David. *Dave's Way: A New Approach to Old Fashioned Success.* New York: Berkley Publishing Group, 1992.

DAVID GERARD HOGAN

Ketchup

The word "ketchup" conjures up an image of the thick, sweet, tomato-based condiment that American teenagers deploy indiscriminately on most of their foods. Although almost every restaurant and café in the United States provides easily accessible bottles of tomato ketchup—often standing on each table next to the salt and pepper shakers—Americans did not invent ketchup, which was originally not thick, or sweet, or made from tomatoes.

The concoction takes its name from the Mandarin word *kē-tsiap,* which refers to a fermented sauce made from soybeans. British explorers, colonists, and traders came into contact with the sauce in Southeast Asia, and upon their return to Europe they attempted to duplicate it. As soybeans were not grown in Europe, British cooks used such substitutes as anchovies, mushrooms, walnuts, and oysters. British colonists brought ketchup to North America, and Americans continued experimenting, using a variety of additional ingredients, including beans and apples.

Tomato ketchup may have originated in America. It was widely used throughout the United States in the early nineteenth century, and small quantities of it were first bottled in the 1850s. After the Civil War commercial production of ketchup rapidly increased and while other ketchups were manufactured, tomato ketchup became the most important version. In 1891 a writer in the *Merchant's Review* declared it to be the "sauce of sauces." In 1896 the *New York Tribune* reported that tomato ketchup was America's national condiment, available "on every table in the land." A 1901 study found ninety-four different brands of tomato ketchup being sold in Connecticut alone. The authors reported that ketchup was the "most popular bottled table sauce" in America, that it was "found on the tables of nearly every hotel and restaurant" and was "consumed in large quantities in families." More than eight hundred different ketchups have been identified as manufactured prior to 1915, and

Ketchup. Advertisement for Blue Label ketchup, early twentieth century. *Collection of Andrew F. Smith*

Company, which first sold tomato ketchup in 1873. By 1890 Heinz had hit upon the famous brand-image combination of keystone label, neckband, screw cap, and octagonal bottle. The ketchup bottle itself has become a culinary icon throughout the world. In the early years of the twentieth century, the H. J. Heinz Company was the largest tomato ketchup producer, and when the century ended it was still in that position.

Another ketchup manufacturer, the Del Monte Corporation of San Francisco, had begun bottling ketchup by 1915 and rapidly expanded production during the 1940s. Yet another producer was the Hunt Brothers Packing Company, which began making ketchup during the 1930s. Heinz, Del Monte, and Hunt are the three largest ketchup producers in the world.

Virtually all ketchup was originally packed into glass bottles, except for commercial ketchup, which was sold in large cans. This changed in the 1970s when the H. J. Heinz Company introduced the Vol-Pak, a plastic bag filled aseptically with ketchup. Designed for food-service operations and restaurants, the bag was kept on a rack to refill plastic bottles conveniently. The Vol-Pak soon replaced cans. During the 1980s two additional packaging innovations appeared: the single-serving ketchup pouch, which increased in sales from half a million cases to 5 million cases in just ten years; and the squeezable plastic ketchup bottle, which was easier to use than a glass bottle and almost unbreakable. By 2000, 60 percent of all ketchup in the United States was sold in plastic containers.

The consumption of ketchup has expanded along with the proliferation of fast food restaurants, where it is dispensed in single-serving pouches or in large plastic reservoirs with push pumps. Americans alone purchase 10 billion ounces of ketchup per year, averaging out to about three bottles per person. Worldwide, more than 840 million fourteen-ounce bottles alone are sold annually.

By the end of the twentieth century, ketchup was ubiquitous. Its usage had expanded rapidly throughout Latin America, Europe, Australia, and East and Southeast Asia. Few other sauces or condiments have transcended local and national culinary traditions as thoroughly as tomato ketchup. With the global growth of fast food chains, the consumption of ketchup is likely to escalate. Some denounce it as an American culinary atrocity and others condemn it as a promoter of global homogenization. Still others view it as the Esperanto of cuisine.

this is probably only a fraction of the total number actually bottled in America.

Up until about 1900, ketchup was mainly used as an ingredient for savory pies and sauces, and to enhance the flavor of meat, poultry, and fish. It then became famous as a condiment following the appearance of three major host foods: hamburgers, hot dogs, and french fries. A leading commercial producer at the time was the H. J. Heinz

[*See also* Aseptic Packaging; Bottling; Condiments; Fast
   Food; Packaging; Soybeans; Heinz Foods; Tomatoes.]

BIBLIOGRAPHY

Smith, Andrew F. *Pure Ketchup: A History of America's National
   Condiment*. Columbia: University of South Carolina Press,
   1996.

                                    ANDREW F. SMITH

Kettles

The term "kettle" appears most often in early cooking
manuscripts referring to pots used for preserving and
candying that were generally made of earthenware,
bronze, or copper, materials that did not darken acidic
food. They were open pots with straight or slanted sides
and swinging or "falling" bail handles for suspension
over coals or flames, and they were well suited for efficient evaporation. Other kettles made of cast iron worked
better for long, slow, moist cookery of stews, soups, and
porridges. By the late seventeenth century, the term was
sometimes used synonymously with "pot," and thus
either word might have referred to the same utensil. For
the most part, kettles had flat bottoms. Kettles sometimes
were made with a pouring lip on one edge and a tipping
handle partway down the opposite side.

In the 1830s a manufactory of brass kettles—Israel
Coe and Company—thrived in America's brass-produc-
ing state, Connecticut. In 1851 H. W. Hayden, of
Waterbury, Connecticut, patented a new method of manufacturing brass preserve kettles. His process for spinning brass on a wooden form mostly put an end to the
pieced-brass kettles with dovetailed joins. The Hayden
spun-brass kettles were made in sizes from two to fourteen gallons and they retained the old-fashioned
wrought-iron bail handle. By the 1890s many kettles
were made in enameled sheet iron that had been
stamped into shape before enameling; others were produced in cast iron with enameled interiors, which made
them almost impervious to acidic foods. From about
1900 on, spun- and cast-aluminum kettles were made,
but these are only satisfactory when heavy enough to
accommodate the long, slow cooking for which kettles
are still needed.

[*See also* Material Culture and Technology, *sidebar on*
   The Technology of Cooking Containers; Pots and Pans;
   Preserves.]

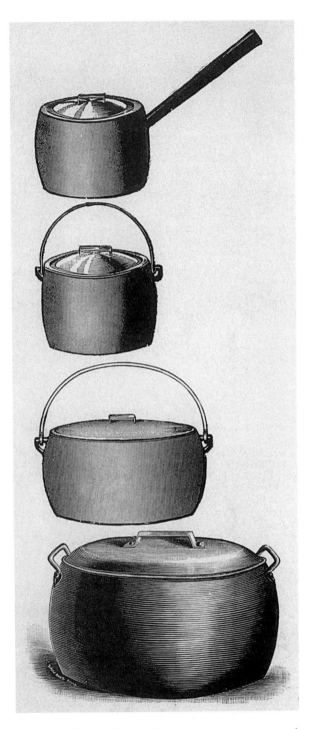

Cast Iron Hollow Ware. *Top to bottom*, saucepan, round
boiler, oval boiler, and oblong kettle. From the Duparquet,
Huot, & Moneuse Co. catalog (Boston, 1915), p. 166.

BIBLIOGRAPHY

Franklin, Linda Campbell. *300 Years of Kitchen Collectibles*. 5th
   ed. Iola, WI: Krause Publications, 2003.

Greguire, Helen. *The Collector's Encyclopedia of Graniteware Colors, Shapes, and Values.* Book 2. Paducah, KY: Collector Books, 1993.

Smith, David G., and Chuck Watford. *The Book of Wagner & Griswold.* Atglen, PA: Schiffer Books, 2001.

LINDA CAMPBELL FRANKLIN AND ALICE ROSS

KFC, *see Kentucky Fried Chicken*

Kitchen Gardening

A steadfast symbol of sustenance, well-being, and American self-sufficiency, kitchen gardening has played a vital role in the evolution of America's cultural and culinary heritage for nearly four hundred years. As the American diet has evolved over time to accommodate ever-shifting priorities and the introduction of a variety of new foods, so has the kitchen garden followed suit.

Early American Kitchen Gardens

The kitchen garden was a mainstay of early American life and was mandated by law as early as 1624. A necessity for enduring the many hardships common to life in the New World, the kitchen garden, along with the hearth, served as the hub of the early American colonial home. A no-nonsense food production area designed for function rather than aesthetics or pleasure, the kitchen garden produced plants used for food and flavorings, in herbal medicines, for dyes, for air freshening, and for insect repellent. The division of labor mandated that women of the time feed and attend to their families' medical needs while the majority of men practiced large-scale crop farming.

The early American culinary garden was typically divided into four (or more) symmetrical square or rectangular raised beds divided by two narrow intersecting paths in the tradition of the English cottage garden, known as the four-square design. The raised beds helped warm the soil for early planting and encouraged drainage. Traditionally, the food garden was planted within close proximity to the home and to a water source, and the garden was surrounded by a protective enclosure, such as a fence, in order to keep animals out. Kitchen gardens varied in size from one-fourth of an acre in the North to six or more acres in the South. Planting and harvesting were done according to the phases of the moon and the astrological calendar.

Many of the seeds and plants used in early American kitchen gardens were brought from the Old World in an effort to duplicate the gardens left behind. Culinary gardens of the time often contained lettuce, beets, peas, asparagus, celery, cucumbers, radishes, sorrel, kidney beans, broccoli, and cauliflower. Culinary herbs included chives, leeks, mint, fennel, marjoram, tarragon, savory, parsley, borage, and thyme. Such pharmaceutical herbs as chamomile, hyssop, angelica, betony, clary sage, feverfew, licorice, rue, and valerian were grown. Kitchen gardens of the northern colonies relied heavily on root vegetables, such as turnips, parsnips, onions, carrots, and (eventually) potatoes, as they could be preserved through the cold winters in the mandatory root cellar. Cabbage was among the most highly prized plants for its hardiness and keeping qualities. The more temperate climate of the South allowed for greater flexibility in plant selection, which included such greens as spinach and collards. The indigenous populations had also introduced the settlers to such important native foods as corn, runner beans, pumpkins, squash, and Jerusalem artichokes, which were gradually integrated into their diet.

Thomas Jefferson's kitchen garden at Monticello in Charlottesville, Virginia, and that of George Washington at Mount Vernon, Virginia, are two examples of formal, early American kitchen gardens that have remained under cultivation.

African Slaves and the Kitchen Garden

Enslaved Africans were frequently allocated personal garden plots, enabling them to supplement their food rations while growing the foods they preferred. African cooks were also responsible for food preparation in the

Mail Order Seeds. Order envelope of Aaron Low Seed Grower, Essex, Massachusetts, 1880s. Low's catalogs included illustrations of vegetables, an order form, and advertisements from agricultural implement sellers.

large southern plantation houses, allowing them to introduce a variety of new foods to the American table. These included peanuts, black-eyed peas, sesame (also known as benne), okra, sweet potatoes, yams, watermelon, rice, sorghum, eggplant, and tomatoes. Over time, these foods became integral parts of the American diet while contributing to the development of a distinct cuisine.

The Good Life

The importance of kitchen gardening declined in the later nineteenth century as the dominant agrarian way of life gave way to rapid urbanization. Consequently, for the first time in U.S. history, the population began buying produce from retail grocers rather than cultivating it themselves. Many people left the cities for the newly created post–Civil War suburbs, seeking relief from such urban problems as crime and epidemics. Gardening was promoted as a therapeutic activity while vegetables were recognized for the contribution they made to good health. Thus the opportunity to cultivate a kitchen garden was an acknowledged factor in the appeal of the suburban "good life." However, hybrid seeds sold by new commercial seed catalogues and chemical fertilizers now replaced the time-honored practice of seed saving and using composted manure.

"Planting for Freedom"

Escalating prices, food shortages, and economic hardships of World War I triggered a major wave of kitchen gardening across the United States. The National War Commission, created in 1917, encouraged citizens of all economic classes to contribute to the domestic war effort by growing liberty gardens (later known as victory gardens). Liberty gardens (1917–1920) frequently took the form of community gardens, also known as allotment gardens, cultivated on large, open spaces, such as vacant city lots or railroad yards. Despite its enormous success, the end of the war prompted the demise of the liberty garden program.

The Great Depression of the 1930s also inspired a revival of culinary gardening as rampant unemployment and widespread poverty among the middle classes spurred the development of government-sponsored community "relief" gardens (1930–1939).

During World War II, kitchen garden cultivation was regarded as a patriotic duty. Providing a way for the population to feel involved in the war effort, the victory gardens also served as a self-help solution to deal with food shortages and rationing. Americans were urged to

Liberty Garden. Poster distributed by the National War Garden Commission around 1919. *Prints and Photographs Division, Library of Congress*

grow and preserve as much of their own food as possible in order to make commercially grown produce available to the troops overseas. It is estimated that nearly 20 million victory gardens were planted during World War II. In 1944 alone, more than one-third of the country's vegetables were grown in victory gardens. The end of the war, coupled with the return of national prosperity, signaled an end to the kitchen gardening movement.

Back to Nature

In the early 1960s, growing concern over the environmental impact of chemical fertilizers and pesticides gave birth to the organic gardening movement. The energy crisis, high food prices brought about by inflation, and widespread disenchantment with mass-produced foods all contributed to a renaissance in both culinary and community gardening in the early 1970s.

Modern Kitchen Gardening

A 1998 Harris Poll ranked gardening as America's most popular leisure activity. With over 31 million Americans taking part and thousands of books, articles, and

Victory Garden, World War II. *Prints and Photographs Division, Library of Congress*

television programs devoted to the subject, kitchen gardening has become a significant influence on modern American popular culture. In addition, a worldwide movement seeks to preserve genetic diversity by restoring to their former prominence heirloom seeds thought to have been lost through hybridization. Cooking creatively with vegetables and herbs from the kitchen garden remains an important culinary trend among restaurant chefs and home gardeners alike.

[*See also* Heirloom Vegetables; Organic Gardening.]

BIBLIOGRAPHY

Shapiro, Howard-Yana, and John Harrisson. *Gardening for the Future of the Earth*. New York: Bantam, 2000.
Tucker, David. *Kitchen Gardening in America: A History*. Ames: Iowa State University Press, 1993.
Weaver, William Woys. *Heirloom Vegetable Gardening: A Master Gardener's Guide to Planting, Seed Saving, and Cultural History*. New York: Holt, 1997.

ELYSE FRIEDMAN

Kitchens

This entry has two subentries:

Early Kitchens
1800 to the Present

Early Kitchens

The English term "kitchen," used in many variations for over a thousand years, has always meant the place where cooking was done, and American colonial kitchens have been largely understood in that light. But in fact, the idea of one room (in an average home) devoted entirely to cookery is relatively new. For thousands of years the vast majority of people lived in small one-room shelters in which the central hearth was the place where most human needs (including food) were met, where work of all kinds was performed, and where significant social interactions occurred. Only the very wealthy set aside dedicated spaces and maintained separate kitchens under the direction of professional cooks. With the gradual development of material culture, the average house expanded and began to devote special-purpose rooms to sleeping, dining, business, or entertaining. The kitchen itself was the one of the last to give up its general function.

In the earliest American settlements, limited by time, technology and means, relatively small "kitchens" were truly the heart of a one-room house. Everything hinged on the fire, and everyone had the skill to light one quickly by means of flint stones, forged-iron strikers, and fine tinder, all kept dry and ready at hand in small tinder boxes. Many dwellings incorporated the fireplaces of stone, brick, or wattle and daub (stick and mud or clay) that were increasingly available to average families of the time. This was a clear improvement over the earlier European style in which fires were built directly on the dirt floor in the center of the room, allowing the smoke to escape erratically through thatched roofs. The air in both kitchens was often hazy with smoke, and the light dim. Cleanliness was limited, as it depended on water hauled in buckets from wells or springs. However, the earlier, primitive form was logically the colonists' first frontier house, if only temporarily, and was to be found on the frontiers of American expansion for well over two centuries. The styles of these hut-like homes varied according to regional climate and resources: for example, sod houses and thatched-roof dugouts on the plains, or adobe structures in the Southwest.

As farm families became established (more than 95 percent of Americans were farmers at the time of the American Revolution), homesteads enlarged. Succeeding generations added rooms and built new, more substantial homes. Larger barns and special-purpose sheds relieved the kitchen of much work.

The architecture of a house and its kitchen depended on a number of factors. Apart from basic shelter needs and climate conditions, it responded to social views, economic status, and the familiar European traditions brought by the colonists. For example, eighteenth-century English Americans located their fireplaces and chimneys on interior walls, on the concept that one could have back-to-back hearths in adjoining rooms, sharing a common chimney and heating the house more efficiently. The fireplace's back wall and jambs (side walls that protruded into the room) contained the fire, controlling smoke, heat, and danger, and provided a place to locate shelves and hang equipment. The floor of the fireplace and its protruding hearth tended to be at the same level as that of room's floor, offering additional space for gentle-heat cooking. By the early 1700s, swinging cranes were installed into fireplace jambs. Their system of hooks and adapted trammels made hearth cooking processes safer, more comfortable, and more efficient.

The Dutch used a basically similar concept, but their fireplaces were built on an exterior wall. Although the house itself may have been a wood frame construction, one of the side walls was built of stone and supported the chimney. The fireplace was situated inside the room against this stone wall, but was jambless. Instead, a fender or shallow canopy attached to the stone wall protruded above the fire area. It gathered the smoke and channeled it into the chimney. This had the advantage of more efficient house-heating in winter, and it worked well in temperate climates.

Other groups continued to use the special features of the kitchens they had known in Europe. German kitchens in America followed English designs in their use of jambed fireplaces, but with variations in the hearth height. Their hearths were more likely to be raised above the level of the kitchen floor, a feature that relieved the cook of some bending and heavy lifting. The Spanish, in what would become the U.S. Southwest, brought their traditions of clay and tile,

Early Kitchen. Kitchen at the Governor's Palace, Williamsburg, Virginia. *Culinary Archives & Museum at Johnson & Wales University, Providence, R.I.*

building thick walls of adobe to protect against the heat and applying their use of clay ovens and built-in clay "stoves," or rows of individual charcoal burners.

Regional and Social Variations

Conditions in the colonies also determined the direction taken by kitchens. Southern plantations developed an architecture of their own. Their kitchens were often separate buildings, in order to reduce heat and fire risks in the main house and to distance the owners from the physical and social evidence of both the work and those who did it. Kitchens in slave dwellings were very much like the one-room huts of the early colonies, utilizing fireplaces for simple family cooking. Sometimes permanently equipped outdoor areas were designated for the preparation and serving of field hands' daily one-dish noon dinners. In the Louisiana dogtrot cabins, kitchens were separated from other rooms by a breezeway, although they all shared a common roof.

In northeastern cities and in places where land and plot size were limited, kitchens were frequently removed to a cellar area, where once again the work, noise, smells, heat, and servants were kept at a distance from the family living space. For a family with servants, this arrangement offered advantages. Kitchens remained cooler in summer heat. The cook herself was conveniently near other food-related cellar areas devoted to food, among them spaces or rooms for the processing and storage of staples, root vegetables, and fruits, butter, and cheese; for butchering and meat processing; and for wine, cider, and beers. Needless to say, such cellars needed large double bulkhead doors to the outside through which great amounts of food and equipment could be moved. Traffic patterns within the house were appropriately redirected.

Bake ovens were important kitchen features. Although sometimes built free-standing out of doors, they were more often within the house, constructed behind the fireplace wall as large oval brick cavities enclosed in their own spaces between the walls of adjacent rooms. Access to the oven was through a framed opening in the back fireplace wall, at about eye height. Ovens were heated by fires built directly in the baking chamber, the smoke leaving through

Clock Jack. The clock jack was the epitome of cooking equipment of the eighteenth century. This version was wound up manually and lasted for some twenty minutes. Its pulley drove the spitted meats on the earth—an early rotisserie. Handmade by a skilled blacksmith, it commanded high prices and was available only to the wealthier or commercial kitchens of the time. *Collection of Alice Ross*

the door into the fireplace and then directly up the chimney. Oven rakes were used to scrape out the embers and ash onto the fireplace floor below. Once heated, ovens held their heat by use of a tight-fitting door of lined wood or iron. Getting the food into and out of the oven required a long-handled peel of forged iron or wood.

By the late 1700s the oven door had moved to the side wall of the fireplace, perhaps freeing up more cooking space on baking days. By the early 1800s it was removed from the hearth itself and instead occupied an extension of the jamb wall alongside the hearth. This oven often had its own interior flue, a smoke channel that connected the top of the oven to the chimney directly, as well as an ash channel that opened into the hearth or an area below. For ovens without flues, overhead fenders or canopies (following the Dutch design) caught the smoke as it rose and redirected it through the fireplace into the chimney.

Utensils and Furnishings

The basic cooking implements of these early kitchens was simple. People made as many utensils of their own as they could of wood, bone, or leather. As iron was expensive in the early colonies, it was owned in limited quantities and according to means. Far more common was earthenware, inexpensive and easily manufactured locally and well suited to simple frying and stewing. During the eighteenth century, inexpensive tin utensils were equally common. A minimal kitchen also required an all-purpose cast-iron cauldron-shaped pot; it had a bulging shape that narrowed and flared at the top, three legs to hold it above hearth embers, and a swinging bail handle to hang it above the flames. These were available in a number of sizes, and very likely a modest house kept a small assortment for boiling and simmering. In addition, frying pans and griddles on legs were important, as were posnets (saucepans) and a water kettle (what is thought of today as a tea kettle, but used for providing boiling water for a number of purposes). Forged gridirons served as broilers; toasters of various designs were important to the English. Families of means had these in various sizes, along with more specialized (and expensive) salamanders—thick plates of cast iron on legs and a long handle that were heated to glowing and passed over food to brown it. And the very wealthy who required roasted meats in quantity were likely to own a wall-mounted clock jack, a geared wind-up mechanism that turned spitted meat before the fire. This required spits fitted with wheeled ends to receive the connecting pulley, special andirons (turnspit dogs) on which to rest the spits,

and drip pans. As the eighteenth-century tin industry progressed, reflecting ovens achieved equally fine roasting and became available to the average household. Everyone cooked with long-handled utensils, often hand-forged but sometimes of wood, such as meat forks, ladles, skimmers, turners, and spoons.

Kitchen furnishings expanded just as the cookware did. At first a pioneering family had few tables and chairs, and children ate sitting on the floor. Before very long tables and chairs accommodated the entire family and its servants, if any, the same table at first serving as both work and dining space. For those with only a few utensils, simple, open shelving served as storage; for those of means there were locked cabinets (food safes) in which to secure expensive spices, sugar, or meats. By the 1700s many had dressers—free-standing tables or cabinets that supported open shelves above—used both to store and display important pieces and as an adjunct to work spaces. Closets were rare. Farm kitchens were extended with "dirty kitchens," lean–to enclosures behind the fireplace in which were stored work tools, bulky cooking equipment, and occasionally food.

By the early 1800s, American cities were on the rise and beginning a transition to the new urban culture that was to replace rural ways. Urban homemakers were no longer so deeply involved in subsistence production but were steadily drawn into the cash economy and consumerism. As families increasingly bought what they needed from nearby shops or caterers, their kitchens changed in character; and as new technology became available, there was a long period of overlap in which both fireplace and cookstove were in use. In most cases kitchens remained large and the family center of home. The range of equipment, storage, and furnishings began to reflect industrial changes that would escalate during the antebellum period. The first waves of mass immigration, beginning with the Irish, became a source of hired kitchen help. At first the shifts were a simple matter of owning more things and maintaining a higher standard of living (within the same system), but this period also saw the first steps toward major changes. As the male workplace moved from home to office, factory, or shop, and as children's now-compulsory education took them away from home, the kitchen became women's territory. Still a social gathering point, it was no longer a family work space.

[See also Cupboards and Food Safes; Dutch Influences on American Food; Frying Pans, Skillets, and Spiders; Hearth Cookery; Stoves and Ovens, subentry Wood and Coal; Turnspit Dogs.]

BIBLIOGRAPHY

Beecher, Catharine E., and Harriet Beecher Stowe. *The American Woman's Home or, Principles of Domestic Science; Being a Guide to the Formation and Maintenance of Economical, Healthful, Beautiful and Christian Homes*. New York: J. B. Ford, 1869.

Celehar Jane H. *Kitchens and Kitchenware*. Radnor, PA: Wallace-Homestead, 1985.

Crump, Nancy Carter. *Hearthside Cooking: An Introduction to Virginia Plantation Cuisine Including Bills of Fare, Tools and Techniques, and Original Recipes with Adaptations for Modern Fireplaces and Kitchens*. McLean, VA: EPM Publications, 1986.

Harrison, Molly. *The Kitchen in History*. New York: Scribner's, 1972.

Phipps, Frances. *Colonial Kitchens, Their Furnishings, and Their Gardens*. New York: Hawthorn, 1972.

Plante, Ellen M. *The American Kitchen, 1700 to the Present: From Hearth to Highrise*. New York: Facts on File, 1995.

Smallzried, Kathleen Ann. *The Everlasting Pleasure: Influences on American Kitchens, Cooks, and Cooking from 1565 to 2000*. New York: Appleton Century Crofts, 1956.

Williams, Jacqueline. *Wagon Wheel Kitchens*. Lawrence, KS: University Press of Kansas, 1993

Williams, Jacqueline. *The Way We Ate: Pacific Northwest Cooking, 1843–1900*. Pullman: Washington State University Press, 1996.

ALICE ROSS

1800 to the Present

By the early nineteenth century, American cities were on the rise, and Americans were beginning a transition to an urban culture that was to replace rural ways. Urban homemakers were no longer deeply involved in subsistence production but were increasingly drawn into consumerism and the cash economy. Because consumers were buying most of what they needed from nearby shops or caterers, kitchens changed in character. As the men's workplaces shifted from home to office, factory, or shop, and as compulsory education took children away from home, kitchen space became women's domain. Still a social gathering place, the kitchen was no longer a family work space. The first waves of mass immigration (beginning with the Irish) provided the urban middle class with a source of hired kitchen help.

In most cases, urban kitchens remained large and the family center of home, but early industrial growth and technologies escalated during the antebellum period, crowding kitchens with equipment, storage, and furnishings. There was a long period of overlap during which both fireplaces and cookstoves as well as their attendant utensils were in use, sometimes in the same room, because each one offered advantages and disadvantages. For example, roasting and brick oven baking gave superior results at the hearth, whereas griddle foods were easier to prepare on the stove. Thus the kitchen often was crowded by two sets of pots and utensils, the new and the old. By the 1840s and 1850s, cookstoves had been enlarged and perfected and were commonly accepted in urban middle-class households.

Rural kitchens did not change a great deal in the early nineteenth century because most farmers were faced with the problems of low cash flow. Even prosperous farmers had their capital tied up in land, buildings, equipment, animals, and crops and saw their profits as cash only when the harvest was sold. People in rural areas consequently were slower to obtain new cookstoves and modernize their kitchens. They continued to work in the traditional cooperative way at subsistence farming. Their kitchens remained the center of a variety of activities, still an important gathering and work place.

1850–1900

In the face of social, economic, and cultural changes, urban middle-class women began to see their role differently and for the first time defined themselves as homemakers. It became women's task to create a pleasant, orderly, and efficient home environment that would serve as a calming influence on their men and children, presumably overstimulated and made ill by city life. Kitchens became centers of the women's world and changed to accommodate both the new image and expanding cookery responsibilities.

In the city and the country, summer kitchens were added to the backs of houses and were used seasonally. Large and airy, these kitchens were spacious enough for equipment, storage, and workspace. They were sometimes fitted with small "oil" (gasoline) stoves and sometimes temporarily housed the main kitchen's large cookstove, which had been moved in for the summer.

With the onset of the American Industrial Revolution (ca. 1850), the numbers of manufactured kitchen goods continued to rise. Gadgetry became extremely desirable, and many inexpensive tools, from apple peelers to canning equipment and egg beaters to shaped baking pans, competed with reasonably priced tableware for storage space. The storage problem urgently required solutions in the face of more complex and stylish cooking, baking, and newly instituted home canning.

One of the earliest figures to shape women's new roles and responsibilities was Catharine Beecher. Beecher's seminal works (*Treatise on Domestic Economy*, 1841, and *The American Woman's Home*, 1869) promoted the new notions and espoused acceptance of a new social ideal. Beecher's innovative theories on kitchen management, design, and efficiency sought to remedy the problems of unnecessary, difficult, and time-consuming tasks engendered by unorganized workspaces. She suggested rearranged workspaces, new furnishings, and simplified traffic patterns to reduce the number of steps taken in a day. In a similar work, *The Philosophy of Housekeeping,* published in 1869, Joseph B. and Laura E. Lyman contributed the notion of the L-shaped kitchen plan, charting an imaginary "triangle" between major workspaces. This plan resulted in a shortened path for the cook, a principle that allowed maximum convenience and use of space.

One effect of such writings was a new plan for furnishing kitchens. In addition to the central, all-purpose work table, kitchens were furnished with free-standing jam cupboards and food safes filled with homemade products and staples stored in earthenware or wooden containers. Most elaborate in the late nineteenth century was the Hoosier cabinet, which offered a combination of efficient workspace and storage. This freestanding cabinet had special shelves, drawers, and compartments for cutlery and linens; dispensing bins for staples such as flour, sugar, spices, cereals, dishes, coffee, and tea; and a pullout work shelf.

Another major step in the evolution of kitchens was a mechanically operated water supply. Cast iron hand pumps, which sometimes were installed indoors, eliminated the heavy work of hauling well water. Special sinks of iron, soapstone, or granite, often without plumbing, replaced the old bucket system. In addition, the refrigerator, invented in the 1830s, was improved and marketed widely in association with the new ice industry.

Few of these innovations were incorporated into the kitchens of New York City's immigrant tenements. There, as in other poor neighborhoods and remote rural areas, fireplaces and hand-carried water, minimal furnishings, and limited open shelving remained the rule.

1900–1945

The early twentieth century continued in the transitional character of the previous century. Wood- and coal-burning cookstoves were replaced with gas and electric ranges. Wood ranges wasted much more fuel than gas ranges, and the risk of household fires was greater. Gas stoves, sold in cast iron and a combination of iron and wood, burned cleaner and did not require the carting of fuel. Combination ranges fueled by either gas or wood were popular because in the summer gas added little heat to the room, whereas coal and wood stove fires heated the house in winter. Electric ranges became available in 1910 but

were not easy or practical to use until 1913, when the automatic oven temperature regulator was invented. Electric ranges were not in general use for another two decades.

Electricity was added to kitchens slowly but steadily. A good deal of work—beating and mixing, for example—was still done manually. In the 1920s and 1930s, sinks, refrigerators, and ranges were freestanding, but most urban kitchens had electricity, and electric stoves gained favor. The first automatic dishwashers, although not common in average homes, were built in next to the sinks of the well-to-do.

Although closets and cabinets were used in modest kitchens, upper-class kitchen pantries housed most cooking utensils and ingredients, but these pantries were often not large enough and were often inconveniently placed. Christine Frederick (*Efficient Housekeeping,* 1914) approached the new problems by advocating a smaller, step-saving kitchen over a large kitchen space. Although kitchen storage was increasing, appliances such as stoves were becoming smaller. In addition, the kitchen was no longer the family multiple-purpose room and was given a smaller space in the house. Frederick's revolutionary concept was to

Refrigerator. Advertisement for Frigidaire refrigerators that appeared in *Good Housekeeping,* 1929.

devote the modern kitchen to food preparation alone. To this end, and in the face of overwhelming choices of newly available mechanized kitchen equipment, Frederick recommended that purchasing decisions depend on the duration of cleanup and how often the item would be used, rather than the usual economic factors.

From the 1920s on, kitchen design began reflecting the concern for sanitation promoted by home economists. The new discipline of science had found its way into cookbooks and kitchen furnishings, and fashion drew on the look of white, sterile laboratories. Walls were made of easily cleaned materials: improved paints made them easier to maintain, and the wooden wainscoting popular in the 1880s and 1890s was done away with. Instead of oilcloth, sheets of decorative linoleum were used throughout the kitchen like throw rugs to cover less sanitary brick and wood flooring. Those who could afford it applied shining tile to their kitchen floors and walls. Before furnishings became secondary to built-ins, most kitchens with adequate space had a second worktable in the middle of the room. The top surface was made of an easy-to-clean material, such as zinc, enamel, or porcelain.

The fascination with science affected middle-class kitchen decor. A new concept in the previously utilitarian workspace suggested that a degree of socializing might be conducted in the kitchen. Designers and manufacturers recommended the use of color in the kitchen to add warmth and a note of personal style, and sponging, a decorative painting technique, was used on kitchen floors. Kitchen aesthetics were central to sales campaigns and advertising. In 1927 Westinghouse offered a selection of new porcelain-enamel ranges that had no legs and came in a variety of colors. Art nouveau curves of the early twentieth century were replaced in the 1930s and 1940s with the classic straight lines of art deco. By 1930 the eastern cities had been introduced to built-ins, sinks installed in countertops to creating a continuous surface. Older wall-hung sinks were improved with adjacent countertops and cupboards underneath. These kitchen fashions spread slowly, reaching middle-class homes of the Midwest after World War II. One response to the desire for increased storage and access was the lazy Susan, a rotating round shelf invented in 1933. Refrigerators of the 1940s had freezing compartments, two-door access, moveable shelves, and egg compartments.

In the 1930s, time-and-motion studies conducted by Lillian Gilbreth, an efficiency engineer, reexamined the organization and design of the kitchen. Following Beecher and Frederick, Gilbreth studied the motions

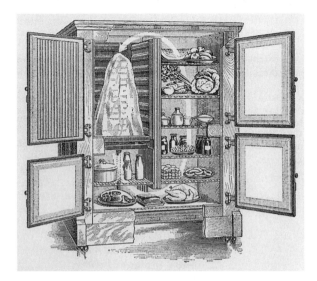

Ice-cooled Refrigerator. From *Woman's Institute Library of Cookery: Essentials of Cookery, Cereals, Breads, Hot Breads* (Scranton, Pa., 1924), sec. 2, p. 24.

used by a housewife to complete certain kitchen tasks and then rearranged them, reducing the time needed. Gilbreth's conclusions—that despite many advances, the kitchen lacked efficient organization—prompted many manufacturers of kitchen equipment to "streamline" the kitchen. Gilbreth's legacy remains the basic reorganization of kitchens. Designs continue to use the triangle arrangement of sink, refrigerator, and stove.

1945–2000

After World War II, every kitchen needed increased electrical service to meet the demands of new stoves, refrigerators, freezers, kitchen fans, dishwashers, clothes washers, garbage disposals, and a host of small equipment. Old kitchens were rewired. New kitchens built with apparently adequate power supplies were, before long, in need of more outlets. Gas continued to be a fuel of choice but was not available everywhere.

The postwar kitchen renewed its social function. After the war, women left their wartime jobs to raise families and reverted to their earlier kitchen orientation. In the new American suburbia, housewives welcomed an open floor plan that allowed them to supervise children. In their new automobile-centered communities, homeowners wanted their kitchens to be near the driveway for unloading groceries and to be a pretty place for "koffee klatching"—informal neighborhood visiting. The do-it-yourself method of home improvement on a low budget helped to beautify this space.

Informal kitchen islands surrounded by stools became an alternative to breakfast nooks. "Warm" wood replaced "cold" metal. The 1970s brought built-in ovens, countertop ranges, and countertop microwave ovens. The new style of informal entertaining moved the kitchen (or some parts of it) almost into the living room and added cooking to the entertainment of guests. The postwar decades also saw advances in the creation of new materials for kitchen countertops: plastic laminate (Formica), vinyl, and synthetic marble.

A long period of economic affluence permitted faster-paced fashions. The bicentennial of 1976 inspired the country look—idealized and romanticized images of colonial life. The 1980s revived the Victorian look. Soon thereafter came high tech, a spin-off of the industrial images of commercial kitchens, and a modernist style known as "city slick," which featured the most advanced kitchen technology.

Kitchens of the late twentieth and early twenty-first centuries reflect a range of tastes and are among the most frequently remodeled rooms in the house. For the affluent, the kitchen is a symbol of luxury, replete with state-of-the art appliances and design. New technology has created practical wood floors. Previously limited to the privileged, marble countertops, restaurant stoves with powerful exhaust fans, convection ovens, garbage disposals, and dishwashers have become commonplace and are marketed as having quiet operation and ecological advantages. Such kitchens are often the domain of hobbyists who entertain on weekends with well-prepared gourmet dishes. Despite the preoccupation with kitchen design, a large part of the population uses their kitchens less. Many families no longer eat meals together and rarely use their kitchens as social family centers. With little time to cook, adults turn to weekend cooking and meals of leftovers. The rise of frozen foods, fast foods, convenience foods, take-out foods, and restaurants has added to the decline of the kitchen as the place where cooking is done.

[*See also* Beecher, Catharine; Cupboards and Food Safes; Dishwashing and Cleaning Up; Gender Roles; Home Economics; Iceboxes; Microwave Ovens; Refrigerators; Stoves and Ovens.]

BIBLIOGRAPHY

Barlow, Ronald S. *Victorian Houseware, Hardware, and Kitchenware*. El Cajon, CA: Windmill, 1992.

Beecher, Catharine E., and Harriet Beecher Stowe. *The American Woman's Home or, Principles of Domestic Science; Being a Guide to the Formation and Maintenance of Economical, Healthful, Beautiful and Christian Homes*. New York: J. B. Ford, 1869.

Celehar, Jane H. *Kitchens and Gadgets 1920–1950*. Radnor, PA: Wallace-Homestead, 1982.

Celehar Jane H. *Kitchens and Kitchenware*. Radnor, PA: Wallace-Homestead, 1985.

Conran, Terrence. *The Kitchen Book*. New York: Crown, 1977.

Franklin, Linda Campbell. *Three Hundred Years of Kitchen Collectibles*. 5th ed. Iola, WI: Krause, 2003.

Harrison, Molly. *The Kitchen in History*. New York: Scribners, 1972.

Lyman, Joseph B., and Laura E. Lyman *The Philosophy of Housekeeping*. Hartford, CT: S. M. Betts, 1869.

Plante, Ellen M. *The American Kitchen: 1700 to the Present—From Hearth to Highrise*. New York: Facts on File, 1995.

Smallzried, Kathleen Ann. *The Everlasting Pleasure: Influences on American Kitchens, Cooks, and Cooking from 1565 to 2000*. New York: Appleton-Century-Crofts, 1956.

Williams, Jacqueline. *Wagon Wheel Kitchens*. Lawrence, KS: University Press of Kansas, 1993

Williams, Jacqueline. *The Way We Ate: Pacific Northwest Cooking, 1843–1900*. Pullman: Washington State University Press, 1996.

LYNN MARIE HOUSTON

Kitchen Equipment. Mixers like those used in restaurant kitchens at the Institute of Culinary Education, New York.

Kitchenware, *see Frying Pans, Skillets, and Spiders; Pots and Pans; Sieves, Sifters, and Colanders*

Kiwis

Native to East Asia, the kiwifruit (*Actinidia deliciosa*), or Chinese gooseberry, was first commercially cultivated in the early twentieth century in New Zealand and has been exported to the United States since the 1960s. Domestic plantings of kiwi vines began in the late 1960s, chiefly in California, where there were 4,500 bearing acres in 2002. The leading variety, Hayward, is a bit larger than an egg, with tan, fuzzy skin, and green, tart-sweet flesh. The harvest is in late autumn, but the fruits store well and are available throughout the year. They are eaten fresh, in fruit salads, and in desserts such as tarts and cakes.

A closely related species, *A. chinensis*, has yellow flesh. Sweeter and more complex than the Hayward, with hints of mango, melon, and citrus flavor, it was first exported from New Zealand in 2000 and was soon being planted by California farmers. There are also several species of hardy kiwis with grape-size fruits that are grown on a small scale from Oregon to Pennsylvania.

BIBLIOGRAPHY

Hasey, Janine K., and R. Scott Johnson, eds. *Kiwifruit Growing and Handling*. Oakland: University of California Press, 1994.
Warrington, I. J., and G. C. Weston, eds. *Kiwifruit Science and Management*. Wellington, New Zealand: Ray Richards, 1990.

DAVID KARP

Knives, *see Silverware*

Kool-Aid

Kool-Aid concentrated soft-drink mix was created by Edwin Perkins, head of the Perkins Products Company of Hastings, Nebraska. The firm manufactured a wide array of products and sold them through mail order. In 1920 Perkins marketed his first soft-drink concentrate, Fruit Smack, a syrup that consumers mixed with water and sugar to produce a sweet beverage. It proved successful, but the four-ounce glass bottles were heavy and often broke in the mail. Inspired by the tremendous success of Jell-O dessert powder, Perkins decided to sell a powdered beverage concentrate in paper packets. All the customer had to do was mix the powder with water and sugar.

In 1927 the first Kool-Aid packets sold through the mail for ten cents apiece. The original six flavors were cherry, grape, lemon-lime, orange, raspberry, and strawberry. As the sales of Kool-Aid increased, Perkins phased out his other products and concentrated on marketing Kool-Aid. By 1929 it was sold in stores throughout the United States. During the Depression, Perkins lowered the price of Kool-Aid to five cents a packet and launched a major national advertising campaign aimed at children. Perkins subsequently developed additional Kool-Aid products, including pie fillings and ice cream mixes, but they were not successful. During World War II, sugar rationing restricted the consumption of Kool-Aid, but after the war, sales of Kool-Aid took off again, and the product enjoyed its heyday in the 1950s.

In 1953 Perkins sold his company to General Foods Corporation, which added root beer and lemon flavors in 1955 and sweetened Kool-Aid in 1964. In 1988 General Foods merged with Kraft Inc., and the merged company launched new product lines, such as Kool-Aid Slushies and ready-to-drink Kool-Aid Splash. When Kool-Aid celebrated its seventy-fifth anniversary in 2002, a permanent exhibition of product memorabilia and history was inaugurated at Hastings Museum of Natural and Cultural History, in Hastings, Nebraska.

For many Americans, Kool-Aid evokes images of childhood, refreshment, and innocent summer fun. Its longtime advertising image, a smiling face drawn in the condensation on an icy pitcher of Kool-Aid, has become a national icon.

[*See also* Flavorings; General Foods; Jell-O; Kraft Foods.]

BIBLIOGRAPHY

Hastings Museum of Natural and Cultural History, Hastings, NE. http://www.hastingsmuseum.org/koolaid/history.htm

ANDREW F. SMITH

Korean American Food

Korean cuisine is richly endowed with fermented foods, hundreds of vegetable and wild greens dishes, grains, soups, teas, liquors, confections, and soft drinks. Traditional *hanjongshik* literally means "full course Korean meal." It is invariably accompanied by a huge, steaming bowl of soup or stew and features grilled fish or meat and many vibrant side dishes. Korean food is seldom deep-fried like Chinese food; it is usually boiled or blanched, broiled, stir-fried, steamed, or pan-fried with vegetable oil. Vegetables are parboiled and seasoned with spices that specifically complement the main dish. It is said that the vegetables ought to be mixed, seasoned, and soaked by hand to improve the taste. Unlike Western cuisines, where courses are served one after the other, Korean dishes are served all at once—some at room temperature, others piping hot, and many in fact, while still cooking, as anyone who has seen the giant clam in a spicy Korean stew (*chigae*) can attest.

Types of Korean Food

Boiled rice, often mixed with barley, corn, or other grains, is a staple of the Korean diet. Rice and grains can be cooked together into gruel, then served as a choice delicacy. Along with ginseng, porridge has served as a medicinal dish for the ailing for thousands of years.

Soups, known as *guk* or *tang*, are usually composed of meat, vegetables, fish, seaweed, clams, and beef bones, tripe, and other internal organs. Stews and casseroles contain less water and feature more ingredients than soups.

Gui and *jeon* are dishes prepared by either broiling on a spit or directly on a grill. The notorious *bulgogi*, which literally means "fire beef," is thinly sliced and marinated beef and ribs. *Jeon* is a popular pan-fried dish. Chopped meats, fish, or vegetables are covered with flour, dipped in beaten egg, then pan-fried. Koreans are fond of raw meat and fish on special occasions. Raw and parboiled dishes are said to complement sturdy Korean libations, especially *soju*, or potato vodka, and beer.

Tteok is steamed rice flour in the form of a cake. These traditional cakes are used in ceremonial rites honoring ancestors during holidays and festivities. *Hangwa* are light and crispy traditional sweets made of rice flour and mixed with honey. *Hwachae*, served as refreshments with dessert, are traditional Korean fruit-based drinks. A sweet rice drink or a cinnamon fruit punch are common palate refreshers after a spicy Korean meal.

Kimchi

A Korean meal without kimchi is unthinkable. Today there are more than 160 kimchi variations, differentiated by regional specialties and by season. Fresh and lively flavors are preferred for a light summer kimchi, while more intense, often garlicky or briny flavors, are suitable for winter kimchi. One question, however, persists: is the kimchi in the United States comparable to the authentic version found in the homeland?

One native Korean recently traveling in Texas observed: "The kimchi I am having at the hotel has less pickled shrimp and clams in it, so it tastes very plain, which means . . . terrible. A good kimchi should have that strong smelly socks stink. And kimchi is not a hot food. It may look hot. Some Mexican food here is hotter."

And that is just one kimchi style. Not surprisingly, kimchi styles vary greatly across the United States. Korean Americans have brought different kimchi recipes from their native Korean regions and then have adapted them with available regional ingredients.

In early Korea, kimchi was simply a mass of pickled vegetables. Salt-preserved vegetables are assumed to have very long history according to Korean literature, which suggests that Koreans had pickled vegetables as early as the seventh century. Later, around the twelfth century, various additives began to flavor kimchi. Then, in 1592, red peppers were introduced to kimchi during Hideyoshi's invasion of Korea. It is assumed that red pepper was used in an effort to conserve valuable salt. Hot red pepper contains capsaicin, which accelerates the process of fermentation and implants a particular taste and texture. Around the nineteenth century, cultivation of cabbage for winter kimchi became systematized. The tradition continues in the twenty-first century, as Korean cooks still prepare winter kimchi from late November through early December during a nationwide annual event called *kimjang*.

Fermentation has long played a role in the preservation of nutrients in vegetables and fish in Korea. The Korean peninsula is largely mountainous, home to hundreds of wild vegetables. The Korean climate ranges from the dry and frigid winters of the north to the nearly tropical conditions in parts of the south. Accordingly, early Koreans developed methods of preserving food with salt. One process, known as *yumjang*, had been developed to keep vegetables during cold winters when fresh vegetables were scarce. In the cold northern regions, kimchi was traditionally prepared with powdered red pepper and strong salted fish. In the warmer southern areas, kimchi was typically prepared with simple powdered red pepper and salt. The purity and quantity of salt, the salinity of the brine, the duration of the salting process, and the temperature of the pickled mass all influence the taste of kimchi.

Tropical conditions of the South also perfected a brining technique. Koreans still preserve fish, their internal organs and eggs, and clams with salt until they become fermented. *Jjim* is prepared by putting ingredients and seasonings into an earthenware pot and steaming at low heat. Glazing in soy sauce, or in *gochuchang*, a red pepper paste, is a time-honored technique that preserves food for weeks. These intensely salty but tasty side dishes are also unique base flavorings for kimchi and other dishes.

Korean Americans

Aside from having introduced so-called Korean barbecue and kimchi to Americans, Korean immigrants have contributed *doenjang*, a paste made of soybeans, and *gochujang* to Asian markets in the States. These fermented staples, along with soy sauce, are indispensable to Korean cookery. Immigrants often chuckle as they recount stories of stowing jars of *doenjang* and *gochujang* in their luggage during their migration overseas. By 1888, a small number of Korean students, political exiles, ginseng merchants, and migration laborers began to arrive on American shores. The first major wave of immigrants reached Hawaii from 1903 to 1905, when a total of 7,226 Koreans arrived in as contract laborers for sugar plantations. The second wave of Koreans arrived between the Korean War of 1950–1953 and 1965, as war orphans or wives and relatives of American servicemen who had been stationed in Korea. Koreans began to immigrate to the United States in larger numbers after the Immigration Act of 1965 removed quotas based on national origin. From 1976 to 1990, an annual average of 30,000 to 35,000 Koreans immigrated to the United States.

Korean Americans have found employment as greengrocers in the United States and also operate a fair number of liquor stores, fish markets, and restaurants. Koreans happened to enter the fish market business as an extension of the their greengroceries. In New York City during the 1980s, ownership of fish markets began to change hands, along with the selection of fresh fish. As a result, fried shrimp, clam, fish and chips, and even sushi and sashimi became widely available at Korean fish markets. Typically, the owner serves as the cashier, while two or more workers clean and slice the fish. The experience has been the training ground for many who go on to become sushi chefs in Japanese and Korean restaurants.

Even with thirty or so Korean cookbooks published in the United States, Korean cookery has yet to truly influence American cuisine. Korean restaurants are generally clustered in Korean neighborhoods around the country, satisfying Koreans who crave comfort foods. In the last several years, Pan-Asian and Asian fusion restaurants have started to offer such Korean staples as kimchi and *bulgogi*. These restaurants, found in hip metropolitan enclaves, cater to a smattering of adventurous eaters. In Manhattan, the area around Thirty-second Street between Broadway and Fifth Avenue, known as K-town, boasts a

Korean Greengrocer. Daniel's Food Market, Brooklyn, New York. *Photograph by Joe Zarba*

wide array of restaurants, markets, and coffeehouses, featuring talents of Korean chefs from every region. Han Ah Reum Asian Market in Manhattan is a leading Korean American food retailer, with fifteen outposts in New York, New Jersey, Pennsylvania, Maryland, and Virginia, which has served the Korean American community since 1982. At Korean greengrocers in New York City, kimchi is often found as an international delegate at the salad bar, next to, say, German potato salad or Italian lasagna. Go to any Korean American household for Thanksgiving dinner, and inevitably, kimchi stands as a proud side dish, as important to the family as the turkey itself.

[*See also* Fermentation; Fusion Food; Pickling; Salt and Salting; Soy Sauce.]

BIBLIOGRAPHY

Hepinstall, Hi Shooshin. *Growing Up in a Korean Kitchen: A Cookbook*. Berkeley, CA: Ten Speed Press, 2001.

Min, Pyong Gap. *Changes and Conflicts: Korean Immigrant Families in New York*. Boston: Allyn and Bacon, 1998.

Park, Kyeyong. *The Korean American Dream: Immigrants and Small Business in New York City*. Ithaca, NY: Cornell University Press, 1997.

The Wonderful World of Korean Food. Seoul: Korean National Tourism Organization. 2001.

HYON JUNG LEE

Kosher, *see Jewish Dietary Laws*

Kraft Foods

In 1903, James L. Kraft noticed that grocers traveled daily to the cheese market to buy cheese for their stores.

Recognizing an opportunity, he started a wholesale cheese distribution business in Chicago that brought the cheese to the grocers. His four brothers joined him in 1909, and they incorporated the fledgling business as J. L. Kraft and Brothers Company.

Kraft used innovative and aggressive advertising to promote its line of thirty-one varieties of cheese. Kraft was one of the first food companies to use color advertisements in national magazines. In 1914, the company opened its first cheese factory. At the beginning of the twenty-first century, Kraft Foods had evolved into the largest food company in the United States.

When James Kraft started his business, cheese was produced in large wheels. When cut, cheese has a tendency to spoil quickly at room temperature, which was a problem at a time when most grocers and consumers had little access to refrigeration. In 1915, Kraft came up with the idea to produce a cheese that did not spoil as quickly. He created a blended, pasteurized cheese, which he called "process cheese," and packaged it in small tins. The sale of 6 million pounds of cheese to the U.S. Army during World War I ensured the fortunes of the company.

The company changed its name to Kraft Cheese Company in 1924 and soon after merged with the Phenix Cheese Corporation, the maker of Philadelphia Brand cream cheese (introduced in the United States in 1880). In 1928, the company introduced Velveeta pasteurized process cheese spread and Miracle Whip salad dressing, adding Kraft caramels in 1933. In 1937, Kraft's famous macaroni and cheese dinner was launched, followed by Parkay margarine in 1940. Kraft again became a major food supplier to the armed forces during World War II. To market their growing list of products the company sponsored the *Kraft Musical Review* on radio in 1933, which evolved into the *Kraft Music Hall* hosted by Bing Crosby. In 1947, the company created the *Kraft Television Theatre*, the first network program on television.

New products continued to appear in the postwar era. In 1952, Kraft introduced Cheez Whiz, which for some replaced the provolone cheese that was a traditional topping for a Philadelphia cheesesteak. In 1965, Kraft introduced individually wrapped cheese slices. Light n' Lively yogurt came on the market in 1969.

In 1988, the Philip Morris Company, because of a shrinking tobacco market, purchased Kraft, just as they had purchased the General Foods Corporation in 1985. In 2000, Philip Morris acquired the Nabisco Company. In the early 2000s, there is probably not a refrigerator or cupboard in America that does not have one or more brand name products distributed by Kraft Foods. Some of these brands include Post cereals, Oscar Mayer meat products, Maxwell House coffee, Life Savers, Kool-Aid, Jell-O, Planters Nuts, Ritz crackers, and Snackwells low-fat cookies and crackers.

[*See also* Cereal, Cold; Cheese, *subentry on* Later Developments; Crackers; General Foods; Jell-O; Kool-Aid; Maxwell House; Nabisco; Philadelphia Cheese Steak Sandwich; Post Foods; Velveeta.]

BIBLIOGRAPHY

"Kraft Foods Inc." In *International Directory of Company Histories*. Vol. 45, edited by Jay P. Pederson. Chicago: St. James Press, 2002.
"Kraft General Foods Inc." In *International Directory of Company Histories*. Vol. 2, edited by Lisa Mirabile. Chicago: St. James Press, 1990.

JOSEPH M. CARLIN

Krispy Kreme

"When Krispy Kremes are hot, they are to other doughnuts what angels are to people," quipped southern humorist Roy Blount Jr. in the *New York Times Magazine*. Krispy Kreme doughnuts are marketed at retail shops with the familiar green roof and red-glazed brick exterior and the distinctive sign, "Hot Doughnuts Now." When the sign is lit, freshly made doughnuts can be seen moving along an overhead conveyor belt.

Joe LeBeau, a French chef in New Orleans, is credited with developing this yeast-raised doughnut sometime before the Great Depression. He sold the business in 1935 to Vernon Rudolph who took the business to Winston-Salem, North Carolina. For a short time in the 1970s, the Beatrice Foods Company operated Krispy Kreme without success. Krispy Kreme was purchased from Beatrice in the 1980s by one of Krispy Kreme's largest franchisees. In 2003, the company had 310 stores in 41 states, Canada, and Australia. Their doughnuts were never hotter!

BIBLIOGRAPHY

Blount, Roy, Jr. "Southern Comfort." *New York Times Magazine*. September 8, 1996.
"Krispy Kreme Doughnut Corporation." In *International Directory of Company Histories*, edited by Tina Grant and Jay P. Pederson. Vol. 21. Detroit: St. James Press, 1998.

JOSEPH M. CARLIN

Kroc, Ray, *see McDonald's*

Kvass

Kvass, from the Russian word for "leavened," is the quintessential Russian beverage. It is brewed from traditional fundamentals of the diet, either black rye bread or beets, and provides a significant secondary source of nutritionally rich foods in a drinkable form. Similar to beer, kvass is thinner and only slightly fizzy, with a flavor that is both sweeter and tangier. Black-currant leaves, caraway, mint, and fruit such as lemons and raisins are sometimes added. The technique for brewing kvass dates back to ancient Mesopotamia, when ale was prepared from baked grain loaves. Because of the short fermentation period, two to three days, the alcoholic content of kvass is low, typically 0.7 to 2.2 percent.

Kvass has been made in Russia and surrounding eastern European nations for centuries. It was originally a home-brewed beverage associated with the poor, consumed with meals, and added to some dishes, such as soups. Its popularity increased during the early 1900s as small-scale commercial production began. It became widely available from small, truck-mounted kegs on urban corners, especially in summer. Some Russians consider kvass good for digestion and a cure for hangovers. In the United States kvass concentrate is available for home use; kvass is also sometimes found in the refrigerator section of Russian delicatessens, sold in used two-liter soda bottles.

[*See also* Brewing; Ethnic Foods; Fermentation; Russian American Food.]

BIBLIOGRAPHY

Volokh, Anne. *The Art of Russian Cuisine*. New York: Collier Books, 1983.

PAMELA GOYAN KITTLER

Kwanzaa

Kwanzaa is a nonreligious, African American cultural holiday celebrated annually from December 26 through January 1. The word "Kwanzaa" is derived from the Swahili phrase "*matunda ya kwanza*" (first fruits of the harvest), and the nomenclature for the holiday comes from this East African language as well. The holiday was created in 1966 in Southern California by Dr. Malauna Karenga, an African American scholar who later became a professor of African Studies at California State University, Long Beach. Karenga's inspiration for Kwanzaa drew from the time before Africans were enslaved on American soil. The holiday reclaims and affirms lost cultural traditions, imagery, history, symbolism, philosophy, values, and spirituality. The unifying week of commemoration that Karenga created serves to instill seven core African-inspired values. These seven principles are known as the *Nguzo Saba* and uphold the holiday's main purpose, which is to strengthen familial and communal bonds. The *kinara* (candleholder) is a main icon in which a different colored candle (three red, three green, and one black in the middle) is lit daily to illuminate each principle: *Umoja* (Unity), *Kujichagulia* (Self-Determination), *Ujima* (Collective Work and Responsibility), *Ujamaa* (Cooperative Economics), *Nia* (Purpose), *Kuumba* (Creativity), and *Imani* (Faith). On each of Kwanzaa's seven days, the corresponding principle is the central theme for daytime and evening activities, including crafting and giving gifts (*zawadi*) or making and sharing memorable meals (*karamu*). In the early twenty-first century Kwanzaa was embraced by an estimated 28 million people of African descent around the globe honoring a common heritage, and its popularity continues to grow.

Kwanzaa and Harvest

The concept of Kwanzaa is linked to sustenance and agrarian rites, as it is a creative synthesis of the many African harvest rituals practiced across the continent during ancient and modern times. At these "first fruits celebrations" people come together to harvest crops (*mazao*) of fruits, vegetables, and other produce and to give thanks for the bounty of their efforts. Like Kwanzaa, these African festivals typically last seven to nine days, occurring at the end of one year and the beginning of a new.

Food imagery is woven throughout the fabric of the holiday and shows up prominently on the Kwanzaa table. An African basket or wooden bowl of fruits and vegetables represents the crops and serves as the centerpiece. Another symbol, *muhundi* (corn) has special relevance in many African societies as a fundamental food staple that also represents the human life cycle. During Kwanzaa, ears of corn represent the children of a household, extended family, or community. The unity cup (*Kikombe cha umoja*) is used for the ancient African practice of pouring libations for the ancestors using water, juice, or wine.

The Kwanzaa Feast

People celebrate Kwanzaa in unique and creative ways, using food to cultivate and share old and new traditions. Some try a different cuisine each day, highlighting regional fare from the African diaspora: the African continent, the Caribbean Islands, Central and South America, and the American South. Families or groups of friends might take turns hosting an afternoon brunch or a dinner each night of the week. Community organizations host banquets in major cities throughout the nation, notably the annual Kwanzaa *Karamu* in Los Angeles, traditionally hosted and attended by Dr. Karenga himself, along with representatives from his organization, Us.

The holiday culminates in a glorious *Karamu* feast that takes place on December 31, the evening of the sixth day (*Kuumba*/Creativity). This is when extended family, friends, and neighbors come together for a ceremonial, communal meal. Most *Karamu* festivities begin or end with the candle-lighting ceremony amid an African motif with a red, black, and green color scheme. The decor usually features tables covered with African fabrics, woven table and floor mats, the *mazao* centerpiece, and African masks and art on the walls. Guests often dress in African attire representing many nationalities. More elaborate events might incorporate African drumming, music, dancers, storytelling, and history lessons. Participants might also forgo Western dining protocol, opting for floor seating and a traditional African etiquette of eating with one's hands or using flatbreads and other food items for gathering up bite-size portions.

The Kwanzaa Menu

While there is no set menu, it is customary to serve African and African-influenced foods for any Kwanzaa meal. Indigenous African foodstuffs and those introduced to the Americas from Africa are common: black-eyed and pigeon peas, cassava, yams or yuccas, chilies and peppers, coconuts, dates, eggplants, figs, leafy greens, okra, peanuts or groundnuts, rice, sesame seeds, sweet potatoes, tomatoes, watermelons. A full-course meal could highlight one national cuisine, a broader or regional theme (soul food, Caribbean cuisine, West African dishes), or a multinational selection of African-influenced dishes from different continents.

Hearty stews, one-pot dishes, and rice pilaus resonate throughout the African diaspora and as main courses for Kwanzaa. Ghanaian groundnut stew, West Indian or South African curry dishes, Philadelphia pepper pot soup, Louisiana jambalaya, Nigerian *jollof* rice, and Senegalese *thiebou dienne* (national fish and rice dish) are among the many examples. Fish and shellfish (indicative of coastal origins) are popular, as is chicken served in a variety of international ways, such as Jamaican jerk, Senegalese *yassa*, or southern fried. Starch or vegetable side dishes might consist of cabbage, couscous, or candied yams, baked or fried plantains, and fritters made from flour mixed with minced fish, meats, or pureed beans. A wide variety of breads can accompany the Kwanzaa meal from buttermilk biscuits to Ethiopian *injera*, Native American fry bread, and numerous breads made from cornmeal (spoon bread, hush puppies, corn pone, cornbread, hoe cakes, cracklin' bread, johnnycakes, ash cake, batter bread). Popular beverages include (mostly tropical) fruit juices and drinks, Jamaican ginger beer, and rum punch for adults. Fruit-based desserts are quite common, ranging from simple pieces of fruit to ambrosia or fruit salad and apple, berry, or peach cobblers.

Sweet potato and bean pies, bread puddings, and *benne* (sesame seed) or coconut cakes likely find their way onto the Kwanzaa menu, like New Orleans seafood gumbo at Christmas, Puerto Rican *pasteles* for the holiday season, or Cuban tamales for New Year's.

Dishes with folkloric significance are eaten, like the Gullah and southern black food traditions of eating collard greens with black-eyed peas or hoppin' John (black-eyed peas with rice) on New Year's Day for good luck and prosperity throughout the new year. Pork dishes are sometimes not appropriate for Kwanzaa meals because of the strong influence of black American Muslim dietary laws that render pork taboo. However, religious diversity does not interfere with the Kwanzaa ideal of promoting Unity (*Umoja*) and Collective Work and Responsibility (*Ujima*) by having dishes prepared by many different cooks or organizing the meal as a potluck that enriches an already festive holiday season.

[*See also* African American Food; Cajun and Creole Food; Caribbean Influences on American Food; Rice, *sidebar* Hoppin' John and Other Rice Dishes.]

BIBLIOGRAPHY

Copage, Eric V. *Kwanzaa: An African-American Celebration of Culture and Cooking.* New York: Morrow, 1991.
Goyan Kittler, Pamela, and Kathryn P. Sucher. "Africans/African-Americans." In *Food and Culture*, 175–197. 3rd ed. Belmont,

CA: Wadsworth/Thomas Learning, 2001. Provides thorough and insightful academic overview of culturally rooted food habits of various ethnic groups in the United States.

Grosvenor, Vertamae. *Vertamae Cooks in the Americas' Family Kitchen.* Hong Kong: Window to the World Communications, 1996.

Harris, Jessica B. *A Kwanzaa Keepsake.* New York: Simon and Schuster, 1995.

Karenga, Maulana. *The African American Holiday of Kwanzaa: A Celebration of Family, Community, and Culture.* Los Angeles, CA: University of Sankore Press, 1988.

Karenga, Maulana. *Kwanzaa: A Celebration of Community and Culture: Commemorative Edition.* Los Angeles, CA: University of Sankore Press, 2002. Provides official information directly from the source and creator of the Kwanzaa holiday.

Official Kwanzaa Website. http://www.OfficialKwanzaaWebsite.org. Provides official information and updates (where relevant) on the origins, values, principles, and practices of Kwanzaa.

Smith, Barbara. *Entertaining and Cooking for Friends.* New York: Artisan Publishers, 2000. See esp. chapter on Kwanzaa foods.

TONYA HOPKINS

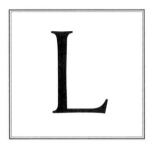

L

Ladles, *see Silverware*

Ladyfingers

Ladyfingers are dry, airy cakes, often with a sugary crust, which are made by piping a stiffly whipped egg-and-flour batter into diminutive oblongs. The sponge batter used for ladyfingers was developed in Europe by the seventeenth century to produce Naples or Savoy biscuits. Introduced to colonial America under those names, the cakes often were baked in specially designed tins or paper cases of varying sizes and shapes. The term "ladies' fingers" was used in America no later than the 1820s, although recipes continue for Savoy biscuits, in which one puts the batter "into the biscuit funnel, and lay it out about the length and size of your finger."

Ladyfingers have no strong ethnic identity and can be used in most recipes requiring sponge cake, from trifle to charlotte to tiramisu. They substitute for chemically leavened biscuits in fruit shortcakes, garnish ice cream, and grace trays of petits fours.

[*See also* Cakes; Desserts.]

BIBLIOGRAPHY

Carson, Jane. *Colonial Virginia Cookery: Procedures, Equipment, and Ingredients in Colonial Cooking.* Williamsburg, VA: Colonial Williamsburg Foundation, 1985. Distributed by the University Press of Virginia, Charlottesville.

Lee, Mrs. N. K. M. *The Cook's Own Book.* 1832. Reprint, New York: Crown, 1982.

Weaver, William Woys. *The Christmas Cook: Three Centuries of American Yuletide Sweets.* New York: HarperPerennial, 1990.

CATHY K. KAUFMAN

Lagasse, Emeril

Emeril Lagasse (1959–) is a popular television chef and has been a star of the Food Network since 1993. Noted for his theatrical cooking style and audience rapport, he has hosted several cooking series and made regular appearances on network television. *Emeril Live!*, with its live audience and studio band, has the elements of a late-night entertainment program. In many ways Lagasse is the embodiment of the age in which chefs have become as famous as rock stars. His catch phrases—"Bam!" and "Kick it up a notch"—are as familiar to Americans as Julia Child's "Bon appétit" was to television viewers in the 1960s and 1970s.

Of Portuguese and French Canadian descent, Lagasse was born in Fall River, Massachusetts. He began his culinary arts education at a vocational high school and completed it at Johnson and Wales University in Providence, Rhode Island, in 1978. After training in restaurants in France and the northeast United States, Lagasse settled in New Orleans and became the executive chef of Commander's Palace. There he adopted Creole cooking, which became the basis for the menu at his own successful restaurant, Emeril's, opened in 1990. His infusion of Portuguese and Vietnamese influences into Creole and Cajun cooking was a style he defined in his first cookbook as *Emeril's New New Orleans Cooking* (1993). He has established restaurants in New Orleans, Las Vegas, Orlando, and Atlanta and published numerous cookbooks.

Lagasse was the first professional chef to star in a television sitcom. His overwhelming popularity has resulted in a stream of enterprises and commercial partnerships, including signature lines of cookware and knives, sauces, salad dressings, and wines.

[*See also* Celebrity Chefs.]

LYNNE SAMPSON

Lamb and Mutton

Lamb and mutton are the meats of the domesticated sheep (*Ovis aries*). The meat is termed "lamb" from birth until about eighteen months, when the characteristics of the flesh, bones, and joints begin to change. By about two years, the meat becomes mutton, with a higher percentage of fat and a richer flavor. Like all red meats, lamb and mutton are high in proteins, amino acids, B vitamins, niacin, zinc, and iron. Despite their many positive culinary and nutritional characteristics, the meats have never found much favor with American palates.

Domestic sheep were first brought to the New World by the Spanish conquerors of Florida and New Mexico. Settlers also carried them to the English and Dutch colonies in Virginia, Massachusetts, and New York. Although the first sheep were dual-use breeds producing both meat and wool, for the next three centuries American sheep were bred primarily for their wool. The early colonists were poor shepherds, and their sheep ran wild, allowing many to be taken by Indians or eaten by wolves and other predators. Sheep that survived were harvested mainly for their wool. Their meat was poor and never became as popular as it remained back in Europe. When it was cooked, mutton (it was not economical to slaughter lambs) was usually prepared in the English style, in chops, roasted or boiled, often covered with a sour sauce. Martha Washington's *A Booke of Cookery* includes a roast or boiled leg of mutton served with a sauce made from currants, barberries, herbs, verjuice (the sour juice of grapes, crab apples, or other unripe fruit), and sugar.

In 1801 a handful of Merino sheep, a breed known for its fine wool, were smuggled out of Spain and taken to the United States. Within decades, the majority of American ewes had merino blood in them, the wool industry boomed, and sheep covered states like Massachusetts, Vermont, and Pennsylvania. Unfortunately, merinos were inferior mutton sheep and did not improve the quality of the meat on American tables. Travelers from England, where mutton was a staple, often complained of the poor quality of what mutton they could find. Mrs. Harriet Martineau said of her fare in Tennessee, "The dish from which I ate was, according to some, mutton; to others, pork. My own idea is that it was dog."

Nevertheless, as wool production rose, there were more sheep to harvest for meat. Sheep farmers even had large enough flocks to cull some of the young ones, and for the first time numbers of "spring lambs" (probably from six months to a year old) began to appear in the market. The meat cost about 50 percent more than mutton and at first was mainly a seasonal specialty sold in expensive restaurants. In elite New York City restaurants like Delmonico's, the roast saddle of mutton was joined by spring lamb with mint sauce and *cotelettes d'agneau à la jardinière*.

By 1900 the United States was home to a record 61 million head of sheep, the vast majority used solely for wool production. The center of sheep production moved westward, first to Illinois and Iowa and eventually to Texas, California, Wyoming, and other western states. The merino breed, which was notoriously delicate, had been strengthened by the introduction of Rambouillets, larger and hardier French merinos. (Today nearly all American sheep contain at least 50 percent Rambouillet blood.) The Rambouillets also produced better meat, which was advantageous because the wool market tended to go through cycles of boom and bust. In wartime, soldiers needed wool for their uniforms, and business skyrocketed. During peacetime, however, foreign wool was more competitive, so sheep producers were glad to have meat as a secondary product.

After World War I, Americans developed a taste for lamb, while mutton was considered coarse, stringy, and "woolly." More delicate than mutton, lamb needed gentler cooking methods, such as those that produced roasted leg of lamb, broiled lamb chops, or Irish stew. At the table, the roast or broiled meat was usually served with mint sauce or jelly, which American palates seemed to like because it masked the distinctive flavor of the meat. During the 1930s lamb and mutton rose to over 6 percent of American red meat consumption, a record but still far behind pork and beef. Most of this was in the urban Northeast, where Americans of Jewish and Mediterranean ancestry kept up Old World culinary and religious traditions that included lamb. Greek Americans served baby or suckling lamb six to ten weeks old at their Orthodox Easter celebrations, while lamb dishes were the main course at Jewish Passover feasts.

Lamb and mutton consumption rose even further during World War II, although not always willingly. Sheep production had skyrocketed owing to wool demand, while tons of pork and beef were being sent to soldiers and allied nations. Because of rationing on the home front, often the only meat sold by butchers was low-grade lamb and mutton. By the end of the war, many consumers had vowed to swear off both of them. During the postwar economic boom, consumption of sheep products plummeted. Prosperity meant people could afford beef, and so steak and hamburgers appeared on every American table. Meanwhile, the American wool market crashed in the face of cheap imports, and the number of sheep fell from 57 million in 1945 to less than 5 million by the beginning of the twenty-first century. Sheep producers adapted their flocks to this new reality by cross-breeding them with mutton breeds, so that they would be primarily mutton sheep with wool as the secondary product. (There is also a small but growing dairy sheep industry producing mainly artisanal cheeses.)

But paralleling the decline in the wool market, by the early 2000s Americans were consuming less than a pound of lamb a year per capita. That decline was tied to the decline of consumption of all red meats, as a result of their perceived health risks. What lamb and mutton does get to American tables comes increasingly from Australia and New Zealand, the world's largest lamb producers. Most of the meat is served as chops or roasts in individual homes, but lamb has also found a niche as a luxury item in the nation's "white tablecloth" restaurants. Chefs offer it as chops or rack of lamb or in nouvelle cuisine preparations that emphasize the delicateness of the meat. Unfortunately for aficionados of its rich flavor, mutton has almost vanished. It retains a tiny foothold in a few old-style steakhouses where it usually appears as mutton chops. It is the preferred barbecue meat of Owensboro, Kentucky. And it survives in the culinary traditions imported by recent immigrants from the Middle East and South Asia.

[*See also* Meat.]

BIBLIOGRAPHY

American Meat Institute. "Meat and Poultry Facts." Washington, DC: American Meat Institute, 2001.

Clemens, Rudolf. *The American Livestock and Meat Industry*. New York: Ronald Press Co., 1923.

Elie, Lolis Eric. *Smokestack Lightning*. New York: Farrar, Straus, and Giroux, 1996.

Hess, Karen, ed. *Martha Washington's Booke of Cookery*. New York: Columbia University Press, 1981.

Olney, Richard, ed. *Lamb: The Good Cook*. New York: Time-Life, 1981.

Romans, John R., William J. Costello, Wendell C. Carlson, Marion L. Grease, and Kevin W. Jones. *The Meat We Eat*. Danville, IL: Insterstate Publishers, 2001.

Root, Waverley, and Richard de Rochemont. *Eating in America*. New York: Morrow, 1976.

Skaggs, Jimmy. *Prime Cut*. College Station, TX: Texas A&M University Press, 1986.

Wentworth, Edward Norris. *America's Sheep Trails*. Ames, IA: Iowa State College Press, 1948.

Wing, Joseph E. *Sheep Farming in America*. Chicago: The Breeder's Gazette, 1912.

ANDREW COE

Lard, *see Fats and Oils*

Latin American Food, *see Cuban American Food; Iberian and South American Food; Mexican American Food; Puerto Rican Food; Southwestern Regional Cookery*

Law

The production, distribution, and sale of food in the United States is controlled by a complex structure of interrelated federal, state, and local laws and regulations. These laws and regulations are designed to ensure that the American food supply is safe and that consumers are not defrauded. With the exception of home consumption of homegrown food, all food in the United States is subject to some type of law or regulation.

Scope of Federal Legislation

The federal government's power to regulate food comes from the U.S. Constitution. When the Constitution was written in 1787, the founders wanted the federal government to promote and encourage commerce among the states. To prevent individual states from setting up unreasonable barriers to commerce, the commerce clause of the Constitution gave the federal government the right to control interstate commerce. By statute, interstate commerce is defined as commerce between any state or territory and any place outside the state or territory. Federal control starts when food enters into interstate commerce and ends when food is delivered to the ultimate consumer. The federal government also has the right to control all foreign food imports, all American food exports, and food commerce within the District of Columbia.

Because the courts interpret interstate commerce broadly, the power of the federal government over food is virtually complete. For example, in the 1999 case of *United States v. Varela-Cruz*, when dairy farmers in Puerto Rico, a U.S. territory, adulterated their milk by unlawfully increasing its volume with water and salt, the federal government prosecuted them even though the adulteration and sale of the milk occurred completely within Puerto Rico. The dairy farmers asked the court to dismiss the case, arguing that the milk was not in the stream of interstate commerce and that they therefore could not be prosecuted under federal law. The federal government prevailed, however, because the salt that the farmers used to adulterate the milk had been imported into Puerto Rico. Since the salt was in interstate commerce, milk illegally adulterated with the salt was also in interstate commerce, regardless of its ultimate destination or ultimate consumer.

The federal government's broad right to regulate food in interstate commerce also extends to animal feed and pet foods. In the 1993 case of *United States v. Strauss*, a Federal Bureau of Investigation covert dog-food-purchase operation led to the federal criminal convictions of pet store owners for selling dog food that had false and misleading labels. When their inventory was low, the defendants simply relabeled wholesale "Lite & Lean" dog kibble as "Supreme Stew," "Special Puppy Blend," "Special Adult Blend," or "Special Senior Blend," as needed.

Development of Federal Food Laws

Because the United States did not have a significant interstate commerce in food until after the Civil War, the first federal food laws concerned the export and import of food products. An act to prevent the import of "adulterated and spurious Teas" was passed in 1883. Adulterated tea included tea having exhausted leaves or "spurious leaf." Tea that had chemicals "or other deleterious substances" that made it "unfit for use" was also banned. All tea was held at a customhouse for inspection and not released until it had received an examiner's approval. In 1897 this law was repealed and replaced by another that authorized the secretary of the treasury to adopt uniform standards of purity and quality for tea. Imported teas that were "inferior in purity, quality, and fitness for consumption" to federal tea standards were prohibited entry into the country.

The first federal meat law was an 1884 act designed to study livestock that had "pleuro-pneumonia, or any contagious, infectious, or communicable disease" and eliminate its export. In 1890 a law was passed authorizing the inspection of salted pork and bacon intended for export. This law also prohibited the importation of any "adulterated or unwholesome food or drug or any vinous, spirituous or malt liquors, adulterated or mixed with any poisonous or noxious chemical drug or other ingredient injurious to health."

The Meat Inspection Act of 1891 was the first food law specifically regulating interstate commerce. The law authorized federal inspection of all cattle, sheep, and hogs in interstate commerce "prior to their slaughter" and, thereafter, the marking or stamping of those meat products

from animals "found to be free of disease, and wholesome, sound, and fit for human food." The scope of this law was narrow. It did not give federal inspectors the power to address the generally unsanitary conditions in the meat processing and meatpacking industry. The description of these conditions in Upton Sinclair's novel *The Jungle* led to passage of the Meat Inspection Act of 1906.

Although Congress was aware of the movement of adulterated food in interstate commerce, the first comprehensive Pure Food and Drug Act was not passed until 1906. Passage of such a law by Congress did not go unchallenged. Many people thought that the federal government did not have the authority under the commerce clause of the Constitution to regulate adulterated food. They argued that only states had the right to set standards and regulate the quality of food. That dispute was resolved in a series of cases decided by the United States Supreme Court in 1911, 1913, 1916, and 1918. The Supreme Court confirmed that Congress had the power to regulate interstate commerce in food and seize adulterated products that were "outlaws of commerce." The Court stated that Congress "has the right not only to pass laws that regulate legitimate commerce among the states and with foreign nations, but has full power to keep the channels of such commerce free from the transportation of illicit or harmful articles, to make such as are injurious to the public health outlaws of such commerce and to bar them from the facilities and privileges thereof." Although there were some problems with enforcement and interpretation of the Pure Food and Drug Act of 1906, the power of the federal government to prohibit the introduction, movement, and delivery of adulterated and misbranded food in interstate commerce was never again seriously questioned.

The full extent of the federal government's power over interstate commerce in food found expression in the Federal Food, Drug, and Cosmetic Act of 1938. For most foods in interstate commerce, this comprehensive law explicitly authorized the establishment of federal definitions and standards of identity, federal standards of quality, and federal container standards for the amount of fill. Adulterated foods were broadly defined to prohibit any food that was "injurious to health" from entering into interstate commerce. In addition, fraudulent substitutes and all other forms of economic adulteration were prohibited. The act mandated that certain minimum information be printed on a label, and it prohibited false or misleading labeling and the use of names of foods not represented in a product unless labeled "imitation." While there have been some substantive amendments since its passage, including the Miller Pesticide Amendment of 1954, the Food Additives Amendment of 1958, and the Color Additive Amendment of 1960, the 1938 act remains the backbone of federal regulation of U.S. food.

State and Local Regulation

Although the federal government regulates imported food and all food moved in interstate commerce, states still retain the right to pass laws governing foods that are placed into interstate commerce. Any state rule or regulation that does not conflict with federal law is allowed to stand. A state is therefore free to pass laws and regulations prohibiting the use of certain additives, for example, even though the use of those additives is allowed under federal law.

In the 1919 case of *Weigle v. Curtice Bros. Co.*, a Wisconsin law prohibiting the sale of any food containing benzoic acid or benzoates was challenged by a ketchup and bulk-sweet-pickle manufacturer that used benzoate of soda as a preservative. In upholding Wisconsin's right to prohibit benzoate of soda as an additive, Justice Oliver Wendell Holmes wrote: "When objects of commerce get within the sphere of state legislation, the state may exercise its independent judgment and prohibit what Congress did not see fit to prohibit."

The extent of the state's power to regulate food may not always be this clear, as illustrated by *Grocery Manufacturers of America, Inc. v. Gerace*, a 1985 case. New York had passed a law that required printing the word "imitation" on any package containing artificially made cheese. In addition, New York ordered restaurants in the state to display a sign near a proprietor's cash register notifying purchasers of any products containing artificial cheese, and to add the words "contains imitation cheese" to menu listings and cheese shakers that featured such products. A federal court reviewing the validity of the New York law ruled that requiring the package to have "imitation" on the label conflicted with federal law (the label "imitation cheese" is not required under federal law) and struck down that portion of the New York law. The cash-register signs and menu and container provisions were found to be valid, however, since they were a local state matter, not placing any significant burden on interstate commerce.

Many states have laws and regulations designed to protect economically important local food products, such as the New York laws pertaining to imitation cheese,

which protect the state's dairy industry. California, as another example, has specific laws and regulations that protect its avocado, navel orange, and Valencia orange industries. California also has specific regulations for bottled water, butter, eggs, honey, ice, olive oil, organic foods, tomatoes, and wine grapes.

Local government regulation of food focuses primarily on food safety at local retail food facilities and establishments. Food facilities may include vending machines, produce stands and farmers' markets, ice cream and taco trucks, and any other stationary or mobile food-preparation unit. Food facility permits are required, and the permit application, issuance, and inspection process is designed to ensure that a local retail food establishment conforms to all local and state food safety laws. A facility that violates the laws may be cited and risk having its permit to operate revoked.

State and local retail food safety laws direct that food be pure and free from contamination, adulteration, and spoilage. Regulations therefore establish standards for food storage, food handling, sanitation, and hygiene. For example, most state and local regulations require that potentially hazardous foods, like meat, seafood, and eggs, be held at or below 41°F or at or above 140°F (to prevent the growth of bacteria), that certain foods be cooked to minimum temperatures (for example, ground beef to 155°F), that utensils and cutting boards be cleaned and sanitized when switching between foods to prevent cross-contamination, and that food handlers wash their hands with hot water and soap for at least twenty seconds at specified times (before starting work, when switching between foods, and after eating).

There are, however, some significant limitations on the right of a state or local government to regulate food. For example, the establishment clause of the Constitution precludes the government from promoting or prohibiting any religion. New York passed a kosher fraud law that required that foods labeled "kosher" be prepared "in accordance with Orthodox Hebrew religious requirements." A kosher meat dealer was fined for not following this law. In his defense, the meat producer explained that a rabbi who followed Conservative Hebrew religious requirements actively supervised his kosher operation. In *Commack Self-Service Kosher Meats, Inc. v. Weiss*, a 2002 case, a federal court threw out the New York law as unconstitutional in violation of the establishment clause because the kosher fraud laws entangled the government in religious matters, promoted the Orthodox Hebrew position on kosher, and enforced the Orthodox view of kosher food over those of other branches of the religion.

[*See also* Adulterations; Pure Food and Drug Act.]

BIBLIOGRAPHY

Levenson, Barry M. *Habeas Codfish: Reflections on Food and the Law.* Madison: University of Wisconsin Press, 2001.

ROBERT W. BROWER

Leeks

Leeks (*Allium ampeloprasum porrum*) are cylindrical onions with a white base that bleeds into green leaves. They can be fried as a vegetable, braised or boiled as a vegetable or salad, and used to flavor soups, stews, and stocks.

Colonial Americans seem to have made little use of cultivated European leeks. John Josselyn's *New England's*

American Flag Leeks. From the 1894 catalog of Peter Henderson & Co., New York.

Rarities Discovered (1672) praised indigenous "wild Leekes," probably *Allium canadense*, "which the Indians use much to eat with their fish," and other early sources talk about gathering the wild plant. Some early American cookbooks may have envisioned leeks, wild or cultivated, in braised onion recipes, as they specify "the white kind" or suggest cooking the onion with some of the tender green attached. Mrs. N. K. M. Lee's *Cook's Own Book* (1832) uses them for seasoning but asserts, "they are very rarely brought to table." Only two varieties of leeks appear in Bernard M'Mahon's 1815 seed catalog.

Leeks grew modestly in popularity in the later nineteenth century, when numerous French cultivars were introduced and more recipes appeared in French-influenced cookbooks. Although easily found at supermarkets, leeks remain bit players in American cookery.

[*See also* Heirloom Vegetables; Onions.]

BIBLIOGRAPHY

Faccioli, Stephen. *Cornucopia: A Source Book of Edible Plants.* Vista, CA: Kampong, 1998.
Weaver, William Woys. *Heirloom Vegetable Gardening.* New York: Holt, 1997.
Phipps, Frances. *Colonial Kitchens, Their Furnishings, and Their Gardens.* New York: Hawthorne, 1972.

CATHY K. KAUFMAN

Legal Issues, *see Law*

Lemonade

Lemonade, which in its simplest form is a drink made from lemon juice, sugar, and water, has a history dating back to at least the thirteenth century, when Arab cookery books offered recipes for drinks made from lemon syrup. The Mongols enjoyed a sweetened lemon drink preserved with alcohol, and the Persians enjoyed *sharbia*, from which the English "sherbet" derives. By the mid-seventeenth century the drink was popular in Europe when *limonadiers*, street vendors in France, sold lemonade at modest prices. A lemonade recipe appears in the 1653 English translation of LaVarenne's *The French Cook.*

Lemonade arrived in America no later than the eighteenth century, imported from the various European cultures of immigrants. Recipes varied widely. One might begin by bruising sugar and lemon rind together; another added a single sliced lemon directly into water; yet another required a large quantity of juice. Many started off with lemon and sugar syrup, which could be bottled and stored for later use. Some added milk, and others clarified cloudy lemon juice by adding an egg and then straining the liquid. Mary Randolph's *The Virginia House-wife* (1824) included an iced lemonade recipe that is actually a sherbet. The popularity of homemade aerated, or effervescing, lemonade paralleled the rise of commercially available lemon-flavored soda water. By the 1860s several bartender's guides contained "lemonade" recipes that packed a wallop from the various wines and spirits added to the sweetened lemon juice.

But lemonade's image underwent a transformation engendered by the temperance movement, which turned lemonade into a genteel Victorian drink. The First Lady Lucy Webb Hayes, a teetotaler, forbade virtually all alcohol in the White House of the 1870s, thus garnering the moniker "Lemonade Lucy." Modern technology also helped the juice flow: household juice extractors, a vast improvement over the gadgets of the past, appeared in the second half of the nineteenth century. Hostesses conspicuously served front-porch visitors from pitchers specifically designed for the beverage. They also brought the beverage along on picnics. Lemonade's popularity rose unabated, prompting the 1901 New Orleans *Times-Picayune's Creole Cook Book* to proclaim, "Lemonade is among the most delightful and most commonly used of all Fruit Waters."

Lemonade also was considered a tonic, served to those suffering from colds (hot "flaxseed lemonade") or to invalids. The Shakers, an American religious sect, read in the April 1881 issue of their *Manifesto*, that "lemonade is one of the healthiest and most refreshing drinks of all drinks; suitable for almost all stomach and bowel disorders and excellent in most sicknesses." Lemonade also proved useful in the westward expansion, particularly in the forms of dried "portable lemonade" and "lemon sugar," for which recipes appeared in many cookbooks. A photographer along the Union Pacific noted in his 1869 diary that he "used a good deal of 'portable lemonade' " to counter the brackish taste of the local river water.

As the twenty-first century opens, lemonade flourishes at all points along a commercial and culinary spectrum: from instant powder and imitation lemonades that historically relied for tartness on essence of lemon, lemon oil, and tartaric or citric acid, to the frozen concentrate introduced in 1950s, to ready-to-drink supermarket varieties, to homemade "front-porch lemonade," to flavor variations such as ginger, blackberry, or pineapple.

[*See also* Fruit Juices; Homemade Remedies; Temperance.]

ROBIN M. MOWER

Lentils, *see Beans*

Leslie, Eliza

Although Eliza Leslie's cookbooks were reprinted dozens of times, Leslie maintained that her first love was fiction, finding herself drawn to it even as a child. Born the eldest of five children in Philadelphia in 1787, she was educated primarily at home by her father, a self-taught watchmaker and mathematician, who counted Thomas Jefferson and Benjamin Franklin among his friends and fellow members of the American Philosophical Society. When he died in 1803, he left the family virtually penniless, and the sixteen-year-old Eliza and her mother opened a boardinghouse in order to support the family.

Leslie's first commercial success resulted from attending the Philadelphia cooking school of Mrs. William Goodfellow, where she took copious notes. At her brother's behest, she collected them in *Seventy-five Receipts for Pastry, Cakes and Sweetmeats* by "A Lady from Philadelphia." Published in 1827, this became one of America's earliest and most popular cookbooks.

Leslie took great pleasure in writing fiction, particularly juvenile stories about American children. Her stories for adults, which often punctured America's social pretensions and pointed out the defects of American manners, appeared in most of the day's leading magazines. Despite her preference for fiction, she admitted that most of her income came from the many editions of her books on domestic economy. After the success of *Seventy-Five Receipts*, she published *Domestic French Cookery* (a translation, 1832), the *Domestic Cookery Book* (1837), *Directions for Cookery in Its Various Branches* (1837), *The House Book* (1840), *The Ladies' Receipt Book* (1846), *Miss Leslie's New Cookery Book* (1857), and several volumes on etiquette. Although Leslie never acknowledged her cooking teacher in her books, the publication of *Mrs. Goodfellow's Cookery as It Should Be* in 1865 is widely believed to be the work of Eliza Leslie.

Leslie's success depended in large measure upon her concern for American housewives. She declared that all the ingredients and utensils necessary for her recipes were available in the United States. She drew heavily on such easily obtained foods as pumpkin, cranberries, clams, wild grapes, green corn, and Indian meal, with recipes for baked Indian pudding, flannel cakes, johnny-cakes, and Indian bread. She professed to believe in accurate measurements and provided tables of equivalencies, recommending an accurate scale and a set of tin cups in graduated sizes, but sometimes violated her own precepts, however, calling for "a teacup of sugar" or "a small wineglass of brandy." Lists of ingredients preceded each recipe in her early books, but she later strayed from this model and reverted to the more conventional style of combining ingredients and directions into one or two paragraphs. Some of her recipes were clearly British and French in origin, but each book remains firmly American in style, with recipes for Federal cake, Connecticut cake, election cake, catfish, Yankee tea cakes, and okra.

Leslie never married, supporting herself by her writing. She lived the last few years of her life at the U.S. Hotel in Philadelphia, holding court for a wide variety of celebrities, friends, and relatives. Leslie had a reputation as a somewhat difficult curmudgeon, since she was often abrupt and critical, yet she devoted much of her time to charity and those close to her described her as warm and loving.

[*See also* Cookbooks and Manuscripts, *subentry* From the Beginnings to 1860.]

BIBLIOGRAPHY

Hale, Sarah Josepha. *Woman's Record; or, Sketches of All Distinguished Women from "The Beginning" till A.D. 1850*. New York: Harper & Bros., 1853.

Hart, John S. *Female Prose Writers of America*. Philadelphia: E. H. Butler & Co., 1852.

Haven, Alice B. "Personal Reminiscences of Miss Eliza Leslie." *Godey's Lady's Book* (April 1858): 344–350.

James, Edward T., ed. *Notable American Women*. Vol. 2. Cambridge, MA: Belknap Press, 1971.

VIRGINIA K. BARTLETT

Lettuce

Lettuce is any plant of the genus *Lactuca*. Its wild ancestors were commonly distributed in Europe and Asia in prehistoric times. A semiwild type called spindly lettuce grows in the Mediterranean, which suggests that lettuce cultivation probably began there. Ancient Egyptians, Greeks, and Romans cooked lettuce and also served it raw. Cultivated lettuce (*L. sativa*) was grown throughout Europe during the Middle Ages and the Renaissance, and it was among the first Old World plants introduced into the New World.

Both leaf and head lettuces were commonly grown in colonial and early American times. Lettuce was highly perishable and was available only locally in season. However, lettuce became more readily available in the twentieth century with the development of crisphead lettuce (iceberg is the most familiar). With sturdy leaves forming a compact, round head, these lettuces can be transported over long distances without damage. Distributed by railroad from California and Arizona, lettuce became an important year-round food in America. During the 1920s and 1930s its production tripled.

Lettuce was the main ingredient in salads, from the ubiquitous lettuce and tomato salad to the Caesar salad, and in sandwiches, from the BLT to the hamburger sandwich.

The most commonly consumed varieties are iceberg and the long-leaved romaine (also called cos). With salads becoming more prominent in the American diet, butterhead lettuces, such as Bibb and Boston, and loose-leaf lettuces, such as red leaf, are gaining a wider audience. Most recently, the gourmet "mesclun" mixes of baby lettuces have become common in restaurants and even supermarkets, where industrially produced, prewashed bags of mesclun and other lettuces offer consumers unprecedented ease in preparing salads at home.

[*See also* Salads and Salad Dressings.]

BIBLIOGRAPHY

Book of Lettuce and Greens. rev. ed. Burlington, VT: National Gardening Association, 1985.

Davis, R. Michael, Krishna V. Subbarao, Richard N. Raid, and Edward A. Kurtz, eds. *Compendium of Lettuce Diseases*. St. Paul, MN: American Phytopathological Society, 1997.

Ryder, Edward J. *Lettuce, Endive, and Chicory*. New York: CABI Publishing, 1999.

ANDREW F. SMITH

Library Collections

Libraries in the United States that contain major culinary collections vary greatly in their holdings. Some concentrate on contemporary material, while others have very old material or collections focused on specific areas. Large culinary collections suitable for serious research most often reside at major universities or independent research libraries, though a few exceptions are found in public libraries and professional culinary schools.

Collections of culinary literature and books on cookery and food have been built in various ways. While some institutions set out to build culinary collections for specific purposes, others received donations of large private libraries that reflect the areas of concentrations of the original owners. Many of the collections grew to their current size in land-grant universities in support of home economics departments. Only a sampling of these collections is given here; many other fine collections exist.

Collections in Universities and Public Institutions

The Arthur and Elizabeth Schlesinger Library on the History of Women in America at the Radcliffe Institute for Advanced Studies at Harvard University, Cambridge, Massachusetts, maintains a collection of more than sixteen thousand cookery books. This is an excellent culinary research resource, especially when supplemented by the holdings of the Widener Library in history, anthropology, and sociology and the early and rare culinary material in the collection of the Houghton Library, both at Harvard. The Schlesinger collection has much material on the history of cuisines and in regional cooking, especially that of New England.

The University of Iowa holds a large portion of the great library of the late chef Louis Szathmary of Chicago, which includes many rare and unusual works. This major research collection is rich in books and ephemera also, with particular strength in nineteenth-century Americana.

Hale Library, on the campus of Kansas State University in Manhattan, Kansas, is rich in early materials, which are housed in its Special Collections Department. The collection contains early English works, including several editions of Hannah Glasse's *The Art of Cookery Made Plain and Easy*, which first appeared in England in 1747. The general collection of the library is also strong in cookery books and related material that make possible studies in the social history of food.

There are culinary collections at two libraries that are part of Indiana University in Bloomington, Indiana. The Lilly Library has both depth over several hundred years and breadth in areas of concentration. It is especially strong in American, English, French, German, and Italian material from early times to the present. The main library at Indiana University at Bloomington has significant holdings in Chinese, Japanese, and Korean cuisines.

The Library of Congress, in Washington, D.C., serves the same function for the United States that the British Library does for the United Kingdom and the Bibliothèque Nationale for France. Like these two, the Library of Congress is considered the library of last resort for researchers, who are expected to try all other resources first. The Library of Congress holds an extraordinary collection of community cookbooks and also much locally specialized material. It is rich in regional American works and has a strong representation in both classic and contemporary cooking. The library also holds an excellent collection of books on early and contemporary French, English, and Italian cookery and a substantial number of books on French Canadian cookery.

Along with community cookbooks, recipe booklets produced for inclusion in cooking appliances and food products are a significant part of the history of home cooking in the twentieth and twenty-first centuries. The culinary collection of Michigan State University holds many of these. The collection also has an unusual profile, holding some early English and French works in the original and is also strong in the cooking of Africa and in Jewish cookery. The library holds a complete run of the scholarly journal *Petits propos culinaires*.

The Los Angeles Public Library, the library for the City of Los Angeles, California, Science and Patents Division, has substantial holdings in Pacific Rim cookery, as well as many books on Mexican and African cookery and a wide representation of books on barbecuing that cover aspects from slow-cooked pit barbecue to grilling and smoke cooking. America's California-style cookery is also a strong feature of the collection, as are the foods of the American South and Southwest and the Caribbean. Also well represented are Italian, French, Indic (referring to the cookery of the Indian subcontinent), and Russian cuisines.

The collection of the New York Academy of Medicine in New York City contains material on the history of cookery, gastronomy, nutrition, and dietetics. The collection contains some very old and rare materials, including a ninth-century manuscript written by Apicius, *De re culinaria Libri I–IX*, on vellum. The library has later, print editions written by Apicius as well. The library holds other old manuscripts and incunabula relating to cookery and gastronomy. Items in more than twenty languages date from 900 C.E. to the present and focus on the Western world.

The New York Public Library, the library of the city of New York, has extensive culinary holdings in its Research Division. The collection is especially strong in American cookery and in early and contemporary African, English, French, and Italian cuisines. The library also has complete runs of *Petits propos culinaires* and *Gourmet* magazine, along with many other periodicals.

The Blagg-Huey Library on the campus of Texas Women's University at Denton, Texas, is strong in general cookery of the late twentieth and early twenty-first centuries, including American, English, French, and Mexican works. The collection focuses on cooking in the home and contains broad representations of community and organization cookbooks, recipes accompanying equipment and products, and the publications of county extension services. The collection was begun in 1960 with the Marion Somerville Church Collection and was built further with the addition of the Julie Benell Collection and the Margaret Scruggs Collection of regional cookbooks. A number of seventeenth-century collections of recipes and related medical information are to be found here. The library includes a large representation from the American Southeast, Louisiana, and Texas.

The Penrose Library of the University of Denver in Denver, Colorado, holds over eight thousand volumes of culinary material, divided between the main stacks and the Special Collections Department. The Special Collections holdings are strong in nineteenth- and twentieth-century American materials and the collection has some very early European works in excellent condition. Because of its focus on home cooking, the library is a fine resource for those researching the social history of food and cooking in the home.

A large number of works related to food and cooking are dispersed throughout the collections of the University of Michigan. The collections are especially strong in American foodways and American culinary literature. It also has online access to all of the culinary material in the Early English Books Online collection. But what are most remarkable are the large holdings in original languages pertaining to Japanese, Chinese, and other East Asian cuisines.

The University of Pennsylvania libraries, home for the culinary collection of the late Esther Aresty, hold many pre-1800 American works, including some very early volumes and manuscripts. There are also early works on English cooking. Other cuisines especially well represented are Mexican, Brazilian, and Indic.

Library Collections at Culinary Schools

The City College of San Francisco's Alice Statler Library has been assembled to serve students in the hospitality program. It contains considerable material on management of food, beverage, and hospitality establishments, but in addition it actively supports studies in food and culture. The library has begun a large project to provide a body of digitized rare texts that will eventually be available online.

The Conrad Hilton Library at the Culinary Institute of America in Hyde Park, New York, displays exceptional breadth in modern-day cuisine and books on ethnic and regional cookery. Much of this information is available in translation for the student who does not read languages other than English, although some books are in other languages. The library provides an excellent base for a comparative study of cuisines of the early 2000s. Modern editions of some early texts are also available.

The Culinary Archives and Museum of Johnson and Wales University in Providence, Rhode Island, holds a vast number of books, periodicals, and ephemera valuable to a culinary researcher. Among these are the collection of rare books donated by Paul Fritsche and many books and ephemera from the collection of the late chef Louis Szathmary and other prominent persons in the culinary field. In addition, the Culinary Archives and Museum features a wealth of objects related to culinary work. The entire collection comprises, by the estimate of the archive staff, more than 400,000 items. Because of the size and complexity of the collection, arrangements should be made ahead of time to use it. The Culinary Library, a separate facility at Johnson and Wales, is designed for the use of students in its culinary program. It focuses on contemporary and recent cooking and management issues.

Many other libraries in the United States have fine culinary collections. An examination of their online catalogs is the place to begin for readers interested in working in one of these libraries. Many require special permission for visitors to use them. As at the University of Michigan, many works produced outside the United States and England are in their original languages. Considerable fluency may be required to use them.

Another consideration in using these collections is that of accessibility. As collections have grown and the space to house them has become more expensive to build, many libraries store books that are not often used in premises away from the library itself. It is therefore necessary to determine the location of a book and verify how long it may take to retrieve it from off-site storage before setting out to use the library.

[*See also* Cookbooks and Manuscripts.]

BIBLIOGRAPHY

Aresty, Esther B. *The Delectable Past: Notes on the Author's Collection.* New York: Simon and Schuster, 1964.

Bitting, Katherine Golden. *Gastronomic Bibliography.* San Francisco, 1939.

Cagle, William R. *A Matter of Taste: A Bibliographical Catalog of International Books on Food and Drink.* 2nd ed. New Castle, DE: Oak Knoll Press, 1999.

Cagle, William R., and Lisa Killion Stafford. *American Books on Food and Drink.* New Castle, DE: Oak Knoll Press, 1998.

Feret, Barbara L. *Gastronomical and Culinary Literature.* Metuchen, NJ, and London: Scarecrow Press, 1979.

International Association of Culinary Professionals Foundation. http://www.iacpfoundation.com. Contains a more detailed description of library collections.

Oxford, Arnold Whitaker. *English Cookery Books to the Year 1850.* London: Oxford University Press, 1913.

MADGE GRISWOLD

Lime Rickey

The lime rickey is a nonalcoholic, sweet, refreshing lime soda, sometimes made with actual lime pulp, and sometimes augmented with cherry or raspberry. The term can also refer to a drink of rum, coconut syrup, cream, and lime juice shaken with ice and served in a half-coconut, but this recipe is less common. The nonalcoholic lime rickey was sold at soda fountains and ice cream shops possibly as early as the 1920s. (Other lime drinks, such as lime cola and green river, were particularly popular around 1918.) In the 1940s Seaman's Beverages began selling a mass-market, bright-green bottled version of the lime rickey that was still available in Canada in 2002. In the United States by that time, lime, raspberry-lime, and cherry-lime rickeys were generally available only in Boston and New England ice cream shops and diners. For a time, the lime rickey was served at the American chain restaurant Friendly's.

Originally, a rickey was any iced alcoholic drink mixed with lime and carbonated water, the most popular being the gin rickey. That drink owes its name to Colonel Rickey, an 1890s lobbyist in Washington, DC, who fre-

quented a tavern called Shoemaker's and liked lime juice with his liquor. By 1906 bartenders were serving gin, brandy, whiskey, and vermouth rickeys.

[*See also* Cocktails; Soda Drinks.]

JESSY RANDALL

Lincoln, Mrs.

Mary Johnson Bailey Lincoln (Mrs. David A. Lincoln), cooking teacher, cookbook author, and first principal of the Boston Cooking School, was born July 8, 1844, in South Attleboro, Massachusetts. Hired in 1879 by the Cooking School Committee of the Women's Education Association to teach at the Boston Cooking School, Mary J. Lincoln had no professional training as a cook or a teacher. She had been a Boston homemaker until she was suddenly forced to earn a living to alleviate financial difficulties caused by her husband's ill health. Mrs. Lincoln rose to the occasion by translating her experience in running a kitchen in her own home into a career as one of the most famous late nineteenth- and early twentieth-century American cooking teachers.

When the committee hired her, they stipulated that she take two weeks of classes at the school before starting her job. Lincoln did take several classes in "fancy dishes" from Joanna Sweeney and attended a single demonstration by Maria Parloa, the previous term's teachers, before assuming the positions of both principal and teacher at a salary of seventy-five dollars a month. She remained at the school until 1885, when she resigned to devote all of her time to writing, editing, and lecturing.

The Boston Cooking School never attracted home cooks from immigrant neighborhoods, as had been its intended purpose, but during Mrs. Lincoln's tenure it became a Boston institution training a small number of household cooks and a greater number of their bosses in "plain cooking," "richer cooking," and "fancy cooking." In addition, the "normal" course (referring to normal schools) produced many cooking teachers, supervisors of school and hospital kitchens, tearoom operators, private caterers, and nutrition lecturers. A pioneer of household economics, Mrs. Lincoln offered her students orderly, clearly written, detailed, and extremely thorough information on nutrition, table service, teaching, and "rational cooking." She promoted the movement toward scientific measurement during her tenure at the school. Indeed, her first cookbook,

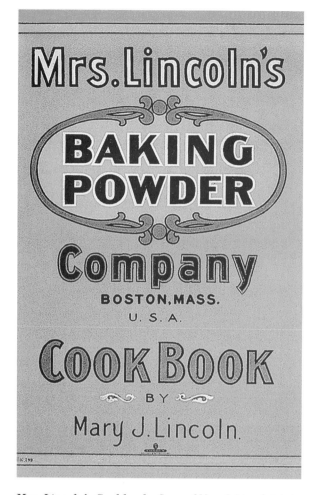

Mrs. Lincoln's Cookbook. Cover of Mary J. Lincoln's baking powder cookbook (Boston, 1899). *Collection of Andrew F. Smith*

which became the school's primary text, contained detailed directions for using the measuring equipment available at the time. Fannie Farmer, who graduated from the Boston Cooking School and later became its most famous principal, had studied from that text and built on Mrs. Lincoln's foundation when she perfected and popularized the system of level measurements with standard cups and spoons that is still used in America today.

After leaving the Boston Cooking School, Mary J. Lincoln wrote for *American Kitchen Magazine*, was co-editor of *New England Kitchen Magazine* with Anna Barrows, and promoted products that she felt were "pure foods." Her books include *Mrs. Lincoln's Boston Cook Book* (1884), *Mrs. D. A. Lincoln's Boston School Kitchen Text-Book*; *Lessons in Cooking for the Use of Classes in Public and Industrial Schools* (1884), *Mrs. Lincoln's Cook Book: What to Do and What Not to Do in Cooking* (1896), *The Home Science Cookbook* (1902), *What to Have for Luncheon* (1904), and *Home Helps: A Pure Food Cook Book* (1911). Most were reissued many times, and the textbook Mrs. Lincoln wrote for the Boston public school system's cookery classes set the model for domestic science programs in schools all across the country.

[*See also* Boston Cooking School; Farmer, Fannie; Measurement; Parloa, Maria.]

BIBLIOGRAPHY

Krondl, Michael. *Around the American Table: Treasured Recipes and Food Traditions from the American Cookery Collections of the New York Public Library*. Holbrook, MA: Adams, 1995.
Shapiro, Laura. *Perfection Salad: Women and Cooking at the Turn of the Century*. New York: Farrar, Straus and Giroux, 1986.

JOANNE LAMB HAYES

Liquor Cabinets

Liquor cabinets were introduced in Europe during the fifteenth century as a means of keeping alcohol under lock and key in public houses or as a way to transport small quantities of alcohol. In colonial America, cellarettes—freestanding cabinets or chests—crafted from wood and fitted for bottles were among the more common objects for storing wine, Scotch, whiskey, and rye. During the Revolutionary War, officers' cellarettes were outfitted with more elaborate accessories, such as hand-blown crystal decanters, pitchers, glass funnels, shot glasses, and drinking goblets. Cellarettes remained in use through the Civil War and well into the twentieth century in public houses and private homes.

During the federal period (1788–1825), liquor cabinets began to give way to more conventional storage facilities that would become a standard for design: upright cupboards, sideboards, and breakfronts. These were crafted from mahogany and sometimes included marble tops. "Pedestal-end" sideboards incorporated a separate, freestanding cellarette.

Prohibition (1920–1933) generated an active underground movement of illegal alcohol consumption, as well as new methods for keeping illegal alcohol safe. Storage facilities ranged from subterranean storerooms to revolving faux walls ("libraries") in drinking establishments and private homes. Cellarettes enjoyed a renaissance, in the form of new variations that included trompe l'œil cabinetry designed to transform ordinary household furnishings—drop-leaf tables, bookshelves, and end tables—into objects that could conceal contraband substances.

The beverage cart was invented in the 1930s as a means of serving alcohol to passengers traveling by rail, cruise ship, and air or to guests enjoying hospitality in private homes. Upright cupboards, sideboards, and breakfronts were transformed into lavish lacquered wooden (burled walnut or bird's-eye maple, for example) objects with mirrors, etched glass, and halogen lights. Cabinet doors folded out into drop-down shelves; ample space was provided for the storage of alcohol and bar accessories, chrome or silver juicers, and Bakelite "martini-picks."

[*See also* Cocktails.]

BIBLIOGRAPHY

A Dram of History presented by Dr. David "The Scotch Doc" McCoy. http://www.scotchdoc.com/tsd/seminars/dramhist.html. Provides photographs and descriptions of cellarettes.

Montgomery, Charles F. *American Furniture: The Federal Period (1788–1825), in the Henry Francis du Pont Winterthur Museum.* New York: Viking Press, 1966.

Wilson, Richard Guy, Dianne H. Pilgrim, and Dickran Tashijian. *The Machine Age in America, 1918–1941.* New York: Brooklyn Museum in association with Harry N. Abrams, 1986.

JANE OTTO

Literature and Food

Americans consume stories the way they consume food, voraciously, and American fiction reflects this gastronomic and literary passion with its artistic, symbolic representations of food production and consumption, of food rituals and feasts. The Canadian novelist Margaret Atwood explains in *The CanLit Foodbook* that "eating is our earliest metaphor, preceding our consciousness of gender difference, race, nationality and language. We eat before we talk" (p. 2). Food becomes the social basis of most human interchanges, experiences, and communication, and, as symbol, encodes multiple languages of signification that examine power, gender, value, and creativity in literature.

In both real life and literature, food is oftentimes more than nourishment; Joyce Carol Oates notes in *(Woman) Writer* that "food . . . is a kind of poetry . . . it seems scarcely to exist in itself but rather as an expression of metaphor" (p. 310), functioning as a symbol of success or failure, of wealth or poverty, of civilization or savagery; sometimes it displays a taste of the sacred in the profane

and is frequently a text of self-discovery. The language of food-as-symbol in literature allows the reader to get at the uncertainties and unknowns of life by examining food tropes about power, self, and cultural expressions. As Kim Chernin observes in *The Hungry Self*, "an obsession with food is always, at heart, an expression of some attempt to bring about either profound personal transformation or entry into collective life and its spiritual meanings" (p. 168).

Food-as-metaphor in literature comes to symbolize America's collective life. Just as specific regions become known for special foods, regional fictions reflect the race, class, gender, and geopolitics of each place.

Immigrants: Anzia Yezierska

America and American literature began as a melting pot of other nationalities and narratives. The best example of food-as-metaphor is found in the New World fictions of Anzia Yezierska, an eastern European, Jewish immigrant. Food procurement, preparation, and consumption function as a symbol of self-development and identity formation for her characters. Writing in a tenement on the Lower East Side of New York during the early decades of the twentieth century, Yezierska announces her predilection for food in such titles as *Hungry Hearts* (1920) and *Bread-Givers* (1925). For her, cultural assimilation is mirrored in the adoption of American food and foodways; mealtimes and table manners symbolically measure one's integration into the New World. For Yezierska's heroines, to be American is to abandon Old World energetic cooking and relishing of food and to conform, instead, to a stereotype of simpering ineffectuality and fasting; ironically, to become an American is to be hungry in the new land of plenty for her characters.

The Northeast: Edith Wharton and Gloria Naylor

In a reverse immigration movement, the American novelist Edith Wharton transplants Americans from the New World to the Old; in *The House of Mirth* (1905) her Americans remain Americans no matter what the geography. In the heart of the gastronomically rich European scene, they search for un-foreign food, which underscores their Yankee snobbery. Descended from Old World Puritan stock, Wharton's Yankees devour whatever is not new as they eat well-cooked, Old World style peas and terrapin. They remain powerful in their isolationism. Yezierska's characters forget their birth nationalities to become Americans; Wharton's always remember they are Americans no matter where they are geographically.

Gloria Naylor, a black writer from New York, urges her protagonists to define themselves racially by the foods they do not eat. In her 1985 novel, *Linden Hills*, her characters remove themselves from their African American heritage by binging and purging or starving themselves to death. In order to assimilate into the white world, they must erase their blackness and their appetites for black food; instead of greasy pork ribs, collard greens, deep-fried catfish and the like, her characters nibble lettuce and cucumbers, dabs of fish, and cottage cheese. Maxwell Smyth in *Linden Hills* so controls his food that he lives his life in the bathroom, a prisoner to his elimination of clear, white foods in his attempt to negate his natural blackness. Bulimia and anorexia define Naylor's African American characters.

Southern Women Writers

African American foods and identity also filter into southern literature. Perhaps more than in any of the other regional literatures, the southern narrative is a story of growing up, and it is defined by its symbolic food matrix of southern plenty and well-being; the self-discovery narratives and the tables of these rites of passage stories groan with the antebellum comfort foods of fried chicken, ham, greens, gravy, and gumbo. It is southern women writers especially who put their signature on this regional literature. For Eudora Welty, Carson McCullers, Flannery O'Connor, Gail Godwin, Josephine Humphreys, Ellen Gilchrist, Lee Smith, Ellen Douglas, Fannie Flagg, Anne Tyler, Kaye Gibbons, and Sheila Bosworth, to name the most prominent, the kitchen becomes the heart and soul of the southern narrative and the female narrator its fertile nurturer.

The Midwest: Willa Cather and Ernest Hemingway

Plains narratives also reinscribe the feminine. The archetypal author here is Willa Cather, who examines the relationship between immigrants, the land, and the self in her many novels. Her descriptions of food are as detailed as any aesthetic description of a work of art, and her theme is always food as a gesture of love. *My Ántonia* (1918), for example, opens and closes in a kitchen; three of its five sections are organized around food production: growing crops in a wild land; establishing a community that will provide these crops to the world; and creating a secure home in this

new country. Like Yezierska, Wharton and others, Cather defines the narrating self in terms of the region and its food.

The most American of accents, the most American of foods, and perhaps the most American of narratives come from the heartland of America: the Midwest. The quintessential figure here is Ernest Hemingway, who was born in Illinois. He incorporates all regions and all accents in his fictions and uses food as a code to heighten or intensify a moment of adventure in his fiction. From celebratory food in *The Sun Also Rises* (1926) to last suppers in *A Farewell to Arms* (1929), from the meals in *A Moveable Feast* (1964) to the nonexistence of meals in *To Have and Have Not* (1937), the shared communion of food or lack thereof symbolizes the relationship between the characters and the world. Hemingway's archetypal protagonist, Nick Adams, celebrates his union with himself and nature with a meal by the Big Two-Hearted River, thus providing one of the quintessential food-as-self metaphors in American literature.

To examine food as metaphor in American literature concisely is to look to the geography of the United States. Like William Butler Yeats's observation that one cannot tell the dancer from the dance, so one cannot separate American literature from its regional food roots; foodways and literary byways become one.

[*See also* Midwestern Regional Cookery; Settlement Houses; Southern Regional Cookery.]

BIBLIOGRAPHY

Atwood, Margaret, comp. *The CanLit Foodbook: From Pen to Palate: A Collection of Tasty Fare.* Toronto: Totem, 1987.

Chernin, Kim. *The Hungry Self: Women, Eating and Identity.* New York: Harper, 1985.

Oates, Joyce Carol. "Food as Poetry." In *(Woman) Writer*, pp. 310–315. New York: Dutton, 1988.

MARY ANNE SCHOFIELD

Low-Calorie Syrup

For centuries people mixed sugar with water or fruit juice to create syrups used as sweeteners or flavorings or to deliver medications. Artificial sweeteners opened the door for the low-calorie and sugar-free market, starting with saccharin, discovered in 1879. Its use became widespread when sugar was rationed during World War I and II.

Before the 1960s, dietetic products were sold to people on medically restricted diets, such as diabetics. But during the 1960s, when people became more health conscious, and during the 1970s fitness boom, so-called light products, meaning low calorie or low fat, became more popular. By 2003 with over 65 percent of Americans, more than 135 million people, overweight, both dieters and low-calorie converts had incorporated light products into their lives.

Low-calorie breakfast syrups often use artificial maple flavoring. Other low-calorie syrups for desserts and beverages, for instance, include flavors ranging from chocolate and vanilla to fruit, liquors, nuts, and spices. Food and beverage manufacturers have many newer artificial sweeteners with a wide range of sweetness, supplying few or no calories, to choose from. They may combine them or use them singly. Syrups made from these artificial sweeteners satisfy a strong demand for safe, low-calorie, tasty foods and beverages, because Americans still want to eat their favorite foods but without the calories.

BIBLIOGRAPHY

The Calorie Control Council. http://caloriecontrol.org. Describes how to reduce dietary calories and fat to lose and maintain weight and how multiple ingredients, including low-calorie sweeteners, improve food and beverage taste. Describes trends and statistics, recipes, exercise recommendations, and FAQs.

ELISABETH TOWNSEND

Lowenstein, Eleanor

Eleanor Lowenstein (1909–1980) was a definitive bibliographer of culinary Americana and seller of rare cookery books. A native of New York City, she held forth many years in the Corner Book Shop on lower Fourth Avenue, a mecca for cooks and food historians. A chosen few were occasionally invited to browse in her fabled private holdings.

[See also Cookbooks and Manuscripts, subentry From the Beginnings to 1860.]

BIBLIOGRAPHY

Lowenstein, Eleanor. Bibliography of American Cookery Books, 1742–1860. 3rd ed. Worcester, MA: American Antiquarian Society, 1972. Based on American Cookery Books, 1742–1860 by Waldo Lincoln.

KAREN HESS

Lüchow's

In the 1880s, when New York City's Union Square was a cultural crossroads—home to the Academy of Music, Steinway Hall, and Tony Pastor's Music Hall—Lüchow's German restaurant was the haunt of musicians, actors, and writers who came for the pigs knuckles, sauerbraten, bratwurst, roast goose, schnitzel, and Würzburger beer and stayed for the gemütlichkeit. Notables who were seen at Lüchow's included O. Henry, H. L. Mencken, Theodore Dreiser, Lillian Russell, John Barrymore, Enrico Caruso, Richard Strauss, and Victor Herbert, who for four years led the resident string ensemble in Viennese favorites. Even when the beer stopped flowing—Prohibition spelled the end for many establishments—Lüchow's hung on. The day Prohibition was repealed, one thousand guests came to quaff seidels of Würzburger.

Lüchow's was founded by August Guido Lüchow, who came to New York from Hanover, Germany, in 1879. Within a few years he had bought the beer hall at 110 East Fourteenth Street where he had worked as a waiter. Part of Lüchow's charm was its decor. The oak-paneled walls were covered with European paintings, photographs of celebrated customers, and elaborate mirrors. The Hunt Room had twenty-one mounted deer heads, and in the Nibelungen Room there were murals representing scenes from Wagnerian opera. Hundreds of beer steins lined the walls. At holiday time, the restaurant hosted the city's tallest indoor Christmas tree.

In the 1950s a number of old-fashioned dishes that had not been served since the 1920s were reinstated by the new owner Leonard Jan Mitchell, who also revived the old festivals—Bock Beer, May Wine, Venison, and Goose—with special menus and music. Mitchell also compiled Lüchow's German Cookbook, published in 1952. Like many old-fashioned German restaurants across America, the restaurant closed its East Fourteenth Street doors in 1982. Following a brief revival in a midtown location, Lüchow's closed for good.

[See also German American Food.]

BIBLIOGRAPHY

Mitchell, Leonard Jan. Lüchow's German Cookbook. Garden City, NY: Doubleday, 1952.
Patrick, Ted, and Silas Spitzer. Great Restaurants of America. Philadelphia: Lippincott, 1960.

BONNIE J. SLOTNICK

Lunch, see Meal Patterns

Lunch Boxes, Dinner Pails, and Picnic Kits

In the eighteenth and early nineteenth centuries, farmers, miners, laborers, schoolchildren, and city workers carried meals (especially the midday dinner now called lunch) in wooden boxes or wrapped in oiled paper or cloth. Tinplate boxes made by tinkers were used in the early 1800s, as were reused tin biscuit boxes.

In the 1850s meals began to be carried in fitted metal pails and boxes. Most of these containers were made of sheet metal, tin-plated to be sanitary and resist rust, and formed into stacked compartments or pails within pails. They had metal handles and bands or leather straps. Most contained a drinking cup. Workers carrying their tin-boxed meals were referred to in a trade newspaper (*The Metal Worker*, 1882) as the "tin pail brigade." Miners sometimes used large fitted tin trunks, which held meals for a whole crew. Some city workers of the 1880s and 1890s carried small stamped and decorated lunch or sandwich carriers, which were disguised to look like books or little satchels. In the 1880s and later, biscuits and tobacco were sometimes sold in colorful lithographed tin boxes, which could be used for lunch boxes after their original contents were gone. Invented in 1892, glass-lined vacuum bottles or thermoses kept liquids hot or cold. Children's lunch kits with thermoses and the familiar workers' lunch kits shaped like little barns with a pullout drawer for the thermos and cup were in wide use by the 1920s.

Picnic kits—usually baskets fitted with tin plates, cups, flatware, and thermoses—became common by about 1910, as automobiles gave people an easy way to travel into the countryside for recreation. Children's lunch boxes were decorated amusingly with appealing characters as early as 1902, but most were made after 1930. The first children's lunch box with a cartoon character on it appeared in 1935 and depicted Mickey Mouse, but it was not until 1950, with decals of television's Hopalong Cassidy, that decorated children's lunch boxes became hugely popular. Decades later many lunch kits were made either of plastic or insulated fabric. Take-out fast food made lunch boxes for workers largely obsolete.

[See also Containers; Picnics; Tailgate Picnics.]

BIBLIOGRAPHY

Aikins, Larry. *Pictorial Price Guide to Metal Lunch Boxes and Thermoses*. Gas City, IN: L-W Book Sales, 1994.

Franklin, Linda Campbell. *300 Years of Kitchen Collectibles: A Price Guide for Collectors, with 60 Color Pictures and 400 Black and White Illustrations*. 5th ed. Iola, WI: Krause, 2003.

Woodall, Allen, and Sean Brickell. *The Illustrated Encyclopedia of Metal Lunch Boxes*. West Chester, PA: Schiffer, 1992.

LINDA CAMPBELL FRANKLIN

Luncheonettes

Strictly speaking, luncheonettes are small restaurants, the suffix implying size, where light meals are served at lunchtime. The term does not always refer to freestanding dining spots but could mean food service counters within other establishments, such as Woolworth's five-and-ten stores.

Restaurants specializing in midday meals appeared in America with industrialization and the intensification of office work in cities and towns. In the early to mid-nineteenth century the concept of lunch, dining away from home during the workday, became regulated by the clock as was work itself. Eating fast had long been an American characteristic, but quick service was now required when lunch breaks might last only thirty minutes.

Lunch service for people engaged in business dates to the mid-eighteenth century, when a New York City tavern offered it, only to be accused of destroying home life. The real progenitors of the fixed-location lunch places were street vendors who served urban populaces, as they still do, notably in New York City. They served varieties of raw and cooked foods, from oysters to sausages. Quick service counters may have emerged with railroads in the 1850s; food counters were introduced in Chicago in 1852 or 1854 with the new connections to its western hinterlands. The food counters were typically horseshoe shaped, later with high stools, to minimize the number of servers needed.

The idea spread to cities, especially catering to middling class people and to the growing numbers of women who were entering workforce as clerical staff. H. M. Kohlsaat opened a "dairy lunch room" in the Loop in Chicago specifically as a safe place for young women to dine quickly and cheaply. His restaurant featured swivel stools, the later standard for the industry. By the early twentieth century, entrepreneurs, such as John Raklios, had set up chains of "luncheonettes" in Chicago and across urban America. The name, coming from "luncheon," suggested a better grade of dining than the blunter "lunch" or "lunch counter."

The food served in early luncheonettes was hot, mostly meats (chicken à la King and chipped beef on

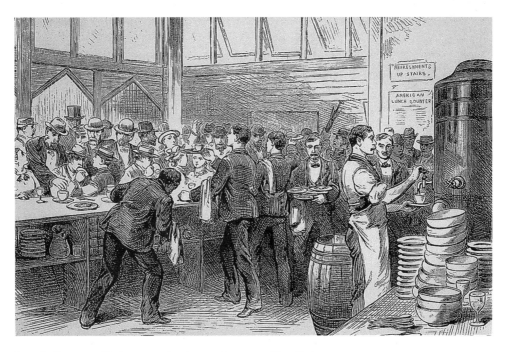

Lunch Counter. Eating scene in nineteenth-century New York.

toast after World War I), but with cheese and egg dishes along with coffee and teas. By the 1920s menus had begun to offer lighter fare. A 1934 pulp novel describes one such as place "a roadside sandwich joint, like a million others." Ham, grilled cheese, BLT, egg salad, tuna salad, perhaps grilled hamburgers (with or without cheese), tuna melts, and others were sandwich staples. Many were served on toast, not available until commercial toasters came into use in the 1920s. Soups, from chicken noodle to tomato, reheated from food service cans, were also featured. For healthier fare, salads—such as ham, chicken, macaroni, and tuna—were served with iceberg lettuce and unripe tomatoes.

However, some dishes were regional; grits were almost always on southern luncheonette menus. Some lunch places, drugstore lunch counters especially, became soda fountains serving national or regional soft drinks and ice cream creations.

With the advance of national fast food chains, beginning in the later 1950s, classic luncheonettes have mostly disappeared from the American dining scene. Some remain as nostalgic reminders of a past life, but usually with modernized menus.

[*See also* Restaurants; Sandwiches; Soda Fountains.]

BRUCE KRAIG

Macadamia Nuts

The macadamia nut tree (*Macadamia integrifolia*) originated in the rain forests of Queensland, Australia, and was first domesticated in 1858. In 1882 William Purvis brought the first macadamia nut trees to Hawaii, where they were widely planted. The horticulturist Walter Storey introduced macadamia trees to California, and other states have attempted to grow them. However, most of the world's commercial macadamias are still grown in Hawaii. Creamy-fleshed macadamias are the highest in fat and calories of all tree nuts; they are usually enjoyed on their own but are also incorporated into candies, cookies, and luxurious desserts.

[*See also* Hawaiian Foods; Nuts.]

ANDREW F. SMITH

Mai Tai

Victor Bergeron, also known as Trader Vic, tells the following story about the mai tai in his book *Trader Vic's Bartender's Guide*. He was experimenting at the bar of his original *Trader Vic's* location in Emeryville, California with a fine sixteen-year-old Jamaican rum he had purchased. When he finished, he served the drink to his friends from Tahiti, Ham and Carrie Guild. After tasting the drink, Carrie raised her glass and said, "*mai tai roa ae,*" which means out of this world, the best, in Tahitian. "That's the name of the drink," replied Bergeron. He often said it was "one of the finest drinks I ever concocted."

Many years later in 1970 over drinks with Jim Bishop, a syndicated newspaper columnist, and Donn Beach, his biggest competitor and the pioneer of the tiki drinks craze, Bergeron admitted that Donn had come up with the original mai tai. In actuality the two recipes are completely different.

Bergeron's mai tai is a sweet and sour rum drink; the sweet ingredients are orange curacao and orgeat syrup, a milky almond flavored syrup used extensively in Italian baking. The sour ingredient is fresh lime juice. Don the Beachcomber's recipe calls for a Jamaican and a Cuban rum mixed with grapefruit, lime, Cointreau, and falernum along with a dash of bitters and a dash of Pernod. To make Trader Vic's mai tai, combine 2 ounces of aged rum, ¾ ounce of orange curaçao, ¾ ounce of lime juice, and ¼ ounce of orgeat syrup. Shake well with ice and strain into an old-fashioned glass filled with ice. Garnish with mint sprigs and a piece of lime.

[*See also* Cocktails; Rum.]

BIBLIOGRAPHY

Bergeron, Victor J. *Trader Vic's Bartender's Guide*. New York: Doubleday, 1972.
Bergeron, Victor J. *Trader Vic's Rum Cookery and Drinkery*. New York: Doubleday, 1974.

DALE DeGROFF

Manhattan

One of the most important drinks in the world of the cocktail-mixing bartender, the Manhattan, created by an unknown mixologist, probably in the 1870s, was one of the first cocktails to utilize vermouth as a balancing agent. Originally made with straight rye whiskey, sweet vermouth, bitters, and a dash of curaçao or maraschino liqueur, the recipe has changed, though not substantially, over the past century or more.

The first cocktail book to be printed, *How to Mix Drinks; or, The Bon-Vivant's Companion* (1862) by Jerry Thomas, contained no mention of the Manhattan, but his next book, *The Bar-Tender's Guide; or, How to Mix all Kinds of Plain and Fancy Drinks* (1887), contained a recipe for the drink, and this time span coincides with the growth of sales of vermouth in the United States. Sweet vermouth became popular before dry vermouth, to the point where many recipe books prior to 1900 called for "vermouth" without differentiating between the two types. After that time, cocktail books started to call for either vermouth or dry vermouth, thus indicating that the sweet variety was more commonly known.

Thomas's recipe calls for twice as much vermouth as whiskey, but in 1906 a book by Louis Muckensturm, *Louis' Mixed Drinks with Hints for the Care and Service of Wines*, reversed the ratios, and the whiskey became the base of the drink. Since then, apart from myriad variations on the theme, the Manhattan has not changed a great deal.

After the repeal of Prohibition in 1933, Americans started to refer to blended Canadian whiskey as rye, since the Canadians used much rye in their formula at that time, and it was far easier to find than straight American rye. Blended Canadian whiskey became the base of the drink, but the formula stayed pretty much the same. During the 1980s and 1990s, when bourbon was enjoying a resurgence in popularity, many people started to order bourbon Manhattans and shied away from the Canadian version. This was also the period when bitters began to be omitted from the formula, but for no apparent reason other than perhaps a little laziness on the part of American bartenders.

The Manhattan is one of the most difficult drinks to make correctly, mostly because, in order to achieve proper balance in the cocktail, the mixologist must take into consideration the style of whiskey being used and also the brand of vermouth. Whiskeys and vermouths vary fairly drastically from one bottling to the next, so a keen knowledge of ingredients is required in order to make a good Manhattan cocktail.

[*See also* Cocktails; Vermouth.]

BIBLIOGRAPHY

Behr, Edward. *Prohibition: Thirteen Years That Changed America*. New York: Arcade Publishing, 1996.

Grimes, William. *Straight Up or On the Rocks: The Story of the American Cocktail*. New York: North Point Press, 2001.

Johnson, Harry. *New and Improved Illustrated Bartender's Manual*. New York: Harry Johnson, 1900.

GARY AND MARDEE HAIDIN REGAN

Maple Syrup

During the six-week "maple moon" of consistently warm, sunny days and cold nights in late winter, sap flows through sugar maples (*Acer saccharum*) and black maples (*Acer nigrum*) from eastern Canada to Minnesota and as far south as Kentucky. Since at least the mid-1500s, North American Indians and early European forest travelers drank the clear, barely sweet liquid, which was at times their only source of nourishment.

Anthropologists and historians debate the point, but it is probable that the Indians were the first both to tap maple trees and to distill their sap into syrup. Sap was collected through carved wooden spigots ("spiles") inserted into ax cuts in the tree. The colonists learned both the method of making syrup and an appreciation for the sweetener from the Indians.

Maple sugar takes a lot of work to produce. Sap is less than 3 percent sugar; thirty-two to forty gallons of sap boil down to just one gallon of syrup, and eight gallons of syrup boil down further to make one pound of maple sugar. But, historically, maple sugar may have been more useful than maple syrup.

Early colonists liked their desserts sweet, but they also liberally doused savory dishes with sweeteners. However, even muscovada, the coarsest brown cane sugar, was costly. Pragmatic Americans used the cheapest source available, maple sugar or syrup from nearby woods, to appease a sweet tooth. To many seeking a more neutral alternative, this "Indian melasses," also known as "Indian sugar," was avoided because of its relatively strong taste. To other mid-eighteenth- and nineteenth-century settlers, such as the Quakers, maple sugar was a morally acceptable alternative to cane sugar, which they boycotted. They abhorred the New England–African–Caribbean triangle trade of sugar and molasses, rum, and

Collecting Maple Syrup. Nineteenth-century print. *Culinary Archives & Museum at Johnson & Wales University, Providence, R.I.*

slaves on which they believed many East Coast fortunes were based.

It was not until the eighteenth century that maple syrup and sugar gained widespread use. These remained popular until the end of the nineteenth century. Several factors then conspired to restrict the use of these sweeteners. Among them were a decline in the price of other competing sugars, increased labor costs, a preference for commodity foods, and the introduction of cheaper imitation syrups.

This quintessential North American sweetener (Canada is by far the largest producer) has captured the imagination of pancake eaters but not their taste buds or their wallets: an estimated 90 to 95 percent of Americans have never tasted the real thing. Today's pancake syrups are far removed from maple sap. By law only syrups containing at least 2 percent of maple syrup may use the words "maple syrup." Some so-called maple syrups contain only artificial flavorings. Pure maple syrup is graded according to color (and, at least in Vermont, by depth of flavor). Grades are variously named, from light and delicate (Fancy Grade A Light Amber, for example) through a more robust midrange (Grade A Medium Amber, Grade A Dark Amber, and Grade B) to a commercial grade.

Recipes featuring maple syrup include the favorite of New England schoolchildren: hot maple syrup poured over clean snow to congeal into "sugar on snow," "wax sugar," or "gum sugar." Maple syrup sweetened New Englanders' baked beans, was drizzled over 1880s flannel cakes, and flavored a 1913 Texas ice cream recipe. Maple walnut pie rivals the South's popular cane- or corn-syrup-sweetened pecan pie.

Maple syrup has a unique—and delicious—character. As early tasters noted, it cannot be used as a generic sweetener. It can be tricky to cook with; some cooks suggest treating it as a flavoring rather than a sweetener. But it remains prized. As the Vermont senator George Aiken is said to have observed, "You can bribe anyone in Washington with a quart of maple syrup."

[*See also* Native American Foods; New England Regional Cookery; Sweeteners.]

BIBLIOGRAPHY

Lawrence, James M., and Rux Martin. *Sweet Maple: Life, Lore, and Recipes from the Sugarbush*. Shelburne, VT: Chapters, 1993.
Nearing, Helen, and Scott Nearing. *The Maple Sugar Book*. New York: John Day, 1950.

ROBIN M. MOWER

Margarine

Since its inception, margarine has had to define itself in opposition to butter, at first as a cheaper and then as a healthier alternative. Hippolyte Mège Mouriès, a French chemist, concocted the first margarine out of beef suet and milk in 1869. Two years later he sold his process to Jurgens (later merged with Unilever), a Dutch dairy company that found a ready market for its synthetic butter in industrial Europe's working class. These early margarines were made mostly of imported American animal fats, a cheap by-product of the booming midwestern meatpacking industry. In 1873 an American patent was granted to Mège Mouriès, who intended to expand production to the United States. There was, however, already competition in New York, where the U.S. Dairy Company had begun production of "artificial butter" by that same year.

The butter substitute was so successful that state laws were passed as early as 1877 to protect state dairy interests.

Cooking with Margarine. Jelke Good Luck Margarine recipe booklet, 1927. *Collection of Andrew F. Smith*

Within ten years, even Congress got into the act, passing a bill taxing and regulating the margarine industry. By this point more than thirty factories were churning out margarine. It was particularly the yellow dye added to the many ersatz butters that drew the lawmakers' ire. As a consequence, by 1902 thirty-two states had banned yellow margarine. And once again Washington followed suit, this time by increasing the tax on tinted margarine fivefold. In order to bypass government regulation, purveyors began to provide little capsules of food coloring to knead into the fat. By the 1930s even the armed forces and other federal agencies were barred from using margarine for anything but cooking purposes. Though the campaign against margarine began to let up during the food shortages and rationing of World War II, it was not until 1967 that Wisconsin became the last state to repeal restrictions on margarine.

The composition of margarine has changed with technology. Early margarine got its butterlike texture from naturally occurring, highly hydrogenated animal fats and tropical oils, which remain firm at room temperature. By 1910 the chemistry of hydrogenating vegetable oils had been perfected, and soon it was possible to produce margarine from virtually any oil. In the United States, peanut and cottonseed oil led the way, but tropical oils, milk, and even a little real butter might be added to the mix. Not surprisingly, some of the earliest producers were companies that had a firm grasp of the chemistry of fat from their experience manufacturing soap, like Lever Brothers of New York.

Margarine consumption received a tremendous boost in the late 1960s, when butter and other fats high in cholesterol were deemed practically homicidal and the public was enjoined to turn to margarine as a healthier alternative. As a result, millions of people made the switch. In 1930 per capita consumption of margarine was only 2.6 pounds while butter was 17.6 pounds. On the cusp of the twenty-first century, the average American ate 8.3 pounds of margarine and only 4.2 pounds of butter.

At the moment that margarine's ascendancy over butter seemed unassailable, new research in the 1990s once again muddied scientific opinion. It appeared that the trans-fatty acids, which result when oils are hydrogenated to form solid stick margarine, might pose even greater health hazards than the naturally occurring, saturated fat in butter. What little agreement existed steered the health-conscious consumer toward margarines that are the softest in consistency because they are the least likely to raise the levels of cholesterol associated with heart disease.

As the twenty-first century opened, margarine continued to see gains as producers tinkered with their formulas. The grocery dairy cases were full of butter substitutes: some that actually included butter or other dairy products, most made from some half dozen edible oils, while others even contained pharmaceuticals that promised to lower cholesterol. Chemistry clearly held sway over the fat of the land.

BIBLIOGRAPHY

"Hearty Food." *Newsweek*, November 16, 1998.
International Margarine Association of the Countries of Europe. http://www.imace.org/margarine/history.htm.
National Association of Margarine Manufacturers. http://www.margarine.org.
"Say It Ain't So, Oleo! Even Margarine May Be Bad for the Heart." *Time*, August 27, 1990.
Tanner, John. "Unilever's History." *New Internationalist*, June 1987.

MICHAEL KRONDL

Margarita

The margarita, a cocktail made of tequila, triple sec, or Cointreau, and lime juice served in a salt-rimmed glass, was popularized by Victor J. Bergeron in his chain of Señor Pico restaurants in California during the 1960s. Bergeron went to Mexico to find a recipe but concluded that Mexicans drank tequila straight and did not like tequila cocktails. So Bergeron adapted recipes borrowed from other American restaurateurs. By 1973, his Señor Pico restaurants sold more tequila than did any other restaurant in the world.

While Bergeron popularized the margarita, he did not invent it. Several different origin stories for margaritas have circulated. According to Marion Gorman and Felipe de Alba's *The Tequila Book*, one story traces the margarita to the bar at the Caliente Race Track in Tijuana, Mexico, about 1930. Another credits Doña Bertha, owner of Bertha's Bar in Taxco, Mexico, with the invention of a drink that later evolved into the margarita. The former Los Angeles bartender Daniel Negrete claims to have originated the cocktail in 1936 at the Garcí Crespo Hotel in Puebla, Mexico, naming it after a girlfriend called Margarita. While the margarita may have started out in bars, it quickly spread to Mexican restaurants. Los Angeles's El Cholo café served margaritas a few years after opening in 1927. Another contender for the title of originator was Margarita Sames, who made the drink for houseguests in 1948 while living in Acapulco, Mexico.

Yet another story credited Pancho Morales, a bartender in Tommy's Place in Juárez, with the invention of the drink in 1942.

Whatever its origins, the margarita cocktail quickly spread throughout America during the 1960s. It became a staple in Mexican restaurants in the United States. In Mexico, restaurants that attracted the American tourist trade adopted margaritas. From the original margarita, Anglo tastes encouraged adaptations. Mariano Martinez Jr. purportedly assembled the first frozen margarita with crushed ice in 1971 at Dallas's El Charro Bar. In an attempt to hide tequila's taste, since not everyone liked it, the strawberry margarita and other flavor sensations appeared in bars and restaurants. As the twenty-first century opened, the margarita was one of America's most popular cocktails.

BIBLIOGRAPHY

Bergeron, Victor J. *Trader Vic's Pacific Island Cookbook with Side Trips to Hong Kong, Southeast Asia, Mexico, and Texas.* Garden City, NY: Doubleday, 1968.

Gorman, Marion, and Felipe de Alba. *The Tequila Book.* Chicago: Contemporary Books, 1978.

Smith, Andrew F. "Tacos, Enchiladas and Refried Beans: The Invention of Mexican-American Cookery." In *Cultural and Historical Aspects of Foods,* edited by Mary Wallace Kelsey and ZoeAnn Holmes. Corvallis: Oregon State University, 1999.

ANDREW F. SMITH

Markets, *see Farmers' Markets; Grocery Stores*

Mars

Mars Inc., one of the largest family-owned businesses in the United States and a global confectionery giant, began when Frank C. Mars (1883–1934) launched the Mar-O-Bar Company in 1911, making buttercream candies in his home in Tacoma, Washington. In 1920, Mars moved his company to larger quarters in Minneapolis, introducing Snickers (minus the chocolate coating) and Milky Way (1922) candy bars. Relocating again outside Chicago and renamed Mars Candies in 1926, the company prospered even during the Depression, when it successfully introduced Mars Almond Bar, chocolate-covered Snickers, and 3 Musketeers.

Forrest Mars (1904–1999) worked with his father at Mars Candies, but they had a tumultuous relationship. The younger Mars was sent to England in the early 1930s to start his own company, aided by a sum of cash and the world rights for Milky Way candy bars from his father. Forrest, a driven perfectionist, first worked incognito in Swiss chocolate factories to learn more about candy making. In England he produced a sweeter Milky Way, called a Mars Bar, building a successful candy company in addition to a canned pet food company, Pedigree.

Forrest returned to the United States in 1940, founding M and M Limited in Newark, New Jersey, with Bruce Murrie, the son of a Hershey executive. Borrowing the idea of a hard sugar shell from the British candy, Smarties, they created a chocolate candy—M&M's—that could be sold during the warm summer months when melting was a problem. M&M's became so popular that they were included in soldiers' rations during World War II. The company began using the ad slogan "Melts in your mouth, not in your hand" in 1954, the same year they introduced Peanut M&M's.

The 1960s were a decade of expansion. New plants were built in New Jersey and in Europe. Frank Mars's original company, Mars Candies, was merged with his son's in 1964. The consolidated company was named Mars, Inc. Although it was already the largest dog-food packer in the world, in 1968 Mars acquired another dog food company, Kal-Kan Foods Inc.

During the 1970s and 1980s, Mars fought Hershey Foods for the leadership of the candy industry, a fight ultimately won by Hershey's in the United States. The era also saw the introduction of many new products: Bounty Bars, Combos, Starburst, Skittles, and Twix Cookie Bar. Mars also acquired the Dove Bar in 1985 (a hand-dipped ice cream bar with a thick chocolate coating developed by Leo Staphanos in Chicago in 1956) and created ice cream versions of 3 Musketeers, Milky Way, and Snickers. The company, which also owned Uncle Ben's Rice, successfully introduced Uncle Ben's Rice Bowls (frozen microwave dinners) in the late 1990s.

At the start of the twenty-first century, remaining family owned and notoriously secretive, the company, based in McLean, Virginia, was jointly run by Forrest Mars Sr.'s children, John and Jacqueline Badger Mars. (Another son, Forrest Jr., retired in 2000.) The Mars family had become one of the richest families in the United States.

[*See also* Candy Bars and Candy; Chocolate.]

BIBLIOGRAPHY

Brenner, Joel Glenn. *The Emperors of Chocolate.* New York: Random House, 1999.

Grant, Tina, ed. *International Directory of Company Histories.* Vol. 40. Farmington Hills, MI: Gale, 2001. A continually updated series highlighting major events and histories of large corporations.

JOY SANTLOFER

Marshmallow Fluff

Marshmallow Fluff is a spreadable marshmallow cream developed in the Boston area around 1915 and produced since the 1920s at Durkee-Mower Incorporated in Lynn, Massachusetts. Marshmallow confections were first made by the French, who in the nineteenth century added whipped egg whites and sugar to the sticky sap from roots of the marshmallow plant (*Althaea officinalis*). The gooey result was called *paté de guimauve.* Before that, the sap, harvested from the roots of the plant, was used in northern Europe as a type of gum. During the eleventh century and through the Middle Ages, the mallow sap was also dispensed as a cure for colds.

The original Fluff recipe came from Archibald Query, a Boston-area man who made batches of it in his kitchen. He sold it door to door until the ingredients became too scarce during World War I. After the war, veterans H. Allen Durkee and Fred L. Mower pooled their savings and bought the recipe from Query for five hundred dollars. Durkee and Mower called their early product "Toot Sweet Marshmallow Fluff," a pun on the French expression *tout de suite,* which translates as "right away," and sold it door to door. The "Toot Sweet" was dropped, but the "Fluff" caught on with customers. In the late 1920s, Durkee and Mower began selling their product at retail stores and advertising in Boston newspapers. The first factory opened in 1929. From 1930 through the late 1940s, the company's *Flufferettes* show on the Yankee radio network attracted listeners from around New England.

Though Durkee-Mower also made Sweeco hot chocolate mix (originally Rich's Instant Sweet Milk Cocoa) for nearly thirty years, Fluff has remained its primary product. Recipes that use Fluff have become American classics. Never Fail Fudge, developed with Nestlé in 1956 from First Lady Mamie Eisenhower's recipe, is still reprinted on Fluff labels. The peanut butter–Fluff combination, officially named the "Fluffernutter" in the 1960s, is still a lunchbox favorite in the early twenty-first century. Fluff is also made in raspberry and strawberry flavors, sold around the United States and internationally.

Marshmallow Fluff. Recipe booklet. *Culinary Archives & Museum at Johnson & Wales University, Providence, R.I.*

[*See also* Fudge; Peanut Butter.]

BIBLIOGRAPHY

McLaughlin, Michael. *The Back of the Box Gourmet.* New York: Simon and Schuster, 1990.
Richardson, Tim. *Sweets: A History of Candy.* New York: Bloomsbury USA, 2002.
Marshmallow Fluff. http://www.marshmallowfluff.com. History and current information about Fluff and Durkee-Mower Incorporated.

CLARA SILVERSTEIN

Martini

During the 1990s the word "martini" became synonymous with the word "cocktail" and, in the early 2000s, was used to describe almost any drink served in a V-shaped cocktail glass, also known as a martini glass. The original martini appeared in cocktail recipe books during the

1880s and was made with Old Tom gin (a sweetened spirit), sweet vermouth, bitters (often orange-flavored bitters), and sometimes a little maraschino liqueur. A drink calling for identical ingredients, known as the Martinez, also appeared in cocktail books of that same era.

Some recipes for the Martinez instructed only that one should make it "like a Manhattan substituting Old Tom for the whiskey," indicating that the drink was merely a variation on the Manhattan. Dry martinis, made with dry gin, dry vermouth—usually in equal proportions—and orange bitters, did not appear in cocktail books until the years surrounding the turn of the twentieth century. There are many theories about why the name "Martinez" was changed to "martini," but the most likely answer is that the company marketing Martini and Rossi vermouth changed the name by advertising the drink in American newspapers. Sales of that brand of vermouth were massive compared with sales of other brands at the time, and the company has in its archives a 1906 newspaper advertisement that substantiates this claim.

Orange bitters remained an ingredient in the dry martini right up to, and even after, the years of Prohibition (1920–1933). Even during the so-called Great Drought, at least one book, printed in 1926 and "issued for the St. Botolph Society," detailed a martini that called for two parts gin to one part vermouth. This ratio was adhered to in many cocktail books published shortly after Prohibition was repealed. The bitters did not disappear from the drink in most books until the 1950s. This was also the time when gin became by far the main ingredient of the martini—sometimes comprising as much as seven-eighths of the drink. In 1958 *The Fine Art of Mixing Drinks*, by David Embury, mentioned that some bartenders were merely coating the interior of the cocktail glass with vermouth, shaking the vermouth out so that hardly any remained, and then adding cold gin; still others were employing atomizers to add minuscule amounts of vermouth to the dry martini.

The same book by Embury also states that the vodka martini had reared its head by this time and comments: "It is hard to conceive of any worse cocktail monstrosity than the Vodka Martini." According to Barnaby Conrad III, author of 1995's *The Martini*, the earliest written mention of the vodka martini occurred in Ted Saucier's cocktail book *Bottoms Up* in 1951. Conrad wrote, "The recipe for a 'Vodkatini' was contributed by Jerome Zerbe, photographer and then society editor of *Town and Country*. Zerbe called for 4/5 jigger of Smirnoff vodka and 1/5 jigger of dry vermouth to be stirred with ice; the garnish was a twist of lemon peel." Substituting another liquor for the gin in a martini was also detailed by Embury, who allowed that martinis could be made with spirits such as rum and even tequila, and he included recipes for variations on the drink that called for other ingredients, such as sherry, curaçao, and crème de cassis.

The martini has often been used in literature and film to bring a sense of sophistication to a character. Lowell Edmunds's book *Martini, Straight Up*, published in 1998, explores this use in depth. Some famous people have used the drink to express how "American" something is. For example, President Gerald Ford said in a 1978 speech to the National Restaurant Association, "The Three Martini lunch is the epitome of American efficiency. Where else can you get an earful, a bellyful, and a snootful at the same time?"

Writers have also been known to wax lyrical on the subject of martinis. Bernard DeVoto claimed in his 1948 book *The Hour* that "you can no more keep a Martini in the refrigerator than you can keep a kiss there. The proper union of gin and vermouth is a great and sudden glory; it is one of the happiest marriages on earth and one of the shortest-lived." And the poet Ogden Nash gave us his take on the drink in his famed verse, "A Drink with Something in It":

> There is something about a Martini,
> A tingle remarkably pleasant;
> A yellow, a mellow Martini;
> I wish that I had one at present
> There is something about a Martini,
> Ere the dining and dancing begin,
> And to tell you the truth,
> It is not the vermouth—
> I think that perhaps it's the gin.

The 1971 edition of *Playboy's Host and Bar Book*, written by Thomas Mario, included recipes for martini variations that called for strawberry liqueur, sambuca, pineapple juice, lime juice, and even cream, so it is hardly surprising that by 2000 the word "martini" had become an acceptable substitute for the word "cocktail." But the debate on the question whether "martini" was a logical synonym for "cocktail" raged in the barrooms of America. At the turn of the twenty-first century, it was not uncommon to be offered a menu full of all manner of cocktails when ordering a martini at a bar, and the so-called purist who desired a mixture of gin and dry vermouth had to specify a dry gin martini. The vodka martini, meanwhile, grew in popularity until by the 1990s many bartenders claimed that the vodka version outsold the gin-based variety by at least ten to one.

Garnishes for the martini have varied over the years, but the 1906 book *Louis' Mixed Drinks with Hints for the Care and Service of Wines*, by Louis Muckensturm, suggests a twist of lemon peel, and the 1912 book *Hoffman House Bartender's Guide: How to Open a Saloon and Make It Pay* calls for a cherry or an olive as well as a lemon twist, although the recipe in that book is for a martini made with Old Tom and sweet vermouth. The Gibson, a dry gin martini garnished with cocktail onions, was reportedly created at New York's Players Club in the 1930s, but recipes for the drink without the onion garnish appeared in Jacques Straub's *Drinks*, published in 1914, as well as Tom Bullock's 1917 book *The Ideal Bartender*. By the beginning of the twenty-first century, all manner of garnishes had made their way into martinis, and it was possible at some bars to order the drink served with caper berries, cornichons, or even pickled quail eggs.

[*See also* Cocktails; Gin; Vermouth.]

BIBLIOGRAPHY

Connrad, Barnaby, III. *The Martini: An Illustrated History of an American Classic*. San Francisco: Chronicle Books, 1995.

Embury, David A. *The Fine Art of Mixing Drinks*. New rev. ed. New York: Doubleday, 1958.

Mario, Thomas. *Playboy's Host & Bar Book*. Chicago: Playboy Press, 1971.

GARY AND MARDEE HAIDIN REGAN

Mason Jars. Advertisement for Payne's fruit preserver, which used Mason jars. Reprinted in *Mason Jar Centennial, 1858–1958*.

Mason Jars

The Mason jar—a glass canning jar with a sealable metal lid—revolutionized fruit and vegetable preservation in the home, freeing Americans from earlier, more complicated and less reliable processes of preserving fruits and vegetables. It was the invention of John L. Mason of New Jersey, who had a metalworking shop on Canal Street in New York City. On November 30, 1858, when he was twenty-six years old, Mason patented a self-sealing zinc lid to fit preserving jars. A rubber gasket between the glass lip and zinc lid completed the seal. The inexpensive screw-on lid greatly simplified the canning process and made jars genuinely reusable. As the jars had wide mouths, they were easy to fill. Although his name remained on the jar, Mason's control of his invention was short lived. In 1859 he sold his patent to Lewis R. Boyd, who owned the Sheet Metal Screw Company of New York. Boyd made additional improvements, one of which separated the zinc lid from the contents of the jar. As the jars were easy to use and comparatively inexpensive to produce, their popularity soared, and Mason jars were shipped throughout the United States during the 1860s.

In 1871 Boyd's company was merged with others to form the Consolidated Fruit Jar Company. Since then, numerous companies have manufactured Mason jars, and containers very similar to Mason's original are still in use. Several improvements to Mason's design have been developed over the years. The most important is credited to Alexander H. Kerr, who founded the Hermetic Fruit Jar Company in 1903. Kerr invented a two-piece lid composed of a flat metal disk with a rubber gasket attached to its underside; a threaded metal band, which overlapped the disk, screwed onto the jar and held the lid in place. Once the jar was filled, sterilized, and cooled, the disk was sealed to the jar, and the threaded band could be removed and used for canning another batch. This innovation was employed in the "economy" jar, which has been manufactured ever since.

In additional to improving home canning, the Mason jar also provided the inspiration for major advances in commercial canning. Commercial food processors confronted problems similar to those of home canners. In the late nineteenth century, commercial canners, who packed food into metal cans, began using thick rubber gaskets similar to those used in Mason jars. The rubber rings, however, were cumbersome and costly. Charles M. Ams came up with the idea of lining the rim of the tin can with a rubber cement. This innovation greatly reduced the amount of rubber required and sped up the canning process. The result contributed to the creation of the "sanitary can," which simplified and sped up the sealing process, revolutionizing can manufacture and use.

[*See also* Canning and Bottling; Packaging.]

BIBLIOGRAPHY

Creswick, Alice. *The Fruit Jar Works*. 2 vols. North Muskegon, MI: Leybourne, 1995.

Cruess, W. V. *Commercial Fruit and Vegetable Products: A Textbook for Student, Investigator, and Manufacturer*. 2nd ed. New York: McGraw-Hill, 1938.

Mason Jar Centennial, 1858–1958. New York: GCMI, 1958.

Toulouse, Julian H. *Fruit Jars*. Camden, NJ: Nelson, 1969.

ANDREW F. SMITH

Material Culture and Technology

This entry contains two subentries:

Social Aspects of Material Culture
The Technology of Cooking Containers

People have been fascinated by objects of the past for centuries. This fascination with objects has been concerned with their technology, form, properties, and usage. The linking of material culture and social history is a relatively new academic approach to history that has broadened vistas of American social history and has

contributed to the useful integration of all social sciences. It is a vital part of the cyclical nature of historical change—that is, the ways in which culture determines its own material advances (demand) and the ways in which new materials redirect culture.

Although the following approaches to material culture are discussed separately, it should be understood that, in fact, they were always inextricably interwoven and are impossible to understand any other way.

Social Aspects of Material Culture

It is not possible to separate the materials of cookery and dining from the cultures that produced them. These issues—the constructs of regional and cultural worldviews, value systems, environmental, social, cultural, and physical influences—provide the backdrop for this analysis of food-related objects from the point of view of their users.

Worldview

The prevailing philosophies of a society determine the significance of its material objects. Among many American colonists materialism was a high priority, and ownership of more objects of good quality was an important goal. Unfettered desire for wealth existed early among southern English tobacco, corn, and rice planters, the Spanish of the deep South, the Dutch in the Northeast, and the French throughout the Mississippi River Valley, to name a few.

Culture dictated their choice of objects, and from group to group they did not carry the same value. For example, English American colonists traditionally rejected the "excessive" richness and sensuality of French cookery and its accoutrements. Thomas Jefferson, of English descent, imported a French ice cream maker, a pewter *sorbétière*, drawing the admiration of his cosmopolitan peers, who valued sophisticated dining as a cultural ideal, and the scorn of those with plainer orientations.

Another example of a culture's influence on cooking objects is found in the teachings of the eighteenth-century Amish, who believed that life should be led in surroundings that permitted full attention to the relationship to God. Food was an important bond within their strong families and communities, and their kitchen hearths were equipped abundantly for ambitious cooking and baking, according to the standards of the time. However, as the great industrial innovations of the nineteenth and

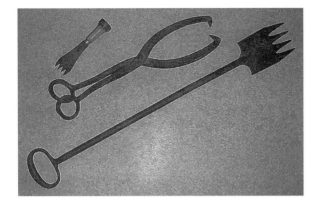

Ice Tongs and Chipper. Tools used for ice at home in the nineteenth century. *Collection of Alice Ross*

twentieth centuries changed the American kitchen, Old Order Amish objects remained largely the same, in the belief that earlier simplicity would be less distracting. Their material culture now appeared out of date and valueless to modernizing contemporaries, who had no such cultural constraints and preferred, among other things, the benefits of electricity.

Other American colonists who emigrated for religious reasons included English Puritans and Quakers (and later Shakers), German and French Huguenots, and French Jesuits, each of whom arrived with differing views on materialism. Puritans believed that prosperity was a divine reward, although the piety and deeds that had presumably earned it were not always obvious. They felt little conflict about enjoying what their wealth could buy and followed the current fashions of menu, table furnishings, or kitchenware as they could.

Among the Dutch, who were early in achieving high levels of international trade, wealth, and culture, riches and possessions were a test of spirituality because of the ongoing conflict between ostentation and humility. The faith of Dutch Calvinists supported frugal daily meals. In contrast, Dutch festive observances revolved around excessive feasting, and they particularly enjoyed the elaborate and complex specialties of commercial bakers, confectioners, and caterers whose services made home ownership of specialized equipment unnecessary. Although they took pride in displays of gleaming copper and brass (and, in later periods, fine porcelains), their kitchens were often modest and their cooking artless.

Shakers were unencumbered by such dualities, were eminently practical, and limited themselves to few possessions. However, their communal kitchens were well stocked with modern (for the time) technologies, often of their own invention. Concerned with efficiency, their equipment accomplished quantity cookery without unnecessary work, and included "arch kettles" (large built-in stew pots of different sizes), "griddle stoves" (also over their own enclosed fires), and specialty ovens for pie or bread, sometimes with permanent shelving built in. In addition they were famous for their fine design and craftsmanship in such kitchenwares as bentwood food storage boxes.

Economics

A family's economic place within a community may be analyzed according to its possessions. Seventeenth- and eighteenth-century American estate inventories, the required listing of each taxable object owned by a newly deceased head of household, offer a way to visualize economic levels. Analyses of these inventories have led to the suggestion that a hearth qualified as a kitchen when it contained a minimum number of cooking utensils—perhaps a hot water kettle, a stew pot, and a frying pan. Then, with increased means, the presence of additional gridirons (broilers) or toasters may have indicated an average kitchen (depending on ethnicity), while chafing dishes, sugar nippers, and spice grinders were associated with those few who could afford the regular acquisition of costly sugars and spices.

The presence of abundant luxurious equipment or tableware is clear evidence that a family occupied a place in the upper economic levels of society. Only the wealthy few owned quantities of silver spoons, imported China bowls, and hot water plates that kept food warm during serving. Also expensive (and of limited use) were salamanders, or heavy, long-handled iron disks, heated in embers and passed over the surface of foods to toast or broil them.

Certain objects are not categorized so easily, as their value was culture-related. For example, in a colonial household maintaining a staunchly English cuisine, the repeated use of toast required a hearth toaster, and it may

---

EXCERPT FROM "A WELCH RABBIT"

Put a Salamander in the Fire, or a large Poker, or the Bottom of a Fire-Shovel heated red hot will do.

—Martha Bradley, *The British Housewife* (London, 1756), used in the American colonies.

COMPARISON OF ESTATE INVENTORIES

LOWER AND UPPER CLASS KITCHEN AND DINING ROOM OBJECTS

Gavin ?ludge, Hempsted, NY, 1735

	Pounds	Shillings
to pewter brass tin earthen and		
knifes & forks	08	03
To 5 Iron Pt & kettle two trammils		
& other Iron things	02	18
1 case of bottles and other		
glass things	01	10

Mordacay Gomez, New York City, 1750

		ounces
1 Large Silver Tankard		44 1/2
1 Ditto		30 1/2
1 Ditto		242 1/8
1 Large silver Cup & Cover		358 7/8
1 Large Coffe Pott & handle		25
1 Silver Tea Pott & handle		11 1/2
1 Silver Mugg		9
1 Silver ?		49 3/4
1 Large Silver Salver		29
2 Salters		
1 Porringer		
1 Spice Box		
1 Milk Pott		
1 Sugar		
1 Small Tea &		
2 Tea spoons & Shovel	[the group]	32 oz 1/4
11 Large Spoon		
3 Tea Spoons		
1 Salt Shovel	[the group]	22 oz 1/2
1 Table Silver spoon		
1 Punch strainer		
1 Punch ladle & wood handle		
1 Supe spoon large		
1 Silver chafingdish & handle	[the group]	41 oz 3/8

1 paire bellows
1 Doz Pewter Plates
1 Brass Toggin Iron
12 New Knives
12 New forks
2 Iron Pott hooks
3 Tea Kittles
2 fry pans
2 Grid Iron
2 frying pans
1 Brass Morter & Pestle
1 Wooden ditto
1 Little brass sauce pan
1 Old brass Skiullet
1 Chaffin Dish
1 Copper ... pot
1 ? chocolate ditto
1 Old Tin Coffee pott
6 Pewter Dishes old, large & small
24 Plates
4 Iron Potts
1 Brass Ladle
Two Brass   ? of the Potts
4 Brass Kittles large & small
1 Iron Chopping knife
2 tinned pooding pans
3 Old Iron potts
3 Pewter porringers
2 Funnels
1 Small brass pepper boc
35 knives
25 forks
1 Pewter bason
1 Large China Pott. broaken
21 China plates, broken & whole
16 Chocolate Cups, ditto
25 Tea Cupps
27 Sawcers
1 China sugar box
1 Tea Pott broek d

Courtesy of the Gomez Mill House Museum, Newburgh, New York

have seemed a necessity regardless of income. Among the Dutch, for whom toast was less significant, such a possession may have been more discretionary and may have represented a luxurious expense.

The economic value of objects also relates to the time they were used and their shifting value over time. For example, a pewter plate in the possession of a seventeenth-century New Netherland family (here a mark of wealth) had an almost opposite meaning from one belonging to a mid-nineteenth-century New York family. The plates were similar, but as they were replaced by later fashionable tableware, their financial value decreased.

Geography, Ethnicity, and Folk Art

Rural and urban wealth took different forms and thus require different standards for interpretation. Before the nineteenth-century growth of cities, the vast majority of colonial Americans were farming, an economic venture in which there may have been wealth but an incommensurate cash flow. Preindustrial farm wealth, traditionally locked up in land, buildings, stock, and equipment, was not always available to expend on basic kitchen or dining room furnishings. The success of farming in various regions of the nation depended on local conditions, among them soils, weather patterns, and water access. For example, bottomland in river valleys was richer than that of the hills and mountains. Natural transportation routes, such as rivers, enabled the ready sale or barter of surplus and the opportunity to acquire more objects.

On the ever-changing frontier a few manufactured goods were supplemented by large numbers of handmade objects. Regardless of the date of settlement and their location, new emigrant homes began with bare necessities, if only temporarily, until further settlement and new trade routes brought access to additional manufactured goods.

Urban areas, even in the earlier colonies, functioned under a different economic system. By definition they were densely populated communities, usually situated on an important body of water that had been instrumental in their original growth and that continued to facilitate the flow of marketable objects to people with cash. Operating on a mercantile and cash-based economy, urban residents had more flexibility in the use of discretionary income than did farmers. Most had less need to invest so heavily in their work, owned more things, and were, according to their means, more attuned to fashion. With nineteenth-century industrialization and rapid growth, city dwellers were faster to acquire new technological advances—refrigerators, cookstoves, canning supplies, and gadgetry—and were more sensitive to changing kitchen and dining room styles.

Geographical location was often associated with ethnic settlements, in which food-related objects were shaped or decorated distinctively. For example, universal redware pottery was slip-painted by Pennsylvania Dutch (Germans) in heart, tulip, and bird motifs, while the English of New York, New Jersey, and Connecticut were known for using wavy lines. The Dutch of New York and New Jersey favored bulbous shapes in their copper and brass teapots, in comparison with the slimmer curves of English and German wares. Some ethnic American communities also required specialized utensils for making

Redware. Redware plate with a slip pattern dating from the eighteenth century. *Collection of Alice Ross*

their own specialties. Germans used sauerkraut stompers and large copper kettles, ring stands, and stirrers for apple butter production. The English, who preferred light or no bread crusts, scraped them off with bread rasps and stocked molds for their traditional puddings. French cuisine required iron or copper *daubières* for potted ragouts, or stews. Baskets were especially regional: the so-called Rice Kingdom worked by Carolinian African Americans used disk-shaped, flat, rice fanners, different from New England winnowers with handles and uneven rims.

These differences started to blur by the 1750s, when widely distributed English imports began to replace local forms. This process was accelerated by successive innovations, especially the improved late-eighteenth-century roads and vehicles and nineteenth-century canals and railroads. Early cultural isolation and local material cultures, first weakened by colonial consolidation against the British, gave way further during the American Industrial Revolution with burgeoning far-flung general stores that had almost identical inventories.

History and Fashion

Fashion and its timing are closely tied to economics. Throughout history most fashion has started at the socioeconomic top, often inspired by expense and scarcity, but gradually becoming available to lower levels when prices moderated. Less often it has been inspired by the sentimentalization of originally modest artifacts, exemplified by the Colonial Revival decor of the 1870s. By the 1880s American industrialization was providing considerably more objects than had been possible one hundred years earlier. Numerous newly patented and ingenious kitchen tools extended the movement toward specialization and saving labor. Women's nineteenth-century homemaker image was enhanced by up-to-date cookery that required specialized equipment, table furnishings, and cookbooks.

In light of the perpetual evolution of technology and fashion, the date at which a possession was owned had a good deal to say about its desirability. For example, the replacement of the kitchen hearth with a new cookstove in 1835 suggested a family on the cutting edge of change, as opposed to one making the change thirty years later. Nineteenth-century gentry, desiring to differentiate itself from lower levels of society, adopted *service à la Russe*, a new style of serving meals. Monumental sets of specialized dinnerware, flatware, and stemware proclaimed exclusivity. Specially designed and shaped dishes displayed designated foods, among them asparagus dishes, celery vases, pickle dishes, and wine glasses. As enterprising manufacturers copied the forms, the new service was eventually embraced by middle- and lower-class households.

Even before the twentieth century, nationwide catalog shopping brought numerous food objects to the most remote kitchens. Such visionaries as Sears, Roebuck and Company and Montgomery Ward educated the public and provisioned homes with a succession of objects, exemplified by simple gas and electric appliances, tins, and agateware. The increasing pace of changes brought a succession of status and convenience objects, among them chafing dishes (1920–1950), fondue pots (1960s and 1970s), powerful electric mixers, bread bakers, and professional knives (1980s and on). Dishwashers and microwave ovens have been elevated to necessity status, and elaborate outdoor cooking equipment became a basis for informal entertaining. As the twenty-first century opened, kitchens furnished with state-of-the-art appliances and cabinetry were the ideal.

[See also Chafing Dish; Dining Rooms, Table Settings, and Table Manners; Fondue Pot; Food Processors; Glassware; Iceboxes; Microwave Ovens; Plates; Refrigerators; Silverware; Stoves and Ovens.]

BIBLIOGRAPHY

Belden, Louise Conway. *The Festive Tradition: Table Decoration and Desserts in America: 1650–1900.* New York: Norton, 1983.

Cowan, Ruth Schwartz. *More Work for Mother: The Ironies of Household Technology from the Open Hearth to the Microwave.* New York: Basic Books, 1983.

Franklin, Linda Campbell. *Three Hundred Years of Kitchen Collectibles.* 5th ed. Iola, WI: Krause, 2003.

St. George, Robert Blair. *Material Life in America 1600–1860.* Boston: Northeastern University Press, 1988.

Schlereth, Thomas J. *Material Culture Studies in America.* Nashville, TN: American Association for State and Local History, 1982.

ALICE ROSS

The Technology of Cooking Containers

The technology of cooking utensils—their materials and design—changed during the course of American history. The changes affected the quality of cookery and were important components of evolving cuisine.

The technology of working basic materials changed little during the eighteenth and early nineteenth centuries despite strong stylistic changes. Objects were made by individual craftsmen with the same kinds of hand tools their great-great-grandfathers had used. Even in large workshops, production revolved around hand methods and hand power. While local craftsmen often made pieces to order for local customers, larger workshops employed many highly skilled workmen capable of tremendous speed, and precision developed through constant repetition. The contrast between local work and large-scale production was not so much a difference in manufacturing technology as a difference in skill level and experience.

Like any other kind of tool, equipment for the hearth is made out of various materials, which are chosen for a variety of characteristics; among these might be cost, availability, performance, desirability, and fashion. Raw materials may be divided into three categories: metals, clays, and organics (animal components and wood).

Metals can be worked in three ways: casting (pouring into a mold while molten), forging (hammering solid metal while it is either hot or cold), or cutting (stock removal). Each method has its benefits and drawbacks. And different metals lend themselves more easily to one method or another. (It is important to keep in mind that since metal objects were usually priced by weight, there was great incentive to minimize use of material.)

Casting can be used to make repeated shapes quickly, though pouring thin pieces is difficult and the metals that lend themselves to casting (lead, pewter, brass, bronze, cast iron) are weaker, meaning that pieces must be made heavier to ensure adequate strength. Forging is generally a freehand process but produces the strongest results. Iron, steel, and copper are usually forged. Light, yet very strong pieces are possible. Brass, although often cast, is much stronger when forged. Cutting produces too much waste to be a viable shaping method but is often used to finish the surfaces of castings and forgings (by filing, grinding, turning, and polishing).

Wrought Iron

Of all the metals used in cooking, the most common was wrought iron, historically called simply "iron." Wrought iron is almost pure iron but contains slag filaments trapped in the bar, giving it a linear grain sometimes visible on the surface. Wrought iron's advantages are high strength, low cost, toughness (because it can bend without breaking), and abundance. It also has the highest melting point of the common metals. Unfortunately, it is only a moderate heat conductor, will not heat evenly enough for dry cooking or sauces, and runs the risk of scorching. Thin pans can heat very quickly and are good for frying or warming liquids. Iron is excellent for andirons, fire tongs, trivets, grills, forks, and spoons. It is worked by forging at the anvil in a typical blacksmith's workshop. Eighteenth-century workmanship ranged from simple and crude to very sophisticated and elegant. Simpler pieces were often left as they came from the anvil, with the texture of forging and occasional hammer marks. Better work was carefully filed bright after forging, leaving smooth and sometimes polished surfaces.

Wrought iron has no dangerous effect on food, although leaving an iron spoon in acidic foods for extended time can alter flavor. Iron will readily oxidize (rust) if left in wet conditions, but keeping pieces dry or oiled between use can prevent this.

Cast Iron

The second ferrous metal in common use is cast iron, or pig iron. It is composed of iron with 2 percent to 4 percent carbon added. As the name implies, this metal is usually worked by casting, either ladled out of the furnace or run from the furnace mouth directly into sand molds. This was the cheapest metal available in the eighteenth century because it is the first stage in smelting iron. Its low cost made it appealing in spite of its greatest drawback—extreme brittleness. But this lack of malleability makes cast iron resistant to warping, and it withstands high heat extremely well. However, cast iron pots are actually fragile and can break if dropped on a hearth. Sudden thermal shock, or expansion of contents during freezing, can also cause breakage. Once broken, cast iron is very difficult to fix. Cast iron is the slowest

heat conductor of all the common metals. This can be problematic except when heating thin liquids or frying. The pieces commonly made from cast iron are pots, griddles, firebacks, stoveplates, Dutch ovens, teapots, and occasionally andirons.

Cast iron is quite benign in its effect on food. Since it is somewhat porous, cast iron will gradually absorb oil and grease until eventually it develops a smooth, nonstick, durable surface. This so-called seasoning is almost unique to cast iron.

The range of use expanded dramatically in the nineteenth century as steadily dropping costs overshadowed the deficiencies. In addition, advancements in casting technology helped eliminate some of the brittleness associated with earlier cast iron, leading to the gradual replacement of wrought iron as the primary metal.

Steel

The third ferrous metal found in the preindustrial kitchen is steel. This was the strongest metal available. It is composed of iron and carbon, like cast iron, but the carbon range is 0.5 percent to 1 percent. Steel is forged to shape just as wrought iron is, though at a lower heat. Since it has almost the same color and texture as iron, it frequently eludes identification. Pieces can be left rough from the anvil or finely finished just like iron. However it can be hardened dramatically by quenching in water or oil. This gives it excellent edge-holding ability and stiffness.

The main drawback of steel was its high cost, so the amount used was limited in each piece. Usually a small amount of steel was welded to the end of an iron tool, giving the advantages of both the economy of iron and the hardness of steel. Cleavers are a good example, since most of the tool could be iron as long as the edge was steel. Common table cutlery is another good example. Each knife and fork had an iron tang, or handle connector, welded to the steel working end.

Articles such as nutcrackers or sugar nippers were frequently offered in iron or steel, with the steel versions being more expensive. The steel pieces are stronger, take a higher polish, and resist rust extremely well. Examples of steel utensils include knives of all sorts, scissors, toasting forks, corkscrews, bread rasps, and sharpening steels.

Tin

Pure tin oxidizes very slowly and imparts very little flavor to foods, making it desirable in the kitchen. However, it is also very soft and therefore has limited use. Tin

Cookware. Advertisement for Lalance and Grosjean Agate Nickel-Steel Ware, ca. 1903. *Collection of Alice Ross*

melts at approximately 450°F, rendering it useless near high heat.

For this reason, tinware, or "tin" as it is often called, is actually composed of wrought iron sheets with a thin coating of tin on the surface. The iron is rolled out very thin, carefully cleaned, and finally dipped in a bath of molten tin to produce the coating. This combination of tin over iron makes a material that is light, strong, and stable. When new, tinplate is silver in color, very shiny, and retains a rippled surface from the dipping. After several years, the surface oxidizes to a dark gray. Tinplate is shaped cold. The sheets are cut with shears and worked over iron and steel stakes with wooden mallets. Finished pieces are made of several parts, either soldered or riveted together. Solder melts at lower temperatures than the tin itself, making exposure to high heat risky.

Tin was well suited to vessels and containers, such as washpans, storage canisters, teapots, inexpensive saucepans, drinking cups, funnels, and molds. It was also used for reflector ovens, though some care was needed to avoid melting the solder. In addition, tin was often chosen for field use, both military and civilian, because of its light weight.

Tinware had been in common use in English kitchens since the late seventeenth century, but its great increase in use came early in the nineteenth century as advances were made in rolling technology. Just as important, many small machines were developed that enabled tinsmiths to speed the process of cutting and forming joints and seams, making tinware very economical.

Pewter

Pewter is a relatively soft metal, composed mostly of tin. The addition of small amounts of antimony and copper produce a somewhat stiffer alloy, but it is still easily bent or dented. Historically, pewter was made in two grades: fine or hard pewter, which was lead free, and common pewter, which had some lead substituted for tin to lower the price. Pewter has little effect on food flavor and oxidizes very slowly. This makes it a popular choice for plates, tankards, teapots, spoons, and other common eating utensils. Its low melting point and softness make it unfit for cooking utensils.

The alloy pours very well, which means that pewter is an excellent choice for casting in permanent brass or bronze molds. Some pieces are made of multiple parts that are soldered together. Pewter is also easily forged cold. After forming, pieces are usually filed and polished to make them smooth and shiny. When new, pewter is a bright silver color, but slightly darker than tin. As is the case with tin, pewter eventually develops a dark gray patina.

Copper

Copper is one of the few pure metals used in the kitchen. It is strong and easy to forge either hot or cold. This metal is one of the fastest heat conductors, making it ideal for saucepans, water boilers, and teapots. However, its relatively high cost limited extensive use to more prosperous kitchens.

Because it is so ductile, copper is often beaten out into thin sheets and made up into vessels of various sorts. Typically, the side of a pot is made of one sheet and the bottom another. The edges of the pieces are notched, interlocked, and soldered with brass, which has a high melting point. Afterwards, the seams are hammered flat and smooth. This produces the characteristic dovetail seams found in coppersmith's work.

Like a number of metals, copper can be stiffened or work-hardened by hammering it while cold. After forming, the piece is systematically hammered all over its entire surface, leaving a regular pattern of planishing marks. This stiffening produces thin yet strong vessels, which keeps costs lower. Frequently an iron rim is used to strengthen a copper vessel, enabling even further lightening.

One serious drawback to using copper is the toxic nature of copper oxide. To avoid health risk, vessels are usually coated inside with tin. Even a thin coating will last many years, and pieces are easily re-tinned when necessary.

Brass and Bronze

"Brass" was the name given to a range of copper-based metal alloys. The two main categories include copper-zinc alloys and copper-tin alloys. Both types normally contain a small amount of lead to improve working characteristics. The zinc alloys are usually softer and yellower in color while the tin alloys are reddish. Both are normally cast in sand molds and subsequently filed, scraped, or polished to give a smooth surface. These alloys are good heat conductors and are well suited for use in saucepans, skillets, and posnets. Forged brass sheeting (copper-zinc alloy) is used for lighter vessels, such as teapots, kettles, and small utensils like ladles, graters, and tinderboxes. Brass is also used in combination with other metals (such as knobs or finials on iron tools). As the end of the eighteenth century approached, the technology for rolling thin sheets improved dramatically, leading to machine stamping as an economical production method.

Ceramics

The earliest American settlers brought and used their own ceramic traditions. English, Dutch, French, and German imports of ceramics were available, but colonial potters manufactured most of the hand-built, inexpensive redware (earthenware), as well as smaller amounts of expensive stoneware. Although redware was fragile, it was easily replaced and was used kitchenwide for cooking, storage, tools, implements, and tableware.

Cookware Redware, so called because of the natural red-brown color of the clay it was made from, was the lowest-fired pottery and the most porous. It was sealed with glazes that required lead, known in the eighteenth century to be a health hazard when in contact with acidic mixtures. It nevertheless had the distinct advantage of easy cleaning, and its even heat transmission reduced thermal-shock breakage caused by uneven expansion. It required gradual introduction to the fire but, once heated

through, it sustained fairly high cooking heats. It performed well in stew pots, small three-legged frying pans, posnets and pipkins (small saucepans), cups and dishware, storage containers, bowls, churns, pie plates, pitchers, and decorative molds.

In the early 1800s, lead-glazed, molded yellowware began to replace redware. Its popularity was attributed to its light color and strength, a product of white, slightly higher-firing clays. Throughout the century, it remained in use in baking pans and pie plates (uniform oven heat avoided thermal shock), mixing bowls, and storage containers.

Stoneware, made of an expensive high-fired clay, was dense, durable, and lead-free, but a poor conductor of heat. More likely to crack when heated, it was suitable for storage jugs and drinking steins. Although its American manufacture dated from the 1630s, its great popularity began in the mid-nineteenth century, when such commercial potteries as Bennington (Vermont) and Wilcox (Pennsylvania) produced gray salt-glaze stoneware crockery, often used for pickling and storage.

Albany slip, a high-fired, New York red clay with a high flux content (improving its ability to adhere to other clay) was used as both a clay and a glaze. It found its most important kitchen applications in pitchers and containers.

In the twenty-first century, ceramic cookware is increasingly available as commercial and hand-crafted casseroles, stove-top teapots, and small skillets, strengthened against thermal shock by the addition of perlite (grit) or lithium.

Dinnerware In addition to early earthenware (redware), the wealthiest households of the eighteenth century sought more colorful, decorative, and delicate styling. European, and then American, potteries produced low-fired majolica, faience, and creamware, often boldly stenciled and painted in intricate patterns. The sometimes-colorful imported tableware was prized for its strength, thinness, and lightness. Among the favorites were Chinese porcelains and Dutch Delft. English Wedgwood and Staffordshire were available in different qualities at different prices.

Nineteenth-century industrialization introduced mechanized methods of decoration that included detailed transfer-printing. Mechanization increased the production of high-fired porcelain, made of kaolin clays, into thinner, finer, and whiter dinnerware. Imported white English ironstone, a porcelainlike, albeit heavy stoneware well suited to simple, everyday dishware, was copied by American potteries and maintained popularity beyond the Victorian era.

In the early 1900s, reoccurring movements that attempted alternately to embrace technological innovation or to celebrate nostalgia, or even to synthesize both, brought a new kind of ceramics to the dining table. Influenced by the early Bauhaus movement and its explorations of modernistic shape and glaze, ceramics appeared as hand-constructed bowls and platters. Succeeding styles evolved into art nouveau, art deco, and, after World War II, a domestic artist-craftsperson movement. Since the 1960s there has been a focus on natural materials and ethnic handcrafts, produced as casseroles, serving bowls, platters, mugs, pitchers, and tea sets.

Wood

One of the earliest materials adapted to kitchen use, wood has been whittled, carved, and turned by foot- or water-powered lathes. For centuries, settlers in various parts of America have valued wood's relative sturdiness, ease of home production and repair, versatility, and low cost, and it was so widely used that historians refer to the "American Wooden Age." They reason that without the availability of wood in American forests, those who explored and settled remote territories could not otherwise have survived, since they could not have carried all their necessities.

Early kitchens were furnished with a wide range of hand-fashioned wooden utensils. The most common included implements (cooking spoons and paddles), bowls (all-purpose, butter-working, chopping, kneading, and dough-raising), containers (butter firkins, spice boxes, barrels for spirits, flour, vinegar, or molasses), tools (mortars and pestles, churns, cookie boards), baskets, tubs, cabinetry (food safes, dressers), or common tableware.

Before the nineteenth century, small "factories" had increased production of uniform wooden kitchenware, and by the 1830s, vestiges of handwork were slowly disappearing. Industrialization standardized such items as chopping bowls, wooden spoons, and handles. In combination with metal, wood provided knife or chopper handles, knobs, butter-working tables, beater blades, sausage grinders, and apple peelers.

Cutting boards and wooden spoons continue to be produced; however, in the late twentieth century such synthetic materials as plastics became common. Most exotic woods were being reserved for serving platters and bowls.

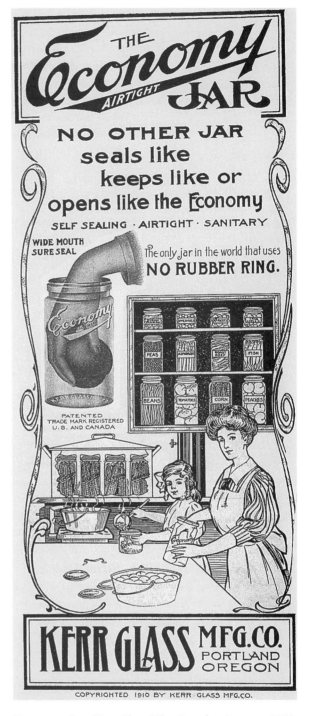

Economy Jar. Kerr Glass Mfg. Co. advertisement, 1910. *Collection of Alice Ross*

Glass

Glass-blowing techniques were brought from Europe in the seventeenth century and developed commercially in eighteenth-century New Jersey, where good-quality silica sand abounded. Limited by fragility and little heat tolerance, glass was used for wine and spirits bottles, carafes, pitchers, drinking tumblers, stemware, punch bowls and cups, decorative serving pieces, and jelly glasses. Home canning jars (the first were produced by Mason in 1858) and inexpensive glassware were introduced by the 1860s. Heat-tolerant Pyrex (1915) was used for bakeware and mixing bowls, followed mid-century by Anchor Hocking and Fire King ovenware.

[*See also* Apple-Preparation Tools; Beer Barrels; Biscuit Cutters; Bread-Making Tools; Butter-Making Tools and Churns; Cabbage Cutters and Planes; Cheese-Making Tools; Cherry Pitters or Stoners; Chopping Knives and Food Choppers; Containers; Corn-Preparation Tools; Doughnut-Making Tools; Dutch Ovens; Egg-Preparation Tools; Frying Pans, Skillets, and Spiders; Kettles; Mason Jars; Pancake Pans; Pie-Making Tools; Potato-Cooking Tools; Pots and Pans; Sieves, Sifters, and Colanders; Silverware; Waffle, Wafer, and Pizelle Irons; Wine Barrels.]

BIBLIOGRAPHY

Barons, Richard, and Devere Card. *The American Hearth.* Binghamton, NY: Broome County Historical Society, 1976.

Cullity, Brian. *Slipped and Glazed: Regional American Redware.* Sandwich, MA: Heritage Plantation of Sandwich Museum, 1991.

DeVoe, Shirley Spaulding. *The Art of the Tinsmith.* Exton, PA: Schiffer, 1981.

Fennimore, Donald L. *Metalwork in Early America.* Wilmington, DE: Henry Francis DuPont Winterthur Museum, 1996.

Garvan, Beatrice B. *The Pennsylvahia German Collection.* Philadelphia: Philadelphia Museum of Art, 1982.

Gentle, Rupert, and Rachel Field. *Domestic Metalwork 1640–1820.* London: Elek, 1975. Revised by Belinda Gentle. Woodbridge, UK: Antique Collectors Club, 1994.

Ketchum, William C., Jr. *American Stoneware.* New York: Holt, 1991.

Lindsay, J. Seymour. *Iron and Brass Implements of the English House.* London: Tiranti, 1970.

Neumann, George. *Early American Antique Country Furnishings.* New York: McGraw Hill, 1984.

Pinto, Edward H. *Treen or Small Woodware Throughout the Ages.* London: B. T. Batsford, 1949.

Roberts, Hugh D. *Downhearth to Bargrate.* Wiltshire, UK: Wiltshire Folk Life Society, 1982.

PETER ROSS

Matzo

Matzo is the unleavened bread baked in great haste by the children of Israel on the eve of their flight from Egypt (Exodus 12:8). Every year at Passover, or the Feast of Unleavened Bread, the eating of matzo and the purging of all leavened products from the home commemorate this flight (Exodus 12:15–39, 13:6–7, and 23:15). Unleavened bread is the only food the children of Israel are actually commanded to eat in the Hebrew Bible. In this sense, matzo is the most Jewish food there is. The foods that are called Jewish foods are almost always the regional foods from areas where Jews have settled in large numbers. These Jewish foods may be different from the local non-Jewish food, but they bear more resemblance to non-Jewish food of their own region than to Jewish food from far away. The exception is matzo. Every Jewish community has some variation of matzo. The variations in shape and thickness, however, are minor, since the laws of matzo manufacture are so very specific. All matzo must be prepared in less than eighteen minutes from the moment water comes into contact with flour to the moment the fully baked matzo emerges from the oven.

For most of its three-thousand-year history, matzo was made only by hand in an exhausting and very expensive process. Because matzo was so expensive, it was generally eaten only on Passover and only by Jews. In the middle of the nineteenth century, with the invention of machinery for matzo manufacture, matzo producers promoted their product as suitable for the whole year.

The first major American matzo concern was started in 1883, when Regina Horowitz Margareten and her husband, Ignatz Margareten, immigrated to Manhattan from Hungary. Their families opened a grocery store on Willett Street on the Lower East Side of New York City. They baked their own matzo for themselves their first year, and the next year they produced extra matzo for sale in their store. A few years later, they abandoned the grocery store to devote themselves to the baking of matzo.

In 1888 Rabbi Dov Ber Manischewitz opened the B. Manischewitz company in Cincinnati, Ohio, to provide reliably kosher matzo in the West. A few years later he opened a second factory in New Jersey and made Manischewitz a national brand. Manischewitz matzo became the best-known and best-selling American matzo, thanks to the company's aggressive campaign to market matzo as a year-round food. The hallmark of this campaign was the commercials on Yiddish-language radio written and recorded by the great Yiddish lexicographer, playwright, and performer Nahum Stutchkoff. In these brilliant spots for Manischewitz American Matzos. Stutchkoff always emphasized the combination of Jewish and American virtues that made Manischewitz matzo

Matzo Advertisement. Horowitz Margareten matzo advertisement that appeared in the 13 March 1953 newsletter of Congregation Shaare Zedek, New York.

unique. In one memorable ad for Tam Tam crackers, Stutchkoff noted that the crackers had two great virtues: a Jewish heritage and an American upbringing. He could have been speaking about his listeners' own children.

By the end of the twentieth century, the Streit's company, founded in 1925, was the only major American matzo company still located in Manhattan.

Most of the matzo consumed in the Americas and worldwide is machine made. There are, however, still matzo bakeries in New York, Montreal, and Israel that make hand matzo. This matzo is called *shmura matzo*, or guarded matzo, to reflect the fact that it is under rabbinic supervision at every point in the process from the harvesting and milling of the wheat to the baking of the matzo.

[*See also* Jewish American Food; Jewish Dietary Laws; Passover.]

EVE JOCHNOWITZ

Maxwell House

Maxwell House Coffee, one of the two dominant mass-market American coffees, was the creation of Joel Owsley Cheek, a rural Kentucky native who served as a "drummer," or traveling salesman, for a wholesale grocery firm. In 1884, he moved to Nashville, Tennessee, and in 1892 approached the Maxwell House, a prestigious Nashville hotel, with his special blend of coffee. Impressed with consumer reaction, the hotel manager allowed Cheek to name his blend after the establishment.

Cheek quit his job in 1893 and formed a partnership with John Neal. The Cheek-Neal Coffee Company established a successful business in the Nashville area, opening additional roasting facilities in Houston, Texas; Jacksonville, Florida; and Richmond, Virginia, by 1916. Six of Cheek's eight sons joined the firm. Cheek was a gracious boss who truly cared for his employees and believed that coffee was a boon to humankind. He was also a master marketer. He adopted the slogan "Good to the Last Drop" in 1920, claiming that Teddy Roosevelt had used the phrase in reference to Maxwell House Coffee. General Foods purchased Maxwell House in 1928, taking the brand national with ads featuring southern hospitality. During much of the Depression the *Maxwell House Show Boat* was the top-rated radio show, with favorite characters slurping the coffee audibly throughout the program.

During World War II, Maxwell House produced patriotic print ads extolling the lift the troops got from instant and regular coffee. In the postwar era Instant Maxwell House ads claimed that its crystals "burst instantly into that famous good-to-the-last-drop flavor," though it tasted only remotely like regular coffee. General Foods also began to put cheaper robusta beans into the regular Maxwell House blend.

In 1960, television viewers saw the now-classic Maxwell House percolator ad, with its perky theme music. The company introduced Maxim, the first freeze-dried instant coffee, in 1964. The following year saw the introduction of the sexist "Be a Maxwell Housewife" commercials, in which a patronizing husband taught his wife to make coffee. Later, the down-home Aunt Cora character touted Maxwell House to counter Folgers's Mrs. Olson.

Despite some heartwarming commercials over the years, General Foods failed to understand or to take advantage of the specialty coffee movement. It pulled innovative 1983 spots featuring the comedian Jerry Seinfeld, and it mishandled the 1985 introduction of whole beans in supermarkets, in part because it distributed to warehouses rather than following the lead of small specialty roasters, who sent out individual supervisors to put freshly roasted beans directly on shelves. Late in 1985, the tobacco giant Philip Morris, looking to diversify in the face of hostility to cancer-causing cigarettes, bought General Foods. Philip Morris also owned Gevalia, a high-quality Swedish coffee roaster, and Jacobs Kaffee, the major German brand, among others.

[*See also* Coffee; Coffee, Instant.]

BIBLIOGRAPHY

Pendergrast, Mark. *Uncommon Grounds: The History of Coffee and How It Transformed Our World*. New York: Basic Books, 1999. Comprehensive business and social history.

MARK PENDERGRAST

Mayonnaise

Mayonnaise is a thick sauce traditionally composed of egg yolk beaten with oil, vinegar, and seasonings. How mayonnaise acquired its name has been debated for years, and the only general agreement is that the word "mayonnaise" was popularized by the French. Historically, mayonnaise was based on aioli, a Catalan and Provençal sauce that combined olive oil, eggs, and garlic. In the late eighteenth century, the French whipped the egg and slowly added oil. The lecithin in the egg yolks acted as an emulsifier and broke the oil into droplets. Mayonnaise became one the five foundation sauces of classical French

cookery. It is an adaptable ingredient, used in many dishes and other sauces.

Mayonnaise was mentioned in cookbooks published in the United States by 1829, but it did not become an important condiment until the end of the nineteenth century. The major reason for this delay was the high cost of imported olive oil. Several factors contributed to the increase in the popularity of mayonnaise in America during the last few decades of the nineteenth century. One was the use of mayonnaise in upscale American restaurants, such as Delmonico's in New York, by French chefs during the latter part of the nineteenth century. Another factor was a decrease in olive oil's price, owing to production of domestic olive oil in Florida and California. Yet another reason was that mayonnaise was used to make salad dressings and other condiments, such as tartar sauce. Indeed, the main use of mayonnaise during the late nineteenth century was on salads and as an accompaniment to cold fish and meats. There had been a vast increase in American interest in fresh green salads, caused in part by a transportation revolution that made it possible to grow salad vegetables in California and Florida and transport them long distances year-round. During the twentieth century, mayonnaise replaced butter as a sandwich spread. Along with the hamburger, American mayonnaise rose to global prominence.

Recipes for making mayonnaise and for using it as an ingredient in other dishes began to appear regularly in American cookbooks by 1880 and in cookery magazines shortly thereafter. Depending on the ingredients, the results of these recipes differed in color (white, yellow, green, or red), taste (garlic, horseradish, or red pepper), and content (salmon, lobster, or chicken). Mayonnaise recipes were targeted for specific use on salads, poultry, fish, shellfish, and meats.

Mayonnaise separates and easily spoils and does not survive the bottling process. Commercial mayonnaise therefore differs greatly from that which is made fresh. The first known attempt to make a commercial mayonnaise occurred in 1907, when a delicatessen owner in Philadelphia named Schlorer mixed up a batch of his wife's mayonnaise in the back of his store and added preservatives. He marketed it as "Mrs. Schlorer's Mayonnaise," and it led to the creation of the Schlorer Delicatessen Company, which produced commercial salad dressings, including mayonnaise. In 1911, Schlorer trademarked his mayonnaise. The company began producing advertising cookbooklets featuring mayonnaise during the 1920s.

Schlorer's competition came from four major firms: Hellmann's, Best Foods, Kraft, and Blue Plate. The German immigrant Richard Hellmann opened a delicatessen in New York City in 1905, and his wife's recipe for mayonnaise was featured in salads sold in the store. In 1912, Hellmann began to sell mayonnaise in wooden containers. Later, he marketed two versions of mayonnaise in glass jars, around one of which he put a blue ribbon. There was such a great demand that Hellmann designed a Blue Ribbon label, which was trademarked in 1926. In the same year, Hellmann produced his first advertising cookbooklet, which encouraged customers to incorporate his mayonnaise into various dishes. In 1932, Richard Hellmann Inc. was acquired by Best Foods Inc.

Around 1912, Gold Medal Mayonnaise Company began producing mayonnaise in California. In 1923, it merged with Nucoa to form Best Foods. Best Foods began publishing advertising cookbooklets featuring its mayonnaise by 1927. When Richard Hellmann's firm was acquired by Best Foods in 1932, Hellmann's mayonnaise was sold east of the Rockies and Best Foods mayonnaise in the west. Both Best Foods and Hellmann's are now part of Unilever. In New Orleans, the Southern Cotton Oil Company, a subsidiary of Wesson-Snowdrift, produced mayonnaise in 1929 under the name Blue Plate Food. Through several mergers, Blue Plate Mayonnaise remains a regional product marketed in the South.

Kraft introduced Miracle Whip at the 1933 Century of Progress World's Fair in Chicago. The company was founded in 1903 by James L. Kraft, who sold cheese in Chicago, Illinois. By 1914, the company had begun manufacturing its own cheese. When Miracle Whip was introduced, Kraft launched a major food advertising campaign, including a weekly two-hour radio show. At the end of this introductory period, Miracle Whip outsold all brands of mayonnaise. In the late 1980s, Kraft introduced Miracle Whip Light and Miracle Whip Cholesterol Free. In 1991, Miracle Whip Free, with no fat at all, was launched. Mayonnaise is a major American condiment: in 2000, Americans purchased more than 745 million bottles of mayonnaise. American mayonnaise is increasingly sold in other countries, which can be attributed, in part, to the global spread of American fast food.

[*See also* Advertising Cookbooklets and Recipes; Condiments; Salads and Salad Dressings.]

BIBLIOGRAPHY

Association for Dressings and Sauces. http://www.dressings-sauces.org/index.html.

Mrs. Schlorer's Salad Secrets. Philadelphia: Schlorer Delicatessen Company, 1924.

SBI Market Profile: Salad Dressings and Mayonnaise. New York: Specialists in Business Information, 1996.

A Treatise on Mayonnaise. Philadelphia: Mayonnaise Products Manufacturers Association of America, [n.d.]

ANDREW F. SMITH

McDonald's

When Ray Kroc, a salesman, met two drive-in restaurant operators, Richard and Maurice McDonald, in 1954, America's foodscape changed forever. Richard and Maurice McDonald, born in New Hampshire, moved to southern California to make their fortune in 1930. After several jobs, they opened a hot dog stand and later graduated to a barbecue drive-in.

The Origins

In 1948, the brothers opened a hamburger drive-in in San Bernardino, California, which applied assembly-line efficiency to the restaurant business. They eliminated carhops and waitresses and did not have indoor tables. Customers ordered their food at an outdoor window and ate it in their cars. The menu was limited to a few items: fifteen-cent hamburgers, nineteen-cent cheeseburgers, french fries, milkshakes, and sodas. Their hamburgers came with ketchup, mustard, chopped onions, and two pickles. All food was served in disposable paper wrappers and paper cups. The brothers sped up the process of making hamburgers through a series of innovations; for example, they assigned some workers to make and wrap the food while others took orders, prepared the drinks, and packed the food into paper bags. They purchased Multimixers, which made five milkshakes simultaneously, to speed up the preparation of drink orders.

The McDonald brothers called this the Speedee Service System. It reduced expenses, permitting the McDonald brothers to sell hamburgers at a lower price. The brothers believed that the increased volume of customers would lead to greater profits. Their efforts to streamline their system and mass-produce hamburgers paid off. In 1951, they grossed $275,000.

As efficient as their internal operation was, the McDonald brothers concluded that they could do even better with a new floor plan. They also wanted a more distinctive exterior architectural design to distinguish their drive-in from the hundreds of other fast food establishments in southern California. Their new plan called for a forward-sloping front and walls painted in red and white stripes. Richard McDonald came up with the idea of constructing yellow or "golden" arches right through the building's roof.

Even before their new design was constructed, the McDonald brothers franchised their operation. This permitted others to build McDonald's drive-ins based on the model developed in San Bernardino. Those receiving franchises paid the McDonald brothers an up-front fee and a percentage of their sales. In 1953, newly designed franchises opened in Phoenix, Arizona, and Downey, California.

Ray Kroc

All the early McDonald's drive-ins attracted crowds. One visitor to the San Bernardino operation was Ray Kroc, born in 1902 in Oak Park, Illinois. After a variety of odd jobs, he had settled on selling Lily paper cups. After seventeen years of selling cups successfully, he launched the Prince Castle Sales Corporation. Its main product was the Multimixer for soda fountains and restaurants. He also sold Multimixers to many fast food franchisees, including Dairy Queen and Tastee Freez. These customers had given Kroc a deeper understanding of the fast food business and some knowledge of the problems related to franchising. In the early 1950s, increased competition had reduced the sales of Multimixers and Kroc needed new outlets. He was surprised to learn that a small San Bernardino drive-in had bought eight Multimixers. His curiosity aroused, Kroc visited the McDonald brothers in 1954.

Kroc saw the potential of the McDonald's operation immediately. Ever the optimist, Kroc met with the brothers and signed an agreement allowing him to sell McDonald's franchises nationwide. In the mid-1950s, franchising consisted mainly of assigning territories to franchisees for huge up-front fees. Kroc had a better idea. He avoided territorial franchises by selling one store franchise at a time, thereby controlling the number of stores a licensee could operate. He also required strict conformity to operating standards, menus, recipes, prices, trademarks, and architectural designs.

On April 15, 1955, Kroc opened his first McDonald's in Des Plaines, Illinois. It was intended as a model operation to attract franchisees. It worked. By the end of 1957, there were thirty-seven McDonald's. Two years

McDonald's. A McDonald's drive-in, sometime after 1958, when 100 million burgers had been sold. *Culinary Archives & Museum at Johnson & Wales University, Providence, R.I.*

later, the total had reached over one hundred. In 1961, Kroc bought out the McDonald brothers for $2.7 million.

The early success of McDonald's rested in part on the managers selected to oversee operations. Kroc's mantra was "Quality, Service, Cleanliness, and Value," which he tried to instill in every franchisee. Kroc was also so committed to training managers that he established Hamburger University, which offered a degree in "Hamburgerology." The first class of fifteen graduated in February 1961. By the early 2000s, sixty-five thousand managers had graduated.

Kroc expanded his operation throughout America. Within a decade of his first encounter with the McDonald brothers, Ray Kroc had revolutionized fast food service through further automation, improved franchising, and national advertising, which began in 1966. The company's promotional campaigns have primarily targeted youth. Ronald McDonald, a clown character, was invented to be the national spokesperson in 1966, and McDonald's began opening children's Playlands shortly thereafter. It has tied in much of its marketing with major children's motion pictures. McDonald's Happy Meal, inaugurated in 1979, packages its food with toys. At the beginning of the twenty-first century, 96 percent of American children recognize Ronald McDonald, and McDonald's is the world's largest toy distributor.

Kroc's success encouraged the growth of other fast food chains, which readily adopted McDonald's methods. To keep ahead of the competition, McDonald's has developed new products regularly, such as the Big Mac with its two patties, introduced in 1968. Other innovations include the Quarter Pounder, the McDLT, and the

McLean Deluxe, a 90 percent fat-free hamburger. In 1983, McDonald's introduced Chicken McNuggets, consisting of reconstituted chicken delivered to franchises frozen and then reheated before serving.

Globalization

McDonald's opened its first Canadian drive-in in 1967. Its success convinced Kroc that McDonald's should expand aggressively to other countries. It has continued to expand abroad ever since. Kroc had originally envisioned one thousand McDonald's operations in the United States. When he died in 1984 at the age of eighty-one, there were 7,500 McDonald's outlets worldwide.

By 1994, McDonald's counted more than 4,500 restaurants in 73 foreign countries. At the opening of the twenty-first century, there were more than 30,000 restaurants in about 121 countries. McDonald's operated over 1,000 restaurants in Japan alone. The most popular restaurant in Japan, measured by volume of customers, was McDonald's. In the early 2000s, the world's largest McDonald's was in business near Red Square in Moscow, where a Big Mac lunch cost the equivalent of a week's paycheck. McDonald's boasted 127 restaurants in China—one of which overlooked Tiananmen Square in Beijing. McDonald's international sales were $15 billion out of a total of almost $32 billion.

In part because of McDonald's success, the company has been criticized on a variety of issues. When it was charged with promoting junk food, the company began selling salads, reduced the fat content of its hamburgers, and changed the way it made its french fries. When charged with causing harm to the environment, McDonald's encouraged recycling, purchased more than $4 billion of recycled materials for its own operations, replaced its Styrofoam containers with a more biodegradable material, and refused to buy beef from Brazil, thus helping to protect the rain forests.

McDonald's has also been charged with having adverse effects on local cultures and businesses around the world. McDonald's success abroad has caused deep resentment in others who see the company as a symbol of the United States and who believe that the expansion of McDonald's threatens local culinary traditions. In France, the sheep farmer José Bové demolished a McDonald's restaurant that was nearing completion. Similar actions have occurred in other European countries. McDonald's has pointed out that its foreign operations are locally owned and most ingredients used in McDonald's restaurants are produced in the country where the franchise resides.

The study of McDonald's has become a hot academic topic. Many popular works have tried to dissect the company's success and examine its influence. Among the more famous studies are George Ritzer's *The McDonaldization of Society* (1993), which examines the social effects of McDonald's in the United States; Benjamin Barber's *Jihad vs. McWorld* (1995), which uses McDonald's as a global symbol for modernization; and Eric Schlosser's *Fast Food Nation: The Dark Side of the All-American Meal* (2001), which looks at the seamier side of fast food. Dozens of other works have examined McDonald's worldwide impact.

By the end of the twentieth century, one of every eight American workers had, at some point, been employed by McDonald's. Globally, McDonald's served an estimated 20 million customers every day. It was the world's largest purchaser of beef, and its french fries required 7.5 percent of America's entire potato crop. McDonald's was one of the world's most famous brand names.

[*See also* Drive-Ins; Fast Food; French Fries, *subentry* Twentieth Century; Hamburger; Ronald McDonald.]

BIBLIOGRAPHY

Barber, Benjamin R. *Jihad vs. McWorld*. New York: Times Books, 1995.

Boas, Max, and Steve Chain. *Big Mac: The Unauthorized Story of McDonald's*. New York: Mentor/New American Library, 1977.

Gould, William. *Business Portraits: McDonald's*. Lincolnwood, IL: VGM Career Horizons, 1996.

Kroc, Ray, with Robert Anderson. *Grinding It Out: The Making of McDonald's*. Chicago: St. Martin's, 1987.

Love, John F. *McDonald's: Behind the Arches*. Rev. ed. New York: Bantam, 1995.

McDonald's Corporation. http://mcdonalds.com/corporate.html.

Ritzer, George. *The McDonaldization of Society*. Newbury Park, CA: Pine Forge Press, 1993.

Schlosser, Eric. *Fast Food Nation: The Dark Side of the All-American Meal*. Boston and New York: Houghton Mifflin, 2001.

ANDREW F. SMITH

Meal Patterns

American meal patterns over the past four centuries have varied across different regions of the country and have been determined by an individual's occupation, social class, gender, ethnicity, and personal preferences. Seasons, holidays, and the weekly round of activities also played a part in determining what is eaten when.

All meals, whether served at home or in a restaurant, are structured events. Seating arrangements often reflect status. Rituals, including prayers and other formal components of meals, are often observed. Etiquette rules for eating became commonly accepted, and divergence from these rules reflects badly on the rule breaker. Most dinners follow a typical pattern from savory to sweet. Meals also move from simple salads to more complex foods, the desserts often being the most difficult dish to prepare. Dinners served on special occasions, such as birthdays, weddings, and holidays, often connect the individuals to the wider social fabric.

Colonial Times

In colonial times, American meal patterns followed European practices, in which the extended family participated in meals, which occurred three times a day: the standard meals were breakfast, dinner, and supper. As the first meal of the day, breakfast literally broke the fast. It was eaten immediately upon rising or a few hours later, after the earliest chores had been completed. A summer breakfast might consist of dishes like bread, rice, milk-pudding, cheese, cold meat, smoked fish, fowl, and fresh berries; milk, cider, coffee, tea or chocolate were common breakfast beverages. Cold weather called for a heartier meal that might include toast soaked in milk, warm muffins, barley cakes, buckwheat cakes, waffles, mush, hominy, or baked pumpkin.

Working men and schoolchildren returned home for dinner, the main meal of the day, which was traditionally served in the early or late afternoon. For the upper classes, this could be a formal and lengthy meal replete with multiple courses of meats, poultry, seafood, vegetables, followed by lavish sweets such as flummeries, trifles, or whipped syllabub. Middle-class dinners would be somewhat pared-down versions of the upper-class meal. The lower classes, poor farmers, indentured servants, and slaves ate what they could produce on their own or afford to buy, usually simple fare such as a pudding or mush, game, stews, soups, and home-grown vegetables.

Supper, the last meal of the day, was light and, sometimes, optional. It was eaten in the early evening. In some regions and at certain times of year, supper was similar to breakfast; in New England, for example, pie was eaten at both meals. In other settings, supper was composed of dinner leftovers, or a simple soup, plus dessert.

For women who kept house, and for the servants and slaves of those who did not, this traditional meal pattern required hours of hard work. They had to rise early (4 a.m. was not unusual) to prepare the hearth or stove fire, cook and serve breakfast, and clean up afterward; preparation for the next meal began almost immediately. To keep food on the table there was also marketing, gardening, baking, and preserving to be done—in addition to other rigorous household chores such as keeping the stove clean and doing the laundry.

The Nineteenth Century

The traditional meal pattern began to change during the mid-nineteenth century, due in part to the growth of cities and the shifting occupations of American men. The first meal to change was dinner. As towns and cities grew, it became more difficult for workers to return home for dinner at midday as the distance between the home and the place of work increased. Workers earning an hourly wage did not have paid lunch breaks, so they tended to eat as quickly as possible. And if a husband and wife both worked, a relaxed noontime meal at home with the family was out of the question.

Dinner, the most important meal of the day, moved to the evening, when the family could dine together at a more leisurely pace. The midday repast came to be called lunch (shortened from "luncheon") and evolved into a small, light, and frequently rushed meal—often something brought from home in a tin pail or a brown bag, or a quick bite in a workplace cafeteria. Sandwiches, soups, and salads became common luncheon foods.

Although somewhat more the masters of their own schedules, professionals, such as doctors, lawyers, and businessmen, rarely had time to return home for a long afternoon meal. So they ate large, hearty breakfasts and big dinners, and skipped lunch or ate something light at work. On the other hand, sometimes business was conducted over an extended lunch similar to the dinners of earlier years, but these meals were eaten in restaurants, not at home. Middle- and upper-class women, once they no longer had to spend the morning preparing the family dinner, were free to seek out their own social activities, such as women's clubs, which frequently met at a member's home for lunch. These ladies' lunches—usually dainty fare because there were no men present—became a field for social competition as each hostess attempted to outdo the last with clever table decorations, color-coordinated foods, and favors.

To fill the void between lunch, usually consumed at noon, and dinner, usually eaten at 8 p.m. in upper-class homes, afternoon tea was served at 4 or 5 p.m. Having the main meal of the day served late in the evening necessitated a shift in breakfast, as many people who eat a late and heavy dinner were not hungry for a big breakfast. Lighter breakfasts, consisting of fruit, bread, coffee, or tea, became common at the end of the nineteenth century. For those of the leisure class who were inclined to sleep late, a hybrid meal called "brunch" became popular. Eaten in late morning or early afternoon, brunch could consist of breakfast foods such as eggs and waffles, or could be made up of heartier foods such as would normally be served at lunch. Alcoholic beverages made with breakfast juices (mimosas, Bloody Marys, and screwdrivers) became a standard accompaniment. Brunch became a meal for relaxing on weekends, whether eaten in a restaurant or enjoyed with guests at home.

By the late nineteenth century, the evening meal became the major meal of the day; it evolved into an occasion for entertaining. Among the affluent, dinner was served later and the offerings were much more sumptuous than they had been. Most meals contained meat, particularly beef, which became abundant as cattlemen in the western states and territories began raising and transporting cattle to markets thousands of miles away.

The Twentieth Century

Yet another major shift in American meal patterns was caused by the rise of commercial food processors. The breakfast food industry challenged the traditional morning menu with quick-cooking and ready-to-eat cereals such as granola, rolled oats, grape nuts, and corn flakes. These new products, promoted as healthful, began to replace the traditional, heavier breakfast foods. During the 1920s, the orange juice industry used the same technique of stressing the healthful qualities of orange juice as a breakfast drink and within a decade, fruit juice became a major breakfast food fad throughout America.

The rise of the snack food industry around the turn of the twentieth century wrought a major change in American eating habits. Eating between meals was a new option. Confections, candy, and roasted nuts, which had previously been available only at fairs, circuses, and other special events, were now widely available for on-the-spot consumption and to keep on hand at home. As the twentieth century progressed, breakfast often became a quick downing of a commercial drink like a milk shake or the consumption of a breakfast bar while running out the door.

After World War II, the American meal pattern changed yet again. With men away at war and women taking their places in the work force, getting a family meal on the table was a challenge. Prepared, processed, canned, frozen, or dehydrated foods requiring little kitchen time were a boon to the working mother. Toward the end of the twentieth century, the microwave oven took center stage as the source of hot meals at home and in the workplace. At the same time, Americans were increasingly eating their meals away from home, and cafeterias, lunch counters, cafes, restaurants, and fast food outlets flourished.

Snacking became increasingly common as the century progressed, and the "three squares" diminished in importance. Eating a series of small meals and snacks throughout the day—"grazing" or "noshing"—became popular in some circles in the 1980s; it was thought to be more healthful than sitting down to three heavy meals a day.

BIBLIOGRAPHY

Haber, Barbara. *From Hardtack to Home Fries: An Uncommon History of American Cooks and Meals.* New York: Free Press, 2002.

Levenstein, Harvey A. *Revolution at the Table: The Transformation of the American Diet.* New York and Oxford: Oxford University Press, 1988.

ANDREW F. SMITH

Meals on Wheels

There is an old folk saying that goes, "Old John would half-starve were there no woman to prepare his meals; old Nellie would starve if she had no one to share her cooking." Until the middle of the twentieth century many elderly people, living alone and isolated from families and friends, died prematurely from hunger and malnutrition. The situation changed for the better for some elderly people in January 1954, when a group of volunteers at the Lighthouse, a settlement house in the Kensington area of Philadelphia, started to deliver noontime meals, five days a week, to elderly, isolated shut-ins. They modeled their program after a civil-defense program started by the Women's Voluntary Services in Great Britain to feed the aged during the blitz. As word about Philadelphia's so-called meals-on-wheels spread, communities across the country began their own volunteer programs. More than three hundred of them started over the next twenty years.

The idea for using federal dollars to expand this service took root at the 1961 White House Conference on Aging. The deciding event that finally prompted action was the publication in 1965 of the shocking findings from a national food-consumption survey conducted by the

U.S. Department of Agriculture. This study found that as many as 6 million to 8 million older persons might have deficient diets. A task force on nutrition was created to develop both administrative and legislative recommendations for correcting the problem. In 1968 Congress appropriated $2 million to fund a national demonstration to determine whether a nationwide model for feeding older people was feasible. Twenty-three demonstration programs tested two potential models for providing meals to older people: meals taken to the home, called home-delivered meals, and meals served in group settings, called congregate meals. The home-delivered–meals model was clearly derived from existing meals-on-wheels programs. The congregate program took as its model the meals programs operated in the Jewish settlement houses located on the Lower East Side of Manhattan.

On March 22, 1972, a law was passed creating the Elderly Nutrition Program to be administered nationwide by the Administration on Aging, then part of the U. S. Department of Health, Education, and Welfare, now the Department of Health and Human Services. The purpose of the program was to provide lifesaving meals to elderly people at nutritional risk. Meals were to be both served in a congregate setting and delivered to the home. This new program grew out of the social activism that paralleled America's soul-searching in the 1960s during America's involvement in the Vietnam War and the struggles of the civil rights movement. Providing nutritious meals to America's elderly was viewed as just one of the many actions society needed to take to provide a safety net for America's most vulnerable.

In 2003 more than 300 million meals were delivered to the elderly under this program. About half of these meals were delivered to people at home. Since the creation of Meals on Wheels as a federal program in 1972, it has continued to grow, as an army of volunteers carries out the work of Little Red Riding Hood, delivering meals to America's elderly.

[*See also* Hunger Programs.]

BIBLIOGRAPHY

Administration on Aging 2002 Annual Report, *What We Do Makes a Difference*. Washington, DC: U.S. Department of Health and Human Services, 2003.
Bechill, William D., and Irene Wolgamot. *Nutrition for the Elderly: The Program Highlights of Research and Development Nutrition Projects Funded under Title IV of the Older Americans Act of 1965*. Washington, DC: U.S. Department of Health, Education, and Welfare, Administration on Aging, 1973.
"Meals on Wheels: A New and Progressive Step in the Care of the Aged." *What's New*, no. 203, (1957). Special Christmas Issue published by Abbott Laboratories, North Chicago, IL.

JOSEPH M. CARLIN

Measurement

Throughout history, food measurements have had more to do with experience and judgment than objective amounts. However, when needed in the English-American colonies, they followed a loose and variable adaptation of the English imperial system. Originally based largely on weight, they gave way to volume measurements by the late nineteenth century, at about the same time a single American standard was adopted.

Weight and Volume

Colonial food measurements in the commercial and household arenas were developed to meet different needs. Commercial transactions were regulated by law to ensure honest dealings and depended on carefully calibrated equipment. Eighteenth-century tavern owners, for example, were legally obliged to buy and use sets of official measures for dispensing cider, wine, beer, ale, and spirits in familiar volume units—gallons, half gallons, quarts, pints, cups, and gills.

Likewise, seventeenth- and eighteenth-century barrels were required to meet regional standards of size and were labeled appropriately. In New York, City pipes contained at least 120 gallons of wine, hogsheads 60 gallons, and quarter casks 30 gallons. Molasses hogsheads held 63 gallons and the casks for dried salt fish held 31½ gallons. Others, equally specific, held meat, cider, beer, salt, rum, bread, ship's biscuit, and flour.

EIGHTEENTH-CENTURY MEASUREMENT BY WEIGHT

French Biskits: "Having a Pair of clean Scales ready, in one Scale, put three new-laid Eggs, in the other Scale put as much dried flour, an equal Weight with the Eggs, take out the Flour, and as much fine Powder-sugar. . . ."

Glasse, Hannah. *The Art of Cookery, Made Plain and Easy.*
London: 1747.

Home cooking was more concerned with ensuring desired amounts and achievable quality. Colonial American cooks measured with a kinesthetic system that suggested amounts and depended on the cook to adjust them according to experience, the knowledge of flavor principles, and the properties of food. As both measuring equipment and ingredients were inconsistent, cooks learned to determine the correct amounts pragmatically, according to the look, feel, smell, taste, and even sound at various steps of the recipe. The food itself indicated when quantities, handling, or timing were sufficient; a competent cook achieved consistently good results. Cooks' training, whether involving a professional master and apprentice or home-based mother and daughter, relied on close supervision, oral instruction, demonstration, and hands-on practice. The written recipes of period cookbooks, invoking the same methods, were used chiefly by the affluent and literate.

Another factor in the success of the measurement system lay in the fact that local foodways were dominated by a single ethnic tradition and their cooking repertoires were familiar, limited, and fairly standard. English or Dutch cookbooks were used by those already versed in basic preparations. For example, the common instruction, "Put in flour until it is enough," although inadequate for modern cooks, made sense to someone of the right cultural grounding.

This system of sensory measurement was entirely appropriate to home-based cultures with limited technology, familiarity with foodstuffs, enough time for daily cooking, and a high regard for meals. The favored measurement technique for solids was by weight, as balances and steelyards (arm and fulcrum) required minimal technology and had calibrated weights. Liquids were estimated by volume, using drinking cups and eating spoons of inconsistent sizes, and small amounts were gauged by tasting.

Nineteenth-century cookbook authors faced the challenge of transmitting an oral tradition in written form. Unable to instruct by demonstration, they refined their measurement systems. For example, a recipe for bread in Mary Randolph's *The Virginia House-wife* (1824) requires one quart of flour and then, as an afterthought, explains that a quart of flour weighs 1¼ pounds.

An exponential rise in the number of printed recipes followed. Cookbooks, women's magazines, newspaper columns, and advertising handouts disseminated large numbers of unfamiliar recipes and an expanding, evolving cuisine, reinforcing the need for dependable, clear instructions. At the same time, more women, unschooled

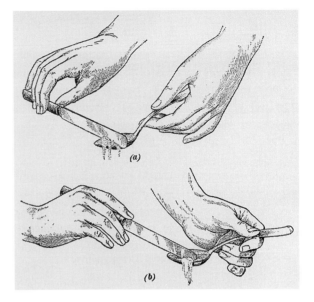

Measuring Ingredients. How to use a spoon and knife to measure ingredients. From *Woman's Institute Library of Cookery: Essentials of Cookery, Cereals, Breads, Hot Breads* (Scranton, Pa., 1924), sec. 2, p. 14.

in cookery at home, were involved in education and jobs. New authors, increasingly writing for inexperienced brides, recognized the importance of complete and accurate measurements and measured by volume, finding it easier to use.

It was not until the mid- to late nineteenth century that standardized equipment for volume measuring was mass-produced and distributed. Influenced by the new field of science and early nutrition research, cooking schools rewrote traditional American recipes in more precise volume units. Mary J. Lincoln's *Boston School Kitchen Text-Book* (1887), one of the most important pioneering efforts, defines a standardized cup as "just half a pint (beer measure)," a clear adaptation of legal volume, and instructs, "A cupful is all the cup will hold without running over,—full to the brim." Her "scant cupful is within a quarter of an inch of the top," and various spoon measurements are defined as rounded or level. Fannie Merritt Farmer's 1896 revision further recommends the use of inexpensive (and then widely available) graduated tin or agate measuring cups and spoons.

In the early twentieth century, newly required public-school classes in home economics taught scientific measurement methods to generations of boys and girls. Lincoln and other early proponents of standardization knew the value of cooking by experience and believed the consistent use of measurements was a stepping-stone toward that

HISTORICAL AMERICAN MEASURING

4 even saltspoons = 1 teaspoon
4 teaspoonfuls = 1 tablespoon
4 teaspoonfuls = 1 wineglass, or ¼ cup
8 tablespoons = ½ cup, or ½ gill
2 gills or 1 cup = ½ pint
4 gills or 2 cups = 1 pint
2 pints = 1 quart
4 quarts = 1 gallon
1 even tablespoon of butter or lard = 1 ounce
1 heaping tablespoon of butter or lard = 2 ounces
butter the size of a walnut = 1 ounce
butter the size of an egg = 2 ounces

1 even cupful of butter = ½ pound
1 pint of liquid = 1 pound
1 pint finely chopped meat = 1 pound
1 cupful raisins (stemmed) = 6 ounces
5 nutmegs = 1 ounce
1 teaspoon (heaping) ground spice = ¼ ounce
2 teaspoons (rounded) mustard = ¼ ounce
The standard cup in all cooking recipes is the ordinary kitchen cup, which is larger than a teacup, but not so large as a breakfast cup. It holds exactly half a pint.
Taken from *Served in Sayville*, published by the Sayville Congregational Church in Long Island, New York, 1909.

experience, but later practitioners focused with such zeal on the new scheme that it became the only correct way. Although it overshadowed a tried-and-true system for achieving good results, it nevertheless served home cooks exploring new cuisines, ethnic and international cookery, and the sophisticated creations of gifted chefs.

At the end of the twentieth century, the "outdated" measuring systems began to be reinstated. Involvement with international cooking brought weight measurement and kitchen scales to American homes, particularly as many cooks believed them to be more accurate. American descendants of immigrants, eager to recreate the ancestral foods of their childhoods, learned the sensory techniques

of their aging relatives. It seems that Americans are using the best of all systems.

Heat and Time

Heat measurement is another aspect of cookery. For millennia cooks have judged the heat of the hearth by its feel on the skin, the look of embers and flames, the bubbling sounds of frying, the telltale indication of white brick-oven walls after the soot burns off, and how long it takes to brown a cube of bread. Thermometers and then thermostats were largely twentieth-century advances and permitted the cook almost to ignore stove or oven progress.

Time measurements have long depended on experience and estimations, the desired result, an inner time sense, clocks and watches, perhaps even the position of the sun. Modern timers have freed the busy cook from close watching. Timing has taken on new meanings: menu construction often is based on the time available in a busy day; the twenty-minute meal has restructured family dinners.

[*See also* Cookbooks and Manuscripts; Home Economics; Recipes; Timers, Hourglasses, and Egg Timers.]

BIBLIOGRAPHY

Carlin, Joseph M. "Weights and Measures in Nineteenth-Century America," *The Journal of Gastronomy* 3, no. 3 (Autumn 1987).

ALICE ROSS

MODERN AMERICAN MEASURES

DRY MEASURES BY VOLUME

3 teaspoons = 1 tablespoon
2 tablespoons = 1 ounce
8 ounces (or 16 tablespoons) = 1 cup
2 cups = 1 pint
2 pints = 4 cups = 1 quart
4 cups = 1 quart
4 quarts = 1 gallon

LIQUID MEASURES

1 gallon = 4 liquid quarts
1 liquid quart = 2 liquid pints
1 liquid pint = 4 liquid gills

AVOIRDUPOIS WEIGHT

16 ounces = 1 pound

Meat

America has been a meat-eating nation from the days of the Native American hunter-gatherer societies, blessed as it was by extensive fertile lands and (at least in most parts) a benign climate that supported a variety of wildlife. Selectively harvested wild animals, from squirrels to birds to bison, were integral parts of the diet of early European settlers and of successive waves of American migrants who pushed back the fringes of the wilderness. The expansion of farming in the seventeenth and eighteenth centuries stabilized the consumption of meat by ensuring a steady supply of domesticated livestock. The scattered and incomplete information available indicates that annual per capita meat consumption reached approximately 150 pounds in the early 1700s and remained at that level, give or take 20 percent, until the 1950s.

Such persistence implies a consistency that obscures dramatic shifts in the patterns of meat consumption over American history. Americans have continued to eat meat, but the kinds of meats they eat have changed significantly since the 1700s. At the same time, these apparent cultural changes have been constrained by meat's irreducible physical qualities.

Meat consumption has been—and remains—tethered to the exigencies of moving this perishable product from the farm to the dinner table. Changes in the technology of production, transportation, and preservation have dramatically altered the character and categories of meat eaten by Americans over the past 250 years. The cycle of the seasons and their extremes of temperature affect the natural deterioration of meat, while technology seeks to even out climate, speed distribution, and package meat conveniently for sale. Livestock—as the vessel in which meat incubated—embodied these conflicting forces. Arriving in odd, irregular shapes, growing and fattening in their particular ineffable manner, animals stubbornly resist transformation into mere expressions of human will. The shifts within the category called meat took place between species, among the different parts of an animal, and in the form in which meat reached the consumer. These variations highlight the persistence of Americans' demand for animal flesh as an integral part of their diet.

Rural Pork and Urban Beef

Pork was America's favorite and most widely consumed meat from the time of European settlement well into the twentieth century. Pigs were well suited to farming families who lived near woodlands or who grew corn (or both). Pigs required little management and fattened easily on the leftovers of human consumption and the leavings of the annual harvest. They were easier for farmers to handle than cattle because their relatively small size simplified killing and curing. Their flesh could be preserved through materials that were easy to obtain and use—salt, sugar, and smoke—and thus pork could be stored for later consumption in an era without home refrigeration. Processing hogs fit into the family division of labor, with men performing the killing and cutting operations outside and women and children handling the meat that needed more detailed care to be turned into a usable product.

American farmers used well-established European methods to cure pork. For home curing the limbs of pigs were separated from the trunks, which in turn were cut into pieces small enough to place in a barrel filled with a brine solution that was usually composed of salt, saltpeter, and sugar or molasses. Salt did the actual curing, while sugar and molasses helped with taste and saltpeter improved the meat's color. The cure was intended to keep the meat for six months to a year.

Complementing barrel pork were cuts cured with a combination of salt and smoke. Hams (rear legs) and shoulders often were dry-cured (sprinkled with salt, saltpeter, and sugar rather than immersed in a liquid solution), then smoked to complete the curing process. Smoke added flavor and the dry-cured meat could last well over a year without spoiling. Sometimes farmers separated the ribs from the pig's belly and cured the latter as bacon.

While dinner tables of families from all classes and regions offered pork for dinner, consumption of particular products were markers of America's social hierarchy. Barrel salt pork was a poor family's meat, whether the families were slaves, farmers, or wage earners. Bacon was especially popular among rural southern whites. Elites favored hams and other choice dry-cured products in warm weather and fresh roasts during the colder months. Upper-class preferences aside, wet-cured pork was widely consumed and highly valued among eighteenth- and nineteenth-century Americans.

Fresh pork remained a highly seasonal dish, unlike the cured products. Roasted or stewed pork generally was a fall or winter treat that accompanied the slaughtering and curing of the rest of the animal for later use. This cyclical consumption pattern, originating in climate's natural influences, assumed a cultural life of its own and induced suspicion among nineteenth-century Americans toward fresh pork eaten out of season.

For fresh meat, eighteenth- and nineteenth-century Americans vastly preferred beef. While appetizing when eaten fresh, beef was cumbersome to preserve because of the large size of cattle. And cured beef generally did not taste as good as cured pork because of its tougher fibrous nature. In most rural areas, beef was only an occasional treat, with the slaughtering of cattle becoming a celebratory ritual that brought members of a community together for a special feast. Fresh beef became more available in settled regions of the countryside when itinerant butchers established set routes and sold meat to dispersed homesteads. Limited transportation and the absence of refrigeration nonetheless remained impediments to developing a large rural clientele.

The growth of towns generated more stable demand for meat. As in Europe, fresh meat consumption was predominantly an urban phenomenon until the late nineteenth century. In these concentrated settlements, fresh beef was the most desirable form of meat. Urban areas with sufficient populations to create a consumer demand for beef in turn stimulated cattle- and livestock-raising in rural areas capable of supplying these markets. New England farmers plied the livestock markets astutely, investing in equipment and land for these purposes well before the Revolutionary War. As the new republic took control of first the Ohio and then the Mississippi valleys, market-oriented livestock-raising expanded apace. Farmers aggressively imported new breeds from Europe, bred and crossbred new varieties, experimented with fattening techniques, and shared their husbandry experiences at county fairs and competitions for the finest, largest, and most delicious meat-producing cattle.

Before the Civil War, most urban areas assumed responsibility for monitoring meat retailing through municipally regulated public markets. While America never had guilds similar to the butcher organizations of early modern Europe, the antebellum butchers were a protected group who oversaw beef production from slaughter to sale. Killing took place in small sheds scattered through towns and cities usually located close to the retail markets. The filth that accompanied such practices led to nuisance regulations and eventually to a public health movement that pushed slaughterhouses to the edges of settled areas. Retailing remained a highly personal and individualized process, with direct bargaining between consumer and butcher, and considerable variation in the size and character of the cuts that ended up on city dwellers' dinner tables.

The varieties of beef sold in urban settings meant that most nineteenth-century townspeople could obtain this meat in some form. Travelers' accounts document the

opulent beef consumption habits of upper-class families, who could easily consume several types of roasts at one meal. But it was the quantity and type of cuts, not beef consumption as such, that distinguished elite eating habits from common practices. For example, a food budget from a Philadelphia working-class family in 1851 indicated that with the cost of meat averaging ten cents a pound, annual per capita consumption of "butcher's meat" by family members was 146 pounds. This budget probably reflected conventional usage of cheaper cuts for stewing and boiling, employment of bones to make soup stock, and an occasional roast or steak purchased for special occasions. While not distinguishing between beef and pork, the reference to "butcher's meat" attests to the availability of fresh meat, including beef, to urban residents of modest means.

If beef was an urban meat, class was inscribed into the varieties consumed by city-dwelling Americans. At the pinnacle of the beef hierarchy were roasts, such as the so-called baron of beef, a cut of English origin formed by separating the loin from the rear hindquarters, which had not been split down the middle, forming a large, square, and boneless piece often weighing more than one hundred pounds. Americans, even in elite circles, found this cut extremely unwieldy to prepare and instead were fonder of cuts that separated the baron of beef into smaller sections to form sirloin or rump roasts, often weighing more than twenty pounds. Roasts cut from the first nine ribs of the forequarters were almost as popular. Costing between fifteen and twenty cents a pound, such roasts were generally the province of the upper class.

Most urban residents could not afford the pricey broiled steaks and roasts for home consumption. Other,

Meat Market. Nineteenth-century print. *Culinary Archives & Museum at Johnson & Wales University, Providence, R.I.*

less desirable forms sufficed for the stews and soups that constituted more conventional cuisine. Tougher cuts of beef, such as the flank, rounds (both from the hindquarters), brisket, and plate (from the forequarters), generally served for stews, as longer cooking times in water softened them sufficiently. Bony meat, such as the neck, shoulder, and thigh, were used for soups and stews, as were internal organs, such as livers and hearts.

Lean beef, principally the brisket and plate, were the typical sources of eighteenth- and nineteenth-century cured beef. These were low-grade products in comparison to cured pork. Most cured beef was corned through a wet-cure method similar to barrel pork, where it was placed in a salty brine solution and kept in the liquid until ready for eating. Wet-cured beef could last for close to one year, similar to pork. To keep beef wholesome for longer periods it was dried or jerked. Although nutritious, this hard, tasteless product was one of the least desirable forms of meat.

Industrial Meat

Beginning in the 1820s, entrepreneurs discovered that whenever possible, it was cheaper to move the slaughterhouses and meat-processing facilities to the animal than to ship live animals to major population centers. As long as the meat could be kept from spoiling and could be transported economically, large-scale production facilities near livestock sources permitted economies of scale in meat production. Until well after the Civil War, these processes were limited to cured pork, as the meat still had to be transported considerable distances to population centers under nonrefrigerated conditions. (Well into the 1870s it remained easier to transport live cattle by moving them "on the hoof" than to try to convey fresh meat very far.) Fragmenting the labor processes to increase productivity and centralizing distribution reduced costs significantly—and eventually changed the types of pork consumed in America.

Climate and geography were the principal determinants of the early meatpacking industry's location. Growth of internal transportation after 1815, principally roads, canals, and steamboat shipping on inland and coastal waterways, allowed nodal points to emerge for packing cured pork. So long as water remained the principal transportation mode, river cities like Cincinnati led as packing centers. The rise of the railroad, offering year-round transportation among other virtues, allowed Chicago to best all its rivals shortly after the Civil War.

Industrialization systematized the categories of pork consumed by Americans. Vernacular styles became regulated varieties, as Boards of Trade in meatpacking centers sought consistency in the terms applied to meat sold to the public. In the nineteenth century, particular care was devoted to the categories of barreled pork, the chief product of these packing centers and the variety most vulnerable to bastardization and deception.

By the 1830s, Cincinnati packers had agreed to regulations carefully delineating among barrel-pork products and in so doing facilitated selling their goods to distinct market segments. Among barreled meat (defined as at least 196 pounds in each container), clear pork was the best class, composed of the sides of large hogs, with the ribs cut out. Mess pork came next in quality (and price), as it included two rumps as well as the sides. A barrel of slightly less desirable prime pork typically contained sides from lighter hogs along with two shoulders and two jowls. Bulk pork was the lowest grade, as it could contain any part of the hog (including the head and feet). Stable farming families were the strongest consumers of the better varieties, while southern slaves received most of the bulk pork.

Distinction among barrel-pork varieties grew along with the centralization of the industry in Chicago. By the 1880s, the Chicago Board of Trade had doubled barrel-pork varieties to eight. The elite clear pork, for example, was now a regular variety that had the backbone and half of the ribs removed from the sides of well-fattened hogs, and an "extra clear pork" version was completely boned and limited to fourteen large pieces. Prime pork metamorphosed into regular prime, extra prime, and prime mess. Only regular prime could contain heads, and prime mess meat had to be in four-pound square chunks and packed so that for every twenty shoulder pieces there were thirty from the side.

Meat's perishable nature still restricted the industry in the decade after the Civil War; it was Chicago that turned meatpacking into a year-round business. By the mid-1870s, Armour and other large Chicago packers had invested in cold storage facilities kept cool through the summer with ice from the Great Lakes. Able to run meat operations year-round with refrigeration, Chicago's packers produced one-third of all meat sold commercially in 1890.

The application of refrigeration to production and distribution also altered the status of fresh meat—principally beef. Developing cold storage techniques using natural ice allowed for year-round slaughtering and processing of meat. Extending refrigeration into transportation in the

1880s with the ice-cooled railroad car permitted the radical separation of slaughter from consumption of fresh meat. Not only did fresh meat prices decline in large urban centers, but fresh meat became more generally available in small towns and rural areas throughout the American hinterland. Firms, such as Swift, set up branch houses that provided meat to urban butcher shops and established refrigerated railroad car routes that reached deep into the American countryside. By World War I, the distribution networks of the five dominant Chicago-based meatpacking firms touched 25,000 American communities.

Growth of a commercial meatpacking industry encouraged farmers to find ways of enhancing the commercial value of their livestock. The practice of fattening pigs and cattle for slaughter by feeding them corn and other high carbohydrate foods can be traced back into the eighteenth century and became increasingly widespread as industrial meat firms expanded their scope of operations. By the late nineteenth century "corn-fed" animals fetched the best price in the livestock markets and the meat they produced became the standard for the complex evaluation methods that later would lead to retail grading systems.

Nationalizing beef production made beef more widely and consistently available for Americans. With the branch houses and refrigerated car routes extending throughout the nation, consumers no longer had to rely on local livestock sources to obtain beef. An exhaustive 1909 consumption study showed that beef had surpassed pork consumption among all northern urban white groups (immigrant and native born) and had pulled even with pork among urban southern whites. While southern African Americans evinced a clear preference for pork, northern blacks ate almost as much beef as pork.

Traditional nineteenth-century preferences persisted even as beef spread in popularity. In practice, Americans remained willing to eat meat from all parts of the cattle. Yet steaks and roasts remained intractably perched on the top of the status hierarchy despite persistent efforts from meat-producing firms, retailers, and home economists to stimulate more diverse use of cuts.

Beef producers, the packinghouse firms, had an attenuated relationship with consumers and little ability to directly influence their preferences. Beef was a commodity obtained anonymously through butcher shops, unlike pork whose predominant processed forms were clearly branded with their manufacturer. Beef left packinghouses in the form of animal quarters weighing around two hundred pounds, not as consumer-size cuts characteristic of cured pork. Butcher shops obtained beef from the branch houses of packing firms, either by visiting personally or through deliveries made to their store. Retail butchers either cut pieces to order, or, if displayed already cut, then wrapped the meat in brown paper at the request of the customers. Meat firms learned of consumer preferences through retailers, who in turn were influenced by their interactions with consumers.

Beef cuts varied regionally in accordance with butchers' sense of local traditions. Mid-twentieth-century butcher handbooks explained in intricate details the variations between New York, Boston, Philadelphia, and Chicago cuts, as well as among such cities as Spokane, Minneapolis, and New Orleans. New York cuts were "shorter" (cut nearer to the backbone) than in Chicago, hence with less of the "tail" characteristic of Chicago-style steaks and roasts. Boston varied even more dramatically, as butchers there traditionally left three ribs in the hindquarters, creating especially "short" roasts and chops.

The women who bought meat were discerning shoppers. In consumer studies shoppers consistently ranked meat quality as the principal reason for patronizing a particular store, though equaled by price concerns among poorer customers. Looking for meat that was red, fat that was white, and a smell that was fresh were, for most shoppers, the first steps in making a beef purchase.

These preferences posed a problem for the local butcher shops. Since beef came to them as cattle quarters, the character of consumer demand forced them to accentuate price differences among beef varieties in order to not be left with parts of the animal. Elite beef, such as porterhouse steak, sold for fifty-five cents a pound in Pittsburgh around 1930 and a rib roast went for forty cents, while flank steak sold for a mere thirty-three cents and boiling beef just twenty-six cents a pound. Such pricing strategy further reinforced the place of steaks and roasts as the most elite and desirable meats.

These variations among consumer beef cuts, depending on region, reflected how industrial meat production had not standardized beef to the same degree as it had pork. Beef was consumed in fresh forms, while pork was far more fully processed to prepare it for increasingly efficient curing operations by industrial methods.

Modern Meat

Industrializing pork changed the character of this meat, as well as the types favored by Americans. At the same time that they were improving production technologies and systematizing barrel-pork varieties, national packing companies were seeking to expand the consumption of

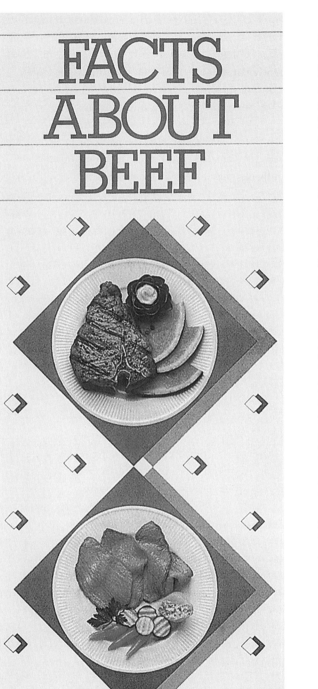

Facts about Beef. Pamphlet published by the Beef Industry Council, 1984. *Collection of Andrew F. Smith*

branded pork meats, principally ham and bacon. By pursuing this branding strategy, meatpacking companies transformed the pork Americans ate.

The focal points for innovation, bacon and ham, occupied different places in the pork hierarchy. Hams were the elite pork products. Fine differences among hams could be produced by the foods fed to the pigs, the cut and trim of the raw meat, and the ingredients in the curing solution. Most nineteenth-century hams were fully cured in a liquid brine solution after an initial dry-curing period. Consistently, though, hams were subsequently dried and smoked.

Bacon, on the other hand, was a common meat, perhaps slightly better than bulk pork, but still a rough provision. Consumed throughout the country, bacon was especially popular in the South where local production was widespread. Clearly a low-status meat, bacon remained widely popular because, preserved through dry-cure methods, it lasted longer than salt pork soaked in brine and could be purchased in smaller quantities.

Contradictory definitions of what constituted bacon reflected the incomplete confluence of traditional rural practices with the commercializing meat economy. While Cincinnati and Chicago packers defined bacon as cured pigs' bellies, a specific part of the pig, in traditional country parlance "bacon" referred to the dry-curing method of impregnating the meat with salt followed by smoking and drying. Virtually any part of the pig could become bacon if cured in this manner.

Dry-curing techniques were not convenient for high-volume bacon production. A liquid "sweet pickle" solution, in addition to more reliably imparting the right flavor, also reduced handling and material costs. Thousands of pounds could be wet-cured in the vats that were standard packinghouse equipment in the early twentieth century. Once the meat went to the smokehouse, the remaining liquid could be reused for the next batch.

With all these advantages, it was little wonder that packing firms began to cure bacon using wet methods similar to hams. By the early twentieth century, only "fancy" bacon was made through dry-cure methods. In so doing the firms turned the definition of this form of pork upside down; rather than referring to meat cured a particular way, "bacon" now referred to a part of the pig, regardless of how it was cured.

Meat industry firms continued to search for ways to shorten the two- to three-month curing periods that saddled them with large meat inventories. Nitrite emerged as a leading candidate in the 1910s, with the federal government authorizing its use in 1925. Combined with new methods for imparting the cure, industrialization of pork made new strides in the 1920s and 1930s. After 1920, firms moved to using "artery" pumping to impart water-based cures into the hams, plugging nozzles into the joint's circulatory system to speed delivery of the curing agent. Artery pumping greatly magnified nitrite's impact on curing times; mid-1920s advertisements made astounding—and accurate—claims that hams cured with these methods were ready in just five to ten days.

Fast cure methods also changed hams' taste. They may have saved firms a great deal of money, but the methods met with heavy criticism for creating bland, water-logged hams. Meat flavor was in large part due to slow ripening under conditions that inhibited uncontrolled bacterial growth. The fast cure did not give sufficient time for the meat to age and for the taste to develop. Government regulations limited the water-added component of ham, and curing-agent suppliers tried to refine their products in order to restore traditional cured taste.

The hams of the 1960s might not have seemed like hams to eighteenth-century consumers. Wet-cured and less inoculated with salt than their predecessors, hams became softer and sweeter—or blander, depending on taste preferences. But if their character changed, their elite place in the pork hierarchy did not.

Hams may have remained in the same cultural space, but bacon experienced a second transformation that altered its appeal across regional and socioeconomic lines. In so doing, bacon broke with its past association as a poor person's meat. Changes in production and packaging technology fueled bacon's makeover. Until the 1910s, bacon left the packinghouse as cured slabs weighing four to ten pounds. Packaging was limited to wrapping in waxed paper embossed with the firm's name. Beginning in 1915 packing firms began to incorporate slicing machines into bacon operations. In so doing they were accommodating themselves to evident consumer preferences for a more manageable form of this meat. Creating a bacon-slicing and -packaging operation entailed substantial capital investment and employment of more workers, as well as prolonged retention of this product in the plant. The return, packers hoped, would be higher value added with sliced bacon and, above all, an upgrade of the meat's reputation. In the 1950s, "needle-cure" injection methods similar to artery pumping reduced the still-considerable curing time to a few days, while packaging (first cellophane, and then polyvinyl chloride materials) protected the meat from the deterioration caused by air and light.

The cumulative effect of these innovations was dramatic. By the mid-1960s, bacon was a true national meat

whose appeal crossed income levels. Nationally, slightly over 60 percent of all families purchased bacon, with higher income groups slightly more likely to do so than lower. Bacon had been remade as a form of meat.

Barrel pork, once America's preeminent meat, simply disappeared as a consumption option. By 1963, the U.S. Census of Manufacturers no longer included it as a category. Barrel pork's decline was probably a good thing for the American diet. In addition to whatever the problems of curing agents, such as nitrites, the fatty, salt pork (cured at a ration of one pound salt to four pounds meat), which typified eighteenth- and nineteenth-century meat consumption, doubtless was not good for the heart or for digestion.

Fresh pork rose from the ashes of barrel pork's demise. As the refrigerated distribution networks of packing firms provided alternatives to keeping pork wholesome in salty brine solutions, pork processors began to think of pig meat in different forms and shapes. Not surprisingly, pork chops became widely available after 1900 as the loin (from which they are cut) no longer ended up in barrels of salt pork and instead could be kept fresh. Cuts that had previously been cured, or that had been available fresh only at certain times of the year, were widely obtainable by the 1960s.

While the very nature of pork changed, beef's physical form remained relatively stable. The consumer hierarchy favoring well-marbled rib and loin cuts over rounds and chuck, while affected at the margins in regional variation of cuts, did not change much over two hundred years. Consumed fresh rather than processed, beef remained anonymous, its human purveyors invisible. The grading systems, especially those of the federal government, followed traditional preferences for fattened beef, inscribing taste into law and regulation.

Beef consumption soared in the 1950s and 1960s, aided immensely by new means of delivery and preservation. Previously, refrigeration had unchained slaughter from distribution; now its expansion in the home opened new vistas to fresh beef. Electrification in the 1930s, followed by the expansion of mechanical refrigeration, relieved consumers of the tedious daily search for a piece of meat. Cellophane producers adapted their packaging from cured to fresh products, permitting retail food stores to create self-serve meat departments in the 1950s and 1960s. Hidden from consumers, major changes in the methods of beef processing moved the cutting operations previously performed in butcher shops by skilled labor back to the packinghouses where a close division of labor reduced labor costs. Beef boned and placed in boxes for shipment by trucks displaced the old system pioneered in the 1880s of cattle quarters transported by refrigerated railroad cars. Beef consumption peaked in the late 1970s at eighty-one pounds per capita annually. While the beef cuts may have looked similar to those of a century before, the meat came to consumers by utterly different means.

There were significant changes in consumption patterns of types of beef. Heavily marbled rib steaks that cooked so well on the charcoal grill replaced elaborate oven-cooked rib roasts. Boxed beef left most of the bones in packinghouses, so the shins and other classic sources of beef stock faded from stores. Chopped meat, the source for the ubiquitous hamburger, took the place of stewing meat at the lower end of the beef hierarchy, made available both through the new vast food chains for home consumption and also through institutional sales. A massive secondary market in beef scraps emerged as leading beef packers specialized in consumer cuts and shipped trimmings and bones to packinghouses devoted to the production of chopped beef. By 1980, beef had completely established its dominance over pork in American cuisine.

At the apogee of its success, however, beef faced a new challenge from chicken, an upstart that most Americans traditionally did not consider a meat. Since the colonial period, chicken generally had been a luxury meat served only on special occasions. Dramatic changes after World War II resulted, by the 1990s, in chicken challenging beef as America's favorite meat.

Categories changed along with consumption habits. At least through the 1940s, chicken was part of a larger category called poultry or fowl that contained many distinct breeds. Most farmers relied on White Leghorns for egg production, but many other varieties circulated through the nation's farms and meat markets. Broilers referred not to a type of chicken, but to a stage of development that suited the animal to a certain kind of cooking. Aggressive crossbreeding of chicken following the war largely eliminated breeds outside of poultry fanciers, in favor of distinctions by the form in which the animal would be used: layers, broilers, and roasters, differentiated by age and weight rather than lineage. Breeding practices and technological advances in animal medicine and nutrition accelerated maturing times and improved efficiency in feed conversion, creating in effect a new kind of chicken.

Preparing Meat. Cooking class at Institute of Culinary Education, New York. *Courtesy of the Institute of Culinary Education*

Not only did the chicken change, so too did the experience of consumers with the varieties available in stores. Until the 1960s, most chicken appeared on the shelves whole, along with occasional packages of legs or thighs. To broaden chicken's appeal, firms emulated beef by creating a new range of cuts available in self-service stores, principally boned, skinned, and cut-up varieties. Branding strategies similar to pork also attached consumers to particular firms, who claimed that their special processing methods imparted a distinctive character to their product. From an item consumed seasonally, and generally as part of a special Sunday meal, chicken became a meat that could be adapted to many forms of food.

Conclusion

In 2000, Americans ate more meat than at any point in American history by consuming 195 pounds per person. However, the composition of their preferred meats was quite different from that of the eighteenth century. On an annual per capita basis, beef still led, but at 64.5 pounds per person had dropped 30 percent from its peak in the 1970s. Chicken was close behind at 53 pounds per person, three times more than its 1960 level. Pork, once America's leading meat, trailed behind at 47.7 pounds per person. Fish accounted for 15 pounds per person, turkey another 13.5 pounds, and lamb barely 1 pound. Boned skinless chicken breasts covered with countless sauces and spreads had become as ubiquitous as the nineteenth century's barrel pork, while quick hamburgers became the public's cheap beef where once stews had ruled.

Meat's annoying natural qualities persist even as firms develop more sophisticated means to overcome the organic elements of this food with ever more aggressive human intervention. Factory farming designed to standardize animals' bodies generated so much waste that human communities fought to shut them down. Efficient processing methods yielded massive food contamination as commingling meat gave bacteria an enlarged surface on which to propagate. Food panics involving meat have followed a repetitive cycle of exposé, revulsion, short-term consumption decline, followed before too long with the renewed, if somewhat altered, prominence of meat in the American diet. Yet despite all the anxieties concerning its wholesomeness, Americans like their meat, they always have, and evidence indicates they will continue to in the foreseeable future.

[See also Adulterations; Armour, Philip Danforth; Aseptic Packaging; Burger King; Butchering; Chicken; Chipped Beef; Corned Beef; Drying; Freezers and Freezing; Game; Goetta; Hamburger; Lamb and Mutton; McDonald's; Pickling; Pig; Popeyes Chicken and Biscuits; Poultry and Fowl; Refrigerators; Salt and Salting; Sanders, Colonel; Sausage; Scrapple; Sinclair, Upton; Smoking; Soups and Stews; Spam; Stuffed Ham; Swift, Gustavus Franklin; Transportation of Food; Vienna Sausage; White Castle.]

BIBLIOGRAPHY

Broadway, Michael, and Donald Stull. *Slaughterhouse Blues: The Meat and Poultry Industry in North America.* New York: Wadsworth, 2003.

Clemen, Rudolf Alexander. *The American Livestock and Meat Industry.* New York: Ronald Press, 1923.

DeVoe, Thomas F. *The Market Book: A History of the Public Markets of the City of New York.* New York: Augustus Kelley, 1970. First published 1862.

Economic Research Service of the U.S. Department of Agriculture. http://www.ers.usda.gov/.

Garrison, J. Ritchie. "Farm Dynamics and Regional Exchange: The Connecticut Valley Beef Trade, 1670–1850." *Agricultural History* 61, no. 3 (Summer 1987): 1–17.

Hilliad, Sam Bowers. *Hog Meat and Hoecake: Food Supply in the Old South, 1840–1860.* Carbondale: Southern Illinois University Press, 1972.

Hogan, David. *Selling 'em by the Sack: White Castle and the Creation of American Food.* New York: New York University Press, 1997.

Horowitz, Roger. *Meat in America: Taste, Technology, Transformation.* Baltimore: Johns Hopkins University Press, 2005.

Horowitz, Roger. *"Negro and White, Unite and Fight!": A Social History of Industrial Unionism in Meatpacking, 1930–1990.* Urbana: University of Illinois Press, 1998.

Horwitz, Richard P. *Hog Ties: Pigs, Manure, and Mortality in American Culture.* New York: St. Martin's Press, 1998.

McMahon, Sarah F. "'All Things in Their Proper Season': Seasonal Rhythms of Diet in Nineteenth Century New England." *Agricultural History* 63, no. 2 (Spring 1989): 130–151.

McMahon, Sarah F. "A Comfortable Subsistence: The Changing Composition of Diet in Rural New England, 1620–1840." *William and Mary Quarterly* 42, no. 1 (January 1985): 26–65.

Schlosser, Eric. *Fast Food Nation: The Dark Side of the All-American Meal.* New York: Houghton Mifflin, 2001.

Smith, Page, and Charles Daniel. *The Chicken Book.* San Francisco: North Point, 1982.

Wade, Louise Carroll. *Chicago's Pride: The Stockyards, Packingtown, and Environs in the Nineteenth Century.* Urbana: University of Illinois Press, 1987.

Walsh, Margaret. *The Rise of the Midwestern Meat Packing Industry.* Lexington: University Press of Kentucky, 1982.

Williams, William H. *Delmarva's Chicken Industry.* Georgetown, DE: Delmarva Poultry Industry, 1998.

Yeager, Mary. *Competition and Regulation: The Development of Oligopoly in the Meat Industry.* Greenwich, CT: Jai Press, 1981.

ROGER HOROWITZ

Melons

Melons originated in Africa and have been cultivated in the Middle East and Europe since prebiblical times. They were introduced to the New World by Christopher Columbus in 1494. The term "melon" refers to members of the species *Cucumis melo*, which sometimes are referred to as muskmelons, cantaloupes, or winter melons. The term does not include other species such as watermelon (*Citrullus lanatus*) or jelly melon (*Cucumis metuliferus*).

Charles Naudin, a French botanist, determined in the mid-nineteenth century that various melons previously considered to be different species easily can be crossed and therefore all belong to the same species. He classified them into different groups, including the group commonly called cantaloupe in the United States and the group *inodorus*. Cantaloupes have a netted rind and a separation layer on the stem that causes an abscission or the natural separation of the fruit from the vine when it is mature. Melons of the *inodorus* group have a smooth rind and lack a separation layer for abscission. Cantaloupe

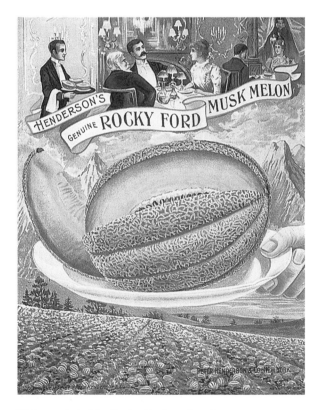

Melons. Label for Rocky Ford musk melon.

varieties are about twice as popular with growers and consumers as those of the *inodorus* group.

The disease-resistant cantaloupe variety PMR 45 was popular throughout the second half of the twentieth century, but has been superseded by Top Mark and other F_1 hybrid varieties that also have heavy fruit netting, which enables them to be shipped across the country. Varieties that have large fruit with sparse netting, such as Iroquois, do not ship as well but often are grown in eastern states and marketed locally.

Varieties of the *inodorus* group include honeydew, casaba, and canary. Most have green or white flesh. They are called winter melons because they have a long storage life, enabling them to be shipped from growers in western states to markets thousands of miles away. The French variety white Antibes was introduced to America in 1911 and renamed honey dew in 1915. It has been an important commodity in America ever since. Honeydew fruit have a smooth, cream-colored rind and green flesh with a high sugar content and delectable flavor. Honeydew melons can be stored for two weeks or more at 45°F and 85 to 90 percent relative humidity.

Orange-fleshed cantaloupe varieties predominate, but in the early 1900s melons of this group with green flesh were more popular. The orange color is caused by the presence of beta-carotene, a precursor to vitamin A that is an antioxidant and has nutritional and health benefits. Orange-fleshed melon varieties provide much more vitamin A than melons with green flesh. Melons are mostly water (more than 90 percent) but have significant amounts of niacin and vitamins A and C.

Melons are most often served fresh as a dessert, sometimes à la mode, and are a colorful addition to salads. They are occasionally processed by being frozen in syrup and are even used in soups, salsa, ice cream, and alcoholic drinks.

All melons are of inferior quality if they are harvested before full maturation. Looking at the separation layer of cantaloupes in the market can provide an indication if they were harvested too soon. When melons are fully mature, they have a smooth, round area where the fruit formerly was attached to the plant. Melons harvested before the half-slip stage, when more than half of the stem attachment area is jagged, seldom are of desirable flavor. The appearance of the stem attachment area for melons that abscise is one indication of maturity. Others include aroma, softness, and the color of the fruit.

An important quality attribute is sugar content. The total soluble solids measurement, mostly sugars, needs to be above 11 percent to meet U.S. Fancy and 9 percent for U.S. No. 1 grades. Honeydew melons generally have more sugar than cantaloupes and California requires by law that they have at least 10 percent soluble solids. Melons are grown in every American state, but the leading states for commercial production are California, Arizona, Texas, and Georgia. Most melons are produced in the spring and summer months. Prices received by growers are significantly lower in the summer. The consumption of melons in the United States is increasing.

[*See also* Fruit; Watermelon.]

BIBLIOGRAPHY

The Cucurbit Network. *The Cucurbit Network News.* Biennial publication with information about melons and other cucurbits.

Decker-Walters, Deena S. "The Origin of New World Melons." *Cucurbit Network News* 9, no. 1 (Spring 2002) and 9, no. 2 (Fall, 2002).

Goldman, Amy. *Melons: For the Passionate Grower.* New York: Artisan, 2002. Heritage varieties of melon and watermelon are beautifully illustrated and described, with information on their culture from a home gardener's viewpoint.

Robinson, R. W., and D. S. Decker-Walters. *Cucurbits.* New York: CAB International, 1997. Reprint with corrections, 1999. Botany and culture of melons and other cucurbits.

RICHARD W. ROBINSON

Mexican American Food

The foods of Mexican Americans belong to one of the oldest regional cuisines in the United States and are simultaneously one of the newest immigrant contributions to this multicultural nation. Native American and Hispanic influences survive in the corn tortillas and chiles rellenos (stuffed peppers) prepared in and around Santa Fe, New Mexico. Meanwhile, Mexican food displays its endless novelty wherever immigrant communities spring up; for example, exotic Oaxacan specialties appear in established barrios of Los Angeles and Chicago at the same time that familiar foods from the conventional migrant-sending regions around Guadalajara and Puebla spread to new parts of the country, such as Atlanta and New York City. Yet most people in the United States encounter Mexican food neither in isolated New Mexico towns nor in urban immigrant enclaves but rather in suburban restaurants and fast-food outlets where the cooking bears little resemblance to dishes served south of the border. Between settled tradition and immigrant adaptation, appropriation and commercialization, the experience of Mexican Americans encompasses the entire history of food in the United States.

For Mexican Americans, fusion cuisine is not a trendy new discovery but a historical process reaching back for centuries and reflecting broader social currents. Following the conquest of Mexico, Native American and Spanish cooking traditions blended to form a mestizo cuisine, even as race mixture spread through colonial society. Racial boundaries were particularly fluid along the northern frontier of New Spain, stretching from Texas to California, as the threat of Indian raids made mestizo settlers appear European by comparison with nomadic Apaches and Comanches. When the United States invaded the region, Anglo newcomers seized land and wealth while imposing inflexible Northern European racial categories in which "white" meant the absence of a single drop of "colored" blood. To avoid discrimination, residents claimed Spanish ancestry and shunned more recent Mexican migrants. Although scornful at first of so-called Spanish foods, Anglos gradually acquired a taste for them. Predictably, nonethnics from William Gebhardt to Glen Bell made most of the profits from industrializing and marketing these foods to mainstream consumers. New waves of Mexican migrants in the second half of the twentieth century gradually began to reclaim the land and culture that they had lost a hundred years earlier.

This entry begins with a historical description of Mexican foods in general and of the peculiar nature of southwestern dishes. The second section provides a brief overview of the Mexican experience in the United States, with attention both to settlers who arrived before the U.S.-Mexican War and to immigrants who crossed the border after 1848. Next follows a discussion of how Mexican foods changed in order to appeal to mainstream consumers and how Mexican Americans asserted claims to United States citizenship based on the value of their foods. There is also a look at the regional nature of southwestern cuisine, including historical definitions of Tex-Mex, Cal-Mex, New Mexican, and Sonoran foods. The entry concludes with a look at contemporary trends of the early twenty-first century, including the globalization of Mexican cuisine, and a consideration of the social contradictions that have persisted.

Historical Origins

The cuisines of Mexico comprise a complex mixture of regional and ethnic influences that have been blending for centuries. After the conquest, sophisticated Native American cuisines, based on the staple grain maize (corn) and on stews made with chilies, combined with

Spanish foods, particularly with wheat and meats. In some regions, such as Oaxaca and Yucatan, indigenous dishes remained ascendant, while along the Gulf Coast and in the central highlands Spanish culture had more influence. In the arid north, which was only lightly settled by nomadic peoples, European foods became predominant. This *norteño* cuisine, which later became "Mexican American," was characterized by the use of wheat flour instead of corn, tortillas, large amounts of meat, especially beef, and a relatively limited variety of vegetables, herbs, and chilies.

When the Spanish arrived in Mesoamerica, they found not a single "Aztec nation" but rather many diverse cultures including the Maya, Nahua, Totonac, and Zapotec. These societies nevertheless shared a common, basically vegetarian cuisine in which the combination of corn and beans provided a source of complementary protein that ensured a sound diet. Simmering the corn with lye to make hominy and then grinding and cooking it as tortillas or tamales offset the threat of pellagra. The addition of squash, avocados, and greens, as well as turkeys, small dogs, fish, and rodents also helped round out the nutritional balance. Finally, chilies provided the basis for elaborate festive stews called *mollis* and made even the everyday tortillas and beans tasty.

The indigenous peoples of the Southwest relied on a variety of strategies to make optimum use of plant and animal life in the arid region. They hunted deer as well as smaller game, such as rabbits, mice, and snakes, and gathered edible desert plants including prickly pear, mesquite bean pods, maguey, and roots, herbs, and greens. In some areas nature provided so abundantly that the inhabitants had little incentive to cultivate the land and lived a nomadic existence gathering acorns in California or fish and sea turtles along the Pacific coast. Pueblo communities on the upper Rio Grande, by contrast, developed sophisticated corn and bean agriculture.

The Spanish conquest of Mexico and the introduction of African slaves produced a social hierarchy known as the system of castes, which theoretically separated elite Spaniards from Native American villages. In practice, however, the races had become completely intermingled and colonial status derived more from ethnicity and wealth than from genetic differences. Thus, Spanish dishes such as *arroz con pollo* (chicken with rice) and *puchero* (stew) gained high status while Native American enchiladas, tamales, and gorditas were more plebeian. Nevertheless, culinary blending occurred as the Spaniards began eating chilies and frijoles while the indigenous people gained a taste for European livestock. Dishes such as *mole poblano*, which blended Old World spices with New World chilies, later became the basis for Mexico's mestizo national cuisine.

Settlers on the northern frontier of the Mexican states (that is, in the present-day southwestern United States), although generally mestizos from central Mexico, attempted to construct a Spanish society. This culture included the medieval Iberian tradition of raising cattle using herdsmen mounted on horseback—the vaquero culture later taken over by Anglo cowboys—as well as irrigated agriculture. Cooking techniques often consisted of methods of preservation, such as making cheese and sausage. The colonists also produced large amounts of *carne seca*, a form of jerky made by cutting beef into long strips and drying it in the desert sun, under cages to keep the flies out. To preserve pork, they made a vinegar marinade called *adovo*, heavily spiced with chilies and quite different from Spanish preparations with the same name.

Whenever possible, the settlers cultivated European wheat, although the expense of operating mills and ovens often forced women to grind wheat by hand and cook it in the form of tortillas rather than bread. The pervasive use of chilies in stews and salsas likewise demonstrated the Native American influence on Spanish cuisine. The rich agricultural land of California allowed settlers there to produce those Mediterranean staples, wine and olives, unavailable elsewhere in New Spain, but even the wealthiest settlers ate a generally Spartan diet with only an occasional luxury, such as imported chocolate. These sturdy frontier foods later became the foundation for southwestern cuisine and a bulwark of Mexican American identity.

The Legacy of Guadalupe Hidalgo

When U.S. conquistadores imposed the Treaty of Guadalupe Hidalgo in 1848, Mexicans living in the frontier region from Texas to California became subjects of a hostile power. The Anglo newcomers looked on Mexicans with disdain based on recent war memories, old stereotypes from the sixteenth-century "Black Legend" of the Spanish as cruel, and simple racism. Many Mexicans fled, and those who stayed fought a losing battle for half a century to preserve their land and wealth. As the border economy developed in the late nineteenth century, northward migration resumed, and although it halted briefly during the Depression, the onset of World War II and the postwar boom brought ever-greater numbers of Mexicans into their old frontier. Meanwhile established Mexican Americans fought an ongoing battle to gain the rights of citizenship and equality promised not just in the Treaty of 1848 but also in the Constitution of 1789.

The displacement of Mexican Americans followed an uneven but inexorable course in the second half of the nineteenth century. Ranchers in Texas were often lynched by land-hungry Anglos, who looked down on Mexicans as "chilis," "greasers," and in the case of women "hot tamales." The relative isolation of New Mexico and Arizona allowed Hispanics there to preserve more of their wealth and culture, but the indignities visited on the Californio, or original Spanish-descended, elite led to the first great work of Mexican American culinary literature, ironically entitled *El cocinero español* (The Spanish Cook, 1898). The author, Encarnación Pinedo, heiress of the prominent Berreyesa clan, suffered the loss of the family estate and the lynching of eight uncles and cousins. Her cookbook nevertheless sought to preserve classical Mexican dishes such as moles and tamales, even though she disguised them with Spanish titles.

Mexican migration to the United States began at the end of the nineteenth century and continues with greater or lesser intensity in the early twenty-first century. The mining industry attracted many workers to the Southwest, while railroad construction carried them to more distant centers, such as Kansas City and Chicago. The dangers of the Mexican Revolution of 1910 increased the flow of migrants, while the Great Depression brought restrictions and even the forced repatriation of many Mexican American citizens. The bracero program was established in 1942 to provide substitute agricultural laborers needed to replace those who had gone to fight in World War II. Mexican guest workers often complained about their inability to get familiar foods, but they also acquired a taste for Idaho potatoes and Carolina barbecue. When Congress finally ended the program in 1964, migrants continued informally along familiar routes and in ever-greater numbers as economic crises of the 1980s and 1990s made it difficult to earn a living at home.

Mexican Americans meanwhile firmly established their rights as citizens. Military service in World War II inspired a generation of Mexican American politicians to win office throughout the Southwest. When Frito-Lay launched their Frito Bandito advertising campaign, the threat of a lawsuit by the National Mexican American Anti-Defamation Committee forced the company to dis-

continue the commercial and its offending stereotype in 1970. Although a nativist backlash arose in the late twentieth century, for example, in California's Proposition 187 that would have denied basic medical and educational services to migrants, Mexican Americans continued to consolidate their political and economic power.

The Americanization of Mexican Food and Vice Versa

Immigrant food vendors inevitably had to adapt their cuisines in order to appeal to mainstream consumers. In the case of Mexican Americans, the most obvious barrier to acceptance by Anglos lay in the piquancy of chilies. The process of industrializing labor-intensive cooking techniques posed more profound dilemmas, and nonethnics, who were ignorant of the subtleties of Mexican cuisine but skilled in techniques of high-volume cooking, often reaped the initial profits from mass-marketing. Nevertheless, appeals to authenticity allowed Mexican

Americanization of Mexican Food. *Mexican Cookery for American Homes*, published by Gebhardt Chili Powder Company (San Antonio, Texas, 1943). *Collection of Andrew F. Smith*

Americans a measure of control over the popularization of their foods, thus defying simplistic notions of cultural hegemony and appropriation.

The process of cultural appropriation is best illustrated through the history of San Antonio chili. This dish originated with eighteenth-century settlers as a simple mole spiced with red chilies, cumin, and oregano, which are still the distinctive flavors of the Tex-Mex kitchen. By the 1880s women known as "Chili Queens" had begun setting up tables in San Antonio plazas to sell their spicy stew, while being carefully chaperoned by male relatives. The dish became a prominent tourist attraction and gained national attention at the 1893 World's Columbian Exposition in Chicago. A few years later, in 1896, chili powder was industrialized by the German immigrant William Gebhardt, whose company later began selling packaged dinners, including canned chili and tamales, by mail throughout the country. Already tamed down for Anglo palates, chili underwent further alterations when a side order of beans was dumped into the mixture and spread on hot dogs. In Cincinnati in the 1920s, the Macedonian immigrant Tom Kiradjieff added cinnamon and allspice to the stew and served it over spaghetti, with multiple layers of beans, onions, and cheese. Meanwhile, back in San Antonio, after a long struggle with city inspectors, the original chili stands were closed down as a supposed health hazard in 1936. After a brief revival in 1939, they closed for good in 1943.

Despite these indignities, Mexican Americans insisted on the value of their food and used the home economics movement as a way of claiming U.S. citizenship. This campaign began in New Mexico, where the descendants of colonial settlers still retained social prominence. In 1939 Cleofas M. Jaramillo published *The Genuine New Mexico Tasty Recipes* in order to counter inaccurate descriptions of local foods. A decade later Fabiola Cabeza de Vaca Gilbert, a graduate of the New Mexico College of Agriculture and Mechanic Arts, wrote a larger volume, *The Good Life: New Mexico Traditions and Food* (1949). Meanwhile in San Francisco, a courageous, blind Mexican immigrant named Elena Zelayeta, who supported her family by teaching cooking classes, published *Elena's Famous Mexican and Spanish Recipes* (1944). These works sought to counter stereotypes of Mexican food as unhealthy and unsanitary and to gain acceptance for this cuisine within the broader society.

Yet at the same time, Mexican American foods were changing in order to appeal to Anglo customers. The combination plate, rarely seen in Mexico but one of the mainstays of Mexican American restaurants, may have originated in Texas early in the twentieth century. Tacos, enchiladas, and tostadas, known collectively as *antojitos* (little whimsies), had long provided quick meals, often eaten while standing on a street corner, to working-class Mexicans. Mainstream diners required a more formal meal, including a plate and silverware, so Hispanic cooks complied, perhaps spreading quantities of red chili sauce and cheese on top because the customers were using forks anyway. Anglo expectations for a quick plate filled with food, as opposed to the Mexican preference for separate, smaller courses, encouraged cooks to combine the main dish with rice (usually eaten prior to the main course) and beans (after). Numbering the combination plates relieved non-Spanish speakers of the need to pronounce what they were eating, a strategy also used by Chinese cooks seeking a crossover clientele.

Small restaurants have high mortality rates, and Mexican American establishments are no exception; nevertheless a few have survived through the years to attain the status of enduring monuments. The names of these restaurants have become local legends: in Los Angeles, El Cholo, founded in 1923 as the Sonora Café; Tucson's El Charro Café, dating back to 1922; La Posta, which opened in Mesilla, New Mexico, in 1939; and Mi Tierra, located on San Antonio's Market Square since 1951. The fame of these culinary monuments spread far beyond ethnic enclaves, in part because of celebrity endorsements. El Cholo became a watering hole for Hollywood stars from Clark Gable to Jack Nicholson.

Another form of word-of-mouth advertising came through culinary legends, endlessly repeated and debated, about which southwestern restaurateur named Ignacio invented nachos, or who created the original margarita or the first green enchiladas with chicken and sour cream. These tales often reveal a desire for the broader society to accept ethnic foods; for example, the owners of El Charro Café in Tucson recall a visit in 1946 by Thomas E. Dewey in which the presidential candidate supposedly mistook one of the soft, thin flour tortillas for a napkin and tucked it into his collar. These urban legends gently chide Anglos for their unfamiliarity with Mexican food and by extension Mexican society. Perhaps the most famous story tells of President Gerald Ford eating a tamale without taking off the husk.

Another route to financial success for Mexican American restaurants came from the development of franchise chains. The largest of these, Texas-based El Chico, began in 1931 with Adelaida "Mama" Cuellar's tamale stand at the Kaufman County Fair. After losing a number of small-town cafes in the Depression, the family moved to Dallas and opened the first El Chico in 1940. When the World War II ended, the Cuellar brothers began expanding, locally at first, and eventually throughout the South and Southwest before selling the restaurants in the 1990s.

Despite the success of culinary monuments and southwestern chains, Mexican American food did not attain a national presence until taken over by nonethnic corporations such as Taco Bell. The founder of this chain, Glen Bell, began running a hamburger stand in Downey, California, in the 1950s, but rather than compete with McDonald's in nearby San Bernardino, he decided to seek out a new market niche, tacos. His breakthrough came when he pre-fried corn tortillas in order to speed up production, thus creating the prototype for the hard taco shell. Mexican-style food was thereby released from the need for fresh tortillas, which had tied it to the ethnic community, allowing the chain to expand throughout the country. Founded in 1962, Taco Bell went public in 1969, was bought by PepsiCo in 1978, and then spunoff as Tricon Global Restaurants with Pizza Hut and KFC in 1997. With more than 4,600 locations worldwide, and with look-alike competitors such as Del Taco, Taco Time, and Taco Tico, the company defined a whole new architecture of Mexican food consisting of a layer of homogenized meat topped with shredded lettuce, chopped tomato, incandescent cheese, and hot sauce served on a carbohydrate platform, whether old-fashioned taco shells or burrito wrappers or newfangled gordita and chalupa packets.

Supermarket sales of tortillas, chips, salsas, and other Mexican American foods had grown into a $3 billion market by the mid 1990s. The industry, at the beginning of the twenty-first century, was dominated by Anglos, at least since Elmer Doolin had purchased the formula for Fritos corn chips from a nameless Mexican American in 1932 and Dave Pace began bottling salsa in 1948. Although sales of salsa surpassed ketchup in the 1990s, just three corporations controlled more than half the market: Pace, owned by Campbell Soup Company, Tostitos, a brand of Frito-Lay, and Old El Paso, a subsidiary of Pillsbury.

Manufacturers have likewise stripped tortillas of their original ethnic character by adding cinnamon or pesto flavoring and marketing them as "wraps." In an ironic twist, one of the great corporate champions of authentic Mexican food in the United States has been the Mission brand, a subsidiary of the Maseca Corporation, which has been a major force in displacing "mom and pop" tortilla factories in Mexico. Not to be confused with Maseca, Pancho Ochoa, founder of the Pollo Loco chain, showed the possibility for marketing Mexican food to mainstream consumers. Even the Taco Bell dog, Madison Avenue's creation, has been subverted on T-shirts that show a very proletarian Chihuahua urinating on a police car labeled "Migra"—the border patrol.

Tex-Mex and Other Border Cuisines

Although the cooking of the Southwest forms part of a broader *norteño* culture, common to both sides of the border, considerable variety exists from one state to the next. Tex-Mex cooking, found in northeastern Mexico as well as Texas, is noted for the predominance of beef and tiny, lethal *chiltepín* peppers. The foods of the Sonoran desert, including the Mexican state of the same name and southern Arizona, likewise emphasize beef but accompanied by mild Anaheim peppers. New Mexico, which as a region also encompasses Chihuahua, southern Colorado, and northern Arizona, is built on eponymous chilies and pork instead of beef. In contrast to the deep roots of other southwestern styles, Cal-Mex cooking is a relatively modern offshoot, cultivated primarily by new immigrants, not all of them from Mexico, and flavored by memories of the Californio ranching society that existed before 1848.

Fajitas are perhaps the best-known example of Tex-Mex cooking and paradoxically one of its most recent inventions. Their novelty lies not in the cooking technique used for fajitas but rather in their presentation and their success among mainstream diners. The method of pounding meat paper-thin, marinating it for additional taste and tenderness, then cooking it quickly on a hot fire is used in the classic northern Mexican carne asada. This elaborate treatment is needed because Mexicans prefer the taste of freshly slaughtered meat, rather than aged Omaha steaks that have been tenderized by the onset of decomposition. The technique was used by Mexican Americans in the lower Rio Grande valley, who could afford only cast-off cuts, such as the diaphragm muscle, originally known as *arrachera*. Other popular meats included *aldilla* (flank steak), *machitos* (organ meats), *tripitas* (tripe), and *barbacoa de cabeza* (pit-roasted cow's head). The transformation of humble *arrachera* or *aldilla* into fashionable fajitas probably began about 1970 in the lower Rio Grande valley with the adoption of the more appetizing name "fajita" from the diminutive of "belt," which refers back to skirt steak and diaphragm muscle. By the mid-1970s, fajitas had become a signature dish in Mama Ninfa's restaurant in Houston, although as late as 1980, *Jane Butel's Tex-Mex Cookbook* did not use the term. Once the fad caught on in the early 1980s, the price of skirt steak rose beyond the reach of the working-class Mexican Americans who invented the dish and also led to such oxymorons as chicken and shrimp fajitas.

Despite the fajita craze, the true heart of Tex-Mex cooking is the chili gravy. Although many people think of chili as a beef stew, it is the pan gravy made with chili powder, cumin, and small amounts of ground beef that imparts the distinctive Tex-Mex taste to enchiladas, tamales, and even Frito pies (a concoction made by adding chili gravy and cheese to individual packages of Fritos). Among Mexican Americans, chili con carne stew is often referred to as *carne guisada*. Another Tex-Mex favorite is *cabrito al pastor*, although it is more often eaten in Mexico, where tender young goats are more easily available.

The foods of Sonora resemble those of south Texas, although with a milder flavor, because of the use of Anaheim peppers. Mexican Americans in Arizona, as in Texas, often prepare the colonial style jerky called *carne seca* or *machaca*, for the pounding needed to reconstitute it. Communal dinners of carne asada are also a favorite for festive occasions. Flour tortillas, while common throughout the Southwest, reach the peak of artistry in Sonora, where cooks often roll them out to perfectly round, paper-thin disks a foot and a half in diameter. When wrapped around beef or bean fillings they form the basis for burritos, which in turn take the name "chimichanga" (basically meaning "thingamajig") when deep-fried.

The soul of Mexican cuisine has always been the chile. While the cooks of Old Mexico experimented with blending different chilies to make mole, the cooks of New Mexico perfected the cultivation and cooking of a single chile. The New Mexico chile forms the basic ingredient for both *chile verde* (green) and *chile colorado* (red), which can be served thick as an enchilada sauce or with broth and vegetables as a stew, although in the latter case the green variety is more common, sometimes with the name *carne con chile verde* or *chile verde caldo* to distinguish it from the sauce. For those unable to choose between the two sauces, restaurants in New Mexico offer a combination of red and green known as Christmas.

Another local twist is the technique of stacking enchiladas like pancakes with only cheese as a garnish. Other New Mexico dishes include the celebrated blue corn and the little-known *chicos* (roasted green ears). Pork rather than beef became the most common meat, used both for chile stews and the colonial dish *carne adovada*, which remains a local favorite. Meals end with such distinctive desserts as fried sopaipillas with honey.

When classically trained chefs began searching for a distinctive national cuisine in the 1980s, Santa Fe became the epicenter of upscale southwestern food. John Rivera Sedlar, an expatriate New Mexican living in Los Angeles, started this trend in 1980 when he began introducing Mexican street foods to the classical French menu of his restaurant, St. Estèphe. Soon such upstarts as caviar on blue corn tortillas and lobster tamales had shouldered aside the creations of Escoffier. This new style returned to Santa Fe a few years later when Mark Miller opened the Coyote Café and from there spread throughout the Southwest.

Cal-Mex cooking is perhaps the most difficult kind of southwestern cooking to define historically, although Encarnación Pinedo's *El cocinero español* offers glimpses of the pastoral society of colonial Alta California. Many recipes were common throughout the Southwest, such as *carne con chile* and *barbacoa de cabeza*, but there were also directions for adding olives and raisins to tamales, an example of the unique combination of California's agricultural bounty with Mexican culinary traditions. The old ranchero class of colonial settlers has largely been overwhelmed by later migration, and much of the repertoire of modern Cal-Mex is likewise of recent arrival. The fish taco, for example, now a specialty of San Diego, was discovered by surfers, such as Ralph Rubio, while vacationing in Baja California. Steak burritos, often flavored with citrus marinades, were also subsumed under the Cal-Mex banner.

Fajitas in the Global Village

Contradictory images of Mexico and of Mexican foods persist. Lower-class stereotypes have made it difficult for even highly rated Mexican restaurateurs to charge prices comparable to those of their French and Italian colleagues, although they use the same quality of ingredients. The supposed primitivism of Mexican cuisine has also encouraged large-scale culinary tourism to Native American regions of Mexico by aging hippies eager to re-create peasant foods on their Viking stoves. Cheap alcohol attracts hordes of college students to

Cancún for spring break, even as top-shelf *añejo* tequilas compete with the finest Scotch whiskys and cognacs. Tex-Mex food has spread around the world, distorting global perceptions of Mexican culture, at the same time that increasing numbers of Mexicans migrants have been transforming American culture. The trends established since the Treaty of Guadalupe Hidalgo in 1848 thus seem likely to continue into the future.

The globalization of Mexican cuisine has resulted less from migration, as was the case with Chinese and Italian foods, than from the process of Americanization. Although Mexican expatriates introduced their food to Europe at least as early as the 1950s, some of the oldest surviving restaurants, including the Pacifico Café chain, which first opened in Amsterdam, were established in the 1970s by expatriate members of the very American California counterculture. At about the same time, U.S. military commissaries began to create the business infrastructure for supplying Mexican ingredients to servicemen and servicewomen stationed around the world, thus giving a whole new meaning to the term "cultural imperialism." For a few decades, the expatriate-founded basically Tex-Mex and Cal-Mex restaurants maintained a pretense of Mexican identity, but that had passed by the mid-1990s when American regional foods became an international fad and corporate chains began establishing overtly Tex-Mex restaurants throughout Europe and Japan. As a result of their travels, these already Americanized foods underwent further changes; in Paris, for example, chicken fajitas began to taste like coq au vin.

Tex-Mex influences even spread to Mexico City in response both to tourist demands for familiar ethnic food and to Mexican travel to the United States. The archetypal example of this cultural clash came about around 1992 when Taco Bell opened an outlet in Mexico City. Fearing rejection by local aficionados, managers took care to offer authentic tacos al carbon served with fresh corn tortillas, but as a result they disappointed middle-class Mexican customers who nostalgically expected the standard tomato, lettuce, and cheese combination they had encountered on vacation in the United States. The franchise soon closed, but more mundane Tex-Mex influences, such as chips and salsa, continued to spread through Mexico. At the turn of the millennium, fashionable restaurants in suburban San Angel and Polanco began a new trend of serving fajitas, complete with sizzling plates, grilled onions, green peppers, and sour cream. The irony of wealthy Mexicans imitating Tex-Mex food is compounded by the origins of the dish among poor Mexican Americans in South Texas.

Further ironies arose from the quest of North American foodies for a pristine version of Mexican cuisine, untainted by Tex-Mex influences, and referred to somewhat ambiguously along the border as "interior Mexican." This trend dated back at least to the 1920s, when Anita Brenner published indigenous recipes in her journal *Mexican Folkways*. The foodies' desire to experience authentic Mexican cooking began in 1972 with the publication of Diana Kennedy's *The Cuisines of Mexico*. Disdaining border foods, Kennedy concentrated on the regional dishes of south and central Mexico, such as moles from Oaxaca, seafood from Veracruz, and roasted pig from the Yucatán. By the 1980s, the interest in regional Mexican cooking had led to the opening of upscale restaurants, some of the first of which were the Frontera Grill in Chicago and Rosa Mexicano in New York City. Meanwhile, culinary tourism became a thriving industry, with a dozen cooking schools and tour groups in Oaxaca alone. One college graduate signed up for a private cooking class in Oaxaca and found himself in a rather proletarian home, preparing a large pot of turkey mole under the direction of a Mexican woman, while her family hovered outside the kitchen waiting to eat his leftovers. The sharp señora thus briefly reversed the international division of labor, turning a hapless gringo tourist into a migrant worker—even getting him to buy the groceries.

For Mexican migrant workers, kitchen work is more likely to be a way of life than an afternoon's diversion. Spanish has become the lingua franca of the restaurant world, as Mexicans and Central Americans provide essential labor in French, Chinese, and American, as well as Mexican restaurants. Yet hardworking busboys, dishwashers, and prep cooks have little opportunity, as the twenty-first century begins, to advance into well-paid positions as executive or sous-chefs. The exploited condition of undocumented kitchen workers in upscale fusion restaurants is matched by the self-exploitation of families struggling to maintain taquerias in ethnic barrios and of commissary van drivers who deliver Mexican food to factories across the country. Workers like these do not appear on the Food Channel, but they nevertheless represent the future, not just of Mexican American but of all American cuisine.

[*See also* Batidos; Chili; Chorizo; Frito-Lay, *sidebar on* Frito Pie; Navajo Tacos; Pinedo, Encarnación; Salsa; Southwestern Regional Cookery; Taco Bell; Tequila.]

BIBLIOGRAPHY

Arreola, Daniel D. *Tejano South Texas: A Mexican American Cultural Province.* Austin, TX: University of Texas Press, 2002.

Bentley, Amy. "From Culinary Other to Mainstream American: Meanings and Uses of Southwestern Cuisine." *Southern Folklore* 55, no. 3 (1998): 238–252.

Cabeza de Baca Gilbert, Fabiola. *The Good Life: New Mexico Traditions and Food.* Santa Fe, NM: Museum of New Mexico, 1982.

Campa, Arthur L. *Hispanic Culture in the Southwest.* Norman, OK: University of Oklahoma Press, 1979.

De León, Arnoldo. *The Tejano Community, 1836–1900.* Dallas, TX: Southern Methodist University Press, 1997.

Gabaccia, Donna R. *We Are What We Eat: Ethnic Foods and the Making of Americans.* Cambridge, MA: Harvard University Press, 1998.

Garcilazo, Jeffrey Marcos. "*Traqueros*: Mexican Railroad Workers in the United States, 1870–1930." Ph.D. diss., University of California, Santa Barbara, 1995.

Jaramillo, Cleofas M. *The Genuine New Mexico Tasty Recipes.* Santa Fe, NM: Ancient City Press, 1981.

Limón, José E. *Dancing with the Devil: Society and Cultural Poetics in Mexican-American South Texas.* Madison, WI: University of Wisconsin Press, 1994.

Martin, Patricia Preciado. *Songs My Mother Sang to Me: An Oral History of Mexican American Women.* Tucson, AZ: University of Arizona Press, 1992.

McWilliams, Carey. *North from Mexico: The Spanish-Speaking People of the United States.* Philadelphia: J. P. Lippincott, 1948.

Montaño, Mario. "Appropriation and Counterhegemony in South Texas: Food Slurs, Offal Meats, and Blood." In *Usable Pasts: Traditions and Group Expressions in North America*, edited by Tad Tuleja, 50–67. Logan, UT: Utah State University Press, 1997.

Pilcher, Jeffrey M. *¡Que vivan los tamales! Food and the Making of Mexican Identity.* Albuquerque, NM: University of New Mexico Press, 1998.

Pinedo, Encarnación. *El cocinero español.* San Francisco: Imprenta de E.C. Hughes, 1898.

Ruiz, Vicki L. *From Out of the Shadows: Mexican Women in Twentieth-Century America.* New York and Oxford: Oxford University Press, 1998.

Smith, Andrew F. "Tacos, Enchiladas, and Refried Beans: The Invention of Mexican-American Cookery." In *Cultural and Historical Aspects of Food*, edited by Mary Wallace Kelsey and ZoeAnn Holmes, 183–203. Corvallis, OR: Oregon State University Press, 1999.

Valle, Victor M. *Recipes of Memory: Five Generations of Mexican Cuisine in Los Angeles.* New York: New Press, 1995.

Valle, Victor M., and Rodolfo D. Torres. *Latino Metropolis.* Minneapolis, MN: University of Minnesota Press, 2000.

Zelayeta, Elena. *Elena's Famous Mexican and Spanish Recipes.* San Francisco: Prentice Hall, 1944.

JEFFREY M. PILCHER

Microbreweries

The microbrewery industry, as we know it in this country, began in July 1965, when Fritz Maytag purchased an interest in the Anchor Steam Brewery (est. 1896) of San Francisco, California. Maytag's rescue of the company and its turnaround into a thriving firm were to prove an inspiration to an entire generation of followers. In January 1983 the United States could boast of just fifty-one companies operating only eighty breweries that provided fewer than twenty-five nationally distributed brands. Not before or since has the United States had fewer commercial breweries in operation. Just thirty years later there were more than twelve hundred breweries, producing some five thousand different beers. There are more different styles of beer made in the United States than in any other country in the world, and it all happened over a remarkably short period of time.

As Maytag said, "We are all friends in fermentation," and so it was in California in the mid-1960s. People with money and an appreciation of fine wine began investing in California real estate, developing vineyards. They invested, they planted, and they waited for California to become another Bordeaux. The vines grew and produced fine grapes, the weather was predictable, and then the Internal Revenue Service revised the "Limited Partnership" provisions that made investing in ventures like cattle futures and boutique wineries very profitable. Even with the shakeout of financially distressed wineries at the end of the twentieth century, there was a good amount of world-class wine flowing from the Napa, Sonoma, and Mendocino valleys of California. The success of the wineries caught the attention of others. These were people who knew what well-made, fresh beer tasted like. It was a demand waiting to be satisfied.

Jack McAuliffe was stationed at a military base in Scotland while on active duty with the U.S. Navy in the mid-1970s. His appreciation of the local ales was restrained by the size of his paycheck. To compensate, he took up the local custom of home brewing. When he returned to the United States, he continued home brewing. He got so good at it that in 1977, just one year before federal legislation was passed legalizing home brewing, he was toasting his partners Suzy Stern and Jane Zimmerman, of the New Albion Brewing Company in Sonoma, with the first pints of ale that marked the rebirth of the small-brewing industry in the United States, lost because of Prohibition. That year the first U.S. microbrewery, with an annual production of two hundred barrels, began producing British-style ale and a stout. Their market was limited, but their reputation flourished in the friendly climate of the California wine country.

The Microbrew Boom

In fact, import beers were beginning to find increasing favor with consumers who were returning from their travels overseas and demanding the same full-flavored beers they had enjoyed in Europe. These consumers demanded foods and beverages of quality, and they knew quality. They defined "quality" by a product's ingredients, not by the brand name. This search for quality continues unabated.

If Jack McAuliffe was the father of the U.S. microbrewing industry, then Bert Grant gets the credit for making the brewpub, a brewery with a restaurant or a restaurant with a brewery, part of the North American food service business. It was in 1982 when, for the first time since Prohibition, Bert Grant's Yakima Brewing and Malting Company was permitted not only to sell beer at the brewery but also to serve food. The brewpub was born. Two years later, in 1984, the small breweries (breweries that produce fewer than fifteen thousand barrels of beer annually) began to spread, including Riley-Lyon in Arkansas, Boulder in Colorado, Snake River in Idaho, Millstream in Iowa, Columbia River in Oregon, Kessler in Montana, and Chesapeake Bay in Virginia. That same year, on the East Coast, New York City could boast of a microbrewery when Manhattan Brewing Company opened its doors in the SoHo neighborhood and Jim Koch established the Boston Beer Company in Boston.

The growth of the microbrew industry in 1990 included the opening of the Dock Street Brewing Company in Philadelphia, Pennsylvania. That year the Sierra Nevada Brewery, in Chico, California, became the first microbrewery to break into the regional ranks when its production reached 31,000 barrels of beer. The Association of Brewers, a trade association of brewers, reckons that the term "microbrewery" is applied to breweries producing less than 15,001 barrels of beer annually. The "regional" breweries produce between 15,001 and two million barrels of beer annually. In 1990, Wendy Pound and Barbara Groom opened the Lost Coast Brewery & Café. Just four years later, in 1994, California could boast of eighty-four microbreweries or brewpubs, more breweries than were in operation in the entire United States in 1984. By 1995 approximately five hundred breweries were in operation in the United States, and the numbers continued to grow at a pace of three or four per week. The next year there were more than one thousand microbreweries and brewpubs rolling out over 5 million barrels annually. That was also the year that a record 333 new brewpubs and microbreweries opened for business.

According to statistics provided by the Association of Brewers, by 1977 the opening of 218 new microbreweries pushed the total number of microbreweries to 1,320 and

Microbrews. The Park Slope Ale House in Brooklyn specializes in microbrews. *Photograph by Joe Zarba*

total production to 5,573,427 barrels of beer. However, one year later, 77 new breweries were only able to increase total production by 1,844 barrels, as larger microbreweries closed at the same time smaller "pub-breweries" opened their doors. The growth of pub-breweries (restaurants with on-premise breweries producing beer for on-premise consumption) would soon outpace the traditional microbreweries that brewed, bottled, and kegged beer for consumption in restaurants, taverns, and the home. The result was an interesting situation of more breweries opening while the total number of barrels of beer produced would remain stable. The result of the shakeout was a slowing down in the growth of the number of breweries and brewpubs. By 1999 there were 1,147 microbreweries producing 5.8 million barrels of more than five thousand brands of beer. One year later the number of breweries remained stable, but the amount of beer they were brewing had grown by 300,000 barrels. From those first pints of ale served by Jack McAuliffe in 1977, the microbrewing segment of the U.S. brewing industry grew over twenty-five years to include more than fourteen hundred breweries and brewpubs producing more than 6 million barrels of beer and maintaining a $3 billion share of the $51 billion annual U.S. production.

[See also Beer; Beer Barrels; Brewing.]

BIBLIOGRAPHY

Baron, Stanley. *Brewed in America.* Boston: Little, Brown & Company, 1962.
Baum, Dan. *Citizen Coors: An American Dynasty.* New York: Harper Collins, 2000.
Burrows, Edwin G. *Gotham: A History of New York City to 1898.* New York: Oxford University Press, 1999.
Jackson, Michael. *Beer Companion.* Philadelphia: Running Press, 1993.
Ronnenberg, Herman. *Beer and Brewing in the Inland Northwest, 1850–1959.* Moscow: University of Idaho Press, 1993.
Salem, F.W. *Beer: Its History and Its Economic Value as a National Beverage.* Hartford, CT: F. W. Salem & company, 1880.
Skilnik, Bob. *The History of Beer and Brewing in Chicago (1833–1978).* St. Paul, MN: Pogo Press, 1999.
Smith, Gregg. *Beer in America: The Early Years, 1587–1840.* Boulder, CO: Siris Books, 998.

PETER LaFRANCE

Microwave Ovens

The microwave oven emerged from radar experimentation during World War II. Percy Spencer, an employee of the Raytheon Corporation of Waltham, Massachusetts, walked in front of a magnetron that was emitting microwaves and discovered that microwaves had heating properties. After the war Spencer patented the process of heating food by conveying it under two parallel magnetrons. Two years later William M. Hall and Fritz A. Gross, who were coworkers of Spencer's, patented a microwave heating device enclosed in an oven. The prototype microwave oven constructed by Spencer in 1946 cost approximately one hundred thousand dollars. In 1947 Raytheon began constructing commercial ovens, calling them Radaranges. The main use of these ovens was heating cold sandwiches and other foods. Because these early microwave ovens cost in excess of three thousand dollars, sales were mainly limited to restaurants, railroads, cruise ships, and vending-machine companies.

Home Use

In the 1950s Raytheon dominated the microwave oven field. It was the principal manufacturer of magnetrons, but it licensed other companies, such as Hotpoint, Westinghouse, Kelvinator, Whirlpool, and Tappan, to manufacture ovens. In 1952 Tappan Company engineers who were experts in cooking developed an experimental commercial microwave oven intended for home use, but it proved impractical. Tappan continued to experiment and in October 1955 introduced the first domestic microwave oven. Designed to fit on top of a conventional oven, the microwave oven retailed for $1,295. It was marketed as an "electric range" with a cool oven that had the unique ability to reheat food. The Hotpoint division of General Electric unveiled its electronic oven in 1956. Both the Tappan and the Hotpoint ovens generated enthusiasm, but sales were dismal mainly because of the high price. In addition, specially packaged microwavable foods did not yet exist.

What turned the microwave oven into a common kitchen appliance was the invention in 1965 of a compact, low-cost magnetron by Keishi Ogura of the New Japan Radio Company. Raytheon acquired Amana Refrigeration, which developed the first affordable household Radarange, in 1967. The $495 unit was well received, and it launched a microwave oven revolution in American kitchens. In 1965 Litton caused a similar revolution with its Model 500, which was used on TWA airplanes. By 1970 Litton dominated the sale of microwave ovens to restaurants.

Obstacles to Adoption

Despite the early successes, the microwave oven industry faced serious challenges. The first involved persuading the American public that microwave ovens were safe. Safety concerns were raised after a federal government report issued in 1970 stated that microwave ovens leaked microwaves. New standards were developed, and microwave oven manufacturers developed safer ovens, but consumers remained concerned about potential risks. However, by 1975 microwave ovens were outselling gas ranges.

The second challenge had to do with food packaging. Microwave oven manufacturers had to persuade food processors both to take advantage of microwave technology in their product development and to repackage products for microwave use. Foil wrappers, for example, blocked microwaves and damaged ovens. When Americans began to purchase microwave ovens in the 1970s, food processors began producing microwave-safe cookware and microwavable food products. By the early twenty-first century, most American kitchens had microwave ovens, and thousands of microwavable products were being sold in the United States. The two major uses of microwave ovens are to reheat food and to pop popcorn. Several culinary experts have encouraged broader use of microwave ovens because of findings that vegetables retain more nutrients cooked in a microwave oven than when cooked in conventional ovens.

[*See also* Airplane Food; Dining Car; Popcorn; Ship Food; Stoves and Ovens, *subentry* Gas and Electric; Vegetables; Vending Machines.]

BIBLIOGRAPHY

Behrens, Charles W. "The Development of the Microwave Oven." *Appliance Manufacturer* 24 (1976): 70–72.

Buderi, Robert. *The Invention That Changed the World: How a Small Group of Radar Pioneers Won the Second World War and Launched a Technological Revolution.* New York: Simon and Schuster, 1997.

Smith, Andrew F. *Popped Culture: A Social History of Popcorn in America.* Columbia: University of South Carolina Press, 1999.

ANDREW F. SMITH

Mid-Atlantic Region

The melting pot of the Mid-Atlantic states—Pennsylvania, New Jersey, New York, and Delaware— has absorbed the flavors of millions of immigrants of hundreds of ethnic backgrounds over three centuries and blended them into a rich, diverse cuisine. The Mid-Atlantic region stretches from the Atlantic Ocean southwest of New England to

Lake Erie and Lake Ontario on the northwest border. Two of the most prominent rivers of the region are the Delaware River, providing the western boundary of New Jersey and linking Delaware to the other Mid-Atlantic states, and the Hudson River, separating New York from New Jersey. All the states in the Mid-Atlantic region share an early history of Native American tribes (Iroquois, Lenape, and Delaware) whose lives centered on the waterways until these early peoples were uprooted by European settlements, colonization, and immigration. The unique Mid-Atlantic cuisine is Native American fare combined with the adaptations and preferences of the European immigrants.

Mid-Atlantic cuisine is one of the most varied of any of the traditional colonial regional cuisines. The European settlers of the region were diverse in nationality and food customs, and the foods that they introduced flourished in the temperate climate and fertile farmlands of the region. Apples, pears, cherries, peaches, strawberries, and tomatoes were easily grown. In stark contrast was the cuisine of the New England region, which was restricted by harsh weather and poor land. The earliest European settlers in the Hudson and Delaware River valleys came from the Netherlands (Dutch) and Sweden in the seventeenth century. The English soon gained political control but did not dislodge the earlier Dutch settlements that continued their customs and traditional foodways. When William Penn, an English Quaker, was granted a charter for Pennsylvania in 1681, his liberal attitude of religious freedom attracted a variety of immigrants from central Europe, the Germans (Pennsylvania Dutch), and the Scotch Irish (Protestant Irish who had previously moved to northern Ireland from lowland Scotland) with their distinctive eating styles. In contrast, the Quakers of the West Jersey colony (southern New Jersey) had migrated from England and desired, as did other British immigrants to the Mid-Atlantic region, to replicate their traditional diet in the new land.

As they arrived in the Mid-Atlantic region, Europeans found the Native Americans thriving on the bounty of the indigenous foods of the region. The forests provided wild turkey and deer. The coastal shores with long, sandy beaches provided clams, oysters, mussels, scallops, and crabs, and the estuaries provided shelter to ducks, geese, and turtles. The waterways were filled with catfish, eel, salmon, shad, trout, and sturgeon. Wild fruit included blueberries, cranberries, grapes, and beach plums. In the villages gardens were prosperous with corn, beans, and squash. Food was bountiful and varied, and there were more meat and protein foods than the average European colonist had been accustomed to. To many of these new settlers, much of the Mid-Atlantic food was strange. In the short term, many of the Europeans adapted to the Native American foods, but the long-term goal was to bring European farm crops to the new land.

Native Shad and Sturgeon

When an anonymous Englishman visited the Delaware valley in the sixteenth century, he was amazed by the variety of fish. In a letter to England, he wrote about the four months of the year starting in the early spring when there was a bountiful amount of both shad (the largest fish of the herring family) and sturgeon (an exoskeleton fish known for caviar). Both the shad and the sturgeon would ascend the Delaware, Hudson, and Susquehanna Rivers every year from the Delaware, Hudson, and Chesapeake bays to spawn and then return to the bays. The Native Americans caught shad in weirs by the thousands, and archaeological evidence of shad bones documents the use of shad in their diet. The Swedish and Dutch settlers borrowed the Native American practices of drying and smoking shad and sturgeon and added European preservation processes such as pickling and salting. A typical Dutch feast of the mid-seventeenth century might include strips of smoked shad and sturgeon.

The earliest records of the shad runs are found in the eighteenth-century diaries of the Moravians, who settled the area around what became Bethlehem, Pennsylvania. The Moravians were using old bush nets of the Lenape to catch shad. The largest documented seasonal catch was 8,385 shad in 1772 (Scholl, *Return of a Native*). During shad season, March 1 to June 1, shad (especially the female fish with the roe) was the favorite fish in Philadelphia and dominated the market. American shad was the largest commercial fishery in the Mid-Atlantic region until the early twentieth century. American shad was also both a cultural and an economic mainstay of the Mid-Atlantic waterways, much like the cod of Massachusetts and the salmon of the Pacific Northwest.

European Introductions of Food

One of the first European introductions to the Mid-Atlantic region was wheat. In 1626 the Dutch planted wheat in New Netherland (New York). The Native American corn was a better crop for the new land, but the desire for the staff of life (wheat bread) was too strong,

and wheat was viewed as essential. Wheat thrived in the Mid-Atlantic region. Wheat was the chief agricultural product in New York State from the first Dutch settlements until the building of the Erie Canal in 1821 and was considered New Jersey's staple crop in the eighteenth century. Wheat growing in New York began on Long Island but moved to the river flats of the Hudson because of soil exhaustion on the island. The Mohawk River valley, central New York, and finally the Genesee valley in turn became the principal areas of wheat production. During the first half of the nineteenth century, New York and Pennsylvania were the two leading states in wheat production, but after the introduction and expansion of the railroad by the 1860s, less expensive, better wheat became available from the western states and dominated the market.

Apples were introduced to the Mid-Atlantic region in the seventeenth century. Apple seeds imported from England were planted in New Jersey as early as 1632. By the mid-eighteenth century, many types of European fruit trees other than apples were commonplace in orchards in New Jersey—apricots, peaches, plums, pears, medlars, almonds, and English cherries. Apple trees were by far the most economically important because the fruit was used for the production of cider. When the Swedes first arrived, beer was their common beverage, but by the time Peter Kalm (a Swedish botanist who wrote a travel diary in 1748) made his observations, apple trees were common, and cider was the preferred beverage. Other Mid-Atlantic colonies grew apples and made cider, but New Jersey's reputation for cider making was unique. An immigrant from Scotland, William Laird, in 1698 began to distill cider into apple brandy, better known as applejack. Commercial production of applejack was begun in 1780 by Robert Laird. Laird and Company in Scobeyville, New Jersey, is recognized as the oldest operating distillery in the United States.

Europeans wanted not only the grains, fruits, and vegetables with which they were familiar but also cattle for beef and milk. The raising of beef cattle began in New York with the Dutch in New Netherland. There are accounts of black and white cattle having been brought to New Netherland by Dutch settlers in the seventeenth century. The cuisine brought to the Mid-Atlantic region by the English-speaking immigrants who came primarily from England and Wales was based on dairy products. The most important sauce was the white sauce that incorporated butter or milk thickened with flour. It was not until the nineteenth century that dairying became an industry. All the Mid-Atlantic states are leading producers of milk. With dairying came cheese making, and New York leads all other states in the production of cheese. The New York State dairy industry was assisted greatly when native son Gail Borden developed a process to boil off the water from milk in an airtight vacuum that would concentrate milk so it would not spoil. This 1856 patent, which led to condensed milk, was of great value to the Union army in the Civil War and spread to general use in the aftermath of the war.

European Food Customs and Influences: The Pennsylvania Dutch

Small colonies of Dutch and Swedes settled in the Hudson and Delaware river valleys during the seventeenth century. Swedish settlers along the lower Delaware never numbered more than a few hundred and had little influence on Mid-Atlantic foodways. The early Dutch settlements were larger in number and had an influence on the cuisine of the region. In addition to bringing wheat, the Dutch also grew barley, buckwheat, and rye. Those were the preferred grains of the Dutch, but the indigenous corn of the Native Americans was incorporated into Dutch cuisine when the settlers arrived in the region. The Dutch used the "turkey wheat" (corn) to prepare sappaen (also spelled "supawn") for supper. In the Netherlands, the evening meal was typically gruel made from leftover bread soaked in milk. The Mid-Atlantic adaptation of this gruel was to prepare cornmeal with milk rather than water, as the Native Americans did. With the addition of meat and vegetables, the sappaen base became the dinner *hutspot*. In the Netherlands, *hutspot* was a stew containing finely minced beef or mutton. Many Dutch specialties of the Mid-Atlantic region have become part of the regional cuisine: *kool sla* (Dutch for "cabbage" and better known as cole slaw), headcheese, *oliekoecken* (doughnuts), pancakes, and waffles.

The Germans, or Pennsylvania Dutch (a corruption of the German word *Deutsch* for "German"), sought religious tolerance in the colony of Pennsylvania at the end of the seventeenth century and left an enduring and distinctive imprint on the foodways of Mid-Atlantic cuisine. The cooking of the Pennsylvania Dutch flourishes remarkably intact within a limited region in Pennsylvania (a rectangle approximately eighty miles long and thirty-five miles wide with Lancaster at its southwest corner and Allentown at its northeast corner)

but has had considerable influence on the entire state of Pennsylvania and surrounding states.

Almost everything the Pennsylvania Dutch ate came from the land they lived on. They grew their own fruits and vegetables and butchered their own pigs. Their cooking was an amalgam of the foods of their ancestors and the food they found or grew in their new country. The protein choice of their German ancestors was pork. In German-speaking Europe, pork was the most favored meat among the farming class because pigs did not require pasture land, which belonged to the nobility. The Pennsylvania Dutch continued the pork-raising tradition in the New World despite the wealth of available land. The pig was the basic ingredient of Pennsylvania Dutch cuisine. The butchering of pigs was a German family affair and resulted in hams, pork chops, schnitzel (pork pounded into thin slices), bacon, salt pork, pickled pigs knuckles, *souce* (jellied pigs feet), maw (a stomach stuffed with sausage and vegetables), and headcheese. Every part of the pig had some culinary use. One excellent example of the complete use of the pig was scrapple. The primary reason for preparing scrapple was use of leftovers after butchering. Typical recipes started with a pig's haslet (liver, heart, and other organs) and offal (the entrails normally discarded). These ingredients were thickened with half buckwheat and half Indian flour (corn flour, an example of incorporation of a New World product) and shaped into a loaf shape. At mealtime scrapple was sliced into slabs and fried in butter.

Dinner, the midday meal, was the largest meal among the Pennsylvania Dutch. The focus was on pork and dumplings, noodles, or potato dishes accompanied by the appropriate sweets and sours to make the meal more digestible. Chicken also was prominent in Pennsylvania Dutch cuisine, and chicken was inseparable from the homegrown spice saffron. Chicken corn soup (chicken, noodles, fresh corn, and parsley) and chicken potpie (fortified with squares of noodle dough) flaunted both the flavor and golden color of saffron, the world's most costly spice. Saffron is the dried stigmas of a fall-blooming crocus that was native to southern Europe. The German ancestors in the Rhineland were familiar with the spice. Saffron was brought to the Mid-Atlantic states with the Schwenkfelders, a group seeking religious freedom who came to America in 1734. Their traditional saffron-flavored yeast cake is referred to as "Schwenkfelder cake."

One of the most characteristic aspects of Pennsylvania Dutch cuisine was the use of seven sweets and seven

Pennsylvania Dutch Tradition. Amish couple cutting up beef for canning, near Honey Brook, Pennsylvania, March 1942. *Prints and Photographs Division, Library of Congress/John Collier*

sours on the table. Apple orchards provided the basic ingredients for two important sweet and sour products. Apples were sliced and cooked with cider for hours in large kettles that required constant stirring to prepare the sweet apple butter. Apple cider was allowed to ferment into vinegar as an essential ingredient for preparing the necessary sour pickles and spiced fruits for the sours at the table. Other sours included chowchow (a mixed vegetable pickle), spiced and pickled vegetables (onions, beets, mushrooms, cucumbers, and Jerusalem artichokes), dilled beans, and pickled watermelon rinds. In addition to apple butter, sweets were dried fruit, jams, jellies, conserves, sweet preserved fruits, cakes, cookies, and puddings. These sweets were not desserts but were eaten either with the main course or between courses. Dessert for the Pennsylvania Dutch was frequently pie. Many pies of all varieties would be baked on baking day—apple, pumpkin, rhubarb, peach, vinegar, and green tomato. But unique to the Pennsylvania Dutch is shoofly pie—a liquid filling of boiled molasses and water in a pastry crust topped with a crumb mixture and baked.

The culinary traditions of the Pennsylvania Dutch have stood the test of time but not without the effects of industrialization. The primary meat animal of the Germans was the pig, but the Pennsylvania Dutch also raised cattle in America for milk and plowing. When their milk production or work productivity waned, the cattle were sold to the English, who loved beef. With the introduction of the railroad into Pennsylvania in the 1830s and 1840s, the Pennsylvania Germans needed to consume their own beef

because the English had other sources. The necessity for the inclusion of more beef, which did not require the contrasting flavors of acidic fruits and vinegar as pork did, started a transformation of the German diet in the nineteenth century that progressed throughout the century. By the end of the Civil War (1865), with the increase of industrialization in the state, more beef was brought from the West, decreasing the pork intake further and influencing the Pennsylvania Germans to use more sweet pickles than sour. Lebanon bologna, a smoked beef sausage named for its hometown in Pennsylvania, is an example of the inclusion of beef in the Pennsylvania Dutch diet that has become a state specialty.

The Germans made culinary contributions to beverages as well as to food. Beer was the traditional beverage of the English, but English beers were dark, heavy-flavored beverages. German beer was lighter, and the lighter German lagers ultimately replaced the heavier British brew. A German brewer in Philadelphia began selling a lighter, bottom-fermented beer in 1840. The lighter lager and pilsner beers had become the standard of American beer by the mid-nineteenth century, and Philadelphia was the nation's first great beer-producing city.

Philadelphia

In the Pennsylvania Dutch region, the cooking of the German farmers who migrated to Penn's colony remains relatively unchanged. Within miles of this tradition, however, is Philadelphia with its culinary tradition based initially on the foodways of the English Quakers and later influenced by the foods of the French, Pennsylvania Dutch, and Italian Americans.

The early Quakers who founded Philadelphia were not drab in either appearance or foods. Their foods had a distinctly British flavor appropriate for the city's heritage, and the dishes reflected Britain's colonial days with the use of ingredients imported from Europe and the West and East Indies. Succulent turtle from the West Indies, the finest Madeira, burgundy, and claret wines were available. Philadelphia food in the eighteenth century was flavored with spices, sugar, rose and orange flower water, almonds, and currants.

Along with the affinity for spices went a sweet tooth. Philadelphians loved desserts and sweetmeats (food with sugar as its main ingredient) and were early introduced to ice cream. Philadelphia became noted for its excellent ice creams, which were influenced by French ice cream but different in that they were not based on eggs.

Philadelphia first had public notice of ice cream in July 1782, when the treat was served at a party given by the French envoy. The European influence helped to spread the image of ice cream as an elegant luxury. There was an enthusiastic promotion of ice cream during the 1876 exposition in Philadelphia, and this helped to foster ice cream as a Philadelphian tradition. Philadelphia-style ice cream, as opposed to French style, which has a custard base, continues to be made in Philadelphia with no compromise on quality of ingredients. With the city's proximity to dairy country, Philadelphia has been able to meet the increasing demands of ice cream lovers. By 1909 the city had forty-nine ice cream manufacturing plants. Bassett's Ice Cream, an original 1892 tenant of Reading Terminal Market, continues to serve Philadelphia-style ice cream.

Other Philadelphia specialties continue to survive. The Pennsylvania Dutch scrapple is so associated with Philadelphia that in spite of its rural origins, the dish is referred to as Philadelphia scrapple and frequently served for breakfast. Philadelphia pepper pot, which was hawked in the city's streets in milk cans in the nineteenth century and consists of tripe, veal knuckle, vegetables, and herbs and spices, is still a desired Pennsylvania Dutch dish. Another Philadelphia specialty with French influence is snapper soup, which contains tender morsels of snapping-turtle meat in a thick liquid flavored with sherry or Madeira. Some of the old delicacies, such as terrapin, have not fared well with the passage of time. Terrapin, a smaller species of turtle than snapper, once was common in the coastal waters of Delaware Bay and was a staple of Philadelphia dinner parties but is rarely found in the early twenty-first century.

Common on the Philadelphian scene are two food traditions: the Philadelphia soft pretzel and the Philadelphia cheesesteak. The origins of the Philadelphia soft pretzel are attributed to the Pennsylvania German pretzel-making tradition. A true Philadelphia soft pretzel must be soft and chewy, must be detached from the adjacent pretzels in the batch, must be sprinkled with coarse salt, and preferably is purchased from a street vendor. Most Philadelphians use a liberal coating of yellow mustard as the finishing touch.

The essential and irreplaceable ingredient of a Philadelphia cheesesteak is the Italian roll. The Italian Americans settled in South Philadelphia in the late nineteenth century, and one of their culinary gifts to the city was the crusty, yeasty Italian roll. A true Philly cheesesteak outside of Philadelphia is almost impossible without a South Philadelphia Italian roll. The birth of the Philadelphia cheesesteak is attributed to Pat Olivieri, a proprietor of a hot dog stand in South Philadelphia in the 1930s. Olivieri decided to try something new for lunch and put chopped beef on an Italian roll with onions. The Philly cheesesteak had some Philadelphia Quaker roots, however. The traditional "Quaker gravy"—dried beef gravy served on toast—had a chopped beef and onion version that could be characterized as the forerunner of the cheesesteak sandwich. It is true that the first cheesesteak did not contain cheese. What came to be known as the true Philly cheesesteak, however, consists of an Italian roll loaded with thinly sliced beef grilled with fat, caramelized onions, and Cheez Whiz pasteurized process cheese sauce.

Quietly surviving in Philadelphia is the English tradition of eating clubs. These clubs flourished from the earliest beginnings of Philadelphia. The most venerable of all the clubs is the state in Schuylkill Fishing Club, or Fish House. Fish House punch, consisting of light rum, cognac, peach brandy, lime or lemon juice, and sugar steeped together for three to four hours, was concocted in 1732 at this club and was served at each meeting.

New Jersey: The Garden State

New Jersey has been a garden state from the time of the first European settlers in the seventeenth century (the Dutch and Swedes). The seeds and plants that were early European agricultural experiments thrived in the temperate climate and fertile farmlands of New Jersey. Because of its location, soil, climate, markets, and natural resources, New Jersey, even with its industry and high population density, offers agricultural opportunities not equaled by any other area in the United States. No part of the state is more than 125 miles from New York City or Philadelphia, two of the three largest consuming centers in America. Thus historically most of the garden produce has been grown for these two excellent markets. More than 150 crops are grown commercially in New Jersey, tomatoes being the state's leading crop. Peaches are the most valuable fruit crop in the state; major peach orchards are found in the southern part of the state. New Jersey also ranks among the leading states in the production of blueberries and cranberries.

In the middle of this agricultural and industrial state is a region known as the New Jersey Pine Barrens, which covers 1,700 square miles, approximately one-third of

The Garden State. Scenes of garden farming in New Jersey by Paul Frenzeny, *Harper's Weekly*, August 25, 1883: conveying goods to market (*top left*), berry vendors waiting for a train at Carlstadt (*top right*), gathering watercress (*middle left*), gathering mushrooms above (*middle center*) and below ground (*bottom left*), hotbeds and a greenhouse (*bottom center*), and preparing celery for market (*bottom right*). *Collection of Alice Ross*

the state. This region, characterized by sandy soil and cedar swamps dotted with scraggly pine trees, is unsuitable for conventional agriculture and development. The term for the self-sufficient inhabitants of this area is "Pineys." The foodways of the pinelands are much like the rural cookery in other parts of the United States, but they are unique to New Jersey within a sprawling megalopolis. The food of the Pine Barrens comes from four sources: the woods, the water, the garden, and the store. The customs of traditional hunting and gathering are valued, and the family garden plot is the next best source of food. The least desirable is the general store or, even worse, the supermarket. The basic pines diet is venison, waterfowl, shellfish, chain pickerel, catfish, and eel. Waterfowl (wood duck, black duck, mallard, and green-winged teal) is the most esteemed of these foods. The key virtues of the Pineys are attachment to the land and self-sufficiency.

In striking contrast to the New Jersey Pineys, who live a simple, traditional life, are the New Jersey–born scientists who have made the state famous for discoveries in agricultural research. Scientific work on hybridization has resulted in new, improved varieties of peaches, tomatoes, and sweet potatoes. These improved varieties have increased yield, but fewer of New Jersey's vegetables go directly to the markets of the nearby cities and more go to canning and frozen food processing plants. New Jersey is one of the leading states in the canning of vegetables. The largest single canned item in volume is canned tomatoes in their several forms—whole, puree, ketchup, pulp, juice concentrate, and soup.

The Campbell Soup Company, noted for its advertisement that housewives could not keep house without Campbell's tomato soup, was born in Camden, New Jersey. The company started as a poultry canning company in 1862, but when Joseph Campbell was acquired as a partner, the new company concentrated on vegetable processing. By 1891, with Arthur Dorrance at the helm, mincemeat and beefsteak (tomato) ketchup, not soups, were the company's two most important products. When he visited in 1895, Arthur Dorrance's nephew John changed the future of the company forever with his development of five condensed soups—tomato, vegetable, chicken, consommé, and oxtail. The company soon developed twenty-one soups and was selling more than sixteen million cans of condensed soup per year by 1921. Although new soups were developed, the number was limited to twenty-one for almost a century. Soup became such an integral part of the company's self-image that the name was changed to the Campbell Soup Company.

Campbell's condensed soup was originally marketed as a luncheon food to be served to children in the winter. John Dorrance was convinced that with some encouragement, Americans would add a soup course to the evening meal. The company's first cookbook, *Help for the Hostess*, was published in 1916 with this goal in mind. But the first real advertising success was the introduction of the Campbell Kids. These children symbolized the core market that has continued in spite of the company's efforts to add a soup course to the dinner meal. The publication of *Cooking with Condensed Soup* in 1952 had enormous influence on American cooking with the promotion of such favorites as Perfect Tuna Casserole. Sales of condensed soup increased to an estimated one million cans per day just for use as a sauce in preparing these new recipes.

New York

The European settlers and immigrants in New York State found fertile fields and a climate conducive to many crops. Apples have been especially successful, as have grapes, and these two are the leading fruit crops in New York. The grapes grown in the four regions of the Finger Lakes, Lake Erie, the Hudson valley, and Long Island support a flourishing wine industry. New York State is second only to California in the production of wine, including white (chardonnay, white Riesling, and Seyval-Villard), red (cabernet sauvignon and merlot), and sparkling wines as well as fortified wines, such as sherry and port. New York is also a leading producer of maple syrup, ranking just behind Vermont and Maine.

The cooking of New York has been influenced by immigrant fare. The Dutch, English, and Germans settling in the region had foodways similar to those of Pennsylvania settlers. Another English influence on New York was Mother Ann, the founder of the Shakers (the United Society of Believers), who arrived in Watervliet in 1774. As a celibate sect, believing in the Second Coming of Christ, the Shakers established isolated communities dedicated to regular and simple living habits. Plain, wholesome food eaten in moderation was considered a preventive against indigestion and was central to the Shaker faith. The Shakers were among the first to advocate the greater inclusion of fruits and vegetables and whole grains in the diet. Shakers extended the growing season by means of a unique rotation of crops—beans, peas, spinach, beets, and turnips—so that they would have fresh vegetables available for more months of the year. Shakers used herbs profusely and advertised herbs to "world's people" (non-Shakers) to improve the flavor of food, to stimulate the appetite, and to add charm and variety to ordinary dishes. Shakers were also among the first to insist on the inclusion of the whole-wheat kernel when flour was ground because of the health-promoting qualities of whole wheat. Shakers were on the forefront of the struggle against millers who removed the live germ from wheat.

Many central Europeans arrived in New York during the late 1800s, including the Poles, who settled in the Buffalo area. Bagels, introduced by the Poles, were paired with an 1872 New York invention, cream cheese, and popularized throughout the nation in the 1890s. The Buffalo area is also attributed with the evolution of Buffalo wings—chicken wings that are deep-fried, highly spiced, and traditionally served with celery and blue cheese dressing. These wings became popular in Buffalo-area bars beginning the 1960s.

Delaware

In the eighteenth century agriculture was the dominant activity in Delaware, and grain was the main agricultural product. Corn and wheat were the primary crops then, but as the population grew and new agricultural lands were opened in the West, grain farming declined. Some new crops were introduced, but unlike in the other Mid-Atlantic states, most attempts at diversification of agriculture in Delaware were unsuccessful until the nineteenth century, when peaches became the money crop for the state. At that time Delaware became known as the Peach State. The peach-growing boom peaked in approximately 1870 and declined steadily after 1900. In the twentieth century, broiler chickens replaced peaches as the dominant agricultural product.

Pennsylvania: The Snack Food State?

The state nickname is the Keystone State, but Pennsylvania is a major producer of snack foods and leads the United States in sales of potato chips, pretzels, and chocolate and cocoa products. The Tasty Baking Company, located in Philadelphia and Oxford, is one of the largest independent baking companies in the United States and is the leading snack cake provider in the Mid-Atlantic region. The Tastykake cake is distributed in forty-nine states.

Even more nationally known is the Hershey's chocolate bar. The originator of Hershey's chocolate, Milton Hershey, was born in 1857 in Derry Church, Pennsylvania. After becoming fascinated with the German chocolate-making machinery exhibited at the 1893 World's Columbian Exposition in Chicago, Hershey returned to Derry Church to build what was to become the world's largest chocolate manufacturing plant. Hershey's goal was to make a product similar to the Swiss chocolate luxury product that would be affordable to the American public. Hershey's milk chocolate quickly became the first nationally marketed product of its kind. Derry Church, Pennsylvania, has become Hershey, Pennsylvania, and the streets are lighted with replicas of Hershey's Kisses candies.

[*See also* Applejack; Apples; Bagels; Beer; Borden; Campbell Soup Company; Campbell Soup Kids; Candy Bars and Candy; Canning and Bottling; Cheese; Chesapeake Bay; Chicken Cookery; Chocolate; Cider; Dairy; Dairy Industry; Dutch Influences on American Food; Fish, *subentries on* Freshwater Fish; Saltwater Fish, and Saltwater Shellfish; German American Food; Herbs and Spices; Hershey Foods Corporation; Ice Cream and Ices; Molasses; Native American Foods; New York Food; Philadelphia Cheesesteak Sandwich; Pickles; Pickles, Sweet; Pickling; Pies and Tarts; Pig; Scrapple; Supawn; Tomatoes; Wine, *subentry on* Eastern U.S. Wines.]

BIBLIOGRAPHY

Barnes, Donna R., and Peter G. Rose *Matters of Taste: Food and Drink in Seventeenth-Century Dutch Art and Life.* Albany, NY: Albany Institute of History and Art, 2002.

Benson, Adolph B., ed. *Peter Kalm's Travels in North America: The English Version of 1770.* New York: Dover, 1964.

Cohen, David Steven. *The Dutch-American Farm.* New York: New York University Press, 1992.

Gerstell, Richard. *American Shad in the Susquehanna River Basin: A Three-Hundred-Year History.* University Park: Pennsylvania State University Press, 1998.

Gillespie, Angus K. "A Wilderness in the Megalopolis: Foodways in the Pine Barrens of New Jersey." In *Ethnic and Regional Foodways in the United States: The Performance of Group Identity*, edited by Linda Keller Brown and Kay Mussell, 145–168. Knoxville: University of Tennessee Press, 1984.

Kittler, Pamela Goyan, and Kathryn P. Sucher *Cultural Foods: Traditions and Trends.* Belmont, CA: Wadsworth/Thompson Learning, 2000.

Micklow, Timothy. "Cheesesteaks Glorious Cheesesteaks." *Today's Dietitian* 4, no. 10 (October 2002): 32–35.

Pillsbury, Richard. *No Foreign Food: The American Diet in Time and Place.* Boulder, CO: Westview Press, 1998.

Scholl, Dennis. *Return of a Native: Shad in the Lehigh River.* Available at http://mgfx.com/fishing/assocs/drsfa/history.htm

The Sensible Cook: Dutch Foodways in the Old and the New World. Translated and edited by Peter G. Rose. Syracuse, NY: Syracuse University Press, 1989.

Wacker, Peter O., and Paul G. E. Clemens *Land Use in Early New Jersey: A Historical Geography.* Newark: New Jersey Historical Society, 1995.

Weaver, William Woys. *Sauerkraut Yankees: Pennsylvania Dutch Foods and Foodways.* 2nd ed. Mechanicsburg, PA: Stackpole Books, 2002.

SUSAN MCLELLAN PLAISTED

Middle Eastern Influences on American Food

The Middle East is where so many crops, such as wheat, barley, onions, peas and lentils, were domesticated in ancient times, as well as animals, including sheep and probably cattle, that its influence on America's European heritage was immense, if hard to trace. It is generally agreed that Egypt gave the world leavened bread, and beer was the everyday beverage of both Egypt and Mesopotamia. In the Middle Ages, the Arabs carried sugar, the techniques for the making of candy and syrups, and probably also the idea of rice pudding from India. They passed on the eggplant from India too, adding their own technique of salting it before frying (a dish they called *badhinjan buran*).

The Persians invented the favorite medieval Arab sweet *lauzinaj*, which we know as marzipan, and the Moors experimented with various ways of making puff pastry, some with Arab names and some with Spanish, reflecting the lively cultural interaction of Moorish Spain. In Anna Martellotti's study of *Il Liber de ferculis di Giambonino da Cremona*, an Arab recipe collection that a Spanish cleric translated into Latin in the thirteenth century, Martellotti argues that the word "aspic" comes from the Arabic *as-sikbaj* through Latin forms, such as *assicpicium*. *Sikbaj* was a dish of meat stewed with vinegar, and its broth certainly does become a jelly when it cools. The Arabic source of the *Liber de ferculis* even defined jelly (*hulam*) as the broth of *sikbaj*.

Coming to America

Some Middle Eastern dishes—pilaf, for instance—came to America by way of other countries and cuisines. The English had developed a taste for this Persian dish (spelling it "pillaw") in India, where they learned to wash the rice scrupulously to remove surface starch, boil it until nearly done, and then steam it for up to half an hour so that all the grains fluffed and separated. They brought it to South Carolina when they started rice plantations there. (They also brought a sweet drink called julep, from the Persian Arabic "*jullab*.") Pilaf is the origin of the Carolina dish perloo, and what southern cooks call dry rice is also pilaf.

Buying Nuts and Dried Fruit. Sahadi's Middle Eastern food market in Brooklyn, New York. *Photograph by Joe Zarba*

Middle Eastern Food Shop. Interior of Sahadi's Middle Eastern food market, Brooklyn, New York. *Photograph by Joe Zarba*

Stuffed cabbage came from central Europe, which very likely got it from the Turks. The Swedes even borrowed their word for it, "*dalma*," from the Turkish "*dolma*." Strudel seems clearly descended from Turkish filo pastries, such as baklava. The most widely traveled dish was the Moorish *samak munashsha*, fish dipped in batter before frying. In the seventeenth century, Sephardic Jews brought the recipe to England, where it became known as Jewish fish (Thomas Jefferson admired the recipe), and eventually it became one half of the favorite English fast food, fish and chips. Meanwhile, Portuguese missionaries had taken batter-fried fish to Japan, where it metamorphosed into a variety of seafood and vegetable tempuras.

Immigrants started coming to the United States from the Ottoman Empire in the 1870s; the vast majority at that time were either Armenians or Arab Christians from Syria and Lebanon. On the whole, their foods remained confined to their own communities, though some influenced their neighbors' cooking without Americans' realizing that these were Middle Eastern foods.

The 1960s

Conscious borrowings from the Middle East began around 1960, when Greece became a fashionable tourist destination (and setting for movies). This was the era of shish kebab marinated in red wine (Americans usually made it with beef, rather than lamb, but always included onions, peppers, and tomatoes on the skewer in the Greek manner), stuffed grape leaves, and a particular recipe for moussaka, which covered the meat and eggplant stew with a thick, custardy béchamel sauce. This was when avant-garde American cooks discovered filo pastry and made not only baklava but also a host of novel hors d'oeuvres and finger foods with it.

Later in the 1960s, tourists visiting Israel encountered a number of Middle Eastern dishes that had been brought there by Jewish refugees. Among them were sandwiches wrapped in pocket bread (always known in America by its Hebrew name, "pita"); the sesame-flavored chickpea paste, hummus; the parsley and bulgur salad, tabbouleh; and the fried bean paste balls called falafel. Over the years they have become standard cafeteria and fast food dishes, and in the late 1990s there was a craze for wrap sandwiches that were as often made with pita as with tortillas.

Vegetarians and health-foodies seized on these Israeli dishes passionately, helping to popularize them. The health-conscious were also enthusiastic about bulgur wheat, often under the misapprehension that it was a form of whole wheat when, actually, the bran and germ have been removed. But bulgur is certainly a convenient food. Having been cooked and dried before being cracked, its starch has already converted into a digestible form so that it does not even have to be cooked again (it is used raw in tabbouleh). In the 1990s, Americans discovered couscous, a grain that is also quickly cooked; however, in this incarnation it was typically cooked by boiling, rather than steaming it in the North African way.

Anonymous Borrowings

There had already been Middle Eastern borrowings on an unconscious, folk level. Rice-A-Roni is a dish of rice mixed with toasted pasta that has been popular since the Middle Ages under such names as *rizz bi-sha'riyya* and *sehriyeli pilav*. The founder of the Rice-A-Roni company had learned to make the dish in childhood from his Armenian neighbors. In the Midwest, there is a positive cult for a dish variously called taverns, maid-rights, or loosemeats. It is ground beef fried loose, not in a patty but in such a way that all the tiny bits of meat are separate. This is an ancient dish that every Turkish-speaking nation from the Mediterranean to western China cooks; the Turkish word for it, "*kiyma*," shows up in the names of various dishes on Greek and Indian menus. It was introduced to the Midwest by an Arab restaurateur.

According to a well-known story, the ice cream cone was invented at the 1904 Columbian Exposition (popularly known as the St. Louis World's Fair) by a Syrian immigrant named Ernest Hamwy who ran a booth selling a pastry called *zalabiya*. Unlike the coiled fritter of this name, which in most Middle Eastern countries is made by pouring a thin stream of batter into boiling oil, Hamwy's Syrian version was a flat wafer with a grid-patterned surface that was cooked between hot irons. The story continues that a neighboring ice cream vendor on the midway ran out of serving cups and Hamwy obliged by rolling up *zalabiyas* into cones. The ice cream cone is claimed by many fathers, however. Other Syrian or Turkish immigrants (little distinction was made at the time) named Abe Doumar, Nick Kabbaz, and David Avayu also said they invented the ice cream cone. They were not the first to serve ice cream in a cone—the prominent English ice cream maker Agnes Marshall had been using ice cream cones made from rolled-up wafers since the 1880s—but the ice cream cone craze that swept the country began at the World's Fair, and all those claiming to have invented the cone were Middle Easterners.

There may be even more unrecognized Middle Eastern influences, because immigrants from the Middle East have generally preferred not to stress their ethnic identity. The father of the dancer Robert Joffrey was a refugee from Afghanistan who ran a chili parlor in Seattle during the early twentieth century using a recipe that had touches of Middle Eastern spicing. Joffrey's father sold his popular recipe to one of the major canning companies (the family no longer remembers which one), so countless people have had, in effect, Afghan chili without ever knowing it.

[*See also* Almonds; Apricots; Chickpeas; Coffee; Ethnic Foods; Health Food; Jewish American Food; Muslim Dietary Laws; Pistachios; Rice; Sugar; Vegetarianism; World's Fairs.]

BIBLIOGRAPHY

Anawalt, Sasha. *The Joffrey Ballet: Robert Joffrey and the Making of an American Dance Company.* New York: Scribners, 1999.
Denker, Joel. *The World on a Plate: A Tour through the History of America's Ethnic Cuisines.* New York: Westview, 2003.
Marlowe, Jack. "Zalabia and the First Ice Cream Cone." *Aramco World Magazine,* July/August 2003.
Martellotti, Anna. *Il liber de ferculis di Giambonino da Cremona: La gastronomia araba in Occidente nella trattatistica dietetica.* Fasano (Brindisi): Schena Editore, 2001.

CHARLES PERRY

Midwestern Regional Cookery

The conceptual boundaries of the Midwest are both variable and changing as James R. Shortridge (1989) has so well demonstrated. Boundaries of cultural regions only coincidentally correspond with those of political units or even geographical zones. Geographically, the Midwest is often thought to be that area between the Ohio River and the Great Plains. Some would include the Great Plains states. Others exclude the nonagricultural northern areas of Michigan, Wisconsin, and Minnesota. Despite the abundance of midwestern agriculture, much of the region is industrial, which contributed to its early prosperity and to its growth (thanks to the many immigrants who supplied the labor for production). However the region is defined, it is an area of good, hearty eating: meat and potatoes; meals of all-white food; more plain than fancy, given to substantial meat dishes, dumplings, home-baked breads, and pies; the land of casseroles and Jell-O salads. Much of this picture is stereotype, of course, especially in this time of global franchising. But in terms of traditional eating, there is enough truth to legitimate the image. In any case, regional foodways are not just a collection of recipes but also ideas about food, erroneous or not.

Meat on the Hoof. Chicago Stockyards, late nineteenth century. *Culinary Archives & Museum at Johnson & Wales University, Providence, R.I.*

Establishing absolute boundaries for a culinary region is quite impossible. There is nothing, after all, that all midwesterners eat in common and that only they eat. Rather, midwestern foods are those of the many communities—ethnic, occupational, local—that constitute the Midwest. *Bierocks*, also called "runsa" and, commercially, "runza" (a savory pastry of Volga Deutsch origin made of beef and cabbage encased in yeast dough and baked), are common in Nebraska but lap over into adjacent parts of Iowa, Kansas, and the Dakotas. They also became a local specialty in some pockets of Volga Deutsch settlement outside the region, such as Fresno, California. Butter tarts (individual-size tarts filled with custard, sometimes including currants, raisins, or nuts) are a specialty of Ontario, Canada, but are also a part of the traditional cuisine of some parts of eastern Michigan along the Canadian border. *Saucijzenbroodjes* (pigs-in-a-blanket) are a popular festive food in and around Dutch communities scattered from western Michigan to Iowa. *Booya*, a stew of chicken and fresh vegetables, can be found in scattered pockets from Minnesota to southern Indiana. Simmered for hours in large pots over outdoor wood fires, *booya* is served at family reunions, church picnics, community celebrations, and fund-raisers. Wisconsin's chicken *booyah* (with an added "h") is said to be Belgian in origin and can also include beef, corn, and beans.

Still, it is possible to make a few generalizations about traditional food and the ways that midwesterners eat. The Midwest is an area where fresh, high-quality ingredients can be found not far from the fields, stockyards, or lakes of origin, prepared expertly but usually in simple ways. There is an emphasis on meat, especially pork, except in locales like Omaha and Chicago, where, for historic reasons, the beefsteak reigns supreme. Throughout the region, but especially across the northern half, fish is a dietary staple. Consumption of milk and milk products is probably higher per capita in the Midwest than elsewhere in America. Milk is frequently served with meals, even to adults, and cheese has become emblematic, particularly in Wisconsin, whose residents are jokingly called "cheeseheads." Cheese curd is especially popular in Wisconsin, where it is eaten as a snack out of hand, sometimes dipped in cocktail sauce, and even floured, breaded, or batter coated and deep fried as a bar food.

Throughout the farmlands, a favorite dinner, especially on Sunday, is fried chicken with mashed potatoes and cream gravy. In some areas this was known as "parson food," because it was what was inevitably served the visiting preacher after Sunday church service. Fried chicken is a must for potlucks and family picnics. It is also a favorite restaurant meal, and many establishments specialize in it, some offering the meal family style, eat all you want. Usually the meal is accompanied either by biscuits or sweet rolls.

How do culinary generalizations such as these, as well as the many more localized food traditions, develop? Two factors are most significant: physical environment and history, particularly immigration history. Both factors are complex and highly interrelated, and their persistent interaction over time is of critical importance.

History

A great many of the people who originally settled this area came from New York, New Jersey, and Pennsylvania, or they had paused there long enough to carry with them the cooking and eating patterns of the original British, German, and Dutch colonists. The same was true of Scotch Irish settlers coming from southern Appalachia to southern regions of the Midwest. Immigrants coming directly from northern Europe, especially Germans, Scandinavians, and Irish, soon followed. Many of the features that define the Midwest's traditional foodways are due to the early northern European, especially German, influence. Some of this influence is general, affecting food preferences, cooking styles, and taste combinations. More specifically, the emphasis on pork in much of the region probably relates to the heavy settlement of Germans during the formative period, when eating patterns were being established. These patterns were bolstered by the traditions of later arrivals, for example, East Europeans. Similarly, the heavy influx of Scandinavians, with a high per-capita milk consumption, probably shaped the Midwest's love of dairy products. By the late nineteenth century, new waves of immigrants from origins farther south and east were enriching the cuisine with their diverse styles.

Environment

Physical environment includes the topography, soil conditions, climate, wildlife, undomesticated resources, and crops and livestock adaptable to the region. Because of geographic variability, areas within the Midwest produce unique wild foods traditional to local foodways. Thimbleberries grow in small pockets for a limited season in Michigan's Upper Peninsula and are a favorite of that area, especially of the numerous Finnish Americans living there. From southern Ohio and Indiana to Kansas, the wild persimmon grows in private yards and untended in pastures, along fences, and at the edge of woods, and its sweet orange fruit is highly coveted for cooking (pie, pudding, bread, cake, cookies, ice cream) and eating out of hand. Pawpaw and hickory nuts are also native to a broad area of the Midwest, but they are especially associated with Ohio. Wild cranberries, a fruit native to North America, once grew abundantly in the marshes of Wisconsin. The domesticated varieties are descendants of the wild berries that sustained Indian people and have appeared on settlers' tables in sauces, baked goods, and beverages since the early nineteenth century. Wild blueberries, too, abound in forest clearings and other disturbed areas that have plenty of sunlight and dry, sandy soil. Another North American native, these berries were dietary staples for Native Americans and are traditional in others' diets as well. Berrying was a major seasonal activity for the area's native people, and families across the cutover forests of the northern Midwest continue to enjoy berry-picking outings.

Just what specific use Midwesterners make of the abundance of foods in their environment depends greatly on the culture the inhabitants and their forebears brought with them to the area. It is this interaction between tradition and available food that led to the development of current foodways. The original Native American inhabitants first cultivated corn, among other crops, but perhaps the best examples of Native American influence on Midwestern foodways are maple syrup and wild rice. A large number of small-scale maple syrup producers exist in Michigan, Wisconsin, and Minnesota, the most important syrup-producing area in the United States after New England. They work with better tools perhaps but otherwise harvest syrup much like Native Americans did before Europeans arrived. Wild rice, growing in northern lakes in Minnesota and Wisconsin (as well as Ontario) and hand harvested, is regarded as a gourmet food, especially outside the region, but it is also used in everyday soups, salads, and casseroles. Its popularity has spawned commercial growers, who farm and mechanically harvest "paddy rice." A broad variety of mushrooms grow wild in the fields and forests of the Midwest. Morels, however, with their distinctively furrowed and pitted caps, are the all-time favorite. A subculture of morel hunters gathers these delicious, nutty mushrooms, keeping secret their growing places and perpetuating the folklore of when and where to hunt them.

Fruit

Although cultivated across the nation, certain fruits have become specifically identified with the Midwest. With the felling of forests in the 1800s, farmers planted fruit trees, especially apple trees, and soon orchards appeared throughout the region. The Midwest is where the legend of Johnny Appleseed is rooted and remembered; John

Chapman scattered his apple seeds across Ohio, Indiana, Illinois, and Iowa. Apple cider is an all-time favorite, and making apple butter is an old tradition maintained in kitchens throughout the Midwest and as a part of historic reenactments at local living-history museums. Cider mills and pick-your-own orchards are scattered through the area and provide popular excursion sites, especially in the fall. Sour cherry orchards, established by early homesteaders in northwest Michigan, spawned a range of foods and traditions—preserves, dried cherries, juice, pies, soups—maintained in local family foodways and prized throughout the region. Since 1988 cherries have even been utilized as an extender in ground meat to improve its nutritional value. The climate tempered by Lake Michigan makes Michigan the leading producer of tart cherries, supplying approximately 75 percent of the total United States crop. This same climate also makes Wisconsin's Door Peninsula an important cherry-growing area. Families flock to pick-your-own cherry orchards in the summer to stock up, just as they go to apple orchards in the fall.

Pie is one of the dishes most frequently associated with the Midwest. Local and regional specialties include sour cream raisin, buttermilk, vinegar, and fruit, especially apple, cherry, blueberry, and rhubarb. The fried pies of southern cuisine are also traditional in areas of the Midwest adjacent to the South. Pie is eaten not only for dessert and snacks but is also regarded by many as the best breakfast food. Pie-making, pie-eating, and pie-throwing contests are popular components of county and state fairs.

Dry Beans

Dry beans are closely associated with Michigan, whose farmers in the "Thumb" and central regions produce 40 percent of the nation's dry beans. Navy beans account for the majority of production. Not surprising, beans are important ingredients in Midwest cookery. Senate Bean Soup, for example, is one of the hallmarks of Michigan and often represents Michigan food in American cookbooks. Baked beans, bean casseroles, and bean soups are ubiquitous in the Midwest.

Corn

Corn farming extends through most of the region. The Midwest's productivity is rivaled only by the adjacent Great Plains. A nice ear of boiled or roasted corn, slathered with butter, minutes away from the field where it grew, is one of the great Midwestern culinary treats and is paid proper respect in regional culture. In season, corn is one of the most popular items offered at roadside stands, and a pickup truck parked by the side of the road, loaded with ears of corn for sale, is a common sight. A frequent component of family meals in season, corn is also the focus of corn roasts and corn boils held as community events by churches, service organizations, and

Mitchell Corn Place
World's Only Corn Palace
Mitchell, South Dakota.
Sept.26 to Oct.1 1938

Corn Construction. The Corn Palace, Mitchell, South Dakota, 1938. *Collection of Alice Ross*

fraternal orders. And it is no coincidence that the corn dog (invented as the "cozydog" in Springfield, Illinois, in 1947) and cornflakes (by Kellogg's in Battle Creek, Michigan, in 1902) both originated in the Midwest, and that corncob jelly is a traditional specialty in Indiana.

The Corn Palace in Mitchell, South Dakota, is a monument to corn. Annually since 1892 the municipal auditorium is completely covered with ears of colored corn grown by local farmers. The building, with minarets, Moorish towers, and twelve elaborate murals, requires more than fifty thousand ears plus four thousand pounds of other grains. The work begins each year in June and concludes in September with a festival.

Pork

Because corn is excellent feed for pigs, a good proportion of the nation's hogs are raised and butchered in the region. Pork is frequently the meat of choice, and this "other white meat" receives much attention in the culinary culture. It is significant that large numbers of people from Germany, Scandinavia, and east Europe—all places where pork is an important meat—settled the area. Pigs are slaughtered in winter, and headcheese, country ham, bacon, and many kinds of sausage are prepared in kitchens, sheds, and butcher shops across the region. Goetta, a specialty of the greater Cincinnati region, is a mixture of ground pork (and sometimes beef) scraps, steel-cut oats, and seasonings that is cooked, molded, cooled, and then sliced and fried. Like Pennsylvania Dutch scrapple, which it resembles, goetta is German American in origin. Pork roast is the frequent centerpiece of Sunday dinners, with applesauce its common side dish. Whole pigs are spit roasted at community and extended-family events in rural and semirural areas throughout much of the region. For a fee, professionals will come to an event and cook a pig. Some pig chefs split a fuel-oil tank in two, install a spit, and mount it on wheels, making an enclosed roaster that can be towed from one pig roast to the next.

Barbecue, too, is plentiful in homes and restaurants and at community festivals and cook-offs. Across the northern portion of the Midwest, barbecue means ribs with a sweet, mildly spiced, ketchup-based sauce, a style particularly associated with Chicago. When other regional styles are offered commercially—Texas brisket, North Carolina and Memphis pulled or sliced pork—they are usually labeled as such. In northern cities barbecue is often the province of African Americans. Chicago has a particularly well-developed culture of barbecue, brought there by the great migration of African Americans from South to North during World War I and during and after World War II.

Although the South has a more highly developed barbecue culture and, as a region, is better known for barbecue, the city most renowned for barbecue, Kansas City, Missouri, is in the Midwest. Missouri has a distinctive barbecue tradition, a consequence of being the meeting point for the beef barbecue tradition of Texas, carried along by post–Civil War cattle drives, and the pork barbecue traditions of the South, brought by the dispersal of African Americans. East Saint Louis, Missouri, has a local barbecue tradition that is unique to that area. Snoots (actually a hog face, mostly composed of cheeks) are well grilled, then doused liberally with barbecue sauce and eaten as a sandwich.

The pork chop—grilled, fried, baked, smoked, or stuffed—also constitutes a popular home and restaurant meal. Some restaurants feature one-pound pork chops. There is even a special double-thick cut called the "Iowa chop." A favorite lunch all across Iowa, and extending into Nebraska, Illinois, Indiana, and parts of neighboring states, is the tenderloin sandwich: a slice of tenderloin (conscientious cooks slice their own) pounded very thin (the thinner the better) and dipped in flour (some add a bit of cornmeal for crunch) before frying. It is most often eaten on a hamburger bun with the usual sandwich condiments, but at dinner the same tenderloin is offered as an entrée with mashed potatoes. Size is important: A tenderloin should extend beyond—far beyond—the edge of the bun. In eastern Wisconsin, outside the usual range of the tenderloin, a traditional specialty is the butterfly pork chop: a similar boneless slice of pork pounded flat before grilling and served in a sandwich. In Indiana there is even pork cake, a moist spice cake traditionally made at Christmas in which ground pork or finely chopped salt pork is added to the batter.

Bratwurst (or more often "brat") is found throughout much of the Midwest, but it is especially associated with Sheboygan, Wisconsin, where it is the focus of much local pride and cultural elaboration. The Sheboygan brat is a charcoal-grilled, coarsely ground pork sausage, customarily served on a hard roll with butter and fried onions. It is often ordered as a pair, two brats on a single roll. There are numerous variants: some parboil in beer before grilling, some even make it into a patty, sans casing. It is a popular bar food and a common picnic food,

---

THE BEST SINGLE RESTAURANT IN THE WORLD?

African American Henry Perry opened Kansas City's first barbecue establishment about 1908. Working out of an old trolley car, he practiced the art of making slow-smoked ribs. Texas-born Charlie Bryant and his son Arthur learned these techniques from Perry and opened their barbecue establishment, named Charlie Bryant's, in 1927. Charlie died in 1952, and the restaurant was continued by Arthur, who became known as the "Barbecue King" in Kansas City. The restaurant was located near Kansas City's Municipal stadium-

later the home of the Kansas City Chiefs-and became a popular eating establishment. It received national recognition in 1974 when Kansas City native Calvin Trillin declared in a tongue-in-cheek *New Yorker* article that Arthur Bryant's barbecue was the single best restaurant in the world. Arthur Bryant died in 1982, and his restaurant was eventually sold to a management group, which has subsequently opened a second establishment at the Ameristar Casino.

ANDREW F. SMITH

---

and it is offered by numerous streetside carts, stands, and restaurants. Fairs and carnivals of the region always include at least one bratwurst stand.

Fish

All along the Mississippi River, fried catfish is an especially popular dish. In the northern half of the Midwest, the site not only of the five Great Lakes but also countless smaller lakes, rivers, and streams, fish takes center stage. Fish was a crucial resource for both the original Native population and the settlers who intruded on them. Commercial fishing is an important part of the regional and local economies of Michigan, Wisconsin, Minnesota, and Ohio, and sport fishing is one of the most popular pastimes. Ice fishing and smelting are major seasonal activities with important social and culinary dimensions. Fish is an important part of the daily diet as well as the centerpiece of special events, including Lenten fish fries and Christmastime lutefisk dinners, held as church fundraisers, and festivals celebrating fish sandwiches, catfish, trout, smelt, carp, and eelpout.

Midwesterners use a wide variety of fish, including whitefish (the principal commercial fish); lake, brook, and rainbow trout; perch pike; pickerel; burbot; mullet; catfish; muskellunge; sturgeon; chub; suckers; bass; bluegill; and smelt and salmon (both introduced from saltwater), prepared in an even wider variety of ways: fried, baked, grilled, planked, smoked, pickled, boiled, and steamed, using innumerable specific recipes, but more often with no recipe at all. Planked whitefish, for example, is a traditional manner of preparation still offered in some upscale restaurants in the Great Lakes area. Those fish that are not eaten immediately are pre-

served. Drying is less common than it was historically, but canning and pickling are still common household methods of preservation. Most important is smoking. Smoked fish is one of the traditional delicacies of the region, appreciated by tourists, visiting sports enthusiasts, and local inhabitants. Smoked lake trout, chub, and whitefish are the most popular, but even suckers, little used otherwise, are good smoked. Fish smoking is both a commercial and a private enterprise. Small-scale commercial outlets are numerous along lakeside roads throughout the upper Great Lakes region. Private smokehouses range from elaborate, custom-built structures to gutted refrigerators, the latter being particularly common. The selection of fish, the source of smoke, the length of time the fish is allowed to cure, the strength of the salt solution, and the heat and duration of the smoking process are all choices that express individual taste and creativity. The liver and roe of whitefish are special delicacies. Few whitefish livers make it to market, however, because commercial fishermen tend to keep them for themselves. They dredge them in flour and sauté them in butter, perhaps with onions or mushrooms.

Fish boils are important group activities around the Great Lakes, much like pig roasts in the southern part of the Midwest. An organization or an extended family will set a huge pot atop a campfire (or, more commonly, a propane burner) and fill it with water for boiling large chunks of fish with potatoes and onions. Some cooks add tomato juice. A combination of local fish varieties is thought best. Fish boils are the most institutionalized in Door County, a peninsula in northeastern Wisconsin. Fishermen host smaller events, often cooking the results of that day's catch in camp. When done at home, a fish boil is usually women's work, but at larger communal events—fish for more than one hundred is not uncommon—men usually take over.

The region's significant Catholic population has further strengthened the historic emphasis on fish. The Friday fish fry is an important institution throughout much of the area. Restaurants and a wide variety of service organizations and fraternal orders offer a Friday night special, often all-you-can-eat. During Lent the choice in some communities is even greater, as many Catholic churches (even after relaxation of the abstinence rule) offer Friday fish fries as fund-raising events. The battered, deep-fried fish (cod, whitefish, and, best of all, lake perch) is most often accompanied by french fries, coleslaw, tartar sauce, and a roll, though side dishes can vary considerably. There is no clear correspondence between those who attend Friday fish fries and Catholic affiliation, but, in any case, relaxed church stricture on Friday meat-eating had little effect on the popularity of the Friday fish fry. It is as much a social event as it is a fund-raiser.

Game

Hunting is a way of life for many in the Midwest. Many varieties of game are most plentiful in the woods of the region's northern reaches, and hunters from Indiana, Ohio, Illinois, and throughout the Midwest and beyond make their pilgrimage in droves to hunt there, especially during deer season. Venison is eaten as stew, steaks, roast, barbecue, and burgers and is incorporated into many regional and ethnic dishes, including pasty, Swedish potato sausage, jerky, summer sausage, *cudighi*, Italian pork sausage, Christmas mincemeat, and German sauerbraten. Pheasant is more common in the corn and grain fields that predominate in the southern and western parts of the region. Waterfowl hunters flock to the region's many wetlands and flyways in season. Roasted goose and duck, sometimes smoked, sometimes stuffed, are enjoyed at any time and are often a special treat at Christmas. Wild game dinners in the fall and winter are popular social events.

Some game is associated with specific locales. Muskrat is one such example. Although consumed by many throughout the region who trap it, muskrat (called "mushrat" by locals or, more affectionately, "rat") in season is the center of family, restaurant, and club dinners in Monroe, Michigan, where it has been the symbol of this Lake Erie community since the early twentieth

century. It had been eaten by the French-Canadian trappers who first settled the region and was maintained by their descendants as a symbol of their ethnic identity, until it was adopted by the area as a whole. Muskrat is trapped only in the cold winter months, when the flesh is firm. It is consumed more by men than by women. According to local legend, church officials once declared muskrat to be the same as fish, because it too lives in water and therefore could still be eaten on fast days. Once skinned and the musk sacks removed, the animal is parboiled with vegetables and then finished in various ways. A traditional method of final preparation still popular is to roast the whole animal with sweet and creamed corn and to serve it, one to a diner, with applesauce, mashed potatoes, pickled beets, and coleslaw.

Local Specialties

All across the Midwest culinary specialties associated with a particular town or limited region can be found. These, too, comprise Midwest food. A very large proportion of such local specialties are related to the particular immigrant history of the locality. They are immigrant foods that have over time been adopted by the entire community, being altered, sometimes substantially, in the process. Often origins can be traced back to single persons, immigrant entrepreneurs who made use of their own culinary traditions in combination with the new American traditions they were learning in order to make a living.

Cudighi, a specialty of the Negaunee-Ishpeming area of northern Michigan, is a good example of both how an ethnic food becomes a local food specialty and the degree to which it can absorb the local imagination. In 1936 an Italian immigrant opened a sausage stand between the family barbershop and the bar from which came many of his customers. He served homemade Italian sausage with a "secret" spicing in a sandwich with an American-style sandwich dressing of mustard, ketchup, and chopped onions. He called it "gudighi." His son opened a bar in the post–World War II period, when pizza was first becoming universalized, and he distinguished his sandwich from his father's by forming the meat into a patty and dressing it with pizza sauce and mozzarella cheese. He kept the same secret spices. In this form it became ubiquitous, being offered in nearly every restaurant in the area except franchises, as well as by many home cooks. At some point most people came to call this sandwich and the meat "cudighi," though some still use the original "gudighi," just as a few still dress it with the original mustard and onions. New versions of the secret spice recipe were developed. Butcher shops and grocers offer a variety of *cudighi*-related products: *cudighi* meat either in bulk or already formed into patties, in three degrees of spiciness; turkey *cudighi;* cold and hot *cudighi* sandwiches; packages of *cudighi* buns; store-made sauces to dress *cudighi* sandwiches; and packages of mixed spices to combine with meat for *cudighi.*

An earlier, more widespread but otherwise similar process made the pasty a regional specialty of the entire iron-mining district stretching across the Upper Peninsula of Michigan and northern Wisconsin and Minnesota. Originally Cornish, the pasty was brought to the region by tin miners who came from Cornwall in the mid-nineteenth century to develop new mines. Finns, Italians, Poles, and South Slavs, who arrived around the turn of the twentieth century to supply cheap labor in the mines, adopted the pasty as their own. It was a perfect meal to be taken into the mines: a hearty meal-in-one eaten with the hands that was easily transported, kept warm for a long time, and could be reheated over a miner's candle. Finns, the largest ethnic group of the region, played an important role in the pasty's dispersal. Although there had been many variants of the pasty in Cornwall, in this region it became standardized: chopped or ground beef, or beef and pork, potatoes, onions, and rutabaga or carrots baked in a pie-crust turnover. New variants, including chicken and vegetarian, have become common. The pasty is ubiquitous throughout the region and has taken on great symbolic significance as a marker of regional pride.

Toasted ravioli, a specialty of Saint Louis, Missouri, are beef ravioli that have been deep fried instead of boiled. They have no precedent in Italy but are the creation of an Italian American restaurateur and have spread throughout the community. Similarly, deep-fried sauerkraut balls are a specialty of northern Ohio and apparently were developed by members of the large German American population there, although nothing like them exists in Germany. Likewise, Italian beef sandwiches are a local specialty of Chicago, though there is little about them that is Italian other than the ethnicity of those who owned the earliest sandwich shops. They consist of thinly sliced beef au jus on a crusty roll, usually dressed with spicy *giardiniera* or roasted peppers.

It is important to note that the foodstuff that eventually becomes regionalized is seldom the same as any

antecedent in the Old Country but has been substantively changed, or creolized, in the transformation from immigrant to ethnic. In some cases the immigrant contribution consists of something as nebulous as a seasoning style. Sometime during the first two decades of the twentieth century, Macedonian immigrants in the industrial cities of the northern Midwest—a group in Flint, Michigan, take credit—began to season American chili with the sweet spices of the eastern Mediterranean and to serve it as a sauce, along with chopped onions and mustard, on a hot dog sandwich. They called this a "coney," after Coney Island, although hot dogs are served there in quite a different style. The coney has become the dominant hot dog style throughout the northern Midwest, except in Chicago, which has its own distinctive hot dog (an all-beef wiener on a poppy seed bun, dressed with mustard, onions, bright green piccalilli relish, tomato and lettuce, celery salt, and a couple of "sport" peppers). Coney stands are abundant across the area, the vast majority owned by Macedonians, Greeks, or Albanians.

Cincinnati chili is a close relative to this coney sauce but is served in a manner unique to Cincinnati. In 1922 another Macedonian immigrant, after working several years in coney stands, developed his own version of chili, utilizing a similar eastern Mediterranean mixture of sweet and hot spices. He served his chili on hot dogs or by the bowl, but most popularly on spaghetti, topped with grated yellow cheese. This came to be known as "three-way Cincinnati chili." Four-way is with added chopped onion. Five-way includes a layer of boiled kidney beans. Cincinnati chili is served in more than two hundred area establishments, including several chains of franchised chili parlors, independent chili parlors, and restaurants that do not specialize in chili, as well as in private homes. Each business has its own secret recipe. Homemakers can purchase frozen or canned chili, but many prefer to develop their own versions.

Yet another variant of chili is a local specialty of Green Bay, Wisconsin. It is similar to yet different from the chili prepared in Cincinnati, consisting of spiced ground meat atop layers of spaghetti and beans, doused with a ladleful of oil skimmed from the top of the chili pot.

Stability and Change in Midwestern Foodways

In this context of a highly diverse population and continued immigration, other ethnic foods are still being adopted as regional specialties in the early twenty-first century. Arab foods, for example, are quickly becoming regionalized in metropolitan Detroit, home of the largest Arab American community outside the Middle East. Polish food has become so ubiquitous in midwestern cities with heavy Polish settlement, such as Chicago, Hamtramck (Detroit), Milwaukee, and Minneapolis, and even in rural areas with large Polish populations, that some elements of the Polish kitchen have become accepted by the surrounding general populace. No Polish food, however, has been more embraced by the general population than *paczki*, the Polish version of the jelly doughnut, which are eaten at Carnival before Lent. *Paczki* are made of a yeast dough rich with eggs and butter and best fried in lard (though vegetable oil is usually used). Traditionally, they were made to use up all the lard and eggs in the home before Lenten fasting. They are still made for the pre-Lenten season, but eating them no longer has anything to do with being either Polish or Catholic. Available until the 1980s only at Polish bakeries and church and community celebrations, *paczki* can be found at non-Polish bakeries and even at most chain supermarkets in the area. Traditionally prepared without filling or filled with prune butter, *paczki* are also made in the Midwest with a half-dozen different fruit jam fillings and custard. More frequently, *paczki* are becoming the focus of local annual festivals and parades on Shrove Tuesday, or Paczki Day.

Culture is always changing, always evolving; so, too, are food and foodways. While many food traditions of the early inhabitants of the Midwest are still intact, the region continues to attract new settlers who bring with them new resources, ingredients, and cuisines. Sometimes a process of culinary adoption, adaptation, or amalgamation may occur; new foods may be integrated into family, community, and, finally, regional foodways, such as happened with the pasty and Cincinnati chili. On the other hand, although food traditions can be quick to adapt and change in new contexts, they also are resistant to change and held onto tightly. Thus, newer food traditions coexist with foods and food habits dating from an earlier time. However Midwestern food is described, the picture will look somewhat different in the future.

[*See also* Barbecue; Beans; Cheese; Cincinnati Chili; Corn; Cranberries; Dairy Industry; Fish, *subentry on* Freshwater Fish; Fund-Raisers; German American Food; Goetta; Grapes; Maple Syrup; Middle Eastern Influences on American Food; Milk; Mushrooms; Myths and Folkore, *sidebar on* Johnny Appleseed; Pasties; Persimmons; Pig; Polish American Food; Russian American Food; Scandinavian and Finnish American Food; Soybeans.]

BIBLIOGRAPHY

Algren, Nelson. *America Eats.* Iowa City: University of Iowa Press, 1992. Research done under the Works Progress Administration in the 1930s. Although the author was not a trained social scientist, this is one of the first studies of regional food in the United States.

Allen, Therese. "Goodness Gracious! For Local Flavor and Fellowship, You Can't Beat a Church Supper." In *Wisconsin Folklife: A Celebration of Wisconsin Food Traditions*, edited by Marshall Cook, 44–49. Madison: Wisconsin Academy of Sciences, Arts, and Letters, 1998. An excellent, accessible study of church suppers in Wisconsin. Much here applies to church suppers throughout the Midwest.

Allen, Therese. *Wisconsin Food Festival.* Amherst, WI: Amherst Press, 1995. Food festivals that express connections between communities and local food.

Bennett, John. "Food and Culture in Southern Illinois." *American Sociological Review* 7 (October 1942): 645–660. A classic study of the class and ethnic boundaries of local foods.

Brown, Linda Keller, and Linda Mussel, eds. *Ethnic and Regional Foodways in the United States.* Knoxville: University of Tennessee Press, 1984.

Fussell, Betty. *I Hear America Cooking.* New York: Viking Penguin, 1986. A section on "The Great Lakes of the Midwest" (pp. 327–405) includes informational text and recipes that often reflect the author's touch.

Gilmore, Janet. " 'Pretty Hungry for Fish': Fish Foodways among Commercial Fishing People of the Western Shore of Lake Michigan's Green Bay." *Midwestern Folklore* 29, no. 1 (Spring 2003). A thoroughly researched study.

Hachten, Harva. *The Flavor of Wisconsin.* Madison: State Historical Society of Wisconsin, 1981. Historical and cultural study, including recipes attributed to individuals.

Isern, Thomas D. "Bierocks." In *The Taste of American Place*, edited by Barbara G. Shortridge and James R. Shortridge, 135–137. Lawrence: University of Kansas Press, 1998. Brief and descriptive.

Kaplan, Anne R. " 'It's All from One Big Pot': Booya as an Expression of Community." In *"We Gather Together": Food and Festival in American Life*, edited by Theodore C. Humphrey and Lin T. Humphrey, 169–198. Ann Arbor, MI: UMI Research Press, 1988. An ethnographic study of *booya* in Minnesota.

Kaplan, Anne R., Marjorie A. Hoover, and Willard B. Moore. *The Minnesota Ethnic Food Book.* St. Paul: Minnesota Historical Society Press, 1986. Includes chapters on both the cultural history of twelve ethnic communities and their foodways.

Lloyd, Timothy. "The Cincinnati Chili Culinary Complex." *Western Folklore* 40, no. 1 (1981): 28–40. The definitive study on the cultural history of Cincinnati chili.

Lockwood, Yvonne R., and Anne R. Kaplan. "Upper Great Lakes Foodways." In *Smithsonian Folklife Cookbook*, edited by Katherine Kirlin and Thomas Kirlin, 172–211. Washington, DC: Smithsonian, 1991. A survey with recipes of foods prepared by selected participants from the Upper Great Lakes region at the Smithsonian Folklife Festival.

Lockwood, Yvonne R., and William G. Lockwood. "Pasties in Michigan: Foodways, Interethnic Relations, and Cultural Dynamics." In *Creative Ethnicity*, edited by Stephen Stern and John Allan Cicala, 3–20. Logan: Utah State University Press, 1991. The creolization of the pasty; its change from mono-ethnic to regional specialization.

Paddleford, Clementine. *How America Eats.* New York: Scribners, 1960. Includes a section on the Midwest (pp. 287–390). Brief text between recipes, some of which are widely shared in discrete locales; others are those of specific cooks and chefs.

Perl, Lila. *Red Flannel Hash and Shoo-Fly Pie: American Regional Foods and Festivals.* Cleveland: World, 1965. Includes a section on the Midwest and the Great Plains (pp. 148–185), with text and recipes.

Shortridge, Barbara G., and James R. Shortridge, eds. *The Taste of American Place: A Reader on Regional and Ethnic Foods.* Lanham, MD: Rowman and Littlefield, 1998. Intended as a textbook for college classes. Articles selected to demonstrate the role of region and ethnicity in food culture.

Shortridge, James. *The Middle West: Its Meaning in American Culture.* Lawrence: University of Kansas Press, 1989.

Sokolov, Raymond. *Fading Feast: A Compendium of Disappearing American Regional Foods.* New York: Farrar, Straus, and Giroux, 1981. A section on the Midwest includes essays, with some recipes, on persimmons, wild rice, morels, goose, pasty, and an Iowa county fair.

Stern, Michael, and Jane Stern. *Real American Food.* New York: Knopf, 1986. A popular publication with a section on the Midwest (pp. 182–255) divided into "Café Society," "Where Nice People Eat," "Chicken Dinner Halls," "Chicago's Deep Dish Delirium," "Upper Peninsula Pasty Shops," and "Rude Food." Includes brief texts on history and context, with recipes.

Vennum, Thomas, Jr. *Wild Rice and the Ojibway People.* St. Paul: Minnesota Historical Society Press, 1988. The definitive study of wild rice in Ojibway culture.

Weaver, William Woys. *America Eats: Forms of Edible Folk Art.* New York: Harper and Row, 1989. An important contribution to the analysis of the regionalization of foods.

Wilson, José, and the editors of Time-Life Books. *American Cooking: The Eastern Heartland.* New York: Time, 1971. Lengthy discussions of the regional cooking of Ohio, Indiana, Illinois, and Michigan, with some recipes.

YVONNE R. LOCKWOOD AND WILLIAM G. LOCKWOOD

Military Food, *see Combat Food*

Milk

A Chicago Department of Health brochure from the mid-1920s declared milk "the modern Atlas supporting the world." For many nutritionists at the time, milk was nature's perfect food, to be promoted and protected at all costs. Ideas about milk, however, have become less sanguine. Concerns about bovine growth hormone and lactose intolerance abound. An antimilk movement is epitomized by the 1997 book *Milk: The Deadly Poison*, in which the author blames a variety of ailments on milk, including many forms of cancer, early maturation, and even osteoporosis. Milk incites emotional reactions, both positive and negative, among Americans.

Milk was not always the American staple that it became in the twentieth century. Native Americans did not habitually drink milk, and cows, goats, and sheep are all Old World animals. Although cows were present in Jamestown by 1611, milking in early America was a seasonal event, occurring almost entirely in spring and summer, when vegetation was abundant. The milk itself was mainly turned into longer-lasting products, such as cheese and butter. For the next two centuries, fresh milk was somewhat of a seasonal luxury. Until the development of refrigeration, fresh milk was a rarity in the South, because of warm temperatures. Southerners continue to drink small amounts of milk compared with other Americans. Even in New England, although milk was consumed by children, most milk produced on farms was used for butter and cheese.

Until the nineteenth century, most of the cows providing cities with milk were primarily pastured behind urban homes, in neighborhood pastures such as Boston Common, or on nearby farms. As cities grew and became more densely settled, lack of room and sanitation problems led to a decline in pasture space. The first milk transported by rail arrived in New York City in 1842. Most of New York City's milk at the time, however, was provided by in-city "swill dairies." These dairies were attached to breweries and distilleries. The cows were fed the grain mash that was left over after distilling and fermentation. These cows were often kept in dark barns and rarely saw the light of day. Although this practice was an effective way for brewers and distillers to recycle waste, the swill process soon came under fire. New Yorkers objected to both the dreadful conditions in which the cows were kept and the idea that their children were drinking milk produced by "drunk" cows.

The swill milk issue was a point of focus for one of America's first consumer advocates, Robert Hartley. In *An Historical, Scientific, and Practical Essay on Milk as an Article of Human Substance* Hartley set the tone for future milk treatises, treating milk as a pure, almost perfect, food that could be easily tainted by misuse. The solution was to promote the development of market milk production in surrounding "grass regions" and the transportation of country milk to the city by train. Hartley considered the city no place for the production of a pure food. Although Hartley did not immediately get his way, in 1862 the New York state legislature passed a law prohibiting the sale of adulterated milk and the maintenance of swill stables. Many other cities followed suit.

Dairy Farm. Illustrations by Paul Frenzeny in *Harper's Weekly*, September 2, 1882. *Collection of Alice Ross*

The Perfect Food

By the end of the nineteenth century, almost all the milk drunk in the largest U.S. cities arrived from surrounding areas by rail (smaller cities, particularly in the South, were still directly supplied by local producers). The increased distance from which this milk was sourced and the increased awareness about both the nutritional benefits of milk and its ability to act as a vector for disease made milk a focus of Progressive-era urban reformers. Milk was chosen as "the perfect food" because of a combination of its ability to provide numerous nutritional benefits at a relatively low price and the cultural meaning attached to it. In growing cities, there was a need for inexpensive foods that could provide a variety of nutrients to new immigrant populations. At the same time, the development of new nutritional research techniques led to analysis of foods in a search for the essential components needed for a healthful diet. Milk contained many of these components at a relatively low price. One of the chief proponents of milk was E. V. McCollum, the discoverer of vitamin A.

The ties between milk and western European culture and the connection between milk and motherhood and purity helped it to become a part of standard Americanization techniques. Progressive-era social advocates, such as Jane Addams in Chicago, advocated teaching immigrant and African American mothers to drink milk, for both health and socialization reasons. Milk was promoted as an almost magical food, able to make children healthier and more vigorous. In 1924 a Chicago Department of Health bulletin specifically devoted to milk stated that strength and attractiveness were tied to milk consumption. Girls were advised to drink milk with every meal to help maintain a face that "glows with health and animation," and boys were told that sports heroes "consider milk their most valuable training food."

Adulteration, Contamination, and Pasteurization

Moving farms outside the city made farmers more anonymous to urban consumers and more difficult to control by urban authorities. Problems with adulteration began to appear. An example was that milk was skimmed and then whitened with chalk. In a time in which many people were malnourished, fat was considered one of the most important nutrients in milk. Even worse cases involved tainting milk with formaldehyde so it would not sour.

Outlawing skimming, chalking, and other forms of adulteration was the focus of most early milk laws. Additional laws in the late 1800s and early 1900s controlled the selling of "loose" milk—milk sold from pails and poured with a ladle into the customer's container. The first milk bottles were developed in the 1870s and came into general use during the next two decades. At the same time, milk delivery services became widespread and dominated milk distribution during the first three decades of the twentieth century. These services were increasingly controlled by large milk dealers.

During the first three decades of the twentieth century, the amount of milk drunk by the average American increased markedly. In New York City, for example, between 1890 and 1930 sales of milk and cream rose at approximately double the rate of population growth. Such success would not have been possible if public health officers and the dairy industry had not dealt with the fact that milk was a vector of disease. During the late 1800s researchers such as Robert Koch and Louis Pasteur, staring through newly developed microscopes, had discovered microbes and developed the germ theory of disease. It came to be realized that diseases could be transmitted by ingestion of contaminated food. Milk, which arrived from the country daily and was consumed raw, was a frequently cited culprit. Numerous epidemics were linked to milk. In Chicago in 1907, for example, an epidemic of scarlet fever was tied to an epidemic in a town in Wisconsin that had provided the Chicago victims with milk.

Two remedies appeared to solve the problem of contaminated milk: certification and pasteurization. Certification involved the creation of a long list of strict requirements for farmers providing milk to a city. A "medical milk commission," usually composed of physicians, inspected farms and certified them as pure milk producers. Pasteurization involves the heating of milk to kill pathogenic bacteria. Pasteurization of milk was first developed in 1886 by Franz Ritter von Soxhlet, a German biochemist. Soon thereafter, in 1893, Nathan Straus, a New York philanthropist, heard about the method and opened a "pure milk station" on the East Third Street Pier in New York City. Straus provided pasteurized milk for a minimal price to all comers and was extremely successful in promoting pasteurized milk production. Soon some milk dealers began to pasteurize milk on their own accord. In 1909 Chicago passed the first law requiring pasteurization of milk sold within the city limits.

The price of certified milk was the crux of the conflict between promoters of certified milk and promoters of pasteurization. Although both movements influenced regulation, the pasteurization movement was ultimately more popular with public health departments because pasteurization was less expensive than certification and did not impose heavy restrictions on farmers, restrictions that often might not be met and that required a large staff for enforcement. Promoters of certified milk considered pasteurization not beneficial in itself because the process decreased the germicidal quality of milk—a charge that continues to be made—and promoted unsanitary methods of milk production that could be covered up by pasteurization. In general, public health experts increasingly viewed pasteurization as a necessary evil. These experts supported the ideal of certified milk but believed pasteurization was needed as a stopgap measure. The cost of certified milk simply put it beyond the reach of most urban consumers.

Federal Regulation

Until the 1930s milk markets were locally regulated. States and cities set regulations for market milk producers, such as controls on milking methods, the cleanliness of the barn, and the manner in which the cows were kept. In the 1910s and 1920s many states and cities began to require testing of cattle for bovine tuberculosis, which can pass from cow to human. Dealers were required to pasteurize milk. These regulations were not without controversy. Tuberculosis legislation, for example, often was resisted because it required farmers to destroy cattle that had positive test results. Although farmers usually received an indemnity, the amount was not always enough to cover the loss. At the same time, smaller farms and dealers found it difficult to invest in new technology. Many left the industry, beginning a process of concentration that has continued into the early twenty-first century.

In addition to being involved in controversies surrounding health regulations, farmers providing milk to cities often were upset by the terms of milk contracts. The need for farmers to have daily buyers for their milk forced them into annual contracts, often at what they considered unfavorable terms. The Capper-Volstead Act of 1922 gave farmer cooperatives antitrust protection, which soon allowed farmers to demand higher prices for milk. These better terms became more difficult to receive during the Great Depression as prices and demand fell. Many cooperatives also found it necessary to close membership or

Drink Milk. Poster produced by the Federal Art Project for the Cleveland Division of Health, 1940. *Prints and Photographs Division, Library of Congress*

take other drastic actions to artificially raise prices for their members. Cooperatives learned that negotiating prices for a product that went through an annual surplus period in the spring and summer and an annual drought in the fall and winter was not an easy endeavor. Dealers also were under pressure from upstarts who sold to "cash and carry" stores and did not have to pay for home delivery. This situation led to numerous "milk strikes" during the 1930s whereby farmers withheld their milk from the cities. It is a testimony to the importance of milk in the American diet of the time that these strikes were of national importance. The National Guard often was called into action to guard strikebreakers bringing milk into the cities.

The federal solution to the problem of milk pricing was the milk marketing order program, authorized by Congress in 1937. This program allows dairy farmers serving particular cities to agree to be federally regulated. The federal government then sets a floor on the price received by farmers for fluid milk within that "milkshed" (the area that provides a city with milk). This program, greatly revised, continues in the early 2000s to guide the milk market in much of the United States (a notable exception is California, which has its own state system). Although it has increased the price of milk for consumers somewhat, the milk marketing order program has steadied the price of milk for both consumers and farmers. In addition to the milk marketing order system, the government has periodically strengthened the price of farmers' milk by buying up quantities of milk and distributing dried milk powder, cheese, and butter for public aid programs and for the military.

At the same time it was attempting to control the milk economy, the U.S. government was becoming more directly involved in protecting milk purity. In 1936 the federal government developed a suggested ordinance for cities and states for fluid milk, which it called "grade A." Manufacturing grade was "grade B." Most milk produced in the United States, even that destined for manufacturing markets, meets the grade A standards.

Milk since World War II

With the establishment of the milk marketing order system, the appearance of large cooperatives, and the development of the main sanitary laws during the first four decades of the twentieth century, milk faded from the headlines and became a trusted staple of the American diet. It seemed that the goal of providing a reliable, inexpensive food source to all Americans had been reached. Dairy products, milk in particular, were a cornerstone of the four food groups nutrition model. Children were urged to drink four glasses of milk a day. Later, in the food pyramid model, milk was placed on slightly less equal footing with vegetables and grains, but milk still was one of the components of a healthful diet. The sometimes dirty, sometimes dangerous, sometimes not available product of the early 1900s has been replaced by a product that was safe and reliable.

Despite the apparent stability of milk production, many changes did occur. Homogenization, the breaking apart of fat molecules in milk to retard separation, became standard in the 1940s. Many Americans lamented the disappearance of the cream that floated to the top of the milk bottle and often was used for the morning coffee. Milk packaging also changed, glass bottles being replaced with paper cartons and then plastic cartons. Home delivery steadily decreased and by the 1960s had almost disappeared.

Despite the prominence of milk in mainstream nutrition and the increased safety and reliance of the product, per capita consumption of milk has declined since World War II. Estimated consumption of milk in 1946 was approximately 267 pounds a year per person, increasing from approximately 151 pounds in 1926. Consumption was steady throughout the 1950s and 1960s but then declined to 233 pounds in 1981, 217 pounds in 1991, and 190 pounds in 2001. The type of milk sold also has changed. Whereas in 1946 most milk sold was whole milk, in 2001 more reduced and lowfat milk was sold than whole. The amount of whole milk drunk per capita has declined one-half since 1981.

The decline in milk consumption per capita is due at least in part to increased immigration from Latin America and Asia, both of which are low–milk-drinking areas. However, such a steady and large decline probably has additional sources, including a declining focus on milk drinking as an "Americanization" tool and increased consumption of soda, particularly among children. In response to this trend, the dairy industry has developed new flavored and sugared milks in easy to "chug" containers and developed new marketing techniques directed at younger consumers, in particular the "Got Milk?" advertising campaign. Per capita consumption of flavored milk has increased approximately one-third since 1995. Total per capita milk consumption has continued to decline.

Another possible cause of the decline in milk consumption is frustration with the mainstream American food system in general. Current industrial dairying methods, in particular the use of bovine growth hormone, have inspired outcry among consumers that parallel the "dirtying of a pure product" discussions of the late nineteenth century. The very precautions that have protected milk have distanced consumers from producers. Milk is safe but generally arrives at markets from unknown places and unknown farmers. As a result, new, usually more expensive milk products, such as organic milk and premium delivery services, have become increasingly popular.

Evaporated, Sweetened Condensed, and Dried Milk

One of the most notable characteristics of fluid milk is the lack of general success industry has had with substituting new products for fresh milk. Fresh milk is bulky and perishable. Transporting nonperishable dried or condensed milk is much easier than transporting fresh milk. Fresh,

Condensed Milk. Advertisement for Grandmother's A&P Condensed Milk. *Warshaw Collection of Business Americana, Archives Center, National Museum of American History, Behring Center, Smithsonian Institution*

uncondensed fluid milk, however, remains the most commonly used variety among consumers, at least in the United States—probably because of federal involvement in promoting fluid milk and the success of the industry in protecting fresh fluid milk from health problems.

Milk substitutes have had their eras of popularity. Sweetened condensed milk was developed by Gail Borden in the 1850s and proved to be a highly successful product, particularly canned. Condensed milk was one of the standard food items for the Union Army in the Civil War. Evaporated milk, developed in the 1880s, was a sanitary improvement on condensed milk and was very popular, sparking the development of two large food companies—Pet and Carnation. As fresh milk and refrigeration improved, however, the demand for condensed and evaporated milk declined. These products are used mainly at home in recipes for sweets. U.S. production of evaporated and condensed milk peaked in 1945 (the U.S. military continued to be a good customer) at more than 4 million pounds. By 1975 only one-fourth of this amount was produced. This figure has decreased even further, probably because of the declining amount of baking done at home. Per capita consumption of evaporated and condensed milk has halved since 1980.

Dried milk, a somewhat later invention than evaporated and condensed milk, was a successful industrial food ingredient but has not proved popular for home use. Of the 935 million pounds of dried milk produced in the United States in 2000, only 8 million pounds was packaged for retail sale. Most dried milk is used in a variety of industrial food production processes, including the manufacture of other dairy products, baking mixes, confections, and pharmaceuticals.

[*See also* Adulterations; Borden; Dairy; Dairy Industry; Milk, Powdered; Milk Packaging; Pure Food and Drug Act; Transportation of Food.]

BIBLIOGRAPHY

Bailey, Kenneth W. *Marketing and Pricing of Milk and Dairy Products in the United States.* Ames: Iowa State University Press, 1997.

Block, Daniel R. "Purity, Economy, and Social Welfare in the Progressive Era Pure Milk Movement." *Journal for the Study of Food and Society* 3 (1999): 20–27.

Bundesen, Herman N. "Milk in Your Life." *Bulletin of the Chicago Department of Health* 18, no. 16 (1924).

Bundesen, Herman N. "The Growing Child." *Bulletin of the Chicago Department of Health* 21, no. 44 (1927).

Cohen, Robert. *Milk: The Deadly Poison.* Englewood Cliffs, NJ: Argus, 1997.

DuPuis, E. Melanie. *Nature's Perfect Food: How Milk Became America's Drink.* New York: New York University Press, 2002.

Hartley, Robert Milham. *An Historical, Scientific, and Practical Essay on Milk as an Article of Human Substance.* New York: Arno, 1977. The original edition was published in 1842.

International Dairy Foods Association. *Milk Facts.* Washington, DC: International Dairy Foods Association, 2002.

Manchester, Alden C. *The Public Role in the Dairy Economy: Why and How Governments Intervene in the Milk Business.* Boulder, CO: Westview, 1983.

McIntosh, Elaine N. *American Food Habits in Historical Perspective.* Westport, CT: Praeger, 1995.

Parker, Horatio Newton. *City Milk Supply.* New York: McGraw-Hill, 1917.

Roadhouse, Charles Linwood, and James Lloyd Henderson. *The Market Milk Industry.* New York: McGraw-Hill, 1941.

Rosenau, M. J. *The Milk Question.* Boston: Houghton Mifflin, 1912.

Selitzer, Ralph. *The Dairy Industry in America.* New York: Dairy and Ice Cream Field and Books for Industry, 1976.

Straus, Nathan. *Disease in Milk: The Remedy Pasteurization—The Life Work of Nathan Straus.* Compiled by Lina Gutherz Straus. New York: Arno, 1977. The original edition was published in 1917.

DANIEL BLOCK

Milk, Powdered

Marco Polo gets the credit for introducing powdered milk to Europe. His journals contain a lively account of thirteenth-century Mongols dehydrating skimmed mare's milk in the sun, creating a transportable, durable food. Modern technology has mechanized production, but the process of reducing milk to a powder has not changed. Defatted milk has its water content removed through evaporation, leaving a residue containing the proteins, vitamins, and minerals present in whole milk. Properly stored, powdered milk will keep its maximum nutritional value for up to four years. Because of its long shelf life, its portability, and the ease of reconstitution, it is a favored ration for hunters, hikers, survivalists, relief agencies, and the military.

Britain issued a patent for manufacturing dried milk in 1855. In 1869 Henri Nestlé perfected the process in Switzerland, and the United States issued a patent for producing it in 1872. The product was initially unpopular because of the food adulteration scandals that rocked the last part of the nineteenth century. Consumers were leery of how easily the powder could be cut or replaced entirely by other substances, like plaster of Paris. However, necessity brought it into wide use during World War II both on the battlefield and on the home front. Powdered milk became a staple of relief agencies operating in the postwar world.

Powdered milk found its niche in America in partnership with other ingredients to make foods like bread, instant cereal, and a variety of other convenience and ready-made foods. It achieved what is arguably its starring role in Pennsylvania in 1895, when the entrepreneur and candy maker Milton Hershey applied Henry Ford's assembly line to the formula for milk chocolate he had created based on the Swiss method of combining conched chocolate with powdered milk. The result was a smooth, consistent flavor of chocolate that is still a mass-market best seller.

Powdered milk is a mainstay of chocolate milk mixes, instant breakfast drinks, and numerous "instant" puddings, dips, and dressings, as well as a major supplement to livestock feed.

[See also Breakfast Drinks; Dips; Hershey Foods Corporation; Milk; Nestlé; Puddings.]

BIBLIOGRAPHY

Tannahill, Reay. *Food in History*. Rev. ed. New York: Crown Publishers, 1989. An excellent overview of the cultural history of food; first published in 1973.

ESTHER DELLA REESE

Milk Packaging

For most of human history, milk was kept in its original package, the cow's udder, until it was needed. On the farm this meant that the cow was milked daily. In the city, cows were walked to the customer's door and milked on the spot. Some cows were milked at a central location in the city, and the milk was quickly delivered in metal pails. Customers came out with pitchers and bowls to receive the milk. During hot weather some of this milk spoiled, became contaminated, and in some places was a major source of milk-borne diseases, such as tuberculosis, diphtheria, and dysentery.

As populations grew, particularly in the cities, the pressure to find more efficient methods of packaging and distributing milk became a priority. The New York Dairy Company is thought to have been the first dairy to use a factory-made milk bottle around 1875. In 1878 the Lester Milk Jar received a patent as a milk container. In 1880 a glass milk bottle with a glass lid held in place with tin clips was patented. But the bottle that was to be the standard for most of the twentieth century was a milk bottle with a cap seat, which permitted the user to reseal the bottle with a paper disk. Milk bottles were embossed with the name of the dairy in order to ensure that they found their way back to be reused. Until the 1960s the cream in the milk floated to the top of the bottle and was used in coffee or reserved for making whipped cream. Homogenization (breaking up the butterfat into particles that stay in suspension) became standard at this time, and the layer of cream at the top disappeared.

Through the 1950s it was the milkman who delivered milk in heavy glass bottles. With a car, the modern housewife could purchase milk in paper cartons at convenient supermarkets. These containers were at first covered with wax to make the carton waterproof. These paper-based milk containers first appeared in California around 1906, but it was not until 1915 that John Van Wormer, a toy factory owner, received a patent for his paper milk carton. It took him ten years to develop a machine that could fold, glue, fill, and seal the cartons at the dairy. He called his paper milk container Pure-Pak, "pure" because it could be discarded after one use. By 1934 the Ex-Cell-O Corporation owned the rights to the Pure-Pak system. They introduced the tab on the side of the gable so it could be lifted for pouring. Prior to this innovation, consumers had to use a knife to open the top of the container. By the 1970s the one-gallon plastic jug had become the standard milk container. The paper carton, its waxing replaced by a polyethylene laminate, is still widely used for half-pint servings, mostly in schools and vending machines.

[See also Aseptic Packaging; Milk.]

BIBLIOGRAPHY

Moyer, Judith. "From Dairy to Doorstep." *Historic New England*, Fall 2001. The magazine of the Society for the Preservation of New England antiquities.

JOSEPH M. CARLIN

Milkshakes, Malts, and Floats

In the late nineteenth century soda fountains all over the United States offered a variety of sweet concoctions. Among the most popular from the late nineteenth century on, were malteds, milkshakes, and ice cream floats.

Malted milk powder was introduced in 1887 by William Horlick of Racine, Wisconsin, who marketed the powder in association with his brother James, an English apothecary. Malted milk, consisting of whole dried milk, malted barley, and wheat flour was intended to be dissolved in hot water and was used as a dietary supplement for infants. It was also considered useful for treating intestinal problems.

Soda fountain operators began adding malted milk powder to their flavored beverages, selling cold malted milk shakes in the summer and hot in the winter. Malted milk beverages were viewed as healthy, complete meal drinks that had particular appeal for men who preferred hearty, rich beverages to dainty ones. The temperance movement helped promote malteds as a good alternative to alcoholic beverages and thus as a draw for male customers at soda fountains.

Another invention that promoted the popularity of malteds was the development of various types of blenders in the late nineteenth and early twentieth centuries The blender allowed soda jerks to create smoother, richer drinks than they could by hand and added to the showmanship that was integral to the soda fountain experience. In the 1920s one malted milk powder manufacturer offered a free blender to any soda fountain that ordered a substantial amount of its malted milk powder.

Malteds were so popular that some soda fountains were called malt shops. Soda jerks used a special lingo when malts were ordered. "Twist it, choke it, and make it cackle" was an order for a malted with an egg, or malted nog. Among the most popular malteds and their code calls were "black and white," a chocolate malted with vanilla ice cream; "burn one," a chocolate malted milk; and "burn one all the way," a chocolate malted with chocolate ice cream. As with other soda fountain beverages, the varieties were limitless.

Like malteds, milkshakes became popular in the late 1800s. They were also viewed as health drinks because they contained syrup along with the milk or the milk and ice cream. In different parts of the country milkshakes were called by different names. For example, a shake in most of New England was called a "frappe," but in Rhode Island it was a "cabinet." The variety of shakes was endless, chocolate and strawberry being the most popular. A more complex shake was the brown cow, which included chocolate syrup, milk, and root beer, and an unusual one was the prune juice shake. The basic soda fountain call for a milkshake was "shake one," modified by the flavor, such as "shake one in the hay"—a strawberry milkshake. Milkshakes could be shaken by hand, but as with malteds, the blender provided a thicker, smoother shake—and a show.

Ice cream floats are a form of ice cream soda. The differences lies in when the ice cream is added to the beverage. In a float the syrup is put into the glass, milk, if being used, is added, and then soda water is drawn into the glass so that a small amount of space is left at the top for the floating of ice cream and a bit more syrup . In making an ice cream soda, the ice cream is added when the glass is half to three-quarters full, and topped off with carbonated water. The most familiar popular floats were made with root beer or Coca-Cola. A black or brown cow was a root beer float.

[*See also* Batidos; Blenders; Egg Cream; Frappes; Ice Cream and Ices; Ice Cream Sodas; Milk; Phosphates; Root Beer; Seltzer; Slang, Food; Soda Drinks; Soda Fountains.]

BIBLIOGRAPHY

Funderburg, Anne Cooper. *Sundae Best: A History of Soda Fountains*. Bowling Green, OH: Bowling Green State University Popular Press, 2002. Well researched and documented. Good bibliography.

Kelly, Patricia M., ed. *Luncheonette: Ice-Cream, Beverage, and Sandwich Recipes from the Golden Age of the Soda Fountain*. New York: Crown, 1988.

PATRICIA M. KELLY

Miller Brewing Company

In 1855 Frederick Miller, an immigrant from Germany, bought the Menomonee Valley Brewery, a Milwaukee brewery also known as the Plank Road Brewery, which had been founded seven years earlier by Frederick Charles Best. The company remained in the hands of the Miller family until the late 1960s, when the head of the family was killed in an airplane crash. Philip Morris and Company purchased Miller in 1970. In 1972 Miller bought rights to the Meister Brau line of products, including one called Meister Brau Lite beer. Although Lite Beer cost less to produce than conventional beer,

Miller positioned the product as a premium beer. The formula for Lite Beer from Miller continued to prove a winner, especially because of widespread, aggressive marketing. Miller's goal was to persuade the public that the low-calorie beer was as suited for men as it was for women. Miller not only achieved this goal but also broke ground in the brewing industry by developing low-calorie and low-*carbohydrate* beer and making it a national best seller.

In 1973 Miller's advertising agency, McCann-Erickson, was given the Lite Beer account. The usual brand research found that the beer drinkers of Anderson, Indiana, where the product was test marketed, gave Lite Beer an extremely high approval rating. The decision was made to conduct a nationwide campaign with a television advertisement that is considered a classic. The commercial featured lovable Matt Snell, a well-known former football player, and the slogan "New Lite Beer from Miller is all you ever wanted in a beer . . . and less." That was the start of an advertising campaign that turned Miller Lite into a national institution and started the revolution in "light beer"—beer low in calories and carbohydrates.

By 1978 Miller passed Schlitz and Pabst to take second place to Anheuser-Busch, which had become the first brewer to sell 40 million barrels of beer a year. Soon the two top brewers were producing more than 50 percent of the beer sold in America, largely at the expense of smaller, independent breweries. In 1993 Miller test-marketed a clear beer, which failed in every way. In 1995, an attempt to expand the market and distribution of imported products with established reputations, Miller acquired a stake in Canada's Molson and Mexico's FEMSA breweries. In May 2002 South African Breweries bought Miller Brewing Company from Philip Morris for $3.6 billion in stock, renaming the company SABMiller. This transaction allowed SABMiller to begin importing South African Breweries Pilsner Urquell beer to the United States and SABMiller to promote Miller products internationally.

[*See also* Advertising; Beer; Brewing; Budweiser; Coors Brewing Company.]

BIBLIOGRAPHY

Baron, Stanley. *Brewed in America*. Boston: Little Brown, 1962.
LaFrance, Peter. *Beer Basics*. New York: Wiley, 1995.
Rhodes, Christine P., ed. *The Encyclopedia of Beer*. New York: Henry Holt, 1995.
Van Wieren, Dale E. *American Breweries*. West Point, PA: East Coast Breweriana Association, 1995.

PETER LAFRANCE

Mimosa

The mimosa is one of America's first designer cocktails. It is the American version of a Buck's fizz. Invented in Britain in the 1920s, the Buck's fizz is made up of equal parts orange juice and champagne plus another, disputed ingredient, such as gin, brandy, or Cointreau. Sometime in the 1940s or 1950s, the drink appeared in the United States without the disputed extra ingredients and was called the mimosa. One Hollywood legend has it that the mimosa was introduced to the United States by the British film director Alfred Hitchcock. As the story goes, Hitchcock added champagne to orange juice at a luncheon and presented it to fellow guests as a hangover cure. Perhaps this is why the mimosa is the drink of choice for brunch. The sweet and effervescent cocktail has proved the perfect accompaniment to everything from croissants and muffins to eggs and smoked salmon. In an interesting twist, as the designer cocktail reemerged on the scene in the late twentieth century, bartenders across the United States once again began to put their signatures on the mimosa by adding an additional ingredient such as tangerine juice or Cointreau.

[*See also* Champagne; Cocktails.]

BIBLIOGRAPHY

Miller, Anistatia, Jared Brown, and Don Gutterdam. *Champagne Cocktails*. New York: HarperCollins, 1999.

HOPE-MARIE FLAMM

Mint Julep

Far from their Kentucky home, two men traveling to the California gold mines in the early 1850s gathered snow left over from the past winter and prepared "mint juleps in abundance"(Morgan, 1959). They were, like so many others in Kentucky, Virginia, Georgia, and elsewhere, planning on carrying on the tradition of banishing the cares of the day with a frosty drink made with mint, ice, sugar, and whiskey. In the antebellum South, a mint julep was compared with sipping the nectar of the gods. Although the recipe sounds simple, preparing it requires a carefully observed ritual.

"Julep," according to the *Oxford English Dictionary*, comes from the Arabic *julab* or Persian *gul-ab* (rose water). The French adapted the word to *julep*. A citation in the *OED* from as early as 1400 describes a julep as a medicinal "syrup made only of water and sugar." Americans in Virginia, according to Richard Barksdale Harwell, the author of *The Mint Julep*, added spirits in 1787 and mint in 1803 and originated the mint julep. Deciding that the English might like this new version, Captain Frederick Marryat, who had been traveling in America, reintroduced the mint julep to the English in 1837. Marryat noted that the mint julep is "one of the most delightful and insinuating potations that ever was invented."

The first mint julep recipes called for brandy or rum, but local whiskey, frequently home-distilled rye and bourbon soon became the spirits of choice. Charles Joseph Latrobe, who described the mint julep in 1833 at a meeting of the Anti-Temperance Society in Saratoga, Florida, declared the mint must be unbruised. Jerry Thomas, in *How to Mix Drinks*, which was published in 1862, called for bruising the mint. The issue is still being debated. Both Latrobe and Thomas called for filling a tumbler or glass with shaved ice. Preparation of mint julep is seeped in ceremony and is a symbol of southern hospitality. Harwell quotes Judge Soule Smith, a Lexington, Kentucky, attorney in the late nineteenth century, praising the drink as "the very dream of drinks, the vision of sweet quaffings. The bourbon and the mint are lovers."

Although the mint julep is appreciated throughout the South, Kentucky, proud of its bourbon, popularized the drink in the twentieth century. The year and date are unknown, but a letter written by Judge Soule Smith in the late nineteenth century makes clear that Kentucky bourbon should be the whiskey of choice for a mint julep. The tradition is upheld each year at the Kentucky Derby. Mint julep in a glass marked "Kentucky Derby" was first served in the dining room at Churchill Downs, home of the derby, in 1938. The vessel was an ordinary water glass, but patrons kept it as a souvenir and established a tradition. The next year proper julep glasses were used. Official Kentucky Derby glasses are collectors' items. Kentucky distilleries vie for the distinction of having their bourbon poured into the mint juleps served on derby day.

[*See also* Bourbon; Cocktails.]

BIBLIOGRAPHY

Harwell, Richard Barksdale. *The Mint Julep*. Charlottesville: University of Virginia Press, 1975. A history of mint julep; includes source notes.

Morgan, Dale L., ed. *The Overland Diary of James A. Patterson*. Denver: Old West Publishing, 1959.

JACQUELINE BLOCK WILLIAMS

Mr. Peanut

Planters Peanuts was launched in 1906 by two Italian immigrants, Amedeo Obici and Mario Peruzzi. In 1916 Planters conducted a contest to develop a trademark, offering a prize worth five dollars for the best-designed symbol. The winner was a fourteen-year-old boy named Anthony Gentile, who submitted a drawing of "a little peanut person." With this image as a starting point, Planters hired a Chicago art firm, which commissioned a commercial artist named Andrew Wallach to draw several different caricatures. Planters selected the peanut person with a top hat, monocle, cane, and the look of a raffish gentleman, which was subsequently named "Mr. Peanut." At least, this was the story that Planters circulated. Similar peanut figures, complete with top hat, monocle, cane, and gloves, had illustrated an article in *Good Housekeeping* magazine in 1902.

Mr. Peanut. The Planters Peanuts mascot on the cover of a cookbooklet issued by Standard Brands, 1970. *Collection of Andrew F. Smith*

Whatever the origin of Mr. Peanut, the character was a solid advertising success aimed at America's youth. Planters applied for a trademark on March 12, 1917. During that year, Mr. Peanut made his debut in New England newspapers and on advertising posters in New York City subway trains. This debut was followed by a national advertising campaign in which Mr. Peanut appeared in the *Saturday Evening Post*. These campaigns were so successful that Planters increased its advertising budget for each succeeding year, spending hundreds of thousands of dollars on advertisements in the best newspapers and magazines in the United States. In advertisements, Mr. Peanut proclaimed that peanuts were a perfect food for picnics and baseball games and for use as an ingredient in main dishes served at lunch and dinner. The company used other media as well, including Mr. Peanut paint books.

Planters print promotions moved from commonplace advertising to novel schemes that drew in readers, and the advertising paid off. Sales rose from $1 million in 1917 to $7 million five years later. Within these few years, salted peanuts and confections bearing Mr. Peanut's picture became known all across America. Planters opened a store on the boardwalk in Atlantic City, New Jersey. A man dressed in a Mr. Peanut outfit greeted visitors outside the store and became one of the most memorable figures along the boardwalk. In New York City, Mr. Peanut, complete with hat and cane, appeared on a dazzling sign at Forty-sixth Street and Broadway, in Times Square. By the mid-1930s, Mr. Peanut had become the symbol for the entire peanut industry.

Since his origin, Mr. Peanut has been on almost every Planters package, container, premium, and advertisement. As a result, the Mr. Peanut caricature has become one of the most familiar icons in advertising history. His likeness graces mugs, pencils, pens, and tote bags, which are available by redemption of product wrappers. Planters offered a variety of premium items with its products: glass jars, charm bracelets, clocks, metal tins, wristwatches, ashtrays, plastic whistles, and display figures with monocles that lit up. At the beginning of the twenty-first century, Mr. Peanut is an American culinary icon known the world over.

[*See also* Advertising; Kraft Foods; Peanuts; Snack Food.]

BIBLIOGRAPHY

Lindenberger, Jan, with Joyce Spontak. *Planters Peanut Collectibles since 1961*. Atglen, PA: Schiffer, 1995.

Lindenberger, Jan, with Joyce Spontak. *Planters Peanut Collectibles 1906–1961*. 2nd ed. Atglen, PA: Schiffer, 1999.

Smith, Andrew F. *Peanuts: The Illustrious History of the Goober Pea*. Urbana: University of Illinois Press, 2002.

ANDREW F. SMITH

Mock Foods

Mock foods provide an insight into America's national heritage. This culinary genre was introduced to colonial America by European cooks versed in the ancient arts of presentation and food substitution. American mock foods were created when colonial cooks plied these skills to reconcile Old World recipes with New World ingredients. Recipes evolved according to immediate need, technological advancement, cultural advancement, economic necessity, and health concerns. In the eighteenth and nineteenth centuries American mock foods centered on practical substitutions. In the late nineteenth century creations featured more complicated, showy foods. In the twentieth century mock foods often showcased manufactured products promoted by food companies. What makes a food "mock" is not a simple question to answer.

Mock can denote substitution of a primary ingredient. Perhaps the most famous mock food is mock turtle soup, immortalized by Lewis Carroll in *Alice's Adventures in Wonderland*. Mock goose (leg of pork), mock duck (leg of lamb), and mock oysters (corn fritters) were known to Americans in the nineteenth century. In the twentieth century recipes for mock chicken were variously composed of pork, peanuts, tuna, or veal.

Mock can mean that a food tastes like another. The mock apple pie known to most Americans was introduced in the 1930s by the National Biscuit Company (Nabisco) as a promotion for Ritz crackers. This recipe evolved from mid-nineteenth-century imitation apple pies and mock mince pies, which were made with soda crackers, sugar, and spices. Crackers have a history of approximating apple pie in both texture and taste.

Mock foods may look like other foods. Upscale caterers throughout time have used food to create complicated, edible works of art. American culinary artists have been known to disguise entire hams as Easter eggs, create fantastic beasts from bread, and sculpt national icons from pâté. In the twentieth century American homemakers decorated holiday tables with pineapple peacocks and cheese ducks.

MOCK FOODS

SOUPS

Mock bouillon—canned tomatoes, diced vegetables, and spices, 1923

Mock fish chowder—fish chowder without the fish, 1918

Mock St. Germain soup—diced salt pork, canned condensed pea soup, and bouillon, 1942

Mock turtle soup—calf's head, 1824

SAUCES AND DRESSINGS

Mock hollandaise—hot cream cheese, egg yolks, lemon juice, and mayonnaise, 1958

Mock maple syrup—brown sugar, water, salt, and vanilla, 1939

MEATS AND EGGS

Mock chicken—breaded & fried peanuts and sweet potatoes, 1925

Mock chicken drumsticks or "city chicken"— veal and pork on skewers, 1946

Mock chicken salad—cubed pork, 1923

Mock chicken salad—cubed veal, 1956

Mock chicken sandwiches—tuna, 1931

Mock duck—shoulder of lamb, the shank shaped to look like a duck's bill, 1884

Mock duck—stuffed tenderloin or flank steak,1958

Mock goose—leg of pork, 1877

Mock sausages—pureed lima beans, cracker crumbs, heavy cream, and spices fried in oil, 1923

Mock veal cutlets—baked lentils, peanuts, graham cracker crumbs, tomatoes, and spices, 1925

Mock venison—mutton served with gravy and currant jelly, 1844

SEAFOOD

Mock crab sandwich—grated cheese, creamed butter, mustard, and anchovy paste served hot, 1929

Mock crabs—canned corn, cracker crumbs, milk, and spices baked in butter, 1923

Mock oysters—corn fritters shaped like oysters, 1844

Mock oysters—mushrooms dipped in egg and bread crumbs and then fried, 1902

Mock scallops—halibut cut in the shape of scallops, breaded and deep fried, 1939

Mock terrapin—chicken, white sauce, eggs, sherry, and spices, 1939

VEGETABLES AND STARCHES

Mock artichokes—white turnips, 1902

Mock macaroni—crackers soaked in milk and used for casseroles, 1828

Continued

Mock foods can be economical approximations of more expensive foods. Depression-era and wartime cooks relied on mock foods to stretch budgets. American cookbooks printed in these lean years were filled with less expensive alternatives to traditional favorites. In some cookbooks, the word "mock" was featured in the index, facilitating recipe identification. Fannie Farmer's 1939 *Boston Cooking-School Cook Book* listed nineteen recipes under this heading.

Mock can mean less of a key ingredient, acknowledging a substandard product. Fannie Farmer's 1923 recipe for mock angel food called for two egg whites rather than eight.

Mock can mean a vegetarian alternative. In the 1920s the American vegetarian movement created mock sausage (puréed lima beans) and mock veal cutlets (lentils and peanuts). Tofu burgers were promoted as healthy protein alternatives in the 1970s. American vegetarians in the 1980s celebrated Thanksgiving with "tofurkey" (tofu shaped like turkey).

Mock foods have been known by other names. In 1796 in a recipe for "a tasty indian pudding" in *American Cookery* (considered the first American cookbook) Amelia Simmons substituted cornmeal for wheat flour. In the 1884 edition of the *Boston Cooking-School Cook Book*, Mrs. D. A. Lincoln provided detailed instructions for meat porcupines (molded meat with bacon quills) and mutton ducks (artfully reconstructed bones and meat). Betty Crocker promoted emergency steak (T-bone–shaped

MOCK FOODS (Continued)

Mock olives—unripe plums preserved in brine, 1918

DESSERTS

Mock angel cake—two egg whites instead of the usual eight to ten, 1923

Mock charlotte—cornstarch, sugar, eggs and water served with custard sauce, 1902

Mock cheese blintzes—cottage cheese, Uneeda biscuits, eggs, milk, and butter, 1958

Mock cherry pie—cranberries and raisins, 1923

Mock cream—milk, cornstarch, eggs, and butter, 1910

Mock cream pie—eggs, flour, and milk poured over puff paste and cooked in the oven, 1847

Mock Devonshire cream—cream cheese, cream, and sugar, 1956

Mock Indian pudding—whole wheat bread, milk, molasses, and butter, 1923

Mock mince pie—crackers rolled fine, water, vinegar, molasses, sugar, currants, and spices, 1877

Mock pistachio ice cream—vanilla with almond extract and green food coloring, 1931

Mock toasted marshmallows—gelatin, water, sugar, egg whites, vanilla, and stale macaroons, 1939

CANDY

Mock almonds—stale bread cut in almond shapes, brushed with butter, and baked; croutons, 1923

Mock candy—ground nuts and fruits pressed together and cut like caramels, 1902

SOURCES

1824 and 1828, *The Virginia House-wife*, Mary Randolph

1844, *The Improved Housewife*, Mrs. A. L. Webster

1849, *Directions for Cookery in Its Various Branches*, Miss Eliza Leslie

1866, *Mrs. Crowen's American Lady's Cookery Book*, Mrs. T. J. Crowen

1877, *Buckeye Cookery and Practical Housekeeping*, Esther Woods Wilcox

1884, *Boston Cooking School Cook Book*, Mary J. Lincoln

1902, *Mrs. Rorer's New Cook Book*, Sarah Tyson Rorer

1910, *Hand-book for the Kitchen and Housekeeper's Guide*, Flora Neely

1918, *Jewish Cook Book*, Florence Kreisler Greenbaum

1923, *The Boston Cooking-School Cook Book*, Fannie Merritt Farmer

1924, *Mrs Allen on Cooking, Menus, Service*, Ida C. Bailey Allen

1925, *How to Grow the Peanut and 105 Ways for Preparing It for Human Consumption*, George Washington Carver

1929, *Seven Hundred Sandwiches*, Florence A. Cowles

1931, The *Joy of Cooking*, Irma S. Rombauer

1939, *Boston Cooking-School Cook Book*, Fannie Merritt Farmer

1942, *Woman's Home Companion Cook Book*

1956, *Picture Cook Book*, Betty Crocker

1958, *The Jewish Cook Book*, Mildred Grosberg Bellin

LYNNE OLVER

---

meat loaf) during World War II. In the 1950s residents of Pittsburgh consumed "city chicken" (skewered pork and veal), adopting it as a local favorite.

[See also Betty Crocker; Cookbooks and Manuscripts, *subentries* From the Beginnings to 1860, From the Civil War to World War I, *and* From World War I to World War II; Crackers; Nabisco; Thanksgiving;Vegetarianism.]

BIBLIOGRAPHY

Allen, Ida C. Bailey. *Mrs. Allen on Cooking, Menus, Service: 2500 Recipes*. Garden City, NY: Doubleday, Page, 1924.

Bellin, Mildred Grosberg. *The Jewish Cook Book*. New York: Bloch, 1958.

Carver, George Washington. *How to Grow the Peanut and 105 Ways for Preparing It for Human Consumption*. Bulletin no. 31 June 1925, 7th ed. Tuskegee, AL: Tuskegee Institute Experimental Station, 1940. Reprinted 1983 for Tuskegee Institute National Historic Site, George Washington Carver National Monument by the Eastern National Park and Monument Association. http://aggie–horticulture.tamu.edu/plantanswers/recipes/peanutrecipes.html.

Cowles, Florence A. *Seven Hundred Sandwiches*. Boston: Little, Brown, 1929.

Crocker, Betty. *Picture Cook Book*, 2nd ed. New York: McGraw-Hill, 1956.

Crowen, Mrs. T. J. *Mrs. Crowen's American Lady's Cookery Book*. New York: Dick and Fitzgerald, 1847.

Farmer, Fannie Merritt. *The Boston Cooking-School Cook Book*. New edition, revised and enlarged. Boston: Little, Brown, 1923.

Farmer, Fannie Merritt. *Boston Cooking-School Cook Book*. 6th ed. Boston: Little, Brown, 1939.

Greenbaum, Florence Kreisler. *The International Jewish Cook Book*. New York: Bloch, 1918.

Leslie, Eliza. *Miss Leslie's Complete Cookery:* Directions for Cookery, in Its Various Branches. Philadelphia: Baird, 1849.

Lincoln, Mary J. *Boston Cooking School Cook Book: A Reprint of the 1884 Classic.* With a new introduction by Janice Bluestein Longone. Mineola, NY: Dover, 1996.

Neely, Flora. *Hand-book for the Kitchen and Housekeeper's Guide.* 3rd ed, revised. New Rochelle, NY: Paragraph, 1910.

Randolph, Mary. *The Virginia House-wife.* With historical notes and commentaries by Karen Hess. Columbia: University of South Carolina Press, 1984.

Rombauer, Irma S. *The Joy of Cooking.* New York: Scribner, 1998. Facsimile of 1931 edition.

Rorer, Sarah Tyson. *Mrs. Rorer's New Cook Book: A Manual of Housekeeping.* Philadelphia: Arnold, 1902.

Webster, Mrs. A. L. *The Improved Housewife or Book of Receipts: Or, Book of Receipts; with Engravings for Marketing and Carving, by a Married Lady.* 5th ed. Hartford, CT: Hobbs, 1844.

Wilcox, Esther Woods. *Buckeye Cookery and Practical Housekeeping, Compiled from Original Recipes.* Bedford, MA: Applewood, 2000. Facsimile of 1877 edition.

Woman's Home Companion Cook Book. Foreword by Willa Roberts. New York: Collier, 1942.

LYNNE M. OLVER

Molasses

Molasses, like honey, is a liquid sweetener. The term "molasses" has several meanings. In the rural South and in parts of Appalachia, "molasses" refers to a homemade syrup produced from farm-grown sugarcane. The sugarcane is cleaned and then manually crushed by rollers in a mule-powered mill or press. Milling extracts juice and water from the cane. The extracted liquid is boiled down in an open kettle to evaporate some of the water, making a syrup. This very sweet sugary syrup is pure cane syrup or more commonly, "molasses." In Louisiana, this syrup is called *la cuite.* Farther to the north, including most of the Midwest, farm-produced molasses is made from sorghum, a cereal grass, by the same open-kettle technique.

In the refined-sugar industry, molasses is a by-product of the sugar-extraction process. After most of the water is removed from sugarcane juice by evaporation, raw sugar is crystallized from the syrup. These sugar crystals are mechanically removed by first spinning the syrup (centrifugation) and then passing it through very fine screens. The liquid that remains after some or all of the sugar has been removed from the syrup is molasses.

There are three primary types of commercial molasses because the sugarcane juice can be processed three times. After the initial boiling of the juice and the first removal of sugar crystals from the syrup, the remaining liquid is sweet and thick. This by-product is first, or

light, molasses. When the syrup is processed a second time and more sugar crystals are removed, the remaining liquid is darker and less sweet. This product is called second, or dark, molasses. The third processing produces blackstrap molasses, a dark, bitter, nonsweet syrup. First or second molasses that has been bleached with sulfur dioxide is called "sulfured" molasses.

Molasses first came to America from the Caribbean. The British started sugarcane cultivation in Barbados in 1646, and by the late 1670s there was a flourishing two-way sea trade between Barbados and the American colony at Rhode Island. The colonists shipped agricultural and forest products, such as pork, beef, butter, cider, barrel staves, and shingles, to the West Indies, and the ships returned with cargoes of cotton wool, rum, molasses, and sugar. The large volume of sugar and molasses going to Rhode Island could not be used there, so much of this cargo was resold in Boston.

Molasses. *Forty Ways to Use Molasses,* cookbooklet published by the American Molasses Company, 1923. *Collection of Andrew F. Smith*

The New England colonists used molasses not only as the primary sweetener in cooking and baking but also as an ingredient in brewing birch beer and molasses beer and in distilling rum. In the early 1700s rum made in New England became an essential element in a highly profitable triangular trade across the Atlantic. The colonists exported rum to West Africa in trade for slaves; the ships brought the slaves from Africa to the French West Indies, trading them for more molasses and sugar; these products were then shipped to New England to make more rum.

Because importation of molasses to New England from the French West Indies seriously harmed British farmers in the Caribbean, the British government passed the Molasses Act in 1733. This law imposed a duty on "foreign" molasses or syrup imported into the American colonies or plantations. In addition, some shipments of American rum were subject to forfeiture and confiscation of the vessel of transport. The Molasses Act of 1733 and the Sugar Act of 1764 caused the price of molasses to rise, leading to the use of less expensive maple sugar as a sweetener. When the cost of refined sugar dropped at the end of the nineteenth century—as a result of increased production from manufacturing advances and huge increases in the amount of imported refined sugar—molasses lost its role as an important sweetener in the American diet.

In the early twenty-first century, molasses is not an important sweetener in cooking. It is, however, an essential flavor ingredient in a number of traditional American baked goods, such as anadama bread, gingerbread, gingersnaps, hermits, Indian pudding, molasses cakes, molasses cookies, and shoofly pie. Molasses is also an important flavor ingredient in Cracker Jack, a popcorn-and-peanuts snack food. Specific regional dishes, such as Boston baked beans and Boston brown bread, require molasses. Because molasses complements pork dishes, it is commonly found in ham glazes and barbecue sauces.

Molasses, like many other food words, has entered American slang. People who are lethargic or not efficient are called "slow as molasses" or "slow as molasses in January." American children are introduced to molasses and its very sticky nature in *Candyland*, a board game for children who have not yet learned to read. *Candyland* is played with gingerbread-men game pieces. The unlucky child whose game piece lands on a certain penalty spot on the way to finding the Lost Castle becomes stuck in the molasses swamp.

[See also Anadama Bread; Birch Beer; Cajun and Creole Food; Cracker Jack; German American Food, *sidebar on* Shoofly Pie; Rum; Sorghum Syrup; Sugar; Sweeteners.]

BIBLIOGRAPHY

Bienvenu, Marcelle. *Who's Your Mama, Are You Catholic, and Can You Make a Roux? A Family Album, Cajun/Creole Cookbook.* Lafayette, LA: Times of Acadian, 1991.
Farr, Sidney Saylor. *More Than Moonshine: Appalachian Recipes and Recollections.* Pittsburgh, PA: University of Pittsburgh Press, 1983.
Woloson, Wendy A. *Refined Tastes: Sugar, Confectionery, and Consumers in Nineteenth-Century America.* Baltimore: Johns Hopkins University Press, 2002.

ROBERT W. BROWER

Mondavi, Robert

Robert Mondavi (b. 1913) is a leading figure in the transformation of the American wine industry, notably the Napa Valley in California. The Robert Mondavi corporation, now a public company, has expanded from its base in the Napa Valley to joint ventures with international wine producers such as the Frescobaldi in Italy and Eduardo Chadwick in Chile. The best known of Robert Mondavi's strategic partnerships was that with Baron Philippe de Rothschild to create the wine Opus One. This partnership and the quality of the wine gave new cachet to the wines of California, specifically those of the Napa Valley.

The Mondavi dynasty began when Robert's father, Cesare, came to the United States from Italy in 1906. Cesare ran a boarding house in Minnesota and left there in 1922 for the San Joaquin Valley of California. Like the Gallo family, who lived nearby, Cesare became involved in the sale of grapes to home winemakers, a questionable enterprise in a nation that was still in the midst of Prohibition. The sale of grapes in limited quantities for personal winemaking was, however, legal. Also like the Gallo family, Cesare Mondavi began to produce wine at the end of Prohibition. He later chose to leave the hot Central Valley, where grapes for sweet wines thrived, for the cooler Napa Valley to concentrate on quality varietal wines. The Gallos remained in the Central Valley and built the world's largest winery, a cornerstone of their empire.

In the cooler climate of the Napa Valley sometime after 1936, Robert Mondavi began to make wine. He worked at the Sunny St. Helena Winery and later was involved in the operation of the Charles Krug Winery, which the Mondavi family acquired in 1943. At the Krug winery Mondavi became acquainted with the work of André Tchelistcheff (1901–1994). Tchelistcheff, a Russian émigré, was an enologist whose work was a major contribution to the California wine industry.

Tchelistcheff was working for Charles de Latour of the Beaulieu Vineyard but acted as a consultant to many Napa vineyards. Mondavi and Tchelistcheff's mutual vision was the production of grapes suited to the soil and climate with the goal of making fine wine. Mondavi believed that cabernet sauvignon was ideally suited to the region and conducted experiments with the grape. When Cesare Mondavi died in 1959, his brother Peter, whose vision for the winery was at odds with Robert's, cut Robert out of the operation. Family acrimony was not uncommon among the great California wine makers, and families such as the Gallos and the Sebastianis had highly publicized disputes. After a difficult legal struggle Robert Mondavi obtained compensation and in 1966 founded his own winery on the Oakville Highway in Napa Valley. Among the first winemakers whom Mondavi consulted was the venerable André Tchelistcheff.

Thirteen years after founding his winery, in 1979, Mondavi entered into the historic partnership with Baron Philippe de Rothschild. The wine created was Opus One, a partnership of the old world and the new that was highly regarded and introduced the wine world to the possibilities of the Napa Valley. Unlike the Gallo family, who relied on keeping the company private and controlling the many aspects of wine production, Mondavi became a pioneer in joint ventures worldwide and acquired numerous properties. The company expanded to include labels such as Woodbridge, Vichon, and Byron. In 1993 the Robert Mondavi company began selling shares to the public. In his early nineties, Robert Mondavi continues active participation in the company, serving as a goodwill ambassador. Mondavi's children, R. Michael, Timothy, and Marcia manage the company.

[See also Wine, subentry Later Developments; Wineries; Wines, California.]

BIBLIOGRAPHY

Laube, J. "Play or Pass on Mondavi Stock." *Wine Spectator* (July 31, 1993).
Mondavi, Robert. "Scenes from a Life in Wine." *Wine Spectator* (March 18, 1993).

STEVEN M. CRAIG

Mondavi Wineries

In 1966, one year after he left Charles Krug Winery, his family's business, Robert Mondavi founded his eponymous company on the Oakville Highway in the Napa Valley of California. The Charles Krug Winery had been purchased by his father, Cesare, in 1943, and Robert was associated with it until his brother Peter, having a different vision for its future, removed him from active participation. The result of this was lengthy litigation finally awarding compensation to Robert Mondavi, after which he decided to form his own winery. His company became known for its research and production of wines based on European grapes, notably, Cabernet Sauvignon. It also was one of the first California producers to recognize the importance of wood and conducted many experiments on the variations of barrel size, manufacture, and wood type on its wines.

In 1979 the company formed a partnership with Philippe de Rothschild to produce a wine in the Napa Valley; the success of that wine, Opus One, is now legendary. This success came despite the fact that Mondavi, in a break with the tradition of using estate-grown grapes for ultra-premium wines, used sourced grapes to produce their wine. The company built its own winery at a cost of $17 million in 1992. Since 1992 all grapes used to make Opus One have been estate-grown from Opus-designated vineyards. This strategic partnership set the stage for other international alliances with prestige producers around the globe—notably, with the Frecobaldi family in Italy to produce the Super-Tuscan Luce and with the Chadwick family in Chile to produce Sena, one of South America's most expensive wines. While these partnerships gave the winery more prestige, it was the lower-end wines, particularly those of the Woodbridge label, that were the financial workhorses that provided the most revenue and profit in the last decade of the twentieth century.

In 1993 the Robert Mondavi Company was producing about 500,000 cases of wine in the Napa Valley. Mondavi's substantial land holdings there were estimated at 1,500 acres, and the winery also acquired the Byron and Vichon properties, in the Santa Maria Valley of California and in the Languedoc region of France, respectively. Nonetheless, the company was struggling with a massive debt load and in 1993 Mondavi went public, selling stock at $13.50 per share; this offering raised $70 million for 28 percent of the company. Little changed in management, however; Robert Mondavi remained as chairman and his two sons shared the responsibilities of chief executive officer. But the offering gave the public a rare look into the books of a prestige producer, and many were surprised that the aforementioned Woodbridge line accounted for 85 percent of sales and 65 percent of net revenues. Since then the winery, while reaping substantial publicity for its luxury wines, has expanded its relationship with the Chadwick family of Chile to include inexpensive wines marketed under the Caliterra label (in addition to the premium Sena). Mondavi also discontinued the Vichon Napa line in favor of operating as a negocient (or middleman) in France's Languedoc region, where in 1995 the company began buying bulk "unfinished" wine that had matured to a certain point and finishing the maturation process in California. It later arranged to produce the wine entirely in France and purchased its own vineyards for a percentage of the label's wines. The company also created the La Familiglia line of Italian varietals and began to make "district" wines under the Robert Mondavi label.

The Robert Mondavi Company continues to innovate and was among the first in America to use a capsule-less bottle design and synthetic stoppers for some of its labels. Unlike its neighbor in California's Central Valley, the privately held and secretive Gallo wine empire, the Mondavi clan has risked its future on public markets, global ventures, and strategic partnerships. Whatever the future may bring, Mondavi is an American success story that has had an effect on the global wine industry through its innovations and quality wine making and marketing.

[*See also* Gallo, Ernest and Julio; Mondavi, Robert; Wine, *subentry on* Wines, California; Wine Barrels; Wine Bottles; Wine Casks.]

STEVEN M. CRAIG

Monte Cristo Sandwich

The Monte Cristo sandwich is composed of white bread, slices of ham, turkey, or chicken, and Swiss cheese. The sandwich is dipped in egg batter, deep-fried in oil or fried in butter, and then dusted with powdered sugar and served with strawberry or raspberry jam for dipping. The Monte Cristo is a variation of the American grilled-cheese sandwich that evolved from the French *croque monsieur*. The sandwich was first mentioned in an American restaurant industry publication in 1923. The origin of the Monte Cristo has been traditionally attributed to California, and it was featured on a 1941 menu in Gordon's, a restaurant once located on Wilshire Boulevard in Los Angeles. Although no explanation of the name has been determined, the sandwich may have been named after the popular movie *The Count of Monte Cristo*, produced in four adaptations between 1908 and 1934. By the early 1950s a Monte Carlo version of the sandwich was being made with sliced tongue, and both sandwiches, cut into small squares for serving with cocktails, were called Monte Benitos.

[*See also* Sandwiches.]

BIBLIOGRAPHY

Brown, Helen Evans. *West Coast Cook Book*. New York: Knopf, 1991.
Mercuri, Becky. *Sandwiches That You Will Like*. Pittsburgh, PA: WQED Multimedia, 2002.

BECKY MERCURI

Moonshine

Moonshine is illicitly distilled liquor. In the rural southern United States it is most commonly corn whiskey. The word "moonshine" was in use as early as 1785, but at that time it meant smuggled liquor. The current meaning came into use about 1875. Americans were distilling homemade whiskey much earlier than that, of course, for both medicinal and recreational purposes.

Moonshine, also known as angel teat, Kentucky fire, squirrel whiskey, swamp dew, white lightning, or white mule, had its heyday during Prohibition. It is made by fermenting water, yeast, malt, sugar or molasses or sorghum, and almost any sugary or starchy edible including, among many other possibilities, cornmeal, hog feed, blackberries, rose hips, potatoes, pumpkins, or raisins in a still. By definition, moonshine is unregulated, so it may be poisoned or unsanitary. It is often cut with water, glycerin, food coloring, extracts, or caustics, and its most dangerous side effect is lead poisoning, which can lead to blindness or death. Unlike regular whiskey, which goes brown from aging in barrels made of charred oak, moonshine is clear and is usually not aged at all.

During Prohibition, moonshiners enjoyed a huge profit margin, making four gallons of whiskey for about $4 and selling them for about $160. The drink is generally tasteless and harsh; many compare its flavor to grain alcohol. There are commercially produced, imitation versions of moonshine available, like Georgia Moon and Platte Valley, packaged in jelly jars and ceramic jugs, respectively.

[*See also* Alcohol and Teetotalism; Bourbon; Homemade Remedies; Prohibition; Stills; Temperance; Whiskey.]

BIBLIOGRAPHY

Kellner, Esther. *Moonshine: Its History and Folklore*. Indianapolis: Bobbs-Merrill, 1971.

Lender, Mark Edward, and Martin, James Kirby. *Drinking in America: A History*. The Revised and Expanded Edition. New York: The Free Press, 1987.

JESSY RANDALL

Mortar and Pestle

Smashing and grinding into fine particles is the job of a mortar and pestle. Mortars are the vessels; pestles are the handheld tools that do the work. The concept and form are probably the earliest of all cookery tools anywhere in the world. The earliest American mortars were probably stone, although other materials—cast iron, cast bronze, and heavy ceramic—would have been brought with immigrants from the beginning. Mortars made of the hardest, densest wood available, *lignum vitae* (wood of life), from a tropical tree, were probably in very early use too. Local hardwoods that resist splintering, such as maple, were also used. Even if set into wooden handles for comfort, the business end of a pestle was made of the same material as its mortar. Since the mid-nineteenth century, most mortars and pestles have been made of thick, white stoneware that resembles marble, with wooden handles for the pestles. Stoneware is impervious to acids and alkalies, and it does not interact with foods. An all-wood implement like a pestle, used with any kind of vessel, is called a beetle.

[*See also* Grinders.]

BIBLIOGRAPHY

Franklin, Linda Campbell. *300 Years of Kitchen Collectibles*. 5th ed. Iola, WI: Krause Publications, 2003.

LINDA CAMPBELL FRANKLIN

Moxie

Moxie, which originated in New England, is the oldest carbonated soft drink and outsold Coca-Cola until the 1920s. Aficionados describe Moxie as extremely potent root beer, although it is a cola drink, but detractors find it unappealing and medicinal. Perhaps because of its strong flavor, Moxie became known as a drink with an attitude, and the word "moxie" has come to mean a "can-do" character. Calvin Coolidge is said to have used Moxie to toast his swearing in as president in 1923.

Moxie was invented as a patent medicine in 1876 by a pharmacist, Augustin Thompson, who sold it over the counter as Moxie Nerve Food in his Lowell, Massachusetts, drug store. Thompson claimed that Moxie, made with gentian root, a nerve-calming ingredient, cured everything from upset stomach to dullness of the brain. In 1910, however, the newly formed U.S. Food and Drug Administration put a stop to the claims.

Moxie advertising was aimed at people with discerning taste, such as the "Moxie Man." The Boston Red Sox star Ted Williams promoted the drink with "Make Mine Moxie" baseball cards. Despite the advertising, Moxie never caught up to Coca-Cola in sales. Nevertheless, every July approximately 25,000 "Moxie heads" gather in Lisbon Falls, Maine, for Moxie Days, which are celebrated with parades, floats, booths of memorabilia, and foods made from Moxie. Although it is considered a New England institution, Moxie is now made by the Monarch Beverage Company, in Atlanta, Georgia.

[*See also* Coca-Cola; New England Regional Cookery; Soda Drinks.]

BIBLIOGRAPHY

Funderburg, Anne Cooper. *Sundae Best: A History of Soda Fountains*. Bowling Green, OH: Bowling Green State University Popular Press, 2002.

Schlozman, Danny. "Make Mine Moxie." Cambridge, MA: *Perspective* (November 2001).

MARIAN BETANCOURT

Muffaletta Sandwich

The muffaletta sandwich is composed of a round loaf of crusty Italian bread containing layers of mortadella (Italian salami), ham, Genoa salami, mozzarella and provolone cheeses, and olive salad. It reflects the influence of Italian immigrants on the cooking of New Orleans, a city noted for its Cajun and Creole cuisine. Arriving in significant numbers around the turn of the twentieth century, many of the immigrants were from Sicily, and they found employment in the French Quarter's food industry. One such person was Signor Lupo Salvadore, who established Central Grocery in 1906. It is said that Lupo, taking a cue from Italian workers who would scoop broken olives from barrels onto the bread they brought for lunch, created the muffaletta sandwich. It is named for a bread called muffaletta that was first made in New Orleans around 1895 by a baker of Albanian descent from

Palermo, Sicily. The bread is still produced, in the early 2000s, by at least one old-fashioned neighborhood bakery in Piano degli Albanese, near Palermo, home of an Albanian colony since the fifteenth century. A signature sandwich of New Orleans, the muffaletta has become so popular that it appears on restaurant menus throughout the United States.

[*See also* Hoagie; Italian American Food; Po'boy Sandwich; Sandwiches.]

BIBLIOGRAPHY

Mercuri, Becky. *Sandwiches That You Will Like*. Pittsburgh, PA: WQED, 2002.

BECKY MERCURI

Mulberries

Three distinct tree fruits are known as mulberries. The white mulberry (*Morus alba*) is a native of western Asia. The two-inch fruits are used dried more commonly than they are fresh. The leaves of the white mulberry are used as feed for silkworms, for which James I of England and his successors offered a subsidy. For this reason, the white mulberry was introduced to America in early colonial times. The plant seeds prolifically, and some of the early trees and their wilding progeny are extant in the Carolinas and Georgia.

The red mulberry (*M. rubra*), native to the eastern seaboard of North America, bears fruits smaller than those of the white mulberry and appreciated more by Native Americans than by Europeans. The black mulberry (*M. nigra*), which is unknown in the wild state, was introduced to Europe and then to North America from warmer areas of western Asia. It fruits reliably only in the Pacific Coast states. Popular usage misapplies the names "white," "red," and "black" to the fruits of mulberry trees. In fact the names indicate the bud-scale colors of the respective species in winter.

Both dark and colorless white forms of white mulberry are grown in the United States. In America, white mulberry is planted as feed for free-range hogs. The high reputation of the flesh of these hogs is attributed to seasonal mulberry and acorn feed. White mulberry also is used to produce feed for free-run chickens. White mulberry is otherwise limited to dooryard culture. Because the pigment of white mulberry fruit causes stains, paler and colorless berries are more popular. The flavor of white mulberry fruits is sweet but never rich, and many find the flavor cloying when the berries are consumed in quantity.

The fruit of the black mulberry is finer for dessert purposes than is that of the white mulberry. Black mulberry fruits are exquisitely fragile and juicy. It is not possible to harvest the fruit without breaking the skin. Highly acid, the juice acquires sugar only in the last day or two before the fruit drops from the tree. For this reason the fruits are highly variable in flavor when harvested. The best berries confirm the reputation of the black mulberry as the richest flavored of all temperate-zone fruits.

Because of the fragility and perishable nature of all mulberries, the market for these fruits is strictly local. Even in California, sales are limited to occasional farmers' market stands. The fruits of the black mulberry are so exquisite that most are consumed fresh. They are unsuited for cooking. There is no American industry for production of mulberry syrup or juice. Such industries do exist in central Asia.

[*See also* Desserts; Fruit.]

BIBLIOGRAPHY

Hedrick, U. P. *Cyclopedia of Hardy Fruits*. New York: Macmillan, 1922.

TODD KENNEDY

Mushrooms

"Mushroom" is the colloquial name for approximately 38,000 varieties of fungi that have mycelia (threadlike roots) and often a distinctive cap and stem structure. Most varieties grow only in the wild, although mycologists are increasingly unlocking the mysteries of mushroom cultivation. Mushrooms are marketed fresh, dried, canned, and frozen. Some important families of culinary mushrooms include the Agaricaceae, home to *Agaricus campestris*, the field mushroom, and its cultivated "white" or "French" mushroom counterpart, *A. bisporus*; Boletaceae, whose most popular member, *Boletus edulis*, travels as the cèpe, or porcini; and Polyporaceae, in which the Asian favorites *Lentinus edodes*, or shiitake, and *Grifola frondosa*, or hen-of-the-woods, are grouped.

With such a selection, it may seem surprising that mushrooms entered the American culinary limelight only in the late nineteenth century. Until the 1890s most mushroom recipes were for ketchups, sauces, and pickles, with occasional stewed mushrooms or French-influenced dishes

HOW TO RAISE MUSHROOMS, FROM HANNAH GLASSE, *THE ART OF COOKERY MADE PLAIN AND EASY* (1805)

Cover an old hot-bed three or four inches thick with fine garden mould, and cover that three or four inches thick with mouldy long muck, of a horse muck-kill, or old rotten stubble; when that bed has lain some time thus prepared, boil any mushrooms that are not fit for use, in water, and throw the water on your prepared bed; in a day or two after, you will have the best small button mushrooms.

named "champignons." Few Americans included mushrooms in kitchen gardens, which was understandable given Hannah Glasse's rare and unappetizing instructions for mushroom cultivation in *The Art of Cookery Made Plain and Easy* (1805). Mushroom gathering was fraught with danger, for no reliable American guides distinguished between gustatory pleasure and peril. Typical is *The Kentucky Housewife* (1839) by Lettice Bryan, which simply warns the cook to "be careful to select the esculent mushrooms, as some of them are very poisonous."

Mushroom cultivation began in seventeenth-century France as mushrooms became an important component of France's emerging haute cuisine. The techniques were perfected in the 1870s and spread abroad, just as French cookery became fashionable in America.

By the 1890s a veritable fungus frenzy was sweeping America, both as a fad food and as a scientific curiosity. Mushrooming clubs, where foragers swapped tips, sprang up quickly. Meticulously illustrated literature educated amateurs and professionals in identifying and cooking mushrooms. The highly technical *Studies of American Fungi* (1911) by George Francis Atkinson contains 250 extraordinary photographs along with recipes by Sarah Tyson Rorer. Rorer differentiates among a dozen genera, each with distinct culinary characteristics. The cultlike adulation of mushrooms is shown by her recipe (similar to others beginning in the 1890s) for baking *A. campestris* on toasts with a bit of cream under a glass bell, "to retain every particle of the flavor. The bell is then lifted at the table, that the eater may get the full aroma and flavor from the mushrooms." This scientific precision in identifying preferred

species for different preparations had become common by the early twentieth century, as seen in one of America's first cookbooks devoted exclusively to mushrooms, *One Hundred Mushroom Receipts* (1899) by Kate Sargeant.

The first professional information on mushroom cultivation in America was disseminated on a large scale in the 1890s, mainly through the efforts of William Falconer. Falconer encouraged both hobbyists and industry with detailed explanations of mushroom houses used on successful farms in the vicinity of New York City. By the early twenty-first century, the basics of mushroom cultivation had changed little, although the scale had exploded. There has been some limited success in cultivating mushrooms from families other than Agaricaceae, but most of the domesticated industry still grows different strains and hybrids developed in the twentieth century from *A. bisporus*. In 2002 Pennsylvania led the nation's production with a crop valued at more than $390 million, representing 59.2 percent of the American output.

BIBLIOGRAPHY

The American Mushroom Institute. http://www.americanmushroom.org/.

Facciola, Stephen. *Cornucopia II: A Source Book of Edible Plants.* Vista, CA: Kampong Publications, 1998.

Falconer, William. *Mushrooms: How to Grow Them: A Practical Treatise on Mushroom Culture for Profit and Pleasure.* New York: Orange Judd, 1891.

Gibson, W. Hamilton. "A Few Edible Toadstools and Mushrooms." *Harper's New Monthly,* August 1894.

Mushrooms for All: How to Grow and How to Cook Them. Philadelphia: Burpee, 1896.

CATHY K. KAUFMAN

Muslim Dietary Laws

Islam is a religion that permeates a Muslim's life; and food, recognized as one of God's great gifts, is naturally regulated according to Islamic law. The dietary laws of Islam are based upon the Koran, the holy book of Islam, and the Hadith, the collection of the sayings of the prophet Muhammad. Muslims in America, like Muslims everywhere, are expected to follow these dietary laws. And in a predominantly non-Muslim culture, this can lead to certain problems for Muslims, as well as new opportunities.

Muslim dietary law places most food into two broad categories: *halal* and *haram,* meaning, in Arabic, permitted (lawful) and prohibited (unlawful). Eating *halal* essentially means not eating any unlawful or *haram* food.

Haram foods are foods that come into contact with, or are in whole or part:

Pork, or meat from dogs, donkeys, or carnivorous animals, taloned birds, amphibians, reptiles, insects, rats, or other vermin

Bodies of dead animals that have died due to strangulation, a violent blow, natural causes (carrion), pagan rituals, or being gored or killed by another animal

Animals not slaughtered in accordance with Islamic law (excepting fish)

Alcoholic beverages, poisonous or narcotic drugs

Meat cut from a live animal

Food additives derived from any of the above.

Many *haram*, or prohibited, foods are rarely found in the normal American diet (carnivorous animals, insects, donkeys, dogs, amphibians, taloned birds) and cause no problems for the Muslim eating in the United States; but three aspects of *haram* in particular are of more concern to Muslim Americans.

Pork and alcohol are both *haram*, and thus prohibited; and both are very common in U.S. diets. In addition, most animals are not slaughtered in accordance with Islamic law. Finally, many products contain additives that may include *haram* items. For example, soy sauce may contain alcohol as a product of fermentation, while muffins or other bread products may include lard from pork. And in general most American food is not prepared in accordance with *halal*.

Halal foods are those foods which are:

Free from any *haram* component.

Processed, prepared, and stored with apparatus and equipment that has been cleansed in accordance with Islamic law and is thus free from things unclean (*najis*). *Najis* means dirt (such as feces, urine, and blood) that must be cleaned according to Islamic law, generally by clean water.

More specifically, *halal* foods include:

Milk from cows, sheep, and goats

Honey

Fresh or naturally frozen vegetables

Grains, legumes, and nuts

Fish

Non-*haram* animals (such as beef, sheep, and other hoofed animals, as well as poultry) slaughtered in accordance with Islamic rites, called *Zabidah*.

Zabidah slaughter of animals is an integral part of *halal* eating. The slaughter must be of live animals or birds, the butcher must be a mature, pious, and knowledgeable Muslim, and the animal's throat must be slit (through the respiratory tract, esophagus, and jugular vein) while the butcher recites in Arabic that this is done "in the name of God, God is most great" (*Bismallah Allahu Akbar*). The knife must be sharp, and the animal must be dead before skinning or dismembering takes place.

All healthy and able Muslims over age twelve are also expected to practice *sawm*, or fasting, during the daylight hours of Ramadan, the ninth lunar month when the Koran was first transcribed. The fast is broken after sunset, with a meal known as *iftar*. During Ramadan especially, the Muslim dietary guidelines of *halal* and *haram* are most carefully followed.

In addition to these general dietary guidelines, some American Muslims, such as those of the Shia branch of Islam and those from Anatolia, recognize some foods as *makrouh* or doubtful; this category includes shellfish and some birds. But the biggest category of food facing all U.S. Muslims in a predominantly Christian or secular society is what is called *mushbooh* in Arabic, meaning uncertain, doubtful, or suspected. Simply put, the typical American Muslim when shopping in a supermarket or dining out must frequently ask himself or herself: is this food *halal*?

Given these strictures, it is no surprise that *halal* foods are fast becoming a major social and political issue, as well as a growing industry in the United States. Food has been increasingly labeled as *halal*. However there were few regulations concerning these labels, and it was estimated by the California based *Minaret Magazine* that up to 65 percent of stores in Los Angeles were selling non-*halal* foods as *halal*. But this situation is changing rapidly in the early 2000s.

The U.S. Department of Agriculture has approved an addition to the Standards and Labeling Policy Book on the use of *halal* labeling on food and poultry products. Several accrediting groups, such as the Islamic Food and Nutrition Council of America (IFANCA), have been authorized. California, Illinois, and New Jersey, among other states with large Muslim populations, have enacted laws making it illegal to sell meat or other foods that are falsely represented as *halal*. Still, for a Muslim wishing to remain *halal*, problems persist. Even in 2001, most *halal* certification was still local; local clerics from nearby mosques certified local foods, leading to questions about reliability and standards. And even more difficult is the problem of food additives. For example, many com-

***Halal* Meat and Live Fish.** A market in Brooklyn, New York. *Photograph by Joe Zarba*

mon foods contain gelatin; the question for the Muslim is from what was the gelatin rendered—a pig or a cow? One Muslim tells of a typical episode while eating in a fast food restaurant. Tempted by the muffins, he ordered some takeout, only to hesitate before eating: were they made with *haram* ingredients such as pork lard? After a series of phone calls to the chain headquarters and the local store, he determined they were not *haram*, only to find another problem: they were now stale.

But in the early 2000s books and websites exist listing thousands of common supermarket products and indicating whether they are *halal* or *haram*. And U.S. restaurants, particularly in Muslim communities, are getting into the picture: McDonald's in Michigan began offering *halal* McNuggets. Big Boy has begun offering *halal* hamburgers in the same state. Kroger has begun selling *halal* chicken. Independent *halal* butchers have seen a dramatic rise in business as the Muslim population has grown, and national chains are now interested as well. *Halal* in America, as kosher before it, is becoming big business.

[*See also* African American Food, *subentry* Since Emancipation; Jewish Dietary Laws; Middle Eastern Influences on American Food.]

BIBLIOGRAPHY

Ali, A. Yusuf. *An English Interpretation of the Holy Qur-an: With Full Arabic Text.* Lahore: Muhammad Ashraf, 1975.

Sakr, Ahmad H. *Understanding Halal Foods: Fallacies and Facts.* Lombard, IL: Foundation for Islamic Knowledge, 1996.

SYLVIA LOVEGREN

Mustard

The mustard plant, an annual belonging to the Cruciferae family, has been one of the most widely grown and used spices in the world. There are three main types of mustard seeds, whose powders are often blended: white or yellow mustard (*Sinapis alba*); brown mustard (*Brassica juncea*), which has a slightly mustier flavor; and black mustard (*B. nigra*), the most pungent of all. In addition to the seeds, the leaves of mustard plants are often used in salads and as flavorings.

In ancient Roman times, mustard was made from seeds of a variety of plants in the genus *Brassica*. The word "mustard" in Latin means the "must" of new wine, which suggests that mustard seeds were combined with wine or vinegar. The Romans used the plant for both food and medicine and called it *mustem ardem*, or "burning juice." The French word *moutarde* and the English word "mustard" are derived from Latin. The Romans introduced mustard into France and England. Mustard was manufactured in Dijon at least by the thirteenth century.

Mustard was well integrated into French and English cookery by the Middle Ages.

Although several mustard companies flourished in England, it was not until 1814 that Jeremiah Colman, a miller of flour in Norwich, first sold mustard flour. He began to export the flour worldwide around 1830. Coleman's mustard was imported into the United States from a factory in Toronto, Ontario, Canada.

Mustard has been manufactured in America since colonial times. The most important American manufacturer of mustard was Robert Timothy French (1823–1893). French was born near Ithaca, New York, and at the age of twenty-one went to work for a spice merchant and relocated to New York City. In 1883 French and his son, George J. French, purchased a small flour mill and a bakery, creating the R. T. French Company. They moved their operation to Rochester, New York, where they sold spices, including powdered mustard with turmeric. The business became extremely successful after the introduction of their French's cream salad mustard in 1904.

Sold as a condiment in glass jars, French's cream salad mustard was milder than other brands and was used mainly as a salad dressing and as a condiment for hot dogs, a food commonly served in baseball stadiums. The company's association with baseball was symbolized by its adoption of the pennant its official logo in 1915. By this date, French's mustard was America's largest selling prepared mustard, outselling all other brands combined. The competition was not far behind, however, and the R. T. French Company began advertising nationally during the 1920s and published advertising cookery booklets, such as *Made Dishes: Salads and Savories with French's Cream Salad Mustard* (1925). The following

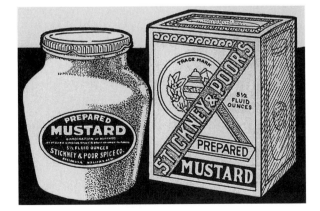

Mustard. Advertisement from January 1921 issue of *American Cookery*.

year, the R. T. French Company was purchased by Reckitt and Colman, the successor company to Jeremiah Colman's operation in England.

Reckitt and Colman expanded its mustard product line. French's squeeze package was introduced in 1974, French's Bold 'n Spicy in 1982, and French's Dijon mustard in 1983. In 2000 Reckitt and Coleman merged with Benckiser to form Reckitt Benckiser, Inc. An estimated 80 percent of American households buy mustard each year. By 2002 the total mustard market in America was approximately $280 million. French's mustard remains America's largest selling branded mustard, followed by private labels and Kraft Grey Poupon.

[*See also* Advertising Cookbooklets and Recipes; Condiments; Herbs and Spices; Hot Dogs; Ketchup; Salads and Salad Dressings.]

BIBLIOGRAPHY

Jordan, Michele Anna. *Good Cook's Book of Mustard*. Reading, MA: Addison-Wesley, 1994.
Man, Rosamond, and Robin Weir. *The Compleat Mustard*. Bury St Edmunds, Suffolk, UK: St. Emundsbury, 1988.
Roberts-Dominguez, Jan. *The Mustard Book*. New York: Macmillan, 1993.
Stone, Sally, and Martin Stone. *The Mustard Cookbook*. New York: Avon, 1981.

ANDREW F. SMITH

Myths and Folklore

In popular terminology, the myths and folklore of food frequently refer to superstitions, or nonscientifically based beliefs about food and eating habits. These beliefs are usually holdovers from the past, come from undocumented sources, and are often seen as preludes or additives to advice from trained professionals. Such beliefs are numerous throughout American culture, and their veracity and worth are debated in medical journals and domestic living magazines. More scholarly understandings of the concepts of "myth" and of "folklore" shed light on the significance of these beliefs and help to explain their tenacity. Generally, definitions approach myths as beliefs concerning overarching truths by which we live. Beliefs normally are expressed through sayings, anecdotes, narratives, material objects, and rituals. Similarly, folklore refers to artistic communication in small groups, and to socially constructed connections of meaning between an individual and his or her place, past, and other people. Folklore also includes foodways, that is, the system of beliefs and habits surrounding all aspects of food production and consumption.

Myth and Folklore of Food as Superstition

Food myths surround those areas of our lives that tend to worry us—gender and sex; body image; health and food safety; childbirth, pregnancy, nursing, and proper care of the young; and social stereotyping of ethnicity, region, and social class.

Although American culture does not have gendered food taboos per se, there are certain expectations for what constitutes a manly meal and what is dainty enough for a lady. Men eat beef, preferably in the form of large slabs of steak still dripping with blood, although men do eat beef in the form of meat loaf, sloppy joes, or hamburgers. Men also can prove their manhood by eating hot peppers, downing large quantities of beer, and sticking to stick-to-the-ribs foods like baked or fried potatoes, beans, eggs, biscuits, and sauces, such as gravy, ketchup, or hot sauce. In the 1960s and 1970s the saying "real men don't eat quiche" summed up gender expectations: men ate hearty, plain foods that were straightforward and loaded with protein and carbohydrates. Their cooking was limited to the outdoor grill or to large public gatherings. Though these beliefs persist, modern men can delve into exotic and gourmet cooking, and the well-rounded man is expected to know his way around the kitchen. Meanwhile, females have always been associated with smaller portions and lighter foods, such as salads and soups, and with cooking that emphasizes family, home, and nutrition as well as a prescribed artistic style in arranging and presenting food.

Beliefs about food are closely related to those about body image and what foods and ways of eating best construct the desired physique. The folklore of dieting and maintaining weight abounds with fads and rituals, some of which have been adapted from nutritionally sound systems. Drinking a glass of water before every meal, eating only while sitting at a table and with an attractive place setting, chewing each bite one hundred times, eating primarily carbohydrates, eating no carbohydrates, and weighing each serving have become folk beliefs in that they are transmitted informally, reside alongside "official" advice, and carry the weight of tradition.

Folklore about body image and gender leads to folklore about sex, such as how to use foods in a sexually attractive way, as well as what foods are best to use before, during, and after sexual acts. Bananas are obviously subjects of folklore, especially humor and anecdotes

about their resemblance to, and possible substitution for, male genitalia. Other foods are believed to be aphrodisiacs (oysters and chocolate), to enhance one's sexual abilities (ginseng, beef, peppers, and chocolate), or to limit those abilities (alcohol, large meals, and beans).

A great deal of folklore is also attached to food and eating during pregnancy, childbirth, and lactation. Unusual food cravings by pregnant women are legendary and are fodder for anecdotes (a husband driving two hours in the middle of the night to a particular pizza outlet, trying to hunt down out-of-season fruit, or strange combinations, such as pickles and ice cream). The consumption of a particular type of mud by African slave women in the American Southeast was a part of folk tradition that some scholars now say has a sound nutritional basis. Advice on what to eat (dairy products and leafy, green vegetables) and what to avoid (caffeine, alcohol, hot peppers, and chocolate) is passed along both as "scientific" prescription and as folklore. Of particular interest is folklore surrounding breastfeeding—how to do it, when and where to do it, what clothing to wear in order to nurse discreetly, what foods should be avoided (anything that might upset the child's more delicate system), and at what age weaning is appropriate. There are numerous family stories (usually passed around only among women) concerning children weaning themselves or nursing after learning to talk, and then talking about it.

Health and sickness are also common subjects of food folklore and myths. Adages such as "eat like a king in the morning, like a duke in the afternoon, and a pauper in the evening"; "an apple a day keeps the doctor away"; and "wait half an hour after eating before swimming" relate traditional wisdom for eating to keep oneself healthy and to avoid danger. Food also shows up in folk remedies: chicken soup and oranges for colds; Popsicles for sore throats; "stuff a cold; starve a fever"; bean burritos or a "hair of the dog" for hangovers. Also, there are beliefs concerning the effects of particular foods or ingredients—sugar makes children hyperactive; caffeine stunts their growth.

Related to health is a subgenre of urban legends surrounding commercial foods, particularly the fast food industry and ethnic restaurants. Stories of Kentucky fried rats, rat tails in the french fries, mice in Coke bottles, and fast food workers spitting into food represent our trepidation in handing over control of our food to complete strangers. Similarly, stories of neighborhood cats disappearing around Chinese restaurants, of Southeast Asian immigrants in California adopting suspiciously large

JOHNNY APPLESEED

Johnny Appleseed is the name legend ascribes to John Chapman, an apple-tree nurseryman and frontiersman who was born in Leominster, Massachusetts, on September 26, 1774, and died near Fort Wayne, Indiana, on March 18, 1845. His father, Nathaniel, was a carpenter and farmer who served in the Continental army during the Revolutionary War; his mother, Elizabeth Symonds, died when John was two years old, and he was raised by relatives.

During the 1790s Chapman and his half-brother, Nathaniel, traveled westward into Pennsylvania a number of times, planting small nurseries of apple trees from seeds collected at commercial cider presses in Pennsylvania. In the first decade of the nineteenth century, John Chapman, then in his middle twenties, traveled alone into Ohio to plant nurseries ahead of settlers encouraged to develop the West by federal homesteading policy.

In 1798 Congress had granted public land ranging from 160 to 2,240 acres to settlers who indicated they would permanently occupy it. One sign of such intention was the planting of an orchard. Chapman, as a land developer, selected dozens of suitable nursery sites, fenced them in, sowed the apple seeds, and returned periodically to maintain the nursery and to sell or give trees to the homesteaders. These seedlings enabled the development of profitable orchards in the Ohio Valley.

Chapman did not develop particular varieties of apples by grafting but used a method of seeding orchards based on the Van Mons theory, which claimed to improve the apple quality. The theory named for Jean Baptiste Van Mons (1765–1842) was based on seed selection and successive planting generation after generation to regenerate a rapid, uninterrupted, direct line of descent. He may have also rejected grafting on the religious principle that grafting or budding interfered with the work of God.

As every seed in every apple represents a potential new variety, Chapman's selection of seeds from successful strains produced hundreds of new varieties, including Black Annette, Franklin, Ohio Nonpareil, Western Beauty, and Ingram. Orchardists and newcomers in developing towns along the Ohio and Mississippi Rivers bought and established orchards of these new acclimated varieties.

Early in the 1800s Chapman became a self-ordained missionary of the Church of the New Jerusalem, a Christian church based on the biblical writing of Emanuel Swedenborg, the Swedish philosopher and theologian. The dress, demeanor, and behavior that generated many myths about Chapman probably resulted from this spiritual expression.

Chapman was a highly organized businessman who would, at the same time, bury money for future use, barter for clothes that did not fit him, give trees to those who could not pay, and converse with Native Americans in their languages. Many of the legends about him come from an article, "Johnny Appleseed, a Pioneer Hero," by W. D. Haley, in an 1871 issue of *Harper's New Monthly Magazine*. Along with many nonlegendary nurserymen in the same business, Johnny Appleseed took the seeds from the apple presses of the East and established the foundation of the orchards of the West.

[*See also* Apples; Fruit.]

BIBLIOGRAPHY

Haley, W. D. "Johnny Appleseed, a Pioneer Hero." *Harper's New Monthly Magazine* 63, no. 258 (November 1871).

Leominster Historical Commission, Leominster, MA. Johnny Appleseed Marker: "Near this site was born John Chapman known as Johnny Appleseed, September 26, 1774–March 18, 1845. The Leominster Historical Society 1963"; "Located by Florence Wheeler 1935."

Price, Robert. *Johnny Appleseed: Man and Myth.* Bloomington: Indiana University Press, 1954.

THOMAS BURFORD

---

numbers of dogs from humane societies, and of those same immigrants enthusiastically buying cans of dog food, believing that they are purchasing dog meat, express fears of cultures that appear different and threatening.

Folk Foods

Another way of approaching the folklore of food is to explore the foods traditionally associated with specific groups of people. Historically, folk foods were thought of as peasant foods. Since peasants in the European sense of a close-knit kinship group with generations tied to the same land did not exist in the United States, scholars in the late 1800s considered folk groups to be groups that were isolated in some way from the mainstream culture. This isolation could be created by region, ethnicity, race, religion, or even occupation. Each of these groups then had its own folk foods. The Amish and the Pennsylvania Dutch had scrapple, shoofly pie, custard, and apple butter; New Englanders had boiled supper, lobster rolls, and clambakes; Cajuns had crawfish and jambalaya; Southerners had grits, biscuits and gravy, salt-cured ham, fried chicken, and pecan pie; Southern blacks had fried chicken, mashed potatoes, turnip greens, and cornbread; Appalachian mountaineers had cornbread, leather britches (dried green beans), and moonshine (corn whiskey); lumberjacks of the northern United States had "mooseturd pie"; cowboys on the ranges of the Southwest had chili and beans. Groups of people were also stereotyped negatively by the foods they were thought to consume that did not fit within the mainstream, British-based model: Italians were called "spaghetti-eaters," French ate frogs and horses, Asians ate dogs and cats, and Mexicans ate tacos and tortillas filled with beans and questionable animal parts.

Contemporary folklore scholarship sees any group of people with common traditions as being a folk group. Any food that is traditional to a group, that represents the group's identity, and that is used in aesthetic ways to express the interests and values of the group can be considered a folk food. American college students, for example, constitute a folk group, with their foodways characterized by pizza, ramen noodles, cafeteria food, and beer.

Folk Cookery and Foodways

A shift toward exploring the processes of making food was represented in scholarship on folk cookery, "traditional domestic cookery marked by regional variation." In the 1970s the folklorist Don Yoder developed the study of folk cookery, drawing from European ethnology, which involved detailed observation of all aspects of peasant life. Yoder introduced the term "foodways" to refer to "the total cookery complex, including attitudes, taboos, and meal systems—the whole range of cookery and food habits in a society." Folklorists developed the foodways model further, using it to refer to the extended network of activities surrounding the procurement, preservation, preparation, presentation, performance, and consumption of food. This model also involves the beliefs, aesthetics, economics, and politics involved in food behaviors.

Procurement involves obtaining the ingredients and items needed for a meal. Preservation involves strategies used for keeping foods frozen or fresh and storing them until needed. Preparation involves selecting menus and recipes as well as chopping, marinating, and using other techniques to turn raw ingredients into culturally acceptable food. Preparation leads directly to the product, the food itself, and includes the actual recipes and ingredients used. Presentation of food refers to how it is physically displayed, brought to the table, and served to consumers. It includes the artistic placement of dishes and the laying out of the various food items.

Performance in foodways includes the place of those foods within the usual meal system and cuisine. The meal system involves the larger framework of the overall daily, weekly, annual, and celebratory meal cycles. The social roles and functions of a meal are defined within this framework. For example, people have different expectations of breakfast and lunch, not only of what foods will be offered and at what times, but also of whom those meals can be shared with, the kinds of interactions that might occur, and the formality of the event. Consumption refers to how people eat the meal—what utensils they use, what mixtures they create, and the order in which items are consumed. Last in the foodways model is the cleanup after food preparation and consumption. Cleanup includes questions of storage and the use of leftovers; it is highly significant in that it may determine what foods and preparation methods an individual might choose.

"Foodways" suggests the full meaning of food in people's lives and why it carries such significance; the activities surrounding food are integrated into all aspects of daily life. Looking at a group's foodways reveals where subtle differences can arise and where meaning is placed. For example, a bagel purchased from the neighborhood deli has an entirely different set of foodways behind it than one purchased from the frozen foods section of a chain supermarket. Similarly, two dinner menus may be identical, but the processes by which they were put together, who cooked them, and who eats them make them two very different experiences. Using the foodways model helps to distinguish and delineate the traditional or folk aspects of a food event from those that are mass produced, popular, or elite.

Food as Artistic Communication (Folklore)

Another approach to the folklore of food utilizes theories that developed in the 1960s and 1970s that define folklore as "artistic communication in small groups." This definition focuses on how individuals draw upon tradition as a resource for expressing their identities and interests and how those expressions are shaped by both the aesthetics of

ROBERT GIBBON JOHNSON AND THE TOMATO

On Sunday, January 30, 1949, the CBS radio network broadcast a "reenactment" of Robert Gibbon Johnson eating the first tomato in the United States, an event that supposedly took place in Salem, New Jersey, in September 1820. According to the broadcast, which was on the CBS *You Are There* series, until Johnson's moment in 1820 Americans considered the tomato poisonous. Johnson, one of Salem's most prominent citizens, had imported tomato seeds from South America and planted them in his garden. When the plants produced fruit Johnson announced that he intended to eat a tomato on the courthouse steps. On the appointed day, as the CBS version told it, hundreds of onlookers gathered to watch Johnson eat a tomato—and die a painful death. Johnson sank his teeth into the tomato but did not die. His brave act shocked the crowd and changed the course of American culinary history. Thanks to Johnson's courage, Americans started eating tomatoes—or so the story went.

The CBS broadcast was not the first telling of this tale. The earliest known version of it appeared in the *Salem County Handbook* (1908), when William Chew, who was to become publisher of the *Salem Standard and Jerseyman*, asserted that Johnson brought tomatoes to Salem in 1820. That unremarkable fact might have remained a simple, obscure nugget of Salem lore had not Joseph S. Sickler, an amateur local historian, added something to it and recounted the story to Harry Emerson Wildes, who included it in his nationally acclaimed book *The Delaware* (1940). Using Sickler's account, Wildes wrote that Johnson had dared to eat a prize tomato publicly on the courthouse steps. Stewart Holbrook, in his *Lost Men of American History* (1946), dramatized Wildes's version by creating imaginary dialogue for the event. Then Sickler, as historical consultant to CBS for the broadcast, embellished the story further.

Versions of the legend have appeared in professional and scholarly journals; in several publications of historical societies; in *Scientific American*, *Horticulture*, the *New Yorker*, and similar magazines; and in prestigious newspapers, including the *New York Times*. Dozens of cookbooks and food books have retold it. Yet no primary evidence has surfaced indicating that this story has any basis in fact.

The myth of Johnson and the tomato became enshrined as legend for several reasons. First, it rings true and is difficult or impossible to disprove.

Tomato Fakelore. Historical reenactors in historically inaccurate costumes outside the house of Colonel Robert Gibbon Johnson in Salem, New Jersey, commemorate a non-event: According to legend, Johnson proved that tomatoes are not poisonous by eating a basket of them on the steps of the Salem County courthouse in 1820. He didn't. *Collection of Andrew F. Smith*

Second, the story seems to explain why Americans, who formerly thought that the tomato was poisonous, began eating it. Third, some residents of Salem believed the story would make their community famous, and they therefore kept telling the tale to

Continued

ROBERT GIBBON JOHNSON AND THE TOMATO (*Continued*)

reporters and authors. Finally, the writers found the story attractive: as there were no primary sources for it, writers could—and did—embellish the narrative to give punch to their writing. The story of Johnson eating the first tomato in America made good reading—and bad history.

[*See also* Tomatoes.]

BIBLIOGRAPHY

Smith, Andrew F. "The Making of the Legend of Robert Gibbon Johnson and the Tomato." *New Jersey History* 108 (Fall/Winter 1990): 59–74.

Smith, Andrew F. *The Tomato in America: Early History, Culture and Cookery*. Columbia: University of South Carolina Press, 1994.

ANDREW F. SMITH

that individual and the context of the expression. In this sense, food as folklore is used to communicate feelings, opinions, relationships, social status, relationships, and power. Food folklore appears in three forms: material, oral, and customary.

Material foodlore is the actual food itself as a physical object; oral foodlore involves narratives, songs, names, and talking about food; customary foodlore includes the rituals, habits, and patterns of interacting surrounding food. Similar to foodways, this approach to the folklore of food embeds food in every aspect of life and sees eating as a multifaceted activity, rich with emotional, symbolic, and artistic potential. It also emphasizes the aesthetic nature of food—the tastes and textures of foods and how people manipulate food and cooking simply for artistic pleasure. People often manipulate their food simply because they find the process satisfying on an aesthetic level, such as the ways in which they eat Oreo cookies or ice cream cones, or arrange different foods on their plate, or spread relish and mustard on their hot dogs. Most meals are a mixture of traditional components, variations on those components, and complete innovations. This mixture offers a key to the identities of the producers and consumers and the ways in which their meal is expressive of their culture, their values, their food aesthetics, and their immediate contexts for eating. Also, certain forms of food carry emotive and symbolic connotations. Garnishes signify a special occasion, as do elaborate dishes requiring sauces and extensive preparation. Raw fruits and vegetables may be carved into artistic designs—radishes into roses, carrots into curlicues, or cucumbers into geometric patterns. Everyday foods may be dressed up with little extras, such as nuts (almonds to green beans), spices (ginger to carrots), and other sauces (pecan butter to brussels sprouts). Gelatin molds can be varied to fit the holiday with the use of appropriate colors (orange or yellow for Thanksgiving, red for Christmas, green for St. Patrick's Day) or fillings (apples and nuts for Thanksgiving molds).

Food as folklore also opens up issues of politics in the sense of individuals and groups having the power to construct their foodways and shape the ways in which they are presented to others. Competitions over whose recipe to use for the Thanksgiving pie, the choice of "stuffing" or "dressing," or who gets to sit where at the table are the source of much folklore, particularly personal experience narratives about such incidents, and they reflect the potential for emotional meaning that food holds for us. "Commensal politics" refers to those issues of power surrounding eating together; "gastropolitics" refers to issues of access and distribution of food; and "cultural politics" refers to issues over what foods mean and symbolize.

Holiday Meals and Foods

Most holiday celebrations have strong food traditions. Some of these foods come from traditional sources; others have been introduced by marketing but have become so associated with the holiday as to have become traditional. Most dry cereals now appear in the colors and symbols specific to major holidays. Christian-based holidays have permeated American culture, and, regardless of actual religious beliefs, many individuals participate in the foodways associated with them. Christmas includes candy canes, fruitcakes, seafood supper on Christmas Eve for many Italian Americans, brunch on Christmas morning, and turkey dinner on Christmas Day. Easter includes a wide variety of special candy (chocolate rabbits and eggs, jellybeans, and marshmallows in symbolic shapes) along with boiled and decorated eggs. Some ethnic traditions, such as paczki (*paschke*), an eastern European pastry

THE ICE CREAM CONE AND THE SAINT LOUIS WORLD'S FAIR

The sweet equivalent of the sandwich, the ice cream cone belongs to one of America's favorite food categories, the hand-held wrapped dish in which filler and wrapping are eaten together. Like many other iconic American dishes, ice cream cones were made for public eating and became popular in venues such as seaside resorts, fairs, and carnivals at the turn of the nineteenth century.

The classic cone is a wheat-based wafer baked in an iron mold and then rolled into a cone shape with a pointed bottom. The wafer is a venerable dish, dating to the European Middle Ages. Its more immediate antecedent in the United States is the waffle, which was brought to North America by Dutch immigrants in the seventeenth century. As in Europe, ice cream, which had become popular throughout colonial America, was often eaten with sweet wafers. The earliest written recipe yet discovered for a "cornet with cream" comes from England and appears in *Mrs. A. B. Marshall's Cookery Book* (1888), written by an expert on French cookery. Marshall's recipe calls for flour, eggs, ground almonds, and orange water, and suggests that the ice cream should be eaten from the cone with a utensil.

The other style of ice cream cone, a plain wafer baked with a flat bottom, was introduced to the general public in 1904 at the Saint Louis World's Fair (which celebrated the centennial of the Louisiana Purchase), although it may not have been invented there. The most common tale about the origin of the ice cream cone says that a Syrian immigrant named Ernest A. Hamwi had a concession at the fair for *zalabia*, a waffle of Persian origin. His stand was set up next to an ice cream stand, and Hamwi (or a Lebanese acquaintance named Abe Doumar) suggested rolling the waffles and filling them with ice cream. Thus was the "cornucopia" born. Hamwi soon thereafter worked with a Cornucopia Waffle Company and set up several other companies in later years.

The first cone-making mold to be patented was invented in New York City in 1903, the year before the Saint Louis World's Fair. Italo Marchiony, an Italian ices maker and pushcart vendor, wanted a replacement for the glass cups in which he sold his ices in the area around Wall Street. His device made flat pastries that were rolled on the spot by pushcart vendors. Marchiony later claimed that he had come up with the idea in 1896, and this is generally conceded to be the date of the origin of the cone.

Nevertheless, the Saint Louis fair made the ice cream cone popular, and, despite Hamwi's invented history, it appears that there were so many waffle vendors and ice cream makers cheek by jowl at the event that the idea of the cornucopia, which already existed in New York, probably occurred to many vendors, perhaps Hamwi among them. Paper cones for ice cream had appeared by at least the 1850s.

Within a few years, ice cream cone making had become industrialized. Frederick Bruckman patented a machine to make rolled cones in 1912, and in the 1920s molded cones with flat bottoms, modeled on Marchiony's design, were perfected by the Maryland Baking Company in Baltimore. By the late 1920s, at least one-third of all ice creams sold in the United States were in industrially made cones.

BIBLIOGRAPHY

Dickson, Paul. *The Great American Ice Cream Book*. New York: Atheneum, 1972.
Liddel, Caroline, and Robin Weir. *Ices: The Definitive Guide*. London: Hodder and Stoughton, 1994.

BRUCE KRAIG

---

similar to a jelly doughnut, are becoming more commonplace. In many cases these religiously based holidays overlap with seasons, and their foods reflect this phenomenon. Christmas celebrates winter with eggnog, hot chocolate, and other foods to warm one up; Easter foods celebrate spring and new life: dinner menus usually include new potatoes, young peas, and fresh asparagus.

Thanksgiving officially celebrates feasting and food. Although meant to mark the survival of the Pilgrims in the New World and their appreciation to God and to the Native Americans who helped them, the holiday now tends to celebrate the abundance of food most Americans are thought to have (as represented by the cornucopia spilling over with fruits and nuts). The ubiquitous turkey dinner appears in a variety of regional forms—bread stuffing in New England, oyster stuffing on the Atlantic Coast, and cornbread dressing in the South. The main dishes are almost always accompanied by mashed potatoes and gravy, vegetables (green beans, peas, carrots, or mashed turnips), breads (dinner rolls, cornbread, muffins, and zucchini or pumpkin bread), and desserts (traditionally pies, particularly pumpkin, apple, pecan, and custard). Families vary this menu according to their own tastes, resources, and circumstances. It is common for an ethnic specialty (sauerkraut, lasagna, egg rolls, sushi, or tamales) to appear on the table, symbolizing the specific heritage of the family while also celebrating national unity. The theme of unity is also represented in the collective preparation of the meal, in the presentation of the turkey as a single large food, and in the expectation of families and friends sitting and consuming the meal together. Innovation is possible within this theme, however. The more traditional roasting of the turkey has given way to smoking in a covered outdoor grill (a West Coast innovation) or deep-frying in large vats of boiling oil (introduced in the American Southeast). The holiday also frequently celebrates the harvest and fall season, utilizing "harvest" decorations such as corn sheaths, pumpkins, and autumn colors.

Sweet foods are also central to Halloween, a holiday originally brought to the United States by Irish immigrants. Trick-or-treat involves children acquiring vast amounts of candy from strangers, and mass-produced specialty sweets have been developed for this purpose (bite-sized candy bars, candies shaped in Halloween symbols—jack-o'-lanterns, ghosts, and bats—and candies representing the scary, dark side of the holiday, such as bloody fangs, eyeballs, and popcorn balls dyed green or black). These foods have replaced the traditional apples, homemade taffy, fudge, and popcorn balls that were historically associated with the holiday.

The passing of seasons as well as the seasons themselves are frequently marked by food folklore. On New Year's Day, it is common among Pennsylvania Germans and other German Americans to eat pork and sauerkraut. Southerners traditionally eat hoppin' John, a black-eyed peas and rice dish, usually with pork sausage mixed in or on the side. The arrival of summer is marked by taking out the grill and setting up for outdoor cooking and picnics and grilling.

Food is central to our physical existence and adds to our emotional and social well-being. It is no surprise, then, that folklore surrounds it, providing ways of expressing identity, value, and meaning through food. Food as folklore helps bind us to one another, gives us connections with past and place, and adds an aesthetic dimension to this functional necessity of life.

[*See also* Christmas; Diets, Fad; Dutch Influences on American Food; Easter; Ethnic Foods; Fast Food; Gender Roles; German American Food; Halloween; Picnics; Thanksgiving.]

BIBLIOGRAPHY

Brown, Linda Keller, and Kay Mussell. *Ethnic and Regional Foodways in the United States: The Performance of Group Identity.* Knoxville: University of Tennessee Press, 1984.

Camp, Charles. *American Foodways: What, When, Why and How We Eat In America.* Little Rock, AR: August House, 1989.

Counihan, Carole M., and Penny Van Esterik, eds. *Food and Culture: A Reader.* New York: Routledge, 1997.

Gabaccia, Donna R. *We Are What We Eat: Ethnic Food and the Making of Americans.* Cambridge, MA: Harvard University Press, 1998.

Haber, Barbara. *From Hardtack to Home Fries: An Uncommon History of American Cooks and Meals.* New York: Free Press, 2002.

Long, Lucy. "Holiday Meals: Rituals of Family Tradition." In *Dimensions of the Meal: The Science, Culture, Business, and Art of Eating,* edited by Herbert L. Meiselman, 143–160. Gaithersburg, MD: Aspen, 2000.

Long, Lucy, ed. *Culinary Tourism.* Lexington: University Press of Kentucky, 2004.

Newstadt, Kathy. *Clambake: A History and Celebration of an American Tradition.* Amherst: University of Massachusetts Press, 1992.

Shortridge, Barbara G., and James R. Shortridge, eds. *The Taste of American Place: A Reader on Regional and Ethnic Foods.* NY: Rowman and Littlefield, 1998.

Wilson, Donald Scofield, and Angus Kress Gillespie, eds. *Rooted in America: Foodlore of Popular Fruits and Vegetables.* Knoxville: University of Tennessee Press, 1999.

Yoder, Don. "Food Cookery." In *Folklore and Folklife: An Introduction,* edited by Richard M. Dorson, 325–350. Chicago: University of Chicago Press, 1972.

LUCY LONG

Nabisco

The Nabisco brand is perhaps best known for the cookies and crackers it manufactures and sells, among them Uneeda Biscuits, Oreos, Fig Newtons, Social Tea Biscuits, and Premium Saltines, but the company also contributed to the development of mass marketing in America by making freshness a selling point and distributing products directly to retailers. In 1898, at Adolphus W. Green's urging, the National Biscuit Company (NBC) was incorporated in Jersey City, New Jersey, established through the merger of the American Biscuit and Manufacturing Company, the New York Biscuit Company, and the United States Baking Company. Green sought to maximize profits through high-volume business, an unusual concept at a time when few food manufacturing companies sold nationally. This merger unified much of the biscuit business and led to the creation of a national brand name.

The National Biscuit Company's incorporation in 1898 signaled the end of the cracker barrel as an American institution. When buying from a barrel, it was the first customers who got the freshest crackers from the top of the cracker barrel. As sales proceeded and the barrel emptied, the crackers became broken, soggy, and dirty, sometimes tainted with the odor of an adjacent kerosene tank or befouled by vermin that lived inside the barrel.

To provide the consumer with a crisp, fresh, and sanitary cracker, the National Biscuit Company devised a package that would keep crackers clean and unbroken. A piece of waxed paper was put on a cardboard carton blank, and both were folded into an airtight and moisture-proof box. The packaging was introduced with Uneeda Biscuits, the company's first product. The distinctive packaging's name, *In-er-seal*, was printed on one end of the box. The carton gave wholesomeness and freshness commercial value that consumers began to seek out and did much to destroy confidence in the cracker barrel. As a consequence, many other food products, such as pickles, tea, cheese, flour, and rice, followed suit, moving out of bulk boxes and barrels into clean, convenient packaging. The new approach to packaging started a revolution that began with a new era of packaged food and self-service markets and ultimately helped pave the way for the emergence of chain stores and supermarkets.

In addition to innovations in packaging, Green's focus on promotion and advertising influenced how food is marketed in the United States. The National Biscuit Company advertised on billboards, sides of buildings, and in newspapers. NBC foods were used in early product placements in movies. With the rise of radio ads in the 1930s, the company started using the word "Nabisco" in its advertising to make its products easier to remember.

NBC acquired the Shredded Wheat Company in 1928 and in 1931 added Milk-Bone dog biscuits. Some thirty years later, in 1962, it bought the Cream of Wheat Company. In 1971 the National Biscuit Company changed its name to Nabisco, Inc., and in 1981 merged with Standard Brands Incorporated to become Nabisco Brands, Inc. The merger added Planters nuts and snacks to the portfolio. In 1985 RJ Reynolds Industries, Inc., in an attempt to reduce its reliance on tobacco, acquired Nabisco Brands, Inc. A year later, in 1986, RJ Reynolds Industries, Inc., changed its name to RJR Nabisco, Inc., and RJR's Del Monte and Nabisco Brands operations were combined to form Nabisco Brands, Inc. In 1999 RJR Nabisco broke up, splitting the U.S. tobacco business off from Nabisco's food division in a bid to shield the food company from liability for smoking-related lawsuits associated with the tobacco side of the company. In 2000 Philip Morris Companies, Inc., acquired Nabisco Holdings Corporation; Nabisco, Inc.; and its subsidiaries. Nabisco was then integrated into the Kraft Foods business, creating one of the largest food companies in the world.

[See also Historical Overview, *subentry* From Victorian
    America to World War I; Kraft Foods; Packaging; Waxed
    Paper.]

BIBLIOGRAPHY

Cahn, William. *Out of the Cracker Barrel: The Nabisco Story, from Animal Crackers to Zuzus.* New York: Simon and Schuster, 1969. A comprehensive history of Nabisco. Valuable for historical context and discussion of the historical significance of the company in packaging, merchandising, and brand development but lacks substantive discussion of competition.

Kraft Foods. http://www.kraft.com/newsroom/. Press releases on acquisition of Nabisco and the resulting new corporate structure.

SANDRA YIN

Native American Foods

This entry contains three subentries:

Before and After Contact
Spiritual and Social Connections
Technology and Sources

Before and After Contact

The study of Native American foodways is immensely large and complex. It involves vast tracts of land with varied geographical terrain and weather systems and consequent regional differences in foods, fuels, and implements. Indigenous history spans many thousands of years, encompassing a long period of precontact, dramatic and often devastating encounters with Europeans, and evolving adaptations to foreign modernization. Foodways are equally complicated and depend on the moment and place of European encounters, the ethnicity of the settlers, and gradual encroachments on ancestral lands. Indian foods—never static historically—continue to evolve today.

The great diversity of political and cultural divisions adds another dimension to the study of Native American life. At the point of European contact, one thousand to two thousand native languages were spoken in North America. Estimations are clouded by similarities and overlapping forms of tribal languages. The foodways of nations, tribes, and clans are based on political and social structures, culture, and worldview. Another obstacle to documented research is the absence of Native American written records. This problem has been addressed to some degree by the investigations of archaeologists and anthropologists, careful analysis of early travelers' reports, new evidence in the fields of linguistics and genetics, and Native American oral histories and mythologies, but large gaps remain.

Despite the many opportunities for differences, the foods and foodways of the various groups of Native Americans have a good deal in common, including indigenous plants and animals, staple foods, technological exploitation of natural materials, and cooking styles. Isolated from the world's cuisines and technologies, Native American directions were unaltered by outside forces. Low-density populations coexisted in an immense and often well-endowed land. Long-range trade routes facilitated the spread and exchange of wild and domesticated plants, especially corn, beans, squash, and pumpkin; animal products; salt; and tool-making materials, such as regional stone and shell. The wheel, iron working, and substantial use of domesticated animals were unknown. The common technologies of cooking utensils produced specialized, efficient, and well-crafted tools.

Long before European contact, Native American foodways existed in a perpetual state of evolution. Europeans added new foods and technologies, redistributed land, and changed land use. As the frontier moved to new territories, this process was repeated, bringing change to increasing numbers of tribes, always according to the time of contact and conquest. In the first periods after contact, those who survived decimating population losses maintained their cultural identities, general access to traditional food, and inherited foodways.

A major shift in foodways came about in the middle to late nineteenth century. As the Indian wars came to a close, large numbers of indigenous peoples were moved to government-run and poverty-stricken reservations, where their foodways were forcibly "Americanized" by government and missionary schools. At the same time, commercially manufactured and distributed foods and kitchenware brought modernizing change as American women everywhere used recipes published in food columns and cookbooks. Without their inherited resources, many Native Americans adapted commercial foods into traditional recipes and used the traditional foods at hand in developing pies, cakes, leavened white breads, and home canning. Cultural erosion was so rapid that anthropologists of the period hastened to record what information they could before it was entirely lost.

Today Native Americans dine in any numbers of ways. Less segregated from mainstream culture and identifying increasingly with it, many embrace the standard American fast and convenience foods and changing trends, or fads. The number of traditional foods in cooking repertoires is narrowing. Use of traditional foods has more to do with cultural identity than basic cuisine, and the foods have become part of a new Indian effort to promote and strengthen Native American cultures.

Early and postcontact food adaptations followed basic culture. Organized socially and politically according to nation, tribe, clan, and family, Native Americans functioned with complex patterns of land ownership and usage privileges. Daily life was often communal. Food-related work was generally divided by gender. Basic spiritual concepts and worldviews of food and its sources reinforced the interconnectedness of animate and inanimate forms and the need to maintain respectful relationships with them. Such governing concepts were integrated into daily life and are the basis for understanding food practices.

Geography was one basis for differentiating tribes. Well-defined Native American regions had their own balances of horticulture, hunting, and gathering, and their own array of indigenous foods. These regions included the Northwest Coast, the Northwestern Plateau, the Great Basin just to the south of the plateau, Coastal California, the Plains, the Prairies, the East (east of the Mississippi), and the Southwest. Among the numerous tribes of these regions the following are representative because of their size, prominence, and characteristic foodways.

The eastern tribes depended largely on horticulture, followed by abundant hunting of game and fish and gathering of wild foods, especially nuts and berries. Tribes of this region included the Iroquois, Algonquian, Catawba, Cherokee, Choctaw, Creek, Delaware, Menominee, Ottawa, Penobscot, Potawatomi, Seminole, Susquehanna, and Winnebago.

Sometimes considered one region, the Prairie-Plains areas overlap considerably. The plains were relatively flat and grassy and were the home of the buffalo. Plains Indians subsisted largely on buffalo hunting and secondarily on wild plant foods and traded corn. The Plains Indians included the Blackfoot, Cheyenne, Comanche, Crow, and Sioux (Dakota), but the land often was peopled by Prairie Indians and others on extensive hunts. The Prairie Indians sometimes moved permanently to the plains because of encroaching white expansion. Situated between the East and the Plains, Prairie tribes practiced a combination of hunting and farming, traveling long distances from their planting fields to reach the buffalo. Prairie tribes included the Illinois, Iowa, Menominee, Omaha, Osage, Pawnee, Potawatomi, and Winnebago.

The Southwest Indians—Apache, Mojave, Navajo, Pueblo (Hopi and Zuni), and Yuma—were largely devoted to farming, foraging of numerous wild plants, and the hunting of game.

The western Great Basin, a dry region between California and the Southwest, was the home of the Paiute, Shoshone, and Ute. This region offered sparse food, large animals in the mountains, and vegetation in the lowlands.

The California tribes—Maidu, Miwok, Pomo, and Yokut—were hunters and gatherers who used a great abundance of naturally existing foods, especially coastal fish and seafood. The foodways of the California tribes were based on the acorn and complemented by wild plants and small game. The foods of southern California tribes—Cahuilla, Cupeño, and Luiseño—were similar to those of the tribes farther north but were adapted to arid conditions and included pine nuts, chia (*Salvia columbariae,* a kind of sage), and cactus.

On the Northern Coast and Northwestern Plateau, the Chinook, Coo, and Tillamook subsisted primarily on the abundant salmon and other saltwater fish and secondarily on gathered roots, acorns, and berries.

"INDIANS" VS. "NATIVE AMERICANS"

There is confusion over the correct term for the indigenous peoples of what became the United States. When it became clear that the term "Indians" had been a misnomer, incorrectly identifying New World people with Asian Indians, many adopted the more accurate name "Native Americans." In general, the terms used by the peoples themselves are preferred. However, as new terms are sometimes cumbersome, and as many indigenous people today still use earlier terminology, a variety of terms are commonly in use. Likewise, in some contexts there is confusion over the appropriate word for settlers, historically called "Americans," because the term has frequently been used to exclude indigenous peoples. The terms "white," "red," "Old World," and "New World" carry misleading connotations, implying a European-based point of view, and are avoided.

A good deal of this essay has been written in the past tense because it focuses on events from the time of contact, with appropriate attention to ongoing change. This should not be understood to mean that the foodways discussed existed only in the past—many are still alive today.

Prehistory

Christopher Columbus's discovery of what was called the New World was a globe-shaping event. Others had preceded Columbus—among them Vikings and Basques—but their influence was slight. America, having had a long and rich history of major civilizations comparable with those on the other side of the Atlantic, was a new world only from the perspective of Old World Europeans.

Archaeologists debate the dates of the first settlement of the Western Hemisphere. Evidence strengthens the case for a succession of waves of migration, the first as early as forty thousand years ago, during which both large mammals and hunting Siberians crossed the Bering Strait to Alaska by way of a land bridge. Usually under water, the bridge surfaced during ice ages, when an immense amount of ocean moisture was redistributed into frozen glaciers, causing the sea level to drop. The land bridge likely was used most recently during the last Ice Age (ca. 10,000 B.C.E) but may not have been an easy traversal for nomadic Asians. Rather, because of massive deposits of ice that blocked the land, many Asians probably came to North America by sea, probably hugging the coast and making landfall at several sites along the West Coast. Newcomers of this period spread through large areas of the Americas, leaving archaeological evidence of their presence and their hunting and gathering methods of procuring food. The mammoth-hunters were called the Clovis people (ca. 11,000–6000 B.C.E.), named for the type of stone points they made. The Clovis left remains on the Great Plains and in the American Southwest and the Southeast. Their successors developed preagricultural cultivation of wild plants. These plants later became secondary to the domesticated plants of Mexican agriculture (ca. 6000 B.C.E.), which slowly made their way north. The descendants of the Clovis over the course of many thousands of years and after much interaction evolved from hunting and gathering societies to sophisticated agricultural systems and achieved sufficiently large-scale production to support the growth of highly developed civilizations. These peoples influenced the North American cultural and culinary development of the large Adena and Hopewell cultures of the east of the Mississippi and of the Anasazi, the ancestors of the pueblo dwellers.

Precontact cultures also hunted and fished. The ratio of meat to vegetative material differed considerably according to time and place, but in most areas meat was supplementary and not always available. The most important exception was the Plains region, where game was paramount. The only domesticated animals of North America were the dog and the turkey. The fishing and seafood groups of the western, southern, and eastern coasts thrived on ocean products and complex fishing systems supplemented with gathered vegetation. Of these, the salmon tribes of the Northwest were different from the other tribes in origin and culture and survived for thousands of years as hunting, foraging, and fishing cultures.

Depending on regional conditions, the early groups gave rise to distinct Native American nations, tribes, and cultures, each with its own variations of the food encountered by the first Europeans. Native American agriculture evolved. The balance between wild, cultivated, and domesticated plants shifted with major climate swings. After 2000 B.C.E. weather conditions favored domestication, and the practice spread rapidly to enable the development of the Anasazi, the Mogollon, and the Pima in the Southwest and the River Yuman of the Colorado River. Preagriculture was based on cultivation, that is, the selective tending of wild plants, a system that provided substantial quantities of seed and root foods. In later Hopewell and Mississippian cultures, cultivation included early forms of barley, amaranth, sumpweed, sunflowers, maygrass, goosefoot, knotweed, cactus pear, and maguey. By the time of first European contact, Indians were cultivating more than one hundred wild plants.

Domesticated Mexican maize (*Zea mays*, or corn), beans, squash, pumpkins, and chilies supplemented by cultivated Jerusalem artichokes and sunflowers were the basis of the first American agriculture. Evidence that these crops were grown supports the idea of long periods of settlement in one place and of intelligent horticulture—careful seed selection from only the best plants. Archaeological remains include the seeds of cultivated wild plants, the stone mortars and pestles (*metates y manos*) used to process them, and evidence of irrigated corn fields. The gradual spread and proliferation of Mexican agriculture into the American Southwest encouraged the growth of sedentary farming. From there agriculture followed several routes north, one up the Mississippi River and its tributaries, one to the southeast, and one through the eastern woodlands, reaching coastal areas last. Thus the people living near Mexico and along the Mississippi River, being well situated for tribal interchange and the communication of ideas, reached levels of foodways that impressed the Spanish explorer Hernando De Soto, the first European to investigate the American interior (1539–1542). One hundred years after De Soto's expedition, the French explorers in the northeastern woodlands and prairies were similarly impressed (although agriculture had made its way there somewhat later), and the Dutch and English on the East Coast were finding newly established farms.

At the first points of contact, Native American subsistence included the complex corn-beans-pumpkin-and-squash horticulture of Mexican origin and continued with cultivation, foraging, and hunting. Most food resources were highly seasonal and depended on intermittent availability. Menus were built on a rotation of garden crops in summer, hunting and harvesting in fall, use of stored and processed foods in winter, fish in spring, and berries in early summer. Acquiring food sometimes required seasonal moves. After spring planting, when most of the stored winter foods had been exhausted, most Eastern Woodlands Indians (among them the Iroquois) left their more permanent winter and farming settlements to live temporarily on the shores of rivers, lakes, and oceans. There they subsisted on the fish migrating into shallower waters and on early berries and shoots, drying large quantities of each for later use. The Indians returned to their inland homes when the first green corn (in the milky stage) was ready to eat.

Some ocean coasts were so richly endowed year-round with fish, game, and vegetation that there was little need to advance beyond highly local hunting and gathering, making it unnecessary to engage in agriculture and undertake seasonal removes. Peoples who enjoyed this lifestyle were exemplified by the salmon cultures of the Pacific Northwest (Chinook, Tillamook) and the Algonquians before 1600 on the Atlantic coast. By 1600 the coastal Algonquians had added agriculture to their food-producing efforts (for uncertain reasons) and sometimes occupied separate winter and summer sites. Seasonal removes also were undertaken for hunting. Prairie-Plains tribes followed the buffalo, traveling for months to procure enough hides and dried meat for months of subsistence and trade.

Contact and Ongoing Change

Intertribal contact was common throughout America. Tribes changed locations, traveled long distances for trade and social events, and engaged in both warring and peaceful relationships. Despite regional, tribal, and language differences, a common worldview and basic sign language facilitated Indian transactions. Long-distance trade routes and contacts spanned the continent. For example, long before European encounters, Pueblo Indians, unrestrained by modern political borders,

---

TRADE ROUTES

Major trade routes often followed waterways. The Mississippi River and its tributaries allowed an exchange of coastal and inland products, and the Great Lakes traffic brought copper to the East. Cross-country routes required carrying heavy loads but were nevertheless active as well. Archaeologists studying the Hopewell mounds in Ohio (200 B.C.E. to 400 C.E.) unearthed both raw and dressed points of obsidian that could only have come from the Rocky Mountains, more than one thousand miles away. Likewise, there is early evidence of salt trade between coastal and inland agriculture-based tribes throughout the southern regions. By the time of contact, hunt-centered Plains tribes, among them the Apache, bartered with their agricultural Hopi neighbors, exchanging dried buffalo meat for corn, beans, and pumpkins. Acorns were traded for pine nuts in the Southwest and California, and throughout the South people continued to trade long distances with and for salt. Some people traded for food with currency, that is, eastern wampum, northwest dentalia shells, and clamshell disk beads of California, but most transactions involved direct barter of commodities.

---

established exchange with Mexican trade centers. (Vikings and Basques had followed the fishing to the Newfoundland Banks long before Columbus but had little, if any, effect on cooking.)

The rate of culinary change was fastest among the disenfranchised. Early encounters with Europeans decimated Indian populations through the spread of smallpox, influenza, and syphilis. Survivors sometimes regrouped and joined forces with the remnants of other bands, forming new communities and probably sharing foodways. Some new groups became allied with religious factions, for example, the largely Iroquois Kahwanake community with the French Jesuits (ca. 1700). Other Indians moving west joined different tribes; still others were forcibly removed to special territories and reservations. The mixing of indigenous groups sometimes resulted in blended regional foods, but many tribes held to their own traditions. For example, the Navajo adjustment from nomadic hunting to settled herding increased their use of southwestern corn, beans, squash, and sunflowers. The Navajo, however, did not embrace the domestic turkey of their Hopi neighbors or the Muscovy duck brought from the

TOOLS

Iron tools enabled the continuation of old ways with more efficiency and without change to traditional foodways. Other tools altered peripheral tasks without affecting food. Axes, for example, allowed Native Americans to fell large trees more efficiently, to cut and process large trees, and to change fuel-gathering processes without affecting fires or cooking principles. The use of other European goods implied a change in foodways and some acceptance of European culture. These tools included shallow and deep frying pans that added frying to Native American repertoires, portable braziers for broiling, and forks, which changed table manners.

Southeast. At the other extreme, those who successfully hid from invaders (Cherokees and Creeks, for example) sustained their own ways far longer than other peoples. Some peoples, such as the Iroquois, both hid and resisted.

The degree to which Indians adopted new foodways differed from tribe to tribe and from person to person. Some believed that eating the foods of foreigners was subversive and weakening and that the use of trade goods such as tea and sugar would weaken native identity and lead to dangerous and traumatic changes. At the same time, many peoples, among them the Secotan of Roanoke Island (Chesapeake Bay area, 1585), enjoyed interaction and food exchanges.

Contact introduced cooking articles, such as durable metal pots, kettles, and knives, that were immediately appreciated and sought after for their durability and heat transmission. Among the most important early trade foods were salt, wheat flour, coffee, tea, whiskey, and rum. The introduction of wheat and leavenings led to the use of light raised breads, one version of which was prepared in the new frying pans and eventually became fry bread. Use of other new foods, especially meat from domesticated animals, certain milk products, rice, molasses, and sugar, began the shift toward modernization throughout the Indian world.

Factors of Change

Encounters and changes after 1492 varied according to several factors. Timing was paramount. For example, each moment of contact (that is, late fifteenth and early sixteenth centuries in the East and South to the late nineteenth century in the Northwest) brought to bear the influences of the European world of the time. The tribes that first met Europeans were the first to undergo decimation, dispersal, and acculturation, and their foodways are far more difficult to retrieve. Those with fairly recent contact have lost less, as their cultures are more intact and their foodways are still part of their oral tradition.

Some changes were slow, gradual, and often partial; others were fast and pervasive. Spanish peaches and melons, introduced very early in the South, spread so quickly and were adopted so readily by inland tribes that later Anglo-American arrivals believed these foods were indigenous. As the nineteenth-century Indian wars progressed, more tribes were forced from their traditional hunting and gathering areas and were quickly "Americanized" in mission and government schools that taught Anglo-American cookery.

Some changes resulted from passing time, new centuries, and modernization. For example, the Ojibwa of Minnesota traditionally dried blueberries in large quantities for winter use. With the introduction of cookstoves, inexpensive sugar, canning technology, and eventually freezers, preserving methods were updated and with them the character of many products. Moreover, the Ojibwa integrated berries into an evolving mainstream diet by preparing them as European-style pies, cobblers, puddings (no longer slow-cooked and thickened with whole or pounded corn), and preserves.

Geography also affected changing foodways. The first areas explored and settled were situated on easily traveled waterways that were accessible to indigenous people and newcomers alike. Thus the earliest encounters occurred in the coastal East, the Mississippi River and its tributaries, and the Great Lakes region, whereas large inland areas such as the Plains did not encourage early interaction. The expedition led by Francisco Vásquez de Coronado in 1540–1542, skirted the Plains and found buffalo but turned aside when it found the terrain and the Apaches inhospitable. Explorers who followed were likewise intimidated, thus Native Americans of this region experienced far later contact than did others. The Plains remained largely isolated until the nineteenth century, when the land became economically viable for eastern entrepreneurs and for settlers taking advantage of government offers of free land.

The climatic systems of different regions also determined contact. Northern fur trading encouraged inland exploration and the early establishment of European trading posts. Sometimes the conditions of new geographical regions were so different from those of ancient home grounds that traditional skills of hunting, fishing, and farming were no longer appropriate. For example, the people of the seacoast who had survived on richly endowed waterfronts were at a dietary loss when moved inland. They not only lost seafood but also were often faced with new varieties of food plants, different soils and weather systems, and changed availability of the materials needed for cooking—clay, wood, and stone.

Conflicting worldviews of indigenous peoples and newcomers had repercussions in foodways. Out of respect for all natural forms, Native Americans believed they had the rights to natural substances but not to the land on which the substances were found. This belief applied to agricultural and hunting lands, fishing rights, and waterfront use. Europeans believed in land ownership and little spiritual connection between the land and its inhabitants. Thus in the seventeenth century when the English "ceded" lands from the Long Island Shinnecock, the parties had very different concepts of the agreement. The English, believing they had control of the land itself, fenced it and legally forced the Indians to refrain from "digging holes" throughout the area. The Indians had expected to retain harvesting rights and therefore to dig (spring and fall) the important tuber the groundnut (sometimes called "the Indian potato"), an essential year-round staple. Christianized Indians gave up beliefs in the sanctity of animal life and land use and were more open to what had been considered wastefulness and overeating.

Adaptability to change, or its lack, was an important factor. For example, the Apache originally were Plains hunters who benefited from the introduction of the horse.

INDIAN PUDDING

Europeans fit indigenous foods into their cooking styles. At first early settlers exchanged foods with Native Americans as a means of establishing good relations and ate indigenous corn to survive. Before long, the culinary assets of New World foods made these foods appear more desirable, and they became standard ingredients in colonial dishes, but without changing the European character of the dishes. Thus Indian pudding, which became an American icon, was made with Native American cornmeal and Caribbean molasses but was a variation of the English baked milk and egg custard pudding.

When forced from the Plains, the Apache settled in the Southwest, where they learned agriculture and herding and adjusted their cooking. Likewise, the Navajo, famous for their adaptability, took on herding and, as evidenced by their rapid population growth, thrived.

Changing Cuisines

The first Europeans arriving on American shores were impressed by the large numbers of foods they had never before seen or eaten. Similarly, indigenous Americans were introduced to European foods that were equally foreign to them. The resulting interchange began what has been called the Columbian Exchange, a global redistribution of foodstuffs. The lists are long. The most important European contributions were wheat and other European grains, domesticated root vegetables, leafy kitchen garden plants, orchard fruits, and domesticated animals. Traffic in seeds, root stock, and animals distributed these foods throughout Native American settlements; sometimes they were simply left behind when an army departed.

In a period of change, foodways are the last cultural phenomena to disappear, and in that spirit Indians made consistent efforts to maintain their familiar and significant eating patterns. The first introduced foods were sometimes adapted into Indian cooking and used in the same manner as familiar ingredients. For example, in the eighteenth century when tribes in the South traded their foods to the French, they did not choose to use European chickens immediately.

Many new foods had clear advantages. The products of the domesticated pig, previously unknown in the New World, resembled those of the indigenous bear. Rendered pork fat (lard) replaced essential fats and oils obtained from bear fat, and the meats were comparable. Chickens and other barnyard fowl were often acceptable because they resembled wild game birds. Dairy and beef cattle met with more resistance, because most Native Americans had no experience with domesticated animals (apart from dogs) or inclination to consume unfamiliar dairy products. Cattle were difficult to raise, did not easily accommodate seasonal and nomadic moves, needed fencing, and sometimes needed substantial amounts of winter feed. To some peoples cattle were more of a hindrance than a benefit, to others just the reverse. The agricultural Iroquois raised cattle in New York in the seventeenth century. The gradual shift from wild game to beef, pork, mutton, goat, and poultry required a more sedentary existence and a change in orientation to land ownership.

COMMON FOODS OF THE COLUMBIAN EXCHANGE, BEGINNING IN 1492

This is not a complete list of indigenous foods, but rather a guide to changing Native American cuisines. The foods brought to America are identified according to those who brought them, not necessarily where they originated.

Foods native to America	Taken to	Foods brought to America	From
		Staple grains	
Corn	Universal	Wheat	Europe
Wild rice	Europe	Oats	Europe
		Rye	Europe
		Barley	Europe
		Millet	North Africa
		Rice	Africa, Europe
		Staple starches	
Assorted beans,	Universal	Soybeans	Asia
e.g., navy, cranberry,		Adzuki beans	Asia
black, kidney, and lima		Mung beans	Asia
		Fava beans	Europe
		Cowpeas	Africa
Peanuts (South America)	Africa	Peanuts return	Africa (slaves)
		Vegetables	
White potatoes (Peru)	Europe	White potatoes	North America
Sweet potatoes	Europe	Yams	Africa
Pumpkins	Europe, Africa	Cucumbers	Europe
Winter squash	Europe	Tomatoes (Mexico)	Spain
Summer squash	Europe	Lettuce	Europe
		Cabbage	Europe
		Turnips	Europe
		Onions	Europe
		Carrots	Europe
		Parsnips	Europe
		Broccoli	Europe
		Collards	Africa
		Okra	Africa
		Fruits	
Blueberries, huckleberries	Europe	Apples	Europe
Cranberries	Europe	Pears	Europe
Persimmons		Peaches	Europe
Paw-paws		Citrus fruits	Europe
		Figs	Europe
		Olives	Europe
Strawberries*	Europe	Strawberries	Europe
		Melons	Europe
		Water melons	Europe, Africa
Cherries*		Cherries	Europe
Grapes		Grapes	Europe
Raspberries,* blackberries		Raspberries, blackberries	Europe
Currants, red and black		Currants	Europe
Mulberries		Mulberries	Europe
		Nuts	
Black walnuts		Almonds	Europe
Hickory nuts		English walnuts	Europe
Beechnuts		Pistachios	Europe
Hazelnuts	Europe		

Continued

COMMON FOODS OF THE COLUMBIAN EXCHANGE, BEGINNING IN 1492
(Continued)

Foods native to America	Taken to		Foods brought to America	From
Pecans				
Chestnuts	Europe			
Chinquapins				
Pine nuts				
		Meat		
Turkey	Universal		Dairy cattle (milk, butter, cheese, cream)	Europe
			Beef cattle	Europe
			Lamb	Europe
			Pig	Europe
			Goat	Europe
			Barnyard poultry (chickens, geese, and ducks and their eggs)	Europe
			Horse (meat, work)	Europe
		Beverages		
			Tea and coffee	Europe
			Wine and spirits	Europe
			Beer and ale	England
			Cider	Europe
		Seasonings		
Allspice	Universal		Cinnamon	Europe (colonies)
Juniper	Europe		Cloves	Europe (colonies)
Sassafras	Europe		Nutmeg	Europe (colonies)
Chilies	Universal		Ginger	Europe (colonies)
			Pepper	Europe (colonies)
			Sesame	Africa
			Coconut	Europe
		Sweets		
Chocolate (Mexico)	Universal		Sugar	Europe
Vanilla (Mexico)	Universal		Honey	Europe
Maple and hickory sugars			Sorghum	Africa
Honey, locust				

* Some considered better quality than European equivalents.

The all-important horse, which had been introduced to the American Southwest by the Spanish in the sixteenth century, changed cultures outright. Escaped horses formed wild herds and became a major asset. At first horses were used for food, but their increasing value as transportation saved them from the stew pot. The hunts of Prairie-Plains Indians became more efficient with horses, and these peoples turned from a mixed agriculture and hunting culture to a nomadic lifestyle that was less vulnerable to European attack. Horse culture, however, added the need to provide fodder, exemplified by the Navajo use of spider flower (genus *Cleome*) and panic grass (genus *Panicum*).

Tribal foodways gave way in the face of the gradual appeal of European foods and the increasing unreliability of producing native food. The timing of such shifts differed according to the moments of contact and the rate at which Native Americans were disenfranchised.

Sixteenth Century

Native American foods of the sixteenth century changed relatively little, but they were enhanced with European trade items. In the sixteenth century Europeans found Native Americans to be avid traders. The Europeans established what would become vast fur-trading empires and bought salt for European markets. After settlement this kind of trade intensified and was extended to staple foods, such as corn, for survival. Europeans bartered with metal cookware, implements, and a few foods. As Eastern Woodlands trade increased, Europeans added to their

HOSPITALITY

The reactions of the first Europeans to visit an area (1500–1700) give mixed impressions of what early Native American foods were like. Native American worldview prescribed hospitality, and visitors were well fed. The visitors' reactions to the ingredients and cookery they encountered varied, presumably depending on the degree of ethnocentrism and gastronomic adventurousness of the observer, the food's resemblance to familiar flavors and textures of home cookery, the type of occasion and meal being shared, the skill of the cook, and the time of year and its effect on food availability. Opinions ranged from delight, "as good as any feast I have had in England," to "inedible," suggesting that the indigenous cuisine sometimes reached the heights of sophistication and variation known in Europe at the time.

trading posts on coastal and inland waterways, exposing inland Indians to their products.

The Spanish, seeking to extend their successful colonization of Mexico, made the first broad inland explorations of what became the United States. De Soto approached from Florida and crossed the Appalachians and the Mississippi River (1539–1543). Coronado, traveling north from the Southwest (1540–1542), met nomadic Plains Indians, traded with them, and withdrew from what was for the explorers an inhospitable countryside. The trade was an exchange of buffalo robes for the corn of neighboring agriculturists and of salt and hides for axes, hoes, fishhooks, knives, kettles, rum, and beer. During the sixteenth century Native American staples of corn, beans, pumpkins, squash, and sunflower seeds were extended by European domesticated pigs, cattle, and wheat. The hunters of the Plains, quick to take advantage of the Spanish horse, enlarged their staples of buffalo and wild turnips with dried horse meat, fat, and dressed hides.

Seventeenth Century

The first pockets of permanent European settlements increased contacts and accelerated change, although in relatively small areas of North America. With contact came population decimation due to disease (at times as much as 90 percent of a tribe), colonial policies of dispersal, and aggravated frontier and intertribal warfare. In the course of the seventeenth century, the early

NEW COMMUNITIES

In response to decimation and harassment, some Native American survivors banded together into new towns and communities. Among these was Conestoga, Pennsylvania, a community of 150 persons that drew many others from within walking distance. Kahwanake, a largely Iroquois community in Montreal, Canada, attracted Indians from the northern American tribes. Another community formed near Camden Plantation, Virginia. Native Americans in these communities maintained cultural and culinary continuity to the extent that limited available resources allowed. Members did trade outside the community, however. The Nanzatico women of Camden Plantation produced and sold their pottery to colonists for the price of as much corn as would fill the vessels. Some Indians also settled in early towns and took jobs within the local cash economy but with unclear food adaptations. Others moved westward to regroup.

European outposts expanded, increasing problems and tensions.

Europeans controlled increasing amounts of land and resources for their own aggrandizement and survival. At first, having arrived with few subsistence skills, the settlers depended heavily on the begged, bartered, and stolen food of local tribes. In time Europeans learned to feed themselves, but newcomers to the changing frontier continued to need help, for which they supplied trade goods, such as copper, brass, and iron pots, iron hoes, axes, and guns. Lightweight and durable brass and copper kettles became increasingly common among Indians, especially for travel. By the end of the seventeenth century, pottery and stone tools in areas of contact had been abandoned in favor of imported cookware. In the eastern woodlands, however, watertight splint baskets continued to be common because of the efficient European draw knife. The

They had large kettles which they traded for with the French long since, and do still buy of the English as their need requires. Before they had substantial earthern pots of their own making.

—William Wood, *New England Prospect* (1634)

result was an intermingling of Native and European cooking materials at the hearth but minimal change in diet.

As the seventeenth century drew on, trade increased. Agreements between the French and the Huron in the Northeast, the Iroquois and the Dutch in early New Netherland and Albany (later replaced by the English), and the French and Choctaw in Louisiana provided Indian staples for Europeans. Some tribes grew extra corn to trade, and Europe manufactured trade items targeted for the Indian market. European foods began to make their way into some Native American communities. For example, the agricultural Algonquian Mohegans in Connecticut began to keep pigs, beef cattle, and sheep during the 1660s and 1670s, and the Iroquois planted orchards of European fruits, among them apples and pears.

Contact sometimes advanced far beyond the settlements as European traders pushed inland from coastal communities. Following trails and streams with pack animals for deer hides in the south and furs in the north, many traders lived in tribal communities for much of the year. Their influence on Indian cuisine was probably variable and is difficult to assess.

Eighteenth Century

By 1700 the Indians of the central Eastern Seaboard were far outnumbered by colonists. European settlement of new lands repeated patterns of disease and loss of land established in the seventeenth century and were particularly evident in densely populated Indian areas. Continuing declines in population were due to deportations of enslaved Native Americans to the Caribbean and voluntary moves westward as people hoped to escape general anti-Indian harassment and violence. Only a few precontact Indian groups survived on the coasts and maintained their traditions, among them the Pamunkey community in Virginia. Others were able to maintain small tracts near ancestral homes, among them the Piscataway of coastal New Hampshire. The strong tribes and nations (Creek and Iroquois) who had maintained

---

Thin cakes mixt with bear's oil were formerly baked on thin broad stones placed over a fire, or on broad earthen [earthenware] bottoms fit for such a use, but now they use kettles.

—James Adair, *The History of American Indians* (1747)

---

their sovereignty maintained access to traditional food and foodways.

In general, Native Americans, having survived generations of contact, disease, and land loss, fell into a pattern of transition that included increasing erosion of their foodways. Although many western tribes were intact on ancestral land, Indians of the East had been resettled onto reserved lands, such as the town of Mashpee on Cape Cod, Massachusetts, and remote areas where they were unable to maintain earlier subsistence economies. Many Indians worked as laborers, farmhands, servants, fishers, hunters, and trappers. Increasing intimacy wore away traditions. Some people acculturated, took European names, were converted to Christianity, married Europeans, Africans, and Native Americans of other tribes, and moved in varying degrees into mainstream life. At one extreme, the children of mixed marriages had the choice of community, indigenous or colonial, and, depending on the directions they took, sometimes lost their Indian foodways entirely.

The East was, in many ways, a pattern for what would happen throughout America, according to the time of contact. For example, the first encounters on the Northwest Coast, beginning in the 1770s with coastal fur traders, did not lead immediately to major change until the late nineteenth century, when white land ownership became an issue. The coastal trade hardly affected native cuisine, apart from the introduction of the potato to the Makah. Traded tools and pots, however, were to become an important factor in the development of the Kwakiutl potlatch, a status-seeking ritual of feasting and social interaction in which an extended family distributed its goods throughout the community.

Not all eighteenth-century encounters were devastating, because trade thrived. Several tribes capitalized economically on newcomers' need for food. For example, the French established themselves in the Mississippi area in a series of forts and small communities. Their concerns were religious conversion, conquest, a military presence, and trade, and at first they produced little of their own food. The French found native foodways desirable, describing them as rich cuisines, and traded for both ingredients and fully prepared dishes. With appreciation of local diversity—both wild and cultivated food sources—the French traded for smoked buffalo, rendered bear meat and oil, deer, fish, various melons (which had been introduced earlier), and wild fruits, berries, and nuts; pumpkins, beans, and corn grown on the river's natural levees; and prepared foods such as persimmon bread. Native Americans who provided these foods bartered for trade goods and were drawn into the European economic systems. These Indians enlarged their fields and expanded their food production to meet growing European demand.

Despite flourishing trade, Native Americans did not immediately embrace European foods. For example, the Louisiana Houma, recognizing the market potential, bred chickens left by the Spanish and grew European salad greens for the French but did not eat these foods themselves. The French, who did not want to farm themselves, bought indigenous game and produce from Native Americans and sometimes sold them to other French, undertaking a chain of transactions that originated with Native Americans. Indians in the interior sold corn, poultry, and vegetables. Those near the coast sold salt, corn, fish, and game. The French bartered with guns, gunpowder, kettles, and knives. Trade was lucrative, and around 1760 some Indians from British West Florida moved closer to French settlements to further their commercial ventures.

Similar trade patterns spread throughout the colonies, among them the fur trade between the Iroquois and the Dutch, once again depending on national or tribal worldview. The Ojibwa of the Great Lakes area, in response to growing numbers of French traders and missionaries in the area, in the late eighteenth century harvested more wild rice than they needed and sold the surplus at the rate of one keg of rum for twenty fawn skins of rice. Ironic as it may seem, during the early stages of contact, Native Americans enabled colonial survival, albeit acting from cultural orientation and self-interest. By the middle of the eighteenth century, trade had transformed the technology of precontact cookery. Eastern central Native Americans were committed to European imports, as were the settlers. By 1783 Native Americans were as dependent on European-style materials, both imported and domestic, as were the colonists.

Nineteenth Century

In the nineteenth century Anglo-American hegemony and major transformations in native culture and foodways accelerated. At the beginning of the century, trade continued. Native Americans offered the products of their heritage, such as corn, reflecting continuity with their traditional foodways. Until the demise of the buffalo late in the nineteenth century, the mobile Apache traded buffalo products for the products of Pueblo agriculture. Indians increasingly traded for cash. As the fur trade decreased,

transactions were more likely to resemble the Ojibwa practice of supplying local wild blueberries to local stores. The eastern Cherokee, still strongly identified with tradition in the early 1830s, were growing enough corn to sell and only a small amount of wheat for their own consumption.

At the beginning of the nineteenth century, western Native Americans had had little contact with newcomers. Meriwether Lewis and William Clark, traversing the area from the Missouri River to the Pacific coast between 1804 and 1806, had passing encounters with local tribes who knew little about white culture. These tribes may have had only brief prior contact, and there had been little pressure to make dietary changes. By the end of the nineteenth century, most Native Americans had been settled on reservations and were controlled by U.S. law.

Several factors brought about changes. Eastern commercial interests saw opportunity in the West, in 1833 buying the last of the Indian lands on Lake Michigan to create the gateway city of Chicago. The city became a central trade depot from which to ship western products such as beef and grain to eastern markets. The western Plains were made even more accessible with the extension of the railroads and the deliberate and systematic destruction of vast buffalo herds. The herds had numbered 40 million head in 1800 and were reduced to approximately five hundred head by 1880. Nomadic hunters, dispossessed of their livelihood, sometimes became cowboys or ranchers. Agriculturists, repeatedly deprived of fertile lands, struggled to feed themselves on poor soil and sought jobs in the modernizing world. At the same time, native tribes in the East were resettled in the West, further crowding the land. Defensive wars further decimated western Indian populations and reduced autonomy, playing havoc with a good part of Native American culture and its cuisine.

The most sweeping dietary changes resulted from the new U.S. control of indigenous populations. In 1830 the Indian Removal Act, the new Bureau of Indian Affairs, and powerful private interests established federally funded and governed reservations and forced the tribes to relocate to them. After decades of resistance, wars, and treaties, the tribes were resettled onto government lands, the last of these in the Northwest in the 1890s. A series of mass removes, marches, and "trails of tears" compelled Native Americans to live without autonomy or access to traditional subsistence and cooking styles and to increase the use of commercial mainstream food.

After 1850, for reservation Indians who had ceded their land through treaties, the government provided periodic food rations as "compensation" for the loss of hunting, foraging, and farming lands. Allotments of beef, sugar, wheat flour, and coffee were supposed to replace game, honey and maple syrup, cornmeal, and hot herbal beverages. Although they staved off hunger, these foods also directed home cooking away from inherited cuisines. Often forced to farm on inappropriate and unproductive land, Native Americans needed to patronize trading posts and reservation stores.

One result of the reservation experience was the emergence of a new Native American tradition, one strongly oriented to inexpensive white wheat flour and sugar. The foods made with these ingredients included fry bread, white wheat bread, bread pudding, iced and filled cakes, sweet puddings, cobblers, and pork sausage. Some traditional foods remained, but they were adapted to mainstream techniques. For example, women of many tribes replaced dried berries with home-canned jams and jellies and used them in English-American pies. Reservation schools, meant to deliberately "Americanize" Native Americans, in part through foodways, taught the dishes of then-modern America. These dishes often were prepared at home with traditional corn, beans, pumpkin, sunflower seeds, salmon, acorn flour, and berries. In many cases, these dishes were made with the cast-iron cook stove that had replaced, at least in part, the stone-lined hearth and pit oven.

Native Americans were exposed to modernizing cookery through newspapers, magazines, and cookbooks, which were standardizing cookery throughout the United States. Along with inexpensive commercial ingredients, Indians expanded their use of what had been, for them, nontraditional foods. For example, access to sugar dramatically increased the desire for sweetened foods; broadened the diet with sweet snacks, pies, pastries, puddings, preserves, and candies; and introduced the concept of dessert. The idea of drinking hot herbal drinks was not new, and Asian teas, which contained caffeine, and coffee were easily accepted among some tribes. Alcohol, originally used ritualistically only in some tribes of the Southwest, proved to have disastrous effects. To these were added other deleterious new foods, among them milk products, which created problems because many Native American adults were lactose intolerant. The poverty imposed by reservation life resulted in diets overbalanced with carbohydrates and poor-quality fats, and the result was a high incidence of diabetes.

ISHI AND COOKERY

The first moments of encounter are almost impossible to reconstruct, but the carefully documented experience of one Native American may provide insight into the native view of changing foodways. In 1911 in central California a Yahi Indian named Ishi, the sole survivor of a small, secluded nomadic band, made his first contact with Anglo-Americans. He spent the remaining five years of his life working with anthropologists. Ishi's reactions to American life and food reflected many common native food preferences, the kinds of European foods that were most acceptable, and those that were resisted. His reactions also typified the integration of spiritual belief and cookery and the successful technology that achieved standards held by modern food professionals.

The native predilection for low-temperature steaming and boiling was accomplished by the addition of small, hot rocks to the cooking pot. This technique produced firmer textures and stronger flavors in vegetables, stews, soups, and mushes. Ishi preferred these cooking methods to modern stoves, which he found were too hot and overcooked food. Ishi preferred clear soups—the clarity of liquids was desirable and viewed as a symbol of clarity of vision—and disliked milk and butter (on the basis of a mythological principle), soft-cooked eggs, custards, and thickened gravies—all cloudy or opaque liquids. He readily accepted foods that resembled those of his former life—potatoes; beans; rice; dried, fresh, and canned fruits; and fresh vegetables. To Ishi's tastes, the meat of an ideal stew was firm, the broth clear, and the vegetables firm to the tooth, not soft or mushy. Ishi's standard dinner choices consisted of roasted, baked, or broiled beef or fish accompanied by a potato in its skin, plain rice or cereal, and a vegetable eaten raw, baked, roasted, or boiled gently. After a period of acculturation, Ishi learned to like bread, jelly, honey, tea (because it was clear), ice cream, and after a while, sweetened coffee (although this drink was cloudy, Ishi believed it important because of its popularity among his new associates). Ishi's eating style was much like the ones reported by the first European observers and continues among surviving traditional cuisines.

People adhered to their cultures and cuisines as long and as completely as the new conditions would allow. Under the new laws, Native Americans retained certain hunting and fishing rights. For example, they were allowed to hunt large game such as deer year-round in contrast to the specific hunting seasons that limited whites. The salmon-based tribes in California were allowed to leave the reservation to fish and to dry their staple food. The resulting conflict between the reservation agriculture imposed by the whites and traditional subsistence fishing was sometimes resolved in favor of tradition. Government Indian agents complained that well-sown and tended native crops were lost when the tribes moved to the Pacific coast for two or three months of extended fishing, but the agents could not prevent the migration.

Twentieth and Early Twenty-First Centuries

In the twentieth century a large part of Native American cooking was eroded by the same problems that had been established earlier: relocation, government control of cookery in government schools, the poverty and lack of opportunity associated with much of reservation life, the difficulties of minority status and racism, the passage of time, and the progress of the modern world. A new movement to relocate Indians in cities further weakened the cultural reinforcement often associated with reservation life. At the same time, many attempts were made to dissolve Indian governments and close reservations to open land to commercial interests. Indian reaction began a pan-Indian movement in which tribes came together to strengthen political power and culture.

Dietary changes and adaptations have been associated with a number of health problems. Nutritionists are concerned with modification of eating habits to reduce the high incidence of obesity and diabetes, recommending daily intake balances based on scientific findings. There is some evidence of improvement when Indians with diabetes consume traditional foods, that is, wild foods and heirloom plant varieties. This diet apparently results in considerable weight loss and cessation of the need for insulin therapy. Heirloom corn apparently is digested more slowly than newer varieties. Other problems seem to tie traditional diet to health and genetics. It has been suggested by such researchers as J. S. Carter that the high incidence of obesity and diabetes is related to a "thrifty gene." This gene connects obesity and the Indian ability to overeat on special occasions and store the surplus against times of scarcity and starvation.

While this mechanism was helpful in the past, it leads to health problems in the modern world of year-round plenty. Similarly, genetic inability to process alcohol is being investigated by such groups as American Indian and Alaska Native Genetics Research.

Despite five centuries of immense pressure to change inherited cuisine, a surprising body of Native American foodways has survived. Much of this success is due to the elemental importance and strength of the Native American oral tradition. Some credit also belongs to late-nineteenth- and early-twentieth-century social scientists, who believed that the weakened Indian culture was on the verge of disappearing. Among these works were important anthropological food studies that recorded Iroquois and Zuni food in great detail. Native Americans themselves began to write about and publish their own foodways. For example, *The Indian Cook Book* (Oklahoma, 1933) compiled by a group of Native American women offered eighteen pages of authentic old recipes unchanged by mainstream ingredients, as did *Choctaw Indian Dishes* (Oklahoma, 1935) by Amanda Hudson. Orally transmitted instruction that survived across the United States continues to be recorded in print. Increasing determination to keep alive and record the old foods and their meanings is reflected in contemporary tribal dishes, among them Hopi blue corn piki bread. Lakota grape dumpling stew, Cherokee ramp-and-egg feasts, Wampanoag clambake, and its northwestern equivalent, pit-roasted salmon and camas root. Such recipes are exchanged across the United States through powwows and active channels of media communication and appear in various combinations of Indian and modernized versions.

A large number of Native Americans are assimilated. Their eating preferences and habits are those of most mainstream Americans. The pressures of modern life and long work days have created the same need for frozen, fast, and convenience foods that exists throughout the United States. Many Native Americans, however otherwise acculturated and modern, continue cooking traditional dishes from time to time and to one extent or another. For example, in one contemporary Long Island family of mixed ancestry, an Indian man cooks traditional foods, weather permitting, at an outdoor hearth while his wife prepares meat dishes from her heritage on a modern indoor stove. For others, traditional foods are most important symbolically as culture references at holidays and celebrations. The same kind of variation exists among people living on the "res," although there is more likelihood that recognizable cultural food themes exist.

In some communities, inherited use of regional foods and cookery is still valued and maintained with pride. Tribes and individuals are working to maintain or reinstate inherited foodways. For example, some Paiute Wada Tika continue traditional patterns of hunting and gathering and cooking camas root, bitterroot, biscuitroot, chokecherries, berries, and small game. Efforts to keep the past alive are also bringing Native American products to the mainstream market. Often the work of individual tribes and entrepreneurs, Indian products are promoted by a few small companies. In one case Senecas are growing, processing, milling, and selling Tuscarora corn. They are concerned with keeping their local agriculture viable, being economically supportive of their tribal farming families, and maintaining an heirloom variety of corn with ancient genetics that does not increase the risk of diabetes. Companies in the Southwest are marketing special chilies and blue corn flour. Ojibwas are engaged in wild rice ventures, and Apaches offer hunting and fishing tourism on reservations. Buffalo, which are increasing in number, are protected in national parks and are raised commercially for the table.

Native American cuisine is being saved in print. Native American communities are producing their own cookbooks, pointedly working to keep the old ways alive for the younger generations. Published personal memoirs are preserving the handed-down family cooking and garden lore of past generations. Children's books on indigenous food are being used in public schools with mandated curricula in Native American history and culture. Health specialists are devising culturally appropriate diets for diabetes-prone Indians. Efforts to promote and legitimize native foodways are found at public festivals and powwows, where foods such as fry bread and cooked beans are sold. Historical societies and Indian museums have begun to focus on Native American histories, offering not only pottery and stone artifacts but also food traditions based on archaeological and anthropological research.

In accordance with popular interest in ethnic foods and concepts of cultural pluralism, there is a growing movement toward bringing traditional native foodways to the palates of modern gourmets. Handsomely illustrated cookbooks do credit to the culture and offer creative uses of important Indian foods. Innovative restaurants and Native American chefs have begun presenting sophisticated recipes that highlight precontact ingredients and flavors.

[See also Beans; Buffalo; Corn; Mid-Atlantic Region; Midwestern Regional Cookery; New England Regional Cookery; Pumpkins; Southern Regional Cookery; Southwestern Regional Cookery; Squash.]

BIBLIOGRAPHY

Bartram, William. *Travels through North and South Carolina, Georgia, East and West Florida*. Philadelphia: James Johnson, 1791. Reprint edited by Mark Van Doran as *Travels of William Bartram*. New York: Dover, 1955.

Beverley, Robert. *The History and Present State of Virginia*. London: Parker, 1705. Reprint edited by Louis B. Wright. Chapel Hill: University of North Carolina Press, 1947.

Bradbury, John. *Travels in the Interior of America in the Years 1809, 1810, and 1811*. London: Sherwood, Neely and Jones, 1819. Reprint, Lincoln: University of Nebraska, 1986.

Brain, Jeffrey P. *Tunica Treasure*. Cambridge, MA: Peabody Museum of Archaeology and Ethnology, and Salem, MA: Peabody Museum, 1979.

Carter, J. S., J. A. Pugh, and A. Monterrosa. "Non-Insulin-Dependent Diabetes Mellitus in Minorities in the United States." *Annals of Internal Medicine* 125, no. 3 (1996): 221–232.

Dixon, E. James. *Bones, Boats and Bison: Archaeology and the First Colonization of Western North America*. Albuquerque: University of New Mexico, 1999.

Drimmer, Frederick, ed. *Captured by the Indians: Fifteen Firsthand Accounts, 1750–1870*. New York: Dover, 1985. Reprint of *Scalps and Tomahawks: Narratives of Indian Captivity*. New York: Coward-McCann, 1961.

Driver, Harold E. *Indians of North America*. 2nd ed. Chicago: University of Chicago Press, 1961. Reprinted 1972.

Fagan, Brian M. *Ancient North America: The Archaeology of a Continent*. New York: Thames and Hudson, 1991.

Gelb, Norman, ed. *Jonathan Carver's Travels through America 1766–1768: An Eighteenth-Century Explorer's Account of Uncharted America*. New York: Wiley, 1933.

Grumet, Robert S. *Historic Contact: Indian People and Colonists in Today's Northeastern United States in the Sixteenth through Eighteenth Centuries*. Norman: University of Oklahoma, 1995.

Hoebel, E. Adamson. *The Cheyennes: Indians of the Great Plains*. 2nd ed. New York: Holt, Rinehart, and Winston, 1978.

Hulton, Paul. *America 1585: The Complete Drawings of John White*. Chapel Hill: University of North Carolina Press, 1984.

James, Sydney V., Jr., ed. *Three Visitors to Early Plymouth*. Plymouth, MA: Plimoth Plantation, 1963.

Kraft, Herbert C. *The Lenape-Delaware Indian Heritage: 10,000 BC–AD 2000*. Stanhope, NJ: Lenape Books, 2000.

Kroeber, Theodora. *Ishi in Two Worlds: A Biography of the Last Wild Indian in North America*. Berkeley: University of California Press, 1961.

Lawrence, Bill. *The Early American Wilderness as the Explorers Saw It*. New York: Paragon, 1991.

Mails, Thomas E. *The Cherokee People: The Story of the Cherokees from Earliest Origins to Contemporary Times*. New York: Marlowe, 1996.

Oehler, Gottlieb F., and David Z. Smith. *Description of a Journey and Visit to the Pawnee Indians*. Fairfield, WA: Ye Galleon Press, 1974. The original edition was published in 1914.

Quinn, David B., and Alison M. Quinn, eds. *The First Colonists: Documents on the Planting of the First English Settlements in*

North America, 1584–1590. Raleigh: North Carolina Department of Cultural Resources, 1982.

Sauer, Carl Ortwin. *Sixteenth Century North America: The Land and the People as Seen by the Europeans.* Berkeley: University of California, 1971.

Super, John C. *Food, Conquest, and Colonization in Sixteenth-Century Spanish America.* Albuquerque: University of New Mexico, 1988.

Wallace, Paul A. W., ed. *The Travels of John Heckewelder in Frontier America.* Pittsburgh: University of Pittsburgh Press, 1958. Reprinted 1985.

Will, George F., and George E. Hyde. *Corn among the Indians of the Upper Missouri.* Lincoln: University of Nebraska, 1964. The original edition was published in 1917.

ALICE ROSS

Spiritual and Social Connections

The Native American worldview conceived of a balance among all forms, including plants, animals, water, wind, earth, stone, and sun. Each had a place in the total scheme, offered spiritual and practical aid to people associated with them, and each needed respect for its contributions. Taking the life of a plant or animal, even though for food, was a serious matter. The spirits of plants and animals presumably offered themselves as food, but only on the condition that they would not be treated cruelly or wastefully. Each food spirit required rituals to express honor and thanks to it and imposed penalties if the gift of itself was abused. These penalties ranged from a species' refusal to make itself available for human sustenance to the punishment of a single offender by the infliction of bad luck or disease. These issues were of paramount importance to people whose welfare depended on the forces of the natural world and they fostered the ideal of a harmonious universe.

Staple foods were central in Native American mythologies. Creation stories focused on the introduction of important foods. Legends described "first people" as hungry, ignorant, and unhappy. They were then transformed by a supreme god or goddess who brought the significant new food and taught its use. Among agriculturists, the Corn Goddess (blonde to represent corn tassels) was a major figure. The northeastern Senecas told of the Earth Mother (also called Corn Mother), whose breasts produced the first corn, and who, in some versions, brought beans, squash, and general fertility. One Apache benefactor was Turkey, who ended hunger by shaking plant foods out of his feathers, introducing wild fruits, plants, and two varieties of corn. The Ojibwe boy

FOOD MYTHOLOGY

Food-related mythologies were part of daily life. Southwestern Zuni women sang the adventures of the Corn Goddesses as they ground corn. Hopi babies were presented to the sun at birth, along with two perfect ears of corn, a reference to the Corn Goddess and the child's two mothers (spiritual and temporal). Lenape men, when hunting deer, or Lenape women, when gathering nuts and firewood in the forests, asked for the approval of Mësingw, the bearlike "Keeper of the Game" who was the chief protector of animals and their environment. In addition, annual festivals such as the Corn Dance, the Green Corn Festival, the Strawberry Festival, the First Salmon Ceremony of the Northwest, or the Cheyenne Sun Dance were meant to ensure the survival of humankind and its cultures with sufficient food.

In the areas where hunting predominated, legends tell of creation spirits who brought the game. The Northwest, one of the few regions in which corn was not grown, told creation stories about Salmon Boy and Bear Mother. White Buffalo Woman, of the Lakota Sioux, was the bringer of hordes of buffalo and appropriate instruction. She also taught the women how to make hearth fires, to do stone cooking in buffalo paunches, to make pemmican, corn, and wild turnip, all dishes that were central to Lakota cuisine.

Winaboozhoo found wild rice through a series of visions; Wunzh learned about corn from the god Mondawmin.

In addition to the large consumption of these iconographic foods, most tribes followed a series of taboos. These were sometimes related to life stages and gender issues. Many women avoided eating meat for fear of offending hunted animals; during menstruation some avoided all contact with meat lest it spoil. Men, on the other hand, ate meat to make themselves more difficult to kill. Sometimes a particular animal was thought to have negative powers; the Iroquois believed that eating a chickadee would make one a liar.

Like so much of Indian culture, mythologies changed with the presence and power of Christian colonists, and the rather vague Creator of precontact myths became a stronger, more personal and immediate figure.

Social and Ritualistic Foods

Socialization was a large part of group living but was often structured by gender. Men and women were divided by complementary work and spiritual roles and developed strong same-sex ties through food. Women spent a good deal of the day in the company of other women, planting and harvesting, cooking for special celebrations, gathering food and fuel, or processing winter provisions. Men worked closely together on extended hunting and fishing trips and the extensive advance preparations needed for them. Men and women sometimes crossed the gender lines to provide help when necessary or to honor male spirits; some men (Osage, for example) cooked meat on special occasions. Certain foods were associated with one gender or another, for example, saskatoon berries (*Amalanchier alnifolia*) of the Blackfoot Indians were a snack food reserved for men. Salmonberry (*Rubus spectabilis*) parties were an event specific to Makah women, who traveled by canoe to the stand of fruit, gathered and pit-steamed it on the beach, and engaged in appropriate women's songs and dances until the fruit was ready.

The taking of animal life also required a ritual in which some part of the animal was returned to the earth, prayers were offered giving thanks, requesting forgiveness, and promising to waste nothing. Some believed that if these rituals were neglected, the spirit of the animal would follow the hunter home and afflict him with disease or poor hunting. Cherokee hunters sacrificed the melt (large fat deposits) of an animal. Sometimes they sacrificed the first animal caught during an extended hunt to express

CEREMONIES

Key foods were incorporated into ritual dishes for important ceremonials. For example, pit-baked Navajo cake was made for weddings, squaw dances, and womanhood ceremonies. The mixture of roasted cornmeal, raisins and, after contact, European sprouted wheat and brown sugar was precooked, placed on circles of corn husks, sprinkled with cornmeal of four different colors, and pit baked. Colored corn had special meanings. Among the Navajo, white symbolized the East and the rising sun; among the Cherokee it meant happiness and peace. When it was served, the center of the cake, or the "heart," was buried in the ground to feed Mother Earth. In similar fashion, Hopi women making blue corn piki threw the first piece of flatbread into the fire to "feed it," asking the baking stone "not to be lazy and to work well." Mooseberry (*Viburnum*) was eaten only at feasts by the Kwakiutl, who also boiled huckleberries mixed with red salmon spawn and oil for their winter ceremony feast.

FESTIVALS

Elaborate food preparations with spiritual references were common. The calendar year was punctuated by annual festivals in which plants and animals were asked to provide generously, or thanked for good harvests. For example, the Shinnecock Strawberry Festival was a "first-food" homecoming in which the fruit and gratitude for it were paramount. For agriculturists the most important festival of the year was the Green Corn Festival, a new year celebration of the first edible corn (the often-sweet "milk" stage) and the promise of enough food for another year; festivities involved some ten days of feasting and ritual. Similar ceremonies were performed by the eastern foragers of such wild foods as ramps (*alliums*) and strawberries. At the time of the first harvesting of northwest salmon, men fasted and women and children ate out of sight of the river.

gratitude for recovery from illness or to ensure success in the hunt. Cherokee women routinely threw a piece of fat into the cooking fire before and during meals, as a way of protecting the family from evil and inducing good luck. The northwestern tribes sang to welcome the salmon. The first ritualistic cuts of salmon were made by female shamans. Others burned the salmon heart to prevent it from being defiled by dogs. Dog meat was often used ceremonially, sometimes offered to the god of war to ensure good hunts.

Food taboos and prescriptions were often associated with origin mythologies. One of the injunctions against drinking milk came from the story of the Corn Mother, whose breasts had provided the first corn to the Senecas. Foods to be shunned were often believed to have specific health dangers. The Cherokees avoided eating a number of animals, including dogs, eels, foxes, wolves, snakes and snakelike water eels, and catfish, in the belief that such would bring bodily contamination. The Cayugas believed that the flesh of pregnant animals would produce diarrhea if eaten and avoided allowing the skinned bodies of trapped animals to touch the ground, lest the animal be offended and refuse to offer itself for human use in the future.

In some cases, the foods associated with festivals do not appear to have such strong symbolism. For example,

POTLATCH

One of the most unusual of Native American feasts was the Kwakiutl potlatch, in which the host family not only fed everyone with ample high-quality food, but also distributed all its accumulated wealth among the guests. In this economic show of power, the quantity and quality of the prepared foods earned commensurate community status.

the California Cahuilla use of acorn and meat stews or Iroquois and Chippewa use of blackberry beverages may have more to do with availability and desirable flavor.

One of the most elusive areas of knowledge about Native American foodways is that of dining etiquette—there is no physical evidence from indigenous records, and most sources come from early European impressions. There is, however, a fair degree of consistency in the descriptions offered by the English in the Chesapeake (1585) and Virginia (1705), the French in Louisiana (early 1700), and the German Moravian John Heckewelder in the northern Eastern Woodlands (1754–1813). Many commented on the principle that it was insulting to thank a host for food, as feeding a guest was considered to be nothing that required extra effort and was simply an everyday interaction.

It would appear that at the time of contact, good manners required that all visitors be offered food soon after arrival, and that guests eat everything offered. People ate sitting on woven grass mats on the ground or floor. Each person owned a bowl and spoon (for soups), brought them to meals, and was responsible for their cleanliness. Most food was eaten with fingers, although there were some ladles and dippers for serving liquid foods. Daily meals were cooked by women for their families, but in their sometimes-communal system much food was also shared, and it was considered quite acceptable for people to help themselves from the cooking pots of other families.

Gluttony was considered reprehensible, in keeping with the proper attitude of respect toward the spirit of the food and a general value on abstemiousness, self-denial, and Spartan strengthening. These general manners were, under certain circumstances, set aside for the greater value of survival. Overeating was common at times of fresh kills (especially when food was scarce or a rarity). It was sometimes a means of surviving periods in which

there might be no food at all for days, or it occurred at Iroquois feasts when it was expected that everything placed before a guest, throughout the day, would be completely consumed.

[See also Beans; Buffalo; Corn; Myths and Folklore.]

BIBLIOGRAPHY

Gill, Sam D., and Irene F. Sullivan, eds. *Dictionary of Native American Mythology*. New York: Oxford University Press, 1994.
Leeming, David, and Jake Page. *The Mythology of Native North America*. Norman: University of Oklahoma Press, 1988.
Storm, Hyemeyohsts. *Seven Arrows*. New York: Ballantine, 1972.

ALICE ROSS

Technology and Sources

Basic Food Preparation

Meals and recipes are elusive constructs; they are difficult to describe and analyze. Archaeologists have identified plants and animals by their seeds and bones, but they have not found a sense of what the food tasted or felt like or how it fit into the day's nourishment. In addition, cookery, like other aspects of culture, is in a constant state of change, and food historians use caution when applying modern foodways to the past. A good deal of what is known or surmised depends on firsthand accounts—the oral history of Native Americans and the observations of early European travelers, a sometimes contradictory base.

[They] accustom themselves to no set Meals, but eat night and day, when they have plenty of Provisions, or if they have got any thing that is a rarity. They are very patient of Hunger. . . . Fashion of sitting at meals is on a mat spread on the ground, with their Legs lying out at length before them, and the dish between their Legs . . . never sit more than two together at a Dish. . . . Spoons which they eat with, do generally hold half a pint; and they laugh at the English for using small ones, which they must be forc'd to carry so often to their Mouths, that their Arms are in Danger of being tir'd, before their Belly.

—Robert Beverley, *Report on the True State of Virginia* (1705)

CONTACT ATTITUDES TOWARD NATIVE AMERICAN FOODS

The reasons for disagreement over Native American meal patterns—whether they reflected tribal differences or the personal tastes of the observer—are not clear. For example, the flavors and textures of certain foods (buried, aged, and "rotted") were foreign to Europeans, were not equated with comparable European fermentations such as aged wines and cheeses, and would have elicited negative reactions. Seasonality and intermittent available resources were not taken into account consistently, nor was the variability in quality and quantity due to the time of year. Native Americans categorized some foods as "starvation foods," implying that they prepared for times of scarcity when more desirable foods were in short supply. Observers might have seen Native Americans eating less appealing foods without understanding that such foods prevented starvation. In addition, the quality of food observed may have depended on the time of day, whether the foods described were snacks or the large meal of the day, whether the meal was a feast or an ordinary meal, whether eating had been scheduled to accommodate special projects, and whether the people were in a permanent encampment with access to stored food or in a temporary encampment with fewer resources. In addition, observers were not always sensitive to underlying standards of manners. For example, what may have seemed like carelessness or dirtiness to Europeans was often a strict native injunction against using food that had dropped to the ground, because such items were considered food for the dead.

Meals Many observers thought meals were informal affairs, often one-dish preparations like those the Iroquois simmered in large pots and usually served at noon. According to the memories of an Onondaga, supported by the testimony of James Smith, a 1755 visitor, there was no concept of regular meals, but rather food was available all day and eaten as one became hungry. The Delaware and Huron apparently scheduled two daily meals, morning and evening. Other meals were described in which a series of separate dishes were served, sometimes not at the same time, according to an ethic against mixing foods. When certain foods were scarce, their sudden availability brought on feasting that may have lasted for days. These feasts might have celebrated fresh meat in wintertime and maple syrup and first fruits in the spring and summer. Such meals may

have been related to the Indians' genetic ability to store vast quantities of nutrients and to draw on them during times of hunger.

Food Patterns Although the tribes shared basic recipe genres, their foods varied somewhat from region to region. What the various peoples had in common was the ability to use the natural environment as a source of enjoyable and nutritious foods. The more tribes exploited the wild food of the natural world, the healthier they were; nomads fared better than agriculturists. Tribal differences had most to do with nomadic as opposed to agricultural orientation and the available foodstuffs. For example, the Menominee viewed fresh raspberries as less important than dried ones, probably as a result of their agricultural and sedentary lifestyle that depended on stored wintertime resources. The nomadic, hunting Cheyenne, who customarily ate the berries fresh and out of hand, did not have the time, place, or harvest for preservation and storage and were likely to consume such food as they moved.

Most tribes depended chiefly on their basic grain and starch preparations, which, according to region, were dishes of corn, wild rice, or acorn. In some regions these key grains or starches constituted 60 percent of the day's eating; in other regions, more. These dishes were cooked as breads—steamed, stone baked as flatbread and bannock, and boiled as dumplings and porridge—and commonly enriched with beans, nuts, seeds, and fruit. Ground, parched (roasted), green, or ripe corn was a favored component of festive dumplings, breads, and pemmican. For puddings, the grains (whole or pounded) were simmered at length and thickened into a sweet mass. Appearing in some form at every meal, such "breads" may have composed an entire meal; they were also integral to basic soups and stews and were sometimes supplemented by other dishes. Agricultural peoples often combined grain with beans in boiled dishes and breads. Dried meat and fish were as important to hunting and fishing tribes as corn was to agricultural peoples.

Before contact with the European settlers and depending on the season, almost all Indians roasted and stewed meats, pit-steamed or boiled vegetables and starches, and then dressed them with animal fat, nuts, and seasonings. Fruits were used in and out of season—raw or boiled in season and dried to be reconstituted in sauces for meats and fish or as flavorings in grain and starch breads, dumplings, and porridges. The northwestern Makah, for example, used pit-steamed dewberries with

Native American Technology. Papago woman picking cactus fruit with stick, Arizona, 1907. *Prints and Photographs Division, Library of Congress/Edward S. Curtis*

salmon, and the Ojibwa cooked blueberries with corn or venison. Cooked and eaten alone, fruit was frequently dressed in animal fat. Assorted vegetables contributed to the meal and were treated similarly to fruits throughout the year, although vegetables played a larger role in soups and stews. Many young foods were enjoyed raw, among them the roots of young cattail, which were peeled, chewed, and sucked.

Water was the common beverage, but regional teas were infused with leaves or blossoms, pine needles, fruit, or sap syrup from trees and young corn canes. Fermented alcoholic drinks were rare, although there is some evidence that alcohol was used in religious ceremonies in the Southwest. Hot drinks were made from numerous vegetable sources, among them eastern teaberry (*Gaultheria procumbens*), Oswego tea or bee balm (genus *Monarda*), roasted acorns (genus *Quercus*), and honey locust beans (*Gleditsia triacanthos*).

Special Occasion Foods Every tribe used specific foods and preparations to meet a variety of needs, among

them seasonality, travel use, winter storage, and provision for times of shortage. There were even special foods for children—oxalis root (*Oxalis montana*) among the Pawnee and butternuts (*Juglans cinerea*) among the Iroquois. The foods of celebrations and festivals were often related to specific new foods of the year, whether in preparation for planting and hunting or as an expression of gratitude that followed success.

Seasonal Dishes The Native American calendar was marked by a succession of seasonal foods. Although the basic cooking techniques remained the same, availability determined the combinations of foods that were possible. For example, winter succotash was made by the Cherokee from dried corn, beans, and sometimes dried pumpkin, but summer succotash was made with juicy green corn and soft, immature beans and was more likely to be flavored with fresh garden vegetables or meat. On the northwestern coast, salmon and camas root (genus *Camassia*) available at the same time in spring, were cooked together for major feasts. The highly valued combination of dried chokecherries (*Prunus virginiana*) and deer liver was a favorite of the Paiute in winter. The dried fruit was a favored travel food and was at hand at the time of a kill to flavor the perishable and cherished liver, which was usually eaten immediately.

Travel and Hunting Foods Most tribes carried the dried berries and fruit of their regions when traveling. In northern areas processed blueberries and chokecherries, for example, were mixed with parched corn (roasted corn, either as whole kernels or flour). Complete on its own, the mixture was sometimes converted into pemmican with the addition of pounded, dried meat (jerky) and enough fat or marrow to form it into a thick paste. Variations of this basic recipe were made according to the available meat: Plains Indians used dried buffalo and antelope; the eastern tribes used dried deer and bear; and the northwestern groups used dried fish. Eating it necessitated consumption of periodic drinks of water, but pemmican was sustaining enough, even in small amounts, to fuel a long-distance runner.

Starvation Foods The foods used in times of shortages varied according to region, availability, and intrinsic desirability. These foods often were not much prized or eaten when more favored foods were available, but they could be depended on in emergencies. The Seminole, for example, turned to elderberries (*Sambucus canadensis*), and the Comanche to acorns. In the Northwest, the Shoshone and

Paiute stored giant wild rye (*Leymus condensatus*) for times of famine.

Regional Specialties

Before contact, each region used local products and technologies in representative dishes. However, after the first encounters with Europeans, available foods and technologies changed, and the divisions of local cooking styles started to blur. European ingredients were added gradually, and modernizing technology replaced use of earlier hearths and pit ovens and other methods of cooking and preserving. The original balance between the numerous local wild and the few domesticated foods reversed, becoming more heavily oriented to commercial foods and limited choices that were available everywhere. In later times many tribes combined local precontact specialties and those of more recent origin. Regional distinctions are sometimes highlighted and sometimes tempered by the creative skills of gourmet chefs and cookbook authors. In the movement to strengthen a pan–Native American culture, some regional foods have been adopted by tribes everywhere. Regionalism continues to be a factor but is a smaller one. The following representative dishes suggest the character of each region.

The Southwest The cuisine of the Pueblo tribes, who have lived in the same place for more than one thousand years, maintained its culinary character longer than that of other regions. Pueblo cuisine remained close to the early Mexican culinary origins of the area—corn, particularly blue corn, beans, pumpkins, and squash. The use of Central American chilies and tomatoes, which were

Making Bread. Zuni woman making bread. From *In Field and Pasture*, a volume in Dutton's World at Work series, 1906. *Collection of Mark H. Zanger*

especially favored by the Navajo, was facilitated by the Spanish, who carried these products north. Corn dishes included stone-baked tortillas called "piki," the paper-thin blue corn bread of the Hopi and Zuni. Blue-corn breads leavened with juniper ash were baked in embers. Posoles—stews with hominy corn, meat, and chilis—were simmered in clay pots, as were various versions of sweet corn pulp, mush, and soup. Squash and pumpkin in various stages of ripeness were cooked similarly and added to composite dishes along with their blossoms. Beans were eaten boiled, mashed, and frequently in combination with corn; under the Spanish influence beans were flavored with pork. Products of wild cacti, among them the leaves, buds, roots, and fruit, were eaten seasonally. For example, the Mescalero Apache pit-baked great quantities of roots of the mescal century plant (genus *Agave*) and dried them for later use. Small desert game was sometimes available and and was roasted or used in soups and stews. Pumpkinseed oil, wild lamb's-quarter leaves (genus *Chenopodium*), and juniper berries were important flavorings, as were the many chilies used fresh, dried, roasted, and smoked. Although the cuisines of southwestern tribes were quite similar to one another, there were small differences. The Hopi and Zuni ate turkey, as appropriate for sedentary farmers, but the Navajo, perhaps because of their nomadic origins or as a way of distinguishing their culture, often did not. The early Spanish brought lamb, and the Navajo on the high desert became sheepherders. Their diet then included lamb and mutton that was roasted, broiled, or stewed, and posole-like stews contained larger amounts of meat than in the past. Earlier ash leavening was eventually replaced with baking powder and soda in cornbread.

Introduced wheat flour and yeast stimulated the baking of European-style oven breads. Kneel-down bread, so called because of the cook's position at the stone metate, was a mashed sweet-corn filling wrapped in corn husks and then baked in hot embers. This bread has evolved into one enriched with eggs and tomatoes and then baked in a conventional oven. Baked pumpkin is filled with piñon nuts and corn. Pueblo Indians (Hopi, Zuni, Acoma, and Tewa) make a wild sage bread shaped flat and round like Wampanoag bannock. These archetypal dishes are recognizable in later southwestern cooking but have been updated by breakfasts of Spam and potato wrapped in tortillas, the substitution (especially in tortillas) of wheat for corn, and a raft of sweet desserts that include bread pudding and the products of new orchard fruit.

THREE SISTERS AGRICULTURE

Three sisters agriculture was messy by English standards, but it was highly productive and efficient. Irregular hills were hoed up, some of them ten feet across, in which were planted corn (*Zea mays*), beans (genus *Phaseolus*), and pumpkins and squash (genus *Cucurbita*). This symbiotic system allowed each plant to thrive more than it would have alone, because each plant benefited the others. The corn stalks were poles on which the beans could climb for increased sunlight. The nitrogen-fixing beans absorbed nitrogen, a plant nutrient, from the air and released it into the soil around the roots. The squash and pumpkin vines spread out between the hills, shading the soil with their large leaves, keeping the moisture in and weeds out. The hills were tended rigorously through the first two or three hoeings, after which they required little work beyond careful guarding against marauding tribes and hungry birds and animals. At critical moments just before ripening and harvesting, family members guarded the crops day and night.

The East The vast East was chiefly characterized by a rich seasonal mixture of agriculture, hunting of large and small game, and foraging in woodlands and on the seacoasts, and therefore was favored with considerable variety. Much of the East was dominated by the Iroquois, who used the "three sisters" agriculture of corn, beans, and pumpkin as well as sunflowers and was a relatively settled culture. For example, various cornmeal preparations were cooked into cornbread, dumplings, soup, and porridge, which were enriched with beans, pumpkin, and wild fruit and nuts and then combined with large and small game in stew and soup. Southern tribes varied mainly in their addition of the few fruits, including pawpaw and persimmon, that grew in gentler climates. The tribes of coastal areas from Maine and Narragansett Bay to Chesapeake Bay originally were hunters and gatherers but developed numerous fish dishes, clambakes, and beach plum (*Prunus maritima*) flavoring in conjunction with introduced agriculture. The Wampanoags pride themselves on wheat-flour bannock. Corn soups have been modernized into chowders made with bacon, onions, green peppers, potatoes, butter, and milk. Maple syrup with cornmeal pancakes is a representative dish of the eastern peoples.

The Southeast Characterized by the corn, pumpkin, and bean tradition as well as hunting and fishing, the cuisine of the Southeast is distinctive because of the availability of warm-weather plants and ocean foods. It has a strong African American component (black-eyed peas, for example) from the days when southern tribes adopted escaped slaves. The Lumbee, one of the tribes to incorporate African Americans, integrated early and in many cases relocated to cities where their cooking expanded to include European-based cuisines. Lumbee cooking is likely to reflect this urbanization, as does that of a great many acculturated Indians, and features a combination of early and late elements: blueberry cake, Indian fry bread, sweet potato dishes, southern fried chicken, and pecan pie.

The Creek, Seminole, and Miccosukee are known for *sofkee*, a liquid version of hominy grits cooked into a beverage and enjoyed throughout the day. These Indians use the dried root of wild coontie (genus *Zamia*) to make bread flour and are famous for pumpkin bread, a sweet version of fry bread. Local stews incorporate the products of local fishing and hunting, among them alligator and octopus. Also typical are cabbage palm hearts, citrus fruit, guava products, and numerous uses of sweet potatoes.

The Prairie-Plains Corn, beans, and squash and an agricultural lifestyle predominated in much of the prairie. The Prairie-Plains Indians supplemented their crops with gathered and hunted wild foods. The strong early tradition of hunting large game (often buffalo and antelope on the plains) was curtailed when nineteenth-century Americans resettled and was augmented with domestic meats. In the Great Lakes region wild rice was the primary grain and was used (sometimes alongside corn) as a staple in breads, stews, and soups. The dishes often were prepared with fish or small game, including beaver, from this wet terrain and perhaps with eggs and bacon. Maple syrup was the common sweetener.

Contemporary cooking includes evolved dishes such as Potawatomi baked corn, an oven preparation of canned cream-style corn and whole-kernel corn, egg, butter, milk, sugar, and saltine crackers or sweet potato biscuits (of southern origin). Roasted pumpkin is stuffed with wild rice, dry mustard, rendered fat, venison, buffalo, or beef, onion, eggs, sage, and pepper. The Shuswap make bannock, a small, flat bread fried in a pan, with flour or cornmeal and assorted flavorings.

The plains were peopled by the large Sioux nation, originally sedentary farmers from the prairie. After contact and a series of displacements, the Sioux adopted the horse and became a nomadic buffalo and antelope culture. Meat in its many forms was a key component of the diet, but the tribes traded skins for corn, particularly with prairie peoples. Some Sioux undertook small gardens and continued their original cuisine, although with a change in balance among meat, vegetables, and grain.

Game meats were served roasted, broiled, stewed, simmered in soup, dried, and added to numerous dishes as flavoring. Fry bread, a postcontact addition, was an important meal component, as were "popovers," a stuffed variation of fry bread. Sioux plum cakes are flour and hazelnut cakes mixed with pureed plums and spices and then sweetened with maple syrup or honey. A long, complex procedure is needed to make *tinpsula*, a soup of dried turnips, dried corn, and dried buffalo or beef. *Wahuwapa wasna*, balls of toasted cornmeal, dried chokecherries or juneberries, tallow or lard, and sugar are shaped and fried. In newer versions, these corn balls are spread in frying pans, baked, and then cut into wedges. This dish exemplifies a fairly old recipe that is made with minimal modernization.

The Pacific Northwest and the Plateau The hunting and gathering cuisine of the Pacific Northwest and the Plateau was based on halibut, euchalon (a small, oily fish also called candlefish), herring, and other fish; acorns; numerous berries; camas and yellow pond lily roots; and tender buds of pine. The most important food in the Northwest, salmon, was fished and eaten year-round, although it was consumed in heavier concentrations during spawning time. Berries were also an abundant and basic component of the northwestern diet. Varieties included salal berries, (*Gaultheria shallon*), blueberries, soapberries (genus *Sapindus*), buffalo berries (genus *Shepherdia*), salmonberries (*Rupus spectafilis*), dewberries (genus *Rupus*), and saskatoons (genus *Amelanchier*). Camas root was a staple starch. *Yal*, a favorite dessert, was made by whipping soapberries into a frothy mixture; in later times the dish is sweetened with sugar. The late-eighteenth-century coastal trade brought potatoes, and they became another staple.

California California tribes were discovered early, but the relatively late arrival of Spanish missionaries from Mexico in 1779 began the catastrophic decimation of the tribes that continued with the influx of gold prospectors in 1848. Many Native Americans were lost to disease, conversion and assimilation, and newcomers' hunger for land. Relatively

---

SALMON

Salmon was the center of northern California and northwestern foodways. This fish figured in origin stories, spiritual rituals, and cultural identity. Air- or sun-dried salmon (and more recently smoked salmon) was pounded into a meal for storage, and the roe was sometimes fermented. Salmon meal was used in porridges, soups, and other dishes. All parts of the fish were used, particularly the flesh, cheeks, gut, and stomach. The fish was prepared in a number of ways: broiled, baked directly on embers or heated stones, spit-roasted over fire, pit-steamed with seaweed or thimbleberries, and simmered in stews and soups—and it was eaten raw. Seaweed of the genus *Porphyra* was rotted, fermented, and dried for use as an accompaniment to salmon at important events such as the feasts of the Kwakiutl. Salmon products were also important items for trade.

---

little remains of many of the original tribes of the coastal Southwest, although several small tribes have retained strong cultural identity. The precontact foodways of California locales were substantially different from one another and included coastal, inland plateau, and southern deserts. Fish and shellfish dominated the foodways of coastal hunting and gathering tribes. Foodways of the inland plateau and basin were characterized by plant gathering and, to a lesser degree, the hunting of large and small mammals, particularly rabbits, and water birds, all eaten in the usual variety of methods. Insects, trapped in "surrounds" (a method similar to that used to hunt plains buffalo) or smoked out of trees, were a major source of animal protein and often were roasted. Acorn-based breads and camas roots provided staple starches along with roots and seeds of wild cattail (in wetlands) and a grassy rice. Pine nuts were not only used as seasonings but were also ground into meal for cooking and baking. Rose hips were a common food. The cuisine of Southern California reflected coastal fishing, inland arid conditions, and Mexican influences. Desert cacti provided a number of important foods, among them nopal leaves (genus *Nopalea*), barrel cactus buds (genus *Ferocactus* and *Echinocactus*), and yucca flowers (genus *Opuntia*), that were often cooked over mesquite.

CRAFTING THE TOOLS

Throughout most early Indian culture, cooking equipment was crafted by part-time specialists, men and women. In communally oriented cultures, utensils were obtained from others in the community, often by informal barter. Individual cooks, hunters, gatherers, and farmers did not make all their own tools. Flint napping, the deliberate shaping of stone by controlled chipping, was often men's work. Pottery and basketry were often women's work. Full-time crafters lived primarily in the southern coastal areas, from the Chesapeake region to New Orleans, and then only in areas of dense population. Materials and designs were a factor of regional resources. Designs were eminently pragmatic, and exemplified the aesthetic of form follows function.

These dishes have survived alongside Mexican *atole* (a corn porridge or drink), which was brought from Mexico by early missionaries.

Technology

The dishes cooked and eaten by Native Americans resulted from regional resources—available foods, fuels, and materials for cooking utensils. They consequently varied to some degree, but shared basic forms and processes. The following discussion focuses on foodways at the point of contact and ensuing changes. Native American skills and their food-related artifacts began to change after European contact. Seventeenth-century stone knives, for example, were replaced with bartered iron knives, and clay pots were replaced with brass and copper kettles. Nineteenth-century cookstoves replaced hearth fires. Recipes evolved similarly. Indians in closest contact with newcomers changed faster. Those in remote and secluded areas or in large tribal communities maintained their early technologies longest. To keep old philosophies and foodways alive, some Native Americans, especially in the Southwest, continue to cook with fire in traditional pots. The dishes usually are prepared ritualistically on special occasions.

Cooking Technologies and Processes Native Americans mastered the technologies of a late Stone Age culture and were proficient in making implements of stone, clay, wood, shell, bone, and leather. They did not use iron, although they occasionally used copper, a softer and more malleable metal. Their cooking technologies and processes were simple and straightforward.

Fuels and Fires Fire making was the source of all cookery, and fires were made from the fuel at hand. Wood was chosen according to the heat produced, perhaps the flavor imparted by the smoke, and the dish. Wood gathering was a chore for women, who hauled dead and dried branches from their surroundings. Among some tribes (the Hidatsa, for example) dogs were harnessed to a travois, or hauling frame, and transported the collected branches and logs. Relatively small cooking fires and slow cooking were most common, whether in boiling pots or pit ovens. Among the tribes of the eastern woodlands, hardwoods such as oak, nut woods, and fruit woods produced moderate temperatures and long-lasting heat. Juniper and mesquite were favored in the Southwest. Large trunks were rarely felled or split, because stone axes were inadequate to the job. On the often-woodless plains, women collected "buffalo chips," or dry dung, which ignited fast, burned well (although quickly), and produced low to moderate heat. In some areas dried grass was burned. The plains offered cottonwood, which was used as fuel by the Kiowa.

STARTING A FIRE

Friction was the source of ignition, which was achieved with a bow drill. The user twirled a hardwood shaft, pressing it down against a thin, softwood platform. The resulting accumulations of fine sawdust were heated to the point of glowing. The resulting ember was placed in a "nest" of fine tinder—dried grass for the Prairie Indians and shaved oak for the California Costanoans—that was brought to ignition by blowing. After the first flame appeared, increasingly larger twigs and branches were added to the fire. Large trunks were rarely burned, because stone axes were inadequate for the job of cutting them up, but modest-sized branches were manageable. The introduced European method of fire making with flint and steel replaced bow drilling. To start a fire, the user produced sparks by striking the steel piece forcefully against the flint, which sometimes was made of the mineral chert. In the nineteenth century, Native Americans, along with most of the United States, adopted matches.

> They bake their Bread either in Cakes before the Fire, or in Loaves on a warm Hearth, covering the Loaf first with Leaves, then warm Ashes, and afterwards with Coals over all.
>
> —Robert Beverly, *The History and Present State of Virginia* (1705)

Permanent outdoor hearths were usually long, shallow depressions that frequently were lined with stone to absorb and reflect heat and keep the food clean. The hearth held one central fire or a series of small ones, each for a different preparation. Small tripod stones, sometimes permanently installed, held round-bottom clay pots above the heat. Wooden spits held meats at an angle over the heat. Some hearths were unlined, particularly those of the nomadic groups of the Colorado mountains or in temporary encampments. Hearths held enough ash and hot embers to broil meats and root vegetables directly on their surface or to roast them buried. Breads such as corn "cakes" were baked covered with live embers. After being roasted in embers, parched corn kernels (Algonquian *nokake*) were cleaned by sifting to remove the ash. The Paiute made dough of processed corn, acorns, and cattail seeds, kneaded and shaped the dough into flat cakes, and then roasted the cakes under hot coals. Surfaces were sometimes protected from ash with leaf wrappings but often were simply washed after baking.

Baking stones, flat slabs of smoothed stone placed in or near the hearth, were heated over small fires and used to bake flatbread (such as Hopi piki) or for roasting of acorns. Some tribes (the northwestern Chehali, for example) used baking stones to steam and soften their dried elderberries in winter. The California Pomo baked bolete mushrooms (genus *Boletus*) on stones. The stones were chosen for their shape and their density. Porous rocks such as shale and sandstone absorbed water and were more likely to burst in the heat. These issues were less critical in arid climates. Baking stones were important family possessions, often generations old, and were greased periodically for a nonstick finish.

Indoor hearths varied. In small one-family dwellings, such as the poled tepees of the Plains Crows, or the wood frame, domed, and bark-covered wigwams of the East, inclement weather drove the cooking indoors. A stone-ringed fire was situated in the center of the floor, the smoke escaping through one or more smoke holes in the roof. In the multiple-family dwellings of the Northwest and the longhouses of the Iroquois in the East, indoor hearths were situated at intervals on ground level down the central hall of the building. Cooking sites in temporary encampments were simplified versions of those in permanent sites; for example, rock linings were used less frequently. In the case of seasonal encampments, such as those for annual maple sugaring, hunting, and fishing, year-to-year permanence was maintained, because hearths and specialized tools were used repeatedly.

Pit Ovens and Steaming   Pit ovens were adjuncts to the hearth and were used extensively. Fairly large pits could service a group event; a small pit served one family. Small cooking pits were valuable to those traveling unencumbered by heavy or breakable pots. Some pit ovens were dug into clay-rich soil that underwent a kind of firing during the cooking, thereby sealing in flavor and moisture. Pits sometimes outnumbered hearths. Pits were used for steaming shellfish in permanent coastal Massachusetts sites.

Pit cooking was a low-temperature, slow-cooking, steaming process, sometimes requiring a full twelve hours, usually overnight. This method was ideal for special

---

PIT OVENS

The simplest pit ovens were modest holes into which food and heated stones were placed. More elaborate permanent pit ovens were lined with stone, sometimes several layers thick, and were capacious enough to accommodate a substantial bed of coals at the bottom, the food (often wrapped or layered in special leaves chosen for their toughness, fragrance, and moisture content), and a topping of more coals. Sometimes the entire pit was sealed with additional layers of leaves and soil to keep in the steam. In pits without stone linings, layers of leaves were used around the walls. The choice of leaves depended on availability—for example, in coastal areas seaweed was favored, and inland the Apache chose sweet and sturdy grasses, among them spike muhly (*Muhlenbergia wrightii*). Leaf-wrapped foods were protected against dirt, ash, and water.

festival food and allowed travelers substantial morning meals without drawing on travel time. The gentle, moist heat worked well for vegetables, which were sometimes cooked in combination with game or fish. Traditional recipes expanded after contact to include meat from domesticated animals (chicken and pork) and imported root vegetables. The Wampanoag clambakes in coastal Massachusetts still use traditional clams, lobster, and corn as well as introduced sausage, onions, and potatoes. Similar evolutions are found at Rhode Island clambakes and with southern pit-roasted barbecue.

Cooking Implements

Wood, Basketry, and Gourds Wooden cooking and eating implements were common everywhere. Native Americans used shaped dishes, bowls, platters, spoons, dippers and ladles, stirrers, spits and skewers, and cooking and drying racks. After contact, tin sometimes replaced some wooden tools and became common in reservation life. The kind of wood used depended on local availability. Sometimes the choice was made on the basis of imparted flavor—pine and juniper in the Southwest, oak and maple in the North, and cedar in the Northwest. The densest woods were difficult to carve, the hardest being the knot or burl formations of a tree, but they produced stronger and longer-lasting implements. Bowls and platters were shaped and sized according to use. The original shaping tools— beaver teeth, clam shells, and stone—were replaced with iron blades soon after contact with European settlers.

BASKETRY

Indian basketry influenced that of many newcomers, among them the Germans of the Mid-Atlantic region, the Shakers of the Northeast, and British of the Appalachians. In addition, the Native Americans learned from the work of newcomers such as African Americans in the Southeast. The adoption of new foods inspired new styles of food baskets; for example, cheese baskets, required by the new dairying, were adaptations of sifters but had an extremely open weave for draining. By the late nineteenth century some sifters had been replaced with purchased sieves of horsehair or wire mesh. Basketry continues to be a well-developed art form, has continued to represent Native American culture, and is being practiced by regional specialists.

CLAY COOKING POTS

Clay cooking pots and containers were constructed and fired by hand. In many cases they were handsome, thin walled, symmetrical, and decorated regionally, characteristically painted in the Southwest and inscribed in the East. The pots were invariably shaped with round or rounded-point bottoms, sometimes set into loose soil and ringed with fire, and sometimes propped and leveled over the fire with small easel stones. Pots with projecting ears and flaring rims were wrapped with cordage and suspended over the heat. Clay pots were made in all sizes. Some held more than twenty gallons and were used for boiling quantities of festival dishes, for reducing tree sap into syrup, and for storage. Clay pots were often admired by Europeans and were considered as well-formed and handsome as any being thrown on European potters' wheels of thze time

---

Bark was used to make bowls, the popular sources being hickory, elm, pine, basswood, and buttonwood. For example, the Iroquois made large bread-making bowls of elm bark that was cut in warm weather while supple and bent into shape. The rim was strengthened with lashed hickory strips. Pine and birch bark were folded into shape and the ends tied.

Basketry, important everywhere, was one of the few crafts practiced by both men and women with great regional variation. Baskets were inventively designed for special functions. In the Eastern Woodlands, splits— narrow strips of hardwood or river cane—were woven into sturdy pack baskets, wood-gathering baskets, or bottle-shaped fish traps. The openwork tops of hominy baskets allowed loosened hulls to float away. Sifters were open-weave, flat-bottomed trays of oak or hickory splits used for ash, flour, or popcorn.

In clayless or treeless regions such as the Pacific Northwest, California, and the Great Basin, basketry was the equivalent of much pottery. Complex, finely and tightly made waterproof baskets of twined and coiled grasses, hazel shoots, or conifer roots were used for stone-boiling staple dishes such as acorn mush. Other baskets served largely nomadic cultures as carrying, gathering, and storage containers, trays, water jars, seed beaters, winnowing trays, bottles, and bowls. Nomadic groups of Plains and Plateau Indians used hemp and husks to make soft, collapsible baskets that traveled and stored well. Other baskets were constructed of folded sheets of bark that were pinched and tied at the ends and sometimes sealed with pitch.

In addition to these crafted utensils and containers, Native Americans also grew several varieties of gourds (family Cucurbitaceae) to be used as bowls, spoons, and dippers. Once grown and dried, they required relatively little preparation for use, as the outer shell was thick and hard, there was no pulp to speak of, and only the seeds and a little fibrous matter needed removing. Some were rubbed with preserving fats.

Pottery and Boiling Equipment Boiling and simmering were extremely common forms of cooking. Clay pots were used by sedentary and agriculture-centered tribes in areas that had good-quality clay deposits (particularly the East and Southwest). In addition to clay, a number of soft containers were used for boiling. Cooking pots of watertight baskets, leather bags, large animal bladders and stomachs, and baskets were used for a heating method called "stone-boiling." The receptacle was supported in a shallow hole near the fire, and water and food were placed within. Springy wooden tongs were used to add a succession of small, hot stones to the pot and to remove them as their heat dissipated. Stone-boiling was common everywhere; it was efficient and easily controlled and was the chief form of boiling (in wood and basket containers) among western coastal tribes. In another boiling technique, foods were wrapped in leaves to preserve their shape and to prevent their disintegration in water. Southwestern tamales, for example, were wrapped in corn husks and tied before boiling. The Cherokee used green corn leaves and husks or dried hickory leaves to wrap a mixture of corn dough and pounded nuts. After contact, many clay pots were discarded, supplemented, or replaced by iron and brass trade kettles, which had clear advantages of durability and improved heat transmission but did not change basic preparations.

Broiling, Roasting, and Drying Equipment Meat and fish were commonly roasted or broiled on sticks propped over a fire. Branches of springy wood, often hickory, were split part way and tied around flattened twig-supported food. The pointed end of the stick, secured in the ground at an angle, held the food end over the heat. This combination of smoking and broiling achieved moist and flavorful results. Sometimes pieces of

> The Indians killed a bear and two does that day. . . . They brought the meat of all to the camp that evening, and some of them was busily engaged in cutting the meat off the bones and drying it on a little rod or stick over the fire to make what the Indians call Jerk—dried meat to carry with them. . . . One of the . . . Indians . . . attended . . . continually throughout the night to drying their meat, making Jerk of it so as to carry it with them.
>
> —Peter Henry, *Accounts of His Captivity and Other Events* (1780)

meat or whole fish were skewered onto slender sticks and positioned the same way. Broiling and roasting racks were constructed of forked legs and lashed sticks and required that the meat be turned regularly. Wooden drying racks held meat strips (jerky) and fish for drying, sometimes in the smoke of special wood.

Pounding and Grinding Equipment

In the eastern areas where wood abounded, hardwood tree trunks, sometimes still rooted in the ground, were hollowed out by alternating charring and scraping. Corn was pounded in these giant mortars with long, heavy, and often dumbbell-shaped wooden pestles. When possible, the pestle was hung from the springy branch of a nearby aspen or hickory, saving considerable labor.

In the Southwest, corn and acorn flours were ground with *metates y manos*, traylike grinding stones with rolling crushers sometimes in a series with different degrees of coarseness. A stone surface was universally used for grinding. These tools sometimes were shaped from rocks into shallow bowls or slightly scooped surfaces. Handheld pounders, or mullers, were smoothed pieces of stone that fitted the hand comfortably. Celts were common stone pounding tools. These handheld pieces often were blunt on one end for pounding and had a thin scraping edge on the other end. Some had grooved finger ridges for greater control. Celts had to be made of nonbrittle material, such as metamorphic rock like basalt or granite in the East and limestone and sedimentary sandstone in the Southwest. Early grinding and pounding implements were eventually replaced by commercial milling and small home grinders, although some continue to be used for ritual or ceremonial events.

Grinding and pounding apparatuses were made in different sizes, according to the need for transportation and the kind of food being processed. Hard, dry corn and acorns required large containers. Small amounts of seed, dried leaf, and ash seasonings were easily managed in smaller sizes, which had the additional advantage of portability. Many dried foods were pounded, among them pumpkin and sunflower seeds, meats, and nuts.

Cutting Tools and Stone Working

Knives and hunting points (arrowheads and spearheads) were flaked or flint-knapped from jasper, fine-grained chert, flint, obsidian, and quartzite. These brittle stones formed long-lasting and extremely sharp edges. The best stones were mined from deposits in specific localities, were shaped, and were traded over long distances.

Softer stone had other uses. Steatite, or soapstone, was commonly used for thin pots and containers and sometimes for flat baking stones. It was easily shaped and conducted heat fairly evenly. As steatite deposits were localized, particularly in Vermont and Virginia, it was one of the desirable trade stones.

Animal Material Implements Many small tools were made from animal material. Bone husking pins, which were thin, curved, awl-like tools, were used in every agricultural region to pry hard corn kernels from the cob. Bone skewers and fishhooks were also used for this purpose. Deer jaws, their imbedded grinding teeth intact, worked admirably for scraping juicy corn from the cob. Deer ribs were used to scrape the edible cambium layers from flavorful trees. Turtle shells made platters, and large clam shells made hoes, spoons, or ladles. Beaver teeth had good cutting edges. Meat sinews provided lashing for bows and arrows, and the shoulder blades of deer made workable digging tools. Skins made stone-boiling receptacles, storage containers, and traveling food pouches.

Preserving and Seasoning

Subsistence required preservation of seasonal foods. Most foods were dried with equipment that allowed free air flow. Some foods were dried with the direct heat of the sun or small fires; for other foods, the wind sufficed. Among the Iroquois, ripe corn ears were braided by their husks into long strings and hung indoors to finish drying. Shelling of kernels for storage was accomplished with strong bone or wood husking pins. Meat and fish were processed in strips for drying; small fish were split open and dried flat. Small fruits such as berries were dried on bark trays, open mats of rush or grass, and baskets. The mats were sometimes propped over low fires to keep flies away. Fruits were often mashed raw or stone-boiled, shaped into small cakes, and then sun-dried for storage. At the time of use, the fruits were soaked and then boiled into sauces. Whole fruits with waxy skin, such as blueberries, huckleberries, cranberries, grapes, and cherries, were sometimes blanched first to hasten drying. Larger fruits such as peaches and plums were opened for pitting and drying. Some tribes cooked elderberries and wrapped them in skunk cabbage leaves for winter. Vegetables were handled in much the same way as fruit. In many cases they were cut into strips or rings for drying. Wild turnips were scraped and dried, and leafy plants were dried without special preparation.

Storage Food storage was determined regionally. Most tribes used underground caches or protected shelters. In the Northeast these storage areas may have been as deep as six feet. The sides and bottom of these pits were usually lined, sometimes with stone or bark and often with fragrant, durable grasses. Sometimes the food being stored was paired with compatible vegetation; for example, the Iroquois used sumac leaves with squashes and hemlock

With so much of the year's food preserved for lean times, it was essential to use large storage containers, among them large pottery jars, wooden bowls, baskets, and gourds. The Pomo used large coiled baskets for storing dried blueberries, and the Cree kept cranberries in pitch-sealed birch bark. The Menominee kept wild rice in containers made from the outer layers of birch or woven from the inner bark of cedar. Eastern Algonquians made grass sacks for corn. Hunting societies used animal products for their containers. The Apache stored dried, pounded acorn and meat mixtures in skins; the Paiute used buckskin bags to hang dried elderberries; and the Menominee stored wild rice in muskrat skins, fawn skins, and raccoon sacks. In some cases animal bladders were inflated and hung over a fire to harden into bottle-shaped containers.

branches with corn. Pits were roofed and made watertight and then disguised with coverings of soil or brush. In many ways similar to European root cellars, storage areas after contact were occasionally made of wooden planks and straw. Northern tribes sometimes took advantage of cold and perhaps freezing streams: the Makah submerged alder-bark cones containing elderberry clusters into cold creeks. Indoor granaries served short-term needs. In the Northeast, granaries tended to be large, chestlike constructions of elm or birch bark that may have held sixty bushels of shelled corn. The granaries of the Luiseño held acorns. Outdoor above-ground corn cribs for drying and storing ears of corn were built by the Iroquois.

Early traditions gave way to nineteenth-century home canning and twentieth-century freezing. Like others in America, Indians put up their vegetables in glass canning jars and used the preserving qualities of sugar to make fruit syrup, preserves, jams, jellies, conserves, and marmalades. After the early introduction of pigs and the European techniques of salt curing and smoking, Native Americans sometimes added salt and black pepper to cure game and fish. In the Southwest, adobo, a blend of chilies, was used for this purpose.

Uses of Ash   Ash, the residue of burned wood and vegetation, had many uses. In addition to its function in ash baking, perhaps most important was the production of hominy. The alkali composition of ash acted on corn to "lime" or soften it. Hard flint corn did not release its hulls easily but when boiled or soaked with ash (or ash water, better known as lye), the hulls slipped off easily. The lye was then removed by several washings, and the hominy corn was ready for cooking, pounding, or grinding.

The kind of wood ash chosen varied from tribe to tribe, according to local flora. The Navajo liked juniper, and the Creek and Seminole used hickory. The Hopi preferred ash made from green plants, because they were more alkaline, saltbush (*Atriplex canescens*), and chamisa or rabbitbrush (*Chrysothamnus nauseosus*), which had a high mineral content. The Pawnee, Omaha, Ponca, and Winnebago used basswood (genus *Tilia*) ash in the same way, but with the purpose of leaching out the bitterness of certain acorns.

Sometimes ash was used to control color. Chamisa ash intensified the blue in blue corn products and functioned like litmus paper by indicating acid (red) and alkali (blue). Ash sometimes was used as cornbread leavening. The Tewa used chamisa, and the Hopi used the combined ash of bean vines, dried, empty bean pods, and

> [The tribes in his area] have no Salt among them, but for seasoning use the Ashes of Hiccory, Stickweed, or some other Wood or Plant, affording a Salt ash.
>
> —Robert Beverley, *The History and Present State of Virginia* (1705)

corn cobs. These methods predated the eighteenth-century European-American use of pearl ash, an early form of baking soda, but could not have produced substantial lightness without the gluten found in wheat.

Seasonings   Native Americans had access to numerous flavorings, and it is likely that their food was not dull. Most flavorings were vegetative and specific to one part of the plant. Examples include the berries of juniper and red sumac (lemonlike), the root and bark of sassafras and birch, the roots of wild ginger, the leaves of alliums, the flowers of Oswego tea, the fruiting bodies of chilies, and the seeds of roasted pumpkin. Nuts also were a major source of flavoring. Nuts were used as they came from the shell or were roasted, pounded, or boiled into nut milk and oil. The Iroquois fancied acorn nutmeats boiled and ground or nut oil mixed into cornbread and pudding.

Rendered animal fat was a prime source of flavoring and was commonly used with fruits, vegetables, and grain preparations. For example, the Chippewa seasoned boiled blueberries with moose fat and deer tallow. The ashes of particular trees and leaves also were used to influence flavor. The Huron sometimes used pieces of cinders to season sagamite (a kind of gruel made of cornmeal) and the ash of basswood to sweeten acorns.

Sweetness was prized but was not a dominating force in precontact cuisine. Sugar cane and sugar making were unknown to indigenous Americans, who sweetened their foods with ripe fruits and berries widely collected and dried for that purpose. *Staninca*, the Osage "cake," was sweetened with ripe persimmon. Tree sap syrup of maple or hickory also provided sweetening, sometimes in large quantities, as did a few sweet blossoms, such as elderberry. Among northern sugaring tribes, small quantities of maple syrup were used instead of salt to intensify flavor. In some cases a starchy food, often corn or roots, was chewed and used as a source of sweetening, the starch having been converted to sugar by the salivary enzyme amylase. Wild bees existed in the precontact New World but were not strong honey producers. Sweetening played a larger role after the arrival of Europeans. Maple sugar technology improved, sugar became a trade item, and imported honey-producing bees spread through most regions. With increasing exposure to European-American cuisines and decreasing costs in the late nineteenth century, Native Americans (like everyone else) embarked on the sugar-heavy pursuit of pies, cakes, cookies, candies, and beverages and began sweetening preserved fruits.

Sugaring Both hard and soft maple syrups as well as walnut and hickory syrups were prepared annually in late winter when the tree sap began to run. Native Americans tapped the trees, collected sap, and then boiled the sap down into a mildly concentrated syrup. The boiling pots were of clay, animal skins, or sealed bark, and the cooking often was accomplished by the hot stone method. The resulting syrup was stored in bark containers that were sealed and waterproofed with pitch. It is unlikely that a full year's supply was produced, considering the precontact technology. Northern tribes often used the occasion of syrup-making to socialize and probably consumed a fair amount of the product on site. After contact, Native Americans took advantage of iron pots and European familiarity with cane sugar production to crystalize syrup into sugar, making transportation and storage far simpler and production higher.

Salt Agricultural and hunting lifestyles determined which tribes ate salt. Meat contains more salt than vegetables do, and those who ate meat (Plains Indians, for example) or saltwater fish (coastal tribes everywhere) consumed enough salt to satisfy bodily needs. Peoples who subsisted largely on vegetation did not ingest enough salt, and therefore it was added to cooked foods by inland tribes of California, the Great Basin, the Southwest, and some parts

---

SALT

Salt was obtained by different methods. In the Southeast, peoples on the coast evaporated salt water and traded the surplus to peoples some distance away. In the Great Basin, most salt was gathered from dry surfaces and salt lake-bed deposits. Indians of California gathered their salt from the eastern slopes of the Sierras, where it was plentiful. Inland salt licks (surface deposits) were scraped, and the water of natural salt springs was boiled and evaporated to produce crystalline salt.

---

of the Prairies. Salt was sometimes obtained by use of special plants. The southwestern saltbush and eastern coltsfoot (*Tussilago farfara*) were used in pit ovens to flavor steaming corn, as winter fodder for sheep, in puddings, and as a general seasoning for meat and vegetables.

Salt was an important trade article in the Southwest and California. Native Americans of the Southeast traded widely, first with Hernando De Soto during his sixteenth-century explorations and later with European settlements on the Mississippi River. In the East, the Onondagas' abundant deposits of fine salt figured in their terms in the treaty of 1786, which required that Anglo-Americans be provided with five thousand pounds of salt yearly.

Fermenting Fermentation was used, but only rarely to make beverages. More likely, fermented liquids were used as a necessary intermediate step in the production of something else. For example, eastern tribes made vinegar, an important flavoring and tenderizing aid, by fermenting maple sap. The Ojibwa cooked meat in combinations of fermented and sweet saps to produce a sweet and sour effect. One version of a Seminole soup is made with fermented *sofkee* (corn porridge). Certain foods were buried for storage, sometimes for long periods, during which time they fermented. This method was used by the Huron to cache wet corn, by the Sioux to process wild rice in water, and by Indians of the Northwest to preserve salmon roe. The goal appears to have been a combination of preservation and desirable flavor. Although early European visitors rarely found them attractive, these foods were used with great pleasure by Indians.

Techniques Used after Contact

Modern Native American traditions include foods that were not related to precontact patterns, were instituted after contact, and represent Indian readiness to take advantage of the changing world. These foodways did not completely overshadow earlier traditions; the two often blended.

Deep-Frying and Fry Bread There is little evidence that Native Americans used deep-frying before contact. Available fuels and low-temperature pottery materials could not support intense cooking fires, and the technique was at odds with a worldview that valued restraint. There was an insufficient supply of oil, considering Native Americans experienced regular depletions of fat in the diet. Shallow frying (sautéing) in small amounts of fat was possible, but even so, cooking preferences favored

FRY BREAD

Fry bread, the most important of the foods of the pan-Indian movement and the symbol of intertribal unity, does not represent precontact indigenous foods or cooking style. The origins of this dish are apparently in the nineteenth century and reflect the ongoing cultural change that happens everywhere. Fry bread usually is made with a dough of wheat flour and milk or water. The dough is leavened with yeast or baking powder, kneaded, flattened into individual patties of varying sizes, and then deep fried. Fry bread is served with a variety of accompaniments, such as honey, maple syrup, and sugar, and sometimes is wrapped around a hot dogs or other filling in place of a bun or tortilla. The Lakota today sometimes eat fry bread topped with pureed and sweetened fruit pudding. In a variation, popovers (stuffed fry bread) are made by piling raw bread dough with a mixture of cooked beef, chili, onion, tomato sauce, and taco seasoning and then folding and deep frying the result. This dish sometimes is likened to tacos. Whatever the combinations, fry bread has a central role at powwows.

Some historians believe that fry bread originated as a result of Navajo incarceration in Fort Sumner, where the Indians had access only to flour and lard. Others see a connection to Spanish deep-fried churros and sopaipillas, which are flat, lard-fried, breadlike

treats often served with sugar. According to another theory, the Plains Indians were among the first to make fry bread, having been influenced in the early nineteenth century by the French, who were particularly noted for their fine yeast-leavened breads and who, more importantly, maintained influence and contact with tribes throughout the Mississippi area from Canada to Louisiana. Still another claim is that fry bread resulted from the creative efforts of inventive reservation women faced with government rations.

NAVAJO FRY BREAD

Fry bread is made with small variations from kitchen to kitchen. Here is one version.

2 cups flour

1 tablespoon baking powder

½ teaspoon salt, or to taste

Warm water

Vegetable oil for frying

Mix dry ingredients. Add water gradually, stirring as you go, until the dough is no longer sticky but still quite soft and workable. Knead for 5 minutes. Cover and let rest.

Divide dough into eight portions. Shape each portion into a ball and pat or roll until one-half inch thick. Toss between hands to stretch into a circle 8 inches or more in diameter. Poke a hole in the center.

low-temperature cookery. Vegetables and fruits were most often boiled gently or steamed before the addition of fat or oil, which appear to have been used more as flavoring agents than as cooking media.

Contact brought new pots, ingredients, fuels, and processes. European metal frying pans allowed increased cooking temperatures, and pigs, cattle, and sheep added to fat supplies. Nineteenth-century commercial products (lard, cottonseed oil, Cottolene, and Crisco), wheat, milk, and yeast were the ingredients, and fry bread became popular. By the middle to late nineteenth century, a time of changing cookstoves and dietary patterns, fry bread had been adopted by relocated tribes and became a reservation staple. Today it is used by most tribes to represent Native American culture and tradition and is eaten regularly in many traditional homes. Some forms are called "bannock."

Oven Baking Oven-baked foods, as distinguished from ash-baked "breads," stone-baked flatbreads, and boiled dumplings, became traditional comparatively recently. Baking, in the modern sense of the word, did not exist in precontact America—there is no archaeological evidence of ovens. The enclosures that resembled ovens—pit ovens—were steaming chambers and did not produce the crisp texture and intense flavor associated with baking. Sixteenth-century Spanish explorers brought *hornos* (Spanish for "ovens") to the Southwest along with the concept of baking yeast-leavened wheat bread. The tribes of this region built large adobe ovens outdoors and small ones indoors to bake the new breads and to dry foods such as chilies.

A number of factors brought baking to Native American kitchens. In the late nineteenth century the cast-iron cookstove and reservation instruction were critical, as was the decreasing cost of ingredients. In addition, the emerging publishing industry disseminated fashionable American recipes nationwide. Pies, cakes, cookies, wheat-thickened and sweetened puddings, and raised wheat breads were added to daily meals. Gas and electric ovens were used where energy was available. The pots and cooking techniques of precontact and early contact years are no longer the center of Native American cookery, as Indians have modernized like everyone else. However, they are not entirely gone and are used to strengthen cultural identity at traditional ceremonial feasts.

Food Plants

Since ancient times America's greatest culinary strength has been its abundance of edible plants growing naturally according to regional conditions. Domesticated animals were rare (only the dog and the turkey in North America), and wild fish and animals were secondary apart from hunting and fishing centers such as the Plains and the West Coast. Knowledge of wild plants was extensive. It has been estimated that each tribe knew about and used more than one hundred species. The vast reaches of North America held numerous varieties of plants and trees, each with distinct culinary assets. Some plants grew only in specific locations and under limited conditions, exemplified by the century plant (genus *Agave*) of the southwestern dessert and wild rice (*Zizania aquatica*) of northern prairie waterways. Other plants, such as shadbush and serviceberry, Juneberry, or saskatoon as they are variously known (genus *Amelanchier*), were adaptable. The many regional varieties produced sweet fruit cross country, north to south.

Most native plants were gathered from the wild. Others were cultivated—that is, moved from wild areas to home gardens and improved by careful seed selection. Cultivated plants include the ubiquitous tuberous Jerusalem artichoke (*Helianthus tuberosus*), amaranth (genus *Amaranthus*), and a variety of related seed-bearing sunflowers (genus *Helianthus*). Other plants were available only through agriculture, being produced and sustained by human intervention and millennia-long and perhaps inadvert hybridization. These included corn, certain beans, and the cucurbits—pumpkins and squash. The following association of plants with native tribes is not intended to be complete, but rather to offer examples of their usage, and were selected for familiarity and common applications.

FORAGING

Understanding, identifying, gathering, and foraging for plants have been one of the earliest human means of obtaining nourishment. The legendary skills of foragers included their excellent memories and substantial knowledge of extraordinary numbers of plants—where to find them and when to gather the desired roots, shoots, stems, bark, leaves, fruit, and seeds. It was necessary to differentiate safe plants and those that were poisonous at particular seasons or that had one or two poisonous structures. Many plants were treated in specific ways to remove poisonous elements or undue bitterness to make them palatable and entirely safe. Tribal lore regarding edibility sometimes differed. For example, among the Hesquiat of the Pacific Northwest, elderberries (*Sambucus canadensis*) were always cooked and were considered potentially poisonous when eaten raw. The Dakota, on the other hand, commonly ate the same species of elderberries fresh. It is likely that regional strains may have been different.

Wild Foods and Foraging Indigenous women, like those of most ancient cultures, were the traditional foragers and the repositories of essential information. They knew hundreds of plants as well as their locations and seasons. The women knew how to identify, cook, and preserve quantities of gathered material for immediate use or storage. Skills were transmitted orally by older women to girls. This work, like much food-related work, required strong bodies for walking long distances while carrying substantial loads. The women often used specially designed backpack baskets supported securely with head straps and foraged in groups. Some nonfood plant material was used tangentially. Wood ash of specific trees provided alkali for softening the tough hulls of hominy corn and for maintaining color. Some leaves were durable and flavorful and were used as protective wrappings for foods cooked in embers or as lining for cooking pits.

Basic Wild Plants Native Americans used the nutritious, sometimes delicious, bounty from the environment. Some foods required little preparation, others were more labor-intensive.

Staple Grains and Starches Apart from domesticated corn, staple grains and starches were gathered from the wild and in some cases were cultivated. Acorns (genus *Quercus*) were used universally but in greatest concentration among the western tribes, especially those of the hunter-gathering cultures of the Northwest, for whom they were staples. America's sixty-nine native oak varieties produced acorns of different qualities. Acorns of the white oak (*Quercus alba*) were sweet, flavorful, and highly prized as an important staple starch. Other acorns, such as those of the northern red oak (*Quercus rubra*), contained large amounts of bitter tannic acid. The Paiute, Winnebago, Dakota, and Apache, among others, removed this acid by treating the acorns with basswood or hardwood ash, rinsing them, or cooking them in repeated changes of water. Some tribes leached or "ripened" acorns by storing them in mud. Some acorns, such as those of the interior live oak (*Quercus wisilzeni*), were considered inferior.

Many tribes used acorns as broadly as corn was used in the East. Acorns were a key ingredient in the same kinds of dishes as corn. For example, Potawatomi acorn porridge was called "samp," the same term used for eastern corn and bean porridge. Acorns were used in a full range of dishes, among them mush and porridge, bread and cakes, soups, and hot beverages. Acorns also were used as enrichments to bread and accompaniment to deer meat. They were boiled as vegetables or roasted whole, and acorn oil was valued as flavoring. The Iroquois used raw acorns as special foods for babies and young children. Acorns were widely preserved and stored for year-round use, whole or as flour. Other nuts, particularly the American chestnut of the East (*Castanea dentata*) and the

---

ACORNS

Certain plants were sometimes held in different levels of esteem from area to area. The Cahuilla of California and the Iroquois of the Northeast considered acorns delicacies and feast fare. For the Miwok and Pomo of the Northwest, acorns were staples used in a variety of preparations. The Comanche believed some local acorns were edible only in times of starvation. The Luiseño of California made distinctions between the California black oak (*Quercus kelloggii*) and the Engelmann oak (*Quercus engelmannii*), staples they ate year-round and stored in granaries for winter use. The Luiseño chose acorns of the California scrub oak (*Quercus dumosa*) only when more desirable varieties were in short supply.

---

pine nut of the Southwest (genus *Pinus*), were used as staple starches in a similar way.

Seeds, another source of staple starches, were pounded into flour or boiled whole. In the Southwest amaranth seeds were favored by the Navajo, Papago, and Yuma. In the northern and eastern regions lamb's-quarter and pigweed (genus *Chenopodia*) were used. The seeds of cattails (*Typha latifolia*) as well as their pollen and roots were used fresh or dried throughout America by tribes such as the Lakota, Yuma, and Cherokee. Wild rice (*Zinzania acquatica*, botanically considered a seed) was the chief starch of the Winnebago. Harvested in canoes and later in flat-bottomed boats, this tall marsh plant was pulled over the boats and beaten to release the seeds.

Roots and tubers, such as groundnuts (*Apios americana*), camas root, and cattail roots were important staples. Gathered with a digging stick, these foods were eaten at different seasons in different ways. For example, groundnuts (called "wild potato" by the Potawatomi), which grew throughout the eastern and northern regions, were harvested in the spring and eaten raw or lightly roasted (sometimes with maple sugar). In the fall, however, groundnuts were dried and pounded into flour for winter use. The roots of King Solomon seal (*Polygonatum biflorum*) were dried, beaten into flour, and then baked into bread by the Cherokee. Among the many families of root vegetables, Liliaceae includes onions, asparagus, camas lilies, sorrel (genus *Oxalis*), yampah (genus *Perideridia*), and wild turnips (*Pediomelum esculentum* and others).

Wild Fruits and Berries   Fruits were among the most important wild foods throughout America. Highly seasonal, they were dried and stored for year-round use and then served as an important source of flavor, sugar, and vitamins. Fruit generally was eaten raw in season and incorporated into beverages, soups, dumplings, and sauces. Preserved fruit, often dried, was used in winter. Fruit was often stewed briefly, mashed, formed into small cakes, and then dried in the sun to be reconstituted by stewing in water. Some fruits, particularly less juicy tree fruits such as black cherries (*Prunus serotina*), were sun- or fire-dried by many tribes, including the Iroquois. Fruits with larger seeds were pitted before drying, for example, the early Spanish peach (*Prunus persica*), which was adapted to local climates by the Lakota, Navajo, and Hopi. Chokecherries were widely used small

FROM ROOT TO BLOSSOM

Native Americans found culinary uses for every plant structure.

Seeds were used as starches, as a source of oil, and as flavoring. Wild tepary bean (*Phaseolus acutifolius*) seeds were a basic starch. Leaves from widely different plant forms were used everywhere. In the Southwest the Havasupai used the leafy greens of southwestern purslane (genus *Portulaca*), lamb's-quarters (genus *Chenopodium*) and poverty weed (genus *Monolepsis*), and evergreen needles such as piñon needles (*Pinus monophylla*) for flavoring pit-roasted meats. The Cahuilla boiled the fleshy pads of cactus leaves (*Opuntia basilaris*).

Shoots and stems of young pokeweed (*Phytolacca americana*) were enjoyed steamed or boiled by the Iroquois and Cherokee, and those of cattails (*Typha latifolia*) were eaten raw by the Apache.

Buds and blossoms were consumed in a variety of ways. Milkweed buds (*Asclepias speciosa*) were simmered into soup by the Apache. Elderberry flowers (*Sambucus canadensis*) were used in drinks by the Dakota. Blueberry blossoms (*Vaccinium myrtilloides*) were eaten fresh by the Iroquois.

The pods of the honey locust (*Gleditsia triacanthos*) were used in drinks by the Cherokee, and the pods of unripe beans were eaten by all agriculturists.

Assorted roots and tubers often were important staple starches. Camas roots (genus *Camassia*) were basic elements of northern and northwestern diets. Groundnuts (*Apios americana*) were favored in eastern and prairie areas. Lotus roots (*Nelumbo lutea*) were consumed in the northern prairies and plains, and cattail roots were eaten almost universally wherever they grew. Desert roots were so important in the Southwest that some tribes were named for the ones they used, among them the Mescalero and the Jicarilla Apache.

The sap and juice of maple, walnut, hickory, and other hardwood trees as well as those from young cornstalks were used as sweeteners.

---

cherries. Although they are very tart, chokecherries sometimes were eaten raw. More often, they were dried and stored in cakes and then used later in sauces or jerky. Chokecherries figure in rituals such as the Navajo Mountain Way Ceremony. Fruiting bodies such as rose hips (genus *Rosa*) were eaten raw, cooked, and dried throughout America by tribes such as the Montana, Lakota, Chippewa, Pomo, and Cherokee. Ground cherries and husk tomatoes (genus *Physalis*) were common in the Southeast and Southwest.

Many trees provided fruit, often of superior quality. These trees included serviceberry or Juneberry, dogwood (genus *Cornus*), plums, cherries, pawpaws (genus *Asimina*), persimmons (genus *Diospyros*), and mulberries (genus *Morus*). Apples (genus *Malus*) were small, of the crabapple type, and were used relatively infrequently. Peaches (genus *Prunus*), often thought by Europeans to be native, were actually established by the Spanish long before permanent settlements in the Southwest and were acclimatized to local conditions. Grapes (family Vitaceae) grew in several varieties in many regions of northern America. Some varieties were considered superior to those in England. Grapes were often used for juice, eaten raw, and dried for winter use.

Berries were eaten everywhere, often in large quantities, and their numbers were legion. Berries were used raw and for juices, were ingredients in soups and sauces, and when dried were an important component of travel food. According to early visitors, America's eastern strawberries (genus *Fragraria*) were far superior to the European *fraise de bois*, as were many members of the genus *Rubus*: raspberries, blackberries, cloudberries, dewberries, thimbleberries, and salmonberries. Blueberries, huckleberries, and lingonberries (genus *Vaccinium*) were used extensively and were highly favored in the North. Because they

BERRIES

Tribes gathering the same fruits sometimes differed in methods of using the fruit. Among the Menominee, eating fresh raspberries was not considered important, although the Cheyenne generally enjoyed the berries raw. Nannyberries (*Viburnum lentago*) were eaten from the hand (but not gathered in quantity) by the Dakota, Ojibwa, Omaha, Pawnee, Ponca, and Winnebago, but the Iroquois harvested nannyberries in great quantity for drying, storing, and cooking.

remained on the plant in usable condition until winter, cranberries (*Vaccinium oxycoccos* and *Vaccinium macrocarpon*) enjoyed a long season, but they were also dried. Black and red currants (genus *Ribes*) were numerous and found throughout America in high quality. Salal berries (*Gaultheria shallon*) and soapberries (*Shepherdia canadensis*) were common on the West Coast, and wolfberries (genus *Lycium*), sometimes called tomatillos, were eaten in the Southwest.

Vegetables In addition to starchy root vegetables, seasonal leafy vegetables were common. The season often began with a spring tonic from the onion family, among the Cherokee a dish of ramps, or wild leek (*Allium tricoccum*), and progressed to other spring and summer greens. Examples of the greens most widely used are mustard, cabbage, turnip (genus *Brassica* and *Pediomelum esculentum*), amaranth, purslane, lamb's-quarter (*Chenopodium*), nettles and nightshades (genus *Solanum*), wood sorrel, and watercress (*Rorippa nasturtium-aquaticum*). The immature seed pods of some plants, among them milkweed (genus *Asclepias*), were steamed or boiled and then served as vegetables.

Nuts Nuts were a significant and underestimated addition to the Native American diet. Perhaps most important were the nutritional value of nut oil and the delicious flavors. Nuts were valued as snacks, and ground nutmeats were used as seasonings in grain and starch dishes. The nuts native to America were eastern beechnuts (*Fagus grandifolia*), black walnuts (*Juglans nigra*), butternuts (*Juglans cinerea*), hickory nuts (genus *Carya*), chestnuts (genus *Castanea*), and hazelnuts (*Corylus*) in the East; pine nuts (genus *Pinus*) and chinquapins in the Southwest, California, and the plains; and pecans (*Carya illinoinensis*) on the plains.

Incidentals, Flavorings, and Delicacies Mushrooms were gathered in season, dried, and used as flavorings in soups and stews. Although mushrooms abounded throughout America, especially in the Northwest, reported use was limited to clearly identifiable, safe varieties. These varieties included bracket fungus (family Polyporaceae), which was prized by the Pueblo Indians; oyster mushrooms (genus *Pleurotus*) and timber mushrooms (genus *Boletus*), prized by the Pomo and eastern tribes; field mushrooms (genus *Agaricus*), by the Delaware and Pomo; and hen-of-the-woods and chicken-of-the-woods (family Polyporaceae), by eastern tribes. Corn smut, a large, black,

irregularly shaped fungus appearing on an ear of corn, was especially prized. Even now, the southwestern Hopi simmer corn smut and then crisp it in fat.

Seaweeds (genus *Porphyra*) were used by the salmon people of the northwestern coastal areas. They were sometimes eaten raw, dried and used as a snack food, or cooked in soups and stews. The Pomo made seaweed into a cake, cooked it in earthen ovens, and then stored it for winter. For other peoples seaweed was an important accompaniment at salmon feasts.

A large number of wild plants were used as seasonings. They include many members of the onion family (Alliaceae), such as assorted leaves, wild garlic bulbs, and wild leeks. The sage leaf (genus *Salvia*) was widely used in the Southwest, and sassafras root and bark (genus *Sassafras*) were favored by the Cherokee, Chippewa, and Choctaw. Sumac berries (*Rhus hirta*, *R. ovata*, and *R. trilobata*) were used as a lemony flavoring throughout America. Sap syrup and, later, sugar were a major source of sweetening. The boiled and reduced juices of sugar maple (genus *Acer*), hickory (genus *Carya*), and walnut trees (genus *Juglans*), among others, were storable.

Cultivated Plants The cultivation of wild plants—that is, transplanting or encouraging the seeding of wild plants in concentrations that made tending and harvesting easier

CLEARING THE LAND

Planting fields were often used for periods of approximately ten years, during which time the resources of an area—firewood, food plants, soil, and game—became depleted. At such times, some tribes, among them those in the Eastern Woodlands region, moved a few miles away and started again. A year or so before the move was scheduled, an area of land was selected with an eye to available water, fuel, plants, and animal populations, and the process of clearing the land was begun. Trees were girdled near the base—that is, the bark was cut away in a complete ring, causing the tree to die. A year later people returned to remove much of the dead wood, using a slash-and-burn system that returned a good many minerals to the soil. The "cleared" land still had large, dead tree trunks here and there. The hills in which corn, beans, and pumpkins were planted were scattered irregularly among the tree trunks. This method of agriculture was possible because of the existence of large tracts of woodland and a low population density.

Garden foods were consumed and preserved in various stages of ripening. In addition to providing variety, this method was one way to ensure a crop large enough to survive the winter. Young sweet corn, unripe bean pods (string beans), still-green beans (for summer succotash), and immature pumpkins were part of the summer diet and sometimes preserved in that stage (as parched corn, for example). Most crops were allowed to mature in the fields, brought to the villages for additional drying and shelling, and then sometimes were processed—as dried pumpkin strips and green-bean pods, for example—before being stored for winter use.

and harvests fuller—was an intermediate step between plant gathering and agriculture. Before contact, seed selection and tending of plants such as marsh elder (*Iva annua*), also called sumpweed, sometimes produced crops of seeds that were three times the size of those growing untended. Stands of cultivated plants at contact included wild lamb's-quarter, Jerusalem artichoke, amaranth, and elderberry (genus *Sambucus*).

Agriculture In addition to their responsibilities for foraged and cultivated plant foods, Native American women were the primary agriculturists, selecting seeds, planting, cultivating, and harvesting. Male-conducted agriculture occurred in only a few pockets of the Southwest, the extreme Northeast, and the Lake Superior region. Individual women often had land rights inherited matrilineally and produced their family's crop foods. Despite this somewhat formal distribution of land, women frequently worked communally, helping each other as needed. Men participated in the work by clearing land and occasionally helped to bring in harvests. Because the survival and welfare of the group depended on sufficient plant food, general cooperation was a necessity.

In the agriculture of the Native Americans, as in earlier Mexican horticulture, corn, beans, and pumpkins and squash were planted together. The Iroquois called these crops the three sisters, a reference to both the plants and the female agriculturists who bore traditional responsibility for their care. Varieties of corn, many beans, cucurbits, and sunflowers evolved through human selection to suit local conditions. Evolving strains adapted to the length of

growing seasons, temperature ranges, amount and timing of rainfall, altitude, and soil, and their use spread throughout most of America. For example, Hopi corn varieties developed deep tap roots to reach scarce moisture in an arid climate, whereas northeastern varieties, which received ample rainfall, were shallow rooted. At contact with the European settlers there were more than one thousand varieties of corn, one hundred varieties of beans, and many cucurbits. These foods were the staples of agricultural people, were supplemented by products of hunting and gathering, and were grown, eaten, preserved, and stored for year-round eating. Of these three basic plants, corn was entirely dependent on humans for survival, because dried kernels remaining in the field would die before the next planting season. Some beans (wild tepary beans, for example), pumpkins, and squash reseeded themselves, but many tribes ensured good strains by selecting and saving the seeds of plants that had produced well.

Corn, the most important American food crop, was grown selectively to serve a number of purposes. Soft corn varieties such as "dent corn," which dented when dried, were ground into flour for bread, dumplings, pudding, and thickening. Hard corn varieties, among them flint and some varieties of hominy corn, were treated with ash (alkali) to soften and remove extremely tough hulls, a process that added calcium and allowed greater absorption of niacin. This corn was often used whole or cracked in porridge, soup, and stew and was ground, in the Southwest, into masa harina, the essential flour for flatbread (tortillas) and tamales. Sweet corn and popcorn varieties also were grown (although many kinds of corn pop). Sweet corn was a botanical strain or simply any corn harvested when it was "in milk." Some strains of corn were developed in colors—red, blue, yellow, white, and variegated. Some varieties of colored corn were used in ritualistic ceremonies, and some

CORN AND MAIZE

The word "corn" was brought to the colonies by the English, who used it to mean grain of any kind. Only the Native American word "maize" specifically meant what became known as corn among Americans. The English indicated that they meant *Zea mays* by calling it "maize," "turkey corn," "Indian corn," or just plain "Indian."

were highly edible and preferred for their flavor, (such as Hopi blue corn in piki breads).

Beans (genus *Phaseolus*), originally Mexican, existed in numerous varieties. Among the earliest were the tepary beans (*Phaseolus acutifolius*) of the Southwest tribes, scarlet runner beans (*Phaseolus coccineus*) of the Iroquois, sieva beans (*Phaseolus lunatus*) of the Cherokee, Havasupai, and Iroquois, and kidney beans (*Phaseolus vulgaris*), which were used almost everywhere. Beans were eaten as immature pods, green beans, and dried beans.

Cucurbits—squash, pumpkins, and gourds—were also Mexican products that made their way north. Crookneck squash and field pumpkins were eaten young, ripe, and dried by the southern Navajo and the northern Iroquois. The flowers and seeds also were consumed. Seeds were eaten fresh or roasted, were easily stored, and provided an important source of oil. Eastern and southern tribes ate cucurbit pulp fresh or dried, cooked with fat, or incorporated into bread. Cucurbits were staple foods of the Pima and festival foods among the Iroquois.

Sweet and hot peppers (genus *Capiscum*) were another legacy of Mexican horticulture, brought to southwestern Pueblo Indians by the first Spanish visitors. Some peppers naturalized and grew wild, but most were produced by farming and were used almost everywhere in many forms.

Tribal farms also cultivated plants that grew in the wild and benefited from less sophisticated genetic selection. Most common were Jerusalem artichokes and sunflowers, although in some areas plants such as amaranth and lamb's-quarter were grown for their leaves and seeds. In areas where growing conditions were unreliable, these plants produced more consistently if protected and tended—watered and hoed—throughout the season.

Introduced Foods Columbus' second voyage to the Americas carried European plant foods and established them on Caribbean islands. The list included sugar cane, melons, wheat, chickpeas, large onions, radishes, salad greens, grapevines, and fruit trees. Not long after this voyage, Spanish conquistadors and explorers brought food plants to Mexico and the American Southwest, and the slave trade brought African plants to the southeastern coasts. When planted in the appropriate soil and climate, the crops flourished, were carried long distances on established Native American trade routes, and were quickly adopted by other tribes. Thus a number of introduced foods, among them wheat, peaches, and melons, were growing profusely in the Southwest at the time of

English encounters many decades later and were misinterpreted as indigenous plants. These foods had become integral to local agriculture and were part of the ongoing dietary change that would characterize changing Indian foods throughout North America. In the course of centuries, other European and African foods were introduced to local agriculture with the same results. Among these were the potato, carrot, turnip, eating apples and pears, and okra. In addition to these domesticated plants, a number of European species often planted in colonial kitchen gardens "escaped" to grow wild and thrived across the continent. Explorers entering "new territory" sometimes found dandelions, certain varieties of purslane, cresses, violets, and burdock already in Native American diets.

Animals, Fish, and Insects

Native Americans obtained their animal proteins, fats, and oils from large and small game, fish, and insects. Protein built the muscle so essential to physically active people. Consumption of large quantities of fat, considered desirable and delicious by indigenous people, reflected the need for calories, essential oils, and appealing flavor. The dietary balance of vegetative and animal foods differed by region and availability. The tribes of the plains and many coastal areas, who had seemingly inexhaustible supplies of game and fish, remained hunters and gatherers, undertook only minor agriculture, if any, and traded surpluses for the grain they needed. Most regions supported combinations of agriculture and hunting and fishing. Staples—corn, acorns, and wild rice—were supplemented seasonally by smaller quantities of meat, fish, and insects.

Large Game Among game animals, American bison, or buffalo, were probably the most important. They existed in most of America and were hunted throughout most of the nation. The largest concentrations lived on the plains. Buffalo provided the chief sustenance of more than twenty tribes of Plains Indians and were the most important figures in their cultural worldviews and mythologies. The early introduction of the horse by the Spanish strengthened buffalo cultures. Also of considerable universal importance were deer, antelope, bear, elk, and moose.

Hunting strategies were developed according to season, region, terrain, and the size, power, and fleetness of the animals. One problem was getting close enough to prey. The projectile weapons of early hunters were ineffective from a distance. Large game animals not only were

HUNTING SEASON

The hunting season, usually autumn or winter, was a time during which large numbers of people left their settlements, sometimes for several months. The hunters followed the game and provided a substantial amount of meat for winter. Extended hunts were complex, often requiring the establishment of one or a series of temporary hunting camps. Runners carried processed meat and hides to permanent encampments and then brought fresh supplies of food and equipment back to the hunters. Hunts were generally planned and executed by a large number of a tribe's men, but it was also customary for some women and children to participate, both as hunters and as cooks. Solitary hunts were of shorter duration, requiring the hunter to haul his prey home alone. Because a dressed deer may have weighed more than one hundred pounds, transporting the kill required considerable strength or the decision to transport only the choicest parts. In either case, women were generally responsible for the processing—butchering, drying, and cooking.

dangerous but also moved quickly. These obstacles were overcome by driving animals into immobilizing marshes or bodies of water or over cliffs. Many tribes constructed funnel-shaped "fences" that forced the game into "corrals," or small enclosures. Once trapped, the game was dispatched with bows and arrows or spears, which were the most common weapons.

The Plains Indians hunted buffalo with additional schemes. The technique called the "surround" required mounted hunters to cut out a section of the herd by riding around it noisily in narrowing circles. The selected animals were pressed together and rendered inactive and then were killed efficiently and in large numbers, sometimes as many as three hundred at one time. Buffalo killed by these hunts provided fresh and dried meat (jerky), fat, hides, and tool materials to be shared among the participants. In a variation of the surround technique, fire was used to consolidate groups of animals. Small encircling fires were set a distance from a section of the herd. The fires burned steadily toward the center of the ring and compressed the group of animals. This method worked well for smaller numbers of hunters. Sometimes a fire ring was set with a small opening, through which the

buffalo, attempting to escape, were ambushed. In a second hunting system, called "impounding," animals were stampeded into a previously built enclosure. "Buffalo jumps" also involved stampeding or crowding animals over cliffs to hunters waiting below.

Herds of deer were caught with techniques similar to those used for buffalo, but more often deer were hunted singly, as were antelope, bear, elk, moose, and, in the Colorado uplands, bighorn sheep. Large game was sometimes located by tribal dogs, which were most effective in detecting solitary animals, or was attacked by dogs in small groups. Hunting in the snow had many advantages: The game was easier to find (by tracks), to see (trees were leafless), and to immobilize.

A number of auditory lures were developed to attract game, among them bark trumpets for calling moose, ribbon reeds for calling deer (blowing on a grass leaf to imitate the cry of fawns), and antlers struck together to suggest fighting males, which attracted females in rut. Certain plants were also used as lures for attracting wild game. The Blackfoot used smallwing sedge (*Carex nebrascensis*) to lure buffalo.

Small Game Acquisition of small game did not require the extraordinary coordination and organization of hunts for large game. Depending on locale, small game included raccoons, opossums, rabbits (western jackrabbits and eastern cottontails), squirrels, badgers, beavers, and muskrats. Small mammals were available year-round and could be found near permanent encampments. Both men and women trapped and killed small game with concealed pits, deadfall traps, snares, and nooses. In addition to spears and bows and arrows, atlatls (sling and spear apparatuses) worked well and were commonly used wherever wood for their manufacture was available.

Traveling many days over those plains they came to a rancheria [community] of about two hundred houses, with their people. The houses were of buffalo hides, for these neither sow nor harvest maize. . . . The stomachs served as jars and cups for drinking: they live on the meat which they eat half broiled over buffalo chips [dried manure, burned as fuel].

—Juan Jaramillo, firsthand account of the expedition of Francisco Vásquez de Coronado (1540–1542)

FISHING METHODS

Fish of all sizes and varieties were caught with different strategies. In addition to using fishhooks, cordage lines, and nets, the Lenape "poisoned" pond water with black walnut hulls to momentarily stupefy the fish, which then floated and could be gathered into boats or nets. The closely related Delaware in Oklahoma used the Ohio buckeye (*Aesculus glabra*) to the same effect.

Birds Birds were hunted in the fall, often during their migrations, because they were most tender and flavorful after the summer's fattening. Flocks of geese, ducks, cranes, and pigeons were netted and lured, sometimes with decoys. Other birds were shot from blinds with bows and arrows. Birds were roasted, stewed, steamed, and added to soup and porridge, as were wild turkeys, partridge, pheasant, grouse, and western prairie chickens. Bird eggs were a seasonal treat, because they were available only during times of egg laying.

Water Mammals, Fish, and Seafood Fish and saltwater mammals were a major source of food and were, throughout regions with enough waterways, more important in diet than hunted game or gathered plants. Often concentrated in large numbers and apparently available endlessly, seafood was the chief food for some tribes and was second only to agriculture for others. In all, seafood was the major source of protein and oil for tribes living on the shores of the Atlantic and Pacific Oceans, the Gulf of Mexico, Chesapeake and San Francisco bays, and the lower reaches of the Mississippi and Hudson rivers. Whales, the largest of the sea animals, were highly prized. Although beached or stranded whales were easiest to obtain, tribes of the coastal East and Northwest mastered hunting techniques with harpoons and bows and arrows. Seals and porpoises were harpooned. (Harpooning skills made many Native Americans valuable to the Anglo-American whaling industry.) Oil was a major contribution of these mammals, but meat and sometimes skins were important as well.

Migrating fish were especially important. In early spring, just as winter supplies were finished, fish left their winter depths for the warmer shallows, where they were speared and netted or taken with hook and line. Some tribes, among them the Kwakiutl, fashioned rakes with sharpened tines that impaled herring when they ran. Also prized were salmon, cod, halibut, and sturgeon. The largest sources of migrating fish spawned, that is, they left the oceans annually to swim upstream and lay eggs. Fish that spawned were salmon, eastern shad, and alewives. These fish were caught by Indians in systems of woven nets and weirs and were often speared. Most of the catch was dried for the following winter. The northwestern tribes had year-round access to salmon, although the fish were of varying quality. Salmon were so plentiful that they were the most important staple food (comparable to corn among agriculturists) and a cultural icon. Although the Northwest was, and is, noted for salmon fishing, salmon proliferated in many other coastal waterways as well. In the Great Lakes and rivers of the Northeast, salmon were also plentiful. "In this river there are six or seven or even 800 salmon caught in one day. I saw houses with 60, 70, and more dried salmon." (H. M. van den Bogaert, *A Journey into Mohawk and Oneida Country* [1634–1635])

Freshwater fish abounded in rivers and lakes. Large bodies of freshwater—the Great Lakes, for example—held whitefish, muskelunge, sheepshead, and lake salmon. Small lakes and ponds supported perch, bass, bluegill, sunfish, and catfish. Trout and salmon abounded in streams and small rivers, as did pike and pickerel.

Turtles from oceans, freshwater, and land were caught for their meat and their eggs and were often cooked whole in the shell. Freshwater and saltwater eels were also caught by spearing, sometimes in basket traps. In the winter, hunters sometimes used their bare feet to locate eels hiding dormant in the mud and then caught them with their bare hands.

Shellfish was easy to obtain. Quahog and soft clams, razor clams, whelks, and oysters abounded and were simply available for the taking. The presence of large middens (shell deposits) along the East Coast and eastern rivers attests to the mammoth quantities of shellfish eaten, dried, and traded. Lobsters and crabs were prepared by fire and pit roasting and sometimes broiled on spits. These crustaceans were frequent additions to soups, stews, and porridges.

Insects A major source of protein, insects were used in varying degrees by all tribes. Enjoyed as a delicacy as boiled or roasted snacks and stews, many insects were rich in flavor and desirable fats. In regions such as coastal California, where large and small game were sparse, insects were staple foods. Insects consumed

---

INSECTS

Insects were a large part of the diet in many areas and were often delicacies. Even in areas such as Virginia, where game was plentiful, Robert Beverley (1705) described Indians eating "Grubs, the Nymphae of Wasps, some kinds of Scarabai, Cicadae, &c." In Pennsylvania wasps were mashed and served on flatbread and considered a flavorful and sweet-tasting dish. The Iroquois enjoyed raw, acid-flavored ants as well as the roasted larvae of seventeen-year locusts served with grease. The Huron, wrote Beverley, added a "a handful of little waterflies to their sagamité, esteem them highly, and made feasts of them," and Cherokee parched (roasted) yellow jackets and made yellow jacket soup.

---

included caterpillars, grasshoppers, maggots, wasps, ants, bee larvae, and beetles. Earthworms, not insects but annelids, were eaten as well. Insects sometimes were hunted. Grasshoppers were trapped in "surrounds" as were the Plains buffalo. Other insects were forced from trees with smoke. The sweet secretions of aphids (collected by rinsing them from leaves) were made into a honey-like drink.

Domesticated Animals Domesticated animals contributed little to the Native American diet and were often more important for other uses. The dog, for example, played a number of roles in tribal life, among them as alarm and dray animals. Dogs performed the important physical work of hauling heavy loads, managing as much as fifty pounds. Dogs were not abused; Native Americans worked as hard as their dogs. Many tribes were loath to eat dog, and in most cases it was served only at special feasts. The meat was highly esteemed and usually was stewed. Before contact, domesticated turkeys were bred and used in the Southwest, where they were as important for their feathers as they were for their meat.

European introduction of domesticated animals brought major changes to New World diets. These animals were received differently among tribes and according to the time of contact. At first, the more easily accepted animals were those that were largely self-supporting and adapted easily to life in communities, regional conditions, and suitable grazing material. Sheep, which were acclimatized to the Southwest by early Spanish settlers, became a basic herd animal of the Navajo, who used the

meat and wool. Along with cattle, sheep had been adopted into the diet of the eastern Mohican by 1670. Packs of Spanish horses, running wild and finding ample forage on the plains, were quickly adopted by tribes of that area. Horses were at first used as a source of meat, but their dietary value was soon outweighed by their advantages as transportation.

Pigs, which were adopted early, fed themselves on scraps or foraged woodland mast, and were sometimes as tame as dogs. The early allure of pigs was due, in part, to their resemblance to previously used bear in flavor and fat. The Seneca word for pig was "bear-that-walks-around-in-the yard." Chickens were adopted but vulnerable to marauding wolves, foxes, and coyotes. Chickens, however, when protected, provided predictable year-round supplies of eggs, previously available only from wild birds and turtles in egg-laying season.

Beef cattle needed considerable care, ample grazing land, and a sedentary lifestyle. Beef generally was not eaten until the eighteenth century, somewhat late after introduction, possibly because Indians generally associated the animals with human diseases attributed to improper reverence, hunting, and wrathful spirits. In the mid-eighteenth century, in line with a general movement toward accepting the material aspects of European culture, Iroquois on Ohio farms and in the Susquehanna Valley were establishing beef cattle herds. Today, domesticated meats have largely replaced wild game, although a symbolic association with hunted animals is an important cultural expression.

[See also Buffalo; Corn; Mid-Atlantic Region; Midwestern Regional Cookery; New England Regional Cookery; Pacific Northwestern Regional Cookery; Southwestern Regional Cookery; Squash.]

FEEDING THE SHEEP

When Native Americans began to include domestic animals in their subsistence projects, they experienced changes in diet and lifestyle. Some tribes undertook the production or gathering of plants for their animals—a new concept and responsibility. For example, the Montana used the bulbs of spring beauty (genus *Claytonia*) to fatten pigs. The Navajo used spider flower (genus *Cleome*) to feed their horses and Nebraska sedge (*Caryx nebrascensis*) to feed their sheep.

BIBLIOGRAPHY

Cox, Beverly, and Martin Jacobs. *Spirit of the Harvest: North American Indian Cooking*. New York: Stewart, Tabori, and Chang, 1991.

Cronon, William. *Nature's Metropolis: Chicago and the Great West*. New York: Norton, 1991.

Cushing, Frank Hamilton. *Zuñi Breadstuff*. New York: AMS, 1975. The original edition was published in 1920.

Dary, David A. *The Buffalo Book: The Saga of an American Symbol*. New York: Discus and Avon, 1975.

Frank, Lois Ellen. *Foods of the Southwest Indian Nations*. Berkeley, CA: Ten Speed, 2002.

Hesse, Zora Getmansky. *Southwestern Indian Recipe Book*. Palmer Lake, CO: Filter, 1973.

Hudson, Amanda, and Peter J. Hudson. "Choctaw Indian Dishes." In *Southwestern Cookery: Indian and Spanish Influences*, edited by Louis Szathmary. New York: Promontory, 1974. The original edition was published in 1933.

Indian Women's Club of Tulsa, Oklahoma. "The Indian Cook Book." In *Southwestern Cookery: Indian and Spanish Influences*, edited by Louis Szathmary. New York: Promontory, 1974. The original edition was published in 1933.

Jennings, Bertha W., ed. *American Indian Society of Washington D.C. Cook Book*. Washington, DC: American Indian Society of Washington, D.C., 1975.

Kavasch, E. Barrie. *Enduring Harvests: Native American Foods and Festivals for Every Season*. Old Saybrook, CT: Globe Pequot, 1995.

Keegan, Marcia. *Southwest Indian Cookbook*. Weehawken, NJ: Clear Light, 1987.

Kimball, Yefee, and Jean Anderson. *The Art of American Indian Cooking*. Garden City, NY: Doubleday, 1965.

Martin, Calvin. *Keepers of the Game: Indian-Animal Relationships and the Fur Trade*. Berkeley: University of California, 1978.

Moerman, Daniel E. *Native American Ethnobotany*. Portland, OR: Timber, 1998.

Niethammer, Carolyn. *American Indian Food and Lore: 150 Authentic Recipes*. New York: Macmillan, 1974.

Ortiz, Beverly R. *It Will Live Forever: Traditional Yosemite Acorn Preparation*. Berkeley, CA: Heyday, 1991.

Parker, A. C. *Iroquois Uses of Maize and Other Food Plants*. 1910. Ohsweken, Ontario, Canada: Iroqrafts, 1983. The original edition was published in 1910.

Peters, Russell M. *Clambake: A Wampanoag Tradition*. Minneapolis, MN: Lerner, 1992.

Raine, Carolyn. *A Woodland Feast: Native American Foodways of the 17th and 18th Centuries*. Huber Heights, OH: Morningstar, 1997.

Speth, John C. *Bison Kills and Bone Counts: Decision Making by Ancient Hunters*, edited by Karl Butzer and Leslie G. Freeman. Chicago: University of Chicago Press, 1983.

Stewart, Hilary. *Indian Fishing: Early Methods on the Northwest Coast*. Seattle: University of Washington Press, 1977.

"Traditional Navajo Foods and Cooking." *Tsa' Aszi'* 3, no. 4 and 4, no. 1 (1983).

Vennum, Thomas, Jr. *Wild Rice and the Ojibway People*. St. Paul: Minnesota Historical Society, 1988.

Waugh, F. W. *Iroquois Foods and Food Preparation*. Ottawa, Ontario: National Museums of Canada, 1973. The original edition was published in 1916.

Wilson, Gilbert L. *Buffalo Bird Woman's Garden: Agriculture of the Hidatsa Indians*. St. Paul: Minnesota Historical Society, 1987.

Young, Joyce LaFray. *Seminole Indian Recipes*. Tampa, FL: Surfside, 1987.

Zanger, Mark H. *The American Ethnic Cookbook for Students*. Phoenix, AZ: Oryx, 2001.

ALICE ROSS

Navajo Tacos

Originating in the southwestern states of Arizona, New Mexico, and Utah, Navajo tacos are a type of Native American snack food served at rodeos, fairs, gatherings, powwows, and even Southwest fast food restaurants. Instead of using tortillas as in a typical Mexican taco, the Navajo taco starts out with a sopaipilla (also known as Navajo fry bread). A sopaipilla is made from wheat dough that is shaped into a plate-sized flat disk and deep-fried in lard. Once fried, the sopaipilla is topped with refried beans, lettuce, tomato, scallion, cheese, avocado, sour cream, and taco sauce or salsa. The origins of the Navajo taco reflect the diversity of southwestern cuisine. The beans, tomato, oregano, and cilantro used in the dish are Aztec ingredients brought to the region from Mexico by Spanish conquistadores, while the use of flour and lard is a Spanish contribution. The chilies used to make the salsa for the taco are native to the area, as are the preparation techniques. Currently, the Navajo taco is sold throughout the Southwest at the Mexican fast food restaurant chain Taco Time. The Navajo Nation has not given consent for the use of its name in selling the product.

[*See also* Mexican American Food; Native American Foods; Southwestern Regional Cookery.]

JEAN RAILLA

Nestlé

There are few kitchens in America that do not contain at least one product manufactured by the Nestlé Company. Headquartered in Vevey, Switzerland, Nestlé is the largest food company in the world, with almost five hundred manufacturing plants worldwide. The company has had a presence in North America since 1900, when Nestlé opened its first factory in the United States. Nestlé's products are distributed under hundreds of brand names and include Crosse and Blackwell preserves, Stouffer's frozen foods, Poland Springs bottled water, Libby's fruit juices, Carnation Instant Breakfast, and Maggi bouillon cubes.

NESTLÉ COFFEE PRODUCTS

In 1938, after eight years of experimentation, Nestlé launched Nescafé, a powdered instant coffee superior to previous efforts. It was produced by spraying brewed coffee into heated towers, where it turned to powder almost instantly. The venerable Swiss firm had been founded by Henri Nestlé in 1867, when he invented an infant-feeding formula. With subsidiaries for its chocolate and confectionery products already in place all over the world, Nestlé was ideally situated to promote its new instant coffee, while the advent of World War II provided the perfect American market when the U.S. military bought all the instant coffee it could.

In the postwar era Nestlé tried to sell Nescafé in America with lackluster reason-why ads about no fuss and no coffee grounds, and it lost its lead to instant Maxwell House. In the late 1960s, however, when freeze-drying techniques were introduced that produced a better-tasting coffee, ads for Nestlé's Taster's Choice freeze-dried coffee claimed to offer "all the deep, rich flavor and hearty coffee aroma you used to have to perk up a pot for," and with a $10-million-a-year marketing campaign, Taster's Choice pulled ahead of Maxwell House's Maxim. Nestlé was wise to choose a completely new name for the product so that it was not associated with the low-quality image of Nescafé.

In the 1980s Nestlé expanded its North American business beyond instant coffee by purchasing once-famous brands, then down on their luck, such as Hills Brothers, MJB, and Chase and Sanborn. Seeking a toehold in the specialty whole-bean market, the firm also purchased California-based Sark's Gourmet Coffee in 1987.

In the early 1990s, Nestlé ran innovative Taster's Choice ads cribbed from its equivalent British brand, Gold Blend. In the serial soap opera–style commercials, suave Tony wooed sexy Sharon by mixing up seductive cups of Taster's Choice in a variety of situations. The commercial in which they finally kissed made the national news.

As the twenty-first century opened, Nestlé was the world's largest coffee company, primarily owing to global sales of instant coffee. In the United States, however, it roasted less coffee than Philip Morris's Maxwell House or Procter & Gamble's Folgers.

BIBLIOGRAPHY

Heer, Jean. *Nestlé: 125 Years, 1866–1991.* Translated by B. J. Benson with Constance Devanthéry-Lewis. Vevey, Switzerland: Nestlé, 1991.

Pendergrast, Mark. *Uncommon Grounds: The History of Coffee and How It Transformed Our World.* New York: Basic Books, 1999. Comprehensive business and social history.

MARK PENDERGRAST

The history of the company began with Charles Page in 1866. Page had recognized the potential of Gail Borden's condensed milk product, which was first produced in the United States in the decade before the U.S. Civil War. After his experiences as the American consul in Zurich, Page believed that Switzerland, with its central location and abundant milk supply, was the ideal site for developing and marketing a condensed milk product. He called his new business the Anglo-Swiss Condensed Milk Company to make it easier to market his Swiss-made products in England.

In 1867, Henri Nestlé, a pharmacist, was asked by a friend to make something for an infant who could not digest fresh cow's milk. Knowing that the child would die without his intervention, Nestlé created a milk food from crumbs made from baked malted wheat rusks mixed with sweetened condensed milk. This granular brown powder was the first instant infant weaning food. He called his alternative to breast-feeding Farine Lactée Henri Nestlé and adopted his family's coat of arms, a bird's nest, as a trademark. The symbol of the nest suggested maternity, nature, security, and nourishment.

Nestlé sold his company to Jules Monnerat in 1874. The following year another Swiss citizen, Daniel Peter, found a way to combine cocoa powder with milk to create chocolate milk. This company also merged with Nestlé. Five years after opening its first U.S. factory, in 1905 Nestlé merged with Page's Anglo-Swiss Condensed Milk Company. The merger of the two companies made it possible for the new firm to expand.

In 1938, Nestlé added Nescafé, a soluble powdered coffee, to its product line. Nescafé became an American staple after servicemen tasted it in Europe and Asia during World War II. Based on the success of Nescafé, the company developed a freeze-dried coffee in 1966 called Taster's Choice.

During the 1970s, Nestlé aggressively expanded the marketing of its baby formula in developing countries. A boycott against the company started in the United States in 1977; it was claimed that, because of poverty and illiteracy, the company's formula products would be diluted with polluted water, resulting in disease or starvation. The boycott cost Nestlé millions of dollars. In a textbook example of crisis management, the managing director of the company met with the boycotters and agreed to follow the World Health Organization's guidelines for advertising and marketing baby formula in developing countries.

[*See also* Borden; Chocolate; Coffee, Instant.]

BIBLIOGRAPHY

Mirabile, Lisa, ed. *International Directory of Company Histories.* Vol. 2, *Electrical and Electronics—Food Services and Retailers.* Chicago: St. James Press, 1990.

Toussaint-Samat, Maguelonne, et al. *2 Million Years of the Food Industry.* Vevey, Switzerland: Nestlé S.A., 1991. Published on the 125th anniversary of the company's founding.

JOSEPH M. CARLIN

New England Regional Cookery

The English colonists who named the northeastern most corner of America after their home country brought with them the expectation of maintaining their familiar English yeoman foodways based on wheat bread, peas, dairy products, beef, mutton, pork, and orchard and bramble fruits. The climate, the soil, and the fiscal requirements of being a colony funded by a joint-stock company all affected the food that the settlers ultimately could produce and gradually came to choose.

The six New England states—Massachusetts, Rhode Island, Connecticut, Maine, Vermont, and New Hampshire—cover a large enough area to be divided into smaller subregions, some of which have distinctive foodways, distinctions blurred in later times by mass consumption and popular culture and possibly retained only by self-conscious effort. New England contained some of the country's earliest urban and industrial centers and so absorbed great numbers of immigrants who contributed to the region's foods even as they gave up many of their own. Out of New England came many settlers who moved to western parts, taking with them their food preferences and laying down the basic diet over and through which subsequent influences from other regions and ethnic groups would be laid.

National Food. Uncle Sam assures John Bull that minced codfish is the American national dish. Advertising card distributed by Henry Mayo and Co., Boston, late nineteenth century. *Collection of Alice Ross*

Something in the New England character affected food choices and cooking habits. Practical, frugal, and almost always interested in something other than what they were eating, New Englanders were susceptible to a simplified cuisine speedily prepared. The reformist tendencies that came with a colonizing effort bloomed later into the temperance movement, the cause of abolition, and the domestic science movement, which brought with it diet reforms in the late nineteenth century. With the exception of some reformers, the average New Englander of the early nineteenth century, the time by which the cuisine of the region had been established, was less hostile to fine and careful cuisine than careless of it.

The Colonial and Federal Eras

New Englanders developed their regional cuisine over the two hundred years of initial settlement through the

Revolution and into the early nineteenth century. The process was hardly uniform throughout the region or the society. Urban foodways close to the southern and eastern coasts of New England in the early eighteenth century were different from those on the newly settled frontiers to the west and north. Market forces always had an effect, and truly self-sufficient subsistence was rare. Even the earliest settlers were supported in part by shipments of food from England, and they turned to producing marketable products, including the famous salt cod, to pay for the imports. The New England gentry ate and drank differently from the tradespeople and poorer farmers, even within a few years of settlement.

Through the colonial era new immigrants, many from the British Isles, reinforced the basic Anglo diet and looked to England for trends, even as they desired political independence. During the fifty or so years after the Revolutionary War, America became more aware of itself as a separate culture. New Englanders, like other Americans, when asked what constituted a New England diet, probably would have named many dishes that had evolved during the previous one hundred years, although they would have been equally at home with standard English dishes.

The English Diet   Each English settler was accustomed to the daily consumption of nearly one pound of grain flour or meal in the form of porridge or bread or peas in a pottage; close to one pound of cheese and butter; and approximately one gallon of dark ale. Meat was a smaller proportion of the diet, approximately one-fourth of a pound being consumed each day. This diet—approximately six thousand calories per day—powered a labor-intensive agriculture. It helps explain why the first few years of the Plymouth colony were so hard on the settlers. Eating foods they could gather, such as fish and shellfish, wild fruit, and greens, merely filled in a few empty places in stomachs accustomed to a great deal of grain. When barley, peas, and wheat did not thrive, the settlers depended on corn. The plentiful codfish had more value as a source of cash for repaying the joint-stock company than it had as food.

Shifting from Wheat to Rye and Maize   In New England, wheat suffered from a rust that greatly limited its production. After trying for a couple of decades, the English largely gave up trying to grow enough wheat for bread and baking and adopted what they called "Indian corn," that is, maize. The English word "corn" denoted "grain," hence the phrase "Indian corn" literally meant "Indian grain." Rye thrived and was combined with maize, in accordance with an earlier tradition of mixing coarse grains and sometimes even ground legumes to make an everyday bread called "rye and Indian." Mixed crops of grains included oats, rye, barley, and sometimes even wild plant seed to yield "maslin," which was made into bread.

When wheat crops did succeed, the flour was often reserved for pastry and fine baking. As they pressed inland from the coast, settlers found more ground suitable for wheat cultivation. Western Massachusetts, parts of the Connecticut River valley, and sections of Maine proved suitable for wheat cultivation. Some homesteads were able to grow enough wheat for the family's consumption. Additional wheat was obtained from the Mid-Atlantic and southern colonies.

Cornmeal proved useful for sweet and savory dishes. In addition to bread, grain-based dishes, particularly porridge, were adapted to corn. The old hasty pudding based on wheat became a cornmeal mush also called hasty pudding. Because of its culinary similarity to oatmeal, cornmeal was used to make bannock, a flat, unleavened bread made of grain and water and baked before a fire. In Rhode Island this bread was called "jonnycake," without the "h," harking back to "jonniken," a term used in the north of England for oat bannock. The pudding that emerged was based on milk and cornmeal sweetened with molasses and called "Indian pudding." The dish was named for the meal used, not for the originators. Versions of Indian meal dumplings and pound cake appear in early cookbooks. Unsweetened Indian puddings boiled in bags provided filling starch as an accompaniment to meat.

Animals for Increase   The first few years of settlement in any newly begun colony usually meant eating less meat than the colonists would probably have preferred. Waiting for both natural increase and time to clear sufficient pastureland to support animals delayed meat consumption. Prolific animals, particularly pigs, could be harvested sooner than cattle. Although English colonists generally preferred surer results than hunting afforded, for a short time, as on any frontier, hunting for deer, moose, small animals, and water and land wildfowl helped supplement the diet.

Many colonists came from a countryside where hunting was an activity conducted by the gentry on land reserved for that purpose. Some settlers enjoyed the opportunity to eat venison in relative abundance after having been forbidden to eat it for so long. A lingering sense that hunting and fishing were leisure activities, sport for the gentry, meant colonists tended to regard Native American hunters a little less well than they did the women, who were, like the English, cultivators of the soil. Hunting, especially in cold weather, was strenuous and took time for proficiency. A fine balance had to be kept between energy expended for gathering wild food and the nutrients gained from it. By the eighteenth century, New England, particularly the southern part, was producing enough sheep and cattle to have a surplus for trading to the sugar-producing West Indies.

Waiting for Apples English settlers had a fondness for stone, bramble, and pip fruits but were obliged to wait sometimes a decade or more to enjoy apples, pears, cherries, and others, although strawberries, blueberries, cranberries, and blackberries grew wild and could be gathered. Apples took well to the New England soil and climate. In the eighteenth and nineteenth centuries, orchards were established, and hundreds of varieties of apples were cultivated.

Just as they had adapted corn to create familiar dishes, colonists turned to pumpkin, using its sweet flesh as they had formerly used apples. Cooked slowly, pumpkins made a sauce to accompany meat, were put into pastry as apples had been for tarts, or what New Englanders ultimately called "pie." Pumpkins were used in puddings and even baked whole.

In some parts of New England, freshly squeezed apple cider was boiled into apple molasses and used in place of molasses, which came from cane sugar. Apple and pear sauces were cooked by the cask-full for household use. Apple butter was not used until there was a larger German presence in the area. Apples dried well, as did pumpkin, for home consumption and later for sale.

The wait for apple, pear, and peach trees to bear fruit was repeated as settlers advanced westward into the hill country of New England and even farther into the Midwest. In the nineteenth century one proof that a homestead claim had been fulfilled was that an orchard had been planted. The New Englander John Chapman, better known as Johnny Appleseed, moved in advance of settlers into Ohio, Indiana, and Illinois planting nursery stock of apple and other trees to shorten the wait for fruit and home ownership.

Beer and Cider That apples succeeded so well helped offset the discouraging returns on grains that were widely used in brewing. New England settlers liked their ale, and brewing was an essential housewifely task that accompanied bread baking with yeast. The English culinary repertoire included cider making, which took full advantage of New England's apple abundance. Gallons squeezed and fermented provided a family beverage and a way to preserve apples. Many families continued brewing ale and eventually beer, adding apple cider to the selection.

Dairying as Women's Work In addition to baking and brewing, housewives raised garden vegetables, tended poultry, and conducted dairying, from twice daily milking to butter and cheese making. By the late eighteenth century, New England's farmwives were producing enough cheese for it to be an article of commerce with developing urban centers, such as Boston and even Mid-Atlantic cities, including Baltimore, Philadelphia, and New York. Dairying expertise stood the region in good stead in the later nineteenth century, when dairying became a farm activity for supplying developing industrial centers.

Peas to Beans Hot, humid summers were hard on the peas that many English settlers had been accustomed to growing as a field crop and had relied on as a staple legume. Native Americans introduced the colonists to the beans that were suited to the New England climate. Thus the culinary emphasis switched from peas to beans. The customary pottage, a slowly stewed mixture of peas and meat, often salted meat, gradually gave way to one made of beans. The bean pottage, a substantial dish because of the salted meat, evolved into the region's famous, sweet version of baked beans.

The Native American combination of dried beans and corn in a dish called "succotash" sufficiently resembled other familiar pottages that settlers readily adopted it. Early succotash usually contained meat, often salted. In Plymouth, Massachusetts, an elaborate variation appeared in the nineteenth century that included substantial chunks of corned beef and even fresh chicken. In the nineteenth century, succotash often consisted only of corn and beans.

Beans were boiled as peas were, in a bag suspended in a pot with a piece of boiling salt meat and sometimes with other vegetables. Beans were used fresh in summer and dried in the winter. Beans replaced peas in seafarers' rations. Early New England colonists cultivated hundreds of varieties of bean, some of which have been preserved as heirlooms, because they were so important and widely grown.

Abundant Hardwood Many settlers came from parts of England that had been inhabited for so long that fuel wood was scarce. In the new region, trees stood in the way of pastures and fields. The abundance provided wood for homes and shipbuilding, for heating and cooking, and for export. Wood also was burned for charcoal and potash. European travelers in New England commented on the huge fires blazing on New England hearths. The abundance of wood meant that many homes had their own ovens for baking, an unusual feature in England and elsewhere in Europe. Not all of the first homes had ovens, as evidenced by diary and journal entries describing exchanges made for oven use, but the large number of ovens that were available promoted domestic bread baking. The abundance of wood also meant that many households were able to roast meat before the radiant heat of a fire. Even moderately prosperous households enjoyed roasted meat more often than they would have in England and the rest of Europe.

Much Meat By the end of the eighteenth century, New Englanders' meat eating was a feature of life commented upon by travelers. Timothy Dwight, the eighth president of Yale University, serving from 1795 to 1817, traveled throughout the region keeping journals of what he observed. Dwight noted in the early nineteenth century that it was not unusual to find that in many households meat was eaten at least twice if not three times a day. Once farms were established, beef was the preferred meat, followed by pork, mutton and lamb, and veal. The quality of meat consumed by any household depended a good deal on income and status. Fresh meat was always at a premium winter or summer. Those who produced meat, and their nearest relatives, benefited from exchanges of better cuts. Cheaper cuts and organ and salted meats were apportioned to poorer associates and given to tradespeople in payment for labor or products. City markets received meat driven in from the countryside, and as in the country, the wealthy acquired the freshest meat and better cuts.

Fish Once a Week Even though Protestant Christians shook off the required fasts of Catholic life during the Reformation, a desire for variety in diet found New Englanders continuing to eat fish for dinner at least once a week and to use fish to accompany other viands at breakfast and supper. The long association between fasting, hard times, and the salt fish allocated to the general population in old England meant that fresh fish was preferred, although New Englanders also acquired for home use the best quality salt cod, called "dunfish" because of its buff color.

Evidence in archaeological digs shows that in the seventeenth and eighteenth centuries there was was probably an active inshore fishery for species such as bluefish, pollack, haddock, and bass caught for fresh-market sales in cities such as Boston. Shad and salmon were caught in season, and smaller fish, such as mackerel, alewife, and herring, were salted and smoked. Shad and salmon were smoked when the catch exceeded what could be consumed quickly. Shellfish, particularly oysters and lobsters, found a ready enough market that oyster harvesting had to be curtailed in the early nineteenth century to prevent overfishing. Clams and mussels, if eaten at all, were consumed in small quantities. Clams were valuable as bait.

Fast and Thanksgiving English settlers were accustomed to a seasonal pattern of fast and thanksgiving. Although either event could be called at any time for purposes of supplication in times of duress, such as in war, or to express gratitude, the traditional spring observation of Lent was reduced by the early nineteenth century to one day, often falling in March or April. A fall harvest festival eventually was established as a day of thanksgiving. This festival was a moveable feast for more than two hundred years, usually occurring in late November or early December. In the mid-nineteenth century the feast was codified as a national holiday. Because Christmas was too closely associated with the Catholic Church, the Calvinist settlers avoided the holiday and prohibited its observance, including the making of foods such as mincemeat, which marked the day. Until the mid-nineteenth century, most New Englanders conducted business, attended school, and went on with everyday activities on December 25. The old English celebratory spirit and energy of the day and some of the food, which few colonists wanted to give up entirely, were shifted to the thanksgiving holiday.

Spirits, Sweets, and Spices Although the gentry and other prosperous New Englanders followed their seventeenth- and eighteenth-century English peers in their taste for Madeira, port, and other fortified wines, using them both as a beverage and in cooking, the general public drank gin and rum. New Englanders obtained molasses in trade with the West Indies and made their own rum. (Southerners, by contrast, preferred to buy rum made in the West Indies.) By the end of the colonial period, what seems to modern Americans an astonishing quantity of alcoholic beverages was being consumed— three or four gallons per capita per year, the highest level of alcohol consumption in American history.

Molasses not distilled into rum became the common sweetener throughout New England. Refined sugar, an expensive import for most of the seventeenth and eighteenth centuries, was reserved for fine cooking, baking, and preserve making. Less refined brown sugar and molasses were daily sweeteners for many, and the sturdy flavor of molasses characterizes many regional New England dishes. When inland and upcountry people tapped maple trees and boiled sap, they were seeking a locally available version of brown sugar and molasses. In the early days of New England most maple sap was processed into sugar, as it was in other areas of America.

New Englanders came to the region with a preference for late medieval spicing and the complex flavors of the sixteenth century. Through the eighteenth century, the colonists gradually simplified seasoning. In the nineteenth and early twentieth centuries, New Englanders ate the plainest fare in their history, but they ended the twentieth century with the more vibrant flavors of the southwestern United States, Japan, China, Vietnam, Thailand, and the Mediterranean countries. The original Puritans ate more highly flavored foods than did the Victorians who followed them. In later times the preference for bland food was mistakenly attributed to the Puritans.

Nineteenth Century

The era between 1840 and the 1890s saw both change and continuity in New England foodways. The change was less in kind than in the source and production of food. New Englanders continued to prefer beef, pork, and mutton. They ate beans, succotash, molasses-sweetened dishes, and pumpkin and apple pies, and fish once a week. By the mid-nineteenth century in urban New England, beef increasingly came from the West, and by century's end, the beans and succotash may have come from cans. One substantial change was the shift from the old rye-and-Indian bread back to wheat bread. Another was the dramatic turn to nonalcoholic beverages by many middle-class households.

Shifting Back to Wheat Once the Erie Canal was completed, connecting the port of New York and southern New England with western New York State and newly settled lands around the Great Lakes, the cost of wheat dropped, and the quantity available increased. New Englanders seemed glad to give up rye-and-Indian as the daily loaf in favor of bread made in part or entirely of wheat. Forms of bread included loaves made of one-third each wheat, corn,

> ## COFFEE GELATIN
>
> Coffee gelatin is one of the original recipes at Durgin-Park, a Boston restaurant that dates back to 1827—"Established before you were born," as the slogan goes. The restaurant used to serve straightforward Yankee fare to workers at Boston's Faneuil Hall, and still serves classics like prime rib, Yankee pot roast, baked beans, and Indian pudding.
>
> Originally, coffee gelatin was considered a poor person's dessert, because it used leftover coffee. The recipe is nothing more than reheated coffee, sugar, and unflavored gelatin stirred together and refrigerated until firm. It is served in bowls with homemade whipped cream on the side. Customers, especially old-timers, also like to pour cream on top and gently stir for a café au lait effect. Eaten plain, the coffee gelatin is much less sweet than any fruit-flavored gelatin from a packaged mix, a humble ending to a traditional New England meal.
>
> **BIBLIOGRAPHY**
>
> Stern, Jane, and Michael Stern. *The Durgin-Park Cookbook: Classic Yankee Cooking in the Shadow of Faneuil Hall.* Nashville, TN: Rutledge Hill Press, 2002.
>
> CLARA SILVERSTEIN

and rye or from wheat and cornmeal. When more refined wheat made white loaves possible and desirable, bread containing other grains or whole, unbolted wheat, were called "brown bread" or "Graham bread." The old combination of rye-and-Indian with or without wheat flour or meal evolved into a steamed pudding by the middle to late nineteenth century. Sweetened with molasses and mixed with sour milk and baking soda this concoction became known outside the region as "Boston brown bread" and within New England simply as "brown bread."

When refined wheat was joined by a more plentiful supply of white sugar and with the invention of the rotary egg beater, New Englanders, like other Americans, took to cake. People in the Northeast, particularly New England, adopted chemical leavenings, which promoted the preparation of cakes and quick breads, more quickly than did those in the Mid-Atlantic region and the South. Pearlash (potassium carbonate) was the main chemical leavening agent from the 1790s into the 1830s and 1840s. It was followed by saleratus (sodium carbonate) and baking soda (sodium bicarbonate), used with cream of tartar through the mid-nineteenth century, and eventually baking powder. There were chronological overlaps in the use of all these ingredients. Where the population was generally less prosperous, for example, coastal and interior Maine and the remote Vermont and New Hampshire hill country, molasses continued to be the major sweetener. Molasses doughnuts and a version of molasses blueberry cake are found in some Maine bakeries.

The Temperance Movement and Other Diet Reforms Between the end of the Revolution and the first decades of the nineteenth century, American annual alcohol consumption peaked at approximately three and one-half gallons per capita. Some historians attribute the high consumption to the stresses of a rapidly changing society and the combined pressures of uncertainty and opportunity as the new country expanded. A need for a sober workforce to labor in New England mills combined with the millenarianism of the first half of the nineteenth century to create a backlash against heavy drinking. The temperance movement took hold in reform-minded New England, and the old household habit of combining baking and brewing ceased. Many more apples were dried than were squeezed into cider, and it became a sign of refinement to eschew rum, punch, and wine.

One energetic campaigner for temperance was Sylvester Graham, who added diet reform to his list of causes, which included encouraging people to reduce their sexual activity. Graham believed that if one altered one's diet to exclude what he termed "stimulating" foods, such as meat, spices and heavy sauces, refined sugar and flour, and beverages other than water, it would be easier to cease longing for spirituous liquors. Graham also believed that a vegetarian regimen combined with great sexual restraint would allow people to live long and healthy lives. Most Americans in the nineteenth century were not ready to become vegetarians. Although one hundred years earlier New England–born Benjamin Franklin had briefly adopted the practice, vegetarians were considered peculiar.

Graham promoted the use of grains, especially wheat flour still containing the bran and germ, which by the 1830s and 1840s were being routinely removed. Graham's name still clings to the flour he promoted, especially when it is baked into the sweet cracker named for the flour. Graham was followed by many nineteenth-century diet reformers. Some espoused diet reform for religious reasons, but others were students of the growing fields of nutrition and domestic science.

The notion that certain foods and beverages were "stimulating" gained sufficient currency to affect nineteenth-century ideas of good nutrition and suffused cookbook writing for much of the nineteenth century. The

New England Tea Room. Vusper Country Club in Tyngsboro, Massachusetts, early twentieth century. *Prints and Photographs Division, Library of Congress*

belief helps account for but does not entirely explain the simplification of seasoning in the period. Dislocation, even if deliberate migration to the frontier, and hard times often disrupted supplies of food and broke people's culinary habits, factors that may have contributed to the abandonment of earlier foodways.

Refinement and Gentility During the nineteenth century, a combination of prosperity and education brought ideas of refinement to a growing middle class. In the kitchen and dining room these changes were played out in the elaboration of table settings, the widespread adoption of fork use, attention paid to manners, and proliferation of gentry-style dishes among the middle classes. Adoption of temperance principles also was a sign of refinement.

Victorian New Englanders, like other Americans of the era, especially in urban and the new suburban areas, lived farther from their sources of food than they previously had. Many continued to eat organ meats, but the old-style presentations of entire meat and fish fell from fashion. The less a dish looked like its raw ingredients, the more genteel it was considered to be. This trend included shortening the legs of poultry and wildfowl, trussing the birds neatly, and consistently removing the heads of small animals, birds, and eventually, fish.

Certain labor-intensive dishes of earlier times, such as jelled and whipped egg- or cream-based dishes, were eased into middle-class use with egg beaters and commercial gelatin. Mimicking French dishes was another sign of refinement. Even cookbooks such as *The Boston Cooking-School Cook Book* which was aimed at a middle-class audience as well as those who expected to cook for a living, contained recipes for sauces, puddings, and entrees with French names.

Food and Industry Another influence on food habits in New England and nationwide was growing commerce and industry related to food. Although it did not begin in New England, the canning industry found opportunities there. Many farms added to the general production of meat, milk, grain, and vegetables, and they began to grow crops such as tomatoes, sweet corn, beans, and squash for the canneries that were springing up in cities and towns close to the growers. Along the coast, clams, lobster, and sardines joined the list of canned foods.

In the late nineteenth century Gloucester and Boston fish producers, to help support New England fisheries, which were competing with West Coast fisheries, began selling prepared fish—boneless salt cod, even salt cod

shredded and ready for quick freshening in hot water; canned chowder; codfish cakes; and crab and salmon ready for salad or heating in cream sauce. These products were among the nation's earliest convenience foods.

Immigration During the nineteenth century and into the beginning of the twentieth, New England cities, seaports, and industrial centers attracted large numbers of immigrants. The first were Irish fleeing the potato famine, followed by Italians, Germans, Swedes, middle Europeans, Portuguese, freed blacks, and French Canadians. A combination of the desire of newcomers to become Americanized and the desire of native Yankees to remain apart meant that many food habits were only slowly exchanged. Some ethnic groups were numerous enough to support local grocery stores, which carried favorite foods. Even in a small city like Portsmouth, New Hampshire, there was large enough Jewish population to support kosher butchers. Italians in Boston fished for and sold varieties of fish to other immigrants that most other New Englanders had ignored. In New Bedford, Massachusetts, and Providence, Rhode Island, Portuguese bakeries were established that survived into the late twentieth century.

Some immigrants were glad to adopt New England food habits, particularly meat eating. Gradually, and mostly in the twentieth century, Yankees learned how to eat and cook a few ethnic foods, usually adapting them to suit their own palates. Many found, for example, the smell and flavor of garlic reminded them of poor, urban immigrants with whom they did not wish to associate. Diet reformers took up the cause of teaching immigrants American ways of cookery, which often included meat, potatoes, dairy products, and bread to replace what would, in the late twentieth century, be recognized as a healthier diet of more fish, more vegetables, small quantities of meat, and fewer sweets.

Twentieth and Early Twenty-first Centuries

Two World Wars and a Depression Three major events disrupted New England foodways in the twentieth century. Two world wars brought periods of rationing of meat, butter, and sugar for most citizens, and the Depression caused hardship for many New Englanders. That these events occurred within thirty years meant that some people spent most of their lives getting by. Others grew up during the Depression, endured World War II, and entered the 1950s with strong memories of hard times and making do or doing without. With meat consumption curtailed during rationing, some families ate more fish than they once had. Many families had victory gardens, and, encouraged by government agencies, patriotically canned fruits and vegetables.

The result seems to have been that with the interruptions caused by hard times, it was easier for New Englanders to forget old ways and to adopt new and, by the 1950s, often commercially introduced foods. In remote and less prosperous sections of New England, old foodways persisted, but in more affluent urban and suburban areas, national brands and mass distribution overwhelmed many traditions.

Food Production Leaves the Region   Even before the Depression, New England farmers were feeling pressure from the Midwest, where larger farms achieved an economy of scale practically impossible in the Northeast. Many smaller canneries in rural areas went out of business by World War II, and during the war, labor shortages, even when alleviated by the work of prisoners of war, closed down others. Dairy farming and fruit growing with some market gardening kept some food production within the region, but rising land values and a growing regional population looking for house lots starting in the 1970s have forced many more farms out of existence. In the early twenty-first century, most food consumed in New England comes from other regions in the United States and the world.

Later Ethnic Introductions   The variety of ethnic fare shared by groups who had been in New England for decades became absorbed through the influence of mass communication and restaurant offerings. In addition, new immigrants have arrived in the region and brought their foodways. Even small inland cities are likely to sport a Thai, Mexican, Vietnamese, or Caribbean restaurant.

Food, Festivals, and Regional Identity   New England food traditions are kept alive by self-conscious means. Festivals and food tourism have proved popular vehicles for both curious visitors from outside the region and long-time New Englanders seeking reaffirmation or reacquaintance with their food traditions. Seasonal observances begin with maple syrup making in the spring; continue through strawberry and blueberry festivals in early and mid summer and lobster festivals in late summer; and end with apple and pumpkin celebrations in the fall. Religious, grange, and civic organizations hold baked bean and ham suppers and, along the coast, chowder suppers. Vacationers and locals both hold clambakes or lobster bakes, a leisure-time activity that dates to the mid-nineteenth century and recalls an even earlier supposed connection to the original settlers and Native Americans. In northern New England, bean-hole bean suppers recall the lumber industry of the region. Ethnic groups hold festivals at which food is sold. Some festivals are held merely to celebrate the existence of the group; others are held in connection with older observances, such as Blessings of the Fleet (Italian) and old religious holidays. New England tourism fosters regional specialties, such as Vermont cheese and maple sugar candy and Maine lobster. Locally landed seafood offered in restaurants, clam shacks, and lobster pounds similarly hark back to the New England fishing history

To provision the dense New England population, food from outside the region continues to supply most of the region's diet. A countervailing impulse comes from regional restaurants featuring locally grown food and from chefs, food writers, and cooking schools who encourage consumers to support regional agricultural by patronizing farmers' markets and community-supported agriculture operations and by demanding locally grown food in supermarkets. Trading on New England's traditional dishes and specialties, locally grown foods, and new cultural influences may freshen the fare of the region.

[*See also* Apples; Beans; Boston Cooking School; Brweing; Cakes; Cheese; Christmas; Cider; Cider, Hard; Clambake; Corn; Dairy Industry; Ethnic Foods; Fish, *subentries on* Saltwater Fish *and* Saltwater Shellfish; Food Festivals; Graham, Sylvester; Molasses; Myths and Folklore, *sidebar on* Johnny Appleseed; Native American Foods; Pudding, *sidebar on* Hasty Pudding; Rum; Temperance; Thanksgiving; Vegetarianism.]

BIBLIOGRAPHY

Albion, Robert, William A. Baker, and Benjamin W. Labaree. *New England and the Sea*. Middletown, CT: Wesleyan University Press, 1972.

Child, Lydia Maria. *The American Frugal Housewife*. Columbus, OH: Friends of the Libraries of the Ohio State University, 1965. Reprint of the 12th edition, published in 1833 by Carter, Hendee, Boston.

Conroy, David W. *In Public Houses: Drink and the Revolution of Authority in Colonial Massachusetts*. Chapel Hill: University of North Carolina Press, 1995.

Farmer, Fanny Merritt. *The Boston Cooking-School Cook Book*. Boston: Little, Brown, 1895.

Larkin, Jack. *The Reshaping of Everyday Life, 1790–1840*. New York: Harper and Row, 1988.

Neustadt, Kathy. *Clambakes: A History and Celebration of an American Tradition*. Amherst: University of Massachusetts Press, 1992.

Nylander, Jane. *Our Own Snug Fireside: Images of the New England Home. 1760–1860*. New York: Knopf, 1993.

Oliver, Sandra L. *Saltwater Foodways: New Englanders and Their Food at Sea and Ashore in the 19th Century*. Mystic, CT: Mystic Seaport Museum, 1995.

Rorabaugh, William J. *The Alcoholic Republic: An American Tradition*. New York and Oxford: Oxford University Press, 1979.

Russell, Howard S. *A Long Deep Furrow: Three Centuries of Farming in New England*. Hanover, NH, and London: University Press of New England, 1982.

Shapiro, Laura. *Perfection Salad: Women and Cooking at the Turn of the Century*. New York: Farrar, Straus, and Giroux, 1986.

Simmons, Amelia. *The First American Cookbook: A Facsimile of "American Cookery," 1796 by Amelia Simmons*. New York: Dover, 1984. Includes an essay by Mary Tolford Wilson.

Ulrich, Laurel Thatcher. *A Midwife's Tale: the Life of Martha Ballard, Based on Her Diary, 1785–1812*. New York: Knopf, 1990.

SANDRA OLIVER

New Orleans Syrup

New Orleans syrup is a gold-colored sweetener derived from sugarcane juice. In New Orleans the product is most commonly known by the brand name Steen's 100% Pure Cane Syrup or ribbon cane syrup. In southern states, it became known as New Orleans syrup because of the large quantities produced in the New Orleans area.

The sugarcane plant used for syrup production came from India by way of the Caribbean islands. It was first introduced to Louisiana in the mid-eighteenth century and thrives there in the high temperatures and constant moisture required for cultivation. Farmers often raised patches of sugarcane and took their harvests to local sugar mills for processing. During harvest season, the cane is cut down, and its outer leaves are stripped away. At the mill, the stalks are pulverized, and the cane juice is boiled to remove impurities. The resulting syrup is canned and cooled.

Before the prevalence of cane sugar, cane syrup was the primary sweetener. An old-time southern Louisiana desert called "syrup soppin'" consisted of cane syrup poured onto the plate after a finished meal and sopped up with bread. New Orleans syrup is used as a condiment, is poured over biscuits and *pain perdu* (French toast), and is used as a sweetener in baking and other cooking methods.

[*See also* Cajun and Creole Food; Sugar; Sweeteners.]

BIBLIOGRAPHY

Steen, Mrs. J. Wesley, ed. *The Story of Steen's Syrup and its Famous Recipes*. Abbeville, LA: Steen's Syrup Mill, n.d.

Gutierrez, Paige C. *Cajun Foodways*. Jackson: University of Mississippi Press, 1992.

JENNIFER MINNICK

New Year's Celebrations

Although champagne has become de rigueur as midnight strikes, no single food epitomizes the contemporary New Year's holiday. The menu may be luxurious caviar at a New Year's Eve bacchanalia or sobering hoppin' John on New Year's Day. Celebrations marking the inexorable march of Father Time often involve foods imbued with symbolism, such as in the Pennsylvania Dutch New Year's tradition of sauerkraut (for wealth) and pork—the pig roots forward into the future, unlike the Christmas turkey, which buries the past by scratching backward in the dirt.

Seventeenth-century Dutch immigrants in the Hudson River valley welcomed the New Year by "opening the house" to family and friends. The custom was adapted by English colonists, who used brief, strictly choreographed, January 1 social calls for gentlemen to renew bonds or repair frayed relationships. Ladies remained at home, offering elegantly arrayed collations laden with cherry bounce, wine, hot punch, and cakes and cookies, often flavored with the Dutch signatures of caraway, coriander,

New Year's Cider. Advertising card for Weber's bread products, early twentieth century. *Collection of Alice Ross*

cardamom, and honey. Embossed New Year's "cakes," from the Dutch *nieuwjaarskoeken*—made by pressing a cookie-like dough into carved wooden boards decorated with flora and fauna—were a New York specialty throughout the nineteenth century.

Politicians embraced—or were embraced by—the New Year's open house. George Washington inaugurated a custom of presidential New Year's levees in 1791. The levees, which continued until the Franklin D. Roosevelt administration, were a powerful statement in the fledgling democracy: Any properly dressed person with a letter of introduction, could—without an invitation—drink punch and nibble cake with the president. The diarist Philip Hone reported in 1837 that "scamps" with muddy boots stormed the home of the New York mayor, shouting "huzzas" for the mayor and demanding refreshment. The police restored order only after the celebrants had drained the mayor's bottles, devoured his beef and turkey, and wiped their greasy fingers on his curtains.

Heavy drinking, especially among the young and the disadvantaged, was widely reported from the late eighteenth century on, when servants and slaves pounded on doors in the middle of the night demanding New Year's drinks. Alcohol continues to assume a prominent place in New Year's parties, notwithstanding the efforts of nineteenth-century temperance advocates, who pointedly poured effervescent sarsaparilla, coffee, and tea.

The New York custom of open house spread westward in the nineteenth century. Although the Dutch palimpsest continued in the "cold-slaw" found in Eliza Leslie's menus for New Year's dinner in *New Receipts for Cooking* (1854), other influences shaped the holiday, particularly in the South. In the eighteenth and nineteenth centuries those of French and English backgrounds celebrated the twelve days of Christmas with gifts of food and festive dinners on January 1. Antebellum plantation owners sometimes gave slaves oxen to slaughter on New Year's Day as well as liquor for the slaves' parties. African Americans in the eighteenth and nineteenth centuries made one of the most enduring contributions to the modern holiday. Starting in the Carolinas but extending throughout the South, hoppin' John and greens became traditional New Year's fare, black-eyed peas bringing luck and the rice (which swelled in the cooking) and greens (like money) bringing prosperity. In the early twentieth century Japanese Americans adopted the open house tradition, serving glutinous rice dishes, soups, boiled lobsters (signifying health and happiness), and fish specially prepared to appear alive and swimming.

[*See also* Christmas; Thanksgiving.]

BIBLIOGRAPHY

Barnes, Donna R., and Peter G. Rose. *Matters of Taste: Food and Drink in Seventeenth-Century Dutch Art and Life*. Albany, NY: Albany Institute of History and Art, 2002. Beautifully illustrated museum catalog exploring Dutch and New Netherlands foodways, including holiday foods, with essays.

Nissenbaum, Stephen. *The Battle for Christmas*. New York: Random House, 1997. A thoughtful social history of the nineteenth-century domesticity revolution as it changed the way in which the Christmas season was celebrated, with some helpful references to journals, diaries, and popular literature.

Weaver, William Woys. *America Eats: Forms of Edible Folk Art*. New York: Harper and Row, 1989. Well-illustrated and informative descriptions of mainly historical foods. Special holiday dishes are identified.

CATHY K. KAUFMAN

New York Food

A vast natural web of food resources in the region now occupied by New York City was quickly obliterated when Europeans arrived. The Dutch West India Company, which founded the town of New Amsterdam on Manhattan Island in 1624 as the launching point for New Netherland colony, saw fur trading as its chief interest in the lower Hudson River valley. The colonists brought with them the region's first European field crops, garden vegetables, orchard fruits, and livestock, but the low priority given by the company to establishing self-sufficiency in food meant a slow start for farming.

New Amsterdammers initially relied on dried peas and other legumes, salted meat or fish, butter, cheese, beer, salt, and flour, all carried from the Netherlands or other Dutch New World holdings and sold, often at extortionate prices, from the company's storehouse on what is now Whitehall Street, close to the East River. They drew heavily on the fish and shellfish that were the region's greatest resource and obtained game and sometimes maize from the Indians.

After farming was established, most food was either grown at home or bought at the public market on the Strand, an open area near the company's storehouses to which farmers brought produce in season as well as milk, eggs, and livestock or dressed meat. The Indians also brought game and fish to market until they began to be crowded out of their settlements.

The colony was a place of simple foodways. The kitchen, where it existed as a separate room, contained little more than a fireplace with a few cooking pots of tin-lined brass or cast iron, a few implements, and some wooden or pewter dishes. Few home ovens existed, except in farmhouses. The cooking was largely a replica of contemporary Dutch cooking with the addition of New World maize, squash, and *Phaseolus* beans. One-pot stews and soup-stews with various meat-vegetable combinations were usual main dishes. The Dutch taste for cereal porridges hastened their adoption of the local Indian cornmeal mush (*sapaen*). An anchor of the Dutch diet was milk in different forms (fresh, soured, or made into buttermilk, whey, and cheeses). The crafts of baking and brewing were soon established, and special decorative holiday breads became well known in the colony. Eventually, the colonists were sending their own wheat, flour, salt meat, and pickled oysters to the slave plantations of the West Indies, which in turn sent sugar and rum.

Ale or beer was a frequent accompaniment to all daily meals (including breakfast) as well as refreshment at other times. Wine, gin, brandy, and rum were consumed in large enough amounts to occasion regular scandals about public drunkenness. Neither restaurants nor hotels existed, but public accommodations in the form of taverns and inns with simple meals cooked to order were quickly founded in New Amsterdam starting with a large stone building known as the Stadts Herbergh (City Tavern), erected on Pearl Street around 1640.

England's conquest of the colony (renamed New York) in 1664 paradoxically gave Hudson Valley Dutch settlers greater stability than they had known before. For many generations, Dutch-descended Brooklyn farmers and the "Jersey Dutch" of Bergen County, New Jersey, were among the principal suppliers of the city's public markets. Here and there, local Dutch held on to some of their characteristic foodways until the twentieth century. Among the foods that they bequeathed to a later America were coleslaw (often originally made with a melted butter dressing), waffles, doughnuts (called *oliekoecken*), and *koekjes* (later anglicized to "cookies").

In many ways, the colonial English cuisine resembled that of the Dutch. Both cuisines were products of damp northern climates with a fairly heavy use of animal fats, both relied on bread and cheese as plain people's everyday fare, and both had a taste for sugar that was gradually spreading from the elite throughout society. The English, however, were already known as Europe's great specialists in roasted and grilled meats.

Food in Commerce

English New York acquired an increasing social and economic complexity—along with pronounced English-derived class divisions—as a greater volume of Caribbean and Old World trade channeled more money, goods, and people into the colony. Much locally raised food was shipped abroad, including salt pork and beef as well as wheat and flour destined for the West Indies; a political football of the day was a New York City monopoly on the lucrative business of bolting flour (sifting it through cloths) from all wheat grown in the province, from 1680 to 1696.

New York became, and remained for close to two centuries, one of America's major sugar towns, with large sugar mills and rum distilleries. By the early eighteenth century, African slaves brought to the colony through local extensions of the infamous triangular trade involving the Caribbean, Europe, and North America constituted more than a fifth of the city's population, though little African influence was visible in the Anglo-Dutch cuisine.

The chief source of perishable foods was the public markets, whose offerings were mostly ferried over the rivers from New Jersey or the Long Island towns; livestock were often driven overland from the King's Bridge across Spuyten Duyvil Creek between southern Westchester (now the Bronx) and the northern tip of Manhattan. Meat was more plentiful than in early days, though by now game had to be sought from farther away. Clean water for drinking and cooking became scarcer in the course of the eighteenth century. The most important food-related professions remained baking and brewing. Among the wealthy merchant classes it is likely (though not documented) that French-influenced cooking was, as in England, on the rise by the time of the Revolution.

The number of taverns and inns increased along with New York's commercial importance. The new European hot beverages—coffee, tea, and chocolate—reached the colony late in the seventeenth century. The makings of these (along with sugar, spices, and sometimes wine and liquor) were sold by retail merchants called "grocers" whose operations were still sharply distinguished from those of the markets. Many coffeehouses, serving a range of food and drink along with coffee and tea, sprang up close to the docks and warehouses at the southern tip of Manhattan and quickly became the usual venues of merchants' business meetings. After about 1750, political activity also flourished in the city's taverns and coffee-houses, and several became associated with different factions in the events leading up to the Revolution. During the war itself, New York, as headquarters of the occupying British army, suffered repeated food shortages because of the interdiction of supplies from England and the constant pilfering from surrounding farms by both armies. Manhattan's growth into the new nation's first metropolis began in earnest early in the nineteenth century. The narrow island acquired a concentration of business establishments at the southern end that pushed residential housing farther and farther away, rearranging people's work and mealtime schedules so that many had to take the midday meal away from home. The growing volume of wealthy business transients and other people temporarily based in the city also led to a demand for suitable accommodations. From about 1825, these needs began to be met by eating places, hotels, and boarding houses that gradually replaced the older coffeehouses, taverns, and inns.

The foundations of New York's restaurant culture were laid through an array of choices including chophouses, coffee shops, confectioners' or pastry shops, "ice cream saloons," and oyster houses—these last among the few business opportunities then open to free blacks; Thomas Downing's Broad Street establishment was considered the finest of many. The elegant food of Delmonico's Restaurant (which began as a small confectioner's shop in 1827 and had several prosperous branches by the end of the century) and the Astor House (which opened in 1836) was the admiration of both American and European travelers, many of whom found American food generally regrettable. A novelty of the pre–Civil War era was establishments suitable for women whose shopping activities—something that became a fashionable pursuit from about the 1830s on—made a midday pause for refreshment attractive. Throughout the century, further changes in family schedules occasioned by new work and school patterns continued to expand the role of places for eating out or buying prepared foods (e.g., candy or snacks) and to diminish the importance of home kitchens, formerly the source of almost all the day's meals for virtually everyone.

Canal and railroad transport confirmed New York's role as the great national port of exit and entry for commercial food shipments. These included exports of grain, salt meat and fish, and Hudson Valley table fruits and imports of "fancy trade" luxuries (such as Mediterranean citrus fruits and Caribbean tropical fruits) destined for affluent Manhattan consumers.

Decline of the Markets

By the time of the Civil War, farming around the metropolis was being displaced by real-estate pressures. The

Delmonico's. Interior of Delmonico's Restaurant in the late nineteenth century.

public markets, formerly the site of retail sales by individual farmers to an inclusive cross section of New York humanity, were entering on changes that would shrink their numbers and, by the early twentieth century, convert most of the survivors into wholesale depots for Midwestern and Pacific Coast food shipments. By then, the earlier distinction between "markets" and "groceries" had blurred, the latter assuming most of the functions of the former for household shopping.

From about the 1840s on, dwellings gradually acquired running water from the new Croton reservoir project (completed in 1842), coal- or wood-burning iron kitchen ranges, and ice-cooled "refrigerators." These amenities, however, did not reach all classes at once and were not common in the first homes of the immigrants who began arriving by the thousands after the late 1840s.

Of the first two waves, the Irish (who largely replaced American black women as domestic cooks) brought no characteristic national foodways, but the Germans possessed an unmistakable culinary culture. Their local settlements (the largest being *Kleindeutschland*, or "Little Germany," on the East Side below Fourteenth Street) had distinctively German bread bakeries, breweries specializing in the refreshing lager beer, (instantly popular with the locals), *Delikatessen* selling a large range of both imported and locally made German "delicacies" (the literal meaning of the word), and beer halls or outdoor beer gardens—soon to be copied by American restaurateurs—that dispensed food like fresh hot sausages and pickled-fish salads to German parties along with musical entertainment.

After the Civil War, New York's expanding national and international stature as a hub of finance and manufacturing was accompanied by the rise of a wealthy elite able to command lavish gastronomic displays that drew on a food supply of increasingly global dimensions. Some installed French chefs at home; they also supported the growth of restaurants like Delmonico's, its splashier rival Louis Sherry's, the Waldorf-Astoria Hotel Palm Garden, and, by the end of the century, the gaudy big shot–and–showgirl hangouts dubbed "lobster palaces" (Rector's was the most famous). The city's role as a center of journalism, book publishing, and the arts helped attract a diverse population of transplants from all regions of the country, who formed a lively restaurant clientele.

Several large new immigrant communities emerged, mostly concentrated in lower Manhattan. The major groups were eastern European Jews, southern Italians, and a much smaller but highly visible Chinese group (hindered from

Pretzel Man. Peddler selling pretzels on the sidewalk in New York City, 1917. *Prints and Photographs Division, Library of Congress*

growth by the Chinese Exclusion Act of 1882). The cooking of all these communities initially kept some continuity with their original foodways. Jewish and Italian preferences, however, were increasingly shaped by new factors like cheap, plentiful meat and other formerly unattainable luxuries, as well as by a process of hybridization on these shores among members of immigrant communities who would not have been exposed to each other's food in the old country. All these groups eventually developed restaurant versions of their original cuisines (the Chinese being the most self-consciously adapted to outside tastes) that played to a diverse American-born audience and enhanced New York's growing image as a gastronomic tourist destination. Chop suey, spaghetti and meatballs, and delicatessen sandwiches—indeed, much of the Jewish or Jewish-style delicatessen food that came to be synonymous with New York in many minds—were fundamentally American constructs for Americans.

Lunchtime

Population growth and economic development continued at a furious pace after the 1880s, leading up to the 1898 consolidation of Manhattan and four adjoining counties into the five boroughs of New York City; further immense population increases in the boroughs were made possible by subway transport. The changes also meant a vast expansion of employment that created a demand for simple, conveniently located, inexpensive eateries open to a wide social spectrum. By the early twentieth century, much of the New York white-collar workforce was eating lunch and sometimes other meals at popular chains such as Childs (begun here in 1889), Schrafft's (which was expanding from tiny beginnings by 1906), and the Horn & Hardart Automats (which arrived from Philadelphia in 1912). All offered unprecedented accommodation for the city's many female office and clerical workers, opened up an important new source of low-level employment for

New York Business Lunch. Hot dog vendor's cart at Twenty-third Street and Fifth Avenue in Manhattan. *Photograph by Joe Zarba*

women, and heralded the modern emergence of food service as one of the city's main job sectors.

After World War I, another surge in New York's global importance (as world investment-banking capital, arts mecca, hub of communications technology, and national nerve center) enabled its restaurant culture to keep on deepening, broadening, and diversifying. Ethnic population increases, however, were largely stalled by the discriminatory quotas of the 1924 National Origins Act at a time of other disruptive changes. Highways and other public works projects were destroying neighborhoods in the boroughs, a large influx of southern blacks and a smaller one of Puerto Ricans were rearranging the racial makeup of Harlem and other neighborhoods, and the city was undergoing some retrenchment in manufacturing jobs. The city's foodways responded variously to these and other factors.

Restaurants generally, and the much-remarked array of ethnic restaurants and food shops, became a New York pride and joy as well as a tourist drawing card. The old elite among city dining places (Delmonico's, Sherry's, and many temples of French-inspired cuisine) were put out of business after Prohibition began in 1919. But for members of New York's professional classes as well as its arts and communications circles, a glamorous night life continued unabated at a plethora of speakeasies and clubs supplying bootleg liquor. In the ethnic neighborhoods of the boroughs, bars and taverns sometimes survived under the guise of social-athletic clubs. Various kinds of establishments not dependent on alcohol sales expanded during Prohibition, while eating places of most varieties became friendlier places for unescorted women. Inexpensive ethnic restaurants—particularly those offering a vaguely bohemian atmosphere and a version of Italian cooking tailored to American taste—became New York perennials; chains and cafeterias catering to the lunch crowd solidified their presence.

By the time of the Depression, the New York public markets had almost wholly ceased to handle local produce or retail sales. Neighborhood grocery stores were the principal shopping places for most residents except in some ethnic neighborhoods where vegetables, fish, and fruit were generally bought from pushcart vendors. City Hall tended to regard these as street nuisances and herded most of the pushcarts into enclosed market buildings during the administration of Mayor Fiorello La Guardia (1934–1945). In Manhattan, an ever-tighter real-estate squeeze kept retail food stores from following

Pressures of Space. Narrow aisles in Park Slope Food Coop, Brooklyn, New York. *Photograph by Joe Zarba*

a national trend toward greater square footage and forced supermarkets (which began in 1930 in Jamaica, Queens, with King Kullen) into tiny, crowded premises.

The same pressures of space caused even fairly successful professionals to make do with kitchens of minuscule dimensions with few amenities in Manhattan apartments incompatible with families, and led to frequent curtailment of cooking activities among sophisticates. Yet at the same time New York was becoming the national center of a corps of food journalists who patronized and publicized a wide spectrum of city eateries (and drinking spots, after the repeal of Prohibition in 1933). They laid the foundations of a gourmet home-cooking movement that achieved full visibility with the 1941 debut of *Gourmet* magazine and that throughout the country would be seen as essentially directed from, though not limited to, New York.

The last half of the twentieth century saw New York's role as the American culinary capital first amplified, then impinged on, by massive demographic changes. The forces that intensified New York's affluence (a large concentration of international corporate headquarters with much ancillary professional activity leading to a golden age of expense accounts) and the forces that aggravated poverty (steep local manufacturing job losses and a shrunken labor market at a time of huge southern black and Puerto Rican influxes) all too often made the New York food story into a tale of two cities.

For the many sharers of privilege and prosperity, the years immediately after World War II brought a rising tide of interest in gourmet home cooking; by the mid-1960s and early 1970s, many fashionable urban professionals were regularly preparing elaborate meals, usually French in character, using recipes from cookbooks like the influ-

ential *Mastering the Art of French Cooking* by Julia Child, Simone Beck, and Louisette Bertholle (volume I, 1961; volume II, 1970), or *Michael Field's Cooking School* (1965). The vogue for cooking complex, time-consuming dishes from scratch had somewhat faded by the 1990s (to be replaced by a vogue for *buying* such dishes from a burgeoning array of gourmet takeout shops and caterers), but the market for cookbooks only increased. Cookbook publishing, massively dominated by New York editors and editorial groups, grew explosively, with an intense concentration on specialized market niches and on large, photograph-filled books by another product of the era: celebrity chefs. The latters' work was also often displayed on television cooking shows and publicized in the new food magazines that were launched (mostly from New York) in the 1970s and 1980s.

Critics and Cults

A marked cult of restaurants had begun building in New York in the 1950s, when professional think-tank teams started developing splashy dining spots that represented huge real estate speculations for corporate backers. The Forum of the Twelve Caesars and the Four Seasons, created by the pioneering Restaurant Associates group, were early examples of this trend. After 1957, Craig Claiborne, as the *New York Times'* influential food critic, contributed greatly to the mythos of haute cuisine strongholds like Le Pavillon (founded in 1941 by staff members of the French restaurant pavilion at the 1939–1940 New York World's Fair who were stranded here by the outbreak of war in Europe). With other restaurant reviewers, Claiborne helped invest the subject of dining out with weighty importance and launched a series of trends that swung during the late 1960s and 1970s through the vogues of nouvelle cuisine (supposedly a break with ponderous French *grande cuisine* traditions); *cuisine minceur* (high style with low fat); elegant, expensive versions of Italian food; a "New American cuisine" especially associated with the innovative restaurateur Larry Forgione at An American Place; and a colorful amalgam known as "Mediterranean cuisine." By the end of the 1980s, a highly disparate "fusion cuisine" evincing contemporary chefs' new interest in Far Eastern and other non-European culinary motifs propelled a sophisticated urban public into an increasing fascination with restaurant dining as theatrical experiment.

At the same time, however, observers of the general American culinary scene were noting that more and more new developments were being absorbed everywhere in the

Greenmarket. Greenmarket at Grand Army Plaza, Brooklyn. *Photograph by Joe Zarba*

country without special reference to New York tastemakers. The chefs who now appeared to be freshest and most original in their approach were principally Californians drawing on a wealth of genuinely local, seasonal produce that had vanished from Greater Metropolitan New York generations ago—though a farmers' market program, founded in 1976 by the Council on the Environment of New York City under the name of "Greenmarkets," was making valiant inroads on this situation.

Far from the ken of those who made a cult of food fashion (often dubbed "foodies" after the mid-1980s), the most decisive alteration in twentieth-century American foodways was initiated by the 1965 Hart-Celler Act. This groundbreaking legislation, which (with a few later adjustments) abolished prior restrictions on immigration from all of the Third World as well as southern and eastern Europe, would eventually revitalize huge chunks of the metropolis that had suffered job loss and blight. The newcomers arrived in many parts of America at once rather than being funnelled through New York, so that the city's earlier role as immigration gateway was only partly reprised. They included people from all regions of China (who broadened the previously Cantonese slant of New York Chinese food), Koreans, Southeast Asians of many nationalities, Indians, Pakistanis, Bangladeshis, assorted Middle Easterners, Russian Jews, West Africans, West

Indians, and a vast spectrum of Latin Americans. Within a few years, recent immigrants from developing countries constituted much of the labor force for the brilliant mainstream restaurants of Manhattan.

While home cooking yielded in many parts of New York to frozen microwave dinners or takeout meals and the old, inclusive city chain eateries were replaced by national fast-food franchises, the new ethnic enclaves, in (especially) Queens, Brooklyn, and nearby New Jersey became the metropolitan region's prime strongholds of home cooking and affordable, community-based restaurant food.

Because of computer-age technology and an easy global movement of capital, the new immigrants were able to maintain uninterrupted, virtually instant communication with their first homes as they swiftly created local support systems including food-manufacturing businesses, small groceries, supermarkets, and gigantic pan-Asian or pan-Latin emporiums supplying a panoply of foodstuffs either canned, frozen, or fresh. After about the mid-1990s, the New York food press and the foodie community became increasingly aware of the ongoing ethnic revolution and began exploring the culinary resources of neighborhoods such as Flushing and Jackson Heights in Queens or Sunset Park and Brighton Beach in Brooklyn.

By the late 1990s, a few bridges were opening between the culinary establishment's New York and demotic New

York. In the midtown and Wall Street office districts, an expanding street-food business (which had become many people's solution to the lunch question as the old coffee shops and chain restaurants dwindled) took on a robustly multiethnic character, offering such fare as tacos, falafel, souvlaki, Pakistani kebabs with naan, West Indian curried chicken with roti, or Chinese roast pork buns. Takeout sushi from a tribe of "gourmet delis" in the same areas (unrelated to the earlier New York delicatessens) also had become thoroughly naturalized. As *New York Times* restaurant critic from 1993 to 1999, Ruth Reichl helped ease some foodie prejudices about the gap between ethnic food and elegant cuisine.

Superstar chefs, super expensive Manhattan restaurants, and elaborate culinary contrivance continued to dominate local food news without serious interruption even through the fiscal ills of the 1970s and the 1987 stock market collapse. From the early 1980s, however, leading figures in local gastronomic circles were responding to the plight of the homeless and disabled by spearheading food-relief efforts like Citymeals on Wheels and Share Our Strength. Some signs of a weakening restaurant market were apparent even before the terrible events of September 11, 2001. The destruction of the beloved Windows on the World (in which seventy-three employees and several hundred patrons died) in the collapse of the World Trade Center ushered in a grave citywide crisis in the restaurant business, leaving the future of the high-end gastronomy so long identified with New York in much doubt.

[*See also* Automats; Beer Gardens; Beer Halls; Brady, Diamond Jim; Cafeterias; Celebrity Chefs; Chinese American Food; Claiborne, Craig; Coffeehouses; Delicatessens; Delmonico's; Doughnuts; Dutch Influences on American Food; Ethnic Foods; Farmers' Markets; Fusion Food; German American Food; Indian American Food; Italian American Food; Jewish American Food; Lüchow's; Nouvelle Cuisine; Prohibition; Restaurant Critics and Food Columnists; Restaurants; Taverns; Transportation of Food; Tschirky, Oscar.]

BIBLIOGRAPHY

Batterberry, Michael and Ariane. *On the Town in New York: The Landmark History of Eating, Drinking, and Entertainments from the American Revolution to the Food Revolution.* 25th Anniversary Edition. New York and London: Routledge, 1999.

Burroughs, Edwin G., and Mike Wallace. *Gotham: A History of New York City to 1898.* New York: Oxford University Press, 1999.

DeVoe, Thomas F. *The Market Assistant.* New York: Hurd and Houghton, 1867.

DeVoe, Thomas F. *The Market Book.* New York: Franklin, 1969. Facsimile of 1862 self-published edition.

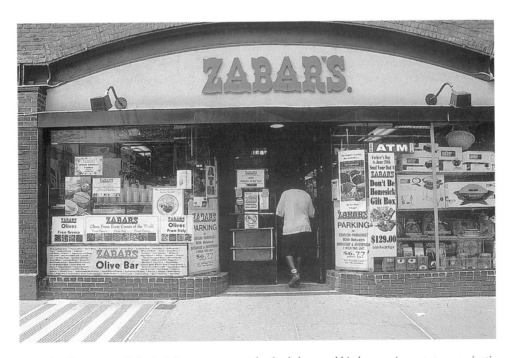

Zabar's. Entrance to Zabar's delicatessen, specialty food shop, and kitchen equipment store, an institution on the Upper West Side of Manhattan. *Photograph by Joe Zarba*

Evans, Meryle R. "Knickerbocker Hotels and Restaurants 1800–1850." *New-York Historical Society Quarterly* 36 (1952): 377–410.

Jackson, Kenneth T., ed. *The Encyclopedia of New York City.* New Haven, London, and New York: Yale University Press and the New-York Historical Society, 1995.

Mariani, John. *America Eats Out: An Illustrated History of Restaurants, Taverns, Coffee Shops, Speakeasies, and Other Establishments That Have Fed Us for 350 Years.* New York: Morrow, 1991.

Rose, Peter G., tr. and ed. *The Sensible Cook: Dutch Foodways in the Old and the New World.* Syracuse: Syracuse University Press, 1989; paperback, 1998. Contains an annotated translation of the seventeenth-century Dutch cookbook *De Verstandige Kock, of Sorghvuldige Huyshoudster,* Amsterdam, 1683.

ANNE MENDELSON

North American Free Trade Agreement

Entered into on December 17, 1992, the North American Free Trade Agreement, or NAFTA, is a multilateral agreement among the United States, Canada, and Mexico to eliminate barriers to trade, to facilitate cross-border movement of goods and services, and to promote conditions of fair competition in the free trade area. Where food and agriculture are concerned, critics have claimed that NAFTA's free trade provisions present potential risks to the safety of the United States' food supply and significant threats to the existence of America's small farms and small food-producers.

NAFTA superseded the 1989 Canada–United States Free Trade Agreement (CUSFTA), an agreement that significantly increased trade between the two countries by reducing and removing certain tariffs and trade barriers. The free trade area was expanded to include Mexico after that country expressed interest in gaining increased access to the Canadian–United States market. NAFTA was ratified by Congress and implemented in the United States when President George H. W. Bush signed the North American Free Trade Agreement Implementation Act on December 8, 1993. It went into effect on January 1, 1994.

Under NAFTA and the NAFTA Implementation Act, trade is not completely free. There are significant limitations on unrestricted free trade among the NAFTA countries concerning food safety. NAFTA gives each country the right to implement and enforce "sanitary" measures to protect its consumers from unsafe food and food products exported by either of the other countries. The NAFTA Implementation Act definitions of the terms "sanitary measures" (protecting animal and human health) and "phytosanitary measures" (protecting plants) are very broad. They include, in part, any law, regulation, or procedure adopted "to protect human or animal life or health in the United States from risks arising from the presence of an additive, contaminant, toxin, or disease-causing organism in a food, beverage, or feedstuff." Further, the NAFTA Implementation Act states that nothing in the law "may be construed (1) to prohibit a Federal agency or State agency from engaging in activity related to sanitary or phytosanitary measures to protect human, animal, or plant life or health; or (2) to limit the authority of a Federal agency or State agency to determine the level of protection of human, animal, or plant life or health the agency considers appropriate."

This clause means, for example, that under the NAFTA Implementation Act, California retains the right to set its own food safety standards and can test, sample, and inspect at its border all fruits and vegetables imported from Mexico to determine if they comply with California's laws and regulations. Unsafe foods are not allowed to enter the state. Thus, given adequate border inspections, fruits and vegetables imported from Mexico will be as safe as those grown in California. Although there have been some reports of unsafe foods entering the United States from Mexico, it appears that increased food trade under NAFTA has not contributed to the amount of food-borne illness in the United States.

NAFTA's primary impact on food trade has been on the production of food. It is generally agreed that NAFTA has played an important role in the decline of the number of small farms and food producers in the United States. Small farmers, heavily regulated in the United States, cannot compete with the corporations running unregulated, large industrial farms in Mexico. For example, in the United States many farmworkers must be paid more per hour than farmworkers in Mexico earn in a day. Consequently, fruits and vegetables from Mexico can sell in American markets for less than those grown and harvested domestically. As a general rule, however, the maturity and quality of Mexican fruits and vegetables are not comparable to the maturity and quality of those grown by small farmers and food producers in the United States.

It is not a coincidence that since the implementation of NAFTA in 1994 many small farmers and food producers have turned to direct marketing for survival. Such face-to-face marketing at certified farmers' markets or retail food stands near the place of production benefits small farmers by providing a profitable way for them to sell their products, and it benefits American consumers by supplying high-quality agricultural products at reasonable prices. As a result of NAFTA, many Americans can choose between buying low-cost, low-quality imported fruits and vegetables at large chain supermarkets or more expensive, better quality, fresher local produce directly from growers at farmers' markets.

[See also Department of Agriculture, United States; Farm Subsidies, Duties, Quotas, and Tariffs; Farmers' Markets; Food and Drug Administration.]

BIBLIOGRAPHY

McDonald, James H. "NAFTA and Basic Food Production: Dependency and Marginalization on Both Sides of the US/Mexico Border." In *Food in the USA: A Reader*, edited by Carole M. Counihan, 359–372. New York: Routledge, 2002.

ROBERT W. BROWER

Nouvelle Cuisine

Perhaps no trend in cookery has incited as much controversy and confusion as nouvelle cuisine, called "one of the splashiest social and artistic events of the postwar period" by the restaurant critic Henri Gault. Developed in France in the early 1960s and exported to America by the 1970s, nouvelle cuisine seemed a bit like pornography: hard to define, but people knew it when they saw it. Although it sounds trite (and a bit pompous) in retrospect, nouvelle cuisine was more an approach to cooking than a tightly structured cuisine. It encouraged each chef to invent personally distinctive dishes, artistically presented, showcasing the best-quality, seasonal ingredients.

Nouvelle cuisine's roots are in the French town of Vienne in the 1950s and the chef Fernand Point's renowned Michelin three-starred restaurant, La pyramide. While largely cooking the classic haute cuisine codified fifty years earlier by the master French chef Auguste Escoffier (1846–1935) in *Le guide culinaire* (1903), the inventive Point (1897–1955) and one of his cooks, Paul Bocuse (b. 1926), deliberately undercooked the green beans and committed other seeming culinary heresies. When Bocuse opened his own restaurant outside Lyons in 1962, he continued his experiments and soon dubbed his cooking and that of other like-minded French chefs "la nouvelle cuisine française." Cynics viewed the nomenclature as impresario hype, while those mesmerized by the cooking (especially Gault and his business partner, Christian Millau) lauded it as revolutionary.

The polemics sparked the famous "Manifesto of Nouvelle Cuisine," published in the October 1973 issue of *Le nouveau guide Gault-Millau*. Aping the Ten Commandments, it identified ten trends in the finest contemporary cooking. The manifesto ignited a firestorm in both France and America, with articles bearing such eye-popping titles as "French Cooking Is Dead; The New French Cooking Is Born," (*Esquire*, June 1975) or "*La Nouvelle Cuisine*: Is It Really New?" (*House Beautiful*, January 1976).

The cognoscenti hailed nouvelle cuisine for breathing life into a moribund French cookery that was suffocating under the dead weight of Escoffier's invariable rules. Detractors lambasted the vaunted rule breaking as a mask for poor technique (undercooking fish so that it was still raw at the bone was a typical nouvelle conceit) and as an excuse for ill-conceived combinations of incongruous ingredients, such as the ubiquitous kiwi paired with veal. They denigrated hamster-sized portions tortuously arranged on Frisbee-sized plates as "gastro-porn." To add financial injury to gastronomic insult, the food was expensive: one American chef admitted that he charged a lot more for soup simply by following Bocuse's model of crowning it with puff pastry.

Nouvelle cuisine was elitist, targeted to well-heeled, urbane (and urban) audiences. Upscale, fashion-conscious publications such as *Vogue* and *Harper's Bazaar*, as well as the intellectually oriented *New York Review of Books*, *New Yorker*, *Natural History*, and *New York Times*, all prepped their readers to sample the cuisine on European vacations or in expensive restaurants in major American cities, such as New York's Dodin-Bouffant, Washington's Jean-Louis, Chicago's Le perroquet, or Los Angeles's Ma maison (with the pre-Spago Wolfgang Puck at the stove). Nouvelle cuisine's notoriety led middle-market *Redbook* to publish a "how-to" article in February 1981 (beginning with the phonetic "noo vell kwee zeen"), helping housewives "create a dazzling dinner party" just a few short years after their hip *Vogue*- and *Esquire*-reading siblings. Significantly, the *Redbook* article was the lone middle-market voice: the skilled labor required to prepare a nouvelle meal and the expense and difficulty of procuring many of the ingredients in the 1980s, such as pink peppercorns or foie gras, made nouvelle cuisine all but impossible to reproduce in most homes or to find in middle-class, suburban restaurants.

Although no longer the chic cuisine of the moment, nouvelle cuisine has profoundly shaped contemporary

American cooking. Its French progenitors, Bocuse, the Troisgros brothers (also Point disciples), and Michel Guérard, published American editions of their cookbooks in the mid-1970s. They toured the United States, teaching and promoting their work as the first cadre of celebrity chefs, influencing a generation of young American cooks. When Guérard opened the Manhattan outpost of Paris's Régine's in 1977, both Larry Forgione and Michael Romano worked under him. They subsequently applied nouvelle cuisine's central tenets of impeccable ingredients, creatively manipulated, to existing American culinary traditions, pioneering "New American Cooking" at Forgione's An American Place and Romano's Union Square Café. Another "New American" pioneer, the Santa Monica–based chef Michael McCarty, trained in France during the height of the nouvelle revolution and incorporated its ideas of "freshness and lightness" into his California riff on new American cooking at the eponymous Michael's.

Nouvelle cuisine's legacy is visible in restaurant presentations of individual plates (rather than the carefully composed platters shown in classic French cookbooks through the 1950s) that have become edible art, often with fragile, almost architectural constructions. Kitchens outfitted with legions of squeeze-bottles holding brightly colored sauces "paint" Jackson Pollock–like squiggles on oversized plates that the Troisgros brothers first used and that the French porcelain maker Limoges now calls "American plates." The American magazine for professional chefs, *Art culinaire* (despite the French name, it covers global cuisine), founded in 1986 at the peak of nouvelle presentations, has never deviated from its luscious high-fashion photographs of plated dishes.

Contemporary menus, with their playful culinary puns, such as savory "napoleons" made from layers of carefully grilled vegetables or lobster *navarin* (the classic stew à la Escoffier could only be made with mutton), debuted as nouvelle cuisine. Lengthy descriptions of each offering on the menu are also a nouvelle legacy, as Escoffier's conventional terms no longer adequately communicate the dish. Restaurant reviewers evaluate innovation in addition to skillful cookery, and the demand for innovation has trickled down to the home cook, whose magazines proudly boast of recipes "with a twist," that is, some clever variation on an established dish. That twist may be as minor as substituting cilantro for tarragon in béarnaise sauce, yet it is something that simply was not done prior to nouvelle cuisine.

By prizing creativity above all else, nouvelle cuisine redefined the standards by which great cooking was judged. It uncorked chefs' imaginations and opened the dining public's eyes to experimentation, helping to account for the popularity of fusion cooking. As Christian Millau said in 1983, "The best proof that nouvelle cuisine is not a passing fashion, is that in America you are now trying to create your own." Larry Forgione concurred: "What that movement left was a feeling to pursue our goals without the pressure of conforming. A sense of freedom was felt by every culinary artist throughout the world. That is why nouvelle cuisine should be recognized as one of the most powerful culinary movements of our time."

[*See also* Celebrity Chefs; French Influences on American Food.]

BIBLIOGRAPHY

Brown, Ellen. *Cooking with the New American Chefs.* New York: Harper and Row, 1985. A "New American" cookbook with interviews with the chefs describing the influences in their cooking.
Cockburn, Andrew. "Gastro-Porn." *New York Review of Books*, December 8, 1977. A thoughtful review of cookbooks, including the scathing critique of Bocuse's work as "gastro-porn." A time capsule for cookbooks in the mid-1970s.
Cooke, Phillip S., ed. *The Second Symposium on American Cuisine.* New York: Van Nostrand Reinhold, 1984. See especially Larry Forgione's "American Cooking: Revolution or Evolution?" and Christian Millau's "The Influence of *Nouvelle Cuisine*." A very interesting collection of presentations by chefs, restaurateurs, and food writers struggling to define "American" food in 1983.
Gault, Henri. "Nouvelle Cuisine." In *Cooks and Other People: Proceedings of the 1995 Oxford Symposium on Food and Cookery*, Prospect Books, 1996. Retrospective analysis of nouvelle cuisine by one of the shapers of the movement.
Puck, Wolfgang. *Modern French Cooking for the American Kitchen.* Boston: Houghton Mifflin, 1981.
Urvater, Michele, and David Leiderman. *Cooking the Nouvelle Cuisine in America.* New York: Workman, 1979. Helpful examples of nouvelle cookery, specifically written for the American home kitchen. The Urvater-Leiderman book contains a detailed history of nouvelle cuisine through the late 1970s that is fascinating, as the authors, like Gault and Millau, are completely seduced by the cooking style at that moment.

CATHY K. KAUFMAN

Nutcrackers and Grinders

Some nutcrackers consist of a small hammer and an anvil; most use levered jaws or screw-clamp jaws to crack nuts. Earliest are cast metal or hardwood, with two hinged arms, corrugated near the hinge to secure the nut before squeezing the handles. Small silver-plated versions for table use, which cracked small nuts one way and larger nuts when the handles were reversed, came with nutpicks beginning in the 1880s. Corrugations look like animal teeth, and since the 1870s a menagerie of fully figural nutcrackers (including squirrels, dogs, or alligators) has been patented. The lower jaw lever sticks out behind like a tail.

Screw-clamp varieties include handheld nutcrackers with opposing fixed and screwed jaws to crush the shell. Some are strictly utilitarian; some are shaped like nuts. Inventors applied themselves to cracking specific nuts, too: a horizontal screwed cracker on a board was patented in 1914 for pecans. Since the 1930s small nut grinders with glass jars and cranked teeth in a screw-on hopper have facilitated the chopping of nutmeats for baking.

[*See also* Grinders; Nuts.]

BIBLIOGRAPHY

Franklin, Linda Campbell. *300 Years of Kitchen Collectibles*. 5th ed. Iola, WI: Krause Publications, 2003.

LINDA CAMPBELL FRANKLIN

Nutmeg Graters

A nutmeg's two usable parts are an outer husk called "mace," which is used in powdered form in baking and cannot be grated, and the inner kernel, the nutmeg, which when dry is hard and easily grated into food or drink. The simplest nutmeg grater is nonmechanical. One type used in Europe and in the early days of America was a portable or pocket-size cylinder with a grating surface and a storage compartment for the nutmeg. Also simple was the nineteenth-century tin coffin-like grater with hinged compartment and curved grating surface. This is the only type still made.

So popular had nutmeg become by the mid-nineteenth century, when world trade from Grenada made it easily available, that immediately U.S. inventors started patenting mechanical graters. The first came in 1854; sixteen were patented between 1866 and 1868. Most were cranked devices that held the nutmeg firmly (many with springs) against a grating surface while the grater revolved and scraped the nutmeg.

[*See also* Herbs and Spices.]

BIBLIOGRAPHY

Franklin, Linda Campbell. *300 Years of Kitchen Collectibles*. 5th ed. Iola, WI: Krause Publications, 2003.

LINDA CAMPBELL FRANKLIN

Nutrition

For millennia, humans have been aware of the relationship between food and health. At the most basic level, even primitive peoples knew that a lack of food led to sickness or even death and that eating certain plants or animals could bring illness, while other foods could be protective or curative. This collected wisdom was passed down orally, but physicians in ancient Greece, Rome, and China began to assemble this wisdom in herbal manuscripts that were hand-copied for hundreds of years. Herbals were collections of assertions about the relationships between specific foods and health. These assertions were based on contemporary medical theories.

During the late eighteenth and early nineteenth centuries, studies of human digestion began to offer insights into how the body processed food. William Beaumont (1785–1853), an Army surgeon, examined the process of digestion through the examination of a gunshot victim, who had wounds that exposed his stomach. Through this wound, Beaumont was able to observe the operations of the stomach.

By 1840, chemists had classified food into three categories: carbohydrates, fats, and proteins. Carbohydrates, mainly sugars and starches, make up the bulk of the diet of *Homo sapiens* and constitute the chief source of energy. Dietary fats, now generally called lipids, include vegetable oil and animal fat. Lipids are highly concentrated sources of energy, furnishing more calories per gram than either carbohydrates or proteins. Proteins are the major

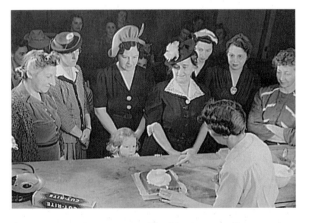

Nutrition Demonstration. Nutritionist spreading sugarless frosting on a sugarless, butterless cake, Alexandria, Virginia, March 1943. *Prints and Photographs Division, Library of Congress/Ann Rosener*

source of building material for the body; they repair and replace worn tissue.

Justus von Liebig of the University of Giessen in Germany is often identified as the father of the scientific approach to nutrition. During the 1820s, he measured and examined foods consumed by animals and the products that were excreted and exhaled. Based on this quantitative research, he proposed theories about intermediate processes in the body in his *Animal Chemistry* (1842).

By the late nineteenth century, many American scientists were focusing on nutritional research. The agricultural chemist Wilbur O. Atwater, who had founded the Office of Experiment Stations for the U.S. Department of Agriculture in 1888, systematically tabulated the caloric compositions of different foods. He calculated the energy yields of carbohydrates, protein, and fat and developed the first American human calorimeter, an apparatus for measuring the amount of calories in food. Using Atwater's methods, other scientists established standards for the energy needs of healthy individuals. Other important work on nutrition was done by Russell Henry Chittenden, head of the Sheffield Scientific School at Yale.

The application of these new findings to the daily diet and home cooking was championed by Ellen Richards, whose *Chemistry of Cooking and Cleaning: A Manual for Housekeepers* (1882), which went through several editions, became a defining work. Food chemistry became an important component of many cooking schools that thrived during the latter part of the nineteenth and early twentieth centuries. Graduates of these schools were often referred to as "dietitians." They applied the principles of nutrition in hospitals, the military, public schools, and other institutional settings. Dietitians became leaders in the home economics movement and founded the American Dietetic Association in 1917.

Vitamins and Minerals

The first ailment clearly associated with a specific food was scurvy (caused by a vitamin C deficiency), which was common among sailors on long voyages. By the seventeenth century it was known, although the reason was not understood, that eating fresh fruit and vegetables could cure scurvy; years later, following scientific studies, British sailors were supplied with lemon juice, and the men remained healthy. During the first decade of the twentieth century, several other diseases, such as beriberi, rickets, and pellagra, were linked to dietary shortcomings. Scientists began to investigate the

unknown factors at play in these cases—substances that came to be called vitamins.

Casimir Funk, a chemist at the Lister Institute in London, crystallized an amine substance from rice bran in 1911. Funk used the word "vitamine," constructed from "vital amines," to apply to these previously unknown substances that prevented specific diseases. Since it was soon discovered that many of the substances were not amines, the spelling was changed to "vitamin." Through the course of the century, many other vitamins were isolated and identified. By the early 2000s, seventeen vitamins had been identified as "essential," which meant that the human body could not synthesize them and they had to be ingested for the body to function properly.

Minerals were also found to be essential for the proper functioning of the human body. They had begun to be identified during the late nineteenth century, but it was not until the twentieth century that their functions were determined. Minerals act as catalysts in many biochemical reactions of the body and are also vital to the growth of bones, muscular contractions, digestion, and many other functions. Calcium, for instance, is essential for proper heart rhythm, iron for blood formation, and phosphorus for healthy bones and teeth. Some minerals, such as calcium, iron, and sulfur, are required in relatively large amounts, while others, such as zinc, copper, iodine, and fluoride, are required in smaller (trace) amounts. In the early 2000s, twenty-four minerals were identified as essential. One of the first uses of micronutrients to enrich food occurred in the 1920s; once it was determined that dietary iodine could prevent goiter, it was added to commercial table salt and cases of this thyroid disorder dropped markedly.

Nutrition in Public Policy

Prior to the discovery of vitamins, food processors had concluded that the way to prevent illness caused by food was to sterilize and mill their products to reduce the danger of consumers being exposed to bacteria, mold, and toxins. Beginning in the 1880s, wheat milling removed the bran, germ, and oil from the flour, which was then bleached to a bright white color. But by the 1920s, it was understood that the milling process eliminated much of the nutritional value of the wheat. Nutrition experts attacked flour millers and commercial bakers for white bread's lack of vitamins and minerals. During World War II, the Federal Drug Administration encouraged the enrichment of white bread with vitamins. In 1943, the War Foods Administration temporarily required enriched bread. Most white flour and bread sold in the United States in the early 2000s is enriched with several nutrients.

During World War II, the federal government first published nutritional standards—called Recommended Dietary Allowances (RDA)—for energy, protein, and eight essential vitamins and minerals. These were the levels of nutrients required by the average adult for good health. During the war, the U.S. Department of Agriculture also promoted the "Basic Seven" food groups, which showed people dealing with wartime food shortages how to maintain proper nutrition. These guidelines were modified after the war to the "Basic Four," which stressed dairy products, meats, fruits and vegetables, and grain products. As new research demonstrates additional requirements, RDAs were replaced in the late 1990s with a concept called the Dietary Reference Intakes (DRIs).

DRIs are the basis for assessing and planning diets of healthy people. They are also used as a basis for federal nutrition and food programs. The DRIs include: estimated average requirements (EAR), Recommended Dietary Allowance (RDA), and adequate intake (AI). The DRIs are established by the Food and Nutrition Board, the Institute of Medicine, and the National Academy of Sciences.

In the interest of promoting better eating habits among Americans, the Department of Health and Human Services and the Department of Agriculture jointly developed *Dietary Guidelines for Americans* in 1980; it has been regularly updated ever since. Because of an increase in heart disease during the second half of the twentieth century, in 1992 the U.S. Department of Agriculture unveiled the new "Food Pyramid," which broke from the recommendations of previous food-group charts to emphasize more consumption of complex carbohydrates and less consumption of animal protein, fat, and sugar. In 1994, following years of discussion, the Nutrition Labeling and Education Act was passed by Congress requiring nutrition labels on all processed foods sold in the United States. This measure had been supported for many years by the Center for Science in the Public Interest, which insisted that Americans could not make enlightened food choices—and frequently made the wrong ones—because they did not know the nutritional value of the foods they bought at the supermarket.

The chemist Linus Pauling, the recipient of two Nobel prizes, concluded that huge doses of certain micronutrients—particularly vitamin C—could cure some diseases and prolong life. He published his findings in a 1970 book entitled *Vitamin C and the Common Cold*. Some studies suggested that megadoses of vitamin C could help

terminal cancer patients. Based on findings such as these, manufacturers of vitamin and mineral supplements began making claims for the effects of their products. In 1994, the Dietary and Supplement Health and Education Act was passed by Congress, limiting what vitamin manufacturers could claim about abilities of their supplements to prevent or cure diseases.

Developments in Nutrition

During the late twentieth and early twenty-first centuries, the major focus of nutrition has shifted from concern over which foods are required to avoid deficiencies and illness, to what foods and supplements may be consumed to promote health. Nutrition studies are spread over the fields of medicine, biochemistry, physiology, and the behavioral and social sciences, as well as the public health sciences. The issues of special focus among nutritionists include topics related to functional foods, pediatrics, geriatrics, obesity, chronic diseases, malnutrition, and nutritional deficiencies.

[*See also* Adulterations; Baby Food; Chemical Additives; Combat Food; Department of Agriculture, United States; Eating Disorders; Food and Nutrition Systems; Health Food; Hunger Programs; Meals on Wheels; Pioneers and Survival Food; Politics of Food; Prison Food; Pure Food and Drug Act; Richards, Ellen Swallow; School Food; Ship Food; Soup Kitchens; Vegetarianism; Vitamins.]

BIBLIOGRAPHY

Beeuwkes, Adelia M., E. Neige Todhunter, and Emma Seifrit Weigley, comps. *Essays of History of Nutrition and Dietetics*. Chicago: American Dietetic Association, 1967.

Berdanier, Carolyn D., et al. *Handbook of Nutrition and Food*. Boca Raton, FL: CRC Press, 2002.

Cassell, Jo Anne. *Carry the Flame: The History of the American Dietetic Association*. Chicago: The Association, 1990.

Desai, Babasaheb B. *Handbook of Nutrition and Diet*. New York: Marcel Dekker, 2000.

Kamminga, Harmke, and Andrew Cunningham. *The Science and Culture of Nutrition*. Amsterdam: Rodopi, 1995.

McCollum, Elmer Verner. *A History of Nutrition: The Sequence of Ideas in Nutrition Investigations*. Boston: Houghton Mifflin 1957.

Nestle, Marion. *Food Politics: How the Food Industry Influences Nutrition and Health*. Berkeley: University of California Press, 2002.

JOSEPH M. CARLIN

Nuts

Tree nuts have been an important part of the human diet since prehistoric times. While there is extreme diversity among tree nuts, most have in common an edible kernel enclosed in a hard outer shell. (Peanuts, though called "nuts," are actually legumes.)

North America is abundantly supplied with indigenous nut-bearing trees, and their fruit has been gathered and consumed since humans arrived thousands of years ago. Acorns and pine nuts, for instance, were an important constituent of the diet of Native Americans, especially California Indians. Pecans were prized by Native Americans in the Midwest and South, and East Coast Indians used butternuts to thicken their soups. Other Native Americans consumed American chestnuts, filberts, hickory nuts, and black walnuts.

European colonists in North America adopted many indigenous nuts into their diets. The most important of these came from three trees in the walnut family: the pecan, the butternut, and the hickory. The nuts were pressed to make oil and were used in baked goods and confections. Although they were sold well into the twentieth century, only the pecan has survived as a commercial crop. European colonists also introduced into America such Old World nut-bearing trees as the English walnut and the European chestnut. Later, nuts that could not be grown in America, such as cashews and Brazil nuts, were imported and became important additions to the American diet.

By the beginning of the nineteenth century, nut vendors were selling roasted nuts on the streets of major American cities; at the time, few other foods could be so easily produced, transported, distributed, and prepared for sale. By the 1840s nut vendors appeared at circuses and fairs. At first, children were their main customers.

From 1865 to 1900 nuts made the transition from a snack and dessert food to an important component of the American diet. Clearly, the most influential early work in this field was accomplished by vegetarians such as John Harvey Kellogg. His attempt to produce an alternative to "cow's butter" by grinding various nuts ended in the creation of nut butters, the most famous of which is peanut butter. *Guide for Nut Cookery* (1899) by Almeda Lambert reflects the progress made in nut cookery by vegetarians during the late 1890s. It includes over a thousand nut recipes, most of which had never before been published. It eased nut cookery into the American mainstream and inspired others to include more creative nut recipes in their cookbooks and in cookery magazines. Subsequent vegetarian cookbooks, such as the second edition of *Science in the Kitchen* (1900) by Ella E. Kellogg and

Vegetarian Cook Book: Substitutes for Flesh Foods (1904) by E. G. Fulton, promoted nut cookery and encouraged its use by nonvegetarians.

Nut cookery was also publicized in the recipe booklets published by commercial nut processors, nut butter manufacturers, and equipment makers. The recipes were often developed by professional cooks, and they represented the pinnacle of nut cookery. These publications helped to bridge the geographically diverse and heterogeneous nut industry, and one of their functions was to encourage nut cookery. Recipes from commercial sources were regularly republished in other magazines and mainstream cookbooks. Specialty cookbooks on specific nuts were published, such as *800 Proved Pecan Recipes* (1925); *A Treasury of Prize Winning Filbert Recipes from the Oregon Filbert Commission* (1973); Carole Bough, *Cooking with Black Walnuts* (1995); Lucy Gerspacher, *Hazelnuts and More* (1995); Jean-Luc Toussaint, *The Walnut Cookbook* (1998); and Annie Bhagwandin, *The Chestnut Cookbook* (2003).

Additional influences on nut cookery were the U.S. Department of Agriculture, the federal and state agricultural experiment stations, and the county extension services, which published recipes and booklets encouraging farmers to grow nut trees and American consumers to eat more nuts. These sources provided thousands of diverse recipes with nuts as ingredients. In addition to roasted nuts served as a snack food, tree nuts appeared as ingredients in recipes for baked goods, beverages, brittle, butters, fudge, ice cream, ketchup, meat substitutes, salads, sauces, and stuffings.

The most important nuts consumed in the United States, are almonds, Brazil nuts, cashews, macadamia nuts, pecans, pine nuts, pistachios, and walnuts.

[*See also* Almonds; Brazil Nuts; Cashews; Chestnuts; Filberts; Macadamia Nuts; Peanuts; Pecans; Pine Nuts; Pistachios; Walnuts.]

BIBLIOGRAPHY

Bhagwandin, Annie. *The Chestnut Cookbook*. 2nd ed. Onalaska, WI: Shady Grove Publications, 2003.

Bough, Carole. *Cooking with Black Walnuts*. Stockton, MO: Missouri Dandy Pantry, 1993.

Carder, Shirl. *The Nut Lovers' Cookbook*. Berkeley, CA: Celestial Arts, 1984.

Frank, Dorothy C. *Cooking with Nuts*. New York: Potter, 1979.

Gerspacher, Lucy. *Hazelnuts and More*. Portland, OR: Graphic Arts Center, 1995.

Keystone Pecan Company. *800 Proved Pecan Recipes: Their Place in the Menu, by 5,083 Housewives*. Manheim, PA.: Keystone Pecan Research Laboratory, 1925.

Lambert, Almeda. *Guide for Nut Cookery*. Battle Creek, MI: Lambert, 1899.

MacPherson, Mary. *Completely Nuts: A Cookbook and Cultural History of the World's Most Popular Nuts*. Ontario, Canada: Doubleday Canada, 1995.

Manaster, Jane. *The Pecan Tree*. Austin: University of Texas Press, 1994.

Oregon Filbert Commission. *A Treasury of Prize Winning Filbert Recipes*. 3rd ed. Tigard, OR: Oregon Filbert Commission, 1973.

Rosengarten, Frederic, Jr. *The Book of Edible Nuts*. New York: Walker, 1984.

Toussaint, Jean-Luc. *Walnut Cookbook*. Berkeley, CA: Ten Speed Press, 1998.

ANDREW F. SMITH

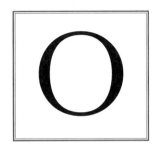

Oats

The origins of oats (*Avena sativa*) are obscure. They were cultivated in Switzerland and northern Europe by 2500 B.C.E., and two millennia later they were widely cultivated in Europe by the ancient Romans, Germans, and Celts. The advantage of oats was that they could be grown in higher altitudes and in colder climates than could wheat or other common grains. Oats were mainly used to feed horses, cattle, and other animals, but hulled oats were used in broths, porridges, and gruels. They were particularly important in the Scottish kitchen, which led Samuel Johnson to define oats as "a grain which in England is generally given to horses, but in Scotland supports the people" in his *Dictionary of the English Language* (1755).

Oats were introduced into North America by early European explorers including Captain Bartholomew Gosnold, who planted them on Elizabeth Island off the Massachusetts coast. The Dutch grew oats in New Netherland by 1626, and they were cultivated in Virginia prior to 1648. Oats were generally grown throughout colonial America, mainly for animal feed, but Scottish, Dutch, and other immigrants used them in their traditional porridges, puddings, and baked goods. Hannah Glasse's *Art of Cookery Made Plain and Easy* (1747 and subsequent editions), although initially published in England, was one of the most popular cookbooks in colonial America. It included oats in recipes for haggis, flummery, and hasty and other puddings, as well as for cake. Similar recipes were published in America through the nineteenth century. Other oat recipes published in the United States included Scotch burgoo, an oatmeal hasty pudding in which the rolled oats were stirred into boiling water until the mixture thickened; gruel, which was a thinner porridge frequently identified as invalid food; and oatmeal blancmange. Baked goods included Scottish and English oaten cakes baked on a griddle, muffins made from cold cooked oatmeal, and bread and biscuits, for which the oatmeal was usually mixed with flour, because on its own, oatmeal or oat flour does not develop enough gluten to support a rising loaf.

By the nineteenth century, grocery stores sold oat products in bulk. Customers could choose from groats, the whole oat with its outer shell; grits, hulled oat kernels, coarsely ground; and oatmeal, which was milled into several different grades of fineness. In 1877, rolled oats were developed and trademarked by Henry D. Seymour and William Heston, who had established the Quaker Mill Company. The product was packed in cardboard boxes bearing the reassuring image of an elderly Quaker man and promoted via a national advertising campaign, making it the first cereal to advertise nationally. In 1901, the Quaker Mill Company merged with other mills, and became the Quaker Oats Company.

Directions for cooking oatmeal were printed on the outside of the Quaker box. These recipes, in turn, were reprinted in community and other cookbooks, and oatmeal became more popular as a cooking ingredient. During the twentieth century many new oatmeal recipes were published, including ones for soup, cakes, cookies, wafers, drops, macaroons, quick breads and yeast breads, muffins, scones, and pancakes. Oatmeal was also used as a filler and binder in meatloaf, hamburger, and sausage. The growing interest in healthy diet and vegetarianism in the 1970s saw new interest in oats and other whole grains. Instant oatmeal, which was more finely ground so that it was ready as soon as hot water was added, was introduced in 1966 and made hot cereal as convenient as cold. The announcement in the 1990s that the soluble fiber in oats could reduce cholesterol levels caused a tremendous boom in sales of oatmeal, oat bran, and products made with oats. But by far the most enduring recipe was for oatmeal cookies, which accounted for the most important noncereal use of oatmeal in the early 2000s.

At the beginning of the twenty-first century, the United States was one of the world's largest producers of oats. In 2003, America produced 148 million bushels of oats with the largest production in Minnesota, North Dakota, Wisconsin, South Dakota, and Iowa.

[*See also* Bread; Breakfast Foods; Cookies; Quaker Oats Man.]

BIBLIOGRAPHY

Hedrick, U. P., ed. *Sturtevant's Edible Plants of the World*. 1919. Reprint, New York: Dover, 1972.

Hinman, Bobbie. *Oat Cuisine*. Rocklin, CA: Prima, 1989.

Marquette, Arthur F. *Brands, Trademarks and Good Will: The Story of the Quaker Oats Company*. New York: McGraw Hill, 1967.

Ward, Artemas. *The Grocers' Hand-Book and Directory for 1883*. Philadelphia: Philadelphia Grocer, 1882.

ANDREW F. SMITH

Obesity

The high rate of overweight and obesity in America in the twenty-first century has attracted worldwide attention. How U.S. society reached this point is a story of the conflict between excess and restraint and of the relative values Americans place on what they eat, how much and how often they eat, and physical activity. Over the centuries, American culture has moved toward ever slimmer ideals, increasing anxiety about weight but not keeping it down. The link between excess pounds and health means that many more Americans are at risk for serious illnesses and conditions.

Cultural Underpinnings

Early European colonists, facing the hardships of adapting to a new land, necessarily adopted an austere diet. With the need for heavy labor and farming, weight was not an issue. Once the colonists moved past subsistence, however, ideas about diet and weight underwent a change. Girth became synonymous with good health, prosperity, and status. Around the beginning of the twentieth century, social changes forced concern about weight on the middle class, partly as the result of changing fashions. Women cast aside their corsets, dress sizes were standardized, and men's clothing began to emphasize good build. At the same time, minor technological changes propelled anxiety. Scales, introduced in 1891, were often used at fairs for public weighing. The calorimeter, invented in 1894, made it possible for the first time to measure calories, the value of foods for producing heat and energy in the body. Ideas about appropriate weight were not equally applied to all classes. The

U.S. Department of Agriculture developed recommended daily calorie counts and the cheapest food sources for workers to perform certain tasks.

A major force in shaping a link between weight and health was life insurance companies. In the 1890s they started to track clients' heights, weights, life spans, and causes of death. The charts were based almost exclusively on white, urban, middle-class, Protestant men. By 1898 the companies dropped the idea that the weights were averages and instead labeled them "ideals." The tables quickly assumed the air of authority. Statistics about health consequences became influential. Actuaries reported that men as little as 10 percent overweight could not expect to live as long as those at ideal weight, while men 30 percent or more overweight had a 34.5 percent greater mortality rate.

Remarkably, the medical establishment did not consider these risks reasons for losing weight. Physicians recognized that obesity put stress on organs and reduced longevity by as much as two years, but generally they believed that obesity was glandular or hereditary, which meant that little could be done. Only after 1900 did doctors focus on overweight as an adult degenerative disease.

The insurance companies periodically modified their ideal weights downward. A 1914 insurance association study reported that there should be no weight gain after age thirty-five; above age forty, even average weight was pronounced excessive. Commercial interests took advantage of the new anxiety by opening reducing salons and launching a diet products industry.

Introduction of a Moral Dimension: 1920s

During the Roaring Twenties weight consciousness acquired a new intensity. In *Fat History: Bodies and Beauty in the Modern World* (1997), the social historian Peter Stearns suggests that this increasing preoccupation during the 1920s was related to increased prosperity, consumerism, and sexual permissiveness. It seemed as if some social restraint was required to balance excess and luxury. For the first time, weight control took on a moral dimension as Americans struggled with guilt over self-indulgence.

Disproportionate attention was paid to women's weight (a trend that would continue through the 1950s). Most diet books and commercial reducing programs were aimed squarely at females, partly, it seems, as a check on women's growing independence, particularly in the sexual area. The tyranny of the height-weight

Obesity Remedy. The effects of a weight-loss patent medicine. Illustration from an advertisement for Richard Hudnut, a New York pharmacist, that appeared in *Harper's Monthly*, August 1894. *Collection of Georgia Maas*

tables continued. In the 1920s the insurance companies began to require physical exams for policies, a process that focused more attention on weighing by an authority figure, the doctor. More than half of all people over thirty-five were pronounced overweight. This era marked the beginning of an ever-widening gap between ideal cultural size standards and actual eating and weight patterns, a discrepancy that has yet to be reconciled.

National Health Problem

In the 1930s public health authorities became increasingly convinced that overweight was a national health problem. Physicians determined that the previous maximum intake of 3,000 calories a day for men was too high; it should be 2,400 or even 2,035. A shift in thinking in the medical community occurred when doctors began to view excess weight as a character flaw, signifying lack of self-control and willpower. Physicians were increasingly

hostile to fat patients, blaming them for their malady. This mind-set marked the beginning of the identification and stigmatization of a deviant subculture of the obese, who were regarded with disdain and disgust.

When Metropolitan Life revised its tables again in 1942–1943, ideal weights for women were included for the first time. Recommended pounds for men were once again reduced. The company suggested that a five-foot, four-inch woman should weigh between 124 and 132 pounds, and a medium frame, five-foot, eight-inch man between 145 and 156 pounds.

After World War II there was an explosion of diet paraphernalia. Between 1950 and 1955 the sale of diet soft drinks increased three thousandfold. Throughout the 1950s the pressure to reduce focused primarily on females, even where overweight children were concerned. Disdain for fat women was common in popular publications, and women's magazines filled their pages with weight-loss articles, often with before and after pictures, and fashion layouts featuring models so thin that the average woman could never hope to compete. The illusion of the reward for shedding pounds went beyond improved health and longevity to an almost mythical belief that all good things would magically be conferred—a glamorous job, wealth, sexual attractiveness, and marriage. By 1959 recommended weights had been pared down to 113 to 126 pounds for women and 138 to 152 pounds for men. African American women escaped the white middle-class standards. Popular material aimed at the black female audience defined obesity more liberally (about 50 percent over recommended weights for whites).

National Obsession

By the 1960s weight loss had become an American obsession for both genders; men were included because the data on heart disease suggested a greater health risk for males with overweight classified as a risk factor. Anxious dieters placed their faith in behavioral approaches, including weight-reducing chains like Weight Watchers, Jenny Craig, and Overeaters Anonymous, which enrolled millions. Fad diet books based on scant science sold millions of copies. These strategies, which thrived on recidivism, only enhanced desperation as people repeatedly tried and failed to lose weight. Even overweight children became targets. Through the 1960s physicians and parents perceived plumpness in children as evidence of being loved. When research found that an overweight child had up to an 80 percent greater chance of becoming obese in adulthood than a thin child, that view changed. Overweight children were taken to doctors for early medical attention and preventive care.

Inevitably, perhaps, the obsession triggered a backlash. As the women's movement gained momentum during the 1960s, feminists decried chronic dieting as a constraint on female independence, designed to force women to conform to patriarchal cultural standards. A pathological consequence of anxious dieting was the increasing diagnosis of the eating disorders anorexia nervosa and bulimia, occurring primarily among middle- to upper-class adolescents and young adult women. The most ironic backlash came from the "afflicted" group itself. Overweight activists organized their own subculture to defend their right to a fat lifestyle and fight employer discrimination.

Dietary Fat: A New Culprit

In the early 1960s the entire discussion of weight loss took a turn that contributed to a paradoxical effect. Overweight had by then been linked to increased risk of heart disease, type 2 diabetes, and some types of cancer. Based on little scientific evidence, private health organizations—including the American Heart Association, the American Cancer Society, and the American Diabetes Association—began to condemn dietary fat as the culprit for adverse health consequences and weight. They recommended cutting back fat to no more than one-third of daily calories. By the late 1970s the government had added its sanction to the low-fat message, promoting a diet based primarily on carbohydrates. Eventually, these groups made distinctions among various fats (saturated fats and trans-fatty acids were bad; others, like monounsaturated fats, were beneficial for blood lipids).

Still, the prevailing message that the public grasped was that all fat was bad. Members of the middle and upper classes began to regard the classic indicators of material success—slabs of beef, butter, eggs, rich cream—with fear, while the lower classes continued to perceive them as symbols of the good life. Part of the problem was that the formerly high-status foods had become so easily available that the upper classes began to disvalue them.

The antifat movement spawned an irrational phobia, particularly among upper-class women. In 1999 about 35 percent of all Americans labeled fat—even a trace amount—as a "toxin" or "poison." The paradox of high-status high-fat food is that the appeal exists only when the foods can be rejected. The elite upper classes elevated the nobility of austerity in diet and the simplicity of fat avoidance as evidence of refinement, a moral and virtuous life. This process of moralization of eating high-fat foods has been associated with certain cultural markers: a health link (the association of fat with heart disease and cancer); behavioral prescriptions from government and private health agencies; the association of the behavior with a socially stigmatized group (namely, the obese); a Protestant culture; and the presence of disgust, an emotion termed a "moral amplifier."

Obesity Epidemic

Despite the designation of the low-fat diet as the gold standard, Americans continued to gain weight, and rates of heart disease did not decrease. Apparently, the dietary fat–heart health link applied only to a small subgroup who were at risk. In the early 1980s, the obesity rate—constant during the 1960s and 1970s—went up by eight points. By the end of the decade, one in four Americans was obese. As of 2002, 64.5 percent of adults (120 million people) were overweight, defined as ten to thirty pounds over healthy weight, and 33 percent of women and 28 percent of men were obese, defined as thirty or more pounds over healthy weight. At the same time, about 15 percent of children age six to age nineteen (9 million) were overweight. Those people with obesity problems were most likely to be poor, concentrated geographically in depressed rural areas of Mississippi and West Virginia, and among ethnic groups of African, Asian, and Hispanic Americans in the inner city.

The health implications of the obesity epidemic are staggering. Between 1990 and 1998 there was a 33 percent rise in type 2 diabetes, 76 percent among people in their thirties, and for the first time, the condition was diagnosed in adolescents. The risk of heart failure was 34 percent higher in 2002 in those overweight and double in obese people. The estimated health-care costs for all complications of overweight in 2000 were $117 billion.

The reasons for the surge of obesity are complex. First, there is the failure of the low-fat diet. For 30 to 40 percent of the population, according to one estimate, low-fat diets may be counterproductive because they encourage unlimited consumption of carbohydrates and fat-free products, often made from calorie-laden sugar. Ultimately, it is calories—no matter what their source—that cause people to gain weight.

The simple explanation for the unprecedented rise in overweight—the highest level ever recorded in

America—is too much food and too little physical activity. More people eat their meals in restaurants, where large portions of high-calorie food are the norm. The $112 billion fast-food industry provides easy access to inexpensive, calorie-dense, super-size servings. The soft-drink industry—the single major source of added dietary sugar—induced Americans to drink five times as much soda in 2002 as they had in the 1950s. Few Americans spend the recommended allotment of one hour a day in moderate exercise. School physical education programs have been severely cut back. Watching television—a common sedentary activity—encourages simultaneous eating with its annual bombardment of ten thousand food ads. Americans may simply be seeing the end point of a process that takes place in the developed world as food moves from subsistence to abundance, and conveniences encourage a sedentary lifestyle. It seems that nothing short of an overhaul of our food environment can stem the tide of obesity in America. Persuading people to eat less in our culture has never been a successful enterprise; the United States is a nation of overeaters.

[*See also* Diets, Fad; Eating Disorders; Fast Food; Food and Nutrition Systems; Nutrition.]

BIBLIOGRAPHY

Levenstein, Harvey. *The Paradox of Plenty: A Social History of Eating in Modern America*. Rev. ed. Berkeley: University of California Press, 2003. Explores the paradox of the need for cutting down on dietary fat in the midst of food abundance.

Powdermaker, Hortense. "An Anthropological Approach to the Problems of Obesity." In *Food and Culture: A Reader*, edited by Carole Counihan and Penny Van Esterik, 203–10. New York: Routledge, 1997. Sets the problem of obesity in the context of culture.

Rozin, Paul, and C. Fischler, S. Imada, A. Sarubin, and A. Wrzesniewski. "Attitudes to Food and the Role of Food in Life in the U.S.A., Japan, Flemish Belgium and France: Possible Implications for the Diet-Health Debate." *Appetite* 33, no. 2 (1999): 163–80. Documents fat phobia among American women in particular.

Schwartz, Hillel. *Never Satisfied: A Cultural History of Diets, Fantasies, and Fat*. New York: Free Press, 1986.

Shell, Ellen Ruppel. *The Hungry Gene: The Science of Fat and the Future of Thin*. New York: Atlantic Monthly Press, 2002. Provides the inside story on scientific research on obesity and the race among the pharmaceutical companies to devise a lucrative pharmacological treatment.

Stearns, Peter N. *Battleground of Desire: The Struggle for Self-Control in Modern America*. New York: New York University Press, 1999. Chronicles the historical progression of weight standards with periods of sexual permissiveness.

Stearns, Peter N. *Fat History: Bodies and Beauty in the Modern West*. New York: New York University Press, 1997. Explores fat's transformation from a symbol of health and well-being to a sign of moral, psychological, and physical disorder.

Taubes, Gary. "What If It's All Been a Big Fat Lie?" *New York Times Magazine*, July 7, 2002. Good on the flaws of the low-fat diet.

LINDA MURRAY BERZOK

Oils, *see Fats and Oils*

Okra

Okra (*Abelmoschus esculentus*, formerly *Hibiscus esculentus*) is an Old World plant that was widely disseminated in Africa and Asia in prehistoric times. Some evidence suggests that it may have originated in Ethiopia. The ridged, seed-filled pods are eaten in a variety of ways. Okra's chief distinction among vegetables is its mucilaginous nature; when cooked in liquid, it releases a gluey substance that thickens the broth.

The word "okra" clearly derives from West African *nkru ma*, which indicates that the plant was brought to the Americas through the slave trade directly from Africa or indirectly through the Caribbean. Slaves grew okra in gardens on southern plantations and introduced its cookery into mainstream America. The Swedish scientist Peter Kalm reported in his *Travels into North America* (1748) that okra was growing in Philadelphia. Thomas Jefferson, in his *Notes on the State of Virginia* (1785), recorded that okra was cultivated there. Extensive directions for growing okra were published in Robert Squibb's *The Gardener's Calendar for South Carolina, Georgia, and North Carolina* (1787).

The pod of the okra plant is steamed, boiled, fried, pickled, and cooked in soups and stews, notably gumbo. The seeds are also ground into meal for use in making bread and oil. Southerners used ground okra seeds as a coffee substitute, especially during the Civil War, when coffee was unavailable due to the northern blockade. The leaves and flower buds are also edible and are cooked as greens. The pods and the leaves are dried, crushed into powder, and used for flavoring and thickening soups, including pepper pot, and stews.

Although recipes for okra appear in early American cookery manuscripts, Thomas Cooper's edition of the *Domestic Encyclopedia* (1821) includes the first published recipe with okra as an ingredient. Mary Randolph's *Virginia House-wife* (1824) offers recipes using okra: "Ocra and Tomatoes" calls for stewing sliced okra with tomatoes, butter, and onion, and "Gumbs, A West India Dish," calls for cooking whole pods "in a little water" and serving them with melted butter.

The word "gumbo" or "gombo" is another African name for okra. In New Orleans it was applied to both the vegetable and the complex Creole stew made with it. Gumbos frequently contained okra and filé (powdered, dried sassafras leaves), a seasoning and thickener thought to have originated with the Choctaw Indians in Louisiana. Okra is just one ingredient in gumbo, which may be based on meat, such as chicken, turkey, squirrel, or rabbit, or shellfish, such as crabs, oysters, or shrimp.

Gumbos migrated quickly throughout America. The first gumbo recipe published in an American cookery book appeared in an edition of Eliza Leslie's *Directions for Cooking* (1838). She identified it as "a favourite New Orleans dish." Will Coleman, the publisher of Lafcadio Hearn's *La cuisine Creole* (1885), described gumbo as the "great dish of New Orleans." So it remains.

Since the 1960s, okra has entered the American culinary mainstream, although as many writers point out, it is an acquired taste. It is a significant component of soul food and southern cookery in general. Pickled okra is sold in many supermarkets. Okra is generally grown in Florida and Mexico and is sold fresh in many grocery stores and farmers' markets. While boiled okra is the norm from Louisiana and points east, in Texas and Oklahoma it is most commonly served fried (usually rolled in cornmeal and flour, often seasoned with cayenne) or pickled whole with caps intact. Both methods yield products that are devoid of the slimy, viscid quality that some Americans disparage and others love.

[*See also* Hearn, Lafcadio; Jefferson, Thomas; Leslie, Eliza; Randolph, Mary; Southern Regional Cookery.]

BIBLIOGRAPHY

Raymond, Dick, and Jan Raymond. *The Gardens for All Book of Eggplant, Okra, and Peppers.* Burlington, VT: Gardens for All, 1984.

Smith, Andrew F. *Souper Tomatoes: The Story of America's Favorite Food.* New Brunswick, NJ: Rutgers University Press, 2000.

ANDREW F. SMITH

Old-Fashioned

"Don't muddle with an old-fashioned" could be this cocktail's motto, as the name itself indicates its adherence to tradition. Muddling, however, is precisely one of the traditions to which the drink adheres; the old-fashioned is, in fact, probably the best known of the few remaining cocktails whose authenticity depends upon the technique, which involves mashing together certain (generally solid) ingredients with a wooden muddler, or pestle, to release their flavors. In this case, orange, lemon, cherries, and sugar are muddled with bitters—the storied flavoring agent whose inclusion is another nod to tradition—before the key ingredient, whiskey (typically bourbon), is added. According to legend, the drink was created in the late nineteenth century at the Pendennis Club in Louisville, Kentucky, at the behest of a member, Colonel James Pepper, who must have had a stake in the outcome; Pepper was a distiller of bourbon under the label "Old 1776." For the record, however, rumors of an even older-fashioned version of the cocktail persist among some rye drinkers. At any rate, eclipsed though it may be by more modern, flashy libations, the old-fashioned shines on through the stout, cylindrical, much-used tumbler that bears its name.

[*See also* Bourbon; Cocktails; Whiskey.]

BIBLIOGRAPHY

Foley, Ray, ed. *The Williams-Sonoma Bar Guide.* San Francisco: Time-Life Books, 1999. Smart and thorough reference guide.

Grimes, William. *Straight Up or On the Rocks: The Story of the American Cocktail.* New York: North Point Press, 2001. Provides a full historical overview.

International Bartender's Guide. New York: Random House, 1996.

Lanza, Joseph. *The Cocktail: The Influence of Spirits on the American Psyche.* New York: St. Martin's Press, 1995. Lively account placing the drink within a pop cultural context.

RUTH TOBIAS

Olestra, *see Fats and Oils*

Olive Oil, *see Fats and Oils*

Olives

The olive (*Olea europea*) is the fruit of a Mediterranean tree that has been cultivated since the dawn of history. The olive tree grows to a great age; the trees in the Garden of Gethsemane, on the Mount of Olives in Jerusalem, are reputed to be two thousand years old. The

Olives. A few of the many varieties for sale at Sahadi's in Brooklyn, New York. *Photograph by Joe Zarba*

ripe fruits are more or less oval and are green at first, later turning black. They are extremely bitter because of the glucoside oleuropin. Olives are eaten green and black and are highly nutritious, but they must first be processed to eliminate the bitterness. Processing can be done in several ways, but it always involves steeping the olives in a water solution containing a strong alkali, usually lye or wood ash.

The olive has played a pivotal role in world history, its valuably oily fruit warding off famine in times of want, which is why the three major monotheistic religions—Judaism, Christianity, and Islam—have given it a symbolic significance. Monarchs have traditionally been anointed with olive oil at their coronations.

The olive was brought to California in the late eighteenth and early nineteenth centuries by the Spanish missionaries and grown in the only part of the United States with a suitable climate, the Southwest. The number of olive varieties is enormous, though sometimes the same variety is grown under different names, depending on the country from which it originates.

The Mission olive is still grown in Arizona, New Mexico, and Texas, with a few outposts in Nevada and even Oregon, but the commercial crop comes almost exclusively from northern California. Southern California land values are now prohibitive (the profitability of an olive grove is only one-tenth that of other fruit trees). The Mission olive is the most widely-grown California olive. It is a shiny, wrinkly-skinned fruit, originally planted for processing and canning, though some olives are picked early and processed for oil.

The Sevillano is another olive grown in California. It is eaten green and has thick flesh. It is usually salted and canned—and sometimes pitted, its cavity filled with a blanched almond or red pimiento.

Unlike European olives, commercially grown California olives are almost always sold pitted, and they have a milder flavor than olives imported from the Mediterranean. This flavor results from their being soaked in a ferrous gluconate solution to fix the pigment, then soaked in lye and immediately pickled in brine. Mediterranean olives are normally preserved in olive oil after curing. Olives are imported into the United States from Spain, Italy, and Greece (the Kalamata olive). These olives are sometimes crushed and mixed with spices, such as chili pepper.

Olives are generally eaten as a cocktail snack, but they can be cooked—chicken with olives is a popular Moroccan dish. They are highly nutritious, as is evidenced by their oil content. They contain valuable amounts of protein and trace elements, and their oil (as much as one teaspoon in a serving of seven olives) is monounsaturated and cholesterol free. Ten small olives are said to have the equivalent nutritional value of one hen's egg.

Californians who find olive trees on their property may want to pick and process their olives and make their own olive oil. There is plenty of online help for amateur growers from the Olive Oil Source (at http://www.oliveoil source.com), which publishes the *California Olive Oil News.*

[*See also* California; Fats and Oils.]

BIBLIOGRAPHY

Knickerbocker, Peggy. *Olive Oil: From Tree to Table.* San Francisco: Chronicle Books, 1997.
Rosenblum, Mort. *Olives: The Life and Lore of a Noble Fruit.* New York: North Point Press, 1996.
Taylor, Judith M. *The Olive in California: History of an Immigrant Tree.* Berkeley, CA: Ten Speed Press, 2000.

JOSEPHINE BACON

Onions

Most of America's early settlers brought with them whatever they needed to reestablish their gardens on the new continent. And they always brought onions (*Allium cepa*). Onions could make people weep, but they made any dish taste better. The bulbs were resistant to decay and could last all winter in the root cellar.

Onions are very climate and soil sensitive, so European onions had to be adapted selectively to local growing

Onions. From Reeves & Simonson's *Descriptive Catalogue of Choice Selected Seeds*, 1874.

American cookbook. She called for roasting the turkey on a spit and serving it up "with boiled onions and cramberry [*sic*] sauce, mangoes, pickles and celery." And she had other onion advice: "If you consult cheapness, the largest are the best; if you consult taste and softness, the very smallest are the most delicate, and used at the first tables." Few American recipes were specific: people used whatever onions they could grow or buy.

The contemporary onion scene is kaleidoscopic. Onions can be yellow, red, white or brown, as small as a grape or as large as a cabbage. They can be round or oval, or shaped like a torpedo, a spinning top, or a disc. There are slender green onions, or scallions. While some onions are especially strong, there are sweet onions—Vidalias, Walla Wallas, Mauis, and Texas 1015s—that have so little of those alliaceous or sulfurous compounds that they can be eaten like a peach.

The great breakthrough in the development of all of these varieties was the discovery in 1925 of a male-sterile onion by the botanist Henry Alfred Jones of the University of California. Until then there had been selective breeding of new varieties, but the process was slow. Jones planted sixty-three Italian Red onions to create seed for future propagation. When they bloomed, he put paper bags over each to ensure self-fertilization. One of them did not produce seed; its pollen had failed to develop genetic material. Instead it produced 136 bulbils, tiny replicas of the sterile plant. Jones used them to propagate the male-sterile specimen, which became the blank canvas on which he could create new cultivars specially adapted to growing conditions like climate, day length, altitude, and soil conditions. If he found a characteristic that might help a variety resist a disease or pest, he could more easily breed it into a new variety. What followed was the explosive development of a great range of onions.

The Americans have been creative with their onions in other ways. The dehydration industry grew up in this country during World War II, and dried and powdered onions were used to spice up the rations being shipped to soldiers abroad. About 7 percent of the American crop is dehydrated for use in the food processing industry. Jerry Bass, a bandleader and businessman in Akron, Ohio, first developed and took to market the precut and prebreaded onion ring that became, for a time, a universal accompaniment to a restaurant steak.

Commercial onion farming dates back to at least 1788, when the Wells Brothers opened their farm in Wethersfield, Connecticut. Farmers in the United States grow 3,350,000

conditions. Kitchen gardens of the eighteenth century tended to rely on imported onions for seed stock because seeds saved from domestically grown onions often deteriorated. After the Revolutionary War, growers started adapting varieties to different American climates. Many of the onion varieties in the eighteenth and nineteenth centuries were derived from the imported English globe onion and were suited for the cooler New England and Mid-Atlantic climates. Other varieties, successful in southern conditions, were developed from Spanish, Portuguese, and Italian stock. A few of these heirlooms are still grown.

Colonists and pioneers also used some of the dozens of onion cousins that grew wild in America. People in the Appalachians discovered the now fabled spring treat, the ramp (*A. tricoccum*).

American cookbooks were full of onions, first showing up in 1796, when Amelia Simmons published the first tons of onions on 160,000 acres. California produces more than a quarter of the onions grown in the United States. Idaho and Oregon are also major onion states, and Washington, New York, Michigan, Wisconsin, Nevada, Utah, Nebraska, Ohio, Georgia, and Texas are also important producers. Texas, Georgia, and Washington are especially well known for the so-called "sweets," but most of what Americans consume are the pungent, tear-producing storage onions. U.S. onion consumption averages 19½ pounds per person. The total value of the onion crop in America is approaching $1 billion per year.

There are myriad suggestions for avoiding tears when cutting up a hot onion. Chill them first. Cut them under water. Hold a piece of bread in your mouth. Use a food processor. Keep your knife sharp. Cover the chopped onions with a wet towel. Wear goggles. But the best advice is just to grin and bear it with the knowledge that the onions are always worth the tears.

[*See also* Garlic; Simmons, Amelia.]

BIBLIOGRAPHY

Bacheller, Barbara. *Lilies of the Kitchen*. New York: St. Martin's Press, 1986.
Griffith, Fred, and Linda Griffith. *Onions, Onions, Onions*. Shelburne, VT: Chapters, 1994.
Morash, Marian. *The Victory Garden Cookbook*. New York: Knopf, 1982.
Weaver, William Woys. *Heirloom Vegetable Gardening*. New York: Henry Holt, 1997.

FRED GRIFFITH AND LINDA GRIFFITH

Orange Flower Water

Orange flower water, also called orange blossom water, is a flavoring distilled from the flowers of sour orange trees, such as Seville and bergamot, usually as a condensed-steam by-product of distilling the oil, known as neroli. It is made primarily in Lebanon and France.

In the nineteenth century, orange flower water flavored many English desserts. It migrated in cake and custard recipes and in *capillaire*, a sugar syrup. Either orange flower water or rose water was a key ingredient in orgeat, originally a beverage and later a syrup used to sweeten other beverages. (In 1828 the cookbook writer Mary Randolph deemed orgeat a "necessary refreshment at all parties.") Orange flower water also piques a boiled orange pudding found in *How To Keep a Husband, or Culinary Tactics* (1872), a cookbook from California.

Except for a star turn in the Ramos gin fizz (the famous cocktail from New Orleans) and Mardi Gras cake, orange flower water in America remains primarily an ingredient of the cuisines of Spain (for example, *turron*, or nougat) and the Middle East (for example, baklava). It is often used interchangeably with rose water.

[*See also* Rose Water.]

BIBLIOGRAPHY

Brown, John Hull. *Early American Beverages*. Rutland, VT: C. E. Tuttle, 1966.
Randolph, Mary. *The Virginia House-wife*. Columbia: University of South Carolina Press, 1984. "A facsimile of the first edition, 1824, along with additional material from the editions of 1825 and 1828, thus presenting a complete text." Includes historical notes and commentary by Karen Hess.
Randolph, Mary. *The Virginia Housewife, or, Methodical Cook: A Facsimile of an Authentic Early American Cookbook*. New York: Dover Publications, 1993. Includes a new introduction by Janice Bluestein Longone.

ROBIN M. MOWER

Orange Juice

Few Americans drank orange juice before the mid-nineteenth century, mainly because oranges, which were imported from the West Indies, were so expensive. Many of those who did drink orange juice did so in the form of "orangeade" (sweetened, diluted juice, like lemonade). With the completion of the transcontinental railroad in 1869 and the subsequent construction of railroads to Florida, orange growers greatly expanded their groves, and the price of oranges dropped during the late nineteenth and early twentieth centuries.

In the late 1920s, vitamin C was isolated by the Hungarian scientist Albert Szent-Györgyi, and oranges were identified as an excellent source of the vitamin. Although its function was not fully understood at the time, vitamin C is an antioxidant and thus helps prevent disease and encourage healing. Shortly thereafter, orange growers in Florida and California launched a major campaign to promote orange juice as a healthful drink and a breakfast necessity. Orange juice sales skyrocketed as Americans became convinced that their health depended on drinking a glass of the juice every morning. Rarely has a food habit been adopted so quickly by so many people.

Fresh-squeezed orange juice remained a luxury through the early twentieth century, and most Americans consumed less-expensive canned juice. Frozen orange juice

CONCENTRATED ORANGE JUICE

Oranges must ripen on the tree, between December and June, before they can be picked. In Florida, 98 percent of all oranges are harvested by hand after testing determines that the ratio of Brix (soluble sugar content) to acidity is just right. The ripe oranges are transported to a processing plant, washed, and graded and the juice is extracted. Next the peel, pulp, and seeds are removed. The juice can be pasteurized for "not from concentrate" products or it can go into vacuum evaporators, where most of the water is removed. The concentrated orange juice is then chilled and frozen. It is packaged into cans for sale in supermarkets or shipped by tanker truck to dairies, to be reconstituted with fresh water and packaged into cardboard cartons, glass bottles, or plastic jugs.

John M. Fox, the founder and president of the Minute Maid Company, is credited with developing frozen orange juice concentrate in the 1940s. He used a technique he had seen demonstrated during World War II to dehydrate penicillin and blood plasma. Fox intended to make a soluble orange juice powder but it had a bad taste. However, by adding water to the reduced concentrate, the juice had a fresh-squeezed taste. An advertising agency in Boston, the city famous for its minutemen, created the name "Minute Maid," to emphasize the product's convenience and ease of preparation. The company was sold to Coca-Cola in 1960.

BIBLIOGRAPHY

Encyclopedia of Consumer Brands. Vol. 1 Consumable Products. Detroit: St. James Press, 1994.

JOSEPH M. CARLIN

was first marketed during the early 1930s, but it was unsuccessful until research showed that concentrating the juice (removing much of the water) before freezing improved the taste. After World War II, frozen foods became big business: Grocers devoted more space to freezers, and appliance makers enlarged the freezer compartments of home refrigerators. By the early 1950s, orange juice accounted for 20 percent of the frozen food market.

Orange juice is used as an ingredient in several drinks, including the Orange Julius, the screwdriver (vodka and orange juice), the mimosa (champagne and orange juice), the orange blossom (gin and orange juice), and the tequila sunrise (tequila, orange juice, and grenadine).

The largest commercial producers of orange juice in the United States are Minute Maid, owned by Coca-Cola, and Tropicana, owned by PepsiCo. Americans drank on average 4.7 gallons of orange juice in 2003.

[*See also* Citrus; Fruit Juices; Orange Julius; Mimosa; Screwdriver; Tequila Sunrise.]

BIBLIOGRAPHY

Frank, M. G. *Keeping Well with Oranges and Grapefruit.* Tampa: Florida Citrus Exchange, 1931.
McPhee, John. *Oranges.* New York: Farrar, Straus and Giroux, 1967.

ANDREW F. SMITH

Orange Julius

In 1926 the real estate agent Willard Hamlin helped to secure a downtown Los Angeles storefront for the fresh-squeezed orange juice stand owned by his friend Julius Freed. Hamlin, who had a background in chemistry, thought there might be a market for more interesting orange-based drinks, and he began experimenting with combinations of fresh orange juice and crushed ice blended with various food powders. The result was a fruit drink with a creamy, frothy texture. The formula is proprietary, but published "copycat" recipes for home consumption consist of orange juice blended with such additives as milk, sugar, vanilla, egg whites, powdered whipped topping mix, and vanilla pudding mix. In many ways, the Orange Julius was the forerunner of the smoothie.

Freed adopted Hamlin's recipe, and the business was so successful that Hamlin gave up the real estate business and concentrated on marketing and franchising Orange Julius operations. By 1929 he had opened about one hundred stores from Los Angeles to Boston. The Depression and World War II curtailed expansion, but the company rapidly expanded during the 1950s. In 1967 the company was acquired by International Industries, which also controlled the International House of Pancakes (IHOP) and other restaurant operations. Orange Julius later became part of the Dairy Queen Corporation. By the beginning of the twenty-first century, there were about three hundred Orange Julius outlets in the United States (many in shopping malls), Canada, and other countries.

BIBLIOGRAPHY

Orange Julius of America. http://www.orangejulius.com/en-US/default.htm. Official website.

ANDREW F. SMITH

Oranges, *see Citrus*

Organic Food

The term "organic" has been both a socially and a legally defined category of food that is claimed to be more natural than artificial in both its production and its preparation. Organic foods are now the central element of American health foods. Some would argue that until the industrial agricultural complex of the twentieth century, all foods produced were essentially organic and their purity up to that point had been tainted primarily by the food processing industry. Although some federal oversight of food quality had been in effect since the Lincoln administration, it was the Progressive Era legislation promoted by Theodore Roosevelt that led to the Pure Food and Drug Act (1906) and the establishment of the Food and Drug Administration (FDA). Numerous consumer protection laws followed, and most Americans assume that their food supply is safe and pure. Most notable to its relationship to organic foods was the Delaney Clause, part of the 1958 food additives amendment to the Food, Drug, and Cosmetic Act (1938). In short, the Delaney Clause states that any additive in any amount that is demonstrated to cause cancer in laboratory animals will be banned from the market. Even with such a restricted definition there is still some allowance for "acceptable risks" if the chance is extremely remote that someone may be harmed by a product.

This clause introduces an organic food conundrum. If our food is deemed safe by government oversight, then why do we need to have a separate category of organic food? Is organic food any safer, more nutritious, or better tasting than conventional food? The answer is not a simple yes or no. A brief overview of the development of the organic food and farming movement will help to illuminate some of the concerns about conventional foods and government oversight that were initially raised in the early to mid-twentieth century. The movement involved not only individuals who questioned the ways in which food was being produced and its impact on the land, but also those who were wary of the safety and quality of the food that eventually made its way to the table.

The history of the organic movement has its early roots in English founders such as Sir Albert Howard. In his book *An Agricultural Testament* (1940), Howard argues that the growing scientific agriculture of the early to mid-twentieth century was out of touch with nature. The imbalance that was emerging was damaging to both the environment and human health and well-being. In that same year Lord Northbourne (Walter Ernest Christopher James) is said to have been the first explicitly to use the term "organic farming," in his book *Look to the Land* (1940). He stressed the biological completeness of the farm as a living entity that must be in balance with organic life.

Lady Eve Balfour, another of the early English founders of the organic movement, emphasized the importance of soil fertility and was concerned with the increased use of petroleum-based, or "artificial," chemical fertilizers. She promoted the adage that healthy soil meant healthy plants and in turn that translated into healthy people. Her book *The Living Soil* (1943) was the impetus for the formation in 1946 of the Soil Association, over which she presided as its first president. Dedicated to alternative and sustainable agriculture based on the use of renewable sources of soil fertility that do not harm the environment, the association has become a leading advocacy and organic certification organization in England.

Emerging from the U.S. dust bowl of the Depression of the 1930s—witness to a failure of soil conservation—the works of individuals like Howard inspired the beginnings of the American organic movement. The movement was popularized most by the writings of Jerome Irving Rodale. In the early 1940s Rodale purchased sixty acres of land near Emmaus, Pennsylvania, to experiment with Howard's ideas. Combining his interests with magazine publishing, in 1942 he put out *Organic Farming and Gardening*, which popularized the American organic food and agricultural movement. He also founded *Prevention*

Certified Organic. Bananas with organic and fair-trade stickers, Park Slope Food Coop, Brooklyn, New York. *Photograph by Joe Zarba*

magazine, which continues to be a primary source of information on organic health foods.

A crucial impetus to the organic movement came with the book *Silent Spring* (1962), in which Rachel Carson highlighted the dangers of pesticides in our ecosystems and inevitably on our tables. Her work was seen as being symbolic of all that was wrong with modern agriculture. The mass popularity of her work, the writings of the English founders of the organic movement, and the ongoing research by Rodale were quickly incorporated into the counterculture society of the 1960s and 1970s. With communal living and "free love," plots of organic land sprouted up across the United States, especially along the Pacific coast. For older generations organic foods conjure up images of earthy, granola-crunching, vegetarian hippies and counterculture gurus. Still, it is during this period that organic agriculture and foods became firmly established in U.S. society as an alternative to mainstream agribusiness, which had come to dominate the American food system in the late twentieth century.

The initial interest in organic foods in the United States was primarily limited to pesticide-free fresh fruits and vegetables grown on small garden plots. In time this focus spread to the large-scale raising of grains and other plant foods, which reflected the important relationship of the movement with vegetarianism. As the appeal for organic foods grew, the movement expanded into the raising of antibiotic-free animal products that were fed organic grains. To clarify what "organic" meant to the consumer, several states established their own organic standards for food products and their production in the 1970s and 1980s.

To provide a national uniformity, the Organic Foods Production Act (OFPA) was implemented as Title XXI of the 1990 Farm Bill. It set national standards for how organic food was to be produced, handled, and labeled. It also established the National Organic Standards Board (NOSB), which recommends a list of products that cannot be used in organic production. Products used in organic farm production cannot have a negative effect on human health or the ecosystem and must be compatible with a system of sustainable farming.

With more than a decade of development, the National Organic Rule went into effect on October 21, 2002. Since that time all standards have been fully implemented with the use of criteria established and modified since OFPA. States that may have had even stricter standards may still use them, but the standards must be approved by the

U.S. Department of Agriculture (USDA) and cannot restrict products from other states that only meet the USDA standards. Some products now also carry labels that include specific state certifications for those who feel that a particular state is even more compliant with organic standards than the federal criteria.

The organic rule applies only to the food producer or handler who receives more than $5,000 a year in revenue from the sale of the products. These producers must be certified by a USDA-accredited, independent third party, usually a state or a private agency. For certification organic farmers must submit a plan of operation that documents its compliance with regulations, and they must be prepared to undergo audits by the certifying agencies. The real key to making a product organic is that land used must not have been subjected in the past three years to any of the substances on the NOSB prohibited list of products. For organic plant foods, farmers are to use organic seeds when feasible and utilize a number of soil and environmentally friendly methods of production, such as crop rotation, natural fertilizers (animal and vegetable manures), and integrated pest management. For the production of meat, dairy, and egg products, the animals must be raised in conditions that are open and more closely resemble a natural habitat, generally referred to as "free-range" conditions. This emphasis on animal welfare also excludes the use of antibiotics and growth hormones in healthy animals.

In terms of labeling what the consumer may be eating as organic, the National Organic Rule has very specific parameters. It should be noted that the terms "natural" and "organic" cannot be used interchangeably. Organic labeling laws are as follows: Labeling a product "100 percent organic" requires that the product contain only organic ingredients; this product can carry the official USDA organic seal, but use is voluntary. Labeling a product "organic" requires that at least 95 percent of the product, by weight or by volume, contain organic ingredients; this product can carry the official USDA organic seal. Labeling a product "contains organic ingredients" or "made with organic ingredients" requires that at least 70 percent of the product contain, by weight or volume, organic ingredients; this product, however, cannot carry the official USDA organic seal.

Again, since both organic and conventional foods must meet federal health and safety standards, why should organic food carry a different label? It has been shown that organic foods do contain less pesticide residue, but even the amounts found in conventional foods are far below the levels allowed by the current government standards. In addition some have voiced concern over some natural contaminants (for example, bacteria and fungi) that are not regulated in organic foods. Perhaps the real key is that people would rather err on the side of caution than assume the additional risks of unknown factors that might lie in conventional food production and sources coming from around the world. It also becomes an ideological commitment to sustainable food production, for which many are willing to pay the extra cost as an investment in the future.

The advantage of organic agriculture to farmers is that it lowers production costs, relies more on renewable resources, reduces energy costs, fosters both biodiversity and sustainability, and decreases farmers' direct exposure to toxic substances. It also produces a product that captures high-value markets compared to conventional foods, which boosts farm income. This fact has not gone unnoticed by the large-scale food producers and processors.

Although organic farms now produce less than 2 percent of the U.S. food supply and utilize less than 1 percent of American farmland, during the 1990s the organic food market began to grow more than 15 to 20 percent each year. The preoccupation of the aging baby boomers and the children of the 1960s with health and environmental concerns has no doubt contributed to this substantial growth in the organic food market. Organic foods are generally more expensive and have a greater appeal to middle-class America. Without their support, as reflected in the rapid increase in the organic market, it is highly unlikely that the 2002 labeling plan would have gone into effect.

The reasons for eating organic foods vary, ranging from health issues to environmental concerns and from preferences for taste to nutritional advantages. Many do claim that organic foods taste better and are more nutritious. However, at the beginning of the twenty-first century, no scientific studies had substantiated that claim. Still, most would argue that the demands of the food processing industry to increase shelf life for conventional foods can have a real impact, at least on taste. In addition, reading the label on any food product can be a daunting prospect for consumers who are intimidated by the listing of chemical additives and unsure about their long-term health effects, even if they are deemed safe by law. Organic food choice represents a complex intersection of traditional perceptions, ideology, and scientific fact.

Many consumers also seek out organic foods as an alternative to the industrial agricultural complex and factory food production of conventional foods. While the early twenty-first-century trend, an estimated $10 billion in annual sales and rising, is great news for the organic food industry overall, hard-line organic food advocates are alarmed by a number of changes that are taking place. They feel that as organic foods become more mainstream, many of the traditions of organic farming will be left behind. The traditional small farm is beginning to lose out to the larger corporate farms and food companies. A number of traditional organic food product lines have already been bought up by the major food companies. Organic foods are no longer confined primarily to the natural food stores, either. Most large grocery store chains across the United States have been devoting specific sections to organic foods, often alongside other "health food" products. Organic foods can also be found mixed among the conventional foods as well, including organic microwaveable macaroni and cheese, potato chips, ketchup, and ready-to-eat bags of salad.

Traditional organic food producers feel that, even though the larger companies, often monopolizing and multinational, will follow the rule of the law when it comes to organic certification, the legislation is full of loopholes, with an oversight process that has little room for ongoing public response. In the end, the convenience of the widespread availability of organic foods may be compromised with the ability to support local organic producers who still advocate for a world in which we "think globally and eat locally."

[*See also* Organic Gardening.]

BIBLIOGRAPHY

Greene, Catherine, and Amy Kremen. "U.S. Organic Farming in 2000–2001: Adoption of Certified Systems." USDA Economic Research Service, 2003. http://www.ers.usda.gov/publications/aib780.

Lampkin, Nicholas. *Organic Farming*. Alexandria Bay, NY: Diamond Farm Book Publishers, 2000.

Lipson, Elaine Marie. *The Organic Foods Sourcebook*. Chicago: Contemporary Books, 2001.

Nabhan, Gary. *Coming Home to Eat: The Pleasures and Politics of Local Foods*. New York: Norton, 2002.

The National Organic Program. http://www.ams.usda.gov/nop. This USDA website provides updates and regulations related to organic food production in the United States.

The Organic Alliance. http://www.organic.org. This comprehensive website, sponsored by the nonprofit organization Organic Alliance, promotes the environmental and economic benefits of certified organic food production to farmers, processors, distributors, retailers, and consumers.

BARRETT P. BRENTON AND KEVIN T. MCINTYRE

Organic Gardening

Organic gardening is based on a human relationship with nature. From this flows a system of growing food or cultivating plants that maintains and regenerates the fertility of the soil without the use of synthetic pesticides and fertilizers. An organic gardener strives for a balance with nature, using methods and materials that will meet the needs and desires of the gardener with the least possible impact on the environment. Gardening has become a popular pursuit and a thriving industry around the world. By the early twenty-first century, approximately 80 million households were participating in lawn and gardening activities, representing a $40 billion industry. Roughly 10 percent of this industry is organic.

All gardens and farms remained essentially organic until the early 1800s. Changing cultural attitudes brought on by the Industrial Revolution began to threaten the limits of nature in the nineteenth century. In 1840 the German scientist Justin von Liebig sought to produce artificially the major nutrients that plants absorbed naturally from the soil. At the same time, John Bennet Lawes discovered that adding sulfuric acid to phosphate rock would more rapidly release phosphorus to soil for plant use. He opened a fertilizer factory in London in 1842, and within a decade manufacturers had opened similar chemical factories in Baltimore and Boston. This development marked the entrance of chemical fertilizers into soils of farms and gardens in the United States.

During World War I and World War II, the fear of food shortages combined with patriotic impulses turned many Americans into gardeners. Over the same period, chemists were devising deadly biological weapons for wartime use that would eventually find their way onto gardens and farms and have devastating impacts not only on weeds and insects, but on the environment as well. Ammoniated fertilizers sprung from the explosive industry in Germany during World War I. By 1918 victory gardens in the United States had become a part of everyday life, and garden chemicals were becoming readily available. In 1939 DDT, which had been used as an insecticide during the war, was being heralded as a miracle for gardening and farming. Four years after World War II began, Eleanor Roosevelt urged Americans to grow victory gardens once again. In 1942 there were 21 million victory plots in the United States, producing 40 percent of the nation's vegetables. Organophosphate insecticides were first used for human extermination during World War II and became available for garden and agricultural

Organic Products. Food stand at the Grand Army Plaza farmers' market, Brooklyn, New York. *Photograph by Joe Zarba*

use after. In response to the popularity of gardening and the growing acceptance of garden chemicals, the organic movement began to heat up on both sides of the Atlantic.

The organic movement came to life for the public in the United States via J. I. Rodale's magazine *Organic Gardening and Farming*, in which Rodale coined the word "organiculture" to describe organic agriculture. Rodale was greatly influenced by the studies and writings of both Sir Albert Howard and Lady Eve Balfour of England. He believed that healthy, humus-rich soil would grow healthy crops and improve public health. He started the first organic gardening experimental farm near Allentown, Pennsylvania, and founded the Soul and Health Foundation in 1947.

In 1962 Rachel Carson published *Silent Spring*, which describes the environmental damage caused by the use of synthetic, "toxic" chemicals. Her descriptions sounded an alarm in the hearts of Americans. This unease spurred new interest in alternatives. Horticultural innovators in the last quarter of the twentieth century included John Jeavons with his biointensive approach; David Holmgren and Bill Mollison with permaculture; and Robert Rodale (J. I. Rodale's son), who realized that growing food was about health and survival for the world, not just about an alternative lifestyle for a few. While conventional economists viewed all the resources of the earth as being available for personal profit, these practical organic visionaries saw stewardship of the living world as a sacred duty.

Rodale saw that organic agriculture could be successful by integrating organic scientific research with the organic farmer and gardener's personal relationship with the soil: nature could heal itself, be productive without chemicals, and meet the needs of both feeding humanity and preserving the land. Robert Rodale called this renewal process "regenerative agriculture," and it has become not only the basis for the methods used by many organic gardeners, farmers, and environmentalists, but also a personal way to improve life now and for future generations.

Cutting-edge organic gardeners use organic-regenerative gardening techniques that combine traditional wisdom and innovative discoveries. They use plants suited to local weather and soils that are insect and disease tolerant but are not genetically modified or engineered. With heirloom varieties they can preserve seed for use in the next growing season and protect genetic diversity and crop quality for years to come. Organic practitioners know that adding chemicals to the soil depletes it of the essential nutrients and living organisms that help it to

regenerate itself. Soil becomes dependent on chemical inputs to foster plant growth as its natural, biologically based recycling mechanisms are disrupted by chemical use. This process is analogous to drug addiction, in which the input disrupts natural processes, leading to ever greater reliance on the chemical and decreasing response to its use. Regenerating soil means replenishing its nutrients and living systems by subtracting disruptive, unnatural chemical inputs and adding what will feed a healthy living soil community—for example, organic compost, beneficial microbes, enzymes, and earthworms.

Adding compost to soil improves its structure and its ability to retain both air and moisture needed for vigorous plant growth. Organic gardeners recycle their garden material instead of buying compost. Mulching by laying organic materials on the soil surface combats adverse weather by holding in additional moisture and preventing the beating action of heavy rain that compacts the soil and breaks down its structure. Organic mulches also control weeds and add nutrients to the soil while greatly aiding a robust soil biological community. Dried grass clippings, instead of commercial mulch that may contain unwanted coloring or chemicals, are often used by organic gardeners. Crop rotation, cover cropping, and companion planting improve the soil, discourage weeds and unwanted pests, and attract beneficial insects.

Organic agriculture and gardening can still sometimes be more costly and labor intensive initially. Organic growing requires more initial labor input for natural fertilization, pest control, and weed control methods, and it sometimes results in smaller yields. But, as soil improves, the need for input decreases, while in chemically based gardening, more and more fertilizer is needed over time as soil declines in quality. Findings at The Rodale Institute Farming Systems Trial have shown that the cost of fertilizer and pesticides makes up three-fourths of the total energy input into conventional, chemically based gardening or farming, while organic biological (natural) input makes up three-fourths of input into organic gardening or farming, which is much more cost effective. Prices for organic produce are higher and help farmers and gardeners to convert to organic production profitably.

The cost of gardening and farming organically is really an investment in the future for several reasons. There are mounting studies on the dangers of garden pesticides—the hidden costs of growing food using chemicals. The U.S. Environmental Protection Agency (EPA) estimates that pesticides contaminate the groundwater in thirty-eight states and pollute the primary source of drinking water for more than half the country's population. The EPA estimates that on average, each American uses over four pounds of chemicals per year on lawns and gardens. These chemicals reduce the diversity of essential soil life, contribute to soil compaction, intensify soil acidity, and increase thatch buildup in lawns. They also lead to an increase in algae growth in lakes, which reduces oxygen levels, killing fish and other organisms. Studies also report an increased incidence of cancer and other health problems among families who use these products. Children and pets may be particularly susceptible because they are especially sensitive to toxic chemicals and they often spend time playing in the yard. Also, the food choices that people make now will have an impact upon their children's health in the future. The average child receives four times more exposure than an adult to at least eight widely used cancer-causing pesticides in food.

By the beginning of the twenty-first century, only 19 percent of Americans were more inclined to purchase organic foods regardless of the price, and only 10 percent of the 80 million U.S. households that participated in lawn and gardening activities were organic gardeners. Studies showed that 70 percent of Americans listed the higher prices of organic foods as a major factor for not buying organic. The majority of Americans want the best-looking produce at the lowest immediate cost. Consumers, gardeners, and farmers need to be educated about organic produce and its benefits to both health and the environment. As organic production scales up, premiums will narrow, and prices will fall as economies grow. The expansion of organics lies in continuing to develop innovative, cost-effective ways to work within the intricate bounds of nature and to develop public education programs that will eventually change perceptions and attitudes toward organic produce's higher prices, which will eventually begin to subside.

Whether they grow healthy vegetables for food, fragrant herbs for aromatherapy, culinary herbs for cooking, or simply attractive plants to add aesthetic beauty to a yard, organic gardeners know that they are working in harmony with the rhythms of nature—the air, seasons, wind, soil, sun, and rain. Healthy soil is the foundation of the organic movement, and organic gardeners and farmers are the cornerstones. Within the soil exists not only the key to the future of organic gardening, but the vital connection to the health of the planet and the health of people.

[See also Organic Food.]

BIBLIOGRAPHY

Bartholomew, Mel. Square Foot Gardening. Emmaus, PA: Rodale Press, 1981.
Brummond, Brad. "Organic Gardening Tips." North Dakota State University Extension Service. http://www.ext.nodak.edu/extpubs/plantsci/hortcrop/h1106w.htm.
Dominé, André. Organic and Wholefoods: Naturally Delicious Cuisine. Cologne, Germany: Könemann Verlagsgesellschaft, 1997.
Ellis, Barbara W. Rodale's Illustrated Encyclopedia of Gardening and Landscaping Techniques. Emmaus, PA: Rodale Press, 1990.
Fairbairn, Neil. A Brief History of Gardening. Emmaus, PA: Rodale, 2001.
Hynes, Erin. Rodale's Successful Organic Gardening: Improving the Soil. Emmaus, PA: Rodale Press, 1994.
Jesiolowski Cebenko, Jill, and Deborah L. Martin. Insect, Disease, and Weed I.D. Guide. Emmaus, PA: Rodale, 2001.
Kimbrell, Andrew. Fatal Harvest: The Tragedy of Industrial Agriculture. San Rafael, CA: Foundation for Deep Ecology by arrangement with Island Press, 2002.
Kuepper, George. "Organic Farm Certification and the National Organic Program." ATTRA (October 2002), http://www.attra.ncat.org.
"New and Improved National Organic Standards." Rodale, 2003. http://www.organicgardening.com/watchdog/food.html.
"Organic Gardening 1942–2002, 60 Years of OG: Our 60 Greatest Garden Secrets." OG (September-October 2002): 26–33.
Rodale, J. I. How to Grow Vegetables and Fruits by the Organic Method. Emmaus, PA: Rodale Press, 1961.
Rodale, J. I., and Sir Albert Howard. Pay Dirt: Farming and Gardening with Composts. New York: Devin-Adair, 1946.
Rodale, Maria. Maria Rodale's Organic Gardening. Emmaus, PA: Rodale Press, 1998.
Rodale, Robert. Our Next Frontier: A Personal Guide for Tomorrow's Lifestyle. Emmaus, PA: Rodale Press, 1981.
Shapiro, Howard-Yana, and John Harrisson. Gardening for the Future of the Earth. New York: Bantam Books, 2000.
Spitzer, Eliot. "Home and Garden Pesticides: Questions and Answers About Safety and Alternatives." April 1999. http://www.oag.state.ny.us/environment/home_pesticides.html.
Stell, Elizabeth P. Secrets to Great Soil: A Grower's Guide to Composting, Mulching, and Creating Healthy, Fertile Soil for Your Garden and Lawn. Pownal, VT: Storey Communications, 998.
Stoner, Carol. The Organic Directory. Emmaus, PA: Rodale Press, 1974.

ANTHONY RODALE AND SUSAN FEAKES DORSCHUTZ

Ovens, see Stoves and Ovens

Oyster Bars

The shucking and serving of oysters has been a downstairs-upstairs phenomenon in the history of American restaurants. As early as 1763 a cellar on Broad Street in New York City featured oysters on the half shell, as did a handful of other basement saloons, which were occasionally called parlors or bars. As time passed and the number of these establishments grew, they were recognized by certain distinctive features. A balloon of red muslin, which could be illuminated at night by a candle within, beckoned the oyster aficionado down a short flight of steps. In the nineteenth century, these 25-by-100-foot cellars were ornately furnished with mirrors, gilded paintings, gaslights or chandeliers, carpeting in the center aisle, and a handsome bar at one end of the room. Oysters became the incentive for consuming alcoholic beverages, and the atmosphere of these clubby, all-male cellars led to the invitation "Let us royster with the oyster—in the shorter days and moister" (*Detroit Free Press*, October 12, 1889). One of the most prestigious of these oyster cellars was Downings at 5 Broad Street in New York. Because of its proximity to the U.S. Custom House, the Merchant's Exchange, banks, and stores, it also became a meeting place of politicians and office-seekers. By 1874 over 850 oyster establishments existed in New York City alone. Not limited to this major commercial seaport, but also located in other cities along the Atlantic coast and as far west as the railroads extended, oyster cellars, saloons, and bars displaced coffeehouses as meeting places.

When it became essential for businesspeople to spend the workday away from home, aboveground oyster stalls located in busy market areas and the more leisurely oyster houses and lunchrooms gained in popularity. The stalls offered freshly shucked oysters, instantly prepared stews, and oysters roasted in the wood fire that also kept the vendors warm. The back-of-the-house cooks of the more elaborate oyster houses served oysters in a variety of recipes, with shellfish and fish entrées as well as with steaks and chops. In 1826 the Union Oyster House in Boston, reputed to be the country's oldest restaurant still in operation, introduced a semicircular oyster bar where Daniel Webster was reputed to have eaten three dozen oysters, accompanied by brandy and water, at one sitting. Other cities along the East Coast, as well as Chicago, Pittsburgh, and St. Louis, boasted well-appointed oyster houses decorated with marble and mahogany, offering first-class service and tempting food. In New Orleans, special oyster preparations—Bienville, Roffignac, and Rockefeller—became the distinguishing dishes of famous restaurants, and during the gold rush days, the infamous mining town of Placerville, California, known for its frequent hangings, served an oyster omelet appropriately named the Hangtown fry, later a signature dish of Maye's Oyster House in San Francisco.

Eating Oysters. Oyster stands in Fulton Market, New York City, around 1870. *Culinary Archives & Museum at Johnson & Wales University, Providence, R.I.*

The continuing popularity of restaurants like the Grand Central Oyster Bar in New York City, which opened in 1913, proves that the tradition of the oyster bar has not faded. Whether serving a platter of half shells, an oyster stew or panfry, or, in the contemporary mode, offering a selection of shellfish from a pristine raw bar, restaurateurs know that the celebration of the oyster never ends.

[*See also* Oysters.]

BIBLIOGRAPHY

Fisher, M. F. K. *Consider the Oyster*. San Francisco: North Point Press, 1988.
Foley, Joseph, and Joan Foley. *The Grand Central Oyster Bar and Restaurant Seafood Cookbook*. New York: Crown, 1977.
Gordon, David G., Nancy E. Blanton, and Terry Y. Nosho. *Heaven on the Half Shell: The Story of the Northwest's Love Affair with the Oyster*. Portland, OR: WestWinds, 2001.
Reardon, Joan. *Oysters: A Culinary Celebration*. Orleans, MA: Parnassus, 1984; rev. ed. New York: Lyons Press, 2000.

JOAN REARDON

Oyster Loaf Sandwich

The oyster loaf sandwich is composed of a hollowed-out loaf of french bread that is buttered and toasted, then filled with oysters that have been lightly breaded in cornmeal and deep-fried. It was created during the late nineteenth century, when oysters, plentiful and cheap, were a popular American food. In New Orleans, Louisiana, husbands who spent the evening carousing in the French Quarter often brought home an oyster loaf in the hope of pacifying a jealous wife; the oyster loaf was thus known as *la médiatrice*, or "the mediator." Also laying claim to the oyster loaf is San Francisco, where it is said that Mayes Oyster House, established in 1867, created it. Various versions of the sandwich can typically be found in oyster-harvesting areas throughout the United States.

[*See also* Oysters.]

BIBLIOGRAPHY

Mercuri, Becky. *Sandwiches That You Will Like*. Pittsburgh, PA: WQED, 2002.

BECKY MERCURI

Oysters

A subject of still-life paintings, a source for metaphors and lyrics, and a legendary aphrodisiac, the oyster is scientifi-

cally an edible bivalve mollusk. *Ostrea* and *Crassostrea* are the main genera of the edible oyster, and within both groups there are at least fifty species, each with hundreds of varieties specific to the bays, coves, and estuaries where they grow. *Ostrea edulis* is the flat, smooth, European oyster commonly called Belon, which is now cultivated on both the Atlantic and Pacific coasts of the United States. *Ostrea lurida*, or the Olympia oyster, is indigenous to the waters of the Pacific Northwest. *Crassostrea virginica*, sometimes called the American oyster, is native to the waters of the U.S. Atlantic and Gulf coasts. *Crassostrea gigas* is indigenous to Japan, but since the early 1900s it has been highly cultivated along the Pacific coast from San Francisco to British Columbia. Such familiar commercial names as Lynnhavens, Blue Points, Cotuits, Wellfleets, Chincoteagues, Tomales Bays, and Apalachicolas derive from the waters where the adult oysters are harvested.

Oyster shells found in remnants of barrier reefs along the coast of France and Portugal and into the Mediterranean as far as Greece indicate that oysters were plentiful in the ancient world. As early as the fourth century B.C.E., the cultivation of oysters and the probable origins of aquaculture were also evident in China. On this side of the Atlantic, mounds of shells along the eastern seaboard gave ample evidence of the huge storage pools that the Indians used for oysters and other shellfish. Along the coast of Maine, 7 million bushels of shells were found, while remnants of weirs were located in Boston in the marshes now known as Back Bay. Oyster place-names like Osterville, Oyster Harbor, and Oyster Lane distinguished Cape Cod in Massachusetts. Ellis Island, New York, was known as Oyster Island when the Dutch purchased Manhattan, and the Indians named Long Island Sewanahaka, or Island of Shells.

The changing role that oysters played in American cuisine, from the wigwams of the Wampanoags to the famous New York City oyster saloons and gradually to dining rooms from Boston to San Francisco, is a saga that progressed from sheer necessity to serendipity. The Indians taught the colonists to harvest and cook oysters in a stew that staved off hunger, and in 1610 food shortages in Jamestown, Virginia, led settlers to travel to the mouth of the James River, where oysters sustained them. Two centuries later, a feature of the American diet became a between-meal snack at a vendor's stand, and a dozen or two half shells became a prelude to a more substantial oyster pie or, on the West Coast, an oyster omelet known as the Hangtown fry. Another dish utilizing the mollusk was roasted fowl stuffed with oysters. By 1840, annual shipments of oysters from the Chesapeake Bay to Philadelphia had reached four thousand tons. By 1859, residents in New York City spent more on oysters than on butchers' meat. The oyster craze of the nineteenth century spread across the country by stagecoach, by boat when the Erie Canal opened to barges, and by rail when the railroads traveled westward.

By the 1880s the demand for oysters was so great that the beds that stretched along the Atlantic and Gulf coasts began to be depleted, and the near extinction of the indigenous Olympias of the Pacific Northwest necessitated the importation of oysters from Japan and the cultivation of eastern oysters in western waters. Human consumption, however, was not the only threat to the supply of oysters. Industrial waste began to pollute the waters, storms and hurricanes ravaged the beds, and predators wasted the young oyster spats. In the early twenty-first century, these threats are balanced by new methods of aquaculture, and oysters are available but not plentiful. Along with caviar and foie gras, they are considered to be in a class apart.

[*See also* New England; Oyster Bars; Oyster Loaf Sandwich; Pacific Northwestern Regional Cookery.]

BIBLIOGRAPHY

Gordon, David G., Nancy E. Blanton, and Terry Y. Nosho. *Heaven on the Half Shell: The Story of the Northwest's Love Affair with the Oyster*. Portland, OR: WestWinds, 2001.

Mariani, John F. *The Dictionary of American Food and Drink*. New York: Ticknor and Fields, 1983.

Reardon, Joan. *Oysters: A Culinary Celebration*. Orleans, MA.: Parnassus Press, 1984; rev. ed. New York: Lyons Press, 2000.

JOAN REARDON

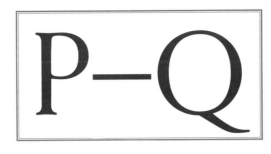

Pacific Northwestern Regional Cookery

When the last glaciers receded from the Pacific Northwest ten thousand to fourteen thousand years ago, people moved in. The aboriginal peoples were the first to feast on an abundance of salmon, halibut, clams, crabs, deer, and venison; young shoots and leaves of green plants (*Heracleum lanatum*, or cow parsnip); root vegetables (camas and wapato); and a variety of berries (salmonberry, huckleberry, and blackberry). In the nineteenth century, when explorers and settlers added nonnative foods, such as wheat, potatoes, apples, and grapes, agriculture was on its way to becoming a prominent industry. It has been aided by large-scale irrigation using runoff from the melting snowcaps of the Cascade Mountains and water released by Grand Coulee Dam as well as a unique combination of soil, moisture, and climate.

In Oregon and Washington, the Cascades, majestic rugged mountains, slice the area into two distinct climate zones. The west side is home to alluvial soil, coastal mountains (the Olympics) and plains, undulating hillsides, dense forests, meandering rivers, and a temperate maritime climate. A variety of berries thrives in the cool marine climate. On the east is the arid and semiarid region of hot summers and cold winters. It too has mountains and plains, but the soil in many areas is derived from basalt, a volcanic rock. With help from irrigation, its warm, dry summer days, cool nights, and nutrient-rich volcanic soil are perfect for growing crops such as wheat, potatoes, dry peas, and lentils. The Columbia River, with its abundance of salmon and other fish, flows 1,270 miles from Canada through Washington and along most of the border that separates Washington and Oregon before emptying in the Pacific Ocean. Idaho and the southwest corner of Montana are often considered part of the Pacific Northwest region.

The native people who moved camps to follow the migration of animals and the emergence of plants, such as ripening berries, lived on both sides of the mountains. Though all tribes had their own dialects and "tribal" identities, they had similar methods of preparing food. Native people cooked with boiling water heated with hot stones in a watertight coiled basket, steamed food in a hot pit filled with grasses and/or dirt and covered with mats, or roasted over a smoldering fire. Seeking food and preparing foods for winter storage were major activities and involved the entire tribe. However, because the landscape provided such an array of edibles, the first people remained hunter-gatherers. Over the years, with the arrival of explorers and large numbers of immigrants, their foodways began to resemble the predominant culture. Sugar instead of berries was used as a sweetener, and wheat replaced camas and fern roots for making bread. In the twenty-first century few people, native or nonnative, subsist on wild plants and game. Seafood remains popular although much is now farm raised.

The settlers, mostly white Protestants from the midwestern and southern states, began arriving in the Pacific Northwest in the 1830s. Beginning in the 1880s ethnic populations, such as the Chinese, Germans, Irish, Japanese, Jews, Mexicans, and Scandinavians, moved in. Most of the people made their homes on the west side in the alluvial plains of the Willamette Valley in Oregon and the Puget Sound region in Washington. Portland, Oregon, and Seattle, Washington, the largest cities, are located there.

Many of the newcomers who settled in the Pacific Northwest were skilled farmers eager to provide their families with food as well as make a profit selling the surplus. Though in the beginning shortages forced the family cook to adapt and substitute, the immigrants strove for a customary cuisine and did not familiarize themselves with native cooking. The pioneers had no desire to use unfamiliar cooking methods or native plants, such as camas or fern roots.

The ethnic settlers also brought their foodways and when possible prepared native dishes, such as the Scandinavian lutefisk (fish preserved in lye), Japanese *satsumage* (fish cake), Chinese bean curd, and German tortes. They also introduced new foods or incorporated the local fare in their traditional foods. For example, the Japanese

WAPATO

Wapato (*Sagittaria latifolia*) is a semiaquatic perennial with starchy walnut- to golf ball-size edible rhizomes. It grows wholly or partially submerged in lakes, ponds, and marshes. The leaves have a characteristic arrowhead shape. It was once an important food plant for the Indian tribes, especially the Chinooks, on Sauvie Island at the mouth of the Willamette River in Oregon and along the lower Columbia. Families gathered the tubers by wading in the water and dislodging the plants with their feet so that they could be easily pulled up, or they hauled up the plants with their hands from a canoe. Wapato plants are harvested in late fall or early winter. The botanist Nancy Turner notes that wapato was baked in hot ashes and has a sweetish flavor similar to chestnuts.

BIBLIOGRAPHY

Pojar, Jim, and Andy MacKinnon. *Plants of the Pacific Northwest Coast: Washington, Oregon, British Columbia, and Alaska*. Vancouver, British Columbia: Lone Pine Publishing, 1994.

Smith, Harriet L. *Wonderful Wappato: The Wild Potato*. Lake Oswego, OR: Smith, Smith, and Smith Publishing Company, 1976. A collection of quotes from explorers who first described the wapato; includes bibliography.

planted daikon to make *takuan* pickles, the Chinese grew bok choy (a type of cabbage), and the Jews used salmon in their gefilte fish instead of the traditional carp.

Small neighborhood stores, usually operated by members of the ethnic community, were the main source for these unique ingredients. Uwajimaya, which is now a large supermarket in Seattle with several branches offering a variety of Asian goods as well as basic grocery staples, began in 1928 selling fresh fish cakes to Japanese laborers.

Agriculture

The diversity of products and its high ranking in agriculture production make the Pacific Northwest a special place. In the year 2000 this high-tech territory, especially Washington, ranked number one in the United States in the production of hops, spearmint oil, seed peas, lentils, dry edible peas, apples, hazelnuts, sweet cherries, pears, Concord grapes, processing carrots, sweet corn, and red raspberries. The region also ranks high in production of potatoes, wheat, apricots, tart cherries, prunes, plums, asparagus, strawberries, broccoli, and onions. Among other states, only California comes close.

Explorers planted the earliest gardens. In 1792 Salvador Fidalgo, a Spanish marine explorer, supervised the planting of gardens at Nunez Gaona (Neah Bay, Washington). The gardens, the first in the Pacific Northwest, were used by the Spanish to provide food for crews going north into Canada and Alaska, but misgivings about the site soon surfaced, and within six months the Spanish abandoned Neah Bay.

The British employees of the Hudson's Bay Company established several forts and planted large gardens at Vancouver (1824), Colville (1825), and Nisqually (1833). Under the supervision of George Simpson the gardens thrived, and for the first time large amounts of nonnative foods became available. "We are now at [Fort] Vancouver, the New York of the Pacific Ocean," wrote Narcissa Whitman, a missionary wife who came with her husband, Marcus Whitman, in 1836 and was the first white woman to settle in the Pacific Northwest. "Here we find fruit [all nonnative] of every description. Apples peaches grapes Pear, plum and Fig trees in abundance; Cucumbers melons beans peas beats cabbage tammatoes, & every kind of vegitable, to numerous to be mentioned." In effect, Hudson's Bay started the commercialization of agriculture. Beginning in 1825 major crops, such as wheat and potatoes along with barley and oats, were planted and given or sold to the pioneers.

Wheat and Bread

The settlers missed bread more than any other food and pleaded for merchants to increase the supply of flour. Although by 1846 wheat had become a major crop in the Pacific Northwest, the large influx of immigrants, plus the orders coming from those participating in the California gold rush of 1849, meant supply could not keep up with demand. For homeowners, planting wheat and building a gristmill was as important as constructing a house. Rebecca Ebey, who came to the Northwest in 1853, recorded in her diary that "a grist mill there [Coveland on Whidbey Island, Washington] will be a great advantage . . . and our farmers have some wheat coming on, and will be able before another year to make their own bread in place of having to bring it from California and pay twenty dollars per hundred for it."

The pioneers preferred to plant hard red winter wheat, best suited for breads. Red winter and hard red spring wheat are still grown, but soft white winter wheat, perfect for pasta and pastry, has become the dominant variety. The rolling hills of eastern Washington, particularly the southeast quadrant called the Palouse country, is the leading U.S. producer of soft white wheat. Most of it, 85 to 90 percent, is exported.

The large mills use rollers to grind the wheat berries into flour. Only a few, such as Bob's Red Mill in Milwaukie, Oregon, and Cedar Creek Grist Mill in Woodlawn, Washington, grind with century old stone millstones. Since the 1980s, a proliferation of bakeries throughout the Pacific Northwest has been offering tasty artisan breads that would challenge the best French *boulangerie*.

Potatoes

In the 1850s immigrants often encountered Native Americans selling potatoes. Most likely, the Indians added the potato to their diet in the late eighteenth century and obtained their first seed potatoes from the Spanish gardens on Vancouver Island and Neah Bay, the European ships that sailed along the coast, or the early forts managed by the fur traders. An early variety was called the "ship potato," giving credence to the idea that ships brought the first potatoes to the Northwest.

The tuber was successful among the native tribes because it could be harvested and prepared like the camas. Tools used in harvesting the camas root made perfect implements for digging potato holes at planting time and for removing tubers at harvest time. Steaming in pits seemed to be the preferred method of cooking potatoes. The Makahs, a tribe that lives near Neah Bay at the tip of Washington, peeled off the skins and dipped the potatoes in fish oil. The Makahs still raise potatoes that some people believe are the progeny of the first potatoes raised at Neah Bay. Called Anna Cheeka's Ozette, Haida, or Kasaan fingerlings (tests show they are all same variety), these potatoes have creamy-yellowish flesh and an unusual number of deep-set eyes.

Rich volcanic soil and a long growing season made the potato a profitable crop on the western side of the mountains. But lack of sufficient rainfall delayed potato growth east of the mountains until the Grand Coulee Dam released water from the Columbia River. Several million acres of well-irrigated land in Washington and Oregon have made the Pacific Northwest one of the largest and finest potato-producing areas in the country. The Idaho potato is the most popular baking potato. Modern, climate-controlled storage facilities ensure the availability of fresh potatoes all year.

Apples and Other Fruits

The first apple tree planted in the Pacific Northwest allegedly came from English seeds planted at Hudson's Bay Company's Fort Vancouver in 1826. But most of the grafted apple and other fruit trees (cherry, pear, plum, and quince) that pioneers planted in their yards or orchards came from stock that made the journey in 1847 in a covered wagon owned by an Iowa Quaker, Henderson Luelling. To transport the seven hundred grafted trees across the prairie and plains, Luelling packed them in boxes filled with charcoal and dirt. Within four years, the nursery at Milwaukie, Oregon, began to expand and prosper.

Over the years a profusion of orchards has successfully produced a wide variety of apples. Most of the orchards in Oregon are in Umatilla, Hood River, and Wasco counties, which border the Columbia River. The orchards in Washington are nestled in the eastern foothills of the Cascade Mountains and irrigated with cool mountain water. Growers use dwarf trees in high-density plantings to bring new orchards into production faster. Washington leads the nation in apple production and in the percentage of apples going to the "fresh" fruit market. In the nineteenth century, Gravenstein, Winesap, and Northern Spy were the varieties of choice. In the early twenty-first century, Red and Golden Delicious, Fuji, Granny Smith, Gala, and Braeburn head the list.

Native blueberries (*Vaccinium*) and trailing types of blackberries (*Rubus ursinus*) still grow on the western slopes of the Cascade Mountains, but it is the cultivated varieties of caneberries (raspberries, blackberries, marionberries, and boysenberries) that display a cornucopia of colors on northwestern farmlands. Washington is number one in the production of red raspberries, sweet cherries, pears, and Concord grapes. Washington is also one of the top five growing states for apricots, other grapes, tart cherries, prunes, peaches, and plums. Oregon accounts for 95 percent of black raspberries and loganberries (grown mainly for juice, pies, and wine) and is a large producer of wine grapes, pears, and cherries. A new berry, the marionberry, named after Marion County, Oregon, was introduced in 1956 by George Waldo. It was developed from a cross between cultivated and wild blackberries. Bing, Lambert, Royal Ann, and Willamette cherries bursting with flavor began life at the Luelling nurseries in the nineteenth century. Plump, golden Rainier cherries are a more recent variety.

Fish

When the fishing industry is added to agriculture, the importance of the Pacific Northwest to the world's food supply achieves even more fame. The waterways presented a veritable fish market to the native peoples as well as the explorers and settlers who followed them. People might dine on whale meat, trout, sturgeon, smelt, herring, halibut, clams (including geoduck, the largest bivalve along Puget Sound), oysters, crabs, and salmon. What could not be eaten fresh was smoked or dried for winter use.

But of all the seafood, the wild Pacific salmon, shimmering with significance, has had the most "cultural, economic, recreational and symbolic importance" of any food in the Pacific Northwest. Early explorers were astonished at the numbers of salmon the Indians caught at Kettle Falls, Washington, or Celilo Falls, Oregon, principal Indian fisheries and commercial trading centers. At Ceilo Falls, which is now submerged by the backwaters of the Dalles Dam, Meriwether Lewis and William Clark, the first explorers to cross the United States (1804–1806), described baskets of fish containing from ninety to one hundred pounds of dried salmon. At one point Clark counted 107 baskets, which he estimated contained ten thousand pounds of dried salmon.

Archaeological deposits indicate that salmon have been part of the native diet for at least nine thousand years. Five species of Pacific salmon (*Oncorhynchus*) make their home in the Pacific Northwest. They are chinook (tyee, king), sockeye (red), coho (silver), chum (dog), and pink (humpback). Of the five, chinook is the largest—some reach sixty pounds—and richest in oil. The salmon's incredible life cycle with its regularity—freshwater birth and ocean growth (anadromy) and behavior (homing)—may be why salmon are so venerated and are thought to be magical.

The Indians awaited the beginning of the salmon fishing season with keen anticipation. Each tribe developed rituals to celebrate the first catch of the season and assure a bountiful run. When fish sellers in front of an appreciative audience at the famous Pike Place Market in Seattle toss ten- to twelve-pound resplendently colored salmon high in the air, they, like the Indians, are proclaiming that the salmon embodies the essence of the Pacific Northwest.

The Indians roasted salmon by grilling on a two-foot stick split in half to about three-fourths of its length. The salmon would also be split, backbone and entrails removed, and stuck lengthwise onto the split stick. Short sticks inserted crosswise kept the fish flat so the heat could cook the whole piece. The long stick was stuck into the ground in a slanted position and a fire built under it. Similar methods are still used although the grill is probably a black box and the heat comes from charcoal or

Packing Salmon. The 1941 salmon run was so huge that the Columbia River Paking Association in Astoria, Oregon, put up more than 125,000 cases in the first five days of the run. *Prints and Photographs Division, Library of Congress/Russell Lee*

propane gas rather than alder wood. The salmon are often served with a slice of lemon and a sprig of cilantro, an herb-enhanced butter, or a tart huckleberry conserve.

The Hudson's Bay Company began the commercialization of salmon when it began salting and selling the fish in the 1820s. In 1866 Hapgood, Hume, and Company opened a cannery on the lower Columbia River and filled cans with salted chunks of chinook salmon. Spectacular profits drew in other companies, and within twenty years more than fifty canneries had established plants on the Columbia River and its tributaries. With the coming of the railroad and other industrial innovations, such as better refrigeration, Pacific salmon could be found in kitchens all over the world. Unfortunately the "still abundant salmon population" would be forever altered.

Hatchery fish, introduced in 1870 as a way to maintain salmon in the Columbia River, make up a large portion of the salmon sold to consumers. Over the years people have criticized the hatchery fish, which are less genetically diverse than wild populations. Though many problems have been solved, their use remains controversial.

The immense supply of chinook and coho salmon created a false sense that salmon would be running forever. Unfortunately, salmon, native to the Pacific Northwest waterways, are declining as much as 40 percent in some areas. Urbanization and the many natural and man-made environmental fluctuations are taking their toll.

Though wild salmon is considered the king of the waters, Dungeness crab, a hard-shell crab that is unique to the West Coast, receives much praise. It has been harvested since the late 1800s. Only prime males over 6¼ inches are delivered to the processing plants, where they are prepared for live shipment. In the Northwest, most fishmongers sell the crab after it has been cooked. It is also available frozen or canned.

Quantities of oysters greeted the early settlers. The tiny native oyster, *Ostrea lurida*, flourished in the pristine waters of Willapa Bay. Portland restaurants featured it on the menu as early as 1862. Seriously depleted in the 1950s due to water pollution, oysters are being reestablished in Hood Canal and other coastal areas. The heartier Pacific oyster (*Crassostrea gigas*) is the principal oyster harvested commercially in the Pacific Northwest. Oysterville, Washington, now a national historic site, honors the memory of those nineteenth-century people who harvested oysters.

Since 1975 oysters, along with clams and mussels, have been farmed at Penn Cove on Whidby Island in Washington. The sweet-tasting Penn Cove mussels (*Mytilus trossulus*) are naturally prevalent from Alaska to Washington. They are shipped fresh across the city, the country, or the ocean within twenty-four hours.

Breweries and Wineries

"It's the Water," the Olympia Brewing Company, located in Tumwater, Washington, advertised in 1902, six years after Leopold Schmidt set up what would become one of the largest and best-known breweries in Washington. It was also what drew earlier experienced German brewers like Henry Saxer, who opened the territory's first brewery in 1852. The German brewmasters had come just in time to take advantage of the heightened popularity of lager beer. Throughout the territory a thirsty population greeted their arrival with joy. Within a few years a burgeoning saloon industry happily opened the tap of wooden kegs filled with local beer.

Most of the early breweries were small and soon disappeared or were absorbed by larger concerns.

Three—Blitz-Weinhard (1862), Rainier Beer (1878), and Olympia Beer (1896)—achieved national fame, although all are now part of national companies.

Besides benefiting from an abundance of good water, the breweries had quick access to flourishing hop fields, which provided a key ingredient of good lager beer. The Willamette Valley began producing hops in the 1860s, and soon twelve-foot poles all over the territory supported the blossoming green vines of the hop plant. By 1943 Washington had become the leading hop producer in the United States. About 60 percent of the harvest is exported.

The proliferation of microbreweries, begun in the 1980s by people looking for beer with character, has once again given rise to numerous small breweries in Oregon and Washington. Ina Zucker, the author of *The Brewpub Explorer of the Pacific Northwest* (2000), calls the area the craft beer capital. Yakima Brewing Company and Redhook Ales of Seattle rolled out Washington's first kegs in 1982. BridgePort Brewing Company, established in 1984, is Oregon's oldest.

Grapes are grown in Washington and in Oregon. Between the two states there are eleven viticultural appellations, each a specific geographic region. Oregon ranks second in the United States for number of wineries; Washington is second in the United States in premium wine production.

Hudson's Bay Company started it all in 1825, but the pioneers quickly realized that the unique growing conditions in the Pacific Northwest were similar to the wine-growing regions of Europe, and by the 1850s the settlers were planting hybrid varieties of grapes. Isabella, a hybrid developed by William Meek, won an award in 1859.

Until the 1960s most of the wineries were small and family owned. Founders of commercial wineries include Richard Sommer of Hill Crest Vineyards in Oregon and André Tchelistcheff, a pioneering enologist who guided Chateau St. Michelle in Washington. Acres of prestige vineyards planted to Chardonnay, Pinot Noir, Cabernet, and Zinfandel grapes enhance the states' revenues.

Specialty Foods

The Pacific Northwest had coffee saloons in the 1860s, but Starbucks Coffee Company made Seattle a coffee capital when in 1971 it began introducing superior roasted coffee beans. The company rose to fame under the direction of Howard Schultz, who acquired Starbucks in 1985. In 2001 Starbucks sold a variety of coffee beans and coffee drinks at 4,709 locations.

While continuing to till the large farms, farmers in the 1980s began developing and marketing specialty foods such as white Oregon truffles (*Tuber gibbosum*), golden Rainier cherries, Yukon Gold potatoes, Oregon hazelnuts (*Corylus avellana*), Walla Walla sweets (onions), and loganberry wine. Thanks to modern technology that is able to freeze, can, dry, and puree foods without losing flavor; a transportation system that promises next-day delivery; worldwide advertising; and instant ordering via the Internet, people all over the world now have access to produce from the Pacific Northwest.

[*See also* Apples; California; Camas Root; Cherries; Coffeehouses; Fish, *subentries on* Freshwater Fish *and* Saltwater Fish; Native American Foods; Oysters; Peaches and Nectarines; Potatoes; Raspberries; Seafood; Starbucks; Wineries.]

BIBLIOGRAPHY

Caditz, Mary Houser. *Wandering and Feasting: A Washington Cookbook*. Pullman: Washington State University Press, 1996. Regional recipes featuring local foods and historical sketches of communities.

Committee on Protection and Management of Pacific Northwest Anadromous Salmonids. *Upstream: Salmon and Society in the Pacific Northwest*. Washington, DC: National Academy Press, 1996. A review of and commentary on Pacific Northwest salmon, authorized by the governing board of the National Research Council. Text includes genetics, history, management, production by hatcheries, as well as federal, state, and tribal regulations.

Cone, Joseph, and Sandy Ridlington, eds. *The Northwest Salmon Crisis: A Documentary History*. Corvallis: Oregon State University Press, 1996. A series of essays explaining the origins of the current salmon crisis.

Elliott, T. C., comp. *The Coming of the White Women, 1836*. Portland, OR: Oregon Historical Society, 1937. Letters written by Narcissa Whitman. Originally published in *Oregon Historical Quarterly*, 1936–1937.

Haeberlin, Hermann, and Erna Gunther. *The Indians of Puget Sound*. Seattle: University of Washington Press, 1930. A detailed study of the customs and foodways of the Snohomish and Snoqualmi Indian tribes of Washington.

Hibler, Janie. *Dungeness Crabs and Blackberry Cobblers: The Northwest Heritage Cookbook*. New York: Knopf, 1991. Recipes and historical tidbits emphasizing the Northwest's culinary heritage.

Irvine, Ronald. *The Wine Project: Washington State's Winemaking History*. Vashon, WA: Sketch Publications, 1997.

Judson, Phoebe Goodell. *A Pioneer's Search for an Ideal Home: A Book of Personal Memoirs*. Lincoln: University of Nebraska Press, 1984. Diary of pioneer who came to Washington in 1853. Forward by Susan Armitage, Professor of History, Washington State University.

Kirk, Ruth. *Exploring Washington Archaeology*. Seattle: University of Washington Press, 1978. Archaeological surveys of Washington's past. The origins of salmon in the Northwest.

McClintock, Thomas. "Henderson Luelling, Seth Lewelling and the Birth of the Pacific Coast Fruit Industry." *Oregon Historical Quarterly* LXVIII, no. 2 (June 1967), pp. 153–174.

Meier, Gary, and Gloria Meier. *Brewed in the Pacific Northwest: A History of Beer-Making in Oregon and Washington*. Seattle, WA: Fjord Press, 1991. Detailed account of the people and companies that made the area's beer. Illustrations.

National Agricultural Statistics Service (NASS). http://www.usda.gov/nass. Gathers official statistics for each state. Ranks states according to crop production.

Schwantes, Carlos Arnaldo. *The Pacific Northwest: An Interpretive History*. Rev. ed. Lincoln: University of Nebraska Press, 1996. A look at the people, places, and land that are part of the Pacific Northwest. Illustrated with historical paintings and photographs.

Smith, Marian Wesley. *The Puyallup-Nisqually*. New York: Columbia University Press, 1940. Includes a detailed chapter on the foodways and cooking practices of two Indian tribes in the Pacific Northwest. One of the best.

Suttles, Wayne. "The Early Diffusion of the Potato Among the Coast Salish." *Southwestern Journal of Anthropology* 7 (1951): 3.

Swan, James Gilchrist. *The Indians of Cape Flattery, at the Entrance to the Strait of Fuca, Washington Territory*. Washington, DC: Smithsonian Institution, 1870. Swan lived among the Indians and regularly sent reports describing their activities.

Thwaites, Reuben Gold, ed. *Original Journals of the Lewis and Clark Expedition, 1804–1806*. vol. 3. New York: Antiquarian Press, 1959. Journals, letters, maps, and notebooks printed from original manuscripts in the library of the American Philosophical Society.

Trafzer, Clifford E., and Richard D. Scheuerman. *Renegade Tribe: The Palouse Indians and the Invasion of the Inland Pacific Northwest*. Pullman: Washington State University Press, 1986.

Williams, Jacqueline. *The Way We Ate: Pacific Northwest Cooking, 1843–1900*. Pullman: Washington State University Press, 1996. Foodways of the pioneer families who settled in the Pacific Northwest.

Zucker, Ina, Hudson Dodd, and Matthew Latterell. *The Brewpub Explorer of the Pacific Northwest*. 2nd ed. Medina, WA: JASI, 2000. Includes bibliographical references and guidebook to breweries.

JACQUELINE BLOCK WILLIAMS

Packaging

Food packages—vessels that facilitate food transportation and trade—began early in human development as shells, gourds, and animal skins. As human societies became more complex, so did packaging. Packages transformed from purely functional to decorative objects and from vessels whose sole purpose was transportation to containers that helped preserve, protect, and increase the appeal of their contents. As the early food packages became more sophisticated, they were made of increasingly diverse materials, including pottery, wood, and cloth.

Similarly, modern food packaging was originally devised as a method for transporting and extending the shelf life of foods. Prior to the later nineteenth century, most food was distributed only in bulk. Bulk foods were commonly associated with spoilage and related sanitation and disease problems.

Toward the end of the nineteenth century, the Industrial Revolution produced key packaging advances, including the use of metal cans for heat-processed foods, the collapsible tube, the folding carton, the corrugated shipping case, crown closures for sealing bottles, and the ubiquitous paper bag. These advances should not be underestimated in their importance; for instance, the availability of canned and bottled milk is credited with reducing disease and infant mortality.

Advances in food packaging were also key to the growth of the U.S. food industry. The commercial success of Quaker Oats beginning in 1886 and Uneeda Biscuits from the National Biscuit Company in 1899 triggered the explosive concept of packaging as a marketing communicator, known as the "silent salesman."

Meat had been canned since the early nineteenth century, and by the turn of the twentieth century automated machinery turned out thousands of cans per hour. Brand names such as Wilson, Armour, Swift, and Libby, McNeill and Libby were national in scope. But problems of food safety in the meatpacking industry, revealed in 1906, led President Theodore Roosevelt's administration to create the Food and Drug Administration. The seeds for food packaging regulation were planted.

With World War I came the demand for more preserved goods; the War Department bought three-quarters of all canned goods produced. Early packaging processes and methods were hardly safe, however, and in 1918 the appearance of botulism resulted in the recognition that safer, more scientific methods of preserving in cans were needed.

Meanwhile, the demand for more and better packaging was growing, thanks to the advent of supermarkets and readily available refrigeration—and the concomitant expectation of more and better individually packaged goods. The packaging revolution, which Daniel J. Boorstin called "one of the most manifold and least noticed revolutions in the common experience," was now in full force.

By the late nineteenth and early twentieth centuries, the race was on to win consumer attention with attractive, distinctive containers made of paper, paperboard, glass, and tinplate. Many famous brands arose, from Kellogg's Corn Flakes and Aunt Jemima Pancake Mix in the 1890s to the naturalist-explorer Clarence Birdseye's first frozen foods in 1930, the result of his observations (while on expedition to Labrador) that fish retained its flavor and freshness when frozen.

Major food packaging advances came in 1927, when DuPont perfected waterproof cellophane, and in 1936 with the discovery of polyethylene. These discoveries, combined with the shortages that arose from World War II, led to major advances in plastics, which in turn refocused the way many foods were packaged in the postwar era.

By the 1950s packaged foods of every kind had become commonplace in U.S. households, and by the last decade of the century, packaged foods had all but replaced fresh in many homes. Packaging became an integral part of a product's profitability, and the marketing component of packaging came under fire as individually packaged portion sizes increased and were suspected of contributing to a national epidemic of obesity.

Food packaging has many functions. At its heart, a package is still a vessel by which food is more easily transported, and the package also importantly often serves to protect its contents. Packaging is invaluable in helping to sell products and can often cost far more than its contents to produce.

In food packaging, four basic materials are used, either alone or in combination: metal, plant (paper and wood), glass, and plastic. Each material has unique characteristics as well as advantages and disadvantages. Metal is strong and creates a good barrier between food and potential spoilage agents such as light, but it is heavy and can corrode. Paper, often an economical choice, is a good medium on which to print manufacturers' messages, but it can disintegrate when it absorbs liquids. Glass is transparent, which can add visual appeal, but it breaks easily. Plastics, which take many forms, are versatile, but they tend to be more costly.

Most packaging is a combination of materials. A milk box, for example, is made of paper, which is economical but which must be lined with a thin layer of plastic in order to create a stable barrier. A peanut butter jar may be glass or plastic, and the lid is usually metal lined with plastic. Most packages such as these are placed in a larger, secondary package or container that facilitates shipment. These secondary containers are often made of paper, but they may also be plastic.

One of the most important challenges facing food packagers is balancing the needs dictated by product characteristics and food safety, the marketing needs of manufacturers, consumer convenience, and the effect the packaging may have on the environment.

Recycling is one approach to the problem of discarded food packages. Part of what is called postconsumer recycling, aluminum cans make up the largest category. Although most recycled plastics come from the container manufacturing process, postconsumer recycling is growing. Polyethylene terephthalate (PET) products, marked by a triangle on the bottom, are the standard for bottled beverages. Recycling has been instituted by governments across the country, but overcoming the traditional American attitude of using and discarding things, fast food packages for instance, has been difficult.

[*See also* Birdseye, Clarence; Bottling; Canning and Bottling; Kellogg Company; Milk Packaging; Plastic Bags; Plastic Covering.]

BIBLIOGRAPHY

Beniger, James R. *The Control Revolution: Technological and Economic Origins of the Information Society.* Cambridge, MA: Harvard University Press, 1986.

Boorstin, Daniel J. *The Americans: The Democratic Experience.* New York: Random House, 1965.

Hine, Thomas. *The Total Package: The Evolution and Secret Meanings of Boxes, Bottles, Cans, and Tubes.* Boston: Little, Brown, 1995.

Institute of Food Science and Technology. http://www.ifst.org.

Institute of Food Technologists. http://www.ift.org.

National Food Processors Association. http://www.nfpa-food.org.

MARGE PERRY

Pancake Pans

Pancakes are one of the universal foods of the world and were brought to the American colonies as early as European crepe-style delicacies. Their preparation at the hearth required flat, cast-iron griddles, usually with legs and swinging bail handles for hanging, or small, flat-bottomed frying pans. They were extremely popular as a colonial French, Dutch American, and English festive food.

Raised American pancakes, an offshoot, became the lighter "flapjack" in the late 1700s, leavened with yeast and later baking soda. Made with wheat flour, cornmeal, or buckwheat, they were also baked on even-cooking soapstone griddles. Earthenware batter jugs with spouts, bail handles, and tin covers for spout and top held yeast batters for overnight rising and easy pouring at breakfast time. By the later 1800s the cookstove and the gadget craze provoked the invention of hinged, multiple griddles of cast iron or tin. The batter was poured into individual circlets and flipped, one or all at a time, onto the facing open griddle plate. It is likely that the perfectly circular pancake shape was the attraction.

During this period waves of immigrants also brought pans for their own ethnic pancake versions. The Danes used *ebelskiver* pans (sometimes porcelainized), usually with sets of seven attached cast-iron cups that produced a globular pancake form (flipped with knitting needles); the Swedes and Russians had *plett kakers*—pans with individualized shallow indentations.

Pancake equipment remains in American kitchens. Heavy griddles of iron or soapstone are required for Sunday breakfast treats, and French crepe pans of thin iron produce the delicate wrappings for many sweet and savory fillings.

[*See also* Aunt Jemima.]

ALICE ROSS

Pancakes

The basic American pancake (also called a flapjack, slapjack, griddle cake, or hotcake) is a flat, round breadstuff made from a simple batter that blends flour, milk, and eggs. The batter is poured onto a lightly greased griddle or into a skillet and the cake is flipped over when the underside is done. American pancakes are most commonly made from wheat flour, buckwheat flour, or cornmeal; like other quickbreads, they lend themselves to additions such as berries and other fruits. A pat of butter along with maple or another sweet syrup are traditional accompaniments. More elaborate toppings include whipped cream and fresh fruit.

Pancakes are common to many peoples throughout the world. The prototypical American pancakes probably arrived with the earliest English and Dutch settlers, whose pancake traditions dated back to at least the fifteenth century, and possibly as far back as prehistoric times. Later immigrants to the United States brought their own pancake recipes, such as the Russian *blini*, French *crêpes*, eastern European Jewish *latkes*, Norwegian *lefse*, and Austrian *palatschinken*. Most of these are not breakfast fare, but holiday specialties, party foods, or desserts.

The wide appeal of pancakes is attested to by the popularity of pancake restaurants, or "pancake houses," such as the International House of Pancakes (IHOP), launched in 1958 in a Los Angeles suburb. These establishments serve pancakes to suit every taste and time of day, from sweet to savory, breakfast to dinner. Some Episcopal churches hold pancake breakfasts on Shrove Tuesday, even including a British-style pancake race, in which the contestants must flip a pancake in a skillet as they run. Pancake breakfasts are also traditional fundraisers for nonprofit organizations and other good causes.

Somewhat surprisingly, American inventors saw potential for a convenience food in a recipe as simple as pancake batter. In 1899, Chris L. Rutt and Charles G. Underwood introduced the first ready-mixed commercial food product, which was later renamed Aunt Jemima Pancake Mix.

The first located American cookbook focusing exclusively on pancakes is Ruth Ellen Church's *Pancakes Aplenty* (1962); it was followed by Myra Waldo's *Pancake Cookbook* (1963) and many others.

[*See also* Aunt Jemima; Breakfast Foods.]

BIBLIOGRAPHY

Church, Ruth Ellen. *Pancakes Aplenty: Tasty, Tempting Recipes for Pancakes Plain and Fancy Including Waffles, Fritters and Omelets.* Chicago: Rand McNallay, [1962].
Messer, Betty, ed. *A Collection of Maple Recipes: Pancakes, and More!!! / from Members of New Hampshire Maple Producers' Association.* Lebanon, NH: Hanover Printing Co., 2001.
Pappas, Lou Seibert. *Pancakes & Waffles: Great Recipes.* San Francisco: Chronicle Books, 2004.
Waldo, Myra. *The Pancake Cookbook.* New York: Bantam Books, 1963.

ANDREW F. SMITH

Panini

"Panini" is the Americanized version of the Italian word *panino*, which means little sandwich and refers to a class of sandwiches that became popular in the United States in the late 1990s. Flavor is key to panini, which are based on high-quality Italian artisan breads like focaccia or *ciabatta*. The sandwiches are layered, but not overstuffed, with flavorful combinations of cheeses, meats, or roasted vegetables. Various dressings or condiments are added, and the sandwich is pressed and lightly grilled. Panini-style sandwiches are popular in trendy restaurants throughout the United States.

[*See also* Italian American Food; Sandwiches.]

BIBLIOGRAPHY

Mercuri, Becky. *Sandwiches That You Will Like.* Pittsburgh, PA: WQED, 2002.

BECKY MERCURI

Pans, *see Pots and Pans*

Parers, *see Apple Preparation Tools*

Parloa, Maria

Maria Parloa is now nearly forgotten, but in the latter part of the nineteenth century she was well known as a respected cooking authority, teacher and lecturer, author of many popular cookbooks, founder of cooking schools in Boston and New York City, and editor of women's magazines. She was one of the innovative superstars of her field, addressing her material to the training of both cooking teachers and the growing group of urban, middle-class women who had the leisure and desire to improve their cooking and maintain fashion. Parloa's fame was such that her name and recipes were effective

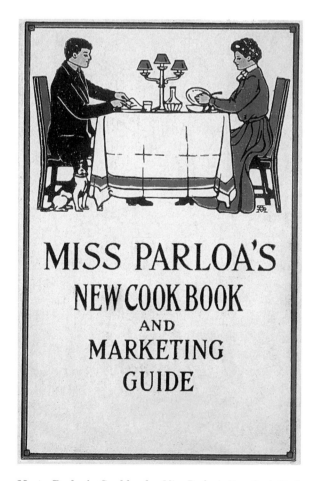

Maria Parloa's Cookbook. *Miss Parloa's New Cook Book and Marketing Guide. Culinary Archives & Museum at Johnson & Wales University, Providence, R.I.*

endorsements of several commercial products. In her own words, "having had years of experience as a cook in private families and hotels, I know the wants of the masses and feel competent to supply them."

Parloa was born of English parentage in Massachusetts in September 1843. Although little is known of her early life, she apparently attended school in Maine, and at some point she gained important experience working as a pastry cook in noted New England hotels. Her lifelong association with food and cooking had begun. By 1872 she had produced her first comprehensive cookbook, *The Appledore Cook Book: Containing Practical Receipts for Plain and Rich Cooking* (1872). Encouraged by favorable comments on her early fund-raising food demonstrations, she repeated the success in New London, Connecticut (1876).

These activities served as the springboard for her long, New England–based career as a teacher, lecturer, and author. After only two years in Boston, her reputation was such that she was engaged to teach a series of classes on cooking-teacher training at Tremont Temple in Boston (May 1877). In October of that same year, she expanded her teaching scope, opening her own cooking school nearby (on the corner of Tremont and Mason Streets). She also began directing the scientific teaching of cooking at Lesell Seminary in Auburndale, Massachusetts, and offered lectures at Miss Morgan's School in Portsmouth, New Hampshire.

Classes and lectures led to additional publications, among them a slim volume called *Camp Cookery* (1878). Intent on expanding her credentials and skills, she traveled abroad, where she studied methods of teaching cooking at the National Training School for Cookery in London and French cuisine in Paris, visiting local schools as she went. Parloa's ambitious training, unusual for a woman at that time, set her apart from many other American cooking authorities.

Once back in the United States, she instituted the first training course in cookery for teachers at the prestigious Chatauqua summer schools (summer 1879). She was one of the first two teachers at the soon-to-be prestigious Boston Cooking School (1879) and continued to be involved: subsequently she called herself variously the founder or the principal of the school. She taught the school's first normal course, a teacher training program. In that same year she began a lecture tour to such cities as Chicago and Milwaukee, and she taught at the New York Cooking School. According to William Alexander, writing in *Good Housekeeping*, "her engagement was a most

successful one, the auditorium being crowded every day." A popular figure and a good businesswoman, she commanded an unusually high salary for a woman at that time.

Parloa was also well known as an expert on household management. Once more she traveled abroad, this time for two years, to study Europe's best methods of housekeeping. She again followed her studies with a series of lectures at home. Because many cookbooks of the time included such homemaking instruction, she was able to expand the scope of her own writings. According to Alexander, she gave about seven hundred lectures or public demonstrations in addition to her private instruction. He estimates that she taught courses in forty or fifty towns and cities in a dozen states.

Parloa continued to be active professionally in her later years. As a firm believer in and practitioner of lifelong learning, she attended the first Summer School of Food and Nutrition at Wesleyan University in Middletown, Connecticut. Although she was then close to retirement, she also attended the 1903 Graduate Course in Nutrition. Her valued contributions to the fields of cookery and household management earned her an invitation to participate in the Lake Placid Conferences. As a result of the conference, the American Home Economics Association was established, and needless to say, Parloa was a charter member.

Parloa retired to Bethel, Connecticut, where she is still remembered for her gracious hospitality and generosity to the community. She died there in August 1909 and was buried in Boston.

Parloa's publications include *The Appledore Cook Book: Containing Practical Receipts for Plain and Rich Cooking* (1872); *Camp Cookery: How to Live in Camp* (1878); *First Principles of Household Management and Cookery: A Text-book for Schools and Families* (1879); *Miss Parloa's New Cook Book, A Guide to Marketing and Cooking (1881)*; *Practical Cookery, with Demonstrations* (1884); *Miss Parloa's Kitchen Companion: A Guide for All Who Would Be Good Housekeepers* (1887); *Miss Parloa's Young Housekeeper: Designed Especially to Aid Beginners: Economic Receipts for Those Who Are Cooking for Two or Three* (1893); *Home Economics: A Guide to Household Management, Including the Proper Treatment of the Materials Entering into the Construction and Furnishing of the House* (1898); *and Home Economics: A Practical Guide in Every Branch of Housekeeping* (1910).

In addition to these voluminous writings, she prepared two widely circulated Farmers' Bulletins for the Office of Experiment Stations of the U.S. Department of Agriculture. One was *Preparation of Vegetables for the Table*; the other was *Canned Fruit, Preserves, and Jellies, Household Methods of Preparation* (1917).

As with many prominent cookbook authors and teachers, her name was considered enough of a draw to feature her work in commercial promotional pamphlets. Notable among these was a series for Walter Baker and Company entitled *Choice Receipts*. In some of these she shared authorship with other famous food writers; some booklets are attributed to "Miss Parloa and other Noted Teachers." In at least one, the work was entirely her own, "specially prepared for the Walter Baker & Co. Exhibit at the World's Columbian Exposition in 1893." Likewise, she contributed to advertising booklets on cocoa, coffee, meat extract, and tableware.

[*See also* Cookbooks and Manuscripts: From the Civil War to World War I; Cooking Manuscripts; Cooking Schools.]

BIBLIOGRAPHY

Alexander, William V. "Maria Parloa: What She Has Done and Is Doing to Improve American Cookery." *Good Housekeeping* 11 (July 1885).

Shapiro, Laura. *Perfection Salad: Women and Cooking at the Turn of the Century*. New York: Farrar, Straus, and Giroux, 1986. Intermittent references.

MARY MOONEY-GETOFF

Parsnips

Parsnips, *Pastinaca sativa*, are creamy white root vegetables resembling their carrot cousins (both belong to the family Umbellifera), but they often taste sweeter and nuttier. Best dug and eaten after the fall frosts, they store well in root cellars or controlled environments where their starches convert to sugars. They remain alive in the ground during cold winters and are sometimes preferred as early spring vegetables.

Parsnip consumption began with wild plants of the European Stone Age. Cultivated in ancient Greece and Rome, they became central to the medieval diet and (with fava beans) structured many Catholic fast day and Lenten (meatless) meals. The first American seeds were planted in 1609 by the English, followed by German, French, and Dutch settlers. Following ethnic custom, parsnips were served boiled and buttered, baked, mashed, in sweetened rich puddings and fritters, and candied as sweetmeats.

Henderson's Hollow Crowned Parsnip. From the 1894 catalog of Peter Henderson & Co., New York.

European parsnip seeds "escaped" and grew wild in the East; a western wild strain may have been indigenous. Both were dug and eaten by Native Americans and European travelers. Early-nineteenth-century hybridization furthered the parsnip's already substantial popularity, but by the early 1900s it was being largely eclipsed by the carrot and used by most as soup flavoring. Experimental cooks have since returned them to fine restaurants and adventurous diners.

[*See also* Carrots; Vegetables.]

BIBLIOGRAPHY

Weaver, William Woys. *Heirloom Vegetable Gardening: A Master Gardener's Guide to Planting, Growing, Seed Saving, and Cultural History*. New York: Holt, 1997.

ALICE ROSS

Partridge

Two varieties of this game bird, the red-legged partridge (*Alectoris rufa*) and the gray partridge (*Perdrix perdrix*), were introduced from England to the thirteen colonies for sport. They are now farmed for their meat and eggs mainly in Oregon. The chukar partridge (*Alectoris chukar*), native to Turkey, the Mediterranean, and Asia, was introduced to North America in the twentieth century as it is better suited to the warmer U.S. climate. At game bird farms in North America it is reared by the thousands for hunting and for its meat and eggs. The meat of partridges resembles that of chicken in color and texture, and it has a chickenlike shape with plenty of meat but a stronger flavor. All varieties have a similar flavor and are treated the same for culinary purposes. Unlike other types of game, partridges do not need to be hung for more than forty-eight hours to tenderize the flesh. To prevent their flesh from drying out, young birds are first covered with strips of fat pork or bacon, trussed, and roasted in a hot oven. Older birds are stewed with root vegetables or with cabbage in the French style. The eggs should be hard cooked and can be served as an appetizer.

[*See also* Chicken; Game; Poultry and Fowl.]

BIBLIOGRAPHY

Marrone, Teresa. *Cookin' Wild Game: The Complete Guide to Dressing and Cooking Big Game, Small Game, Upland Birds and Waterfowl.* Minnetonka, MN: 2002.
McClane, Albert Jules, and Donna Turner. *A Taste of the Wild: A Compendium of Modern American Game Cookery.* New York: Penguin, 1991.
Youel, Milo A. *Cook the Wild Bird: An Erudite Treatise on the Joy of Hunting, Cooking, and Eating Game Birds.* New York: A. S. Barnes, 1975.

JOSEPHINE BACON

Passenger Pigeon

In 1600 the passenger pigeon, *Ectopistes migratorius*, was possibly the most numerous bird in the world, with population estimates of 3 to 5 billion. The birds traveled in vast flocks from northern Mississippi up to Nova Scotia and from coastal Massachusetts west to the Great Plains, taking as long as three days to pass over. Hunters did not let this bounty pass unmolested. After a pigeon hunt in 1813, the naturalist John James Audubon said of the slaughter, "The Pigeons were picked up and piled in heaps, until each had as many as he could possibly dispose of, when the hogs were let loose to feed on the remainder."

The dark flesh was good roasted or braised, but the birds were also salted down for later consumption. Another method was described in an 1843 Michigan newspaper: "When I shoot my rifle clear, to pigeons in the skies, I'll bid farewell to pork and beans, and live on good pot pies." Pies filled with squab, the juvenile pigeon, were frequently served when Benjamin Franklin visited Thomas Jefferson at Monticello.

Unfortunately, the passion for squabs, the wholesale slaughter of the birds, the destruction of habitat, and perhaps the pigeon's own biological need for large nesting colonies had caused a catastrophic collapse of the passenger pigeon population by 1880. The last passenger pigeon died at the Cincinnati Zoo in Ohio in 1914.

[*See also* Game; Poultry and Fowl.]

BIBLIOGRAPHY

Marshall, Ann Parks. *Martha Washington's Rules for Cooking Used Everyday at Mt. Vernon.* Washington, DC: Ransdell, 1931.
Matthiessen, Peter. *Wildlife in America.* Rev. ed. New York: Viking, 1987.
Ponting, Clive. *A Green History of the World: The Environment and the Collapse of Great Civilizations.* New York: St. Martin's Press, 1992.
Quammen, David. *The Song of the Dodo: Island Biogeography in an Age of Extinctions.* New York: Scribners, 1996.
Taylor, Dale. *The Writer's Guide to Everyday Life in Colonial America.* Cincinnati, OH: Writer's Digest Books, 1997.
Wuepper, Jon. *Niles (Michigan) Republican, April 29, 1843,* in *Passenger Pigeon Records.* Berrien, MI: 2001. Available at http://www.ulala.org/P_Pigeon/NewPaper.html.

SYLVIA LOVEGREN

Passover

The Jewish festival of Passover (Pesach) falls in spring, after the first full moon following the vernal equinox. Passover, a weeklong festival, commemorates the flight of the Hebrews from slavery in Egypt. This celebration has special significance in the United States, traditionally a haven from persecution, for Jews as for many others. For this reason, Passover is the best-known Jewish holiday in the wider community.

Symbolic foods are eaten at all Jewish festivals, but in the case of Passover, they are part of the story. When Pharaoh finally let the Hebrews go, they had to leave so quickly that there was no time to let the bread rise before baking. They carried the dough on their backs, so it baked in the heat of the sun. Therefore, only unleavened bread, known as matzo, may be eaten for the eight days of the festival. All leaven (*hametz*) is forbidden during Passover. This directive includes not only yeast-risen and fermented foods, but also others that might be liable to ferment. Beer and whisky are banned, but not wine. Among Orthodox Jews, not only must every food product be kosher for Passover, toothpaste and even cleaning agents, such as pan scourers and detergents, must be guaranteed leaven free.

On the day before the festival, a ceremony is performed, called the examination of the leaven (*bedikat hametz*), in which any bread crumbs found are burned. The highlight of Passover is the communal meal of family and friends held on Passover Eve, the first night of the festival, and among Orthodox Ashkenazic Jews also on the second night; the meal is called the seder (order). Certain foods, referred to in the Hagaddah, the order of service used for the occasion, must be present on the seder table. These foods include a bitter herb (*maror*), usually horseradish; a roasted lamb or chicken bone (*pesakh*), to symbolize the burned offerings made in the Temple; a roasted egg (*beitza*); a sweet herb (usually parsley); and a paste called *haroset*, made with honey, apples, almonds, and wine, to represent the mortar used by the Hebrew slaves to bind bricks. Three ceremonial pieces of matzo are also on the table, symbolizing the three layers of ancient Jewish society: Cohanim (high priests), Leviim (Levites, priests), and Israel (everyone else). Half of the middle cake, known as the *afikoman*, from the Greek word for dessert, is hidden by the organizer of the seder. The other item on the table is a bowl of saltwater to represent the tears shed by the Israelites. At certain points during the seder service, pieces of matzo are passed around, in one case eaten with parsley, in another eaten dipped in saltwater, in a third eaten as a sandwich with horseradish, and in a fourth eaten with *haroset*. Four ritual glasses of wine are drunk. Persian Jews "whip" each other with scallions (green onions), at one point, to symbolize the scourges and whips of the Egyptians. Ashkenazic Jews begin the meal with a hard-cooked egg in saltwater. The egg is a sign of mourning and of the spring (renewal and the life cycle). Soup containing *kneidlach*, matzo dumplings or matzo balls, is essential. After the meal, there is a hunt for the *afikoman*. In some families, the parents hide it for the children to find, but nowadays, it is mainly the children who hide it from their parents or the host of the seder. In either case, the adults reward the children with prizes.

A communal seder banquet may also be held at a synagogue or hotel. As a communal feast celebrating freedom from slavery, the format was loosely adopted by African Americans for the Kwanzaa holiday.

[*See also* Jewish American Food; Jewish Dietary Laws; Matzo.]

BIBLIOGRAPHY

Amster, Linda, ed. *The New York Times Passover Cookbook*. New York: Morrow, 1999.

Frances R. AvRutick. *The Complete Passover Cookbook*. Middle Village, NY: David, 1981.

Nathan, Joan. *The Children's Jewish Holiday Kitchen*. New York: Schocken, 1995.

Sisterhood of Temple Beth Hillel-Beth El, Wynnewood, Pennsylvania. *Passoverama, A Cookbook for Passover*. Wynnewood, PA, 1978.

JOSEPHINE BACON

Pasta, *see Italian American Food*

Pasties

Also called "Cornish pasties" or "Cousin Jack pasties," pasties (pronounced PASS-tee or PAHS-tee) are beef-and-vegetable-filled pastries originally eaten by mine workers as a warm noontime meal. They were an ideal food for men working in deep, dark, damp mines. Pasties were brought to America in the mid-nineteenth century from Cornwall, England, by immigrant mine workers. At that time, though depleted tin mines in Cornwall were closing, new mines were opening in America: copper and iron mines in the Upper Peninsula of Michigan, iron mines in northeastern Minnesota, and lead mines in southwest Wisconsin.

Pasties were made at home by hand. First, flour, salt, shortening, and water were mixed to form a piecrust. Some recipes specified using inexpensive ground suet or lard for the shortening, which made a very sturdy crust. The piecrust was divided into individual portions, and each portion was rolled out into a circle. Diced beef, sliced potatoes, rutabagas (or turnips), and onions were placed in layers on half of the piecrust and seasoned with salt and pepper. After the filling was dotted with suet or butter, the crust was folded into a semicircle, like a calzone or an empanada, and the edges were crimped. The miner's initials were carved in the crust for easy identification. The pasties were baked in a moderate oven for an hour, timed to finish as a miner left for work. To keep the pasty hot and clean until lunchtime, it was wrapped in oilskins, paper, and cloth.

Pasties are primarily a Michigan-Wisconsin-Minnesota regional food. Specialty bakeries make and sell several sizes with various fillings. Pasties not only make good picnic fare but also sell by the thousands at church fund-raisers every month.

Pasties gained national and international recognition in the late twentieth century after they received prominent mention in two best-selling murder mysteries by Lilian Jackson Braun: *The Cat Who Played Brahms* and *The Cat Who Said Cheese*. In these stories, the protagonist prefers tourist-style pasties, ones made with flaky pastry, no turnips, and some juicy sauce.

[*See also* Pastries; Pies and Tarts.]

BIBLIOGRAPHY

Clayton, Bernard. *Bernard Clayton's Cooking across America: Cooking with More than 100 of North America's Best Cooks and 250 of Their Recipes.* New York: Simon and Schuster, 1993.

ROBERT W. BROWER

Pastrami

"Pastrami" is a Yiddish word derived from the Romanian *pastram* (a preserved food), from the Latin *parcere* (to save or be thrifty). It is a cured cut of beef, usually brisket, but plate and round are also used. Although not originally a specifically Jewish food, pastrami is exclusively Jewish in the United States (and unknown in other English-speaking Jewish communities). It is very rarely home cured but is served in restaurants and available in supermarkets in Jewish neighborhoods. Because it is usually a preprepared dish, it is rarely mentioned in Jewish cookbooks or books about the history of Jewish food. As with so many traditional foods, there are variations in the preparation method in that the meat may be dry cured or soaked for several weeks in brine and spices, as is corned beef. However, in the case of pastrami, after salting, the meat is always smoked. The technique originated in Romania but spread throughout the former Ottoman Empire, where it was also used for curing pork. Indeed, throughout the former Ottoman Empire, *pastrama*, *basturma*, or variations of these words can mean cured beef, cured ham, or bacon, depending on whether the community is Muslim or Christian. Pastrami was brought to the United States by Romanian Jews, most of whom immigrated following the Kishinev Pogroms of 1903 and 1905.

Pastrami is made from a quality cut of boneless beef brisket, chuck, or round weighing at least three to five pounds. The surface of the meat must be rubbed with kosher (coarse) salt and with a spice mixture that includes brown sugar, garlic, black and white peppercorns, allspice

berries, cinnamon stick, hot and mild paprika, bay leaves, and possibly coriander seeds and gingerroot. Naturally, there are variations in the mixture. The meat is dry rubbed and refrigerated for seven to ten days; it must be turned frequently and rubbed with more spice mixture and more coarse salt. Pastrami can also be pickled in brine flavored with the same ingredients used in the dry rub, in which case it should be left for around two weeks in a cool, dark place or in the refrigerator and turned every two days.

When the beef has been cured, it should be left to dry out in a cool, dark place for two days, then placed in a smoker and smoked according to the manufacturer's instructions. When ready, it should be vacuum-packed or wrapped in plastic wrap and refrigerated until ready for cooking.

To serve pastrami, rinse it with cold water to remove excess salt and place it in a Dutch oven or casserole. Cover it with four inches of unsalted water and bring to a boil. Bring the pot to a simmer, but do not allow it to boil hard, for two hours or until cooked through. Pastrami is best served hot, straight from the pot, but it can also be served cold. Pastrami is eaten in a sandwich, usually on rye bread with mustard, with pickles on the side, or on a water or egg bagel with pickles and mustard. It can also be served as an entrée with latkes (potato pancakes) and coleslaw or sauerkraut. As a nod to the current obsession with lower fat foods, turkey meat is now processed into pastrami.

[*See also* Corned Beef; Jewish American Food; Jewish Dietary Laws; Meat; Pickling.]

BIBLIOGRAPHY

Ayto, John. *A Gourmet's Guide: Food and Drink from A to Z.* New York: Oxford University Press, 1994.
Bartlett, Jonathan. *The Cook's Dictionary and Culinary Reference: A Comprehensive, Definitive Guide to Cooking and Food.* Chicago: Contemporary Books, 1996.
Fitzgibbon, Theodora. *Food of the Western World: An Encyclopedia of Food from Europe and North America.* New York: Quadrangle/New York Times Book Company, 1976.

JOSEPHINE BACON

Pastries

The term "pastry" traditionally denoted any sweet or savory dish that had the slightly antiquated sounding "paste," a dense dough made from flour, fat, and liquid, as a key ingredient. In current parlance, "pastry" loosely embraces most sweet foods (candy is a notable exception) that are eaten for breakfasts, desserts, or snacks, regardless of whether "paste" is an element of the dish. Starting in the 1970s, "pastry" chefs built architecturally complex desserts from cakes, creams, spun sugar, fruits, nuts, or molded chocolates, often with nary a paste foundation. "Pastry" maintains its older meaning of "crust" when applied to savories.

Recipes for paste vary greatly, but classically paste is made only from flour, liquid, and fats, such as butter (either melted or solid), lard, suet, and drippings. By the early twentieth century, margarine, hydrogenated vegetable shortenings, and occasionally oils were added as the tenderizing fat. The proportions of liquid and fat, and the techniques for incorporating the fat into the flour, determine the paste's flavor and texture, from unpalatable luting paste to ethereal puff pastry, in which a single piece of baked dough separates into nearly one thousand delicate layers. Although flour-liquid mixtures may also make "pasta" (with its obvious etymological link to "paste"), the two categories differ in their cooking techniques: by the twentieth century, most pastries were baked or fried, whereas most pasta is boiled. Some doughs are yeasted, giving rise to Danish, croissants, and certain doughnuts, while other doughnuts, scones, and biscuits are chemically leavened. All are considered pastries for breakfasts and coffee breaks.

Early Forms of Pastry

Virtually every culture has some form of pastry, stretching back at least to early recorded history. The first known written recipes, cuneiform-incised clay tablets dating from 1700 B.C.E. Mesopotamia, include ones for birds served in pastry. Until the development of relatively inexpensive sources of sugar, most pastries were savory pies. England, from whence much of America's pastry tradition derives, had bustling pie markets by the Middle Ages. In fourteenth-century London, statutes governed "pastelers" who "baked in pasties rabbits, geese and garbage [offal]" for sale to the public. Pies were a convenient "take-out" meal for urban dwellers, especially those too poor to have kitchens. The "pasties" were often inedibly tough, for the crust was designed to serve as a vessel for cooking, transporting, and storing the meats, rather than as a delectable contrast to the filling. Cooks pieced together "standing" pastes that could be baked, unsupported by a pan, without collapsing and that could preserve for days, or even weeks, the meats within by sealing out air with melted fat.

Pie making was changing by the seventeenth century, and those changes would be exported to the American

Pastry Kitchen. *Culinary Archives & Museum at Johnson & Wales University, Providence, R.I.*

colonies. First, sugar became more available. Although still something of a luxury, sugar and its cheaper derivative, molasses, created highly sweetened fruit fillings. Second, baking dishes made from earthenware or metal became increasingly common. With dishes to support the crusts in the oven, the paste could become thinner, more tender, and actually edible. This innovation transplanted easily to clay-rich areas. Colonial Pennsylvania was especially noted for its redware pie dishes, sent throughout eastern America.

American towns had pastry shops (sometimes under the rubric "confectioners") by the eighteenth century but many viewed commercial baked goods as unnecessarily expensive luxuries. Pastries tended to be homemade until after World War II, although pastry making was considered challenging. Homemakers learned to make paste not only from their mothers but also from a number of additional sources. Pastry teachers advertised classes in the colonies as early as 1731, and cookery books burst with paste recipes.

Pastry in America

Among the first published pastry recipes to reach the colonies were those in Hannah Glasse's influential *The Art of Cookery, Made Plain and Easy* (London, 1747; Alexandria, Virginia, 1805). Her pastries included puddings baked or boiled in crusts, and pies with sweet or savory fillings. The single-crust puddings actually are akin to custard-filled tarts; this "pudding" nomenclature endured through the nineteenth century in English-influenced American kitchens. Many of Mrs. Glasse's savory pies reveal medieval roots: the upper crusts were removed during baking; gravy, wine, vinegar, or butter

A BRIEF CATALOG OF AMERICAN PIES

Among the many varieties of pies are those made from New World foods that are uniquely part of the American repertoire, such as pumpkin, squash, sweet potato, green tomato, pecan, blueberry, and cranberry. Florida's key limes make a revered curd filling. Other pies that have evolved in decidedly American versions include creams (most popularly coconut, banana, and chocolate) and their cousins, the chiffons (creams or fruit curds lightened with whipped egg whites); rhubarb (sometimes called "pie plant" and often combined with strawberries); shoofly, crumb, and gravel (Pennsylvania Dutch treats made with molasses, brown sugar, and cake or cookie crumbs); black bottom and Mississippi mud (chocolate custard layered with rum custard or cream cheese); vinegar and cider (nineteenth-century specialties from the Midwest and New England, respectively, in which egg custards were flavored with a healthy dose of vinegar or cider, used because of the expense of transporting lemons to the hinterland); and President Tyler pie, the most patriotically named of the so-called transparent pies, made from a high proportion of sugar or corn syrup, butter, and eggs baked to a translucent gel. Confederate Jefferson Davis pie is a sweetened, spiced custard, sometimes containing dried fruits and nuts, lightened with or covered by meringue. Similar to the South's beloved chess pie, both have discernible British ancestors, although the thick layer of meringue topping is an American tradition. Buttermilk also was thickened into custard and baked in crust.

Mincemeat pies, mixtures of finely chopped meats (often including leftovers or variety meats, such as tongue and heart), suet, vegetables, fruits, spices, and brandy, although originating in England, were so ubiquitous and had so many different recipes in the eighteenth and nineteenth centuries that they must be considered an essential American pie. When mince lost its suet and meat in the twentieth century, it was soon exiled to Thanksgiving and Christmas tables as a nostalgic, old-fashioned dessert. Potato pies also originated in England but found ready acceptance in sweet and savory forms on colonial and nineteenth-century tables.

Boston cream pie and Martha Washington pie are misleadingly named, for they are actually layered cakes filled with pastry cream or raspberry jam, respectively. Angel pies, claimed by James Beard to be one of the most frequently printed pie recipes in the early to mid twentieth century, take a bit of a nomenclature license: the crust for these "pies" was a meringue shell filled with a lightened fruit curd. Moon pies similarly are cookies sandwiching a marshmallow filling.

CATHY K. KAUFMAN

---

was poured in; and the crusts replaced, to be removed at table so the diner could exhume tidbits of venison, goose, oysters, or other savories from the pastry "coffins." These standing pies largely disappeared in nineteenth-century America, although sturdy paste lingers in a few enclaves. In the Upper Peninsula of Michigan, descendants of emigrants from England's Cornwall continue to bake Cornish pasties, meat turnovers notorious for durable crusts that enabled miners to tote them into shafts. Pâté en croûte, a medieval holdover in which finely ground and seasoned meats are baked in dense paste and sealed with fat or gelatin under the top crust, is a classic preparation in gourmet shops and French restaurants.

Some of Mrs. Glasse's other recipes, including a very workable recipe for buttery puff pastry, use modern techniques. Early American cookery writers followed English examples in propounding rich, tender piecrust recipes. Amelia Simmons's *American Cookery* (1796) has nine different pastes, most with high ratios of fat to flour. Others offered painstakingly detailed instructions for making paste, as if a cascade of theory could remedy the practical critique that pastries were tough or indigestible. Among the most pedantic are Lydia Maria Child's *The Frugal Housewife* (1829), Lettice Bryan's *The Kentucky Housewife* (1839), and the anonymous *American Home Cook Book* (1854), with its illustration of a meat pie mold and its helpful reminder that its "common paste for meatpies . . . is intended to be eaten."

Not all pastries were baked: the original "potpies" were stews boiled in pastry-lined pots over hearths or stove tops and then inverted onto a platter for serving. Unlike baked meat pies with solid lids (called meat "patties" when baked in individual portion size, a common practice among the well-to-do from the eighteenth century on), the lid of potpies had a convenient hole for adding more liquid should the stew begin to dry out. Recipes for boiled potpies faded by the end of the nineteenth century, as pastry dumplings replaced crusts in simmering stews. The old-fashioned grunt is a fruit version of a pot-pie: fruits were buried under a layer of grunts (a New England term for a dough somewhere between a dumpling and a biscuit), the pot covered, and the dish cooked by a mixture of steaming and simmering.

Rustic baked pastries filled with fruit were a staple of both the middle and working classes, as well as of rural dwellers. Mrs. Bryan deemed her sloppy-to-serve peach potpie, for which she gives an alternative name of "cobbler," as "not a fashionable pie for company," but "very excellent for family use." During the twentieth century, many cobbler recipes substituted absorbent biscuits for the denser paste. Slumps are traditional fruit cobblers that are not inverted but are served from the baking dish. Pandowdies are pasted cobblers in which the crust is submerged in the cooking fruit juices, leading to a soft crust. Betties and crisps employ breadcrumbs, cookie crumbs, or sweetened oats for the pastry.

American recipe collections geared to the more affluent are filled with techniques for adorning pastries. Elite tables in the eighteenth and nineteenth centuries copied the European tradition of intricate centerpieces made from sugar and paste. Pastry-eating etiquette, a social marker in the mid-nineteenth century, engendered many controversies: authorities disagreed as to whether spoons, forks alone, or knives and forks should cut pies and pastries. American silver manufacturers solved the dilemma in the 1860s by introducing specialized pastry forks to penetrate crusts. The desired appearance of paste also changed, from the "genteel" pale pies popular through the first half of the nineteenth century, darkening to golden brown in the twentieth century.

Pastry Case. La Bagel Delight, Brooklyn, New York. *Photograph by Joe Zarba*

Savory pastries were used as appetizers and miniaturized into hors d'oeuvres in the late nineteenth century. New pastries developed, such as the three variations on cheese straws, or puff pastry flavored with cheese and cayenne, found in *Mrs. Seeley's Cook Book* (1902). Twentieth-century cocktail parties relied on "finger foods" conveniently packaged in pastry wrappers. Standing guests could sip cocktails held in one hand and nibble morsels from the other, such as bouchées, bite-size pastry cups holding anything from creamed oysters to chicken salad, or more down-home pigs in a blanket, tiny hot dogs wrapped in flaky dough.

Ethnic Contributions

Virtually all immigrant groups have contributed pastries to American foodways. Beyond the nearly limitless pies and tarts, signature ethnic specialties include fried Spanish churros sold as street food in Latino communities, along with savory empanadas, cornmeal turnovers. Pennsylvania Dutch funnel cakes appear at fairs. Central Europeans introduced gossamer strudels, while Greeks use similar, papery filo dough in nutty, honey-drenched baklava. French *chou* paste creates éclairs and cream puffs, while puff pastry is deliberately restrained in baking to yield crisp napoleons or allowed to explode for patty shells called "vol-au-vents," literally, "soaring on the wind." Among the many pastries of the Italians are fried cannoli and baked *sfogliatelle*. Even the Chinese, with a relatively limited range of sweet pastries, brought almond cookies and invented the Chinese American fortune cookie.

Pastries connote indulgence and often are forsworn by Lenten observers. Pastries have also long been considered a health hazard or nutritionally unsound. Sarah Josepha

Making Pastry. Making tarts at the Institute of Culinary Education, New York. *Courtesy of the Institute of Culinary Education*

Hale's *The Good Housekeeper* (1841) intones, "Pies are more apt to prove injurious to persons of delicate constitutions than puddings, because of the indigestible nature of pastry." Pierre Blot's *Hand-book of Practical Cookery* (1869) echoes the growing concern that, "It is well known that the poorer class of Americans eat too much pie and pudding. . . . We do not mean to do away with them entirely, but we advise every one to . . . 'use, but do not abuse.'" Contemporary warnings about obesity, saturated fats, and refined carbohydrates, the building blocks of calorie-dense pastry, fall on deaf ears: the commercial baking industry valued its annual output of fresh pies and pastries (excluding the large, separate category of frozen products) at over $2.5 billion in the late 1990s.

[*See also* Appetizers; Breakfast Foods; Crullers; Desserts; Dumplings; Pasties; Pies and Tarts; Puddings.]

BIBLIOGRAPHY

Beard, James. *American Cookery*. Boston: Little, Brown, 1972.
Belden, Louise Conway. *The Festive Tradition: Table Decoration and Desserts in America, 1650–1900*. New York: Norton, 1983.
Fertig, Judith M. *All-American Desserts*. Boston: Harvard Common Press, 2003. Recipes interwoven with thoroughly researched culinary history; good, but abbreviated, bibliography.
Hibben, Sheila. *American Regional Cookery*. Boston: Little, Brown, 1946.
LeDraoulec, Pascale. *American Pie: Slices of Life (and Pie) from America's Back Roads*. New York: HarperCollins, 2002. Entertaining memoir of a road trip seeking the best old-fashioned American pies still being baked in the twenty-first century.
Leslie, Eliza. *Seventy-five Receipts for Pastry, Cakes, and Sweetmeats*. Boston: Munroe and Francis, 1828. Traditional pastries and other desserts for well-to-do kitchens in the early to mid-nineteenth century.
McIntyre, Nancy Fair. *Cooking in Crust*. North Hollywood, CA: Gala Books, 1973. The state of savory pastries in the 1970s.
Pastry Art and Design. A bimonthly magazine reflecting trends in contemporary pastry for the professional; "pastes" typically play very minor roles in these constructions.
Pies and Pastries. The Good Cook series, edited by Time-Life Books. Alexandria, VA: Time-Life Books, 1981.
Weaver, William Woys. *America Eats: Forms of Edible Folk Art*. New York: Harper and Row, 1989.

CATHY K. KAUFMAN

Pawpaw

The North American pawpaw (*Asimina triloba*) has a well-established place in folklore and rural culture. "Way Down Yonder in the Pawpaw Patch" is an American folk song that was quite popular once, and fall hunting for pawpaws in the woods is still a cherished tradition for many rural families. Interest has grown in the pawpaw as a gourmet food.

Pawpaws grow wild in the understories of hardwood forests in the eastern United States, ranging from northern Florida to southern Ontario in Canada and as far west as eastern Nebraska. The fruit of the pawpaw can weigh from three or four ounces to a pound and may be borne singly or in clusters. Pawpaws are highly nutritious, with a strong aroma and a unique flavor that resembles a combination of banana, mango, and pineapple. Pawpaws are ripe when soft and are usually harvested from September to October across their native range. When ripe, skin color ranges from green to yellow and flesh color ranges from creamy white to shades of orange. The fruit should be harvested prior to the first frost.

Pulp from the fruit can be eaten fresh or cooked. The flavor of the fruit can intensify when it is overripe, as with bananas, resulting in pulp that is excellent for use in cooking. The seed and skin are generally not eaten. Local delicacies made from fruit pulp include ice cream, compote, jam, pie, custard, and wine. In the early 2000s, most fruits for sale were collected from wild stands in the forest and sold mainly at farmers' markets, directly to restaurants, or through entrepreneurs on the Internet.

[*See also* Fruit; Fruit Wines.]

BIBLIOGRAPHY

Layne, D. R. "The All-American Pawpaw. Part 1: Revival Efforts May Bear Much 'Fruit'." *The Fruit Gardener*, May–June 1996.
Reich, Lee. "Pawpaw: Banana of the North." *Uncommon Fruits Worthy of Attention: A Gardener's Guide*. Reading MA: Addison-Wesley, 1991.

KIRK W. POMPER AND DESMOND R. LAYNE

Peaches and Nectarines

The peach and its smooth-skinned form, the nectarine, were once thought to be native to Persia since the Romans first imported the peach from Persia, giving rise to its botanical name, *Prunus persica*. In fact, the fruit originated in China, where as early as 550 B.C.E. it was depicted in art and literature as a symbol of immortality. It still grows wild in eastern Asia, exhibiting many of the variant forms found in modern cultivars, including freestone and clingstone, white, yellow, and red-fleshed types. From south China comes the *pen-t'ao*, or flat-shaped peach, as well as the *mi-t'ao*, or honey peach, with its very sweet, low-acid flavor. Nectarines were less common in China proper but flourished in eastern Turkestan, an early extension of the peach's natural range. The Romans spread the peach throughout their empire, especially around the Mediterranean, where warm to hot summers favor ripening.

Introduction of the peach to America occurred during the period of European exploration and colonization in the New World, especially through the Spanish conquest of Mexico and exploration of Florida in the sixteenth century. The peach eventually naturalized and became wild in parts of Mexico, the American South, and the Southwest, where the Indians cultivated various seedling strains called "Indian peaches," leading botanists several centuries later erroneously to suppose that the peach was a native of the New World. Most of these trees, including clingstones and red-fleshed peaches, were planted as seedlings through the mid-nineteenth century, but several named freestone varieties, such as Early Crawford, Late Crawford, and Oldmixon, also became popular. These peaches and others of their day were noted for their soft, juicy, delicate flesh with a tendency toward bruising. It was not until after the Civil War, when hybrids involving a strain of peach from northern China were introduced, that modern hybridization of peaches began in America.

In 1850 Charles Downing introduced the Chinese Cling variety, which led to the development of many standard American commercial varieties, such as Elberta, J. H. Hale, and Redhaven, all forerunners of modern hybrid peaches characterized by large, round shape; highly blushed skin; and firm, yellow flesh. These kinds of peaches are often harvested when they are not fully ripe so that they can be packed and marketed with minimal bruising.

More recently, there has been a resurgence of white-fleshed varieties of both peaches and nectarines. In the past, white-fleshed fruit were often much too delicate for marketing beyond the orchard where they were grown, but firm-fleshed hybrids, initially developed for export and ethnic markets, are showing up more and more in America's mainstream retail markets. These new white-fleshed types are often what are called "subacid" (properly "low-acid") types, having very sweet to mildly sweet flavor with little complementary acidity.

Also increasing in popularity are the so-called "flat" peaches, shaped like a doughnut or a bagel; these distinctive fruits actually represent a revival of an ancient form, the favorite of Chinese emperors because they could eat around the pit without suffering the indignity of dripping juice onto their beards.

Peach Label. Jones Yerkes label, ca. 1867. *Warshaw Collection of Business Americana, Archives Center, National Museum of American History, Behring Center, Smithsonian Institution*

The clingstone is also a characteristic found among the older strains of peaches. The ripe flesh is often much firmer and less juicy than that of freestone peaches, and for this reason it is preferred by commercial canners because the fruit holds up better after processing. California growers have therefore specialized in the production of cling peaches to supply the state's large canning industry.

The newest trend in developing peaches for the fresh market is to incorporate the cling, or nonmelting, flesh characteristic into market peaches. Fruit breeders in Texas, Georgia, New Jersey, and Florida are developing new varieties that can be tree ripened yet remain firm enough to withstand the rigors of harvesting, shipping, and marketing.

Still others are looking back to the old heirloom varieties of peaches for old-fashioned flavor and juicy texture. Smaller artisanal growers are creating niche markets for these varieties that can be found mostly at fruit stands, farmers' markets, and specialty stores.

It seems that the English invented the word "nectarine" about the middle of the seventeenth century to distinguish the nectarine from the peach. This distinction has sometimes led to the assumption that the nectarine is a unique fruit, perhaps even a cross between a peach and a plum. In fact, the nectarine is no more than a smooth-skinned peach, a single recessive gene (homozygous for smooth skin) separating it from the peach. In many old-world cultures, there is no distinction beyond making reference to nectarines as "naked" or "hairless" peaches.

The older nectarine varieties imported from Europe to America were not of commercial quality, being smaller, often of poorer flavor, and more prone to rot and insect damage than peaches. It was not until the breeding work of Fred W. Anderson of California, the father of the modern nectarine, that commercial nectarine production was possible. In the 1940s and 1950s Anderson developed many new varieties that were much larger and better in quality for the fresh market. California now leads the nation in the production of the nectarine, and it may overtake the peach in volume of California production because of consumers' preference for fuzzless skin.

While the nectarine finds its special domain in California and in parts of the Northwest and Florida, the peach is adaptable to a wide range of climates, and commercial production exists along the Pacific coast, the eastern seaboard, and the gulf states, from as far north as Michigan to as far south as Florida. Some varieties are extremely cold hardy, while others require very little winter chill and can be grown in subtropical climates. Among the minimum requirements for growing peaches, however, is the need for heat during the growing season to ripen the fruit satisfactorily and the need to protect it from very hard freezes and spring frosts, which can destroy a crop or even kill trees.

Both peaches and nectarines are excellent when consumed fresh. They also have many culinary uses, mainly as desserts, but also in pickling and in chutneys and preserved in brandy.

Both fruits are high in vitamins A and C and have fewer calories than apples and pears. For dessert, they are great in compotes, ice creams, smoothies, jams, and pastries. Indeed, peach cobbler rivals traditional apple pie as the classic all-American dessert.

[*See also* California; Fruit.]

BIBLIOGRAPHY

Childers, Norman F., ed. *The Peach, Varieties, Culture, Pest Control, Storage*. Rev. 3rd ed. New Brunswick, NJ: Horticultural Publications, 1975. A compendium of articles by experts on the various topics related to the peach industry.

Hedrick, U. P. *The Peaches of New York*. Albany, NY: New York Agricultural Experiment Station, 1917. Contains much valuable historical information.

Janick, Jules, and James N. Moore, eds. *Fruit Breeding*. New York: Wiley, 1996. Section on peaches is a thorough treatment of the history, progress, and prospects of peach improvement.

Okie, W. R. *A Handbook of Peach and Nectarine Varieties, Performance in the Southeastern United States*. Byron, GA: USDA, 1998. Regional analysis of varieties grown in the Southeast, but valuable information for growers throughout the nation.

ANDREW MARIANI

Peach Parers and Stoners

Because the immediate pleasure of eating a ripe peach is delayed by peeling, we can sympathize with the words of a certain 1872 editorial writer: "A continuous and urgent inquiry for a machine for Paring Peaches has been ringing in our ears . . . for five years." He then praised the cast-iron, cranked Lightning Peach Parer, which had been manufactured by an apple-parer company since 1869. A parer that did not waste the fruit was desirable for canneries and home cooks. Merchants' price sheets in the 1860s quoted peeled-peach prices that were twice those for unpeeled.

Also important is removing the pit or stone. Several devices that were available from the 1860s to 1900 pushed the pit out by force with a plunger. Another type, a sort of curved knife, came in different sizes for different pits. With this device, one would first cut the peach in half and then slip the blade around the pit and cut it out. Even in canneries this method was used as recently as the 1930s.

[*See also* Peaches and Nectarines.]

BIBLIOGRAPHY

Franklin, Linda Campbell. *300 Years of Kitchen Collectibles*. 5th ed. Iola, WI: Krause Publications, 2003.

LINDA CAMPBELL FRANKLIN

Peanut Butter

For centuries peanuts have been ground and consumed by indigenous peoples of South America and by Africans, but peanut butter was not popularized in America until the vegetarian John Harvey Kellogg endorsed it as a substitute for "cow's butter." In the early 1890s Kellogg crushed various nuts between two rollers and claimed the results to be "nut butters." At the time, peanuts were less expensive than nuts, and they soon became the most significant "nut" butter. Kellogg was an excellent promoter. He extolled the virtues of peanut butter throughout the nation. To commercialize his discovery, Kellogg created the Sanitas Nut Food Company and placed his brother, Will Kellogg, in charge. Nut butters quickly became a fad among other health-food manufacturers in America. Vegetarians adopted peanut butter, and recipes for making and using it appeared in almost all vegetarian cookbooks from 1899 on.

Dainty tearooms and upper-class restaurants proudly announced that peanut butter was an ingredient in numerous salads, soups, and entrées. Confectioners made candy with peanut butter fillings. Peanut butter recipes filled cookery magazines and cookbooks. Among its earliest and most common uses was in making sandwiches; by 1900 the peanut butter sandwich had quickly spread throughout the United States. Peanut butter sandwiches were also filled with a variety of other foods, such as raisins, jelly, marmalade, cheese, cucumbers, grapefruit, celery, apricots, dates, bacon, and bananas.

Peanut butter sandwiches moved down the class structure as the price of peanut butter declined, owing to the commercialization of the industry. They took another leap forward, however, during the Depression, when this low-cost sandwich spread became one of the top luncheon items.

Peanut Butter Ad. From *Peter Pan Peanut Butter in Your Diet*, published by Derby Foods, Chicago. *Collection of Andrew F. Smith*

Commerce and Industry

Within two decades of its invention, peanut butter was being manufactured in virtually every large and middle-size city in America. Since the 1920s, however, the peanut butter industry has become centralized, and three companies dominated the peanut butter market by the early 2000s. The first was launched by Joseph L. Rosefield of Alameda, California, in 1922. He developed a process of hydrogenation of peanut butter, which prevented oil separation, made spoilage less likely, and increased the shelf life of peanut butter. Rosefield selected the name "Skippy" for his new product. The second major peanut manufacturer was the E. K. Pond Company, which began to manufacture peanut butter in 1920. Its sales were limited until the company changed the name of its peanut butter to Peter Pan. The third was Procter and Gamble, which introduced Jif in 1958. Procter and Gamble operates the world's largest peanut butter plant, churning out 250,000 jars every day.

Peanut butter was born at the end of the nineteenth century as a health and vegetarian food, but by the 1920s it was a major mainstream staple used in recipes for many types of food, from soups, salads, and sauces to desserts and snacks of every description. Few other products in American culinary history have achieved such influence in so many ways in such a short period of time. In the early years of the twenty-first century, peanut butter was ensconced in 85 percent of the kitchens of America.

[See also Candy Bars and Candy; Health Food; Kellogg, John Harvey; Sandwiches; Vegetarianism.]

BIBLIOGRAPHY

Smith, Andrew F. "Peanut Butter: A Vegetarian Food That Went Awry." *Petits Propos Culinaires* 65 (September 2000): 60–72.
Smith, Andrew F. *Peanuts: The Illustrious History of the Goober Pea*. Urbana: University of Illinois Press, 2002.

ANDREW F. SMITH

Peanuts

There is something quintessentially American about peanuts. While people in other areas of the world eat them, nowhere else are they devoured in so many diverse ways or with the same gusto as in the United States. The peanut (*Arachis hypogaea*), which is a legume rather than a nut, originated in the Guarani region of Paraguay, eastern Bolivia, and central Brazil. In pre-Columbian times, peanuts were disseminated throughout South America, the Caribbean, and Mexico. When European explorers arrived in the New World, they discovered peanuts and introduced them to Africa, where they were quickly adopted, particularly for use as food in the slave trade. Through the slave trade, peanuts were introduced into the British North American colonies, where they were grown by slaves in their gardens. Although some children and teenagers consumed peanuts occasionally at Christmas, they were mainly considered a trash food inappropriate for "genteel" society.

Peanut Cookery and Uses

By the 1830s peanuts entered mainstream cooking and recipes featuring them began to appear in cookbooks. Peanut cookery probably was introduced into Philadelphia by French Creole refugees, who had settled there after escaping the 1791 slave insurrection in Haiti. Recipes for peanut cakes and other peanut dishes were featured in cookbooks a few decades later. Eliza Leslie's *Directions for Cookery* (1837), for instance, included a recipe for "Cocoa-nut Maccaroons" with peanuts. Subsequently, similar recipes were published by many other authors. The first cookbook printed in the South that contained peanut recipes was Sarah Rutledge's *Carolina Housewife* (1847). Her peanut soup recipe likely derived from African culinary traditions.

The American Civil War (1861–1865) greatly accelerated the adoption of peanuts throughout the United States. When the war broke out, white Southerners soon discovered the peanut's value, as the northern blockade prevented the importation of goods to the South. Peanut oil was used as a substitute for whale oil in southern industry. At least four factories were established in the South to convert peanuts into oil, which was used as a lubricant for industrial machinery and railroad locomotives. Southern housewives substituted peanut oil for lard as shortening in bread and pastry and for olive oil in salad dressings. Peanuts were ground to make beverages and served as a substitute for coffee and chocolate.

When northern armies occupied the peanut-growing areas, Union soldiers were introduced to this "new" food. After the war, peanut cultivation skyrocketed, and peanuts became a fad food throughout the country. Peanuts were mainly consumed roasted in the shell as a snack food at fairs, circuses, and other social events, but cooks and chefs soon began exploring the peanut's broader culinary potential. Beginning in 1916, George

Peanut Roaster. Hand-turned peanut roaster and warmer. From the 1922 catalog of the Crandall Pettee Co., New York, p. 83.

Washington Carver began to popularize the peanut. His efforts greatly increased peanut consumption in America.

Peanuts are used in soups, salads, and confections as well as in peanut flour, bread, cookies, cakes, and biscuits. Other peanut dishes are local specialties, such as boiled peanuts in some of the southern states of America. Finally, peanuts are also a major source of oil, which is a common ingredient in many processed foods.

Modern Peanut Industry

During the late nineteenth century three major peanut companies were launched. The first was started by two Italian immigrants who specialized in roasted peanuts. They named their company Planters Peanuts. In 1917 they created "Mr. Peanut," which became an American culinary icon within a few years. The second company was initiated by John Harvey Kellogg, who popularized peanut butter beginning in 1894. During the early twentieth century peanut butter companies were started in many medium-size cities in the United States. Peanuts are often employed in making candy. Several of the most popular candies include peanuts, such as Baby Ruth bars, Reese's Peanut Butter Cups, Butterfingers, Clark candy bars, and Peanut M&M's.

During the last decade of the twentieth century, American peanut production hovered between 3.6 and 4.9 billion bushels. By 2002 peanuts ranked eighth among primary field crops produced in the United States, with an average farm value of $1.2 billion. The American retail market for peanuts and peanut products totaled $2.5 billion annually at the dawn of the 2000s, when consumption had increased 2 to 3 percent over the last few years of the twentieth century.

Peanuts are one of the leading causes of food-allergic reactions. The diagnosis of peanut allergies has been increasing at a disturbing rate among young children. The problem is that allergic reactions may be generated not only by ingesting peanuts but simply by coming into contact with them or consuming dishes made with peanut products. Simply removing peanuts from a dish does not remove the contaminating protein. Steps have been taken to remove peanut products from school lunches and airplanes.

[*See also* Candy Bars and Candy; Carver, George Washington; Fats and Oils; Health Food; Kellogg, John Harvey; Mr. Peanut; Peanut Butter; Sandwiches; Snack Foods; Vegetarianism.]

BIBLIOGRAPHY

American Peanut Research and Education Association. *Peanuts— Culture and Uses: A Symposium.* Stillwater, OK: American Peanut Research and Education Association, 1973.

Carver, George Washington. *How to Grow the Peanut and 105 Ways of Preparing It for Human Consumption.* Bulletin 31. Tuskegee, AL: Experiment Station, Tuskegee Institute, 1925.

Johnson, F. Roy. *The Peanut Story.* Murfreesboro, NC: Johnson Publishing, 1964.

Lambert, Almeda. *Guide for Nut Cookery.* Battle Creek, MI: Joseph Lambert, 1899.

Smith, Andrew F. "Peanut Butter: A Vegetarian Food That Went Awry." *Petits Propos Culinaires* 65 (September 2000): 60–72.

Smith, Andrew F. *Peanuts: The Illustrious History of the Goober Pea.* Urbana: University of Illinois Press, 2002.

ANDREW F. SMITH

Pears

The pear is among the several fruits whose origin is attributed to the Caucasus and Elburz mountains of western Asia and which spread in the footsteps of Caucasian civilization to all the temperate zones. Pears arrived in seventeenth-century eastern America chiefly as seeds or seedlings; improved stocks and named varieties as scions

and dormant trees did not come to the colonies until the mid-eighteenth century. Thus, the American colonies had evolved their own pear varieties for some 150 years, outside the influence of English and Continental sources.

Progress in developing a good eating pear suitable for American conditions was slow, not least because the initial genetic material was most likely perry pear seedlings from the West Country of England. These made up in vigor what they lacked in fruit quality; the trees grew well despite long tropical summers and arctic winters, not the conditions dessert pears experience in western Europe.

By 1750 the American colonies had evolved numerous pear varieties local to the three chief centers of horticulture: the neighborhoods of Boston, Long Island, and the hinterland of Philadelphia. An industry in perry, the drink of fermented pear juice, had developed, but it was a small trade compared with that in cider, the comparable ferment of apples, which grew much more readily everywhere in the colonies. Perry has never developed any commercial importance in America, which seems odd, since the origin of American pear commerce lay in perry pears.

Most notable and still foremost among the early American pears was Seckel, a small fruit ripening in mid-autumn, originating perhaps from Rousselette or perry pear seed and recovered circa 1780 from the near-wild in Pennsylvania. Seckel has been the parent of uncountably many varieties of small pears of quality in America, from the early nineteenth century to the present. It is the country's most versatile pear and suitable for conditions in all the Middle Atlantic states and along the northern Atlantic seaboard.

The variety known as Bartlett is a late-colonial introduction from England, by scion or dormant tree. It is the eighteenth-century English variety Williams Bon Crétien

Pears. *Photograph by Joe Zarba*

and was "discovered" in 1817 in the orchard of Enoch Bartlett in Massachusetts, propagated by many nurserymen in the succeeding decades, and subsequently sold bearing his name. It is known in all the rest of the world under its original and true name.

Seckel and Bartlett were the chief pears of the nineteenth-century American market. Other varieties were commercially successful to the degree they approximated these two, at least in appearance; furthermore, under American conditions, trees of Seckel and to a lesser degree of Bartlett have a survival rate superior to that of European imports. Hence, Seckel and Bartlett were the most important parents of modern pears, and introductions of greater merit from Europe never approached their commercial success.

Among the most lasting of nineteenth-century European varieties were Doyenné du Comice and Beurré Bosc—the former a luxury winter fruit, the latter a coarse, very sweet fruit resistant to both the insults of machine handling and the climate of eastern states. Beurré d'Anjou is an undistinguished but nearly indestructible fruit in controlled atmosphere storage, from which it is available nearly year-round.

Fireblight, a bacterial disease first noticed in the Hudson Valley in New York State about 1780, spread rapidly in the United States starting in the 1860s. A ferocious devourer of entire pear trees, especially in climates with warm, humid spring and summer seasons, fireblight devastated the pear orchards of the eastern states. Thereafter, commercial pear growing shifted to the three states of the Pacific coast, where the disease was not so destructive.

Modern Production and Uses

In the early twenty-first century, Bartlett pears come from the counties of Sacramento, Mendocino, and Lake in California. The largest production of main-crop pears, however, comes from the high-desert districts of central Washington, chiefly bulk Bartlett, Beurré d'Anjou bound for cold storage, Beurré Bosc, and various red-skinned mutations of common varieties, which have had novelty value. Most sought are the Bartlett and related types from the Hood River district and Doyenné du Comice from the Rogue River district of Oregon. Winter Nelis has vanished from American production, and only Beurré Hardy (under the generic name French Butter Pear) has a limited following among pear fanciers. It is unfortunate that meritorious cultivars such as Gorham, Magness, Beurré Superfin, and Belle Lucrative, though no more costly to produce than Bartlett, are not found in American

markets. And purely culinary varieties, such as are sold in Europe for cooking, are unknown in America.

Many, perhaps most, Americans are unaware that pears are to be eaten after softening, and indeed treat the pear as an odd-shaped, coarse, and gritty variant of the apple. Thus pears have found no place in institutional feeding or in popular culture. American culinary skill has been applied to the preserving of pears, however, and tinned Bartlett pears and Bartlett juice are the basis for the truly American invention, the fruit cocktail. Occasional culinary use of whole-pear preserves, chutneys, and dried pears in various forms can be observed in the American home, and there is a small trade in dried Bartlett pears from California. In these uses, the pears must be still firm, or they will decompose in processing. Pears appear occasionally in open tarts, according to European principles and recipes.

In the early 2000s, the most important industrial use of pears has been for juice, as a highly concentrated syrup to serve as a sweetener of "sugarless" breakfast cereals and confectionery and as a neutral base for various "all-fruit" beverages.

Nashi and Li

Close relatives of the pear are the *nashi* of Japan and the *li* of China, complex hybrids of several centuries' standing between the species *Pyrus pyrifolia*, *P. ussuriensis*, and *P. bretschneideri*, quite distinct from both pear and apple. The *nashi* are round, coarse, and juicy fruits of late summer and autumn—often with more or less russet skin, which is invariably peeled before consumption of the fruit. The flavor of *nashi* is refreshing but rarely complex and quite ruined by heat, so the fruit has no culinary use except as a canned product. Favorite varieties are Nijiseiki (Twentieth Century), Shinseiki (New Century), and Hosui. Both *nashi* and *li* are produced and common in California, whence they are despatched to Asian markets elsewhere in America. The fruits of *li* are elongated and pear-shaped, with clear green to yellow skin. *Li* are the nearest rivals to apples in the world production of fruits. Practically unknown outside China, where they are ubiquitous, *li* (in the forms Ya Li and Tsu Li) are grown in the Western world chiefly in California. *Nashi* and *li* are unflatteringly called "apple pears" and "sand pears" in the rest of the United States.

Asian Pears *Nashi* is better appreciated as one parent, with the European pear, of the true Asian pears. These hybrids have inherited resistance to fireblight from *nashi* and are common in the southern states and the Midwest of

America in the varieties Kieffer, Le Conte, and Pineapple, which are truly impervious, as both tree and fruit, in those climates. The hybrid Asian pears are in common use for home canning while immature, though if they are allowed to ripen on the tree in a long season, the fruits can develop a most extraordinary aroma and a near-melting texture approaching that of the true pear and become a legitimate contribution to the dessert repertoire of American fruits. Indeed, these hybrids are among the few truly American contributions to the tree fruits.

[*See also* Condiments; Fruit; Fruit Juices; Pies and Tarts; Preserves; Sweeteners.]

BIBLIOGRAPHY

Hedrick, U. P. *The Pears of New York*. Albany, NY: New York Agricultural Experiment Station, 1921.

C. T. KENNEDY

Peas

The pea (*Pisum sativum*) is a legume domesticated in prehistoric times in western Asia. Peas can be divided into two categories: sweet or green peas, which can be eaten raw or briefly cooked, and field peas, which are dried for storage and require fairly long simmering to soften and cook them. Peas were widely distributed throughout the Old World in ancient times, and field peas were commonly eaten by the Greeks and Romans.

Peas did not become an important food in England until after the Norman Conquest in 1066 Thereafter, for the lower class, pea soup or gruel was a staple dish for hundreds of years. For the upper class, peas with salt pork was considered a fashionable dish, to be consumed at feasts.

Both field and green peas were introduced into America by European explorers and colonists in the early seventeenth century. At first, dried peas were used in soups, porridges, and puddings; during the nineteenth century, fresh peas were served as a side dish with poultry and meat. Since green peas are among the earliest vegetables picked from the garden, they became a symbol of the advent of summer.

Unusually among vegetable recipes in the nineteenth century, instructions for cooking peas often included an admonition not to overcook them. Usually peas were simply boiled and served up with butter, but the French cooked them cloaked in layers of lettuce leaves, and English- and Spanish-style recipes also appeared. Peas were incorporated into omelets, soufflés, dumplings, frit-

Peas. Bliss' American wonder pea, from *Aaron Low's Illustrated Retail Seed Catalogue and Garden Manual*, 1887, p. 27.

ters, and salads. Green peas, with their delicate flavor and short growing season, were popular fodder for home canners. Field peas were dried, and directions were given for converting them into powder. Split peas (they split naturally after drying) became popular for soup making because they cook much faster than whole dried peas.

Peas were among the first vegetables to be canned commercially. By the late nineteenth century, peas, along with corn and tomatoes, ranked highest in sales among canned foods. Peas were first frozen in the 1920s, but they did not become popular until the 1950s.

The edible-podded peas, such as snow peas, were introduced to the American table by Asian Americans in the twentieth century and have become mainstream enough that they are now sold frozen. Snow peas are not shelled; rather, both their crisp, flat pods and diminutive peas are cooked and eaten. Sugar snaps, introduced in the 1970s, have fleshy pods and peas that grow comparatively large while remaining sweet; they are eaten whole, either raw or cooked.

[*See also* Canning and Bottling; Soups and Stews.]

BIBLIOGRAPHY

Bitting, A. W. *Appetizing; or, The Art of Canning*. San Francisco: Trade Pressroom, 1937.
Facciola, Stephen. *Cornucopia II: A Source Book of Edible Plants*. Vista, CA: Kampong Publications, 1998.
Unwin, Charles W. J. *Sweet Peas: Their History, Development, Culture*. New York: Appleton, 1926.

ANDREW F. SMITH

Pecans

The word "pecan" originated from the Algonquian *paccan*, but its pronunciation is somewhat controversial since in the northern United States it is pronounced **pee**-kan, with the accent on the first syllable, while to Southerners this pronunciation evokes a mildly scatological image ("pee can"), and they therefore pronounce it with the accent on the second syllable: puh-**kahn** or puh-**kan**.

Pecan trees (*Carya illinoinensis*) are indigenous to a roughly south-north rectangle extending from the Gulf of Mexico to southern Illinois and Iowa, covering the valley of the Mississippi River, its tributaries, and the major rivers of Texas and Oklahoma. There are also several areas in northern Mexico where pecan trees are indigenous.

Native Americans had been eating pecans and using them as stew thickeners for several millennia before the arrival of Europeans. The first European to encounter pecans was the Spanish explorer Cabeza de Vaca, along the northern shores of the Gulf of Mexico and adjacent hinterlands in 1528.

The French colonization of Louisiana at the end of the seventeenth century resulted in a pecan confection called "pralines," which to this day are sold all over New Orleans. In the eighteenth century pecans were brought to the northeastern colonies by fur traders who obtained them from the Illinois Indians of southern Illinois, Missouri, and Arkansas. The fur traders called these nuts "Indian nuts" or "Illinois nuts." These nuts subsequently came to the attention of F. A. J. Von Wangenheim, a Hessian forester who served with the troops hired by King George III to squelch the rebellious colonists led by George Washington. It was Wangenheim who, in recognition of their common name "Illinois nuts," gave pecans their species name *illinoinensis*.

Pecans grow on stately trees up to seventy to one hundred feet in height and forty to seventy-five feet wide and have smooth, relatively thin shells, generally ovoid in shape and three-quarters of an inch to two inches long. The kernel somewhat resembles an elongated walnut but its taste is much milder, with a distinct trace of sweetness.

In the second half of the nineteenth century, pecans were grown primarily in Texas and Louisiana, and trade in pecans was somewhat limited because trees grown from seed yielded unpredictable results, since seedlings are not exact copies of the parent tree. The development of successful cultivars through budding or grafting changed all that. The first grafts were achieved in 1846 or 1847 by a slave named Antoine who was owned by J. J. Roman, a Louisiana plantation owner. While Antoine's success had very little effect on the industry, the work of Emil

Bourgeois, starting in 1877 on the Rapidan Plantation in Louisiana, resulted in wide acceptance of the vegetative propagation of pecan trees and laid the foundation for modern pecan orchards.

At the end of the nineteenth century tree nurseries used Bourgeois's techniques to develop cultivars that combined good taste, large kernel size, high yield and resistance to insects, diseases, and adverse climatic conditions and, of great importance for economical harvesting, enabled the simultaneous maturing of all the nuts on the tree. It was this development that triggered the start-up of pecan orchards in Georgia and led to that state's current position as the largest producer of pecans from cultivars, with Texas being the largest producer of pecans from the combined harvests of cultivars and seedlings. The main uses for pecans are in raw nut mixtures, confections, and pastries. Pecan pie is a very popular, and, unlike apple pie, a truly all-American dessert.

[*See also* Nuts.]

BIBLIOGRAPHY

Hume, H. Harold. *The Pecan and Its Culture.* Petersburg, VA: American Fruit and Nut Journal, 1912.
Manaster, Jane. *The Pecan Tree.* Austin: University of Texas Press, 1994.
Sparks, Darrell. *Pecan Cultivars: The Orchard's Foundation.* Watkinsville, GA: Pecan Production Innovations, 1992.
Stuckey, H. P., and Edwin Jackson Kyle. *Pecan Growing.* New York: Macmillan, 1925.

EDGAR ROSE

Pennell, Elizabeth

Elizabeth Robins Pennell (1855–1936) could not cook, yet she wrote a newspaper cookery column for five years, authored two books related to cooking, and amassed an extensive collection of rare cookbooks, which is the second largest of the holdings in the Rare Book and Special Collections Division of the Library of Congress.

Pennell, a resident of London from 1884 through World War I, was born in Philadelphia. After the death of her mother, her father sent both Elizabeth and her sister to a Catholic convent outside Philadelphia. Pennell remained there until her graduation in 1872; she then moved to her father's home and reluctantly acceded to her family's demands to blend into Philadelphia's social milieu. A reacquaintance with her uncle, Charles Godfrey Leland, a journalist with ties to the intellectual community of writers and artists in the United States and Europe, stimulated her imagination and introduced her to a world outside of Philadelphia. Under his tutelage Pennell began to write.

A commission to do a story about Philadelphia led to her introduction to the illustrator and graphic artist Joseph Pennell. Within a few days of their meeting Elizabeth and Joseph began a lifetime collaboration, which led to marriage. A commission in 1884 from the *Century Magazine* sent the Pennells to London. They remained there for thirty years, enjoying the company of notable artists and writers and working together on books.

Although Pennell admitted that she could not boil an egg, she agreed to write weekly cookery essays for the *Pall Mall Gazette*, a London newspaper. Her column ran for five years and launched her culinary career. A selection of some of the best essays was published in 1896 as *The Feasts of Autolycus* (later changed to *The Delights of Delicate Eating*). The book broke new ground in venturing beyond the details of recipes to the delights of dining; one reviewer considered it "one of the wisest and wittiest of the literary products of the famous [18]90s." It set the stage for cookery books filled with wit, wisdom, and humor.

Pennell was far ahead of her time in urging women to take pride in mastering their role in the kitchen and, as she wrote in *The Delights of Delicate Eating*, to "be bold, defy convention." *Delights*, with its descriptions of local dishes in Europe and America and tidbits of historical information, gives us a unique glimpse into the nineteenth-century world of cookery.

Pennell stumbled into her career as a serious cookbook collector when a friend presented her with a copy of Alexandre Dumas's *Le grand dictionnaire de cuisine*. From its pages she helped herself to dishes and menus that would amuse and instruct her readers. To enhance her essays and not bore her followers with Dumas, Pennell bought a few more cookbooks and began to seriously collect. She recounts her collecting activities and describes the books in *My Cookery Books* (1903).

The large Library of Congress collection, which includes such rarities as *Apicus de re Coquinaria* (1498) and *Acetaria: A Discourse on Sallets* (1699), enables scholars to pursue centuries of culinary cuisine and is a significant contribution to culinary history). Originally comprising over one thousand books, Pennell's collection suffered water damage during World War I and now includes 433 cookbooks and 299 books on other topics, such as fine printing, bibliography, and literature.

[*See also* Cookbooks and Manuscripts, *subentries* From the Beginnings to 1860, From World War I to World War II, *and* From the 1970s to the Present; Library Collections.]

BIBLIOGRAPHY

Beck, Leonard N. *Two "Loaf-Givers"; or, A Tour through the Gastronomic Libraries of Katherine Golden Bitting and Elizabeth Robins Pennell*. Washington, DC: Library of Congress, 1984. Beck, curator of special collections at the Library of Congress, examines and analyzes Renaissance and early-modern publications, such as the *Libro de arte coquinaria* of Maestro Martino (1450–1460) and John Murrell's *A Daily Exercise for Ladies and Gentlewomen* (1617). Photographs of title pages and manuscript illustrations accompany the text.

Pennell, Elizabeth Robins. *The Feasts of Autolycus: The Diary of a Greedy Woman*. London, 1896. A collection of cookery essays that Pennell wrote for the *Pall Mall Gazette*. Essays discuss menus, foods, and wines, as gleaned from her travels and from the pages of noted cookbooks.

Pennell, Elizabeth Robins. *The Delights of Delicate Eating* (originally published as *The Feasts of Autolycus*). Reprinted with an introduction to Pennel's life and career by Jacqueline Williams. Urbana, IL, 2000.

Pennell, Elizabeth Robins. *My Cookery Books*. Boston: Houghton, Mifflin, 1903. Pennell provides a personal account of her collecting activities along with a description of many of the books.

JACQUELINE BLOCK WILLIAMS

Pennsylvania Dutch Food, *see German American Food; Mid-Atlantic Region*

Pepper, Black

Black pepper (*Piper nigrum*) is said to have originated on the Malabar coast of India, where it grew on vines attached to trees. The spice migrated east with Indian traders following the monsoons, and became established as a crop in Java and the Sunda Islands and then in Malaysia, Borneo, Sumatra, Sri Lanka, and Penang. Today it is also grown in Thailand, tropical Africa, the South Sea Islands, and Brazil.

Pepper vines bear white flowers on spikes, becoming peppercorns that look like small clusters of berries. The peppercorns ripen from green to red and then to brown; green peppercorns become black peppercorns when dried in the sun. Black pepper owes its pungency to a resin and its flavor to a volatile oil. Most of the pungent flavor of the black peppercorn is in its skin. Green peppercorns are picked unripe, and sold dry or pickled in vinegar or brine. White pepper is formed by soaking fresh berries in salt water, removing their red shells by hand, and then drying them. Some say white peppercorn is milder than black and is a more favorable spice. Gray pepper is most often a ground mix of black and white peppercorns.

Throughout history, pepper has been the most widely used spice. Pepper entered written Western history during the Roman Empire. The Romans established trade routes to India through Alexandria and the Arabian Peninsula. After Portugal's navigations to India in the sixteenth century, and for the next two centuries, pepper became a source of economic competition between the Portuguese, the English, and the Dutch.

Pepper was available in the United States in the colonial period, but it was only after the American Revolution that the United States became a player in the global pepper trade. This trade began in 1793 when Jonathan Carnes, a Salem, Massachusetts, sea captain, set sail for the East Indies. He was successful in finding pepper, but on his way home his ship was wrecked off Bermuda. He sailed to the Indies in 1795 on a new ship, the Rajah, and returned with his hold full of peppercorns—which he sold at a 700 percent profit. Others followed, and Salem became the pepper port of note in the new United States—nearly one thousand voyages were completed in one two-year period—and remained so until 1873. By that time other ports such as New York and Boston had grown larger and took in pepper from the British and Dutch. Earlier, Jefferson's embargo of U.S. shipping in 1807 greatly hindered the pepper trade, as did the War of 1812. Today, much of the pepper supply arrives through various global importers, such as McCormick.

In the early nineteenth century some regarded pepper as a cause of insanity. Pepper was in any case shunned by food purists, who thought that the spice should be avoided or, at least, used in moderation. By the post–Civil War period, pepper was considered more acceptable, but it was still to be avoided by children or by those who already had a "sound digestion" and did not need condiments.

Pepper, usually preground, has become, with salt, one of the two basic spices found in American kitchens and on American tables. The three basic types of peppercorns—black, green, and white—have entered American cuisine from other cultures and evolved, in some cases, into unique American dishes.

[See also Herbs and Spices.]

FRED CZARRA

Pepperoni

Pepperoni, or peperoni, is essentially a variety of air-dried salami that derives its name from the word "pepper," alluding to the spicy red pepper that is its principal spice. Pepperoni's origins can be traced to ancient Roman times, when butchers chopped and dried mixtures of meat and fat, which had been seasoned with black pepper and other spices, to make a food that was convenient for soldiers to eat during marches. In modern times, Italian immigrants introduced pepperoni to the United States, where pepperoni is rarely consumed alone; it is most commonly served on pizzas. About 1900 pizzerias were established in New York, and pepperoni and cheese were tied as the favorite toppings. More than a century later, pepperoni still heads the list of toppings for pizza.

Pepperoni, like most American foods, is not indigenous to the United States. But no other country has done as much to produce and popularize this highly seasoned salami. The method of making pepperoni had changed little over two millennia, but when pepperoni arrived with the immigrants, American ingenuity introduced several innovations in both manufacturing and ingredients. In the early 1900s, Armour and Company in Chicago pioneered automated production of pepperoni. Refrigeration and humidity-control technologies enabled year-round manufacture, changing the Old World practice of producing pepperoni only in late fall and early winter.

The traditional recipe for pepperoni included pork trimmings, beef chucks, hearts, cheeks, and pork jowl seasoned with ground red pepper and other spices. These highly seasoned mixtures were stuffed into pig casings and air-dried or smoked at relatively low temperatures (not exceeding 140°F). The finished product was aged in cool, dry temperatures for a period of six to ten months to help develop its characteristic pepperoni flavor. Americans introduced lactic acid cultures to help optimize the development of flavor and shorten the curing time from months to days or even hours. Whey and soy-based ingredients helped enhance pepperoni flavor and bind moisture, and they also significantly shortened drying and curing processes.

In the 1950s, the U.S. Department of Agriculture issued a Standard of Identity for pepperoni and mandated a moisture-to-protein ratio of 1.6:1 for retail markets. Pizza makers found that manual peeling and slicing of pepperoni was expensive because of the labor involved—and because of the injuries. Better safety and easier slicing were facilitated, first by the invention of slicing machines for pepperoni in the late 1960s and then by the development of edible protein films to replace the traditional pig casings.

Pepperoni is probably the only salami that is heated to help bring out its flavor. Americans use pepperoni as pizza topping, as filling in calzones, and in sauces for pasta. Reduced fat and turkey pepperoni developed by Hormel Foods Corporation are popular with those conscious of fat in their diets. Annually, Americans consume twenty-four pounds of pizza per capita, more than two pounds of which is pepperoni. American children rate pepperoni pizza highest of all the foods in the school lunch program, and the general American population loves pepperoni flavor, rating it next to cheese and seasonings as the flavor of choice for savory snacks. Pepperoni popularity is further evidenced by the increasing number of references in treats for pets—Pepperoni Nawsomes and Pupperoni Treats.

[*See also* Armour, Philip Danforth; Drying; Italian American Food; Pizza; Pizzerias; Salami; Sausage.]

BIBLIOGRAPHY

Dowell, Philip, and Adrian Bailey. *Cook's Ingredients*. New York: Morrow, 1980.

Toussant-Samat, Maguelonne. *History of Food*. Translated by Anthea Bell. New York: Barnes and Noble, 1998.

KANTHA SHELKE

Pepsi-Cola

Like many other pharmacists at the end of the nineteenth century, Caleb Bradham, of New Bern, North Carolina, experimented with various blends of fruit flavors and other extracts, hoping to create a new drink. One of Bradham's concoctions became especially popular with local patrons. This nameless drink eventually became known as Brad's Drink, named after Bradham. As the popularity of Brad's Drink rose, so did the need to give it a proper name. In 1898, Brad's Drink became Pepsi-Cola, and one of the most important beverages in soft drink history was born. It is believed that the name Pepsi-Cola was chosen because, like pepsin, Pepsi-Cola aids in digestion. At the same time, it provides the refreshment of a cola drink.

Over the next few years, demand for Pepsi-Cola spread well beyond New Bern. On December 30, 1902, the Pepsi-Cola Company was formed; the first Pepsi-Cola trademark was registered in 1903. At first Pepsi-Cola

was sold exclusively as a fountain drink, but by 1905 it was also available in bottles. At the same time, Bradham began offering franchises to bottle Pepsi-Cola. By 1910 there were 280 bottlers in twenty-four states producing bottled Pepsi-Cola.

The company continued to grow and prosper until the sugar crisis of World War I. Sugar rationing and price controls resulted in an unstable sugar market; since sugar is a primary ingredient in soft drinks, this was a severe blow to the entire soft-drink industry. Pepsi-Cola became desperate to find enough sugar to keep operating. At one point, they tried using sugar substitutes, such as molasses. But the molasses gave Pepsi-Cola an unpleasant taste, which resulted in lower sales. Bradham did not want to take the chance of running out of sugar again. So once the sugar restrictions eased, he purchased a large supply of sugar at a very high price. Months later the cost of sugar tumbled to a fraction of what Bradham had paid. Years of sugar rationing and price controls, combined with slumping sales, were too much for the Pepsi-Cola Company. By 1923, Bradham was forced into bankruptcy.

For the next eight years, the Pepsi-Cola Company was located in Richmond, Virginia, where it struggled through reorganizations and a second bankruptcy before being bought by a Long Island candy company called Loft Candies. By this time, the famous Pepsi-Cola trademark had all but disappeared from public view.

In New York, Charles Guth, president of Loft Candies, was embroiled in a dispute over the price of Coca-Cola syrup, which was dispensed at Loft stores in the New York area. Unable to resolve this dispute, Guth decided to purchase the trademark and formula of Pepsi-Cola, which would then be sold in place of Coca-Cola at Loft soda fountains. But the results Guth had hoped for never materialized. The people of New York were not familiar with the Pepsi-Cola name. Furthermore, Coca-Cola was filing lawsuits that claimed that Pepsi-Cola was misleading consumers as to which cola drink they were getting.

Finally, in desperation, Guth decided to sell Pepsi-Cola in bottles rather than from the fountain. To make these bottles more distinctive, he decided to use twelve-ounce bottles rather than the standard six-ounce bottle, and to sell them for ten cents. This made a bad situation worse. People were not used to paying more than a nickel for a soft drink—even if it was twice the usual size. Faced with the prospect of failure, Guth decided to cut the price of Pepsi-Cola to five cents in a final attempt to revive the drink. His timing could not have been better: in 1934, the country was in the midst of the Great Depression. This new twelve-ounce bottle for a nickel was just what people were looking for. Success came immediately; over the next five years, Pepsi-Cola sales skyrocketed. New Pepsi bottling franchises were popping up all over the country.

Charles Guth did not share in the success of Pepsi-Cola. Believing he owned the rights to Pepsi-Cola, Guth left Loft and took Pepsi-Cola with him. In a subsequent lawsuit filed by Loft, Guth was forced to give back all rights to Pepsi-Cola. Walter Mack, a financier who had financed the lawsuit against Guth, was now president of the Pepsi-Cola Company.

One of Mack's first actions as CEO was to take control of Pepsi-Cola advertising. Perhaps Mack's greatest contribution to Pepsi advertising history was the popular Pepsi jingle, the first "stand-alone" radio jingle of its day. Mack was also responsible for the creation of "Pepsi and Pete, the Pepsi-Cola Cops," and in 1940 he replaced the plain bottle with a standardized, custom-embossed twelve-ounce bottle.

In 1941, to show its support for the war effort, Pepsi changed its bottle crown colors to red, white, and blue. These colors soon became an integral part of the Pepsi logo.

The World War II era was difficult for the Pepsi-Cola Company, which had to deal with everything from raw material shortages to postwar inflation. The inflation issue was the more serious problem because it reduced profits, and it eventually forced Pepsi to raise the five-cent price that had made it famous.

In 1950, Alfred Steele was appointed CEO of Pepsi. Steele's greatest achievement was in modernizing Pepsi-Cola, both in image and in operation. The formula was changed to include less sugar, and a new advertising campaign was launched with the slogan "The Light Refreshment." A new bottle was commissioned, and in 1958 the swirl bottle was introduced to coincide with the "Be Sociable" advertising campaign. Pepsi had moved from the kitchen to the dining room.

The 1960s saw the emergence of the baby boomers. To tap into this market, Pepsi created what would become its most successful advertising campaign to date: "The Pepsi Generation." Pepsi's move into the growing youth market would eventually give it the number one position in soft-drink popularity. In 1965, President Donald Kendall engineered a merger between Pepsi-Cola and Frito-Lay to form PepsiCo.

The 1960s also brought many changes in packaging and products. The American consumer was now more concerned with convenience rather than price. To respond to this new trend, Pepsi introduced nonreturnable bottles and cans. Additionally, Pepsi began brand expansion with the introduction of Diet Pepsi and Mountain Dew.

The 1970s and 1980s saw more of the same, with more nonreturnable packaging—especially the two-liter bottle and the twelve-ounce can. The returnable Pepsi bottle was nearly extinct. Brand extension continued with flavors like Pepsi Light, Slice, and Mug Root Beer.

[*See also* Cola Wars; Soda Drinks; Soda Fountains.]

BIBLIOGRAPHY

Enrico, Roger. *The Other Guy Blinked: How Pepsi Won the Cola Wars.* New York: Bantam Books, 1986.
Martin, Milward W. *Twelve Full Ounces.* New York: Holt, Rinehart, 1962.
Stoddard, Bob. *Pepsi: 100 Years.* Los Angeles: General Publishing Group, 1997.

BOB STODDARD

Periodicals

The doctor's waiting room and the beauty parlor are full of them. Flea markets thrive on them, and many attics and basements are stacked with those too interesting to throw away. Food magazines, an integral part of American life, are a ready source of information and pleasure.

Filled with full-color photographs of mouthwatering dishes, food magazines are hard to resist, promising tempting family meals or elaborate gourmet feasts. Travel articles highlight recipes from exotic places. Magazines appealing to almost every taste continue to flood the newsstands, yet many twenty-first-century cooks admit they never use food magazines to cook with. They admire the photographs and read the recipes with pleasure but never take the book into the kitchen.

As technological improvements began finding their way into the kitchen in the nineteenth century, magazine editors declared themselves ready to help readers deal with the newest appliances and the latest food products—many of them advertised in the periodical's own pages. Advertisers were quick to take advantage of magazines that would be welcomed into the homes of prospective buyers. Although editorials averred that their aim was to help their readers perform household tasks more quickly and more efficiently, increasing advertising revenue was at least as important. As advertisements began to proliferate in magazine pages, they frequently blended with editorial content, making it difficult to differentiate one from the other. Magazine columnists like Fannie Farmer and Sarah Tyson Rorer, respected cookbook writers and cooking-school directors, had no qualms about recommending advertised products in their recipes. In a 1930 editorial *Woman's Home Companion* asked its readers to patronize their advertisers. In 1932 in *American Cookery*, the popular cookbook author Ida Bailey Allen asked her readers to "read these directions, please—for they tell you how to use Mazola for all your frying, shortening and especially Salad Dressing." In 1973 James Beard wrote *Cook with Corning: Selected Recipes*, promoting the advantages of Corning glass cookware.

Early Magazines

The earliest magazines dealing with food were "educational" periodicals, heavy on fiction, fashion, and needlework but with a minimum of cooking and other household information. These magazines were teaching women to be good and economical housewives and to expand their horizons with literature. *Godey Lady's Book*, founded in 1837 and edited for forty years by Sarah Josepha Hale, set the model for many future publications, featuring generous helpings of advice for young families plus some food and household hints, along with fiction, poetry, and fashion. Mrs. Hale was strong minded and opinionated and bent on instruction; her motherly style appealed to upper-middle-class women, and she was able to edit the magazine successfully while promoting an agenda for the better education of women.

Just one year after *Godey's* appeared, Caroline Gilman published *The Lady's Annual Register and Housewife's Memorandum Book*, featuring advice on numerous domestic topics. In 1843 the cookbook author Eliza Leslie launched a new publication, *Miss Leslie's Magazine*, that was virtually indistinguishable from other women's magazines; it failed after only one year. *The Cottage Hearth*, published in the 1860s, followed the *Godey's* pattern, as did *Frank Leslie's Monthly Magazine; Peterson's Magazine; The Household: A Monthly Journal Devoted to the Interests of the American Housewife; The New Lady's Magazine, or Polite, Useful, and Entertaining Monthly for the Fair Sex; The Farmer's Wife*, appealing to rural women; and *Demorest's Monthly Magazine*, primarily a fashion magazine that paid some attention to food and other household topics.

Berney's Mysterious Magazine may have been the first magazine devoted solely to cooking. Appearing in 1868, *Berney's* offered hundreds of recipes, many of them test-ed by Mrs. Prudence Winslow, allegedly an experienced cook and homemaker. The magazine promised many more recipes to come, but *Berney's* lasted only one issue.

By the 1870s more magazines devoted primarily to food and the art of dining began to appear, some only briefly. *The Table: A Monthly Publication Devoted to the Refinements of the Table* lasted only eight months in 1873. Dedicated to an upscale audience, the magazine promised attention to the "art of good living" and published articles on public banquets and social breakfasts. In 1876 *American Cookery: A Monthly Dining Room Magazine* (no connection to the later journal of the same name), less sophisticated than *The Table*, cautioned its readers to make allowances for visitors from "the country" who might not be used to the refinements of urban society. James Parkinson, a well-known Philadelphia caterer, published *The Caterer and Household Magazine* in 1882, with information for both professional and home cooks.

The Cook, lasting just a year (from 1885 to 1886), provided important marketing information to its readers, including the prices, quality, and abundance of produce, meat, and fish. Decidedly upscale, the magazine printed letters about the food preferences of famous New Yorkers, such as Jay Gould and William Vanderbilt.

In 1886 *Table Talk* appeared, filled with information on menus, recipes, etiquette, fashion, and children's topics and in-depth discussions of food. Lasting until 1920, *Table Talk* was edited in its early years by Sarah Tyson Rorer, who left her own magazine, *Household News*, to take on this new assignment. *Table Talk* featured monthly menus and recipes; in 1893 it published articles on the Chicago Columbian Exposition, where the magazine set up an experimental electric kitchen to demonstrate new appliances, and a gossipy feature, "Capricious Washington."

In 1896 the handsomely illustrated *National Food Magazine* took a more proactive stance than had its predecessors, lobbying vigorously for a pure-food law. Besides running articles on food history, the magazine also reported on food fairs and expositions around the country. It continued publication until 1920.

Home Economics: The Education of the American Housewife

The same year that the *National Food Magazine* appeared, the *Boston Cooking School Magazine* made its debut. The editor, Fannie Farmer, Boston's well-known cooking-school director, had revolutionized home cooking by standardizing measurements; no longer did the housewife need to rely on "a teacup" of flour or "a heaping dessert spoon" of sugar. In addition to advice on food preparation, her magazine was filled with solid information on stoves and sinks, servant problems, health, nutrition, and sports. The name was later changed to *American Cookery: Formerly the Boston Cooking School Magazine of Culinary Science and Domestic Economies*. The latter magazine, edited by Janet McKenzie Hill, was a useful compendium of menus, recipes, and essays on laundry work, table etiquette, and the joys of a well-run home; during World War II it published articles on meat rationing, refrigeration and home freezing, the nutritional value of grain, and "Breakfast for Victory," and it helped home cooks cope with wartime shortages. *American Cookery* ceased publication in 1947, its legacy a remarkable record of the changes in American society and in women's lives over half a century.

New England Kitchen Magazine, later called *The American Kitchen*, appeared in 1894, edited by Mary J.

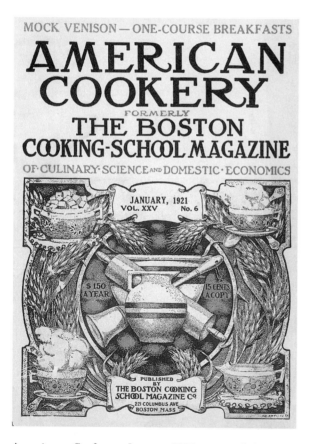

American Cookery. January 1921 cover of *American Cookery*, which was the successor to *Boston Cooking School Magazine*.

Lincoln and Ann Barrows. Mary Lincoln, a well-known cooking teacher, writer, and lecturer, wrote a monthly column, "From Day to Day." A strong supporter of the home economics movement, which stressed efficiency and scientific principles in the kitchen, *New England Kitchen Magazine* extolled the virtues of cooking schools while lamenting the slow pace of change in cooking techniques. Home economists taught that kitchen "drudgery" could be virtually eliminated by applying scientific principles to routine kitchen work, and *The American Kitchen* lobbied vigorously for change. But new ideas, always a challenge in any field, were slow to take hold in the home, where many housewives clung to the familiar ways of their mothers and grandmothers, much to the dismay of home economists striving to make the home kitchen more scientific.

In 1895 *The Cooking Club, by Every Day Cooks Who Cook Every Day: The Only Culinary Publication Adapted to Use of Families with Limited Incomes* offered recipes and menus, many from other cultures. Published in Goshen, Indiana, for twenty-one years, it was one of the few cooking magazines that did not choose the eastern United States as its home base.

"The Big Six"

The 1870s witnessed the beginnings of the major service magazines, popular periodicals featuring fiction by well-known writers, articles on current issues of concern to women, and departments emphasizing food preparation and other household information. Called "The Big Six," they were *McCall's, Woman's Home Companion, Delineator, Ladies' Home Journal, Pictorial Review,* and *Good Housekeeping*.

Eighteen seventy-three saw the launching of a small fashion sheet designed to advertise clothes, called *The Queen: Illustrating McCall's Bazar Glove-Fitting Patterns;* not until 1883 did the magazine become merely *McCall's*. Although still emphasizing patterns and fashions, *McCall's* slowly changed its identity, adding fiction by well-known writers like Zane Grey and Mary Roberts Rinehart and, later, service features for the homemaker. By 1932 the editor, Otis Wiese, had redesigned the magazine, dividing it into three parts—Fiction and News, Home-Making, and Style and Beauty—with each section carrying its own advertising. By this means *McCall's* sought to increase its readership among ordinary middle-class subscribers, and it succeeded well enough to survive the Depression without major losses. During World War II the editors offered guidelines for cooking under rationing and tips on juggling home and wartime jobs; after the war *McCall's* turned its attention to suburban women, and the food pages reflected this, with more entertainment tips and recipes designed to save time. At the same time it took increasing notice of the working woman and her needs. Wiese will perhaps be most remembered for coining the slogan "Togetherness," which Americans made an integral part of the language, both praising and mocking the concept.

McCall's stopped publishing patterns more than one hundred years after the first fashions appeared in *The Queen*. The company changed hands and editors several times in the 1980s and 1990s, and circulation figures dropped; television and other sources of information and recreation made serious inroads on all service magazines as they scrambled to meet the needs of a changing population. In 2001 *McCall's* published its last issue.

Two other major service magazines appeared in the same year as *McCall's*. *The Home*, published in Cleveland, Ohio, went through several incarnations before becoming the *Woman's Home Companion*, with fiction and articles from some of the country's best writers: Bret Harte, Jack London, Charlotte Perkins Gilman, and Jane Addams. Fannie Farmer, with her sister Cora Dexter Perkins, edited the magazine's cooking department for ten years, followed by Alice Bradley, also an influential cookbook writer and teacher. In 1930 Bradley encouraged women to use the new electric grills and toasters, the better to prepare dainty toasted mushroom sandwiches for afternoon refreshments. Her recommendations for party sweets were, she said, worked out at Miss Farmer's School of Cooking. In 1911 Sarah Tyson Rorer resigned from the *Ladies' Home Journal* and became head of the *Woman's Home Companion* culinary department.

In 1929 the *Companion* often devoted a page to the "Men's Cooking Club," soliciting recipes and cooking experiences from its male readers. One such contributor sent in an "original" recipe combining spaghetti, ground beef, onions, and tomatoes, topped with cheese and baked until brown. "The Children's Page" featured the Junior Cooking Club, with appropriate recipes "if mother will allow," and included directions for a candy pull.

Gertrude Battles Lane served as *Companion* editor from 1911 to 1940, and the magazine reflected her concern with women's issues—among them women's right to work, even during the Depression, and their duty to run for public office, even though they were unable to vote. She trusted her readers and enlisted a cadre of two thousand of them,

from all over the country, to advise her on all phases of the magazine. When she retired in 1940, subsequent editors opted for a somewhat harder edge, publishing articles on divorce, abortion, breast cancer, and birth control, which some critics said contributed to the *Companion's* decline. Corporate financial problems, intense competition, cash flow problems, and a decrease in advertising revenue all served to weaken the *Companion's* market position, and the January 1957 issue was the last.

The *Delineator*, known for its fashion pages, short stories, and serialized novels, also carried substantial homemaking pages. From 1873 until 1937 the magazine featured suggestions concerning home decoration, vegetable gardening, canning techniques, and food preparation. The January 1898 issue discussed "False Economy in the Home" and also gave instructions on how to give a successful tea party, including advice on the kind of candy to serve so as not to soil the ladies' gloves. Party suggestions in the September 1921 issue included "Cooking with the Gipsies [*sic*]" and included directions on building a campfire and preparing recipes purporting to come from English gypsies.

Over the years the personality of the magazine changed, from an emphasis on fashion and fiction to muckraking articles on important social issues such as child labor, women's rights (including property rights), cleaning up slums, and sanitary food processing. By 1928, however, the *Delineator* had returned to its original fashion magazine identity. The Depression cut heavily into its advertising revenues and circulation dropped; in April 1937 the *Delineator* merged with *Pictorial Review*.

The first issue of *Pictorial Review* appeared in 1899, designed exclusively to sell dress patterns. By 1929 it boasted advertising revenue and circulation figures on a par with rivals *Ladies' Home Journal* and *Good Housekeeping*. A series of editors changed the magazine's direction to social reform and muckraking issues, added fiction and improved graphics, and emphasized the importance of American values such as family and education. Reader polls were conducted on divorce, child labor, and birth control. During the Depression, circulation rose to more than three million subscribers, but advertising revenues began to slip. Another change of editors failed to stem the loss of income, and in 1937 *Pictorial Review* shut down suddenly, without a word of explanation to its readers or to the public.

With the advent of the *Ladies' Home Journal* in 1883, serious competition among major service magazines increased. Edward Bok became editor in 1890 and shaped the magazine into a service vehicle for the growing middle-class family: he expanded the departments offering practical advice on child rearing, health, and food, hiring Sarah Tyson Rorer in 1893 to edit the food pages. Her column offered such treats as "baked apples Creole style," "strawberry blanc mange," and "lobster salad garnished with the empty claws," and "menus for picnics, garden parties, and excursions." Her other column, "Mrs. Rorer Answers Questions," offered advice on every conceivable household subject.

Essentially conservative, Bok editorialized against woman suffrage and lobbied vigorously against the sale of patent medicines containing alcohol; he opposed the prohibition movement but wrote editorials recommending sex education for women. When he retired in 1919, the *Journal* acquired a series of new editors, each of whom put his or her stamp on the magazine. But Bok's essential conservatism still permeated the editorial content. Beatrice Gould, part of a husband-and-wife team of editors in 1935, set forth the magazine's philosophy in an editorial, declaring that a woman's job was to be as womanly as possible, as pretty as possible, and as loving as possible in order to hold her family together cheerfully with warmth and comfort and good sense.

Part of this good sense required skills in the kitchen, and the *Journal*'s food departments tried to provide the information housewives needed. During the Depression the magazine was hit hard by declining advertisements and subscription sales, but it tried to assist housewives in getting through the hard times by publishing money-saving recipes and urging families to have confidence in their government.

Despite the many editorial changes in the magazine over more than 120 years, food features still remain in the forefront. The full-time housewife is less visible today than in 1883, and the majority of *Journal* readers work outside the home; many have small children. The food pages reflect these realities, with shortcuts and time-savers for all household chores as well as attention-getting color photographs and recipes.

Good Housekeeping began publishing in 1885, incorporating the same mix of fiction, recipes, and household advice offered by the other "Big Six" magazines but with one major difference: the "Good Housekeeping Seal of Approval." In 1900 the magazine established the Good Housekeeping Institute Experiment Station, with a small staff charged with researching household practices. In 1902 *Good Housekeeping* offered a money-back guarantee on any item advertised in the magazine and began inspecting food products, creating an "honor roll" of food that passed its tests. This evolved into the Seal of Approval, praised by many but attacked by others—primarily the competition, which accused *Good Housekeeping* of false and misleading practices. The Federal Trade Commission took an interest in the matter and determined that the Seal of Approval must go; in its place, the magazine introduced a "Guaranty Seal," promising to refund readers' money if an advertised product proved unsatisfactory.

In the first issue of *Good Housekeeping* an article titled "How to Eat, Sleep and Drink as Christians Should" shared space with an article on dealing fairly with servants and information on how to bake bread. Maria Parloa's department, "Gustatory Thought and Suggestions," began in 1886, the same year cookbook author Catherine Owen began her column, "Keeping House Well on $10 a Week." The editors have always tried to maintain a close relationship with their readers, soliciting articles and stories, printing family photographs, requesting ideas for the magazine's content, and taking polls, such as the popular "Ten Most Admired American Women" (later expanded to include men). In more than one hundred years of publication *Good Housekeeping* has maintained the mix of recipes, articles on home decoration, attention to health and children's issues, celebrity interviews, and information features that has appealed to readers from the very first issue.

Better Homes and Gardens

In 1924 a new kind of magazine appeared. *Better Homes and Gardens* grew out of *Successful Farming*, when founder and publisher E. T. Meredith decided that America needed a magazine devoted to traditional values and to providing the ideas, information, and inspiration that families needed to help them live a better life. This translated into a service magazine addressing middle-class families who were interested in their homes, their kitchens, and their gardens. The food page editor, Josephine Wylie, presented ethnic dishes, recognized the housewife's need to save time by introducing "Six Twenty Minute Meals," published articles on food allergies and diet long before Americans considered their weight to be a health issue, and was the guiding light behind *The Better Homes and Gardens Cookbook* in 1930, the enormously successful all-purpose cookbook that sold forty thousand copies within three months.

The Depression and World War II slowed the magazine's growth temporarily, but as servicemen returned, Meredith understood their keen interest in home and family. *Better Homes and Gardens* provided information to help make their dreams come true: innovative building plans and gardening techniques, new kitchen designs, and recipes celebrating the return to nonrationed foods. The magazine is credited with introducing the concept of the "family room," and it promoted outdoor entertaining and barbecues. In the 1960s advertisers were urged to develop precooked meals to appeal to working women. *Better Homes and Gardens* has remained firmly committed to its middle-class readers, and its formula for providing information and products designed to enhance family life has proved successful for more than one hundred years.

New Food Magazines

The launching of *Gourmet* magazine in 1941 coincided with World War II, seemingly an inauspicious time to begin a magazine dedicated to good food and good living. But the publisher, Earl R. MacAusland, managed to demonstrate to his readers that despite rationing, his philosophy could benefit America by promoting "a fine appreciation of good food, less waste, and an even smaller expenditure of food." He lived with his family and personal chef in a penthouse at the Plaza Hotel and moved the *Gourmet* office there as well.

After the war, circulation increased as did upscale advertising, and accomplished writers like James Beard, Samuel Chamberlain, Craig Claiborne, and Louis Diet of the Ritz-Carlton Hotel were regular contributors. Magnificent color photography enhanced first the food pages and later the travel articles as *Gourmet* expanded its editorial content to include stories on exotic destinations in Europe and America and in little-known areas of the world.

Early popular features still remain: "Specialties de la Maison," restaurant reviews first from New York, then from other cities; "Sugar and Spice," letters and recipes from readers; "The Last Touch," the final page in the magazine, always on a single subject, such as apples or walnuts or chocolate; and "You Asked for It," answers to readers' queries about recipes from restaurants they had visited.

Advertising is handsome and upscale, with beautiful women driving expensive automobiles or subtly recommending perfume, wine, or hotels in exotic locales. *Gourmet*'s editor, Ruth Reichl, retains and improves on MacAusland's philosophy, "Good food and good living have always been a great American tradition."

Gourmet's major competitor, *Bon Appétit*, evolved from a liquor store throwaway into a full-fledged magazine in 1956. Aiming for an over-thirty, somewhat affluent audience, the magazine was less sophisticated than *Gourmet*, with features on easy-to-find, affordable ingredients (rather than, the editors maintained, some of the exotic items called for in *Gourmet*) and easy-to-make meals; the magazine was also among the first to promote healthful, low-calorie dinners. Its color photographs rivaled those of *Gourmet*, and the editors seemed constantly to be tinkering with and making over the magazine, usually with success. They too added travel stories, complete with handsome photographs, and in 1990 they began special collector's issues concentrating on one country or city. Advertising was also upscale, but *Bon Appétit* accepted ads for less expensive products, such as vegetable oils and Uncle Ben's rice. By 1987 *Bon Appétit* had overtaken its rival in circulation. As of 2004 both magazines are owned by Condé Nast, but each retains its unique identity.

Food and Wine, published by the American Express Company, follows the pattern established by *Gourmet* and *Bon Appétit* but in a more relaxed style, with more emphasis on consumer information. Stories on the best canned tomatoes, features such as "75 Best Food Buys" and "8 Superfast Pastas," and surveys of readers' favorite foods, restaurants, and TV chefs keep the magazine in touch with its subscribers.

Saveur concentrates on the heritage and tradition of food throughout the world, describing itself as a definitive culinary and culinary travel magazine. In-depth articles may cover exotic locales in Asia or the food specialties available in hidden pockets of the United States.

Cuisine at Home specializes in teaching a culinary technique, then providing several recipes that draw on that technique. "All about Spinach" discussed the varieties of the vegetable and how to clean, store, and cook it; recipes for four different dishes using spinach followed. Utilizing the same format, the magazine has dealt with pizza, all kinds of meat cutlets, and homemade pasta.

Consumer information is paramount in *Cook's Illustrated*. Reports on kitchen tools, food products, and small appliances share space with details of cooking techniques, basic recipes such as chicken cutlets or lemon pie, or a two-page spread on eggs. *Cook's Illustrated* carries no advertisements, a decision that the publisher hopes will encourage consumer confidence in the magazine's product judgments.

Supermarket Magazines

In 1932 *Family Circle* began life as a giveaway at Piggly Wiggly stores and later throughout the Safeway and Kroger's chains. Designed to sell products that these supermarkets stocked, *Family Circle* printed articles on child care and beauty but always emphasized food preparation. Women were quick to pick up the free copies at the checkout counter, and the magazine's popularity continued even when readers were asked to pay two cents a copy.

The supermarket and newsstand single-copy distribution system offered many advantages to the publisher, not the least of which was the savings in postage costs. *Family Circle* added new features over the years that would appeal to young readers with families: health and environmental issues were explored, along with changing lifestyles. But in the wake of declining sales and advertising revenue, in the 1980s the publisher began offering subscriptions in the hope of increasing readership. As of December 2003 only 23.4 percent of the magazine's sales still came from newsstand and supermarket sales.

When *Woman's Day* began publication in 1937, it quickly became a major competitor of *Family Circle*. Also beginning its life as a free giveaway (from the Great Atlantic and Pacific Tea Company), it shortly became a full-fledged magazine, printing features very similar to those of its rival on food preparation, child care issues, beauty, and money- and time-savers. The editors sought to make the magazine indispensable to the reader month after month, and circulation climbed, but it never reached the figures *Family Circle* achieved. As with that magazine, copies were originally sold only in supermarkets and on newsstands, but in the 1980s declines in sales and advertising revenues forced it to follow *Family Circle*'s strategy of offering subscriptions.

Diet-Conscious Magazines

The recognition of obesity as a national health problem has proved a challenge to food magazines. Confronted with the realization that many readers are increasingly concerned about their weight, editors feature foods rich in butter and cream less frequently in recipes, and scaled-down versions of favorite dishes are common. The interest in diet and fitness has also spawned several magazines devoted entirely to healthy lifestyles.

In 1950 J. I. Rodale, a pioneer in the organic gardening movement, published the first issue of *Prevention: The Magazine for Good Health*, featuring fitness and diet information. *American Health: Fitness of Body and Mind* began publication in 1982, with articles on nutrition and dietary habits as well as on general health issues. In 1986 appeared the first issue of *Cooking Light*, an information-filled magazine written in an easy conversational style that bills itself as the world's largest epicurean magazine. Dozens of delicious and nutritious recipes along with down-to-earth fitness tips appeal to readers who prefer not to give up good food in order to maintain a healthy lifestyle. Recipes provide nutritional breakdowns along with accurate and useful culinary information and are accompanied by beautiful photographs designed to show that low-calorie dishes can be appealing. Articles feature healthy exotic vegetables like *edamame*, the young green

---

GASTRONOMICA

Launched in February 2001, *Gastronomica: The Journal of Food and Culture* offers an innovative approach to the study of food and its role in our lives. This quarterly journal, published by the University of California Press under the editorship of Darra Goldstein, seeks to make readers aware of food as an important source of knowledge about different cultures and societies. Combining the latest scholarly research in the social sciences, humanities, and sciences with an appreciation for the pleasures and aesthetics of food, *Gastronomica* provides a forum for sharing ideas, provoking discussion, and encouraging thoughtful reflection on the history, literature, representation, and cultural impact of food.

Because of its interdisciplinary approach, *Gastronomica* offers a wide range of perspectives and includes articles from many fields, such as anthropology, cultural studies, environmental studies, and history. Each issue of *Gastronomica* also aims to be visually stunning, with illustrations that are both sensuous and arcane. The journal intends to stimulate discourse on a broad range of topics related to food and gastronomy and to encourage the general population to think seriously about food: where it comes from, how it is produced, and how it affects the world. Going beyond the recipes and attractive photographs presented in commercial magazines, *Gastronomica* brings scholars in the arts, anthropology, sociology, health, science, environmental studies, history, nutrition, and other disciplines into discussion with researchers in food studies and culinary professionals to offer food for thought.

DARRA GOLDSTEIN

beans of the soy plant, and sautéing techniques that don't sacrifice flavor to nutrition.

Eating Well, a handsome magazine filled with recipes, nutritional breakdowns, and stunning color photographs, promises to keep its readers informed of new trends in the health field and to help allay the confusion concerning ever-changing food warnings. Articles on such topics as winter vegetables, the mystique of green tea, and an apple primer, and commentary on the nutrition pyramid, provide practical information for cooks.

First published in 2001, *Light n' Tasty* takes on its competitors by declaring its goal to be keeping its readers' caloric intake and fat, cholesterol, and sodium levels lower than those of readers of other magazines. Written in a straightforward, conversational style, *Light n' Tasty* offers meatless dinners, recipes with reduced fat and cheese, a feature called "A Pinch of Salt or Less," and straightforward nutritional information.

Elegance vs. Simplicity in the Home Kitchen

The cooking magazine with the highest circulation in 2003 was *A Taste of Home,* a modest, unsophisticated collection of recipes reminiscent of a national community cookbook. Signed recipes are solicited from readers and supplemented by a volunteer group of one thousand "field editors" and a small in-house staff. To describe its content, the magazine uses words like "down-home" and "country favorites"; recipes come from "editors, readers—and their moms." Pictures of the contributors often appear with their recipes, and regular features include "Men Who Run the Range" and "Touring Country Kitchens"; a family grace is included in each issue. Readers' favorite feature is "My Mom's Best Meal." Typical recipes have included cheesy mashed potatoes, Swiss pot roast, peanut butter chocolate cake, hot cross buns, and "Mom's bean medley."

An upscale version of *Taste of Home* is one of the newest entries in the Martha Stewart media empire, *Everyday Food.* Positioned to offer recipes for family meals that call for basic supermarket staples rather than the traditional Martha Stewart exotic ingredients, *Everyday Food* is the compact size of a *TV Guide* and specializes in healthful thirty-minute meals that are easy to prepare. This is a far cry from *Martha Stewart's Living,* the sophisticated magazine edited and marketed so successfully by Martha Stewart Living Omnomedia. There, seviche *verde,* chocolate-pistachio brittle with praline dust, and baked oysters and *pescado* are photographed on

---

> ## FOOD HISTORY NEWS
>
> *Food History News (FHN),* first published in June 1989, is one of the longest-standing publications dealing with the subject of food history. With a small circulation, it has an influence far beyond its size, enjoying an eclectic readership consisting of food writers, historic cooks, military reenactors, chefs, academics, and food professionals of all sorts, as well as a substantial general readership.
>
> The publication explores topics dealing with North American food history since the early seventeenth century. Topics have ranged from fairly esoteric discussions—for example, traditional uses of mutton or wild fowl—to those with a wider interest, such as food and health, gentility and refinement, and popular foods such as apples and doughnuts. *FHN* typically includes a section devoted to food in military history, another for announcements and reader queries, and an ongoing column dedicated to the history of a particular dish or ingredient, ranging from bran muffins to salt-rising bread, from chemical leavenings to sugar.
>
> With the growing use of the Internet, *FHN* established a website, www.foodhistorynews.com, with a calendar of events, food history resources, a guide to products and services for food historians, and a searchable directory of international food and beverage museums. The weekly updated "Editor's Notebook" offers news about people and events, book reviews, and links to sites related to food history. *Food History News* is published four times a year.
>
> SANDRA L. OLIVER

tables set with expensive china and linens. Recipes often call for ingredients not easily found on supermarket shelves and require lengthy preparation time.

Food Magazines in an Evolving Society

Unless one is required to prepare family meals day after day, it is difficult to realize what a boring and backbreaking task that can be. Nineteenth-century housewives or their cooks must have found inspiration in the pages of the *Boston Cooking School Magazine* or the *Ladies' Home Journal* and concluded what the magazines intended: that they had a "friend" to help them.

After World War I returning soldiers wanted home-cooked meals again, and *Good Housekeeping* was there to assist. Servicemen also were more open to the ethnic foods they had sampled overseas, and magazines like *Gourmet* and *Bon Appétit* provided the recipes.

As women's roles changed, so did food magazines, which gave more attention to shortcuts and timesaving recipes. When health and fitness became watchwords, magazines like *Cooking Light* and *Eating Well* responded. *Martha Stewart's Living* understood the need for elegance at the same time that the yearning for a simpler life was recognized by *Taste of Home*.

Over several generations, American lifestyles have changed dramatically. Did food magazines play a leadership role in this change, or did they merely respond to changes already taking place? Whatever the answer, we can be certain that America's love affair with food has been sustained by the imagination and enthusiasm of our food magazines.

[*See also* Boston Cooking School; Farmer, Fannie; Good Housekeeping Institute; Home Economics; Rorer, Sarah Tyson; Stewart, Martha.]

BIBLIOGRAPHY

Brown, Kathi Ann. *Meredith: The First 100 Years.* Des Moines, IA: Meredith, 2002.

Endres, Kathleen L., and Therese L. Lueck, eds. *Women's Periodicals in the United States: Consumer Magazines.* Westport, CT: Greenwood, 1995.

Langone, Jan. "Berney's Mystery of Living and Other Nineteenth Century Cooking Magazines." *Gastronomica: The Journal of Food and Culture* 2, no. 2 (Spring 2002): 97–102.

Mott, Frank Luther. *A History of American Magazines.* 5 vols. Cambridge, MA: Harvard University Press, 1957–1968.

Shapiro, Laura. *Perfection Salad: Women and Cooking at the Turn of the Century.* New York: Farrar, Strauss and Giroux, 1986.

Tebbel, John, and Mary Ellen Zuckerman. *The Magazine in America, 1741–1990.* New York: Oxford University Press, 1991.

Woodward, Helen. *The Lady Persuaders.* New York: Ivan Obonlensky, 1960.

Zuckerman, Mary Ellen, comp. *Sources on the History of Women's Magazines, 1792–1960.* New York: Greenwood, 1991.

VIRGINIA K. BARTLETT

Persimmons

The two main persimmon species are *Diospyros virginiana*, native to the American states south of a line from Connecticut to Kansas, and *D. kaki*, indigenous to China. The name "persimmon" comes from the Algonquian word "pessemmin."

The native American persimmon, a round orange fruit that ranges up to the size of a small plum, is fiercely astringent when unripe because of soluble tannins in its flesh, but rich, sweet, and custardy when soft. Some improved selections were made in the late nineteenth and early twentieth centuries, but traditionally the persimmon is harvested from wild seedlings and used for puddings and breads. Although the fruit is important in American lore, it has been supplanted in commercial cultivation by the larger-fruited Asian kinds.

Of these there are two main types: the tomato-shaped Fuyu (the common name for several similar varieties), eaten crunchy-hard like an apple, and the acorn-shaped Hachiya, which like the native American species is edible only when soft and gelatinous. Both turn bright red-orange when ripe and are honey-sweet, with mild pumpkiny flavor. The season runs from late September through December. Fuyus are chiefly consumed as fresh fruits; Hachiyas can be eaten fresh, with a spoon, but are mostly used in puddings, ice creams, breads, and cookies.

The cultivation of Asian persimmons, chiefly in central and southern California, began with the importation of grafted trees from Japan in the 1870s and soared to three thousand acres in the 1920s, as part of a general boom in subtropical fruits. Plantings later declined, but in the 1970s and 1980s Asian immigration sparked a second boom. The U.S. Department of Agriculture's 1997 Census listed 3,459 bearing acres in California.

[*See also* Appalachian Food; Southern Regional Cookery.]

BIBLIOGRAPHY

Condit, Ira J. *The Kaki or Oriental Persimmon.* Berkeley: University of California Press, 1919.

Kitagawa, Hirotoshi, and Paul G. Glucina. *Persimmon Culture in New Zealand.* Wellington, New Zealand: Science Information Publishing Centre, 1984.

DAVID KARP

Philadelphia Cheesesteak Sandwich

The Philadelphia cheesesteak sandwich consists of very thinly sliced beefsteak that is grilled with onions and served on an Italian roll with a choice of cheese and a garnish of fried hot or sweet peppers. According to legend, the cheesesteak sandwich was created in 1930 by Pat Olivieri, operator of a hot dog stand at the Italian Market in South Philadelphia. Tired of hot dogs, Olivieri cooked up some thinly sliced beef and onions on his grill and piled it all into a crusty roll. As he was eating his sandwich, a cab driver and longtime customer arrived and asked for one, too. Upon tasting it, the cabbie advised Olivieri to forget hot dogs and sell the new beef sandwich instead. Cheese was added during the 1940s. Pat's King of Steaks, still owned and operated by the Olivieri family, is known for its Philadelphia cheesesteak sandwiches. The sandwich is served by a host of competitors in Philadelphia as well as restaurants and vendors throughout the United States.

[*See also* Sandwiches.]

BIBLIOGRAPHY

Mercuri, Becky. *Sandwiches That You Will Like*. Pittsburgh, PA: WQED, 2002.

BECKY MERCURI

Philanthropy, *see Fund-Raisers*

Phosphates

Phosphates are a class of soft drink flavored with phosphoric acid, which imparts a distinct but flat sourness. Chemists use various methods to produce phosphoric acid, also called acid phosphate, from phosphorus or phosphate rocks.

Phosphates first appeared in the late 1870s as the result of a patent medicine craze. Companies promoting the healing properties of nostrums like Horsford's Acid Phosphate discovered that consumers liked the powder's sour taste, particularly when mixed with sugar and water. Somebody tried adding it to a fruit syrup soda drink, and the phosphate quickly made the leap from the drugstore's medicine counter to its soda fountain. The chemical was usually added to the soda in the form of a solution of acid phosphate mixed with water.

During the 1880s and 1890s, phosphates had a reputation as a "man's" drink (as opposed to "feminine" milk-based concoctions). The basic phosphates were the lemon or orange phosphate (fruit syrup, phosphate, soda water) and the egg phosphate (a regular phosphate with raw egg added). Soda parlors in the downtown business districts served phosphates mixed with malt extracts for indigestion and with wine for a pick-me-up. After 1900, the sex preferences largely disappeared, and phosphates became one of the most popular soda fountain drinks, generally blended with fruit syrups and soda water. Their heyday lasted until the 1930s, when ice cream–based concoctions began to dominate the soda fountain. In the twenty-first century, classic phosphates have all but disappeared except at a handful of "old-time" soda fountains mining the nostalgia craze.

Nevertheless, some of the most popular soft drinks still contain phosphoric acid. Almost all colas are blended with phosphoric acid to impart a hint of flat sourness (while fruit sodas and ginger ales use the more rounded acidity of citric acid). During the 1950s and 1960s, foreign countries like France and Japan tried to ban Coca-Cola as dangerous, because phosphoric acid can block the absorption of calcium. These efforts failed when it was shown that the amounts of the acid were too small to have an effect.

[*See also* Homemade Remedies; Soda Drinks; Soda Fountains.]

BIBLIOGRAPHY

Bonham, Wesley A. *Modern Guide for Soda Dispensers: Introducing New Methods and Modern Ideas*. Chicago: A. O. Ellison, 1897.

Dubelle, George H., ed. *Soda Fountain Beverages; A Practical Receipt Book for Druggists, Chemists, Confectioners, and Vendors of Soda Water*. New York: Spon & Chamberlain, 1917.

Fenaroli, Giovanni. *Fenaroli's Handbook of Flavor Ingredients*. Boca Raton, FL: CRC Press, 2002.

Mitchell, Alan J., ed. *Formulation and Production of Soft Drinks*. New York: AVI, 1990.

Saxe, D. W. *Saxe's Guide, or Hints to Soda Dispensers: Complete and Modern Formulae for the Manufacture and Dispensing of All Carbonated Drinks*. Omaha, NE: Phospho-Guarano, 1890.

Woodroof, Jasper, and G. Frank Phillips. *Beverages: Carbonated and Noncarbonated*. Westport, CT: AVI, 1974.

ANDREW COE

Pickles

The word "pickle" derives from the Dutch *pekel* or German *Pökel*; the method of pickling was brought to North America with the arrival of Dutch colonizers from the Netherlands in the early 1600s. Throughout history, pickles and other preserved foods have made world exploration possible by providing palatable, mobile foods for sailors to eat. They have helped people survive during winter months when many fresh ingredients were not available.

Pickles date from as far back as ancient Mesopotamia (now Iraq), where a variety of foods were preserved in salt-water brine and regarded as delicacies. In the United States cucumber pickles are the most common pickle; but a variety of fruits, vegetables, meats, and fish have been preserved in a liquid combination of brine or vinegar, herbs, or spices—often in sugar or even oil. Pickles can be sour or sweet, salty, hot, or spicy—even pungent.

Although pickles are a favorite snack all over the country, there are many different recipes and traditions for pickles in America. Since pickles can be sweet or sour, made with vinegar or without, pickle enthusiasts do not necessarily agree on one definition. During the height of immigration into New York City around the turn of the last century (from the late 1800s to the early 1900s), an influx of Jews from Eastern Europe arrived and brought with them a specific method of kosher pickling, which was applied mainly to cucumbers but also to sauerkraut (white cabbage), tomatoes, and peppers. The home craft of pickling turned into a lucrative business within the Yiddish-speaking community.

In the practice of koshering (preparing edible foods in compliance with Jewish dietary laws), a rabbi supervises all ingredients and equipment used to make pickles. He ensures that the pickling cucumbers are washed, placed in large wooden barrels, and covered with a combination of kosher salt, dill, spices, and, finally, clean water. The supervising rabbi also sees that the barrels and equipment are not used for anything else. These "kosher" pickles sit, covered in a cool, dark place, for between a few weeks and several months—until the pickles ferment to the desired flavor, color, and texture. Depending on the length of fermentation, the result will be either what are called "fresh pickles" (bright green and mild—almost like salty cucumbers) or "sour" pickles (dull green and highly flavorful). There is also a "half-sour" or "medium-flavored" pickle, whose fermentation time is halfway between that for fresh and sour pickles. Outside New York, America refers to all three as "kosher dills."

Before the opening of Hunts Point Market in the Bronx in 1967—the city's central port for all fresh food distribution—all cucumbers for the pickle trade used to be sold on Ludlow Street on the Lower East Side, a predominantly Jewish neighborhood. Delicatessens abound in New York City, and today a kosher pickle spear is still served alongside deli sandwiches across the city. It remains a strong symbol of New York's culinary heritage.

The English brought with them to America a love for sweet pickles: the cucumbers are first salted, to leech out the bitterness of the peel, then rinsed and covered with hot vinegar, sugar, and spice syrup. The Czechs, Poles, Slavs, and Germans brought with them a passion for mustards and salt-brined and salt-and-sugar-brined cabbage (sauerkraut and sweetkraut, respectively) and for cucumbers made with spices, herbs, and either salt brine or vinegar. The French brought a passion for *cornichons* (gherkins)—tiny, delicate cucumber pickles, heavily flavored with vinegar and spices and served with pâtés, cold meats, and cheeses.

In the early twenty-first century, pickle varieties from all over the world could be made at home or purchased in specialty stores. Some of the most common international pickles popular in America come from Japan, China, and India, where a variety of pickles are served throughout the day at mealtimes.

Home pickling remains a part of fast-paced American family lives, even though it has long been a luxury rather than a necessity; but in the United States most pickles are processed and manufactured commercially and distributed internationally. Pickles are a popular complement to savory foods such as hamburgers, hot dogs, and barbecue; pickled red beets, carrots, cauliflower, and cabbage are also served on their own as appetizers and in salads. In many families, having a plate of pickles at Thanksgiving and Christmas completes a meal.

Although they are not as common as they used to be, homemade pickle prize contests are held annually at county and state fairs across the United States. More than twenty known pickle festivals are held in United States cities where pickle farming and manufacturing directly influence the local economy and help maintain cultural stability; some of the more notable festivals are held in New York, Arkansas, Pennsylvania, Michigan, and North Carolina. Many of these hometown pickle festivals also include live music and theater performances, 5K running races, baby pageants, pickle-eating contests, and cultural and historical exhibits.

As in many countries around the world, pickles have played a role in the history of American folk medicine and dietary practices. For instance, there seems to be an association between pregnancy and eating pickles: pregnant women in America are believed to crave unlikely food combinations such as sour pickles and ice cream. Pickle "juice" (brine) has been used to combat dehydration during extremely hot weather—an old remedy brought to national attention in 2000 by the head athletic trainer for the Philadelphia Eagles football team, who used pickle juice in an elixir he learned from his father, a high school football trainer, to help the Eagles combat heat to win a game. Administering pickle juice to football players during extreme heat has been used by athletic trainers for years, though recent studies have shown that unless the juice is diluted, dehydration, cramping, and fatigue increase. Too much consumption of pickle juice combined with the stress of competition can also make someone ill or aggravate hypertension and heart disease.

Pickles have gone in and out of fashion in the United States, where many fear the sodium in pickles and hence exclude them from their diet. In other countries, especially in Asia and parts of eastern Europe, pickles became an important accompaniment to meals owing to their historical significance in preventing mass starvation and disease during famines and harsh weather. Pickles provided something rich in vitamins for people to eat with staple foods, and they also pleased the palate. It is no wonder that people's relationship to pickled foods runs very deep in those cultures that have relied on them throughout the centuries as a major part of both their diet and their cultural identity.

[See also Delicatessens; Jewish American Food; Jewish Dietary Laws; Pickles, Sweet; Pickling; Preserves.]

BIBLIOGRAPHY

Davidson, Alan. *The Oxford Companion to Food.* Oxford: Oxford University Press, 1999.

Norris, Lucy. *Pickled: Preserving a World of Tastes and Traditions.* New York: Stewart, Tabori and Chang, 2003.

Shephard, Sue. *Pickled Potted and Canned: The Story of Food Preserving.* London: Headline, 2000.

Ziedrich, Linda. *The Joy of Pickling.* Boston: Harvard Common Press, 1998.

LUCY NORRIS

Pickles, Sweet

The noun "pickle" applies to that which pickles as well as to that which gets pickled; hence, a sweet pickle is both a fruit or vegetable that has been preserved in a sugary solution and the sugary solution in which the fruit or vegetable has been preserved. Known the world over in one form or another—for pickling is an ancient solution to the problems of food storage and spoilage, one that has had a lasting impact on virtually all foodways—sweet pickles reach their peak in condiments like mango chutney from India, northern Italy's *mostarda di frutta*, and *umeboshi*, the exquisitely sour Japanese pickled plum.

In the United States, pickles are primarily the products of central European tradition. Pickling begins with vinegar or brine and just about anything deemed edible; American Indians themselves produced a maple-sap vinegar to preserve game in preparation for the winter. Still, the story of American pickles does not really take shape until the early eighteenth century, with the arrival

of the Pennsylvania Dutch. These were mostly "plain people" from Germany ("Dutch" is a misnomer) who managed to settle the countryside around Philadelphia with their Mennonite customs largely intact—including a style of cooking that relied heavily on sweet-and-sour flavor combinations. In fact, Pennsylvania Dutch cookery fairly rests on the notion of the seven sweets and seven sours thought requisite to any feast; sweet pickles made from small cucumbers, particularly gherkins, are just one of many options—but the one Americans have collectively chosen to adopt and to adapt (along with the vocabulary, for both "pickle" and "gherkin" come from the German). Even cursory glances at regional cookbooks reveal a slew of recipes for what are in kind if not always in name sweet pickles, from Refrigerator Pickles, Icicle Pickles, Ripe Pickles, and Chunk Pickles to Candied Dills and curious Garlic Sweet Dills—as well as, of course, Bread and Butter Pickles (so named either for their compatibility with bread and butter, or, as the food critic Craig Claiborne has contended, for the income they bring in). Such recipes contain not only copious amounts of sugar but also spices both sweet and savory, including cinnamon, cloves, celery seed, and mustard seed.

There are, furthermore, numerous variations on the sweet pickle theme more or less popular in American cuisine. Pickled fruits (including strawberries, grapes, and even watermelon rinds) may be less relevant in the twenty-first century than they were in the nineteenth when home canning and preserving was the norm; elaborate, piquant mixed-vegetable relishes like chowchow (adapted from a Chinese preparation) and piccalilli (a gift from India by way of England) are also less popular, but simpler relishes are crucial to an all-American menu of hamburgers and hot dogs; even ketchup, America's sugary version of yet another Chinese invention, captures the essence of the medium. The production of such condiments built corporate giants like H. J. Heinz Company—which, beginning in the 1870s, was the world's first mass manufacturer of sweet pickles.

[See also Condiments; Cucumbers; German American Food; Heinz Foods; Ketchup; Pickles; Pickling; Preserves.]

BIBLIOGRAPHY

Claiborne, Craig. *Craig Claiborne's The New York Times Food Encyclopedia.* Compiled by Joan Whitman. New York: Times Books, 1985.

Shephard, Sue. *Pickled, Potted, and Canned: How the Art and Science of Food Preserving Changed the World.* New York: Simon and Schuster, 2001.

Weaver, William Woys. *Pennsylvania Dutch Country Cooking*. New York: Abbeville Press, 1993.

RUTH TOBIAS

Pickling

Using some sort of liquid or brine—typically a combination of salt, acid, and seasoning—is common to all pickling. It is an old technique for preserving food—older than freezing. Pickling may have begun when people discovered that spice added to salt and vinegar or citrus juice was highly flavorful and could mask foods too bland or rotten to eat.

Pickling is a preservation process that occurs when fresh raw food is introduced into a moderately acidic liquid or brine that denatures fresh foods to the extent that they are no longer raw though not necessarily cooked, thereby temporarily halting spoilage. The acidity in vinegars and citrus juices, or that produced naturally by fermentation, is what "pickles" a food.

In fermentation, safe bacteria in food—for example, *Leuconostoc mesenteroides* or *Lactobacillus plantarum*—break apart sugars to create acid (mainly lactic acid). Moderate acid production helps to preserve food for an extended time in its partially decomposed form by inhibiting the growth of harmful food-borne pathogens. Too much acid, on the other hand, halts the fermentation process.

Acids from fermentation, citrus juice, and vinegar add flavor but also discourage the growth of harmful microorganisms. Food-borne pathogens, such as *Clostridium botulinum* (which causes botulism) and *Escherichia coli*, cannot survive in extreme environments—for example, in pH levels from 2.6 to 4.0.

Refrigeration and freezer storage slow bacteria, often killing them. Canning or processing pickle jars in a hot-water bath with a temperature of 160°F to 180°F for ten to twenty minutes also kills bad bacteria. Airtight containers prevent oxidization and the growth of molds in foods, so pickles should be kept covered or tightly sealed. (Nonreactive bowls, glass jars with lids, and sturdy plastic receptacles are best.) Storing pickles in the sunlight activates fermentation in some pickles but is harder to control, while darkness protects foods from overheating and processing.

Salt is an indispensable ingredient in pickling; indeed, without salt one can hardly be said to have a pickle. Salt controls fermentation, fosters the progression of good bacteria, draws excess—often bitter—liquid from food, firms the texture of food, and concentrates and balances a host of herbaceous, sweet, and spicy flavors. Without salt, fermentation progresses too quickly, and food never becomes sour enough.

The most common pickles in the United States are either brined or fermented. The acid essential for eliminating harmful bacteria (which cause food to rot) in pickles comes from fermenting with salt, or using citrus juice (like lemon juice) or vinegar. Many pickles are salty. Although there are many sweet varieties known in the United States, they still contain a fair amount of salt and nitrites. Pickling retains most of food's original nutrients if they are processed soon after harvesting.

In the last century, during the Great Depression, pickled home-grown food kept many American families from starvation. Home pickling reached its peak of popularity during World War II, when it was people's patriotic duty to grow Victory Gardens and put away their own canned and pickled foods. The United States government even relegated 40 percent of all commercially made pickles to feed the armed forces here and abroad; those who wanted pickles during this time most likely made their own at home. The decline of home pickling has occurred since the 1950s because most Americans believe that they do not need the skill. It is easier to buy commercially made pickles, though many claim they are inferior to homemade.

[*See also* Pickles; Pickles, Sweet; Preserves; Salt and Salting.]

BIBLIOGRAPHY

Davidson, Alan. *The Oxford Companion to Food*. Oxford: Oxford University Press, 1999.
Norris, Lucy. *Pickled: Preserving a World of Tastes and Traditions*. New York: Stewart, Tabori and Chang, 2003.
Shephard, Sue. *Pickled Potted and Canned: The Story of Food Preserving*. London: Headline, 2000.
Tannahill, Reay. *Food in History*. New York: Three Rivers Press, 1988.
Ziedrich, Linda. *The Joy of Pickling*. Boston: Harvard Common Press, 1998.

LUCY NORRIS

Picnic Kits, see Lunch Boxes, Dinner Pails, and Picnic Kits; Picnics

Picnics

Picnics are leisurely outdoor gatherings at which people meet to eat, at tables or on the ground, and socialize.

American picnics are known by other names such as clambakes, corn roasts, corn boilings, oyster roasts, fish fries, wiener roasts, bean suppers, cookouts, and barbecues.

Who goes on a picnic? Everyone picnics: the rich and the poor, loners and more gregarious folk, old-fashioned couples spooning and modern couples libidinously romancing, parents and children, church congregations, and company workers.

When do people picnic? On the Fourth of July, celebrating national independence and the unofficial beginning of summer. On Labor Day, anticipating the fall and the start of the school year. On days off.

As a rule, people go on picnics mostly for the fun, the freedom, and the charm of it. Americans, like other picnickers, prefer the outdoors and hope for that "perfect day for a picnic." Picnics are held in backyards and parks, on beaches and rooftops—wherever a space can be found to spread a blanket or set a table and chairs. American food critic James Beard, an aficionado of picnics, distinguishes picnicking from simply eating alfresco: in *Menus for Entertaining* (1965, revised 1997), he stresses that a picnic requires that you *travel* somewhere to eat, even if you eat while traveling in a car.

Picnicking requires more than a setting, however, for there is the ritual of food preparation and the selection of receptacles for carrying food, supplies for cooking, and the requisite items for serving—and except for modern technologies (thermos containers, insulated baskets, propane stoves, plastic utensils, and the like), these elements have changed little over time. The preparation and service of picnic foods may be casual or cosmopolitan, regardless of social class, wealth, or education: sandwiches, canned soda, and beer thrown into a paper bag, or elaborate baskets fitted with coolers for pâté and roasts and crystal stemware for wine or champagne.

Naming and Representing Picnics

Strangely, given its universality and popularity, the origins of picknicking are unclear, and even the etymology and spelling of the word "picnic" are uncertain. The English word "picnic" is probably a loan word derived from the French *piquenique*—a word of unknown origin that signifies a meal at which each diner pays his share for food to be eaten outdoors (see Gilles Ménage's *Dictionnaire étymologique de la langue Françoise*, 1692). The *Oxford English Dictionary* records 1748 as the first use of "picnic" in English—by Lord Chesterfield, who used it in the sense of an assembly or salon gathering. According to Georgina Battiscombe, whose *English Picnics* is authoritative, by the beginning of the eighteenth century picnics were common events involving an outdoor party during which it was customary to eat a meal of some kind.

The earliest mention in America is of "picnic silk stockings," a satirical phrase used by Washington Irving (or one of his coauthors) in *Salmagundi* (1807) to signify the silliness of women's fashion. Irving's 1855 memoir, *Wolfert's Roost*, suggests that his lunch breaks at school in the 1790s were picniclike, but he does not use the word "picnic." During the eighteenth and nineteenth centuries, the French preferred *pique-nique*, and the English "pic-nic" or "picnic." Irving uses "picnic," but Mark Twain uses both spellings, "pic-nic" in *The Adventures of Tom Sawyer* (1875) and "picnic" in *The Adventures of Huckleberry Finn* (1885).

In the arts, a picnic may be presented as a symbol and a leisure activity. The American artist Thomas Cole's painting *Pic-Nic* (1846), depicts a family and friends picnicking in the Catskill Mountains. The simplicity of the scene conveys a sense of being out of doors that is particularly attractive to city dwellers, while suggesting the grandeur of nature and its spiritual impact on the intellect and passions. A picnic in Louisa May Alcott's *Little Women* (1868) is a pleasant and practical event at which the sisters work and relax outdoors: according to Jo, "Mother likes to have us out of doors as much as possible; so we bring our work here, and have nice times. For the fun of it we bring our things in these bags, wear old hats, use poles to climb the hill, and play pilgrims, as we used to years ago."

The English travel writer Frances Trollope complains, in *Domestic Manners of the Americans* (1832), that

Picnic. From a lithographed advertisement for Royal brand canned fish.

American picnics are too rare and that picnickers are often too rowdy and drunk. Her attempt at picnicking in the forest outside of Cincinnati, Ohio, is a fiasco; the day begins well with packed books and sandwiches but ends poorly with heat, insects, and a lost forest path. The American novelist James Fenimore Cooper refers to a June picnic in his *Home as Found* (1838) as a "rustic fete"; the "customary repast" (whose contents are never divulged) is served, by domestics, on cloths spread on the ground. Picnic debris discarded without care, the precursor of fast food trash, constitutes the "picnic pots and cans" that Owen Wister complains about in *The Virginian* (1902).

Fourth of July picnics are usually celebrations of the United States's national birthday, except in Joyce Carol Oates's novel *Black Water* (1992), in which celebration of the holiday is subordinated to a sexual escapade. Guests feast on a traditional menu of grilled meat; slabs of marinated tuna; chicken pieces swabbed with Tex-Mex sauce; huge, raw red patties of ground sirloin; corn on the cob; buckets of potato salad, coleslaw, bean salad, and curried rice; and quarts of ice cream passed around with spoons.

Labor Day, originally a celebration of the American worker, is often a cause for Picnicking that also marks the end of summer. But in William Inge's play *Picnic* (1953) the picnic is, ironically, not shown, and the food of choice, fried chicken, never gets eaten. When Madge says to Hal, her seducer, that they must get to the picnic, he embraces her and says that the fried chicken will have to wait.

Picnic Customs, History, and Fare

June 10 is celebrated with picnics by African Americans in remembrance of the signing of the Emancipation Proclamation. Angela Shelf Medearis's *The African-American Kitchen: Cooking from Heritage* (1997) suggests a picnic menu of jerk pork, potato salad, pickled beets, red rice, roasted potatoes, and pecan cake.

Two company picnics were held in Henry Louis Gates Jr.'s hometown—one for whites and another for African Americans. In *Colored People: A Memoir* (1994), Gates recalls that there was a traditional meal of fried chicken, and he is nostalgic about how corn was cooked in a huge black cast-iron vat, set on cinder blocks and fueled by pinewood. Gates fondly recalls sipping coffee doused with sweet cream while waiting for the water to boil.

"Dinner on the Grounds" is a midday picnic meal served during revival meetings of Methodists and Baptists in the South and Midwest. Usually held in August, the meal is served at tables covered with white cloths and set up outside the church, though contemporary meals are now often served indoors in air-conditioned splendor.

Other occasions for picnics are homecomings, reunions, and gravecleanings (events at which families meet to socialize and pay tribute to the dead, as described in Clyde Edgerton's *The Floatplane Note Books*, 1988). In the South, picnickers are served traditional meals—a good selection of which is provided by Edna Lewis in *A Taste of Country Cooking* (1977): baked Virginia ham, southern fried chicken, braised leg of mutton, sweet potato casserole, corn pudding, green beans with pork, sliced tomatoes, various pies and cakes, and lemonade and iced tea. More selections are found in Albert Brumley's *All-Day Singin' and Dinner on the Ground* [sic]: *A Collection of Favorite Old Time Songs and Hymns and Choice Recipes from Days of Yesteryear* (1972).

Urban charity picnics for children of the poor were held in post–Civil War New York City in Central Park, and in 1872 the *New York Times* began a series of picnics for the poor children of the working class in the lower wards of New York. Before the summer was over, it was expected that ten to fifteen thousand children would be treated to picnics that included lunches of sandwiches, cake, ice cream, and lemonade.

A "Hoosier barbecue," described by William E. Wilson in Elizabeth L. Gilman's *Picnic Adventures*, was a community picnic. Food was served on wide boards set up on sawhorses that sagged under the weight of roasted corn with butter, potato salad, deviled eggs, ham, cold fried chicken, and burgoo (a stew made with chicken, veal, corn, okra, peas, butter beans, peppers, onions, garlic, and spices). Desserts included layer cakes with chocolate, lemon, and strawberry icing as well as old standbys among pies.

A most unusual picnic was W. C. Fields's three-day southern California picnic tour. As reported by biographer Robert Lewis Taylor in his *W. C. Fields: His Follies and Fortunes* (1949), the picnic began when Fields had his staff fill big wicker hampers with watercress; chopped olives and nuts; tongue; sandwiches of peanut butter and strawberry preserves; deviled eggs and spiced ham; celery stuffed with Roquefort cheese; black caviar; pâté de foie gras; anchovies; smoked oysters; baby shrimps and crabmeat; tinned lobster; potted chicken and turkey; swiss, liederkranz, and camembert cheeses; a bottle of olives; three or four jars of glazed fruit; angel food and devil's food cakes; and a variety of combination sandwiches. There was a case of Champagne (Lanson 1928), several bottles of gin, six bottles of fine dry sauterne, and a case of beer.

On their departure, Fields is purported to have said, "What we've missed, we'll pick up on the way."

Marian Cunningham's thirteenth edition of the *Fannie Farmer Cookbook* (2000) suggests that "a picnic, or just eating out of doors, is a holiday from our daily table." She suggests a variety of basic foods for a picnic basket, such as cold vegetables, scallions, tomatoes, hearts of celery, avocado, cold meatloaf, fried chicken, cold cooked shrimp, and breads. More elaborate picnicking is suggested by James Beard, who believes that at an elegant picnic one might serve stuffed tomatoes, veal and pork terrine, beef à la mode gelée, potato salad or green salad, french bread, butter, cheese, fruit, and angel food cake, all accompanied by lightly cooled Beaujolais or California red wine, cognac, kirsch to go with the cake, and a great vacuum bottle of hot or iced coffee.

Beard's idea of a picnic beer party includes sausage board, Westphalian ham, boiled or baked ham, cold meat loaf, deviled eggs, caviar eggs, pungent eggs, coleslaw, dill pickles, emmenthaler cheese, rye bread, pumpernickel, and butter, and apple kuchen. This contrasts neatly with tailgating picnics held in parking lots before a sporting event, at which spectators gather around their trucks and car trunks, even in subzero or heat-scorching weather, to drink beer and enjoy barbecued meats with names like Beer Butt Chicken, Turducken, Pickled Salmon Burgers with Tartar Sauce, and Garlic Gizzards. (See John Madden and Peter Kaminsky's *John Madden's Ultimate Tailgating* [1998].)

Alice Waters, the renowned American chef who combined French recipes with California ingredients, begins her *Chez Panisse Menu Cookbook* (1982) with an homage to Elizabeth David, the English food critic, who loved French food and picnics. Waters begins with a summer menu, inspired by David, that calls for roasted pepper with anchovies, potato and truffle salad, hard-cooked quail eggs, marinated cheese with olives and whole garlic, roast pigeon with purple grapes, sourdough bread with parsley butter, almond tart, and nectarines, served with red or white Provençal wines with the meal and muscatel with dessert.

The case has been made that picnicking is the inalienable right of every American man, woman, and child. Writing for *Appleton's Journal* in 1869, an unknown writer aptly suggested: "What the full requirements of a picnic may be admits of some range of opinion, but the great charm of this social device is undoubtedly the freedom it affords. It is to eat, to chat, to lie, to talk, to walk, with something of the unconstraint of primitive life. We find a fascination in carrying back our civilization to the wilderness."

[*See also* Barbecue; Clambake; Fourth of July; Lunch Boxes, Dinner Pails, and Picnic Kits.]

BIBLIOGRAPHY

Battiscombe, Georgina. *English Picnics*. London: Harvill Press, 1949.

Craigie, Carter W. "A Movable Feast: The Picnic as Folklife Custom in Chester County, Pennsylvania, 1870–1925." Ph.D. diss., University of Pennsylvania, 1976.

Craigie, Carter W. "The Vocabulary of the Picnic." *Midwestern Language and Folklore Newsletter* 1978: 2–6.

Eyre, Karen, and Mireille Galinou. *Picnics*. London: Museum of London, 1988.

"Picnic Excursions." *Appleton's Journal*, August 14, 1869, 625.

Wilson, William E. "Hoosier Barbecue: Rescue on the Banks of the Wabash." In *Picnic Adventures*, edited by Elizabeth L. Gilman. New York: Farrar & Rinehart, Inc., 1940.

WALTER LEVY

Pie-Making Tools

Pies are a particularly English form dating back to the Middle Ages. Originating throughout Europe as very deep, free-standing meat pies with tough, often inedible crusts that needed no additional support, they came to the colonies as delicate pastry pies that required shaped ceramic pie dishes, or pie plates. These were usually dinner plates of a slightly scooped, rounded shape that helped support the shallow, often sweet fillings. With the expansion of tin manufacturing in the eighteenth century "pie plates" evolved into pieced-tin flat-bottomed pans with flared straight sides. Little jagging wheels were used to cut zigzag edges for lattice tops, and rolling corrugated crimping wheels sealed and decorated the rims of top and bottom crusts. Small hollow pie funnels, later "pie birds" in the shape of blackbirds, were inserted in the top crust to allow steam to escape. Ceramic pie birds have become a popular collectible, and editions of blackbirds, bluebirds, chefs, cartoon characters, and the like have been produced since the 1940s. One-piece rolling pins were fashioned of hard woods both on lathes and by hand and were either evenly cylindrical or tapered at both ends.

ALICE ROSS

Although mass-produced pie pans have been made for well over one hundred years—of stamped tin (then aluminum), enamelware, ceramic, and glass—there has been no need to change their shape. They are still made in shallow and deep-dish versions, usually ranging in diameter between eight and ten inches. Many early to mid-twentieth-century stamped metal pans have embossed advertising; printed underglaze advertising decorates some early twentieth-century spongeware or stoneware pie plates. Inventors have focused on accessories, some of which were meant for the bakeries that began to flourish toward the later nineteenth century. Inventions included pie markers that marked off segments of a pie and stamped a letter on the top crust ("P" for Peach, "H" for Huckleberry). Pie cutters and crimpers were patented as early as the 1860s, along with "improved" jagging wheels; some crimpers effected the look of pinched or twisted crust edges if the crimper was simply rolled once around the rim of the pie.

Inventors of kitchen tools have taken great interest in rolling pins, constantly seeking the perfect coolness, weight, ease of use, and nonsticky surface. A pin with double rollers was patented in 1867 by Albert Taylor of Vermont, who also in 1867 patented a flour-sprinkling rolling pin, which dusted flour over the dough as you rolled it. Glass pins that could hold ice water were tried, and a number of combination-tool pins were sold widely: Some pins made mostly of tin came apart into components including a funnel, a doughnut cutter, a nutmeg grater, and a pie crimper. Sets of matching pins and pastry "boards" (made of tin or enameled sheet iron) from the 1890s on were made to hang on the wall between uses. Probably the strangest rolling pin ever made was the "Magnus," a round-framed red-and-white plastic affair with eight hotdog-like rollers and an arched handle, made in the 1940s by the Magnus Harmonica Company.

LINDA CAMPBELL FRANKLIN

Pies and Tarts

As a favored dish of the English, pies were baked in America as soon as the early settlers set up housekeeping on dry land. Beyond mere preference, however, there was a practical reason for making pies, especially in the harsh and primitive conditions endured by the first colonists. A piecrust used less flour than bread and did not require anything as complicated as a brick oven for baking. More important, though, was how pies could stretch even the most meager provisions into sustaining a few more hungry mouths.

Without the resources of brick ovens, or even the open-sided metal boxes known as Dutch ovens or tin kitchens, colonial cooks often made cobblers—also called slumps or grunts—and their cousins, pandowdies, in pots over an open fire. In these types of pies, a filling made of fruit, meat, or vegetable goes into a pot first; then a skin of dough is placed over the filling, followed by the pot's lid. As cobblers cook, the filling stews and creates its own sauce and gravy, while the pastry puffs up and dries. After the cobbler is served, the diner has a choice of breaking the dough and stirring it into the filling or eating it separately on its own. Pandowdy is made the same way—and almost exclusively with fruit—but differs in that, after the crust is partially baked it is pushed into the filling, where it swells with the filling and becomes much like a dumpling.

The surrounding countryside offered the newcomers a rich array of fillings, not only fruits and berries that were akin to those the settlers knew back home, but also unknown vegetables and game they discovered with the help of Indians. When the apple spurs the Pilgrims brought with them matured into flourishing fruit-bearing trees, apple pie quickly dominated the American table, because the abundant fruit was easy to dry and store in barrels during the winter. On many a farm and across miles of pioneer trails, breakfast, lunch, and dinner were often composed of little more than a thick slice of dried-apple pie.

The Evolution of the American Pie

No one, least of all the early settlers, would probably proclaim their early pies as masterpieces of culinary delight. The crusts were often heavy, composed of some form of rough flour mixed with suet that resulted in what one visitor to the colonies reported was a crust that "is not broken if a wagon wheel goes over it" (Bennington, 1992). Pie refinement had to wait until the arrival of new immigrants—most notably religious sects from Germany, who came in search of William Penn's tolerance, and aristocratic Frenchmen and their followers fleeing the French Revolution.

The German Amish and Mennonite immigrants, who were soon lumped together under the misleading designation "Pennsylvania Dutch," have contributed to the country's pie history recipes that are distinguished for their resourcefulness and ingenuity in the use of indigenous ingredients—not so much sweet as aromatic—and eloquently spiced. The most famous of Pennsylvania

Dutch pies is the shoofly pie: thick with molasses, its crust as dense as a cookie, and made most often for the breakfast table. While they took pride in their thrift, the Pennsylvania Dutch were robust gourmets, inventing crumb pie, made with little more than flour, sugar, and nutmeg; cheese pie, which is actually a cheesecake in a pie shell; and, for special occasions, goose liver pie, which blends rich foie gras with lemons, Madeira, veal, and wild mushrooms.

The French may be thanked, first, for introducing butter into American piecrusts, thereby turning the pie from a mere subsistence food into an elegant dessert. In addition, although tarts, galettes, and pâtés were known and enjoyed by many colonists before the guillotine drove so many highborn French and their partisans to American shores, as the French lingered here these pie variations became more popular. Tarts are essentially open-face pies (though occasionally they may sport a lattice top) and are shallower than ordinary pies, with straight instead of sloping sides. More often than not they contain a sweet and delicate filling made of fruit, preserves, or custard (and sometimes all three). Galettes are flat round French cakes, the most celebrated in France being the so-called Twelfth Night cake. In America, a galette is often a free-form open-face rustic tart, but it may also be considered the missing link in the murky evolution of the Boston cream pie, that much beloved half-cake, half-pie mutt comprising a cake topped with vanilla pastry cream and satiny chocolate icing. Pâté is easily defined as any forcemeat devised of meat or fish entirely encased in dough; it is the only French export that has not become completely assimilated into American cuisine.

Regional Variations

The common pie continued to sustain people from many nations as they poured into the new country and spread westward over virgin territory. Dried apples played an essential role in both wagon trains and cattle drive mess; and when the apple barrel was empty, canny cooks came up with mock apple pie, the best known being one made from crushed crackers. (Even in our more established times, the makers of Ritz crackers continue to tout this creation by printing the classic recipe for mock apple pie on its box.) Vinegar-soaked potatoes also made an acceptable apple substitute. Other equally ingenious mock fillings invented on the westward trails included sour green tomatoes (substituted for mincemeat) and soft-shell river turtles (substituted for everything from oyster to chicken pie).

CHESS PIE

A chess pie (or tart) is a single-crust pie with a filling made from eggs, sugar, and cream or buttermilk. It belongs to a long English tradition of sweet, egg-rich, custard pies. As to the origin of the name "chess pie," explanations abound. According to the culinary historian Karen Hess, the most plausible is that "chess," an archaic spelling of the word "cheese," derived from so-called cheesecakes, which were common in England from the seventeenth century. Many early cheesecakes did not contain cheese, and this was the tradition that was infused into "chess pie." The earliest located reference to a recipe with the name "chess pie" dates to 1866. During the late nineteenth century, chess pies became common, particularly in the South. There is a great diversity among chess pie recipes, which can include such flavorings as chocolate, lemon, vanilla and vinegar.

BIBLIOGRAPHY

Randolph, Mary. *The Virginia House-Wife*. With historical notes and commentary by Karen Hess. Columbia: University of South Carolina Press, 1983. 1824 edition in facsimile with additional material from the editions of 1825 and 1828.

BARRY POPIK AND ANDREW F. SMITH

Once pioneers came to a stop and found a piece of land to call their own, their pies reflected certain regional differences. Some were due to a region's economy—such as the lingering hold of molasses-sweetened pies in southern states, which was influenced by the proximity of the molasses trade and the rum-and-slave trade with the Caribbean Islands, while pies made with maple syrup ruled across the northern states, where Indians taught the newcomers how to tap the syrup from surrounding trees. On the great dairy farms of the Midwest, cream and cheese pies became favorites; blessed with groves of native pecan and black walnut trees, the Southwest won renown for nut pies. Swedish immigrants in the upper plains states made fish and tart berry pies plentiful, while Cornish and Finnish immigrants in Michigan's Upper Peninsula region established a certain reputation for pasties and meat pies. Florida bakers turned native limes into Key lime pie, while those in Kentucky took chess pie, a silky classic of the southern plantation's table, and added bourbon to the rich mix of sugar, cream (or buttermilk), and egg filling. In northern states, where pumpkins have always been plentiful, a preference for pumpkin pie generally holds; below the Mason-Dixon Line, where sweet potatoes have been commercially grown since the mid-1600s and were a vital source of nutrition for African American slaves, the populace dreamed of creamy sweet potato pie.

The Diminishment of Pies

The hold that pies had on America's diet began to loosen in the 1870s, coinciding with a growing social concern for the poor and working class. The new science of nutrition, especially as it was embraced by Wilbur O. Atwater, a chemist on the faculty of Wesleyan University, set about attacking the poverty and social ills afflicting both slum dwellers and the hordes of immigrants flooding into the cities by trying to change how and what the populace ate. Atwater argued that much of what the underclass suffered could be mitigated if they turned away from the prevailing American diet—which was based on too many carbohydrates, especially in the form of sweets—in favor of a diet rich in protein. His ideas materialized in the New England Kitchen Movement, which began setting up communal kitchens and conducting cooking classes in settlement houses. Unfortunately, the movement's menu was based on bland soups, chowders, and beans, and even the hungry poor could not see the attraction. The movement fared even worse with immigrants when it attempted to steer them away from native foods toward more insipid dishes.

Atwater and his followers did succeed in securing an acceptance of domestic science as a legitimate field. The new nutritionists, as they came to be called, found a tireless advocate in Sarah Tyson Rorer, a noted cooking teacher and the food editor of the influential *Ladies' Home Journal*. In article after article, she championed the forward-thinking virtues of the new science and warned her middle-class readers about consuming food that took a lot of energy to digest—which often resulted, she wrote, in "nervous prostration and headaches." She expressed particular indignation about pies and took pains to condemn them at every opportunity.

The food fads that rattled the country throughout the 1890s and into the next century magnified the harmful effects of the country's reliance upon pies. But new realities in the twentieth century also helped to lessen the number of pies baked and eaten in American homes. Industrialization and urbanization had quickened the pace of life and resulted in more women working outside the home. Women joined the workforce in record numbers after World War I, and except on farms, where the presence of homebound women was crucial, pie making became only an occasional undertaking. Concerns about ingesting so much fat and flour lingered long after most of the nineteenth-century food crazes vanished—though as attitudes about beauty changed, Americans were more obsessed with the size of their waists than with the health of their internal organs.

Pies in the Modern World: A National Emblem Reclaimed

Yet even while pies were relegated to an occasional Sunday treat and appearances at holiday meals, they lingered as an abiding symbol of the American home. Through the various world struggles of the twentieth century, popular culture continually invoked pies as the embodiment of the nation's abundant goodness. With the end of World War II and with women, reluctantly or happily, returning to the home, pies experienced a small rebound in fashion.

There was one difference, however: Advances in food science and technology had hatched all manner of ingredients that caused the making of a pie to become less of a challenging art form. Delicate cream and chiffon fillings became foolproof with the availability of instant-pudding mixes. Fruit, in heavy syrup that would readily congeal, was sold in cans. That age-old stumbling block to a flawless pie, the crust, was made easier to achieve as well. Joining the ranks of ready-made crusts already available in stores, frozen in an aluminum tin, or sold in a box to be mixed with a little water, women's magazines and newspapers' "lifestyle" sections divulged recipes for quick crusts constructed out of little more than cookie and cracker crumbs. Well into the 1960s and 1970s, crusts shaped from the likes of potato chips, popcorn, and canned fried onion rings graced many a dinner-party table. If crusts were no longer flaky (or even very tasty), if fillings were not as delicately redolent of cream, eggs, and butter—or of the bracing savor of freshly picked fruits and the simmer of stewed meat—at least pies were once again being baked and enjoyed on more of a regular basis than they had been in a century.

Giant food corporations were responsible for some of the stranger pie creations of the later twentieth century. Companies hired teams of nutritionists to concoct ways to make their brand-name products into pies, giving birth to such infamous offspring as the Jell-O and Cool Whip pie, the Frito-Lay corn chip pie, Bisquik's series of "miracle" pies (the ingredients for the crust and the filling were all mixed together right in the pie pan), and the Hershey Bar pie.

It is a marvel, perhaps, that a country so burdened with inferior pies would continue to yearn for them at all. Perhaps what kept them alive were the fine examples often stumbled upon in family restaurants and roadside diners, where impeccable renditions of lemon meringue, coconut cream, or banana cream pie always seemed to be waiting. And across the land, there is hardly a state or county fair at which a table or two isn't laden with the blue-ribbon pride of local bakers, each a perfect sphere suffused with personal and provincial history.

By the early 1980s, when a renewed interest in exploring America's culinary roots took hold, pies were being rediscovered. The overarching theme of pies today is their universality, embracing a dizzying array of cross-cultural influences. Pies may no longer play such an essential role in America's diet, but their sublime place in our collective heritage assures that they will always be savored.

[See also Desserts; Pasties; Pastries.]

BIBLIOGRAPHY

Levenstein, Harvey A. *Revolution at the Table: The Transformation of the American Diet*. Berkeley: University of California Press, 2003.

Luchetti, Cathy. *Home on the Range: A Culinary History of the American West*. New York: Villard, 1993.

Nichols, Nell B., ed. Farm Journal's *Complete Pie Cookbook*. Garden City, NY: Doubleday, 1965.

Purdy, Susan G. *As Easy as Pie*. New York: Ballantine, 1984.

Root, Waverly, and Richard de Rochemont. *Eating in America*. New York: Ecco Press, 1981.

Sokolov, Raymond. *Fading Feast: A Compendium of Disappearing American Regional Food*. New York: Farrar, Straus and Giroux, 1981.

Willard, Pat. *Pie Every Day: Recipes and Slices of Life*. Chapel Hill, NC: Algonquin Books of Chapel Hill, 1997.

PAT WILLARD

Pig

Pigs belong to the order Artidactyla, hoofed and even-toed animals, and the family Suidae, which is subdivided into five genera, nine species, and many subspecies. Pigs are not native to America. They arrived as immigrants who had accompanied human travelers from the Old World. Only one species is widespread on the American mainland, the European *Sus scrofa* or *Sus domesticus*, the domesticated pig. The peccary, an animal resembling the pig and occu-

pying similar ecological niches, is indigenous to the Americas. Its distribution is mainly South American, but the collared peccary (*Tayassu tajacu*) or javelina has a range extending into the southwestern states.

Early History

The earliest swine domestication appears to have been in mainland Southeast Asia sometime in the eighth millennium B.C.E. Versions of these pigs were brought to Polynesia by Asian migrants and were the first in what is the twenty-first-century United States when Polynesians entered Hawaii about 1000 C.E. European domesticated pigs came later. These descend from wild boars that were bred in the Mediterranean region and the Continent. By the era of the Roman Republic two breeds had emerged: short-legged pigs kept in small spaces; and long-legged animals that lived in forests and were kept by swineherds. It is unclear which of these was first brought to the New World, but most likely the Spanish pigs were long-legged and the French and English pigs were the more domestic versions.

Pigs came to North America along with Spanish explorers and settlers in the sixteenth century but not directly from Europe. Until the introduction of canned foods, long-distance sailing ships carried live animals destined for the galley. For Spaniards of the time, pigs were the meat of choice. Christopher Columbus brought eight pigs to Hispaniola on his second voyage (1493–1496) and within a decade pigs had spread to every new Spanish colony in the Caribbean. When Hernando de Soto set out across the southern states to find gold in 1538, he brought thirteen pigs from Cuba. By the time of his death in 1542, his herd had grown to seven hundred. Some escaped and formed the basis of a vast colony of feral pigs, sleek, swift animals with large tusks, later known as "razorbacks." These were to be an important food source for native peoples and European explorers and settlers. With the Spanish colony at Saint Augustine in Florida (1565) and settlements in New Mexico around 1600 the pork-rearing industry was established.

French and English colonists brought their own pigs in the seventeenth century. Jamestown, founded in 1607, eventually had so many "swarm like Vermaine upon the earth," that attempts were made to sequester them on "Pig Island." Foraging pigs decimated shellfish beds in the Massachusetts Bay Colony's tidal flats, while in New York a wall was built to control feral porkers. Pigs routinely wandered the streets of Boston, Philadelphia, and New York well into the nineteenth century. Nativists,

RAEDER ON THE PIG

Ole Munch Raeder was a jurist sent by the Norwegian government to America to study the jury system in 1847. His observations in newspaper articles and dispatches were read by an avid Norwegian public back home. This is one of them about the glorious pig:

I cannot refrain from saying a few kind words on behalf of the favorite pet of the Americans, the swine. I have not yet found any city, county, or town, where I have not seen these lovable animals wandering about peacefully in huge herds. Everywhere their domestic tendencies are much in evidence, no respectable sow appears in public unless she is surrounded by a countless number of beloved offspring. These family groups are a pleasing sight to the Americans, not only because they mean increasing prosperity, but also because a young porker is a particularly delicious morsel. Besides, the swine have shown certain good traits which are of real practical value; in the country they greedily devour all kinds of snakes and the like, and in the towns they are very helpful in keeping the streets clear "cleaner than men can do" by eating all kinds of refuse. And then, when these walking sewers are properly filled up they are butchered and provide a real treat for the dinner table.

As with everything else that is typically American, this fondness for pork is most noticeable in the West.

BRUCE KRAIG

such as the Know-Nothings of the 1850s, blamed the new Irish immigrants for this deplorable situation, while happily gorging upon pork themselves. As Ole Munch Raeder, a Norwegian visitor in 1847, put it:

In New York war has been declared against these animals; it was decreed that any pig found walking the streets of New York after the first of July of this year should be outlawed and become the property of anyone who could catch it. I do not know if the law was dropped or if a common feeling of sympathy prevented its execution, but at any rate I have seen pigs wandering about just as freely as ever, even after that ominous day, on Broadway itself, and evidently with perfect peace of mind, just as though no one had ever thought of depriving them of life, liberty, and the pursuit of happiness.

Pig Ecology

Three qualities made pigs so successful in the New World: their extraordinary adaptability, their fecundity, and their intelligence. The pig's natural habitat is varied, consisting mostly of forests and moors, but also open land thickets, brush and grasslands, dry savannas, and rain forests. Having no sweat glands, pigs need shaded areas, water, or wet mud to cool off. Like humans, they are omnivores, eating wide varieties of vegetable material, from roots and fungi to bulbs, nuts—especially acorns—and even leaves. Animal proteins in the pig diet include insects and larvae, worms, eggs, frogs, mice, snakes, young birds, and carrion. Contrary to popular lore, pigs are picky if voracious eaters (they must eat frequently because they have small stomachs), and only in dire circumstances do they eat garbage. The pig's nose is a highly sensitive food finder. The pig's sense of smell is so keen that it can find delicacies hidden under the earth and readily root them up. Brought to the New World where there were only a few predators to hunt them—wolves, some larger cats, and humans—pigs adapted rapidly to the propitious environments. In the warmer South with its greater biomass, its water, and its pine and deciduous forests, pigs flourished. That pork is a traditional staple of the regional diet is not surprising. Even in the North, with cold winters, pigs also did well. Their remarkable foraging abilities and herd societies allowed them to survive and increase.

Wild pigs have considerable reproductive capacities, even more so in farming situations. With individuals living from twelve to fifteen years and producing litters of three to eight young each year, sometimes more, populations can

Pigs in the Street. Engraving, nineteenth century. *Culinary Archives & Museum at Johnson & Wales University, Providence, R.I.*

grow exponentially. Pigs are social animals with a matriarchal social structure, strength in numbers being a key survival strategy. Animal ethologists estimate that among mammals pigs rank fourth in intelligence, at least by human standards. In the wild they are wily, learn rapidly, and have long memories, as pet pig owners know. The Barnum and Bailey Circus featured a troupe of musically trained pigs described as "showing almost human intelligence and reason." Further anecdotal evidence of pig intelligence from hunters and farmers is voluminous.

Visitors to the United States in the eighteenth and nineteenth centuries often commented on the enormous herds of swine they saw in town and country. However useful pigs were to colonist and traveler alike, they cause damage to ecological systems in areas to which they have been introduced. In places like Hawaii and Michigan's Upper Peninsula feral pigs have driven out native species by eating their food and sometimes eating their young. Rooting has caused erosion along waterways and has disturbed plant communities almost everywhere, especially in Appalachian regions. By wallowing in fresh waterways pigs have been known to spread *E. coli* and other pathogens. The concentrated density of pigs in twenty-first-century factory farms has caused a number of environmental problems, ranging from pollution of groundwater by manure to appalling odors from the decomposition of pig wastes. Valuable as pigs have been to humans, in massive numbers they pose problems.

Pig Breeds

Europeans did not import pigs as cherished pets, but as food animals. In America semi-domesticated pigs were the rule into the nineteenth century depending on the region and were dubbed "hogs" once reaching maturity regardless of gender. Living on mast, or nuts that accumulate on the forest floor, they were prized for their fatty meat and their lard. Purebred pigs created with specific attributes, such as greater reproductive abilities, to produce specific kinds of meat or bacon, appeared in the later eighteenth century and most modern breeds are nineteenth-century creations. Thomas Jefferson may have begun the trend by importing Calcutta pigs (*Sus indicus*) in the early nineteenth century. The same Asians had been imported to England in the 1770s and bred with the native animals to produce the classic Yorkshire. This new breed was lighter, longer, and produced leaner meat and is considered to be the mother breed from which many others emerged. Yorkshires may have been imported to eastern Pennsylvania before 1812 and certainly appeared in Ohio in the 1830s.

Hampshires are probably the oldest non-crossbred race in the United States. They have black and white belts and were common in the northern border regions of England and Scotland. Hampshires were brought to the United States around 1825 and made their way to Kentucky where they flourished. Called "Thin Rind," they were prized for their size, robustness, and foraging abilities. Before long, butchers in Cincinnati (dubbed "Porkopolis") began to buy them in great numbers at good prices and it is quite likely that the celebrated Smithfield hams came from Hampshires.

Other imported breeds include large-bodied Berkshires (1823), bacon-producing Tamworths (1882), Landraces (1895), prolific Meishans from China (1989), and in the 1980s the Vietnamese Potbelly, an Asian dwarf developed about twenty years earlier. The members of this dwarf species average from 70 to 150 pounds and are kept as pets, not usually as potential human food. Except for Potbellies, each of the imported pigs was transformed into a popular American breed.

The two breeds in widest use are the Poland China and the Duroc. Poland Chinas are neither Polish nor Chinese but were developed in Ohio supposedly by a farmer of Polish descent. They were probably a mixture of unknown local pigs and the Kentucky Hampshire. The Poland China is a hardy, lean animal that breeds abundantly. The Duroc, once known as Duroc-Jersey, is a red pig and was developed in New York and New Jersey. It is said that the Duroc descended from African pigs brought both by Columbus and in the slave trade, but that has not been proved. Jersey Reds, dating to at least the 1820s, were prized for their rapid weight gains. Durocs appeared in the 1830s in New York and apparently descend from Berkshires. They, too, are rapid weight gainers and it is this quality that makes both Poland Chinas and Durocs popular with hog farmers.

Pigs as Food

From the colonial era until the mid-twentieth century many farm families who raised hogs did their own slaughtering. Either free-ranging and lured to farms with corn, or fed on corn and skim milk during the whole year and kept in pens, fat hogs were ready for slaughter in the late autumn or winter. In Appalachia, where Hampshires were common, 250 pounds was considered the best weight for meat and lard. In other regions, Poland Chinas

Pig Butchering. Engraving, nineteenth century. *Culinary Archives & Museum at Johnson & Wales University, Providence, R.I.*

BIBLIOGRAPHY

Horwitz, Richard P. *Hog Ties: What Pigs Tell Us about America.* Minneapolis: University of Minnesota Press, 2002.

Malcolmson, Robert, and Stephanos Mastoris. *The English Pig: A History.* London: Hambledon Press, 1999.

"Meat for the Multitudes." *National Provisioner* 185, no. 1 (July 4, 1984).

Pukite, John. *A Field Guide to Pigs.* Helena, MT: Falcon Publishing, 1999.

Raeder, Ole Munch. *America in the Forties: The Letters of Ole Munch Raeder.* Translated and Edited by Gunnar Malmin. Minneapolis: University of Minnesota Press, MN, 1929.

www.factoryfarm.org

www.iastate.edu/outreach/agriculture/pork

BRUCE KRAIG

and Durocs were preferred, and the same weight was considered optimum. Hog-killing time was one of the year's special events. Families and neighbors gathered to share in the festivities. The selected animal was brought to the site, shot between the eyes, then quickly turned over so that a knife could be inserted into its heart. Draining blood was important in obtaining good meat. After scalding in large kettles the hog was debristled and cut up. Families delighted in gorging on various parts of the pig, such as roasted pancreas (called "melt"), brains, and other parts. Various cuts, such as hams, were set aside for curing and smoking. Some of the meat was ground and stuffed into cloth sausage bags or made into patties, fried, set into containers, and covered with lard for use during the rest of the year. Making lard was especially important because it was the culinary fat of choice in rural America well into the twentieth century.

Hogs became a commodity in the nineteenth century with industrialization of slaughtering, rendering, breeding, and rearing. The twenty-first-century hog industry utilizes economies of scale with large farms of two thousand animals or more dominating the market. Scientific research, often done at land grant universities, has optimized every aspect of pigs' lives, from comfortable housing to feeding, optimal breeding, disease control, and waste removal. Like most twenty-first-century foods, pigs have been genetically modified so as to be unable to live in the wild. And, unlike former days when farmers knew their animals by personality and even name, pigs have become anonymous lumps of protein.

[*See also* Butchering; Chorizo; Goetta; Meat; Mid-Atlantic Region; Sausage; Scrapple; Smoking; Southern Regional Cookery; Spam; Stuffed Ham; Vienna Sausage.]

Piggly Wiggly

Clarence Saunders opened the original Piggly Wiggly at 79 Jefferson Street, Memphis, Tennessee, on September 6, 1916. It was the first self-service grocery store in America and changed forever the way Americans shopped for food.

Saunders (1881–1953) was born in Virginia and left school at the age of fourteen to clerk at a general store. In those days customers told clerks what they wanted and the clerks gathered the goods from the shelves. In 1900 Saunders became a traveling salesman for a wholesale grocery distributor where he observed that many small grocers were suffering because of heavy credit losses and high overhead.

Saunders's patented self-serve invention gave each customer a basket into which they placed individually priced items while walking through well-stocked aisles before visiting the checkout counter. Consumers had the benefit of greater variety, lower prices, and quicker shopping.

Saunders enjoyed causing speculation about the source of the name Piggly Wiggly. Some thought the idea may have occurred while he was riding on a train, looking out the window, and saw several little pigs struggling to squeeze under a fence. Or was it inspired by "this little pig went to market"? Saunders never squealed. When asked why the name Piggly Wiggly, Saunders merely replied, "So people will ask that very question."

Clarence Saunders loved the concept of self-service, and so did his customers. The Piggly Wiggly Corporation issued franchises to hundreds of grocery retailers who operated stores according to Saunders's rigid specifications on a strictly cash basis. Stores gave shoppers more for their food dollar through high-volume, low-profit-margin retailing. Refrigerated cases kept produce fresher, employees wore

PIGGLY WIGGLY

San Marcos, Texas

PIGGLY WIGGLY offers within easy reach famous foods from everywhere. Crisp, fresh fruits and vegetables, and the finest quality meats obtainable anywhere. We list only a few of our prices for Friday and Saturday, April 28 and 29.

Banquet—Extra Fancy
TEA, ¼ lb. 15c   ½ lb. 29c
COCOA, Hershey's 1 lb. can 17c
Kellogg's
CORN FLAKES, large pkg. 9c
Stokely's
HOMINY, No. 2½ can 8c
Premier—Vacuum Can
COFFEE, 1 lb.   26c
Fancy Peaberry, lb. 20   Fancy Rio 15c
Libby's
PINEAPPLE, Gallon can 39c
CATSUP, Ruby, 14 oz. 10c
P & G or Crystal White
SOAP, 3 giant bars   10c
Staley's
SYRUP, ½ gal. .....25c   Gallon 45c
PICKLES, quart sour 14c
MEAT, fresh or cured, The Best

Piggly Wiggly. Price list from a Piggly Wiggly store in San Marcos, Texas, 1933. *Collection of Alice Ross*

uniforms, and shelves were stocked with Piggly Wiggly's own national brand.

Saunders began issuing stock in his Piggly Wiggly Corporation and for some time it was successfully traded on the New York Stock Exchange. He began planning the construction of a mansion in Memphis to be built of pink marble from Georgia. Then, in the 1920s, due to unwise investments, Clarence Saunders lost control of his Piggly Wiggly stores and declared bankruptcy. He began another chain, "Clarence Saunders, Sole Owner of My Name Stores," which enjoyed some success but the chain closed during the Depression. Saunders chose the brand name "Keedoozle" (Key-Does-All) for the prototype of an automated grocery store that the indefatigable entrepreneur designed and constructed in 1937. At the time of his death in October 1953, Saunders was working on another

automatic store system that he called "Foodelectric." It never opened.

By 1929, Piggly Wiggly was the second-largest group of grocery stores in the nation. The Piggly Wiggly Company was owned by Fleming Companies Inc., headquartered in Dallas, Texas, at the beginning of the twenty-first century.

The enduring genius of Clarence Saunders is most evident in the familiar logo of the happy pig with the jaunty little, white cap that, in the early 2000s, smiles beamingly on more than eight hundred Piggly Wiggly stores in twenty-one states. The independent retailers of the Piggly Wiggly family recognize their grocery stores as the dream of an American original.

Saunders's ornate, pink Georgian marble mansion, where the entrepreneur never actually lived, was donated unfinished to the city of Memphis for use as a museum in the late 1920s. The Memphis Pink Palace, Tennessee's most visited museum, features a shrunken head, a hand-carved miniature circus, and a replica of the original Piggly Wiggly supermarket.

[See also Food Marketing; Grocery Stores.]

BIBLIOGRAPHY

Piggly Wiggly. http://www.pigglywiggly.com. The official Piggly Wiggly website provides a detailed biography of Saunders and a history of the corporation.
Rath, Sara. *The Complete Pig.* Stillwater, MN: Voyageur Press, 2000.

SARA RATH

Pillsbury

Charles A. Pillsbury (1842–1899) bought one-third of the Minneapolis Flour Milling Company in 1869. By the early 1870s, using modernized equipment to process the local spring wheat at several mills, his company was producing two thousand barrels of flour a day. Renamed C. A. Pillsbury and Company in 1872, it adopted the trademark "Pillsbury's Best XXXX" (the four exes constituting a medieval symbol for top quality).

Pillsbury installed "middlings purifiers" in 1871, implementing a process developed at the Washburn Mills (later to become General Mills) that removed dark specks of hull, producing whiter flour. In the-mid 1870s, Pillsbury began using a Hungarian innovation that he saw on a visit to Europe, involving sets of iron and porcelain steamrollers that crushed and disintegrated the wheat, replacing traditional millstones; all of the bran and wheat germ was removed, producing an even whiter and longer-lasting flour and boosting production by 3 percent. Pillsbury's brother sold the leftover bran as animal feed.

The company was expanding rapidly, and in 1882 it built a huge new facility, called the "A Mill," which was the largest flour mill in the Western Hemisphere. By 1889, the mill was producing almost seven thousand barrels of flour a day. The company continued to innovate and grow throughout the 1880s, helping Minneapolis become the leading flour-producing city in the United States.

An English financial syndicate acquired C. A. Pillsbury in 1889 along with Washburn Mills, creating Pillsbury–Washburn Flour Mills. Led by Charles Pillsbury, it was the world's largest miller, producing fifteen thousand barrels of flour a day. In 1923 Charles's sons and a nephew bought out the English owners and formed Pillsbury Flour Mills.

The new company began producing cake flours and cereals in 1932. Throughout the 1940s it specialized in kitchen staples, introducing the first convenience baking product, Pie Crust Mix, in 1945, and cake mixes in 1948. To celebrate the company's eightieth birthday, a contest, the Pillsbury Bake-Off, was held in 1949 at the Waldorf Astoria Hotel in New York City.

Pillsbury acquired Ballard and Ballard Flour in 1950 and introduced fresh dough products, followed by refrigerated cookie dough in 1957. The Pillsbury Doughboy was introduced in a television commercial for Crescent Rolls in 1965. In the succeeding decades, Pillsbury made many major acquisitions worldwide: Burger King in 1967, Totino's Pizza in 1975, Green Giant in 1979, the Steak & Ale restaurant chain in 1976, and Häagen-Dazs ice cream in 1983.

After twenty-seven years of steady growth, involving over two hundred products in fifty-five countries, losses began to mount in the mid-1980s, particularly in the restaurant sector. Pillsbury was acquired in a $5.75 billion hostile takeover in 1989 by the U.K.-based food and spirits company Grand Metropolitan. Pillsbury's fortunes improved under GrandMet (renamed Diageo after a merger in 1997), and acquisitions continued: Country Hearth bread in 1993, Martha White mixes and flours in 1994, and Pet in 1995, including Old El Paso Mexican foods, Progresso, and Pet-Ritz pie crusts.

In October 2002, Pillsbury was sold to General Mills, its long-time rival, for $10.4 billion, creating the world's fifth-largest packaged food company. After a Federal Trade Commission review, several Pillsbury brands, including Martha White, Pillsbury baking mixes, and Softasilk flour, were sold to avoid antitrust concerns.

[*See also* Pillsbury Bake-Off; Pillsbury Doughboy.]

BIBLIOGRAPHY

American National Biography, s.v. "Pillsbury, Charles Alfred." New York: Oxford University Press [electronic resource], 2000.
International Directory of Company Histories, vol. 13. Edited by Tina Grant. New York: Pillsbury Company, 1996.

JOY SANTLOFER

Pillsbury Bake-Off

Pillsbury's Grand National Recipe and Baking Contest—dubbed the Bake-Off (now a Pillsbury trademark)—was inaugurated in 1949, marking the company's eightieth anniversary and the postwar return to normal home life. Each recipe submitted was required to use a half-cup of Pillsbury's flour, and contestants (mostly women, mostly

Pillsbury Bake-Off Winner. Bake-off winner with Ronald Reagan. *Culinary Archives & Museum at Johnson & Wales University, Providence, R.I.*

homemakers) responded with from-scratch pies, cakes, cookies, crisps, cobblers, doughnuts, dumplings, quick breads, and yeast breads. Submissions were winnowed down by a team of home economists, and the finals were held at the Waldorf Astoria Hotel, where one hundred electric stoves filled the ballroom. The winner, for her No-Knead Water-Rising Twists (that is, sweet rolls) was Mrs. Ralph E. Smafield of Detroit; her $25,000 Grand Prize was presented by Eleanor Roosevelt, who also served as a judge. (The Grand Prize became $1 million in 1996.)

In 1951, Jack Meili became the first male prizewinner, taking second place in the junior division with wiener-filled "Hot Ziggities." (Creative nomenclature is a Bake-Off tradition.). Over the years, the use of Pillsbury convenience products—notably cake, cookie, and frosting mixes and refrigerated dough—was encouraged, and "quick and easy preparation" became a judging standard.

An illustrated booklet published after each Bake-Off affords the winning recipes wide distribution, and early Bake-Off booklets (especially the first one) are sought-after collectibles. Browsing through them yields fascinating insights into a half century of baking in America, and quite a few of the winning recipes have become national favorites.

[*See also* Pillsbury; Pillsbury Doughboy; Recipes.]

BIBLIOGRAPHY

Best of the Bake-Off Collection. Chicago: Consolidated Book Publishers, 1959.

BONNIE J. SLOTNICK

Pillsbury Doughboy

In 1965 Leo Burnett's Chicago ad agency, known for creating many endearing trademark critters to build brands, was assigned the Pillsbury refrigerated-dough account. In search of a character, creative director Rudy Perz whacked a tube of dough on the table and imagined what might pop out. A seven-and-one-half-inch-tall Doughboy, weighing the equivalent of two and one-half cups of flour, did. The little fellow was a natural, an outgrowth of the product itself, who would go on to become the perfect spokesboy.

But first he needed a voice. Perz auditioned fifty actors before choosing Paul Frees, who also provided the voice of Boris Badenov in *The Adventures of Rocky and Bullwinkle* cartoon series. One of the twelve different dialects Frees used featured the catchy "Hoo, hoo" giggle that, along with the tummy poke, would become the Doughboy's signature.

The Doughboy was soon ready for his first TV commercial. In it he jumped out of a container of Crescent Dinner Rolls and danced a two-step on the kitchen counter. He introduced himself as "Poppin' Fresh, the Pillsbury Doughboy" and announced Pillsbury's slogan, "Nothin' Says Lovin' Like Something from the Oven, and Pillsbury Says It Best."

Although the Doughboy has become hipper over the years, at times rapping or playing blues harmonica in commercials, his personality has not changed much. He has always been helpful, trustworthy, likable, friendly, charming, and adorable, some might even say irresistible. His appearance too has remained the same—small and plump, with a doughy white complexion. He always sports a large chef's hat, a neckerchief, and a big smile. In addition to having a delightful personality, he is a versatile, multitalented little guy, having appeared as a ballet dancer, singer, musician, painter, rap artist, teacher, poet, Cupid, business executive, announcer, skateboarder, and even a cuckoo in a cuckoo clock.

The Doughboy's role, however, has changed over time. Originally envisioned as the ideal homemaker's helper, he was the main character in early commercials. He offered encouraging words and helped out in the kitchen. His job was to convince consumers that Pillsbury's products were as good as those made from scratch. In the 1970s and early 1980s, when he was considered dated, he made only cameo appearances in commercials, showing up for a belly poke and a giggle at the end of each ad. By the late 1980s, however, he was found at center stage in starring roles, like strumming air guitar for Pillsbury Cinnamon Rolls. His later tasks were more closely focused on the products. He is likely to highlight a product attribute—for example, to close up a resealable package.

The Doughboy quickly captured the hearts of Americans and held onto them. By 1968 he was recognized in a random sampling by nine out of ten Americans, giving him a recognition factor similar to that of the president of the United States. In 1987 he won *Advertising Age*'s "Whom Do You Love?" contest. *Advertising Age* considers him to be number six of the top ten advertising icons of the twentieth century.

[*See also* Advertising; Pillsbury.]

BIBLIOGRAPHY

Pillsbury Classic Cookbooks. *Poppin' Fresh Recipes: Appetizers to Desserts—The Doughboy Picks His Favorites.* Minneapolis: Pillsbury Co., 1990.

SHARON KAPNICK

Pimiento Cheese Sandwich

Pimiento cheese has often been called the "comfort food" of the American South, where the sandwich filling is usually homemade in either a cooked or uncooked version and served on white bread. The basic mixture includes grated cheddar or American cheese combined with mayonnaise, chopped canned pimientos, salt, and pepper. Various additions include mustard, cayenne or hot red pepper sauce, garlic, lemon juice, Worcestershire sauce, or horseradish. Researchers have been unable to discover the origin of pimiento cheese, but its popularity has been noted since the availability of hoop cheese in country stores. A recipe for Pimento (sic) Sandwich appeared in the *Up-to-Date Sandwich Book* (1909) by Eva Greene Fuller. By the Depression, pimiento cheese sandwiches were served as a popular and economical meal throughout the United States. They were even featured on luncheon menus of some restaurants, including the Hotel Barbara Worth in El Centro, California, where, in 1930, the sandwich was priced at thirty cents. Pimiento cheese remains a favorite homemade sandwich filling, and in the South, it is also a popular topping for hamburgers and hot dogs.

[*See also* Cheese; Sandwiches; Southern Regional Cookery.]

BIBLIOGRAPHY

Mercuri, Becky. *Sandwiches That You Will Like.* Pittsburgh, PA: WQED, 2002.

BECKY MERCURI

Pineapple

The pineapple (*Ananas comosus*) originated in South America, probably in the area around the Orinoco and Negro river basins. Technically, it is not a single fruit but the fruits of a hundred or more separate flowers that grow on a central plant spike. As they grow, they swell with juice and pulp, expanding to become the fruit. There are two major pineapple cultivars: the Smooth Cayenne from Venezuela, which is cultivated for its large, juicy fruit and lack of spines on its leaves, and the Red Spanish from the Caribbean.

In pre-Columbian times, pineapples grew widely in Central America and the Caribbean, where they were called *anana*. Caribbean Indians introduced the pineapple to early Spanish explorers, who, noting that it resembled a pinecone, called it *piña*, from which the English word derives. The Spanish promptly shipped some pineapples back to Spain, where they became an instant sensation. Pineapples were disseminated to Africa and Asia during the sixteenth century. While pineapples thrived in tropical climates, European gardeners had to grow them in hothouses for the wealthy.

In North America, English colonists imported pineapples from the Caribbean beginning in the seventeenth century. The pineapple became a symbol of hospitality in America; pineapple motifs were common in the decorative arts of colonial America, including in architecture, furniture, gateposts, and silverware. Pineapple recipes appeared in English cookbooks during the eighteenth century and in American cookbooks by the early nineteenth century. Mary Randolph's *Virginia House-wife* (1824), for instance, includes a recipe for pineapple ice cream. Over the decades several attempts were made to cultivate pineapples commercially in Florida and California, but growers were unable to compete with lower-cost production in foreign lands.

Pineapples were also canned in small quantities in Florida and the Caribbean by 1882. The major American pineapple industry started in Hawaii. Pineapples had appeared in Hawaii well before it became a U.S. territory in 1898. Plantations grew pineapples that were shipped to West Coast American cities, but this was expensive. Canning in Hawaii began in 1885 but was of little importance until Jim Dole founded the Hawaiian Pineapple Company in 1901. Pineapple production increased dramatically. By 1911, 95 percent of all Hawaiian pineapples were canned and sent to the mainland. By 1921 pineapple was Hawaii's largest crop and industry.

The vast increase in supply created the need to expand the market, and pineapple growers encouraged publication of pineapple recipes, which soon appeared in cookery magazines and cookbooks. For instance, Riley M. Fletcher-Berry's *Fruit Recipes* (1907) included thirty-four pineapple recipes, among them pineapple beer, champagne, muffins, fritters, and omelets. Around 1909 the Hawaii Pineapple Growers' Association issued its first advertising cookery booklet encouraging Americans to serve pineapple in new ways. During the following decade, the cost of canned pineapple decreased until it was affordable to almost all Americans. Cookery magazines and cookbook authors published hundreds of recipes using canned pineapple, including such dishes

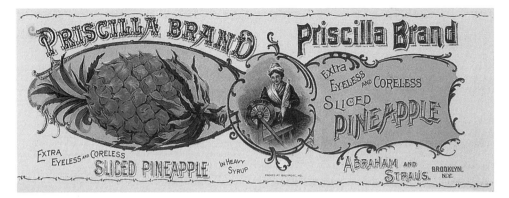

Pineapple Label. Label for Priscilla brand sliced pineapples. *Warshaw Collection of Business Americana, Archives Center, National Museum of American History, Behring Center, Smithsonian Institution*

as hollowed-out pineapple boats for edible presentation of cold salads, vegetables, or fruits; pineapple upside-down cake; and numerous dishes with pork, seafood, and poultry.

Until the 1960s Hawaii supplied almost three-quarters of the world's pineapples, but urbanization and labor costs encouraged Dole and other growers to transfer production to the Philippines, Thailand, and Costa Rica. By 2002 Hawaii produced less than 10 percent of the world's pineapple crops. But pineapple remains a staple in the American diet.

[*See also* Advertising Cookbooklets and Recipes; Canning and Bottling; Fruit; Randolph, Mary.]

BIBLIOGRAPHY

Hale, Marion Mason. *The Kingdom that Grew Out of a Little Boy's Garden.* Honolulu, HI: Hawaiian Pineapple Company, 1929.

Hyles, Claudia. *And the Answer Is a Pineapple: The King of Fruit in Folklore, Fabric, and Food.* Burra Creek, NSW, Australia: Milner, 1998.

ANDREW F. SMITH

Pinedo, Encarnación

Encarnación Pinedo (1848–1902), cookbook author, wrote the first cookbook by a Hispanic in the United States. *El Cocinero Español* (The Spanish Cook) is a landmark, the only contemporary record of what Californios (the original Spanish colonists in California and their descendants) ate and how they prepared it. Through the nineteenth century the Californios lost their social, political, and economic dominance to the Anglo Americans. Encarnación Pinedo deliberately attempted to keep her cultural foodways from disappearing by compiling this cookbook, printed in San Francisco in 1898.

Encarnación Pinedo's family suffered considerably during the Anglo takeover of California. Her first ancestor in California was her great-grandfather Nicolas Berreyesa, who arrived in the San Francisco Bay area with the De Anza expedition in 1775. His son, her grandfather José Berreyesa, received a land grant for the Rancho San Vicente. It included the very valuable New Almaden quicksilver mine, which was to become a source of tragedy and litigation for the prominent family. José married Maria Bernal, and their daughter, Maria del Carmen, was born in 1811. As the Americans established control over California, they lynched or shot eight Berreyesa men, including Encarnación's namesake uncle. José himself was murdered by Kit Carson in 1846.

Maria del Carmen married an Ecuadoran, Lorenzo Pinedo, and they had two daughters, Dolores, born April 29, 1845, and Encarnación, born May 21, 1848. Lorenzo died suddenly of cholera in 1852 when Encarnación was only four. Encarnación received a secondary education at a well-regarded convent school, the Notre Dame Academy in San Jose, but she then conformed with Mexican custom and devoted her life to caring for her widowed mother. When Maria del Carmen died in 1876, Encarnación was twenty-eight, considered too old to marry. Her sister, however, had married an Anglo, much against the family's wishes. We know that by 1880 Encarnación was living in her sister's household and cooking for the family. Her book was published when she was fifty, and on April 9, 1902, she died at fifty-three.

In *El Cocinero Español* Pinedo comments on the insipidity of English food, and we may infer that she feels the same way about the American foodways familiar to her brother-in-law. Her book is one of the most comprehensive cookbooks published in California in the nineteenth century. Most California cookbooks of the period were much smaller. Her book includes some 880 recipes in which she demonstrates a liberal use of spices, chilies, vinegars, and wines. No American cookbook of the time includes more than a few Mexican (usually called "Spanish") recipes. The sophistication of her recipes is striking, their range remarkable. Pinedo includes recipes not only from Mexico and Spain but from France and Italy as well. The nuns of her convent school may have had a library of cookbooks, and San Francisco was certainly a bookish city with European connections.

Pinedo was not a professional writer. She took some of her recipes from published sources; some recipes are detailed while others are sketchy, and they are written in different and inconsistent voices. Nonetheless, *El Cocinero Español* is a major culinary work, clear evidence that the Mexican community in California harbored cooks of great sophistication showcasing a wealth of flavors that were not widely known in the Anglo community until decades later.

[*See also* California; Mexican American Food.]

BIBLIOGRAPHY

Pinedo, Encarnación. *El cocinero español: Obra que contiene mil recetas valiosas y utiles para cocinar con facilidad en diferentes estilos.* San Francisco: Imprenta de E.C. Hughes, 1898.

Pitt, Leonard. *The Decline of the Californios: A Social History of the Spanish-Speaking Californians, 1846–1890.* Berkeley: University of California Press, 1966.

Strehl, Dan, ed. and trans. *Encarnación's Kitchen: Mexican Recipes from Nineteenth-Century California.* Berkeley: University of California Press, 2003.

DAN STREHL

Pine Nuts

Pine nuts are the seeds of any member of the pine tree family (Pinaceae). Pine nuts were commonly consumed by Native Americans. Piñon nuts (*Pinus edulis*) were particularly important to pre-Columbian Native Americans in the Southwest. They were eaten raw or roasted. Roasted nuts were ground into flour, then mixed with cornmeal to make bread. Pine nuts are an important wild food but have been minimally commercialized. Old World pine nuts have been imported into the United States, and Italian pignoli are the kind most commonly available here. Pignoli are sold shelled and are used in pasta dishes and sauces as well as cakes and cookies.

[*See also* Native American Foods; Nuts.]

ANDREW F. SMITH

Pinole

Pinole is flour or powder made of toasted maize and also the beverage prepared by dissolving the powder in water or milk. Sugar, other sweeteners, or flavorings such as chocolate, vanilla, or cinnamon may be added. Pinole (from the Nahuatl *pinolli*) belongs to the category of maize-based *atole* gruels used by native peoples in Mexico and the American Southwest. Because pinole requires no cooking, the Aztecs found it ideal food for travelers. Spanish explorers quickly adopted it, and pinole became a staple among Hispanic settlers as well as Native Americans. In *Commerce of the Prairies* (1844), a classic account of the Santa Fe trade, Josiah Gregg likened pinole to the "cold flour" of the northern Plains Indians, used by hunters and fur-trappers, and noted that some tribes made a similar product from dried mesquite beans. Pinole is still used by elderly people in Hispanic and Native American communities.

[*See also* Corn; Native American Foods, *subentry* Before and After Contact; Southwestern Regional Cookery.]

BIBLIOGRAPHY

Coe, Sophie D. *America's First Cuisines.* Austin: University of Texas Press, 1994.

Gilbert, Fabiola Cabeza de Baca. *Historic Cookery.* Santa Fe, NM: Ancient City Press, 1970. First published 1939.

Gregg, Josiah. *Commerce of the Prairies.* Edited by Max L. Moorhead. Norman: University of Oklahoma Press, 1990. Originally published in 1844.

Santamaria, Francisco J. *Diccionario de Mejicanismos*, 3rd ed. Mexico: Editorial Porrua, 1978.

CHERYL FOOTE

Pioneers and Survival Food

From the arrival of the earliest settlers to the closing of the American frontier, pioneers in the wilderness depended on food supplies for their survival. They prepared by bringing staples, seeds, and as much animal stock as they could transport over difficult terrain, and depended on skills and equipment for foraging, hunting, and fishing. The first stage of life on the frontier often lasted a relatively short time, sometimes only two or three years, before the area's growth could support trade and supplies from the outside. The timing depended largely on available transportation. For example, Ohio River settlements, benefiting from the river's commerce, grew beyond the frontier stage far more quickly than remote areas of the Smoky Mountains.

Survival strategy drove emigrants to arrive at the last possible moment, that is, with enough time to become established before the freezes but not so early as to use up staples needed to get them through the winter. They packed using information from published lists of recommendations. Most brought preserving salt, flours, beans, salt pork, bacon, molasses, and perhaps a little tea and sugar. Those who could also brought draft animals, cattle, pigs, and "dung hill fowl" (poultry). In later years, rice, dried apples, and potatoes were added; these were supplemented by foods from the wild.

Good foraging was essential while waiting for field crops, gardens, and herds and flocks to become productive. Hunting, trapping, and fishing were often the major sources of food, but they provided a boring and scurvy-producing diet. Foraged nuts, fruits, berries, greens, and roots added occasional seasonal diversity—dried cattail roots or processed acorns made palatable starches, and English tea was replaced with infusions of monarda or of red sumac berries.

At first, frontier fields and gardens on newly worked soils yielded uncertain results. Depending on the time of arrival and plant requirements, northern gardens yielded corn, beans, squash, and pumpkins, and assorted root vegetables that dried easily or stored well. Gardens planted late were limited to short-season plants, such as peas and greens. Cabbages and parsnips, which withstood cold when mulched, were wintered in the ground and dug as needed. Southern settlers found longer growing seasons and had more flexibility in what they planted. Ethnic cuisines were perforce adapted to materials at hand. In emergencies it was sometimes possible to obtain corn or meat from Native Americans; eating one's breeding stock or seed was the last resort.

Cooking utensils were also limited—often a large iron pot, a frying pan, some tinware, and a teakettle, supplemented by home-fashioned implements. With little equipment and heavy demands on time, newcomers cooked very simply, frequently making one-dish meals of meats, root vegetables (when at hand), corn, and beans. Improvised cookery made use of hot embers and ash to bake flatbreads and ash cakes, root vegetables, and meats. Roasting methods included planking (securing meat or fish to the face of a split log propped before the fire), string roasting (suspending a roast near the heat from a length of twisting homemade string), or spit-roasting on a green branch. Foods were abundant, and were preserved by drying and smoking; customary preservatives (sugar, vinegar, and salt) were scarce. Although many settlers did not survive this harsh regimen, large numbers of the young and healthy lived to enlarge their holdings and prosper.

[*See also* Frontier Cooking of the Far West; Hearth Cookery.]

BIBLIOGRAPHY

Burlend, Rebecca, and Edward Burlend. *A True Picture of Emigration: or Fourteen Years in the Interior of North America.* London: 1848. Reprint edited by Milo Milton Quaife. Secaucus, NJ: Citadel Press, 1974.

Cooper, William. *A Guide in the Wilderness; or, The History of the First Settlement in the Western Counties of New York, with Useful Instructions to Future Settlers.* Dublin: Gilbert and Hodges, 1810. Reprint, 5th ed. Cooperstown, NY: Freeman's Journal, 1965.

Heckewelder, John. *The Travels of John Heckewelder in Frontier America.* 1817. Edited by Paul A. W. Wallace. Pittsburgh: University of Pittsburgh Press, 1958. Reprint, Pittsburgh: University of Pittsburgh Press, 1985. One of the best of many journals describing the frontier.

Stratton, Joana L. *Pioneer Women: Voices from the Kansas Frontier.* New York: Simon and Schuster, 1981. First-hand memories.

Wilder, Laura Ingalls. *Little House on the Prairie* and others in the series. 1935. Reprint by Harper and Row, 1971. Remarkably accurate details of frontier life.

ALICE ROSS

Pistachios

The pistachio (*Pistacia vera*) is native to central Asia, where it has been cultivated for over nine thousand years. The ancient Greeks consumed pistachios, and the nuts were introduced to Italy in the first century C.E. The first pistachio seeds were planted in California and several southern states in 1854, but the trees did not thrive. Pistachio nuts were imported, and recipes for them published in American cookbooks by the early twentieth century. In 1929, William E. Whitehouse, an American plant scientist, planted pistachio seeds from Persia (Iran) in California's San Joaquin Valley, where they thrived. The nuts became popular during the 1930s, when they were largely sold to immigrant groups and distributed through vending machines. In 1976, the first major crop of pistachio nuts was harvested in California, which, in the early 2000s, was the world's second-largest producer. Roasted pistachio nuts in the shell are an addictive snack; the nuts are also used in pastries, cakes, confectionery, and ice cream, and pistachios appear in some savory dishes as well. The nuts are a good source of protein and several important minerals.

[*See also* California; Nuts.]

ANDREW F. SMITH

Pizza

Also called "pizza pie" or "tomato pie," pizza is a flatbread dough made with flour, yeast, salt, olive oil, and water, topped with various combinations of meats, cheeses, and vegetables, and baked in a very hot oven. In the United States, the combinations of pizza toppings are imaginative and seemingly unlimited.

Pizza came to America at the end of the nineteenth century with immigrants from southern Italy. Italian immigrants built commercial bakeries and backyard ovens to produce breads they had eaten in Italy. In addition, Italian bakers used their ovens for flatbreads: northern Italians baked focaccia, while southern Italians made pizza. Initially, pizza was made by Italians for Italians, but by the late 1930s after the Great Depression many Americans were eating pizza in Italian restaurants and pizzerias on the East and West Coasts.

The first American cookbook recipe for pizza appeared in *Specialità Culinarie Italiane, 137 Tested Recipes of Famous Italian Foods*, a fund-raising cookbook published in Boston in 1936. That recipe, for Neapolitan pie or *Pizza alla Napolitana*, directed that pizza dough be hand-stretched until it was one-quarter-inch thick. The dough was topped with salt and pepper, Scamozza (Scamorza) cheese, tomatoes, grated parmesan cheese, and olive oil, in that order. There were no ingredients for the pizza dough itself; instead, the reader was told that the dough "can be purchased in any Italian bake shop."

Over time, two basic and distinct styles of American pizza appeared. A thin-crust pizza, commonly called "East Coast" or "New York" style, is made with just a few toppings like *pizze* made in Naples. A common type of thin-crust pie is topped with a light tomato sauce, shredded fresh whole-milk mozzarella, and sprinkled dried oregano. After baking, the thin crust should not be too crisp; it should be flexible so that a piece of pizza can be folded in half lengthwise.

The crust of thick- or double-crust pizza, also called "West Coast" style, serves as a foundation for a larger number and amount of toppings. Pizzas with several meats, various vegetables, such as artichoke hearts, zucchini, mushrooms, olives, and onions, with a spicy tomato sauce, and two or three cheeses are not uncommon.

There are several uniquely American pizzas. Deep-dish, or "Chicago style," pizza originated at Pizzeria Uno on East Ohio Street in Chicago in 1943. It is made and baked in a twelve- or fourteen-inch round metal pie pan that has two-inch-deep sides. The pizza dough is placed in the pan, stretched to cover the bottom, and pressed up the sides of the pan. To fill the crust, sliced mozzarella, chunky chopped tomatoes, and sweet Italian sausage are layered on top. "Stuffed" pizza is a type of Chicago deep-dish. After the bottom crust is filled with chopped spinach and mozzarella and parmesan cheeses, a second thinner crust is added. The second crust is topped with a spicy crushed tomato sauce.

California or "gourmet" pizza originated in 1980 at Chez Panisse, a restaurant in Berkeley, California. The Chez Panisse pizzas were lighter; the dough was very thin, often creating a crackerlike crust. Reflecting the philosophy of the restaurant, the pizza toppings were simple combinations of a few fresh ingredients or flavors. Chez Panisse used non-Italian cheeses that came from local suppliers. Many pizzas had no tomatoes and no tomato sauce.

Many Americans make pizza at home. Some people prefer their homemade pizza baked on a square or round thick ceramic tile, called a pizza stone. When a pizza stone is placed in a kitchen oven and preheated, the stone mimics a hearth. For people who do not want to make fresh dough, a premade pizza crust, such as Boboli produces, can be purchased at most food stores. For those who prefer their pizza assembled and ready to bake, most pizzerias sell take-and-bake pizzas, while grocery stores sell unbaked frozen pizzas.

Any doubt about pizza's place in mainstream American culture was erased when pizza was mentioned in an Academy Award–nominated song from the 1953 movie *The Caddy*. "That's Amore," sung by Dean Martin and Jerry Lewis, included the sing-along line: "When the moon hits your eye like a big pizza pie, That's amore."

[*See also* Fast Food; Italian American Food; Pizza Hut; Pizzerias; Take-Out Foods.]

BIBLIOGRAPHY

Bruno, Pasquale, Jr. *The Ultimate Pizza: The World's Favorite Pizza Recipes—From Deep-Dish to Dessert.* Chicago: Contemporary Books, 1995.
Reinhart, Peter. *American Pie: My Search for the Perfect Pizza.* Berkeley, CA: Ten Speed, 2003.

ROBERT W. BROWER

Pizza Hut

Pizza Hut is an international chain of quick-service pizza restaurants, founded in Wichita, Kansas, in 1958. Significant in food history, Pizza Hut was primarily responsible for popularizing pizza, bringing a food item previously available only from pizzerias in urban Italian neighborhoods into American standard cuisine. Through extensive franchising, Pizza Hut successfully introduced pizza to consumers in small towns across the United States, and eventually throughout the world.

The success of Pizza Hut has more to do with the late-1950s revolution in fast-food franchising than with any tradition of Italian immigrant cuisine. With no experience in pizza-making, but looking for income to pay their college tuition, brothers Dan and Frank Carney borrowed six hundred dollars from their mother to open their first pizza restaurant in a rented brick building. The brothers needed a name for their restaurant. On a tight budget, they decided that they could afford only to modify the existing sign on their roof; it had room for eight letters, with the first five already spelling "Pizza" left over by the previous tenant. One of their relatives said that their small building resembled a hut and suggested that the word "Hut" be added to the sign. It fit, and the Carneys had their company name. Pizza Hut's success was immediate. With their new restaurant generating sizable profits, the Carneys abandoned their education, instead expanding their operation and selling franchises. Midwestern consumers loved their pizza, and franchises sold quickly. As their chain grew to eighty-five restaurants by 1965, the brothers established a uniform architecture featuring a sweeping red roof, common marketing strategies, and company-wide standards for customer service. At the peak of their expansion the Carneys were opening a new restaurant every day.

Though Pizza Huts offered inside seating, over half of their business was done on a take-out basis, enabling them to compete with other types of fast food. The appeal of their pizza, however, had its cultural and regional limitations. Consumers accustomed to authentic pizza from Italian pizzerias did not like Pizza Hut's bland fare. Frank Carney quickly adapted his pizza to suit local tastes, sacrificing product uniformity throughout his chain for the sake of profitability. In addition to regional variations, he soon also offered customers a thin-crust pizza, a thick, Chicago-style pan pizza, sandwiches, and several pasta dishes. Heightened competition from a growing number of pizza chains in the 1970s proved to be a greater threat than regional preferences. California-based Shakey's Pizza Parlors and Omaha's Godfather's Pizza spread quickly, competing for eat-in customers, while the streamlined, low-overhead operations of Domino's and Little Caesar's came to dominate the take-out market. Even advances in frozen-food technology undercut the pizza market, providing consumers with a new array of lower-cost pizza choices in grocery store freezer cases.

While still enjoying a comfortable lead in their industry in 1977, with 1,246 company-owned outlets and 1,075 franchisees, the Carneys sold Pizza Hut to PepsiCo Inc. for over $300 million in PepsiCo stock. PepsiCo retained Frank Carney as head of the company, but he soon resigned, first to become a large-scale franchisee for the Chi-Chi's Mexican food chain, and later a franchiser for competitor Papa John's Pizza. The pizza industry was highly saturated by the late 1980s, but Pizza Hut continued to thrive as a PepsiCo subsidiary by offering such new and innovative pizza products as Super Supreme, Sicilian Pan, Priazzo, Calizza, and Hand-Tossed Traditional Pizza. In the 1990s new products included the Personal Pan, the Bigfoot, Stuffed Crust, Italian Chicken, and Big New Yorker pizzas and spicy chicken wings. Expansion into new markets grew even faster than the menu. Still dominating the domestic United States pizza industry, in the early twenty-first century PepsiCo concentrated on spreading Pizza Hut around the globe.

[*See also* Fast Food; Frozen Food; Italian American Food; Pizza; Pizzerias; Take-Out Foods.]

BIBLIOGRAPHY

Gumpert, David E. *Inc. Magazine Presents How to Create a Successful Business Plan: Featuring the Business Plans of Pizza Hut, Software Publishing Corp., Celestial Seasonings, and Ben and Jerry's.* Boston: Inc Pub., 1996.
Luxenberg, Stan. *Roadside Empires: How the Chains Franchised America.* New York: Viking Press, 1985.

DAVID GERARD HOGAN

Pizzerias

Colloquially called "pizza parlors" or "pizza joints," pizzerias are restaurants that have high-temperature ovens specially designed and constructed to bake pizza. The type of oven significantly influences the pizzeria's products and, consequently, helps define the restaurant.

Some pizzerias have wood-burning hearth ovens that can attain temperatures of 850°F. These ovens must be manned by skilled pizza makers who by training and experience know how to form a pizza by hand, how to use a pizza peel (a large, long-handled wood or metal paddle) to load the oven, when to rotate the pizza in the oven for even baking, and when to remove the pizza from the oven. An experienced pizza maker can produce up to one hundred pizzas per hour in a single wood-burning hearth oven. Because of the high temperature of the oven, a thin-crust pizza placed on the preheated hearth cooks quickly. The crust of the pizza will be very dark and crisp from the high heat of the hearth and it may have a distinctive wood-smoke taste.

Gas or electric commercial pizza ovens bake at 600–650°F. Although these lower-temperature ovens are easier to use, they retain the advantage of producing a pizza baked on a solid deck of very hot baking stone or metal.

High-volume pizzerias use conveyor-belt ovens and mechanically formed pizzas. Dough rounds are formed with a press or rollers and then the pizzas are placed side by side on a continuous stainless steel belt that moves them through the oven. The pizzas are cooked by a heat source below the belt. Experience is not necessary; anyone can place an unbaked pizza on the belt at one end of the oven and pick up a fully baked pizza at the other end. Conveyor-belt systems also allow pizzas to be baked and served in nontraditional settings such as snack stands in warehouse discount stores and twenty-four-hour-a-day pizza operations on cruise ships.

The first American pizzerias were started by Italian immigrants who built hearth ovens similar to those they had in Italy. On the East Coast, immigrants from southern Italy built brick hearth ovens, usually fueled by coal, to bake Neapolitan-style pizza. It is generally agreed that Gennaro Lombardi, an immigrant from Naples, opened the first licensed American pizzeria in New York's Little Italy in 1905. Expansion of the pizza business was slow. Anthony ("Totonno") Pero, one of Lombardi's employees, opened Totonno's, a coal-fired brick-oven pizzeria, at Coney Island in 1924. Another Lombardi employee, John Sasso, opened John's Pizzeria in New York's Greenwich Village in 1929.

On the West Coast, northern Italian immigrants built hearth ovens to bake Italian breads and the Ligurian specialty flatbread, focaccia. Commercial Neapolitan pizza arrived much later: the first West Coast pizzeria, Lupo's, opened in San Francisco in 1936. For non-Italians, Lupo's pizza was called "tomato pie."

In the United States there are two pizzeria business forms, independent and franchise. Independent pizzerias are owned and operated by the same person, family, or company and operate within a small, well-defined urban area. It is not uncommon for an independent chain to have two or three locations. The largest American independent pizza chain in terms of gross sales is Amici's East Coast Pizzeria, with seven locations in the San Francisco Bay Area. Founded by two East Coast natives, this independent offers pizza in the styles of New York, Boston, Philadelphia, and New Haven, as well as traditional Italian-style thin-crust pizzas baked in gas-fired hearth ovens. The chain's top ranking among independents reflects an efficient and prompt home-delivery system, which includes ordering via the Internet.

Franchise Standards

Franchise pizzerias dominate American pizza. A franchise is a license that grants to one person (the franchisee) the right to own and operate the franchisor's business and sell the franchisor's brand-name product in a limited geographical area. This territorial limit protects the franchisee from competition within the defined market. The franchisee also obtains the right to operate a facility with the brand owner's distinctive design and signage. The owner helps the franchisee in the operation of the business and usually enforces standards of quality. Thus, franchise products appear to be uniform regardless of who actually makes them or where they are purchased.

Shakey's, in 1954, was the first pizzeria to franchise. Fifty years later the leading franchise pizzerias were Pizza Hut, Domino's Pizza, Papa John's, and Little Caesar's Pizza. These large franchises had thousands of locations and annual gross sales in the billions of dollars.

Franchise pizzerias from America's Midwest turned Italian pizza into American fast food. Pizza Hut, which originated in Wichita, Kansas, and started franchising in 1959, made pizza into a roadside attraction. Pizza Hut restaurants with uniform architectural style and matching logo signage presented a recognizable image to passing motorists. Although Pizza Hut offered sit-down dining, high-speed pizza production in infrared conveyor ovens contributed to a substantial carryout business. Domino's, which started in Ypsilanti, Michigan, in 1960, refined high-speed pizza production with a limited menu of pizza and Coca-Cola. At one time, Domino's promised home delivery within thirty minutes of receiving a telephone order.

Many American pizzerias sell sections or "slices" of a pizza pie, an offering seldom seen in Italy. The pizzeria will bake several different pizzas and cut them into sections. The cut pizzas are placed under heat lamps and the individual slices are sold as fast food. Since the price of all the slices is greater than the cost of a whole pie, selling pizza by the slice is profitable for the pizzeria. From the customers' point of view, there is no waiting for a whole pie to bake, and a couple of slices of different pizza make a quick lunchtime meal. The most successful slice operations are located near schools and universities, catering to students' need for fast food.

[*See also* Fast Food; Italian American Food; Pizza; Pizza Hut; Roadside Food; Take-Out Foods.]

BIBLIOGRAPHY

Jakle, John A., and Keith A. Sculle. *Fast Food: Roadside Restaurants in the Automobile Age.* Baltimore: Johns Hopkins University Press, 1999.
Monaghan, Tom, with Robert Anderson. *Pizza Tiger.* New York: Random House, 1986.

ROBERT W. BROWER

PL480, *see International Aid*

Plastic Bags

Polyethylene, the material from which most plastic bags are made, was developed in 1933 by Reginald Gibson and Eric Fawcett at the British industrial behemoth Imperial Chemical Industries. It evolved into two forms: low-density polyethylene (LDPE), and high-density polyethylene (HDPE). LDPE is the most common plastic used to make wraps, films, and packaging materials. The first plastic bags to be widely used were green plastic garbage bags, invented by Harry Wasylyk for hospital use in his native Winnipeg, Manitoba, Canada. Union Carbide Corporation bought the invention from Wasylyk and his partner, Larry

Hansen, and the company manufactured the first green garbage bags under the name Glad Bags.

Food spoilage, long known to be accelerated by exposure to the elements, was attacked first by use of Saran plastic film (pioneered by The Dow Chemical Company during World War II) and then by the introduction of plastic food storage bags. Baggies and plastic sandwich bags on a roll were introduced in 1957 to compete with waxed-paper bags then in use. The advent of the folded-lip opening in the 1960s made the use of plastic sandwich bags much more practical. By 1966 plastic produce bags had been introduced in grocery stores.

In 1968 the S. C. Johnson Company test-marketed Ziploc polyethylene food storage bags, which sealed airtight using interlocking grooves and a bead along the bag's opening. The food storage bags were officially launched in 1972, followed by sandwich bags in 1975 and various other specialty Ziploc bags for freezing and storing fresh vegetables in later years. A different plastic, polyethylene terpthalate (PET), came into use in the 1980s for pouches in which food can be boiled. In 1977 the first plastic grocery bag was introduced to the supermarket as an alternative to paper sacks. At the end of the century four out of five grocery bags used were plastic.

[*See also* Plastic Covering.]

BIBLIOGRAPHY

Fenichell, Stephen. *Plastic: The Making of a Synthetic Century.* New York: Harper Business, 1996.
Heller, Steven, and Anne Fink. *Food Wrap: Packages That Sell.* Glen Cove, NY: Graphic Details, 1996.
Mossman, Susan, ed. *Early Plastics.* London: Leicester University Press, 1997.
Oswin, C. R. *Plastic Films and Packaging.* New York: Wiley, 1975.

JAY WEINSTEIN

Plastic Covering

Plastic covering serves as a barrier against oxygen, moisture, acids, bases, solvents, and odors and can keep foods, both raw and cooked, fresh longer. One of the first plastics to be used to protect food was polyvinylidene chloride (PVDC), which came to the attention of researchers at Dow Chemical Company in 1933 when Ralph Wiley, a laboratory worker, accidentally found the substance in a vial that he could not scrub clean. Researchers made the PVDC into a greasy film, which Dow named Saran. Initially used to protect fighter jets from salty sea spray and as a stain repellent for car upholstery, Saran was cleared for use in food packaging after World War II. Saran films are best known in the form of Saran Wrap film, the first cling wrap designed for household (1953) and commercial use (1949), introduced by the Dow Chemical Company. Saran Wrap brand plastic film is marketed by chemical products giant S. C. Johnson Company.

Plastic wrap, which is made of plastics of many kinds, including polyvinyl chloride (PVC), is notable for its ability to cling to almost any material, including glass or ceramic dishes, bowls, pots, and even itself for an airtight seal. At the grocery, it seals in the freshness of foods such as meat, cheese, and cut fruit, making it possible to sell such items days after they have been cut. It is also used to seal prepared foods that go from the grocery shelf or freezer to a home microwave. The wrap made it easier for Americans to cook less often by covering leftovers in plastic and reheating them later.

[*See also* Plastic Bags.]

BIBLIOGRAPHY

American Plastics Council. http://www.americanplasticscouncil .org. Contains a history of plastics and its uses.
Plasticsinfo.org. http://www.plasticsinfo.org. Looks at the safety of plastic food wrap and containers.

SANDRA YIN

Plates

Whether made from wood, metal, ceramic, glass, plastic, or paper, the plate has mirrored changing lifestyles over America's four hundred years. Behind this common artifact is a rich history that includes industrial espionage, economic policy, and social competition.

The earliest colonists had a surprisingly diverse array of plates, at least if they were wealthy. Spanish grandees in Florida brought in majolica, which has also been found in the Jamestown and Plymouth settlements. The earliest Chinese porcelain in America seems to have entered California through Spanish settlements.

Imported ceramics were a luxury for the affluent. Apart from what the immigrants carried, most colonists depended on local production until well into the eighteenth century. Wooden trenchers (woodenware was also called treen) were common among the middling classes and could be replaced easily along the heavily wooded Atlantic seaboard. Along with treen, metal plates and porringers (shallow, rimless bowls with flat handles, ideal for the ubiquitous gruels of colonial dining and still produced for babies), were the most common plates for the middling and wealthy in the English colonies until the eighteenth century. Multiple diners might share pewter plates; the more affluent had individual pewter, and the very wealthiest had silver. Prized for their durability, beauty, practicality, and obvious value, metal plates often were displayed on cupboards, following medieval tradition. Metal plates retain heat well (important during a New England winter) and could be easily converted into money or reworked into new forms as styles changed.

Local production of earthenwares started quickly. The Spanish built kilns by the end of the sixteenth century. Expatriate Iberian craftsmen may have produced the glazed wares that have been found in the American Southwest. Many Spanish colonists, however, used functional unglazed earthenware that was influenced by Native American production techniques. Both Jamestown and Plymouth had potteries by the 1620s, and domestic potteries sprang up wherever a good supply of clay could be found. Many southern plantations had small, slave-operated kilns. Although some made charmingly rustic plates, the potteries and plantations excelled at inexpensive, utilitarian earthenwares and stonewares for food preparation, storage, and especially dairying. Early American efforts to produce more elegant tablewares met with little success, as American clays and glazes were often inferior to their European counterparts.

Ironstone Dinner Plate. Such plates were imported from England in the nineteenth century. Ironstone became quite popular and was eventually manufactured in the United States. *Collection of Alice Ross*

THE TRENCHER

TRENCHER: from the French, *tranchoir*, to slice. Originally referring to slices of stale bread used in the Middle Ages as disposable plates, by the sixteenth century trenchers denoted carved wooden plates or platters, frequently with a small niche to hold salt. They were often reversible: One could flip the trencher between main and dessert courses to provide a clean surface. In the earliest American settlements, two or more diners often shared trenchers, a practice imported from England, hence the term "trenchermate"; "trencherman" refers to someone with a hearty appetite. Trenchers could be quite elegant: One seventeenth-century Plymouth inventory lists a dozen very small fruit trenchers, designed for the dessert course, each of which was decorated with an image of one of the twelve months.

CATHY K. KAUFMAN

Wooden Trencher. Trencher typical of plates used in the early eighteenth century. *Collection of Alice Ross*

In the mid-seventeenth century Britain's Navigation Acts of 1651 and 1660, and the Staple Act of 1663, effectively gave England a monopoly over most colonial trade. This protectionism allowed English delftware in the later seventeenth century, its salt-glazed stoneware in the early eighteenth century, and its creamware and white "pearlware" by the 1770s to define taste for many in the British colonies. French, Dutch, and German colonies imported items from the homeland through non-English ports, but relatively few of those pieces entered English colonies. England, through its India trade, also imported Chinese porcelain, which became quite popular in affluent circles by the end of the eighteenth century. In 1772 England's stranglehold over the colonial luxury market was broken when Chinese porcelain was imported directly from Canton to Philadelphia, although open trade would be interrupted during the Revolutionary War. By this time most modest households could boast a few plates made of some type of ceramic, although not enough to set a fancy table. Wooden trenchers were still advertised for sale in New England as late as 1775, and Lydia Maria Child's *The American Frugal Housewife* (1828) contains directions for cleaning treen. Treen continued in personal use through the nineteenth century in poor and frontier areas.

Gentility in a Plate

Owning generous quantities of high-quality ceramics distinguished the elites from everyone else in the eighteenth century, but during the nineteenth century the demarcation lines shifted downward. The middle classes now worried about whether they ate from matched sets of dishes or bits randomly cobbled together and whether they had fancy china in addition to everyday dishware. By the end of the nineteenth century, even the poor had sets of ceramic dishes, so that mere possession was not enough: One's choice in dishes expressed one's good taste and social standing.

Gilded French porcelain was one mark of an elite table in the early nineteenth century, but well-to-do families sent

Feather-edged Leeds Creamware. Such plates were imported into the colonies from England in the late eighteenth and early nineteenth centuries. *Collection of Alice Ross*

CERAMICS DEFINITIONS

Ceramics is the umbrella term for items fashioned from clay and hardened by heat. *Earthenware* is created from clays containing various impurities that limit the firing temperature to between 800°C and 1100°C and often richly color the ware. Earthenware is less sturdy than items fired at higher temperatures, and the vessel that results remains porous unless a glaze is applied. The relatively low temperature allows for a wide range of minerals (including lead) and colors in the glazes, which do not fuse to the body. Earthenware is susceptible to chipping.

Maiolica and *delft* are tin-glazed earthenwares, both of which were imported to America before 1650; very generally speaking, the former originates in Spain or Italy, the latter in Holland or England. *Faïence* is the French equivalent.

Creamware and *pearlware*, created by Englishman Josiah Wedgwood in the 1760s and 1770s, were highly popular cream-colored and white earthenware, widely imported in elegant dinner sets.

Majolica is nineteenth-century whimsical lead-glazed earthenware, frequently molded in floral, vegetal, or animal motifs and glazed to mimic nature's colorings.

Stoneware is fashioned from clay with fewer impurities, permitting a higher firing temperature (1200°C–1300°C), which encourages vitrification. The pieces are nonporous and stronger than earthenware, but not as sturdy as porcelain. Rhenish stoneware was used in the colonies by 1650 (distinct from the salt-glazed stoneware manufactured in England); Huguenot immigrants started domestic production no later than the 1720s. Fine English stoneware was especially popular in colonial America between 1720 and 1770.

Porcelain, originating in China in the fifth century, is a specialized mixture of clays permitting the highest firing temperatures, over 1300°C. True (hard-paste) porcelain contains the china clays kaolin and petuntse. Coveted for its beauty, porcelain was technically challenging to make, and the first efforts in Europe in the early eighteenth century resulted in soft-paste porcelain, which contains little or no kaolin, is fired at a slightly lower temperature, and lacks the translucence of most true porcelain. The demand for Chinese porcelain was so great that Chinese potters made export porcelain specifically for Western consumers. The decoration on export porcelain steadily declined in the eighteenth and early nineteenth centuries, as growing demand tolerated mediocre craftsmanship. American efforts to make true porcelain started around 1738, although none were commercially successful until the late nineteenth century.

CATHY K. KAUFMAN

their own unique designs to China for painting on porcelain blanks. The social competition expressed through personally designed tablewares and the leisured indulgence it implied were lampooned in Eliza Leslie's *Pencil Sketches, or Outlines of Characters and Manners* (1835). An untalented young daughter struggles with art lessons to create an awkward crest for new china. It is shipped with her father's instruction, "This [star] in the middle!" scribbled on the drawing. When the large service is finally delivered, the "literal and exact" Chinese painters have incorporated the father's scrawl as part of the design on every piece.

Etiquette books advised socially aspiring housewives about choosing dishes. A favorite theme was the gentility and self-respect that came from using attractive dishware, a belief that reached the working and immigrant classes by the late nineteenth century. Writers for the middle class in the 1830s critiqued those who used chipped dishes *en famille* and reserved the best porcelain for guests, turning the house topsy-turvy to hide the flaws when unexpected visitors arrived. It was thought more genteel to use for all occasions one set of moderately priced blue and white "India" ware dishes, either Chinese export porcelain, however poorly painted, or copies of it such as the highly popular Willow pattern from Spode. Replacements for broken pieces, even if not exactly matching, could be inexpensively and unobtrusively integrated, preserving the table's harmony. But fashions changed quickly; by the mid-1840s, white dishware had superseded all others as the quotidian tableware, with French or English porcelain gracing elegant meals. These ceramics were geographically widespread: One 1849 bride in California bragged to her sister in Buffalo about her "very nice" white dishes with French "coffee cups and fluted bowls." By the 1870s, though, white china was thought so "ugly and insipid" that a lady would economize on her clothing to afford colorful, decorated ware.

After the Civil War, changes in production and distribution techniques meant that attractive dishware, and lots of it, would soon be part of even tenement dinner tables. English and American potteries began to manufacture modestly priced majolica in the 1880s, displaying a wide array of gaily colored plates with fruit, animal, vegetable, and floral motifs. From precious, three-inch butter pat "pansies" to large serving platters of overlapping begonia leaves with simulated wickerwork borders, majolica captured the riotous color and specialized dining accoutrements that were fashionable in the late nineteenth century. The Great Atlantic and Pacific Tea Company offered majolica and other tablewares as a premium with purchases of teas, spices, and the like. A&P's mail-order business guaranteed nationwide distribution.

Particularly popular at the beginning of the twentieth century was the new "decalcoware," that is, inexpensive plates decorated with printed decals in a one-step process that slashed production costs. These dishes filled the shelves of the emerging chain stores such as F. W. Woolworth & Co., which catered to the "shawl trade," the poor and working-class immigrants who realized that pretty dishes were one sign of an American lady. Mimicking the A&P model, many food stores offered coupons with purchases that allowed customers to redeem decalcoware premiums. By the early twentieth century, cheap plates were universally found in even the poorest homes.

Confronting the Modern Market

As the Depression hit, lower- and middle-class purchases of dinnerware fell. To combat declining sales and make use of the large production capacity that had developed earlier, such middlebrow American producers as the Homer Laughlin China Company gave dinner plates to moviegoers at midweek shows. Another big stimulus came in 1936 with Homer Laughlin's introduction of Fiesta—vibrant, monochromatic earthenware priced for the working classes—which would later command a hefty premium as a collectible. The most popular dinnerware (over 250 million pieces sold between 1939 and 1959) was Russel Wright's American Modern, organically shaped earthenware in muted, natural tones. Wright's innovative design was reissued in 2002.

New home conveniences changed the composition of everyday dishes. Superficial finishings could not withstand the punishing heat and pressure of the dishwasher, and metal-based glazes ruined microwave ovens. Unbreakable plastic plates, some of the finest of them designed by Russel Wright, were integral to the efficient mid-twentieth-century home. Increasingly casual enter-

THE LENOX COMPANY

As one of the founding partners in 1889 of the Ceramic Art Company, Walter Scott Lenox was spurred by President Theodore Roosevelt's complaint in 1902 that he could not buy top-quality dishes for the White House from any American manufacturer. By 1906 Lenox was the sole owner of the renamed Lenox Company of Trenton, New Jersey, where he quickly perfected a fine china comparable to its European rivals. When President Woodrow Wilson went shopping for White House china in 1918, he commissioned Lenox to manufacture the first White House service "designed by an American artist, made from American clay at an American pottery, burned at American kilns, and decorated by American workmen." Since then, Lenox has supplied all state-dinner services to the White House and is widely considered the preeminent American luxury china manufacturer.

CATHY K. KAUFMAN

taining brought guests face-to-face with disposable paper plates: the hostess's only embarrassment in using inferior, unwaxed paper was telltale grease stains.

Individual dinner plates slowly increased in size. An eighteenth-century dinner plate was typically less than nine inches in diameter; by the early twentieth century, ten-and-one-half-inch plates had become standard, and the size continued to increase, with twelve-inch "buffet" plates frequently serving as dinner plates. Popularized in nouvelle cuisine restaurants and fashionable home-design shops, these larger plates generally have undecorated eating surfaces. Such plates beg for the artistic display of individual portions, making decorative food, rather than decorated china, the latest expression of the host's "good taste."

[See also Child, Lydia Maria; Dining Rooms, Table Settings, and Table Manners; Dishwashing and Cleaning Up; Microwave Ovens; Nouvelle Cuisine.]

BIBLIOGRAPHY

Blaszczyk, Regina Lee. *Imagining Consumers: Design and Innovation from Wedgwood to Corning.* Baltimore: Johns Hopkins University Press, 2000. Excellent business history of the post–Civil War American glass and ceramics industries, with considerable information on changing designs and distribution channels.

Levin, Elaine. *The History of American Ceramics.* New York: Abrams, 1988. Well-illustrated, with much attention to early manufacturers.

Mayhew, Edgar deN., and Minor Myers, Jr. *A Documentary History of American Interiors from the Colonial Era to 1915.* New York: Scribner's, 1980. Interesting and concise survey of American interiors, including table artifacts.

Noël Hume, Ivor. *A Guide to Artifacts of Colonial America.* Philadelphia: University of Pennsylvania Press, 2001. A detailed review of artifacts found in British colonial America interlaced with some political and technical information. Some illustrations. The weaknesses are its Anglo-centric focus and relative lack of socioeconomic context for the artifacts.

Quimby, Ian M. G., ed. *Ceramics in America.* Charlottesville: University of Virginia Press for the Henry Francis DuPont Winterthur Museum, 1972. A collection of scholarly papers; important for the specialist seeking detailed information, especially for non-English areas.

CATHY K. KAUFMAN

Plums

Plums are a most diverse group of fruits, varying greatly in size, shape, color, texture, and flavor. Scientists recognize about fifteen species and innumerable varieties grouped according to primary region of origin as American, European, and Asian.

For millennia Native Americans harvested indigenous wild plums, which generally grow on shrubs or shrublike trees. Compared with modern commercial plums, most native fruits are small and tart and have astringent skins; these characteristics are not ideal for fresh fruit but lend character to preserves, sauces, and wines, their chief uses. In the late nineteenth and early twentieth centuries some farmers grew American plums commercially, and fruit breeders used them in hybridizing new varieties because of their adaptation to local environments. Some of the best-known species are the beach plum, *Prunus maritima*, native to the coastal Northeast; the Sierra plum, *P. subcordata*, indigenous to northern California and Oregon; and *P. americana*, native to the central states.

From the colonial era until the early twentieth century most of the plums cultivated in America were European species, chiefly *P. domestica*, which includes prunes, greengages, and egg plums, and *P. insititia*, which includes damsons and bullaces. Although not uncommon, these plums never attained in America the importance they enjoy in Europe, because the plants are less well adapted to American growing conditions. The best European types, such as greengages, have intense, exquisite flavor. However, cultivation of European plums other than prunes faded after the advent of Asian plums, which are generally larger, juicier, and more abundant in bearing.

Prunes—European plums with sufficiently high sugar content that permits them to be dried whole without fermenting—are sold in small quantities as fresh fruits, but are primarily dried. The most important variety, Agen, was imported from France in 1854 and intensively grown in California's Santa Clara Valley, near San Jose; cultivation later concentrated in the Sacramento Valley. A convenience food in an age when fresh fruit was less easily available, especially in winter and spring, dried prunes remained a kitchen staple until the mid-twentieth century, when consumption declined as access to cold-stored and imported fruit increased. Early in the twenty-first century prune sellers tried to reinvigorate the fruit's image by renaming their product "dried plums."

Luther Burbank, a celebrated plant breeder based in Santa Rosa, California, was the father of the American plum industry, which focuses on Asian and Asian-type plums (*P. salicinia*). Between 1885 and his death in 1926, Burbank imported dozens of plum trees from Japan, crossed them with other species of Asian, Eurasian, and native origin, and introduced more than one hundred varieties. Most fell into oblivion, but about half a dozen, including Santa Rosa, Satsuma, Kelsey, and Elephant Heart, are still grown.

Most Asian plums are quite luscious and flavorful when fully ripe. Growers, however, have dramatically increased production of large, firm, black Asian-type plums such as Friar and Blackamber, which look ripe even when they are not, do not show bruises, and withstand rough handling and prolonged storage. Virtually all of the commercially available specimens of these plums have a bland flavor, termed "neutral" in the fruit trade.

A private fruit breeder widely regarded as the Luther Burbank of the modern age, Floyd Zaiger of Modesto, California, revolutionized the plum world in the early 1990s by introducing his trademarked Pluots, Asian plum–apricot hybrids in which plum genes and characteristics prevail. Pluots have seized a quarter of the market for plumlike fruits, largely at the expense of traditional plums. The best varieties, such as Flavor Supreme and Flavor King, are superbly sweet and delicious. Most Asian plums and Pluots are consumed fresh, though they are also canned, stewed, and used in desserts such as puddings and tarts.

In 2002 California, by far the largest producing state for Asian-type plums, Pluots, and dried prunes, had 36,000 acres of plums and 73,000 acres of prunes. The leading growing area for fresh prune plums is the Northwest.

[*See also* Apricots; California; Drying; Fruit.]

BIBLIOGRAPHY

Hedrick, U. P. *The Plums of New York.* Albany, NY: New York
    Agricultural Experiment Station, 1911.
Janick, Jules, and James N. Moore, eds. *Fruit Breeding.* New York:
    Wiley, 1996.
Waugh, F. A. *Plums and Plum Culture.* New York: Orange Judd,
    1901.

DAVID KARP

Po'boy Sandwich

Po'boy sandwiches are based on crusty loaves of Po'boy-
style french bread rarely available outside New Orleans,
where long-established bakeries produce loaves noted
for their extraordinarily light interior encased in a crusty
exterior. Regular french bread is used as a substitute in
other areas. Po'boy fillings range from roast beef with a
deep, rich gravy called "debris," to ham, Creole hot
sausage, and deep-fried seafood such as shrimp or oysters. Legend credits the creation of the Po'boy to Benny
and Clovis Martin, owners of Martin Brothers Grocery in
New Orleans during the 1920s. Some say the Martins
developed the Po'boy as a way to help striking streetcar
workers with an inexpensive meal. Others claim that the
Martins, unable to resist the pleading of hungry young
black boys requesting a sandwich "for a po' boy," would
cut their sandwiches into thirds and hand the portions
out free to the children. The sandwiches in those days
were likely to be filled with french fries and gravy,
accounting for the popular french fry Po'boy still enjoyed
in New Orleans. Po'boys have become well known and
appear on sandwich menus throughout the United States.

[*See also* Bread; Cajun and Creole Food; Sandwiches;
    Sauces and Gravies.]

BIBLIOGRAPHY

Brown, Cora, Rose Brown, and Bob Brown. *America Cooks: Favorite
    Recipes from the 48 States.* Garden City, NY: Halcyon House, 1940.
Mercuri, Becky. *Sandwiches That You Will Like.* Pittsburgh, PA:
    WQED, 2002.

BECKY MERCURI

Poetry, Food

There have probably been poems that speak about food
since there have been poems. Whether frothy doggerel or

considered elucidation of the human condition, poems by
some of the world's most revered poets have dealt with
food. Ancient Roman, Greek, Chinese, and other venerable cultures recorded poetry about food.

Some food poems current in colonial American times
were "rhyming receipts" to help an illiterate population
remember recipes, and they offered enough detail to
cook from. Here is an excerpt from one written in Britain
by Sydney Smith (1771–1845) but popular in the
colonies. It is called "An Herb Sallad for the Tavern
Bowl."

> Of wondrous mustard, add a single spoon.
> Distrust the condiment that bites too soon.
> But deem it not, thou man of herbs, a fault,
> to add a double quantity of salt.
> Fourtimes the spoon with oil of Lucca crown,
> and twice the vinegar procured from town.
> Lastly o'er the flowery compound, toss
> a magic soupspoon of Anchovy sauce.

There were many of these "receipts" used in the new
nation, thus continuing the British tradition. Colonials
soon developed their own to include New World ingredients. This one, author unknown, is a recipe for "Wheat
and Indian Bread," "Indian" meaning corn.

> Two cups Indian, one cup wheat,
> One cup sour milk, one cup sweet,
> One good egg that well you beat.
> Half cup molasses too;
> Half cup sugar add thereto,
> With one spoon of butter new.
> Salt and soda each a teaspoon;
> Mix it up quick and bake it soon.
> Then you'll have cornbread complete,
> Best of all cornbread you'll meet.

Many nursery rhymes originating in England were likewise brought to America and enjoyed great popularity, as
many still do.

> Little Jack Horner sat in the corner,
> Eating a Christmas pie:
> He put in his thumb, and pulled out a plum,
> And said, "What a good boy am I!"

Others that mention food prominently are "Little Miss
Muffet" and "Jack Sprat." The theme of food appears in
what seems the majority of them. Sing-along poems like
"Do You Know the Muffin Man" and "Hot Cross Buns"
are still common child's fare. Children's play chants often
contain food imagery as well. "Pease Porridge Hot" is a
dancing or jump-rope chant about a pot of soup, and the

baby's clapping game "Patty Cake" comes from the older "Pat-a-Cake."

Poems were often published as broadsides in young America, many for political reasons. When the taxes on tea became oppressive before the Revolutionary War, anti-tea poems appeared. An excerpt from one such poem, "A Lady's Adieu to Her TeaTable," lamented:

> No more shall my teapot so generous be
> In filling the cups with this pernicious tea,
> For I'll fill it with water and drink out the same,
> Before I'll lose LIBERTY that dearest name,
> Because I am taught (and believe it is fact)
> That our ruin is aimed at in the late act,
> Of imposing a duty on all foreign Teas,
> Which detestable stuff we can quit when we please.
> LIBERTY'S The Goddess that I do adore,
> And I'll maintain her right until my last hour,
> Before she shall part I will die in the cause,
> For I'll never be govern'd by tyranny's laws.

Many sources have created rhymes for some specific purpose, commercial or public-spirited. Here are excerpts from "'Twas the Night after Christmas," a poem published by the U.S. National Park Service promoting kitchen sanitation through graphic doggerel:

> 'Twas the night after Christmas
> And all through the kitchen
> Little creatures were stirring up
> Potions bewitching.
> . . . . .
> Salmonella were working
> In gravy and soup
> In the hopes they could turn it
> To poisonous goop!
> . . . . .
> Clostridia were nestled
> All snug in the ham
> While Hep A virus
> Danced in the yam.

Advertising has had its share of examples, as well. Rhymes to sell products or services have a long commercial history. Here is part of an advertising poem from 1859:

> It is the cheap Cash Store, my friends:
> At J. W. Renoud's, please call,
> And find things sold at reason's fee,
> To one, to ten, to all!
> . . . . .
> Yes, find things sold at reason's fee,
> Bread, butter, candles, cheese,
> Salt, Onions, Crackers, Coffee, Brooms,
> And choicest, best of Teas!
> . . . . .

> Sugar and Allspice, Flour and Pork,
> And matches, not the kind
> The young folks often, often make,
> So pleasing to the mind.

As broadcast media took a larger role in advertising, poems set to music—jingles—assumed a more important position. Beginning with early radio efforts and continuing through television advertising, jingles hawk goods and services of all kinds.

There are some rather whimsical settings for food poetry. *HaikuSine: 217 Tiny Food Poems by Texans Who Love to Eat and Feed Their Head*, a book by Micki McClelland with Shelby Watson, is a collection of haiku from an annual contest sponsored by Houston's *My Table Dining Guide* (Lazywood Press). It began in 1997 and became a popular annual event. Juvenile literature has its share of food poems as well. Many such volumes exist, and they are generally filled with doggerel, play poems, and tongue twisters.

In serious modern literature, food poetry is a relatively popular area. Many well-known writers have published poetry about food, and there are several published collections. One collection, *O Taste and See: Food Poems*, features the work of more than one hundred authors, including Robert Frost, Gertrude Stein, Louise Bogan, Frank O'Hara, Pablo Neruda, Allen Ginsberg, William Carlos Williams, Diane Wakoski, and Erica Jong.

Internet searches for "food poetry" and "food poems" will turn up more than five million items, including books, individual poems, and sites to help writers create their own poems.

[*See also* Advertising; Humor, Food; Literature and Food; Recipes; Songs, Food.]

BIBLIOGRAPHY

Garrison, David Lee, and Terry Hermsen, eds. *O Taste and See: Food Poems*. Huron, OH: Bottom Dog Press, 2003. More than two hundred poems by more than one hundred of America's best-known poets, novelists, and essayists.

Goldstein, Bobbye S., ed. *What's on the Menu: Food Poems*. New York: Viking, 1992. Juvenile. A collection about food from lumpy bumpy pickles to chunky chocolate cake.

Morrison, Lillian. *I Scream, You Scream: A Feast of Food Rhymes*. Little Rock, AR: August House Little Folk, 1997. Juvenile. Rhymes, street cries, and tongue twisters. Very whimsical.

Nash, Ogden. *Food*. New York: Stewart, Tabori & Chang, 1989. Humorous poems with rich wordplay and wit.

Washington, Peter, ed. *Eat, Drink, and Be Merry: Poems about Food and Drink*. New York: Alfred A. Knopf Everyman's Library, 2003. A very broad collection ranging from the ancients to contemporary, generally rather light verse.

BOB PASTORIO

Poke Salad

Poke salad (*Phytolacca americana*) is a perennial that is native to the eastern United States. It has been suggested that the early white settlers adopted "poke" from the Algonquian name *pocan*. It has also been known as pokeweed, poke salute, pokeberry, inkberry, and numerous other local names. It resprouts early every spring from a tuberous root. By midsummer it has flowered, its main stalk has turned red, and it may be as high as ten feet tall. Grapelike clusters of berries hanging from its limbs turn deep purple by early fall.

When the shoots sprouted in the early spring they were widely used by the colonists. The young leaves were eaten alone or mixed with other spring greens. The tender, young sprouts were prepared and eaten like asparagus; indeed they are said to have tasted like asparagus. These would have been welcome additions to the diet following winter meals of cured meat, salted fish, pickled cabbage, and cornmeal.

It has been reported that the native Indians also used various parts of this plant as poultices for arthritic pain, in other medications, and as dyes. Early settlers on the frontier adopted these uses too.

Because of the plant's hardy nature and popularity it was cultivated in many colonial gardens. It even became popular in Europe for a time, but poke salad's use as a food source dwindled as time passed. Its decline in popularity can be attributed to several factors. The most significant is believed to have been the commercialization of food preservation techniques coupled with a transportation system that makes all foods available at all times, fresh, frozen, and canned.

Another factor that has undoubtedly played a role in poke's passing from the menu is that, at a point in its annual growth cycle, it becomes poisonous. Although a Dr. Dover was quoted as saying, " Anybody that gets sick from eating poke, I'll treat them free," it has now been scientifically established that the root and the berries are poisonous, as are the stalk and stems after turning red. Dr. Dover to the contrary, there always seems to have been near-universal agreement on the poisonous potential of the plant. Even so, there has been no agreement on the proper preparation technique to avoid the effects of the poison. All of the following directions have been given: Never eat a shoot that is more than six inches high; blanch the shoots before eating; boil and discard the water before eating; boil and discard the water twice before eating.

Although there are those who remember that Elvis Presley recorded the song "Polk Salute Annie" in 1973 and although poke salad is still sought as a rite of spring by some natural food enthusiasts, it is now largely remembered as pokeweed in gardening encyclopedias and various treatises of limited interest.

[*See also* Gibbons, Euell; Homemade Remedies; Salads and Salad Dressing.]

JAMES C. LEE

Polish American Food

Polish immigrants came to the United States in three major waves. The first, around the turn of the twentieth century, came for opportunity and was called "*za chlebem*," literally "following the bread." A second wave was spurred by economic and political pressure in the years just before and just after World War II. The third wave in the mid-1980s reflected a desire to escape economic chaos in the homeland. The first immigration waves coincided with industrialization and urbanization. Work in factories and the coal, steel, and shipbuilding industries brought Poles to cities like Chicago; Waterbury, Connecticut; Pittsburgh; Hamtramck, Michigan; and New York City. In the third immigrant wave, laborers, along with well-educated Polish professionals swelled existing Polish neighborhoods and created new ones in Seattle, Houston, Los Angeles, San Francisco, Denver, and Atlanta.

These communities of Polish immigrants and Americans of Polish descent are called "Polonias." Here, many expressions of Polish identity and influence occur. Institutions that support Polish identity are woven into the community fabric: houses of worship, Polish national homes, restaurants, and food stores. It is food that serves as a bridge between the homeland and the new land. Among Polish Americans, foodways, with flavors of the homeland, are practiced in many forms. Throughout the Polonias, markets, restaurants, and rituals in the community support the continuity of ethnic foodways as culture identifiers, albeit in forms translated by the New World.

Polish immigrants arriving in the United States of America experience an abundance and variety of food not known in the homeland, particularly in the types of produce. Yet the diet of newly arrived immigrants often bears a striking resemblance to that in Poland.

Early food resources available in the various turn-of-the-century and mid-century Polonias were consistent with homeland taste preferences and allowed immigrants to raise, cook, and preserve foods in ways shaped by homeland memories. Foods that were typically prepared by women in their transplanted households included *babka* (egg-rich, yeasted sweet bread), *kapusta* (simmered sauerkraut and fresh cabbage), various soups, pierogi (meat, cheese, potato, *kapusta* or fruit-filled dumplings), *kluski* (flour and potato noodles), and *golabki*, also known in the United States as *golubki* (stuffed cabbage). Some kept backyard produce gardens. Huge pickling crocks, fragrant with dill and garlic, were common sights in some backyards. Occasionally, a pig was raised for slaughter, a regular practice on the Polish farms from which many came. Home kitchens were equipped with manual meat grinders that had sausage attachments used for stuffing casing for kielbasa. This homeland specialty was either boiled fresh or, particularly in urban kitchens, strung up on a broom handle and suspended over the kitchen coal stove chimney to smoke.

In the twenty-first century, many of these recipes are prepared from scratch less frequently in home kitchens, in part, because of the laborious preparations required. Still, they are not disappearing. Restaurants and food stores in Polonias provide flavor links to Poland. Polish bakeries sell *chleb* (bread), *paczki*, (jam-filled doughnuts) and *makowiec* (poppyseed-filled strudels). Butcher shops offer hams, *boscek* (rib bacon), *kiszka* (blood and groats pudding, although Polish Jews, following Jewish dietary laws, make *kiszka* without blood), and an array of kielbasa. Groceries also sell ready-made convenience foods that are the equivalent of many labor-intensive traditional dishes: *golabki* (stuffed cabbage), pierogi (filled dumplings), *flaczki* (tripe soup), and *bigos* (hunter's stew).

Some Polish Food Details

Bigos is a type of hunter's stew. Its history goes back to deep-winter hunting expeditions. Hunters set out with their gear, including a kettle, cabbage, and onions. These were the basics needed for an evolving stew. As the hunt progressed, the *bigos* developed, shaped by the catch. As animals were gutted and cleaned, parts were added to the stew, which fed hunters around a warming fire. After dinner, the pot was set outside the tents in the snow. In the twenty-first century, *bigos* is a cabbage-based stew enriched with assorted bits of meat.

Pierogi are the ubiquitous Polish dumplings. In Poland, pierogi are a casual dish, often cooked impromptu using freshly harvested fillings, like berries gathered during a summertime walk. In Poland, pierogi may make up *kolacja*, the light evening meal. In the United States, pierogi are more often reserved for special occasions, in part because of the labor required to make them. Hand-rolled dough rounds are filled and pinched shut, then boiled or fried, and, if savory, tossed with butter and perhaps sautéed onions. Fillings can be as simple as berries sprinkled with sugar or they can be more involved combinations, such as simmered sauerkraut with pork or mashed potato and cheese. Pierogi are staples in Polish restaurants and at community events and holiday meals. The dumplings were once made exclusively in Polish American homes, then cottage industries produced them for sale in local grocery stores, and, in the early 2000s, they are manufactured and sold frozen in supermarkets nationally.

Kielbasa is a Polish-style sausage that has many varieties. Meat is ground in varying degrees of coarseness from chunky to fine, seasoned with garlic or other flavorings or spices, and piped into casing. Thin sausage is known as *kabanosy* and thicker sausage is the better-known kielbasa. Kielbasa that is fresh is boiled before serving. For longer preservation the sausage is smoked. Some Polish American homes and butcher shops have smokehouses in their backyards for smoking kielbasa.

Babka is an egg-rich, yeast-raised sweet bread.

Kapusta is the Polish form of sauerkraut. In Poland, *kapusta* is typically the vegetable preserved in autumn for winter consumption. It is made by shredding cabbage and layering it with salt in a crock or a wooden barrel. Lore exists about the best way to pack down the cabbage. A wooden mallet may be used, but it is least preferred as it seems to bruise the cabbage. A favored method is to press the cabbage down with the palms of the hands. There is tradition that the very best way is to hoist a thoroughly scrubbed child into the barrel to race around and pack down the cabbage with its bare feet.

Chrusciki, or angel wings, are a treat made from deep-fried dough, sprinkled with confectioners sugar. They are sometimes cut into diamond shapes and slit in the center, with the ends pulled through and fried.

Many of these foods are common to Polish Americans of different faiths, but pork is, of course, eschewed by

Polish American Jews. The church influences foodways, particularly around holidays.

Christian Church Holidays and Foods

Wigilia is the Christmas Eve meal. It is a meatless meal whose number of dishes and attendees is often specifically an odd number. An unoccupied place setting may be left open for the arrival of the Christ child. The meal begins with a sharing of wishes and the breaking of the *oplatek*, a thin wafer that sometimes arrives by mail from relatives in Poland and is also sold in Polish stores or distributed through the church.

Swienconka, the blessing of Easter food baskets, is another important holiday ritual. It is celebrated on Holy Saturday and provides a link between the sorrow of the Crucifixion on Good Friday and the joy of the Resurrection on Easter Sunday. Traditionally, a table set with Easter foods was blessed by a priest in a private service that took place in individual homes. Although it may still take place there, in the twenty-first century the blessing is delivered more commonly in a public church service.

For the *Swienconka* ceremony, samples of what will be the crucial components of the Easter meal are gathered, prepared, and assembled into a basket. The mandatory food items in the basket are eggs, meat, bread, and salt. Each has specific symbolic value. The eggs stand for familial strength and for new life. They may appear in any of several forms: in their natural color, solidly dyed in pastel colors, or as *pisanki*, a folk art form that Poland shares with numerous cultures where eggs are waxed with designs using a stylus and dipped in dye repeatedly to form brilliant geometric patterns. Hard-cooked eggs that are more simply dyed may begin the Easter meal in a ritual called *w waletke*, involving the tapping of eggs with one's neighbor at the dinner table. The broken eggshells symbolize Christ's breaking free from the tomb. The person whose egg remains intact is considered a victor.

The meat served at the Easter meal, commonly a piece of kielbasa or a baked ham, represents both the offering of Christ's blood at the Crucifixion and the Old Testament sprinkling of lamb's blood on doorposts to deter the Angel of Death. Meat indicates festivity in the Polish diet, marking the absence of a fast day. The yeast-raised bread, usually rye, pumpernickel, or egg-rich *babka* symbolizes Christ's resurrection. Finally, salt is added to the food basket to acknowledge its life-preserving qualities and the flavor that Christ and Christianity added to the world described in Matthew 5:13.

The basket might also include horseradish to represent the bitter struggles for faith that have taken place. Lambs, shaped from butter, hard sugar, or cake, represent the Paschal Lamb. Chocolate, a reward for the hard work characteristic of Polish people, might be added, as well as any other item that a person wants blessed. Sprigs of pussy willows or spring greens decorate the basket to celebrate the new cycle of life and the fragrance of youth. The straw basket itself uses materials that have sprung from the earth and may be a representative of a folk art form.

At church blessings, priests say prayers that celebrate the symbolic meaning of each of the food items in the baskets and then sprinkle holy water through the church. Once blessed, the foods are considered to be transformed and amplified by the power of the blessing. Traditional Polish beliefs hold that participants consume the blessing, internalizing it when they eat the blessed food.

[*See also* Cabbage; Jewish American Food; Jewish Dietary Laws; Sausage.]

BIBLIOGRAPHY

Goldstein, Elizabeth, and Gail Green. "Pierogi and Babaka-Making at St. Mary's." *New York Folklore Quarterly* 4 (1978): 71–79.

Hoover, Marjorie A., Willard B. Moore, and Anne R. Kaplan. *The Minnesota Ethnic Food Book*. St. Paul, MN: Minnesota Historical Society Press, 1986.

Nagorka, Suzanne, Marie Palowski, and Kathy Zalucki. "Traditional Polish Cooking." *New York Folklore Quarterly* 28 (1972): 271–285.

Nowakowski, Jacek, ed. *Polish-American Ways: Recipes and Traditions*. New York: Harper and Row, 1989.

Obidinski, Eugene, and Helen Stankiewicz Zand. *Polish Folkways in America: Community and Family*. Lanham, MD, 1987.

ANNIE S. HAUCK-LAWSON

Politics of Food

Most people perceive food as a basic biological need, an indicator of culture, a source of enjoyment, and sometimes as a trade commodity or generator of employment, but they rarely view it as political—an element in the mundane realm of power and manipulation in the interests of commerce. Food and politics, however, are inextricably linked. Politics affects every component of the American food system from production to consumption. Much money is at stake, and the principal stakeholders—the food industry, government regulators, public health officials, nutrition educators, and the general public—have different interests in the food system. Although everyone wants food to be plentiful, safe, environmentally sound, culturally appropriate, affordable, healthful, and palatable, the food industry has one additional interest: to sell products. The conflict between the commercial interests of food companies and the widely varying concerns of other stakeholders drives the politics of food.

The term "food industry" refers to any business that produces, processes, makes, sells, or serves foods, beverages, or dietary supplements. It is usually described in sectors. The agribusiness sector raises food crops and animals and produces fertilizer, pesticides, seeds, and feed; it also includes companies that sell machinery, labor, land, buildings, or financial services to farmers, or that transport, store, distribute, export, process, or market their foods. The food-service sector includes restaurants, fast food outlets, bars, and any other business that serves food: workplaces, schools, hospitals, bookstores, and clothing stores, for example. The retail sector comprises outlets such as supermarkets, convenience stores, or vending machines. This vast industry produces a food supply so abundant, varied, inexpensive, and independent of geography or season that nearly all Americans except the very poorest can obtain enough food to meet biological needs. Indeed, the supply is so overabundant that it contains enough to feed everyone in the country nearly twice over—even after exports are considered. This surplus, along with a society so affluent that most citizens can afford to buy as much food as they need, creates a highly competitive marketing environment. To satisfy stockholders, food companies must work hard to convince people to buy *their* products rather than those of competitors, or to entice people to eat more food in general—regardless of the consequences for nutrition and health.

Companies promote sales through advertising and public relations, but they also use the political system to convince Congress, government agency officials, food and nutrition experts, the media, and the public that their products promote health (or at least do no harm), and should not be subject to restrictive regulations. To protect sales, they contribute to congressional campaigns, lobby members of Congress and federal agencies, and when all else fails, engage in lawsuits. Nearly every food company belongs to a trade association or hires a public relations firm responsible for promoting a positive image of its products among consumers, professionals, and the media. Companies form partnerships and alliances with professional nutrition organizations, fund research on food and nutrition, sponsor professional journals and

conferences, and make sure that influential groups—federal officials, researchers, doctors, nurses, schoolteachers, and the media—do not criticize their products or suggest eating less of them. To divert attention from health, safety, or environmental concerns, they argue that restrictive regulations overly involve the government in personal dietary choices and threaten constitutional guarantees of free speech. Much of this political activity is so invisible a part of contemporary culture that it attracts only occasional notice.

In using the political system, food companies behave like any other business—tobacco, for example—in attempting to exert influence. Promoting food raises more complicated issues than tobacco however. Tobacco is a single product, is unambiguously harmful, and requires simple advice: don't smoke. Food, in contrast, is available in more than 300,000 different products, is required for life, causes problems only when consumed inappropriately, and elicits more complex health messages: eat this product instead of that one, or eat less in general. The "eat less" message is at the root of much of the controversy over nutrition advice, as it conflicts with food industry interests. The primary mission of food companies, like that of tobacco companies, is to sell products. Health enters the picture only when it helps to sell food, and food companies rarely consider the ethical choices involved in such thinking. Thus, government advice about healthful eating is especially fraught with politics.

The Politics of Dietary Recommendations

The U.S. government has issued dietary recommendations for more than a century, but its advice did not become controversial until the 1970s. This history reflects changes in agriculture, food product development, and international trade, as well as in science and medicine. In 1900, the leading causes of death were infectious diseases, such as tuberculosis and diphtheria. These conditions were fostered by the nutrient deficiencies and overall malnutrition prevalent at the time, especially among the poor. Life expectancy at birth for both men and women barely exceeded forty-seven years (in 2000, it was seventy-seven years). To improve public health, government nutritionists advised the public to eat more of a greater variety of foods. The goals of health officials, nutritionists, and the food industry were much the same—to encourage greater consumption of the full range of American agricultural products. Throughout the twentieth century, an expanding economy led to improvements in housing, sanitation, and nutrition, and diseases related to nutritional deficiencies declined. By the 1970s, health officials were well aware that the principal nutritional problems had shifted: they were now conditions associated with overnutrition—eating too much food or too much of certain kinds of food. Overnutrition causes a different set of health problems; it changes metabolism, makes people overweight, and increases the likelihood of chronic diseases, such as coronary heart disease, certain cancers, diabetes, hypertension, stroke, and others—the leading causes of illness and death among any overfed population. With this shift in dietary intake and disease patterns, nutritional recommendations also had to change. Instead of promoting "eat more," the advice of nutritionists shifted to emphasize eating less of certain dietary components—or of food in general. Advice to eat less, however, runs counter to the interests of food producers. Hence: politics.

"Eat less" advice also causes conflicts within the U.S. Department of Agriculture (USDA). Although that agency had issued dietary advice to the public since the early 1900s, its "eat more" publications caused no debate. Only in the late 1970s, when Congress designated the USDA as the leading federal agency for issuing dietary advice to the public, did its dual missions cause conflict. One branch of the USDA continued to promote eating more of American agricultural products, while another issued advice to eat less of certain of those products.

The most celebrated example of that conflict occurred when the USDA attempted to release its *Food Guide Pyramid* in 1991. The pyramid displays a recommended pattern of food intake in which most servings are to come from the grain, fruit, and vegetable groups; fewer should be from the meat and dairy groups; and even fewer should be from foods high in fat and sugar (which are high in energy but relatively low in nutrients). USDA nutritionists developed the pyramid over a ten-year period in which they conducted studies to determine the optimal numbers and sizes of servings from each food group

Food Guide Pyramid
A Guide to Daily Food Choices

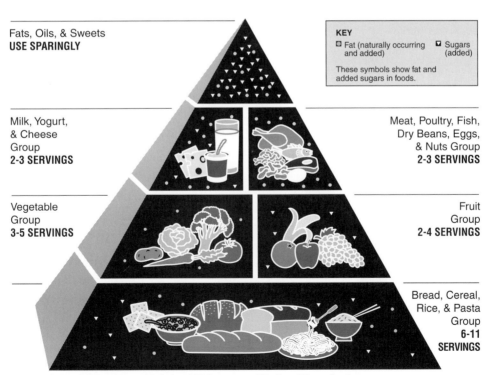

Source: U.S. Department of Agriculture/U.S. Department of Health and Human Services

Food Pyramid. The pyramid as it appeared on the USDA website in 2004. *U.S. Department of Agriculture and U.S. Department of Health and Human Services*

as well as the design that would best convey the most important features of healthful diets: variety (multiple food groups), proportionality (appropriate numbers of servings), and moderation (restrictions on fat and sugar).

Proportionality was the critical factor; the pyramid clearly conveys the idea that people are supposed to eat more of some foods than others. This idea, however, runs counter to the interests of food companies. The food industry much prefers advice based on somewhat different concepts: foods cannot be considered good or bad, and the keys to healthful diets are balance, variety, and moderation. Such advice effectively grants permission to consume *any* food product, no matter where it appears on the pyramid. This preference explains why the National Cattlemen's Association and other producers of meat and dairy foods objected to release of the pyramid and induced the USDA to withdraw it from publication. USDA officials explained this surprising action by announcing that the pyramid had never been tested on low-income women and children and that further research needed to be done. Few observers believed this explanation, however, as it seemed evident that the agency had acted under pressure from food producers. When the new research confirmed the value of the original design, the USDA was faced with a dilemma. It could issue the pyramid against the wishes of the food industry, or issue a different design and face charges that it had yielded to food industry pressure. In a compromise in 1992, the USDA released the pyramid with design changes that met some of the industry objections.

In this case, the controversy resolved satisfactorily for the USDA and for the public. The pyramid survived, and the delay and persistent press coverage gave it much favorable publicity. Subsequently, the pyramid has become widely distributed, well recognized, and iconic. It appears not only in nutrition education materials, posters, and textbooks, but also in food advertisements, cookbooks, board games, and Christmas ornaments. Furthermore, it has spawned a large number of progeny pyramids that illustrate the recommended dietary patterns of one or another cultural, religious, or ethnic group—Mediterranean, Asian, vegetarian, kosher, and soul food, for example.

A second example is that of the U.S. dietary guideline for sugar. Dietary guidelines are nutritional precepts that form the basis of food guides like the pyramid. Since 1980, the USDA and the U.S. Department of Health and Human Services have issued *Dietary Guidelines for Americans* at five-year intervals. Sugars (sucrose and those in corn sweeteners) contain calories but no nutrients. In societies that typically consume excess calories, advice to eat less sugar makes sense. The 1980 and 1985 guidelines for sugar said so explicitly: "Avoid too much sugar." Since then, partly in response to pressures from sugar trade associations, the guideline has become increasingly ambiguous. In 1990, in an effort to state dietary messages more positively, the agencies changed the guideline to read: "Use sugars only in moderation." The 1995 guideline expressed the advice even more positively: "Choose a diet moderate in sugars." The 2000 guideline further weakened the suggestion to eat less sugar: "Choose beverages and foods to moderate your intake of sugars." This peculiar wording is explained by politics.

Sugar was one of the more contentious guidelines in 2000. Sugar trade associations argued that research on sugar and disease did not support a recommendation to eat less sugar, mainly because studies cannot easily distinguish the health effects of sugar from those of the foods in which it is present or from calories in general. The committee reviewing the guideline at first suggested this wording: "Go easy on beverages and foods high in added sugars." This guideline implied a benefit from reducing consumption of sugars, particularly those added to processed and prepared foods (as opposed to those naturally occurring in fruits and vegetables). After further discussion, the committee changed the recommendation to say: "Choose beverages and foods that limit your intake of sugars." The word "limit" troubled sugar lobbyists, who induced thirty senators, half from sugar-growing states, to question the USDA secretary as to whether the agency had the right to make this suggestion. They also objected to singling out individual foods and beverages (like candy, desserts, and soft drinks) as major sources of sugars. Instead, they preferred advice to consume foods containing sugar as part of a total dietary pattern. The USDA agreed and changed the word "limit" to "moderate" in the final guideline. The difference between these two words may be a matter of semantics (and few Americans are aware of the *Dietary Guidelines*), but this incident illustrates the extent of food industry efforts to prevent the government from issuing "eat less" advice.

Food lobbyists are just as concerned about international dietary advice. In 2003, the World Health Organization (WHO), alarmed about rising rates of obesity among its member populations, proposed to recommend intakes of added sugars that did not exceed 10 percent of daily caloric intake, an amount well within the range recommended by the USDA pyramid. Nevertheless, representatives of the beet, cane, and corn sweetener industries objected to this "restriction" and asked the U.S. Department of Health and Human Services to withdraw funding from WHO unless the recommendation was eliminated. Rather than defending sensible dietary advice, the department sided with the sugar lobbyists. Eventually, the WHO acceded to some of the lobbyists' demands, and the final report in 2004 omitted specific dietary targets.

The Politics of Food Marketing

In comparison to the pyramid, American diets clearly are out of balance. Servings of added fats are at least one-third higher than they should be, and caloric sweeteners half again as high. The extra calories in American diets come from eating more food in general, but especially more of foods high in fat (meat, dairy, fried foods, grain dishes with added fat), sugar (soft drinks, juice drinks, desserts), and salt (snack foods). It can hardly be a coincidence that these are just the foods most profitable to the food industry and most promoted by it. To understand this connection, it is necessary to know a bit more about the U.S. food industry.

The American "food-and-fiber" system generates a trillion dollars or more in annual sales, accounts for about 10 percent of the gross national product and employs more than 15 percent of the country's labor force. This industry has been remarkably successful in capitalizing on twentieth-century shifts from small farms to giant corporations, from home cooking to nearly half the meals prepared and consumed outside the home, and from a diet based on locally grown "whole" foods to one based on processed foods transported over long distances. These changes created a farm system that is much less labor-intensive and far more efficient and specialized. In 1900, 40 percent of the U.S. population lived on farms, but in the early 2000s no more than 2 percent did so. Just since 1960, the number of farms declined from about 3.2 million to 1.9 million, but their average size increased by 40 percent and their productivity by 82 percent. Most farms in the twenty-first century raise just a single commodity, such as cattle, chickens, pigs, corn, wheat, or soybeans. Many are part of a system of vertical integration, meaning that one corporation owns all stages of production and marketing. Chickens constitute an especially clear example. In the mid-1950s, farmers raised chickens in small flocks. Today, chickens are factory-farmed in massive numbers under contract to a few large companies.

Economic pressures force food and beverage companies to expand and merge to great size. In 2000, seven U.S. companies—Philip Morris, ConAgra, Mars, IBP, Sara Lee, Heinz, and Tyson Foods—ranked among the ten largest food companies in the world, and others, such as Coca-Cola, McDonald's, PepsiCo, Procter and Gamble, and Roche (vitamins), ranked among the largest one hundred worldwide companies. The very largest of such companies generate $30 billion to $50 billion in annual sales. Similar trends apply to supermarkets and to food-service venues. The most successful food-service chains are sandwich houses and fast food outlets. McDonald's nearly thirteen thousand U.S. outlets bring in close to $20 billion in annual sales, more than twice as much as the nearest competitor.

In an economy of overabundance, such companies can only sell products to people who want to buy them. Whether consumer demands drive food sales or the industry creates such demands is a matter of debate, but much industry effort goes into determining what the public "wants" and how to meet such "needs." Nearly all research on this issue comes to the same conclusion. When food is plentiful and people can afford to buy it, basic biological needs become less compelling, and the principal determinant of food choice is personal preference. In turn, personal preferences are influenced by religion and other cultural factors, as well as by considerations of convenience, price, and sometimes nutritional value. To sell food, companies must be more concerned about those other determinants than about the nutritional value of their products—unless nutritional value helps to entice buyers. Thus, the food industry's marketing imperatives principally concern taste, cost, and convenience. It is no surprise that people prefer foods that taste good, but taste preferences do not occur in a cultural vacuum. Family and ethnic background, levels of education, and income, age, and gender all influence food preferences. Taste is a response to flavor, smell, sight, and texture. Most people prefer sweet foods and those that are "energy-dense," meaning high in calories, fat, and sugar; they also like the taste of salt. Such preferences drive the development of new food products, as well as the menus in restaurants.

The cost issues are more complicated. An overly abundant food market creates pressures to add value to foods through processing. Producers of raw foods receive less than twenty cents on each food dollar spent at supermarkets, and this "farm value" has been declining for years. The farm value is unequally distributed; producers of eggs, beef, and chicken receive as much as half the retail cost whereas producers of lettuce and grapefruit, for example, often receive less than 10 percent. Once foods get to the supermarket, the proportion represented by the farm value declines further in proportion to the extent of processing. The farm value of frozen peas is 13 percent, of canned tomatoes 9 percent, of oatmeal 7 percent, and of corn syrup just 4 percent.

The remaining 80 percent of the food dollar goes for labor, packaging, advertising, and other such value-enhancing activities. Conversion of potatoes (cheap), to potato chips (expensive), and to those fried in artificial fats or coated in soybean flour or herbal supplements (even more expensive) illustrates how value is added to basic food commodities. Added value explains why the cost of the corn in Kellogg's Corn Flakes is less than 10 percent of the retail price. With this kind of pricing distribution, food companies are more likely to focus on added-value products rather than fresh fruits and vegetables, especially because opportunities for adding value to such foods are limited. Marketers can sell fruits and vegetables frozen, canned, or precut, but consumers balk at paying higher prices for such products. Americans pay a smaller percentage of income for food—about 10 percent—than people anywhere else in the world, only in part because of the high average income. The government subsidizes production of sugar and milk through price supports, but also supports farm production through a system of quotas, import restrictions, deficiency payments, lower tax rates, low-cost land leases, land management, water rights, and marketing and promotion programs. The subsidized cost of corn, wheat, and soybeans makes processed foods less expensive to produce and stimulates sales of added-value, top-of-the-pyramid products.

Convenience also drives the development of value-added products. As women entered the workforce and people began to work longer hours, demands for convenience increased. These societal changes explain why nearly half of all meals are prepared or consumed outside the home, why fast food is the fastest-growing segment of the food-service industry, and why the practice of snacking nearly doubled from the mid-1980s to the mid-1990s. They also explain the development of prepackaged sandwiches, salads, entrées, and desserts, as well as power bars, yogurt and pasta in tubes, prepackaged cereal in a bowl, salad bars, hot food bars, take-out chicken, supermarket home meal replacements, McDonald's shaker sal-

ads, chips prepackaged with dips, and foods designed to be eaten directly from the package. Whether these "hyper-convenient" products will outlast the competition remains to be seen, but their success is more likely to depend on taste and price than on nutrient content. Many such products are top-of-the-pyramid foods high in calories, fat, sugar, or salt but marketed as nutritious because they contain added vitamins and minerals, or have eliminated fat or carbohydrates.

Nutritionists and traditionalists may lament such developments, as convenience not only overrides considerations of health, but also the social and cultural meanings of meals and mealtimes. Many food products relegate cooking to a low-priority chore and encourage trends toward one-dish meals, fewer side dishes, fewer ingredients, larger portions to create leftovers, almost nothing cooked from scratch, and home-delivered meals ordered by telephone, fax, or Internet. Interpreting the meaning of these developments is likely to occupy sociologists and anthropologists for decades. In the meantime, convenience adds value to foods and stimulates the food industry to create even more products that can be consumed quickly and with minimal preparation.

Creating an "Eat More" Food Environment

In a competitive food marketplace, food companies must satisfy stockholders by encouraging more people to eat more of their products. They seek new audiences among children, target members of minority groups for special marketing campaigns, and develop international markets for their products. In existing markets, they expand sales through advertising, but also by developing new products designed to respond to consumer "demands." In recent years, marketers have embraced a new strategy—increasing the sizes of food portions. Advertising, new products, and larger portions all contribute to a food environment that promotes eating more, not less.

Advertising operates so far below the consciousness of everyone—the public, most nutritionists, and survey researchers—that rarely is it mentioned as an influence on food choice. The ubiquity of food and beverage advertising is a tribute to the power of its subliminal nature as well as to the sophistication of the agencies that produce it. Extraordinary amounts of money and talent go into this effort. Food and food-service companies spend more than $10 billion annually on direct media advertising in magazines, newspapers, radio, television, and billboards. In 2002, for example, McDonald's spent $1.4 billion, Burger

King spent $650 million, Coca-Cola spent $569 million, and Taco Bell spent $196 million just on direct media advertising. For every dollar spent in that "measured" way, the companies spend another two dollars on discount incentives—for example, coupons for consumers and "slotting fees" for retailers that ensure space on supermarket shelves. In total, food companies spend more than $34 billion annually to advertise and promote their products to the public. The largest part of this astronomical sum is used to promote the most highly processed and elaborately packaged foods and fast foods. Nearly 70 percent of food advertising is for convenience foods, candy and snacks, alcoholic beverages, soft drinks, and desserts, whereas just 2.2 percent is for fruits, vegetables, grains, or beans. The advertising costs for any single, nationally distributed food product far exceed federal expenditures for promotion of the pyramid or of eating more fruit and vegetables. Despite protestations by marketers that advertising is a minor element in food choice, advertising has been demonstrated to promote sales of specific food products and to do so in proportion to the amount spent. Food sales increase with intensity, repetition, and visibility of the advertising message, with promotion of nutritional advantages (low-fat, no cholesterol, high-fiber, "low-carb," and contains calcium), and with the use of health claims ("lowers cholesterol," "prevents cancer," and "supports a healthy immune system"). Advertising is especially effective with children, and advertisers deliberately promote food brands to children, at home and at school.

Added value and convenience drive new product development, and food companies introduce more than 10,000 new products annually. Since 1990, more than 100,000 new products have joined a marketplace containing 320,000 food items that compete for shelf space in supermarkets able to handle about 50,000 products each. The glut of food products means that only the most highly promoted products succeed; even these may encounter difficulties if they do not taste good, raise questions about health or safety, or are too expensive. More than two-thirds of the new products are condiments, candy and snacks, baked goods, soft drinks, and dairy products (cheese products and ice cream novelties). Nearly one-third are "nutritionally enhanced" so they can be marketed as low in fat, cholesterol, salt, or sugar, or higher in fiber, calcium, or vitamins. Some such products, among them no-fat cookies, vitamin-enriched cereals, and calcium-fortified juice drinks, contain so much sugar that they belong with the others at the top of the pyramid, even though they are marketed as "healthy." Developing such foods has one principal purpose: to attract sales.

"Eat more" marketing methods extend beyond billboards and television commercials; they also include substantial increases in the sizes of food packages and restaurant portions. When the pyramid recommends six to eleven grain servings, these amounts seem impossibly large with reference to the actual portions offered by restaurants, fast food chains, or take-out places. The pyramid serving numbers, however, refer to serving-size standards defined by the USDA: a standard grain serving, for example, is one slice of white bread, one ounce of ready-to-eat cereals or muffins, or one-half cup of rice or pasta. A marketplace bakery muffin weighing seven ounces, or a "medium" container of movie-theater popcorn (sixteen cups), meets or exceeds a full day's grain allowances with some left over for the next day. Larger servings, of course, contain more calories. The largest movie-theater soft drink (sixty-four ounces) can provide eight hundred calories if not too diluted with ice. Larger portions contribute to weight gain unless people compensate with diet and exercise. From an industry standpoint, however, larger portions make excellent marketing sense. The cost of food is low relative to labor and other factors that add value. Large portions attract customers who do not need much mathematical skill to understand that the larger units can be 40 percent cheaper by weight.

Advertising, convenience, larger portions, and adding nutrients to foods otherwise high in fat, sugar, and salt, all contribute to an environment that promotes eating more food, more often, and in larger quantities. Because dietary advice affects sales, food companies also conduct systematic, pervasive, and unrelenting (but far less visible) campaigns to convince government officials, health organizations, and nutrition professionals that their products are healthful, or at least do no harm, to avoid any suggestion to the contrary, and to ensure that federal dietary guidelines and food guides will help promote sales

Food Politics: A Matter of Democracy

America's overabundant food system and the consequences of food-marketing practices occur in the context of increasing centralization and globalization of the food industry and of altered patterns of work, welfare, and government. The food system is only one aspect of society but it is unusual in its universality: everyone eats. Because food affects lives as well as livelihoods, the politics of food generates substantial attention from the industry and the government, as well as from advocates, nutrition and health professionals, the media, and the public at large. No matter what the specific area of controversy over food issues, all reflect several recurrent themes central to the functioning of democratic institutions.

One theme is the "paradox of plenty," the term used by the historian Harvey Levenstein to refer to the social consequences of food overproduction, among them the sharp disparities in diet and health between rich and poor. Health habits tend to cluster in patterns, making it difficult to tease out the effects of diet from those of any other behavioral factor. Wealthier people are usually healthier, and they choose better diets. They also tend to avoid smoking cigarettes or drinking too much alcohol and to be better educated and more physically active. One paradox of food overabundance in the United States is that large numbers of Americans lack food security; they do not have enough to eat or cannot count on having enough resources to purchase adequate food on a daily basis. The economic expansion of the twentieth century differentially favored people whose income was higher than average and provided much smaller gains for the poor. In the United States, low-income groups seem to have about the same intake of nutrients as people who are better off, but they choose diets higher in calories, fat, meat, and sugar; they also display higher rates of obesity and chronic diseases. The income gap between rich and poor can be explained by the functioning of economic and related educational systems. The gaps in diet and health are economically based, but they also derive from the social status attached to certain kinds of food—meat for the poor and health foods for the rich, for example. Food and beverage companies reinforce this gap when they seek new marketing opportunities among minority groups or in low-income neighborhoods. The alcoholic beverage industry is especially active in marketing to disenfranchised groups.

A second theme is that of the conflict among belief systems that affect food choices. These systems include scientific beliefs about the value of specific nutrients or foods to health, but many people regard science as just one of a number of belief systems of equal validity and importance. Religious beliefs, concerns about animal rights, and views of the fundamental nature of society also influence food choice, as do vested interests. The conflict between scientific and other belief systems underlies much of the controversy over food issues. Government agencies invoke science as a basis for regulatory decisions. Food and supplement companies invoke science to oppose regulations and dietary advice that might adversely affect sales. Advocates invoke science to question the safety of products perceived as undesirable. Like any other kind of science, nutrition science is more a matter of probabilities than absolutes and, therefore, subject to interpretation. Interpretation, in turn, depends on point of view, but scientists and food producers who might benefit from promoting research results, nutritional benefits, or safety, tend to view other-than-scientific points of view as inherently irrational. When discussing food issues that affect broad aspects of society, scientific proof of safety often becomes the focus of debate whether or not it constitutes the "real" issue, largely because alternative belief systems cannot be validated by scientific methods.

A third theme is the central thesis of this article: diet is a political issue. Because dietary advice affects food sales, and companies demand a favorable regulatory environment for their products, dietary practices raise political issues central to democratic institutions. Debates about food issues nearly always reflect opinions about who should decide what people eat and whether or not a food is "healthy." As a result, food issues inevitably involve differing viewpoints about the way the government balances corporate against public interests. This last issue is revealed whenever a food company attacks its critics as "food police" or justifies self-interested actions as a defense of freedom of choice or exclusion of an Orwellian "Big Brother" from personal decisions. It is expressed whenever food companies use financial relationships with members of Congress, political leaders, and nutrition and health experts to weaken the regulatory ability of federal agencies, or when they go to court to block unfavorable regulatory decisions. Such disputes, of course, are fundamental to the functioning of the American political system. Despite the overwhelmingly greater resources of food companies, consumer advocates can also use the political system to convince Congress, federal agencies, and the courts to take action in the public interest, and sometimes they succeed in doing so.

The Politics of Food Choice

Like other businesses, food companies use lobbying, lawsuits, financial contributions, public relations, advertising, partnerships and alliances, philanthropy, threats, and biased information to convince Congress, federal agencies, nutrition and health professionals, and the public that each of the following precepts holds true: (a) the keys to healthful diets are balance, variety, and moderation; (b) all foods can be part of healthful diets; (c) there is no such thing as a good or bad food; (d) overweight is a result of inactivity, not overeating; (e) research on diet and health is so uncertain that there is no point in trying to eat healthfully; (f) only a small fraction of the population would benefit from following population-based dietary advice; (g) diets are a matter of personal responsibility and freedom of choice; (h) advocacy for more healthful food choices is unscientific; and (i) government intervention in dietary choice is unnecessary, undesirable, and incompatible with democratic institutions—except in situations in which following dietary advice favors their products.

With such statements, food industry officials appeal to fears of totalitarianism and other such emotions to argue against something that no nutritionist, private or governmental, advocates. Some foods are better for health than others. But the food industry fiercely opposes this idea, and uses its substantial resources, political skills, and emotional appeals to discourage attempts to introduce "eat less" messages into public discussion of dietary issues. These tactics are a normal part of doing business; they are no different from those used by such other large commercial interests as drug or tobacco companies. Sellers of food products however do not usually elicit the same level of attention. They should.

Americans cannot make informed decisions about food choice unless they understand how food companies influence their choices. An emphasis on personal choice serves the interests of the food industry for this reason: if diet is a matter of individual free will, then the sole remedy for poor diets is education—not advocating for societal changes that might promote more healthful dietary patterns.

The business press complains that advocates are trying to make food the next tobacco—subject to taxes and lawsuits in the name of health. Such parallels are difficult to avoid. Cigarette companies have long argued that smoking is a matter of individual choice and government has no right to interfere in the private lives of citizens. They use science to sow confusion about the harm caused by cigarettes. They use public relations, advertising, philanthropy, experts, political funding, alliances, lobbying, intimidation, and lawsuits to protect cigarette sales, and they promote cigarette smoking to children and adolescents, minorities, women, and the poor in the United States and internationally. Despite legal judgments against them, cigarette companies continue to lobby government and agencies and become financially enmeshed with nutrition and health experts. Such actions elicited protests that succeeded eventually in getting warning labels on cigarette packages, smoking-restricted areas in businesses and on airplanes, and attempts to regulate tobacco as a drug. The parallel practices of food companies however have not attracted anywhere near this level of protest.

One reason for this difference is that food is more complicated than tobacco. Although poor diets are believed to be responsible for as much illness and death as tobacco, tobacco is a single product requiring one health message: don't smoke. Food comprises hundreds of thousands of products requiring more complex messages: choose this product instead of that one, or eat less in general. Nevertheless, nutrition advocates have much to learn from the tobacco wars. Antismoking advocates based campaigns on four elements: a firm research base, a clear message, well-defined targets for intervention, and strategies that address the social environment as well as the education of individual smokers—age thresholds for buying cigarettes, taxes, and bans on smoking in airplanes, restaurants, and worksites, for example. Such elements could be applied to dietary change also. The evidence for the health benefits of dietary patterns rich in fruits, vegetables, and grains is strong; the message to follow such patterns is more complicated than "don't smoke," but not impossible to understand. If antismoking campaigns succeeded when they began to focus on environmental issues rather than the education of individuals, then promoting more healthful diets means using similar measures to counter food industry lobbying and marketing practices.

[*See also* Advertising; Advertising Cookbooklets and Recipes; Community-Supported Agriculture; Counterculture, Food; Department of Agriculture, United States; Farm Labor and Unions; Farm Subsidies, Duties, Quotas, and Tariffs; Food and Drug Administration; Food and Nutrition Systems; Food Marketing; Food Stamps; Hunger Programs; International Aid; Meals on Wheels; North American Free Trade Agreement; Prohibition; Pure Food and Drug Act; Radio and Television; School Food; Soup Kitchens; World's Fairs.]

Note: This article is based on material published in M. Nestle, *Food Politics: How the Food Industry Influences Nutrition and Health*. Berkeley: University of California Press, 2002. Used with permission.

BIBLIOGRAPHY

Frazão, E., ed. *America's Eating Habits: Changes and Consequences*. Washington, DC: USDA, 1999.

Gerrior, S., and L. Bente. *Nutrient Content of the U.S. Food Supply, 1909–99: A Summary Report*. Washington, DC: U.S. Department of Agriculture, 2002 (Home Economics Research Report No. 55).

Glantz, S. A., and E. D. Balbach. *Tobacco War: Inside the California Battles*. Berkeley: University of California Press, 2000.

Levenstein, H. *Paradox of Plenty: A Social History of Eating in Modern America*. Oxford: Oxford University Press, 1993.

Nestle, M. *Food Politics: How the Food Industry Influences Nutrition and Health*. Berkeley: University of California Press, 2002.

Office of the Surgeon General. *The Surgeon General's Call to Action to Prevent and Decrease Overweight and Obesity*. Rockville, MD: U.S. Department of Health and Human Services, 2001.

Putnam, J. J., and J. E. Allshouse. *Food Consumption, Prices, and Expenditures, 1970–97*. Washington, DC: U.S. Department of Agriculture, 1999.

Salter, L. *Mandated Science: Science and Scientists in the Making of Standards*. Dordrecht, Netherlands: Kluwer, 1988.

U.S. Department of Agriculture. *The Food Guide Pyramid*. Washington, DC: U.S. Government Printing Office, 1992.

U.S. Department of Agriculture and U.S. Department of Health and Human Services. *Dietary Guidelines for Americans*. 5th ed. Washington, DC: U.S. Government Printing Office, 2000.

World Health Organization. *Global Strategy on Diet, Physical Activity, Health*. Geneva, 2004.

MARION NESTLE

Pomegranates

The pomegranate (*Punica granatum*) originated somewhere in the region from Central Asia to Turkey, most likely in Iran, where it has been cultivated for five thousand years. Regally beautiful in its scarlet, leathery skin and turreted crown, it is like a treasure chest inside, with papery white membranes encasing hundreds of glistening garnet gems—seeds embedded in juice sacs. The flavor is sweet-tart and winy, intense but refreshing.

The pomegranate was introduced into Florida by the Spanish no later than the sixteenth century. Almost all of the American crop now comes from the San Joaquin Valley of California, where hot, dry summers mature sweet, attractive fruit. The main commercial variety is the modestly named Wonderful, propagated in 1896 from a Florida cutting. In the late 1990s one huge farm, planted to cash in on the vogue for fruits rich in anthocyanins, tripled California's acreage to 9,500. The season for fresh fruit runs from August through December, peaking in October and November. Pomegranates are used for decoration, eaten fresh (a rather messy affair), and juiced; the juice is used for making jelly, sorbet, cool drinks similar to lemonade, and a kind of wine.

[*See also* Fruit; Fruit Juices.]

BIBLIOGRAPHY

Hodgson, Robert W. *The Pomegranate*. Berkeley: University of California Press, 1917.

Mohnan Kumar, G. N. "Pomegranate." In *Fruits of Tropical and Subtropical Origin*, edited by Steven Nagy, Philip E. Shaw, and Wilfred F. Wardowski, 328–347. Lake Alfred: Florida Science Source, 1990.

DAVID KARP

Popcorn

Pre-Columbian Amerindians domesticated maize (*Zea mays*) by 5000 B.C.E. The earliest variety of maize was popcorn (*Zea everta*), which has small, hard kernels. This hard outer covering, or endosperm, makes unpopped kernels difficult to chew or grind. The easiest way to render them edible is to heat the kernel. Heat converts moisture inside the kernel into steam, which puts pressure on the endosperm. When the outer covering can no longer contain the pressure, the kernel pops, or everts, and exposes the tender inner part of the flake.

Popcorn has been found at archaeological sites in the Southwest, but the earliest record of it east of the Mississippi dates to the early nineteenth century. Popcorn was probably imported into New England from South America by whalers. During the 1840s popping corn became a fad in America. Boys sold popcorn at train stations and public gatherings. In Boston wagonloads of popcorn balls were being sold by street vendors by the late 1840s. Popcorn recipes began to appear in American cookbooks during the 1860s. For instance, E. F. Haskell published recipes for Pop Corn Balls and Pop Corn Cakes in her *Housekeeper's Encyclopedia* (1861). During the 1870s many cookbooks included recipes for Popcorn Pudding, which was a forerunner of cold breakfast cereal, and popcorn confections.

Technology played an important role in popcorn's expansion. The invention of the popcorn popper in the 1830s made it possible to contain the popped corn. (Before the popper, popcorn was placed near a fire, and when the kernels popped, some fell into the fire and others fell onto the floor or ground.) The invention of the steam-powered popcorn wagon by Charles Cretors in 1885 allowed vendors to sell hot popcorn on America's

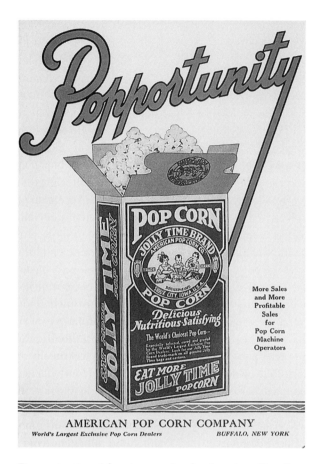

Popportunity. Advertisement for the American Pop Corn Company, 1929. *Collection of Andrew F. Smith*

streets. By the late nineteenth century popcorn was one of America's most popular snack foods. It was sold regularly at fairs, election rallies, circuses, and other large gatherings. When Americans began popping corn in their homes and at festive affairs, such as picnics, sales increased. With the advent of spectator sports, such as baseball, the sales of popcorn and popcorn products—Cracker Jack, for example—zoomed even higher.

At about the time that popcorn wagons disappeared from city streets as the result of zoning restrictions, an unlikely combination of events enhanced the sale of popcorn. The most important was the decision to sell snack foods in movie theaters, which had existed since the late nineteenth century. Early operators, however, had refused to sell popcorn, because it was a mess to clean up. A few independent theaters sold popcorn during the 1920s, but it took the Depression to boost popcorn sales in movie houses dramatically. When Prohibition ended in 1933, cocktail lounges and bars offered complimentary salty popcorn and other salty snacks, which enhanced the sale of alcoholic beverages, thereby greatly improving their profits.

World War II also affected popcorn consumption. Many foods were rationed during the war, but not popcorn. Consuming popcorn became "patriotic" as snack foods made with chocolate or sugar became scarce. During the war, the sale of sugar and chocolate was restricted, which further boosted the sale of popcorn. After the war, popcorn sales continued to increase. Popcorn remains a significant food in the United States.

[*See also* Cracker Jack; Snack Food; Street Vendors.]

BIBLIOGRAPHY

Smith, Andrew F. *Popped Culture: A Social History of Popcorn in America*. Columbia: University of South Carolina Press, 1999.

ANDREW F. SMITH

Popeyes Chicken and Biscuits

Popeyes Chicken and Biscuits is a quick-service restaurant known nationally and internationally for its Cajun-style cuisine. Inspired by the recipes and dishes of New Orleans and southwestern Louisiana, the restaurant features such items as spicy fried chicken, Cajun rice, jambalaya, red beans and rice, and étouffée. It is one of the world's largest fast-food chicken restaurants and the leader in the Cajun segment of the food-service industry. Popeyes has surpassed the billion-dollar mark in annual sales and boasts locations in twenty countries, including Germany, Japan, Italy, China, and the United Kingdom.

The restaurant, originally called Chicken on the Run, was opened in 1972 in New Orleans by Al Copeland. The initial offering was a more traditional fried chicken that did not achieve the desired level of success. As a result, Copeland relaunched the restaurant as Popeyes, naming it after Popeye Doyle from the movie *The French Connection*, and shifted to a spicier, Cajun-based menu. This new approach was very well received, and by 1976 Popeyes had opened its first franchise location in Baton Rouge, Louisiana. Twenty years later the thousandth Popeyes restaurant opened. By the early 2000s there were more than sixteen hundred Popeyes restaurants worldwide, with hundreds more scheduled to open.

Three important social trends have paralleled the growth of Popeyes in the United States: an increase in the size of minority populations accustomed to spicier foods, acceptance of and gradual preference for spicier foods by the U.S. population as a whole, and an upsurge in travel outside the United States. The popularity of Cajun chefs, such as Justin Wilson, a public television fixture for more than twenty-five years, and Paul Prudhomme, also contributed to the mainstreaming of Cajun cuisine.

In 1992 Popeyes was acquired by AFC Enterprises Inc., which also owns Church's Chicken and Cinnabon. Headquartered in Atlanta, Georgia, AFC Enterprises is a leading quick-service restaurant operator and franchiser. In the years following the acquisition, AFC Enterprises took many steps to ensure the continued growth of the Popeyes franchise. The company redesigned the look of the Popeyes restaurants to provide a more modern feel. They also began a more aggressive expansion strategy focusing efforts in the West and internationally.

In 1994 a research facility was opened to allow for the development of new menu items. As a result, Popeyes introduced such dishes as crawfish and chicken po'boys and launched a new menu line named Louisiana Legends. This line featured dishes like gumbo and étouffée, based on the New Orleans tradition of "one pot cooking." The new dishes, combined with the original Popeyes offerings, exemplified the merging of Creole and Cajun cuisines that had occurred in the United States over a number of years.

Responding to changes in the restaurant industry, Popeyes branched out to include new types of locations (convenience stores, grocery stores, mass merchandisers, airports, malls, and food courts) as well as new types of restaurants. One expansion of the franchise's restaurant concept is Cajun Kitchen, an entry into the "fast casual" segment of the dining industry. Throughout its history Popeyes has garnered numerous cuisine and service awards. The restaurant is also known for its popular jingle, "Love That Chicken from Popeyes."

[*See also* Cajun and Creole Food; Chicken; Fast Food.]

BIBLIOGRAPHY

Dwyer, Steve. "Delicious Diversity." *Prepared Foods* 167 (June 1998): 14.

Friedman, Martin. "Brand Extensions Trot to Hot." *Prepared Foods* 163 (November 1994): 61.

Jones, Wilbert. "Cajun and Creole Cuisines." *Prepared Foods* 171 (June 2002): 37–38.

Williamson, Debra Aho. "Foreign Flavors, Mainstream Taste." *Advertising Age* 73 (July 8, 2002): 2.

KRIS KRANENBURG

Pork, *see Pig*

Post Foods

When Charley Post, at the age of thirty-seven, was wheeled into Dr. John Harvey Kellogg's Battle Creek Sanitarium in 1891, he had high hopes that, finally, he would be cured. But the famous doctor's regimen of colon massages, multiple daily enemas, and a severe vegetarian diet were a bust. Frustrated, the man who had seen one enterprise after another sabotaged by his failing digestive tract finally availed himself of a psychic healer. She "vitalized in me the dormant forces," he was to relate later. As a result, it was in mesmerism and the related art of marketing that C. W. Post found his metier.

Post used his newfound health to open La Vita Inn, where he instituted a treatment that combined Kellogg's "scientific" methods with a prescription of mental suggestion. When, in 1895, the doctor turned down his offer to go into business marketing the Sanitarium's coffee substitute, Post holed up in a little horse barn and came up with his own ersatz coffee concocted of toasted wheat, bran, and a little molasses. The resulting Postum was promoted not only as economical, healthy, and natural but also as a builder of nerves, red blood, and all-around health. At the same time, Post's copy vilified real coffee for its "poisonous alkaloids" and implicated it as a cause of everything from blindness to heart attacks. "After all," the master mesmerist was once noted saying, "it's not enough to just make and sell cereal. After that you get it halfway down the customer's throat through the use of advertising. Then they've got to swallow it."

Grape-Nuts, introduced in 1897, was again based on a Kellogg staple called "granola," made by coarsely grinding a whole-grain cracker and then rebaking the resulting pellets. Post's Grape-Nuts was sold in small packages, supposedly because it was "concentrated." It was advertised as an alternative to surgery for an inflamed appendix and recommended for consumption, malaria, and loose teeth. As a result, by 1900 Post was said to be netting $3 million a year. In 1908, one more raid on the Sanitarium larder netted Post Toasties cornflakes. Then, in 1912, an instant Postum was introduced.

Unfortunately for Charley Post, neither his millions nor his mind-over-matter philosophy provided a cure for his troubles. In 1914, the ailing Grape-Nuts magnate shot himself in his California home.

His daughter and sole heir, Marjorie Merriweather Post, steered the company toward further expansion, acquiring over a dozen brands and expanding the product line to some sixty items. The new acquisitions included Baker's chocolate (1927), Maxwell House coffee (1928), and Jell-O gelatin (1925), to name a few. Finally, when the company bought out Clarence Birdseye's frozen food business, Postum was renamed the General Foods Corporation. In 1989, Kraft and General Foods Corporation, now both owned by Philip Morris, were consolidated into Kraft General Foods to form the largest food company at that time in the United States.

Over the years, the company's products have veered from cereals like Raisin Bran (1942) that were decidedly in the granola tradition, to the likes of Cocoa Pebbles (1971), inspired by the Flintstones, an animated sitcom. C. W. Post would most likely have been thrilled at the idea of cross-promoting a cereal with a television show.

[*See also* Birds Eye Foods; Breakfast Drinks; Breakfast Foods; Cereal, Cold; Coffee Substitutes; General Foods; Health Food; Jell-O; Kellogg, John Harvey; Kraft Foods; Maxwell House.]

BIBLIOGRAPHY

Carson, Gerald. *Cornflake Crusade*. New York: Rinehart, 1957.
Hillwood Museum. http://www.hillwoodmuseum.org.
Kraft Foods. http://www.kraft.com.
Lowe, Berenice Bryant. *Tales of Battle Creek*. Battle Creek, MI: Miller Foundation, 1976.
Post. http://www.grapenuts.com/postcereals/heritage.html.

MICHAEL KRONDL

Potato-Cooking Tools

Specialized tools for cutting and cooking potatoes have been used at least since the 1870s. Cranked slicers made continuous curling ribbons of raw potato; these tools appeared aroujnd the 1860s–1870s. Peelers similar in design to apple parers came out in about 1874. Chip slicers, dating to the same period, held a raw peeled potato against a revolving cutting blade. Beetles, wooden pestlelike pounders, are the oldest tool for mashing cooked potato, undoubtedly in use since Americans first grew potatoes. Other beetles of the 1870s have wire or perforated metal heads. A conical sieve, in which a cooked potato is rubbed with a wooden pestle through the holes, also dates to the 1870s. Potato ricers came in two types: a tabletop style with legs (circa 1900) and a handheld press (circa 1940) that forced cooked potato through a perforated hopper to create rice-sized potato pellets.

An 1890s metal rack had folded prongs that pierced potatoes and directed heat toward their centers to speed the baking. Similarly, about 1950 folding racks with thick aluminum nails began to be used; each rack held four potatoes. Stovetop ovens in the 1940s had a built-in thermometer set directly over the burner, and baked potatoes twice as quickly as the stove's oven.

[*See also* Potatoes.]

BIBLIOGRAPHY

Franklin, Linda Campbell. *300 Years of Kitchen Collectibles*. 5th ed. Iola, WI: Krause Publications, 2003.

LINDA CAMPBELL FRANKLIN

Potatoes

Potatoes are native to the South American Andes, whence European explorers brought them to Europe. From Europe they were carried to North America, first to Canada and later to the United States, where potatoes may have been introduced several times. Most sources agree that northeastern U.S. potato production originated with Presbyterian Scotch Irish settlers who brought potatoes with them to Londonderry, New Hampshire, in 1719, and from there the crop spread to the neighboring colonies throughout the Northeast and then westward. Thomas Jefferson and his fellow Virginia planters experimented unsuccessfully with potatoes as a field crop; they fit them into rotations with corn (the major staple food for humans), clover, and other grains, roots, and tubers in the unrealized hope that potatoes would replenish the soils and that animals and workers would eat them.

Potato commerce first entered the U.S. Census in 1840, showed a 20 to 30 percent decline owing to blight by 1843, and then rebounded in the late 1850s and 1860s, as new varieties and cultivation techniques became available. The most important introduction of new seeding material was Rough Purple Chili, which provided the ancestry for the Russet Burbank variety that now accounts for the largest share of U.S. baking potatoes as well as those processed into fries. Idaho and Washington, specializing in Russet Burbank, are the two leading producers; Wisconsin is a distant third.

All potato varieties are vulnerable to attacks by viruses, fungal and other microbial blights, and Colorado beetles. The Interregional Potato Introduction Station in Sturgeon Bay, Wisconsin, maintains a potato germplasm collection used by researchers and breeders to improve pest resistance and quality characteristics. In the 1990s the Monsanto company genetically engineered a line of New Leaf potatoes that were resistant to two viruses and beetles, but they were withdrawn in 2001, after fast food companies refused to buy them, the public resisted them, and farmers who were facing a market glut and low prices were wary of paying a premium for genetically engineered seeding materials.

Culinary Classifications and Nomenclature

Potato varieties are classified, named, and marketed according to their geographic location of production and intended use; for example, Idaho "baking potatoes" or eastern "all-purpose" potatoes. Some also carry particular varietal names, such as Russet Burbank—names that denote color or size, as in White Rose or Gold Rose. Breeders or marketers patent-protect designer heirloom varieties, which are distributed through fine-food stores and seed catalogs that market eyes, cuttings, and minitubers for home gardens, such as the small, elongated, dense, golden-fleshed La Ratte that boasts a nutlike flavor. Breeders at state universities sometimes design new and distinctive varieties for particular niches, for example, Michigan State University's Michigold variety, which is yellow-fleshed, tasty, nutritious, high yielding, and resistant to disease. Such specialty potatoes offer a counterpoint to more insipid potatoes industrially processed for fast food and frozen food markets, which have come to dominate production since the 1940s.

Solids content is the most important culinary characteristic: High-starch, floury potatoes are better for baking, frying, and mashing; low-starch, waxy potatoes are better for boiling, roasting, and salads (because they hold their shape); and medium-starch, all-purpose potatoes can be used for a variety of preparations. In the United States the most common potatoes are low-moisture russets, among which are the trademarked Idaho potatoes (Russet Burbank). These contain the highest percentage of solids, so they make good-quality baked potatoes and also yield better fries, which replace moisture with fat. Potatoes especially bred for standard fries also have a long, oblong shape that maximizes the numbers of fries per tuber. Eric Schlosser, in *Fast Food Nation*, describes how they are sliced; washed; cut into strips; double-blanched, first in water to remove natural sugars then in hot water to precook them; and, finally, dragged through sugar solutions, air-dried, fried, and frozen.

Since the end of World War II, processed products have dominated the market. The development of the frozen-food industry and other food-industry processes and packaging, combined with surging demand for snack and fast (convenience) foods, have contributed to this expansion. By the 1970s, 70 percent of Idaho-grown and 80 percent of Washington-grown potatoes were processed, and 50 percent of potatoes consumed in the United States were dehydrated, fried, canned, or frozen.

Potato in the American Diet

Potatoes fulfill three roles in American cuisine: as a staple of typical American meals, as a main ingredient in various ethnic foods, and as a snack food.

American Food Staple As components of a typical American meal, potatoes are matched with flesh foods (as in "meat and potatoes") and served in casseroles and stews. They also feature as an ingredient in appetizers, soups, salads, and vegetable dishes. By the early 2000s Americans were consuming more potatoes than any other vegetable. In American cuisine, potatoes contribute to distinctive foods of all regions. Randi Danforth's *Culinaria* contains no fewer than sixty-five references to the potato in typical American dishes. These dishes begin with home fries, a basic component of the American breakfast that is served along with eggs, meat, breads or biscuits, and gravies; mashed potatoes, an essential part of the traditional American Thanksgiving dinner, and new potatoes, filling the Fourth of July plate along with poached salmon and fresh green peas.

Ground meat and potatoes, in the form of meat loaf and mashed potatoes (typical "diner" fare) and hamburgers with a bag of fries and a soda (typical "fast food") are considered to be among Americans' favorite comfort foods, whether eaten outside or inside the home. At home the American family increasingly saves time by buying frozen, prepared versions that can be reheated quickly in a conventional oven or even more quickly in a microwave oven. Across America, home cooks have rendered potatoes more elegant by combining them with butter, eggs, cheese, or even stiff whipping cream (which makes them "Chantilly potatoes"). Irma S. Rombauer and Marion Rombauer Becker's *Joy of Cooking* (1964) details the preparation of these various potato dishes.

Potatoes also are basic ingredients in American fish-focused cuisine, in such menu items as New England clam chowder (which incorporates peeled, diced, medium-size

Giant Potato. Parade float in Aroostook County, Maine, October 1940. *Prints and Photographs Division, Library of Congress /Jack Delano*

potatoes), clambakes (which include small whole Maine potatoes or sometimes sweet potatoes), cod and other fish cakes (which blend in the flesh of medium-large boiling potatoes), and the Wisconsin "fish boil" dinner, which contains red new potatoes along with onions.

Potatoes tend to be more important in the cuisines of regions where they are grown—the Northeast, Midwest, and West. They are less popular in the South, but even there the ham and eggs, biscuits, grits, and gravy breakfast typically includes home fried potatoes, and flour-thickened milk gravy joins the flavors of mashed potatoes with fried chicken for dinner. Fried potatoes (chips) are among the popular side dishes eaten with southern barbecue, whereas potato salad is a side dish usually served with Texas barbecue, and mashed potatoes accompany Texas chicken-fried steak.

In the urban East, New York City restaurants famously contributed new potato dishes, among them, Delmonico potatoes, prepared with butter and lemon juice, and vichyssoise, a chilled potato and leek soup concocted by the Ritz Carlton hotel restaurant. The Buttolph Menu Collection of the New York Public Library documents how potatoes fit into the typical dinner meal of the late nineteenth century and the twentieth century.

Like other plant foods (including plain boiled rice and spaghetti), potatoes were put in the vegetable category at restaurants. Patrons often could choose either two vegetables or one potato and one vegetable from the menu. At its simplest, the choice was between boiled or mashed potatoes, two of the eleven "vegetables" on the Astor House (Ladies Ordinary) menu of August 25, 1843 (the oldest menu in the Buttolph Menu Collection). At its most elaborate, as in Fleischmann's Restaurant dinner menu of November 19, 1908, the patron selected from sixteen potato dishes (boiled, broiled, Saratoga fried, french fried, sautéed, fried sweet, mashed, lyonnaise, "maitre d'hotel," hashed or browned, julienne, au gratin, croquettes, stewed in cream, parisienne, or potato pancakes).

Ethnic Food Potatoes are a main ingredient in many complex ethnic foods, such as potato-stuffed pastries, pastas, soups, and stews. Commercial preparations include the "deli" potato knish (pastry enclosing potatoes and onions), potato salads, and potato pancakes, which are claimed by many ethnic groups in America. Potatoes are a central component of Caribbean curried root vegetables, Russian or "ethnic Chicago" pierogi (dumplings), Indian *dosi*, and Pennsylvania Dutch potato

Potato Face. In late-nineteenth-century America, potatoes were still associated with Irish immigrants. Advertising card published by Clay and Richmond, Buffalo, 1886, one of a series of such cards. [For other examples, see the entry for "Vegetables."] *Collection of Alice Ross*

rolls and potato-filled dumplings. Scandinavian settlers made potato flat bread and veal and potato sausage. These ethnic preparations amplified the homesteader diet on the Great Plains, which consisted of bacon and eggs with potatoes and onions fried in the fat.

Snacks Potatoes, particularly fried potatoes, are a snack food that can be eaten apart from the main meal. In this context, potatoes have become a principal menu item for food eaten outside the home. French fries have occupied a class of their own since the 1920s, when demand for fries allegedly soared with soldiers returning from France, where they had developed a taste for them. During World War II, frozen potato foods gained popularity.

Nutritional Dimensions

Potatoes, simply boiled, baked, or roasted, are nutritious. Their dry matter provides easily digested carbohydrate calories from starch and protein that is high in lysine and low in sulfur-containing amino acids and thus complementary to the protein in cereal grains. Even a small tuber (100 grams), boiled in its skin, has 16 milligrams of ascorbic acid, which is 80 percent of a child's or 50 percent of an adult's daily requirement. Potatoes are also a good source of B vitamins (thiamine, pyridoxine, and niacin) and are rich in potassium, phosphorus, and other trace elements. Preparation of potatoes in fried form eliminates the problem that tubers are too bulky to be a dietary staple for infants or children without an energy-rich supplement. In the United States, however, when fried potatoes become the dominant "vegetable" in children's diets, their consumption can pose a nutrition problem in the form of too many calories.

Future of Potatoes

Two countervailing trends in potato production and consumption probably will persist: one favoring uniformity, mass production, and processing and the other favoring a return to greater biodiversity and flavor. Even if genetic engineering is not accepted for comestible potatoes, it will contribute additional nonfood uses for starch, alcohol, pharmaceuticals, and chemical polymers for plastics and synthetic rubbers. In addition, with their strict standards for marketing and processing, potatoes will continue to serve as a model philanthropic crop. The Virginia-based Society of Saint Andrew each year gleans about 20 million pounds of potatoes rejected by commercial markets and processing plants and redirects them to soup kitchens, Native American reservations, food pantries, and other hunger agencies, at a cost of about four cents per pound for the shipping.

[*See also* Diners; Fast Food; French Fries; Heirloom Vegetables; Salads and Salad Dressings; Soups and Stews.]

BIBLIOGRAPHY

Bareham, Lindsey. *In Praise of the Potato: Recipes from around the World.* Woodstock, NY: Overlook Press, 1992.

Betts, Edwin Morris, ed. *Thomas Jefferson's Farm Book, with Commentary and Relevant Extracts from Other Writings.* Charlottesville, VA: Thomas Jefferson Memorial Foundation, 1999.

Bidwell, Percy W., and John I. Falconer. *History of Agriculture in the Northern United States, 1620–1860.* New York: Peter Smith, 1941.

Danforth, Randi, ed. *Culinaria. The United States: A Culinary Discovery.* Cologne and New York: Konemann Publishers, 1998.

Linn, Biing-Hwan, Gary Lucier, Jane Allshouse, Linda S. Kantor. "Market Distribution of Potato Products in the United States." *Journal of Food Products Marketing* 6 (2001): 4.

Marshall, Lydie. *A Passion for Potatoes.* New York: Harper Perennial, 1992.

Messer, Ellen. "Potatoes (White)." In *The Cambridge World History of Food,* edited by Kenneth F. Kiple and Kriemhild Coneè Ornelas. Vol. 2. New York: Cambridge University Press, 2000.

Pool, Robert. "In Search of the Plastic Potato." *Science* 245 (1989): 1187–1189.

Schlosser, Eric. *Fast Food Nation: The Dark Side of the All-American Meal.* Boston: Houghton Mifflin, 2001.

Woolfe, Jennifer A., with Susan V. Poats. *Potato in the Human Diet.* New York: Cambridge University Press, 1987.

ELLEN MESSER

Pot Holders

Pot holders, which have existed in the United States probably since the late eighteenth century, both insulate and decorate. In the 1840s needlepoint holders were used for teapots in the parlor. Most surviving nineteenth- and early-twentieth-century examples are of quilted scrap cloth, such as calico and chintz. Some 1880s Pennsylvania holders look like setting hens whose wings fold around an egg cooker's or tea kettle's handle. By the 1940s booklets produced by yarn companies gave instructions for crocheting colorful pot holders shaped like animals, faces, and houses. Also in the 1940s weaving kits with pronged frames and bright loops of knitted cotton let children make pot holders. The 1950s brought insulated oven mitts.

BIBLIOGRAPHY

Franklin, Linda Campbell. *300 Years of Kitchen Collectibles.* 5th ed. Iola, WI: Krause Publications, 2003.

LINDA CAMPBELL FRANKLIN

Pots and Pans

Pots and pans of surprising similarity have been used throughout the ancient world and have survived, as basic and necessary cookware, to the twenty-first century relatively unchanged. So common as to be idiomatic, their names combine significantly to mean "assorted essentials." The words themselves signify their universality.

The term "pot," in medieval English, referred to a deep and rounded cooking vessel that was deeper than it was wide, stood on three legs, and had a narrowing top and swinging bail handle. Used for such wet processes as boiling or stewing, they have since been known as bulge pots, cauldrons, or "gypsy kettles." The later, more encompassing sixteenth-century term meant almost any deep container for cooking, including straight-sided, long-handled posnets and pipkins (early saucepans).

Pans, on the other hand, were generally straight-sided and flat-bottomed and tended to be shallow. Often three-legged, they were more likely to be used for dry cooking as drip pans (under the roast), baking pans, frying pans, and preserving pans.

By the time of European settlement in America, the iron pot was perhaps the most important and basic of all possible pieces of hearth equipment, though closely followed by the frying pan and water kettle. Its round bottom allowed quick and even heat transmission, and the absence of corners made stirring more efficient. Flat-bottom pots, more commonly made from the softer metals, depended on cooking trivets to hold them high above the hearth's heat. Although they were essential to every kitchen, their numbers, materials, and variations depended on the wealth and social position of their owners.

Emigrants to the New World brought basic pots and pans and re-created them locally. With typical devotion to the food and equipment of their traditional cuisines, the English prepared their stews in stew pots, the French in beloved marmites, and the Spanish in ollas. By the middle of the eighteenth century, the introduction of tin provided a new material for inexpensive cookware, one that would eventually replace earlier ceramics. Increasing availability enabled colonial families to enlarge their stock of pots and pans and to undertake more elaborate cookery.

The American Industrial Revolution (ca. 1850), with its new technologies and production techniques, introduced pots and pans adapted to the new cookstoves. Flat-bottomed, short-handled, and legless, these pots and pans made maximum contact with the new cooking surfaces. Cast-iron goods proliferated and utensils were produced that addressed more decorative and stylish concerns, offering shaped bread pans, such as gem, or muffin, pans and cornbread-stick pans. Tinware was also improved stylistically with coatings of colorful baked-on enamel. It filled kitchen shelves until well into the twentieth century to be superseded by the more durable aluminum and stainless steel.

Americans, in the twenty-first century, have turned to gourmet, ethnic, and health-oriented cookery, and new

Copper Saucepans. From the Duparquet, Huot, & Moneuse Co. catalog (Boston, 1915), p. 160.

pots and pans reflecting these interests and concerns crowd the pantry. Heavy copper pots, once the hallmark of professional chefs, are found in many middle-class kitchens, as are new steamer pots used by the quality-conscious and the health-conscious. Likewise, ethnic cuisines demand that home cooks own such exotica as pasta pots, polenta pots, fondue pots, or paella pans. Looking ahead, pots and pans will continue being adapted to changing food fashion and new fuels, just as they have been adapted to microwaves, magnetic waves, and halogen.

[*See also* Cooking Techniques; Dutch Ovens; Hearth Cookery; Kettles; Material Culture and Technology; Stoves and Ovens.]

BIBLIOGRAPHY

Franklin, Linda Campbell. *300 Years of Kitchen Collectibles.* 5th ed. Iola, WI: Krause, 2003.
Greguire, Helen. *The Collector's Encyclopedia of Granite Ware: Colors, Shapes, and Values, Book 2.* Rev. ed. Paducah, KY: Collector Books, 2000.
Smith, David G., and Chuck Wafford. *The Book of Wagner and Griswold.* Atglen, PA: Schiffer, 2001.
Smith, David G., and Chuck Wafford. *The Book of Griswold and Wagner: Favorite Piqua, Sidney Hollow Ware, Wapak.* Atglen, PA: Schiffer, 1995.

ALICE ROSS

Poultry and Fowl

More than twelve thousand species of birds are dispersed throughout the world, and almost all are edible. Early humans probably took eggs from birds' nests and consumed them, and later they figured out how to capture the birds themselves. Fowl had much to offer, as food and otherwise. Birds provided many advantages: eggs were eaten raw or cooked; poultry flesh was consumed; feathers had practical uses on arrows and as personal adornment, clothing, and ceremonial symbols; and birds such

as ducks, geese, and storks were religious symbols. Chicken eggs and entrails were used for religious ceremonies, divination, and magic. Cock's combs and other body parts were used in medicines, and roosters were used for gaming and entertainment in cockfights.

Poultry

Domestication of fowl began in prehistoric times in both the Old World and the New World. By far the most important domesticated fowl was the chicken (*Gallus domesticus*), which most likely descended from a combination of several species of jungle fowl native to southern and Southeast Asia. Chickens are highly prized because they lay many more eggs than the hens of other fowl and do so throughout the year, providing a steady source of food. In pre-Columbian times, chickens were widely dispersed throughout the Old World and the Pacific Islands. Soon after the beginning of European exploration of the New World in the sixteenth century, chickens were disseminated throughout the Americas. Chickens were kept throughout all the American colonies, and most farms and plantations permitted chickens to roam freely about yards.

European settlers introduced other poultry into the Americas, including domesticated turkeys, Muscovy and mallard ducks, geese, guinea fowl, and peafowl. By the early nineteenth century, chickens and turkeys dominated the poultry yards, and both birds were raised on a large scale for city markets. Little attention was paid to selective breeding of poultry, except for cockfighting purposes, before the 1840s, when traders brought large and exotic chickens, such as the Cochin, Brahma, Shanghai, and Chittagong, from Asia to America. The introduction of exotic fowl contributed to "hen fever," which swept the United States beginning in 1850. Over the next five years, poultry prices increased and fortunes were made in breeding and selling exotic fowl. Poultry exhibitions were held, and new breeds, such as the Plymouth Rock, were developed. By the 1870s, breeds were standardized, and breeding clubs were formed.

During the following decades, the development of refrigerated railway cars allowed producers to ship fresh foods longer distances. Because this system required large amounts of capital, it also led to centralization of the poultry industry in the Midwest. In 1890 two and a half million pounds of dressed fowl were shipped from Kansas City, Missouri, alone. Chickens are the most important form of commercial fowl, followed by turkeys and, a distant third, ducks.

Cookery

Since its introduction in the seventeenth century, the chicken has been America's most important fowl. The mild, neutral flavor of chicken is flattered by any number of different seasonings and companion ingredients. Inexpensive and plentiful, chicken lends itself to an appealing variety of cooking methods and recipes. Chicken—whole or in parts—can be roasted, baked, fricasseed, deviled, fried, hashed, sautéed, made into soups, broths, gumbos, and gravies, and incorporated into pies, puddings, and croquettes. Cold chicken can be served in salads and sandwiches. Poultry can be stuffed with bread, grain, forcemeat, or vegetables or be served with special gravies and sauces, such as oyster and curry sauces. Almost all parts of a chicken, including neck, gizzard, feet, heart, and liver, are consumed in various ways. Recipes for preparing chickens for the table have abounded in cookbooks since the early nineteenth century. These include barbecued chicken, chicken potpie, chicken and dumplings, chicken Maryland, Brunswick stew, jambalaya, gumbo, and chicken à la king.

Chicken was particularly important in the South. Before the Civil War, many slaves were permitted to keep chickens, and they elevated the technique of frying chicken to an art form. After the Civil War, migrations of African Americans out of the South contributed to making "southern fried chicken" a national dish during the twentieth century.

Poultry was used as inexpensive food for servants and slaves, but domesticated and wild birds also appeared on the tables in America's most elegant restaurants. Nineteenth-century cookbooks provided an abundance of recipes for barnyard fowl and wild duck and goose, as well as blackbird, lark, quail, grouse, guinea fowl, peafowl, pigeon, plover, widgeon, and other game birds. There were instructions for buying poultry and for preparing home-grown or purchased birds for the oven or pot. Roasting was a basic method of preparation, but there were also recipes for fricassees, stews, ragouts, potpies, and hashes. The books contained directions for making chicken broth or stock as well as heartier soups and recipes for sauces and stuffings or dressings for specific birds.

Poultry. Brahma Pootra fowls. Frontispiece to Simon M. Saunders, *Domestic Poultry* (New York, 1866).

Commercialization

Chicken remains the dominant poultry in America and the world. In addition to the traditional ways of preparing chicken in the home, fast food establishments have commercialized specific chicken dishes, such as the fried chicken served at KFC and the chicken McNuggets served at McDonald's. Chicken burgers are served at many hamburger establishments, and "chicken dogs" are sold in supermarkets throughout America. Many manufacturers include chicken in frozen dinners. Turkey remains a distant second in the commercial poultry market, but its sales have extended beyond the traditional Thanksgiving and Christmas periods.

[*See also* Chicken; Chicken Cookery; Dressings and Stuffings; Duck; Eggs; Goose; Turkey.]

BIBLIOGRAPHY

American Poultry Historical Society. *American Poultry History 1823–1973*. Madison, WI: American Poultry History Society, 1974.

Davis, Karen. *More than a Meal: The Turkey in History, Myth, Ritual and Reality*. New York: Lantern Books, 2001.

Davis, Karen. *Prisoned Chickens, Poisoned Eggs: An Inside Look at the Modern Poultry Industry*. Summertown, TN: Book, 1996.

Dohner, Janet Vorwald. *The Encyclopedia and Endangered Livestock and Poultry Breeds*. New Haven, CT, and London: Yale University Press, 2001.

National Agricultural Center, National Poultry Museum. http://www.poultryscience.org/psapub/pmuseum.html.

Sawyer, Gordon. *The Agribusiness Poultry Industry: A History of Its Development*. New York: Exposition, 1971.

Smith, Page, and Charles Daniel. *The Chicken Book*. San Francisco: North Point, 1982.

ANDREW F. SMITH

Preserves

Preserves are preparations of fruits cooked with sugar until soft and gelled—delicacies that store well for months without refrigeration. They include the familiar jams, jellies, syrups, fruit butters, and marmalades, as well as the lesser-known conserves (jamlike, but with nuts and raisins and sometimes citrus peels) and preparations of wines, herbs, and spices. Historically, the significance of preserves lay in their ability to provide summertime flavors in wintertime, when such luxuries were beyond the reach of most people.

History of Preserves

From antiquity, preserves were made from fruits wherever there was honey or sugar, the essential preservatives. It was not until the medieval period and the introduction of sugar to Europe that the kinds of preserves later known in America were developed. Among the earliest were a series of quince jams, jellies, syrups, marmalades, and preserves. The quince (an applelike but very sour fruit), sugar, and rose or perfume flavorings were derivatives of still earlier Middle Eastern preparations, exotic to English palates at the time. In addition to its appealing flavor, quince had the benefit of contributing its own pectin, the gelling factor found in the pulp surrounding its seeds. Many preserves also were based on available orchard fruits, berries, currants, and gooseberries. As many of these lacked their own pectin, long cooking and the addition of high pectin fruits or processed gelatinous animal products (isinglass, hartshorn, or calves' feet) were used to achieve the desired thickening.

These basic recipes were brought to the New World, along with the means to establish sugar and fruit production. At first, because of its scarcity and expense, sugar was used only by the wealthy, who prepared some of their own products and imported others from Europe. Using cookbooks and recipes from their mother countries, seventeenth- and eighteenth-century colonists continued basic preparations, sometimes adapting indigenous American foods to their conserves and marmalades. Thus regional specialties evolved based on northwestern salmonberries and dewberries, southwestern hot and spicy tomato mixtures, and coastal northeastern beach plums.

Colonial preserving usually was the province of the mistress of the house, as sugar work and candying were considered special skills. A gift of preserves clearly honored its recipients. Because of their high status, they were featured components of pyramids of sweetmeats or formal teas. Some accompanied meats: Cumberland sauce of jellied currants served with venison, jellied cranberries paired with turkey, mint jelly with lamb, and wild beach plum jams with ham.

By the end of the nineteenth century, a number of converging factors brought home preserving within the reach of middle-class homemakers. Inexpensive sugar, the new cookstove, glass canning jars with screw-on or clamped lids, and abundant fruits reduced the costs and time-consuming labor; home preserving became integral to the domestic calendar year. A homemaker's reputation rested on her clearest jellies, most flavorful jams and conserves, and most innovative combinations of fruits and spices. Home cooks were inspired and guided by single-themed cookbooks such as Sarah Tyson Rorer's *Canning and Preserving* (1887) and Gesine Lemcke's *Preserving*

The Fruits of Victory

Write for Free Book to
National War Garden Commission
Washington, D.C.
Charles Lathrop Pack, President   P.S. Ridsdale, Secretary

Preserves. *Fruits of Victory*, poster by Leonebel Jacobs, ca. 1918. *Prints and Photographs Division, Library of Congress*

and Pickling (1899). Local shops also sold commercially preserved products by companies such as H. J. Heinz and H. K. and F. B. Thurber. Preserves on toast soon became a breakfast standby.

In this era preserving still required long cooking times, which meant a good deal of the fruit's original flavor was lost. Some argued for processing in small quantities. Others shortened cooking times with the introduction of twentieth-century commercial pectins, which were criticized for masking the fruit's flavor. The debate continues. Today only the occasional home cook fills her pantry with homemade specialties. In an era when lack of time is an issue, it is far easier to buy good-quality products, and a homemaker's reputation now is based on other activities.

Methods of Making Preserves

Historically, the standard proportions for preserves were equal weights of fruit and sugar, which were cooked in a shallow brass, bell metal, or enameled iron pan (not uncoated iron, as it darkens the fruit). In some cases the prepared fruit and sugar were allowed to sit overnight before cooking, a process that drew the liquid and maintained a firmer texture. Thickening was achieved by lengthy cooking, often two hours or more. The completed preserve was put up in jelly glasses or stone pots (stoneware), sealed with brandy papers and perhaps melted tallow, and covered with a tied-on paper or cloth. Syrups followed the same procedure, but the fruit was strained and then corked in a bottle.

The cooking time for preserves has been shortened considerably by the use of modern commercial pectin, a product of orange rind. Sealing is accomplished by the use of paraffin, two-piece lids, and sometimes terminal sterilization. Some sweetened, uncooked jams (with wonderfully fresh flavors) are preserved by freezing.

Types of Preserves

Jam is a chunky preservation in which irregular pieces of fruit are cooked in their own juices. This is the most common and simplest form of preserves, in which the fruit preparation involves removing pits and stems (and occasionally peeling) and coarse chopping. Jelly is a clear version of jam. After a brief simmering, the fruit is strained and the juice is processed as for jam. Preserves are a coarse jam, sometimes mixed with other fruits and spices.

Marmalade was historically a simple jam or jelly, and it became associated with orange and lemon rinds in England before 1700. Thinly sliced rinds sometimes were set with sugar overnight to draw the juice and then cooked until translucent. Early orange marmalades used flavorful but bitter Seville oranges, which may have been presoaked or parboiled to reduce bitterness. Early American marmalades sometimes included sliced pumpkin or American citron (a watermelon variety).

Conserves are more complex jams, which combine fruits, nuts, raisins, and spices, and are served on bread or with meats. Syrups are jellylike but ungelled flavorings. Fruit butters are dense, long-cooked jams. They are often fortified with cider and spices. Leathers are sheets of chewy, sweetened semidried fruits. They are prepared like jams but cooked longer, spread on papers on a shallow plate or pan, and further dried over a brazier or in a very cool oven until leathery. These remain popular snacks.

Preserved whole fruits in syrup were used as decorative and flavorful sweet accompaniments or desserts. Small fruits such as crab apples, cherries, or plums were used as edible garnishes. Preserved whole fruits in brandy were a more elegant form of those preserved in syrup. The brandy itself was a preservative. Despite its historical popularity, the temperance movement helped its demise.

[*See also* Canning and Bottling; Fruit; Sugar.]

BIBLIOGRAPHY

Carey, Nora. *Perfect Preserves: Provisions from the Kitchen Garden.* New York: Stewart, Tabori and Chang, 1990.
Plagemann, Catherine. *Fine Preserving: M. F. K. Fisher's Annotated Edition of Catherine Plagemann's Cookbook.* Berkeley, CA: Aris, 1986.

ALICE ROSS

President's Day, *see Washington's Birthday*

Pressure Cookers

Cooking food thoroughly using steam under pressure seems modern, but the French scientist Denis Papin invented a pressure cooker in 1679. Called a "Digester" or "La marmite," it softened bones and otherwise wasted meat parts. Aware of the potential for explosion, Papin incorporated a valve to let off steam when it reached a level of pressure that was dangerous.

A digester available in America was depicted in the 1854 edition of the *American Home Cook Book*. It shows a squat cast-iron kettle, bowed out at its center, with a swinging handle, and a clamp-on lid. Sizes ranged from one quart to eight gallons. Bones and gristle softened for soup gave thrifty cooks full value for any cut of meat. Almost identical was one manufactured in 1909 for hotels and restaurants, with sealing gaskets and lid clamps.

Cast-aluminum pressure cookers began to appear in the 1920s. Always of prime concern was the danger of pressure building up unrelieved until the cooker exploded, so steam escape valves and pressure gauges were standard. Pressure cookers in the twenty-first century are little changed in form, but safety has been greatly improved.

[*See also* Cooking Techniques; Pots and Pans.]

BIBLIOGRAPHY

Franklin, Linda Campbell. *300 Years of Kitchen Collectibles.* 5th ed. Iola, WI: Krause, 2003.

LINDA CAMPBELL FRANKLIN

Prickly Pear, *see Cactus*

Prison Food

The goals and challenges of prison food service are similar to those of other institutional food-service operations. Food must be provided to a large, in-house group in a manner that is efficient, cost-effective, and sanitary. The majority of prisons in the United States are run by individual state Departments of Corrections, which means that prisons differ in their approaches to meeting these goals and challenges. However, on average, the cost of feeding an inmate in a United States prison in 2000 was $2.42 per day.

Prison menus reflect financial constraints, nutrition and safety concerns, and philosophies of the rights of prisoners. Meals reflect the needs and preferences of the institution rather than those of the inmates. Taste, quality, and variety are not major considerations in correctional facilities.

As American prisons become increasingly crowded, states place increased pressure on prisons to cut food-service costs, resulting in reduced food quality and quantity. In Georgia, for example, prisons cut fried foods from the menu to reduce equipment maintenance, sewage problems, and frying-oil expenses. Georgia prisons, in the early 2000s, were adding soy extenders to meat, serving only cold-cut lunches, and preparing only two meals on weekends and holidays. In Texas, prisons reduced daily inmate calories from 2,700 to 2,500, and in Iowa prisons replaced orange juice with vitamin-enhanced orange-flavored liquid.

These changes, however, cannot compromise the nutritional value or safety of inmate diets, both of which are guaranteed to the inmates by the Eighth Amendment to the Constitution. All menus must meet basic nutritional requirements and should be monitored by an in-house or consultant dietitian. Guidelines for preparing healthful meals in prisons are outlined in the *Correctional Foodservice and Nutrition Manual* created by Consultant Dietitians in Health Care Facilities and distributed through the American Dietetics Association.

Early twenty-first-century nutritional improvements to inmate meals include the reduction of fatty, red meats and the increased use of lower-fat poultry items. To make foods safer and reduce instances of food-borne illness, some prisons purchase individually portioned packages of meat to control bacterial growth. Other prisons take temperature readings at the time of food delivery to assure that food is served at the proper temperature. Such changes, however, bring challenges. Prisons report that inmates find higher-calorie menus more satisfying than lower-calorie menus and that lower-fat meals are more expensive than meals containing a greater percentage of fat. For example, a meal composed of only 30 percent fat costs 15 percent more than a meal composed of 40 percent fat.

The preparation and service of food in prisons reflects the institution's role as a place of punishment and rehabilitation. Many prison tensions are played out over food; inmates stage hunger strikes and start food riots, corrections officers tamper with food, and kitchens serve tasteless, unappealing food as punishment. Although the content, preparation, and service of prison meals vary by state, all prison meals reflect the American view of prisoners' rights and the role of American penal institutions.

Twenty-first-century shifts in prison food service include changes in how food is procured, how it is prepared, and what is served. The most common shift in prison food service is from an internally run operation to one that is contracted out to a private company specializing in institutional food service. Although this shift can mean less control over the dietary department, its benefits include increased cash flow and fewer demands on prison staff. Other states tackle prison food service in more creative ways. In Georgia, for example, the Georgia Department of Corrections' Food and Farm Services Division manages a ten thousand-acre growing, processing, and distribution program. This farm includes vegetable crops, dairy production, and meat production; saves taxpayers millions of dollars; and involves the prisoners in the work of growing, harvesting, processing, and preparing of food. In an entirely different approach to feeding prisoners, Victor Valley Medium Correctional Facility in Adelanto, California, implemented the NEW-START vegan program for approximately half of their inmates. In this program, prisoners eat a purely vegan diet (except on weekends) in addition to attending religion and life-skill classes. The prison staff at Victor Valley reports that inmates in this program are better behaved and are less likely to become repeat offenders than inmates not enrolled in the program. Regardless of how prisons choose to feed inmates, decisions made reveal the contradictory role of prisons as institutions of punishment, rehabilitation, and guardianship.

[*See also* Nutrition.]

BIBLIOGRAPHY

American Correctional Food Service Association. http://www.acfsa. org. A professional organization and website for food-service employees in correctional facilities. Includes information about membership, events, products, and other relevant websites.

Consultant Dietitians in Health Care Facilities. http://www.cdhcf. org. A website and professional organization for dietitians in health care facilities. Includes standards of practice, news, products, job listings, and links to related websites.

MIMI MARTIN

Prohibition

Prohibition was a period in U.S. history, between 1920 and 1933, when federal law forbade the manufacture, importation, or sale of alcohol. Brought on by a century-long temperance movement and effected by an amendment to the U.S. Constitution, Prohibition was an attempt by political and religious conservatives to solve what they believed to be the country's social and economic problems. This ban on alcohol during the Prohibition era reduced the drinking of beer, wine, and liquor, but it also became a divisive political issue and helped a network of organized crime to become entrenched in America. Widespread opposition to the law caused its repeal in 1933.

The Temperance Movement

The reasons for Prohibition date back to the beginning of the nineteenth century, when some Christian denominations began a national crusade against alcohol abuse. Drinking alcohol was a common practice for American men, who often congregated in local taverns. Quakers and Methodists were the first groups to speak out against this practice, though they differentiated between distilled spirits, which they cast as evil, and the moderate use of fermented beverages. This temperance sentiment soon spread through other denominations, increasing in intensity with the onset of the Second Great Awakening, a resurgence of religious fervor in the 1830s. Concurrent with this resurgence of religious fervor was the arrival of hundreds of thousands of immigrants from Germany and Ireland. Many of these newcomers in the 1820s and 1830s were Catholic, and most habitually drank much more than their native-born Anglo-American Protestant neighbors. Threatened by the overwhelming numbers of immigrants coming to their cities and offended by immigrant drinking, the native-born Americans, or "nativists," took steps to preserve the status quo. Protestant leaders formed the American Temperance Society in 1826, urging local and state governments to limit or ban drinking. Women's rights groups and abolitionists added their voices to this demand, viewing alcohol abuse as a major social problem. Several northern states responded by passing legislation to prohibit the manufacture and sale of alcohol, laws that remained in force until the 1850s.

The combined efforts of these church groups and restrictive laws did lessen alcohol consumption during this period, but immigrant groups maintained drinking as part of their ethnic cultures. Alcohol consumption briefly rebounded during the Civil War, with millions of American men serving in the armies of the Union and the Confederacy. Protestant temperance groups revived their crusade against drinking immediately after the war's end, starting new organizations, such as the Prohibition Party, the Anti-Saloon League, and the Woman's Christian Temperance Union. These groups lobbied legislators, published numerous tracts on temperance, and often took direct actions against saloons and taverns. Although the Prohibition Party never seriously competed in national elections, the Anti-Saloon League developed a nation-wide network of local church groups, and Woman's Christian Temperance Union members gained notoriety by peacefully invading saloons.

Political Action

These temperance organizations continued their fight into the early twentieth century, patiently building up political and financial support. The business leaders Sebastian Kresge and John D. Rockefeller provided funding, which enabled temperance activists to finance campaigns and educational programs. In 1913 the Anti-Saloon League marched on Washington, D.C., delivering to Congress the draft of a constitutional amendment banning alcohol. That draft soon became the 1914 Hobson-Sheppard bill, which was defeated in the Senate. Responding to that defeat with even greater political funding, temperance leaders gained ground by pushing hard for their "dry" candidates in 1916. Americans quickly became vehemently anti-German with the start of World War I, and temperance supporters turned that anger against large breweries owned by German American families. Also arguing that grain supplies should go to the war effort rather than for alcohol production, they equated sobriety with patriotism. Sensing increasing popular support for the prohibition of spirits, Congress in 1917 passed the Eighteenth Amendment, which was ratified thirteen months later. Next, they passed the National Prohibition Act, commonly called the Volstead Act, which defined the amendment's parameters and enforcement measures. Prohibition became law

on January 29, 1920, criminalizing the manufacture, sale, importation, or distribution of alcohol in the United States.

The Volstead Act banned most alcohol but allowed exceptions for alcohol used in patent medicines, doctor's prescriptions, sacramental wine, cider, syrups, vinegars, and "near beer" with an alcohol content of 0.5 percent or less. These many exceptions became popular conduits for legally acquiring alcohol. Churches often multiplied their pre-Prohibition wine orders, and drinkers injected toxic rubbing alcohol into near beer to create the more potent, though dangerous "needle beer." In addition, many drinkers turned to fermenting grapes or brewing grains at home. Home production of beer and wine was technically in violation of the law, but no government agency attempted to monitor strictly personal consumption.

Federal, state, and local authorities soon realized that the Volstead Act would be difficult to enforce. Consuming alcoholic beverages was a popular activity, and many Americans just refused to stop drinking. Knowing of the ban well in advance, many drinkers stockpiled huge amounts of their favorite beverages. Lacking this foresight or ready cash, others sometimes paid ten times more for a glass of whiskey during Prohibition than they had paid in 1919. Numerous saloons and bars remained open, becoming illegal "speakeasies," even though distilleries, breweries, and wineries abruptly closed or turned to making other products.

Bootlegging and the Rise of Organized Crime

Illicit suppliers immediately replaced the formerly legitimate sources, bringing in Caribbean rum through Florida, Canadian whiskey across the northern border, and higher-priced Scotch whisky and Irish whiskey and European wines onto the Atlantic beaches. Called both bootleggers and rumrunners, these smugglers risked arrest in pursuit of high profits. Domestically, beer production often continued in ethnic neighborhoods and was sold to local residents by the bucket. Rural grain-producing areas also contributed to the alcohol supply by distilling and selling their crude but potent "moonshine." The sheer volume of illicit importation and sale of alcohol overwhelmed enforcement agencies, which were often understaffed and poorly funded. To upgrade enforcement, the federal government established the Prohibition Bureau as an agency of the Treasury Department and ordered the Coast Guard to apprehend smugglers. Despite these best efforts, however, violators far outnumbered the enforcers, and alcohol flowed into the United States unabated.

Smuggling initially was done haphazardly by bold individuals and small criminal gangs. Once the alcohol had crossed the border, ethnic street gangs distributed it to their own neighborhoods, closely guarding their territory against intruding gangs. Gangs of similar ethnicity gradually banded together for greater power and profits, controlling even larger areas of their cities. As profits continued to skyrocket, these gangs became increasingly violent, frequently shooting at and even murdering competitors. Irish, Italian, Jewish, and German gangs fought each other constantly in the effort to dominate the urban alcohol market, resulting in hundreds of deaths. Most infamous among these gang killings was an incident in Chicago known as the Saint Valentine's Day massacre of 1929, when Al Capone ordered the murder of seven rival gang members. Dressed as police officers, Capone's henchmen gunned down the seven at close range, firing more than one thousand machine-gun bullets.

This degree of violence became commonplace between street gangs, until a single mobster consolidated power in a particular city. Capone, for example, emerged from the gang wars as the undisputed kingpin of Chicago crime, enjoying an absolute monopoly on the city's liquor distribution, narcotics, prostitution, and gambling. Capone and others also expanded their operations to include large-scale smuggling networks and manufacturing facilities, totally controlling all facets of the trade. In most cities similar Italian gangs usually came out of the fray as the victors. Taking this consolidation one step further, by the late 1920s the powerful crime bosses of the major cities formed larger syndicates, designed to increase profits and cement their power. These intercity connections among mobsters became the organizational basis for the powerful Cosa Nostra or, as it is more commonly known, the Mafia.

In many cities mobsters met with little or no resistance from law-enforcement authorities. Local police and politicians may have been either indifferent or opposed to Prohibition laws and thus reluctant to enforce them actively. The police forces in the Northeast and Midwest remained disproportionately Irish, an ethnic group that traditionally prized drinking. In addition to ethnic preference, the huge profits from smuggling and distribution operations allowed for substantial bribe money to be paid, often guaranteeing immunity from police interference. Even the federal Prohibition Bureau became wracked by corruption, with 20 percent or more of its agents receiving bribes.

Outstanding among law enforcers was the legendary crime fighter Eliot Ness, whose three hundred Prohibition Bureau agents in Chicago battled against thousands of mobsters. Although he was largely ineffective in thwarting the flow of alcohol, Ness finally succeeded in convicting and imprisoning the notorious mob boss Al Capone.

Repeal of Prohibition and Its Aftermath

Aggressive anti-Prohibition groups began forming by the late 1920s, intent on repealing both the Eighteenth Amendment and the Volstead Act. When the Democratic Party adopted repeal of Prohibition as a major plank of its political platform, it gained the support of millions of thirsty voters who hoped that the ban would soon end. Support grew when the Great Depression hit, with repeal advocates extolling the economic value of restoring jobs in the beer and liquor industries and increasing profits for grain farmers. Franklin Roosevelt easily swept into office in 1932, partly by promising voters that he would solve the government's financial problems by levying a tax on beer. He kept his promise, repealing the Eighteenth Amendment with the Twenty-first Amendment in February 1933 and then legalizing beer that April. By the end of 1933 the national prohibition of alcohol was officially over. Within months, closed distilleries and breweries reopened, though their numbers were a small fraction of the pre-Prohibition industries.

Prohibition achieved some of its goals, in that it reduced per capita alcohol consumption by over half between 1919 and 1933, a trend that remained constant throughout the twentieth century. But the government was never able to end drinking, largely owing to overwhelming public opposition. Moreover, by creating an artificial scarcity of alcohol, Prohibition opened the door for widespread bootlegging, rampant violence, and the entrenchment of organized crime in America. By that measure, the efforts of temperance advocates and legislators proved to be most unsuccessful.

[*See also* Alcohol and Teetotalism; Saloons; Temperance.]

BIBLIOGRAPHY

Fox, Stephen. *Blood and Power: Organized Crime in Twentieth-Century America*. New York: Morrow, 1989.

Kyvig, David E. *Repealing National Prohibition*. Kent, OH: Kent State University Press, 2000.

Rebman, Renne C. *Prohibition*. San Diego: Lucent Books, 1999.

Sinclair, Andrew. *Prohibition: The Era of Excess*. Norwalk, CT: Easton Press, 1986.

DAVID GERARD HOGAN

Paul Prudhomme. *Culinary Archives & Museum at Johnson & Wales University, Providence, R.I.*

Prudhomme, Paul

Paul Prudhomme (b. 1940) is the chef and owner of K-Paul's Louisiana Kitchen in New Orleans. He became the face of Cajun cooking during the 1980s, when Cajun became widely acknowledged as one of America's distinctive regional cuisines. A familiar national television personality, easily recognized by his formidable size and Acadian accent, Prudhomme introduced Americans to the country-cooking traditions of his native Louisiana, popularizing such dishes as gumbo, jambalaya, and dirty rice. His specialty, blackened redfish, prepared by dusting a fillet with a mix of spices and searing it in a dry, hot cast-iron skillet, was widely copied, and blackening as a cooking technique became a 1980s restaurant trend.

The youngest of thirteen children, Prudhomme was raised on a farm in southern Louisiana, the birthplace of Cajun cuisine. He began his restaurant career early, opening a drive-in at the age of seventeen. After working in a variety of restaurants across the country, Prudhomme returned to New Orleans to head the kitchen at Commander's Palace before opening K-Paul's in the French Quarter in 1979.

His first cookbook, *Chef Paul Prudhomme's Louisiana Kitchen*, published in 1984, shared many of the crowd-pleasing recipes from his restaurant and is still considered to be a standard text on Cajun and Creole cuisine. He has published seven additional cookbooks and hosted four cooking series on public television. In 1982 Prudhomme created a signature line of spices, Magic Seasoning Blends, and was one of the first celebrity chefs to market a consumer product in his own name.

[*See also* Cajun and Creole Food; Celebrity Chefs.]

LYNNE SAMPSON

Puck, Wolfgang

He is known as the shy chef who became an industry and the first chef to become a brand name. But there is more to Wolfgang Puck's reputation than just dollars. By showcasing California's bounty of high-quality, locally grown ingredients, Puck helped to create, along with Alice Waters, what is known as "California cuisine." His cookbooks, syndicated food column, Food Network TV show, and restaurant and food-product empire have made Puck as famous as the movie stars he hosts at Spago, his award-winning Los Angeles restaurant.

Born in St. Viet, Austria, in 1949, Puck's first culinary influence was his mother, Maria, who cooked for the dining room of a lakefront hotel. Puck began apprenticing in

Wolfgang Puck. Portrait on the jacket of *Adventures in the Kitchen* (New York, 1991). *Culinary Archives & Museum at Johnson & Wales University, Providence, R.I.*

local restaurants at fourteen, leaving Austria to work in France at seventeen. He eventually became a classically trained French chef in the master kitchens of the Hotel de Paris in Monaco and Maxim's in Paris. His first American stint, in Indianapolis in 1973, taught Puck much about the American eating habits he soon would be influencing. In 1975, after two years in Indianapolis, he moved to Los Angeles, becoming chef and part owner of Ma maison, where he cooked classic French food. The bistro became a magnet for the rich and famous, with Puck as the main attraction. In 1981, Puck's star began to rise rapidly after the publication of his first cookbook, *Modern French Cooking*. Capitalizing on this in 1982, Puck opened Spago, on the Sunset Strip in Los Angeles. The vividly colored eatery, filled with picnic chairs and patio furniture, was designed by his partner and soon-to-be wife, Barbara Lazaroff. The couple was an early leader in the restaurant-as-theater movement, with Lazaroff creating an open kitchen that put Puck in the spotlight. At the same time, Puck also helped pioneer wood-fired gourmet pizza in the United States and is often credited as the father of California-style pizza; his signature pizza is topped with smoked salmon, caviar, and crème fraîche.

In 1983, Puck opened Chinois on Main Street, in Santa Monica. At Chinois, Puck began combining French techniques with Asian ingredients, becoming a pioneer with other chefs like Jeremiah Tower in this hybrid cuisine, and further changing America's eating habits. Meanwhile, Puck's celebrity clientele grew at Spago, and his food came to signify L.A. style. When he began hosting dinners after the Academy Awards, he became a national celebrity himself.

Puck further drew upon his fame by opening other Spago restaurants in Chicago, Hawaii, Tokyo, and Las Vegas, where he was the first star chef to create a fine-dining restaurant. In the 1990s he began opening informal Spago offshoots—Wolfgang Puck Express and Wolfgang Puck Cafes—throughout the United States, after which came a namesake food company, a catering company, and a line of cookware. By 2002 his various companies grossed $375 million annually. Puck also garnered a host of major awards including the James Beard Outstanding Chef in the United States and Outstanding Restaurant for Spago in Los Angeles.

Although Puck appears happiest when he is cooking in the kitchens of his fine-dining restaurants and kibitzing with guests and staff, he has tied his future to his casual dining eateries and to his packaged supermarket foods like frozen pizzas and canned soups. When asked about his success, Puck says he simply did what he loved and got lucky in between. And, he adds, he learned more from his one restaurant that went bankrupt in 1990 (Eureka, a lavish Los Angeles brasserie) than all his successes.

[*See also* California; Celebrity Chefs; Fusion Food; Waters, Alice.]

BIBLIOGRAPHY

Lubow, Arthur. "Puck's Peak." *New Yorker*, December 1, 1997.
Reichl, Ruth. *Comfort Me with Apples*. New York: Random House, 2001.
Schoenfeld, Bruce. "L.A.'s $375 Million Chef." *Wine Spectator*, Aug. 31, 2003.

SCOTT WARNER

Puddings

Ask Americans to name a pudding, and they might mention chocolate pudding or rice pudding; if the respondent is old enough, perhaps tapioca pudding, bread pudding, or even plum pudding will come to mind. If asked to define "pudding," he or she might say that it is a soft, flavored custard made with starch, eggs, and milk. Few people would mention blood pudding, but, in fact, it shares the same roots with all the other puddings.

Nathan Bailey's 1776 dictionary defined pudding as "a sort of food well known, chiefly in England, as hog's puddings, etc." Sheridan's Dictionary (1790) described pudding as "a kind of food generally made of flour, milk, and eggs; the gut of an animal; a bowel stuffed with certain mixtures of meal and other ingredients." In James Barclay's Dictionary, published in 1820, pudding was defined as a "kind of food boiled in a bag; or stuffed in some parts of an animal; or baked. The gut of an animal." These descriptions seem far removed from chocolate pudding.

On close examination, our modern idea of pudding is not that far removed from historical reality. Puddings are composed of starch, eggs, milk, and a flavoring of some kind and are cooked in a container. Today pudding would be prepared in a baking dish or tin mold. In the past the pudding preparation would have been stuffed into a length of intestines or the stomach of an animal and boiled until done. Some puddings were wrapped in a piece of cloth (a pudding bag), tied at the top, and submerged in a large pot of simmering water. The pudding cloth was a substitute for an animal's stomach. As refined

HASTY PUDDING

Hasty pudding was basically a stirred cornmeal porridge that became a symbol of classlessness and independence in eighteenth-century America. It was known at every hearth of the time, regardless of class or ethnic origin. Its reference in "Yankee Doodle," a song of the Revolutionary War period—"And there we saw the men and boys / as thick as hasty pudding."—testifies that it was so widely known that it could be used as a simile.

Likewise, the Connecticut poet Joel Barlow, contributing to the American literary genre born after the Revolutionary War, wrote a long, mock-epic poem, "The Hasty Pudding," extolling the dish. Somewhat tongue in cheek, he not only gave detailed cooking instructions but also sentimentalized the dish's virtues as a wholesome food of the new democracy and the "common man."

The porridge that the American colonists called hasty pudding combined European and Native American traditions. European settlers had been accustomed to making their porridges from the European grains—wheat, oats, rye, and barley—whereas Native Americans used indigenous New World corn (maize) for their sagamite. As corn was easier to grow and more bountiful than the Old World grains, settlers made expedient substitutions and adapted their own cuisines to corn. Everyone, it seems, made cornmeal porridges—the New York and New Jersey Dutch, the Delaware Swedes, the Pennsylvania Germans, and the New England and Virginia English. It was served with milk and molasses for breakfast or supper, according to the tastes of each ethnicity; for example, the Dutch, who loved sour flavors, drowned their *sappaen* in buttermilk.

The English version, also called mush, took the name hasty pudding because of its ancient pudding origins. In a technique conceived in the Middle Ages, a rather complex mixture of assorted meats, grains, fruits, and spices was tied in a cloth or "pudding bag" and boiled in a large pot for as long as twelve or fourteen hours to cook through. With time, the nature of puddings diversified and simplified; one offshoot led to American hasty pudding.

Such transitional puddings as An Excellent Pudding, described in *The Closet of Sir Kenelme Digbie Opened* (London, 1669), required only a manageable hour in a bake oven, a significant change in technology. The pudding bag had been dispensed with, and the dish's character was more like bread pudding. In the next century, Hannah Glasse's Flour Hasty-Pudding (1747) was stirred on the hearth in a process akin to that for making porridge, but it was still called pudding and it cooked faster than the traditional plum puddings that were still boiled in a pudding bag.

The nineteenth century brought American Eliza Leslie's *Directions for Cooking* (1837) and its then-old recipe for Indian Mush, a porridge in fact and name ("Indian" meant cornmeal). She stressed the importance of constant stirring with a "pudding stick," a long, slim, wooden paddle, and up to two hours of cooking. A symbol of patriotic pride at the time of the centennial celebrations, hasty pudding continued as a breakfast staple throughout the nation until the development of still-faster twentieth-century cereals.

[*See also* Cookbooks and Manuscripts, *subentry* From the Beginnings to 1860; Corn; Ethnic Foods; Historical Overview, *subentry* The Colonial Period; Leslie, Eliza; New England.]

BIBLIOGRAPHY

Barlow, Joel. "The Hasty Pudding." In *The Works of Joel Barlow, In Two Volumes*, Volume 2: *Poetry*. Edited by William K. Bottorff and Arthur L. Ford. Gainesville, FL: Scholar's Facsimiles and Reprints, 1970.

ALICE ROSS

---

white sugar, molasses, chocolate, and vanilla became more available, a preference for sweet puddings evolved.

During Roman times blood pudding (Latin: *botellus*) was a sausage made from blood and cereal. The name was altered in old French to *boudin* and in Middle English to pudding. In time, a mixture of chopped organs, vegetables, and cereals, boiled in a sewed-up stomach came to be known as haggis in Scotland. Encased in a pig's stomach, it was called hog maw in Pennsylvania's Lancaster County.

Amelia Simmons's 1796 cookbook *American Cookery*—the first cookbook published by an American in America—contained two recipes for "Pompkin" pudding. We would recognize this dish not as a pudding but as a pie. This is another clue that puddings fall into an extremely broad classification. In America puddings took on regional characteristics. New Englanders preferred hasty pudding, also called Indian pudding (a mush made from cornmeal, molasses, and milk). In the South,

African Americans transformed a pudding made from sweet potatoes into sweet potato pie.

Puddings traditionally have been made from inexpensive or leftover ingredients, such as stale bread, beef suet, organ meats, or drippings from roasted beef, and then boiled, steamed, or baked. They could be served hot or cold at the beginning of the meal, as the meal itself, or as dessert. One type of pudding called for the ingredients to be tied up in a cloth bag and suspended in a pot of boiling water if the housekeeper did not have a proper tin mold. Another method called for baking the pudding in a pottery basin. In Massachusetts some ceramic pots dated to the early nineteenth century were divided into two compartments, one side for pudding and the other for baked beans.

In the United States in the early 2000s, puddings were still part of the culinary repertoire, but as minor players. In the nineteenth century they took center stage. In Mrs. Whitney's 1889 cooking manual, *Just How*, the chapter on puddings is larger than the chapter on vegetables. As puddings evolved in both British and American cookery, there was little attempt to provide stabilization or codification of this class of food. In an attempt to bring some semblance of order, Mrs. Whitney broke down puddings into four general divisions: puddings with crusts, soft-mixed puddings, batter puddings, and sandwich puddings. Puddings with crusts include apple dumplings (boiled, steamed, or baked), Huckleberry hollow and pandowdy, which are deep-dish desserts. Soft-mixed puddings include boiled or baked bread pudding, Indian pudding, and plum pudding and baked rice, tapioca, and lemon pudding.

Mrs. Whitney defined sandwich puddings as being composed of fruit and bread layered in a dish and baked. She stated that this class of puddings could be "varied and multiplied according to one's own pleasure and ingenuity" and with whatever fruit was in season. The fourth classification included custard puddings and pancakes. Pudding recipes are still found in cookbooks, but in fewer numbers.

The word "puddingheaded" came into the language, with the meaning "one whose head was a sack of boiled haggis, or stupid." Mark Twain named one of his classic novels *Pudd'nhead Wilson* (1894; originally published as *The Tragedy of Pudd'nhead Wilson and the Comedy of Those Extraordinary Twins*), the story of two babies, one slave, one free, switched in their cradles. "Puddinghead," as a disparaging term, seems a little old-fashioned today and is seldom heard. One more often hears "mush head" or "meathead," two terms that also trace their roots back to pudding.

[*See also* Custards; Desserts; Pies and Tarts; Sausage.]

BIBLIOGRAPHY

Ciardi, John. *A Second Browser's Dictionary and Native's Guide to the Unknown American Language.* New York: Harper and Row, 1983.
Stone, Robert G., and David M. Hinkley. *The Pudding Book.* Lee's Summit, MO: Fat Little Pudding Boys Press, 1996.
Whitney, A. D. T. *Just How: A Key to the Cook-Books.* Boston: Houghton Mifflin, 1887.

JOSEPH M. CARLIN

Puerto Rican Food

Puerto Rico is one in a chain of islands called the West Indies. Within this island group, Cuba, Jamaica, Hispaniola (Dominican Republic and Haiti), and Puerto Rico together are known as the Greater Antilles. Puerto Rico, the easternmost and smallest of this group, lies 1,050 miles from the tip of Florida and 1,600 miles from New York. On the north it is bounded by the Atlantic Ocean and on the south by the Caribbean.

Native Foods and Early Immigrant Influences

Since its discovery by Christopher Columbus in 1493, Puerto Rico has been enriched by and, in turn, has influenced the culinary styles of the various newcomers who have made the island their home. Caribbean cuisine has a rich and varied history, dating back to the days when the first inhabitants of the island began preparing such native foods as sweet potatoes, root plants, maize, and the fish and fowl that were to become the basis of what is called *cocina criolla* (native cooking).

At the time of Columbus's voyage, the island was inhabited by a tribe of Caribbean Indians known as the Tainos. They were a simple people who had lived for generations on the island they called Borinquen, and they subsisted on what the island provided: fruit, corn, capsicum peppers (especially the large sweet bell peppers known as pimientos), wild birds, and abundant crabs and seafood. Their principal occupation was agriculture, and they cultivated tobacco and cotton. Their primary cooking utensils were made from clay or stone, particularly a vessel called the *caldera*, similar to a kettle. This has become one of the most versatile and popular cooking utensils in Puerto Rican cuisine—a cast-iron or cast-aluminum pot with a round bottom and straight sides, which is used for preparing stews and rice dishes. To the Tainos, food held religious importance. To accompany the dead into the afterlife, the Tainos buried vessels of food and drink so that the deceased would have provisions on their voyage to the next world.

Columbus and his crew came upon foods on the island that they had never seen: cassava bread, native beans, tapioca, maize, and fermented drinks made from fruits. These and other staples were to change the diet of the Old World. Some of these new foods gave rise to new terminology. For instance, the very name "potato" comes from Taino, by way of the Spanish *batata*. Originally, it applied to sweet potatoes, but in time it came to refer to white potatoes as well. The food exchange between the native and immigrant cultures went both ways. The Spanish introduced pigs, chicken, sheep, and the first horses to the island. They also brought with them sugarcane, wheat, chickpeas, and various vegetables. From this interchange a whole new cuisine was to emerge, combining Spanish and native Caribbean cooking techniques and foodstuffs.

When African slaves were brought in to work the sugarcane fields on the island, another dimension was added to this innovative cuisine: the cooking styles of Africa. This influence is all-important. Most likely, the Africans brought with them rice, introducing a prime ingredient to Caribbean agriculture and cuisine. *Gandules* (pigeon peas), also known as congo peas, are also indigenous to Africa.

British, French, and Dutch adventurers added their imprint to the evolving native fare. European adventurers learned from island natives, including the Tainos, how to cook meat on frames of green wood. The natives called the technique *boucan*. To the Spanish, the green wood frame became a *barbacoa*—what is known today as the barbecue. To the French, the *boucan* became the *bucanier*; from this term was derived the name applied to outcasts and adventurers: "buccaneer."

Traditional Dishes and Seasonings

Puerto Rican cooking covers a wide spectrum of styles and methods that have developed over five centuries. The native ingredients of the Tainos have been enhanced and modified with each new influence. Puerto Rican food has incorporated all of them so that *criollo* cooking is replete with unique spices, flavorings, and seasonings:

cilantro, black peppercorns, *aji dulce* (sweet chili pepper), oregano, and *recao* (a small leafy plant used to impart a tangy flavor to food), to name a few.

The main difference between Puerto Rican cuisine and that of the North American mainland lies in three words: *sofrito* (a flavoring), *adobo* (a seasoning), and *achiote* (a coloring). *Sofrito* is a term that has no true English translation. It is a mixture of cilantro, sweet chili pepper, *recao*, garlic, onion, and pimientos that serves as the base ingredient for countless dishes. *Adobo* is a combination of black peppercorns, oregano, and garlic, which is crushed in a mortar and rubbed liberally into meat, fish, or poultry. This seasoning is available in processed form at supermarkets, but nothing can compare to the gusto imparted by the homemade variety. *Achiote* is made of annatto seeds cooked in vegetable oil or olive oil. In the old days, the natives of the island would cook the seeds in lard. Annatto is the pulp of the tropical tree *Bixa orellana*; the dye that comes from this pulp is used as coloring in some cheeses. It was also used by Caribbean and South American Indians as body paint.

Reflecting the diversity of its culture, Puerto Rican foods are called by many Taino and Spanish terms, among them *aguacate* (avocado), *guayaba* (guava), *yautia* (a root plant), *frituras* (fritters), *asopao* (a hearty stew), *caldo gallego* (Galician-style broth), and *biftec* (beefsteak). For centuries Puerto Rican cuisine had remained faithful to its Caribbean heritage. Breakfast had always consisted of the delicious bread known as *pan de agua*, a chewy, water-based bread served with butter. As it had been in Spain, lunch was a minor repast served before the main meal of the day, which was eaten in the early evening. Soups, when they were served, were, and still are, meals in themselves—rich stews cooked with chicken, fish, or rice and usually accompanied by bread or *tostones* (fried green plantains).

The plantain is one of the most important ingredients in Puerto Rican cooking. Contrary to popular belief, plantains are not native to the island—the Spanish brought them. But they have become an important part of the Caribbean diet. There are two basic types: green plantains, called *platanos verdes*, and a ripe variety of yellow plantains, termed *platanos amarillos*. *Platanos* are fried, roasted, stuffed, or baked. Even the plantain leaf is used in one of Puerto Rico's most delicious dishes—*pasteles*, or root plants stuffed with meat, which are then wrapped in plantain leaves and boiled. No Puerto Rican celebration is complete without *pasteles*.

Apart from plantains, other varieties of bananas are served at table—for example, *guineos* (boiled green bananas) or *guineos niños* (little ripe finger bananas). These green bananas are grouped among the *bianda*, or root plants. Early on, European explorers noted that the island natives had a penchant for cooking root plants—*yuca* (cassava), *calabaza* (pumpkin), *yautia* (*tanier* or dasheen), *chayote* (water pear), and *malanga* (taro). The root vegetables remain popular in Puerto Rican cuisine, often simply boiled and served with olive oil and vinegar and no other seasoning or condiment. Other aficionados say they go best with stewed codfish, fritters, or scrambled eggs. Although they are starchy, they are also rich in vitamins A and C as well as thiamine and riboflavin.

Rice, usually the long-grain variety, has always been a mainstay in the Puerto Rican diet. It is prepared in many ways, from yellow rice to rice blackened with squid to plain white rice. Beans, with their complementary protein, make the perfect partner for rice. Beans, too, appear in all sorts of dishes, from garbanzo salad to black bean stew. There is no legume that escapes interest. Puerto Ricans dine on black beans, red small beans, red kidney beans, chickpeas, cowpeas, lima beans, lentils, and navy beans, cooked fresh or dried.

A favorite pairing during the holidays, especially Christmas and Easter, is *arroz con gandules* (rice with pigeon peas). Pork, normally *pernil* (roasted pork shoulder), is a traditional accompaniment to this dish, but the mainland-U.S. influence on the Puerto Rican diet has led to pork being for the most part replaced by roast turkey or some other fowl. Puerto Ricans have given the Thanksgiving dinner their own imprimatur. They serve turkey with all the trimmings, but the bird is highly seasoned, in the manner of traditional pork dishes.

Puerto Rico's North American cousins would feel right at home eating many island entrées: *carne guisada* (beef stew), *carne mechada* (pot roast), *biftec al horno* (London broil), *pescado herbido* (poached fish), and *pollo frito* (fried chicken). Other dishes would be considered odd, even exotic, by mainland standards. Seafood is particularly popular. One of Puerto Rico's premier dishes is octopus salad, but the natives also have a taste for squid and conch meat. Like most people in the Caribbean, Puerto Ricans enjoy rabbit as well.

Influence of the American Mainland

In 1898 the United States took possession of Puerto Rico during the Spanish-American War, ending 405 years of Spanish rule. The mainland influence on Puerto Rico has been manifold. Once a backward Spanish possession, Puerto Rico by the dawn of the twenty-first century had the fourth-highest per capita income in the Western Hemisphere, after the United States, Canada, and Venezuela.

With U.S. control came the next social and culinary transition for Puerto Rico. Puerto Ricans were introduced to new foods and cooking styles and adopted them or adapted them to their needs. They savor such dishes as *butifarron* (meat loaf), *hamburgesa* (hamburgers), *carne de pote* (corned beef), *espinaca en crema* (creamed spinach), and even *budin* (bread pudding).

Fast-food emporiums—McDonald's, Wendy's, Taco Bell, and Pizza Hut among them—dot the island landscape. Before the U.S.-mainland invasion, the Puerto Rican version of the fast-food establishment was the *cuchifrito* parlor. These were small cafés (*cafetines*) that sold a host of fried pork products (*frituras*) along with other savories, such as fried vegetables, some with meat stuffing. It is widely acknowledged that these delicacies were the embodiment of the high-fat, high-calorie snack. With the great Puerto Rican migration to the mainland during the 1950s, *cuchifrito* diners sprang up all along the eastern seaboard, where most of the new immigrants had settled. With a new focus on health-conscious dining beginning in the late twentieth century, *cuchifrito* parlors became a vanishing breed, even on the island. But American fast-food chains remain ubiquitous in Puerto Rico.

The other transformation in Puerto Rican cooking has been through the "Nuyorican" influence. Nuyorican is short for "New York Puerto Rican," Puerto Rican men and women who were either raised or born in New York City. New York was the first great hub of the migration to the mainland, which came about as the result of two factors: an increase in the availability of manufacturing jobs in factories and garment plants in New York City and the introduction of cheap airfares from San Juan to New York. Initially, the only way to get to the mainland had been via seagoing passenger ships across the Caribbean or by taking a flight to Miami and then a long train or bus trip from Miami to New York. In the early days the trip via the propeller-driven DC-6 Constellation took from six to seven hours from San Juan to what was then Idlewild Airport (now John F. Kennedy International Airport) in New York City. With the advent of passenger jets, the time was cut to about three and one-half hours.

Like many before them, the newcomers settled in their own enclaves, mainly in the southern and eastern areas of the Bronx and in the Upper East Side neighborhood that came to be known as Spanish Harlem (or the barrio). Other sections settled by the new arrivals were in northern Queens and Borough Park in Brooklyn. The newcomers transplanted certain aspects of island life to these environs, such as the local social club and the *cafetines*. They added a new dimension, the bodega, or the local mom-and-pop store, where one could purchase American as well as native products.

In a sense, Nuyoricans and islanders shared the same palate and ate the same food. But environmental differences soon showed contrasts. Nuyoricans discovered such food items as bagels, bialys, pasta, and milkshakes, and Chinese, Italian, and Mexican cuisines, among others. They incorporated these new influences, remaining faithful to the basic concepts of the traditional Puerto Rican cooking style. It was not unusual for the Nuyorican family to observe the common New York City Wednesday "spaghetti night" ritual just like their Anglo neighbors. Nuyorican youngsters would munch on pastrami on rye at a local deli or knishes on the boardwalk at Coney Island or canolis in Little Italy. Many of these new tastes and new foods made their way back to the island from the mainland.

Nuyorican food has become a distinct cuisine, a potpourri of Spanish, native Caribbean, and African influences, with a host of North American borrowings thrown into the mix. It still relies on traditional Puerto Rican spices and flavorings, but with a new dash and flair. Stewed chicken might be served with Moroccan couscous, or *pasteles* with a Caesar salad. The old-fashioned dessert of guava jelly with *queso blanco* (a type of farmer's white cheese) has given way to apple pie and even Jell-O. The cultural interchange has been beneficial in other ways. Plantains and papayas can be found in almost any local supermarket in the northeastern United States, and it is not unusual for a New York City resident to enjoy a dish of yellow rice and beans or to have flan as an after-dinner dessert.

Criollo foods were traditionally served with beer or fruit juice. These days, the typical accompaniment is a soft drink, another import from the mainland. Rum is also a popular drink in the Puerto Rican culture. Puerto Rican rums are considered among the best in the world; more than 85 percent of all rum consumed in the United States comes from the island. What distinguishes Puerto Rican rums is their lightness and dryness. They are nothing like their heavy-bodied, sweet counterparts from Jamaica, Martinique, Trinidad, Barbados, and even New England. Rum comes in two varieties: white (or silver) and dark (or gold). A subcategory of gold rum, called *añejo*, is aged for a long period of time. The longer the rum ages in oak casks, the darker, smoother, and stronger it becomes. The strongest of these rums is 151 proof, and it is a prime ingredient in the drink called *coquito*, a coconut-based elixir similar to eggnog that is drunk during the Christmas holidays and on special occasions.

Those who have ever enjoyed a Puerto Rican family dinner find the dishes to be unique and healthful, with an emphasis on fresh vegetables and other fresh ingredients. Evolving over more than five hundred years, Puerto Rican cooking is on a par with the world's great cuisines. This is a cooking style that features warmth and sensuality and is infinitely adaptable.

[*See also* Barbecue; Beans; Caribbean Influences on American Food; Cassava; Chickpeas; Cowpeas; Garlic; Herbs and Spices; New York Food; Rice; Rum.]

BIBLIOGRAPHY

Antonio, Carlos, ed., *The Commuter Nation: Perspectives on Puerto Rican Migration*. Rio Piedras, Puerto Rico: Editorial de la Universidad de Puerto Rico, 1994.
Bender, Lynn Darrell, ed., *The American Presence in Puerto Rico*. Hato Rey, Puerto Rico: Publicaciones Puertorriquenas, 1998.
Brau, M. M. *Islands in the Crossroads: The History of Puerto Rico*. Garden City, NY: Doubleday, 1968.
Davila, Vivian. *Puerto Rican Cooking*. Secaucus, NJ: Castle, 1988.
Middeldyk, R. A. Van. *The History of Puerto Rico*. New York: Arno Press, 1975.
Newman, Ross, and Garske. *International Food Flavors of the Home Economics*. Flushing, NY: Queen's College, 1982.
Valldejuli, Carmen Aboy. *Puerto Rican Cookery*. Gretna: Pelican, 1985.

OSWALD RIVERA

Pullman, George

George Mortimer Pullman (1831–1897), an American industrialist, invented and manufactured a number of luxury railroad passenger cars, including the Pullman sleeping car and the dining car. He was born in Brocton, New York, and was trained as a cabinet-maker. Having acquired skill at carpentry as an apprentice, and at moving buildings from his father's business, he was invited to Chicago (1859) to jack up buildings to a new level as part of a public works project. He invested his earnings from the Chicago project, in partnership with a friend, in the design and construction of the first successful railroad sleeping car, the Pioneer (1865). Pullman, as an experienced rail traveler, had become well acquainted with the deplorable conditions found in rail cars of that day and saw the opportunities for improvement. He established the Pullman Palace Car Company (1865) to build his sleeping cars, then went on to introduce hotel cars (1866), sleeping cars outfitted with small kitchens, and dining cars (1868), which were equipped with a kitchen and a dining room and were intended solely for the preparation and serving of food. In 1880 he established the town of Pullman, Illinois, near Chicago, where his cars were then built. Although intended as an industrial utopia, it became the scene of one of the bloodiest strikes in American history in 1894.

Pullman's sleeping cars, with their well-appointed sleeping compartments and sitting areas, drew the well-to-do traveler willing to pay the extra fare for the comfort of riding in them. The addition of dining cars, as well as of lounge and buffet cars, enabled the railroads that hauled Pullman's cars to offer their passengers both excellent on-board services and faster through trains, which gave them an advantage in the increasingly competitive railroad industry. The introduction of Pullman's equipment revolutionized rail travel.

In the late 1800s Pullman turned his money-losing dining cars over to the railroads themselves. Nevertheless, the Pullman Company continued to manufacture dining cars for the railroads, culminating in the introduction, in cooperation with the Electro-Motive Division of General Motors (EMD), of the streamlined, all-dome, luxury Train of Tomorrow (1947).

George Pullman and his company can be credited with a number of contributions to American culinary history. Pullman's impact on railroad travel, and on dining as a part of that experience, was immediate and profound, while his impact on American culinary practices was less direct. First, his dining car kitchens refined and perfected the concept of cooking in a compact kitchen and served as a model for apartment builders in the early twentieth century. The kitchen that features a long and narrow central floor surrounded on both sides by appliances, but with little counter space, is referred to as a "Pullman kitchen." Among the many space-saving innovations the Pullman Company introduced was the Pullman loaf, popularly known as sandwich bread, wherein baking pans were fitted with lids and produced square, compact loaves. Three

of these loaves would fit into a space that could hold only two loaves of bread with crowns.

Second, the practices Pullman instituted to ensure the consistency of food preparation and service that operating a fleet of dining cars required became the prototype for the uniform standards adopted by national restaurant chains later in the twentieth century. And the dining car meal experience itself, with its emphasis on speedy food preparation and delivery to table, and the need to turn over tables quickly so all waiting passengers could eat—as many as three hundred people in a three- or four-hour period—has been noted by fans and critics alike for its role in reinforcing the eat-and-run mentality associated with fast food.

[See also Dining Car; Harvey, Fred.]

BIBLIOGRAPHY

Leyendecker, Liston Edgington. *Palace Car Prince: A Biography of George Mortimer Pullman.* Niwot: University Press of Colorado, 1992.
White, John H., Jr. *The American Railroad Passenger Car.* Baltimore: Johns Hopkins University Press, 1978.

JAMES D. PORTERFIELD

Pumpkins

The pumpkin (*Curcurbita pepo*) is thought to have originated in Central America about 5500 B.C.E. It was widely disseminated throughout North America in pre-Columbian times. With its thick shell and solid flesh, the pumpkin can be stored through the winter. Native Americans also preserved pumpkin by slicing and drying it.

Pumpkins were introduced into the Old World shortly after the first European explorations of the New World. They are mentioned in European works beginning in 1536. They were originally called pompions, or large gourds, and they were cultivated in England by the mid-sixteenth century, well before Thomas Hariot mentioned them in his *Briefe and True Report of the New Found Land of Virginia* (1588). Hence, English colonists were familiar with pumpkins prior to settling in North America and immediately began growing them when they arrived. Although pumpkins are related to squash, American colonists carefully distinguished between them and used them culinarily in different ways.

Pumpkins proved easy to cultivate, and they became a common food at all meals, particularly in New England. They were baked, fried, mashed, roasted, and stewed,

Pumpkin. Engraving, nineteenth century. *Culinary Archives & Museum at Johnson & Wales University, Providence, R.I.*

and eaten as an accompaniment to meat. A favorite way of preparing pumpkins was to scoop out their seeds, fill the cavity with sweetened, spiced milk, and cook them near a fire. Pumpkins were also used to make puddings, pancakes, pies, soups, stews, and tarts. Less commonly, pumpkins were used as a flavoring in bread, cakes, and muffins and were also employed to make ale. Pumpkin seeds were consumed raw or dried, and pumpkin flower blossoms and buds have been consumed in salads, sandwiches, and in many other ways.

A recipe for pumpkins was among the first cookery recipes to have originated in what is today the United States. John Josselyn in his *New-England Rarities Discovered* (1672) wrote that pumpkins grown in America were sweeter than those he had tasted in England. The common way to prepare them, Josselyn wrote, was "to slice them when ripe, and cut them into dice, and to fill a pot with them of two or three Gallons, and stew them upon a gentle fire a whole day." Butter was then added along with vinegar and spices, such as ginger. The stewed pumpkin was served as a side dish with fish or fowl.

Pumpkin pie recipes appeared in seventeenth-century English cookbooks, such as Hannah Woolley's *The Gentlewoman's Companion* (1675). Culinary fakelore to the contrary, pumpkin pies were not served at the proverbial "First Thanksgiving" and did not become common as a dessert at Thanksgiving dinner until the early nineteenth century. Pumpkin pie recipes frequently appear in American cookbooks beginning in the early nineteenth century. Nineteenth-century cookbooks also offered recipes for baked pumpkin (to be served like mashed potatoes) and pumpkin soup.

The pumpkin is such an important symbol that it frequently appeared in literary works: fairy tales, such as Cinderella and her pumpkin coach, children's nursery rhymes, such as "Peter, Peter, Pumpkin Eater," and poetry, such as John Greenleaf Whittier's "The Pumpkin." In late-nineteenth-century America, the pumpkin became associated with Halloween as a Jack-o-Lantern, most likely as a result of Washington Irving's headless horseman in the "Legend of Sleepy Hollow," first published in 1819. In the twentieth century, Charles Schulz's *Peanuts* comic strip frequently featured Linus waiting in a pumpkin patch for the arrival of "The Great Pumpkin." Halloween is celebrated with sweet treats shaped and colored like pumpkins (which are not usually made with pumpkin) as well as baked goods, such as pumpkin cookies, made with canned pumpkin purée.

In the early 2000s, farmers invite families to come pick their own pumpkins for Halloween, and the pumpkin is celebrated in seasonal festivals, such as that held in Half Moon Bay, California. A pumpkin weigh-off is usually part of the proceedings, with some specimens weighing more than one thousand pounds.

[*See also* Flowers, Edible; Halloween; Heirloom Vegetables; Squash; Thanksgiving.]

BIBLIOGRAPHY

Damerow, Gail. *The Perfect Pumpkin: Growing, Cooking, Carving*. Pownal, VT: Storey Communications, 1997.

Krondl, Michael. *The Great Little Pumpkin Book*. Berkeley, CA: Ten Speed Press, 2000.

Tuleja, Tad. "Pumpkins." In *Rooted in America: Foodlore of Popular Fruits and Vegetables*, edited by David Scofield Wilson and Angus Kress Gillespie, 142–165. Nashville: University of Tennessee Press, 1999.

ANDREW F. SMITH

Punch

Over the centuries punch, as a beverage, has had different definitions. Since the early seventeenth century the British, particularly those who were sailors, knew and enjoyed punch. America's founding fathers enjoyed their punch served in Chinese export bowls at their favorite tavern. Throughout the twentieth century nonalcoholic punch was an essential element at every high school prom, dance, graduation, funeral, and social gathering. To every child born after World War II, Hawaiian Punch was one of the most recognizable fruit-juice drinks in

America. But for most of its existence a punch was a mixed drink composed of rum, water, a citrus fruit juice and peel, sugar, and a dusting of nutmeg. It was served either hot or cold.

The *Oxford English Dictionary* reports that as early as 1698, the word "punch" was believed to be derived from the Hindustani word for five (*pnch*) because the drink was made from five ingredients. These five ingredients were rum, sugar, lemons, water, and spice. This so-called Rule of Five was also expressed as "One sour; Two sweet, Three strong, Four weak, and spices make Five." Benjamin Franklin celebrated punch in 1737 in his publication *Poor Richard's Almanack*, but he did not mention a spice.

> Boy, bring a Bowl of China here,
> Fill it with Water cool and clear:
> Decanter with Jamaica right,
> And Spoon of Silver clean and bright,
> Sugar twice-fin'd, in pieces cut,
> Knife, Sieve and Glass, in order put,
> Bring forth the fragrant Fruit, and then
> We're happy till the Clock strikes Ten.

Some believe that the name "punch" is not derived from an Indian word, but was sailors' talk for a puncheon, the type of cask used for transporting rum at that time. Lending credibility to this theory is that grog, another sailors' drink made by diluting rum with water, was ladled out of a butt, a wooden barrel used for transporting wine. When sailors gathered around the scuttled (full of water) butt, to receive their daily allowance of grog, they would pass on gossip, hence the scuttlebutt. "Scuttlebutt" is just one of the many words to enter the English language as a result of sailors' slang. "Punch" could easily be another.

Punch was one of the first mixed drinks to be served in colonial America. By the early nineteenth century, with the wide availability of mechanically harvested ice, these compound beverages evolved into a separate classification of drinks called cocktails. Punch was usually served in a bowl. For a large gathering it was made in a large bowl and ladled into cups or smaller bowls that were passed from person to person.

A review of punch recipes over the past three hundred years reveals that there is no limit on the number or kind of ingredients that can go into a punch. Some taverns made their punch with rum, brandy, gin, whiskey, wine, tea, sherry, and even milk. Lemons, limes, oranges, pineapples, and guava jelly were frequently added, alone or in combination. Nutmeg was the traditional spice but sometimes a cordial was substituted. Punches might be named after the person who created them, or a town, a historic event, the name of the tavern, or even the name of the tavern keeper. For example planter's punch, made from fruit juices found in the Caribbean, reportedly originated with Jamaican planters. In time milk punches evolved into eggnog. *The Bar-Tender's Guide* from 1887 listed Mississippi Punch made with bourbon whiskey and Claret Punch made with red wine. When consumed in excess the imbiber was considered "punchy" or "punch-drunk."

Hawaiian Punch, a product of Cadbury Schweppes in the early 2000s, was first concocted in a converted garage in Fullerton, California, and trademarked in 1929. It was created as a blend of seven natural fruits— pineapple, orange, passion fruit, apple, apricot, papaya, and guava juices—to be used as a concentrated tropical fruit topping. It was soon discovered that the concentrate, when mixed with water, made a delicious drink. In 1950 Hawaiian Punch was introduced in the familiar forty-six–ounce can. Punchy, the TV cartoon character was created in 1961 with the tagline, "How about a nice Hawaiian Punch?"

Since colonial times prosperous families have had a punch bowl for entertaining. Eighteenth-century Chinese export porcelain bowls were traditionally made in five sizes holding from less than a quart to several gallons. Larger bowls, often decorated as commemorative or presentation pieces, were frequently commissioned. The larger the bowl a household possessed, the more prominent its status in society was likely to be. During the nineteenth century very formal in-home dinner parties were prefaced with a punch. In the twentieth century the punch bowl, made from silver and inscribed, became a trophy piece presented at retirement parties or awarded for sporting accomplishments.

Most American families have a punch bowl, whether a modest one made from glass or plastic for a fruit punch to accompany a backyard cookout or an elegant silver or crystal one for a holiday eggnog.

[*See also* Alcohol and Teetotalism; Drinking Songs; Eggnog; Fruit Juices; Grog; Kool-Aid; Rum; Sangria; Syllabub; Taverns; Temperance; Wine, Hot Spiced.]

BIBLIOGRAPHY

Dubourcq, Hilaire. *Benjamin Franklin Book of Recipes*. Bath, U.K.: Canopus, 2000.

Grimes, William. *Straight-Up or on the Rocks: The Story of the American Cocktail*. New York: North Point Press, 2001.

Lender, Mark Edward, and James Kirby Martin. *Drinking in America: A History*. Rev. ed. New York: Free Press, 1987.

Thomas, Jerry. *The Bar-Tender's Guide; or, How to Mix All Kinds of Plain and Fancy Drinks*. New York: Fitzgerald, 1887.

JOSEPH M. CARLIN

Pure Food and Drug Act

The Pure Food and Drug Act of 1906 marked the beginning of effective U.S. federal regulation of food and drug labeling and assurance of a safe food supply. It prohibited the false labeling or adulteration of foods and drugs transported interstate; as such, it was limited in scope. Items produced and sold within a state or territory came under only local laws. The Pure Food and Drug Act also did not give the federal government the right to require substantive food labels such as the ones Americans enjoy today, but it represented the early efforts toward federal protection for food consumers and substantial and effective federal controls on the safety and purity of the U.S. food supply.

Regulation of the food supply was not new, although earlier efforts were fragmentary, subject to intense (and often successful) lobbying by food and drug industry groups, and ineffectively enforced. In the mid-1800s agricultural chemists under Samuel W. Johnson exposed adulteration in the fertilizer industry, which, in turn, led to attempts to curb adulteration in meat, milk, and other foods. City and state health departments were established, leading to the first general food law, passed in Illinois in 1874. The pure foods movement, a grassroots group that formed in the mid-1870s, also began agitating for change. It was originally a trade movement, some of whose members became concerned that the plethora of local laws and the use of mislabeled adulterants were hindering interstate trade and hurting profits. The first national food-adulteration law, the Oleomargarine Act of 1886, was one outcome; then, in 1889, the United States Department of Agriculture was given the mandate to extend and continue the investigation of the adulteration of foods, drugs, and liquors.

Under the leadership of Harvey Wiley, the jovial and brilliant chief of the department's Bureau of Chemistry, food safety truly reached the public consciousness. Wiley established a "poison squad" of volunteers who ate only foods with measured amounts of chemical additives and preservatives, to test the notion that many adulterants were unsafe. He gave numerous public lectures on his findings, and popular magazines such as the *Ladies' Home Journal* and *Good Housekeeping* took up his cause. Wiley was opposed, in particular, by the patent medicine firms, but the "embalmed beef" scandal that erupted in 1898 over the putrid meat shipped to soldiers during the Spanish-American War and the efforts of the writer Upton Sinclair, whose 1906 novel *The Jungle* exposed unsanitary conditions in the meatpacking plants, pushed Congress on June 30, 1906, to pass two measures protecting the public food and drug supply: the Meat Inspection Act and the Pure Food and Drug Act.

The Pure Food and Drug Act specifically prohibited interstate shipping of adulterated or misbranded goods. Administration of the law fell to Wiley's Bureau of Chemistry. For a complicated regulatory subject, the law as passed was very terse. It fell to Wiley to elaborate upon the law and to test its enforcement. The first case did not involve food, but the manufacturer of a patent medicine remedy with the unlikely name of Curforhedake Brane Fude; after a precedent-setting trial, the verdict was returned: guilty. The fine was small ($700) compared with the manufacturer's profits (a claimed $2 million), but the precedent was set: the federal government was willing and able to promote food and drug safety.

[*See also* Adulterations; Department of Agriculture, United States; Sinclair, Upton; Wiley, Harvey.]

BIBLIOGRAPHY

U.S. Food and Drug Administration. *Federal Food and Drugs Act of 1906 (The "Wiley Act")*. http://www.fda.gov/opacom/laws/wileyact.htm.

Smelser, Neil J., and Paul B. Battles, eds. *International Encyclopedia of the Social and Behavioral Sciences*. New York: Elsevier, 2001.

Pure Food and Drug Act of 1966 (United States Statutes at Large, 59th Congress Session I, Chapter 3915, pp. 766–777).

SYLVIA LOVEGREN

Quaker Oats Man

The Quaker Oats Man is an internationally known trademark figure that has been representing Quaker Oats products since 1877. The story of the Quaker man is more than simply that of a popular trademark character, however. It is also the story of the emergence of the modern American market system and consumer culture.

As the development of mass production in the nineteenth century increased the number of products rolling off production lines, manufacturers faced the challenge of moving goods as fast as they were made. They turned to advertising to increase demand for specific products. Oats, for example, had previously been sold only in bulk and were both unbranded and relatively unfamiliar as a food. When new technology made highly efficient, high-volume production possible at the Quaker Mill in Ravenna, Ohio, the owners of the mill, Henry Seymour and William Heston, set out to develop a brand identity for their product in order to establish a national market for it. In 1877 they registered "a figure of a man in 'Quaker garb'" with the U.S. patent office, becoming the first to register a trademark for a breakfast cereal. Despite the lack of any actual Quaker connection to their product, they claim to have chosen the figure, a full-length picture of a Quaker man holding a scroll with the word "pure" on it, because they felt that the image represented integrity, quality, and honesty.

In 1881 the mill in Ohio and the name "Quaker" were taken over by Henry Parson Crowell, who continued to work toward establishing a national market for his products by pioneering techniques in packaging, promotion, and advertising. In 1882 Crowell launched the first advertising campaign in national magazines for breakfast cereal. In 1885 he began to use the recently patented folding carton for Quaker Oats packaging. Because it lay flat when unfolded, the carton could be printed with the trademark figure and recipes that helped to make the unfamiliar product useful in the lives of new consumers. The Quaker Oats Company remained a leader in national advertising and made the Quaker man a familiar symbol on free samples, billboards, streetcar placards, rural fences, magazines, newspapers, promotional items, such as calendars and match strikers, and booths at fairs and expositions.

The Quaker Oats Company Quaker has remained a popular trademark figure into the twenty-first century, with just three revisions to his appearance. In 1946 a black-and-white image of the familiar smiling-head portrait was designed by Jim Nash to replace the original standing figure. The image was updated to a full-color figure in 1957 by the artist and illustrator Haddon Sundblom. In 1970 the company adopted a one-color "shadow" image of the Quaker man designed by Saul Bass as the registered trademark of the Quaker Oats Company.

The international presence of the Quaker Oats Company Quaker is nearly as old as the figure itself. Quaker Oats were first shipped to Britain in 1877, and by 1908 the Quaker export catalog claimed that the Quaker trademark was the best-known brand in the world. By the early 2000s, the Quaker man was known in nearly every market in the world.

[*See also* Advertising; Breakfast Foods; Oats.]

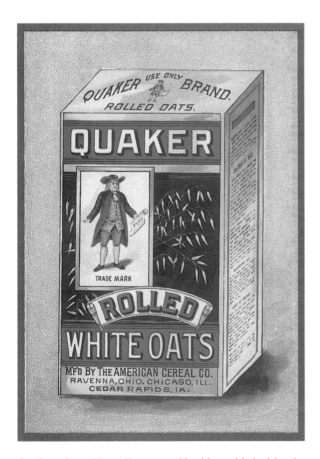

Quaker Oats Man. From a cookbooklet published by the American Cereal Co., 1894. *Collection of Andrew F. Smith*

BIBLIOGRAPHY

Marquette, Arthur. *Brands, Trademarks, and Good Will: The Story of the Quaker Oats Company.* New York: McGraw-Hill, 1967.

Schudson, Michael. *Advertising, The Uneasy Persuasion: Its Dubious Impact on American Society.* New York: Basic Books, 1984. See esp. chap. 5, "The Historical Roots of Consumer Culture." The chapter provides an informative overview of the emergence of consumer culture. Discussion of the role of Quaker Oats can be found on pages 164–166.

CHARLOTTE BILTEKOFF

Quince

The quince (*Cydonia oblonga*) is among the minor pome fruits—relatives of the apple and pear— which are practically unknown in modern America. Probably native to the Elburz Mountains of Iran, the quince figures in the traditional cookery of Persia, Armenia, Georgia, and the Middle East in general. In Roman times the quince was brought to southern Europe, and it spread northward during the medieval period. In the United States, acquaintance with the quince does not often last beyond the first generation after immigration, and the quince has never been a fruit of much notice.

The quince has suffered in popularity because it is not suited for fresh consumption, being hard, rather dry, low in sugars, and high in tannins. However, the tannins are inactivated by cooking, and the flesh breaks down, often turning pink as it does. It is as a cooked product that the quince excels, for it is a supremely aromatic fruit.

Because quince flesh has a pasty quality when cooked, it usually is mixed with apples in pies or sauce or rendered into jellies. A very few sorts of quince in Central Asia and Turkey are edible when raw, but they are not highly attractive.

Quince plantings have historically been small and scattered, near to urban markets; today the quince survives only as occasional trees at the edge of orchards. A very few commercial plantings exist in the San Joaquin Valley of California, mostly tended by families of Armenian origin. Quinces may sometimes be found in urban greenmarkets in autumn.

[*See also* Apples; Pears; Fruit; Pies and Tarts.]

BIBLIOGRAPHY

Hedrick, Ulysses Prentiss. *Cyclopedia of Hardy Fruits*. New York: Macmillan, 1922.
Meech, William Witler. *Quince Culture*. 2nd ed. New York: Orange Judd Co., 1919.

C. T. KENNEDY

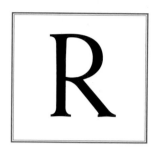

R

Radio and Television

When General Mills launched Betty Crocker's first radio program in 1924, the company could hardly have envisioned the explosion of radio and television food shows in the twentieth and twenty-first centuries. With an audience presented daily with virtually unlimited ideas for every conceivable style of cuisine and cooking technique, advertisers were quick to capitalize on the opportunity to reach millions of potential customers.

Not a real person, Betty Crocker was invented as a spokesperson for General Mills. First broadcast locally in Minnesota, the programs proved so popular that they aired nationally on NBC in 1926 and remained on the air until 1952, moving from NBC to CBS and finally to ABC. In 1936 Betty Crocker acquired a face, a portrait blending the features of several "typical" American women that has been updated through the years to reflect popular tastes.

Early Broadcast Personalities

In radio's earliest days, broadcasts were intimate. Listeners felt close to radio personalities, and women, in particular, relied on food programs not only for information but often also for a sense of community. Advertisers capitalized on this, and the housewife's friendly broadcaster became a supersalesperson.

Aunt Sammy Both commercial firms and public agencies were quick to capitalize on the opportunity to spread their messages by radio, among them the United States Department of Agriculture, which invented Aunt Sammy in 1926. Although the federal agency had kept in touch with farmers through radio beginning in 1920, little or no information was designed to help farmwives, many of whom were isolated and without modern kitchen amenities and appliances such as running water and gas or electric stoves and refrigerators. Aunt Sammy offered advice on virtually every subject of interest to homemak-

ers: cooking and recipes, decorating, child care, sewing, and basic household maintenance.

The fictional wife of Uncle Sam, Aunt Sammy was in reality fifty different women, all reading the same script (provided by the Department of Agriculture) over fifty different radio stations. The primary purpose of the broadcasts was to help housewives produce tasty, healthful family meals. Aunt Sammy took a lighthearted approach with jokes and anecdotes, but she never lost sight of her goal to help women cook simple, nourishing food, especially during the difficult days of the Depression. Her recipes encouraged the use of grain products and milk to supplement expensive cuts of meat. She gave advice on growing vegetables and fruits and then preserving them, and admonished listeners to use up every last scrap of cloth and to save leftover kitchen fats to make soap. Half a million copies of her cookbook were distributed in four years, and it was the world's first cookbook to be printed in Braille. The late 1930s brought many changes to radio. More and more cooking shows appeared, some of them shamelessly copying Aunt Sammy's, and her popularity waned. She "died" in 1944.

Alma Kitchell Advertisers found that their products sold well when they were promoted by a friendly and knowledgeable radio personality. Alma Kitchell, a singer who starred in NBC's first televised opera in 1939, produced a local radio show in 1927 and then moved to NBC, where she broadcast cooking tips along with interviews (1928–1942). Her radio program, *Let's Talk It Over*, was succeeded by *In the Kelvinator Kitchen* on television. She died in 1996 at the age of 103.

Ida Bailey Allen Known as "the Nation's Homemaker," Ida Bailey Allen began broadcasting locally in New York City in 1926, moving to CBS (1928–1935) and then NBC (1935–1936). She founded the National Radio Homemaker's Club in the 1930s, reporting that "little groups of you are meeting in central homes to 'listen in' while you sew and are having Radio Homemakers

Radio Sponsor. Advertisements for three broadcasts sponsored by the Pet Milk Co. in the early 1950s. *The All Star Revue* (originally called *The Four Star Revue*) ran on NBC television between October 1950 and April 1953. Pet sponsored *Fibber McGee and Molly* between 1950 and 1952. *Collection of Andrew F. Smith*

luncheons afterwards." The club was designed to promote happier, better homes and mutual helpfulness. Her dream, she said, had long been to find some way "that women could be united . . . while they kept house. Nursed the babies. Cared for the sick." She authored several popular cookbooks, and on her tenth anniversary as a broadcaster, twenty thousand fans crowded Madison Square Garden for a celebration.

Mary Margaret McBride Mary Margaret McBride, one of radio's best salespersons, began a local interview show in New York City in 1934 under the name of Martha Deane, and then moved to network broadcasts until 1954. She was a graduate of the School of Journalism at the University of Missouri, and her reporting skills and appealing personality enabled her to present a richly textured picture of American life spanning the Depression, World War II, and the cold war.

Her first programs as Martha Deane were chatty and domestic. She played the role of a grandmother who gave household hints and shared anecdotes about her fictional family. Unhappy in this role, she began a new show that brought her fame by just being herself—enthusiastic, natural, loquacious, and a shrewd, intelligent reporter. Her interview subjects included First Lady Eleanor Roosevelt, the architect Frank Lloyd Wright, the poet Carl Sandburg, President Harry Truman, the baseball great Joe DiMaggio, a female test pilot, and the American Mother of 1942, as well as ordinary Americans. On almost every show, she talked about food, whether relating a story from her childhood or discussing a new restaurant she had discovered. Advertisers flocked to her program, in part because she rarely presented a conventional commercial. Rather she gave her personal recommendation of a product, suggesting recipes and ways of utilizing a cake mix or new brand of butter and often discussing the product in depth with the day's guest. Her unconventional approach as well as her charm and enthusiasm built a large and loyal following across the country.

Growth of Food Shows

In 1931 the *G. E. Home Circle* on NBC broadcast recipes along with household advice and etiquette tips. That same year, the *Mystery Chef*, starring John MacPherson, moved to the NBC Blue Network from its local Boston base, and MacPherson continued dispensing his kitchen wisdom on radio until 1945 on CBS, the NBC Red Network, and ABC. (MacPherson shifted from radio to television in 1949 when he appeared in one of NBC's first daytime programs.) Many radio stations employed their own local food experts. Some moved into national and syndicated broadcasts, but others remained fiercely loyal to their local audiences. Roy L. Fruit worked for the *Great Bend Daily Tribune* in Kansas and broadcast over KVBG, soliciting recipes from women in central Kansas and often publishing them in modest cookbooks. Although her home base was Boston, Marjorie Mills's popular programs were heard throughout New England, providing useful information on rationing and conservation during World War II. Louise Morgan and Mildred Carson also broadcast from Boston on WNAC and WBZ, respectively.

Joe Carcione, the "Green Grocer," learned his trade as a teenager in his father's California produce market, and his short radio spots in the 1960s highlighted fresh produce in the San Francisco markets. Brita Griem began radio broadcasts in 1949 over WTMJ in Milwaukee, Wisconsin, and continued her career in television until 1962. Beginning in 1992, Arthur Schwartz, the so-called Food Maven, brought his expertise as a food critic, cookbook author, lecturer, and teacher to his daily program, *Food Talk*, broadcast over WOR in New York; distributed by Talk America, it reached a substantial East Coast audience. Calling himself "the Schwartz Who Ate New York," he attracted both advertisers and listeners with his down-to-earth, everyday preparation of good food.

Minnesota Public Radio's long-running show *The Splendid Table*, hosted by Lynne Rossetto Kasper, brought together the worlds of food in science, history, ecology, health, and many diverse cultures through interviews with writers, chefs, and experts from a wide variety of disciplines, illustrating Kasper's belief that food is the way to delve into almost any field. Distributed by National Public Radio beginning in 1993, her program has won many awards, including the James Beard Award for best radio food program.

Television Food Shows

Although many food lovers are convinced that Julia Child was the first television food chef, James Beard preceded her with *I Love to Eat*, which premiered in 1946 and lasted only a year. This show was followed by Alma Kitchell's *In the Kelvinator Kitchen*. Dione Lucas's *To the Queen's Taste*, broadcast from the Cordon Bleu restaurant in New York (1948–1949), offered a prodigious catalog of subjects, from ravioli and sponge cake to Wiener schnitzel and Monte Carlo soufflé to braised larded liver and crêpes suzette.

Julia Child Living life as an icon, a pioneer, and perhaps the world's most notable cook would faze a less intrepid person than Julia Child, but she has managed to withstand the attention and remain focused on her main goal: sharing the pleasures of French cooking. Her distinctive warbling voice, her relaxed manner, and her ability to cope with major and minor crises on camera have endeared her to generations of food lovers.

Her first television appearance was as a guest on an episode of *I've Been Reading*, broadcast over the Public Broadcasting System's station WGBH in Boston in a makeshift studio following a devastating fire in the station's building. Promoting her book *Mastering the Art of French Cooking*, she decided to demonstrate the proper method of making an omelet, bringing her own hot plate, copper bowl, and whisk to the studio. Station programmers agreed that her relaxed manner and ability to communicate would please viewers, and three pilot programs were produced in the kitchen of the Boston Gas Company in 1963.

With no budget to speak of, Child relied heavily on volunteers, including her husband, Paul, to help with preparations and cleanup. The shows were immediately successful, and soon *The French Chef* was launched. Her first director/producer, Russ Morash, remembers that what he terms the "choreography" was the most difficult problem at the beginning, making sure the right foods were in the right place at the right time. The cooked dish had to come out of the oven as the uncooked one went in, and, lacking an overhead mirror in the early days, Child had to maneuver her dishes so the camera could see them properly.

She is famous for her no-nonsense approach to food and its preparation and delighted her loyal followers in those early days with special "Julia moments," such as the program during which she slammed a cleaver through a chicken as she exclaimed "Whop!" There was also the day she demonstrated how to flip an omelet and dropped a substantial chunk of it in the fire, remarking that sometimes things are not perfect. On another occasion she "mended" a cracked cake by adding a little frosting here and there and suggesting that no one would ever notice. Home cooks could relate to these potential kitchen catastrophes, and her audience continued to grow.

Her techniques and recipes were demonstrated clearly and with enthusiasm, each program ending with a display of that day's dishes and her cheerful farewell, "Bon appétit!" In addition to introducing American cooks to French cooking, Julia Child used television skillfully as a teaching and communication tool and paved the way for many young chefs as well as amateur cooks. Her influence is impossible to quantify, but surely America's love affair with food owes a great debt to the lady Russ Morash called "the supreme TV talent."

Syndication The commercial cook Graham Kerr, popularly known as the "Galloping Gourmet," began his cooking career as a flight lieutenant in the New Zealand Air Force and then moved to Canada in 1969, where he produced a series of programs with his wife, Treena. Syndicated worldwide, his eponymous television show featured the preparation of lavish dishes heavy on butter and cream. After his wife's heart attack, he created a new cooking style called "Minimax," advocating healthy food with a maximum of aroma, color, and taste.

The short, quick-and-easy cooking tips produced by Arthur Ginsberg, known as "Mr. Food," have been syndicated to more than 160 television stations since the 1980s. His "save time" mantra includes spending less time preparing complicated recipes, creating economical, delicious dishes in minutes, and even washing fewer dishes.

Public Television With the great success of Julia Child, PBS had discovered the appeal of cooking shows and quickly added a variety of quality programs to its schedule. The diminutive Joyce Chen, a refugee from Communist China and a successful restaurateur in Cambridge, Massachusetts, launched the first Chinese cooking show in the 1970s. The *Romagnolis' Table* (1974–1976) featured Margaret and Franco Romagnoli, cookbook writers and owners of three Italian restaurants. Justin Wilson, a suspender-wearing, down-home Cajun cook, demonstrated "Louisiana Cookin'," brimming with spices, garlic, and onions, in his show of that name, and Diana Kennedy shared recipes from all the regions of Mexico. Other programs have included Mary Anne Esposito's warm and family-friendly *Ciao, Italia*; Martin Yan's *Yan Can Cook*, a lighthearted demonstration of Chinese cooking; *Lidia's Italian-American Kitchen*, starring Lidia Matticchio Bastianich; and Pierre Franey's *60-Minute Gourmet*, featuring quick but elegant meals with a French accent.

The suave and knowledgeable Jacques Pépin also features in several PBS shows. His programs, *Jacques Pépin's Kitchen: Cooking with Claudine* (cohosted with his daughter), *Today's Gourmet*, *Jacques Pépin Celebrates*, and a series with Julia Child, *Julia and Jacques Cooking at Home*, have taught viewers simple techniques that result in elegant dishes. *The Frugal Gourmet*, one of PBS's most popular cooking shows before its cancellation in 1997, with casual, comfortable Jeff Smith as host, appealed to cooks who appreciated a relaxed attitude toward cooking from a man who made it seem like fun rather than a chore. An ordained minister, Smith emphasized that frugal does not mean cheap. The cook, he said, should waste neither food nor time, and he emphasized that formal training was not necessary to become a good cook. He owed his popularity, he added, to demonstrating, even to people who had never cooked before, that cooking was enjoyable and easy.

Food Network In November of 1993 the Food Network, a new cable channel created by Reese Schoenfeld, began offering twenty-four-hour-a-day programming about food to a seemingly insatiable television audience. The Food Network presented programs with well-known personalities, including Wolfgang Puck, Madhur Jaffrey, Graham Kerr, and Martha Stewart. But new stars have been created, among them Rick Bayless; Bobby Flay; Jamie Oliver; chefs in training from Johnson and Wales University in Providence, Rhode Island; and the most popular chef on the Food Network, Emeril Lagasse.

Lagasse delights his audience not only with his delicious food but also with his ebullient personality. *Emeril Live* features a studio jazz band and an enthralled studio audience, some of whom are selected to sample the results of the day's cooking. When Lagasse puts the finishing touches on his presentation, his signature trademark, an explosive "Bam!" is echoed by the audience. His showmanship and rapport with the audience sometimes obscure his real skill in the kitchen.

The Food Network professes to be about more than just food. The network describes the programs as emphasizing lifestyles. Many are produced in other countries as well as in exotic food markets around the world, often featuring demonstrations of techniques used in barbecues and clambakes and providing in-depth information on a variety of ethnic cuisines. Some shows are produced in-house, and others are acquired from outside producers.

Foreign Imports *The Iron Chef* created a stir when this Japanese-produced program was first shown in the United States in 2002. The show exuded exotic showmanship and ritual, with guest chefs introduced by crashing gongs and pounding drums, flashing knives, and a properly awed host. A theme ingredient is chosen each week and chefs must create a complete meal in one hour, using the ingredient. The appeal of the show lies in part in its resemblance to a sporting event, showcasing the speed, skill, and dexterity of the chefs and featuring play-by-play commentary from the sidelines.

Nigella Bites, starring Nigella Lawson, the "Domestic Goddess" of Great Britain, was an instant success with Americans when the show premiered in 2001. The stunningly beautiful Lawson leads viewers through deceptively simple food preparations. She parts company with many chefs by using frozen peas, advocating bouillon cubes for stock, and casually licking her fingers when a dish tastes especially good. She even does her own washing up.

Public Appetite for Food Shows

The first television food programs appeared shortly after the deprivations of World War II, and their growth in numbers and popularity shows few signs of abating. The genre has been left primarily to PBS and the Food Network, cultivating Americans' interest in new cooking styles and techniques as well as in exotic ingredients from other cultures. Advertisers abound on commercial shows and as PBS underwriters, continuing the tradition of radio and TV chefs as supersalespersons.

[*See also* Advertising; Beard, James; Betty Crocker; Celebrity Chefs; Child, Julia; Cooking Techniques; LaGasse, Emeril; Puck, Wolfgang; Stewart, Martha.]

BIBLIOGRAPHY

Dunning, John. *On the Air: The Encyclopedia of Old-Time Radio.* New York: Oxford University Press, 1998.
Terrace, Vincent. *Radio Programs, 1924–1984: A Catalog of over 1,800 Shows.* Jefferson, N.C.: McFarland, 1999.

VIRGINIA K. BARTLETT

Radishes

Radishes (*Raphanus sativus*) are mainly cool-weather crucifers grown annually for their swollen roots. Though most radishes that make their way to the American table are small, scarlet globes with crisp, peppery white flesh, radishes come in an impressive array of sizes and shapes—from small and round to long and tapered—and colors ranging from pink, lavender, red, and purple to black and white. Amelia Simmons's *American Cookery*

(1796) lists salmon as her favorite radish. Radishes count as one of the earliest garden vegetables and are among the easiest to grow. Most of the radishes in early America came as seed from England.

Early seed catalogs displayed a tremendous variety of radishes and allowed the farmer three different crops: spring, summer, and fall or winter. Yellow summer radishes, called *jaune hatif*, were popular as a heat-tolerant variety during the eighteenth and nineteenth centuries. Among the most intriguing winter radishes are the pungent black varieties, such as the Long Black Spanish and the Round Black Spanish. Found in America since the seventeenth century, the seed was widely dispersed by the Shakers in the nineteenth century.

Parts other than the root were used in the past. Radish leaf salads, made from immature radishes pulled from beds in the normal thinning processes, were a gourmet treat. Radish pods, particularly from the rattail radish introduced from Japan in 1866, were used in pickles and potato salads by the 1880s and were esteemed for enhancing the vibrant green color of pickles. Radishes were occasionally boiled, added to salads, dressed in a dish by themselves, or carved into the ubiquitous flower for use as a garnish. Most connoisseurs consider raw radishes to be the ultimate crudité and pronounce that the best way to eat radishes is to peel off the skin, dip them in salt, and eat them with one's fingers.

[*See also* Heirloom Vegetables; Salads and Salad Dressings; Vegetables.]

BIBLIOGRAPHY

Bittman, Sam. *The Salad Lover's Garden.* New York: Doubleday, 1992.

Facciola, Stephen. *Cornucopia II: A Source Book of Edible Plants.* Vista, CA: Kampong Publications, 1998.

Hessayon, D. G. *The New Vegetable and Herb Expert.* London: Expert Books, 1997.

Murrey, Thomas J. *Salads and Sauces.* New York: Stokes, 1884.

Rubatzky, Vincent E., and Mas Yamaguchi. *World Vegetables: Principles, Production, and Nutritive Values.* 2nd ed. New York: Chapman & Hall, 1997.

Weaver, William Woys. *Heirloom Vegetable Gardening.* New York: Holt, 1997.

KAY RENTSCHLER

Ramps

Ramps (*Allium tricoccum*), also called wild leeks, are members of the onion family. Native to eastern North America, ramps grow in clumps in the rich, moist soil under deciduous trees—sugar maples, birch, and poplar, among others—from New England south to central Appalachia and as far as North Carolina and Tennessee. One of the first spring greens, growing from perennial bulbs in late March and April, ramps have the flavor of sweet spring onions touched with musk and an intense garlic aroma. They are harvested for their young leaves (which resemble lily of the valley) and their small bulbs. Both may be eaten raw—the leaves, for instance, in salads, though the bulbs are frequently fried in smoky fat with eggs or potatoes.

Ramps were part of the Native American diet, valued for their blood-cleansing properties and eaten eagerly at winter's end (ramps are, in fact, high in vitamin C). Over time the ramp harvest became a rite of spring in many Appalachian communities, giving way to community festivals. Ramp consumption and popularity rose steadily in the last two decades of the twentieth century, threatening the wild populations in the forests from which they are gathered. Up to 85 percent of ramps consumed as food come from wild populations, though efforts are under way in North Carolina and elsewhere to cultivate them.

[*See also* Native American Foods; Onions.]

BIBLIOGRAPHY

Elias, Thomas S., and Peter A. Dykeman. *Edible Wild Plants: A North American Field Guide.* New York: Sterling, 1990.

Greenfield, Jackie, and Jeanine M. Davis. *Cultivation of Ramps (Allium tricoccum and A. burdickii).* Raleigh: North Carolina State University, 2001. http://www.ces.ncsu.edu/depts/hort/hil/hil-133.html.

McCormick, M. J. "In Search of the Wild Ramp." *Herb Companion* (March 1991). http://www.foodfinder.com/ramps/ramphistory.html.

KAY RENTSCHLER

Randolph, Mary

Mary Randolph was born in 1762, on the Tuckahoe Plantation at Ampthill, Virginia. In 1824 she published *The Virginia House-wife*, the earliest known southern cookbook in print, regarded by many as the finest work ever to have come out of the American kitchen. Its popularity and influence were such that it had gone through at least nineteen editions by 1860 and only the increasingly general adoption of the kitchen range finally made the work seem old-fashioned. Even so, it continued to be massively plagiarized down through the century. After Randolph's death in 1828 in Washington, D.C., however, the work was seriously compromised by bowdlerization in an effort to make it seem more up-to-date.

As a member of the Randolph family of Virginia, she might be expected to present an aristocratic cuisine, and there is a great deal of that in her work. Much of it was drawn from the same milieu that produced the great culinary manuscripts of sixteenth- and seventeenth-century England, also seen in *Martha Washington's Booke of Cookery*. In addition, many of Randolph's dishes came from the royalist cuisine of France, dishes meticulously described by her cousin Thomas Jefferson in his own hand. Many of her French recipes have entire telltale phrases that are verbatim copies of those attributed to Étienne LeMaire, Jefferson's maître d'hôtel during his years in the President's House (1801–1809), by members of the Jefferson family in their manuscripts. This borrowing was so extensive that she might well be considered the amanuensis of the French aspects of the cuisine of Monticello. But she also presented recipes for more traditional and humble Virginia fare, such as Turnip Tops, boiled with bacon in the Virginia style, Rice Journey, or Johnny Cake, and Cat-fish Soup. Perhaps even more significantly, she published early recipes for a number of products indigenous to Africa, such as Gumbs—A West India Dish, Ochra Soup, and Ocra and Tomatoes, all recipes for okra, as well as one for Field Peas, a general term for black-eyed peas, and many other related ones from Africa. Some of these recipes clearly came from African cooks. An interesting fortuitous section contains a number of Spanish recipes, which came to her from her sister, Mrs. Harriett Hackley, who spent some years in Cadiz. Included among them are directions To Make an Olla—Spanish, Gazpacha—Spanish, and Ropa Veija—Spanish. (The misspelling of *vieja* was to persist in southern cookbooks pretty much through that century.) All in all, this work is wondrously eclectic and not only recorded the cookery of Virginia, but also helped to shape the mythic southern cookery of the nineteenth century.

[*See also* Cookbooks and Manuscripts, *subentry* From the Beginnings to 1860; French Influences on American Food; Southern Regional Cookery.]

BIBLIOGRAPHY

Hess, Karen. *Martha Washington's Booke of Cookery*. New York: Columbia University Press, 1981. An early-seventeenth-century English manuscript that came to be in the possession of Martha Washington.

Randolph, Mary. *The Virginia House-wife*. With historical notes and commentary by Karen Hess. Columbia: University of South Carolina Press, 1983. 1824 edition in facsimile with additional material from the editions of 1825 and 1828.

KAREN HESS

Ranhofer, Charles

Charles Ranhofer (1836–1899) was the chef who brought Delmonico's restaurant to greatness, making the name synonymous with American fine dining for more than a century. More important, he was the author of *The Epicurean* (1893), one of the first, and perhaps the best, of the American encyclopedias of haute cuisine. *The Epicurean* is revolutionary for those who think new American cuisine began in the 1970s. Jeremiah Tower, one of the pioneers of the resurgence of American cooking in the San Francisco Bay Area in the 1970s, described discovering *The Epicurean* after years of exploring other cuisines:

> I saw the title of a soup, Cream of Green Corn a la Mendocino. What struck me about the recipe was that it took its name from a town up the coast from San Francisco. Like a bolt out of the heavens, the realization came to me: Why am I scratching around in Corsica when I have it bountifully all around me here in California? It was American food using French cooking principles. I could not contain my exhilaration over what I beheld as the enormous doors of habit swung open onto a whole new vista.

Although Ranhofer has largely been forgotten, his creations have not—two of his signature dishes are lobster Newburg and baked Alaska, which appears under the name "Alaska, Florida" in *The Epicurean*.

Ranhofer was the son and grandson of chefs. Born in Saint-Denis, France, he was sent to Paris at age twelve to learn his trade, a generation after the master French chef Marie-Antoine Carême had written his grand treatise on French haute cuisine and during the heyday of Carême's successors, most significantly Urbain François Dubois. At age sixteen Ranhofer went into private service for an Alsatian prince. He moved to New York City in 1856, and his first job was with the Russian consul. Then he went to work in Washington, D.C., and New Orleans. After returning briefly to France in 1860 (where he was in charge of the food for the grand balls of Napoleon III at the Tuileries in Paris), he came back to New York City as chef at the new hot spot, Maison Doree.

When Delmonico's restaurant moved from its original Broadway location to one farther uptown on Fourteenth Street, the owner, Lorenzo Delmonico, hired Ranhofer away. "He was perfect in dress and manner, and his attitude was such as to make me feel that he was doing me a great favor by coming into my employment," Delmonico related. "'You are the proprietor,' he said. 'Furnish the room and the provisions, tell me the number of guests and what they want, and I will do the rest.'"

Ranhofer's "rest" was a combination of exquisite French technique melded with fabulous American ingredients. Many of the rules found in *The Epicurean* come straight from Dubois; indeed, Ranhofer graciously acknowledges his debt to Dubois in the preface. These rules of classic cuisine often sound familiar to modern readers: Sauces and meats should not be repeated within a menu; courses should follow in a sensible order; and "offer on the menus all foods in their respective seasons, and let the early products be of the finest quality. . . . Only use preserved articles when no others can be obtained."

Even with Ranhofer's classic French background and abundant borrowing from Dubois's masterpiece *La Cuisine classique* (1856), what is surprising about *The Epicurean* is how decidedly American so much of the cooking sounds. Ranhofer describes local ingredients from avocados and cornbread to Virginia ham and striped bass. Game plays a huge role. There are recipes for canvasback, redhead, mallard, and teal ducks as well as prairie hen. Bear steaks are recommended, with the note that "bear's meat when young can be broiled and after it is cooked has much the same flavor as beef."

There is a truly American assortment of cultural influences as well: blini, kugelhopfen, jambalaya (spelled "jambalaia"), two gumbos, risotto, and borscht (spelled quasi-Polish fashion as "barsch") made with beets you pickle yourself. There is a detailed description of bird's nest soup (he distinguishes between the nests from the Philippines and those from China) and a recipe for a soya sauce that almost sounds like something out of a modern fusion cookbook—basically a red wine stock reduction finished with soy sauce and butter.

Even so, much of the food was just what might be expected from that period. Dishes involved big pieces of meat, usually roasted, and complicated cookery. Consommé Celestine, for example, begins with thin crepes spread with a chicken forcemeat, stacked, pressed, baked, and cut into shapes. The crepes are arranged in the bottom of a bowl with blanched, shredded lettuce, and then hot consommé

is poured over them. Sauces and garnishes play important roles. There are flour-thickened sauces, like béchamel, as well as many "essences" (chicken, fish, game, ham, mushroom, root, duck, and truffle) that actually trace their roots to eighteenth- and early nineteenth-century French practice. These sauces are expensive to make, reflecting a time when cost was no object.

Ranhofer's day was indeed the Gilded Age, when it seemed any man could become an instant millionaire and eat just as he chose. (Although Ranhofer was proud that at his restaurant, a table of six could enjoy "a very good dinner, with an excellent vin ordinaire" for twelve dollars, there was also the banquet put on by the stock promoter Sir Morton Peto that cost twenty thousand dollars—at a time when Ranhofer's annual salary was six thousand dollars.)

Ranhofer often sounded quite the kitchen autocrat, lecturing the American dining public on what he considered its ghastly dining habits: "It is a wonder that you have not ruined the nation's digestion with your careless cooking and hasty eating!" One contemporary article reports Ranhofer as saying, "I must teach you something." Yet in reality he was as amenable to his customers' sometimes curious dinner requests as any modern Beverly Hills chef. "It is a mistaken idea that everyone, willy-nilly, is compelled to take or go with the particular style of cooking that commends itself to the chef," Ranhofer complained.

> The chef may know more about the proper cooking and serving of dishes than the customer, but should the latter have any particular fancies or weaknesses of his own in the eating line, he can, provided his purse dances in close attendance upon his whimsicalities of taste, have set before him dishes which fill the sensitive chef's heart with despair.

Ranhofer was not the last American chef to express such sentiments—but he might have been the first.

[*See also* Delmonico's; Restaurants; Sauces and Gravies *sidebar* Charles Ranhofer's Bread Sauce Recipe.]

RUSS PARSONS

Raspberries

The modern raspberry represents the happy commingling of mainly two botanical varieties of raspberry, one from either side of the Atlantic. Fruits of the European variety

Thompson's Early Prolific Raspberries. From the 1894 catalog of Peter Henderson & Co., New York.

(*Rubus idaeus vulgatus*), are dark red and conical, whereas those of the North American variety (*R. vulgatus strigosus*) are lighter red, round, and have small glandular hairs. The black raspberry (*R. occidentalis*), native to the northeastern United States, also contributes to these hybrids and is a tasty fruit in its own right, being firmer and less prone to rotting than red raspberries. In the past, black raspberries were more popular than today.

Raspberries are grown most extensively where summers stay relatively cool, such as in the Pacific Northwest and coastal California. The canes are biennial, typically bearing fruit in midsummer of their second year, but so-called "ever-bearing" or fall-bearing raspberries begin bearing near their tips toward the end of their first season. This bearing habit has extended the fresh season for this very perishable fruit. Frozen berries are sold as such or are used to flavor juices, yogurts, and jams.

[*See also* Fruit; Fruit Juices.]

BIBLIOGRAPHY

Hedrick, U. P. *The Small Fruits of New York*. Albany, NY: J. B. Lyon, 1925.

McClure, Susan, and Lee Reich. *Fruits and Berries*. Emmaus, PA: Rodale Press, 1996. A volume in the *Rodale's Successful Organic Gardening* series.

LEE REICH

Rastus

In the late nineteenth century, as large-scale manufacturing took hold, it became apparent that the use of images in advertising would enhance the success of a product. Many producers developed logos, often a personification of qualities judged to be most attractive to the consumer audience. In some cases this was an appeal to middle-class homemakers through upper-class images, suggesting that the wealthy could afford the best, and that the middle class could identify itself with the elite by using the same products. In some cases the advertisement reflected the social ideal that middle-class women were efficient and nurturing homemakers, and in others it sentimentalized wholesome and innocent children who would presumably benefit from the product.

Just such a logo was Rastus, who represented Cream of Wheat. Created by Emery Mapes of the budding Cream of Wheat Company of Grand Forks, North Dakota, in 1896, Rastus portrayed a handsome and wise African American chef who symbolized quality cookery, good nutrition (according to the theories of the day), gentility, and geniality. His "portraits" showed him attending to the breakfast table and the children who, presumably, would soon be eating bowlfuls of cooked cereal. Seen within the framework of the overt and common racism of the late nineteenth century, he was the loyal family retainer, someone who could be depended on to guide the family's children with affection, grace, and wisdom.

Alongside the modern view of the political incorrectness of the scene, there is a more noteworthy aspect of the Rastus illustrations. Cream of Wheat used aesthetics innovatively throughout its advertising campaign. In the span between 1902 and 1955, some fifty-eight outstanding artists, each prominent in the new field of illustration, supplied some of the best commercial art of the time. Their steady stream of paintings and drawings appeared in full-color, full-page advertisements in popular periodicals of their time: *Good Housekeeping*, *Woman's Home Companion*, *Colliers*, and the *Saturday Evening Post*.

Rastus. Cream of Wheat advertisement, 1909. *Collection of Alice Ross*

Rastus himself most often appeared in the painting, but was sometimes seen beneath the picture, accompanied by an enlarged message. Either way, he was the thread that connected the art and identified the product. Sometimes he was the central focus, sometimes he appeared subtly in the background, and sometimes his face, almost incidental, was found as a small painting on the wall or half-seen in an open magazine. Finding Rastus in these paintings was sometimes the game that drew the attention of potential buyers.

Throughout the long campaign, Rastus's face never changed, even as the world around him did. As new artists were commissioned, their subject matter and artistic style recorded shifts in social history reflected by the shifting fashions in home decoration and clothing, political and economic events, architecture, and recreation. For example, E. V. Brewer painted Rastus *Standing Back of Uncle Sam* (1918), a recognizable companion piece to his famous Uncle Sam poster of World War I, *I Want You.* The affluence of the later 1920s showed in the well-dressed children of Frederic Kimball Mizen's ice-skating scene, *In High Gear.* The Great Depression and its make-do, chin-up motifs were depicted in the simple, rural amusements of Harry

Anderson's *Gosh All Fishhooks* (1938) and *Going Down!* (1938). H. H. Sundblom's 1920s impressionistic style could be compared dramatically with the promotional Cream of Wheat cartoon strips (still featuring Rastus) of Al Capp in the 1950s.

[*See also* Advertising; Aunt Jemima; Betty Crocker; Breakfast Foods; Nabisco; Quaker Oats Man; Uncle Ben; Wheat.]

BIBLIOGRAPHY

Kern-Foxworth, Marilyn. *Aunt Jemima, Uncle Ben, and Rastus: Blacks in Advertising, Yesterday, Today, and Tomorrow.* Westport, CT: Praeger, 1994.
Stivers, David. *The Nabisco Brands Collection of Cream of Wheat Advertising Art.* San Diego, CA: Collector's Showcase, 1986.

ALICE ROSS

Ratafia

Ratafia is a homemade brandy-based liqueur made with sour cherries, including the stones, which impart a bitter-almond flavor. The name usually is thought to be derived from the Latin phrase *ut rata fiat* or *res rata fiat* ("consider it done"), a late-seventeenth-century toast drunk at the conclusion of an accord but eventually transferred to the liqueur itself. However, some sources indicate that ratafia owes its etymology to French Antilles Creole for a sugarcane-based eau-de-vie (*tafia*), perhaps with the addition of the Malay name for the liquor arrack (*araq*).

Early-nineteenth-century and Victorian-era American recipes flavored ratafias with considerable imagination: currants, chocolate, quince, juniper berries, angelica, violets, and aniseed. The *Picayune's Creole Cook Book* of 1901 provided extended advice on its preparation. Ratafia has all but disappeared; passing along recipes for cherry ratafia, Louisiana Cajun and Creole families remain the keepers of the flame. Cherry ratafia appears to be indistinguishable from cherry bounce. The food historian William Woys Weaver notes in *America Eats* that "American cherry bounce . . . is the folk version of the ratafia."

[*See also* Brandy; Cajun and Creole Food; Cherries; Cherry Bounce.]

BIBLIOGRAPHY

Weaver, William Woys. *America Eats: Forms of Edible Folk Art.* New York: Harper and Row, 1989.

ROBIN M. MOWER

Raw Food Movement, *see Vegetarianism*

RC Cola, *see Soda Drinks*

Recipes

Recipes, in America, as in the rest of the world, are the ideas and the instructions for handling foods and preparing particular dishes. Although directions for cooking exist in oral form, the historical record is derived mainly from those that are written down, and this account of the development of the recipe in America is based on the written record.

From the times of earliest settlement in the New World, the new immigrants brought their recipes with them. Prominent among the early compilations was a seventeenth-century work, *De Verstandige Kock* (*The Sensible Cook*), a book brought by Dutch settlers, whose recipes used the simple, abbreviated forms of the period:

> *To Make Meatballs. Take veal with veal-fat chopped, add to it mace, nutmeg, salt, pepper, knead it together, then you can make [meatballs] from it as large or as small as you please, also all of it is fried in the pan as one large meatball. Many take a few of the outside peels thinly pared of oranges or lemons, cut very fine. It gives a very good smell and flavor.*

The informal, permissive character of the instructions is apparent, based on the assumption that the user of the book was generally knowledgeable about ingredients, about cooking methods, and about the character of a particular dish and the way it should taste. The recipe was basically a set of hints and guidelines, informal in character, often with a suggestion that the reader was being addressed personally—one cook to another. This can also be seen in another major cookbook that immigrants brought with them, Hannah Glasse's legendary *The Art of Cookery Made Plain and Easy* (1747; first American edition, 1805):

> *To Make an Eel Pie. Make a good crust; clean, gut, and wash your eels very well, then cut them in pieces half as long as your finger; season them with pepper, salt and a little mace to your palate, either high or low. Fill your dish with eels, and put as much water as the dish will hold; put on your cover and bake them well.*

Many of the early recipe collections were not published books but handwritten household journals, passed from mother to daughter, each generation adding its own materials and annotations. One of the most famous, which began in England, perhaps in the early 1600s, migrated to America with the Custis family, and it was a widowed Custis daughter-in-law, born Martha Dandridge, who took the book into her second marriage—to George Washington—perhaps making some contributions of her own. The tone, from *Martha Washington's Booke of Cookery* (orthography modernized), is familiar:

> *A Hash of Mutton. Take a boiled leg of mutton and mince both fat and lean together and break the bone to lie in the dish. Stew it betwixt two dishes with water and good store of capers. When it is enough, put in as much salt and verjuice as will season it, and a piece of butter, if you please, with an anchovy, and so serve it up.*

In 1796, the first book written by an American-born woman and published in America appeared. Amelia Simmons's *American Cookery* was a conscientious attempt to offer a "treatise . . . calculated for the improvement of Females in America," but the recipes still shared the brisk, simple, cook-to-cook form of address of many of its predecessors:

> *Baked Custard. Four eggs beat and put to one quart of cream, sweetened to your taste, half a nutmeg, and a little cream—bake.*

As long as cooks were familiar with ingredients and the desired outcome, cooking depended on aide-mémoire—reminders about the food people knew and the observations they had made in their home kitchens as family members

> 370   *Appendix to the Art of Cookery.*
>
> *To make Hamburgh Sausages.*
>
> TAKE a Pound of Beef, mince it very small, with half a Pound of the best Suet; then mix three Quarters of a Pound of Suet cut in large Pieces; then season it with Pepper, Cloves, Nutmeg, a great Quantity of Garlick cut small, some white Wine Vinegar, some Bay Salt, and common Salt, a Glass of red Wine, and one of Rum; mix all this very well together; then take the largest Gut you can find, and stuff it very tight; then hang it up a Chimney, and smoke it with Saw-dust for a Week or ten Days; hang them in the Air, till they are dry, and they will keep a Year. They are very good boiled in Peas Porridge, and roasted with toasted Bread under it, or in an Amlet.

Recipe. Eighteenth-century beef sausage. *Culinary Archives & Museum at Johnson & Wales University, Providence, R.I.*

and servants cooked. What was called for was good taste and common sense. From the 1833 edition of Lydia Maria Child's *American Frugal Housewife* (originally 1828):

> *Bread, Yeast, &c. It is more difficult to give rules for making bread than for anything else; it depends so much on judgment and experience. In summer, bread should be mixed with cold water; during a chilly, damp spell, the water should be slightly warm; in severe cold weather, it should be mixed quite warm, and set in a warm place during the night. If your yeast is new and lively, a small quantity will make the bread rise; if it be old and heavy, it will take more. In these things I believe wisdom must be gained by a few mistakes.*

By the 1840s and 1850s a number of changes came into play that would have profound impact on the character of the recipe. Many of the household helpers who were actively involved in cooking began to abandon domestic service for opportunities in the outside world—factory work and other jobs generated by the Industrial Revolution, in addition to immigration into the expanding frontier as the new nation surged westward. As domestic servants left, those who drew up menus and supervised the preparation of meals found that they were charged with carrying out the kitchen work themselves, and they were often ill equipped to do so.

Increasingly, the details of food preparation were no longer self-apparent, and what was called for were more specific, more instructional recipes—recipes that assumed less and left less to chance. Thus there is in a Civil War–era book, *Mrs. Hill's New Cook Book* (1867), a degree of explicitness seldom seen earlier, even for relatively simple dishes:

> *To Boil Grits. Wash them in several waters, rubbing between the hands well until all the bran is separated from the white of the grain. When perfectly white and clean, pour over boiling water; let it set a few moments. Put the grits to boil in a well-covered stew-pan (lined with tin or porcelain is best); cover with plenty of water. Salt the water to taste; boil until the grain is soft, keeping the cover on. Should there be too much water when the grits are nearly done, take off the cover until the water is sufficiently reduced; if there is a deficiency, supply it by adding hot water. Grits should be boiled slowly, to give them time to swell, and plenty of water used. The hominy when done should be moist, neither very dry nor wet.*

This period also saw the growth of cooking schools to serve the needs of those who could no longer get training at home, and the schools, such as the immensely successful Boston Cooking School incorporated in 1879, committed themselves to produce and teach recipes that "worked"—that were error-free and replicable and that guaranteed uniform quality. This required a distinctly new approach in recipe writing. *Mrs. Lincoln's Boston Cook Book* (1884) by Mrs. D. A. Lincoln, the school's first principal, exemplifies the way in which the cook was now shielded:

> *Break each egg into a cup, being careful not to break the yolk. . . . Cut cold meat into . . . half inch cubes, remove all the gristle and the crisp outside fat. . . . Mix [ingredients] in the order given and divide the dough into four equal parts.*

Many of the recipes provide precise measurements: ¾ cup butter, 2½ cups pastry flour, 1½ teaspoons cream of tartar, white of 8 eggs. This is truly domestic science.

Mrs. Lincoln's successor at the school, Fannie Farmer, developed these principles even further, adding to her own *Boston Cooking-School Cook Book* (1896) a section called "How to Measure," asserting that "correct measurements are obviously necessary to insure the best results." Her recipes frequently reach a new level of detail. Amelia Simmons's recipe for baked custard was just twenty-one words long; Fannie Farmer's runs more than six times that, not including a preceding ingredient list (itself a user-friendly device introduced gradually during the latter part of the nineteenth century).

Another factor that helped bring about longer, more detailed recipes was the expansion of the cooking repertoire in a country that was growing and diversifying rapidly, exposing its citizens progressively to foods that were new and unfamiliar—foods the "correctness" of whose taste could not be judged by the cook against memory or experience. Interestingly, there was probably more exposure to "foreign" foods in culturally heterogeneous Europe than there was in pre–melting pot America, except perhaps in the case of such cosmopolitan figures as Thomas Jefferson and Benjamin Franklin, who had both lived on the Continent.

Beginning in the mid-nineteenth century, however, new immigrant foods began, modestly to be sure, to make inroads into the way Americans ate, and the immigrants themselves were gradually exposed to each other's foods as well as to those that made up America's more traditional diet. Recipes under these circumstances could no longer suggest simply "as you please" but had to say, "do it as we tell you," and such works written for immigrants as *The Settlement Cookbook* (1903 and many editions thereafter) provided newcomers with straightforward, no-questions-asked versions of the mysterious new foods they would be encountering as they made their way in the New World. From the thirteenth edition of the *Settlement* (1924):

Corn Chowder

1 can or 2 cups fresh corn,

4 potatoes cut in slices,

2 onions sliced,

2 cups water,

2 tablespoons flour,

3 cups scalded milk,

3 tablespoons fat drippings,

Salt and pepper.

Fry onion in fat, add flour, stirring often, so that the onion may not burn; add 2 cups water and potatoes. Cook until the potatoes are soft; add corn and milk, and cook corn 5 minutes. Season with salt and pepper, and serve.

Equally explicit are recipes for Old World specialties that the immigrants were beginning to lose as their grandparents and parents were no longer present to provide the memories of methods and tastes that had made it possible to cook from the older style recipes.

Throughout the twentieth century, as cooking and eating habits changed, as more and more women went out to work, as more and more people ate meals outside the home, as the search for new tastes severed reliance on memories of foods "we all know," as new and unfamiliar ingredients came to the market, those who cooked became progressively unable to rely on instinct to guide their hands and their palates in the kitchen. Recipe writing in books, and in due course in women's magazines and in newspapers, began to cater increasingly to this diminution in knowledge, becoming increasingly specific, and in the process rendering the home cooks more and more dependent, undermining their ability to use the recipes as mere guides or reminders.

Recipes at the turn of the twenty-first century were, by far, longer and more explicit than ever before. As distinct from the personal, permissive suggestions to cooks in seventeenth- and eighteenth-century America as hoops and slingshots are from video games are such recipe instructions as:

Lower the heat if the glaze at the bottom of the pan threatens to burn.

In a mortar, crush the peppercorns with a pestle.

Saute the sage leaves in the butter in a small saucepan over medium-high heat 2 minutes, or until crisp.

Add broth, wine, and saffron. Cook uncovered for 6 minutes. Stir well and cook for 6 minutes more.

Peel the avocados and halve them lengthwise, discarding the pits.

Rub the avocados well with the cut sides of the lemon.

½ teaspoon dried thyme, ¼ cup soft fresh white bread crumbs, 1 ounce dried French chanterelles, ½ cup bourbon, 2 tablespoons slivered toasted almonds.

Although it is impossible to know in exactly what direction recipes will develop later in the century, there are some indications that simpler, more intuitive cooking is becoming attractive to increasing numbers of Americans. If this proves to be the case, there may be movement on the part of food writers and editors to provide their readers with more in the way of inspiration and guidance and less in the way of highly specific prescriptions. Certainly recipes that invite people to explore and to grow in their kitchens will, in the long run, produce better and more innovative cooking, thereby contributing to an overall improvement in the ways Americans eat.

[*See also* Advertising Cookbooklets and Recipes; Child, Lydia Maria; Cookbooks and Manuscripts; Cooking Manuscripts; Farmer, Fannie; Lincoln, Mrs.; Rorer, Sarah Tyson; Settlement Houses; Simmons, Amelia.]

BIBLIOGRAPHY

Child, Mrs. [Lydia Maria]. *The American Frugal Housewife*. 1828. A facsimile of the 1833 edition. Bedford, MA: Applewood, n.d.

Farmer, Fannie. *Boston Cooking-School Cook Book*. 1896. A facsimile of the first edition with an introduction by Janice Bluestein Longone. Mineola, NY: Dover, 1997.

Glasse, Hannah. *The Art of Cookery Made Plain and Easy*. 1747. A facsimile of the 1805 American edition with an introduction by Karen Hess. Bedford, MA: Applewood, 1997.

Hill, Mrs. A. P. *Mrs. Hill's New Cook Book*. 1867. A facsimile of the 1872 edition with an introduction by Damon Fowler. Columbia: University of South Carolina Press, n.d.

Kander, Mrs. Simon. *The Settlement Cookbook*. 13th ed. Milwaukee, WS: Settlement Cookbook Company, 1924. First published 1903.

Lincoln, Mrs. D. A. *Mrs. Lincoln's Boston Cook Book*. 1884. A facsimile of the 1887 edition with an introduction by Janice Bluestein Longone. Mineola, NY: Dover, 1996.

Martha Washington's Booke of Cookery. Reprint of an unpublished work compiled between the early sixteenth century and the early nineteenth century. Transcribed and published by Karen Hess. New York: Columbia University Press, 1981.

Rose, Peter, trans. *The Sensible Cook*. [*De Verstandige Kock*]. Syracuse: Syracuse University Press, 1989. Section of a larger Dutch work, edition of 1683.

Simmons, Amelia. *American Cookery*. 1796. A facsimile of the second edition with an introduction by Karen Hess. Bedford, MA: Applewood, 1996.

NACH WAXMAN

Redenbacher, Orville

Born in 1907 in Brazil, Indiana, Redenbacher grew up on a one-hundred-acre farm. He studied agronomy and genetics at Purdue University and conducted research on the first popcorn hybrids. Upon graduation in 1928, he was hired as a vocational agricultural teacher at a high school, a position he held until May 1929. He was then employed as an assistant county agricultural agent in Terre Haute, Indiana. When the county agent moved to Indianapolis, Redenbacher took over his position and conducted a five-minute radio program beginning in 1930. He was the first county agent in the country to broadcast live from his office and the first to interview farmers in the field with a mobile unit.

In January 1940 Redenbacher began managing a twelve-hundred-acre farm in Princeton, Indiana, which was used for seed farming. He built a hybrid seed corn plant and experimented with popcorn hybrids. Under Redenbacher, Princeton Farms' operations grew by 50 percent. While at Princeton Farms, Redenbacher met Charles Bowman, the manager of the Purdue Ag Alumni Seed Implement Association, of Lafayette, Indiana. Redenbacher and Bowman went into partnership in 1951 and purchased the George F. Chester Seed Company at Boone Grove, Indiana. Popcorn was part of their hybrid field seed operation, and within a few years Redenbacher and Bowman became the world's largest supplier of hybrid popcorn seed. They also developed new hybrids. In 1965 their popcorn experimentation came up with a new variety, which expanded to nearly twice the size of commercial brands and left almost no unpopped kernels. This new variety was called Red Bow after the first three letters in Redenbacher's and Bowman's last names. For five years Redenbacher tried to sell his new hybrid to the major processors. Unfortunately, it cost more to harvest, and yields were smaller, and consequently processors were not interested.

Redenbacher traveled at first to local stores in northern Indiana, hawking his popcorn to anyone who would buy it. In 1970 Redenbacher quit producing popcorn seed for other processors and concentrated on selling Red Bow. Redenbacher and Bowman visited a Chicago public relations firm that persuaded them to change the name from Red Bow to "Orville Redenbacher's Gourmet Popping Corn." As the price was higher than that of other popcorn, consumers needed to be convinced that Redenbacher's popcorn was of a better quality than its competitors. The advertising line "The World's Most Expensive Popcorn" emerged. Redenbacher and Bowman achieved regional success through word-of-mouth promotion and virtually no advertising, but they needed assistance to expand nationally. To market their gourmet popcorn, they teamed up in 1973 with Blue Plate Foods, a subsidiary of Hunt-Wesson Foods based in Fullerton, California. This connection permitted national advertising and a widespread distribution system.

When Hunt-Wesson sold Blue Plate Foods in 1974, Redenbacher's gourmet popcorn was so successful that Hunt kept the rights to it. In 1976 Orville Redenbacher's Gourmet Popping Corn business operations and property were sold to Hunt-Wesson, which launched a massive advertising campaign, starring Redenbacher himself, for their newly acquired product. He made hundreds of personal presentations a year and appeared in scores of television commercials. Redenbacher was one of America's most unlikely television stars. His bow tie, dark-framed spectacles, and midwestern accent convinced many that he was just an old country hick. The image worked. Consumers easily recognized the label adorned with Redenbacher's folksy image. Redenbacher's contract for television commercials was not renewed in 1994. While lounging in a hot tub in his home in Coronado, California, Redenbacher suffered a heart attack and drowned on September 19, 1995. His gourmet popping corn stands as his shining legacy.

[*See also* Advertising; Popcorn.]

BIBLIOGRAPHY

Sherman, Len. *Popcorn King: How Orville Redenbacher and His Popcorn Charmed America*. Arlington, TX: Summit, 1996.

Smith, Andrew F. *Popped Culture: A Social History of Popcorn in America*. Columbia: University of South Carolina Press, 1999.

ANDREW F. SMITH

Refrigerators

The mechanical refrigerator was a revolutionary invention that changed life in the United States. No longer were families, restaurants, and businesses inconvenienced by periodic ice deliveries and the necessity of limiting use of the icebox for fear that the ice would melt. Home food costs were reduced because leftovers could be chilled and saved and perishables could be purchased in larger quantities. The diet could be more varied as well. With the advent of mechanical refrigerators, frozen and refrigerated foods became a major factor in the American diet, and refrigerator production became big business.

The United States was the first nation to use home refrigerators widely, but refrigeration technology was an international discovery. In both fourteenth-century China and seventeenth-century Italy, it was learned that the evaporation of salt brine absorbed heat, and, thus, storing food in brine would keep food cold. Throughout the nineteenth century attempts were made to further the idea of practical artificial refrigeration based on evaporation. Inventions centered on two basic ideas, a compression system where a cold, volatile liquid, such as ammonia, was circulated by an electric-powered compressor around a container to be kept cold or an absorption system where refrigeration was accomplished by heating the refrigerant (using gas, steam, or some other source) and so causing evaporation and cooling. A series of inventors from France, Germany, Switzerland, and the United States patented various forms of compression and absorption refrigerators throughout the 1800s. Jacob Perkins, a banknote printer, took out the first patent for mechanical refrigeration in the United States in 1834, and by the late 1800s commercial use by shippers and large food businesses became increasingly common.

It was not until the early 1900s in the United States that these artificial refrigeration systems entered the household kitchen, usually using the compression system, powered by newly perfected small electric motors. The Domelre (Domestic Electric Refrigerator) was marketed in Chicago in 1913, but the first large-scale production came from Kelvinator, an early leader in wooden icebox cabinets; the company began selling mechanical refrigerators in 1916. Frigidaire entered the business shortly thereafter, when General Motors purchased a self-contained household refrigerator developed by Alfred Mellowes in 1915. He called it the "Guardian Frigerator"; General Motors changed the name to Frigidaire, and GM not only mass-produced the household appliance but also gave the public a new vernacular name for the refrigerator: "the fridge."

Prices were initially high, at about nine hundred dollars (at a time when average household income was less than two thousand dollars per year), so use of the refrigerator was very limited. In 1921 about 5,000 mechanical refrigerators were manufactured in the United States; by 1926, 200,000 were sold. With mass production came lowered costs. A 1926 refrigerator sold, on average, for four hundred dollars. By the mid-1930s home refrigerators were not a luxury but a basic household necessity, even during the height of the Great Depression. In 1935 more than 1.5 million were sold, and the average cost was down to just $170. By 1950 over 80 percent of American farms and over 90 percent of urban and suburban homes had refrigerators.

Refrigerators were initially quite ugly, at least by modern standards, often with the round compressor sitting on top of the refrigerator box, undecorated. General Electric, in 1927, was the first company to seal the motor and sell the box as an integral part of the refrigerator. By the 1930s the fashion of "streamlining" came to refrigerators: Kelvinator led the way in 1932 with bulbous round tops and bowlegs, and GE's sleek model became famous. Soon after, even the outline of the compressor was hidden within the steel box surrounding the entire refrigerator, and the rectangular box we know became the standard. Another standard was introduced in 1939, when GE began mass production of the familiar dual-temperature refrigerator, with one section for chilled food and one for frozen.

Early refrigerators were still very rudimentary. The freezing units were small, thin, metal compartments inside the main cabinet of the refrigerator. Instructions were given for the woman who wanted to have both ice cubes (which had to be chipped out of their trays) and a frozen dessert at the same time. For the quickest freezing, the metal freezer tray was supposed to be wet on the bottom. Unfortunately, this often made the tray itself freeze to the inside of the freezing unit; warm cloths or steam had to be applied to remove the tray. To lower or raise the inside temperature, the dealer had to be called. By the 1960s self-defrosting refrigerators became common. In the 1990s sleek, expensive, built-in refrigerators, pioneered by Sub-Zero, became fashionable. And in 2002 the first combination refrigerator-range was introduced.

[See also Freezers and Freezing; Frozen Food; Iceboxes.]

BIBLIOGRAPHY

Hardyment, Christina. *From Mangle to Microwave: The Mechanization of Household Work.* New York: Basil Blackwell, 1988.
Root, Waverley, and de Rechemont, Richard. *Eating in America.* New York: Harper Trade, 1995.

SYLVIA LOVEGREN

Restaurant Awards and Guides

The first American restaurant guides were produced locally in cities with vibrant restaurant cultures, namely, New York, New Orleans, and San Francisco. Among the earliest was *The Restaurants of New York* (1925) by George Chappell, the architecture critic for the *New Yorker* magazine. The first popular national guide to restaurants across the United States was produced by Duncan Hines, a traveling printing salesman who mailed a list of his 167 favorite restaurants to friends as a greeting card in 1935. The following year he published *Adventures in Good Eating*, which, according to his introduction, "let the public know where they might find decent food, carefully prepared by a competent chef in clean surroundings."

Holiday magazine, founded in 1947, began producing an annual national restaurant guide in 1952 under the tight direction of the magazine's food and restaurant editor, Silas Spitzer. Published in the July issue each year (ceasing in the mid-1980s), the 150 or so restaurant reviews that made up *Holiday*'s "Distinctive Dining Awards" were ostensibly the opinions of Spizter, though he relied on input from a network of diners across the country that included Lucius Beebe and James Villas.

During the 1950s American travelers were taking to the road in unprecedented numbers, and several travel guides were produced to help them select hotels and restaurants en route. For large corporations like Mobil Oil—which began rating restaurants in 1958 and published the first *Socony Mobil Guide* in 1960—recommending and rating hotels and restaurants provided a service to consumers, encouraged people to travel by car, and garnered the company respect as an arbiter of taste. In 2002 ten regional ExxonMobil Travel Guides were produced from a database that included more than eleven thousand restaurant listings; only fourteen received the highest, five-star rating. The American Automobile Association (AAA) began listing restaurants in its travel publications in 1937, but AAA did not rate them until 1988. AAA distinguished its ratings with diamonds (one to five) instead of stars—the 2003 guides contain more the twelve thousand rated restaurants, of which fifty-three received the five-diamond rating.

Arguably the most popular guides are produced and published by Zagat Survey. The founders, Tim and Nina Zagat, were lawyers who began by informally surveying colleagues about where they liked to eat. Their first guide to New York City restaurants was self-published and distributed in 1979; by the early 2000s they were producing some forty-five guides covering the United States and a handful of international cities. Ratings out of thirty for food, service, and décor are compiled from surveys completed voluntarily via the Internet by the general dining public.

Increasing interest in restaurants and chefs has led magazines, newspapers, television food shows, and other media into restaurant rating. Magazine features, such as *Food and Wine*'s annual Best New Chefs award and *Gourmet*'s and *Bon Appétit*'s annual restaurant issues, amount to national restaurant guides, as do reader polls. Also popular are industry awards, such as those given annually by the James Beard Foundation, which *Time* magazine called "the Oscars of the food world." Although they are important for chefs and their colleagues, awards given by trade organizations, such as the American Culinary Federation (ACF), are less well known by consumers and therefore have less of an impact on the seemingly unanswerable question of where to eat.

[*See also* Celebrity Chefs; Hines, Duncan; Restaurant Critics and Food Columnists, Restaurants.]

BIBLIOGRAPHY

Hines, Duncan. *Adventures in Good Eating: Good Eating Places along the Highways and in the Cities of America.* 7th ed. Bowling Green, KY: Adventures in Good Eating, Inc., 1940.
Villas, James. *Between Bites: Memoirs of a Hungry Hedonist.* New York: John Wiley and Sons, 2002.

MITCHELL DAVIS

Restaurant Critics and Food Columnists

If the development of a sophisticated gastronomic literature in France can be linked to the democratization of dining that resulted after the French Revolution, as the English sociologist Stephen Mennell has argued, then perhaps a similar development in the United States can be linked to the hiring of the French chef René Verdon to head the kitchens of the White House in 1961, during the administration of John F. Kennedy. Suddenly, an interest in good food took on national political importance. During the 1960s, serious cookbooks—such as *Mastering the Art of French Cooking* by Julia Child, Louisette Bertholle, and Simone Beck—gained cultural currency. Magazines and newspapers also began publishing food features and regular food columns in growing numbers.

Growth and Democratization of Food Criticism

Of course, there was plenty written about food in various media before then. Lucius Beebe, A. J. Liebling, M. F. K. Fisher, and Joseph Wechsberg were among the writers who more than occasionally focused their attention on matters gastronomic in the first half of the twentieth century. *Gourmet* magazine debuted in 1941 and set a new standard for the seriousness with which food and food writing was to be taken. But most of this writing was tailored to a small audience with the financial means and social wherewithal to benefit from advice about which were the best French restaurants in Manhattan and what regional treats to look for while traveling abroad. The alternative was the type of food writing aimed at housewives—publications such as *Good Housekeeping*, *Ladies' Home Journal*, and the food pages of most newspapers, for example—which offered recipes and other advice for women burdened with the daily chore of putting dinner on the table.

One person largely responsible for changing the tenor of food writing targeted to the general public was Craig Claiborne, who was hired as the food editor of the *New York Times* in 1957. Trained at the famed École hôtelière de Lausanne in Switzerland, he applied tough standards to the quality of the food about which he wrote, the recipes he developed, and the restaurants he reviewed. As one example of his reach, the standards and format for his restaurant reviews—many anonymous visits; comprehensive consideration of food, service, and decor; and serious evaluation of the taste, presentation, and authenticity of the food— remain in place at the paper to this day and have been copied by other publications around the country. Of his successors in the role of reviewer at the *Times*, Mimi Sheraton (1975–1983) was known for tracking down out-of-the-way places and for her scathing critiques; Bryan Miller (1984–1993) was known for his love of French food and fancy restaurants; and Ruth Reichl (1992–1999), who went on to become editor-in-chief of *Gourmet*, was known for her ebullient anecdotes and reflexive prose.

Following Claiborne's lead, restaurant critics at other newspapers and magazines asserted themselves as arbiters of taste in important dining centers across the country. Among those who enjoyed the longest tenure and broadest, most loyal readership were Elaine Tait of the *Philadelphia Inquirer* (1962–1997); Gail Greene of *New York* magazine (1968–2000); Phyllis Richman of the *Washington Post* (1976–2000); and Caroline Bates, who was hired by *Gourmet* in 1959, began reviewing California restaurants on a monthly basis for the magazine in 1974, and continued to do so into the 2000s.

Buoyed by the cooking and dining excitement of the 1960s, various national and local media outlets either enhanced or established food sections and food departments during the 1970s. Suddenly, one could not open a magazine or newspaper without reading about the latest restaurant or the newest appliance imported from Europe. In 1974 James Beard began writing a series of cooking lessons for *American Way*, the in-flight magazine of American Airlines. That same year Raymond Sokolov's musings on food history began appearing in *Natural History*. Even *Playboy* gave gastronomy serious consideration in a supplement that was eventually spun off to become *Food & Wine* magazine.

As the proportion of disposable income and leisure time spent on food, cooking, and dining increased, the media and the marketplace expanded to capture as much of both as possible. Food processors, microwave ovens, fondue pots, sandwich grills, and other appliances seduced people into thinking that it was easy to prepare any dish at home as long as they had the right equipment and good advice. Increasingly, that advice came from the people who had come to be called "food writers." New magazines, such as *Bon Appétit*, and *Cuisine*, hit the newsstands, each targeted to a slightly different portion of the food-loving public, some with more money and some with more cooking skill than others.

Multicultural pride, the growing ease of travel, and better distribution of unusual ingredients expanded people's taste for ethnic cuisines. Even the old standbys, such as *Ladies' Home Journal*, began broadening their culinary horizons, including ethnic dishes with ever-more exotic ingredients (or suitable substitutions) as they became available across the nation. By penning hefty, comprehensive cookbooks and narrowly focused articles, experts on specific types of cuisine began to emerge—Paula Wolfert on the food of Morocco and the Mediterranean, Madhur Jaffrey on Indian cooking, Marcella Hazan on Italian food, Richard Olney and Jacques Pépin on French cuisine. When a group of French chefs inaugurated the nouvelle cuisine movement at a conference in 1973, the news was not confined to the food section—it was a front-page story.

Gourmet Food and Regional Cuisines

As the 1980s approached, the consuming public split into camps to satisfy their developing tastes. There were the high-minded, high-living gourmets with the money to cook with expensive ingredients and to eat at the best restaurants. Sybaritic food writers such as James Villas satiated their haute hungers in the pages of *Town & Country*. Neo-traditionalists of the sort that celebrated Chez Panisse wanted their prose simmered with locally grown vegetables and cooked in any number of traditional European styles. These were the people that Ed Behr was addressing when he started his *Art of Eating* newsletter in 1986. Those with academic food interests looked forward to the quarterly arrival of the *Journal of Gastronomy*, published by the American Institute of Wine and Food. Novelty seekers preferred their prose doused with raspberry vinegar and garnished with kiwi, and Sheila Lukins and Julee Rosso, the team behind *The Silver Palate*, were primed to give it to them.

For intrepid gourmets, those hunters and gatherers who ferreted out tasty morsels in such unlikely places as rural American backwaters and ethnic immigrant enclaves, a growing body of literature emerged. To this group spoke writers such as the humorist Calvin Trillin, a *New Yorker* staff writer whose "Tummy Trilogy" of books glorified Kansas City barbecue and take-out Chinese food, among other low-brow temptations. The cross-country travelers Jane and Michael Stern took to the highway with *Roadfood* (1976), a celebration of out-of-the-way, regional, hole-in-the-wall eateries. (They continued to write a monthly column on this subject for *Gourmet* into the early twenty-first century.) John Thorne and his wife, Matt Lewis Thorne, published their first *Simple Cooking* newsletter in the fall of 1980, and in 2004 it was still going strong.

The 1990s saw an ever-increasing number of media outlets for food writing of every type—from the pursuit of authentic ethnic and regional cookery in the pages of *Saveur* to the mastery of home-cooking recipes and techniques in the pages of *Cook's Illustrated* and *Fine Cooking*. Eating healthfully produced its own subgenre of cooking magazines, such as *Eating Well* and *Cooking Light*. Such food columnists as Jeffrey Steingarten in *Vogue* and Alan Richman in *GQ* drew a broad, international audience.

Professionalism in Food Writing

As the cult of celebrity touched the food world during the 1990s, the lines between food writer, chef, cookbook author, entrepreneur, marketer, and television personality blurred. Emeril Lagasse and Martha Stewart are two celebrities who garnered the widest, most varied audiences. The success of his food-as-entertainment, variety-style cooking show and related cookbooks even landed Lagasse a sitcom pilot on CBS. Her media and housewares empire made Stewart one of the most influential women in the country. In 2003, as if to complete the food-writing circle, Stewart, who had built her reputation catering to high society and to hoi polloi yearning for a taste of it, released a magazine more or less targeted to housewives, called *Everyday Food*.

Owing in part to the overwhelming number of people who see food writing as an enticing career option, the last decade of the twentieth century saw a focus on professionalizing the field. In 1996 New York University inaugurated the country's first food studies department, where students can receive undergraduate, master's, and doctoral degrees in the nascent discipline. A large proportion of students who have enrolled in the program hoped to become food writers. Elite universities around the country—from Stanford to Columbia—have made it easier to concentrate on food as a subject of study in a variety of disciplines. Demand for a spot at the prestigious annual Symposium for Professional Food Writers at the Greenbrier resort in West Virginia exceeds availability.

Whereas food writers traditionally have come from diverse backgrounds—among them, journalism, music, literature, and sports—specialization in the subject of food has become a requirement in the industry. A degree from a culinary school program is de rigueur. Industry recognition for food writing, such as the separate food journalism awards administered by the James Beard Foundation and the International Association of Culinary Professionals, also has contributed to the growing professionalism in the field. Of course, it is the quality of the writing that determines the true success of a food writer; the proof of the professionalism of the critic will be in the writing about the pudding.

[*See also* Beard, James; Child, Julia; Claiborne, Craig; Ethnic Foods; French Influences on American Food; Periodicals; Restaurant Awards and Guides; Restaurants; Stewart, Martha; White House.]

BIBLIOGRAPHY

Claiborne, Craig. *A Feast Made for Laughter*. New York: Henry Holt, 1983.

Dornenburg, Andrew, and Karen Page. *Dining Out: Secrets from America's Leading Critics, Chefs, and Restaurateurs.* New York: John Wiley and Sons, 1998.

Robotti, Peter J., with Frances Diane Robotti. *Much Depends on Dinner (The Tablecloth Game).* New York: Fountainhead, 1961.

MITCHELL DAVIS

Restaurants

The fine-dining restaurants of the Western world originated in eighteenth-century France, for myriad complicated political, economic, and cultural reasons. They served a highly articulated cuisine to savvy diners aware of the social status implied by public displays of taste. But in the newly formed United States, dining in public for the sake of the food, let alone the social status that came with it, was slow to catch on. Early food service in American inns and taverns catered to hungry travelers and heavy drinkers. Throughout American history the rise of any sort of restaurant and dining culture can be linked directly to two social phenomena, namely, financial prosperity and immigration. Both have come in waves, and because of their close relationship, enthusiasm for restaurant dining rises and falls with them. As a center of finance, gateway for immigration, and important cultural center, New York City has always been a trendsetter in American food and dining.

New York City

America borrowed its eating-out traditions first from England, then from France, and later from the diverse cultures that made up its population. The early gatherings at Fraunces' Tavern, established in New York City in 1763 and still in operation in the early 2000s, were more notable for the attendees (George Washington and the Revolutionary War officers Henry Knox, Baron Friedrich Wilhelm von Steuben, and Alexander Hamilton, among others), and the toasts made to them than for any of the food served there. Based on reports from foreign travelers, the English naval commander Frederick Marryat and the British naval officer Basil Hall among them, the food served at the English-style inns and taverns in cities and along popular travel routes was copious but inferior to food served in private homes.

Many visitors wrote about the abundance with which the American table was laid—a metaphor for the plentiful resources in the New World—but they strongly criticized the way the food was prepared. While the quality and variety of raw ingredients were impressive, in the hands of uninterested cooks with minimal training, they were transformed into bland and boring dishes—boiled and roasted meats, overly sweet sauces, and other plain fare. These dishes were served at communal tables, where people of every station sat shoulder to shoulder. As rooms were let on the "American plan," which meant all meals were included in the price of the room, there was little incentive for a person to seek food outside the inn. (The "European plan," which allowed for separate payment for meals, was first introduced at the New York Hotel in 1844 and copied at Boston's Parker House Hotel in 1855.)

The age of the tavern as the center of social life was short-lived. As fortunes amassed in the hands of industrialists, inns morphed into hotels with more services, and hotel dining rooms became a center of public social

Bill of Fare. Dishes offered on January 25, 1853, by the Burns Club, Boston. *Collection of Alice Ross*

interaction. Opened in 1794, the City Hotel in New York was the first modern hotel, where the menu for the three daily meals was large, but the quality of the food and communal dining was no different from anywhere else. The Tremont Hotel in Boston, opened in 1829, upped the ante in terms of luxury and attention to food. New York City countered in 1836 with the opening of Astor House, John Jacob Astor's bid to build the most luxurious hotel in America. Meals at the better hotels began with the sounding of a gong. Tables were laid with dishes, and guests were kept to a strict schedule enforced by a militaristic waitstaff. The New York Hotel provided the first à la carte menu, whereby diners could choose and pay for only the dishes they wanted to eat.

By the 1820s the first eating establishments not connected to overnight accommodations began appearing in New York. As the city sprawled and people's homes moved farther away from where they worked, businessmen needed a place to eat lunch. Early cafeteria-style restaurants known as "eating houses" fit the bill and were soon stratified by the quality of the food and the class of the clientele they served. Speed, a recurring theme in the evolution of American restaurants, was a large part of their appeal. A diner could grab a fixed-price lunch, eat it, pay, and be back in the office in a quarter hour. Coffeehouses, oyster cellars, and corner liquor stores also began competing for money spent on food consumed outside the home. Substantial buffet spreads or "free lunches" kept midday bar goers thirsty and prevented them from having to leave to eat.

Dining dollars were being spent in all types of restaurants—from the extravagant Delmonico's to small eateries in Manhattan's ethnic enclaves that served foods catering to the tastes of the local clientele. By the 1840s German beer-hall culture was entrenched in the Bowery's "Little

Waiters. Drawing by Randolph Caldecott. *Culinary Archives & Museum at Johnson & Wales University, Providence, R.I.*

Germany." The 1870s saw prototypical bistros in the French section of Greenwich Village and Chinese restaurants in the same neighborhood as modern-day Chinatown. Spanish and Italian food was available as early as the 1850s. Delmonico's most direct competitor, Sherry's (1881), fought for the same showy clientele, and other famous restaurants, such as Lüchow's (1882) and the ostentatious "lobster palaces"—Rector's (1899) and Café Martin (1899)—also vied for well-heeled customers.

Westward and Southern Expansion

New York City may have been the epicenter of restaurant dining during the nineteenth century, but enthusiasm for eating out spread across the country, in large part owing to the development of the railway and the gold rush. In 1869 George M. Pullman debuted his first luxury dining car, fitted with two rows of booths and a kitchen that prepared delectable hot meals. Such finery en route set a standard for dining nationwide. For less affluent travelers, after 1876, Fred Harvey's "refreshment saloons," located in train stations along popular lines, offered mediocre food enhanced by the warm welcome of the smiling Harvey Girls.

The gold rush hit San Francisco in 1849, and a splendid eatery with an unlikely name, New World Coffee, opened in 1850. In 1887 it became the Tadich Grill, and is still in operation in the early 2000s. Around the same time, Chinese immigrants arrived in the San Francisco Bay area in large numbers and established an early Chinatown with restaurants and food shops to service their needs. In 1864 the French restaurant Jack's opened in San Francisco, and in 1893 Schroeder's served up a taste of German food.

The commodity craze brought a wave of prosperity to Chicago. At the center of the country's meat-processing industry, the city's residents took to an enduring form of high-protein dining, the steakhouse. Areas at the heart of cattle production, such as Kansas City and Oklahoma City, developed local steakhouse variations, and no amount of nutritional information has since been able to dampen the nationwide appeal of eating large portions of aged beef with a selection of side dishes.

Delmonico's and Charles Ranhofer, the restaurant's French chef for more than forty years, established French food as the fine-dining standard. As towns across the country prospered, whether as the consequence of mining, shipping, or industrialization, French restaurants opened to help residents celebrate. According to the historian

At Table. Diners at Café Moutarde, Brooklyn, New York. *Photograph by Joe Zarba*

Harvey Levenstein, by the mid-1870s even small western towns such as Tombstone, Arizona, and Virginia City, Nevada, had fine French restaurants. New Orleans came by its French restaurants naturally, as a result of its large French population. The "Big Easy" earned its reputation for fine dining through establishments such as Antoine's, operating since 1840, serving French, Creole, and Cajun cuisines that derive from the city's unique ethnic mix. At the other end of the dining spectrum, Café du Monde began serving its famous chicory coffee and chewy beignets around the clock in 1862.

Clean, Fair, and Alcohol-Free

At the dawn of the twentieth century, while the upper classes indulged themselves at lobster palaces, steakhouses, and fancy French restaurants, those less flush were turning their attention to more mundane matters, such as efficiency, nutrition, hygiene, and temperance. In Chicago and New York growing chains of "luncheonettes" built their reputations on the purity of their ingredients and the cleanliness of their facilities, typified by the Childs chain of cafeteria-style luncheonettes, which opened in 1898. The Philadelphia-based chain of coffee shops founded by Joe Horn and Frank Hardart in 1888 took the idea of efficiency to a new level with the opening of their first automat in 1902. By 1922 the Chicagoan

John R. Thompson counted 103 restaurants in his citywide chain of modest, clean, and quick eateries. Built on these same themes, the fast food industry took hold in California during the 1950s with the start of chains like McDonald's (1955) and Carl's Jr. (1956).

Prohibition in 1920 devastated fine-dining restaurants. Until then (as now) the business formula that made restaurants viable relied on the high profit margin on alcohol sales. Restaurants such as Delmonico's and Sherry's could not stay afloat. Also gone were the "free

Restaurant Publicity. Publicity photographs for Lindy's restaurant, a notable New York eatery famous for its cheesecake. *Culinary Archives & Museum at Johnson & Wales University, Providence, R.I.*

lunches" in bars and the inexpensive businessmen's lunches that had been subsidized by booze. But other types of restaurants flourished. Soda fountains and luncheonettes took advantage of empty spaces, low rent, and a business model that excluded alcohol. Of course, one could still have a drink with a meal if that meal was eaten behind the locked door of a speakeasy. Opened in 1929 in New York City (and still very much in business), Jack and Charlie's "21" was the epitome of the gourmet "speak."

Perhaps one of the biggest changes wrought by Prohibition was the breakdown of the gender barriers in dining. Generally, women were not welcome in the inner sanctum of fine restaurants or neighborhood saloons. But

THE RISE OF RESTAURANTS

Americans' relationship with restaurants changed dramatically in the decades following World War II. The economic prosperity of the postwar period increased discretionary income, allowing Americans to lavish their extra dollars on professionally prepared foods outside of the home. In addition, the increasing numbers of single-person households, infusion of women into the workforce, decline in cooking knowledge as home economics became a politically incorrect part of high-school curricula, and sheer entertainment, easy availability, and enjoyable sociability of most restaurant experiences all contributed to the waning of at-home dining. Perhaps the most oft-cited reason, proffered in sheepish justification, for the rise in restaurant dining is Americans' popularly bemoaned and irritatingly vague fast-paced lifestyle, which leaves little time, energy, or inclination for cooking. At the turn of the millennium, Americans were on the verge of spending more on food consumed away from home than on food in the family grocery cart.

Since the early 1970s virtually all Americans have spent absolutely and relatively more dollars on food away from home. According to the Food Institute, a trade organization, between 1972 and 1982 American spending at limited menu (fast food) and full menu establishments nearly tripled. Leading the growth in this period were lower-income families. According to the U.S. Department of Labor's Bureau of Labor Statistics, those in the lowest 20 percent of income increased restaurant (including fast food) spending from 18.5 percent of the family food dollar to 24.3 percent. Those in other economic tranches increased their spending as well, with the highest 20 percent of earners spending 37.6 percent of food dollars in restaurants, up from 33.3 percent a decade earlier.

The ratio of spending between fast food and traditional full menu establishments also shifted. In 1972 full-menu restaurants accounted for nearly two-thirds of all restaurant dollars; by 1982 full-menu restaurants had fallen to about 57 percent of restaurant dollars, and this trend continued through 2002, with snack shops and coffeehouses such as the Starbucks chain representing the fastest-growing segment of the restaurant market. In 2002, as frequent restaurant dining for the whole family became a part of American life, so-called fast-casual restaurants such as Applebee's, Red Lobster, and Olive Garden represented a faster-growing market, in terms of the number of new outlets, than McDonald's and Burger King.

Several conclusions emerge. Spending on food away from home rises with income, regardless of age, gender, or family structure. Higher income households spend disproportionately more on food away from home, reinforcing the discretionary nature of the spending. Single-person households spend more per capita than family units on food away from home, probably due to the diseconomies of small-scale cooking for one and the general dreariness of eating alone. The most important audience for restaurants is the dual-earner household. Although they account for approximately one-third of all households, two-career families control approximately 43 percent of restaurant spending.

BIBLIOGRAPHY

Florman, Monte, Marjorie Florman, and the editors of *Consumer Reports. Fast Foods: Eating In and Eating Out.* Mount Vernon, NY: Consumers Union, 1990. An analysis of fast food and chain restaurants by *Consumer Reports*, which ranked restaurants on their speed, service, atmosphere, nutrition, cleanliness, value, and kid-friendliness. Also includes a ranking of quick-to-prepare foods at home.

Food Institute. *Menu for Change: Regional Transition in America's Eating and Drinking Places.* Fair Lawn, NJ: Food Institute, 1984.

Mogelonsky, Marcia. *Who's Buying Food and Drink: Who Spends How Much on Food and Alcohol, at and away from Home.* Ithaca, NY: New Strategist Publications, 1996.

Russell, Cheryl. *Best Customers: Demographics of Consumer Demand.* Ithaca, NY: New Strategist Publications, 2001.

CATHY K. KAUFMAN

In the Restaurant. Waiter and customers at Sotto Voce restaurant, Brooklyn, New York. *Photograph by Joe Zarba*

once the alcohol stopped flowing, the sexes began to mingle over food in soda fountains and tearooms across the country. Although they first appeared in the 1890s, tearooms—small luncheon restaurants operated by and for women with a taste for lighter, more modest fare—peaked in popularity during the 1920s. The tearoom phenomenon spread to every part of the country, both urban and rural, and included every type of establishment, from fine hotels and department stores to dingy gas stations.

Dining Trends after World War II

The Depression and World War II took further tolls on the restaurant industry. An increased demand for low-cost food was met with advances in food-processing technology. Inexpensive eateries across the country, including chains like Schrafft's and Howard Johnson, increasingly took advantage of these new processed foods, serving canned soups, frozen vegetables, and other prepackaged items that minimized food and labor costs. As the food on menus standardized, American restaurateurs began differentiating themselves with extravagant interior decoration. From Portland, Oregon, to Miami, Florida, Venetian gardens, King Tut's tomb, and other kitsch decor became popular in new restaurants, no matter that the menus invariably included steak, roast chicken, mashed potatoes, and peas.

Meanwhile, ethnic dining became fashionable among variety seekers in New York City. Restaurants continued to blossom in the city's immigrant ethnic enclaves, and it was not long before Italian, Jewish, German, Russian, Japanese, and other types of restaurants broke out to other parts of the city. The 1939 World's Fair in the neighborhood of Flushing, Queens, in New York City introduced many Americans to foreign cultures. Among the most popular exhibits was the restaurant in the French pavilion, managed by Henri Soulé, who remained in the United States and opened Le Pavillon in 1941. Le Pavillon ushered in a newfound enthusiasm and set the standard for classic French cuisine, prepared by a mostly French staff that included Pierre Franey, who would become chef in 1952. By mid-century much of the country was eating out with a French accent at fancy places like La Caravelle (1960) and Lutèce (1961) in New York City, Maisonette (1949) in Cincinnati, and all sorts of bistros and brasseries between the East Coast and the Midwest.

Simultaneously, restaurateurs aspired to create a uniquely American fine-dining experience. Joe Baum merged theatricality, theme, and fine food at the grand restaurants produced by his firm, Restaurant Associates. Everything his Forum of the Twelve Caesars project featured in ancient Roman kitsch, his Four Seasons project had in understated modern elegance. Opened in the

Seagram Building on Park Avenue in 1959, the Four Seasons was a lavishly expensive restaurant whose menu—created with the help of the American food champion James Beard—was written solely in English. It featured locally grown, seasonal American produce. The unabashed ambition of the Four Seasons set in motion a celebration of regional American food that continues to this day.

By the 1970s myriad dining trends were heading off in different directions. Opened in 1971, Chez Panisse in Berkeley, California, celebrated the freshest produce simply prepared, an approach that would come to represent California cuisine. The counterculture found its dining model in the Moosewood vegetarian cooperative, which started in Ithaca, New York, in 1973. Ethnic eateries continued to reflect immigration patterns around the country and were stratified to cater to every class of diner. Even the fast food hamburger model has broadened its offerings to include ethnic specialties, healthful alternatives, and items perceived to be "gourmet."

At the turn of the twenty-first century, America experienced an unprecedented economic prosperity that was reflected in a highly diverse dining scene. Unlike most other societies with strong restaurant-dining cultures, for example, France and Japan, America has a unique ability to incorporate both strikingly authentic replications of foreign restaurants and what can only be described as bastardized versions of them. This dichotomy means that there are French, Japanese, Chinese, Italian, Mexican, and other types of restaurants that rival the best in the world alongside others that would be unrecognizable anywhere else. Add to this the openness and creativity that has produced a unique American cuisine, which has begun to challenge French cultural hegemony in matters of food. More than just fast food hamburgers, America has exported an inclusive approach to food and dining that has had an extensive impact on restaurant design and operation around the world.

[*See also* Automats; Bars; Beard, James; Beer Halls; Bistros; Cafeterias; Chinese American Food; Coffeehouses; Delmonico's; Dining Car; Ethnic Foods; Fast Food; French Influences on American Food; German American Food; Harvey, Fred; Hotel Dining Rooms; Italian American Food; Luncheonettes; New York Food; Oyster Bars; Prohibition; Pullman, George; Ranhofer, Charles; Saloons; Soda Fountains; Taverns.]

BIBLIOGRAPHY

Batterberry, Michael, and Ariane Batterberry. *On the Town in New York: The Landmark History of Eating, Drinking, and Entertainments from the American Revolution to the Food Revolution*. New York: Routledge, 1999.

Levenstein, Harvey. *Revolution at the Table: The Transformation of the American Diet*. New York: Oxford University Press, 1988.

Mennell, Stephen. *All Manners of Food: Eating and Taste in England and France from the Middle Ages to the Present*. Urbana: University of Illinois Press, 1996.

Root, Waverly, and Richard de Rochemont. *Eating in America: A History*. New York: William Morrow and Company, 1976.

Spang, Rebecca. *The Invention of the Restaurant: Paris and Modern Gastronomic Culture*. Cambridge, MA: Harvard University Press, 2000.

Whitaker, Jan. *Tea at the Blue Lantern Inn: A Social History of the Tea Room Craze in America*. New York: St. Martin's Press, 2002.

MITCHELL DAVIS

Reuben Sandwich

The Reuben sandwich is composed of thinly sliced corned beef, swiss cheese, sauerkraut, and russian dressing piled between slices of rye bread and grilled. Three separate camps lay claim to the creation of the Reuben. In New York the sandwich is said to have been introduced in 1914 by Arnold Reuben, owner of Reuben's Restaurant on East Fifty-eighth Street. An out-of-work actress named Annette Seelos arrived at Reuben's and asked for something to eat. Mr. Reuben made her an enormous sandwich that consisted of bread, roast beef and other meats, cheese, and spices, and he eventually named it the "Reuben's Special."

In Omaha, Nebraska, legend says that the sandwich, composed of the traditional ingredients, originated in the early 1920s as a snack for a group of hungry poker players at the Blackstone Hotel. Reuben Kolakofsky, a grocer, is credited with its creation, and it was such a hit that the hotel owner, Charles Schimmel, named it in his honor and put it on the menu. In 1956 a former waitress at the Blackstone Hotel named Fern Snider entered the recipe in a national sandwich competition and won. Finally, it is said that the Reuben was created in 1937 at the Cornhusker Hotel in Lincoln, Nebraska. A menu from that establishment, listing the proper ingredients and dated the same year, has been submitted as proof. To date, this menu is the only evidence that has surfaced to substantiate any of the three claims. The Reuben sandwich is a standard offering on delicatessen and restaurant menus throughout the United States.

[*See also* Corned Beef; Delicatessens; Sandwiches.]

BIBLIOGRAPHY

"Reuben and His Restaurant." *American Life Histories: Manuscripts from the Federal Writers' Project, 1936–1940.* At the American Memory website. http://memory.loc.gov/ammem/amhome.html.

Mercuri, Becky. *Sandwiches That You Will Like.* Pittsburgh, PA: WQED, 2002.

BECKY MERCURI

Rhubarb

Rhubarb (*Rheum rhabarbarum*), related to sorrel, grows in a form typical of vegetables, but the U.S. Customs Court at Buffalo, New York, ruled in 1947 that it is a fruit, since that is how it is usually used. A hardy perennial and a pleasant harbinger of spring, rhubarb is also called "pie plant" in the United States. American commercial production of rhubarb is concentrated in Washington, Oregon, and Michigan but also exists in other northern states. About a quarter of the crop is sold fresh; most of the rest is frozen.

Rhubarb originated in Asia over five thousand years ago and was introduced to Maine at the end of the eighteenth century when a gardener obtained seeds or roots from Europe. Cultivation soon flourished in Massachusetts, and by 1822 rhubarb was sold in New England produce markets. In the late nineteenth century, the great plant breeder Luther Burbank developed a mild variety with a long growing season well suited to California.

Early Americans used rhubarb extract and syrup for dyspepsia and a variety of bowel complaints. Most mid-nineteenth-century medical guides recommended the use of rhubarb extracts (an 1866 medical book suggested fifteen drops be given to a constipated child), and tinctures of rhubarb were a standard in medicine chests.

Rhubarb. *Warshaw Collection of Business Americana, Archives Center, National Museum of American History, Behring Center, Smithsonian Institution*

Nineteenth-century American cookbooks carried rhubarb recipes for sweet pies, cobblers, conserves, and tarts. In her *American Frugal Housewife* (1833, twelfth edition), the New England author Lydia Maria Child wrote, "Rhubarb stalks, or the Persian apple, is the earliest ingredient for pies, which the spring offers." But, she mourned, "These are dear pies, for they take an enormous quantity of sugar." However extravagant the pies may have been, eating rhubarb in spring was considered a "broom for the system," and pioneer women took rhubarb seeds west with them on the Overland Trail, where they were eventually sowed beside log cabins and sod houses. Some rhubarb beds dating back a century or more still thrive in the West, although the dwellings they stood by have long disappeared.

Rhubarb leaves contain large amounts of oxalic acid, which makes them inedible. The stalks also contain this poisonous substance, but only in amounts equal to that found in spinach and chard.

[*See also* Child, Lydia Maria; Homemade Remedies; Pies and Tarts; Sorrel.]

BIBLIOGRAPHY

Morse, J. E. *The New Rhubarb Culture.* New York: Orange Judd, 1909.

Schneider, Elizabeth. *Vegetables from Amaranth to Zucchini: The Essential Reference,* 538–542. New York: Morrow, 2001.

SARA RATH

"RHUBARB"

In the early days of radio, when the noise of an angry crowd was needed, actors in the studio were asked to mumble "rhubarb" over and over, which provided that rumbling ambience. A "rhubarb" is also a slang term for a heated fight or argument in a baseball game.

Rice

A staple food of more than two-thirds of the world's population, rice is one of the most important grains in the world. There are two domesticated species: Asian rice (*Oryza sativa*), which has been cultivated for at least seven thousand years in Southeast Asia, China, and India, and African rice (*Oryza glaberrima*), which has been cultivated in West Africa since about 1500 B.C.E. In the sixteenth century *O. sativa* was introduced into West Africa, probably by the Portuguese, and it largely replaced indigenous African rice, mainly because of its higher yields.

Asian rice, the major modern commercial rice, has two major subspecies: *japonica*, a short-grain rice, and *indica*, a long- or medium-grain rice that thrives in hot climates. *Indica* takes longer to mature and is less starchy and mushy when cooked. Historically, *indica* types were first grown in the southern states while *japonica* types were initially cultivated in California in the twentieth century.

Rice Cultivation

The earliest record of rice cultivation in the English colonies is from Virginia in 1647; from the beginning, rice was thought of as an export crop. By the late seventeenth century, as rice production increased in South Carolina, Virginia plantation owners found it more profitable to grow tobacco. Asian rice (*O. sativa indica*) was probably first introduced to South Carolina from Madagascar in the 1680s. The English herbalist William Solomon, who had lived in South Carolina from 1687 to 1690, saw rice "flourish" there, and, he claimed in his *Botanologia* (1710), it was "the best rice which grows on the whole Earth."

"Carolina rice" came to be a generic term for long-grain rice of high quality cultivated in the low country of South Carolina and Georgia. It was frequently cited in British and French cookbooks and won medals at European agricultural fairs and expositions. One of its most attractive attributes was its color—a pure, dazzling white. The term "Carolina gold" was in use by 1700, and it referred to the gold color of the ripe grain in the field.

Commercial rice production—difficult and brutal work—required a large labor force that was supplied through the importation of slaves. Because the early French and British settlers in South Carolina knew nothing about rice cultivation, it was their slaves, from rice-growing areas of West Africa, who prepared the fields; constructed the canals and dikes; planted and cultivated the crops; flooded and drained the fields; and harvested, winnowed, and polished the rice.

Rice cultivation quickly expanded throughout low-country South Carolina and to North Carolina and Georgia. By the early eighteenth century, rice growing had become one of America's most important businesses. South Carolina exported 20,000 pounds of rice in 1698; 394,000 pounds in 1700; and 128 million pounds in 1835. Some rice was shipped to New England and to the West Indies, but most of it was exported to England, where some of it was transshipped to Europe.

Two major innovations contributed to the expansion of the rice industry in colonial and antebellum America. The first was the tidal-flow method of cultivating rice, developed during the 1750s by the South Carolina planter Mckewn Johnstone. Johnstone devised a way to use the ocean tides to flood rice fields, thus opening thousands of additional acres of land for rice growing. The second innovation was the improvement of the rice mills. Initially rice was milled by hand with mortars and pestles. In 1787 Jonathan Lucas of Charleston, South Carolina, developed and built the first water-driven rice mill, from which the tide-driven mill was developed a few years later. It saved on labor and improved the quality of the milled rice. It was marketed along the rice coasts of Georgia and South Carolina.

In South Carolina the rice crop expanded until 1860. During the Civil War rice was difficult to harvest because Union gunboats watched the swampy lowlands, where the rice was grown. After the war, rice production in South Carolina declined slowly until the 1920s, when no rice at all was milled. The decline was mainly due to the loss of the workforce—former slaves—whose children chose other occupations, and to hurricanes, which devastated coastal South Carolina. Also, rice growers had not followed good agricultural practices, and the soil was exhausted.

As rice cultivation declined in South Carolina, it increased in Louisiana and the American Southwest. Rice had been grown in small quantities in French settlements in Louisiana during the eighteenth century. Just before the Civil War, planters along the Mississippi River began to expand rice production, and cultivation exploded after the war. Rice production began in Arkansas and Texas in the 1880s and had begun in the Sacramento Valley in California by the early twentieth century. In 2002 rice production in the United States was concentrated primarily in Arkansas, which produced almost half of the rice grown in the nation, followed by California, Louisiana,

Mississippi, Missouri, and Texas. The United States ranked third among nations with the largest rice exports.

Rice Cookery

Prior to the eighteenth century, English cooks knew little about cooking rice, as few recipes had appeared in manuscripts or cookbooks. When rice began to be imported into England, cooks incorporated it into traditional recipes. Hence rice was used to make gruels and puddings and later bread and pastries. British cookbooks published or sold in America included recipes with rice as an ingredient. For instance, *The Compleat Housewife* (1742) by E. Smith, the first cookbook published in America, includes a recipe "To make a Poloe" (pilaf). *The Art of Cookery, Made Plain and Easy* (1747) by Hannah Glasse offers at least twenty-one recipes with rice as an ingredient, including nine for pudding, four for pilaf, and recipes for soup, curry, and pancakes. While an edition of this cookbook was not published in America until the nineteenth century, so many copies were sold or brought over from England that *The Art of Cookery* was one of America's most popular cookbooks during the colonial period. These cookbooks do not necessarily reflect American practice, although recipes published in British books were titled Carolina Rice Pudding and To make Carolina Snow-balls.

HOPPIN' JOHN AND OTHER RICE DISHES

The sustaining combination of rice and peas—black-eyed peas, cowpeas, or whatever legume is available—is an African dish that took various forms in the Americas, such as Brazilian *feijoada* and Cuban *Moros y Cristianos*. The only specifically American versions of this dish are the hoppin' John of South Carolina and red beans and rice of New Orleans. Hoppin' John may have as its leguminous component cowpeas, or black-eyed peas (*Vigna unguiculata*); Congo peas, or pigeon peas (*Cajanus cajan*); but green or yellow field peas (*Pisum sativum*) are not used. A recipe for hoppin' John appears in *The Carolina Housewife* (1847) by Sarah Rutledge, and it is a signature dish of South Carolina cookery.

Pilau, also known as pilaf, polo, or pullow (there are still more spellings), is long-grain rice that has been washed and presoaked. The rice is briefly browned in fat, and then a flavorful broth is added, usually in the proportion of two parts liquid to one part rice by volume. Other ingredients, such as chicken or seafood, may be added to the rice as it simmers. Pilau most likely originated in Iran, and it traveled to Europe and South Asia after the expansion of Islam. A number of dishes related to pilaf, including arroz con pollo (chicken and rice), paella (a complex dish made with chicken and several types of shellfish), and jambalaya (a spicy dish from New Orleans that might also contain ham, sausage, chicken, or shellfish with vegetables) are all enjoyed in the United States.

Recipes called "rice soup" had been published in England by the late eighteenth century and in America by 1805. Many other soup recipes contain rice, including ones for pepper pot, okra soup, gumbo, and mulligatawny soup.

Rice bread has been consumed for millennia in Europe and Asia. These breads are mainly flatbreads; unlike wheat, rice develops no gluten to support rising dough. These recipes were brought from Europe to America in colonial times. The rice breads, cakes, and cookies of the Carolina lowlands were largely made with rice flour. Rice bread without the addition of flour was dense, even when made with boiled rice flour, which produces a superior loaf. Rice bread was popular in England in the late eighteenth century, and recipes were regularly published in the United States during the nineteenth century. It was mainly used as a substitute for wheat flour in the South. When the price of wheat flour dropped in the nineteenth century, the making of rice bread declined. During World War I it became patriotic to add rice flour to bread so that more wheat could be shipped to European allies and the American armed forces.

Rice cakes and other baked goods were based on traditional English recipes for other grains, such as wheat. Colonists brought them to America and adapted them. Johnnycakes, breads, pancakes, and fritters were all of European origin. In rice-growing areas of America, rice was substituted for oats or wheat.

Sweet rice dishes, classified as puddings, evolved from English and French recipes for blancmange. In rice-growing areas of America, colonists substituted rice for other grains used in these recipes. Many sweet rice dishes died out in the twentieth century, with the exception of rice pudding, which remains a favorite.

ANDREW F. SMITH

In America, English and French rice dishes were augmented by the skills of African slaves, who brought different rice traditions with them. The South was the birthplace of American rice cookery. Rice recipes were regularly published in nineteenth-century southern cookbooks while comparatively few were published in northern cookbooks. The first American recipes with rice as an ingredient appear in South Carolina cookery manuscripts beginning in the second half of the eighteenth century. For instance, *Recipe Book* by Eliza Lucas Pinckney, dated to 1756, includes a recipe on how to boil rice. *Receipt Book* by Harriott Pinckney Horry, dated to 1770, includes four recipes with rice as an ingredient: Rice Bread, Rice Milk, Journey Cake, and "To make a Cassorol or rather a rice pye." Beginning in the early nineteenth century, recipes for rice appeared in many American cookbooks. *The Carolina Housewife* (1847) by Sarah Rutledge, for instance, offers fifty-three recipes with rice as the characterizing ingredient.

The first American cookbook to focus solely on rice (largely a compilation of previously published recipes) was *Carolina Rice Cook Book* (1901) by Mrs. Samuel G. Stoney. The second was *Rice for Breakfast, Dinner, Supper* (1919) by Bessie R. Murphey.

Rice cookery also appeared in cookbooks and recipes associated with other countries or ethnic groups in America. From the early nineteenth century, rice recipes in general cookbooks were identified as Indian, Chinese, Spanish, and Portuguese. Beginning in the late nineteenth century, recipes identified as Mexican contained rice as an ingredient, and recipes for Spanish rice were commonly published in mainstream cookbooks. Rice is a common ingredient in American cookbooks that focus on Chinese, Indian, Italian, Japanese, Mexican, or Spanish cookery.

Rice consumption was encouraged by a variety of groups. For instance, the American Vegetarian Society published *Unpolished Rice, the Staple Food of the Orient* (1905) by Henry Stephen Clubb, and the U.S. Department of Agriculture published several pamphlets, such as *Rice as Food* (1921) and *Cooking American Varieties of Rice* by Mabel Clare Stienbarger. Finally, rice producers distributed publications on rice cookery. The Southern Rice Industry of New Orleans, for instance, published *Rice: 200 Delightful Ways to Serve It* (1934) and *The Use of Rice on the Hospital Menu* (1935) by Millie E. Kalsem.

During the second half of the nineteenth century, many immigrants or new citizens of the rapidly expanding United States came from rice-consuming cultures. When Texas, California, and the Southwest were acquired by annexation, conquest, and treaty, the Mexicans living in these areas automatically became American citizens. They had fully integrated rice into their diets, and recipes for Spanish rice became popular throughout the United States. Puerto Ricans, who became Americans when their island was annexed by the United States in 1898, also relied on rice as a dietary staple. Many Italian immigrants who arrived during the late nineteenth and early twentieth centuries were also familiar with rice, and rice dishes, such as risotto, were common in Italian homes and restaurants. Chinese Americans arriving in California during the gold rush brought their rice-based cuisine. Hawaii, annexed by the United States in 1898, also had a rice-centric cuisine. As Hispanic and Asian immigration to the United States increased, so did the importance of rice in the American diet. The process continues: Asian immigrants have introduced sticky rice into the mainstream American diet. Japanese Americans have made sushi—artistic pairings of raw fish and rice—a common food in America. Mediterranean-style rice pilafs have also become popular, and pilaf mixes are commonly sold in supermarkets. But it was not until after World War II that cookbooks focusing on rice were regularly published in the United States. Dharam Jit Singh published *The Art of Rice Cookery* (1963), and Ellen Blonder and Annabel Low, Chinese Americans, wrote *Every Grain of Rice: A Taste of Our Chinese Childhood in America* (1998). Modern rice cookbooks offer a variety of ethnic recipes and often use less common types of rice, such as Italian Arborio rice and Indian basmati rice.

Hoppin' John. *Collection of Howard Paige*

WILD RICE

Wild rice (*Zizania aquatica*), not a true rice, is the long, brownish-black seed of a wild grass indigenous to North America and Asia. In America it grows in lakes and rivers primarily in areas west and north of the Great Lakes as well as in isolated pockets from New Jersey to Florida and Texas. It was consumed in pre-Columbian times by Native Americans, who harvested it from canoes, beating the grain from the plants with sticks; some wild rice is still harvested in this fashion, and its price reflects the labor-intensive method. As befits its wild origins, the rice is commonly served with game, but it is also served with domestic poultry. Cultivated varieties of wild rice were developed in the 1960s, and California is the largest producer.

BIBLIOGRAPHY

Hauser, Susan Carol. *Wild Rice Cooking: Harvesting, History, Natural History, and Lore with 80 Recipes with 80 Recipes.* New York: Lyons Press, 2000.

Commercial Rice Products

Numerous commercial products made from rice have been manufactured in America. One of the early successful products was Puffed Rice, a cereal developed by Alexander P. Anderson, who in 1902 actually fired the rice out of a cannon to explode the grains. He created the Anderson Puffed Rice Company as a wholly owned subsidiary of Quaker Oats and first introduced Puffed Rice at the St. Louis Exposition in Missouri in 1904. The product's attention-getting slogan was "Shot from Guns!"

The Kellogg Company first marketed Rice Krispies, a cold breakfast cereal, in 1928. Three gnomelike characters, originally drawn by Vernon Grant, were its mascots. "Snap!" first appeared in 1933 while "Crackle!" and "Pop!" were introduced in 1941. Eight years later, the characters were changed to look more elfin and appealing. The recipe for Kellogg's Rice Krispies Treats, made by mixing the cereal with melted marshmallows, was introduced in 1933. Kellogg's produced an advertising cookbooklet, *Creative Cookery Rice Krispies Recipe Collection* (1982).

Uncle Ben's Rice was developed in the 1940s by Gordon Harwell of Texas, who used a British process of treating rice with pressurized steam to drive minerals and vitamins into the kernel. To promote its product, Uncle Ben's Inc. produced several cookbooklets, including *Uncle Ben's Rice Cookery: How to Prepare 231 Delicious Recipes* (1977).

Minute Rice was developed by an Afghan inventor, Ataullah K. Ozai-Durrani, who sold the process to General Foods Corporation in 1941. The process precooked rice, then dried it so that only very brief boiling was needed to reconstitute it. General Foods first marketed Minute Rice in 1946. Rice-A-Roni, composed of rice, pasta, and a dry seasoning mix, was created by Vince DeDomenico of the Golden Grain Company in San Francisco. It was launched regionally in 1958 with a television commercial featuring San Francisco's cable cars accompanied by the jingle "Rice-A-Roni, the San Francisco Treat!" Rice-A-Roni was being sold nationally by 1962.

Later Developments

Rice is a staple food of Hispanic Americans, Creoles, Hawaiians, Asian Americans, and many other ethnic and national groups. Many varieties of rice are available in American supermarkets, each slightly different in texture and flavor. In addition to regular white and brown rice, converted rice, and quick-cooking rice, many stores carry fragrant types, such as Indian basmati rice (both brown and white) and Thai jasmine rice; American-grown fragrant rice varieties, called Calmati and Texmati, are less expensive alternatives to the imported products. Chinese and Japanese rice varieties, imported or grown domestically, are also available. Americans' consumption of rice doubled during the last two decades of the twentieth century, and it will quite likely continue to grow in the twenty-first century.

[*See also* African American Food, *subentry* To the Civil War; Cajun and Creole Food; Cereal, Cold; Chinese American Food; Hawaiian Food; Japanese American Food; Kellogg Company; Mexican American Food; Southeast Asian American Food; Southern Regional Cookery; Southwestern Regional Cookery; Uncle Ben.]

BIBLIOGRAPHY

Carney, Judith A. *Black Rice: The African Origins of Rice Cultivation in the Americas.* Cambridge, MA: Harvard University Press, 2001.
Dethloff, Henry C. A *History of the American Rice Industry, 1685–1985.* College Station: Texas A&M University Press, 1988.

Hess, Karen. *The Carolina Rice Kitchen: The African Connection*. Columbia: University of South Carolina Press, 1992.

Littlefield, David. *Rice and Slaves: Ethnicity and the Slave Trade in Colonial South Carolina*. Baton Rouge: Louisiana State University Press, 1981.

Smith, C. Wayne, and Robert H. Dilday, eds. *Rice: Origin, History, Technology, and Production*. Hoboken, NJ: Wiley, 2003.

ANDREW F. SMITH

Rice Cookers

Toshiba of Japan claims to have released the first electric rice cooker in 1955, but Japan's Ministry of Trade and Technology asserts that the devices first emerged in 1946, around the same time as the Japanese constitution. The earliest automatic rice cookers bear a resemblance to slow cookers used for stewing, with an electric element in a cylindrical base applying heat to a removable cooking vessel. A thermostat triggers a power shutoff when the vessel temperature exceeds the boiling point of water, ensuring that the cooked rice does not scorch. Before the introduction of electric cookers, steamed rice, which requires slow cooking under a tight-fitting lid, was generally made in pots designed for the purpose, heated over fire. Photographic records exist of large, lidded, iron "rice cookers" found by U.S. troops on the Marshall Islands at the end of World War II; they had been used as defensive shields by the Japanese.

America's adoption of the electric devices, which have a 90 percent market penetration in urban China and are ubiquitous in Japan, came with the rising popularity of Asian foods like sushi (Japanese vinegared short-grain rice, usually served with raw fish known as "sashimi") in the late twentieth century. The advantage over conventional rice cookery methods in commercial sushi preparation is gained through keeping the rice warm, important to the formation of the traditional sushi shapes. Technological improvements in rice cookers, such as nonstick linings, computerized timing and temperature control, and childproof safety features, have made the devices more versatile, allowing for preparation of complex dishes like paella and vindaloo with little or no attention from start to finish.

[See also Japanese American Food; Rice; Slow Cookers.]

BIBLIOGRAPHY

Spennemann, Dirk H. R. "Secondary Use of World War II Equipment in the Marshalls: Japanese Rice Cookers. A Photo Essay." Available at http://life.csu.edu.au/marshall/html/WWII/RiceCookers. html.

U.S. Department of Agriculture Economic Research Service. The Economics of Food, Farming, Natural Resources, and Rural America. "Briefing Room: Rice." Available at www.ers.usda.gov/briefing/ rice/.

JAY WEINSTEIN

Richards, Ellen Swallow

Ellen Henrietta Swallow Richards (1842–1911), American chemist, educator, and first president of the American Home Economics Association, was born in Dunstable, Massachusetts. She graduated from Vassar in 1870 and that same year was the first woman to be admitted to the Massachusetts Institute of Technology (as "a special student" pursuing an advanced degree in chemistry). In 1876, with the help of the Boston Women's Education Association, she was instrumental in organizing the Woman's Laboratory at MIT to offer scientific education for women. She served as an instructor in sanitary chemistry at the laboratory, and her first book, *The Chemistry of Cooking and Cleaning*, was published during this period. In 1884, when women were first admitted to the university as regular students, Richards became a member of the MIT faculty, a position she held until her death in 1911.

Richards devoted her life to helping women gain access to scientific education and to the field of chemistry at a time when it was closed to them. By focusing scientific principles on roles that women already filled, she was able to ease the entry of women into applied chemistry laboratories and academic departments in the sciences. She felt that the scientific theories that revolutionized late-eighteenth-and early-nineteenth-century industry could improve the health, happiness, and productivity of the American family if women had access to that information and applied it to their work in the home. With the help of several wealthy Bostonians, Richards founded the New England Kitchen, a cooking laboratory in which recipes for basic New England foods were scientifically formulated and distributed to neighborhood people when they came to purchase the nourishing, low-cost foods that were produced there. A second center was established in Boston and one in New York, but the experiment failed to attract and reeducate the immigrant homemakers of the two cities.

In 1899 Ellen Richards organized the first Lake Placid Conference for people working in the field of home science. The group included educators in chemistry, biology, physics, bacteriology, economics, sanitary science, hygiene, domestic science, and the emerging fields of psychology and sociology. The conferences continued to be held annually in Lake Placid, and in 1903, at a joint session with the National Education Association's manual training session, the group developed a four-year college curriculum in home economics. At the 1908 meeting, the Lake Placid Conference became the American Home Economics Association with Richards as president, a position she held until 1910.

Near the end of her career Richards became interested in the new field of nutrition and wrote some of the first government pamphlets on the subject. She also fostered euthenics, the science of controlled environment, a discipline that dealt with the development of human well-being by the improvement of living conditions. A supporter of the Muckrakers and their campaign to clean up the American food supply, Richards had her students analyze foods for safety and advocated that they do similar tests in their own homes. The theories that she formulated throughout her life came together in the writing of *Euthenics* (1910) and *Conservation by Sanitation* (1911).

[*See also* Food and Nutrition Systems; Home Economics; Nutrition.]

BIBLIOGRAPHY

Shapiro, Laura. *Perfection Salad: Women and Cooking at the Turn of the Century.* New York: Henry Holt, 1986.
Vare, Ethlie A. *Adventurous Spirit: A Story about Ellen Swallow Richards.* Minneapolis, MN: Lerner, 1992.

JOANNE LAMB HAYES

Roadhouses

The roadhouse, as it is popularly conceived in B movies and country ballads, is a rustic saloon where trouble eternally brews. Whether it is a honky-tonk with sawdust on the floor, a seedy neighborhood dive, or even a brothel, and whether the colorful characters within are cowboys, showgirls, or Hells Angels, one thing is certain: the roadhouse is a transgressive space—quite literally, in fact, in that such establishments are often found on the lawless outskirts of town. Technically, however, the term "roadhouse" is rather more prosaic, referring simply to an establishment located on the side of the road to provide some combination of refreshment, lodging, and entertainment; in that sense, it may apply equally well to a colonial tavern, gold rush–era boardinghouse, touristy clam shack, or desolate motel café.

Roadhouses before the Age of Automobiles

The tavern is the clear forerunner of the roadhouse, complete with generally unsavory reputation—although its legality as such, far from being questionable, was actually guaranteed in the seventeenth and eighteenth centuries by ordinances binding many a community to the upkeep of some form of public accommodation. It often served many other municipal functions as well, from post office to meetinghouse. Essentially, though, it was an alehouse; patrons intending to dine as well as drink had better be prepared to do so as, when, where, and if the proprietor saw fit, for the restaurant would not come fully into its own until the dawn of the nineteenth century; flexible hours, waitstaff, menus, and room service in these times were still amenities of the future.

More clearly influential than the coming of the restaurant upon the modern roadhouse was that of rail (and, later, auto) transport; the railroads supplied at once the impetus, the site, and even the model—two, in fact—for its evolution. Depots, after all, were surfacing in the middle of nowhere, with eating places springing up of necessity right alongside them; these soon developed personalities of their own. For instance, there was the Harvey House, a late-nineteenth- to mid-twentieth-century chain of in-station eateries conceived by Fred Harvey to make traveling more palatable through the employment of well-trained chefs, tasteful decor, and comely waitresses known as Harvey Girls. Then there was the dining car of the train itself; the very symbol of luxury for its time, it became, in turn, the inspiration for the kitschy diner, which in its rural rather than urban form is one of the main types of roadhouse today.

Roadhouses after the Advent of Automobiles

Connoting a casual atmosphere and down-home fare, the word "diner" may apply to a variety of roadside venues, many of them veritable warehouses of pop-culture icons, from chrome to Formica; neon jukebox to wise-cracking waitress with beehive hairdo; bottomless cup of joe to mile-high slice of pie. As the twentieth century picked up speed and automobiles progressed from rich man's novelty to everyman's exigency, as highways were constructed and the American way of life became synonymous with mobility, so eateries began to dominate the scenery. At their most basic, they were simply stands or shacks selling a limited number of snacks, such as hamburgers or hot dogs—memorable, especially in the period before World War II, not for their food but for their fanciful architecture, sometimes resembling the very items they served, such as giant coffee pots or cups, frankfurters, and ice cream cones.

More permanent structures, featuring full-service dining—diners, in fact—began appearing too. Truck stops in their mid-century heyday were considered oases of respectable, if meat-heavy, cookery for respectable, if meat-heavy, truckers. The roadhouse in all its forms, like the tavern before it, has been largely the domain of men, just as the travel opportunities that occasioned it were granted primarily to men. Wives and children may sometimes have come along, but they would never, barring unusual circumstances, have set foot on such premises alone. (The exception to this rule was the tearoom of the 1920s, which emerged as a safe country haven precisely for the gentlewoman traveler.) The surprisingly decent truck stop of old has long since made way for the anonymous, corporate-run service plaza.

Coffee shops, whether free standing or set on the grounds of motor inns or motels, are another manifest roadside destination. From this category have emerged some particularly successful chains, such as Howard Johnson, or "Ho-Jo," which spread westward from Massachusetts beginning in the 1930s, making its mark with bright-orange roofs, and Denny's, a round-the-clock operation that extended eastward from California beginning in the 1950s. Appealing, above all, to the virtue of consistency, the menus of such places are generally of a piece: all-day breakfasts feature eggs, bacon, sausage, pancakes, home fries, and hash brown potatoes; lunch items include soups, salads, and sandwiches; and dinner, almost without exception, is a meat-and-potatoes affair.

Of course, for all their notorious homogeneity, even these roadside eateries have been out-systematized, not to mention outnumbered, by the fast food franchises of the early 2000s. Convenience (even to the point of kitchen mechanization), on the one hand, and familiarity (even to the point of monotony), on the other, are the factors most commonly cited to explain the industry's dominance over all other types of road-accessible venues. In response, however, many an American gastronome has made a point of celebrating, or at least commemorating, the roadhouse in print. In books like *Roadfood and Goodfood* and *A Taste of America*, for instance, Jane and Michael Stern have chronicled their years of experience on the nation's byways and back roads, engaged in a never-ending search for the consummate slice of meatloaf or flawless buffalo wing—the very stuff of roadhouse

cuisine (along with beer). The last decades of the twentieth century also gave rise to countless books devoted to roadside architecture, some purely picture books and others scholarly forays into art history and sociology. The American roadhouse may have nothing on, say, the Roman coliseum, but those judging by the enthusiasm for the literature on the topic would never be the wiser.

[*See also* Boardinghouses; Diners; Dining Car; Fast Food; Harvey, Fred; Howard Johnson; Roadside Food; Saloons; Taverns.]

BIBLIOGRAPHY

Jakle, John A., and Keith A. Sculle. *Fast Food: Restaurants in the Automobile Age*. Baltimore: Johns Hopkins University Press, 1999. Thoroughly scholarly without being overly academic.

Mariani, John. *America Eats Out: An Illustrated History of Restaurants, Taverns, Coffee Shops, Speakeasies, and Other Establishments That Have Fed Us for 350 Years*. New York: HarperCollins, 1991. Smart and entertaining both as a written and as a pictorial document.

Pillsbury, Richard. *From Boarding House to Bistro: The American Restaurant Then and Now*. Boston: Routledge, 1990. Judicious use of statistical data balances out the distracting anecdotal sidebars.

Salinger, Sharon V. *Taverns and Drinking in Early America*. Baltimore: Johns Hopkins University Press, 2002. A fascinating, if sometimes appalling, glimpse inside the saloons of the Republic.

Stern, Jane, and Michael Stern. *American Gourmet*. New York: HarperCollins, 1991. A cheery anecdotal collection of recipes gathered from diners nationwide.

Stern, Jane, and Michael Stern. *Roadfood and Goodfood*. New York: Alfred A. Knopf, 1986. *American Gourmet* in guidebook rather than cookbook form.

RUTH TOBIAS

Roadside Food

Roadside food developed in response to the fast-growing American market of hungry travelers. Unlike its culinary cousin known as "fast food," roadside food typically involves a measure of hands-on craftsmanship in its preparation and presentation; though it is still rather fast, the cuisine also requires a modicum of patience from the customer. Fast food, as the saying goes, "waits for you."

America's ability to produce almost anything on an assembly line served it well in the development and adoption of fast food as the unofficial national cuisine. The country's vast expanse cultivated an obsession with travel, facilitated first by the railroads and then by the automobile. Eating habits would necessarily have to conform to this quicker pace of life, now precisely measured by mechanical clocks rather than the sun's passage. Industrialization provided the necessary improvements in food transport, packaging, and storage that would become an absolute requirement for any successful food service operation.

America's roadside food owes much of its existence to the efforts of Fred Harvey, an English-born restaurateur credited with establishing the first chain restaurant. His Harvey Houses greeted railroad passengers traveling through America's Southwest. Harvey's ability to serve hot meals fast in familiar and friendly surroundings made his concept a hit with the itinerant public, who had to adhere to the strict railroad timetables. Harvey enhanced the experience by hiring young, attractive, and wholesome women as servers. The "Harvey Girls" became as much a trademark of the operation as any special on the menu.

As railroad dining became a popular component of rail travel, the design of the railcar kitchens in such cramped quarters would soon play a role on the roadsides as well. The railroads' ability to cook hot meals efficiently for their passengers boded well for the hurried pace of passing motorists. The roadside diner car not only mimicked the style of its railroad counterpart but also shared much of its functional efficiency.

The spread and improvement of the national road network that began in the 1920s inspired thousands of enterprising individuals to set up some of the earliest roadside businesses designed specifically for the automobile trade. In the early years of this trend, spaces between major cities consisted primarily of farms. Resident farmers were the first to seize upon this opportunity to profit from hungry motorists. Already possessing the necessary raw materials—property, beef, pork, and dairy—farmers could easily diversify into this new business, adding a new source of revenue. These early attempts at serving food at the roadside adhered to local culinary traditions, adapted to the quicker pace of this new mobile market.

At about the same time, the White Castle and White Tower restaurant chains opened their first outlets in midwestern cities. Their distinctive buildings clad in white porcelain enamel were designed to counter the negative image of roadside stands as unhealthy greasy spoons, an appellation that many places probably deserved. The chains also capitalized on the rapidly developing efficiency of the meatpacking industry. Able to serve hamburgers at a price of only five cents each, these chains and others promoted their purchase "by the bag."

Though enormously popular in its own right, the ubiquitous hot dog resisted a national restaurant standard and therefore a national chain specializing in them. Easy to prepare and eat, though ever mysterious in its ingredients, the hot dog has become an iconic American meal. While a hamburger has few varieties, hot dogs acquired many regional identities, methods of preparation, and corresponding monikers, such as Coneys, franks, wieners, hots, pups, and tube steaks.

Other popular roadside food alternatives vary in availability. In the Northeast, the proximity of the fishing industry means a broader availability of seafood, usually deep-fried, while fried chicken and barbecue stands have greeted motorists in the South. Barbecue's labor-intensive preparation makes it ill suited for chain restaurants but provides one of the most savory roadside experiences. Barbecue comes in three general regional styles, known as Southern, Kansas City, and Texas, which are distinguished by the use of rubs, sauces, and cooking methods. The Pig Stand in Texas became one of the nation's first drive-in restaurants in the 1920s.

By the 1930s the symbiosis of architecture and advertising hit its stride. Roadside restaurant owners built highly distinctive structures to lure passing motorists, often in the image of their signature product or their name. The Pig Stand venues looked like giant pigs, while an ice cream stand might take the shape of a giant cone. Operators distracted travelers still more with bright neon signs standing sentry over buildings covered with the restaurant's menu. Often-outlandish architectural gimmickry abounded as the owners strove to outdo their competition.

Following the typical American economic business model, the roadside stand spread quickly across the landscape in its early years. The low barrier of entry attracted anyone with cooking abilities willing to work hard. Those staking out the better locations and having savvier marketing and management abilities trumped the competition. Consolidation of the industry followed as people like Howard Johnson perfected the family restaurant concept and its duplication. Other founders of the industry, such as Colonel Harlan Sanders (Kentucky Fried Chicken) and Ray Kroc (McDonald's) famously followed. By the 1950s the industry would set and maintain a standard for family-friendly dining: clean, consistent, inexpensive, and homey.

In terms of dollars, the hamburger chain rules American roadside dining. McDonald's became the world's largest restaurant chain by selling billions of them, and its market dominance has dictated the structure of the entire American food-processing industry, particularly those sectors that supply beef, potatoes, and chicken. Its practice of marketing heavily to children, acknowledged as the real decision makers for family dining, has also skewed American eating habits toward a preference for faster, easy-to-serve finger foods.

By the early 2000s, American roadside food had lost little of its actual variety though much of its ubiquity. Local variations of roadside food have become much harder to find thanks to extremely relentless competition and stricter government regulations. Yet the cuisine still thrives in more remote locations or where operators have upheld high standards of quality and value.

[*See also* Barbecue; Diners; Drive-Ins; Fast Food; Harvey, Fred; Hot Dogs; Howard Johnson; Kentucky Fried Chicken; McDonald's; Roadhouses; Sanders, Colonel; Train Food; White Castle.]

BIBLIOGRAPHY

Anderson, Will. *Where Have You Gone, Starlite Café? America's Golden Era Roadside Restaurants.* Portland, ME: Anderson & Sons' Publishing, 1998.

Gutman, Richard J. S. *American Diner: Then and Now.* 2nd ed. Baltimore: Johns Hopkins University Press, 2000.

Liebs, Chester H. *Main Street to Miracle Mile: American Roadside Architecture.* Baltimore: Johns Hopkins University Press,, 1995.

Pillsbury, Richard. *From Boarding House to Bistro: The American Restaurant Then and Now.* Boston: Unwin Hyman, 1990.

Schlosser, Eric. *Fast Food Nation: The Dark Side of the All-American Meal.* Boston: Houghton Mifflin, 2001.

RANDY GARBIN

Roasters, Coffee, *see Coffee Makers, Roasters, and Mills*

Rolling Pins, *see Pie-Making Tools*

Rombauer, Irma

Irma von Starkloff Rombauer (1877–1962), a leading twentieth-century American cookbook author, was born in St. Louis, Missouri, during the city's nineteenth-century economic and cultural heyday. Rombauer belonged to prominent German American social circles and until middle age had only the knowledge of food to be expected of a sophisticated, well-traveled hostess and clubwoman. When she was widowed in 1930, she decided to support herself by writing a cookbook. *The Joy of Cooking*, published at her own expense in 1931, was initially a modest, fairly conventional recipe collection with assorted contributions from family and friends, but she shortly began planning an expanded version.

Rombauer was able to interest the Bobbs-Merrill Company of Indianapolis and New York in her idea, which featured a recipe-writing format of her own devising, with ingredients introduced in the order of their use rather than as an initial list. The first Bobbs-Merrill edition appeared in 1936. Both Rombauer and the publishers (though they soon fell to quarreling) thought that it might eventually challenge the established kitchen manuals of the day, *The Boston Cooking-School Cook Book* and *The Settlement Cook Book*. Like the first version, it presented a miscellaneous array of recipes (standard American dishes like baked beans and corned beef, German Christmas cookies, as well as many shortcut canned-soup dishes and gelatin salads). It was, however, about twice as long, with more about cooking basics (for example, making soup stocks and working with yeast dough) and new kitchen appliances such as electric mixers. Rombauer also differentiated her work from others by stressing an informal, chatty personal tone—present but less conspicuous in the first edition—that was at the time unorthodox in a cookbook.

The first commercial *Joy of Cooking* was moderately successful, but the book did not become a best seller until 1943, when Rombauer revised it to incorporate the contents of her shorter 1939 work, *Streamlined Cooking* (a collection of hurry-up recipes mostly based on canned and pre-processed foods), and a small selection of recipes meant to help cooks cope with World War II meat and sugar rationing. The resulting version cemented her national reputation and made her highly individual "voice" known to a wide and demographically diverse audience, including people who ordinarily detested cooking and cookbooks but gained confidence through her breezy encouragement.

By the time of this success, Rombauer was in her mid-sixties. It was clear that a serious updating of *The Joy of Cooking*, possibly requiring the contributions of a younger cook, would eventually be needed in order to address rapid changes on the food scene—for example, new appliances such as home freezers, new fashions like Swiss-style fondue and chilled cream soups, and postwar economic adjustments like meat-price inflation. A stopgap revision appeared in 1946, with the wartime-rationing material replaced by a section on one-bowl cakes but little other change; in the same year, Rombauer published her fairly successful *A Cookbook for Girls and Boys*.

In the late 1940s, Rombauer invited her daughter, Marion Rombauer Becker (1903–1976), to work with her on the next revision. The Cincinnati-based Becker had been involved with the production of the 1931 version and was familiar with *Joy* as it had developed. Her participation caused some adjustment of priorities, beginning with the far-reaching revision that appeared in 1951. Reflecting Becker's bent for serious instruction and interest in nutrition and "natural" foods, the new edition somewhat downplayed the earlier emphasis on shortcuts and prepackaged foods; included such new material as meats "roasted" in foil, aspic base made "from scratch," and whole-grain breads (with expanded information on flours); and sought to bolster coverage of weak areas, such as fish.

After 1955, illness prevented Rombauer from further work on the book. Her daughter (assisted by her husband, John W. Becker) prepared two large, ambitious revisions that would long earn *Joy* the reputation of an inexhaustible reference work equally suited to state-of-the-art kitchens and desert islands. The first of these appeared in a garbled version in 1962 (during a battle with the publishers) and in corrected form in 1963. It sought to preserve the lively, personal Rombauer voice while trimming many old convenience-food recipes, broadening the international range of coverage, and greatly increasing the amount of space given to information about ingredients and cooking processes. In 1966 Becker published a small limited-edition history of *Joy* titled *Little Acorn*; in 1975 she completed her last and most ambitious edition of *Joy*. For at least a generation, Becker's two revisions of her mother's cookbook would be the best general source of knowledge about many culinary matters, including unusual herbs and formerly exotic fruits and vegetables.

Becker was succeeded as author by her son Ethan Becker. After some years of uncertainty during the publishing mergers and acquisitions of the 1980s and 1990s, a new publisher, Scribner, issued a dramatically transformed version in 1997. Prepared by a large stable of contributors under the direction of the well-known editor Maria Guarnaschelli, it replaced nearly all of the earlier contents with an up-to-date, eclectic mix of recipes. Guarnaschelli also oversaw a 1998 reprint of the original 1931 edition.

In Rombauer's and, to a certain extent, Becker's lifetimes, *The Joy of Cooking* was exceptional among American cookbooks as a midwestern rather than an East Coast production, as the work of culinary amateurs rather than professional recipe developers, and as a family affair. Its example probably encouraged other cookbook writers to cultivate a certain conversational stance marked by informal asides and anecdotes, but no one (not even her daughter) has managed to duplicate Rombauer's idiosyncratic appeal. The first success of her book had little to do with directing American taste in any particular culinary path. Rombauer's achievement was rather to spontaneously embody or bring to life the state of mid-twentieth-century American taste—in all its extremes and inconsistencies—across many social and culinary fault lines, without lapsing into mere shapelessness. Under Becker the book retained a modicum of its irreverent, inclusive, person-to-person quality while at the same time replicating many aims of the sober turn-of-the-twentieth-century kitchen bibles, to which, ironically, Rombauer's first efforts had been at least partly meant as an antidote.

[*See also* Boston Cooking School; Cookbooks and Manuscripts, *subentries* From World War I to World War II, From World War II to the 1940s, From the 1970s to the Present; Cooking Techniques; Recipes.]

BIBLIOGRAPHY

Becker, Marion Rombauer. *Little Acorn: The Story behind The Joy of Cooking, 1931–1966*. Indianapolis, IN, and New York: Bobbs-Merrill, 1966. Reissued as *Little Acorn: Joy of Cooking. The First Fifty Years, 1931–1981* (1981).

Mendelson, Anne. *Stand Facing the Stove: The Story of the Women Who Gave America the Joy of Cooking*. New York: Scribner, 2003.

ANNE MENDELSON

Ronald McDonald

In 1960 the McDonald's franchise in Washington, D.C., decided to sponsor a local children's television program called *Bozo's Circus*. Bozo was played by Willard Scott, who later gained fame as a television meteorologist and writer. Scott subsequently was asked to play Bozo at the grand opening of another McDonald's outlet in the area. Sales in Washington grew by a whopping 30 percent per year during the next four years. In 1963 the television station decided to drop *Bozo's Circus*, which lagged in the ratings. The local McDonald's franchise chose to produce their own television commercials starring another clown. Previously, McDonald's franchisees had not independently developed television commercials. The owners of this establishment wondered what to name the clown, and an advertising agency proposed "Archie McDonald," which offered an allusion to McDonald's golden arches symbol. But there was a sportscaster in the Washington area named Arch McDonald, so another name had to be found. Using a simple rhyme, Willard Scott came up with the name Ronald McDonald. Scott played Ronald McDonald in the first television commercials, which were broadcast in October 1963.

The national McDonald's Corporation decided to sponsor the broadcast of the Macy's Thanksgiving Day Parade in 1965. They chose to feature Ronald McDonald, but they replaced Willard Scott with Coco, a Hungarian-speaking clown from the Barnum and Bailey Circus. Until then, no fast food chain had advertised on national television; it was considered a risk, especially in autumn, since major sales were achieved largely in summertime. Likewise, Ronald McDonald appealed to children, who were not thought to be an important target of fast food promoters at the time. Nonetheless, the Thanksgiving Day advertisement produced immediate nationwide results, which persuaded McDonald's to expend more funds to target children, thus giving McDonald's an edge in the children's market.

Ronald McDonald became McDonald's official spokesman in 1966. He also became the centerpiece of numerous other advertising activities: His image appeared on television commercials and a vast array of products, including book covers, coloring books, comic books, cups, dolls, masks, Frisbees, games, calendars, mugs, napkins, postcards, puppets, records, toy parachutes, trains and trucks, and the famous "Flying Hamburger," a cartoon McDonald's hamburger with wings.

In addition, McDonald's Playlands, children's recreational spaces designed as part of the restaurant, featured Ronald McDonald and a cast of other fictional characters. While none of the other "McDonaldland" characters achieved the prominence of Ronald McDonald, the Playlands strengthened McDonald's dominance in the children's fast food market. When McDonald's signed a contract to open three hundred outlets at military bases, Ronald McDonald posed for pictures in front of an aircraft carrier. The first Ronald McDonald House, a residence located adjacent to a hospital to provide free or low-cost room and board for families with children requiring extended hospital care, was set up in Philadelphia in 1974. Since then, two hundred more have been constructed in the United States and eleven in other coun-

tries. All are sponsored by local McDonald's operations. Ten years later Ronald McDonald's Children Charities was founded in honor of Ray Kroc, the man who started McDonald's. It is still one of the largest organizations financially devoted to the welfare of children. In 1997 McDonald's published a book "authored" by Ronald McDonald, *The Complete Hamburger: The History of America's Favorite Sandwich*.

As McDonald's expanded to other countries, so did Ronald McDonald. In some countries, adjustments were necessary. In Japan, for instance, the name was changed to Donald McDonald owing to the difficulty the Japanese had in pronouncing the "r" in Ronald. By the early 2000s Ronald McDonald was among the most popular children's characters in the world. Ninety-six percent of American children recognize Ronald McDonald, about the same percentage of children who recognize Santa Claus.

[*See also* Advertising; McDonald's.]

BIBLIOGRAPHY

Losonsky, Joyce, and Terry Losonsky. *McDonald's Pre–Happy Meal Toys from the Fifties, Sixties, and Seventies.* Atglen, PA: Schiffer, 1998.
Losonsky, Terry, and Joyce Losonsky. *McDonald's Happy Meal Toys around the World.* Atglen, PA: Schiffer, 1995.
Love, John F. *McDonald's behind the Arches.* Rev. ed. New York: Bantam, 1995.

ANDREW F. SMITH

Root Beer

Now a sweet soft drink flavored with a mixture of herbal essences, root beer was originally a real beer and a tonic health drink. Small beers, or low-alcohol beers carbonated by the action of yeasts, had been traditional and nutritious drinks for children, women, and the elderly in England and Europe for centuries. Although many of these small beers were flavored with ginger or lemon, another common flavoring and one popular for its antiscurvy properties was that of the bark of spruce or birch trees. When colonists arrived in North America, they found new varieties of the traditional spruce and birch for their beers, but discovered Native Americans using such novel flavorings as the roots of sarsaparilla (*Smilax ornata*) and sassafras (*Sassafras albidum*) as well. Both of these were similar to spruce and birch in taste, and the colonists soon learned to use them in their small beer, often with molasses as a sweetener and fermenting agent.

Exactly when sweetened small beer made with various roots was first called "root beer" is unknown. One of the earliest mentions is in *Dr. Chase's Recipes* from 1869. The doctor's typical recipe calls for the roots of burdock, yellow dock, sarsaparilla, dandelion, and spikenard, along with the oils of spruce and sassafras, and says that "families ought to make it every Spring, and drink freely of it for several weeks, and thereby save, perhaps, several dollars in doctors' bills."

In 1876 Charles E. Hires, who claimed to have invented root beer, began marketing packets of the herbal ingredients necessary to make "the Greatest Health-Giving Beverage in the World" at the Centennial Exposition in Philadelphia. This kit for making root beer was supposed to contain sixteen roots, herbs, barks, and berries, including sassafras, the dominant flavoring, and required home fermentation with yeast. In 1884 Hires decided consumers would be more interested in an easier-to-use product and began selling a liquid concentrate and soda fountain syrup, as well as bottled root beer. By 1892 he was selling 3 million bottles a year. His success, along with the growing temperance movement, brought many others into the marketplace, including Barq's in 1898, A&W in 1922, and Dad's in 1937. The author Tom Morrison has documented over 831 brands since Hires's modest beginnings in 1876. Yet as popular as root beer has always been, it accounts for less than 3 percent of the total American soft-drink market.

The root beer industry was considerably shaken in 1960 when the key flavor component in sassafras, safrole, was found to be carcinogenic and banned by the FDA. Although sassafras treated to remove the toxic safrole is available, most bottlers have substituted other ingredients, such as anise, wintergreen, lemon and orange oils, cloves, molasses, and vanilla, which gives root beer its creamy taste.

Old-fashioned style root beer was coming back into popularity at the turn of the twenty-first century, and the number of small, local brewers had increased dramatically. Home brewing of root beer was again becoming fashionable as well. At a 1998 taste test sponsored by the *Chicago Tribune* fifty different root beers were evaluated, nowhere near a complete sampling of the many root beers on the market.

[*See also* Birch Beer; Brewing; Homemade Remedies; Sarsaparilla; Sassafrasses; Soda Drinks; Soda Fountains; Temperance.]

BIBLIOGRAPHY

Brown, John Hull. *Early American Beverages*. New York: Bonanza Books, 1966.

Jones, Evan. *American Food: The Gastronomic Story*. New York: Dutton, 1975.

Morrison, Tom. *Root Beer Advertising and Collectibles*. West Chester, PA: Schiffer Publishing, 1992.

Rice, William. "Rooting for the Perfect Root Beer." *Chicago Tribune*, July 1, 1998.

SYLVIA LOVEGREN

Rorer, Sarah Tyson

Sarah Tyson Heston Rorer (1849–1937) was a nineteenth-century American culinary superstar—a nationally recognized, respected, and beloved source of kitchen expertise who made her mark well before the advent of mass communication media. Rorer was born in Richboro, Pennsylvania. As a young wife, she countered suburban boredom by attending lectures at the Woman's Medical College of Pennsylvania. Rorer considered becoming a pharmacist or a physician but instead became the first American dietitian.

In 1879 Rorer began attending cooking classes at the New Century Club, a women's club founded in 1877 in Philadelphia. Rorer devoted herself to the classes, becoming the star pupil. When the instructor resigned, Rorer took over teaching duties, which included lecturing at the

Sarah Tyson Rorer. *Culinary Archives & Museum at Johnson & Wales University, Providence, R.I.*

Woman's Medical College. Apprehensive about her qualifications, Rorer devoured nutrition texts and became convinced of the importance of diet in health and disease. Rorer also continued to attend lectures in chemistry, physiology, anatomy, and hygiene.

Rorer's lessons were well received, and over the years she taught a wide range of students: finishing-school girls, residents of a home for wayward children, physicians from prestigious Philadelphia hospitals, professional cooks, society matrons (who were required to do the post-lesson cleanup themselves), and, at a city mission, poor immigrant women—who broadened her palate when they taught her to love garlic.

In 1883 Rorer opened the Philadelphia Cooking School, which operated until 1903. Her husband, an unambitious bookkeeper, came to work for her, and before long Rorer was the sole support of her family—a situation almost unheard-of among women of her class at the time. Rorer's lecture-demonstrations attracted audiences of up to five thousand, and Rorer put her recipes and theories in print in 1886 in *Mrs. Rorer's Philadelphia Cook Book*. Between its waterproof and greaseproof covers lay prescient admonitions: "green vegetables should be freshly gathered, washed well in cold water, and cooked in freshly-boiled water until tender, *no longer*." "Macaroni . . . is the bread of the Italian laborer. In this country, it is a sort of luxury among the upper classes; but there is no good reason . . . why it should not enter more extensively into the food of our working classes."

Also in 1886, Rorer began conducting a question-and-answer column in *Table Talk*, a culinary magazine. Soon she was writing five features, including one on "dietetics." Eight years later, along with two doctors interested in food chemistry and dietetics, Rorer founded *Household News*, which featured articles on pure food, healthy diet, and household sanitation. In its pages Rorer continued (as she had in *Table Talk*) to endorse commercial products ranging from shredded wheat, coffee, and cheese to waffle irons and meat choppers. In 1896 *Household News* folded, and Rorer became domestic science editor of the *Ladies' Home Journal*, a post she held through October 1911.

For a series of pure food expositions held in Philadelphia beginning in 1889, Rorer gave wildly popular cooking demonstrations. Impeccably dressed in silk and lace (to show how mess-free cooking could be) Rorer extolled the virtues of plain, as opposed to "fancy," food, daily eating of salads, and well-made bread and condemned—even as she prepared them—puddings, pies, and candies. At the World's Columbian Exposition in Chicago, in 1893, Rorer presided over the "corn kitchen," where myriad manners of cooking corn were demonstrated six days a week.

Rorer wrote more than fifty books and booklets, including promotional publications for, among others, Cottolene shortening, Wesson oil, Cream of Maize cereal, Tabasco sauce, Cleveland baking powder, and the Enterprise meat chopper. Among her books are *Mrs. Rorer's New Cook Book* (1902); *Bread and Bread-Making*; *Home Candy Making*; *Hot Weather Dishes*; *How to Use a Chafing Dish*; *Ice Creams, Water Ices, Frozen Puddings*; *Made Over Dishes*; *Sandwiches*; *Salads*; *New Ways for Oysters*; and the temptingly titled *Dainties*.

[*See also* Advertising Cookbooklets and Recipes; Cookbooks and Manuscripts, *subentry* From the Civil War to World War I; Cooking Schools, *subentry* Nineteenth Century.]

BIBLIOGRAPHY

Rorer, S. T. *Mrs. Rorer's Philadelphia Cook Book*. Philadelphia: Arnold, 1886.
Weigley, Emma Seifrit. *Sarah Tyson Rorer: The Nation's Instructress in Dietetics and Cookery*. Philadelphia: American Philosophical Society, 1977.

BONNIE J. SLOTNICK

Rose Water

Introduced to Europe from Arab cuisine by the Crusaders in such dishes as marzipan and Turkish delight, rose water is the distillate of rose petals, most famously from the damask rose. Substitutes for the distillate have been made by adding attar of rose, which is the oil extracted from crushed roses, to water.

Colonial Americans used rose water as a flavoring, similar in purpose to the later-introduced vanilla, in confectionery and dessert recipes inherited from Europe and in syrups used to flavor beverages. Rose water also flavored savories, such as chicken pies and creamed spinach. Some housewives, even as late as the 1880s, distilled their own. Others purchased it, perhaps as "Double Distilled Damask Rose Water" from the Shakers, a religious sect respected for the quality and purity of their products and for their rose water apple pie.

Contemporary use is most common in the cuisines of Middle Eastern, Indian, or Sephardic heritage, flavoring desserts and drinks, such as baklava, sorbets, and *lassi*.

Rose water is sometimes used interchangeably with orange flower water and may be sprinkled on fresh fruits.

[*See also* Flavorings; Orange Flower Water.]

ROBIN M. MOWER

Rum

Rum is a consumable spirit derived from sugarcane. Either fresh cane juice or water added to cane syrup or molasses is used as a base, which is then fermented and distilled to an alcohol ranging from 80 to 150 proof (roughly 40 percent to 75 percent alcohol). Unlike spirits made from other sources, such as grains, the conversion of starch to sugar (critical for fermentation to occur) is not necessary when making rum. Rum is also unique in that it can be made either as a white (colorless) spirit, like vodka or gin, or as a brown spirit, like brandy or scotch. Consequently, rum is the most versatile of liquors and is the top-selling distilled spirit in the world.

Rum comes in many varieties. Some of the terminology describes the beverage's color or weight (for example, white, light, silver, gold, dark, or black). Other terms, like "overproof" (150, 151, or full strength), "premium distilled," "aged," *añejo* (Castilian for "aged"), "single marks," "select," "reserve," and "rare," are used to describe alcohol content, age, and quality levels. Fuller-flavored, more complex rums tend to be darker and somewhat heavier and can range in color from light amber to the color of strongly brewed tea. These darker, traditional styles typically start with molasses and are fermented more slowly and aged in charred oak casks to impart deep, rich flavors and color prior to blending. Light (colorless) rum—originally developed in Cuba in the mid-1800s by the Bacardi brand founder Don Facundo, who was seeking to refine the spirit—undergoes faster fermentation in stainless steel tanks and is not aged. This process produces rum that is not only lighter in weight and color but is also drier (less sweet) and more delicately flavored—a style that is considered ideal for mixing into cocktails and that accounts for most modern rum production.

Technological advances in how rum has been made over the centuries are reflected in the progression from traditional copper pot stills (still used by conventional distillers) to the more modern continuous distillation method (enabling production of fine rum at a faster pace). Caramel or another coloring agent is sometimes added for greater color and consistency in certain dark varieties. Rums flavored with spice, vanilla, or fruit essences (like citrus, banana, coconut, or pineapple) are growing in both production and popularity. Other spirits distilled from sugarcane include arrak from the East Indies and *cachaca* from Brazil.

Most commercial rum is produced in the Caribbean, and nearly 80 percent of rum consumed in the United States is from Puerto Rico, the largest exporter and the primary base for Bacardi. While many places produce both dark and light rums, the majority of dark rum varieties (which are in the oldest style) are made in Jamaica, and most light rum is produced in Puerto Rico. A range of such varieties is widely emulated in nearly every part of the Caribbean. Centuries-old formulations and secret family recipes, many of which have never been written down, vary among regions and makers. Hawaii is also a producer and exporter of rum, as are other climates hospitable to the growth of sugarcane, including some southern states in the United States (such as Florida and Louisiana).

Fermenting and distilling beverages from sugarcane dates back thousands of years to China, Egypt, India, Syria, Southeast Asia, and the South Pacific. The Moors introduced sugarcane distillation to Europe via the Spanish and the Portuguese, who later cultivated the tall, weedlike crop on Atlantic islands west of the Iberian Peninsula (Azores). Sugarcane cuttings arrived in the Americas with Christopher Columbus in 1493.

These few initial transplants not only grew into the dominant crop but also became the central economic engine throughout Central America and South America, especially Brazil and the Caribbean Islands, which came to be known as the "sugar islands." This New World industry and its offshoots, the molasses and rum trades, depended entirely on the exploitation of human labor. The arduous toil of millions of captive, relocated Africans was deemed essential for the intense cultivation required for such crops and generated great profits for Europe and the new American colonies. Accordingly, the sugar and rum trade generated the transatlantic slave trade that endured from the fifteenth century through the late nineteenth century.

Rum also played a significant role in early American economic and political development. Imported molasses, primarily from the West Indies, was converted into rum in New England and New York, where distilleries churned out rums described as heavy and full flavored. Small quantities are still produced in some parts of New England. Eventually rum became the most popular distilled beverage during the colonial American era. It was drunk straight, diluted with water, and used in many beverages, including the flip, the sling, the swizzle, the toddy, punch, and grog—a daily ration of which was long served on American naval ships.

This early American rum was also used as a successful trading medium. Some was traded with Native Americans for goods and land, but most was exported to Europe and exchanged along the west coast of Africa to supply the constant stream of slaves working the massive Caribbean and South American sugar plantations. Rum was thus a key component of the "triangular trade"; it was especially important to the economies of Massachusetts, New York, Philadelphia, and Rhode Island and was the top American export well into the early nineteenth century. This heavy maritime trade significantly increased sea traffic and illustrates why barrels of rum have long been associated with pirates, buccaneers, and other swashbucklers sailing the high seas during the seventeenth and eighteenth centuries. "Rum-running" brought easy wealth not only for legitimate shipping companies but also for privateers as well as those engaged in pure piracy.

American rum production was an integral factor in America's independence from England. British duties and taxes on molasses imported into American colonies from non-British territories (Molasses Act of 1733 and Sugar Act of 1764) fueled colonial unrest that ultimately culminated in the Revolutionary War and later the War of 1812. The latter led to the demise of the early U.S. rum industry and gave rise to spirits made from locally grown grains (such as whiskey and bourbon). During Prohibition (1919–1933) rum often synonymously referred to all alcohol and hard liquor with such terminology as "demon rum" and "rum riots." State- and county-run "rum rooms" were designated to hold any type of alcohol seized by the government from bootleggers. During Prohibition, a jet-set crowd, including Hollywood's elite, artists, bohemians, and writers, flocked to Cuba, where there was an established American military presence and where drinking was legal. The original rum and Coke, called a Cuba libre (free Cuba), made and garnished with the juice from a squeezed lime wedge, was introduced at an American military bar in Havana in 1899.

Despite the repeal of Prohibition, spirits production took a while to return to full swing, delayed in part by the Great Depression. By the dawn of World War II, the then-Cuban brand Bacardi was the most readily available spirit imported in bulk to an American public reembracing its cocktail culture. This availability, along with the popularity of the Andrews Sisters' song "Rum and Coca-Cola" (1944), helped establish this drink duo as the official cocktail of America.

Soldiers returning after World War II from Hawaii and the South Pacific brought a Polynesian pop culture known as "tiki," featuring rum as the main spirit in drinks decorated with paper parasols, flowers, and leis. Later, as tourism to places like Hawaii and the Caribbean became accessible to more Americans, so did a seemingly infinite assortment of rum-based concoctions combining both dark and light varieties blended with any combination of tropical fruit juices. Rum continues to be the preferred spirit in colorful cocktails sipped by Americans vacationing in warm locales the world over.

Well-known rum drinks include the blue whale, the daiquiri, the hurricane, the mai tai, the piña colada, rum punch, the yellow bird, and the zombie. Libations mixed with rum are most often paired with Caribbean and nuevo Latino cuisine, with beverages like Jamaican rum punch and the resurgent Cuban *mojito* available on drink menus of many American restaurants serving such fare. Rum is also used as a cooking ingredient for both sweet and savory sauces, cakes, other desserts, and candies.

[*See also* Caribbean Influences on American Food; Cocktails; Cuba Libre.]

BIBLIOGRAPHY

Adlerman, Clifford Lindsey. *Rum, Slaves, and Molasses; the Story of New England's Triangular Trade.* New York: Crowell-Collier Press, 1972.

Arkell, Julie. *Classic Rum.* London: Prion Books, 1999.

Barty-King, Hugh, and Anton Massel. *Rum, Yesterday and Today.* London: Heinemann, 1983.

Captive Passage: The Transatlantic Slave Trade and the Making of the Americas. Washington, DC: Smithsonian Institution Press, 2002. See pages 128 and 151.

DeGroff, Dale. *The Craft of the Cocktail.* New York: Clarkson Potter, 2002.

McCusker, John J. *Rum and the American Revolution: The Rum Trade and the Balance of Payments of the Thirteen Continental Colonies.* New York: Garland, 1989.

Waggoner, Susan, and Robert Markel. *Vintage Cocktails: Authentic Recipes and Illustrations from 1920–1960.* New York: Smithmark, 1999.

TONYA HOPKINS

Russian American Food

Russian American food reflects its two culinary origins, the lowly shtetl and the noble estate. Unlike other waves of immigration, the bulk of Russian immigrants fled either religious or political persecution; fewer came to America purely for economic opportunity. The demographics of the various groups that immigrated in the wake of Russia's social and political upheavals determined the nature of the foods they brought with them.

Immigration Patterns

The first Russian immigrants to contribute significantly to American food culture were Jews escaping the pogroms of 1881–1884 and 1903–1906. They brought foods that Americans now identify more closely with Russian than with Jewish cuisine, namely borscht (beet soup), black bread, and stuffed cabbage.

The so-called first wave of ethnic Russian immigration to the United States occurred following the Russian Revolution of 1917, when the Bolsheviks overthrew the czarist regime and established the Soviet Union. These immigrants consisted largely of aristocrats, whose plight captured the American imagination. They seemed tragic, glamorous, and exotic, and the foods they introduced in lavish restaurants like New York's Russian Tea Room thrilled the American palate. Sophisticated diners came to appreciate elegant dishes like blini (raised pancakes) with caviar, Nesselrode pudding, and beef Stroganoff.

The second wave of immigration occurred in the wake of World War II. Like the first-wave immigrants, these Russians flocked to urban centers, but, unlike the earlier group, they did not bring aristocratic ways. The restaurants they established tended to offer daily fare, as opposed to luxury foods. Especially in San Francisco, where a large community grew up in the Richmond district, Russian groceries and restaurants offered piroshki (little pies filled with ground meat or vegetables), *pelmeni* (boiled Siberian dumplings), and a range of baked goods.

The third wave arrived in the 1970s and 1980s when Jewish refuseniks, who had been denied permission to leave the Soviet Union, were finally allowed to emigrate. Unlike the earlier Jewish immigrants, this group had been highly assimilated into Soviet Russian society. Many settled in Brighton Beach, at the tip of Brooklyn, creating a community that came to be known as Little Odessa. The tastes of this community resembled those of the larger Soviet society. Delicatessens specialized in sausages, smoked fish, and prepared foods and catered to Americans as well as to Russians. The area's restaurants with their loud music and lively entertainment similarly attracted a mixed clientele. Brighton Beach continued to thrive as the twenty-first century opened, thanks to a new influx of immigrants who arrived after the collapse of the Soviet Union in 1991. More entrepreneurial in spirit than the preceding immigrants, most of these Russians came to the United States for economic advantage, rather than as refugees. Their foodways did not differ from those of the earlier Soviet groups.

Russian or Soviet influences are also discernible in other regions of the United States. Alaska boasts one of the country's oldest Russian populations, which dates back to the settlement of Kodiak Island by Siberian fur traders in 1784. Old Believer communities there continue to prepare traditional Russian foods, especially on Russian Orthodox Church holidays. Large cities in the continental United States boast various pockets of ethnic groups who emigrated from the Soviet Union. Even though their foods have little to do with classical Russian cookery, they are associated with Russia in the popular mind. Such groups include Georgians, Volga Germans, Ukrainians, and Karelians.

Dissemination of Russian Food in America

Of the foods brought by the early Jewish immigrants, borscht and kasha (buckwheat groats) became the most popular. Although borscht is widespread in Russia, the soup that Americans consider quintessentially Russian is actually Ukrainian in origin (the Russian national soup is a cabbage soup). By contrast, kasha is deeply Russian—a common proverb holds that "cabbage soup and kasha are our fare." Yet most Americans consider kasha part of Jewish cuisine, not Russian. This association most likely occurred when kasha began to be commercially produced by Wolff's, a company that marketed groats to the Jewish community.

Little Odessa. Russian restaurants along the boardwalk in Brighton Beach, Brooklyn, New York *Photograph by Joe Zarba*

Other Russian foods were introduced to Americans through restaurants. Most large American cities boasted at least one Russian restaurant, and some, like San Francisco's Russian Renaissance restaurant, have been in existence for many years. But the restaurant that for over seventy years defined Russian cuisine for Americans was the Russian Tea Room, located next to Carnegie Hall on West Fifty-seventh Street in New York City. In its ability to create an atmosphere of celebrity and excitement, the Russian Tea Room was ahead of its time. Ballet dancers, musicians, artists, writers, and impresarios all gathered there, while out-of-towners flocked to the restaurant to catch a glimpse of them.

The Russian Tea Room began as a little shop across the street from its Fifty-seventh Street location, to which it moved in 1927. In 1932, after the repeal of Prohibition, the restaurant was bought by Alexander (Sasha) Maeff, whose philosophy of enjoying life became the restaurant's mantra. (Nikita Khrushchev is credited with the line "Life is short, live it up!" but he was not the first Russian to say it.) The Russian Tea Room was not just about good food. It also served up an atmosphere of conviviality; it provided tables where deals were made and hearts were broken. Maeff installed a bar called the Casino Russe, which introduced Americans to specialty vodka drinks like the boyar cocktail (vodka and cherry heering) and the Moscow mule (vodka, lime, and ginger beer). Thanks to the Russian Tea Room's extravagant menu—not least its legendary caviar and blini—Russian food in America came to epitomize luxury. The Russian Tea Room's allure lasted until 2002, when its doors finally closed. By that time Russian food had lost its cachet. Although other Russian restaurants provide fine Russian fare, none is legendary, and only the name of Caviar Russe, a New York City purveyor of caviar, smoked salmon, and foie gras, provides an obvious link to the opulence of aristocratic Russian cuisine.

Cookbooks also helped acquaint Americans with Russian cuisine. In 1941 the Colt Press of San Francisco published a beautiful, limited-edition volume of *The Epicure in Imperial Russia* by Marie Alexandre Markevitch, a noblewoman whose purpose was to present to Americans "the essential character of the culinary art of Imperial Russia." Like the Russian Tea Room, this cookbook represented the glories of an era long past and perpetuated the image of an extravagant table in such recipes as Lark Butter and Crayfish Soufflé. Far more influential, however, was Princess Alexandra Kropotkina's *How to Cook and Eat*

in Russian, published in 1947 by G. P. Putnam's Sons. Written at the beginning of the Cold War, this book sought not only to make Russian food accessible to Americans through easy-to-follow recipes, it also attempted to familiarize Americans with the Russian character in order to make "Ivan" seem less formidable and more friendly.

Russian Dishes in America

By the mid-twentieth century, Americans were familiar with a few of the mainstays of Russian cuisine at both the high and low ends: blini and borscht, caviar and cabbage. The allure of Russian food continued into the 1960s, when one of the era's most popular hostess dishes was beef Stroganoff. Most likely named after the nineteenth-century count Alexander Grigorievich Stroganov, the original beef Stroganoff was basically a French dish. Tenderloin of beef is thinly sliced and briefly cooked in a mustard cream sauce, then served with a garnish of crisp shoestring potatoes. The use of sour cream instead of sweet cream gives it a Russian flair. Beef Stroganoff began to appear on the menus of Continental restaurants throughout the United States. All too often, however, beef Stroganoff in its American incarnation became a thick stew with a heavy sour cream and tomato sauce suffocating a bed of limp noodles. Indeed, recipes for the home cook frequently substituted ketchup for the tomato sauce, resulting in a dish that eventually became a mainstay of mediocre cafeterias and boarding-school dining halls.

Another popular restaurant dish, one that fared better in American hands, is chicken Kiev—chicken breast pounded thin and rolled into a packet around a large pat of butter, then breaded and deep-fried. Unknown in czarist times, this dish is actually a Soviet-era innovation. During the 1970s and 1980s, it was served at the most elegant catered events in America. Eventually some American cooks substituted blue cheese for the butter or pan-fried the chicken instead of deep-frying it, variations that did justice to the original recipe. A third dish that Americans readily adopted is strawberries Romanoff, which bears the name of the royal family. This dessert consists of strawberries macerated in liqueur, then served in meringue shells topped with whipped cream. Because its extravagance reminded Americans of the czars, the dish was dubbed "Romanoff," even though it never carried this name in Russia, neither in Romanov days nor after the royal family had been executed.

Like strawberries Romanoff, other dishes that Americans associate with Russia carry Russian names but are not part of the traditional cuisine. These include russian dressing, a mixture of mayonnaise and chili sauce (or, as in beef Stroganoff, that perennial American favorite, ketchup). Some food writers claim that russian dressing got its name because it once contained caviar, but this is unlikely. The name probably refers to the Russian love of pickles, as pickles or relish are often added to the dressing. Then there are Russian tea cakes, cookies similar to Mexican wedding cakes, and not traditionally Russian at all. Whereas Russian nut cookies are generally rolled before being sprinkled with nuts, Russian tea cakes contain ground nuts that are mixed into a drop-cookie batter. They are probably called Russian in the United States because of their association with tea. The image of a hissing samovar and tea cookies is, in fact, very Russian, and it might also account for the name Russian tea, for which recipes are found in many community and southern cookbooks. Russian tea is simply tea spiced with cinnamon and allspice, and often flavored with lemon. Russian caravan tea, another product associated with Russia, is a commercial name that refers to the trade route from China to Europe, which traversed the great Russian steppe. A blend of fine black China teas and Assam, it has a malty, sometimes slightly smoky flavor.

No discussion of Russian American food would be complete without a mention of vodka and vodka cocktails. More than any foodstuff or dish, vodka may be the item most closely associated in American minds with Russian cuisine. For many years the industry standard was Smirnoff, produced by a noble family that fled to France after the Revolution. In 1980, the year of the Moscow Olympics, PepsiCo signed an exclusive agreement with Stolichnaya vodka to sell Pepsi in the Soviet Union and promote "Stoli" in the United States. Soon Americans were drinking premium vodka in shot glasses, straight from the freezer, in true Russian style. Stoli did not dominate the market for long, however; by the 1990s non-Russian companies had made inroads into the premium vodka market with an array of flavored vodkas. Vodka cocktails continued to be very popular in the early 2000s. One American favorite is the black Russian, a mixture of vodka and Kahlúa, which later gave birth to the white Russian. The latter also contains a splash of cream and plays on the name for the monarchist aristocracy at the time of the Russian Revolution.

Despite the sizeable Russian population in the United States, Russian holiday foods are not generally well known. The two most significant ritual dishes, *paskha* (a rich cheesecake) and *kulich* (a butter-rich yeast bread), are traditional on the Easter table, but more familiar to Americans are the brightly painted Easter eggs that can often be found in specialty shops.

At the beginning of the twenty-first century, Russian food is no longer considered chic in America. The popular conception is of a bland, heavy diet, the result of seventy years of Soviet rule when food was scarce and cooking rudimentary. Americans who traveled to Russia during the Soviet era invariably returned with stories of bad food and even worse service, and this impression has not easily been dispelled. Even so, Americans continue to enjoy the borscht, blini, caviar, and vodka with which Russian cuisine is still most closely identified in this country.

[*See also* Cabbage; Jewish American Food; Vodka.]

BIBLIOGRAPHY

Goldstein, Darra. *A Taste of Russia.* 2nd ed. Montpelier, VT: Russian Life Books, 1999. An overview of Russian food culture, with recipes.

Koehler, Margaret H. *Recipes from the Russians of San Francisco.* Riverside, CT: Chatham, 1974. A collection of recipes from San Francisco's Russian community.

Kropotkin, Alexandra. *How to Cook and Eat in Russian.* New York: Putnam, 1947. The classic cold war volume that made Russian food, and Russians, accessible to Americans.

Russian Cook Book for American Homes. Edited by Gaylord Maddox. New York: Russian War Relief, n.d. Published in the early 1940s, this little book contains recipes from both Russians living in the United States and Americans. The recipes have an American accent despite their origin. A War-Time Edition of the same book appeared in 1943.

Stewart-Gordon, Faith, and Nika Hazelton. *The Russian Tea Room Cookbook.* New York: Marek, 1981. Recipes from the famous New York restaurant.

Visson, Lynn. *The Complete Russian Cookbook.* Ann Arbor, MI: Ardis, 1982. Recipes from the Russian émigré community.

DARRA GOLDSTEIN

Saint Patrick's Day

American Saint Patrick's Day has been described as "Eiresatz: a sentimental slur of imagined memories, fine feeling and faux Irish talismans and traditions" (Dezell, *Irish America*, 17). It is a festival of soda bread, corned beef and cabbage, cardboard shamrocks, and green hats, bagels, and beer. In Ireland Saint Patrick's Day is a religious holiday, but in America it has become a spectacle.

The Irish immigrated to the United States in two distinct waves. In the early eighteenth century, a relatively small number of Scotch-Irish, mostly Presbyterians from Ulster, settled in the agricultural green hills and valleys of the Appalachian region. From 1845 to 1850, Ireland lost 2 million people to starvation and to emigration to the United States. Over the next fifty years, half a million Irish, mostly Roman Catholic, emigrated each decade.

Perhaps because of their experiences in the potato famine and owing to prohibitively expensive farmland near U.S. cities, many immigrants chose not to return to country life. They created new lives in the port cities of the Northeast and Midwest. Saint Patrick's Day evolved in urban America. Like most immigrant groups, the Irish lost some of their traditions as they assimilated American culture. But as they did for many other immigrant groups, poverty and repression led to maintenance as well as modification of holidays that preserve group identity. Simple nostalgia for the "old sod" turned a minor religious event into a major holiday. Saint Patrick's Day evolved from being a feast as in "religious celebration" to being a feast as in "secular celebration, party." Traditional Irish symbols—such as the harp and Celtic cross—were replaced by clichés, like leprechauns and shillelaghs often promoted by non-Irish Americans, that made it easy for all Americans to participate in what a century before had been a parochial event.

The Irish adapted their traditional foodways to their changed circumstances. If there was a national dish in Ireland, it was probably colcannon: boiled potatoes, cabbage, and leeks in buttermilk flavored with wild garlic. Another Irish dish was brown soda bread, made with whole-grain flour. These dishes are recognizable relatives of "authentic" Irish American dishes. Corned beef and cabbage and soda bread made with white flour and currants or caraway seeds replaced colcannon and brown bread as Saint Patrick's Day foods in America. The Irish in nineteenth-century Ireland rarely ate corned beef. For political and economic reasons, the meat was produced primarily for export to England. The immigrants chose to celebrate their holiday in their new country with a food not available to them in the old country. In Ireland white soda bread was reserved for special occasions. It may be that when they arrived in the United States, poor immigrants appropriated the "higher status" bread as their own, adding currants or caraway as signs of their new affluence. These "improved" foods were adopted by the non-Irish in an attempt to "play" at being Irish. Corned beef and cabbage is to authentic Irish cooking as chili con carne is to authentic Mexican food. Both are American dishes in the imagined style of other countries.

[*See also* Bread, *sidebar on* Soda Bread; Cabbage; Corned Beef; Potatoes.]

BIBLIOGRAPHY

Cole, Rosalind. *Of Soda Bread and Guinness: An Irish Cookbook, and a Picture of Ireland as Seen through Its People, Its Places, Its Traditions, and Its Cooking Lore.* Indianapolis, IN: Bobbs-Merrill, 1973.

Dezell, Maureen. *Irish America: Coming into Clover—The Evolution of a People and a Culture.* New York: Doubleday, 2000.

FitzGibbon, Theodora. *Irish Traditional Food.* London and Basingstoke, UK: Macmillan London, 1983.

Johnson, Margaret M. *The Irish Heritage Cookbook.* San Francisco: Chronicle Books, 1999.

McCormick, Malachi. *Irish Country Cooking.* New York: Crown, 1988.

GARY ALLEN

Salads and Salad Dressings

Ancient Greeks picked lettuce (*Lactuca sativa*) in its spindly, wild state and consumed it both raw and in cooked forms. The plant was popularized by the Romans, and many European languages have names that derive from the Latin word for lettuce. The Romans enjoyed a variety of dishes with raw vegetables similar to present-day salad ingredients, such as lettuce, endive, and cucumbers. Roman salad dressing was initially salt (*sal*) or brine—hence the derivation of the word "salad"—and a combination of olive oil and vinegar. The first-century C.E. Roman cook Marcus Apicius gives a recipe for a salad containing ginger, rue, dates, pepper, honey, cumin, and vinegar.

The debate as to when salads should be served began in the ancient world. The medical practitioners Hippocrates and Galen believed that raw vegetables slipped easily through the system and did not create obstructions for what followed, and therefore they should be served first. Others reported that the vinegar in dressings destroyed the taste of wine, and therefore salads should be served last. The debate has continued ever since.

The Emergence of Salet or Salad

The term "salad" was not used in ancient Roman times, but it derives from the Vulgar Latin *herba salata*, literally "salted herb." It was in Renaissance Italy that the word "salad" first appeared. By the sixteenth century many salads were common, including dishes of cress, hops, wild cress, asparagus, and chervil. The saying that a good dressing demands "a miser for the vinegar, a spendthrift for the oil, and a wise man for the salt" predates the seventeenth century. Even at the beginning of the nineteenth century, green salads were not commonly eaten in France, although they were served on the tables of the upper class and in the restaurants that had just emerged. About this time the classic French way of making a salad, with vinaigrette as the most common salad dressing, was established. Demonstrating French culinary power in the nineteenth century, the vinaigrette became known as french dressing in Great Britain and America.

The Old French word *salade* ended up in the late-fourteenth-century English language as "salade" or "salet," a dish that was frequently composed of leafy vegetables served as an accompaniment to cooked meats or poultry. Sometimes salads included flowers. Later, fruits (oranges and lemons) were added, at least in a decorative role. Other salad ingredients included carrots, purslane, marigolds, primroses, violets, cowslips, sorrel, spinach, and borage. Many new plants entered England during the late sixteenth and early seventeenth centuries. Many of them were employed as ingredients in salads.

John Evelyn's *Acetaria* (1699) was the first salad book published in the English language. Evelyn defined "Sallet" as "a particular Composition of certain *Crude* and fresh herbs, such as usually are, or may safely be eaten with some *Acetous* Juice, Oyl, Salt, &c. to give them a grateful Gust and Vehicle." He identified seventy-two ingredients for salads, including roots, stalks, leaves, and buds and flowers, but excluding fruit (although the juice and the grated rind of oranges and lemons are listed among the herbs) and also excluding meat. He offered a recipe for salad dressing: three parts olive oil to one part vinegar, lemon, or orange juice, plus horseradish and a little salt. Evelyn strictly forbade garlic because of its intolerable smell. Although not reprinted until the twentieth century, Evelyn's book and comments were cited in British and American cookbooks well into the nineteenth century.

During the late eighteenth century, the French way of making salads was introduced to England and America by émigrés who had fled the French Revolution. A French émigré named d'Aubignac who grew wealthy in London made a profession out of dressing salads and frequently expressed his own views on the choice of ingredients and new seasoning. He was known as the "fashionable salet-maker" for his salads enhanced by various flavored vinegars, oils, soy, caviar, truffles, anchovies, meat essences, and yolks of eggs.

Salad Ingredients. Lettuce on display at Back to the Land Natural Foods, Brooklyn, New York. *Photograph by Joe Zarba*

American Salad

European colonists brought the concept of salad to the New World. Salad was considered a survival food by many, because salad ingredients were gathered in the early spring before crops matured. Colonial middle- and upper-class Americans enjoyed salads. Most kitchen gardens included salad ingredients, such as lettuce, cabbage, watercress, kale, cucumbers, carrots, parsley, leeks, shallots, onions, spinach, garlic, and chives. In addition, wild greens were collected from fields. In the southern colonies, wider arrays of kitchen garden plants and vegetables were grown. Salad dressings varied, including single ingredients, such as salt or sugar or vinegar or melted butter, or combinations, such as vinegar and egg yolks or salt, vinegar, and sugar or molasses. Occasionally dressings included olive oil, which was an expensive commodity in colonial and early America, as it had to be imported. It was also frequently adulterated and prone to turning rancid easily.

Mary Randolph's *Virginia House-wife* (1824) included a recipe for salads composed of lettuce, peppergrass, cress, and other greens. While the main definition of salad revolved around the leafy green plants, such as lettuce, immigrants and groups had concepts of salad that did not necessarily have any greens in them at all. German immigrants brought potato salad. The Shakers had long made fruit salads. French cookbooks and French immigrant chefs introduced mayonnaise into the United States. It was one of the sauces of classical French cookery and its use introduced chicken and lobster salads to America.

Occasionally, fruits and vegetables were considered unhealthy by some medical authorities. City councils also occasionally prohibited the sale of fruits and vegetables during cholera epidemics. But by the 1840s, the reputations of fruits and vegetables were rehabilitated by many medical professionals, who considered them to be healthy edibles, although some remained concerned about eating vegetables in their raw state. American vegetarians and reformers had mixed views of green salads. The vegetarian Dr. William A. Alcott reported in *Young Housekeeper; or, Thoughts on Food and Cookery* (1839) that lettuce, celery, cabbage, turnips, beets, asparagus, potatoes, and green fruit were much eaten. He concluded, based on an analysis of their contents, that lettuce, greens, and celery had little nutritive value, and he believed that salads were indigestible without condiments, such as vinegar and oil, to which he had strong

objection. The late-nineteenth-century food reformer Dr. Dio Lewis was also strongly opposed to dressing—which he considered a stimulant because it tasted good and stimulated the appetite—as unnecessary. Not until the end of the nineteenth century did debate cease.

Despite these warnings, the American upper class enjoyed European-style salads throughout the nineteenth century. This enjoyment increased as new restaurants opened in the large cities during the early nineteenth century. In New York, for instance, Delmonico's restaurant specialized in salads and salad dressings. Its 1838 menu included six salads based on lettuce, endive, celery, anchovies, lobster, and chicken, and several of them included a dressing of mayonnaise. The literary writer Frederick Saunders reported in his *Salads for the Solitary* (1855) that salads, a "delectable conglomerate of good things—meats, vegetables, —acids and sweets—, oils, sauces, and other condiments too numerous to detail," were highly prized and suitable for all seasons.

After the Civil War, salad experimentation began in earnest in America. Middle and upper classes consumed lettuce salads and others made of potatoes, tomatoes, and cabbages. For balls, evening parties, or formal afternoon teas, lobster, oyster, crab, and turkey salads were highly rated. Chicken salad was a particular favorite. The upper class also served green salads with vinegar and olive oil. Garlic was generally not employed, but it was a frequent component in dressings served in French and other restaurants in America.

This new emphasis on salads appeared in cookbooks by the late 1870s. The first American cookbook devoted solely to salads was Emma Ewing's *Salad and Salad Making* (1883), which was a manual for students in cooking school. Ewing believed that salads were highly nutritious and easy to make. Her goal was to demystify and simplify salad construction. She included thirty-four recipes, dividing the salads into five categories: fruit salads, vegetable salads, fish salads, meat salads, and mixed salads. The cookbook author Juliet Corson, who included lettuce and cream cucumber salads in many of her model menus published in magazines, urged her readers to use such greens as onions, celery, cucumbers, radishes, watercress, lettuce, chicory, and dandelions. For health reasons, Sarah Tyson Rorer, director of the Philadelphia Cooking School, culinary columnist, and cookbook author, engaged in a long campaign to make salads a part of "the dinner-table in every well-regulated house three hundred and sixty-five times a year." She lectured on the importance of salads, included salads in her magazine columns, and published three books on salads.

Iceberg lettuce was developed in 1894. The sturdiness of this green made it easier to transport lettuce long distances. As the price of iceberg lettuce dropped during the early twentieth century, it became the base of most American salads, with romaine lettuce coming in a distant second. By the beginning of the twentieth century, molded or congealed salads, made with gelatin or aspic, had burst onto the culinary mainstream. Frozen salads followed. The ubiquitous lettuce and tomato salad did not appear in cookbooks until 1890 but was not commonly served in restaurants until decades later.

Two places where commercial salad plants grew easily were California and Florida. It is no surprise that a late-nineteenth-century visitor to California found it the "land of salads." He specifically identified the "alligator pear salad" as a San Francisco treat. This salad, renamed "avocado salad," became the rage of the early twentieth century. The first California cookbook entirely devoted to salads was published in 1897. Florida was not far behind. In 1914 Frances Barber Harris published *Florida Salads*, which went through five editions over the course of twelve years. California was also the inspiration for a great number of famous salads, such as the green goddess salad and (via Tijuana, Mexico) caesar salad. So pervasive was the California influence that salad has become a common main-course item in itself, called "chef's salad" and including ham and hard-boiled eggs, on many restaurant menus as well as at many private tables.

Commercial Salad Dressing

Salads had become important enough by the 1870s that salad dressings were commercially bottled and sold by grocers. The most important nineteenth-century manufacturers were the E. R. Durkee Company of New York City and Curtice Brothers of Rochester, New York. Chicago's Tildesley and Company manufactured Yacht Club salad dressing. Durkee began issuing advertising cookbooklets featuring its products by 1875. Other salad dressing manufacturers followed at a later date.

Cookbooks expanded their salad sections to offer recipes using hard-boiled eggs, cabbage, and celery; salmon, beef, tomato, and onion; apple, apricot, banana, bean, celery, and walnut; and cauliflower, orange, aspic, and chicken with walnuts among others. Mayonnaise was mixed with, or surmounted, a variety of fruits and vegetables. The word "salad" continued to be used loosely,

and Sarah Tyson Rorer complained that many cooks joined fruit, sugar, and alcohol and served the mixture as a salad.

Two early salad cookbook writers were Thomas J. Murrey, who published *Salads and Sauces* (1884) and *Fifty Salads* (1886), and Maximilian De Loup, who in *The American Salad Book* (1899), smugly urged Americans to cease believing that foreign countries were ahead in salad making. France had long been so, he wrote, but it did not have the great variety of fruits and vegetables available in the United States. England was still "barbaric" in regard to salads, and German salads were sometimes too powerful for American tastes. Americans, claimed De Loup, were "fast learning that originality and adaptation have given us the best the world affords." He admitted that Americans still ate too few green salads, but they would learn someday to prefer them to "heavy bulky materials." At the time he wrote, celery was used to make "the most popular and abundant" of the winter salads, fruit salads were winning converts, and potato salad, which had been served hot in the conviction that cold potatoes were unwholesome, was now being served cold.

During the twentieth century, warm salads, such as potato salad, were introduced. Awareness of salads from other countries, continents, and cultures was growing. Although the tomato was the queen of the vegetable market in the United States by the mid-nineteenth century, Italian immigrants made the tomato a popular ingredient in salads. Cold pasta salads, particularly those made with tortellini, mayonnaise, and dill, became fashionable.

In 1939, the Boston Oyster House of the Morrison Hotel in Chicago opened what it called a "salad bar" at which customers arranged their own salads. It consisted of thirty glass bowls, packed in ice, containing greens and a variety of cooked and fresh vegetables in season that could be used to make up combination salads. Also on the bar were bowls of julienne chicken, ham, fresh crab flakes, beef, anchovies, tuna, and shrimps, and eight varieties of dressing. During the 1970s, salad bars became a fixture of medium-priced and family restaurants throughout the United States.

Dressings have ranged from the very simple oil and vinegar, called french (or italian) dressing, to elaborate sauces that might contain orange slices and marshmallows. International hotel cuisine, under American influence, in the twenty-first century offers three dressings: oil and vinegar, thousand island, and Roquefort or blue cheese.

Origins of Specific Salads and Salad Dressings

Caesar salad is a combination of romaine lettuce, garlic, olive oil, croutons, parmesan cheese, Worcestershire sauce, and often anchovies. It was purportedly created by Caesar Cardini, an Italian immigrant who opened a series of restaurants in Tijuana, Mexico, just across the border from San Diego. In 1924, Cardini concocted the salad as a main course, arranging the lettuce leaves on a plate with the intention that they would be eaten with the fingers. Later Cardini shredded the leaves into bite-size pieces. The salad became particularly popular with the Hollywood movie in-crowd who visited Tijuana. The salad was later featured at restaurants in Los Angeles. Cardini insisted that the salad be subtly flavored and therefore opposed the introduction of anchovies. He also decreed that only Italian olive oil and imported parmesan cheese be used. In 1948 he established a patent on the dressing, which in the early 2000s was still packaged and sold as Cardini's Original Caesar dressing mix, distributed by Caesar Cardini Foods, Culver City, California.

Cobb salad was introduced in 1926 by Robert Cobb, owner of the Brown Derby restaurant in Los Angeles. It consists of avocado, tomato, watercress, lettuce, bacon, chicken, Roquefort cheese, and a hard-boiled egg arranged in a striped pattern in a flat bowl topped with French dressing.

French dressing is made by mixing three parts oil to one part vinegar, although some other seasonings like mustard and blue cheese may be added.

Green goddess dressing, consisting of many ingredients, including mayonnaise, cream, vinegar, parsley, onion, anchovies, and garlic, was introduced by the Palace Hotel in San Francisco in the early 1920s. It was inspired by the British actor George Arliss, who was a hit in the play *The Green Goddess* then playing in San Francisco.

Lettuce and tomato salad. Although tomatoes had been used in salads for decades, their combination into the ubiquitous lettuce and tomato salad first appeared in the United States in the late nineteenth century. It was popularized by Fannie Merritt Farmer's *Boston Cooking-school Cook Book*. The lettuce and tomato salad did not become common until the mid-twentieth century.

Potato salad is a cold or hot side dish made with potatoes, mayonnaise, and seasonings. It became very popular in the second half of the nineteenth century and is a staple of both delicatessens and home kitchens. Hot potato salad, usually made with bacon, onion, and vinegar dressing, was

associated with German immigrants and is therefore often called "German potato salad."

Salade niçoise is generally a mixture of lettuce, tomatoes, french beans, anchovy, tuna, olives, and hard-boiled eggs with vinaigrette dressing.

Thousand Island dressing is a mayonnaise-based salad dressing flavored with tomatoes, chilies, and green peppers among other things. According to John Ayoto's *Food and Drink from A to Z*, the earliest located reference to it appears in a 1916 advertisement in the *Daily Colonist* of British Columbia, which offered bottles of Mrs. Porter's Thousand Island Salad Dressing. The name presumably comes from the Thousand Islands between the United States and Canada in the St. Lawrence River.

Waldorf salad is a combination of apple, celery, and mayonnaise that dates from 1896. Its invention is credited to Oscar Tschirky, who was in charge of a dining room at Delmonico's before he moved to the Waldorf-Astoria. Walnuts were added during the first decade of the twentieth century.

Ranch dressing, consisting in part of soybean oil, buttermilk, vinegar, sour cream, egg yolk, garlic, and sugar, was introduced in the mid-1970s by Hidden Valley Ranch in a dry dressing mix and later in bottled form. Competitors followed suit and in the early 2000s ranch-style dressing reigned as America's favorite dressing flavor followed in order by Italian, creamy Italian, thousand island, French, and caesar.

[See also Delmonico's; Flowers, Edible; Fruit; Jell-O; Jell-O Molds; Lettuce; Mayonnaise; Poke Salad; Randolph, Mary; Rorer, Sarah Tyson; Tomatoes; Tschirky, Oscar; Vegetables.]

BIBLIOGRAPHY

The Association for Dressings and Sauces. http://www.dressings-sauces.org.

De Loup, Maximilian. *American Salad Book*. New York: Knapp, 1899.

Evelyn, J. *Acetaria. A Discourse of Shallets*. London: Tooke, 1699. Reprint. London: Prospect Books, 1982.

Ewing, Emma. *Salad and Salad Making*. Chicago: Fairbanks, Palmer, 1883.

Green, Olive. *One Thousand Salads*. New York: Putnam's, 1909.

Harris, Frances Barber. *Florida Salads*. Jacksonville, FL: n.p., 1914.

Hill, Janet M. *Salads, Sandwiches and Chafing Dish Dainties*. Boston: Little, Brown, 1899.

Kegler, Henri. *Fancy Salads of the Big Hotels*. New York: Tri-Arts, 1921.

Murrey, Thomas J. *Fifty Salads*. New York: White, Stokes, and Allen, 1886.

The Salad and Cooking Oil Market. New York: Packaged Facts, 1991.

Shapiro, Laura. *Perfection Salad: Women and Cooking at the Turn of the Century*. New York: Holt, 1987.

Toussaint-Samat, Maguelonne. *History of Food*. Translated by Anthea Bell. Cambridge, MA: Blackwell, 1992.

ANDREW F. SMITH

Salami

Originally from Italy, salami is a type of sausage made with ground pork and cubes of fat seasoned with garlic, salt, and spices. The name "salami," from the Italian *salare*, meaning "to salt," refers to the salting process used to make highly seasoned dry sausages with a characteristic fermented flavor.

Salami is usually approximately three to four inches in diameter and often named after the city or region of origin. Salami varies according to country or region of origin, coarseness or fineness of the meat blend, size, and seasonings. Kosher salami is made from kosher ingredients under rabbinical supervision.

Italian immigrants introduced salami to the United States in the mid to late nineteenth century. At the turn of the twentieth century, the immigrants identified the temperate climate of northern California as best suited for dry-curing salami. San Francisco emerged as the leader in salami production and continues to be regarded as the salami capital of America.

In the early eighteenth century Armour and Company, in Chicago, started the first automated commercial production of salami. Salami, in accordance with Old World customs, was traditionally made in late fall and early winter and cured during the cooler season for consumption throughout the year. Refrigeration and humidity control

Salami. A selection at Blue Apron Foods in Brooklyn, New York. *Photograph by Joe Zarba*

technologies did away with the seasonality of salami production and allowed for salami production throughout the year. Salami manufacture initially required five to ten days to ensure optimum curing and flavor development. When lactic acid cultures became available commercially, curing time decreased from days to hours. With advances in ingredient technologies, egg whites and sodium caseinate were used to bind moisture in the product and significantly reduce drying time. Smoke flavoring further helped reduce production time to a matter of hours.

The basic salami-making process—whether the sausage is batch- or mass-produced—consists of stuffing a cured meat mixture into casings and air-drying or smoking the sausages at a relatively low temperature (not exceeding 140°F.). Smoking stops fermentation and adds flavor while drying the product. The finished product is rinsed with water or brine to prevent mold growth and then is chilled or aged.

Salami is consumed without being heated. Salami made from mildly cured fresh meats and cooked before air drying is known as "cooked salami." Cooked salami, such as cotto salami, which contains whole peppercorns, is softer than dry and semidry salami and must be refrigerated.

Convenience, versatility, and low cost helped cooked salami become a staple of snacks and meals among the less affluent and working class of America. Targeted advertising further helped the easy-to-digest and mild-tasting salami and bologna become favorites with children in America.

Salami production and consumption continue to grow in the United States. A high-protein and low-carbohydrate profile makes salami ideal for the popular Atkins and South Beach carbohydrate-restricted weight loss diets. Innovative packaging technologies are adding to the popularity of salami. For example, miniature salami is becoming increasingly popular as a handheld food.

[*See also* California; Italian American Food; Meat; Pepperoni; Sausage; Vienna Sausage.]

BIBLIOGRAPHY

Dowell, Philip, and Bailey, Adrian. *Cook's Ingredients*. New York: Bantam, 1980.

Trager, James. *The Food Chronology*. New York: Henry Holt, 1995.

KANTHA SHELKE

Sally Lunn

Sally Lunn is a delicate, fairly rich bread made with yeast, eggs, milk, wheat flour, butter, and a little sugar, much like the French brioche. Sally Lunn is popular in England, Canada, and New Zealand, where it is served hot as a tea cake, or fork-split and toasted. In the United States, it has many variations, some made with yeast and others with baking powder. Still other variants include cornmeal, sour cream, or buttermilk. It can be baked in a shallow cake pan, a ring mold, a Turk's head mold, a bread pan, a bundt or tube pan, or even in muffin tins. One recipe makes a very light corn bread, baked as a dropped batter on a baking sheet. Whatever the form, Sally Lunn is generally cut into wedges, slices, or squares and served hot with butter and jam. It is a favorite Virginia hot bread and is claimed by Colonial Williamsburg, where visitors can dine on Sally Lunn in the museum's taverns and take home bags of Sally Lunn bread mix.

The origins of Sally Lunn are unclear, but perhaps date to the 1670s in Bath, England, when Bath buns were served in the Pump Room. Over time, Bath buns acquired spices and lemon while Sally Lunn remained a plain and simple kind of bun. Sally Lunn buns were served with morning coffee in the fashionable Bath Pump Room during the eighteenth century. *The Oxford English Dictionary* dates the first citation to 1798: "a certain sort of hot rolls, now, or not long ago, in vogue at Bath." A dictionary published in 1898 also placed the first use of the term "Sally Lunn" at the close of the eighteenth century.

Legend has it that Sally Lunn, herself, was a seventeenth- or eighteenth-century pastry cook who first sold these buns from a basket in the streets of Bath. Nineteenth-century sources credit Dalmer, a baker and musician, who bought her business, made a song about Sally Lunn, and made the bread famous. (The song has been lost.) The Sally Lunn Museum and Restaurant in Bath, England, portrays Sally Lunn as a young French refugee who arrived in England in 1680 and baked the buns to support herself. The bun became a very popular delicacy in Georgian England and was enjoyed with either sweet or savory accompaniments. It can be used as a base for Welsh rabbit, sliced for sandwiches, or used for bread pudding.

Another theory is that the bread's name is a corruption of the French phrase *soleil et lune* (sun and moon), referring to the bread's golden top and white bottom. It is also possible that the name comes from a French word, such as *solimeme* or *solilemme*, for a type of brioche. Proponents of the theory of a French origin believe that the originator of the buns in Bath may have been a French Huguenot who fled from France to escape persecution sometime after the revocation of the Edict of Nantes in 1685.

[*See also* Bread.]

BIBLIOGRAPHY

Beard, James. *James Beard's American Cookery*. Boston: Little, Brown, 1972.

MacDonald, Barbara, Carolyn Boisvert, and Peggy Miller, eds. *The Fifty States Cookbook*. Chicago, 1977.

Perl, Lila. *Red-Flannel Hash and Shoo-Fly Pie: American Regional Foods and Festivals*. Cleveland and New York, 1965.

Sally Lunn Museum, Bath, England. http://www.sallylunns.co.uk/.

Who Cooked That Up? Sally Lunn Bread. http://members.cox.net/jjschnebel/sallylun.html.

VIRGINIA SCOTT JENKINS

Saloons

Swinging doors, player pianos, gunfights, and the Wild West are some of the images that the word "saloon" conjures up. Others think of skid row, red-light districts, drunkenness, and wasted lives when they hear the word. At one time the word embraced all of these ideas and many more. Long before the saloon became associated with debauchery and the Wild West, saloons were watering holes for both the privileged and the poor.

Saloons in America evolved from the public taverns and ordinaries of the eighteenth and early nineteenth centuries. During the colonial period, taverns generally served a broad cross-section of society. It was during the federalist period that these public drinking spaces started to serve a more restricted clientele. The wealthiest found haven in private clubs, and merchants and businessmen retreated to coffeehouses and restaurants. The traveler frequented hotel bars, which had the attributes of both the club and saloon. At first, the saloon (from the French *salon*) catered to wealthy native-born Americans. These saloons, decorated with handsome furniture, woodwork, large mirrors, and carpets, created an ambience of luxury and were associated with the poshest hotels (Boston's Parker House and the Palmer House in Chicago) and restaurants (Delmonico's in New York) in America. It was in the environment of this kind of saloon that the cocktail, a uniquely American invention, had its origins.

After the Civil War, the saloon evolved to meet the needs of urban working-class males. Saloons dominated poor working-class neighborhoods, serving both low-cost food and drink to factory workers. These establishments were mostly frequented by male patrons, who spent many of their nonworking hours drinking beer, cheap whiskey, and in some cases eating free food, providing they purchased a

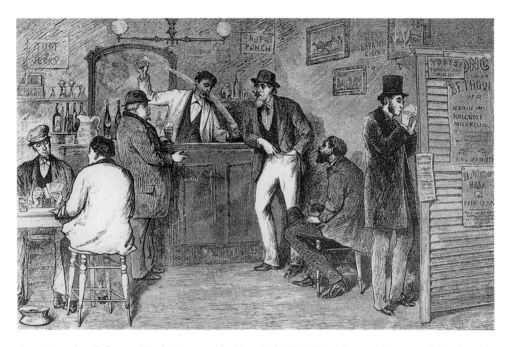

Interior of a Saloon. Mixologist at work, New York City. From George Augustus Sala, *America Revisited*, 3rd edition (London, 1883), vol. 1, facing p. 183.

sufficient quantity of beer. The food was heavily salted to encourage thirst, and the saloon "bouncer" kept an eye on those with too hearty an appetite. Saloons made no pretense of serving fine food.

Because so many of these working-class men were immigrants, saloons have been called "ethnic spaces" and in cities have often been identified with the Irish. It was the saloon that men turned to as a place to meet, eat, take a bath, use a rest room, receive credit, gamble, locate pornography, meet a prostitute, or buy narcotics. In some cities, political bosses recruited saloon regulars to stuff ballot boxes. In Chicago and San Francisco, centers of organized prostitution, the red-light districts, coexisted with the saloon culture. It was also in saloons that bosses found their strikebreakers. Fraternal organizations frequently met in the back room or second-floor halls. Jack London found that in a saloon "life was different. Men talked with great voices, laughed great laughs, and there was an atmosphere of greatness."

Saloons located near factories and places that employed large numbers of men were frequented at lunch, during work breaks, and by apprentices sent to fetch pails of beer for mill workers. Breweries owned many saloons and put pressure on managers to meet quotas. To do this they frequently had to break blue laws (local closing ordinances, such as those forbidding the serving of drink on Sundays) and promote gambling and other underworld activities. The increase in drinking by the poor was identified with the increase in the rise of skid rows in many urban areas. The term "skid" comes from the track made by Seattle's lumbermen to "skid" timber downhill. As Seattle grew, the area around where the lumbermen worked filled up with seedy bars and quarters for unemployed workers, derelicts, and transients. Skid rows developed in other urban areas including New York's Bowery district.

The temperance movement had been concerned with the problem of alcoholism even before the Civil War, but after the war the excesses of saloon culture brought matters to a head. Because of the abuse of alcohol, particularly in saloons, the Woman's Christian Temperance Union (WCTU) made the saloon the target of its hatred, finding in this institution the symbol of women's fears of abandonment. Saloons were associated with drunkenness, prostitution, unemployment, wastefulness, crime, and disease in the minds of many Americans.

The saloon disappeared, except in the form of illegal speakeasies, during the period of Prohibition that lasted from 1920 until 1934. The word is sometimes used today in association with the name of a restaurant or drinking place that attempts to evoke a Victorian, late-nineteenth-century feel or a Western frontier ambience.

[*See also* Alcohol and Teetotalism; Alcoholism; Bars; Beer Halls; Boardinghouses; Cocktails; Coffeehouses; Delmonico's; Drinking Songs; Luchow's; Prohibition; Roadhouses; Temperance.]

BIBLIOGRAPHY

Grimes, William. *Straight Up or on the Rocks: The Story of the American Cocktail.* New York: North Point Press, 2001.

Lender, Mark Edward, and James Kirby Martin. *Drinking in America: A History.* Rev. ed. New York: Free Press, 1987.

Murdock, Catherine Gilbert. *Domesticating Drink: Women, Men, and Alcohol in America, 1870–1940.* Baltimore: Johns Hopkins University Press, 1998.

JOSEPH M. CARLIN

Salsa

Salsa is a condiment made from a variety of ingredients, raw or cooked, usually served at room temperature as a dip for fried corn tortilla chips and as a garnish for other dishes, savory or sweet. Salsas are typically colorful in appearance, chunky in texture, and often (but not always) hot and spicy in taste. In many ways, the salsas eaten in the United States are similar to coarsely textured condiments in other parts of the world, such as the sambals of Southeast Asia and the chutneys of India and Pakistan, as well as the relishes of America's own Deep South.

Salsa is the Spanish word for sauce—an indication of this condiment's origin in Spanish-speaking countries of the Western Hemisphere, particularly Mexico and the countries of Central America. In these countries, the word "salsa" encompasses a wide range of culinary concoctions, from sauces that are smooth, cooked, and served warm or hot, to condiments that are chunky, raw, and served at room temperature.

In the United States, the consumption of condiment salsas began to expand beyond the local Hispanic communities during the 1940s, initially in those parts of the American Southwest where Mexican food was traditionally eaten. The most common type of salsa was—and still is in the early 2000s—a version of Mexican *salsa cruda* (raw sauce), also known as *salsa fresca* (fresh sauce), or *salsa Mexicana* (Mexican sauce), made with chopped tomatoes, onions, and fresh green jalapeño or serrano peppers, their colors a reflection of the red-white-and-green of the Mexican flag. Chopped cilantro (fresh coriander leaves) and a little lemon or lime juice or salt are often added to the mixture to enhance the flavor.

Salsas made at home or in restaurants can be raw, cooked, or made with a combination of both raw and cooked ingredients. Fresh salsas containing raw ingredients are usually eaten shortly after they are made. Bottled salsas, typically sold in widemouthed jars, are always cooked to preserve their ingredients. The first commercially bottled salsas were made in Texas in the late 1940s, and by 1992 salsa had become America's most popular commercial condiment, outselling in dollars the country's other longtime favorite, tomato ketchup.

Salsa's popularity nationwide is generally attributed to Americans' increasing consumption of hot-and-spicy foods during the second half of the twentieth century—first in the Southwest and later throughout other parts of the country—at home, for snacks, in Mexican-food restaurants, and more recently in restaurants featuring fusion foods that combine ingredients and cooking techniques from many places around the globe. Salsas are also perceived as healthy foods, because many of them are low in calories, high in fiber, and full of vitamins. Salsas have become such an accepted part of American cuisine that since 1995 the International Chili Society has hosted hundreds of local, state, and regional salsa cook-offs, where cooks compete for cash prizes and ultimately a world champion title for salsas made from their own personal recipes.

Red, tomato-based salsas are the most common in the United States, followed by green salsas made with tomatillos, green peppers, avocados, and cilantro or other green herbs. But salsas can be made from a wide range of ingredients, including vegetables, fruits, berries, grains, herbs, spices, oils, vinegars, sugars, nuts, seeds, mushrooms, and occasionally even seafood. The chunky texture of salsas comes from their solid ingredients, which can be coarsely or finely chopped. And their piquant, distinctive taste comes from the combination of contrasting flavors—usually hot and spicy, often salty, occasionally sour, and sometimes even sweet.

Almost all salsas in the United States contain mild to hot capsicum peppers, which can be fresh, pickled, or dried and chopped, crumbled, or ground into powder. Although salsa in the United States was originally a hot-and-spicy condiment, the increasing demand for salsas with milder flavors has resulted in the development of new varieties of peppers. These provide the taste of naturally hot peppers, such as jalapeños and habaneros, without the accompanying high levels of capsaicin, an alkaloid present in hot peppers that produces the characteristic burning sensation in the mouth and on the skin.

Salsas turn up on the table as condiments with courses from appetizers to main dishes to desserts. Spicy, hot red or green salsas, typically served as dips for tortilla chips at the beginning of a Tex-Mex meal, are also often used as garnishes for a number of dishes of Mexican origin, including enchiladas, tacos, and tamales. Savory salsas—spicy or mild, with a wide range of flavors and colors—are served as accompaniments to grilled, baked, broiled, or fried meats, fish, and poultry. Some cooks use salsas as an ingredient in marinades, salad dressings, soups, stews, and cooked sauces, and even as a topping for baked potatoes, pizzas, and pastas. In the early 2000s, an emerging trend was to make sweet salsas from fruits, berries, sugars, and spices paired with fruity-flavored peppers, such as habaneros, Scotch bonnets, and datils, for serving with pound cakes, cheesecakes, and frozen desserts.

[*See also* Chili; Condiments; Frito-Lay; Mexican American Food; Southwestern Regional Cookery.]

BIBLIOGRAPHY

Hearon, Reed. *Salsa: Musica for Your Mouth*. San Francisco: Chronicle Books, 1993.
Miller, Mark. *The Great Salsa Book*. Berkeley, CA: Ten Speed Press, 1994.
Schlesinger, Chris, and John Willoughby. *Salsas, Sambals, Chutneys & Chowchows*. New York: William Morrow, 1993.

SHARON HUDGINS

Salsify

Salsify (*Tragopogon porrifolius*) is also known as oyster plant because the pleasant flavor is said to resemble that of an oyster, although it has the firm texture of all root vegetables. The roots of this European vegetable, which can be up to twelve inches long, are grayish-black or brown, and the flesh is white. There is a variety with a black skin known as *scorzonera*. Marion Harland, the pen name of Mary Virginia Terhune (1830–1922; née Hawes), who wrote many cookbooks and books on domestic economy, was very fond of oyster plant and had several recipes for it. It can be cooked like any root vegetable in soups, stews, and so forth. It is in season from early summer through the winter but is most likely to be found in markets in the fall.

[*See also* Soups and Stews.]

JOSEPHINE BACON

Salt and Salting

The chlorine ion bound with a sodium ion forms the chemical compound sodium chloride (NaCl), known as common salt. NaCl is chemically composed of 60 percent chlorine, a gas, and 40 percent sodium, a metal. Purity of salt is dependent on its source and its method of production. For instance, mined rock salt typically ranges between 95 percent and 99.9 percent NaCl, and evaporated salt from purified brine is nearly 99.9 percent pure.

Salt is an essential nutrient. Humans and animals need salt for musculature balance, digestion of food, and proper functioning of the nervous system; salt is lost daily through urination and perspiration. The human body contains about eight ounces of salt. If salt is not replaced, our bodies try to gain an optimum saline balance by discharging excess water. A specific hunger for salt can arise in extreme cases of sodium loss or deprivation. Meanwhile, the presence of too much salt in the diet is thought to be a contributing factor for high blood pressure.

Salt enhances flavor. The human tongue readily detects four main taste sensations: salty, sweet, bitter, and sour. Harold McGee in *On Food and Cooking: The Science and Lore in the Kitchen* explains: "concentration of salt in a food helps determine chemically how many of the other flavors components are going to behave; that is, how available they are to our senses." Many would agree that salty food tastes good. For instance, salt firms the textures of pickles and concentrates and balances a host of herbaceous, spicy, and sweet flavors.

Salt has been known since antiquity as an excellent food preservative. High concentrations of salt preserve food by drawing water out of the cells and destroying bacterial and fungal cells. Salt controls fermentation, wherein the safe, "good" bacteria already existing in the food breaks apart sugars to create an acid. Acid helps preserve the food for extended periods, thereby preserving nutrients.

The United States is the world's largest salt producer, producing 45 million tons a year. The basic methods of producing salt have not changed for centuries—boiling, evaporation, and mining. Salt is available in varying particle gradations and forms and consequently varies in utility. The modern salt industry cites fourteen thousand distinct uses for salt in countless industries, most notably in the manufacture of chemicals, preservation of meats and food products, curing of hides, and deicing of roads.

Cooks are partial to their favorite salt. The texture and flavor of different salts determine their best usage. For purified salt, such additives as iodine (an important preventative for hypothyroidism), fluoride, and anticaking agents influence usage, especially for preservation techniques like curing, brining, and pickling. In unpurified salt, organic remains could potentially react with proteins in the foods being preserved and cause spoilage.

Kinds of Salt

Sea salt has a coarse flake texture. Sea salt may contain impurities, most notably trace amounts of minerals from evaporated seawater. Its mineral content may impart a slight flavor or discolor food and it is thus unsuitable for preserving foods.

Kosher salt has a coarse flake texture. It is often sold in its unaltered crystal form. Kosher salt's large surface area allows for absorption of more moisture than a similarly sized cubic salt crystal. It usually contains calcium silicate or another anticaking agent. It is free of iodine. Many cooks champion kosher salt for its flavor and texture. Kosher salt is generally pure salt suitable for preservation techniques, such as canning, pickling, and meat curing. Like other coarse salts, it can be used in recipes that call for a salt crust. It is to be noted that kosher salt is itself not kosher, but is used in the process of koshering meat. Koshering meat entails soaking meat in water for thirty minutes to remove blood or impurities, then salting it heavily. The salted meat stands and drains for one hour and is then rinsed thoroughly.

Table salt or refined granulated salt is the most versatile and is widely used for cooking and as a condiment. Some critics of the taste of refined salt claim it leaves a bitter and unpleasant taste on the back of the tongue and mouth when compared to salt in a purer form. Table salt contains an anticaking agent and is available with or without iodine.

Fine grain salt, such as canning and pickling salt, is used to make brines for preserved foods like pickles and sauerkraut. Such salt is free of additives, which can cause discoloration or darkening if used for pickling. Popcorn salt has very fine grains, granulated specifically to adhere to popcorn.

Unrefined salt, such as rock salt or water-conditioning salt or agricultural salt, is not food grade and is sold in large chunky crystals. Their grayish cast suggests retention of minerals and harmless impurities. Rock salt and halite are used on roads to melt snow and ice. Rock salt is also used to freeze ice cream by combining it with ice in crank-style ice-cream makers. When salt dissolves in water, the freezing point of the resulting solution is lowered

Salt Container. Salt bag, nineteenth century. *Collection of Alice Ross*

and its boiling point raised. Rock salt is also commonly used as a bed on which to serve baked oysters and clams.

Solar salt is not food grade. It is produced by evaporation of seawater in large ponds. Solar salt is unpurified and may contain the desiccated remains of aquatic life. It is used primarily in water softeners.

Salt in the United States

Where there is salt, there are people. For instance, along the Kanawha River in West Virginia, or near Onondaga, New York, deer and buffalo would travel to salt springs to lick salt. Native Americans followed the animal trails in search of a salt supply. Upon discovery of salt and brine springs, Native Americans set up kettles and boiled brines in order to produce salt.

Salt is an essential commodity. Abundant sources of salt in a region typically led to innovation in searching it out and in production methods, thereby spawning adjunct industries in the area. Salt-producing towns have enriched local history, and many American cities and landmarks memorialize the importance of salt.

For example, salt was a factor in the pathbreaking Lewis and Clark expedition to the Pacific Northwest. President Jefferson instructed Meriwether Lewis to watch for "objects worthy of notice" en route, "such as saltpetre deposits, salines, and such circumstances as may indicate their character." By "salines," Jefferson most likely meant salt flats, salt marshes, salt pans, salt springs, and rock salt deposits. Establishment of early American settlements and demographic shifts of population were determined by continuous and reliable supplies of salt. Plentiful agricultural salt and the mere accessibility of salt contributed to the growth of local fishing and cattle industries. Salt delivered via the Ohio River to the river ports of Louisville and Cincinnati, for instance, stimulated a huge pork and beef industry.

Salt production was so important to the growth and prosperity of America that patents and subsidies were granted to anyone who could produce vast quantities of salt cheaply. In fact the first patent ever issued in America was to Samuel Winslow, a salt maker. Innovation in American salt production was historically encouraged, and lateral improvements in salt production processes were recorded throughout the country. Since the advent of the salt industry, continuous supply has remained the goal. Americans have continuously increased production, refining salt-making processes along the way, while refining the salt itself.

Captain John Smith was among the 105 original settlers of the Jamestown colony in what became Virginia, establishing saltworks around 1607. According to the Salt Institute, the U.S. salt industry formally began in 1614 when the colonists established solar saltworks composed of shallow wooden vats on Smith's Island, Virginia. Large-scale salt production from brine springs was under way in America by 1800, and within a few years drilling for more concentrated brine had begun. Full-scale production in open pits or quarries began in 1862, during the Civil War. By 1869 the first underground salt mine was in operation.

Solar evaporation methods were systemized in New England during the early 1800s. The damp, frigid weather provided less than optimal conditions for salt produc-

tion. Nevertheless, mobile and covered sheds were built over evaporating pans, protecting precious salt and brine from precipitation. Reuben Sears invented a roof that slid open and shut on oak rollers, allowing sea salt to be made efficiently from March to November. By the 1830s on Cape Cod there were 442 saltworks, spawning a fishing industry.

Mechanical evaporation in multiple-effect open "grainer" pans began in about 1833, along with methods to purify the brine before evaporation. Salt producers learned that purification prior to evaporation yielded clean, white salt. Saltwater from the bay or ocean was led into large reservoirs or holding ponds through sluice gates. The gates were then shut, trapping the water. Captured water was left to evaporate naturally and become brine. The brine was then converted to salt either in huge iron sun pans or by boiling. Nathaniel Freeman championed windmills to efficiently pump seawater through pipes to the evaporation pans.

Across the country, solar salt production methods were also recorded in San Francisco Bay, California, in 1770 and in the Great Salt Lake in Utah in 1847. Because of its long, shallow topography and optimal weather of steady breezes and sunshine, San Francisco Bay is an ideal area for salt making. In the early 2000s, solar salt still uses wind and sun to evaporate saltwater in shallow ponds, creating progressively more saline brines. When the salinity of the brine reaches a saturation point, it is introduced to crystallizer beds, where the liquid is evaporated and drained off, leaving salt crystals that are scraped from the bed by a mechanical harvester. The salt is then refined for food or industrial use.

Across America during the 1800s, salt works in Silver Springs, New York, employed the concept of crystallizing salt in enclosed vacuum pans. Salt was produced between 1790 and 1860 in Louisiana, Ohio, Pennsylvania, Kentucky, Indiana, Illinois, and Missouri by boiling brine in salt furnaces. Elisha Brooks leased land on the Kentucky trails and sank hollowed trunks of sycamore trees ten feet into the ground. The three pipes served as wells. Using twenty-four kettles to evaporate the brine by burning almost five cords of wood, he was able to produce the then-enviable yield of three bushels a day.

Making salt for domestic use was deemed as commonplace and necessary as making soap from ash and grease or gathering firewood and lumber from forests. Americans also have a long history of boiling saltwater during salt scarcities. In fact, salt production came to be known as a downright patriotic activity. During lean times, alternative methods for curing meat and preserving foods were experimented with, and salt conservation was a hot topic among neighbors.

On May 28, 1776, Congress announced a "bounty of one third of a dollar per bushel upon all such salt as shall be imported or manufactured." Congress also urged states to make their own salt by reissuing a 1748 book written by William Brownrig titled *The Art of Making Common Salt*. Brownrig's book supported the solar evaporation method of making salt from seawater. This tedious process—about four hundred gallons of salty water is needed to make one bushel of salt—produced a low-quality, coarse salt.

Before 1776, salt could be procured from Massachusetts, Europe, and the West Indies at reasonable rates. During the American Revolution, part of the British war strategy was to deny Americans access to salt. If the salt supply was cut, American soldiers, horses, medical community, fisheries, furriers, and households would invariably suffer. In times of war, salt workers often asked to be paid in salt rather than in money, taking advantage of the inflated wartime prices. In prewar New York, salt cost about twenty pence a bushel; by 1777 it was worth $27 a bushel.

Alarmed by the price escalation and sudden shortages of salt, the state legislatures of Pennsylvania and New Jersey as well as the Continental Congress took strategic measures to ensure the availability of salt. Pennsylvania in the spring of 1776 authorized a committee to establish a saltworks for the commonwealth along Toms River. In that same year, New Jersey passed a saltworks manufacturing and erection act to stimulate the industry.

By the end of 1776, the British Army controlled the area in and around present-day New York City, severing the link between New England salt and also with Pennsylvania and New Jersey. Also at this time the Royal Navy ruled the sea lanes and halted salt imports from Europe and the West Indies. In 1777, the British succeeded in capturing General Washington's salt supply. Loyalist spies on New York Island reported to British army headquarters on the saltworks along the New Jersey coast in Monmouth County, which were supplying the rebel American Army with salt. By destroying the saltworks on the Jersey Shore, the British were waging economic warfare on its former colony.

The coarse salt produced by boiling brine helped tide the Americans over twice more, during the War of 1812

and again during the Civil War. Among the southern heroes of the Civil War were those who supplied the Confederacy with salt. Saltville, Virginia, was the site of an important salt-processing plant critical in sustaining the South's beleaguered armies. Avery Island in Louisiana was also a critically strategic salt resource for the Confederacy during the Civil War.

West Virginia has a rich history of salt production. In 1797, Elisha Brooks erected the first salt furnace in the Kanawha Valley at the mouth of Campbell's Creek. He produced as much as 150 bushels of salt a day and sold it to settlers to be used for curing butter and meats.

The first salt shipment sent west, by river, was on a log raft in 1808. David and Joseph Ruffner succeeded in drilling to fifty-nine feet, where they tapped strong brine. Another Ruffner brother, Tobias, suspected that a vast saline reservoir existed under the Kanawha Valley and, drilling to a depth of 410 feet, tapped even richer brine. This discovery set off a veritable drilling frenzy, and by 1815 there were fifty-two furnaces in operation in the so-called Kanawha Salines. In 1817, David Ruffner experimented with the use of coal in his furnaces, and soon all saltmakers had switched from wood to coal. The saltmakers formed the first trust in the United States, the Kanawha Salt Company, in order to regulate the quality and price of salt and to discourage foreign competition. This cooperative helped the salt industry grow until it reached its peak in 1846, producing more than 3 million bushels that year.

At that time, the Kanawha Valley was one of the largest salt-manufacturing centers in the United States. The salt industry continued to be an economic force in the Valley until 1850, by which time the center of the meatpacking industry had moved from Cincinnati to Chicago, taking salt manufacturing westward as well. In 1861, the valley was struck by flooding. By 1865, floods and the Civil War had destroyed all but one salt furnace in the Kanawha Valley.

As early as 1654, settlers at Onondaga, New York, reported that the local Indians made salt by boiling brine from salt springs. All along New York's inland rivers, forests were cut down, fields were planted, and towns sprang up. Yet the murky swamps around Onondaga Creek were salty. The brine springs in Onondaga and Cayuga counties became critical in mass salt production. In the twenty-first century, salt in the region is used to preserve deer, game, and to make regional specialties such as sauerkraut.

Salt Works. Salt works at Syracuse, New York. Drawing by Frederick Ray, *Harper's Weekly*, November 13, 1886. *Collection of Alice Ross*

With massive quantities of salt being produced in New York, the question became how to transport and distribute it. Syracuse's low, swampy land proved ideal for canal construction. The construction of a canal was deemed a sound enough investment to be financed in part by the state of New York, and taxes and subsequent tolls on salt cargos kept the enterprise profitable. The Erie Canal was opened in 1825, with salt as its principle cargo, and served as a western waterway. The canal quickly established Syracuse's dominance over nearby settlements. When salt manufacturing began to decline in Syracuse in the years after the Civil War, many businesses and diversified industries assured the city's continued economic prosperity. The fruits of American industry—gears, typewriters, electrical devices, shoes, glass and china, to name just a few—were made in Syracuse by companies that took advantage of its superior transportation system, its central location, and its ready, skilled labor force, all made by possible by salt. The "ditch that salt built" continued to run through the heart of the city until the mid-1920s.

Salt as a By-Product, By-Products of Salt

The salt industry has not only advanced infrastructure, but it has also spawned countless adjunct industries. On occasion, salt was accidentally discovered while in pursuit of another resource, such as oil or petroleum. Brine is a source material for the chemical industry. Rock salt or brine serves as a basic component for an array of materials, including plastics, glass, synthetic rubber, cleansers, pesticides, paints adhesives, metal coatings, and chloralkali chemicals. While the Kanawha salt industry declined in importance after 1861, the advent of World War I brought a demand for chlorine, caustic acid and other chemical products, which could be obtained from salt brine. Chemical industries continue to flourish in the Kanawha Valley in the early 2000s. Great chemical industries, like Dow Chemical, among others, are based in and around Detroit chiefly because of the availability of salt.

Salt manufacturing was a by-product of the lumbering industry near metropolitan Detroit. In 1859 the East Saginaw Manufacturing Company discovered brine springs in the rock at a depth of 650 feet and decided that salt manufacturing via kettle evaporation could be made profitable by burning piles of decaying sawdust and lumber waste to produce cheap fuel in the form of steam for the mill. The success of the company led to the rapid development of the salt industry throughout the Saginaw valley, which then spread to all the lumbering towns along the shore of the Saginaw River. While the lumber towns eventually vanished, the salt by-product industry became increasingly important. The industry continued to develop and to utilize brines or artificial brines. In sixteen years Michigan became the leading salt-producing state, a position it has held for most of the time since 1876.

Iconic American consumer packaged goods, such as Morton's Salt, owe their opportunity and rich history to salt production in America. Morton's salt is a prime example of American innovation, offering in one product a purified salt with an anticaking agent and a patented pouring spout. It is also a prime example of clever marketing. The drawing of a girl under an umbrella in pouring rain, with salt pouring freely out of the canister she carries home, has remained an unforgettable image in the American product landscape since 1914.

In the twenty-first century, exotic salt is considered chic. Gourmet markets sell the rock in all colors and gradations from the world over. *Fleur de sel*, for example, is a prestigious ingredient on high-end restaurant menus and commands prices of $60 for a two-pound bag in the early 2000s.

Modern food preservation methods, such as refrigeration, pasteurization, pressure cooking, and hygienic food packaging, have eliminated the need to preserve food with salt. Nevertheless, the United States, with its variety of ethnic groups, continues to employ corning, pickling, and brining, the time-honored salting techniques. Bacon, ham, pickles, and anchovies and other salty foods remain enduring classics in America.

[*See also* Condiments; Drying; Flavorings; Jewish Dietary Laws; Pickling; Snack Food.]

BIBLIOGRAPHY

Collins, John. *Salt and Fishery: 3) The Catching and Curing, or Salting of the Most Eminent or Staple Sorts of Fish, for Long or Short Keeping, 4) the Salting of Flesh, Extraordinary Experiments in Preserving Butter, Flesh, Fish, Fowl, Fruit, Roots, Fresh and Sweet for Long Keeping.* London: A. Godbid and J. Playford, 1682.

Eskew, Garnett Laidlaw. *Salt: The Fifth Element.* Chicago: Ferguson, 1948.

Jordan, Michele Anna. *Salt and Pepper.* New York: Broadway, 1999.

Jorgensen, Janice. *Encyclopedia of Consumer Brands.* Vol. 1, *Consumable Brands.* Detroit: St. James Press, 1994.

Kummer, Corby. "The Cream of the Salt Pan." *Atlantic Monthly,* March 2002.

Kurlansky, Mark. *Salt: A World History.* New York: Penguin, 2002.

McGee, Harold. *On Food and Cooking: The Science and Lore of the Kitchen.* New York: Scribners, 1984.

Norris, Lucy. *Pickled: Preserving a World of Tastes and Traditions.* New York: Stewart, Tabori, and Chang, 2003.

Saltinstitute.org. http://www.saltinstitute.org. Examines the salt industry.

Steingarten, Jeffrey. *It Must Have Been Something I Ate.* New York: Knopf, 2002.

HYON JUNG LEE

Saltwater Taffy

Saltwater taffy is a uniquely American candy made and sold at seaside resorts on the East and West Coasts and in Salt Lake City, Utah. Also known as "saltwater kisses" or "seaside taffy," saltwater taffy is in the class of sweet, chewing candies, along with toffees, nougats, caramels, and other taffies. The bite-size pieces of pastel-colored candy are sold loose by the pound or packed in decorative boxes or tins. A one-pound box of assorted flavors of saltwater taffy is a traditional gift from someone who has vacationed at the seashore.

Saltwater taffy originated in 1883 in Atlantic City, New Jersey. It was merely a saltwater version of hand-pulled molasses taffy, which had existed in America since the 1840s. Initially, molasses was the only flavor of saltwater taffy. Vanilla and chocolate flavors soon followed.

Saltwater taffy is made by boiling sugar, corn syrup, salted water, and butter to a syrup at the hard-ball stage (250°–268°F). The final temperature of the syrup determines the taffy's texture. Syrup cooked to a low temperature is soft and chewy, whereas high-temperature taffy is hard. When the syrup reaches the desired temperature, the hot syrup is poured onto a marble slab or metal table to cool. Then the candy is aerated and expanded by pulling and twisting. Flavor and color are added. When satiny, opaque, and light, the taffy is cut into small pieces and individually wrapped in wax paper. Since the early 1900s these operations have been performed by specialized machines.

[*See also* Candy Bars and Candy; Molasses.]

BIBLIOGRAPHY

Levi, Vicki Gold, ed. *Atlantic City, 125 Years of Ocean Madness: Starring Miss America, Mr. Peanut, Lucy the Elephant, the High Diving Horse, and Four Generations of Americans Cutting Loose.* 2nd ed. Berkeley, CA: Ten Speed Press, 1994.

ROBERT W. BROWER

Sanders, Colonel

Colonel Harland David Sanders was born on September 9, 1890, in Henryville, Indiana, the son of an impoverished butcher. An internationally recognized icon in the twenty-first century, he is famous for founding and developing Kentucky Fried Chicken, an achievement that helped change the way America eats.

When Harland was six years old, his father died. To make ends meet, his mother worked in a tomato-canning plant, leaving the boy to fend for his siblings. Every night Harland cooked and fed them—nurturing, legend has it, his talent as a truly good cook. "The one thing I always could do was cook," he would say years later. The rest of Sanders's early life was spent doing a variety of jobs: farmhand, streetcar conductor, private in the military in Cuba, railroad fireman. Always he dreamed of making it big. He settled with his wife in Kentucky, seizing on business opportunities as a lawyer, an insurance salesman, and a ferry operator, alternating between going up in the world and slipping down. By 1930 Sanders was operating a service station on Highway 25 in Corbin, Kentucky. Noting the lack of anywhere decent to eat, he started cooking traditional southern fare—including fried chicken—for passersby out of a small room in his filling station. Despite the Depression, the Sanders Café did well, even attracting the praise of Duncan Hines in *Adventures in Good Eating* (1939), a book designed to inform Americans where they could eat well on the road.

Though already in his late forties, Sanders still yearned to make real money. He began experimenting, finding a way to make fried chicken faster (and tastier) by using the newly invented pressure cooker. A few years later, he added seasonings—eleven herbs and spices—to the standard eggs, milk, and flour that formed the base of the traditional fried chicken crust. People raved about the chicken, and business grew. In 1949, the governor of Kentucky conferred on Sanders a colonel's commission in recognition of his work. Sanders liked the idea. He began to refer to himself as "Colonel," donning a white suit, a black string tie, and growing a white goatee to match his hair. The creation of an icon had begun.

In 1952, Sanders had a meeting that changed his life. Pete Harman, a restaurateur in Salt Lake City, was a fellow attendee at the National Restaurant Association convention in Chicago. Between them they came up with the idea of franchising the Colonel's recipe and before long, Harman had opened the first franchise. Seeing great potential in Sanders as a marketing image, Harman named the franchise Colonel Sanders' Kentucky Fried Chicken, and painted the Colonel's face on the signboard above his Utah store.

Helped by frequent radio advertising, the franchise was a great success. But the following year, the Colonel faced downfall: Highway 25 was rerouted away from his Corbin café, removing all his potential customers. Undeterred, the Colonel took to the road himself, relentlessly selling his recipe to roadside eateries. His larger-than-life image and his love of self-promotion worked wonders. By 1960, two hundred franchises were selling Kentucky Fried Chicken; three years later, the number had soared to some six hundred.

Colonel Sanders sold his company in 1964 but remained inseparable from his chicken. "He was our ace," said the new owner, the future Kentucky governor John Y. Brown. "He wasn't just a trademark. He wasn't just someone an adman had made up. . . . He was a real, live human being, and a colorful, attractive, persuasive one. My job was to get him before the American people and let him sell his own product." In the late 1960s, the Colonel appeared in national advertising, TV shows, celebrity events, and even a movie. A nationally recognized symbol, he became the emotional connection between the brand and consumers. To the public, he was Kentucky Fried Chicken.

Colonel Sanders died in 1980 and for a while his image receded from view. But his power as a brand icon was undeniable. In 1990, a look-alike actor was used in TV commercials. The ads fell flat. The Colonel, it appeared, could not be imitated. Eight years later he came back more convincingly in an animated format, dancing onto TV screens. In 2002, commercials had the actor Jason Alexander, known for his role on *Seinfeld*, declaring he was on "a mission from the Colonel."

As the twenty-first century opened, KFC was a vast, multimillion-dollar global corporation with nearly twelve thousand outlets worldwide. The Colonel's face embellished every one of them. KFC has kept him as an icon-in-residence quite intentionally. As a company, KFC sells chicken as part of a logistically complex process of mass production and mass-marketing. But by using Colonel Sanders as an icon, the company could at least present the face of a bygone age when times were good and the chicken really was home fried.

[*See also* Chicken; Fast Food; Hines, Duncan; Roadside Food; Pressure Cookers.]

BIBLIOGRAPHY

Jackle, John A., and Keith A. Sculle. *Fast Food: Roadside Restaurants in the Automobile Age*. Baltimore: Johns Hopkins University Press, 1999.

Pearce, John Ed. *The Colonel: The Captivating Biography of the Dynamic Founder of a Fast-Food Empire*. Garden City, NY: Doubleday, 1982.

CORINNA HAWKES

Sandwiches

The fourth Earl of Sandwich was probably not the first person to place food between two pieces of bread and consume it by holding it in his hand, but his doing so launched a culinary revolution that has gained momentum ever since. Sandwiches became popular in London and were first mentioned in a personal diary in 1762. Sandwich aficionados experimented with serving such different foods as ham, cheese, and shrimp in this way. Recipes for sandwiches appeared in cookbooks by the 1770s.

The British introduced sandwiches into the United States. Sandwich recipes were first published in American cookbooks in 1816. Early published sandwich fillings included oysters, potted meats, fish, poultry, cheese, crabs, lobster, prawns, and crayfish. Subsequently, sandwich ingredients expanded to include beef, minced beef, hash, pork, boiled and fried eggs, stewed fruit, chopped nuts, mushrooms, chicken, watercress, sausages, tongue, anchovies, sardines, forced meats, jelly, and jam. In 1861, a sandwich of boned fish flavored with mustard or ketchup was proposed, and five years later another author listed cheese, hard-boiled eggs, stewed fruit, jelly, and preserves as sandwich fillings.

After the Civil War, sandwiches were extremely common in the United States. Pierre Blot in his *Hand-Book of Practical Cookery* (1867) declined to present sandwich recipes, as they were "too well known to require any directions," but other cookbook authors did include them. Most urged that sandwiches be constructed of very thin slices of bread, day-old sponge cake, or small rolls cut in bite-size squares or triangles. These dainty pieces were used for luncheons, teas, suppers, picnics, or the convenience of travelers. They were subsequently sold in fancy teahouses: These sandwiches were taken from a communal plate and the entire sandwich was placed into the mouth, thus avoiding the need for a personal plate.

For the working class, sandwiches were much less dainty. Large rolls were often used to house diverse fillings. These substantial sandwiches were served at taverns and bars. Commenting about these sandwiches, a British observer in 1880 reported that American bar counters were loaded with huge piles of mammoth beef and ham sandwiches, one of which, he claimed, was sufficient for a full meal. He was amazed to see how quickly they disappeared.

Meat spreads for sandwich fillings started as a by-product of the meat canning industry. They were composed of cuttings of minced ham, tongue, and seasonings. By the 1880s sandwich spreads were available in grocery stores. During the twentieth century, sandwich spreads increased in sales and diversity.

The British appear to have been the first to assign names that were not directly associated with ingredients to sandwiches. For instance, "American" sandwiches, as they were known in England, were large, multilayered concoctions. Americans quickly took up the custom of naming sandwiches also. Multilayered ones were called "Club" sandwiches by the 1890s. During the early twentieth century, this custom of naming sandwiches became something of an art. The names were frequently descriptive, the Triple Decker, for example, while others took the names of specific individuals, although the referents are greatly debated, such as the original creator of the Reuben sandwich.

Celebrity chefs also constructed sandwiches in their upper-class restaurants. Charles Ranhofer, the chef at the Waldorf-Astoria restaurant, included sandwiches composed of french rolls filled with foie gras, game, and chopped raw beef in his *The Epicurean* (1893). Many cookbook authors recommended sandwiches for the elite. Professor H. I. Blits in his book *Method of Canning Fruits and Vegetables* (1890) recommended that sandwiches composed of imported gruyère cheese be served with "a fine sherry."

Making Sandwiches. *Culinary Archives & Museum at Johnson & Wales University, Providence, R.I*

Sandwiches could be prepared hours before they were to be eaten. Many sources recommended covering them with waxed paper to keep them fresh. One cookbook author claimed that properly packed sandwiches were good for three or four days, so it is no wonder that complaints surfaced about sandwiches made with stale bread. There were other, more substantive complaints. Many observers pointed out that sandwiches had gone out of fashion because they were commonly composed of offal and odds and ends that could not be sent to the table in any other form.

During the 1890s, sandwiches took another leap forward. In 1893 Mrs. Alexander Orr Bradley published her *Beverages and Sandwiches*. This included twenty-seven sandwich recipes, but Mrs. Bradley reported that she did not bother to include many recipes for beef, turkey, ham, tongue, and others because everyone knew how to make them. Mrs. Bradley also included recipes for unusual sandwiches filled with woodcock, imported Italian tuna, tuna roe, as well as imported Roquefort, gruyère, brie, and neufchâtel cheeses. The following year, Sarah Tyson Rorer published the first American cookbook solely focused on sandwiches. It included fifty-two recipes, divided into general sandwiches, sweet sandwiches, clubhouse sandwiches, scented sandwiches, and canapés—single slices of toast with toppings. Sweet sandwiches were filled with jelly, cherries, figs, and nuts. Scented sandwiches employed roses, violets, and nasturtiums. Her general sandwich section included unusual ones calling for caviar, foie gras, and curry.

By the end of the nineteenth century, salads and sandwiches had become closely associated. This connection was noted in many cookbooks, including Janet MacKenzie Hill's *Salads, Sandwiches, and Chafing Dish Dainties* (1898) and Marion H. Neil's *Salads, Sandwiches, and Chafing Dish Recipes* (1916). Many salads, among them those for chicken, egg, and lobster, became sandwich fillings.

Sandwich diversity dramatically expanded during the early twentieth century. May E. Southworth's *One Hundred and One Sandwiches* was published in 1906. Eva Greene Fuller's *Up-to-Date Sandwich Book* published four hundred sandwich recipes in 1909. She updated her book in 1927, adding 155 sandwich recipes. The following year Florence A. Cowles published *Seven Hundred Sandwiches*; when she updated her book in 1936, it included one thousand recipes.

Sandwich Condiments

From the earliest sandwich recipes, condiments and fillings were listed as ingredients. The most common early sandwich flavoring was butter. Other early fillings and condiments included shredded and leaf lettuce, watercress, ketchup, mustard, and curry powder, as well as a variety of sliced and minced pickles. Homemade mayonnaise appeared as an ingredient by the late nineteenth century, but it did not replace butter until commercial mayonnaise was manufactured during the early twentieth century. Other common sandwich condiments included spices, chopped and sliced onions, mushrooms, chilies, tomatoes, salad dressings, and many types of relishes.

Hot Sandwiches

Until the early twentieth century most sandwiches were served cold. Sandwiches were usually served in the home on thin slices of bread that could not easily contain the juices from hot meat or sausage. The solution was simple: use rolls or buns, but these were not considered delicate enough to be consumed easily in polite company. Before they ever appeared in homes or cookbooks, virtually all large and hot sandwiches were first sold by vendors or delicatessens. While hot sandwiches were most likely sold by the mid-nineteenth century, the first located record of a hot sandwich recipe (Hot Broiled Ham Sandwiches) appeared in Bradley's previously mentioned *Beverages and Sandwiches* cookbook (1893). This innovation was followed by the appearance of toasted or fried sandwiches, such as the ever-popular toasted cheese sandwich.

Sausages and ground meat were another matter. Early-nineteenth-century cookbooks recommended sausages as sandwich fillings. In these recipes, cold sausages were sliced and placed between two pieces of bread. Hot sausages were sold with bread by vendors by the mid-nineteenth century, but frankfurter sandwiches did not commonly appear in cookbooks until the 1920s. The first located mention of the hamburger sandwich occurs in 1904, but, like the hot dog, predecessor recipes to the hamburger sandwich began appearing in the 1870s. For instance, several cookbooks included recipes for finely chopped raw beef on toast or bread. Others recommended that cooked chopped beef be served cold as a sandwich spread. The first located recipe for a hot ground beef sandwich was published in Helen Cramp's *The Institute Cook Book* (1913), but such recipes were not common in American cookbooks until the 1930s. Other hot or large sandwiches, such as grinders, po'boys, Philadelphia cheesesteaks, sloppy joes, and submarine sandwiches, were created by vendors about this time.

Sandwich Revolutions

Several major changes revolutionized sandwich making in America. The first was the removal of the germ in the bread. Rancidity in bread was caused mainly by lipids in the wheat germ. Without the germ, bread stayed fresh-tasting longer. The second was the use of chemical leavening agents, which greatly reduced the time necessary to make bread, as well as the introduction of chemical preservatives that prevented commercial bread from turning stale quickly. The invention of the continuous conveyor oven also made possible the production of bread at a faster pace. Finally, Gustav Papendick invented a process for slicing and wrapping bread in the late 1920s. That each of these changes reduced the taste and nutritional quality of bread was less important than the mass production and national distribution of low-cost bread, rolls, and buns the changes facilitated.

Perhaps the greatest impact of these changes was felt by America's youth and the nation's working class. Sandwiches had been recommended for school lunches as early as 1884. The relationship between children and sandwiches was cemented with the production of commercial sliced bread. Sliced bread meant that young children could make sandwiches themselves without needing to use potentially dangerous knives for cutting through bread loaves. As a consequence of lowered costs, new ease of assembling, and infinite potential variety, sandwiches became one of the top luncheon foods consumed by the nation's working class beginning in the early 1900s. Brought in lunch bags to work or bought in company cafeterias, from street vendors, or at fast food establishments, sandwiches remain one of America's favorite lunch foods in the twenty-first century.

Irena Chalmers and Milton Glaser's *Great American Food Almanac* (1986) estimated that the average American student consumed fifteen hundred peanut butter and jelly sandwiches before high school graduation. They estimated that Americans ate approximately 45 billion sandwiches every year, which averaged out to 193 sandwiches per person. In 2002, this had increased to an estimated 198 sandwiches per American. Through the American military and American fast food establishments, the Anglo-American sandwich went global during the second part of the twentieth century. Sandwiches in the twenty-first century are consumed in some form in almost every country in the world.

[*See also* Bread, Sliced; Club Sandwich; Dagwood
Sandwich; Denver Sandwich; Grinders; Gyro;
Hamburger; Hoagie; Hot Brown Sandwich; Hot Dogs;
Italian Sausage Sandwich with Peppers and Onions;
Monte Cristo Sandwich; Muffaletta Sandwich; Oyster
Loaf Sandwich; Philadelphia Cheesesteak Sandwich;
Pimiento Cheese Sandwich; Po'boy Sandwich; Ranhofer,
Charles; Reuben Sandwich; Rorer, Sarah Tyson;
Sandwich Trucks; Street Vendors; Waxed Paper; Wraps.]

BIBLIOGRAPHY

*Beverages and Sandwiches for Your Husband's Friends by One Who
Knows*. New York: Brentano's, 1893.

Brobeck, Florence. *The Lunch Box in Every Kind of Sandwich*.
New York: Barrows, 1946.

Cowles, Florence A. *1001 Sandwiches*. Boston: Little, Brown, 1936.

Cowles, Florence A. *Seven Hundred Sandwiches*. Boston: Little,
Brown, 1928.

DeGouy, Louis P. *Sandwich Manual for Professionals*. New York:
Derrydale Press, 1939.

Fuller, Eva Greene. *The Up-to-Date Sandwich Book, 400 Ways to
Make a Sandwich*. Chicago: McClurg, 1909.

Fuller, Eva Greene. *The Up-to-Date Sandwich Book, 555 Ways to
Make a Sandwich*. Chicago: McClurg, 1927.

Hill, Janet M. *Salads, Sandwiches, and Chafing Dish Dainties*.
Boston: Little, Brown, 1899.

Marton, Reneé. "Say 'Cheese!' How the Grilled Cheese Sandwich
Evolved in American Culinary History." *ASFS: Association for
the Study of Food and Society* 15 (Fall 2002): 5–8.

*Recipes from the Sandwiches Please: Sandwich Ideas for Every
Occasion*. Chicago: Wheat Flour Institute, 1961.

Rorer, S[arah] T[yson]. *Sandwiches*. Philadelphia: Arnold, 1894.

Shircliffe, Arnold. *The Edgewater Sandwich Book*. Chicago: Willy,
1930.

Southworth, May E. *One Hundred and One Sandwiches*. Rev. ed.
San Francisco: Elder, 1906.

ANDREW F. SMITH

Sandwich Trucks

Sandwich trucks are a type of catering truck, or mobile
food unit, and are referred to in the industry as mobile
industrial caterers. They are designed to cover a route
and sell lunch to people working at construction sites,
industrial parks, or other areas without many food
options nearby.

The idea of taking lunches to where the workers were
employed arose in the early twentieth century, when people began to travel to work in centralized locations, such
as factories, and were unable to go back to their homes to
eat lunch. Local food companies began packing box
lunches in commissary kitchens. These boxes contained
all-inclusive meals that typically included a sandwich,
piece of fruit, cold beverage, dessert, and stick of gum.

The food companies would send workers out to take these
lunches to factories and work sites and have them wait
outside for the noon bell to ring. The factory hands would
come out and purchase box lunches from them.

By the 1940s, the food companies began refining the
process by delivering lunches in holding boxes that had
hot charcoal on the bottom so that hot sandwiches could
be served. Thermoses were used to provide hot coffee.
Eventually the food companies found that selling lunches
from trucks was more convenient than selling them from
holding boxes. This was how the sandwich truck evolved.

The California truck, or cold truck, became popular in
the 1950s. It originated in California and is basically a
pickup truck with a stainless steel body. Its primary purpose is to serve pre-wrapped sandwiches and simple foods,
like hot dogs, that can be prepared on a steam table.
Throughout the years, mobile catering trucks have been
constantly refined and updated. In addition to cold trucks,
there are hot trucks, which are kitchens on wheels that
contain everything from coffee urns to ovens and grills.

According to the Executive Director of the Mobile
Industrial Caterers Association (MICA), sandwich trucks
offer "everything you can imagine" in the way of food
choices. The most popular items are sandwiches, chips,
candy, and soda. Most sandwiches are premanufactured
by specialized companies such as Landshire, Bridgeford,
and White Castle. However, some trucks are equipped to
prepare and sell foods on the spot. These items might
range from grilled cheese and burgers to very popular
Mexican food products.

All mobile food units must be assigned to certified
kitchens or wholesale supermarkets called commissaries.
The trucks are cleaned, stocked, and stored there
overnight. Most of the food for sale on the truck is purchased at the commissary. Individual states have their
own regulations, usually guided by the Department of
Health Services. California, for example, has very strict
rules regarding the purchase of food for trucks, requiring
that it all be obtained from an approved vendor, facility,
or commissary.

The ways of bringing meals to workers have evolved
through the years. The type of truck and the variety of
food choices available may have changed with the times,
but sandwich trucks have remained a mainstay for
employees in need of convenient food choices at
lunchtime.

[*See also* Fast Food; Street Vendors; Take-Out Foods;
White Castle.]

BIBLIOGRAPHY

Custom Mobile Food Equipment. http://customsalesandservice. com. Homepage for the Custom Mobile Food Equipment Company that makes various mobile food equipment products.

Mobile Industrial Caterers Association–International. http:// mobilecaterers.com. Homepage for the Mobile Industrial Caterers Association, which represents food-service professionals who are anxious to improve mobile catering operations.

COLLEEN JOYCE PONTES

Sangria

Sangaree—from the Spanish word *sangría,* which literally means "bloody"—was a common drink in the colonial period of American history, continuing in popularity through the late nineteenth century. It was a punch made of sweetened, diluted red wine spiced with nutmeg. Americans most likely acquired the drink from the Caribbean, where it had been made since at least the late seventeenth century. In North America, sangaree was served either cold or hot, depending on the season. It largely disappeared in the United States during the early twentieth century.

In the twentieth century, sangria became the national iced drink of Spain, and it remained popular in the Caribbean, where American tourists sipped the cool beverage in the tropical heat. During the late 1940s, sangria reemerged in the United States, where it was consumed by Hispanic Americans and was served in Spanish restaurants. In 1964, it captured the attention of other Americans when it was featured at the Spanish pavilion at the New York World's Fair. Sangria's popularity soared in America during the following decade and Yago Sant'Gria, a commercial type of sangria, was imported from Spain in the 1970s.

Sangria is traditionally made with a full-bodied red wine (such as a Spanish Rioja), sweetened with a little sugar, and flavored with orange juice. Sliced lemons and oranges are added and left to macerate in the wine. Still or sparkling water and ice are added when the sangria is served. White sangria is an innovation made using white wine. Some American recipes replace the sparkling water with a lemon-lime soft drink and increase the sugar, thus creating a sweet, bubbly, alcoholic beverage. Americans have also served sangria with a vast array of other fruit (apples, cherries, mangoes, or peaches, for instance), and occasionally brandy is added. Sangria's popularity was most likely the inspiration for the commercial wine coolers, made of white wine and fruit juice, that came on the market in the early 1980s.

ANDREW F. SMITH

Sara Lee Corporation

Sara Lee Corporation is one of the world's largest manufacturers and packagers of branded (as opposed to private-label) goods. Operating in some two hundred countries, its product lines include clothing, household products, and foods—its core business. Sara Lee's corporate history is an example of how aggressive acquisition, combined with technological innovations and keen marketing strategies, succeeded in the new post–World War II global economy.

Sara Lee bears the name of its most celebrated bakery division. Founded in 1950 by Charles Lubin and Arthur Gordon, Lubin's brother-in-law, the Kitchen of Sara Lee was a wholesale baker of high-quality products, such as its celebrated All Butter Pound Cake and All Butter Pecan Coffee Cake, introduced in 1952. Sara Lee, herself, was Lubin's only daughter, who had earlier given her name to either a fruitcake or a cheesecake. As the business expanded in the Chicago area, Lubin realized that frozen products could extend the company's reach. Together with Ekco, a housewares manufacturer, Sara Lee developed the first aluminum foil packages with laminated lids, as well as new formulas for frozen products to go inside them in 1954. Products were shipped nationwide.

This success attracted Nathan Cummings, president of Consolidated Foods. A Canadian, Cummings had built various businesses and in 1939 entered the U.S. market by purchasing a food distribution company in Baltimore, Maryland. Soon other companies were added, including the packager of the well-known Richelieu brand, as Cummings developed an ongoing corporate philosophy— expansion through acquisition both at home and abroad. At one time, Consolidated owned Piggly Wiggly and Eagle supermarkets, long since divested under Federal Trade Commission orders. In the middle 1960s Consolidated began to purchase nonfood companies, and by 1975 about two-thirds of company profits came from these entities.

In 1956 Sara Lee was brought in, with Lubin remaining as president until his retirement in 1965. In 1965 Sara Lee built the largest and most modern baking facility in the country in Deerfield, Illinois (closed in 1990). To go with the increased production and growth in retail and institutional sales, the company hired Mitch Leigh, composer of the hit Broadway show *Man of la Mancha*, to write a new advertising jingle. The result became a part of American popular culture: "Nobody doesn't like Sara Lee."

With John H. Bryan's presidency beginning in 1975, Consolidated Foods saw a huge expansion of sales, a growing presence worldwide, and a new name. In 1985, after considerable market research, the company's name was changed to its most recognizable high-quality brand, Sara Lee Corporation. Bryan came from Bryan Brothers Packing, of West Point, Mississippi, the Southeast's best-known meat packager. By judicious cutting and purchasing, Sara Lee became a profitable company, which, as the twenty-first century began, had never failed to pay shareholders a dividend. Nor should it be surprising that by the 1990s Sara Lee had become America's largest packaged-meat producer. Among its meat brands are Hillshire Farms, Ball Park, Jimmy Dean, Bryan, Kahns, State Fair, Rudy's Farm, Briar Street Market, Trail's Best, Galileo, and Bil Mar. Baked goods, however, remain critical to the company in the form of Sara Lee Bakery, International, Mr. Pita, Manhattan Deli (bagels), Wolferman's English Muffins, and Earthgrains, a newly acquired whole-grain bread company.

[*See also* Bakeries; Cakes; Freezers and Freezing; Meat.]

BIBLIOGRAPHY

Brinson, Carroll. *A Tradition of Looking Ahead: The Story of Bryan Foods*. Jackson, MS: Oakdale Press, 1986.
Gardner, Dorothy. "Lubin's Rolling in Dough." *Chicago American*, December 1, 1957.
Grant, Tina, ed. *The International Directory of Company Histories*. Vols. 15 et seq. Detroit, MI: St. James Press, 1996.
Knoch, Joanne. "Turning Out Sweets a Science at Sara Lee." *Chicago Tribune*, December 2, 1959.
Ramsey, Stewart. "Charles Lubin Knows Cakes—All Kinds of Them." *Chicago Sun-Times*, June 24, 1956.
Sara Lee Bakery Website. http://www.saraleebakery.com/history.shtml.

BRUCE KRAIG

Sarsaparilla

The word "sarsaparilla" may evoke images of languid belles and parched cowboys, but its etymology is decidedly less romantic. An Anglicization of *zarzaparilla*, it refers at once to various New World plant species of the genus *Smilax*, the roots of these vinelike plants, the extracts derived from the roots, the drinks flavored by the extracts—and the subjugation of American indigenes by the Spanish conquistadores who named it. The Spanish

deferred to the native populations, however, in their approach to the plant as a promising medical find (and as an antisyphilitic first and foremost). Meanwhile, their North American counterparts did the same.

In the nineteenth century, as a developing craze for restorative mineral waters slowly took its toll on the long-standing custom of home brewing, apothecaries in Philadelphia and elsewhere began to invent and dispense flavored soda waters that were, of course, the first soft drinks. Among them was sarsaparilla, which became a favorite at the pharmacy-cum-soda fountain not only as a soft drink in itself but also as an ingredient in root beer and ice cream sodas. (One creation myth among many links sarsaparilla to the world's first Black Cow.) Increasingly, however, flavors, such as sassafras, licorice, and wintergreen, were employed to soften the bitterness of sarsaparilla until all that was finally left was the name; and in the twentieth century that too disappeared, perhaps not coincidentally as the medical establishment began mounting challenges to sarsaparilla's therapeutic reputation.

[*See also* Homemade Remedies; Root Beer; Sassafrasses; Soda Drinks; Soda Fountains.]

BIBLIOGRAPHY

Funderburg, Anne Cooper. *Sundae Best: A History of Soda Fountains*. Bowling Green, OH: Bowling Green State University, 2002. Unusually scholarly for a pop-culture analysis of this sort, this book is exhaustively researched and minutely detailed.
Kiple, Kenneth F., and Kriemhild Coneè-Ornelas, eds. "History, Nutrition, and Health." In *The Cambridge World History of Food*. Vol. 2. Cambridge, U.K. Cambridge University Press, 2000. This section provides useful information, both tabular and textual, on the medical uses of roots, especially among indigenous populations.

RUTH TOBIAS

Sassafrasses

The sassafras tree (*Sassafras albidum*) is a New World tree. All parts of the tree are pleasantly aromatic, and its bark and roots can be steeped as a beverage and for medicinal purposes. Large leaves on a single branch of the sassafras tree appear in three different shapes. Sassafras was so prized for a time that it was used as a medium of exchange and offered to guests at weddings.

Before the Civil War, Native Americans and East Coast settlers made sassafras each spring by boiling new maple sugar sap, then adding sassafras roots and simmering for a time. The bark and roots contain the highest

Sassafras. From *Cyclopedia of Useful Knowledge*, 1890s. *Collection of Alice Ross*

concentration of oil. These are steeped to make a deep red sassafras tea given as a diuretic to treat sickness caused from drinking polluted water. It could also be used as a yellow-orange dye. In later years sassafras flavoring became a useful ingredient in the making of root beer and as a scent in perfumes and soaps.

The Choctaw of Louisiana's bayou country discovered that young sassafras leaves and stems, once dried and reduced to a powder, added rich flavor, as well as thickening, to Creole and Cajun dishes, especially as filé (FEE-lay) powder in gumbos. The filé must be added at the end of cooking to prevent it from becoming tough or stringy.

Sassafras oils have been found to contain a carcinogenic substance called safrole. The U.S. Food and Drug Administration has banned many forms of sassafras for human consumption.

[*See also* Food and Drug Administration; Homemade Remedies; Root Beer.]

BIBLIOGRAPHY

Clepper, Henry. "The Singular Sassafras: Fact, Folklore and Fantasy about This Unique Understory Tree with the Mitten Leaves." *American Forests* 95, no. 3–4 (April 1989): 33.

Peeples, Edwin A. "Native Sassafras." *Country Journal* 17, no. 1 (January–February 1990): 18.

MARTY MARTINDALE

Sauces and Gravies

The words "sauce" and "salt" share a common Latin root, suggesting the flavor-enhancing function of sauces. Whether sweet or savory, hot or cold, and spanning textures from brothy liquid through velvety emulsion to chunky salsa, sauces are an "extra," a luxury that in the nineteenth century carried hints of sin and gluttony. Even with this delicious potential, American—like English—sauces historically suffered a poor reputation. An eighteenth-century French visitor allegedly sniped that England was a nation of many religions but only one sauce. Although the tale may be apocryphal, writers such as Sarah Josepha Hale in *The Good Housekeeper* (second edition, 1841) agreed that the "French have a much greater variety of gravies than the English or Americans, who copy the English mode of cookery. Melted butter is with us the gravy for most meats."

Historical Definitions of Sauce and Gravy

"Sauce" has had two seemingly disparate meanings in the American kitchen. Seventeenth- and eighteenth-century Americans used "sauce" to denote, first and consistent with modern usage, fluid embellishments for foods, and, second, garden fruits and vegetables, either raw or cooked. The unifying logic was that both accompany the main victuals. The receipt for pumpkin "sause," in *New England Rarities Discovered* (1672) by the English visitor John Josselyn called for gently cooking diced pumpkin without any liquid until it reached the consistency of "bak'd Apples." Flavored with butter, ginger, and a little vinegar, the dish sounds almost like the cranberry or apple sauces that are considered relishes in later times. This "sauce" was a substantial side dish in the eighteenth century. Popular through the nineteenth century were vegetable sauces in which cooked vegetables, such as mushrooms, chopped onions, celery (some recipes called for pieces as large as one inch), and asparagus tips, were added to a thickened butter or cream base and served with specified meats. Occasionally seen after the eighteenth century, these recipes were linked to the archaic meaning of "sauce."

In the sixteenth century, "gravy" meant simply the natural juices from roasted meat, either collected in a dripping pan during spit roasting or released during carving. By the eighteenth century the meaning of "gravy" had expanded to reflect the increasing, and sometimes begrudged, influence of the French kitchen, which relied on stocks for many dishes. Two basic techniques for making gravies appeared in English sources and hence found their way to America in works such as *The Art of Cookery Made Plain and Easy* (first English edition, 1747; first American edition, 1805) by Hannah Glasse. The more expensive technique extracted a rich gravy from browned meat that was sealed in a pot with aromatics and a bit of water and then gently stewed. The other, lighter gravy, sometimes called "white gravy," was the broth by-product of boiling meat or poultry in water. Both gravies could be thickened for service or briefly kept as a pantry ingredient, depending on the season, in the days before refrigeration.

In more recent times, "gravy" denotes a limited range of finished sauces. They are usually made from flour-bound meat juices and incorporate the fatty drippings left in the roasting pan. Quirky variations include unctuous "cream gravy" and "white gravy." Cream gravy is used with fried chicken and steak and is made by mixing left-over frying fat with flour and water. "White gravy" is the label given to certain fricassees, which are particularly popular in the South. Italian American "spaghetti gravy" refers to tomato sauce with ground meat.

Sauces through the Mid-Nineteenth Century

Seventeenth-century colonists continued the late medieval sauce tradition of thickening broth, wine, vinegar, and fruit juices with bread crumbs. Often seasoned with dried fruits and spices, such as cloves, saffron, nutmeg, and cinnamon, many seventeenth-century sauces were sweet, tart, and piquant. In the New World, sauces had to be adapted to available ingredients, cooking equipment, and the immigrant's pocketbook. As cooking styles were changing in seventeenth- and eighteenth-century Europe to incorporate more butter and cream, the colonies learned of these developments through imported cookbooks, new waves of immigrants, and extended trips to Europe for educating the children of the wealthy.

By the end of the seventeenth century, dairy products were becoming plentiful, starting in more northern colonies. Even in Dutch and German communities, where sweet and sour flavors lingered, many sauces incorporated butter, milk, or cream by the early nineteenth century. The pinnacle of butter and cream sauces, however, was found in English-influenced kitchens. The signature American sauce through the mid-nineteenth century was "drawn" or "melted" butter, composed of a spoonful of water, a dusting of flour, and copious amounts of butter gently melted and swirled into an emulsion. Variations were made by adding herbs, capers, chopped cooked eggs, shellfish, and

Making a Sauce. Making a sauce at the Institute of Culinary Education, New York. *Courtesy of the Institute of Culinary Education*

other flavorings. *The Virginia House-wife* (1824) by Mary Randolph contained the archetypical American receipt (earlier versions are found in English works brought to or printed in America) and reflects Randolph's exasperation with sloppy kitchen technique. Randolph chided inattentive cooks who overheated the butter, causing it "to oil." Frequent, unappetizing descriptions of sauces "composed of little else than liquid grease" confirmed Randolph's lament that no sauce is "so generally done badly."

Table Sauces

Not all sauces came finished from the kitchen in a sauceboat. From the eighteenth century, Americans (who shared this trait with the English) mixed sauces to their taste at table from an assortment of pots, cruets, and casters that were the housewife's pride. The well-stocked table boasted a number of "store sauces" that could be added at table by diners to please their individual palates. Although a few store sauces might have been commercially made (and thus "store-bought"), the term referred to sauces with long shelf lives that were part of the larder. Cookery books through the early twentieth century offered many recipes for homemade ketchup, mustard, chutney, worcestershire sauce, and flavored vinegar, which could add zing to a dish. In her *Domestic Receipt-Book* (1858) Catharine Beecher explained, "*Soy* is a fashionable sauce for fish, which is mixed on the plate with drawn butter." The soy Beecher described was not the true Asian product but rather a homemade concoction of caramelized sugar, salt, anchovies, and flavorings. Beecher's schematic of a properly set table showed a set of casters that would hold such seasonings, including the celery-flavored vinegar that Beecher wrote "is fine to keep in the castor stand." Other authorities loathed the omnipresent casters on the grounds that they destroyed flavor, because spices quickly staled and olive oil turned rancid in the poorly sealed table ornaments. Casters had largely fallen from fashion by the early twentieth century, although commercial "steak sauces," such as A1 Steak Sauce, worcestershire sauce, and ketchup are commonly used.

Table-side cookery (vestiges can still be found in restaurants offering steak diane and crêpe suzette) involved another branch of sauce making. A hostess escaping a hot kitchen in the summer months or a maître d'hôtel with a flair for showmanship could concoct a quick sauce in a chafing dish to season meats. A recipe for sherry sauce for beef steak in *House and Home* (1889) by Marion Harland was typical. The sauce descended from the table sauces of the previous generation in that melted butter was combined with sherry, lemon juice, and catsup and poured over thin slices of seared steak.

The French Influence in Domestic and Professional Kitchens

Direct French influences on American cooking date from Huguenot settlements in the late seventeenth century. Except at rarified tables—such as that of Thomas Jefferson, who had French-trained cooks, or the handful of wealthy urban or plantation households that had cooks skilled enough to use *The French Cook* (1828) by Louis Eustache Ude or *Domestic French Cookery* (1832) by Eliza Leslie—French sauces seemed beyond the ken of Americans. Most cooks accepted the conclusion of eighteenth-century English cookery writers that French cooking was too extravagant for the home, and Menon's best-selling *La cuisinière bourgeoise* (first edition, 1746), although known in the colonies, was seldom cited. According to Sarah Rutledge in *The Carolina Housewife* (1847), the available French (and French-influenced English) cookbooks were designed for foreign servants "and almost always require an apparatus either beyond our reach or too complicated for our native cooks."

One reason for this daunting reputation is that many French sauces require patience and an ever-bubbling stockpot. Although the sauces are not difficult to prepare, hours of simmering, skimming, reducing, and straining are needed. These time-consuming refinements were mentioned relatively infrequently in early American cookbooks. The "housewives" cookery books of the first half of the nineteenth century often eschewed the preparation of meat stocks as a "superfluous waste." In *The Kentucky Housewife* (1839), Lettice Bryan disapproved of the "practice of some cooks to fry pieces of coarse meat for the purpose of making brown gravies" and urged cooks "to avoid expense and trouble" by storing the "white gravy" from boiled meats for her few recipes requiring meat gravy as an ingredient. Bryan's barebones sauce cookery undoubtedly appealed to overworked frontier housewives.

Different styles prevailed in fashionable urban restaurants and affluent homes, where the upwardly mobile expected French cookery by the latter nineteenth century. Two expatriate Frenchmen living in New York, Pierre Blot

---

CHARLES RANHOFER'S BREAD SAUCE RECIPE FROM *THE EPICUREAN* (1893)

American.—Put into a saucepan one ounce of butter with one ounce of finely chopped onions, fry them lightly without coloring and moisten with a pint of boiling milk, add two ounces of bread-crumbs, salt, cayenne pepper and cloves, and when just ready to serve, add a little cream to finish.

English is made exactly the same way, only replacing the fried onions by a raw onion cut in four, and whole peppers instead of cayenne. [Presumably these are strained out before serving. Ed.]

French.—Chop up a shallot and a quarter of a clove of garlic, putting them in a saucepan with two gills of white wine; let simmer and reduce, adding two tablespoonfuls of very fine bread-crumbs, a little fresh butter, a dash of mignonette [pepper] and grated nutmeg and two gills of broth, let reduce to half, then squeeze in some lemon juice and a teaspoonful of chopped parsley.

Fried German.—Melt and heat gradually a half a pound of butter so as to obtain a hazel-nut butter, incorporate into it three ounces of white bread-crumbs, cook it over a slow fire for a few minutes without ceasing to stir, salt it lightly and take off the fire to pour into a hot sauce boat.

and Charles Ranhofer, wrote cookbooks touting extensive sauce repertoires. Blot was the founder of the New York Cooking Academy, and his *Hand-book of Practical Cookery* (1869) was aimed at cost-conscious bourgeois households with a modestly skilled cook. Although the cookbook was not specifically French, many of the sauces had French names and were more complex than most that had theretofore appeared in America. Giving dozens of meticulously detailed recipes, Blot chastised American cooks for failing to make stocks and good quality sauces "through carelessness or prejudice." Blot tilted at the chauvinistic sentiment that America's abundant, high-quality raw ingredients afforded its cooks the luxury of indifferent preparation.

Even more sophisticated was Ranhofer's *The Epicurean* (1893), which contained more than 250 sauce recipes with variations taken directly from the best examples of French haute cuisine. Acknowledging his debt to his contemporary, the French master chef Felix Urbain Dubois, Ranhofer used highly concentrated meat essences and lavishly incorporated truffles and other rare, imported ingredients in his sauces. *The Epicurean* was a bible for classic sauce making in restaurants and wealthy homes with trained chefs.

The Twentieth Century

Several cookery books devoted to sauces, including *One Hundred and One Sauces* (1906) by May E. Southworth, *The Book of Sauces* (1915) by C. Herman Senn, and *Soups, Sauces and Gravies* (1939) by Cora, Rose, and Bob Brown continued efforts to translate "fancy" French sauces into the American vernacular. Only one sauce met with widespread acceptance: the roux-based white sauce, modeled on a debased béchamel, that had started as the darling of Fannie Farmer and the home economics movement. The most wretched form of white sauce surfaced in works such as *Good Meals and How to Prepare Them* (1927) by the Good Housekeeping Institute. Savory sauces were formularized in a chart for a "thin, medium or thick" white sauce made with milk, flour, and butter. With only a few seasoning variations, blandness reigned. In *A Book of Menus with Recipes* (1936), the cookbook author Della T. Lutes thought it no wonder that men cynically likened white sauce to "library paste gone wrong."

Housewives relied on convenience products entering the market. Fully finished sauces, under brand names such as Chef Boiardi, Escoffier, Heinz, and Maison Petitjean, eased cooking burdens for middle-class housewives, who increasingly were doing their own cooking because of the "servant problem" of the early twentieth century. The ever-practical Julia Child in *Mastering the Art of French Cooking* (1961) offered tricks for doctoring canned bouillon when the ambitious home cook did not have time to prepare stock from scratch.

Child, who gave recipes for French mother sauces such as béchamel, velouté, and hollandaise, placed certain sauces beyond the mid-twentieth-century American home cook. Child deliberately omitted a recipe for the traditional brown mother sauce, demi-glace, because it takes "several days to accomplish and the result is splendid, but as we are concerned with less formal cooking, we shall discuss it no further." Given Child's recipes for baguettes with three risings and beef stuffed with foie gras and truffles, this singular omission recalls the nineteenth-century bias against spending too much time making fancy sauces.

The 1970s and After

In the 1970s some sauces started to become lighter. There was a nouvelle cuisine rebellion against "library paste," and a search for lower-fat and lower-calorie sauces often turned to ethnic cuisines for inspiration. "Lightening" sauces did not necessarily mean simplifying their preparation or decreasing their richness. Some of the favorite sauces of nouvelle cuisine were based on time-consuming meat essences and rich melted butter. Intricate sauces intrigued home chefs who viewed cooking as recreation, and American nouvelle cuisine cookbooks included lengthy recipes for the demi-glace that Child had omitted. For cooks short on time, gourmet purveyors sold frozen demi-glace, which could be turned into a sophisticated French sauce with scant effort. This sauce differed from the finished commercial sauces of an earlier generation by providing a foundation for hobbyist cooks, who creatively finished the sauce.

Authors of "diet" cookbooks, a popular niche launched in the mid-1970s, have attempted to revolutionize classic sauce making by substituting lower-fat ingredients, such as farmer's cheese and vegetable puree, for the heavy cream in traditional recipes. These manipulations have frequently been disappointing. The most important addition to American sauce making in the late twentieth century was the broadening spectrum of ethnic influences in both restaurant and domestic kitchens. Reaching beyond urban areas with large immigrant populations to suburban and small-town markets, formerly exotic ingredients have become increasingly common, following each wave of culinary fashion promoted in cooking magazines. Home cooks assemble saucy Chinese stir-fries with hoisin sauce, raw Latin American salsa made with jalapeños, and uncooked pan-Asian dipping sauces redolent of cilantro, ginger, lime, and fermented fish sauce.

[*See also* Beecher, Catharine; Butter; Child, Julia; Cooking Techniques; Farmer, Fannie; French Influences on American Food; Good Housekeeping Institute; Italian American Food; Nouvelle Cuisine; Randolph, Mary; Ranhofer, Charles.]

BIBLIOGRAPHY

Carson, Jane. *Colonial Virginia Cookery*. Charlottesville: University of Virginia for Colonial Williamsburg, 1968. A helpful survey of eighteenth-century cookery as practiced in the English colonies.

Craigie, William A., and James R. Hulbert, eds. *Dictionary of American English on Historical Principles*. Chicago: University of Chicago Press, 1940.

Lehmann, Gilly. "The Rise of the Cream Sauce, 1660–1760." In *Milk: Beyond the Dairy—Proceedings of the 1999 Oxford Symposium on Food and Cookery*, edited by Harlan Walker. Devon, U.K.: Prospect, 2000. A good summary of the shift to dairy sauces in England that sets the context for the shift in the colonies and provides background for the well-to-do colonial kitchen.

Peterson, James. *Sauces*. New York: Van Nostrand Reinhold, 1991. A comprehensive award-winning guide to sauce cookery by a French-trained American chef. The book contains moderately helpful historical notes geared to the classic French kitchen. The recipes show late-twentieth-century modernizations of classic French sauces as well as some contemporary American influences. Useful bibliography and a good glossary for more arcane terminology.

Ranhofer, Charles. *The Epicurean*. New York: Dover Publications, 1971. The original edition was published in 1893. A self-styled Franco-American culinary encyclopedia by the late-nineteenth-century chef at New York City's preeminent restaurant. Many of the sauce recipes derive from the classic cuisine of chef Felix Urbain-Dubois (1818–1901) and show the influence of French haute cuisine at upper-echelon American restaurants.

Renggli, Seppi. *Four Seasons Spa Cuisine*. New York: Simon and Schuster, 1986. By the chef to New York's famous Four Seasons restaurant, the sauce recipes are some of the most extreme, diet-conscious experiments of the period.

Weaver, William Woys. "White Gravies in American Popular Diet." In *Food in Change: Eating Habits from the Middle Ages to the Present Day*, edited by Alexander Fenton and Eszter Kisbán. Atlantic Highlands, NJ: John Donald, 1986. An interesting analysis of dishes incorporating milk- and cream-based pan sauces and their evolution from the English to the American kitchen.

CATHY K. KAUFMAN

Sausage

Sausage was invented as an economical means of preserving and transforming into more palatable forms the less-desirable cuts of meat and components, such as blood and internal organs, that could not be consumed fresh at slaughter. The word "sausage" is derived from the Latin *salsisium*, from *salsus*, meaning "salted" or "preserved meat." Although the etymology indicates that sausage can be made from any kind of salted meat, the term traditionally applies to chopped pork stuffed into a casing.

The origin of sausage making is lost in history. Sausages probably resulted when early cultivators discovered that salt could preserve easily perishable surplus meat. Sausages were reportedly produced from pigs as long ago as 5000 B.C.E. in Egypt and the Far East. One of the earliest documentations of sausage making and consumption is Homer's *Odyssey* (800 B.C.E.). Consumed by the Romans but outlawed by Constantine the Great and forbidden by the early Christian Church because of an association with many pagan festivals, sausages became highly sought after and even gave rise to a black market for distribution.

The history of sausages in the United States is a history of the immigrants who introduced them. American sausages reflect Old World traditions adapted to the prevailing climatic conditions and locally available ingredients. The simple process of salting, smoking, and drying meats to preserve what could not be consumed immediately has evolved into a modern process providing Americans with hundreds of sausage varieties, more than anywhere else in the world.

Early sausage-making directions were clear. "Sausage skins"—the intestines, uterus, stomach, or bladder preserved at butchering time—were used to encase the "stuffing"—meat, scraps, and chopped organs mixed with herbs, seasonings, and fat. The sausages were dried or smoked, and the resulting links were suspended from iron hooks over a fire.

Advances in microbiology and processing technology have transformed the art of sausage making into a precise science. Refrigeration allows flexible production schedules and ingredient choices. Processing innovation and novel ingredient technologies contributed to improvements in both high-speed, large-scale production and small batch-type operations. Modern mass production transforms prime cuts of meat, along with less tender cuts, into delicious sausages that contain seasonings, other ingredients, and extra preservatives, such as sodium metabisulfite and ascorbyl palmitate.

Sausages traditionally are classified as fresh, cured, or heat processed. Fresh sausages are intended for immediate cooking. Cured and heat-processed sausages may be kept and eaten cold or heated before consumption. Because of

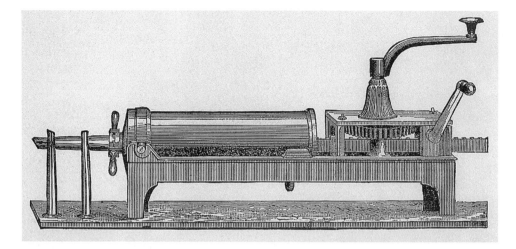

Sausage Stuffer. John Wagner stuffer. From the McArthur, Wirth catalog of equipment for butchers, packers, and sausage makers, 1900.

their convenience and versatility, heat-processed sausages are particularly popular among Americans.

Fresh sausages are made by seasoning and, usually but not always, stuffing into a casing fresh meats, which are not cured, smoked, fermented, or cooked. These products, such as fresh Italian sausages, require refrigerated storage and cooking before consumption. Cured sausages, primarily salami, cervelat, and pepperoni, are made from cured meats that are not heat processed but may be smoked. Also known as summer sausages, these products are classified as semidry or dry, depending on the extent of drying. Characteristically tangy from fermentation, these products are generally stored at room temperature and can be refrigerated for extended shelf life. Heat-processed sausages are further classified as precooked, emulsion type, or cooked. Precooked sausages include knockwurst and some types of bologna. The nonfermented stuffing is cured (brined) and heat treated for reduction of moisture for better keeping quality. These sausages may be eaten as such or further cooked. Emulsion-type sausages, such as wieners and frankfurters, are products of cured meats homogenized with fat, water, and seasonings. These sausages may be pasteurized and may be eaten as such or scalded before consumption. Cooked sausages are ready-to-serve products, prepared from fresh meats that may sometimes be cured or smoked and cooked after stuffing. Some cooked sausages, such as liverwurst and knockwurst, are not stuffed into casings but are molded and therefore are not always considered sausages. In the United States sausages also are classified by primary ingredient—pork, beef, chicken, turkey, or veal. Pork sausage was predominant because beef was more expensive. Beef and veal sausages, introduced when beef became plentiful at low prices, are not as common elsewhere in the world as they are in the United States.

The introduction of mass manufacturing led to inexpensive production of sausages. Small sausage manufacturers, facing immense competition from industry titans, resorted to distinguishing their sausages from mass-manufactured products as a way of maintaining or increasing market share. The small manufacturers added poultry meats to sausages and marketed the products as tasty and more healthful versions of traditional sausage products. When American consumers embraced turkey as a part of a healthful diet, sausage manufacturers introduced turkey sausages. Artisanal sausages abound, incorporating chicken and other exotic game and fowl. Dehydration technologies allowed for the addition of dried fruits and vegetables to produce uniquely American sausages with unprecedented variety and texture. Around 1990 vegetarian imitations appeared. Made of soybeans and textured vegetable protein, these sausages were fashioned to mimic the original product in taste and texture. Americans, aware of the health benefits of soybeans, welcomed soy sausages.

Sausages are usually bought already prepared. Although specialty sausages, such as andouille, blood sausage, bockbier sausage, bratwurst, chorizo, head cheese, kielbasa, knockwurst, and mortadella, are available in the United States, Americans have consumed more than 20 billion hot dogs in recent years. Alternating between decadent and healthful foods, Americans consume sausages as part of meals and as snacks and have even created a similar product, called "Snausages," for

Sausage Stand. *Culinary Archives & Museum at Johnson & Wales University, Providence, R.I.*

their dogs. The sausage in one form or another is a staple in the average American diet.

[*See also* Chorizo; Hot Dogs; Meat; Pepperoni; Salami; Salt and Salting; Vienna Sausage.]

BIBLIOGRAPHY

Dowell, Philip, and Adrian Bailey. *Cook's Ingredients.* New York: Morrow, 1980.

Kinsella, John, and David Harvey. *Professional Charcuterie.* New York: Wiley, 1996.

Montagné, Prosper. *Larousse Gastronomique.* Translated by Nina Froud, Patience Gray, Maud Murdoch, and Barbara Macrae Taylor. New York: Crown, 1961.

Toussant-Samat, Maguelonne. *History of Food.* Translated by Anthea Bell. New York: Barnes and Noble, 1998.

KANTHA SHELKE

Sazerac

The Sazerac is a whiskey-and-bitters drink in the tradition of the earliest cocktails. In the early nineteenth century, the owner of a New Orleans apothecary, Antoine Amédée Peychaud, developed a product called Peychaud's Bitters. He mixed it with cognac and enjoyed serving it to his friends. Sewell Taylor, who owned the Sazerac Coffeehouse, put the drink on the map by mixing it with a popular cognac named Sazerac de Forge et Fils and serving Peychaud's concoction as his house cocktail, calling it the Sazerac.

In 1870 Thomas Handy bought the coffeehouse and the rights to Peychaud's Bitters. He changed the recipe of the Sazerac to appeal to the rye whiskey–drinking crowd of the day. The Sazerac recipe of the mid-nineteenth century was a more complex affair, with many layers of

flavor. The serving glass was seasoned with a splash of absinthe, an anise-based spirit, and then the rye whiskey was dashed with bitters and slightly sweetened with sugar.

Handy began to purchase the rights to other spirit brands and market them. Eventually an employee of Handy's, C. J. O'Reilly, created the company known in the early 2000s as the Sazerac Company, Inc.

[*See also* Cocktails; Whiskey.]

BIBLIOGRAPHY

The Sazerac Company, New Orleans, LA. http://www.sazerac.com.

DALE DEGROFF

Scandinavian and Finnish American Food

Scandinavian food has the reputation of being simple, hearty, and somewhat colorless, with a "meat and potatoes" stereotype. Most of the immigrants to America came from a rural rather than a cosmopolitan background and became farmers and laborers, who were not inclined to become restaurateurs. This is why there are not many Scandinavian restaurants in the United States. The best Scandinavian food has always been found in the home kitchen. It was the woman's job to feed hungry laborers on farms and in logging and mining camps.

Between 1830 and 1930, 2.5 million people emigrated from the Nordic countries to North America. Although the emigrants made up a very small part of the total European emigration, the number amounted to one-third of the total population of the five countries— Iceland, Sweden, Norway, Denmark, and Finland. (Although Finns are technically not Scandinavians, their food and culture are very similar to those of Sweden, Norway, and Denmark. Eastern Finnish food, however, bears resemblance to Russian, particularly the fish and meat pies.) This large-scale emigration was driven by famines in Scandinavia and the dwindling of family farms, which had been traditionally passed down from one generation to another and divided among the sons of the family until they were too small. Those who left their homeland were attracted to the upper Midwest by the offer of free land.

Settling in America

The more to the north the emigrants had originally come from, the more to the north they tended to settle in America. Icelanders settled in Canada, with a few in northern Minnesota. Finns mostly settled in the north and became small farmers, loggers, and miners in Michigan, Minnesota, and Ontario. They retained their heritage, including food traditions and language, longer than did most other Scandinavians.

Swedish settlers were numerous in Minnesota, Illinois, New York, Massachusetts, Washington, and the Canadian prairies. Norwegians settled the prairies to the west and the south and are known for growing high-quality wheat, potatoes, and other grains in the rich soils of the Red River Valley of Minnesota and the Dakotas. This became the foundation of the milling industry that grew in Minneapolis and Saint Paul. At the same time, the Danes were spread in small groups over larger areas in Wisconsin, Iowa, Nebraska, Kansas, and California. Danes were dairy farmers and important in the dairy industry in Wisconsin, southern Minnesota, and Iowa.

Contributions to Cuisine

Finnish women, who trained in home economics schools before emigrating, commonly worked as cooks and maids

Scandinavian Feast. Outdoor festival near Madison, Wisconsin, 1870s. *State Historical Society of Wisconsin*

until they married. They were aided by a bilingual cookbook, *Mina Wallin Keitokirja*, published in New York in the early 1900s in both Finnish and English. The book includes recipes for classic European preparations, from soups to desserts, few of which were common fare in Finland.

The Finns and the Cornish worked together as miners in northern Minnesota and the Upper Peninsula of Michigan. They found common ground in the "pasty," an oval-shaped pie filled with a mixture of beef, potatoes, onions, and sometimes rutabaga, turnips, or carrots, which they carried in their lunch boxes into the mines. The Finns have claimed pasties as their own because of their similarity to the meat pies traditional in eastern Finland. In the twenty-first century pasties are still sold in bakeries throughout the Iron Range of Minnesota and the Upper Peninsula of Michigan. They make great picnic food, and every baker has a personal variation.

The Swedish "smorgasbord" has come to mean a buffet consisting of a variety of foods both simple and elaborate. The American version, however, bears little resemblance to the authentic Scandinavian table. In Sweden and all of Scandinavia "smorgasbord" (or *koldt bord* in Danish, Norwegian, and Icelandic and *voilepapoyta* in Finnish) refers to a bread and butter table. The smorgasbord meal follows a definite pattern. It starts with cold meats, fish, and salads and ends with hot foods. Smorgasbord is served in several courses, and guests never pile their plates high, as is commonly done in America.

Swedish meatballs are often found on the smorgasbord and have become a popular appetizer item on American menus. Authentically they are made of a blend of ground beef, pork, and veal with onions, bread, egg, and seasonings. The mixture is formed into small, one-half-inch balls and sautéed in butter. They are served in a pale brown cream sauce made by combining the pan drippings with cream or milk.

Danes contributed Danish pastry, a yeast pastry that is rolled out and layered with butter in a fashion similar to puff pastry. Known simply as "Danish," they contain a variety of fillings, such as fruit, cream cheese, almond paste, and nuts. In Denmark this pastry is known as "Viennabread."

Norwegian contributions to the cuisine of America are not widely known. *Lefse*, a flatbread that is cooked on a dry griddle, comes from an area in Norway that is small but significant because of the large number of people that emigrated from there. Lutefisk, another contribution of

FINNISH PULLA

For many people of Finnish descent, Christmas is announced by the heady aroma of a cardamom-flavored coffee bread known as *pulla* (boo-la) or *nisu* (nish-oo). Cardamom, which provides most of the festive scent, is the seed that grows on pod-bearing plants of the ginger family in India, where its sweet pungency is favored in curries. (Finns, however, are fond of cardamom in their pastries.) The pods contain black-brown seeds that lose flavor quickly once ground, so seeds need to be ground just before using.

Pulla is made of tender, fragrant dough that is rolled into long strips, then braided and baked. Dry yeast is dissolved in scalded milk that has cooled to lukewarm. Sugar, flour, butter, eggs, salt, and freshly ground cardamom seeds are added. The dough is kneaded and allowed to rise twice. Then it is rolled into thin strands, braided, and allowed to rise once more on a cookie sheet before it is baked. Most bakers use an egg wash before putting pulla in the oven, but some brush the tops of the yeasty braids with creamed coffee, then sprinkle sugar over them, and bake them in the oven until golden brown.

MARIAN BETANCOURT

Norwegians, is also known but in a more limited way by Swedes, Danes, and Finns. Lutefisk translates as "lye fish" and is an air-dried cod, so dehydrated that it resembles a thin slice of firewood. It can be kept without refrigeration until it is ready to be reconstituted. The dried cod is soaked first in a solution of lye and water to open the pores. Then the fish is soaked in fresh water for several days until it is reconstituted into a partially gelatinous consistency. Originally lutefisk (*lutfisk* in Swedish and *lipeakala* in Finnish) was the food of poor people and was eaten throughout the winter. Immigrants brought with them supplies of the dried cod. Because it takes so many days of preparation, the precious store became a special Christmas dish. American fish companies, especially in the upper Midwest, import tons of dried cod from Norway, largely during the holiday season.

Baking is an important part of the Scandinavian kitchen. Crispbreads, flatbreads, spiced coffee breads, cakes, and cookies are universal among Swedes, Norwegians, Danes, Icelanders, and Finns. Butter, sugar, flour, and eggs are the basic ingredients. Swedes and Finns bake saffron-flavored Lucia bread and the spicy *Pepparkakor* cookies for St. Lucia's Day celebrations on December 13.

Butter cookies, such as Swedish *Vaniljhorn, Mandelkakor, and Spritz Sandbakelser,* can be found in Scandinavian bakeries during the Advent season and sometimes throughout the year. Many cookies are known by other names as well; for example, Swedish *Klenater* is also known by the Norwegian name *Fattigman.*

Generally the Scandinavian contribution to the food traditions of the United States is very basic: Finns cleared farmland out of the forests, Norwegians and Swedes tilled the prairie and grew grains, and Swedes and Danes developed food-related businesses, including the all-important dairy and milling industries.

[*See also* Dairy Industry; Midwestern Regional Cookery.]

BIBLIOGRAPHY

Barton, Arnold H. Introduction to "Scandinavian Roots—American Lives." Copenhagen: Nordic Council of Ministers, 2000.

Carheden, Kristina. *Food and Festivals Swedish Style.* Dillon Press, 1968.

Holmquist, June Drenning, ed. *They Chose Minnesota: A Survey of the State's Ethnic Groups.* St. Paul: Minnesota Historical Society Press, 1981.

Kaplan, Anne R., Marjorie A. Hoover, and Willard B. Moore. *The Minnesota Ethnic Food Book.* St. Paul: Minnesota Historical Society Press, 1986.

Norman, Hans, and Runblom Harald. *Transatlantic Connections: Nordic Migration to the New World after 1800.* London: Norwegian University Press, 1987.

Ojakangas, Beatrice. *The Finnish Cookbook.* New York, Crown Publishers, 1964.

Ojakangas, Beatrice. *The Great Scandinavian Baking Book.* 1988. Reprint, Minneapolis: University of Minnesota Press, 1999.

Walli, Mina. *Mina Wallin Keittokirja.* New York: Mina Walli (self-published), 1911.

BEATRICE OJAKANGAS

School Food

The nostalgia for lunch pails and boxes, the 1950s stereotype of food-service workers in cafeterias as hairnetted "lunch ladies," the establishment of National School Lunch Week in 1962, and even the familiarity of institutional food all indicate the impact that school lunch has had on this country's attitudes about childhood nutrition. Traditions, such as the brown paper bag lunch, lunch-pail advertising, and the milk carton, have entered into the national consciousness as a given part of our culture. School meals are a pressing issue for the poor in India, China, South and Central America, and South Africa and are closely linked to literacy in developing countries. As in the United States of 1900, child labor thrives in locations where food is inadequate. For the poor, school meals are a necessary incentive for attendance. Literacy, dropout rates, and overall school performance have been linked to school meal programs in the United States as well.

Most of the school meals in the United States are provided by federally supported breakfast and lunch programs administered by the Food and Nutrition Service (FNS), a branch of the U.S. Department of Agriculture (USDA). The FNS provides a tiered subsidy to school programs for meals that meet certain nutritional criteria. All fifty states, Puerto Rico, and Guam participate in the FNS program to varying degrees, and though participation in the federal program is voluntary, several states mandate school meal programs.

The USDA provides further support with commodity foods—foods bought in large quantity by the USDA to stabilize farm prices on the open market. Most urban areas provide an additional subsidy to offset the higher labor and distribution costs associated with city provisioning. In 2000–2001 the program reimbursed schools for breakfasts for 7.8 million children and lunches for 25.4 million children at a cost of $7 billion in cash and nearly $8 billion in commodity donations. The Special Milk Program served schoolchildren 115.8 million half-pints outside of meals, at a cost of $15.5 million. An estimated 56 percent of the students in these programs were from families of poverty- or near-poverty-level income.

The federal cash subsidy supplies a per-meal reimbursement to states, with additional money for meals served to students whose families are at poverty or near-poverty income levels. Theoretically the base subsidy is enough to cover the costs of food and preparation. To qualify for meal reimbursement, states must fund programs at specified rates and maintain administrative staff at set levels. Breakfast must provide one-fourth, and lunch one-third, of the daily recommended levels of calories, protein, calcium, iron, vitamin A, and vitamin C. Only 30 percent of the calories can come from fat, and only 10 percent from saturated fat. An example of a typical breakfast would be a mixed fruit cup, a biscuit with turkey sausage, a low-fat blueberry muffin, and milk.

In popular culture school food is the introduction to institutional food and is often associated with poor quality, or an institutional aesthetic. As designed by the government, school meals are an opportunity to use targeted farm products and a defense against the problems of poverty. For schools, providing meals is both an administrative burden and an essential element of educational success.

In 1998 a landmark study by Tufts University found that children who ate in the School Breakfast Program had significantly higher Standardized Achievement Test (SAT) scores. Other studies have found improved math grades; less hyperactivity, depression, and anxiety; fewer absences; less tardiness; and improved social behavior. Studies have also demonstrated that low-income children, in particular, do better in schools with meal programs and that early school success and good childhood nutrition have dramatic, long-range impact on later need for government assistance, cost of health care, employment, and overall health and productivity.

History

Public and charity funding of meals in public schools began in Europe in the late 1700s, with most countries having some programs by the early 1900s. School meals have been a practical consideration in individual communities in the United States since the mid-1800s, as educating the working class became a social and governmental priority. The first school lunch programs in the United States were charitable efforts to feed the hungry poor. In 1853 the Children's Aid Society of New York supplied the first recorded school lunches in America. The home economics pioneer Ellen Swallow Richards studied and promoted school nutrition programs in Boston in the late 1800s, and in 1898 the New York City superintendent of schools, Dr. William Maxwell, raised private funds for a pilot program offering meals at the student cost of three cents. Philadelphia, Cleveland, Milwaukee, and Chicago had meal programs by the early 1900s.

Volunteer-based and charity programs grew in the 1910s and 1920s, as food shortages caused by World War I and farm and soil mismanagement brought repeated food crises. The USDA began to develop and disseminate methods of serving school meals, while the U.S. Office of Education coordinated school lunches with home economics departments in public high schools. With the stock market crash of 1929 Congress passed the Agriculture Marketing Act, allocating $500 million to buy surplus crops to stabilize prices and save family farms. By 1931 there were 64,500 community-run school cafeterias and 11,500 school-run programs serving hot meals across the country.

Federal Subsidy

In 1933 Congress set aside 30 percent of import tax revenue to increase domestic consumption and remove farm surplus from the market. The USDA was allowed to operate food assistance programs and purchase farm surplus for school lunch programs in 1935. Thousands of Works Progress Administration (WPA) workers (72,000 in 1942, nearly all women) were hired to oversee health and safety policies, coordinate food supply with community and school gardens, form canning cooperatives in rural areas, and work in food preparation and service. Part-time staff (16,000 in 1941) provided by the National Youth Assistance Program (NYA) served food and made tables, chairs, and equipment. The School Milk Program, or "penny-milk program," offered milk at a reduced price of one cent per half-pint. In 1941 the National Academy of Sciences–National Research Council set the first recommended daily allowances (RDAs) for a variety of nutrients. These guidelines were later used to set nutritional mandates for school meals. Lunch programs in this initial period peaked in 1943, serving 5,277,436 a day and using 56 million pounds of donated food a month.

Soon after the entry of the United States into World War II, the WPA and NYA were eliminated, and women who used to cook at home and with school canning cooperatives were recruited into industry. Food was in short supply. The amount of farm products purchased for school meals dropped from 454 million pounds in 1942 to 93 million pounds in 1944. USDA support switched from supplying labor to supplying cash reimbursement and donated food, while Congress allowed purchase of nonsurplus foods for school meals. Food donations still made up the lion's share of the federal subsidy, but the change from labor to cash eliminated a source of staffing for school lunch programs at a time when labor was already short and, later, put the meal programs in budgetary competition with other school activities. Though demand for school lunches was as high as ever, programs dropped from 92,916 schools serving 6 million children a day in 1942 to 34,064 schools serving 5 million children in 1944. No further decline occurred until the Reagan administration's budgetary cuts in the 1980s.

Until 1946, allocations for school lunch were granted on a year-to-year basis and directly reflected clear, immediate needs. The 1946 National School Lunch Act established school lunch as an ongoing government program, permanently authorizing funds "as may be necessary" for school lunch on a matching basis with states. President Truman positioned the bill as farm support, guaranteeing large purchases of farm products for a domestic market. Congress recognized and debated the funding for the school nutrition program as an anti-hunger and education bill—to give fuel for learning and improve student concentration—but primarily supported it as a national defense measure, citing cases of shell shock in World War II and promoting it as assurance that by the time the next generation came of age, they would be able-bodied and educable and have "sound nervous systems." Introducing the bill to the Senate, Senator Allen Ellender of Louisiana quoted the surgeon general as saying that "one-half of all men rejected for the draft were rejected because of the effects of poor nutrition in childhood." Congress also established the Special Milk Program, a subsidy (three cents) for each half-pint of milk consumed outside of meal programs, to increase the amount of milk drunk in schools and to lessen USDA farm support purchases.

Special Assistance

A major shift in the School Lunch Act program came in the 1960s, beginning with the launch of a pilot special assistance program that consisted of free lunches for children of families whose incomes were at USDA poverty-level rates and reduced-price lunches for children of families whose incomes were 125 percent of poverty level in low-income areas. The program was permanently authorized by the National School Lunch Act and the Child Nutrition Act of 1966, which also funded a school breakfast pilot, as part of President Lyndon Johnson's War on Poverty. It was expanded to needy children in all schools in 1970.

Though the special assistance program was created to help the poor, the administration of special assistance created problems for some students and programs. Family income levels determined eligibility for the increased subsidy and marked students as "poverty" or "near poverty"; many children felt stigmatized by participating. In addition, those that could pay full price frequently dropped out, greatly reducing the available operating cash and thereby lowering the quality of the programs. But perhaps the biggest burden for schools was the dramatic increase in paperwork required to document eligibility of children for the higher reimbursement.

Child nutrition was brought to the fore in the public mind by the 1969 CBS television documentary *Hunger USA*. Throughout the 1970s the USDA expanded and experimented with programs to address the issues of poverty in the United States, including permanent authorization of school breakfast in 1975 and pilot summer meals and snack programs.

1980s Budget Cuts

The federal budget cuts of the 1980s had the single greatest impact on the availability and quality of school meals since the program's inception in 1946. Under pressure from the Reagan administration to cut costs, the USDA proposed abandoning the meal program goal of providing one-third of the recommended calories and nutrients. In the face of studies showing that low-income children depended on the school lunch for up to one-half of their daily nutrition, the proposal reduced serving sizes and nutrients, to supply, at most, 18 percent of a child's daily required calories. Thiamin, vitamin B6, calcium, magnesium and iron—all necessary for normal physical and cognitive development—would fall below one-third of the daily recommendations.

The proposal made headlines by categorizing ketchup and relish as vegetable servings; cake, cookies, and corn chips as bread servings; eggs in cake as a protein serving; and juice in jam as a fruit serving to meet the requirements listed under the subsidy. Proposed cuts would also have affected farmers by reducing the amount of food purchased by the USDA and by individual schools in local markets. After huge public outcry, including Democratic Party slogans of "ketchup is not a vegetable" and fund-raising dinners that served commodity-type cheese and ketchup, the Senate unanimously passed a resolution condemning the changes. The reprieve was short lived. The following year the Senate passed the Omnibus Budget Reconciliation Acts.

The Omnibus Budget Reconciliation Acts of 1986 and 1987 cut school lunch programs by one-third, raising income levels for assistance; lowering subsidies, especially for reduced-price meals; reducing child care food supplements; freezing the milk subsidy; redefining eligibility for additional funding; and removing the Special Milk Program from public schools serving lunch and from most private schools. As a result, an estimated 3 million low-income children were forced out of the school lunch program.

Because schools could no longer meet the needs of their poorest students and because the program's lack of funding meant a serious drop in meal quality, some schools were forced to open campuses at mealtime and offer less-than-ideal alternatives, including closing the meal program, using private services, and selling nonnutritious foods for profit, despite state and federal regulations against the practice. Lunch programs were driven to a greater dependence on federal commodities, which limited food choice and created an additional burden of food processing.

School Meals in the Twenty-first Century

Data gleaned from looking at the effects of school food programs and from related studies on malnutrition have informed the practice of medicine, views on nutrition, and public policy on issues from labor to science spending. In 1998 the Child Nutrition Reauthorization Act made the first substantial program improvements in almost twenty years, reducing meal program paperwork and funding a research pilot on the benefits of universal (free for all students) school breakfast. Changes gave greater flexibility to menu planners while maintaining the previous nutritional standards. Because meal programs frequently run with a goal of break-even finances, any changes in operations or overhead can have a direct and sometimes devastating effect. Meal programs are sensitive to such policies as the 2003 agenda to increase requirements for income verification. Moreover, such plans have been shown to decrease participation for immigrants and some of the very poor.

Ongoing Issues The discussion of school lunch has always been multifaceted, touching on the effect of satiety on learning, the direct contribution of good childhood nutrition to lifelong health, the importance of good health to national defense, the debate over food cost and quality, and direct service to America's poor. Opinions on all these issues determine program funding.

Increasing Emphasis on Childhood Nutrition In the early 2000s studies reported that the quality of childhood nutrition was a major factor in lifelong health and health care costs, with childhood obesity contributing to later incidence of diabetes and heart disease. Poor diet continued to be a risk factor in half of the leading causes of death in America. (Children who bring a lunch from home or who leave campus generally have meals that are lower in nutritional value than the cafeteria meals.)

Food Quality and On-site Cooking Centralized kitchens and the use of precooked meals reheated at schools cut labor costs—one of the biggest expenses in serving lunches. However, these reheated meals are less popular. On-site cooking has been named as the number one determinant of food taste and quality. Kitchens can be expensive to build in a new school and even more expensive to install in an existing school. They are frequently at risk in the increasing debate over cutting costs of school construction and maintenance, as taste, presentation, and acceptance have been equated with expense. Meal advocates insist that, while it is important to be critical of program quality, any school meal is better than none for many children.

Price and Stigma Approximately half of all school meals are served to poverty or near-poverty students (higher in urban areas), and participation in meal programs is extremely price sensitive for all students. Universal meal programs in some districts provide free meals regardless of family income and relieve the stigma of being identified as coming from a low-income family. Universal meals cut paperwork as much as 80 percent, which offsets some of the additional costs. Yet in spite of the 1998 pilot for universal breakfasts, in the early 2000s there was little indication that Congress would make any universal meal a permanent part of the subsidy. Some schools have experimented with ways to reduce or eliminate stigma by using a number of noncash charge systems—such as swipe cards—to keep price structures anonymous.

Lunchroom Conditions Individual schools manage scheduling, safety, cleanliness, noise level, and appearance of lunchrooms. This broad range of responsibilities contributes in large part to the meal program's bad reputation. For example, some overtaxed facilities give children less than ten minutes to eat or allow students to take additional classes during lunch or to leave school early, and hungry.

Privatization In some areas corporations have contracted with public school districts to take over food service on site. Although service privatization has actually led to short-term improvements in the worst lunch programs, studies show that in the long term neither the cost ratio nor the quality is much improved, and in many cases quality and food choice and taste diminish, as does the student participation rate.

Vending and Nonnutritious Foods Vending companies and soft-drink manufacturers offer educational perks and money for exclusive rights to sell drinks. This money is often used by schools to fund clubs, activities, and even core curricula. Some contracts give schools the money up front, based on projected sales in the lunchrooms, student lounges, and hallways, and have asked for it back if projections are not reached, creating a situation in which children and parents actively promote the contracted-for products outside of school. School districts have become "Pizza Hut districts" or "Coke districts," based on contracts with school boards. These competing foods frequently replace meals with nutritional value.

Furthermore, negotiating to get the best contracts can divert the time and attention of parents and administrators from educational goals.

Milk Milk is a source of protein, calcium, and vitamins A and D. Using milk and cheese in school meals supports prices for dairy farmers, and this support played a major part in establishing the lunch program in 1946. Milk also has a high amount of bacteria when compared with soybean milk and can spoil in a matter of hours. Most milk served in schools comes from cows treated with hormones and antibiotics, the use of which has been a major health concern since the beginning of these controversial practices. In addition, one half-pint of whole milk has 26 percent of the daily maximum recommended allowance for saturated fat. Many children cannot digest cow's milk. It is possible that as many as 50 to 80 percent of black, Latin, and Asian schoolchildren are lactose intolerant.

Family farms provide a rapidly shrinking percentage of dairy products. The dairy industry lobby, one of the ten largest lobbies, reported spending $2.25 million in 1999 to promote pro-dairy policies. The USDA itself has recommended the use of hormones and antibiotics to help farmers raise productivity levels, while at the same time buying the dairy surpluses that result. Although milk currently supplies nutrients critical to a child's growth, subsidies, USDA support, and the subsequent ubiquity of milk have limited the practicality of offering alternatives.

Multiculturalism As demographics shift and classrooms become more ethnically diverse, meal programs must pay more attention to varied religious and cultural taboos. Though most dietary requirements can be met with minor shifts in food choices, changes in large-scale food purchases and donated commodities are not as responsive and create additional work for local administrators. Agencies also report the difficulties of filling out assistance eligibility forms for undocumented or non–English-speaking immigrants. Both issues may discourage immigrant participation.

Twenty-first-century Programs Meal programs are seeing innovations. Organic foods, as well as those that have not been genetically modified, may be offered with locally grown and seasonal foods. Student, parent, and staff nutrition committees collaborate. Salad bars may be installed and more food choices may be added. Education can integrate math and life sciences with nutrition, food science, and food history. Cooking classes, guest chefs, lunchtime mentoring, and school gardens may be instituted. These innovative programs have demonstrated some success, especially in food acceptance, but their longevity depends on local resources. In the early 2000s programs remain extremely vulnerable to local administration and funding cuts at every level.

[*See also* Cafeterias; Farm Subsidies, Duties, Quotas, and Tariffs; Hunger Programs; Milk; Nutrition; Politics of Food.]

BIBLIOGRAPHY

American School Food Service Association. *Your Child Nutrition eSource*. http://www.asfsa.org. Primarily for food-service professional staff, this is one of the largest organizations dealing specifically with school meals. Publishes periodicals, studies, and research reviews, many available online.

Center for Ecoliteracy and the Food Systems Project. http://www.ecoliteracy.org. The center has food systems planning documents available online at no charge and publications for sale to provide help in increasing participation in school meal programs, serving organic foods, eliminating harmful food additives and processes, serving meals in a pleasant environment, reducing waste, and ensuring that kitchens are built in every school site.

Center for Science in the Public Interest. http://www.cspinet.org. Nonpartisan breaking news on nutrition issues and governmental policy. Publishes *Nutrition Action Health Letter* ten times per year.

Food and Agriculture Organization of the United Nations. http://www.fao.org. Reports breaking news in food distribution and school meal programs as they become issues for various world populations. Publishes research on world hunger issues in Spanish, French, and English, including the periodical *Food, Nutrition, and Agriculture of the Economic and Social Division of the United Nations.*

Food and Nutrition Service, U.S. Department of Agriculture, School Meals Program. http://www.fns.usda.gov/cnd. Gives many links to purchasing contracts, histories, regulations, press releases, budget and spending reports, and nutrition and meal service resources. USDA and FNS Librarians are particularly helpful and can be reached through this website.

Food Research and Action Center. http://www.frac.org. Publishes reports on federal nutrition programs, hunger statistics, and public policy on nutrition. Most can be downloaded at no cost from the website.

Moffitt, Robert, and Douglas A. Wolf. *The Effect of the 1981 Omnibus Budget Reconciliation Act on Welfare Recipients and Work Incentives in Aid to Families with Dependent Children.* Washington, DC: Urban Institute, 1986.

Schlosser, Eric. *Fast Food Nation: The Dark Side of the All-American Meal.* Boston: Houghton Mifflin, 2001. Discusses the role of fast food and institutional food service.

NANCY RALPH

Scrapple

Scrapple, or Philadelphia scrapple, is a spiced pork breakfast sausage re-fried or re-grilled in slices, and served with ketchup or syrup. Though it is most common in the Pennsylvania Dutch region of eastern Pennsylvania, and the nearby parts of New Jersey, Delaware, and Maryland, it is shipped as a commercial product across America and is sometimes made in rural homes in a number of variations with beef or game substituting for the pork.

Scrapple is the distinctively American descendant of a variety of European slaughtering-day recipes for puddings of pork parts made by simmering them into a gelatinous gruel that is then thickened with meal, spiced, and cooled into a loaf. What makes scrapple American is the substitution of a mixture of buckwheat and cornmeal for European grains, the omission of blood, and the standard use of sage and pepper as seasonings.

The Pennsylvania Dutch name *pawnhas* (or *pawnhoss, panhas, pan hoss*) is recorded earlier than the name "scrapple," even in English-language sources, so its immediate ancestors are most likely black puddings called *panhas*, which are still popular in Germany. But the buckwheat is strongly associated with the New Netherland colony (which briefly included Delaware), and there are similar English recipes as early as 1390.

The name *Panhoss* is usually understood as a variation of *pan haas*, meaning "pan rabbit," by analogy with German terms like "false hare" for meat loaf. But William Woys Weaver has traced *panhas* in Germany back to the 1500s, and suggests that it derives from *panna*, the name of a Celtic vessel, in the same way that dishes like chowder, terrine, and potpie are named for the vessels in which they are cooked. The word "scrapple" is not recorded as naming this food until the 1820s and is usually traced to the English "scrap" and Holland Dutch *scrabbel* as applied to kitchen leftovers. Weaver has argued, however, that "scrapple" came from *panhaskröppel* (literally, a slice of *panhas*) in the Krefelder dialect of the original 1680 Germantown settlers, which was conflated with the English word "scrapple," locally applied to leftovers and three similarly shaped tools: a kitchen scraper, a grubbing hoe, and an ash rake. Supporting this explanation is the fact that scrapple was not originally made from kitchen scraps and quite early became a commercial by-product of slaughterhouse activity. (One explanation of why scrapple went from a black blood pudding to a white pudding, unlike the German *panhas*, is that the blood was being diverted to other industrial uses.)

But Weaver also notes that scrapple was sometimes made from scrapings of meat and sometimes scrapings of bread, and the word "scrapple" had been used for stone or wood chips in Medieval Latin and as a verb for dressing timber in Middle English. The English manuscript *Forme of Curye* (1390) has a recipe for a saffron-flavored scrapple under the title "For to make grewel forced."

Although European preparations range from hot soups and loose hashes to puddings, patés, and sausages, American scrapple is now almost always sliced and pan-fried as a breakfast meat. Scrapple was originally made and traded by farm families in winter and became a commercial product in the early nineteenth century as improved roads and railroads increased the size and scope of slaughterhouses and urban markets. The introduction of the home-size meat grinder in the late nineteenth century meant that scrapple could be made for family consumption in home kitchens and also produced a number of fanciful (and short-lived) recipes, as well as more enduring tastes for meat loaf and peanut butter. In the early twenty-first century, scrapple is again a primarily industrial product with some old and new artisanal producers.

[*See also* Breakfast Foods; German American Food; Goetta; Sausage.]

BIBLIOGRAPHY

Warner, Rev. Richard, ed. *Warner's Antiquitates Culinariae.* London: Prospect Books, n.d. A facsimile of *Antiquitates Culinariae; or, Curious Tracts Relating to the Culinary Affairs of the Old English, With a Preliminary Discourse, Notes, and Illustrations, By The Reverand Richard Warner, of Sway, near Lymngton, Hants.* London, 1791. First print publication of what Warner transcribed as "The Forme of Cury," including recipe for "grewel forced."

Weaver, William Woys. *Country Scrapple: An American Tradition.* Mechanicsburg, PA: Stackpole, 2003. Weaver starts some controversies while settling old ones. Includes historic and contemporary recipes, analogues, such as goetta and Chickasaw *pashofa*, and Pennsylvania Dutch relishes to serve with scrapple.

MARK H. ZANGER

Screwdriver

There is much lore surrounding the cocktail known as the screwdriver. In one story, American oilmen in the Middle East concocted the drink from vodka and canned orange juice, calling it a screwdriver after the one tool on their belts appropriate for use as a stirring stick. The Norwegians—especially the makers of Finlandia vodka—claim that the screwdriver was first concocted in Norwegian oil fields, not the Middle East. Ian Wisniewski and Nicholas Faith in *Classic Vodka* state that a gin drink

commonly known as the orange blossom became the first screwdriver during Prohibition, when bootleggers added canned orange juice to bathtub gin to mask its awful flavor. A screwdriver was needed to pierce the orange juice cans, hence the cocktail's name.

All of these stories aside, John G. Martin, president of Heublein Inc., in the 1940s, used the screwdriver (and the Moscow mule, Bloody Mary, and vodkatini) to promote the introduction of Smirnoff vodka to gin-drinking Americans. It worked. By 1967, vodka sales had pulled ahead of gin sales in the United States.

The screwdriver consists of a shot of vodka mixed with about five ounces of orange juice, over ice, in a highball glass. Notwithstanding the origins of the cocktail, fresh orange juice makes a superior drink. The most famous screwdriver variation was concocted to promote an Italian liqueur, Galliano. A standard screwdriver was topped with a float of Galliano and called a Harvey Wallbanger after an imaginary character, a surfer, who was said to have bumped into walls after consuming several drinks.

[*See also* Cocktails; Prohibition; Vodka.]

BIBLIOGRAPHY

Wisniewski, Ian, and Nicholas Faith. *Classic Vodka.* London: Prion, 1997.

DALE DEGROFF

Seafood

Until modern Americans decided to adopt what has become known as a "heart healthy" diet, seafood generally faced a dubious public. Caught in a series of sometimes contradictory objections, fish and shellfish enjoyed fairly low regard compared with red meat or even chicken. Still, as a natural resource open to anyone with the skill and technology to harvest it, almost all the favored food species have faced overfishing and dangerous levels of depletion. While seafood still does not rank near to meat in frequency of consumption, more people are eating fish more often than ever, and with wild stocks under stress from American and foreign fishing fleets, a wider variety of fish is taken and eaten than earlier in American history. Further, Americans consume a greater-than-ever amount of farm-raised fish. America ranks third in world consumption of fish in the early 2000s.

Nevertheless, ambivalence about fish is self-evident in the use of the word "fishy." In comparison, the words "meaty" and "beefy" are used to indicate substance. Over time there have been several explicit objections to fish to which various fishery producers responded by correcting the problems with fish that the public perceived—only to have new problems emerge. Fish has not, for most of American food history, been considered substantial enough fare to warrant a firm place in the diet. This seems to be changing in the twenty-first century, but the demand is met by problems on the supply end as fishermen, scientists, and the government argue about the real size of, and best way to maintain, fish populations, and as aquaculture sometimes faces challenges from environmentalists and the wild fisheries.

Seafood as Perilous Fare

Fish and shellfish are notorious for their propensity to spoil, the presence of small and pesky bones or tough-to-penetrate exterior shells, and the perceived difficulty of cooking them. Seafood does spoil quickly. The sooner fish can be eaten or preserved after capture, the better. A premium has always been placed on fish sold fresh or even alive. Ponds and pounds that held live fresh- or saltwater fish existed for centuries before settlers brought the technology to America. A vessel design adopted from Europe enabled fisherman to transport live fish by employing wells in boats through which water circulated. Fish could be conveyed considerable distances to market, where they were sometimes further held alive in floating cars until sold.

Barring live sale, the freshest fish brought the best price. Household hint and cookery books abound with advice on detecting freshness, describing how the eyes and gills should look on a newly caught fish and often cautioning about the ways that the fish seller might doctor the product to conceal incipient spoilage. Lobsters and crabs were sometimes cooked shortly after being caught, to avoid their dying before sale or being vended half-alive. Fish were tricky to buy and the consumer had to beware.

Rapid transportation, the practice of icing fish, and the development of artificial refrigeration and freezing technology greatly diminished many of the difficulties of obtaining fresh fish. However, there is some dispute about whether fish that has been frozen, even flash-frozen, can be considered truly fresh. The same railroads that brought western beef to eastern markets in refrigerated cars, beginning in the mid-1800s and continuing through the early 1900s, helped East Coast fisheries sell fresh fish in the Midwest. Fish that had been iced aboard the vessels that caught them remained iced until sale—or at least the consumers hoped so.

Even in the mid-nineteenth century frozen fish were considered preserved fish, no different from salted or canned. Salting fish immediately upon catching them was an ancient practice, often followed by drying. (In some cold and very dry places fish could be dried without salting, though generally that was not done in America.) While New England's salt codfish is its best-known fish product, other species (usually the oilier fish), including shad, mackerel, herring, alewives, and salmon, were also salted, as were some other white-fleshed fish such as pollock and haddock.

Salting and drying were the simplest ways of preserving fish. When the canning industry had developed sufficiently in the nineteenth century to have an impact on the food supply, fish and shellfish joined the seasonal cycle of products being preserved, often alternating with fresh vegetable crops, in the larger plants. Some cannery operations were specifically developed in the later 1800s and early 1900s to handle the product of certain fisheries, such as the West Coast salmon fishery, tuna and sardine fisheries, and even shellfish, such as clams and lobsters in New England, shrimp along the Gulf Coast, and crab and oysters around the Chesapeake Bay.

Canned fish and shellfish seem to have found a more ready market than many fresh fish because they answered questions of freshness and often solved the problem of cooking method. The cook could open the can and have a ready-to-use product. Many late-nineteenth- and early-twentieth-century canned fish and shellfish producers promoted their products with cookery books replete with recipes for salmon loaf, shrimp wiggle, clam chowder, and tuna or lobster salad.

Bones were the bane of the fishery producers' existence. Fresh fish left the bone problem to the consumer, who responded by preferring in many cases larger-boned fish, such as salmon, halibut, and eventually swordfish and tuna, whose bones could be easily found and removed either in the kitchen or at the table. Very bony fish, like shad and alewives, were welcomed in season, but consumers frequently commented upon the inconvenience of eating them. Smaller fish, such as trout and mackerel, cooked whole in a pan and usually yielding up a small portion with a backbone in one piece, were considered suitable for suppers and breakfasts. Canned fish and shellfish diminished the bone and shell problem somewhat. While

Seafood Catch. Fisherman's Wharf, San Francisco, 1943. *Prints and Photographs Division, Library of Congress/Ann Rosener*

the large bones of salmon and jack mackerel did not disappear in the canning process, they were often softened enough to be eaten, and canned shellfish saved the consumer from tedious shucking and picking.

In the nineteenth century, when middle-class eating habits were becoming more refined, thoughtful hostesses did not serve fish from which a guest would be obliged to pick bones. Oysters and lobsters were served already shucked or picked, suitable for eating with a fork so that the diner never had to handle the shell. China oyster plates, imitating the appearance of shells, were available. They underscored the transition from wild to genteel appearance.

To maintain its market share in the face of competition from iced fresh fish, the salt cod industry developed boneless fish products. Consumers bought boxes of neat slabs of codfish, completely boned. They could even buy boned and shredded cod ready for use in codfish cakes or creamed cod.

The most satisfactory solution for the bone problem was commercial filleting. Cooks filleted whole fish domestically and pulled out stray bones left behind when the sides were removed. When Forty Fathom Fish Company in Boston began to offer boneless fillets of fish in 1921, the public responded enthusiastically. Commercial filleting combined with freezing technology paved the way for the ubiquitous breaded fillet.

Wartime Spikes in Seafood Consumption

Commercial filleting also helped move through market the great number of fish caught by steam-powered otter trawl, a new fishing technology introduced in the United States around 1900. This technology caught many more fish than consumers wanted. Fishery producers, noting how much more fish per capita was eaten in Europe than in the United States, often complained that the problem was not overproduction but rather underconsumption. They also noted that a greater variety of species was more readily accepted fare abroad than in America.

The fisheries experienced a discernible spike in fish consumption during the meat rationing of World War I, but the slump that immediately followed the war reminded fishing interests that the American public was not that fond of fish after all. Marketing efforts and industry organization attempted to overcome this consumer resistance. Many households turned to fish—always a low-cost source of protein—more often during the Depression, though the majority continued to eat fish just once a week, a centuries-long habit. During World War II fish consumption rose again until rationing was over and the prosperity of the 1950s once again eased people into eating more red meat.

Seafood as Insufficient Fare

Besides perishability, bones, and lack of confidence about how to cook it, it seems that one past objection to fish centered on its perceived lightness in the diet. Fish had a long association with the practice of fasting. In spite of its being animal food, fish occupied a middle ground between red-blooded animals and vegetables and grains. Many found pleasure and satisfaction eating red meat, while eating the relatively blander and low-calorie fish was less pleasant, a good diet for mortification of the human flesh. That qualified it in the eyes of the Roman Catholic Church for consumption on days dedicated to supplication and prayer and as the diet for people in holy orders, whose life was spent in fasting. Moreover, mandated eating of fish helped a population conserve meat supplies, and the rule was used from time to time to support fisheries even after the Reformation.

Many of America's Protestant settlers were familiar with the idea of fasting for a day at least weekly, and occasionally for two days. While Friday abstinence from meat was a rule among Catholics, Protestants wishing to distinguish themselves from Catholics often chose Saturday as the fish-eating day. This worked until the nineteenth century, when Catholic immigrants arrived in sufficient numbers to create a noticeably ample market for fresh fish sales on Thursday and Friday. Non-Catholics who wanted to buy and consume fresh fish shifted their fish dinners back to Friday.

One way to overcome the lightness and blandness of fish is to cook it with a spicy or heavy sauce. In the American past, small fish were pan fried, and larger fish were served with butter, oyster, or lobster sauce, or sometimes a butter or cream sauce containing mashed, boiled egg. In Maritime Canada, New England, and parts of the country settled by New Englanders fish was served sprinkled with small pieces of salt pork and drizzled with the rendered pork fat. Salt pork fat, cream, or butter added considerable calories, while horseradish, mustard, vinegar, and other sharp ingredients gave fish a livelier flavor. Consumers often prefer deep-fried breaded fish or shellfish. The breading absorbs enough oil to give the fish caloric substance, besides adding a crunchy texture.

Calorie- and fat-conscious twenty-first-century Americans have a hard time understanding the desire for the added fat, but in an era when people labored physically, walked great distances, and, in some parts of the nation, lived in a cold climate without central heating, calories from fat fueled the effort and people craved them. Oilier fish, such as salmon, were recognized as having more substance; salmon was sometimes even described as a red-blooded fish, which its pink flesh suggested. Other oily fish, such as shad, mackerel, and herring, might have been held in higher esteem had they not been so often salted, which reduced their value.

In the nineteenth century the rich sauces that made fish more appetizing made the dish inappropriate for people with digestive problems according to doctors and diet reformers. Fish required rich sauces to make it palatable, but rich sauces were not healthful; therefore fish was not an ideal food. Sarah Josepha Hale, the editor of *Godey's Lady's Book*, believed that salmon was too rich to give to children, though she recognized that those who did not labor hard ought to eat more fish. She even declared in her *New Cook Book* (1857) that "fish is less nutritious than flesh."

In the early twentieth century medical and nutrition experts were much less likely to make the distinction among various forms of animal protein and so did not attempt to dismiss fish as less nutritious. About the worst that anyone could say about fish was that it was less interesting than meat. In the 1970s the medical establishment became concerned about a possible correlation between cholesterol and heart disease. Seafood, as a naturally low-cholesterol food, gained sudden popularity, and whereas it had long been relatively cheap, its price began to rise. Soon after, the United States extended its territorial waters to a new two-hundred-mile limit to allow fishermen larger catches to meet the expanded demand of popular species.

Fish, Foreigners, and Hard Times

As the fishery producers had noted early in the twentieth century, foreign populations ate much more fish per capita than did Americans. Meat-eating was a prerogative of living in the United States, and many immigrant populations gladly took it up, with their seafood consumption declining after a period of residence in America. At the same time their willingness to eat certain species previously underconsumed in the United States taught their American neighbors to broaden their choices some. In early-twentieth-century Boston, for example, albacore, or tuna, appeared in the market, caught and purchased by

Italians who managed to convince Yankee consumers that tuna was a good substitute for pricier beef.

Because many immigrants, especially those from Mediterranean and Asian countries, used a great deal of seafood, and because for a time many of these populations lived in poverty in their new country, some prejudice existed about the connection of seafood, foreigners, and hard times. Italian fishermen selling fish directly from their boats in Boston harbor were allowed to do so despite various health laws because they served the poor, but the practice seems to have offended the sensibilities of more prosperous classes. Further, the American public did not like to confront food in the form of the original whole fish or animal. Fish sold whole in ethnic markets or often still alive in Asian markets remains, in the twenty-first century, too challenging for many mainstream Americans, who find the foreigners' practices unsettling or even disgusting.

Not only immigrants but also other poor Americans turned to fish for subsistence fare or had it forced on them. Much of the salt codfish produced in the first 250 years of American history was sold to feed the enslaved Africans working on sugar plantations in the West Indies. Other salt fish was sold to the South for their slave populations. Archaeological remains from various plantations located on estuaries on the Chesapeake Bay and farther south show that planters incorporated catching fish such as herring and shad into the seasonal work cycle to provide fresh and salt fish for their slaves. Slaves also fished and foraged for themselves to vary and supplement their diets.

Subsistence fishing sometimes sets up odd and seemingly contradictory claims about the value of certain seafood. One such example comes from a Maine family who, according to family lore, was so poor during the Depression, all they had to eat was salt cod and lobster. In other families, children were cautioned against admitting that the family ate clams, since being dependent on foraged food was often a mark of shameful poverty. Similarly, on the West Coast, one story goes that in the mid-1800s the lumbermen in a camp in Washington State protested against being fed salmon more than twice a week. Apprentices in Newcastle, England, and boardinghouse inhabitants in the textile-manufacturing city of Lowell, Massachusetts, as well as in many other places, protested against being fed too much salmon. Yet at the same time lobster and salmon were fetching high prices in the market. Seafood was both a luxury food for those who could afford to buy it and a means of survival for those who could forage for it.

However, many new immigrants to America in the twentieth century, especially since the 1970s, taught Americans new ways of preparing and eating fish. Through ethnic restaurants and cookbooks Americans have greatly expanded their seafood repertoire. Many Americans try a seafood dish at a restaurant and then seek recipes for imitating the dish at home, and with expanded ethnic food sections in large supermarkets, specialty ingredients are available to the home cook for preparing fish in just about every way possible.

Part of the impulse for this has come from the widespread promotion in the twenty-first century of what is known as the new food pyramid, issued by the United States Department of Agriculture (USDA), and the variations on it promulgated by the organization Oldways Preservation Trust. The "new" (it was released in 1992) USDA food pyramid replaces the old four food groups used in nutrition education during the latter half of the twentieth century. The pyramid places foods in relative proportions of their recommended consumption, with cereals and grains at the wide base, followed by fruits and vegetables and then meat, fish, poultry, and other protein sources (such as legumes, eggs, and nuts), at the recommended serving of two to three daily.

Oldways examined the diets of the Mediterranean and Asia in light of the lower rates of heart disease in these areas. Fish plays a more important role in those regional diets, as fishery producers have long observed, and as the Oldways ethnic variations on the food pyramid demonstrate. The Mediterranean food pyramid recommends fish consumption weekly but places meat in a monthly category. Both the Oldways Asian and Latin American food pyramids recommend daily consumption of fish or shellfish, and meat monthly. From having occupied a place in the diet of poor Americans, who often obtained their fish by catching or foraging for it themselves, fish, in the early twenty-first century, has become a high-priced food implying prosperity for those who eat it, while cheap beef has become the food of the working poor.

Prepared Seafood

Fishery producers find that, like many other foods sold to the general American public, the more prepared seafood is, the easier it is to sell. From the later nineteenth century's boneless codfish to the frozen fillet of the early twentieth century, more and more seafood products are presented in market as heat-and-serve fare. In the twenty-first century consumers can buy vacuum-sealed microwaveable packages of salmon in various sauces or plastic bags of frozen shrimp with Asian-style vegetables for stir-fry.

Public desire for precooked seafood has helped the aquaculture industries find a market for their products. Fish processors, who keep their products frozen for sale anywhere in the country or even abroad, buy up surpluses of catfish, tilapia, and salmon, among others. Some seafood products, particularly the breaded fillets, can be produced from whatever whitefish is most plentiful. Consumers buying fish described only as "breaded fillets" or "fish fingers" or "fish nuggets" might be hard pressed to distinguish between tilapia, Alaskan pollock, and even catfish.

Since the 1970s, fish and poultry have become rivals for the low-fat, low-cholesterol market, with precooked fish products competing with ready-to-eat chicken products. Fish processors label breaded fish products as "fingers" or "nuggets" with the understanding that the public will compare them favorably to chicken products of the same name. This marketing ploy was used earlier in the twentieth century for canned tuna, which was styled as "chicken of the sea," interchangeable with canned chicken in popular casseroles, salads, and sandwiches.

Seafood, Leisure, and the Exotic

In America there has long been a correlation between leisure time and seafood consumption. Going fishing, either at the seaside, on lakes and ponds, or along rivers and streams, is a feature of many people's vacations. Seafood restaurants are found in beach and lakeside resorts, and sampling fish or shellfish during foreign travel adds to an exotic experience for many Americans.

In New England a seafood feast called a Squantum, dating to the early 1800s, commemorated a supposed connection of early settlers with the sea, land, and Native Americans. At these all-male, late-summer events, chowder was cooked outdoors. Sometimes lobsters, clams, and corn were served as well. Squantums were also held inland, where trout, perch, or pickerel were cooked up. These events were possibly the progenitors of clambakes, a form of in-ground cookery common around the globe that was not necessarily learned from the Indians.

In the nineteenth century clambakes and chowder parties were common seaside leisure activities that usually entailed the participants catching the fish or digging the clams, which they then cooked outdoors. By the mid-nineteenth century individuals could be hired as chowder- or bake-masters for groups making an event of it. In some seaside towns so-called shore dinners consisting of steamed clams, lobster, corn and other comestibles were offered in an informal restaurantlike establishment. Lobster and clam festivals cropped up along the coast in summer, mostly for tourists.

In the late nineteenth and early twentieth centuries vacationers looking for a rustic experience in New England, where lobstering is done, would go to the pounds and eat lobsters on site. The pounds, which had been used as storage for lobsters about to be transported live to market, also became restaurants where lobsters were boiled to order. In the twenty-first century lobster pounds are sometimes found at a distance from water, but they remain part of leisure-time seafood consumption.

Similarly, along the Chesapeake Bay in Maryland and Virginia, and the coasts and estuaries of North and South Carolina, Georgia, Florida, and the Gulf states, blue crab boils are a feature of leisure activity. Tourists and locals can stop at small shacks, or house businesses, to buy crab cakes, soft-shelled crabs, and boiled crabs to eat in the rough, or other seafood specialties. Blue crab festivals draw vendors who sell the crabs, oysters, and shrimp. Families fish for crabs using fish heads or chicken necks as bait, boil them, and pick them on newspaper-covered tables as a kind of picnic.

In the Deep South, shrimp and crawfish boils are held seasonally. Socializing around jambalaya in Louisiana relies on enthusiasts installing large cooking pots in their fishing camps or summer cottages for the purposes of making large quantities for friends and family.

Where shad run upriver in the spring, mostly through the Middle Atlantic States, along the Hudson, in New Jersey, Pennsylvania, and parts of Maryland, shad bakes featuring planked shad are held. In nineteenth-century Philadelphia shad bakes were held by the State of Schuylkill, a well-known elite men's club, yet another example of men cooking fish as a social activity.

On the Great Lakes and other freshwater lakes and rivers where whitefish and catfish abound, boils and fish-fries fill a role similar to the fish and shellfish events elsewhere. Small roadside eateries featuring local fish appear in some areas. The Mississippi Delta, now famous for catfish farming, has individuals and establishments famous for their fried catfish. Door Country in Wisconsin is famed for its whitefish boils, which some report are derived from the habit of fishermen, who used steam vessels for fishing, cooking whitefish on their steam engines. As in other places and with other seafood, there is a mixture of commercial and private boils and fries that supply locals and tourists.

Independence, Industry, and Wild Food

Fishing or foraging for shellfish is still recreation for many people. A fisherman with a string of trout may expect to have the fish fried up for breakfast or supper, but sport fishing lacks the life-and-death importance it has for commercial fishermen. Commercial and sport fishermen are often at odds, and many people still hold the attitude that fishing is a lazy man's activity. It is an old idea. Hunting and fishing were pastimes of the gentry in old England, as they were in colonial America as well.

Fishing, like most wild-food hunting, is speculative and depends on luck, experience, and intuition. Compared with farming, it seemed very risky to the English settlers in New England when they established the cod fishery that ultimately built fortunes. But the men who preferred to fish liked it because of the independence that working on the water afforded them. An often unruly and independent-minded group, fishermen did not fit into the Puritan expectation of community living. Some three hundred years later, government attempts to manage fish stocks by managing fishermen are the source of much trouble.

Since the mid-nineteenth century, fisheries have endeavored to even out the highly seasonal nature of the work, guarantee catches, and provide year-round work for fishermen. In the nineteenth century vessels were refitted to take advantage of seasonal variations in the fish stocks. Fishermen worked on vessels in northern waters until winter and then went to work in the southern fisheries. Fisheries in the twenty-first century have employed a range of technologies and sophisticated equipment that nearly unerringly find fish, scoop them up, and even process them on board. In only a few days on the water, one vessel can catch what formerly took a season's worth of vessels to harvest. However, older, lower-tech fishing methods, including trolling and long-lining, have been revived to reduce by-catch and also to improve the quality of the product. Conservationists encourage consumers to ask for troll or long-line mahi-mahi and various sorts of tuna in stores and restaurants.

Even with earlier fishing methods it was possible to overfish a popular species. Since the eighteenth century, American fisheries have been driven farther offshore to find stocks of particular fish. They have found themselves competing, sometimes viciously, with their Canadian and Mexican neighbors and agitating the government for treaty protection of certain waters. In turn, the fisheries have been subject to government regulation of vessel size, equipment type, the size of the openings in various nets, and the seasons for catching various species.

Improvements in equipment efficiency have almost always meant that a favored species soon will be overfished. When one stock is reduced, a similar fish replaces it until it also becomes stressed. For example, in the 1990s Chilean sea bass, an ideal commercial fish, replaced cod and haddock as a firm, flaky-fleshed fish that had the added virtue of freezing well for transport. Suitable for just about any style of cooking, it caught on quickly, but the stocks were depleted so much that by the early 2000s conservationists were seeking to protect it.

Wild Fish and Farmed Fish

Aquaculture is one solution to overfishing, but it is also controversial. Fish farmers have grown certain favorites in America—oysters, for example—since the nineteenth century. The fish supply is increasingly global and farmed. Americans eat farmed salmon from Scandinavia, South America, and North America; prawns and shrimp from Asia and Central America; and tilapia from Central America and the continental United States. Mussels, oysters, catfish, and clams are also farmed, many in U.S. waters.

Whenever intensive mono-cropping occurs, disease control and pollution problems appear. Aquaculture's environmental impact includes everything from residue build-up in water around fish pens to damage to third world mangrove swamps, where prawns are raised. Certain farmed species have been subject to genetic engineering, raising concerns about the mixing, even if only accidentally, of wild and farmed fish. The unintended consequences of harvesting certain fish to provide feed for favored farm-raised species raise questions. Aesthetic concerns about fish pens floating in previously wild locations make fish farms a sometimes unwanted neighbor. Finally, there are controversies about the flavors of raised and wild seafood, with many preferring the blander flavor of the farm-raised, while others deplore the loss of more robust wild flavor.

If the past is any indication, any presently nonendangered wild fish, if it finds favor on the American table, will be overfished, more fish will be farmed for human consumption, and efforts will continue to be made to restore and conserve wild stocks.

[See also Clambake; Crab Boils; Fish, *subentries on* Freshwater Fish, Saltwater Fish, *and* Saltwater Shellfish; New England Regional Cookery; Oyster Loaf Sandwich; Oysters; Pacific Northwestern Regional Cookery; Salt and Salting; Tuna.]

BIBLIOGRAPHY

Davidson, Alan. *North Atlantic Seafood.* New York: Viking, 1979.

DeVoe, Thomas F. *The Market Assistant Containing a Brief Description of Every Article of Human Food Sold in the Markets.* New York: Hurd and Haughton, 1867. Reprint, Detroit, MI: Book Tower, 1975.

German, Andrew. *Down on T-Wharf: The Boston Fisheries as Seen through the Photographs of Henry D. Fisher.* Mystic, CT: Mystic Seaport Museum, 1982.

Goode, George Brown, ed. *The Fisheries and Fishery Industries of the United States.* 5 vols. Washington, DC: Government Printing Office, 1887.

Oliver, Sandra L. *Saltwater Foodways: New Englanders and Their Food at Sea and Ashore in the Nineteenth Century.* Mystic, CT: Mystic Seaport Museum, 1995.

Royce, William F. *The Historical Development of Fisheries Science and Management.* http://www.nefsc.noaa.gov/library/history/fsh_sci_history1.html.

SANDRA L. OLIVER

Segmenters, *see Apple Preparation Tools*

Seltzer

Seltzer water is artificially carbonated water to which no flavorings have been added. In the New York City area, seltzer water is often synonymous with soda water. Aside from the bubbles, seltzer's distinct quality is a slightly sour taste caused by the reaction of water with carbon dioxide gas.

Seltzer water takes its name from the German town of Niederselters, the site of a naturally carbonated mineral water spring. With low amounts of minerals and high carbonation, so-called Selters water earned a reputation as a popular table water. In the eighteenth century, Niederselters began exporting its water to North America, where the name became "Seltzer" water. The expense of imported mineral waters led American businessmen to concoct their own domestic water using artificial carbonation, added salts, and other chemicals. By 1810, artificial soda water, including locally made

Selters water, was a popular refreshment in New York and Philadelphia. In the late nineteenth century, however, many soda bottlers stopped adding minerals to their seltzer water. Seltzer became simple tap water that had been filtered and carbonated before being bottled.

Locally made soda bottles occasionally exploded under the pressure of carbonated water. In the 1860s manufacturers, such as Carl H. Schultz of New York, began importing heavy glass bottles from France and central Europe. These were topped with metal siphons that dispensed the liquid without reducing the carbonation left in the bottle. Due to their cost, the siphon bottles remained the property of the seltzer manufacturer, whose name was usually etched or painted onto the glass. Once emptied, the bottles were taken back to the plant for refilling. Because siphons did not work with flavored sodas, the bottles became known as seltzer bottles.

Deliverymen carrying wooden cases of seltzer were common in most American cities and towns. Seltzer water kept people cool in summertime; the wealthy could imitate the English who drank their whiskey with carbonated water; and immigrants could have mineral water on their dinner tables just as they had back in the old country. They called it *Belchwasser* in German, or *grepswasser* in Yiddish, because of the way it aided digestion. Big city seltzer manufacturers tended to be of central European origin, and by the 1920s many German and east European Jews had entered the business. Seltzer's ubiquity in Jewish neighborhoods made it an essential part of the American Jewish experience. On movie screens, the siphon bottle appeared on drink trolleys in elegant drawing room scenes and in the raucous fights of slapstick comedies. In homes, seltzer gained a reputation as a stain remover and as the secret ingredient in the lightest matzo balls.

After 1945, the market for seltzer water began to shrink, as customers moved to the suburbs and women were less often at home to accept deliveries. Supermarkets began to sell carbonated water in throwaway containers. Seltzer water became a novelty, and bottlers either moved into more lucrative lines or were forced out of business. By the 1970s, the refillable seltzer bottle had disappeared from all but a few big cities.

In the early 2000s, there remained less than a dozen bottlers nationwide who still refilled the old seltzer siphons. In the Northeast, supermarkets sold various brands of seltzer water in disposable plastic bottles. There have been attempts to revive the old-style seltzer trade, but, except for a diehard group of customers who enjoy its distinct qualities, seltzer water remains part of the past.

[*See also* Egg Cream; Soda Drinks; Soda Fountains; Water; Water, Bottled.]

BIBLIOGRAPHY

Funderburg, Anne Cooper. *Sundae Best: A History of Soda Fountains*. Bowling Green, OH: Bowling Green State University Popular Press, 2002.

Hiss, A. Emil. *The Standard Manual of Soda and Other Beverages*. Chicago: G. P. Englehard, 1900.

Kuhnigk, Armin. *Niederselters und das Selterswasser in historischen Darstellungen*. Camberg, Germany: M. Neumann, 1972.

McKearin, Helen. *American Bottles and Flasks and Their Ancestry*. New York: Crown, 1978.

Sulz, Charles H. *A Treatise on Beverages*. New York: Dick and Fitzgerald, 1888.

ANDREW COE

Feeding the Hungry. Distributing food at the Five Points Mission, New York, 1880s. From George Augustus Sala, *America Revisited*, 3rd edition (London, 1883), vol. 1, p. 34.

Settlement Houses

Settlement houses were part of a broad endeavor to preserve human values in changing industrial times. The first settlement house, Toynbee Hall, was formed in 1884 by Samuel A. Barnett in the slums of East London. Barnett's idea was to "settle" university men in a working-class neighborhood, where they could apply their intelligence and skills to help relieve poverty while also experiencing the "real world." Barnett's model influenced several Americans who imported ideas from Toynbee Hall to their local communities. The first settlement house in the United States was Neighborhood Guild, formed in 1886 in New York City by Stanton Coit. Three years later College Settlement opened, also in New York City; simultaneously Jane Addams and Ellen Starr founded Hull-House in Chicago.

By 1918 more than four hundred settlement houses thrived in both urban and rural communities across the country. In their early years settlements were financed exclusively through charitable donations and reflected their origins in England, with its state church, by virtue of religious affiliations. Settlement houses became significant facilitators in easing immigrants' adjustment to living in a new culture. Yet immigrants did not escape ethnic stereotypes or prejudice, and most settlements were segregated by ethnicity. Throughout the settlement system the notion of "general welfare"—the conception, associated with emerging social policy of that time, that

individuals had a right to basic assistance, regardless of their religious affiliation—replaced that of charity. The objective was to help each immigrant group become part of the mainstream, to realize the American dream.

In the early twentieth century some settlement houses began to play important roles in the reform movements of the Progressive Era. Settlement houses themselves provided some of the first opportunities for women to become influential leaders in society. Jane Addams and Frances Perkins both carved their way into national affairs through their management of settlement houses. Most settlement activities started with clubs, classes, lectures, and art exhibitions. Settlement house workers pioneered in the kindergarten movement, taught English, and established theaters, courses in industrial education, and music schools.

The best-known commercial product of the settlement house system was *The Settlement House Cook Book: The Way to a Man's Heart*, published for the first time in 1903 by Mrs. Simon Kanter. The cookbook was a response to the need for educational materials to complement the cooking classes Kanter taught at the settlement in Milwaukee, Wisconsin. She believed that if students could take home printed recipes of the dishes they made in class, they would be more likely to utilize them. The settlement board refused the eighteen dollars required to print the books, but the women were undaunted. They solicited advertisements to defray these costs, a form of financing that soon became a model for the multitude of giveaway cookbooks that began to surface with the advent of cooking tools and advanced food product technology in the 1920s.

Accounts of food reform, as told through recipes, instructions, and anecdotes spanning several decades of cookbook publication, tell stories of class, gender, domestic science, and "new philanthropy" movements. (New philanthropy at that time was defined as "an age in which scientific information coupled with social science research suggested cures for a myriad of social ills.") These recipe histories offer a unique perspective on the Americanization of immigrants in the late nineteenth and early twentieth centuries, as traditional recipes were adapted to local ingredients and new dishes were introduced that were thought to be definitively American.

The University Settlement Society, for example, was very concerned with Americanizing the home. Domestic scientists attempted to replace the supremacy of the palate with the rule of scientific law. The rigorous methods of science could bring order to the diversified cultural approaches of immigrants to food preparation. For the reformers, eating was a distasteful but necessary biological function. Food could be civilized only by being controlled, limited, and changed through cooking. The totality of the immigrant homemakers' foodways came under the scrutiny of the reformers. In 1889 a report titled "Food Stores and Purchases in the Tenth Ward" exemplified the scientific observation of culinary habits. Reformers followed the path of food from production to postconsumption, tracing food's place of purchase; its storage, preparation, and consumption in the home; and its removal from the home as waste.

Immigrant women, in their traditional roles as homemakers and mothers, were relied on to achieve the reformers' intended results, but cooking classes for boys and specific classes on hygiene were also held. Reformers encouraged the use of new tools, which were designed for measuring ingredients precisely. Each food item was rigorously analyzed for its properties. The nutritional value of foods could be newly measured in calories and then subdivided further into new categories of protein and carbohydrate. Reformers studied the chemistry of digestion and concluded that the biological process was eased by cooking vegetables until they lost all texture, color, and flavor. Whereas taste was subjective, nutrition was objective and could be strictly prescribed.

Because the settlement movement was defined in the United States by its nonreligious stance, teaching kashruth, the dietary law of religious Jews, was intentionally left out of cooking instruction at many Jewish settlement houses.

The purpose of the cooking classes was to teach American cooking, which consisted of American methods used on American foods. Efforts were made, via recommended menus, to proclaim what foods were American. The nutritionally sound yet benign and bland diet of rural New England was elevated.

The literature of early-twentieth-century Jews in America voices deep resentment and cynicism about attempts to change Jewish food habits. Still, *The Settlement Cook Book* became one of the most popular texts in Jewish immigrant and second-generation kitchens. As the temperance movement spread, further emphasis was placed on the importance of food reform within all settlement houses. Domestic scientists, missionaries, and temperance workers promoted good meals as the solution to what they saw as the drinking problem of the poor.

After World War II, settlement house activities shifted to being more recreational in nature, while the food programs became more service- or convenience-oriented. For example, during this time settlement houses provided the unmarried working woman with an acceptable alternative to living alone or with family. Maid services and the settlement house's public kitchen freed women in the workforce from the need to keep house as well.

The approximately eight hundred settlement houses that exist at the beginning of the twenty-first century continue to provide environments of hope in times of need for new Americans. Settlements provide housing targeted to particular ethnic groups, advocate for policy reform, and facilitate the delivery of government programs as all or part of this ideal. Food continues to be a primary service component, with settlement food programs that include meals-on-wheels for the homebound elderly and after-school and summer meal programs for children, most of which are funded through state and federal sources. The original *Settlement House Cook Book* continues to be revised and reprinted.

[See also Cookbooks and Manuscripts, *subentries* From the Civil War to World War I *and* From World War I to World War II; Cooking Schools; Ethnic Foods; Home Economics; Jewish American Food; Jewish Dietary Laws; Temperance.]

BIBLIOGRAPHY

Berry, Margaret K. *Actual Democracy: The Problems of America.* New York: Prentice-Hall, 1923.

Blank, Barbara Trainin. "Settlement Houses: Old Idea in New Form Builds Communities." *New Social Worker* 55, no. 3 (Summer 1998).

Bryan, Mary Lynn McCree, and Allen F. Davis, eds. *One Hundred Years at Hull-House*. Bloomington, IN: Indiana University Press, 1991.

Davis, Allen F. *Spearheads for Reform: The Social Settlements and the Progressive Movement, 1890–1914*. 2nd ed. Piscataway, NJ: Rutgers University Press, 1984.

Foner, Eric, and John A. Garraty, eds. *The Reader's Companion to American History*. Boston: Houghton-Mifflin, 1991.

Joselit, Jenna Weissman. *The Wonders of America: Reinventing Jewish Culture, 1880–1950*. New York: Hill and Wang, 1994.

Kanter, Mrs. Simon. *The Settlement House Cook Book*. Milwaukee, WI: Settlement Cook Book Company, 1976.

McClymer, John F. "Gender and the 'American Way of Life': Women and the Americanization Movement." *Journal of American Ethnic History* (Spring 1991): 8.

Trolander, Judith Ann. *Professionalism and Social Change: From the Settlement House Movement to Neighborhood Centers, 1886 to the Present*. New York: Columbia University Press, 1987.

KAREN KARP

7 UP

7 UP is a soft drink created by Charles Leiper Grigg of Saint Louis, Missouri. Grigg created his first soft drink, called "Whistle," in 1919. Following a dispute with his employers, Grigg quit his job, leaving Whistle behind, and obtained a new position developing soft-drink flavoring agents for the Warner Jenkinson Company. There he developed his second orange-flavored drink, called "Howdy." Deciding to seek his fortune, Grigg formed a partnership with the financier Edmund D. Ridgway and established the Howdy Corporation in 1920.

Competition from Orange Crush, which dominated the orange soda market, motivated Grigg to develop a new, lemon-lime-flavored drink. By 1929, after testing eleven formulas, Grigg introduced "Bib-Label Lithiated Lemon-Lime Soda." At the time, it actually did include lithium, which was sometimes found in natural spring water and was thought to have curative health effects. The new soft drink, introduced only two weeks before the stock market crash of October 1929, was costly compared with the more than six hundred lemon-lime beverages already on the market, and it bore an unwieldy name; nevertheless, it sold well.

It was not long, however, before Grigg changed the name of his soft drink to 7 UP. The origin of the name is unknown, but various theories have been proposed. At the time, 7 UP contained seven ingredients and was sold in seven-ounce bottles. Another popular Saint Louis soda, called "Bubble Up," may have inspired the "UP" portion of the name. Some speculate that Grigg named his new

7 Up. Advertisement on the back cover of a cookbooklet containing recipes that use 7 Up, 1957. *Collection of Andrew F. Smith*

soda after a card game; others claim that its name is based on a cattle brand that caught Grigg's attention.

The Howdy Corporation fought hard to gain a place for 7 UP in a national market severely affected by the Depression. Lacking national distribution, Grigg instituted a clever marketing strategy by selling 7 UP to the speakeasies that had sprung up as a result of Prohibition, and it quickly became a popular mixer for alcoholic beverages. After the repeal of Prohibition in 1933, Grigg lost no time openly advertising 7 UP as a mixer. In 1936 the Howdy Corporation became the Seven-Up Company, and by 1940 the product had become one of the most popular soft drinks in the United States.

Early 7 UP advertising featured a winged 7 UP logo and the slogan "Seven natural flavors blended into a savory, flavory drink with a real wallop." In 1967 the "UNCOLA" advertising campaign was launched, followed by "No Caffeine" in 1982 and the cartoonlike character of Spot in 1987. In 2002, 7 UP got a new look with Godfrey, the 7 UP Guy who personifies the "Make 7 UP Yours" campaign.

In 1986 the Seven-Up Company merged with the Dr Pepper Company; in 1995 Dr Pepper/Seven Up Companies Inc. was acquired by Cadbury Schweppes of London. In the 1990s the introduction of Diet 7 UP and of various new flavors was geared toward increasing 7 UP's market share. In the United States 7 UP is still widely used as a beverage mixer, and home cooks utilize it as an ingredient in a variety of dishes, including cakes and desserts, molded salads, marinades, and pancakes.

[*See also* Cola Wars; Soda Drinks.]

BIBLIOGRAPHY

Morgan, Hal. *Symbols of America: A Lavish Celebration of America's Best-loved Trademarks and the Products They Symbolize.* New York: Viking, 1986.

Rodengen, Jeffrey L. *The Legend of Dr Pepper/7-Up.* Fort Lauderdale, FL: Write Stuff Syndicate, 1995.

7UP.com. http://www.7up.com. Presents the history of 7 UP, corporate and nutritional information, promotions, a store with 7 UP–related products, and numerous Q & A sections.

BECKY MERCURI

Sherry

Sherry, the afternoon drink of doddering grandmothers and grandaunts, the choice companion to tapas for dedicated Andalusia-admirers, and the inspiration for a short story by Edgar Allan Poe, has a deeper past. Sherry was one of the sweet wines referred to as sack, a commodity that had been heavily traded to the Americas from colonial times. Sack was popular for three reasons. It was inexpensive compared with French wine, it had a high alcohol content because of its fortification with brandy (a practice no longer followed), and it was palatably sweet; all these traits led to its being drunk often by all classes, either alone or as part of a mixed drink. Sherry was used to make a type of American sangria, colloquially called sangaree, and was also the main ingredient of sack posset, a concoction of sherry, sometimes mixed with ale, cooked with sugar, eggs, and cream or milk, and finished off with spices, usually nutmeg or mace, and drunk at weddings in all of the colonies.

Sherry's popularity waned as more whiskeys, jacks, and beers were created in America, but sherry was still used as a mixer as late as the 1867 World Exposition, during which the American pavilion featured sherry cobblers. The twentieth century saw the evolution of two types of sherry.

America developed cooking sherry to circumvent the Prohibition laws. Its flavor was created through cooking or by artificial means, and it was then salted to prevent its being drunk as a beverage. Cheap, fortified sherries were also marketed as inexpensive and potent wines that were often sold in gallon jugs, mainly from California. In contrast, Spanish sherry transformed itself from a fortified wine to one made almost exclusively with the solera system, an aging process that blends several vintages, with distinctions among the four basic styles (in order of dry to sweet, Fino, Manzanilla, Amontillado, and Oloroso). Fino is made with Palomino grapes, is light yellow in color, crisp and dry, and best with savory foods. Manzanilla is Fino aged in Sanlúcar de Barrameda, which, given the proximity to the Mediterranean Sea, lends the sherry a particular (some say salty) taste. Amontillado is oxidized Fino. It is dark brown, nutty, and slightly sweet, and it perfectly balances salted foods like spiced nuts, olives, and other appetizers. Olorosos are made with Ximenez grapes, which are then fortified and sweetened; they complement desserts, cheeses, fruits, and roasted nuts.

[*See also* Prohibition; Sangria; Wine, *subentries* Historical Survey *and* Later Developments.]

BIBLIOGRAPHY

Amory, Cleveland, et al. *The American Heritage Cookbook and Illustrated History of American Eating and Drinking.* New York: American Heritage, 1964.

Gordon, Manuel M. González. *Sherry.* London: Cassell, 1972.

LISA DELANGE

Ship Food

The sea biscuit, salted beef and pork, peas, and beans of shipboard food are popularly known and are often equated with hardship. Throughout most of American maritime history, though, what any seafarer ate aboard a vessel also had a great deal to do with who owned the vessel, what branch of maritime activity it was engaged in, and where in the shipboard hierarchy the seafarer stood.

Most of the rationing schemes employed by American private or naval vessels were based upon British example. Once the voyages of discovery were largely past and regular patterns of transatlantic and coastwise trading, travel, and fishing had been established, sufficient experience informed vessel provisioning. Barring bad weather or a navigator's grave misjudgment, the length of a voyage was relatively predictable. Further, as certain places became established ports, a ship's captain knew where he would be able to restock provisions and take on water. Bakers making ship's biscuits and butchers engaged in barreling salt meat established businesses even in the early 1600s in port towns and cities.

Basic Supplies

The centuries-long practices of carrying hard bread, salted meat (both beef and pork), and staple legumes (peas or beans) formed the baseline of shipboard food. Besides water, many vessels supplied spirits and a brewed beverage, often alcoholic. The British preferred beer, the French and Spanish, wine, but Americans often took beer and cider. Other fare depended a great deal on era and place and included dried fruits, dried fish, rice, cornmeal, wheat flour, cheese, sweetening, and some vegetables to be consumed as long as they lasted. After the 1740s and the experimental work done by Dr. James Lind, a British naval surgeon, it was understood that fresh fruits and vegetables, particularly citrus, prevented debilitating scurvy, although at the time no one knew that it was specifically vitamin C that sailors needed. By the end of the eighteenth century, responsible shipowners took aboard antiscorbutics, usually citrus juice, sauerkraut, and, more likely in American vessels, vinegar.

In the early nineteenth century, basic legal scales of provision on average allowed a pound of beef or pork a day, from fourteen to sixteen ounces of bread, a half-pint of spirits, a half-pound of rice or flour, an ounce of coffee or cocoa, and a quarter-ounce of tea a day per person. Other items like a half-pint of peas or beans might be allowed three times a week, with cheese, pickles, and dried fruit and the like specified once or twice a week. These ingredients were organized into daily menus, or mess bills, repeated weekly. A sailor could tell what day of the week it was by the combination of food that appeared. Seafarers might report that they had pork with beans or peas two times a week, beef three times, potatoes twice a week, rice once or twice a week, salt fish once, and duff, a kind of boiled pudding, twice a week on the days that flour was allowed. Duff was served with molasses and so was rice.

Rations and Hierarchy

A wide range of concerns influenced the provisioning list, the most prominent of which was where the seafarer stood in the shipboard hierarchy, whether a passenger, officer, or foremast hand. The more complex the hierarchy, the greater were the distinctions in food. Naval vessels had more complicated provisioning and dining structures than deep-water merchant vessels, which in turn were more complex than coastwise trading vessels with small crews.

Generally the finest and freshest food was accorded the individuals at the top of the hierarchy: the captain, first officers, and cabin passengers. If, for example, there was any fresh meat, either purchased or newly killed from one of the small animals often carried alive—as pigs, sheep, goats, and chickens often were—that meat was prepared for the cabin, while the sailors before the mast enjoyed such fare only on special occasions. Similarly, fresh vegetables, if in short supply, were cooked for the first officers and passengers, and the fo'mast hands made do with dried peas or beans to go with the salt meat. For sweetening, the occupants of the cabin enjoyed white sugar while the seamen received the cheaper molasses. And if anyone had freshly baked bread, it was those same occupants of the cabin; the rest of the crew ate hardtack.

Niceties, such as preserves, butter, canned fruits or vegetables, and ham, were carried aboard for the cabin, although sometimes the common seamen themselves brought nicer foods from home, received them as gifts, or, when and if they could afford it, bought them in port or from locals in small craft who swarmed newly arriving vessels looking for buyers of fresh produce.

Technology and Nutritional Change

In the last half of the nineteenth century, technological change and growing understanding of minimum nutritional standards gradually made the distinctions in kinds of food provided on board less pronounced. With increased use of steam power, voyages were shorter and ships were reprovisioned more often. At the same time, artificial refrigeration, either using ice or cold generated by other means, enabled vessels to store certain foods longer. Food-processing technology made other kinds of stored food, such as canned fruits, vegetables, and meat, both available and cheaper.

Once it was technologically possible to provide better food for all hands, the expectation of better fare rose as well, as the legal scale of provisions enacted in 1898 revealed. With this scale, canned meat, canned tomatoes, more dried fruit, a greater variety of grains, seasonings, such as pepper and mustard, and butter, cheese, lard, and fresh bread, in addition to hardtack, became minimum requirements. This coincided with smaller crews on steam and sailing vessels of the late nineteenth and early twentieth centuries, which used small engines to do work formerly done manually, so that shipowners spent more on food, but fed fewer personnel.

Good and Sufficient

Yankee shipowners, particularly during the age of sail, often exceeded the legally required rations, providing better food than was found on most European and English ships. A better-fed crew was more energetic, so captains could drive a vessel harder and faster to economic advantage. Also, better fare encouraged sailors' loyalty and served to help recruit crew members. Some seafarers reported that seamen on European ships would jump to American ships in foreign ports in order to be better fed.

When sufficient or good-quality fare was a problem, the problem could usually be traced to the shipowner's parsimony, sometimes aggravated when the captain was also a part owner and in position to control shipboard costs. Whenever various maritime ventures felt economic pressure and lower profits, owners hewed more closely to the legally required minimum rations, to sailors' detriment.

Food in Fishing Fleets

The best food for working seafarers was surely that provided in the offshore fishing fleets in the later 1800s and in the 1900s. Fishing vessels were often owned and outfitted by the fishermen's families and neighbors. Part of the food was provided by the vessel, the rest paid for by the crew. Additionally, the cooks hired were well-paid and skilled individuals, in contrast to the cooks aboard many merchant and whaling ships of the same era, who might have been recruited from the fo'mast crew with little or no prior experience.

Fishermen's fare was notably egalitarian. All hands ate alike, from captain to newest crew member, in kind, quantity, and manner. (Interestingly, the same rule applied aboard vessels engaged in piracy.) Fishermen ate well three times a day, with snacks in between. Cooks made bread, biscuits, cakes, and pies to accompany the best-quality salted beef or pork and potato meals, washed down by gallons of coffee with condensed, or, later, evaporated milk in it. When fishing fleets turned to icing their catches in the latter 1800s, they could carry fresh meat. On many smaller inshore fishing vessels, with only three or four men working aboard, determining who did the cooking might be left to drawing lots, or to the captain's designation. The plentiful fare was simple but usually tolerable for short stretches.

Passengers' Food

In the seventeenth and eighteenth centuries, passengers traveling by sea were expected to provide much of their own food, even when they were served in the cabin in the same manner as the captain and first officers. When transatlantic packet service began in the 1800s, passengers were sorted into a hierarchy according to their accommodations, usually designated by class. Each classification ate at a different time and had its own menu. In some respects, the food resembled hotel fare, increasingly so as the nineteenth century wore on. By the 1880s, a first- or second-class passenger could expect a multicourse meal starting with soup or fish; freshly roasted or baked meat and boiled meats with sauces and gravy; side dishes of organ meats, chops, or poultry; potatoes and other vegetables; a variety of puddings or pies; and for dessert nuts and fruits, tea, coffee, and cheese and crackers.

Many poorer immigrant passengers, occupying steerage, could not have had a more different experience. Responsible for bringing their own provisions, they prepared food for themselves in a usually insufficient cooking area provided for them. Agents recruiting them for passage too often misrepresented the length of the voyage. Consequently many immigrants came aboard undersupplied and when the vessel encountered adverse weather, lengthening the voyage, many suffered terribly, reduced to stealing food anywhere they could find it, or begging the captain for some from the ship's supply. Weakened by hunger and seasickness and crammed together in unsanitary conditions, many immigrants died at sea, victims of disease. Abuses finally led to regulation, but even then only minimal rations were allowed poor emigrating passengers.

Manner of Dining

Eating or dining customs at sea were also governed by hierarchy. In the early days, the men in the fo'c'sle of merchant and whaling vessels were divided into watches that ate, or messed, together. Many provided their own utensils and ate commonly from a container filled at the ship's galley that was brought to them frequently by the watch's youngest member. In the last quarter of the nineteenth century, a table, often collapsible, and simple place settings were provided. A different arrangement obtained in the navy, where smaller groups of men messed together at tables and one of their number dubbed "cook of the mess" fetched the food from the galley. Sailors carefully observed equality among the members of the mess, evenly dividing up the food and sharing losses in the case of spills, not uncommon in rough seas.

In the cabin and among the officers on any ship, a more formal, often homelike, atmosphere was the norm, with table, tablecloths, napkins, and full place settings, including serving dishes. The captain took precedence, followed by the others according to their rank.

Sea Cooks

Sea cooks in working vessels in earlier years could be young boys, especially on small fishing or coasting vessels. In naval vessels, a disabled seaman sometimes was given the berth; he was still fit for service if not for clambering in rigging or manning guns. In larger American merchant and whaling vessels, particularly as the nineteenth century wore on, the cook was most often a black or Asian man, hardly ever trained at cookery. On European vessels the cook was more likely to be a white male. The steward, or stewards, similarly, were often black or Asian, although occasionally women served. They worked in the cabin, serving the captain, first officers, and passengers, and saw to the finer points of cookery, often including bread baking and making whatever desserts were required.

On modern working vessels, most of the old distinctions regarding food have diminished among the crew. Modern food technology and relatively short voyages mean fresh refrigerated and frozen food, making possible even shipboard salad bars and fresh meat or fish every day with vegetables. Cooks are professionally trained for cooking at sea and are often women, though many are still Asian men. And where in the past a crew member's main concern might have been getting a sufficient share, or whack, in the past half century or so, according to one merchant mariner on the Great Lakes, the newest maritime hazard is the good and abundant food, which puts the modern sailor's waistline at risk.

[*See also* Hardtack; Ice; Salt and Salting.]

BIBLIOGRAPHY

Carpenter, Kenneth J. *The History of Scurvy and Vitamin C.* Cambridge, UK, 1986.

Dana, Richard Henry, Jr. *Two Years Before the Mast.* New York, 2001. This is a classic narrative of life at sea in the early 1800s, and Dana often discusses sailors' food.

Druett, Joan, ed. *She Was a Sister Sailor: Mary Brewster's Whaling Journals.* Mystic, CT: Mystic Seaport Museum, 1992. Mary Brewster often mentioned food in her diaries, and this book also quotes from other seafaring women who describe food at sea from the perspective of the cabin.

Garner, Stanton, ed. *The Captain's Best Mate: The Journal of Mary Chipman Lawrence on the Whaler* Addison, *1856–1860.* Hanover, NH, and London, 1966.

Grossman, Anne Chotzinoff, and Lisa Grossman Thomas. *Lobscouse and Spotted Dog: Which It's a Gastronomic Companion to the Aubrey/Maturin Novels.* New York: Norton, 1997. Although the book is a companion to Patrick O'Brian novels of life in the British Navy in the Napoleonic era, it contains recipes for many dishes that would have been served at sea on American vessels.

Harlow, Frederick Pease. *The Making of a Sailor on a Yankee Square-Rigger.* Salem, MA, 1928. Chapter seven, "Salt Horse and Discipline," contains good descriptions of sailors' fare in the 1870s.

Oliver, Sandra L. *Saltwater Foodways: New Englanders and Their Food at Sea and Ashore in the 19th Century.* Mystic, CT, 1995.

Riesenberg, Felix. *Under Sail.* New York: Macmillan, 1918.

SANDRA L. OLIVER

Shoat, *see Pig*

Sieves, Sifters, and Colanders

Utensils with meshes or perforations of different sizes are used for straining solids from liquids, washing and draining fruit, forcing lumpy materials, such as gravy, into smooth homogeneity, pulping ripe fruit, and sifting dry foods into batters. Benjamin Gilbert of Redding, Connecticut, invented wire screening about 1835, after years of making horsehair sieves. Horsehair had to be washed and sorted, woven, set into bentwood frames, and sewed securely with waxed thread. Wire screen was made on special looms and held in metal frames. Gilbert prospered from making screening for meat-safe doors, sieves, and dairy strainers.

Flour sifters differ mostly in the scraper that pushes the flour through the fine screen and in how it moves. Scrapers of revolving wires might be cranked or moved by squeeze action or shaking. Some flour sifters had lids at both ends, making it easy to double- or triple-sift flour for light pastries.

Colanders were first made of copper or tin, then of sheet iron that was enameled to keep the metal from reacting with acidic food, and then of aluminum by 1900. Colanders may be designed like saucepans, or they may have round bottoms that rest in a separate or an attached ring foot. They might also stand on tab feet. Plastic has been used for colanders since the 1960s. In the early 2000s, metal wire screen was still used for strainers and flour sifters.

[*See also* Flytraps and Screens; Frying Baskets.]

BIBLIOGRAPHY

Franklin, Linda Campbell. *300 Years of Kitchen Collectibles.* 5th ed. Iola, WI: Krause, 2003.

LINDA CAMPBELL FRANKLIN

Sifters, *see Sieves, Sifters, and Colanders*

Silverware

Americans often use the term "silverware" with casual, democratic optimism to refer to dining utensils of any material. Properly, the word defines any object fashioned from silver, Sheffield plate, or silver electroplate. Dining silverware includes the vast array of trays, tureens, candlesticks, centerpieces, and other table objects, which can be subdivided into the areas of hollowware (bowls and vases) and flatware (items made from a flat sheet of silver, especially forks and spoons). Cutlery, now used interchangeably with flatware, once signified only those items produced by the Cutler's Guild, especially steel-bladed knives but also scissors and other sharp objects. The American predilection to use "silverware" synonymously with "flatware" or "cutlery" speaks to the enduring popularity and historical importance of silver at the table. Even in the ancient world, hosts wowed their guests with impressive silver platters and elegant spoons. The metal's decorative possibilities have been exploited ever since.

Colonial America

To own a single silver spoon in colonial America was a great luxury; more commonly people owned pewter, latten (a copper alloy similar to brass), or wood. Forks, rare in Europe, were almost unheard of in the colonies. Desire Gorham, a wealthy widow who died in Yarmouth, Massachusetts, in 1683, owned but two silver spoons and one silver beaker. No silver mines existed in New England, so silversmiths created their wares from coins or outmoded objects refashioned into the newest styles. Coin silver, usually made from melting down Spanish colonial *reales*, was not quite .900 pure, compared to the British sterling standard of .925 pure, but silverware could be melted down and converted into cash at any moment.

Matching forks, knives, and spoons did not sit together at place settings until the mid-eighteenth century.

Wealthy colonists might carry their own set of personal utensils in a carrying case. As early as 1669, Antipas Boyse left one such rarity containing a fork, knife, and spoon. By 1728 Governor William Burnet of Boston had amassed a vast collection of domestic silver including a dozen spoons, knives, and forks; three dozen silver-handled knives and forks for dessert; numerous teaspoons; tea, coffee, and punch items; candlesticks; salvers; and other serving pieces. However, an examination of inventories from the Tidewater region of Virginia and Maryland reveals that as late as 1750 roughly one in five households still lacked forks and knives.

By 1800 approximately 2,500 silversmiths were employed in the United States, although English and Continental silver continued to be popular. In 1796, the Reverend William Bentley of Salem, Massachusetts, especially noted that the Prebble family's silver tea service, which he credited as being the best in the city, had been "imported entire." Southerners bought English silver in large quantities, most of which got melted down during the Civil War.

Early American silverware strongly followed English styles and techniques. When, in the late seventeenth century, English spoons grew more elongated and carried trifid handles with three-lobed terminals, so too did their American counterparts. Eighteenth-century American flatware copied the fashion for rattail handles, whose raised rib give them their name; and, later that century, the "Old English" pattern, which was the first laid upward on the table. By the early nineteenth century, Americans had mastered the European technique of making patterned flatware by stamping the blank ingots between two steel dies, cut with the desired shape.

Innovations and the Gilded Age

In 1801, T. Bruff patented a method for manufacturing spoons, which was soon followed by American patents for impressed rollers, bulk casting, water-powered buffing wheels, and forming spoons from flat silver sheets with a drop hammer. Other innovations came from the silver imitators, such as the Britannia metal manufacturers, who by the early nineteenth century produced flatware in various inexpensive white alloys. By the second half of the nineteenth century, entire forks and spoons were made by die stamping.

Electroplating revolutionized the silverware industry. The firm of G. R. and H. Elkington patented the process of coating a thin layer of silver onto finished metal

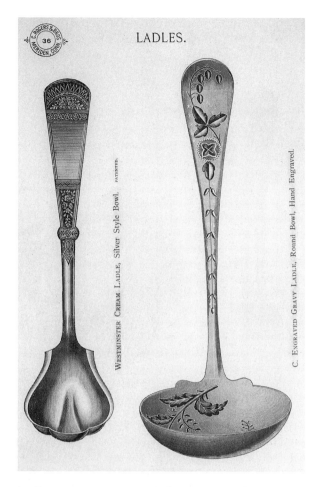

LADLES.

WESTMINSTER CREAM LADLE, Silver Style Bowl. PATENTED.

C. ENGRAVED GRAVY LADLE, Round Bowl, Hand Engraved.

Ladles. Westminster cream ladle and engraved gravy ladle. From C. Rogers & Bros. catalog, 1890.

objects through electrolysis in Sheffield, England, in 1840. John O. Mead, a Britannia-ware manufacturer from Philadelphia, learned of the new technique while abroad in 1837 and within five years developed a plating technique. Almost instantly, numerous American firms produced electroplated flatware. Several grades of plate were quickly developed, a heavy-duty variety marketed as especially appropriate for hotels, boardinghouses, restaurants, railway cars, and steamboats—venues that built public awareness of these elegant wares.

The post–Civil War economic boom fueled Americans' demand for silverware. Americans evolved the practice of mass production by means of using interchangeable parts, a technique showcased at the Centennial Exposition in Philadelphia in 1876. Charles Venable points out that American silver production almost quadrupled between 1875 and 1915, though little of it was exported. The discovery of vast deposits of the precious metal in the

American West significantly lowered its cost, consequently making luxurious dinner services affordable to a broader audience. Households strove to compete with one another over the fineness of their silver. Tiffany and Company, to distinguish its premium quality, adopted the British sterling standard in the 1850s. By 1870 most other American manufacturers voluntarily converted to sterling, although not legally bound to do so until the Stamping Act of 1906.

Among the most astounding American services was the one created by Tiffany for the "silver king" John Mackay as a gift for his wife, fashioned from bullion from Mackay's Comstock silver mine and showcased at the American pavilion in the 1878 Paris exhibition. More than two hundred men spent more than two years laboring exclusively on upwards of twelve hundred articles—tureens, tea trays, enameled napkin rings, a forty-eight–pound punch bowl, and a bewildering array of forks, knives, and spoons. The service was created just as the French fashion for dining à la russe, with numerous individual courses served consecutively, became stylish in America.

Previously, a standard fork, knife, and spoon had sufficed to eat numerous foods. Very elegant homes had had dessert flatware, usually in a fancier pattern than the dinner utensils, as well as such items as fish slices, asparagus tongs, marrow spoons, grape shears, sugar sifters, and carving sets. But with the change in service style, new forms proliferated at a dizzying rate.

Americans far surpassed Europeans in designing specialized flatware. In addition to the vast array of individual dining utensils—lobster picks, nutpicks, and special Victorian moustache spoons with guards to protect facial hair from inadvertently drowning in soup—socially ambitious Americans purchased ice cream saws with ferocious silver blades; macaroni servers whose jagged edge had the proud audacity of a Native American feather headdress; sickle-shaped aspic slicers; and flat servers for the fried oysters that had become a national fetish. The Gilded Age's mania for Saratoga chips, later called potato chips, found expression in silver pieces designed exclusively for dispensing them. Specialized utensils underlined the rarity and luxury of the foods consumed with them while attesting to the wealth and status of their owners.

By 1918 the Chicago wholesaler A. C. Becken distinguished between the forks it sold to serve chipped versus smoked beef. The situation was further confused by the fact that what A. C. Becken called a ramekin fork was a terrapin fork at Tiffany. Even more perplexingly,

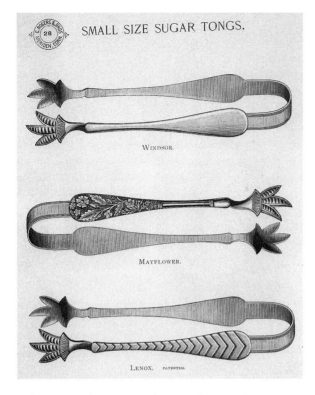

SMALL SIZE SUGAR TONGS.

WINDSOR.

MAYFLOWER.

LENOX.   PATENTED.

Tongs. Sugar tongs in Windsor, Mayflower, and Lenox patterns. C. Rogers & Bros. catalog, 1890.

identical flatware pieces sometimes carried more than one name within the same manufacturer. The escalating costs of producing up to 146 different pieces in a pattern proved burdensome to manufacturers. In 1925 the Sterling Silversmiths Guild of America devised a simplification program, put into place the following year by the Bureau of Standards, which limited the number of pieces in any one pattern and restricted the introduction of new designs.

The large array of flatware, enough to consume a dozen courses, laid out on crammed tables, became not just economically infeasible but also bad form. The streamlined aesthetic of the 1920s simplified the quantity of silverware utilized at formal meals as much as it did the designs. Emily Post and other etiquette authorities decreed that no more than three forks, placed faceup on the left, and two knives on the right, blades facing in, be set on the table at any one time. Additional flatware, if needed, could be brought in with the appropriate course. This arrangement remained correct at the beginning of the twenty-first century.

As the mania for specialized flatware disappeared, new materials and higher working-class standards of liv-

ing brought the basic place setting to every household and roadside diner. Turn-of-the-century experimenters in England, France, and Germany simultaneously discovered that the addition of nickel and chromium to steel significantly lowered its susceptibility to corrosion. Stainless knife blades were common by the 1920s. However, because of the new alloy's challenging hardness, forks and spoons in even the simplest designs remained rare until postwar manufacturers adapted military technology invented during World War II to stainless flatware. Wartime innovation similarly brought about disposable plastic cutlery. These mass-produced, humble, everyday place settings are direct descendants of their more grandiose ancestors, for which reason Americans generously call their stainless flatware "silverware."

Spoons

Indispensable for preparing and consuming liquid foods, spoons hark back to the childhood of civilization. Primitive societies made spoons by attaching shells to a makeshift handle. More than four thousand years ago, the ancient Egyptians had already transformed the utensil into a ceremonial implement of deep meaning and requisite beauty; exquisite ivory spoons were buried in the tombs of pharaohs. Spoons have remained both utilitarian tools and talismanic objects ever since.

The book of Exodus tells that God commanded Moses to make gold spoons for the tabernacle containing the Ark of the Covenant. Numbers 7 relates that the twelve princes of Israel each offered a golden spoon filled with incense at the dedicating of the altar. From the twelfth century, English sovereigns have been anointed with the pearl-encrusted Coronation Spoon. Godparents have gifted their charges with spoons at christenings since at least the early sixteenth century. The custom was imported to the American colonies, as was that of giving funeral pallbearers spoons engraved with the name and death date of the deceased. Welsh brides received spoons upon their betrothal, giving rise to the colloquial term "spooning," which meant making love. Nineteenth-century Americans gave friendship spoons as tokens of affection. Spoons commemorate human events from birth until death, just as they feed us from infancy through enfeebled old age. They are the stuff of nursery rhymes: "The dish ran away with the spoon." And they guard against evil by distancing us from others: "Marry, he must have a long spoon that must eat with the devil," says Shakespeare in *The Comedy of Errors.*

The word "spoon" is derived from the Celtic *spon*, meaning wood chip, the commonest material for early spoons. The Vikings produced intricately carved examples. Nevertheless, the expression "born with a silver spoon" points to the long-standing status of those made from that precious metal.

The earliest American spoons had fig-shaped bowls with a slender, polygonal handle cropped at an angle like a slipped stalk, for which reason they are called "slip-end" spoons. Eighteenth-century colonial spoons came in three basic sizes: porridge, table, and tea. Porridge spoons were largest, then tablespoons; both were also used for preparing and serving meals. Teaspoons were the most decorous because they accompanied luxurious tea. There were also pierced strainer spoons, probably for straining tea; ladles for serving gravy, punch, and soup; basting spoons with elongated handles; marrow spoons; pierced spoons; mustard spoons; sugar spoons and shells; and the occasional sugar crusher.

New Amsterdam silversmiths created distinctive "monkey spoons" imitating Dutch examples. The Dutch referred to drinking as *zuiging de monkey* (sucking the monkey). According to Mary P. Ferris, morning rations of rum were swallowed from the shallow *monkey lepel* (monkey spoon). The form has a hammered, spadelike bowl, often engraved with vignettes, attached to a cast handle with a decorative knop, a kind of finial that frequently depicted a monkey. Given as gifts at betrothals, weddings, christenings, and funerals, some also had fanciful bosses in forms such as a heart, rosette, or mourner at a funerary urn. New England silversmiths, by contrast, invented the coffin-end spoon, whose sober form exclusively commemorated death.

Miniature salt spoons, fancy dessertspoons, and decorative caddy spoons began to appear by 1800. By 1846, Tiffany marketed ice cream spoons and scoops. When the ritual of afternoon tea spread to America in the 1840s, a smaller afternoon teaspoon became fashionable. Delicate after-dinner coffee spoons were also produced, as were chocolate spoons. *Service à la russe* introduced sorbet spoons for between-course palate cleansing; round-bowled spoons for bouillon, chowder, and cream soup; preserve, jam, and jelly spoons; gilded egg spoons; long-handled lemonade spoons, later called iced-tea spoons; and sharp-edged grapefruit spoons. Ladles for cream, mayonnaise, and the ubiquitous oyster stew also appeared.

As spoon forms multiplied, diners were entreated to use them as infrequently as possible. By 1887 American etiquette demanded that spoons be used only for stirring tea or eating soup; even ice cream was to be eaten with a fork.

The generation that disdained using spoons because of their childlike simplicity, perhaps for the same reason collected them at an astounding rate. From the early nineteenth century, colleges and universities offered keepsake spoons to their alumni. Berry spoons were a popular mid-century American invention, often made by redecorating English Georgian spoons. American manufacturers revived the sixteenth-century English fashion for sets of thirteen "Apostle" spoons, representing Jesus and each of the twelve apostles. By the late 1880s souvenir spoons commemorating people, places, and events came into vogue, a fashion imported from Europe. At the 1893 Columbian Exposition in Chicago, spoon frenzy overtook America. Spoons immortalized the Grand Canyon, George Washington, the battle of Gettysburg, Plymouth Rock,

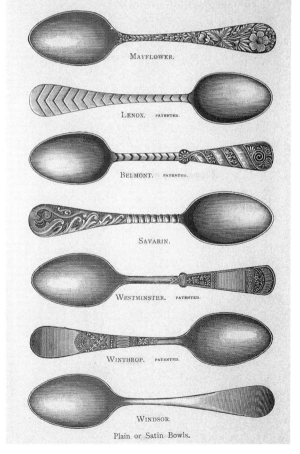

Coffee Spoons. French or after-dinner coffee spoons. From C. Rogers & Bros. catalog, 1890.

Tampa strawberries, and the Milwaukee Indian. Even colorful villains such as Soapy Smith, bad man of the Alaskan gold rush, and Dumbo the Elephant merited spoons. Fanciful silver-spoon holders and racks proliferated to showcase collectible spoons. By 1922 the companies that exclusively produced such items were out of business, although souvenir spoon manufacturers and collecting continue to a much diminished degree. However, use of spoons had made a comeback; it was once again permissible to eat ice cream, puddings, and berries with them.

Knives

Knives are among humankind's first tools. Prehistoric flint examples, which allowed early hunter-gatherers to dismember large animal carcasses, have been unearthed at archaeological sites across Europe. The Copper and Bronze Ages transformed the knife from a sharpened stone into a magnificent metal object, often handsomely decorated, which served as a weapon, multipurpose tool, and critical implement for the preparation and consumption of food. Ritual sacrifice and the ceremonial distribution of meat, facilitated by the knife, flourished at the earliest recorded banquets, with roots as far back as ancient Sumer. These rituals later lay at the center of worship in Homeric Greece, ancient Rome, and the Bible. In medieval Europe, carving became an honorific service performed by noblemen who used slicing and presentation knives of commensurate elegance. Personal knives, carried in a sheath, served as the sole eating utensil. Whenever hands would not suffice, the point of a blade was used to stab food from a platter and place it in the mouth. In northern Europe, where the aristocracy evolved from tribal hunters, the knife maintained its preeminence long after Italians took up the fork. In the United States, knives remained the primary utensil well into the nineteenth century. American knives had wide, rounded blades that conveyed food to the mouth like a kind of individual flat spatula.

By that date, it had been forgotten that Europeans had once eaten from knife blades; the practice was perceived as distinctly American. In *The Young Lady's Friend* of 1837, Eliza Ware Farrar maintained:

> If you wish to imitate the French or English, you will put every mouthful into your mouth with your fork; but if you think, as I do, that Americans have as good a right to their own fashions as the inhabitants of any other country, you may choose the convenience of feeding yourself with your right

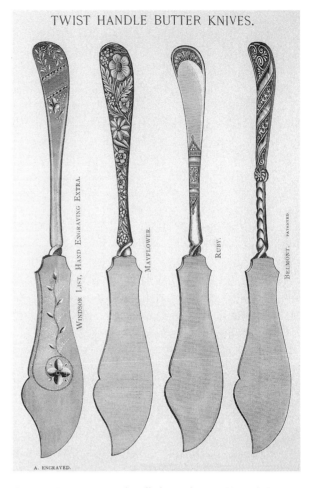

Butter Knives. Twist handle butter knives. From C. Rogers & Bros. catalog, 1890.

hand, armed with a steel blade; and provided you do it neatly, and do not put in large mouthfuls, or close your lips tightly over the blade, you ought not to be considered as eating ungenteelly.

However, by 1845 *The Art of Good Behavior* advised: "If possible the knife should never be put in the mouth at all, and if at all, let the edge be turned downward." Seven years later, *The Art of Pleasing* declared that diners should "eat always with a fork or spoon," though it acknowledged that this was not possible at old-fashioned houses. As late as 1906, a humorous mock etiquette guide published under the pseudonym O. B. Hayve included a letter from a Marion Newlyrich, who complained, "Dear papa insists upon using his knife in eating pie. How can I cure him?"

In his seminal work *The Civilizing Process*, the twentieth-century sociologist Norbert Elias argued that the knife's importance diminished as society deemed it vulgar to brandish a sharp-tooled object at the table. For this same reason, knife blades became as nonthreatening as possible. Fish knives, a mid-nineteenth century European invention, have trowellike silver blades. Butter knives, an American innovation of similar date, likewise sport silver blades, as do salad knives. Conversely, sharp-bladed steak knives are used only when the blunter dinner knife is insufficiently sharp.

Forks

At contemporary meals, the fork reigns supreme, aided by the knife and spoon only when absolutely necessary. It is the newest of the three basic utensils to arrive at the table. The ancient world utilized forks to roast ritually sacrificed meat over the fire, as Homer describes in *The Odyssey*. The Romans made dainty two-tined forks, perhaps for eating seafood. In general, however, ancient forks were used only as cooking tools or weapons—Poseidon's trident and the Devil's pitchfork.

Persian forks made between the second and the sixth centuries hint that perhaps the fork, like many spices, wended its way from Persia to Byzantium before reaching Europe through the gateway of Venice. The earliest known dinner forks in Europe belonged to a Byzantine princess who married the doge of Venice circa 1060. The ecclesiastics called divine wrath down upon her for her excessively refined practice of eating with a golden two-tined fork. When she succumbed to a horrible illness, Saint Bonaventure declared that it was God's just punishment. Venetian courtesans imitated the dogaressa's wanton habit, which had spread through Florence and Venice by the sixteenth century.

Northern Europe continued to deem the fork a vain and pretentious affectation. Around the year 1515, the Protestant Reformer Martin Luther purportedly declared, "God protect me from forks." The earliest Frenchman documented as wielding a fork was Henry III (r. 1574–1589), famous for dressing up in women's clothes. Although by 1672 French etiquette demanded food be consumed with a fork, King Louis XIV (r. 1643–1715) refused ever to use one because he considered it unmanly.

When the Pilgrims sailed for the American colonies, dinner forks had only recently arrived in England. The newfangled affectation of forks was anathema to Puritan culture. Only after worldly and wealthy tradesmen and governors settled in the colonies did forks slowly appear. Captain John Freake, who flamboyantly wore Venetian lace and silver buttons, possessed eight at his death in 1675. Most seventeenth-century American forks were to spear suckett, or preserved ginger and sweetmeats, and had two slender tines with a spoon bowl at the opposite end. Other early forks were convertible fork-spoons, which could be carried by their owners, or cooking forks of iron.

Although silver three-tined dinner forks made in eighteenth-century America survive, most were iron or steel with two sharp tines that steadied a piece of meat while it was being cut with a knife. Morsels were then taken to the mouth with the knife blade. Such forks were produced in England from the late sixteenth through the eighteenth centuries. Americans used them well into the nineteenth century.

Three- and four-tined silver forks gained popularity in America in the early nineteenth century and the two-tined variety came to be regarded as rustic and vulgar. During this transitional period, President Andrew Jackson purportedly offered guests both a silver and a steel two-tined fork, which remained his personal preference. However, by 1860 American etiquette writers declared that three- or four-tined dinner forks were de rigueur.

In America the dinner fork has always been held in the left hand while using the knife with the right, then switching the fork to the right before taking food to the mouth. This method appears to be French in origin, but fell out of use in France in the nineteenth century and came to be regarded as peculiarly American.

Late-nineteenth-century Americans developed a fanaticism for forks. Oyster forks, produced in England from 1790 and retailed by Tiffany from at least 1846, were requisite at smart American dining rooms by 1860. From 1864, etiquette books instructed diners to cut pastry with the edge of a fork, never the knife. However, cheapened production methods resulted in the necessity for new utensils that could withstand such use. In 1869 Reed and Barton patented a "Cutting-Tined Fork," capable of breaking through all kinds of food. By the 1880s pastry forks with a thickened tine were commonly available on the American market. A decade later individual salad and lettuce forks were also sold. Fruit, melons, strawberries, sandwiches, bread, and even ice cream merited their own forks. Turn-of-the-century etiquette books declared, "Never use a knife or spoon when a fork will do." The proliferation of specialized forks fell from fashion after World War I. In 1929 Emily Post declared, "NO rule of etiquette is of less importance than which fork we use." In the era of fast food, people often do without one altogether.

[*See also* Dining Rooms, Table Settings, and Table Manners; Etiquette Books; Material Culture and Technology, *subentry on* Social Aspects of Material Culture.]

BIBLIOGRAPHY

Goldberg, Michael J. *Collectible Plastic: Kitchenware and Dinnerware, 1935–1965.* Atglen, PA: Schiffer, 1995.

Heritage Plantation of Sandwich. *A Cubberd, Four Joyne Stools & Other Smalle Thinges: The Material Culture of Plymouth Colony and Silver and Silversmiths of Plymouth, Cape Cod, and Nantuckett.* Catalog to the Exhibition held 8 May–23 October 1994. Sandwich, MA: Trustees of the Heritage Plantation of Sandwich, 1994.

Hood, William P., Jr., with Roslyn Berlin and Edward Wawrynek. *Tiffany Silver Flatware: 1845–1905, When Dining Was an Art.* Woodbridge, Suffolk, U.K.: Antique Collectors' Club, Ltd., 1999.

Museum of Fine Arts, Boston. *Colonial Silversmiths, Masters and Apprentices.* Boston: Museum of Fine Arts, 1956.

Newman, Harold. *An Illustrated Dictionary of Silverware.* London: Thames and Hudson, 1987.

Philips, John Marshall. *American Silver.* Mineola, NY: Dover, 2001.

Rainwater, Dorothy T., and Donna H. Felger. *A Collector's Guide to Spoons around the World.* Hanover, PA: Everybodys Press, 1976.

Snell, Doris Jean. *Victorian Silverplated Flatware.* Des Moines, IA: Wallace-Homestead Book Co., 1975.

Stutzenberger, Albert. *American Historical Spoons: The American Story in Spoons.* Rutland, VT: Charles E. Tuttle, 1971.

Truman, Charles, ed. *Sotheby's Concise Encyclopedia of Silver.* London: Conran Octopus, 1993.

Turner, Noel D. *American Silver Flatware: 1837–1910.* South Brunswick, NJ: A. S. Barnes, 1972.

Venable, Charles L. *Silver in America, 1840–1940: A Century of Splendor.* New York: Abrams, 1995.

Visser, Margaret. *The Rituals of Dinner: The Origins, Evolution and Meaning of Table Manners.* New York: Grove Weidenfeld, 1991.

CAROLIN C. YOUNG

Simmons, Amelia

Amelia Simmons was the author of *American Cookery*, which first appeared in Hartford, Connecticut, in 1796. The work appears to be the earliest extant published cookbook written by an American. Previously published cookbooks in the colonies had simply been reprints of English works. What is described on the title page as "the second edition" was published in Albany, New York. No date is given, but Eleanor Lowenstein (*Bibliography of American Cookery Books*) cited an advertisement for the work in the *Albany Gazette* of October 31, 1796. Lowenstein listed thirteen appearances of the work; there were also pirated editions.

Considering the importance of *American Cookery*, little is known about Amelia Simmons except that she was "an American orphan" and that she wrote the second edition not only because "the call was so great" but also to free

the work "from those egregious blunders, and inaccuracies, which attended the first: which were occasioned either by the ignorance, or evil intention of the transcriber for the press." Simmons clearly had been forced by necessity to earn her living as a domestic worker, but her home of origin is not known. It has often been suggested that she must have been from Connecticut, but in some respects a more persuasive case can be made for the Hudson River valley. Evidence of the latter likelihood is the early published use in English of a number of words of Dutch origin. The most notable is "slaw" specifically referring to cabbage salad, that is, "coleslaw" or "cole slaw" (from Middle Dutch *kool* and *sla*, meaning "cabbage salad"). Another word of Dutch derivation is "cookie" (from *koekje*, meaning "cookie") rather than either of the corresponding English terms, "small cake" and "biscuit." Although it took some time, both those Dutch terms came to be quintessentially American.

Most of the recipes in *American Cookery* are English. Seven recipes, beginning with "To make a fine sullabub from the cow," are taken verbatim from *The Frugal Housewife*, by Susannah Carter, which had appeared in American editions beginning in 1772. Even Simmons's famous "election cake," the recipe for which did not appear until the Albany edition and so cannot be directly associated with Hartford, as it often is, was simply a "great cake" from historical English baking. Recipes for this cake abound in sixteenth- and seventeenth-century English cookbooks and manuscripts.

Despite the English influence in *American Cookery*, there was a distinctively American use of elements, such as serving "cramberry-sauce" with roast turkey and using "Indian meal" (cornmeal) in place of other types of meal, most typically oatmeal. The book contains three recipes for "a tasty Indian pudding" that describe a strictly traditional English method for puddings made with other types of meal. Likewise, although various hearth cakes made with Indian meal had been made by the colonists from the beginning of settlement and are often cited in literature, Simmons's three recipes for "johny cake, or hoe cake" may be the earliest to actually see print. The very word "johny" comes from "jonniken," a term from northern England meaning oaten bread. Simmons also provided recipes for gingerbread made light with pearlash, a precurser of baking soda, a type of gingerbread that came to be the American style. Simmons's work demonstrates that the use of alkali for leavening in baking must have been a long-standing technique in America.

[*See also* Cakes; Cookbooks and Manuscripts, *subentry* From the Beginnings to 1860; Cooking Manuscripts; Mid-Atlantic Region.]

BIBLIOGRAPHY

Carter, Susannah. *The Frugal Housewife, or Complete Woman Cook*. Boston: Edes and Gill, 1772. Originally published in London. The Boston edition contains plates by Paul Revere.

Lowenstein, Eleanor. *Bibliography of American Cookery Books, 1742–1860*. Worcester, MA: American Antiquarian Society, 1972.

Simmons, Amelia. *American Cookery: Or, the Art of Dressing Viands, Fish, Poultry and Vegetables, and the best modes of making Puff-Pastes, Pies, Tarts, Puddings, Custards and Preserves, and All Kinds of Cakes, from the Imperial Plumb to Plain Cake*. Hartford: Hudson and Goodwin, 1796. In facsimile, as *The First American Cookbook*, with an essay by Mary Tolford Wilson. New York: Oxford University Press, 1958. Reissued by Dover Publications, New York, in 1984.

Simmons, Amelia. *American Cookery*. 2nd ed. Albany, NY: Charles R. & George Webster, 1796. In facsimile, with an introduction by Karen Hess. Bedford, MA: Applewood, 1996.

KAREN HESS

Sinclair, Upton

Before the summer of 1905, food safety was monitored by just two men, who made up the Department of Agriculture's entire Bureau of Chemistry. The Senate had contemplated a pure food and drug bill for three years with little enthusiasm, until a novel, in serial form, was published in the socialist magazine *Appeal to Reason* by Upton Sinclair (1878–1968). Sinclair's depiction of conditions in Chicago's stockyards and packing plants aroused the wrath of the meat-consuming public and forced the creation of the Pure Food and Drug Act of 1906, the Beef Inspection Act, and—ultimately—the Food and Drug Administration. The serial was published in book form in 1906 as *The Jungle*. The book, filled with disturbingly squalid details, was typical of the muckraking journalism of the day. Sinclair had been a student in New York City in the 1890s, and his book was an emotionally charged and convincing extension of Jacob Riis's 1890 exposé of tenement conditions, *How the Other Half Lives*.

The popularity of *The Jungle* caused meat sales to decline so sharply that President Theodore Roosevelt empowered the Neill-Reynolds Commission to investigate conditions in the nation's food industry. The commission confirmed all but one of Sinclair's observations. Nevertheless, influential industry lobbyists succeeded in hamstringing the resulting regulations.

Upton Sinclair. *Prints and Photographs Division, Library of Congress*

The Pure Food and Drug Act, which was concerned primarily with adulteration, contained only one sentence about food quality (other than issues of undesirable additives). According to section 7, a food was considered impure, "if it consists in whole or in part of a filthy, decomposed, or putrid animal or vegetable substance, or any portion of an animal unfit for food, whether manufactured or not, or if it is the product of a diseased animal, or one that has died otherwise than by slaughter." While superficially in the best interest of consumers, the act's penalties for industry violators were light: a maximum of one year's imprisonment or a maximum fine of five hundred dollars per violation or both.

Sinclair was a lifelong defender of lost causes and ethical living and, consequently, an exposer of corruption, writing on slavery, Sacco and Vanzetti, and the Teapot Dome scandal, as well as the healthy alternative diet of vegetarianism. He wrote more than eighty books: novels, nonfiction, an autobiography, a collection of letters, articles, essays, reviews, poems, and countless other works under pseudonyms. He received the Pulitzer Prize in 1946 for a historical novel in his Lanny Budd series. Sinclair tried to manifest his utopian ideals by founding Helicon Hall in Englewood, New Jersey, with royalties from *The Jungle*. The experiment in communal living lasted only one year, collapsing when its building burned in 1907. Sinclair ran unsuccessfully for governor in California in 1934 using the slogan "End Poverty in California." It was five years before John Steinbeck's *Grapes of Wrath* drew attention to the plight of California's migrant farmworkers.

Sinclair had gone to the stockyards to expose brutal working conditions, not the quality of the foods produced there. He complained, at the end of his life, that he had "aimed at the public's heart, and by accident hit it in the stomach."

[*See also* Armour, Philip Danforth; Butchering; Food and Drug Administration; Pure Food and Drug Act.]

BIBLIOGRAPHY

Gaer, Joseph, ed. *Upton Sinclair: Bibliography and Biographical Data*. New York: Burt Franklin, 1935. Reprint New York: Lenox Hill, 1971.
Harris, Leon. *Upton Sinclair: American Rebel*. New York: Crowell, 1975.
Pure Food and Drug Act of 1906. U.S. Statutes at Large, Vol. 34 (1906): 768–772.
Sinclair, Upton. *The Jungle*. New York: Heritage Press, 1965.
Sinclair, Upton. *My Lifetime in Letters*. Columbia: University of Missouri Press, 1960.

GARY ALLEN

Singapore Sling

The first recorded definition of the cocktail, in the May 13, 1806, edition of the *Balance and Columbian Repository*, of Hudson, New York, defined the cocktail as a "bittered sling." The sling, therefore, is an older category of mixed alcoholic drink than the cocktail, so what exactly is a sling? The definition offered in the periodical mentioned is "a stimulating liquor, composed of spirits of any kind, sugar, water, and bitters—it is vulgarly known as a bittered sling." A sling, then, includes sugar, water, and spirits, which corresponds perfectly with the recipe for the sling published by Jerry Thomas in his groundbreaking book *How to Mix Drinks; or, The Bon Vivant's Companion* (1862). The slings and toddies are listed together in Thomas's book; Thomas explains that the gin sling is made

with the same ingredients as the gin toddy, except with a little grated nutmeg on top. The gin toddy recipe, as listed in Thomas's book, is gin, water, sugar, and ice.

The Singapore sling was created in 1915 by Ngiam Tong Boon, a bartender at the Long Bar in the Raffles Hotel in Singapore. The original recipe has been lost. The recipes published in the 1920s and 1930s simply replace the sugar with cherry brandy or liqueur (specifically cherry Heering), replace the water with soda water, and add lemon juice. There is a recipe from 1922 called the straits sling, touted as the "well-known Singapore drink" in *Cocktails and How to Mix Them*, a book by Herbert Jenkins that introduces bitters and Benedictine to these recipes.

The recipe that the head bartender at Raffles provided in 1990 was gin, Cointreau, Benedictine, cherry Heering, bitters, lime, and pineapple juice, with a splash of soda. That recipe has been poured at the Rainbow Room in New York City and has become the modern standard.

[*See also* Cocktails; Gin; Hot Toddies.]

DALE DEGROFF

Skillets, *see Frying Pans, Skillets, and Spiders*

Slang, Food

The vocabulary of American food slang can claim a proud, inspired, and resourceful heritage; slang terms dealing with food enjoyed a truly golden age in the 1930s and 1940s. Nothing has slowed the ever-prolific coining of new alcohol-instigated slang; although much of drinking slang has migrated to the realm of drugs, drinkers have continued to do what drinkers have always done—drink and invent slang.

Food neologisms are abundant thanks to culinary globalization and the insatiable appetite of American eaters for new styles, dishes, and ingredients. However, these newly coined terms are typically standard register, and rarely, if ever, do the innovations in language rise to the level of slang. To be sure, food metaphors abound, with liberal servings of food vocabulary sprinkled throughout idiomatic and colloquial American speech: "American as apple pie" for thoroughly American; "bring home the bacon" for earning the wages that support a family; "baloney" for nonsense; "go bananas" for losing one's temper; "bread" and "dough" for money; "carrottop" for a person with red hair; "cheesecake" for a good-looking, scantily clad woman; "chew the fat" for engaging in idle conversation; "toss your cookies" for vomiting—the food terms used as idioms or metaphors in colloquial speech extend impressively through the lexicon.

In the search for actual food slang, forsake the white tablecloths and tuxedoed waiters and head for the greasy spoon on the other side of the tracks. As a general rule, popular culture, not high culture, produces slang. It should not be surprising, then, that common food eaten by common people, not haute cuisine eaten by the highbrow elite, has inspired America's culinary slang lexicon.

Western and Military Slang

An early example of culinary slang is found in the lexis of the American cowboy. As Ramon Adams, the most famous student of western speech, wrote in *Cowboy Lingo* (1936), "The cowboy did not slight his slang when it came to his 'chuck,' the unpoetic name he gave to food." We can thank the cowhand for such slang terms as "Mexican strawber-

ries" for dried beans; "mountain oysters" for fried cattle testicles; "son-of-a-gun stew" for a medley of calf brain, organs, and parts; and "belly cheater" for camp cook.

A similar flair for culinary slang may be found in the language of the lumberjack, whose appetite for the logging camp food was whetted by demanding physical work. Loggers enjoyed what they claimed were the best "eats" in the world, but like the cowhand, their culinary slang was a bit cynical and thoroughly humorous. Onions were "fruit," the assistant camp cook was a "crumb chaser," oleomargarine was "ole," butter was "salve," eggs were "hen fruit," and a logger was "lanky on the inside," not hungry.

The pinnacle of sarcasm and downright pessimism when it comes to American food slang is found in the mouths of the armed forces. In *Chow: A Cook's Tour of Military Food* (1978), Paul Dickson notes that "like the slang of prisoners, hoboes, college students, summer campers and their counselors, the cant which has emerged to describe military food is fundamentally negative, graphic and colorful." "Armored cow" for con-

---

MILITARY SLANG

army strawberries: prunes
battery acid: coffee
bokoo soused: very drunk
bug juice: Kool-Aid and other powder-based fruit drinks
bullets: beans
buzzard: chicken or turkey
cackleberry: egg
canned cow: canned condensed milk
canteen: a liquor store on a military base
chow: food, a meal
chow down: to eat
chowhound: first in line at the mess
"come and get it": the time-honored call of the mess sergeant
desecrated vegetables: dried or dessicated vegetables
fly light: to miss a meal
gut-packings: food, rations
hardtack: a baked mix of flour and water, soaked in cold water overnight and fried in grease for breakfast
hooch: hard liquor. According to early twentieth-century author and critic H. L. Mencken, it comes from an Eskimo home-brew called *hoochino*.

java: coffee
joe: coffee
kitchen police, K.P.: those assigned to menial clean-up duties
lurp: Long Range Patrol Ration, consisted of precooked freeze dried entrees, could be cold, dry, or warm
meal refusing to exit, meal rejected by Ethiopia: meal ready to eat (M.R.E.)
moo juice: milk
mud: coffee
mystery meat: meat that lacks clear identity
rabbit food: greens, especially lettuce
repeaters: beans, sausages, refers to the gas they produce
shrapnel: Grape-Nuts
tube steak: hot dog

BIBLIOGRAPHY

Dickson, Paul. *Chow: A Cook's Tour of Military Food*. New York: New American Library, 1978.
Dickson, Paul. *War Slang: American Fighting Words and Phrases from the Civil War to the Gulf War*. New York: Pocket Books, 1994.

SANDRA YIN

densed milk, "army strawberries" for prunes, "battery acid" for coffee, "blood" for ketchup, "bug juice" for a powdered fruit drink, "dog food" for corned beef hash, and "SOS" for creamed corned beef on toast are all colorful and dramatic examples of military culinary slang.

1930s and 1940s Slang

The finest examples of American food slang were heard at the lunch counters, diners, and soda fountains of the 1930s and 1940s. The slang of the lunch counter and diner was vibrant and reflected a young and hopeful nation. In his *Hash House Lingo* (1941), Jack Smiley observes that there was no limit "to the lengths to which the bright boys behind the marble counters have extended themselves to outdo the other fellow with fantastic, grotesque or witty labels for food combinations from the kitchen." The witty use of fabricated slang by lunch counter and diner employees in the several decades leading up to World War II was unprecedented in the history of food language and has not been matched since. From "Adam's ale" for water, "cow paste" for butter, "flop two" for two fried eggs over, "guess water" for soup, "hounds

---

SODA FOUNTAIN AND DINER SLANG

Adam and Eve on a raft: poached eggs on toast

angels on horseback: oysters rolled in bacon, served on toast

axle grease: margarine

bad breath: onions

baled hay: Shredded Wheat cereal

bark: a frankfurter

belly busters: baked beans

belly warmer: a cup of coffee

bilge water: soup

board: a slice of toast

Bossy in a bowl: beef stew

break it and shake it: add an egg to a drink

brick: a biscuit

cackle berries: eggs

choker: a hamburger

city juice: water

dogs and maggots: crackers and cheese

drag one through Georgia: a glass of Coca-Cola with chocolate syrup

first lady: spare ribs

glue: tapioca pudding

gold dust: sugar

hash: food

hot top: chocolate sauce

Irish cherries: carrots

jamoka: coffee

looseners: prunes

lumber: a toothpick

maiden's delight: cherries

mug of murk: a cup of black coffee

nervous pudding: Jell-O

O'Connors: potatoes

pause: a glass of Coca-Cola

punk: bread

radio sandwich: a tuna fish sandwich

rush it: Russian dressing

salt horse: corned beef

shimmy: jelly

sinker: a doughnut

squeeze: orange juice

squeal: ham

take a chance: hash

twist it, choke it, and make it cackle: a chocolate malted milkshake with an egg

virgin juice: cherry syrup

wet mystery: beef stew

yard bird: chicken

yum-yum: sugar

TOM DALZELL

---

on an island" for frankfurters with beans, "Mike and Ike" for salt and pepper shakers, "one from the Alps" for a Swiss cheese sandwich, "raft" for a slice of toast, to "yum-yum" for sugar—the smart humor and creativity of the slang slingers is striking. As Smiley notes, those who toiled in the working-class American eateries were "urged on by an appreciative audience" and were thus "induced to bring forth all the fresh expressions "their" wits might concoct."

An equally charming and clever slang was used by the young men who worked behind soda fountains, known without derision as "soda jerks." Their slang vernacular served several functions: It could quickly communicate complicated orders in several condensed words; it was a code understood by insiders only and thus could be used to discuss customers in front of customers; and, most important, it established the soda jerk as a remarkable fellow who accepted the opportunity to flaunt his wit. A glass of Coca-Cola was an "Atlanta special," a chocolate cream soda with vanilla ice cream was a "black and white," to serve a scoop of chocolate ice cream was to "dip a snowball," a banana split was a "houseboat," and to add ice cream to a slice of pie was to "put a hat on it." An innocuous-sounding call of "thirteen" alerted fellow employees that the boss had just walked in, while the innocent "vanilla" announced the presence of a pretty girl.

In the late 1930s, locally owned diners and soda fountains began to give way to national chains whose managers had a decidedly lower tolerance for the linguistic entertainment offered by hash house slingers and soda jerks. The new bosses preferred that corned beef hash be called "corned beef hash," not "the gentleman will take a chance"; that prunes be called "prunes," not "looseners"; and that cherries be called "cherries," not "maiden's delight." The brash, wise-guy speech that had been a fixture in blue-collar restaurants and soda fountains eventually went the way of the restaurants and soda fountains—lost to the hegemony of the national chains.

Today, while food metaphors abound, food slang does not. Admittedly, some slang terms for food may be heard in the speech of young people ("za" for pizza comes to mind as a fixture of modern youth speech), enlisted men and women in the armed forces ("Meals Refused by Ethiopians" for the ready-to-eat meals issued by the military with the official title of MREs), and upscale coffee bars ("why bother" for a decaffeinated, nonfat latte), but the modern idiom is a weak shadow of the glory days of American food slang.

Drink Slang

Leaving the plate and turning to liquid refreshments, the American slang vocabulary of drink is extensive and wide ranging, and demonstrates a clear-cut linguistic creativity. It seems that forms of alcohol and specific drinks ("grape" for wine, "dago red" for cheap red wine, "brewski" for beer, and the all-encompassing "hooch" for alcohol) require slang names. This is also the case with the places where drinking occurs (a "gin mill," perhaps, or a "beer emporium"), with the men and women who serve the drinks ("beer jerker," "doctor," or "mixologist"), and with the actual act of drinking, from "name your poison" for the "antifogmatic," "booster," or "eye-opener" (all describing the first drink of the day) to the "sundowner" or "settler" (the last drink of the night). The slang is, for the most part, jocular and lighthearted, carefully skirting the difficult social issues associated with alcohol. Even the wages of alcoholic sinning—vomiting, hangover, and delirium tremens—are fair game for slang. Rapid-change ephemerality is characteristic of most slang, and the slang of alcohol is no exception to this rule; new terms replace old terms with regularity, and only the catchiest of words survive—"heebie-jeebies" for delirium tremens is an example.

No physical condition or state of health can boast more slang synonyms in American English than the state of inebriation. Over the years, American drinkers have invented hundreds of adjectives to use in place of the plain and simple "drunk." Benjamin Franklin, who is reported to have known something about excess and intemperance, was so impressed with the number of slang expressions meaning "drunk" that in 1733 he compiled and printed the *Drinker's Dictionary*, a glossary of some 228 slang terms for "intoxicated."

In the three centuries since Franklin's compilation, linguistically inclined drinkers have invented new adjectives to use when describing a comrade who has come under the influence of adult beverages. The Washington writer Paul Dickson has amassed a definitive list of slang terms for "drunk." Dickson published a list of 2,231 terms in *Dickson's Word Treasury* (1992) and has since added several hundred entries. The list contains a subtle gradation of degree of intoxication (from "buzzed" to "illuminated" to "high" to "wasted" to "hammered"), but the sheer number of terms suggests something more than a simple attempt to describe with objective precision the level of stupefaction. The large number of words associated with inebriation suggests, it would seem, a society with drinking on its mind.

The most ingenious and appealing American slang alcohol idiom is the slang of the bootlegger and moonshiner. The Eighteenth Amendment criminalized the production, distribution, and consumption of alcohol from 1919 until 1932; the criminal and subversive status bestowed on alcohol by the U.S. Constitution guaranteed an imaginative, smart, and droll vernacular. The moonshiner who illegally distills whiskey has always boasted a rich and vivid slang, thanks both to the criminal nature of his activity and to the expressive leaning of language in the rural, southern Appalachian hills where moonshining is practiced—"Johnny Law" for any law enforcement official, "kitchen" for an illegal still, and the many variations on the end product, from the neutral "alky" to the gentle "balm of Gilead" to the not-so-gentle "panther piss" or "white lightning."

Drinking has always been part of the social fabric of the United States, and the slang vocabulary of drinking is constantly expanding. This imperative to name anew that which has been named by past generations of drinkers reveals the manifest destiny of humans to create new ways of saying old things.

[*See also* Beer Halls; Coffeehouses; Combat Food; Diners; Drinking Songs; Soda Fountains; Taverns.]

BIBLIOGRAPHY

Abel, Ernest L. *Alcohol Wordlore and Folklore: Being a Compendium of Linguistic and Social Fact and Fantasy Associated with the Use and Production of Alcohol as Reflected in the Magazines, Newspapers, and Literature of the English-Speaking World.* Buffalo, NY: Prometheus, 1987.
Bentley, Howard W. "Linguistic Concoctions of the Soda Jerker." *American Speech* 11 (1936): 37–45.
Dalzell, Tom. *The Slang of Sin.* Springfield, MA: Merriam-Webster, 1998.
Dickson, Paul. *The Great American Ice Cream Book.* New York: Atheneum, 1972.
Jones, Michael Owen. "Soda-Fountain, Restaurant, and Tavern Calls." *American Speech* 42 (1967): 58–64.
Keller, Mark, Mairi McCormick, and Vera Efron. *A Dictionary of Words about Alcohol.* New Brunswick, NJ: Rutgers Center of Alcohol Studies, 1982.
Mendelsohn, Oscar A. *The Dictionary of Drink and Drinking.* New York: Hawthorn, 1965.
Smiley, Jack. *Hash House Lingo.* Eaton, PA: privately printed, 1941.
"Soda Fountain Lingo." *California Folklore Quarterly* 4 (1945).
Spears, Richard A. *The Slang and Jargon of Drugs and Drink.* Metuchen, NJ: Scarecrow, 1986.

TOM DALZELL

Slicers, *see Apple Preparation Tools*

Sloppy Joe

The all-American sloppy joe sandwich is typically composed of ground beef that is browned with chopped onions, green pepper, and garlic; combined with tomato sauce and seasonings of choice; and served hot on a hamburger bun. Although it is not known when the sandwich was first called the "sloppy joe," similar ground beef concoctions have been recorded in American cookbooks since the turn of the twentieth century. Some food historians believe that, with the addition of ketchup or tomato sauce, it evolved from the popular Iowa loosemeat sandwich introduced by Floyd Angell, the founder of Maid-Rite restaurants, in 1926. During the Great Depression and World War II, ground beef provided an economical way to stretch meat and ensured the popularity of the sandwich. As for the name "sloppy joe," some say it was inspired by one of two famous bars named Sloppy Joe's in the 1930s—one in Havana, Cuba, and the other in Key West, Florida. The name caught on throughout the United States, and based on the number of establishments that subsequently became known as "Sloppy Joe's" by the late 1930s, it is likely that the messy-to-eat sandwich was named after restaurants that commonly served it. By 1948 the sloppy joe was firmly established in America's sandwich culture.

[*See also* Sandwiches.]

BIBLIOGRAPHY

Mercuri, Becky. *Sandwiches That You Will Like.* Pittsburgh, PA: WQED, 2002.
Smith, Grace, Beverly Smith, and Charles Morrow Wilson. *Through the Kitchen Door: A Cook's Tour to the Best Kitchens of America.* New York: Stackpole, 1938.

BECKY MERCURI

Slow Cookers

The Rival Company introduced the Crock-Pot Slow Cooker in 1971. According to company records, Rival had acquired a smaller company, Naxon Utilities, which manufactured an electric ceramic bean cooker called the "Beanery." It consisted of a glazed brown crock liner housed in a white steel casing. After experimenting with the Beanery, Rival added more wire to the metal housing, found a factory to manufacture the ceramic crocks, came up with the name Crock-Pot, and started selling the appliance with the slogan "Cooks all day while the cook's away."

The slow cooker's emergence in the 1970s coincided with a simultaneous upsurge in American interest in cooking and an economic need to find attractive ways to cook less expensively. Tough stewing meats could be turned into gourmet delights in the slow cooker, with the addition of wine and a few herbs. Eager cooks also discovered that a can of condensed Campbell's soup could be used to make a quick and easy sauce base in the cooker. By 1981 Rival was reporting over $30 million in sales for the homely Crock-Pot. Although "Crock-Pot" is commonly used to mean any electrified ceramic slow cooker, it is still Rival's trademark.

[*See also* Cooking Techniques.]

BIBLIOGRAPHY

Crock-Pot under Links at http://www.rivalproducts.com/.
Lovegren, Sylvia. *Fashionable Food: Seven Decades of Food Fads.* New York: Macmillan, 1995.

SYLVIA LOVEGREN

Slow Food Movement

Probably the only international organization with a snail as its logo, the Italy-based Slow Food International was founded in 1989 in response to the fast-paced, fast food lifestyle that seemed to threaten the "slow" enjoyment of good foods, good wines, and good friends. Its guiding spirit, Carlo Petrini, set about resolving what he saw as several universal problems: the growing uniformity of food tastes, the decline of food quality, the mechanized production of food, and the worldwide loss of crop and livestock biodiversity.

Petrini established Slow Food's headquarters in his northern Italian hometown of Bra, and from this center he set about developing the Slow Food agenda. He encouraged the spread of his fledgling movement by opening national offices in selected countries and by establishing a network of local *convivia*, or groups, in cities worldwide.

Convivia are made up of members who share the same interest in, and passion for, food at all levels—from farmland through the kitchen to the table. *Convivia* leaders plan regular events—such as cooking classes or talks with chefs, food-related outings to visit growers or food producers, dinners or cookouts, and food-wine pairings—that have both an educational and a social component. Because of its localized "convivial" structure of members and friends of Slow Food, this grassroots movement has developed an active global following.

Slow Food International sponsors several formidable global projects, including the Ark of Taste, a commission whose goal is to identify and catalog products, livestock, and food traditions on the verge of extinction. Slow Food's vast biennial Salone del Gusto (Hall of Taste) held in Turin, Italy, is the largest food and wine event in the world and a marketplace for small-scale food and wine producers. With its concurrent onsite food and wine classes, the Salone also functions as a public education opportunity.

Through Slow Food Editore, a publishing house, Slow Food International publishes texts on tourism, food, and wine. Its website, www.slowfood.com, is a valuable resource for learning about the organization and its various events and food and wine recommendations.

[*See also* Fast Food.]

BIBLIOGRAPHY

Kummer, Corby. *The Pleasures of Slow Food: Celebrating Authentic Traditions, Flavors, and Recipes*. San Francisco: Chronicle Books, 2002.

ALEXANDRA GREELEY

Smoking

Smoking is an age-old process used to preserve foods. It was employed to aid preservation of meats, fish, and poultry in conjunction with salting and drying and to develop flavor. Preservation techniques have advanced significantly, but smoking is still used to preserve, impart flavor, and add texture to different foods. The basic process and tools for smoking foods have remained unchanged through the millennia.

Smoking originated in prehistoric times, most likely in several regions of the world independently. That smoke could impart a pleasant flavor and improve the keeping quality of meats and fish was probably discovered in conjunction with dehydration techniques and the use of wood-fueled fire to cook foods. Wood smoke helps dehydrate and sterilize foods and introduces characteristic flavors. The flavor and color of the smoked product depend considerably on whether the wood used is hard or soft, wet or dried, in the form of chips or sawdust. Hardwoods are used predominantly; softwoods are added to enhance color.

Wood selection is a regional preference and is as unique to each region as the smoking technique. Foods may be smoked simply by suspension over an open wood fire or in enclosures that collect the smoke. And the smoking enclosures themselves may be as simple as buckets and barrels or as elaborate as specially built kilns and smokehouses.

The principle of smoking involves exposing food to fat- and water-soluble molecules, steam, and other particles released from burning wood. Foods absorb these compounds, lose moisture, and develop characteristic "smoked" flavors. Woodsmoke components, including acids, aldehydes, and phenols, have distinct roles in the preserving, texturing, and flavoring processes. Smoke acids influence protein coagulation and texture, aldehydes help create networks and influence texture, and phenols contribute to the development of aroma and taste. Smoking temperature and humidity govern the degree to which these reactions occur and, thereby, the extent of cooking, drying, and flavor. Hot smoking also cooks the food, while cool smoking (below 90°F) primarily enhances flavor. The length of smoking also affects the texture and extent of drying.

An important step in the smoking process involves brine—a mixture of sugar, salt, and spices—to cure meats, poultry, and seafood before they are smoked. The mixture may be applied dry as a surface rub, used as a solution for soaking, or injected directly into the food.

Producing the desired smoke flavor, a side effect of a food preservation process, has evolved into an art and a science. In the United States, indigenous hardwoods—hickory (genus *Carya*) and mesquite (genus *Prosopis*)—are used for smoking. Mesquite and hickory smoke flavors are acknowledged universally to be uniquely American and in recent years have evolved as popular flavors for potato chips, cheese, nuts, beer, wine, and even chocolates. American ingenuity is further demonstrated in a product called Wright Liquid Smoke based on E. H. Wright's (Kansas City, Kansas) patent in 1910. It is a water-based solution of smoke flavors and is used extensively as an antimicrobial and to add flavor, color, and texture to commercially processed foods.

As the twenty-first century opened, concerns about the carcinogenic effect of some components of wood smoke were discouraging consumption of heavily smoked foods and favoring lighter smoking and liquid smoke usage.

[*See also* Drying; Meat; Salt and Salting.]

BIBLIOGRAPHY

Toussant-Samat, Maguelonne. *History of Food.* Translated by Anthea Bell, 93–112. New York: Barnes and Noble, 1998.

KANTHA SHELKE

Snack Food

At the beginning of the twentieth century, Americans were likely to choose fruit, unsalted nuts, or bread and cheese if they wanted a snack between meals. At the time, few commercial snacks were available. By the beginning of the twenty-first century, Americans annually consumed almost $22 billion in salted nuts, popcorn, potato chips, pretzels, corn chips, cheese snacks, and other salty snacks.

Many factors contributed to the rise of salty snack foods in America. The first was a packaging and marketing revolution. Prior to 1900, snack foods, such as peanuts, popcorn, and potato chips, were sold from barrels or large glass jars. The grocer dished out the snacks and placed them in a twist of paper or a paper bag. Not only was this a time-consuming process, but often the snacks went stale before they were sold. During the early twentieth century, manufacturers began experimenting with cans, wax paper, glassine, cellophane, and other packaging materials that made possible the sale of individual portions directly to customers. The package kept the snack fresh until the customer opened it.

Other factors that contributed to the increase in consumption of salty snacks were the end of Prohibition in 1933 and food rationing of the World War II era. As bars reopened after Prohibition ended, salty snacks were given free to customers to increase drink orders. The interest in salty snacks increased even more during World War II, as rationing caused a severe shortage of sugar, sweets, and chocolates, making many familiar candies unavailable. Salty snacks based on corn, potatoes, and peanuts were abundant during the war in America. Sales of salty snacks soared.

During the 1950s, salty snacks were promoted on television, and sales skyrocketed. For instance, Lipton wed chips with dips in a major promotion campaign combining its onion soup mix with sour cream to make a snack that became a party favorite. This success launched an ongoing dip revolution with major new dips, such as salsa and guacamole, regularly emerging. Subsequently, similar promotional campaigns were launched on behalf of corn chips, potato chips, popcorn, peanuts, and other salty snack foods.

Nuts and Peanuts

Roasted chestnuts and other nuts have been sold on America's streets since colonial times. Nuts require little preparation and can easily be transported. They are relatively inexpensive and are generally nutritious. The most important nuts sold in America are almonds, walnuts, and pecans followed by chestnuts, pistachios, and macadamias. All are grown extensively in California with the exception of macadamia nuts, which are grown mainly in Hawaii. In addition, cashews and Brazil nuts are imported. In the nineteenth century, nuts were roasted and salted by vendors and homemakers, but the commercial processes of how to salt nuts so that the salt remains on the nut after packaging was not learned until the early twentieth century. Salted nuts were commercially packaged and sold in the United States throughout the twentieth century.

The most important snack nut, however, is technically a legume. The peanut originated in South America but was disseminated to Africa and Asia shortly after the arrival of Europeans in the New World. From Africa, peanuts were brought into North America in colonial times. Peanuts were relatively unimportant as a snack food until after the Civil War, when vendors began selling them on streets in cities. One peanut vendor was Amedeo Obici, an Italian-born immigrant who lived in Wilkes-Barre, Pennsylvania. In 1906 Obici formed a partnership with another Italian immigrant to form the Planters' Peanut Company (later changed to Planters Peanut Company, without the apostrophe). Their products then went through a packaging revolution, permitting Planters to sell fresh peanuts to a larger clientele. Planters also emphasized advertising and marketing, and "Mr. Peanut" quickly became an American culinary icon. The company went from a small vendor operation to a national snack food company in less than two decades. In 2002 Planters was the largest-selling nut brand.

Popcorn

Popcorn exploded onto the American culinary scene during the mid-nineteenth century thanks to the invention of the wire-over-the-fire popper, consisting of a long handle ending in an enclosed wire box shaken over a fire. Street vendors sold popcorn on the streets and at fairs, circuses, and sporting events. The popcorn industry began in the latter part of the nineteenth century. Hundreds of companies were launched, such as the American Pop Corn Company founded in 1914 by Cloid Smith in Sioux City, Iowa. Popcorn kernels were usually sold in cardboard containers, which exposed the kernels to changing levels of moisture, thus affecting their popability. Smith sealed the popcorn in glass jars in 1920. The kernels in

the airtight package did not lose or gain moisture until opened; however, glass was expensive and breakage was high. Smith's second solution was to pack popcorn in hermetically sealed cans, causing a revolution in popcorn packaging. The new techniques were soon applied to other salty snack foods.

Street vendors began selling popcorn in the mid-nineteenth century. Popcorn was not sold in movie theaters until the Great Depression, when owners found that they could make more money on popcorn and other snack food sales than they did on theater admissions. The selling of ready-to-eat popcorn in large bags began before World War II, and sales have increased ever since. When television became important during the 1950s, Americans began watching movies in their homes, and they wanted popcorn in their homes. Popcorn sales expanded rapidly. The invention of the microwave oven and the release of hybrid kernels with tremendous popping volume increased popcorn sales and profits to even greater heights. By the early twenty-first century, popcorn snack food markets were producing about $1.8 billion per year. More than 60 percent of popcorn is microwaved, and 70 percent is consumed in the home.

Potato Chips

George Crum, the chef of the Moon's Lake Lodge in Saratoga Springs, New York, is credited with being the first person to fry thin slices of potatoes and serve them to customers. They were named Saratoga potatoes. In fact, home recipes that called for fried "shavings" of raw potatoes had appeared in American cookery books beginning with Mary Randolf's *Virginia House-Wife* (1824). Recipes named "Saratoga" potatoes and potato chips appeared in American cookbooks during the 1870s.

Early commercial potato chips were less successful. Saratoga potato chips were mass produced during the 1890s by John E. Marshall of Boston. They were initially sold in barrels to grocery stores. Proprietors dished out the chips into paper bags for customers, who warmed them in the home oven before serving. This cumbersome process produced stale chips, which limited sales.

In 1926 the potato chip maker Laura Scudder of Monterey Park, California, experimented with a new potato chip packing idea. She hand-packed the chips into wax paper bags, and her employees sealed the tops with a warm iron. This individual serving container kept out moisture, but it had its limitation in that it was impossible to print on the outside of wax paper. However, in

1933 the Dixie Wax Paper Company introduced the first "preprint" waxed glassine bag, which made it possible for manufacturers to print brand names and other information on the outside of the bag. This mode of packaging promptly became the standard in the salty snack world.

When World War II began, potato chips were initially declared an unessential food, which meant that production would have stopped during the war. Manufacturers lobbied the War Production Board to change this designation for potato chips. Their efforts succeeded. Potato chip sales increased throughout the war. Advertising increased sales even more when the war ended.

The postwar period also saw the introduction of several new potato chip products, such as Ruffles, which were introduced in 1958. In the 1960s, Procter and Gamble introduced Pringles, much to the chagrin of the potato chip industry. Pringles were made from dehydrated potato flakes that were reconstituted, formed, and flash fried. All chips were identical, making possible the packaging of Pringles in a long tube. The potato chip industry went to court to prevent Procter and Gamble from calling Pringles potato chips. This matter was not resolved until 1975, when the U.S. Food and Drug Administration defined Pringles as "potato chips made from dehydrated potatoes."

Pretzels

Pretzels are salted biscuits twisted into a knot or sticks. The word derives from German but probably dates to ancient Roman times. The Dutch probably first introduced pretzels into America, and pretzels were sold during colonial times by street vendors. In 1861 the first commercial pretzel company was launched by Julius Sturgis in Lititz, Pennsylvania. These were twisted by hand and remained a regional product. The first automatic pretzel twisting machine was developed by the Reading Pretzel Machinery Company in 1933. Pretzel manufacturers remained concentrated in Pennsylvania, and pretzels did not emerge as a national snack until the 1960s.

Pretzels are sold in two ways: the large, soft pretzel is perishable and must be sold as a fresh-baked good, usually by vendors, or as a frozen food; the smaller, crisp pretzel has a long shelf life and is sold in plastic barrels or plastic bags. In 2002 the two largest selling pretzel brands were Rold Gold by Frito-Lay and Snyder's of Hanover.

Corn Chips

The success of potato chips created a market for other commercial salty snacks. Corn chips originated as a

---

NACHOS

Nachos, a combination of tortilla pieces with melted cheese and jalapeño peppers, are credited to Ignacio Anaya, the chef at the old Victory Club in Piedras Negras across the border from Eagle Pass, Texas. He assembled the first nachos for some Eagle Pass ladies who stopped in during a shopping trip in the 1940s. Nachos became popular in Texas and throughout the United States during the 1960s. Nacho and other spicy flavorings took the snack food industry by storm, and nacho-flavored corn chips and spicy potato chips were soon on the market. Nachos were also at the spearhead of a national interest in ethnic flavors that were soon applied to corn chips, including jalapeño, cheese, nacho cheese, and other spicy seasonings.

ANDREW F. SMITH

Mexican snack—cut up, fried, or hardened tortillas. Isadore J. Filler, a traveling salesman, ate tostadas—hard tortillas with various toppings—in San Antonio, Texas, and thought they might have wide appeal as a snack food. In 1932 he conceived the idea of manufacturing a rectangular corn chip and applied for a trademark for "Corn Chips," which he received.

At the same time that Filler was trademarking corn chips, Elmer Doolin was also in San Antonio snacking on *friotes*, which were made from fried masa, or corn flour. Doolin purportedly bought a recipe for friotes for one hundred dollars. Doolin began manufacturing them under the name "Fritos," enjoying immediate success. Sales expanded as far as St. Louis, Missouri. In 1945 Doolin met the potato chip manufacturer Herman Lay, who agreed to distribute Fritos. The main target for the advertising of Fritos was children. Fritos became popular nationwide.

Doolin died in 1959, and the company he created merged with Herman Lay's company, creating Frito-Lay, Inc., which continued to grow and acquired other snack foods. In 1965 Frito-Lay was acquired by the Pepsi-Cola Company. The newly merged company launched many new snack foods. A triangular corn chip, Doritos, debuted in 1966 and almost overnight became America's second most popular snack item.

By the end of the twentieth century, the corn chip industry was dominated by Frito-Lay, with the top sellers being Doritos and Tostitos. Fritos do not rank in the twenty top-selling corn chips. The total sales of corn chips exceeds $4.1 billion annually.

Cheese Snacks

Following the lead of popcorn, manufacturers puffed other whole kernels. The most successful examples were in the creation of puffed breakfast cereal, such as Rice Crispies. The process of extruding was invented by accident during the 1930s. While experimenting on animal feed, Edward Wilson noticed that moistened corn kernels, when heated and forced through an "extruder," puffed up when they hit cool air. Wilson cooked them in deep fat, salted them, and ate them. Others liked them as well, and the result was a commercial product called Korn Kurls, which disappeared during World War II due to restrictions on nonessential foods. After the war, Korn Kurls were reintroduced by the Adams Corporation and became popular during the 1950s.

During the late 1940s, the Frito Company invented Chee-tos, which were marketed by Lay in 1948. This extruded snack is covered with an artificially colored powdered cheddar cheese. Similar products were manufactured by other companies. By the beginning of the twenty-first century, Chee-tos dominated the puffed snack market with sales twice as much as all the other top fifteen sales combined.

Junk Food Challenge

During the 1950s the term "junk foods" came to mean snack foods, convenience foods, sodas, and fried fast foods that were high in sugar, fat, salt, and calories, and low in nutritional value. In 1970 the snack world was challenged when Jean Meyer, President Nixon's adviser on food and nutrition, publicly questioned the food value of potato chips. He was quickly joined by Senator George McGovern of South Dakota. Opposition to junk food was voiced by Michael Jacobson of the Center for Science in the Public Interest, the Washington-based watchdog of the food industry.

Junk foods have been an important part of the American diet since the 1920s, but it was not until the vast increase in snack food consumption following World War II promoted by television advertising that American nutritionists became alarmed. Studies reported that about 30 percent of the average American's diet was made up of junk foods. Health advocates' concerns were threefold. First, the increase in consumption of the junk foods correlates with an increase in heart disease, high blood pressure, cancer, and other diseases. Second, junk

Salty Snacks. La Bagel Delight, Brooklyn, New York. *Photograph by Joe Zarba*

food consumption correlates with the increase in obesity in the United States with 23 percent of Americans considered obese.

Finally, as junk food consumption has increased, consumption of healthier foods, such as milk, fruit and vegetables, has decreased, thus reducing nutrients in the diet. This problem is especially of concern for young Americans, whom snack food manufacturers have targeted in their advertising. Some studies suggest that almost 80 percent of food commercials aired on Saturday morning kids' TV shows are for products of low nutritional value. Advertisements for high-sugar products form the majority. Of particular concern to nutritionists is the fact that junk foods, including candy and soda, are now served in schools through vending machines. Junk foods are also advertised on television programs and through sports programs. Many groups have attempted to ban the sale and advertising of junk foods in schools. Others have promoted the notion that junk foods should be taxed and the monies given to the schools to promote nutrition education and offset the funds derived from selling or advertising junk food.

Modern Salty Snack Food

As the twentieth century progressed, the quantity and diversity of salty snack foods proliferated until nearly every grocery store, kiosk, newsstand, and corner shop in America was heavily stocked with bags and packets of chips, crackers, pretzels, and much more. Thousands of salty snack foods have been manufactured in America. Pretzels sell about $1.2 billion per year. Potato chips have experienced steady growth, reaching sales of $6 billion. Sales of America's second favorite savory snack, tortilla chips, have reached $4.1 in sales, particularly due to the growing popularity of southwestern style foods. Collectively, these snack foods comprised a market niche of $21.8 billion in annual sales in 2001. While nutritionists properly complain about the consumption of snack foods, there is no sign that Americans are decreasing their consumption of salty snacks.

[*See also* Almonds; Brazil Nuts; Cashews; Dips; Fast Food; Frito-Lay; Macadamia Nuts; Mexican American Food; Mr. Peanut; Nuts; Peanuts; Pecans; Pistachios; Popcorn; Potatoes; Walnuts.]

BIBLIOGRAPHY

50 Years: A Foundation for the Future. Alexandria, VA: Snack Food Association, 1987.

Fox, William S., and Mae G. Banner. "Social and Economic Contexts of Folklore Variants: The Case of Potato Chip Legends." *Western Folklore* 42 (May 1983): 114–126.

Hess, Karen. "The Origin of French Fries." *Petits Propos Culinaires* 68 (November 2001): 39–48.

Jacobson, Michael F., and Bruce Maxwell. *What Are We Feeding Our Kids?* New York: Workman, 1994.

Matz, Samuel A. *Snack Food Technology.* 3rd ed. New York: Van Nostrand Reinhold, 1993.

Smith, Andrew F. *Peanuts: The Illustrious History of the Goober Pea.* Urbana: University of Illinois Press, 2002.

Smith, Andrew F. *Popped Culture: A Social History of Popcorn in America.* Columbia: University of South Carolina Press, 1999.

"For Your Eyes Only (State of the Industry): Ranking of Bakery Segments by Sales in 2001." *Snack Food and Wholesale Bakery* 91, no. 6 (June 2002): SI 1–71.

ANDREW F. SMITH

Snapple

Snapple was introduced to the soft drink market in 1972 when Leonard Marsh, Hyman Golden, and Arnold Greenberg, three childhood friends from Brooklyn, New York, formed the Unadulaterated Food Corporation and began selling all-natural juices in Greenwich Village, in New York City. Appealing to the health market, Marsh, Golden, and Greenberg used the best ingredients—real fruit flavors and real tea—without preservatives, chemical dyes, or artificial flavorings. At the time no other major soft drink producer could make that claim, and Snapple set the standard for those that followed. The name came from a carbonated apple soda that was part of the original beverage line.

Distributors initially worried that Snapple would not sell or, if it did, would have a limited market. They were wrong. Good nutrition and quirky names, such as Mango Madness and Amazing Grape, which were uncommon in food marketing at the time, intrigued consumers who did not mind paying nearly twice the price of an ordinary soft drink. Snapple was a new-age product that was extremely popular by the second year of production. Stores had begun to call distributors before their next scheduled delivery because they had run out. When stores wanted large orders to stock up, the company refused, because it did not want to limit distribution.

Competitors began to make similar types of fruit juice and tea drinks that eventually cut into the Snapple market. But Snapple had already established itself with a solid name. When the personable and bubbly "Snapple lady" began appearing in television commercials in 1991, more people became fans. As the Snapple lady, Wendy Kaufmann, who had been "discovered" when she worked in the company's order department, received hundreds of letters a week, including marriage proposals.

In 1992 the original owners sold the Snapple company to a Boston-based investment firm that took Snapple public and in three months tripled the value of the stock. Snapple became one of the most popular stocks in the United States. When Quaker Oats Company bought Snapple in 1994, the Snapple lady was dismissed as the commercial spokesperson, and because Quaker Oats had other priorities, Snapple declined. In 1997 Triarc bought Snapple from Quaker Oats for $300 million and brought the company back to the forefront of the market by repairing distributor relationships and appealing to young drinkers. Triarc also returned the Snapple lady to television commercials, claiming that "Wendy is the essence of the brand." In 2000 Snapple was sold to the world's third-largest soft drink maker, Cadbury Schweppes, a company that also handles Mistic, Orangina, Stewart's Root Beer, and Yoo-hoo. By the beginning of the twenty-first century, Snapple had regained its place as the leader in the noncarbonated beverage market.

Snapple offers juice drinks, teas, lemonades, and diet drinks in more than thirty flavors. The highest-selling flavors are lemon tea, peach tea, diet peach tea, kiwi strawberry, diet lemon tea, raspberry tea, diet raspberry tea, Mango Madness, fruit punch, and diet cranberry raspberry. Snapple is available all over the world and claims 28 percent of the premium beverage market in the United States.

[*See also* Fruit Juices; Soda Drinks.]

MARIAN BETANCOURT

Soda Drinks

Soda drinks encompass all carbonated nonalcoholic beverages. At the end of the twentieth century, they were the fastest-growing segment of the U.S. beverage market.

The thirst for soda drinks began with the popularity of naturally carbonated mineral waters, which were thought to have medicinal properties. During the eighteenth century, European scientists, such as Joseph Priestley, developed processes for artificially carbonating water. In 1806 a Yale chemistry professor named Benjamin Silliman purchased an apparatus for impregnating water with carbon dioxide. Within three years, he owned soda parlors in New Haven and New York City that sold his mineral water by the glass and by the bottle. Although the use of these waters was at first strictly therapeutic, soon people realized that these shops could be gathering spots for more than sick people. Everybody seemed to enjoy the refreshing qualities of carbonated water. By 1820 soda makers had started adding flavored syrups to their waters, and a whole new industry was born.

Dispensing

Soda "fountains" dispensed their carbonated water into glasses from urns or pipes. They concealed the machinery for carbonating and cooling water beneath elaborate marble and metal trimmings. To these were added pumps for dispensing syrups, sometimes in dozens of flavors. In addition to being impressive sights, these machines allowed employees to mix and serve their concoctions with minimal effort. Soda parlors soon became centers of urban social life, and temperance advocates promoted them as alternatives to saloons. By 1895 there were an estimated fifty thousand soda fountains across the nation.

Soda drinks were also sold by the bottle, to be enjoyed at home or in restaurants. However, the technology of soda bottling took many years to perfect. Bottles were all handblown and often exploded while being filled. The capping devices, mainly internal stoppers or wire clamps over corks, tended to leak both liquid and carbonation. It was not until the 1890s that American bottle manufacturers invented the technology for producing strong, inexpensive, and standardized glass soda bottles. In 1891 William Painter of Baltimore invented the "crown" metal bottle cap whose corrugated edge crimped around the bottle top. These advances would pave the way for the giant soda companies of the twentieth century.

Flavors

Except for seltzer water, all soda drinks contain added flavoring. Artificial mineral waters were manufactured with blends of salts and other chemicals to duplicate the flavors of natural waters. The earliest sweet flavors were mixtures of sugar syrup and fresh fruit juices (lemon, raspberry, and strawberry) or plant extracts, such as sarsaparilla and spruce beer. By the 1880s, syrup manufacturers had concocted hundreds of often unusual flavors, including allspice, cayenne pepper, champagne, maple, pistachio, and white rose. These were mixed into the glass at the fountain and had to be made almost daily because they tended to ferment quickly. For bottling purposes, the first flavors with shelf life were lemon and ginger ale, joined later by sarsaparilla, root beer, and cream soda.

Through the early 1900s ginger ale was by far the most popular bottled soda flavor. However, soda makers realized that there was more money to be made in proprietary brands than in generic flavors. Their recipes closely guarded, these new syrups were often made from more than a dozen natural and synthetic flavorings. Charles Elmer Hires began in 1876 by selling Hires Root Beer flavorings for mixing at home; through aggressive marketing, the drink was soon being sold at soda fountains nationwide. In the mid-1880s, pharmacists in Waco, Texas, and Atlanta, Georgia, concocted recipes for medicinal tonics that were respectively called Dr Pepper and Coca-Cola. Their therapeutic properties were quickly forgotten as they found a market as soda fountain specialties. Coca-Cola and other companies began selling their syrups to franchised bottlers, and the modern soft-drink industry was born.

Big Business

Between 1899 and 1970 the yearly national consumption of soft drinks rose from 227 million to 72 billion eight-ounce servings. Bottling plants used new mechanized production lines to produce far greater quantities of soda and transported their products on motorized trucks riding along newly paved roads. Manufacturers realized very early the value of advertising, first in newspapers and then on the radio. While regionally distributed sodas boomed (many of them fruit flavors like orange, grape, and cherry), the most phenomenal growth occurred in the cola sector. By 1920 cola drinks had overtaken ginger ale as the most popular flavor. Ten years later, over seven thousand bottling plants were producing 6 billion bottles of soda a year.

After struggling through the Great Depression and then World War II–era shortages of raw materials, the soda drink industry took advantage of postwar prosperity. Indeed, soft drinks became symbols of that prosperity and of the nation's growing role in the world. Wherever American soldiers traveled around the globe, they were sure to bring American-made sodas, Coca-Cola in particular. At home, the big bottlers greatly expanded their plants and began concentrating on fewer, higher-volume brands. They found new outlets in suburban supermarkets, drive-up fast-food restaurants, and improved automatic vending machines. To meet demand from dieters, they developed low-calorie drinks using cyclamates or saccharin as artificial sweeteners. (Cyclamates were eventually banned because they were believed to increase cancer risks, and aspartame became the most widely used artificial sweetener.) Bottlers also broadened their markets with new flavor lines; Pepsi-Cola introduced Diet Pepsi, Teem, Patio, and Mountain Dew. The soda drink industry became big business, causing thousands of smaller bottlers either to sell out or to close. Hundreds of local soft-drink brands disappeared from store shelves forever.

Soda drink packaging evolved rapidly during this era. After supermarkets complained about processing returnable bottles, manufacturers introduced inexpensive "one-way" bottles and, beginning in 1953, metal cans. The popularity of cans skyrocketed after the introduction of pull tabs, and the containers soon littered roadsides across America (eventually leading to laws mandating returnable cans and bottles). Cans are by far the most popular soda container, followed by plastic bottles made of polyethylene terephthalate (PET).

From the 1960s to the 1990s, soda manufacturers tapped into a vast and constantly renewing market through advertising campaigns that effectively linked soft-drink consumption to youth culture. Consumption rose steadily every year, and soda bottles and cups grew ever larger to feed this phenomenal thirst. In the 1980s, manufacturers received a further boost to profits when they replaced sugar with inexpensive high-fructose corn syrup. In 1998 the rate of consumption peaked at a phenomenal fifty-six gallons per person and then began to decline slightly every year. The main culprits are saturation—carbonated drinks have penetrated every possible market—and competition from bottled waters and other forms of noncarbonated beverages.

Americans drink more than fifty-two gallons of soda drinks per person every year, with the highest consumption among consumers between the ages of eighteen and twenty-four. Most sodas are purchased in cans or bottles, while about 25 percent are dispensed in bars and restaurants. The number of bottlers is down to approximately three hundred, producing 450 brands of soda. While these brands include many generics and the remaining regional drinks, major manufacturers like Coca-Cola, Pepsi-Cola, and Cadbury Schweppes still command the market. Although profits may no longer be as high, it is likely that soda drinks will be a large part of Americans' diets for years to come.

[See also Bottling; Canning and Bottling; Coca-Cola; Cola Wars; Cream Soda; Dr Pepper; Ginger Ale; Pepsi-Cola; Root Beer; Sarsaparilla; Seltzer; 7 Up; Soda Fountains; Sweeteners.]

BIBLIOGRAPHY

Beverage World: 100 Year History, 1882–1982, and Future Probe. Great Neck, NY: Beverage World, 1982.

Carbonated Beverages in the United States: Historical Review. Greenwich, CT: Marketing Research–Packaging, American Can Company, 1972.

Funderburg, Anne Cooper. *Sundae Best: A History of Soda Fountains.* Bowling Green, OH: Bowling Green State University Popular Press, 2002.

Paul, John R., and Paul W. Parmalee. *Soft Drink Bottling: A History with Special Reference to Illinois.* Springfield, IL: Illinois State Museum Society, 1973.

Riley, John J. *A History of the American Soft Drink Industry: Bottled Carbonated Beverages, 1807–1957.* New York: Arno Press, 1972.

Woodruff, Jasper Guy, and G. Frank Phillips. *Beverages: Carbonated and Noncarbonated.* Rev. ed. Westport, CT: AVI Publishing, 1981.

ANDREW COE

Soda Fountains

The drug store soda fountain has brought something new into the modern world—a meeting place where both sexes and all ages may enjoy themselves in an atmosphere of decency and charm. . . . They combine an emporium where medicine is dispensed with a community center where the whole neighborhood has its good times. The prescription room for serious business, the fountain for gaiety and refreshment. (*American Druggist*, April 1935, p. 59)

The American soda fountain originated in the early 1800s with the sale of carbonated medicated waters and lasted through the 1960s. During this period, the soda fountain, whether in a drugstore, confectionery, department store, hotel, or sidewalk stand, was a gathering place for families, teenagers, courting couples, women, and, during Prohibition, working men, within walking distance of home or work. The soda fountain provided a clean, wholesome atmosphere in which to enjoy conversation and a tasty concoction. At a time when women did not eat in most restaurants without an escort and when more women were going into the workforce, soda fountains, particularly those offering a light meal in addition to the traditional sodas and sundaes, provided a clean, pleasant, inexpensive dining place.

Taking the Waters

From ancient times people have recognized the healing properties of natural springs, hot or cold, still or effervescent, and scientists have tried to recreate their healing powers. One of the major problems was recreating the effervescence in natural springs. Though Joseph Priestley is often credited with being the first person to create carbonated water in 1767, other scientists preceded him. These waters were intended to be as close in mineral content as possible to the water of famous spas. They were considered medicines to be dispensed by physicians and apothecaries and were touted for curing everything from obesity and dysentery to fevers and scurvy. Bicarbonate of soda was occasionally added to carbonated water for medicinal purposes. The product was known as "soda water," which later became the generic name for carbonated water.

In the early nineteenth century one of the first Americans to produce artificial mineral waters for sale was Philip Physick (aptly named) of Pennsylvania, who sold his water as a cure for obesity. Another was Benjamin Silliman of Connecticut, who created, bottled, and sold soda water. Within a fairly short time, soda water became a popular beverage. Cold soda water was sold everywhere and was inexpensive enough for most people to enjoy.

Though waters were initially sold as medicines, their sale as a pleasurable, thirst-quenching beverage soon superceded their sale as medicine. The shift from drinking soda water primarily as medicine to drinking it for pleasure was due to the addition of flavored syrups. This occurred in the late eighteenth and early nineteenth centuries. One of the first in America to add syrups to his soda water was Eugene Roussel of Philadelphia, who began to sell flavored waters from his perfume shop around 1838. Early flavorings were made by the apothecary, and most had to be used fairly quickly, but by the late 1800s many manufacturers of soda fountains also sold carbonated water and syrups, allowing the soda fountain operator to offer a large variety of flavorings and flavor combinations. Some syrups, such as Coca-Cola and Hires Root Beer, had to be purchased since their composition was a trade secret. These were sold as health tonics.

Soda Fountain and Drugstore

The connection between the soda fountain and the drugstore is natural and of long standing. In the early years of the soda fountain, carbonated medicated waters had to be produced by the druggist. One of the earliest and certainly most influential apothecary shops in America was opened in Philadelphia in 1825 by the French émigré Elias Durand. His apothecary has often been termed the first modern drugstore because it was very ornate with marble and mahogany fixtures. Durand was one of the first to sell medicated waters in a drugstore, and his store became a gathering place for intellectuals, the forerunner of the community social center of later soda fountains.

By the 1940s, 75 percent of all drugstores had soda fountains, and 33 percent of drugstore business was generated by the soda fountain. Mineral waters continued to be sold at soda fountains throughout the history of the fountain, even after the sale of sweet concoctions such as ice cream sodas and sundaes came to make up the bulk of the soda fountain's profits. While there had been ice cream parlors and saloons in America from the early 1800s, with the advent of modern drugstores with their soda fountains, these fountains became the main point of sale for both ice cream and bottled soda waters.

Fountains

The earliest "fountain" was a small, boxlike apparatus for generating carbonated water with a tube to draw the water. The fountain sat on the counter and was connected by tubes to the carbonating apparatus, which was set under the counter or in the cellar. The apparatus was surrounded by ice so that the water would be cold. There was a spigot on the fountain, shaped like a gooseneck in the early years, to draw the water into a bottle. The water was then poured into a glass with or without a flavoring syrup. These early fountains evolved into much more elaborate ones made of marble with mythological figures and a hundred syrups, and the later fountains could cost from a few hundred to thousands of dollars.

One of the first to manufacture an apparatus to make soda water was John Matthews of New York City, who began manufacturing carbonating apparatuses in the early 1830s. Carbonated water was produced by combining sulfuric acid with marble chips. Matthews used the marble scraps left from the construction of Saint Patrick's Cathedral to produce 25 million gallons of soda water. Funderburg notes that when that source dried up, Matthews bought marble from tombstone cutters and sculptors. He later added the sale of syrups and carbonated water to his business and continued to be an innovator in creating ever more elaborate fountains. He promoted his fountains through catalogs and advertising. In one advertisement, Matthews compared a young person's first sip of soda water to the first experience of love.

Another important manufacturer was Gustavus Dows of Massachusetts. In the 1850s he manufactured a cottage-shaped fountain of marble. The addition of marble, adding an ornate touch, was an innovation, as was the device within the fountain to shave ice. Formerly the soda jerk had the time-consuming task of shaving ice for each order. Dows's fountains had silver-plated spigots for drawing syrups with the name of a syrup engraved on each. As had Matthews before him, Dows continued to improve on his apparatuses and was the first to create a fountain that could dispense soda water with two different forces of stream and the first to create an apparatus that dispensed the soda water and syrup into a glass. The earliest soda fountains were placed against a wall, but in 1903 the counter soda fountain was introduced and was quickly adopted throughout the country. The counter fountain allowed people to sit at the counter and watch the soda jerk manipulate the various spigots to create sodas, banana splits, and other concoctions. The counter fountain also enabled the soda jerk to perform facing his audience.

While early soda fountains offered primarily a variety of health-giving mineral waters, flavored waters had become more popular than the medicated waters by the end of the nineteenth century. Cream was also an early addition to flavored carbonated beverages, and after the Civil War, concoctions like ice cream sodas became fountain staples. In their heyday, fountains offered malted milk drinks, flips, phosphates, egg drinks, sundaes, banana splits, milk shakes, ice cream floats, and fizzes created with a large variety of ice cream flavors, syrups, dressings, fruit, and nuts. Many of these concoctions had fanciful names, such as the Knickerbocker glory sundae, Peter Pan soda, and black cow. Some were created and garnished with ingredients that we would not now associate with a sweet treat, such as the tomato milk shake or the prune juice milk shake. The latter certainly reflects on the original role of the fountain as a dispenser of medicine.

Soda Jerk and Soda Fountain Calls

The soda fountain was also a theater with the major role played by the dispenser, also called a "soda jerk," the "professor," "thrower," and, in one place, "licensed fizzician," who by the 1920s was an American folk figure. He dispensed sundaes, sodas, and entertainment. To help him in his task, soda fountain and ice cream trade journals provided him with recipes and diagrams for new concoctions along with tips on how to build them with style and showmanship. The International Association of Ice Cream Manufacturers held a series of seminars around the country called "Sundae Schools," the purpose of which was to share information on the latest treats and how to promote them. This was important for the industry since the soda fountain was the major point of sale for ice cream at a time when most homes had no refrigeration other than an icebox. Trade journals ran articles on successful soda jerks and fountains. Becoming a good dispenser took years of practice and often ensured a good salary. The small-town soda fountain was used as a backdrop for numerous films from the 1930s on and was portrayed as a warm, neighborly, social place to gather and enjoy a leisurely sundae or share an ice cream soda with a date.

In addition to creating soda fountain concoctions and entertaining customers with their artistry, soda jerks provided linguistic entertainment through the use of soda fountain calls. Soda fountain lingo was a type of shorthand used to speed up orders and provide a bit of fun for both dispenser and customer. In some cases this lingo was used to protect customer privacy. If a customer ordered citrus of magnesia, the call was "one Mary garden" or "M. G. cocktail." The lingo also served as a memory aid, and most calls were plays on words. Anything with strawberry flavoring was a "patch," milk was "cow juice," and an order for three of anything was a "crowd." This lingo was not uniform throughout the country with some terms meaning different things in different places.

Prohibition

Soda fountains benefited considerably during the late nineteenth century, when the temperance movement was gaining ground. As the temperance movement grew, it became obvious that there was a need for an alternative to the saloon. This initially posed a dilemma for some fountain operators since a number of their shakes, flips, and sodas contained alcohol. Trade journals began urging operators to eliminate the use of alcohol in their concoctions and began publishing articles on how to attract former saloon customers. They promoted rich drinks, like egg drinks and malted milk beverages, that would appeal to men. Hires Root Beer, Coca-Cola, and Moxie had advertising campaigns promoting their beverages as healthful temperance drinks.

Soda fountains began adding light lunches to their menus around the turn of the twentieth century. These eventually evolved into luncheonettes, which provided full meals, soda fountain treats, and medicated waters for simple remedies. The addition of light meals benefited the soda fountain during Prohibition and the Depression years. Initially these meals were intended to draw female customers, but when men could no longer get the free lunch to which they were accustomed when saloons were open, menu items were geared to draw male customers. Again the trade journals ran articles on how to appeal to men in terms of decor and menu items. Once Prohibition passed and saloons had to stop selling alcohol, many saloons became soda fountains and beer manufacturers transformed their facilities into ice cream plants. The soda fountain lunch was quick and inexpensive enough to maintain business even during the years of the Great Depression.

Decline of the Soda Fountain

The soda fountain weathered two world wars and the Great Depression, and as America emerged from World War II and rationing, soda fountains were still a strong presence and were still found in most drugstores. Several things worked together to bring about the soda fountain's decline. After the war there was a move from towns to the suburbs to newly created housing developments. Low-interest government mortgages allowed returning veterans to purchase housing, and people generally had money to purchase items, such as cars, that were in short supply during the war. In addition, supermarkets began to gain a larger share of ice cream sales once refrigerators and freezers were available for homes. Another factor was the rise of the drive-in restaurant, which began to replace the soda fountain to which everyone had walked as a social gathering place. The old-time soda fountain is more memory than reality.

[*See also* Coca-Cola; Ice Cream Sodas; Luncheonettes; Moxie; Prohibition; Root Beer; Slang, Food; Soda Drinks; Temperance.]

BIBLIOGRAPHY

Bentley, Harold W. "Linguistic Concoctions of the Soda Jerker." *American Speech* 11 (February 1936): 37–45.

Dickson, Paul. *The Great American Ice Cream Book*. New York: Atheneum, 1972.

Funderburg, Anne Cooper. *Sundae Best: A History of Soda Fountains*. Bowling Green, OH: Bowling Green State University Popular Press, 2002.

Kelly, Patricia M., ed. *Luncheonette: Ice-Cream, Beverage, and Sandwich Recipes from the Golden Age of the Soda Fountain*. New York: Crown, 1989.

Riley, John J. *A History of the American Soft Drink Industry: Bottled Carbonated Beverages, 1807–1957*. New York: Arno Press, 1972.

Schwartz, David M. "Sippin' Soda through a Straw." *Smithsonian* 17, no. 4 (July 1986): 114–125. A delightful anecdotal look at the history of the soda fountain.

Stephenson, Howard. "Fountain Profits." *American Druggist* 91, no. 4 (April 1945): 33, 128. *American Druggist* routinely ran articles on how to run a soda fountain.

Weir, Robin. " 'One Leg of a Pair of Drawers': The American Soda Fountain Lingo." In *Disappearing Foods*, edited by Harlan Walker, 215–220. Devon, England: Prospect Books, 1995.

White, E. F. *The Spatula Soda Water Guide*. Boston: Spatula, 1901. This is a good example of a formulary. Boston: Spatula Publishing, 1901.

PATRICIA M. KELLY

Songs, Food

Food songs are almost never really about food. Some songs mention food in the title or in passing in the lyrics, but it is not important to the whole work. Others have more food references but the song is really about something else. Only a few songs are about food as food. In a new twist on the subject, beginning in the twentieth century, songs have been used to sell food in the form of radio and TV jingles.

Americans had songs and nursery rhymes with mentions of food before there was an America. "Hot Cross Buns," "The Muffin Man," and "Pease Porridge Hot" are nursery rhymes that still survive. Humpty Dumpty was an egg.

Yankee Doodle sticking a feather in his cap and calling it macaroni was a food reference once removed. It referred to the practice of calling English dandies in the eighteenth century who affected foreign mannerisms "macaronis." There was a clear British and American scorn for things and mannerisms from the Continent, as shown in a song by Henry Fielding (1707–1754) called "The Roast Beef of Old England." It begins:

When mighty roast beef was the Englishman's food,
It ennobled our hearts, and enriched our blood;
Our soldiers were brave, and our courtiers were good.

The second verse goes on to say:

> Then, Britons, from all the nice dainties refrain,
> Of effeminate Italy, France or Spain;
> and mighty roast beef shall command on the main.

The colonists, in the folk tradition, adapted the song lyrics to be both a bit of cheerleading and a political prod. For the parliamentary elections of 1774, Americans were hoping the Whigs, who were more moderate toward the colonies, would be elected to the eighty-eight open seats. They were not. The Tories remained in power. The song was printed with new lyrics, simultaneously scolding and hopeful, first in Virginia and within a few weeks in Massachusetts, New Hampshire, and Connecticut. Now the song had nine or more verses, depending on the version. Note the inclusion of coffee and tea to imply weakness of character. Some of the verses as printed in the *Virginia Gazette* in November of 1774 were:

> When good Queen Elizabeth sat on the throne,
> Ere coffee and tea, and such slip-slops were known,
> The world was in terror if ere she did frown.
> Our nobles had honour in records of fame;
> Their sons are but shadows, and know but the name,
> Their fathers eat beef, their sons whore and game.
> With beef and their charters, how happy and free!
> Their sons, if they've charters, must live upon tea,
> and cringe to a venal majority.
> The Britons, that once were inured to fight,
> Now tamely sit down their petitions to write;
> Which serve for a laugh, and the boys for a kite.
> The return of the seasons are [sic] settled by fate,
> The Tories may tremble, though now so elate,
> And freedom revive with the new eighty-eight.

Through the colonial period, tavern songs and other songs sung at fairs and markets enjoyed great popularity. The melody of a drinking song, "To Anacreon in Heaven," was used for many patriotic songs around the time of the War of 1812 including America's anthem, "The Star-Spangled Banner," by Francis Scott Key (1779–1843). Anacreon was a Greek poet (ca. 582–485 B.C.E.) whose surviving poetry is devoted to the goddess of love and the god of wine.

In the early eighteenth century, many songs extolled the beauty or bounty of the lands beyond the frontier as the nation was expanding westward. "Hunt the Buffalo" in several variations was popular in America and even enjoyed some acclaim in London. It offered this view of the far lands:

> There are fishes in the river
> That is fitting for our use,
> And high and lofty sugarcanes
> That yield us pleasant juice,
> And all sorts of game, my boys,
> Besides the buck and doe.

In the mid-eighteenth century, one Ole Bull (1810–1880), a Norwegian violinist and well-to-do adventurer, concocted a plan to get Norwegians to come to the United States and homestead farms for themselves. He named his settlement Oleanna after himself. A song was created to promote the idea with a great helping of hyperbole. The song was very much in the spirit of the tall tales about larger-than-life characters that marked the time, like the ones about Paul Bunyan and John Henry. The new land promised that:

> Little roasted piggies
> rush around the city streets
> Inquiring so politely
> if a slice of ham you'd like to eat
> Beer as sweet as Muncheners
> springs from the ground and flows away
> The cows all like to milk themselves
> And the hens lay eggs ten times a day
> In Oleanna land is free
> The wheat and corn just plant themselves
> Then grow a good four feet a day
> While on your bed you rest yourself.

In the turbulent period before and during the American Civil War, songs that contained apparent food references were common. "Follow the Drinking Gourd" gave instructions for runaway slaves and referred to the Big Dipper constellation. It had nothing to do with food. Other songs reflected the black humor that can often emerge in difficult times. "Eating Goober Peas" was popular with the Confederate military and mentioned that uniquely southern crop, peanuts:

> Just before the battle, the General hears a row
> He says "The Yanks are coming, I hear their rifles now."
> He looks down the roadway and what d'you think he sees?
> The Georgia Militia cracking goober peas.

In the early twentieth century, American life was sharply changed by a world war, a dust bowl, a depression, and a general shifting away from the steady life of an agrarian society. That was a perfect setting for a song like "Big Rock Candy Mountain," a traditional hobo ballad that appears in many slightly different versions over the years. Burl Ives popularized his variation in the 1940s and 1950s. It uses food as metaphor for the comfortable life, as in the chorus:

Oh the buzzin' of the bees
In the cigarette trees
Near the soda water fountain
At the lemonade springs
Where the bluebird sings
On the big rock candy mountain.

Radio entered the picture during this period. Songs that had small audiences before now could reach a considerably larger group.

Sometimes songs speak code to the initiates, as in so many sly blues songs where the food references are actually about anatomical parts (jellyroll for female privates), sexual activities, or other sociosexual recognitions like, "That Chick's Too Young to Fry." On occasion, the songs maintain both the food and the sexual reference as in, "It Must Be Jelly ('cause Jam Don't Shake like That)."

Some songs like "Beans and Cornbread" and "Saturday Night Fish Fry" by Louis Jordan (1908–1975) are almost chants against a lively background and can often just be foils for the instrumental work of the artists. The lyrics do mention food, but as novelties or euphemisms. "Beans and Cornbread" has an infectious rhythm, a rather flat melody line, and a lyric that makes little sense:

Beans and Cornbread,
Beans and Cornbread had a fight.
Beans knocked Cornbread out of sight.
Cornbread said, "Now, that's all right,
meet me at the corner tomorrow night."
"I'll be ready, I'll be ready tomorrow night,"
That's what Beans said to Cornbread.
"I'll be ready tomorrow night. . . . "

"Saturday Night Fish Fry" is not about fish at all. It is slang for a rather wild, New Orleans–style raucous party. One of the verses tells it all with references to sex, drugs, and music.

Most often, songs use food as metaphors for other elements of life. They can include political urgings as noted

above, glancing blows of serious romance like, "You're the Cream in My Coffee" and the plaintive note struck by the impecunious boyfriend, "Banana Split for My Baby; Glass of Plain Water for Me."

Some songs are puzzling because they have food-related titles but no lyrics to support the reference, as in the late 1950s and early 1960s hits "Tequila" recorded by the Champs or "Green Onions" recorded by Booker T and the MG's. Or they seem to be saying something but do not, as in "Frim Fram Sauce," which has this nonsensical refrain:

I want the Frim Fram Sauce
With feeossanfay
With shifafa on the side.

Other songs, most notably parodies, go into food in some detail, but are often funny primarily because of the contrast with the original, as in the many contemporary food songs of Weird Al Yankovic like "My Bologna," which parodies a top-forty song called "My Sharona," or "Eat It" to parody "Beat It" by Michael Jackson.

Very often, food songs have simply been novelty ditties. Their hallmarks have been slyness and broad wit. They enjoyed a great vogue during the heyday of radio with such notables as Spike Jones (1911–1965) and his strange recordings of songs like "Cocktails for Two" and "Yes, We Have No Bananas." Songs from the 1940s through the 1960s like Louis Prima's (1910–1978) "Please No Squeeza Da Banana" and "Angelina the Waitress at the Pizzeria" are novelty songs specifically done for a grin. More recently, "Junk Food Junkie" by Larry Groce has kept alive that style.

The very popular song by George (1898–1937) and Ira (1896–1983) Gershwin, "Let's Call the Whole Thing Off," from the 1937 film *Shall We Dance?*, about lovers being too different to stay together very wittily exploited food pronunciations in verses like these:

You like potato and I like potahto
You like tomato and I like tomahto
Potato, potahto, Tomato, tomahto.
Let's call the whole thing off.

Once in a great while, the songs are actually about food, as in many folk songs like "Shortnin' Bread" and "Bile that Cabbage Down," but most of the time, they are about something else. Food in songs can be metaphor, euphemism, code word, or diversion from the real meaning. In this, Americans seem to be like all other cultures.

Virtually everybody sings about the basic human needs and satisfactions. Food references are a socially acceptable substitute for the taboo ones. This is an area of scholarship that has not been extensively studied and holds a promise of richness for future research.

[*See also* Myths and Folklore.]

BOB PASTORIO

Sorghum Flour

Historical records trace the sorghum plant, *Sorghum bicolor* (L.) Moench, to Africa. Benjamin Franklin was thought to have introduced sorghum to the United States in the late 1700s. Sometimes known as one of the "4F" plants, it can be used for fuel, food, forage, and feed. The diversity of the crop has led to many uses: as broomcorn; in building materials, breads, porridges, and alcoholic beverages; for renewable fuel production; and as animal feed. Worldwide, grain sorghum is used for food, and because the plant is drought resistant, it is a predominant cereal in many developing countries, especially in parts of Africa and Asia. In the United States, most sorghums are cultivated for animal feed. Sorghum's popularity as a food item is growing because of its unique nutritional profile and the efforts of several sorghum researchers and marketers.

The whole grain can be cooked liked rice or ground into meal or flour. Unlike wheat, sorghum is gluten free, which is beneficial to people with intolerance to gluten. Some sorghums are even high in antioxidants and can be used in making healthy, whole-grain breads. Not readily available, sorghum can be found in some health food markets and through the Internet.

[*See also* Sorghum Syrup.]

BIBLIOGRAPHY

Bumgarner, Marlene Anne. *The New Book of Whole Grains: More than 200 Recipes Featuring Whole Grains, Including Amaranth, Quinoa, Wheat, Spelt, Oats, Rye, Barley, and Millet.* New York: St. Martin's Griffin, 1997.
Gordon, L. A., J. Awika, L. W. Rooney, R. D. Waniska, and E. L. Suhendro. "Characteristics of Breads Baked with Sorghum Brans High in Phenolic Compounds." Paper presented at the Sorghum Industry Conference and Twenty-Second Biennial Grain Sorghum Research and Utilization Conference, Nashville, TN, February 18–20, 2001.

CHERYL FORBERG

Sorghum Syrup

The sorghum syrup plant, *Sorghum bicolor* (L.) Moench, shares the nomadic heritage of its sister, sorghum grain. Syrup-making techniques came into prominence in the United States around the mid-1800s. Because of the scarcity of sugar during wartime, sorghum syrup was the principal sweetener in many parts of the country. By 1920 the annual U.S. production was nearly 50 million gallons. After World War II, less expensive refined sugar became available, and sorghum syrup use declined. The bulk of production remains in the southeastern United States, Kentucky and Tennessee being the leading producers.

While molasses is a by-product of sugarcane processing, pure sorghum syrup is the goal (and only) product of sorghum cane processing. Like sugarcane, the sorghum plant is harvested and fed into a mill, which crushes the stalks, extracting clear juices. Impurities are removed before the liquid is simmered in an evaporating pan. It is slowly reduced to a viscous amber syrup, which is milder in flavor than molasses and less sweet than honey. Nutritionally, it is rich in antioxidants and minerals.

In the South, sorghum syrup is also referred to as "sorghum molasses." This versatile sweetener is used in beverages, confections, and baking. In the South, too, it is most commonly found on top of hot biscuits. In substituting sorghum for sugar, the general rule is to increase the amount of sorghum by one-third over the amount of sugar and decrease the liquids by the same amount.

[*See also* Molasses; Sorghum Flour; Sweeteners.]

BIBLIOGRAPHY

Sweet Sorghum Production and Processing. Poteau, OK: Kerr Center for Sustainable Agriculture, 1992.
United States Department of Agriculture. *Sorgo for Sirup Production: Culture, Harvesting, and Handling.* Farmers' Bulletin, no. 1619. Washington, DC: GPO, 1930.
University of Georgia College of Agricultural and Environmental Sciences. "Growing Sweet Sorghum for Syrup." University of Georgia, 1999. http//:www.ces.uga.edu/Agriculture/agecon/pubs/sweetsorg.htm.

CHERYL FORBERG

Sorrel

Sorrel (genus *Rumex*) is a perennial herb that originated in Asia and became naturalized throughout Europe and

North America. Closely related to rhubarb, sorrel shares with rhubarb a bright astringency, which comes from a high oxalic acid content (binoxalate of potash). Unlike rhubarb, which is harvested for its stalks but has leaves that are considered poisonous, sorrel is most treasured for its pointed green leaves. Consumed throughout the ancient world, particularly in Egypt, for its tonifying and culinary properties, in modern times sorrel is perhaps most revered by the French.

The name "sorrel" comes from the Old French *surele*, which means "sour." Both major species of cultivated sorrel, the true French sorrel (*Rumex scutatus*) and broad-leaved or garden sorrel (*Rumex acetosa*), have a lemony tartness, but French sorrel is less acidic. Other sorrel species, *Rumex hymenosepalus* (like rhubarb, used for its tart stalks) and *Rumex patientia* (used for its mild leaves), are naturalized in North America. Sorrel is most frequently used in salads, sauces, soups, and pies and alone as a vegetable. None of the varieties has found lasting popularity in American gardens or on American tables.

There is some mystery surrounding the introduction of sorrel to America. Few early American cookbooks contained recipes for sorrel. Mary Randolph, in *The Virginia Housewife* (1824), is an exception, and Thomas Jefferson noted the appearance of sorrel in Washington, D.C., markets. It is possible that Jefferson grew sorrel. Sorrel began to appear more regularly in cookbooks in the last third of the nineteenth century. Most of these books were written by French or French-trained chefs, who viewed sorrel as one of the most "recent additions to our lists of esculent plants." Sorrel's lasting public relations problem was aptly summarized by Mary Henderson in *Practical Cooking and Dinner-Giving* (1877): sorrel "would be popular in America if it were better known."

[See also French Influences on American Food; Herbs and Spices; Jefferson, Thomas; Randolph, Mary; Salads and Salad Dressings; Vegetables.]

BIBLIOGRAPHY

Bittman, Sam. *The Salad Lover's Garden.* New York: Doubleday, 1992.

Facciola, Stephen. *Cornucopia II: A Source Book of Edible Plants.* Vista, CA: Kampong, 1998.

Hessayon, D. G. *The Vegetable and Herb Expert.* London: Sterling, 1998.

McEwan, Barbara. *Thomas Jefferson, Farmer.* Jefferson, NC, and London: MacFarland, 1991.

Murrey, Thomas J. Salads and Sauces. New York: Frederick A. Stokes, 1889.

Schneider, Elizabeth. *Uncommon Fruits and Vegetables.* New York: Harper and Row, 1986.

Spencer, Colin. *Vegetable Book.* London: Conran Octopus, 1995.

KAY RENTSCHLER

Soul Food, *see African American Food*

Soup Kitchens

The earliest references to soup kitchens, in 1826, describe communal areas within cultural venues, such as theaters and charity balls, where meals were served to staff as payment for their services. The term was popularized in 1839 to denote establishments serving minimum dietary essentials to needy people. In 1847 the British government passed the Temporary Relief Act, also known as the Soup Kitchen Act, which replaced public works as the main form of relief to the Irish during the potato famine. As the name implies, the act was to be provisional, for the summer months, ending at harvest.

The Soup Kitchen Act contrasted sharply with earlier relief schemes in Britain, which incorporated various "tests" of need and required labor or internment in return from their recipients. Soup kitchens were initially financed by the government, but many areas did not take advantage of the legislation, which required that funds be paid back, and instead opened private soup kitchens, which were less expensive to run.

Because of the poor quality of the soup served, recipients were not fond of soup kitchens, yet the establishments were heavily depended upon, serving more than 3 million people per day during their peak in July 1847. Despite a significant decrease in mortality while the soup kitchens operated and the hardships of subsequent seasons, soup kitchens in Ireland closed permanently in the autumn of 1847.

In United States during the nineteenth and early twentieth centuries, food assistance, like welfare, was dominated by private and religious organizations whose social concepts were based on the Protestant ethic and liberal values. By the turn of the century new kinds of welfare organizations had emerged with a more scientific and complex way of seeing poverty and its causes; this work was based within neighborhood assistance. New food programs emerged within the expanding settlement house system, at workers' union halls, and through voluntary political organizations.

For more than a decade, beginning in the mid-1900s, welfare capitalism was popular, but the Great Depression, which started at the end of the 1920s, had proved that business could not solve the problems of poverty, including hunger alleviation. Local governments tried to help the needy, but expenditures, which averaged $8.20 per month per person, did nothing to help the thousands more who required federal aid. Thus, following the stock market crash of 1929, organizations like the Red Cross and Salvation Army provided help through soup kitchens and breadlines: 13 million people—25 percent of the population—were unemployed and hungry.

After the Depression, the United States enjoyed many decades of economic growth and affluence, and the need for emergency food declined except among the poorest citizens. Federal food relief programs were established, including the Food Stamp program (1964); Women, Infants, and Children (WIC; 1974); and the National School Lunch, School Breakfast, Special Milk, Child and Adult Care Food, and Summer Food Service programs (all 1969), with the intention of meeting the food and nutrition needs of every citizen.

In the early 1980s another great resurgence of private food programs, including soup kitchens, occurred as a direct result of several factors: a sharp economic recession, interest rate hikes, and cuts in social programs. In the late twentieth century food assistance transformed from the realm of "emergency" to "supplemental." The number of people considered "food insecure"—those who have limited or uncertain availability of food—grows each year. Nearly 11 percent of U.S. households were food insecure during the 2001 calendar year. That year, nearly 3 percent of the population, including 19 percent of households deemed food insecure, received food from a soup kitchen, food pantry, or other program.

The majority of soup kitchens, thousands nationwide, are run by religious organizations. Most of the other agencies that run soup kitchens are private, nonprofit organizations with no religious affiliation. Direct contact between soup kitchen workers—who are mostly volunteers—and guests appeases a natural inclination to help those less fortunate than oneself. This personal contact provides both physical and emotional support to soup kitchen guests.

Food banks, which distribute government commodities, are the principal source of food, providing 43 percent of food resources for soup kitchens. Other food comes through food rescue organizations, private donations, or discount purchases from farmers and commercial distributors. Menus attempt to provide basic nutritional needs but cannot effectively be planned because of the unpredictability of food available and the prevalence of volunteer labor.

More than 58 percent of soup kitchens in major metropolitan areas have seen an increase in patrons since 1998. The kitchens, which have historically served the homeless, also serve poor working families with children. In New York City more than one in five soup kitchen clients is a child. There is no federal standard or procedure for determining recipients' eligibility to receive emergency or supplemental food: patrons are presumed needy if they seek food.

Several political factors indicate that food assistance programs will continue to grow; these include the lack of jobs paying a living wage, the shrinking safety net of federal assistance programs, an emphasis on farming subsidies and food exports, the development of an underclass, the rising cost of housing, and the general acceptance of poverty within an otherwise affluent society.

Soup kitchens and other food assistance programs—and the organizations that support them—are anticipating this growing need by becoming more professional and by accepting their role as permanent providers of ongoing, supplementary sources of food for a growing percentage of the population.

[*See also* Food Stamps; Hunger Programs; School Food; Settlement Houses.]

BIBLIOGRAPHY

America's Second Harvest. "Creating a Hunger-Free America." http://www.secondharvest.org. Website for the nation's largest hunger relief organization.

Church of the Holy Apostles. "Holy Apostles Soup Kitchen: Feeding New York's Hungry and Homeless for Twenty Years." http://www.holyapostlesnyc.org/haskhome.htm. Website for outreach program of the Church of the Holy Apostles in New York City.

"My Grandson's Life and Times." *Escritoir; or, Masonic and Miscellaneous Album* 1, no. 11 (April 8, 1826): 85.

Ohls, James, Fazana Saleem-Ismail, Rhoda Cohen, Brenda Cox, and Laura Tiehen. *The Emergency Food Assistance System— Findings from the Provider Survey, Volume II: Final Report.* Economic Research Service Food Assistance and Nutrition Research Report No. 16-2. Washington, DC: U.S. Department of Agriculture, 2002.

United States Department of Agriculture. "Food, Nutrition, and Consumer Services." http://www.fns.usda.gov/fncs.

KAREN KARP

Soups and Stews

While early humans utilized hot water to heat foods in natural containers, boiling was not a commonly used cooking technique until the invention of waterproof and heatproof containers about five thousand years ago.

Boiling has several advantages over roasting. Water turns to steam at 212°F at sea level. Compared to hot air over a fire, boiling water is denser and comes more fully in contact with the entire surface of submerged foods. Hot water easily and quickly imparts its energy to the food. In addition to consistency, boiling provides a lower cooking temperature than does frying, roasting, or baking. Boiling also permits the fuller use of animal and plant products for food and expands the range of potential edibles. Many animal parts, such as bones, could not otherwise be eaten. Boiling extracts whatever nutritional value these previously unused parts possess. Likewise, some plant parts are inedible in their natural state but become edible after boiling. For instance, acorns are edible only after the tannin has been removed by boiling, a technique employed by Native Americans in pre-Columbian times.

Over the centuries, the terms *gruel, potage, broth, consommé,* and *soup* have vied for culinary supremacy in the English language. These terms have shifted meanings over time, making it difficult to determine what was actually meant by a particular word at a particular time. The English terms *soup* and *stew* did not achieve their overarching status until the late eighteenth century. Soups usually have a predominance of liquids and are served in bowls or mugs. Stews tend to have less water and are frequently cooked in covered containers over low heat for an extended period of time. Stews are often thicker and contain more and larger solids than soups. In a stew, the liquids are frequently boiled down and employed as sauces for the stew. Stews are usually served on plates. But even with these loose definitions, boundaries between soups and stews remain fluid.

Recipes for soups and stews appeared in French and English cookery manuscripts from medieval times. One common term for both dishes was "potages," which were generally hot broths or liquids poured over stale bread or another foodstuff. Some potages were thick stews, while thinner ones would be classified as soups today. The original notion of a potage survives into the modern day in the form of French onion soup or in the vestigial use of croutons in soups. During the eighteenth century, the term *potage* declined in English as *soup* and *stew* gained in popularity.

Early American Soups and Stews

In pre-Columbian America, stone boiling was used by many Native American groups. Hot stones were dropped into waterproof baskets filled with food (mainly vegetables) and water. In parts of eastern North America, for instance, the Chippewa heated water by placing hot stones in clay vessels or freshly cut birch bark baskets containing water. When the stones cooled, they were removed and replaced. To stir the soup, the Chippewa used wooden spoons, and they employed shells as soup bowls.

Some colonial Americans eschewed soup, but evidence indicates that soup was an important culinary component in the diet of the upper class. Even before cookbooks were published in America, newspapers, magazines, and travel accounts mentioned broths and soups. William Parks, a colonial printer in Williamsburg, Virginia, published the first cookbook in America in 1742. It is based on the fifth edition of Eliza Smith's *The Compleat Housewife; or, Accomplished Gentlewoman's Companion* and includes the recipes Soop Sante, Pease Soop, Craw Fish Soop, Brooth, Soop with Teel, and Green Peas Soop, as well as recipes for several bisques. Susannah Carter's *The Frugal Housewife* (1772) contains an entire chapter on soup with nineteen recipes. In addition to British cookbooks published in colonial America, surviving cookery manuscripts attest to the importance of potage, broth, and soup in America—at least among the upper class.

While American culinary traditions were largely based on English cookery, many other national and cultural groups influenced the culinary life of the new nation. For instance, German immigrants have influenced culinary matters in America since the late seventeenth century. Pennsylvania Germans liked soups and were particularly famous for those based on potatoes. When the French revolutionary and journalist Jacques-Pierre Brissot de Warville ate at the home of a wealthy Philadelphia Quaker in 1788, the meal included two soups. German-language cookbooks published in America featured recipes for soups based on chicken, mutton, veal, beef, calf's head, rice, apples, and huckleberries. According to the food historian William Woys Weaver, the Pennsylvania Germans took their commitment to soups seriously. Soup was a "symbol of community, of religious fellowship, and even communion." In two-course meals, soup was the first course; in one-pot meals, soup was the only dish.

French Influences

The second most influential culinary tradition in America was French. As a result of the French Revolution, many noblemen, their families, and their entourages fled France. Chefs were among these refugees. Some found positions as chefs in homes of the wealthy in England and other countries. Others opened up restaurants. The French gastronome Jean-Anthelme Brillat-Savarin, who left France for America at the height of the Reign of Terror, visited a café-tavern in New York City where turtle soup was served for breakfast. While in America, Brillat-Savarin also visited Jean Baptiste Gilbert Payplat dis Julien. In 1794 Julien opened a public eating house in Boston called Julien's Restorator, which was his translation of the French word *restaurant* into English. Julien was famous for his soups and stews, and he was nicknamed the "Prince of Soups." He is credited with introducing to America the julienne soup, a composition of vegetables in long, narrow strips. Julien specialized in making turtle soup.

The pervasive French influence is particularly noticeable through the English words used to describe diverse soups and stews. "Bisque" is a cream-thickened soup, usually containing crustaceans. In English it meant soup from poultry or game birds, particularly pigeons. "Bouillon" derives from the French word *bouillir* (to boil). In France bouillons were produced by slowly simmering bones, aromatics, and usually some flesh, and were frequently augmented by herbs, vegetables, and cereals. Bouillons were considered healthful. Many bouillon recipes originated in New Orleans, Louisiana, which had once been a French colony. The concept of a consommé dates back to at least the Italian Renaissance, but it was popularized by French chefs in the eighteenth century. Recipes for consommés were first published in the United States during the 1830s. "Consommé" came to be defined as a rich, clear broth that has been boiled down, skimmed, and strained. Its base was meat or fish, but not bones. During the nineteenth century, the term was also applied to soup made with vegetables. Names of the stews "fricassee" and "ragout" are French in origin. Fricassee usually involves stewing chicken, veal, or small game, which is cut into pieces and fried. Ragout is a rich stew containing meat or fish and vegetables in a thick sauce. Ragout recipes were published in the United States beginning in 1828.

The French influence also filtered into America through cookbooks, such as Louis Eustache Ude's *The French Cook; or, The Art of Cookery Developed in All Its Various Branches* (1828; an earlier edition was published in London, in 1813), which features over fifty soup, potage, ragout, and related recipes. Subsequent French cookery books that were translated into English and published in the United States kept Americans abreast of the latest soup-making developments. For instance, Louis-Eustache Audot's *La cuisinière de la campagne et de la ville* was translated into English and published in America as *French Domestic Cookery* (1846). It features a recipe for gazpacho, which Audot identified as "a favourite dish with the Andalusians." Many early American restaurants featured French cuisine, and soups became the rage of America's upper class.

Soup was not neglected by American cookbook writers. While the first edition of Amelia Simmon's *American Cookery* (1796) does not contain soup recipes, it does note that parsley is "good for soup." The second edition of this work, published in the same year in Albany, included recipes for soup made of a beef, veal, and lamb's head. In addition Simmon includes a recipe for chowder. Mary Randolph's *Virginia House-wife* (1824) features sixteen soup recipes, such as those for asparagus, beef, veal, bouilli, oyster, and barley. There are two recipes for pea soup; more for hare or rabbit, fowl, catfish, onion, and turtle; and finally, one for mock turtle soup using calf's head. N. K. M. Lee's *The Cook's Own Book* (1832), essentially a compendium of simplified recipes compiled from diverse British and American sources, includes eighty-seven recipes for soups, consommés, and broths. Some are based on asparagus, beef, mutton, beetroot, calf's head, carrot, celery, crawfish, cress, cucumber, eel, giblets, gourds, game, hare, herbs, lobster, macaroni, oxhead, oxheel, oxtail, peas, pigeon, spinach, venison, vermicelli, and barley. Lee also furnished soup recipes for Lorraine, moorfowl, mulligatawny, curry, and cocky-leeky (a Scottish soup made with fowl and leeks).

By the late nineteenth century, America's most famous chefs featured soup on their menus. Felix Déliée, who had served as chef at the prestigious Union, Manhattan, and New York Clubs, recommended soup at the beginning of every meal, and he offered 365 meals with a different soup served each day at the clubs where he worked. His *Franco-American Cookery Book* (1884) features many soup recipes. Thomas J. Murrey, a professional restaurateur in Philadelphia and New York City, believed that the selection of the right soup for the right occasion presented an excellent opportunity for the cook to display good taste and judgment. Arranging and harmonizing a bill of fare was an art form, Murrey believed, and soup was the pivot upon which the meal's harmony depended. The famous chef Charles Ranhofer also published many soup recipes in his monumental work *The Epicurean* (1894). Ranhofer recommended serving two soups—a clear soup and a cream soup—at each meal. His guide to professional cookery includes more than two hundred soup recipes, such as *Consommé à l'Andalouse*, Chartreuse Soup, Chicken Okra Soup, Clam Chowder, and Gumbo with Hard Crabs, Creole Style. Oscar Tschirky, the maître d'hôtel at the Waldorf in New York City, published almost 150 soup recipes in *The Cook Book, by "Oscar" of the Waldorf*, Oscar Tschirky (1896).

As the nineteenth century progressed, recipes for soup making increased in cookbooks. The first known American cooking pamphlet that focused solely on soups was written by Emma Ewing: *Soups and Soup Making* (1882). As an article of diet, soup ranked second in importance only to bread, proclaimed Ewing. Soup was an important part of most Americans' diet by the end of the nineteenth century. As a dish that was both economical and nutritious, soup was prepared for men in prisons and the military, and offered without charge at lunch in saloons.

Stewing as a basic cooking process was noted in American cookbooks from the beginning. In the United States, "stewing" referred to gentle boiling with a small amount of water at a moderate heat for a long time. Recipes for stewing particular foods, such as beef, lamb, poultry, fish and seafood, regularly appeared in American cookery books. Specific stews, however, are usually defined as including two or more solid products. Lee's *The Cook's Own Book* includes several stew recipes, but only her beef stew and Irish stew meet this definition. Regional stews—such as gumbos, bouillabaisse, Brunswick stew, and burgoo—emerged during the nineteenth century. Stews were more common in twentieth-century cookbooks, although many recipes were composed of ingredients at hand, such as mulligan stew, which is made from odds and ends.

Commercial Soup

The first known commercial soup manufacturer was James H. W. Huckins of Boston, who began canning soup about 1858. He first advertised his canned tomato soup in 1876. As Huckins's soups became extremely successful, other canners entered the field.

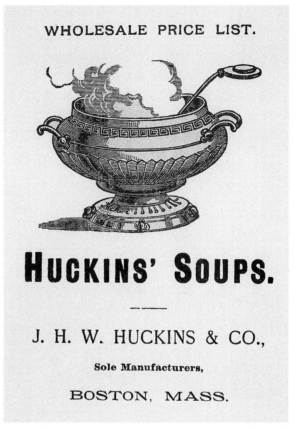

Huckins's Soups. Price list for canned soups sold by J. H. W. Huckins and Co., 1880s. *Collection of Andrew F. Smith*

Huckins began advertising his soup nationally during the 1880s. In these advertisements Huckins proclaimed that his soups were rich and well seasoned, and they "always maintained their excellence." All the consumer needed to do was to heat the contents and serve. The soups were sold in two-quart cans and wholesaled for $3.25 per case of two dozen. Huckins engaged in a variety of promotional gimmicks. He gave away free samples of soup, for instance, charging only for the cost of mailing.

A major reason for Huckins's extensive promotion blitz during the 1880s was the emergence of a major competitor headed by Alphonse Biardot. Biardot had been a soup maker and canner in France. About 1880 Biardot immigrated to the United States, and in 1886 he incorporated the Franco-American Food Company in Jersey City, New Jersey. Franco-American's initial products were canned soups: consommé, bouillon, tomato, oxtail, vegetable, chicken, mock turtle, green turtle, and julienne.

Biardot engaged in extensive advertising. Franco-American distributed several pamphlets beginning in the late 1890s. The company trademarked the phrase "French Soups," which undoubtedly increased the soups' snob appeal. The company's hallmark was a representation of a child cook wearing a white jacket and short pants. The soup cost almost twice as much as some competitors' soup. Biardot's soups were quite popular despite their high cost. They were available in most grocery stores. Biardot was so successful that in 1916 the company was acquired by the Campbell Soup Company of Camden, New Jersey.

Other early companies that manufactured soup were Richardson and Robbins of Dover, Delaware, and Libby, McNeill, and Libby of Chicago, organized in 1868 by the meatpacker Arthur A. Libby. Anderson Preserving Company, also of Camden, and the H. J. Heinz Company of Pittsburgh, Pennsylvania, were also producers of canned soup.

By the 1880s Artemas Ward, a Philadelphia grocer and prolific food writer, reported that "soups of all descriptions are now packed in hermetically sealed cans, and are a very great addition to the comfort of the cook, being prepared for the table almost immediately." There were also extracts, or "dry soups," desiccated packages of ingredients to be reconstituted in water.

Twentieth-Century American Soups and Stews

Many twentieth-century soups and stews derived from non-English culinary traditions that entered the United States with immigrants. Many of these dishes straddled the line between soups and stews; these include minestrone, a thick Italian vegetable soup, and *menudo*, a thick, spicy Mexican tripe-based soup or stew. Others were clearly soups, such as Eastern European borscht, generally a beet-based soup; the Mexican *sopa de albóndigas*, or meatball soup; Japanese miso soup, made with miso (a paste made from soybeans and rice), tofu, and, occasionally, vegetables; and Chinese hot and sour soup, composed of various ingredients, including tofu, corn starch, soy sauce, mushrooms, chili sauce, and meats. These stews and soups proliferated with the success of Hungarian, Italian, Mexican, Japanese, Jewish, and Chinese restaurants and cookbooks, few of which were published in America until after World War II.

Soup is an important commercial enterprise. More than eighty American manufacturers produce soup in some form. Only five produce more than 1 percent of the total soup. The H. J. Heinz Company, for instance, produces 85 percent of the private label soups. Progresso Quality Foods, located in Vineland, New Jersey, makes a full line of ready-to-serve soups, as does Healthy Choice.

The American soup market, however, is dominated by the Campbell Soup Company, which accounts for 60 percent of all soup sales. It boasts four of the five best-selling soups.

Specific Soups and Stews

Following are detailed discussions of certain well-known soups and stews: turtle and mock turtle soup, okra soup and gumbo, bouillabaisse, chowders, borscht, gazpacho, tomato soup, Brunswick stew, Irish stew, pepper pot, burgoo, and frogmore stew.

Turtle and Mock Turtle Soup Turtles were found in abundance in the New World, and they were eaten from the beginning of European settlement. Terrapin turtles were particularly prized. Female turtles, or cow turtles, were treasured for their meat. The male, or bull turtles, had little value and were generally used for making soup. As turtle meat used in soup making was bland, it was usually spiced with red pepper. Turtles were easy to transport long distances and were held in pens until sold. Prior to the Civil War, they were so plentiful as to be considered slave food in the South.

In the North, turtle meat and turtle soup were prized. The French gastronome Jean-Anthelme Brillat-Savarin enjoyed turtle soup in New York City during his stay in America during the 1790s. From the earliest American cookbooks, directions for making turtle soup were included. For instance, the longest and most complicated recipe in Amelia Simmon's *American Cookery* (1796) is for dressing turtles. She also includes a simpler recipe for preparing calf's head in the fashion of a turtle. Randolph's *Virginia House-wife* includes directions for making turtle soup, combining turtle flesh, beef, bacon, onions, sweet herbs, pepper, and salt. If a rich soup were desired, butter and flour were folded in. Randolph recommended that soup be seasoned with wine, ketchup, spice, cayenne, and curry powder.

Turtle soup was difficult to prepare at home. As soon as turtles were killed, they had to be cooked. Because many turtles were extremely large, frequently weighing three hundred pounds, they were sold to cafés, taverns, and restaurants that had a high volume of business. Eliza Leslie's *Directions for Cookery* (1837), for instance, omitted turtle soup because it was a costly, complicated, and difficult dish to prepare: if a family wanted turtle soup, she advised hiring a first-rate cook or buying it at a turtle soup house.

Most cookbooks also offered recipes for mock turtle soup, usually made from calves brains or calves feet, which were thought to have the same texture as turtle meat. Such recipes were regularly published in England in the mid-eighteenth century and later in the United States. Lee's *The Cook's Own Book* contains three such recipes. Similar recipes were regularly published into the beginning of the twentieth century.

Turtle and terrapin soups were among the first to be commercialized. By 1882 canned turtle soup was regularly sold in grocery stores. This commercial production finally depleted the abundant stock of turtles, and prices soared during the early twentieth century. By 1911 turtle had become one of the highest priced foods in America. This shortage led to the creation of turtle farms on which turtles were bred and raised for market. Turtle and mock turtle soup had gone out of fashion by the early twentieth century.

Okra Soup and Gumbos Okra (*Hibiscus esculentus*) originated in Africa. The word is thought to have derived from West African *nkru-ma*. The slave trade brought okra to the Caribbean, where it was cultivated by 1707. From the Caribbean, okra migrated north. Although okra could be prepared in many ways, the early recipes are for okra used as an ingredient in soup. The first published recipe for okra soup appears in Randolph's *Virginia House-wife*. After Randolph's recipe was published, okra soup became a common entry listed in American cookbooks.

Similar to okra soups were the gumbos of New Orleans. At first, gumbos contained okra and filé (dried sassafras leaves), a seasoning thought to have originated with the Choctaw Indians in Louisiana. In addition to okra, cooks prepared gumbos with many other principal ingredients, such as chicken, turkey, squirrel, rabbit, crabs, oysters, shrimp, or even cabbage. The main common element at this stage was the filé powder.

Gumbos migrated throughout America during the early nineteenth century. The first known recipe was published in the *American Farmer* in 1830 and in other publications shortly thereafter. Ingredients in early recipes included okra, tomatoes, and onions seasoned with pepper and salt. The first gumbo recipe published in an American cookery book appeared in Leslie's *Directions for Cooking* (1837). She identified it as "a favourite New Orleans dish." Her recipe included okra but not filé.

Gumbo delighted many admirers. Will Coleman, the publisher of Lafcadio Hearn's *La Cuisine Creole* (1885), described it as the "great dish of New Orleans." According to Coleman, there was "no dish which at the same time so tickles the palate, satisfies the appetite, furnishes the body nutriment sufficient to carry on the physical requirements, and costs so little as a Creole gombo." It was a dinner in itself, the "*pièce de résistance*, entremet, and vegetables in one. Healthy, not heating to the stomach and easy of digestion, it should grace every meal." Most major restaurants in New Orleans presented on their menus three soups and five kinds of gumbo.

Bouillabaisse Bouillabaisse is somewhere between a soup and a stew. In America, New Orleans was famous for its bouillabaisse, the classic Provençal fish stew, which was a specialty of Marseilles, France. The French word *bouillabaisse* derives from the Provençal *bouiabaisso*, which means to "boil and settle." This meant that the cook should boil the stew only for a short period. Bouillabaisse was a fisherman's soup based on fish from the Mediterranean, particularly the *rascasse*, or scorpion fish (*Scorpaena scorfa*), but also the sea bass, bonito, conger eel, and other fish and seafood. During the nineteenth century, bouillabaisse became the rage in Europe. Recipes for bouillabaisse appeared in several British cookbooks in the 1850s. The American cookbook writer Pierre Blot admitted that the real *bouillabaisse* was made in Marseilles. Imitations, claimed Blot, were "very inferior to the real one." However, he offered a recipe based on fish that could be procured in the United States.

By the end of the nineteenth century, bouillabaisse was firmly ensconced in fashionable American restaurants and clubs. Felix Déliée, who had served as a chef at New York City clubs, prepared bouillabaisse. Thomas J. Murrey, a professional caterer at several hotel restaurants, developed a nontraditional recipe for "Bouille-abaisse" that was based on cod fish. Charles Ranhofer's bouillabaisse was founded "on red snapper, one-half pound of lobster, one-half pound of perch, one-half pound of sea bass, one-half pound of blackfish, one-half pound of sheepshead, one-half pound of cod, one-half pound of mackerel."

Chowders Whether chowders were introduced into New England by French, Nova Scotian, or British fishermen is undocumented, but chowders had become important dishes by the beginning of the eighteenth century in America. The earliest known American recipe for chowder was published in Boston in 1751. Chowders were quite distinct from broths and soups. Chowders, originally stews, were composed of fish, seafood, and vegetables of various proportions. The object was to prepare a thick, highly seasoned dish without reducing the ingredients to the consistency of a puree. Hannah Glasse's *The Art of Cookery*, first published in America in 1805, includes a "chouder" recipe, which was adapted by Randolph in her *Virginia House-wife*. Subsequently, similar recipes appeared in other American cookery books, and their popularity expanded.

Several twentieth-century cookbooks presented recipes for vegetable chowder, vegetable clam chowder, and corn chowder. The first located recipe titled Manhattan Clam Chowder was published in Virginia Elliot and Robert Jones's *Soups and Sauces* (1934). This recipe substitutes tomatoes for milk. Despite detractors, Manhattan clam chowder survived and thrived.

Borscht Borscht was originally a soup from Ukraine based on cow parsnips, a plant belonging to the carrot family. Like many other foods, borscht evolved: beetroot became its defining ingredient. The first located American recipe for borscht, or "Polish soup," was published in 1895. Today, hundreds of different types of borscht are available in Ukraine alone. In America borscht was initially an ethnic food particularly associated with Jewish immigrants. So associated were Jewish immigrants with borscht that during the 1930s, Jewish-owned resorts in the Catskill Mountains were referred to as the "Borscht Belt."

Gazpacho Gazpacho originated in Spain, where it was considered a peasant soup. Consequently, recipes for it were not published in early Spanish cookbooks, which were written mainly for the upper middle class. Randolph's *Virginia House-wife* includes the first known recipe for gazpacho, from an Arabic word meaning "soaked bread." As the culinary historian Karen Hess has noted, Randolph probably acquired this recipe from her sister, Harriet Randolph Hackley, who had lived in Cádiz, Spain. It is also interesting to note that the second and third known published recipes for gazpacho were also not published in Spain. *Novisimo Arte de Cocina* (1845), the first known Spanish-language cookbook published in the United States, includes two recipes for gazpacho. This cookbook was printed for a client in Mexico and was probably not distributed in the United States. It had little influence on mainstream American cookery. Several nineteenth-century cookbook authors published similar recipes under the name "Andalusian soup." Gazpacho may have gained general acceptance in Anglo-American high society before it was generally accepted

in Spain. Reports of its excellence had filtered back to the United States. In Spain great diversity exists among gazpacho recipes, but in America the only ones that thrive are those that are tomato based. As gazpacho is served ice cold, it may have been one of the first popular chilled soups. Gazpacho became popular in the United States during the 1960s. Recipes for gazpacho appear in many cookery books and magazines.

Tomato Soup Tomatoes have been grown in the United Kingdom since the late sixteenth century, but they did not become popular as a food until the late eighteenth century. The early culinary use of tomatoes in Britain was as an ingredient in soups. Tomatoes provided coloring and an acidic flavor unmatched by other fruits or vegetables. While references to tomatoes in soups appeared in English medical, agricultural, and botanical works, early recipes titled "Tomato Soup" were really vegetable soups, of which tomato was an ingredient. As the nineteenth century progressed, the amount of tomatoes increased and other vegetables decreased, so that by mid-century, tomatoes had become the major ingredient.

In America tomato soup recipes commonly appeared in cookbooks in the mid-nineteenth century. New types of tomato soup emerged at the close of the nineteenth and beginning of the twentieth centuries: cream of tomato and the combination of tomato soup with other ingredients, such as rice. Milk or cream became an ingredient in tomato soup during the early 1880s. Tomato soup was canned after the Civil War. By the beginning of the twentieth century, tomato soup was America's favorite soup, a position it retained for the next eighty years. Tomato soup remains among the top five soups sold commercially in America.

Brunswick Stew Brunswick stew emerged in the mid-nineteenth century and is claimed to have originated in both Georgia and Virginia. It was commonly made with leftovers or whatever was available, such as squirrel meat, chicken, or other meats along with bacon, green corn, tomatoes, lima beans, potatoes, and other vegetables. The first known recipe for Brunswick stew appeared in Marion Harland's *Common Sense in the Household* (1871). She reported that it derived from Brunswick County, Virginia. Marion Cabell Tyree's *Housekeeping in Old Virginia* (1879) includes four recipes for Brunswick stew, three of which contain chicken or squirrel and one of which is beef based. The cookbook *Housekeeping in the Blue Grass* (1875) includes the recipe Virginia Brunswick Stew, and the author reports that, when the stew is properly made, none of the ingredients dominate. Brunswick stew remains a regional southern stew, and many different recipes claim to be "authentic."

Irish Stew In the eighteenth century, Irish stew was traditionally made of mutton (usually neck), potatoes, onions, and parsley, although some cooks added turnips or parsnips, carrots, and barley. Mutton was the dominant ingredient because of the economic importance of wool and sheep's milk in Ireland: only old sheep ended up in the stew pot, where it needed hours of slow boiling before it was palatable. This stew was recognized as an Irish national dish about 1800.

In the United States, Lee's *The Cook's Own Book* includes a recipe for Irish stew that is made from the same ingredients and in the same way as in Ireland. However, in America, Irish stew evolved. As sheep were not plentiful, other meats were substituted. When made in the traditional manner, Irish stew is cooked so long that the individual ingredients break down, and the result is very thick and hearty broth. Not everyone was pleased with Irish stew. Mark Twain in his *American Claimant* (1892) proclaimed that Irish stew was composed of leftovers. Lamb has become the predominate meat in Irish stew.

Pepper Pot Pepper pot was a savory West Indian stew made with juice of the bitter cassava root with seasoning. This recipe changed in the eighteenth century to include meat, fish, or vegetables, spiced with red pepper. Recipes for pepper pot had been published in British cookbooks by the mid-eighteenth century, and some of these recipes were reprinted in America. However, pepper pot may previously have been brought to America by African slaves who had lived in the Caribbean. American pepper pot was composed of a variety of ingredients, such as fish, mutton, pork, vegetables, lobster, and crab, but all recipes were highly seasoned with crushed peppercorns or red pepper. Pepper pot recipes had been published in America by the early nineteenth century. Randolph's *Virginia House-wife* includes a traditional West Indian pepper pot employing tripe and veal spiced with red pepper. Lee's *The Cook's Own Book* includes two recipes, the first of which is made from spinach, onions, potatoes, lettuce, bacon, suet, dumplings, and cayenne pepper; the second includes beef, ham, onions, potatoes, fowl, pork, and lobster. The pepper pot recipe in *Mrs. Porter's New Southern Cookery Book* (1871) includes tripe, mutton, onions, potatoes, turnips, red pepper, and dumplings. Pepper pot generally disappeared in the twentieth century but lives on in culinary

fakelore, which purports that this dish was first made at Valley Forge, Pennsylvania, by George Washington's army.

Burgoo Burgoo is a thick stew that originated in Kentucky and Tennessee during the nineteenth century but quickly spread throughout the South and Southwest. It could contain almost any combination of meats and vegetables. Squirrel, wild turkey, pigeons, and fish were frequently ingredients, and the vegetables might include tomatoes, celery, turnips, and corn.

Frogmore Stew Frogmore stew, a combination of sausage, corn, crabs and shrimp with seasoning, is attributed to Richard Gay of Gay Seafood Company. Gay claimed to have invented frogmore stew around 1950 while on national guard duty in Beaufort, South Carolina, while preparing a cookout of leftovers for his fellow guardsmen. According to Gay, the Steamer Restaurant on Lady's Island near Beaufort was the first establishment to offer frogmore stew commercially.

[*See also* Cajun and Creole Food; Campbell Soup Company; Dumplings; Native American Foods, *subentry* Before and After Contact.]

BIBLIOGRAPHY

Cameron, Miss. *Soups and Stews and Choice Ragouts: Practical Cookery Recipes.* London: Kegan Paul, Trench, Trübner, 1890.
Hooker, Richard J. *The Book of Chowder.* Boston: The Harvard Common Press, 1978.
Hooker, Richard J. *Food and Drink in America: A History.* Indianapolis, IN: Bobbs-Merrill, 1981.
Peterson, James. *Sauces: Classical and Contemporary Sauce Making.* New York: Van Nostrand Reinhold, 1991.
Smith, Andrew F. *Pure Ketchup: A History of America's National Condiment.* Columbia: University of South Carolina Press, 1996.
Smith, Andrew F. *Souper Tomatoes: The Story of America's Favorite Food.* New Brunswick, NJ: Rutgers University Press, 2000.
Ward, Artemas. *The Grocers' Hand-Book and Directory for 1883.* Philadelphia: Philadelphia Grocer Publishing, 1882.

ANDREW F. SMITH

South American Food, *see Iberian and South American Food*

Southeast Asian American Food

Much of the food of Southeast Asia—Brunei, Cambodia, Indonesia, Laos, Malaysia, Myanmar (formerly Burma), the Philippines, Singapore, Thailand, and Vietnam—is represented in the United States. In pockets where immigrants have formed communities, food helps rebuild culture and identity. In those areas, the food is most likely to be closest to that of the countries of origin. The U.S. mainstream is familiar mainly with the cuisines of Thailand and Vietnam, often in westernized form.

Although Southeast Asian foods share a flavor profile—a balance of hot, salty, sour, sweet, and sometimes bitter—individual cuisines both between and within countries are distinctive. In some cuisines, fish sauce is used for the salty component; in others, salt is used. Palm sugar may provide sweetness, and lime the sour note. Condiments often are provided at the table so that diners can customize dishes to taste. Chilies from the Americas were not added until the sixteenth century. Some cultures eat mostly jasmine rice; others sticky rice. A typical meal is based on a large serving of rice with a scant, flavorful topping of stir-fried meat or fish, vegetables, seasonings, and sometimes coconut milk. Noodles made of rice flour, eggs, or mung beans may be substituted for rice. Leaf wrappers, often of banana or pandanus leaves, are used to package some foods. Soup is essential. Dessert often consists of fresh fruit or sticky rice with bits of fruit.

In immigrant communities in the United States, there is an attempt to re-create the food and ambience of the homeland. Restaurants serve multiple purposes as places for new arrivals to meet, network, and speak the language. Although many Americans enjoy frequenting these ethnic neighborhoods, others do not venture into them. The latter diners prefer upscale versions once the cuisine has gained cachet. Most common in westernizing the cuisines, particularly Thai food, is toning down the heat by decreasing the chili content. Many menus rate the hotness of dishes with a code of chili symbols. American cookbooks may recommend more chilies for "traditional heat" and fewer for medium heat. In Southeast Asian restaurants designed for Americans, the typical ratio of amount of rice to topping is the reverse of that in the country of origin. Westerners prefer a large amount of topping with only a small amount of rice. Some restaurants offer a "pan-Asian" menu that features more than one cuisine alongside the more familiar Chinese. "Big bowl" fast food and noodle shops have become popular.

Thai

The bold, contrasting flavors of Thai food have had the greatest presence in the American dining scene. Thai emerged as an important international cuisine between 1982 and 1992. Despite its popularity, there are a relatively small number of Thai Americans—approximately 113,000 according to the 2000 census, most of whom arrived after 1965 and settled in Los Angeles, Chicago, and New York. Thai is a fusion of Chinese and Malay food ideas with some influences from India (massaman curry), Portugal (deep-fried appetizers), and elsewhere. In the early 1960s, during the Vietnam War, the American military "discovered" this cuisine. In Boston and New York during the 1970s and 1980s, a penchant for spicy Szechwan (Chinese) food paved the way for Thai flavors. This experience was reinforced during the 1980s when millions of American tourists began to visit Thailand, which was promoted as a gourmet paradise and a hub for all travel in Southeast Asia.

The recognizable Thai flavor is produced with a balance of fish sauce, lemongrass, lime, coriander, ginger or galangal, garlic, sweet Thai basil, chilies, and sometimes coconut milk and peanut sauce made with chilies. This combination is the basis for a thriving Thai restaurant business—more than two hundred in Los Angeles alone. Even a Thai Buddhist temple sets up a food court every weekend featuring familiar Thai foods as well as desserts seldom found in the United States. Thai food has become so popular that many immigrants from other Southeast Asian countries have seized business opportunities by opening Thai restaurants. In Boston, for example, Thai food is served in restaurants owned by Malaysians, Cambodians, Chinese, Burmese, and Koreans.

The most familiar Thai dishes are *pad thai*—pan-seared rice noodles with pieces of salty dried shrimp, cooked egg, pork, and sweet preserved turnip; *mee krob*, a crispy noodle dish; *satay*, marinated meat threaded on skewers and served with peanut chili dipping sauce (a catering stock-in-trade for cocktail parties); salad with peanut dressing; various chili-based curries mixed with coconut milk, the most popular being green and red curries; Thai jasmine rice; and Singha beer.

Thai food is made at home with the encouragement of cookbooks, television cooking shows, food magazines, and websites. English-language versions of Thai cookbooks proliferated as early as the 1950s. *Siamese Cookery* by Marie Wilson of Rutland, Vermont, was published in 1965. Wilson's recipes were far from an accurate interpretation. She advised light use of chilies, substitution of soy sauce for fish sauce, and the use of monosodium glutamate (MSG). *The Original Thai Cookbook* by Jennifer Brennan was published in 1981.

Brennan claimed hers was the first authentic Thai cookbook. In the early twenty-first century approximately 575 Thai cookbook titles can be found in American libraries. Ingredients for Thai dishes are available from Asian markets, mail-order and online sources, and local supermarkets. At least one company markets a product line of Americanized Thai ingredients—mostly mixes, including *pad thai*, peanut salad dressing, curry pastes, peanut sauce, lemongrass oil, coconut ginger soup, jasmine rice, and coconut milk in regular and low-fat versions.

Vietnamese

With the fall of Saigon (renamed Ho Chi Minh City) to the North Vietnamese in 1975, refugees began arriving in the United States. In 2000 the U.S. Vietnamese population was 1,112,528, including children born in the United States. Most live in Southern California. The population of Little Saigon in Orange County, California, is approximately 400,000, making it the largest Vietnamese community outside of Vietnam. Other Vietnamese have settled in Houston, Boston, Denver, the Pacific Northwest, and Florida. Some of these concentrations are reflections of resettlement from the original remote locations designated by the federal government.

Vietnamese food is more restrained than Thai with a combination of beef and salads that is closer to American. There is little use of high-fat coconut milk, and a strong vegetarian tradition with an herbaceous trait—basil, mint, and cilantro. Vietnamese food is not very hot, sweet, or pungent. Shaped by French colonization, the cuisine includes a Vietnamese bouillabaisse and sizzling, savory rice-flour crêpes filled with shrimp, pork, and bean sprouts. The blending of fresh and cooked flavors in each mouthful and the combination of meat, fruits, and vegetables in salads are hallmarks of Vietnamese cuisine. Food is often wrapped in lettuce leaves and combined with herbs.

The most familiar Vietnamese foods are spring rolls wrapped in transparent rice flour paper; *nuoc mam*, carrot and daikon pickled salad; *pho bo*, beef broth aromatic with star anise, cinnamon, and ginger slowly simmered and then poured over rice noodles, thinly sliced beef, and fresh basil leaves (traditionally eaten in Vietnam for breakfast); *ga xe phai*, a salad of poached, shredded chicken, bean sprouts, and Vietnamese coriander dressed with tangy, mildly hot, mildly sweet lime juice and fish sauce; *banh mi*, sandwiches of strong-tasting meats, French-Vietnamese pâté, pickled carrots, and

fresh coriander on French-style baguettes with butter and mayonnaise, legacies of the French colonial years; strong, dark coffee layered over condensed milk; *nuoc leo*, peanut *satay* sauce; *nuoc cham*, a dipping sauce of diluted fish sauce, garlic, chilies, lime juice, and sugar; and *mam tom*, fishy dipping sauce served with fish.

Vietnamese restaurants appeared in the late 1970s and became popular partly because of familiar flavors such as beef. The first one in Boston, Rendezvous, opened in 1977. The site of many early eateries was Little Saigon in Orange County, California. At first, the restaurants offered simple, popular dishes, but with competition, new places featuring regional or specialized cuisines sprang up, as did a huge supermarket. A number of restaurants serve *bo 7 mon* (meaning "beef in seven ways"), based on a style of restaurant in Ho Chi Minh City that has also become popular in other North American cities. In Vietnam this dish is a special-occasion meal because meat is not eaten

Southeast Asian Influence. Hmong wedding reception, Saint Paul, Minnesota, 1981. *Minnesota Historical Society*

often. A new American version is the eight-course fish dinner.

Even though the Vietnamese population in the United States is approximately seven times the Thai population, it was not until the 1990s that Vietnamese cuisine began to influence mainstream foodways. The delay stemmed in part from the emotional and political issues surrounding the Vietnam War. By 1999 a franchise of fifty-five noodle shops had been launched in the predominantly Vietnamese communities of Boston, Chicago, Seattle, Houston, Atlanta, and Washington, D.C. A chain of casual Vietnamese eateries aimed at young professionals opened first in Seattle and was slated for replication in California in Santa Monica, Palo Alto, and northern San Francisco before heading east. In Boston a number of Chinese Vietnamese (Chiu Chow speakers who came to the United States after a period in Malaysia) are prominent restaurateurs and grocers in the city's Chinatown. A new generation of "Vietnamese" restaurants in California presents food in a stylized, nontraditional guise. Shredded green papaya salad is made with steamed green beans, large shrimp, and meaty shreds of pork instead of typical dried beef or pounded river crabs. Some soup parlors in cities such as Minneapolis, Minnesota, and New York specialize in *pho bo*, the northern beef broth meal-in-a-bowl.

The preparation of Vietnamese cuisine is encouraged at home by more than 650 cookbooks (more than the number of Thai titles), food magazine articles, websites, and television food shows. Ingredients, including Vietnamese fish sauce (different from the Thai version), are available at Asian markets and from online and mail-order purveyors.

Filipino

Filipinos are unique among Southeast Asian settlers in America, having arrived first and in greatest numbers in several waves of immigration. As residents of a U.S. colonial territory for thirty-five years beginning in 1902, Filipinos held American passports and traveled freely to and from the United States. By 1990 there was a large concentration in New York City. In 1992 Filipinos accounted for 20 percent of the total Asian American population. In 2000 more than 2 million Filipinos were living mostly in Hawaii and on the West Coast. There were large Filipino communities around U.S. naval bases and major hospitals, because Philippine nurses are trained by American protocol and can easily obtain U.S. licenses. Although it is a developed cuisine with potential appeal, Filipino cooking has had less influence than other Southeast Asian cuisines. Some social scientists believe the many years of colonial rule—first by Spain, then by the United States—robbed Filipinos of much cultural identity. In addition, restaurants have not been a major source of mobility for Filipino Americans and are more often basic eateries catering to immigrant workers.

Filipinos are generally more integrated into American society than other Southeast Asians, and some foods have become popular outside their communities. The most familiar food is chicken or pork adobo (Spanish for "marinade"), often described as the national dish, consisting of meat marinated and cooked in vinegar and garlic sauce; *lumpia* (often described as egg rolls), crêpes made of rice-and-egg pastry filled with vegetables and topped with peanut sauce; and *pansit*, sautéed rice noodles with bits of vegetables, sausage, and tiny shrimps. Filipino restaurants in the United States are concentrated in Hawaii, Los Angeles, San Francisco, Chicago, New York City, and Texas. There are nearly 196 Filipino cookbook titles in U.S. libraries.

Indonesian

In the late 1950s, after Indonesian independence, a number of Dutch Indonesians came to America as refugees, settling primarily on the West Coast. Most Indos (Indonesian Europeans) arrived after the 1965 changes in the immigration quota system. Sixty percent of these immigrants live in Southern California and San Francisco, and smaller numbers live in New York City, Houston, Chicago, and Washington, D.C. During the 1960s, Indonesian restaurants helped maintain a network among immigrants. Between 1980 and 1990 the number of Indonesian immigrants more than tripled. The number remained small, however, only approximately forty thousand according to the 2000 census. Indonesians assimilated quickly, and perhaps that is one reason the cuisine is not a major presence in the United States. One of the dishes commonly thought to be Indonesian, rijsttafel, is actually a Dutch colonial elaboration of a native tradition—a buffet in which a rice dish is surrounded by small condiments of various meats, fish, and vegetables.

Other dishes often sampled by Americans in the Netherlands or former Dutch colonies include *nasi goreng* (fried rice), beef *rendang*, *saté* (skewers of meat served with dipping sauces), and several forms of hot *sambal*, made from Indonesian chilies. *Sambal oelek* is a paste of chilies and salt used both for cooking and as a condiment.

Other common ingredients are sweet dark soy sauce, coriander, *blachan* (shrimp paste), and candlenuts (toxic until cooked), which are used as thickening and flavoring agents. There are Indonesian restaurants in Houston, San Francisco, and Madison, Wisconsin. Dutch American enclaves such as Holland, Michigan, are a source of Indonesian-type foods. There are nearly 240 Indonesian cookbooks in U.S. libraries.

Other Southeast Asian

Malaysian restaurants featuring a combination of Thai, Indonesian, Chinese, and Asian Indian flavors have appeared in East Coast cities from Boston to Washington, D.C. Approximately 145,000 Cambodian refugees were admitted to the United States after the war in Indochina, most arriving between 1980 and 1985. The 2000 census showed approximately 172,000 Cambodians living in the United States. Some Cambodian restaurants have appeared in enclaves such as Long Beach and Oakland, California; Lowell, Massachusetts; and the Seattle-Tacoma, Washington, area.

[*See also* Central Asian Food; Chinese American Food; Coconuts; Indian American Food; Japanese American Food; Korean American Food.]

BIBLIOGRAPHY

Alejandro, Reynaldo. *The Philippine Cookbook*. New York: Putnam, 1985.

Alford, Jeffrey, and Duguid, Naomi. *Hot Sour Salty Sweet: A Culinary Journey through Southeast Asia*. New York: Artisan, 2000. Thailand, Vietnam, Laos, and Cambodia. Organization by foodstuff rather than country makes it difficult to get a sense of individual cuisines.

Cost, Bruce. *Asian Ingredients: A Guide to the Foodstuffs of China, Japan, Korea, Thailand, and Vietnam*. New York: Harper-Perennial, 2000.

De Monteiro, Longeine, and Katherine Neustadt. *The Elephant Walk Cookbook*. Boston: Houghton Mifflin, 1998. One of the few books on Cambodian cuisine.

Mowe, Rosalind, ed. *Southeast Asian Specialties: A Culinary Journey*. Cologne, Germany: Konemann, 1999. Part of the Culinaria series. Concentrates on Singapore, Indonesia, and Malaysia.

Smith, Jeff. *The Frugal Gourmet on Our Immigrant Ancestors: Recipes You Should Have Gotten from Your Grandmother*. New York: Morrow, 1990. Companion book to *The Frugal Gourmet* television series on foods and recipes of immigrant groups in the United States.

Zanger, Mark. *The American Ethnic Cookbook for Students*. Phoenix: Oryx, 2001. Features many ethnic American groups and recipes often gleaned from community cookbooks. Also contains general information on how cuisines change during assimilation.

LINDA MURRAY BERZOK

Southern Regional Cookery

The South is often defined as the eleven states that lie south of the Potomac River, or those of the Confederacy (Virginia, North Carolina, South Carolina, Georgia, Florida, Alabama, Mississippi, Louisiana, Texas, Arkansas, and Tennessee), but many inhabitants of Maryland, Kentucky, Missouri, West Virginia, and Oklahoma consider themselves southerners because of shared history and culture if not geography. Though not separated from the rest of the country by dramatic natural borders, the South has, from its beginnings, been a separate region that is divided into several geographical areas with distinct histories. As the population of the South increases at twice the national rate, mostly from interstate immigration, the region no longer resembles the mid-twentieth-century South with its shared bond of the Confederacy.

The distinctive regions within the South include the Tidewater of Virginia and North Carolina; the low country (Atlantic coastal plain) of South Carolina, Georgia, and northeastern Florida; the Gulf Coast; New Orleans, Louisiana, and the Mississippi Delta; the sand hills and piedmont regions between the coast and the mountains; Appalachia; the gently rolling hills of Kentucky bluegrass country and western Tennessee; and the plains and Ozark Plateau, west of the Mississippi. Each area was settled by different peoples at different times in American history, and the regional foods reflect that diversity.

Early Influences

The first settlers were the Spanish, who established a permanent colony in Florida. Though unsuccessful in their attempts to colonize farther north, in what would become Georgia and Carolina, the Spanish nonetheless influenced the cooking of the later British settlers who found figs and peaches from Spain naturalized in the area and wild Spanish pigs roaming the coastal plain. Saint Augustine, settled in northeastern Florida in 1565, was the first European city in North America. Egg custards, rice dishes, and the use of spices unknown in England at the time are some of the lingering culinary traditions of this part of the South, where the early diet was also influenced by a small number of Moors and Africans who came with the conquistadors. In 1768 a group of Minorcans who had been brought to Florida as indentured servants established a colony near the failed plantation; with them, they brought a taste for their own hot pepper variety, the datil, which flavored their pilaus.

In Tidewater Virginia, the British brought pigs with them to Jamestown in the early seventeenth century. Algonquin Indians taught the settlers how to grow and cook corn. Pigs and corn would define much of traditional southern cooking from that point on. Virginia cured hams continue to enjoy an international reputation. Virginia colonists brought cattle, chickens, and sheep; grains, such as wheat and oats; fruit trees, root vegetables, and cabbages; and many types of alcoholic beverages. English tavern food, of roast meats and turnips washed down with beer and rum, was typical home fare as well, supplemented with New World beans, pumpkins, squash, and greens; berries, plums and wild grapes; and a vast supply of wild game and seafood, such as turkeys, deer, rabbits, squirrels, duck, quail, turtles, oysters, shrimp, crabs, catfish, trout, and anadromous fish (such as herring, shad, and sturgeon) that swam from the ocean up into the rivers to spawn. By mid-century, there were three hundred enslaved Africans; with the slave trade had come African foods, such as okra, black-eyed peas, collards, yams, and melons. The foods of the upper class followed mostly English traditions, with recipes varied by African cooks and borrowed from Spanish, French, Dutch, and German traders and settlers. Increasingly, the kitchens of the wealthy were staffed by more slaves.

Plantation System

The plantation system that would come to define much of the South of the eighteenth and nineteenth centuries had its origins in West Indian sugar plantations. On crowded Barbados, a handful of royalists who restored Charles II to the throne of England were granted all of the land south of Virginia. Carolina was settled in 1670 at Charles Town (later Charleston), and quickly the lush, subtropical low country revealed its wealth as rice-growing land. West African rice farmers were enslaved and brought to Carolina by the thousands. By 1708 there was a black majority in the colony, and a Creole cuisine that borrowed heavily from English, French, Caribbean, and African traditions had begun to emerge. Politically and culturally Carolina was different from the other colonies. The English philosopher John Locke had written a constitution for Carolina that established a proprietary government based on an aristocracy of landowners. Locke included religious freedom as a basic right of Carolinians; the religious fugitives of Europe flocked to the colony. By 1750 half of the white settlers were French Huguenots, and Charleston had the largest Jewish population in the

New World. The Jews were Sephardic, and they brought Mediterranean cooking traditions with them, such as sundrying tomatoes and making pasta. A strong settlement of Lutherans from the Palatinate was established seventy miles inland in 1730; they grew wheat and cabbage and raised dairy cattle for the low country gentry, whose rice plantations were becoming enormous operations run by thousands of slaves. Charleston was one of the richest and busiest ports in the New World.

The biggest influence on low country cooking came from the enslaved West Africans, who knew how to grow and cook rice and whose palates had for centuries been enriched by invaders such as the Moors and traders such as the Portuguese. Peanuts, tomatoes, and peppers from the New World were well known along the spice and trade centers of West Africa whence came the enslaved, though they were unknown in the kitchens of northern Europe and Great Britain. West Indian rum and coconuts entered the cuisine, and tropical fruits arrived daily in Charleston harbor. Some tastes from as far away as Java were common enough in the colony to be recorded in plantation journals; for example, *ats jaar*, or *achar*, is a pickle whose recipe traveled from Java to India, Madagascar, and South Africa, then up the coast of West Africa and on to Charleston, along the spice and slave routes. Pickles, relishes, and chutneys accompanied the meals; they are typical at the southern table. African cooks in plantation and town house kitchens prepared hearty one-pot meals, such as gumbo (from a West African word for okra) and rice dishes, such as shrimp pilau and hoppin' john (a bean and rice pilau).

Trade along the Atlantic seaboard and along the old Native American roads was brisk as plantation owners, merchants, and brokers became wealthy. They were well traveled and well educated, and they were avid gardeners and supporters of the arts. Melon seeds were traded between Virginia and Carolina planters; an astounding variety of beans was grown. Cheeses came south from Philadelphia and New York City; pineapples arrived daily from Cuba. Some plantation owners built orangeries to house their citrus trees in winter. Tastes moved inland as the plantation system expanded.

Expansion

By the mid-eighteenth century, other parts of the South were being populated. New Orleans, the Gulf Coast, and Mobile, Alabama, were being settled by the French, whose culinary influence was felt all along the Mississippi River, with its mouth in New Orleans. New Orleans maintains its

French Vegetable Market, New Orleans. From George Augustus Sala, *America Revisited*, 3rd edition (London, 1883), vol. 2, p. 67.

distinctly French flavor, even in its Creole cooking, which was influenced by Africans, West Indians, Spanish, and Native Americans. No other American city can claim a culinary heritage as rich as that of New Orleans, at least partially maintained by the early and continual presence of restaurants—another French contribution. Roux, a cooked paste of flour and fat, thickens and flavors many dishes in New Orleans and in Acadiana, the Louisiana bayou country settled by the exiled Canadian Catholics called "Cajuns." Throughout the state are innumerable foods that are considered truly regional (as well as culinary standards): oyster po'boys, andouille and boudin (two local sausages), jambalaya, beignets, crawfish étouffée, filé gumbo, bread pudding, café au lait, and the commercial brands of Tabasco (hot pepper sauce) and Herbsaint (an absinthelike, anise-flavored liquor). An increase in tourism in the late twentieth century has encouraged a proliferation of even more restaurants, and both Creole and Cajun foods have gained international favor.

West of the Mississippi, northeastern Texas, with its piney woods, cypress swamps, and former cotton plantations, is considered southern; the area includes Dallas and Houston. But Texas did not join the Union until 1845, and its major culinary contributions to the southern diet—beef barbecue and chili—are from the Mexicans and colonial Spaniards who were there early on. Texas shares a border with both Oklahoma and Arkansas, where tamales are regional favorites. Tamales have become local fare in western Tennessee and northern Mississippi as well. Arkansas and Missouri are southern because they are tied to the Mississippi. Arkansas was under mostly French rule until the early nineteenth century when it passed to the United States with the Louisiana Purchase. Cotton farming and slavery quickly came to the area. Highland farmers in the Ozarks of both states have traditionally lived poorly, not unlike the backwoods settlers of much of the Piedmont and Appalachian South. Oklahoma remains largely Native American territory. After the War of 1812, many Native

Americans living east of the Mississippi were forced into what was then considered the Indian Territory. Though Native Americans mostly sided with the Confederacy, prior to the Civil War few white men other than traders or trappers entered the territory. In 1907 the state of Oklahoma was formed by a merger of the Indian Territory and the western Oklahoma Territory. Native American lands were given to white men, and the state entered the nation populated by many disenfranchised Native Americans and African Americans. The Dust Bowl tragedy of the 1930s—a decade-long drought through the Great Plains— helped to form a tighter alliance between Oklahomans and the poor, Depression-era southerners.

The South remained nonindustrial prior the Civil War. Between the coast and the mountains in the Atlantic and Gulf states, cotton plantations thrived. The Cotton Belt united the coastal plains and piedmont regions of the Carolinas, Georgia, Alabama, Mississippi, Louisiana, eastern Texas, western Tennessee, eastern Arkansas, southern Oklahoma, southeastern Missouri, southwestern Kentucky, northern Florida, and southeastern Virginia in a one-crop economy. The same high temperatures, heavy rainfall, and long growing season that cotton required also allowed a vast array of foodstuffs to be grown. The ante-bellum wealth of the planters, with their unlimited slave labor, gave rise to a privileged society that entertained often. The grand style of plantation hospitality mimicked European royalty, with elaborate dishes, particularly desserts, reflecting the neoclassical tastes of the wealthy.

Appalachia

Mountainous southern Appalachia includes parts of Maryland, Virginia, Tennessee, Kentucky, North Carolina, South Carolina, Georgia, and Alabama. No other region of the South was as influenced by the cooking of the Amerindians, with their corn, beans, pumpkins, squash, nuts, and wild game. The region was settled mostly by English, Scots-Irish, and Germans seeking asylum in America, as well as second-, third-, and fourth-generation English, Scottish, and French descendants who moved inland from the coastal plain. A Celtic love of grains fared well in the mountains, where the Cherokees grew a hearty dent corn that could be ground into a meal or grits, or dis-tilled into whiskey. By the 1770s, tens of thousands of set-tlers had flowed down the Great Philadelphia Wagon Road and settled in the region. German Lutherans and Moravians brought with them their great baking and meat-curing skills. Wild greens and corn bread sustained

generations of mountain folk. Cabbage became kraut, apples were dried for use in cakes and sauces, and nut cookery attained unprecedented glory, with the immense quantities of walnuts, chestnuts, and hickory nuts avail-able. Native American grapes and beans remain favored foods in the region. The cooking is typified by the use of cast-iron pots, wood-burning stoves, and food preserva-tion that includes salting, drying, smoking, and burying as well as the pickling and canning found in the rest of the South. While corn was grown and relished throughout the South, the dent corn of the mountains, dried on the stalk in the field, was ground on granite stones and made into corn dodgers, cracklin' bread, hoe cakes, bannocks, frit-ters, muffins, dumplings, mush, grits, spoon bread, hush puppies, and pone—using "Indian meal" in Native American, German, and Scots-Irish traditions. Though many tastes of the South traveled inland from the pros-perous coasts, recipes for corn cookery flowed downhill from the mountains.

The wheat that grows in the South is a soft winter wheat, literally soft to the touch. It lends itself well to the delicate cakes and elegant baked goods for which the South became naturally renowned. To duplicate southern cakes outside the area, cooks often find that they must use a special, light pastry flour or order soft southern flours from venerable millers such as White Lily in Knoxville, Tennessee, in business for over one hundred years. In the middle of the nineteenth century, baking powder was introduced to the market, and the South, with its hot kitchens, developed a permanent love of quick breads such as biscuits and cornbread.

African American Influences

Traditional British and Continental meals, dominated by a large roast of meat, were replaced in the South by a more African meal as slavery spread throughout the region. Soups, stews, rice dishes, and other one-pot meals with little bits of meat (often smoked or cured) strewn in came to be more typical of the southern table. Brunswick stew, jambalaya, gumbo, catfish stew, burgoo (a stew containing mixed game, particularly squirrel meat), pilau, okra soup, and country captain (a tomato-based curried rice dish) are southern dishes that are now beloved beyond the region. Creole cooking emerged wherever African hands stirred the pots: a little hot pepper and the roe of blue crabs were added to a Scottish recipe to make Charleston's classic she-crab soup, for example. Hams were cured in the tra-ditions of the Northumbrian, Black Forest, and Bayonne settlers of the region. Whiskey was made from corn. Rum was served with fruits. Plants such as tomatoes and eggplant were grown on southern plantations decades before they were accepted in other colonies or in England. African words remained attached to certain foods, such as yams, benne (sesame seeds), okra, gumbo, and cooter (turtle).

The hedonism that had early come from the West Indian plantation model became ingrained in the lifestyles of the planters. Their festivities were often directly affected by African folkways, with an exuberance for dance and music. On some plantations, the task system was employed so that the enslaved were free to hunt, fish, garden, and socialize after their individual tasks were done. African celebratory customs, folktales, and expressions of religion entered the vernacular as the enslaved reared the plantation owners' children. The garden became a colorful hybrid of tradition with native plant materials, such as beans and persimmons, coupled with European fruits and herbs, African okra and sesame, Caribbean sweet potatoes, Chinese ginger, Mexican peppers, Mediterranean figs, and Indian cucumbers. By the beginning of the nineteenth century, the South was already a creolized, loosely related society of mostly Protestant, but not Puritan, settlers. Perhaps the most exuberant offerings of that society were from the kitchen.

Condiments

A hallmark of southern tables both rich and poor is the condiment. From its beginnings, the South developed a taste for chutneys in the East Indian tradition to be served with their strongly flavored cured meats, cuts of game, and elaborately composed rice dishes. The East India Company's long history of "country captains" commanding spice ships is preserved today in a dish of the same name, a straightforward chicken curry from northern India. Every large southern seaport claims country captain as a dish of its own. It is served with an assortment of mixed pickles, grated coconut, roasted peanuts, and the sweet-and-sour tang of a homemade chutney made with peaches, pears, or green tomatoes. Preserving was a necessity in the hot and humid South; that necessity begat creativity. After recipes for sweets and drinks, recipes for condiments are generally the most numerous in southern cookbooks, both old and new. Barbecue sauces change hue and tone across county lines: some are little more than vinegar and hot pepper; others are mostly prepared mustard and ketchup, which evolved from a long tradition in the South of homemade ketchups and flavored vinegars. Gravies are offered with both fried and baked meats, as well as with breakfast breads and casseroles. Red-eye gravy, made with coffee and the pan drippings of fried country ham, is common throughout the region. In the backwoods, sawmill gravy is often little more than meat grease, flour, and water (or milk).

Beans are served over rice in South Carolina; a spicy relish of sweetened and pickled ground vegetables or fruits is served alongside the dish. Served with buttered cornbread and a simple salad of sliced tomatoes with a dollop of homemade mayonnaise and thick sorghum syrup as the requisite sweet drizzled over the cornbread, beans become a midsummer meal. Relishes are made from green tomatoes (piccalilli), cabbage (chow chow), pears, sweet peppers, Jerusalem artichokes, and corn. They are usually flavored with aromatic vegetables, such as onions and peppers, as well as spices, such as celery seeds, mustard seeds, and cloves, boiled in a vinegar solution. They dress sandwiches, vegetables, roast meats, rice dishes, and sausages. Other pickled condiments include sweetened watermelon rinds, Jerusalem artichokes, okra pods, green beans with fresh dill, spiced peaches for the holiday table (taking the place of the New Englander's cranberry sauce), and hot pepper vinegar (served with cooked greens). A variety of tomato and pepper sauces, both raw and cooked, is common. Vinaigrettes and mayonnaise-based sauces, such as tartar sauce, are common on the Atlantic and Gulf Coasts. In New Orleans, many sauces, both hot and cold, are purely French, such as rémoulade, hollandaise, and meunière, as well as the white and cream sauces that are based on a roux of fat and flour; brown sauces made with the pan drippings of roasted meats are enjoyed throughout the region. Gravies made with a little of the fat left over from the frying of chicken, pork chops, or cube steak (called "chicken-fried steak," "smothered steak," or "country-fried steak"), with flour and water, milk, or stock, are legion in the South, where they are poured on meats, biscuits, rice, and mashed potatoes. In Arkansas an unusual chocolate gravy made with butter, milk, flour, and sweetened cocoa is served at breakfast.

Poultry

Southern fried chicken is perhaps the best-known dish of the area, and it, too, is a legacy of African cooks in plantation kitchens. A recipe appears in the 1828 edition of *The Virginia House-wife*; *The Carolina Housewife*, published in Charleston in 1847, includes several. Most of the pan-fried versions are succulent homemade dishes made to be served hot, but many southern cooks now leave the deep-fried versions, which remain crispy longer, to the many fast-food franchises that were begun, naturally, in the South, among them, Kentucky Fried Chicken, Popeye's (New Orleans), Church's (San Antonio), Bojangles' (Charlotte, North Carolina), and Hardee's (originally based in Greenville, North Carolina).

Regional poultry dishes include country captain, chicken bog (a rice dish from South Carolina), chicken and dumplings (from German settlers in Appalachia), chicken pilau (claimed by the Carolina low country, Louisiana, and the Minorcans in Florida), and chicken pie (the regional variation being a biscuit top instead of a pie crust). Barbecued chicken is favored in some areas. Chicken and duck are often simmered and added to a world of soups and stews; a gumbo made with duck and sausage is common. In the late twentieth century, the deep-frying of whole turkeys spread from southern hunters' camps across America. Peanut oil has replaced lard as the preferred oil for deep-frying because of its relative stability and tastelessness.

Pork

Pork is said to be the main diet of Southerners, but that was not always so in all parts of the South. On plantations prior to the Civil War, pigs were often allowed to roam the woods to forage. They were hunted as game and killed in the fall and early winter. Much of the hog has traditionally been cured by either smoking or salting. Since the meatpacking industry was not well developed in the antebellum South, most farmers had to raise their own hogs. Some form of pork was served at most country tables, but it was used as flavoring more than substance. The country hams of Virginia, Tennessee, Kentucky, and the Carolinas are salted, smoked, and hung to cure for a year. Slivers of the salty meat are added to biscuits with dollops of chutney and mustard; these "ham biscuits," which are often leavened with both baking powder and yeast, are fancy little sandwiches that are ubiquitous at southern weddings and winter gatherings. Smoked neck bones, hocks, and jowls are added to pots of beans and greens; salt pork or fatback is used in many dishes. On New Year's Day, hoppin' john is eaten for good luck. It is traditionally cooked with a smoked ham hock and served with greens (for financial success), which are cooked with smoked hog jowl (called "butt's meat" in some areas). Blood pudding was once common where the French settled, but it has

almost disappeared from the area (except among backwoods Cajuns). Other sausages, souse or hog's head cheese, and liver pudding (the southerner's version of scrapple, with rice often replacing cornmeal as a binder) have also become rarer commodities but can still be found where Germans settled. Most of the pork eaten at home today in the South is lean meat cut from lean hogs and sold in supermarkets. (After the Civil War, most pork came from the Midwest.) Few butchers survive.

Barbecue restaurants, however, are very popular, from Jacksonville, Florida, to Little Rock, Arkansas. Pork slowly cooked over smoldering hickory or oak, then (more often than not) pulled from the bones, is one of the South's great culinary achievements. The smoked meat is chopped, sliced, left on the ribs, and mopped with thick or thin sauces that might be tomato, vinegar, or mustard based. The sauces can be fiery hot or sticky and sweet. The meat might be piled on plates, served with rice, served on a bun, or topped with pickles; accompanied by coleslaw, potato salad, or baked beans; or simply sucked from the rib bones; but nearly every county in the South has its version of barbecue in which it takes pride. Outside the area, barbecue has come to mean simply grilled meats, but in the South, barbecue is pork. In western Kentucky, mutton has been barbecued at church socials since the first half of the nineteenth century; the tradition has remained. A rich stew is served alongside barbecued pork in some areas: a dense, meaty gravy called "hash" ("liver hash" if organ meats are included) is served over rice in South Carolina; burgoo is offered in Kentucky; Brunswick stew (similar to burgoo) is claimed by Virginians, North Carolinians, and Georgians.

Seafood

With nine states bordering the Atlantic Ocean or Gulf of Mexico and the major tributaries of the Mississippi River flowing through the rest of the southern states, fish and seafood have been prominent in southern cooking since pre-Columbian days. Along the Eastern Seaboard, oyster stew is a simple dish of oysters warmed with milk or cream. In colonial and antebellum days, oysters were more plentiful than meat along the coast; they were added to sausages and stuffings. Oyster dressing is still a favorite holiday dish. Oysters and clams are eaten raw and steamed at "roasts" along the shore. Inland, fancy New Orleans restaurant dishes such as oysters Rockefeller and oysters Bienville have gained popularity. Oysters are fried and served with cocktail or tartar sauce or added to po'boys. They are stirred into jambalayas and gumbos. Shrimp are boiled, steamed, fried, grilled, baked in pies, served atop pasta and grits, ground into pastes, pickled, and added to pilaus and soups. Crabs are steamed and eaten at outdoor tables, or the picked meat, usually cooked with hot spices, is added to soups and salads or transformed into crab dips, deviled crab, crab-meat casseroles, and pan-fried crab cakes. Crawfish are enjoyed regionally, particularly in Louisiana.

Fishing is a popular pastime for young and old of both sexes. Pan fish from freshwater ponds, lakes, streams, and rivers are fried by the ton each year; they are invariably served with hush puppies. Farm-raising of catfish has been a major industry in the South since the 1960s. Freshwater catfish fillets are now enjoyed throughout the country and the world. Mississippi has over 91,000 acres of catfish farms producing more than two-thirds of the national product. Both inshore and offshore fishing are popular on the coast, and commercial fishermen provide restaurants and markets with fresh snappers, flounder, tuna, shad, mackerel, porgies, spots, drums, croaker, whiting, grouper, wahoo, and black sea bass, among other fishes, on a regular basis. Mullet are smoked in northern Florida and made into a dip for crackers. The roe of shad are pan fried in bacon fat, and the fish "planked," or cooked on an oak board. Many fish and shellfish are served as seviche, the Latin American dish of raw seafood marinated in lemon or lime juice.

Side Dishes

Vegetables and side dishes are favorites in the South, where the traditional meal is seldom a series of courses in the French manner but a plate of complementary foods. The mistaken assumption that southerners overcook their vegetables was never true in the homes of the wealthy plantation owners and merchants of the South. Many eighteenth-century cookbooks note that one minute's overcooking can destroy the texture, color, and flavor of vegetables. After the economy of the South was destroyed in the Civil War, most of the region remained poor for a long time. The people often ate poorly, oversalting and overcooking bland dried and canned vegetables. It is this cooking of the poor that fostered the bad reputation. Most vegetables grow well in the South, with its long growing season. Many cash crops—such as tomatoes, corn, and beans—can be grown twice in one year in the southernmost reaches of the area. Eggplant, okra, hundreds of varieties of beans, leafy green vegetables, squash, melons, sweet potatoes, and corn are favored.

Sweet Vidalia onions, grown in southern Georgia, became popular and successful crops in the 1970s.

Side dishes include baked casseroles such as cheese grits, fried apples, numerous sweet potato concoctions, braised greens, corn puddings, succotash (lima beans and corn), stewed okra and tomatoes, pole beans and new potatoes, baked stuffed tomatoes (or squash or eggplant), red rice, dirty rice (with bits of chicken gizzard and liver), red beans and rice, and salads that include avocados, benne seeds, pecans, country ham, or bacon. Congealed dishes were popular in both the nineteenth and twentieth centuries but have recently fallen out of favor, with tomato aspic as the one exception.

Beverages

Iced tea (usually sweet) is often the beverage of choice at many meals, but southerners are also fond of sweetened drinks of many types, from elaborate alcoholic punches to lemonade, sangria, and soft drinks. Most of the major soft drink producers began their operations in the South: Coca-Cola (Atlanta, Georgia), Dr Pepper (Waco, Texas), Pepsi-Cola (New Bern, North Carolina), RC Cola (Columbus, Georgia), and Gatorade (Gainesville, Florida). Bourbon is from Kentucky; sour mash whiskey is from Tennessee. Early settlers enjoyed rum, ale, sherry, Madeira, Marsala, port, and claret. Mint juleps and other cocktails such as the Ramos gin fizz and Sazerac of New Orleans remain popular. Eggnog is still revered, though some of the other old spiked English milk drinks, such as syllabub (frothed milk and wine), have disappeared. Many fund-raiser cookbooks from the South, however, still include dozens of recipes for the famous punches that have been served at balls and weddings for centuries. *Charleston Receipts*, first published in 1950, begins with recipes for four dozen drinks, most of them fruit-sweetened punches; some call for several liquors and champagne. Planter's punch is a summer favorite of rum, brandy, bourbon, and lime juice served in frosted glasses.

Soups and Appetizers

There are few classic first courses in southern cooking other than some soups, such as Spanish (black) bean, she-crab, and consommé. Nevertheless, there are snacks such as pimiento cheese (a spread of grated cheddar and roasted pimientos bound with mayonnaise), roasted pecans (both salted and sweetened), boiled peanuts, cheese straws, and sausage biscuits (an unleavened biscuit enriched with cheese and cooked sausage).

Desserts

The southerner's sweet tooth is legendary. The desserts, candies, pastries, cakes, puddings, pies, cobblers, cookies, creams, ices, meringues, fruits, and nuts of the South have differed from the sweets in more urban settings because they are made by home bakers. Until the end of the twentieth century, any southern cookbook devoted fully half its pages to sweets, especially cakes. *The Southern Heritage Cakes Cookbook*, published in 1983 by the editors of *Southern Living*, includes two hundred cakes, all indigenous to the region. The long growing season and bountiful produce of the region, plus various sweeteners such as cane and sorghum syrup, have broad-ened the southern baker's repertoire. Nowhere else in America are traditional desserts made with beans and loquats. Variety has always been a key to southern sweets: visitors are offered both cake and pie. The oldest recorded uses of pineapples, bananas, and coconuts in America are southern; tropical produce arrived in the old port cities like Savannah, Georgia, and Pensacola, Florida, a mere four days after their harvest in Cuba. Dozens of varieties of berries grow wild throughout the South; they fill cobblers, tarts, and dumplings. Fried sweets reflect the French heritage of the coastal cities of Charleston and New Orleans, and Mississippi's "Confederate soldiers," twice-baked and packed for travel during the Civil War, are Italian biscotti

---

MOON PIE

The Moon Pie is not a pie at all, but a cellophane-wrapped snack consisting of two cookies, four inches in diameter, sandwiched with marshmallow filling and covered with either chocolate, vanilla, or banana-flavored coating. The Chattanooga Bakery in Chattanooga, Tennessee, is the exclusive manufacturer of Moon Pies. The bakery originally started as a business to use excess flour produced at the nearby Mountain City Flour Mill. In the early 1900s the bakery produced more than two hundred different baked goods, but by the late 1950s the Moon Pie was so popular that the bakery's capacity could not handle anything else. The Moon Pie remains the only product the Chattanooga Bakery makes.

According to company lore, Earl Mitchell, a salesman for the Chattanooga Bakery, was the originator of the now-famous snack. In the early 1900s he called on a Tennessee country store that catered to coal miners and asked them what kind of snacks they would like in the lunch boxes they took into the mines. One man replied that they needed a solid, filling snack. Mitchell asked the man how big it should be, and the man, pointing to the sky where a full moon looked down, said, "About that big." With this concept in mind, Mitchell went back to the bakery, where he saw workers dipping cookies into marshmallow. The idea occurred to him to sandwich the marshmallow between the cookies and then coat the whole thing in chocolate. The bakery eventually mastered the technique of making a snack from Mitchell's original idea, and the first Moon Pies were produced and sold in 1917.

Making Moon Pies is a simple process: the dough for the cookies is made in large sheets, then cut into circles, and baked. Marshmallow filling is sandwiched between two cookies and then covered in a coating that hardens while the Moon Pie passes through a refrigerated room on a conveyor belt. The Moon Pies are individually wrapped, boxed, and then shipped all over the United States, Canada, and Mexico.

The phrase "RC and a Moon Pie" is a traditional reference to a convenient and inexpensive snack combination in the South. It is a holdover from the 1920s and 1930s, when a ten-cent lunch meant a nickel for an RC Cola and a nickel for a Moon Pie. In Bell Buckle, Tennessee, the RC and Moon Pie pairing is celebrated with an annual festival that features a Moon Pie toss, a craft fair, and the crowning of the RC and Moon Pie queen. The combination is even recognized in a tune called "RC Cola and a Moon Pie," recorded by the singer Tom Waits in 1986.

The Chattanooga Bakery keeps up with the times, adding microwave instructions to the package (no more than fifteen seconds); producing a smaller, snack-size Moon Pie; and occasionally trying out new flavors. For nearly a century, Southerners have enjoyed the handy, cheap, and tasty marshmallow treat, making it, as the Moon Pie package logo says, "the only one on the planet."

[See also Cookies; Marshmallow Fluff.]

BIBLIOGRAPHY

Dickson, Ron. *The Great American Moon Pie Handbook*. Atlanta, GA: Peachtree Publishers, 1985.
Schmidt, William E. "Moon Pie, Staple of the South." *New York Times*, April 30, 1986.

JACKIE MILLS

by another name. Many of the sweets are based in country English and French traditions—puddings, charlottes, meringues, sweet breads, and fruitcakes; many more are simply the South's own: divinity, Lady Baltimore cake, peach leather, sweet potato pie, pecan pie, peanut butter cookies, benne brittle, and shortenin' bread.

Many southern classics, such as pralines and pecan-bourbon cake, are so widely available that they are no longer considered distinctly southern. Red velvet cake, a cocoa and buttermilk cake colored dark red with food coloring, is a southern classic, as are banana pudding and Ozark pudding (an apple and nut torte). In Tennessee a dried apple stack cake contains many layers. In Woodruff County, Kentucky, the local eponymous pudding is moist with blackberry jam, like the jam cakes known, amusingly, in the Carolinas as "Kentucky jam cake" and in Kentucky as "South Carolina jam cake." There are Moravian sugar cookies and sweet breads in North Carolina and meringues in custard—the French "floating islands" of Mobile, Alabama. Bean cakes and pies have begun to appear in African American Muslim communities. There are chew breads in Texas and Mississippi's famous mud (chocolate) pie. None of the desserts seem to be in danger of disappearing, even as many other traditions do.

The Modern South

After the Civil War, much of the South lingered in poverty for one hundred years. In the second half of the twentieth century, interstate highways and air-conditioning made the area attractive to vacationers from other states. Tourism became a leading industry in the old coastal cities and beaches. Atlanta, a railroad center, became an important transportation hub in the twentieth century, with most airlines and trucking firms using the centrally located city as a hub. The city quadrupled in size in the last half of the century as it popularized the atrium hotel, the convention center, and the shopping mall. Speculators founded Birmingham, Alabama, in 1871 as a manufacturing center, but the city today is better known for its medical and publishing empires and its numerous colleges. In recent years, a New Southern Cuisine has been championed by a handful of prominent chefs in the city. Charlotte became an important transportation hub of the Eastern Seaboard; banking interests and urban development followed quickly. Today the city has more than 2 million inhabitants, many of them highly skilled and highly salaried employees of the financial and high-tech indus-

Southern Cookbook. Savannah Cookbook. *Culinary Archives & Museum at Johnson & Wales University, Providence, R.I.*

tries. New Orleans and Charleston became tourist towns. Country music performers made their style more popular, and people flocked to Nashville, Tennessee. Chapel Hill, Raleigh, and Durham, North Carolina, became home to the Research Triangle Park, attracting thousands of new inhabitants. The region's racial demographics reversed in the twentieth century, which saw African Americans leaving the area until the very end of the century. Television and other media contributed to the homogenization of the South. Women went to work, and home cooking largely disappeared, the way it has in the rest of the country, but the vast rural spaces and continued agricultural importance of the South have offered a buffer from the spread of urban values. Home cooking is still found in rural communities and small towns, at church socials, and at bake sales. In the 1980s and 1990s cookbook authors and chefs throughout the region began, however nostalgically, to call for a return to traditional southern fare.

[*See also* African American Food; Appalachian Food; Barbecue; Cajun and Creole Food; Caribbean Influences on American Food; Chipped Beef; Condiments; Dr Pepper; Fish, *subentries on* Freshwater Fish *and* Saltwater Fish; French Influences on American Food; German American Food; Pepsi-Cola; Po'boy Sandwich; Popeyes Chicken and Biscuits; Rice; Seafood.]

BIBLIOGRAPHY

Bryan, Lettice. *The Kentucky Housewife.* With an introduction by Bill Neal. Columbia: University of South Carolina Press, 1991.

Dabney, Joseph E. *Smokehouse Ham, Spoon Bread & Scuppernong Wine.* Nashville, TN: Cumberland House, 1998.

Egerton, John. *Southern Food.* New York: Knopf, 1987.

The Picayune Creole Cook Book. New Orleans: Picayune Publishing, 1900.

Randolph, Mary. *The Virginia House-wife.* With historical notes and commentary by Karen Hess. Columbia: University of South Carolina Press, 1983.

Taylor, John. *The New Southern Cook.* New York: Bantam Books, 1995.

Wilson, Charles Reagan, and William Ferris, eds. *Encyclopedia of Southern Culture.* Chapel Hill: University of North Carolina Press, 1989.

JOHN MARTIN TAYLOR

Southwestern Regional Cookery

New Mexico, Texas, and Arizona share a culinary heritage based on the foods that indigenous peoples in Mexico and the Southwest exchanged with Spanish settlers. The three states also share a common history rooted in Spanish colonization, Mexican independence, and American Manifest Destiny. Yet the foodways of these states are not identical; New Mexico's are the oldest and most deeply rooted of the regional cuisines, and Texas, as befits its great size, boasts not one but several culinary traditions. Arizona's foodways, of more recent origin, are closely linked to the cookery of the northern Mexican state of Sonora.

Spanish Colonial New Mexico (1598–1821)

Following the conquest of the Aztec empire between 1519 and 1522, Spanish explorers moved north in search of other wealthy civilizations. Six expeditions had visited Indian villages in New Mexico by 1595. Although they failed to find gold, silver, or precious jewels, Spanish chroniclers described the sedentary agricultural people as "Pueblos" (town dwellers), likely candidates for conversion to Christianity. In 1598 Juan de Oñate established New Mexico as a missionary outpost, and Franciscan friars and Hispanic colonists headed north.

Even before Spaniards settled in New Mexico, food exchanges were underway. For centuries the Pueblos had raised corn, beans, and squash—as well as domesticated dogs and turkeys—in villages located along the Rio Grande and its tributaries. Then, in the sixteenth century they began to grow watermelons and cantaloupes, which the Spanish had brought to Mexico. These sweet fruits raced north along indigenous trade networks more quickly than Spanish expeditions. For their part, Spaniards in Mexico had become accustomed to indigenous foods like corn, chilies, and chocolate before they reached the American Southwest.

Although the crops and wild plants of the Pueblos provided the basis of the diet for Pueblos and Hispanic settlers alike, Spanish colonizers introduced their own preferences and food products to New Mexico. Oñate's party brought European livestock (cattle, sheep, goats, pigs, horses, and mules), grain (wheat), and pulses (lentils, garbanzos, and fava beans). By 1680 other European crops—including peas, lettuce, cabbage, carrots, turnips, garlic, onions, artichokes, radishes, and cucumbers—had traveled to New Mexico, though not all were successfully cultivated. European herbs (aniseed, rosemary, lavender, pennyroyal, wild marjoram, coriander, and cumin) and fruits (apricots, peaches, plums, grapes, apples, pears, and cherries) took root in northern New Mexico, and figs were grown at El Paso, a part of New Mexico until 1824.

The Spanish also brought metal tools, including axes, roasting spits, kettles of copper and iron, iron skillets, steel knives, ladles, and metal *comales* (griddles) on which to bake tortillas. Hispanics built the dome-shaped ovens known as *hornos*, flour mills, and *acequias* (new types of irrigation ditches). Equally important, Mexican influences came north in the foods the Spanish had acquired from Mexican natives and from the Mexican natives themselves, who came as servants to the Spanish. Thus, the chili pepper—so much a regional identifier in the American Southwest today—arrived from Mexico with Spanish colonists, along with varieties of Mexican maize and dishes that combined these two important foods.

Once settled in New Mexico, colonists imported favorite food items that they could not produce locally, including sugar, rice, dried fish, shrimp, oysters, almonds, wine, vinegar, pepper, cinnamon, saffron, and chocolate. These coveted goods were often in short supply because Mexico City was fifteen hundred miles away, and supply trains made the journey north only once every three years until the eighteenth century. In exchange, New Mexicans exported food products to Mexico, including piñons, *carne seca* (dried buffalo meat), and cattle and sheep. Agriculture remained at subsistence level throughout the colonial period because New Mexico's aridity, high elevation, and short growing season challenged even the most dedicated farmers. In the frequent droughts of the seventeenth century serious conflicts developed. Hispanic colonists plundered Pueblo stores of corn to stave off starvation and slaughtered breeding stock for food, retarding the growth of the livestock industry. By the mid-eighteenth century, however, the hardy *churro* sheep was New Mexico's major export, furnishing excellent mutton that was prized in northern Mexico and relished as a significant portion of the New Mexican diet. Documentary sources for the Spanish colonial period reveal the variety of plants and animals raised in New Mexico but rarely mention specific dishes. However, archaeological evidence, journals and memoirs dating from the mid-nineteenth century, oral histories, and cookbooks from the early twentieth century furnish additional insights into New Mexican foodways at least as far back as the early nineteenth century. Some dishes from that era may not have been present in the seventeenth century but came north somewhat later as a result of increased trade and communication between New Mexico and northern Mexico between 1776 and 1846.

Mexican New Mexico (1821–1846)

In 1821 Mexico became independent from Spain and opened trade with the United States. Soon heavy freight wagons lumbered west from Missouri along the Santa Fe Trail, bringing new trade goods and reorienting New Mexicans toward the United States. Some food items, like oysters and champagne, entered the region via the Santa Fe trade, but these luxuries were far beyond the means of most settlers, who fed themselves almost entirely on what they raised or gathered. Metal tools remained scarce, and kitchens relied on minimal equipment. Drying was the only form of food preservation, and New Mexicans dried fruits and wild greens as well as corn, beans, chilies, and meat, the mainstays of their diet.

Corn, native to the Americas, was of primary importance to natives and Hispanics. It was most frequently treated with lye made from wood ash to remove the hull. The resulting *nixtamal* was then ground into masa (corn dough) for tortillas or tamales, ancient foods of the Pueblos, who also contributed the blue corn preferred by many New Mexicans. Treated corn kernels were boiled

until they popped in *posole* (or *pozole*, from the Nahuatl *pozolli*), a stew that included meat and chilies. Untreated dried corn was also roasted and ground into fine powders for use in the gruels known as *atole*, *chaquehue*, pinole, and *champurrado*. Whole kernels of dried green corn, *chicos*, were cooked as a vegetable or added to pots of beans.

Dried beans (frijoles), also an indigenous crop, were the second staple in New Mexican homes. In the early years the beans likely were *bolitas*, the progenitors of the pinto bean. Like tortillas, frijoles were eaten every day, cooked alone or added into stews. Dried peas, garbanzos, fava beans, and lentils also frequently appeared in soups or were stewed along with meats.

Chili peppers from Mexico quickly became an important dietary component among both the Pueblos and the Hispanic settlers. By the eighteenth century, the chili was not just a condiment but the primary vegetable in use in New Mexico. Settlers harvested the chili when it was green (sometimes to preserve it in case of an early frost) and when it matured, and they ate it fresh and dried in

Harvesting Cactus. Qahatika harvesting giant cactus, southwestern Arizona, c. 1907. *Prints and Photographs Division, Library of Congress/Edward S. Curtis*

numerous dishes. Fresh green chili pepper was roasted until the skin blistered and then peeled and served raw as a relish or cooked in stews or sauces. Some of it was dried for later consumption. On rare occasions, fresh red chilies were also roasted and peeled and like green chilies were stuffed with a mixture of ground spiced meat or cheese for *chiles rellenos*. More commonly, red chilies were braided into *ristras* (bunches) and dried and then seeded, stemmed, and stewed until the tender pulp slipped free of the tough outer layer. This red flesh, pushed through a sieve or worked into a puree by hand, was combined with water and sometimes a bit of cumin to make a sauce. When meat was added, the dish was known as *chile con carne* (or *carne con chile*). The dried pods were also added to stews or ground into a powder and used for sauces or as condiments. As Americans began to enter New Mexico after 1821, they described the chili as ubiquitous and usually found it too hot for their palates. But those who lingered in the Southwest developed a great fondness for it.

Meat was also an important food. In New Mexico Hispanic settlers carried on the Spanish preference for mutton or goat, with beef a secondary choice. Wild game such as venison accounted for only a small portion of the diet, though *carne seca*, the dried buffalo meat acquired from Plains Indians, occasionally appeared in *higote*, a hash made from pounded, stewed dried meat. Pork was not widely used before 1850 because few pigs were raised in New Mexico; there was little mast for them to eat if they were left to forage for themselves. Consequently, no hams or bacon were locally produced and none was imported. The available pork was used in stews or as *carne adobada* (or *adovada*), in which strips of pork were marinated in red chili pepper sauce, then dried and subsequently stewed or baked. The blood of sheep and goats furnished *morcilla* (blood sausage). Settlers consumed relatively little poultry, either chicken or wild turkey, though they ate fresh fish.

Roasted meats most likely appeared on the tables of the wealthy. The common people ate their meat in the boiled meat dishes known by the Spanish names *estofados*, *cocidos*, or *ollas* when the ingredients did not include the chili pepper and *guisados* or *temole* (based on the Nahuatl *clemole*) when chilies and meat comprised the dish. Some vestiges of medieval Spain, where highly spiced mixtures of meat and fruit were used, may have carried over the centuries. Roast chicken stuffed with a mixture of meat, raisins, spices, and wine was prepared on special occasions or in wealthy homes. A similar stuffing, like mince-meat, also went into small pastries called empanadas. Sweet *chiles rellenos* combined chopped cooked meat with raisins and green chilies to form small fritters that were then fried. Spanish sauces made of ground nuts had been modified in Mexican cookery when pumpkin seeds were substituted for the nuts. New Mexicans used the resulting *pipian* on beef tongue or chicken.

Wheat was a highly significant Spanish contribution to the regional cuisine. Wheat was cultivated early in the colonial era, not only because Hispanic colonists liked bread but also because the Roman Catholic Church required that the wafers used in Holy Communion be made of wheat. Wheat flour was used for bread, for hardtack (useful on military campaigns and trading trips), and for sopaipillas, fried puffs that serve as bread in New Mexico. Tortillas of wheat flour also appeared in Pueblo and Hispanic communities as early as the seventeenth century. Wheat kernels cooked with red chilies and lamb or goat meat provided another stew. Sprouted wheat, dried and ground into flour, made the dessert panocha, a sweet pudding eaten during Lent. Another Lenten dessert, *capirotada* or *sopa*, was based on wheat bread, raisins, and cheese. Various cookies, most likely introduced during the Mexican period, also called for wheat flour.

Spanish livestock provided the eggs, milk, and cheeses that appeared occasionally as main dishes and more frequently in desserts. *Torrejas* or *tortas de huevo*, egg fritters, were served as a meatless main dish during Lent. Popular desserts in the nineteenth century and perhaps earlier included *arroz con leche* (a rice pudding), curds, *chongos* (cheese squares in syrup) and *natillas*, a boiled custard lightened with beaten egg whites. *Marquesote*, a sponge cake, was made of eggs, finely ground corn flour, and anise.

By the nineteenth century, garlic and onions were widely used, though few of the other vegetables introduced earlier were raised; instead, settlers gathered wild purslane and lamb's quarters for *quelites* and *verdolagas*. Fruits were quite popular, either eaten fresh or dried for desserts. Grapes were especially important for wine production, with El Paso producing the best wines in the region. Settlers also manufactured *aguardiente* (brandy) from the grapes. Piñons substituted for almonds, and settlers crushed corn stalks to make corn syrup and sugar. They used local deposits of *tesquesquite* (sodium bicarbonate) for leavening. Chocolate, however, was imported from Mexico and remained a preferred beverage that the wealthy enjoyed much more often than did the poor.

New Mexico and the United States

By 1846 the United States had become interested in New Mexico, in part because of the lucrative Santa Fe trade, in part because the area was en route to the valuable ports in California. During the Mexican War, American forces seized the province, and in 1850 New Mexico, with a population of sixty thousand Hispanic and Native American residents, formally became a territory of the United States. Until 1950 Hispanics accounted for more than 50 percent of New Mexico's residents, but American influences made inroads into the New Mexican diet. New Mexico's sheep industry declined in part because the newcomers preferred beef. The American army was the biggest purchaser of New Mexican products, and army regulations specified rations of beef, bacon, wheat flour, and vinegar, all in short supply in New Mexico. Soon enterprising individuals began to raise more beef, introduced swine, planted more acreage in wheat, and secured contracts to sell these products to the army. In addition, they began cultivating potatoes, virtually unknown in New Mexico in previous years. Large gristmills appeared, and canned goods, including tomatoes, made their way into New Mexico. Fruit production soared with new agricultural techniques. By the end of the century, even the New Mexico chili pepper was undergoing important changes, as Fabian Garcia of New Mexico State University worked to produce bigger, milder, and more standardized chilies from the traditional strains of *pasilla*, *colorado*, and *negro* found in New Mexico. In 1913 he introduced New Mexico No. 9, which became the standard chili in the New Mexico chili industry.

As Garcia had hoped, New Mexican dishes became more popular with Anglos. In 1916 the first New Mexican cookbook appeared, and four others (three by Hispanas) followed by 1939. For the first time, recipes appeared for regional dishes, including meatless enchiladas, *chiles rellenos* with cheese, tamales, and tacos. New Mexico had its own documented regional cuisine.

Texas

Before Spanish explorers visited Texas in the early sixteenth century, Native American tribes lived in the region, most of them nomadic hunter-gatherers or semisedentary peoples. Because they were not settled agriculturalists, they received scant attention for Spanish missionary efforts, and Spain made no effort to colonize until the French explorer René-Robert La Salle attempted to establish a colony along the Gulf Coast in 1685. Galvanized by the threat of a foreign presence in territory that Spain had claimed, Spanish officials determined to settle Texas. By 1693 an early attempt had failed, and settlements in modern Texas date from 1716 to 1731.

Most early colonists in Texas settled at San Antonio, the largest town. Farther east, along the Gulf Coast, was La Bahia (now Goliad), and close to the Louisiana border, Nagodoches. Colonists in these widely separated and sparsely populated areas could not rely on the agricultural produce of Native Americans as settlers had in New Mexico. Instead, *tejanos* relied more heavily on wild game and the livestock they raised than on cultivated crops. In particular, cattle became the center of the livestock industry. By the time of Mexican independence, *tejanos* had driven cattle south to Coahuila and east to Louisiana. Sheep, chicken, goats, and pigs were also raised in Texas, but, in contrast to mutton in New Mexico, beef became the predominant meat in the diet of Hispanic colonists. In addition, settlers raised corn, chilies, beans, pumpkins, melons, peaches, grapes, and figs, as well as sugarcane, which furnished a source of sweetening not available in New Mexico. The New Mexican staples of corn tortillas, *atole*, pinole, frijoles, and tamales also appeared as common foods in Texas. Wheat was not widely cultivated, and colonists apparently traded for it with residents of Louisiana or brought it from Mexico.

After 1821 Americans began to settle in Texas, bringing with them their own food traditions and quickly outnumbering the four thousand residents of Hispanic Texas. In 1836 Americans rebelled against Mexico and created the independent Lone Star Republic, which endured for nine years, until the United States annexed Texas. From the interactions between Americans and *tejanos*, Tex-Mex cuisine emerged, drawing on ingredients and techniques used in Texas in earlier years but modifying them to American sensibilities. By the 1870s "chili queens" in San Antonio sold chili con carne, a dish of beef, red chili peppers, and cumin. Chili became one of the hallmarks of Texas cookery, sparking endless debate over its origins and the authenticity of ingredients and inspiring new convenience foods. In 1896 William Gebhardt began to sell a mixture of ground red chilies and spices known as chili powder. Eight years later his canned chili debuted, and in later years Gebhardt published a cookbook that helped to popularize the Tex-Mex dishes that used his spice mixture.

Gebhardt was one of thousands of Germans who settled in central Texas in the late nineteenth century. Their most important contributions to the foods of Texas were various sausages and other pork-based dishes and a variety of beers. Czechs also migrated to Texas, adding their *kolače* (yeast dough filled with cheese or fruit) and other pastries to Texas cookery. From Louisiana, Cajun and Creole dishes, like gumbo and jambalaya, traveled west, as reflected in the first Texas cookbook, published in Houston in 1883. Most of the recipes in the volume, however, reflect the preferences of Anglo settlers. Many Anglos migrated west from Kentucky, Tennessee, and Arkansas, and they lived on bacon, ham, and corn bread. Eventually they grew wheat and built mills, and biscuits became the preferred form of bread. The southern fondness for sweets is also evident in the book, more than half of which is devoted to dessert recipes. In contrast, none of the recipes are of Hispanic origin, and only one includes chili pepper.

By the end of the Civil War, Anglos began to move into the arid country of west Texas, drawing upon Hispanic and Mexican practices and vast herds of wild cattle to develop a cattle industry. The beef bonanza sent millions of cattle to eastern markets and created a distinctive ranching culture in Texas and across the West. The Texas cattleman Charles Goodnight lashed a cookbox to a wagon and created the chuck wagon that followed the herds. On the "long drives," far from settlements, camp cooks furnished meals of pinto beans, sourdough biscuits, and dried fruit as well as freshly butchered beef, fried, stewed, or roasted. Two Texas favorites originated with these frontier cooks—chicken-fried steak and son-of-a-bitch stew (in polite company, son-of-a-gun stew). For chicken-fried steak, tough steaks were pounded thin, dipped in milk or egg and then in flour, pan fried until crisp, and served with gravy. Son-of-a-bitch stew utilized most of an unweaned calf, including the margut, or marrowgut, the tube that connects the calf's two stomachs, and little else except beef tallow and seasonings, which sometimes included wild *chilepequines*.

Another Texas standard stemming from the cattle boom is barbecued beef brisket, cooked over a wood fire in open pits. Pit-roasting was used on the American frontier as well as in northern Mexico, but the brisket is the centerpiece of Texas barbecue, and it is the cooking technique, not the sauce, that makes the dish distinctive. During the long, slow roasting the meat acquires a smoky taste from the wood fire. Some cooks enhance the dish with dry rubs of herbs before the meat is put in the pit and periodically baste the meat with a "mop" (sauce). Other cuts of beef and pork and hot link sausages may also be cooked in the same manner.

Arizona

Most of Arizona remained unsettled until after 1860. Spanish missionaries in the seventeenth century attempted to convert the Hopis of northeastern Arizona, but they resisted the mission program and had little contact with Spanish settlers in New Mexico. Southern Arizona was the northern region of Sonora known as Pimería Alta, where Jesuit missionaries established missions among the O'odham (Pima) between 1687 and 1711. Settlement of the area proceeded very slowly, and Tucson, founded in 1776, remained the northernmost point of Spanish or Mexican settlement. In northern Sonora cattle raising was the most important industry, and beef played a starring role in the diet. Settlers also raised sheep and chickens but few pigs. They grew corn, beans, lentils, garbanzos, pumpkins, and chilies, and they commonly ate *posole*, *atole*, and tortillas, as well as stews enlivened by chilies. However, Apache raids into the region after 1821 drove most settlers farther south. Fewer than three hundred people remained in Tucson when the United States acquired the area in 1848, but some Anglos married Hispanas, who continued to prepare tortillas, frijoles, and other dishes. Arizona grew slowly, primarily with immigration from the United States, until 1910, when the Mexican Revolution sent thousands of people into southern Arizona. They brought the food traditions of Sonora with them, including large, very thin wheat tortillas, tamales made of green corn rather than the corn flour made from *nixtamal*, and *carne seca*. Beef strips, sometimes unseasoned, other times rubbed with lime juice, salt, and other seasonings, were air dried in the hot sun and dry air of the region. Later, the *carne seca* was pounded or shredded and stewed to make *machaca*.

Modern Southwest

By the mid-twentieth century, *machaca* appeared in chimichangas, a dish popularized in Arizona. Based on *burros*, the packets of meat or beans rolled up in the large, thin flour tortillas popular in the area, chimichangas are deep-fried versions filled with *machaca* and spread with guacamole, sour cream, cheese, and garnishes of lettuce, onion, and tomato. Flour tortillas also are the base for cheese crisps, a flour tortilla topped with cheese, baked until the tortilla is crisp, then topped with guacamole, salsa, or other toppings. Generally Arizona cuisine continues to use more beef, milder chilies, and greater amounts of cheese and sour cream than appear in neighboring New Mexico.

Like Arizona, Texas was also the destination of thousands of Mexican emigrants during the Mexican Revolution of 1910, and immigration has continued into the twenty-first century. As a result, some older food traditions have been revived in Texas, and new dishes of Mexican origin have been introduced. In south Texas, for example, barbecue is not pit-cooked beef brisket but may be *cabrito* (goat) or a pit-cooked beef head. Mexican immigrants also contributed fajitas, the tough cut of beef known as skirt steak, which is marinated, grilled over charcoal, and folded into a flour tortilla.

Additions to Tex-Mex food have also appeared. *Migas* combines eggs scrambled with crumbled corn tortillas, based on the Spanish dish of eggs with bread crumbs. Some Tex-Mex dishes have spread nationwide. In 1932 an entrepreneurial Anglo purchased a recipe for *fritos* (fried tortillas) from a Hispanic resident of San Antonio, which lead to the creation of the Frito-Lay Company. The national craze for salsa likely also began in San Antonio in 1947, when David Pace combined tomatoes, jalapeños, and other ingredients to produce Pace *Picante* sauce. Some years later Ignacio Ahaya (nicknamed "Nacho") spread yellow cheese over tortilla chips and added jalapeños to create his namesake dish. Texans also combined favorite dishes, including enchiladas, tacos, and beans, on a single plate to create the combination plate now popular in restaurants across the Southwest.

In New Mexico the chili pepper—particularly the green chili—remains at the center of the cuisine. The New Mexico chili is available frozen, dried, and canned, and cooks use it in appetizers, breads, casseroles, and stews. Some New Mexicans have even experimented with green chili beer and green chili wine, though neither has developed a large following. Fast food franchises offer small cups of green chilies for customers to add to hamburgers and chicken sandwiches. Many New Mexicans get their daily requirement of the green chili in breakfast burritos, a popular portable breakfast of scrambled eggs, green chilies, and potatoes wrapped in a flour tortilla. Sometimes ham, bacon, sausage, or cheese is included.

A fall tradition in northern New Mexico ties many families to the state's agricultural origins yet also reflects processes of modernization at work. Customers visit farmers' markets or local farms to purchase bushels of chilies. Since the 1980s, though, they do not take them home to roast in their ovens or on their gas grills. Instead, large metal mesh drums are filled with the green pods and then cranked to toss the chilies over propane-powered flames

Texas Specialty. Mexene Chili Powder and Walker's Red Hot Chile Con Carne advertisements. *Culinary Archives & Museum at Johnson & Wales University, Providence, R.I.*

for a few minutes. Customers then carry the chilies home to peel and freeze them. Another sign of fall is the appearance of bags of fresh roasted piñons in the shell, suitable for cracking between the teeth on cold winter evenings.

The blurring of regional lines regarding food occurs throughout the Southwest. Sopaipillas now appear in Texas (though they are served there as dessert rather than as bread), and Texas influences are apparent in New Mexican enchiladas. Originally meatless, enchiladas in New Mexico today usually feature beef, as in Texas, or, in response to health concerns, chicken. Guacamole appears from Texas to Arizona at nearly every festive gathering, along with tortilla chips, *chile con queso*, and salsa. Fresh jalapeños, as well as the smoked and dried version known as *chipotles*, are widely used, and in some settings black beans have nearly replaced pinto beans.

Many of the trends evident in the rest of the United States are also seen in the Southwest. People in the Southwest buy mass-produced foods from tortillas to frozen entrees. Fast-food restaurants have proliferated, offering their versions of regional favorites. Chefs in upscale restaurants vie to enhance regional dishes with exotic ingredients, leading to such creations as lobster enchiladas, smoked duck burritos with prickly pear reduction, and piñon-encrusted halibut in saffron broth. These efforts stem from a broader awareness of other culinary traditions that Americans have experienced over the past fifty years, as well as an eagerness for experimentation, and they often produce results that are pleasing and evolutionary.

Still, Texans continue to hold chili cook-offs and barbecues, while residents of Arizona use fresh corn in green corn tamales at harvest time. In New Mexico *posole* and tamales appear everywhere at Christmas, along with *bizcochitos*, cookies made from lard, flour, eggs, and sugar and flavored with aniseed. To express their pride in their state's culinary heritage, Texans designated chili the state dish. New Mexicans, not to be outdone, enshrined the chili pepper and the pinto bean as state vegetables and made the *bizcochito* the first official state cookie in the nation. In the Southwest the regional folk saying still applies: "*Panza llena, corazón contento*" (Full stomach, happy heart).

[*See also* Barbecue; Cactus; Chili; Corn; Frito-Lay; Iberian and South American Food; Mexican American Food; Pinole; Southern Regional Cookery.]

BIBLIOGRAPHY

Coe, Sophie D. *America's First Cuisines*. Austin: University of Texas Press, 1994.

Engels, Mary Tate, and Madeline Gallego Thorpe. *Corazón Contento: Sonoran Recipes and Stories from the Heart*. Lubbock: Texas Tech University Press, 1999.

Gabaccia, Donna R. *We Are What We Eat: Ethnic Food and the Making of Americans*. Cambridge, MA: Harvard University Press, 1998.

Gilbert, Fabiola Cabeza de Baca. *The Good Life: New Mexico Traditions and Food*. 1949. Reprint, Santa Fe, NM: Museum of New Mexico Press, 1982. An autobiographical account of Hispanic traditions by a New Mexico cookbook author.

Gilbert, Fabiola Cabeza de Baca. *Historic Cookery*. 1939. Reprint, Santa Fe, NM: Ancient City Press, 1970. Recipes.

Gregg, Josiah. *Commerce of the Prairies*. 1844. Reprint, edited by Max L. Moorhead. Norman: University of Oklahoma Press, 1990. The story of the Santa Fe trade, with good descriptions of food and local customs in New Mexico and northern Mexico.

Jamison, Cheryl Alters, and Bill Jamison. *Border Cookbook: Authentic Home Cooking of the American Southwest and Northern Mexico*. Boston: Harvard Common Press, 1995.

Jamison, Cheryl Alters, and Bill Jamison. *Texas Home Cooking*. Boston: Harvard Common Press, 1993.

Jaramillo, Cleofas M. *Romance of a Little Village Girl*. 1955. Reprint, Albuquerque: University of New Mexico Press, 2000. A memoir that places New Mexican food in cultural context.

Jaramillo, Cleofas M. *The Genuine New Mexico Tasty Recipes*. 1939. Reprint, Santa Fe, NM: Ancient City Press, 1981.

Jones, Oakah L. *Los Paisanos: Spanish Settlers on the Northern Frontier of New Spain*. 1979. Reprint, Norman: University of Oklahoma Press, 1996.

Linck, Ernestine Sewell, and Joyce Gibson Roach. *Eats: A Folk History of Texas Foods*. Fort Worth: Texas Christian University Press, 1989.

Martin, Patricia Preciado. *Songs My Mother Sang to Me: An Oral History of Mexican American Women*. Tucson: University of Arizona Press, 1992.

Pilcher, Jeffrey M. "Tex-Mex, Cal-Mex, New Mex, or Whose Mex? Notes on the Historical Geography of Southwestern Cuisine." *Journal of the Southwest* 43 (Winter 2001): 659–679.

Tausend, Marilyn, with Miguel Ravago. *Cocina de la Familia: More Than 200 Recipes from Mexican-American Home Kitchens*. New York: Simon and Schuster, 1997. Primarily recipes, but useful commentary is also provided.

Tolbert, Frank X. *A Bowl of Red*. Garden City, NY: Doubleday, 1983.

Weber, David J. *The Mexican Frontier 1821–1846: The American Southwest under Mexico*. Albuquerque: University of New Mexico Press, 1982.

Weber, David J. *The Spanish Frontier in North America*. New Haven: Yale University Press, 1992. Although this volume contains little about food, it provides a comprehensive overview of the Spanish Southwest.

CHERYL FOOTE

Soybeans

The soybean, *Glycine max*, is an annual summer legume that ranks as one of the world's most nutritious, economical, and protein-rich food sources. Although the soybean is used primarily for animal and human food, it also finds industrial applications in such diverse products as printer's ink, biodiesel fuel, paints, varnishes, plastics, and adhesives.

The soybean plant—a close relative of peas, clover, and alfalfa—is an erect, hairy plant, ranging from two to five feet in height. Also called "soy" or "soya beans," the spherical seeds, which develop in pods, are usually a creamy beige with a black, brown, or yellow hilum (seed scar).

Each bean is composed of about 38 percent protein and 18 percent oil, making the soybean the world's leading source of both edible oil and high-protein feed supplements for livestock. When processed, each sixty-pound bushel of soybeans yields eleven pounds of soybean oil and forty-eight pounds of soybean meal, used to feed livestock. The soybean is one of the few plant foods that supply all of the essential amino acids, important protein building blocks needed for human growth and tissue repair. The soybean's slight deficiency in one of these components, methionine, can easily be offset with the addition of grains to the diet.

Soybeans are also rich in phytonutrients, the naturally occurring substances that serve as hormones, enzymes, pigments, and growth regulators and that give plant foods their distinctive flavors and colors. Phytonutrients help protect plants from assaults by parasites, bacteria, viruses, and insects. When humans eat plants containing these nutrients, especially the ones known as isoflavones, some of the benefits are passed on and may help protect the consumer against certain cancers, heart disease, and osteoporosis.

One of the oldest crops raised by humans, soybeans are believed to have been cultivated first in China some five thousand years ago by farmers who planted the small brown seeds of a wild ancestor. Through careful selection over thousands of years of domestication, the plant grew more upright and the pods bore larger seeds.

Although the soybean, when merely boiled, lacks appeal for the human consumer, the Chinese and later the Japanese ingeniously transformed the legume into myriad appetizing, protein-rich foods, including miso, soy sauce, tempeh, and tofu. So well disguised was the soybean in the Asian diet that the first Europeans who visited the Orient, including Marco Polo, did not realize that the foods they tasted were derived from the soybean.

The merchant Samuel Bowen introduced the soybean to the New World when he brought back seeds from China in 1765. For the next century and a half, American farmers grew soybeans primarily as a forage crop, either baled as hay or preserved as silage. The plant also served as pasture for grazing hogs and sheep. When shipping was disrupted during the American Civil War, ground soybeans slipped briefly into the tin cups of Union soldiers as a substitute for the coffee bean.

In 1904 George Washington Carver discovered that the soybean contained valuable protein and oil. With the onset of World War I, fats and oils became scarce, and America turned to the soybean for these precious commodities. Research soon brought soybean oil into the kitchen in the form of cooking oil, salad oil, and shortening. Shortly after the war the soybean began its industrial career as an oil with many useful properties. The American Soybean Association lists more than 350 industrial products containing soybean-derived materials.

Soybean protein was fed almost exclusively to livestock until World War II, when the powder was used as an extender in sausages and other ground meat products. Research documenting the health benefits of the soybean has boosted American consumption of soybean products.

By the end of the twentieth century some 2,500 soybean products appeared on the American grocery shelf. Soybeans are transformed into tofu (bean curd), soybean milk, soybean butter and cheese, infant formula, roasted and frozen whole bean products, meat substitutes, breakfast cereals, sprouts, and many other foods. In the year 2000 in the United States 1 billion pounds of soybean products were produced for human consumption. This amounts to about four pounds per person.

In 2000 American farmers planted 74.5 million acres (30.2 million hectares) of soybeans, an area roughly the size of Colorado, harvesting 2.77 billion bushels (75.39 million metric tons) of the legume. The trifoliate plants produce white or purple flowers and short pods usually containing two to three seeds. In the fall the leaves turn yellow and drop, and the dry pods can be harvested and shelled with a combine.

Like other legumes, the soybean plant supports colonies of microorganisms that live in root nodules. These specialized microorganisms are able to fix, or capture, nitrogen from the air, making the addition of nitrogen fertilizer unnecessary in a soybean field. A significant portion of this fixed nitrogen, which is an essential plant nutrient, remains in the soil after harvest.

Most of the U.S. soybean crop is grown in the midwestern Corn Belt. The typical farmer will alternate soybeans with corn, taking advantage of the nitrogen contribution of the bean plant to help fertilize the next year's corn crop.

Soybeans can produce more than 33 percent more protein from an acre of land than any other crop and ten times more protein than cattle grazing on a comparable area. Despite the soybean's protein advantage, less than 2 percent of U.S.-grown soybeans are processed for human consumption. This figure is 10 percent worldwide.

The bulk of the soybean crop is converted into feed for cattle, hogs, and poultry. Processors clean and dehull the beans and then run them through giant rollers to crush them into flakes. The addition of a hexane solvent extracts the oil, leaving defatted soybean meal that is used for feed. Cycling soybean meal through animals to produce human food results in a net energy loss because it takes from seven to twenty-one pounds of soybean protein to produce one pound of livestock protein.

[See also Beans; Fats and Oils; Soy Sauce; Vegetarianism.]

BIBLIOGRAPHY

Endres, Joseph G., ed. *Soy Protein Products: Characteristics, Nutritional Aspects, and Utilization.* Rev. ed. Champaign, IL: AOCS Press, 2001.

Greenberg, Patricia. *The Whole Soy Cookbook: 175 Delicious, Nutritious, Easy-to-Prepare Recipes Featuring Tofu, Tempeh, and Various Forms of Nature's Healthiest Bean.* New York: Three Rivers Press, 1998.

Liu, KeShun. *Soybeans: Chemistry, Technology, and Utilization.* New York: Chapman and Hall, 1997. In-depth coverage of nutrition and health benefits, preparation methods, and processing techniques. Information on plant breeding efforts and biotechnological approaches.

Shurtleff, William, and Akiko Aoyagi. *The Book of Tofu: Protein Source of the Future—Now!* Berkeley, CA: Ten Speed Press,

1998. A historical perspective on tofu plus tofu recipes and instructions on making tofu.

PEGGY L. HOLMES

Soy Sauce

Soy sauce is a brown, salty liquid produced from a mixture of fermented soybeans and roasted grain such as wheat or barley. During the production process, the soybean and grain mixture is injected with a yeast mold and salt is added. Following a period of aging, the mixture is strained and bottled for sale.

Soybeans (*Glycine max*) originated in tropical Asia and in prehistoric times were widely disseminated to China, Japan, India, and Southeast Asia. Fermented soybean products were common throughout Asia. British sailors, traders, and colonial administrators encountered soy sauce in the late seventeenth century.

By the seventeenth century, Japan had specialized in manufacturing soy sauce and has been the dominant producer ever since. The Japanese recognize five major types of soy sauce: dark, which dominates the market; light, used for cooking white fish and vegetables; tamari, very dark, used for sashimi; *saishikomi*, twice fermented, darker and thicker, used for sushi and sashimi; and white, used for white fish and vegetables. From Japan, soy sauce was exported to Asia, England, and eventually the United States.

Soy sauce was imported into the United States in small quantities during the early nineteenth century. It appeared in cookbooks published in the United States by 1814 and was important enough in the second half of the nineteenth century to be sold occasionally in grocery stores. Because imported soy sauce was expensive, manufacturers counterfeited it, and several nineteenth-century scientists offered the means of distinguishing imitation soy sauce from the real thing. Manufacturers also used soy sauce to make other commercial sauces. For instance, soy sauce was a component in Worcestershire sauce, which originated in Britain in the 1820s but was imported and later manufactured in the United States. Soybeans were later used in the commercial manufacture of ketchup.

Soybeans were promoted by the U.S. Department of Agriculture during the early twentieth century but were mainly considered an animal feed crop. The shift to human consumption of soybeans began during World War II when the U.S. government recommended soybean products as a meat substitute. After the war, health and nutrition advocates, such as Clive McCay of Cornell University, recommended greater use, as did Ancel and Margaret Keys in *Eat Well and Stay Well* (1959). Probably more significant was the rise in America of Chinese and Japanese restaurants, which featured soy sauce. It became an important American condiment by the 1980s.

In the United States, soy sauce is used in cooking and as a table sauce. Kikkoman, a Japanese food conglomerate, is the largest producer of soy sauce in the world. It also manufactures soy sauce in the United States, as do several other companies.

[*See also* Condiments; Soybeans.]

BIBLIOGRAPHY

Smith, Andrew F. *Pure Ketchup: A History of America's National Condiment*. Columbia: University of South Carolina Press, 1996.

ANDREW F. SMITH

Space Food

On February 20, 1962, John Glenn became the first American to orbit the earth and the first human to eat in space. On his five-hour flight, Glenn carried a menu of freeze-dried powders and spaghetti, applesauce, and roast beef reduced to semiliquids and crammed into aluminum tubes. He also carried a variety of solid foods reduced to bite-sized cubes. Before the historic flight and its experiment in dining, some experts worried that in weightlessness food would be difficult to swallow and would collect in the throat. Glenn found that eating in space was easy—once the food reached his mouth, he had no problem swallowing. The food, however, was far from perfect. The cubes flaked into crumbs that floated around Glenn's capsule, threatening to jam delicate equipment. Other Mercury astronauts endured the bite-sized cubes, freeze-dried powders, and toothpaste tubes, but most agreed that the foods lacked taste and texture, and they disliked squeezing the tubes.

Gemini Food

The two-man Gemini program began in 1965 with a revised approach to space food. For several reasons, including excessive weight (the package was heavier than the contents, and every ounce counts in space), use of the bulky aluminum tubes was discontinued. Gemini astronauts ate bite-sized cubes similar to those Glenn had, but the cubes were coated with an edible gelatin to prevent crumbing. Gemini astronauts also carried freeze-dried foods packaged in special containers to allow better reconstitution. To rehydrate food, the astronauts injected water into the pack through the nozzle of a device that looked like a water pistol. After the contents were kneaded, the food became a puree, which was squeezed through a one-way valve into the astronaut's mouth. Once the food was consumed, a tablet was inserted into the bag to reactivate the leftover food chemically so that it did not rot and emit noxious gases.

The Gemini menu selections were large enough to provide four days of meals before repetition. Menus included shrimp cocktail, chicken and vegetables, butterscotch pudding, and applesauce. Astronauts were allowed to select their meal combinations, as long as the calorie count added up to 2,800 per day. To provide proper balance, 16 to 17 percent of the menu consisted of protein; 30 to 32 percent, fat; and 50 to 54 percent, carbohydrate. Despite the variety, the food was largely unappetizing, prompting a 1965 headline in the Washington, D.C., *Evening Star*: "Space Food Hideous, But It Costs a Lot."

On March 23, 1965, Gus Grissom and John Young became the first to make a manned orbital flight in a Gemini spacecraft. The news of the successful flight was overshadowed somewhat by news of a contraband corned-beef sandwich, purchased at Wolfie's Restaurant in Cocoa Beach, Florida, by Wally Schirra, a fellow astronaut, and handed to Young just before liftoff. Young stuffed the sandwich inside his pressurized suit and later offered it to Grissom in orbit. Grissom took a few bites but quickly rewrapped the sandwich when he saw crumbs floating around the craft. Word of the sandwich leaked out, prompting a congressional scolding and official reprimands—the first ever to astronauts. The press reported on the "$30 million sandwich," citing the cost of the mission, which could have been jeopardized.

Apollo and Skylab

In the Apollo moon program of the late 1960s, the quality and variety of space food improved greatly, especially after the first three manned flights, in which the food seemed to improve with each mission. Hot water was available for rapid reconstitution of freeze-dried foods, and the taste of the foods had improved. The astronauts carried "spoon bowls," pressurized plastic containers that could be opened with a plastic zipper and the contents eaten with a spoon. Because it had a high moisture content, the food clung to the spoon, making eating seem

closer to the earthbound experience. Peas and beans had to be served in sauce lest they escape their spoons. Irradiation of foods for the Apollo missions added more choices to the menu. A pantry stocked with more than one hundred food items (including strawberry and peanut cubes, spaghetti that could be rehydrated, salmon salad, and seventy-five drinks) helped stay the boredom of repetitious menu choices. During the Apollo program, freeze-dried ice cream was provided on one flight, but this product was abandoned because it was not at all like ice cream. Freeze-dried ice cream, however, is sold as space food in the gift shops and visitor centers of the U.S. National Aeronautics and Space Administration (NASA).

The fear of a bad or distracting food odor permeating a spacecraft is a major one, so all new foods are tested by an "odor panel," which has been in existence since 1967. Food odor is no minor concern. In 1976, an unbearably acrid odor caused crew members on a Soviet spacecraft to return to earth before completing the mission.

Flexible Menus

The Skylab program in 1973 and 1974 had larger spacecraft and vast culinary improvements over menus used in Apollo, Gemini, and Mercury flights. Unlike previous space vessels, Skylab had enough space for a dining table—essentially a pedestal on which food trays were mounted. When dining, the three-astronaut teams would sit using foot and thigh restraints and eat in an almost-normal manner. The food trays not only held the food in place but also warmed it; beneath three of the eight cavities in the trays were warmers that could increase the temperature of food to 151°F. Conventional knife, fork, and spoon were used, as was a scissors for cutting open plastic seals. Because it was relatively large and had an ample pantry, Skylab had an extensive menu of seventy-two food items.

Because the Skylab astronauts had to remain in space more than twenty days at a time, food was a critical element of the mission. The spacecraft featured amenities such as a freezer for filet mignon and vanilla ice cream and a refrigerator for chilling fresh fruits and vegetables. Because of the vast amount of energy needed, Skylab was the only program before the International Space Station to feature frozen and cold food. Results of Skylab experiments showed a need for changing the nutritional content of space foods. After long periods in space, astronauts lose calcium and other vital minerals, so all future menus reflected these needs.

Since the inception of the program, Space Shuttle astronauts have been offered a wide array of food items and allowed to choose a standard menu designed around a typical seven-day mission. They also have been allowed to substitute items to accommodate their own tastes. The astronaut-designed menus are checked by a dietitian to ensure that the astronauts consume a balanced supply of nutrients. This flexibility stems in part from the fact that approved foods are commercially available on grocery store shelves. NASA calls these products "natural form foods." These foods, which are low in moisture, include nuts, cookies, candy bars, and crackers. The most popular foods in natural form on shuttle trips are cashews, cookies, and peanuts. Beginning with the fourth shuttle flight, NASA provided fresh foods such as sandwiches, fruits, and vegetables. The sandwiches are eaten as "launch snacks." Fresh items must be stable to avoid spoilage during the flight.

The weight limit for food is 3.8 pounds per person per day, which includes 1 pound of packaging. Diets are designed to supply shuttle crew members with the recommended dietary allowance of vitamins and minerals necessary for performing in space. The standard shuttle menu, which is repeated every seven days, supplies each crew member with three balanced meals plus snacks. Each astronaut's food is stored aboard the shuttle and is identified by a colored dot affixed to the package. Each astronaut has a personal set of silverware, consisting of a knife, a fork, two spoons (large and small), and a scissors for opening pouches and packages. After a meal the empty containers are discarded in a trash compartment below the floor. Eating utensils and food trays are cleaned with premoistened towelettes at a hygiene station.

Special foods have been developed to make astronauts feel more at home. Ethnic foods, such as tortillas, have been processed for meals. Fruit bar snacks designed to be eaten in a space suit without hands cost approximately three hundred dollars each. Astronauts eat these fruit bars before extrashuttle activities.

In space, astronauts drink water provided by shuttle fuel cells. Chemical reactions between hydrogen and oxygen produce electricity for the shuttle, and water is a by-product of the reaction. Nearly two gallons of water per hour are available for drinking, eating, and washing. This is more than enough, so the remainder is released overboard.

Changing Food Systems

Food prepared for the first modules of the international space station had to stay stable at room temperature for nine to twelve months, because there was no refrigerator or freezer on the station. When a habitation module is added to the space station, the food system will be considerably different from those of the space shuttle and early international space stations. Crew members will have frozen and refrigerated foods and be able to eat a menu much like those on earth. The station will have a Safe Haven food system, which can be used to sustain crew members for twenty-two days under emergency operating conditions resulting from onboard failure. A goal of the system is to utilize minimal volume and weight. The Safe Haven food system is independent of the daily menu food and provides each crew member at least two thousand calories per day. The shelf life of each food item is a minimum of two years.

On space missions, flour tortillas are preferred over all other bread items and have been used regularly since 1985. To prevent mold on long missions, NASA developed a shelf-stable tortilla. NASA prefers tortillas over bread because they are almost crumb free. Tortillas also have been used as impromptu Frisbee flying discs. Playing with one's food is a space tradition that dates to the first time an astronaut realized he could spin a shrimp into the air and catch it in his teeth. Reconstituted shrimp is among the most popular entrees. "The shrimp cocktail they fix is very, very good," said seventy-seven-year-old Senator John Glenn on his return to space in 1998, "as good as what you'd get at Delmonico's"—a far cry from applesauce in a tube.

Taco sauce, ketchup, and mustard have long been essential condiments in space, and Tabasco sauce has proved especially popular with shuttle astronauts. Condiments are essential because food generally tastes bland in space. The official explanation from NASA is as follows: "As soon as crew members enter the microgravity environment, they experience a fluid shift. Some of the fluid normally in the lower body shifts to the upper body, leaving the crew members with a slight congested feeling. This affects the way foods taste in much the same way having a cold does." Salt and pepper are important but are supplied in liquid form to avoid the presence of free-floating salt and pepper crystals inside the spacecraft.

Some food items cannot be used in space. Vickie Kloeris, subsystem manager for shuttle and international space station food, reported in 2001:

> Carbonated drinks currently don't make the trip because the carbonation and the soda will separate in microgravity. Some experiments have been done with special microgravity dispensers for soda, but it has not been perfected yet. Ice cream or anything

else frozen can't go up, because we don't have freezers, and try as we might, we just have not been able to come up with a good shelf-stable pizza.

Carbonation is a real challenge, according to Kloeris:

Because there is no gravity, the contents of your stomach float and tend to stay at the top of your stomach, under the rib cage and close to the valve at the top of your stomach. Because this valve isn't a complete closure (just a muscle that works with gravity), if you burp, it becomes a wet burp from the contents in your stomach. I've been told this is NOT pleasant!

One of the great myths of the Apollo program is that it brought the world Teflon nonstick coating, Tang drink mix, and Velcro fasteners. Tang drink mix is a commercial product made by General Foods and initially developed for the Army for prepackaged field rations. Tang mix for the Apollo astronauts, who consumed it on the moon, was purchased by NASA employees in a supermarket. General Foods made much of this fact in its advertising. Although fresh orange juice was introduced on the Apollo 13 mission, Tang is a staple on shuttle missions for use after the supply of fresh oranges is depleted during the first few days in orbit. The shuttle missions use not only the orange-flavor Tang mix familiar in the United States but also the pineapple and grapefruit flavors sold in other countries. Astronauts also use Kool-Aid drink mix, Country Time lemonade mix, instant coffee, and instant tea, because they are all available in powders. Teflon fluorocarbon resin was invented by accident in 1938 in the laboratories of the DuPont chemical company when Dr. Roy J. Plunkett, a chemist, found that this residue of refrigeration gases had unusual properties. First used only in defense projects, Teflon coating became a commercial product in 1948. The Happy Pan, an electric frying pan coated with Teflon material, made its appearance in 1961, about the same time that NASA started using Teflon resin for a host of applications from space suits to nose cones. Velcro fastener was invented in 1948 by George de Mestral. The Swiss engineer, who got cockle burrs caught in his heavy wool stockings, saw the principle of tiny hooks and loops at work and reproduced the effect in woven nylon. The name came from a blend of "velvet" and "crochet," which is French for hook. NASA has always used Velcro fastener, and each space shuttle contains approximately ten thousand square inches of Astro Velcro, which is a special type of the material.

[*See also* Condiments; Food Safety; Freeze-Drying; Freezers and Freezing; Irradiation; Material Culture and Technology, *subentry on* The Technology of Cooking Containers; Refrigerators; Soda Drinks; Tang.]

BIBLIOGRAPHY

National Aeronautics and Space Administration. http//:www.nasa. gov.

PAUL DICKSON

Spam

Spam is a canned luncheon meat manufactured of pork shoulder and ham by the Hormel Foods Corporation. Spam is popular in Hawaii and Guam and among many families in the American heartland but is viewed by many others as the symbol of everything that is wrong with American processed food. Spam, a pink block of fatty, salty pork, became a subject of derision during World War II, when its durability and affordability made Spam a favorite of armed forces food-purchasing offices. Spam became infamous to baby boomers thanks to a skit performed in 1970 on the popular British comedy television program *Monty Python's Flying Circus*. The skit, which was about a restaurant with an all-Spam menu, inspired the Internet term for ubiquitous and unwanted e-mail messages. Spam is as familiar to people who eat it as it is to those who do not. Those who do not eat Spam may wear Spam T-shirts or enter Spam-carving contests.

A Way to Peddle Pork Shoulder

Spam was invented in 1937 by Jay Hormel—the son of George Hormel, the founder of the meat company—as a way to peddle the then unprofitable pork shoulder. The Hormel company, based in Austin, Minnesota, was a pioneer in producing canned pork products. The company introduced canned ham in 1926, and Hormel spiced ham and pork luncheon meats quickly followed. The new product had hardly reached delicatessen cases, however, before competitors produced their own versions. Jay Hormel determined that his company's pork luncheon meat would have to be sold in cans sized conveniently for consumers and with a name that could be trademarked. In late 1936 at a naming party at Jay Hormel's house, Kenneth Daigneau, an actor and the brother of a Hormel vice president, won the top prize of one hundred dollars for "Spam," a portmanteau word that stood for either "spiced ham" or "shoulder of pork and ham" (company sources disagree). Sales were slow at a time when most meat was sold either fresh or cured. Housewives had trouble believing that canned meat could be safe to eat.

Spam and World War II

The U.S. armed forces quartermaster's office had no reservations about the safety of the canned meat. Nutritious, filling, affordable, and shelf stable, Spam was a nearly perfect mess-tent food. Before the war was over, the army alone received 150 million pounds of pork luncheon meat. The result was a chorus of complaints, cartoons, poems, and jokes about Spam. In letters to Hormel and in the military newspapers *Yank* and *Stars and Stripes*, soldiers called the product "ham that didn't pass its physical," "meat loaf without basic training," and "the real reason war was hell." Some of the "Spam" served to soldiers was generic luncheon meat made to government specifications. But because it was the most famous brand before the war, Spam received all the blame. Spam even became part of the language of the war: Uncle Sam became "Uncle Spam," the European invasion fleet was called the "Spam fleet," and the United Services Organizations (USO) toured the "Spam circuit."

England and Russia received Spam as part of American aid packages. In Russia Nikita Khrushchev was grateful. "We had lost our most fertile, food-bearing lands—the Ukraine and the Northern Caucasus. Without Spam we wouldn't have been able to feed our army," Khrushchev recalled in his biography. In Italy and England, a can of Spam was a prized commodity that could be traded for manual labor, intelligence, and even the services of a prostitute.

In the United States, Hormel company executives worried that Spam would become a wartime casualty. But Spam sales increased after World War II. Although many former soldiers had tired of it, many more who had been introduced to Spam during the war soon had their families eating it.

Spam is popular in parts of the world where U.S. troops were stationed, including Guam, Hawaii, and Okinawa. Hawaiian restaurants serve Spam in ramen noodle soup, in box lunches called *bento*, fried with eggs and rice for breakfast, but most commonly in sushi. Made by topping a fried slice of Spam with a block of sticky rice and wrapping them together with a belt of seaweed, Spam sushi, or *musubi*, is as common in convenience stores and take-out stands in Hawaii as hot dogs are in these establishments on the mainland. The world's Spam-eating capital is Guam. Annual per capita consumption in this U.S. territory is eight pounds. Automobile dealers in Guam use trunkfuls of Spam as sales promotions.

Selling Spam

After World War II, Hormel hired former servicewomen to sell Spam and other products. That group grew into a traveling sales force of sixty musically talented women who starred in a radio show as the Hormel Girls. In 1953 Hormel returned to the more conventional and economical sales approach of magazine advertisements featuring Spam recipes. The most popular recipe—for Spam glazed with brown sugar and studded with cloves in the manner of baked ham—was featured on the can for fifty years. In 1997, that image was replaced by a Spamburger—a quarter-pound slice of Spam grilled and served on a hamburger bun. This serving suggestion was designed to position Spam as an alternative to fast food hamburgers. The Hormel Spamburger television advertising campaign in 1992 sent Spam sales soaring.

At a time when fresh and natural foods are extremely popular, Hormel is the only American meat company that advertises processed canned meat on national television. It is also one of few companies whose advertising addresses criticisms of its product, albeit humorously. Hormel's "Surprise" campaign in 1980 recorded the surprisingly positive reactions of people who did not know they were eating Spam. "Okay, so the name's funny. But there's nothing funny about the taste," was the copy in the Spam advertising campaign in 1997. Hormel has addressed concerns about the fat and sodium content of Spam by introducing lower-salt and lower-fat varieties, such as Spam Less Sodium (1986), Spam Lite (1992), and Turkey Spam (2000).

Since 1991 Hormel has sponsored Spam recipe contests at state fairs throughout the United States. Entrants are encouraged to extend their efforts beyond the most popular uses in sandwiches and fried and served with eggs. Grand prize–winning recipes have included Spam-stuffed peppers, Spam manicotti, Spam fritters, and Spam potato cupcakes. Spam dishes served at Spamarama in Austin, Texas, include Spam tequila, Spamores, and ice cream Spamwiches. Spamarama is a fan-sponsored Spam cook-off and athletic event that attracts as many as eight thousand people annually. Spamarama is the oldest and largest of dozens of grassroots Spam celebrations held across the United States every year.

The World Wide Web has many Spam sites, including the Spam Haiku Archive, the mock-religious Church of Spam, and the Spam Cam, which focuses a real-time camera on a decaying brick of Spam. Spam continues to be the butt of jokes in movies and on television by comedians such as Jay Leno. Hormel has joined the fun (or tried to defuse the unauthorized kind) with its own Spam website, annual festival, merchandise catalog, and a 16,500-square-foot Spam museum, which is visited by almost 100,000 persons annually.

[*See also* Breakfast Foods; Canning and Bottling; Combat Food; Food Festivals; Hawaiian Food; Historical Overview, *subentry on* World War II; International Aid; Pig.]

BIBLIOGRAPHY

Corum, Ann Kondo. *Hawai'i's 2nd SPAM Cookbook*. Honolulu, HI: Bess, 2001. Recipes from the most Spam-loving state.

Hormel Foods Corporation. *It's Spam*. http://www.spam.com. Official home page includes a historical time line, recipe database, and a Spam merchandise catalog.

Patten, Marguerite. *Spam: The Cookbook*. London: Hamlyn, 2001. Gourmet Spam recipes and historical tidbits from a British cookbook writer.

Talbott, Strobe, ed. *Khrushchev Remembers*. Boston, MA: Little, Brown, 1970. Soviet premier Nikita Khrushchev's tape-recorded recollections of world events during his lifetime.

Wyman, Carolyn. *Spam: A Biography*. San Diego, CA: Harcourt, 1999. A comprehensive cultural history including information about Spam during World War II, the manufacturing process, festivals and other fan activity, and media references, including the full text of the Monty Python Spam skit.

CAROLYN WYMAN

Spices, *see Herbs and Spices*

Spiders, *see Frying Pans, Skillets, and Spiders*

Spinach

Spinacia oleracea is a leafy vegetable with many cultivars, ranging from light to dark green and from smooth-textured to highly crinkled leaves. Spinach tastes slightly bitter (owing to the presence of oxalic acid), reduces dramatically in volume when cooked, requires several washings before being eaten, delivers few calories, and contains a nutritional powerhouse of beta-carotene, minerals, fiber, protein, and vitamins B, C, and E. Cultivated as early as the fourth century C.E. in Persia, the country to which it owes both its name (from the Persian *aspanākh*) and its highest accolade ("prince of vegetables"), spinach traveled east to China before reversing direction to Europe and thence to America in the seventeenth century.

John Winthrop Jr., the governor of the Massachusetts Bay Colony, bought "spynadge" seed in 1631—perhaps not to universal applause. Bert Greene (1984) referred to a Pilgrim child's prayer to ward off "unclean foreign leaves," that is, "sandy spinach." By the eighteenth century, spinach flourished in colonial Williamsburg gardens as one of many potherbs, round and prickly-seed varieties assuring year-round harvests. Grown predominantly in the gardens of the well-to-do, spinach long retained the aura of luxury shared by cucumbers and shelling peas. Improved varieties, appearing in the late 1800s, broadened the appeal of spinach. Nonetheless, spinach has remained a stranger to most American tables. American annual per capita consumption, only 0.4 pounds by 1977, increased to 1.3 pounds by 2002—lower than that of all other vegetables except artichokes, asparagus, and eggplant.

Recipes from the eighteenth through the mid-twentieth centuries show that spinach was invariably served cooked, sometimes unappealingly overcooked by modern standards. Its juice was used as a food coloring. Although salads became popular around the end of the nineteenth century, the spinach salad of 1915—a cooked spinach mold—would be unrecognizable to aficionados of the raw leaves wilted with bacon dressing that became popular in the 1960s.

An emphasis on nutrition in the early 1900s spooned spinach into children's nurseries, where the vegetable met with much resistance. Carl Rose, a cartoonist for the *New Yorker*, drew a child unhappily faced with a plate of broccoli. E. B. White captioned the 1928 cartoon, "I say it's spinach, and the hell with it!"

Improvements in refrigerated rail transportation and, in 1929, Clarence Birdseye's development of a commercial frozen food process, as well as claims made by the Depression era cartoon character Popeye, encouraged spinach consumption. At the height of Popeye's popularity, children ranked spinach as their third-favorite food—behind turkey and ice cream. The cookbook authors Mollie Gold and Eleanor Gilbert (1930) wrote: "No one has yet been able to crystallize the slanderous rumors concerning spinach . . . Nevertheless, spinach cooked properly, and in moderation, is a highly delectable dish."

Cooked properly means steamed for five minutes without water, chopped, and cooked for five minutes in butter.

Spinach stars in famous American dishes, including some versions of Oysters Rockefeller and Joe's special Hash, a San Francisco specialty. Botanically unrelated New Zealand spinach, Malabar spinach, and wild spinach (also known as mountain spinach and orache) are often substituted for *S. oleracea*.

[*See also* Birdseye, Clarence; Salads and Salad Dressings; Transportation of Food; Vegetables.]

BIBLIOGRAPHY

Economic Research Service, United States Department of Agriculture. Vegetables and Melons Outlook. http://www.ers.usda.gov/publications/.
Gold, Mollie, and Eleanor Gilbert. *The Book of Green Vegetables.* New York and London: Appleton, 1930.
Greene, Bert. *Greene on Greens.* New York: Workman, 1984.
Greene, Wesley. "Salad Greens." Williamsburg, VA: Colonial Williamsburg Foundation, 2004. http://www.history.org/.
Hebert, Malcolm. "Popeye's Vegetable Remains Popular." *San Jose Mercury News*, August 31, 1988.

ROBIN M. MOWER

Spoons, *see Silverware*

Sprouts

"Sprout" is the colloquial name for sprouted seeds and young shoots that are used in raw and cooked salads or as vegetable garnishes; they are also juiced. Sprouts cover many plant genera, including beans, peas, grasses, and bulbs; the most common in America are sprouts from aduki, alfalfa, buckwheat, clover, garlic, garlic chive, radish, sunflower, kaiware, mung bean, soybean, and pea. Growers have also developed a stunning array of sprout blends for the commercial market. Adaptable to a range of climates, sprouts have become a relatively common supermarket staple nationwide. Associated with Asian cuisines as well as health food faddists, sprouts are integral to modern California cookery.

Much of the credit for familiarizing Americans with sprouts must go to the grocer Wallace Smith of Detroit, Michigan, and his Korean partner, Ilhan New, college chums who developed a fresh bean sprout business in the 1920s. The business would mature into La Choy Food Products, selling canned and jarred sprouts.

Notwithstanding sprouts' very contemporary image, sprouts occasionally show up in the culinary patrimony. Lettice Bryan's unusual recipe for "sprouts and other young greens" in *The Kentucky Housewife* (1839) calls for blanching the sprouts and serving them with a hot bacon and vinegar dressing.

[*See also* Health Food; Salads and Salad Dressings.]

BIBLIOGRAPHY

Facciola, Stephen. *Cornucopia II: A Source Book for Edible Plants.* Vista, CA: Kampong, 1998.
Trager, James. *The Food Chronology.* New York: Holt, 1995.

CATHY K. KAUFMAN

Spruce

Ancient Scandinavians and their Viking descendants brewed beer from young shoots of Norway spruce, drinking the beer for strength in battle, for fertility, and to prevent scurvy on long sea voyages. Introduced to spruce beer by the Vikings, European colonists were familiar with the beverage when they arrived in North America. Recipes for spruce beer are in the first American cookbooks. To prevent scurvy, eighteenth-century navies brewed the beer at sea using the decoction essence of spruce.

Native Americans and native Alaskans were the first Americans to use the inner bark, green tips, and new shoots of spruce for medical and culinary purposes. They chewed spruce resin for dental hygiene. In the early twenty-first century, native Alaskans harvest spruce tips as an indigenous vegetable. Alaska exports spruce-tip jelly and syrup as specialty food items.

In the Northeast, sugar maple sap was added to spruce beer for flavor and fermentation. In 1848 John Curtis began selling spruce gum. Sweetened paraffin gum debuted in 1850, and its popularity reduced spruce gum to the status of New England curiosity. Commercial breweries reduced spruce beer to another regional rarity after World War I. The emergence of microbreweries in the late twentieth century reintroduced spruce beer to mainstream consumers.

[*See also* Beer, Corn and Maple; Birch Beer; Historical Overview, *subentry* Colonial Period to the Revolutionary War; Homemade Remedies; Native American Food; Scandinavian and Finnish Food.]

BIBLIOGRAPHY

Alström, Jason, and Todd Alström. *BeerAdvocate.com.* http://www.beeradvocate.com.

Manteufel, Thomas. "Benjamin Franklin's Spruce Beer." *Home Brew Digest*. http://www.hbd.org/brewery/cm3/recs/13_12.html.

Randolph, Mary. *The Virginia House-Wife*, with historical notes and commentary by Karen Hess. Columbia: University of South Carolina Press, 1984. The culture and science of pre-cookstove America. This edition of *Virginia Housewife* is the only complete collection of Mary Randolph's work. The glossary, reading list, and bibliography are comprehensive. A valuable aid in the interpretation of Randolph's recipes.

Simmons, Amelia, with an essay by Mary Tolford Wilson. *The First American Cookbook: A Facsimile of* American Cookery, *1796*. New York: Dover, 1984. In the essay that introduces this facsimile, Mary Tolford Wilson places *American Cookery* and its author in cultural context and explains why certain recipes are more significantly "American" than others in the manuscript.

ESTHER DELLA REESE

Squash

The early European explorers of the New World were delighted to find what they thought were melons growing wild wherever they went. These were not melons but squashes, members of the same family (*Cucurbita pepo sp.*), which also includes pumpkins, cucumbers, gourds, loofahs, zucchini, and chayotes. Remains of squash dating from 7000 B.C.E. have been found in Central and South America.

The word "squash" is believed to derive from the Algonquian words "*askoot asquash*," meaning "eaten green." New varieties of squash are constantly being bred or evolve naturally. That is because squash blossoms can be either male or female and are pollinated by bees and other insects. Squashes are subdivided into summer and winter squashes. Both types are now available throughout the year, but summer squashes are picked at a younger stage, and in general the seeds are smaller and the whole vegetable, including seeds and skin, may be eaten.

Winter squashes are tougher and more fibrous. They are peeled before or after cooking, and larger specimens are cut into chunks and the seeds removed before cooking. Winter varieties include the banana squash; butternut squash, a bulbous, pale-yellow variety with orange flesh; the acorn or Des Moines squash, a small green or yellow, rounded variety; and spaghetti squash, whose flesh falls into narrow spaghetti-like strands when cooked. The magnificently colored red and yellow turban squash is similar to the acorn squash; Hubbard squash is a very warty variety, eaten at the unripe green stage as well as in its mature orange stage. There are also cabocha, delicata, and sweet dumpling squashes.

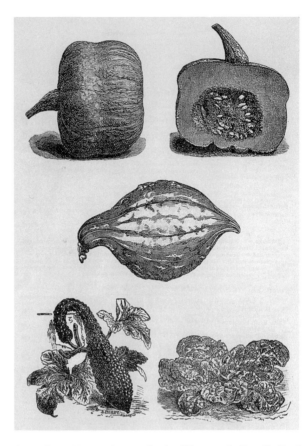

Squashes. From *Aaron Low's Illustrated Retail Seed Catalogue and Garden Manual*, 1887, p. 66.

Summer squashes include the crookneck, an ocher-yellow squash with a long curved neck, and pattypan squash, a small white squash that is given a variety of names in different locations, including Peter Pan, scallops, and scallopini. A miniature version is known as baby boo. In the South, this squash is variously known as simlin, symbling, or cymling.

Squash and pumpkin seeds are salted and sun-dried and eaten as a snack in the Southwest and in Mexico, where they are known as *pepitas*, and are also sold unsalted and skinned in health food stores. The Mexican and southwestern drink known as *horchata* is made by mixing the ground seeds with sugar, cinnamon, and water. Squashes are cooked in stews, pureed and added to soups, or boiled, baked, or broiled and served as a side dish, with a white sauce. Stuffed squash blossom is a popular dish in the Southwest and in Mexico. These flowers are always some shade of yellow or orange-yellow and are generally filled with a savory mixture. Zucchini blossoms are cooked in the same way.

[*See also* Cucumbers; Flowers, Edible; Melons; Pumpkins; Vegetables.]

BIBLIOGRAPHY

Bacon, Josephine. *Exotic Fruits and Vegetables*. London: UPSO, 2004.

Book of Cucumbers, Melons, and Squash. Edited by the staff of *National Gardening*. Rev. ed. New York: Villard, 1987.

McNair, James. *James McNair's Squash Cookbook*. San Francisco: Chronicle Books, 1995.

Ralston, Nancy, Marynor Jordan, and Andrea Chessman. *The Classic Zucchini Cookbook: 225 Recipes for All Kinds of Squash*. North Adams, MA: Storey Books, 1997.

Tarr, Yvonne. *The Squash Cookbook: How to Grow and Cook All Kinds of Squash, from Acorn to Zucchini, Including Pumpkins and Gourds*. New York: Wings Books, 1995.

JOSEPHINE BACON

Starbucks

Starbucks has become a symbol of the modern American specialty coffee movement. Starbucks coffee bars are opening in small towns and major cities alike. Starbucks began in 1971 as one of many grassroots batch-roasting firms started by idealistic, dedicated baby boomers rediscovering the joys of coffee made from freshly roasted, high-quality arabica beans. Jerry Baldwin, Gordon Bowker, and Zev Siegel, three Seattle friends, modeled the first Starbucks store on the Peet's Coffee and Tea shop in Berkeley, California. By the time Siegel sold out in 1980, Starbucks had six retail outlets and was selling beans wholesale to restaurants and supermarkets. By early 2003, there were approximately five thousand stores in continental North America and fifteen hundred elsewhere. Consolidated net revenues were approximately $4 billion annually.

In 1983 Starbucks purchased Peet's. Four years later, frustrated by the commute between Berkeley and Seattle, Jerry Baldwin decided to focus on Peet's, selling Starbucks to Howard Schultz, his former head of marketing. Schultz, a Brooklyn native, was inspired by a 1983 trip to Italy, where he loved the theatrical and communal feeling of espresso bars.

Schultz set about transforming Starbucks into a coffeehouse chain specializing in espresso-based milk drinks, such as cappuccino and latte. The coffee bars spread throughout the northwest then to Chicago and Los Angeles. The company went public in 1992 and continued to advance throughout the United States and Canada. With hardly any advertising, Starbucks became a cultural icon, its green-and-white mermaid logo appearing in movies and its lingo ("That'll be an unleaded grande latte with wings") mocked by comedians. Schultz, the company's chief global strategist, envisions Starbucks as a world brand comparable with Coca-Cola and Disney. The company is opening outlets in Europe, Asia, and Latin America.

[*See also* Coffee; Coffeehouses.]

BIBLIOGRAPHY

Pendergrast, Mark. *Uncommon Grounds: The History of Coffee and How It Transformed Our World*. New York: Basic Books, 1999. Comprehensive business and social history.

Schultz, Howard, and Dori Jones Yang. *Pour Your Heart into It: How Starbucks Built a Company One Cup at a Time*. New York: Hyperion, 1997. First-person account by the Starbucks leader.

MARK PENDERGRAST

Stewart, Martha

Martha Stewart (1941–) is a domestic enhancement industry magnate who began her career as a caterer. Born Martha Kostyra, Stewart was the second of six children born to Polish American parents in Nutley, New Jersey. After an education at Barnard College and early careers as a model and a stockbroker, she entered the realm of professional domesticity as a private caterer. By 1982, with the publication of her first book, *Entertaining*, Stewart had begun her transformation from the white, ethnic, middle-class Martha Kostyra to her trademark persona, the Greenwich, Connecticut, Yankee Martha Stewart. She went on to build a phenomenally successful domestic enhancement empire, Martha Stewart Living Omnimedia, Inc., with cookbooks, magazines, newspaper columns, television and radio appearances, mail-order catalog, and website, all offering material goods and advice on home beautification, including the production, preparation, and proper display of food both for entertaining and for everyday family meals. A controversial figure who evokes strong feelings among fans as well as detractors, as evidenced in a widely reported trial and conviction in 2004 on charges of obstruction of justice and securities violations, Stewart is the latest in a long line of famous American women domestic advice givers, including Sara Josepha Hale, Eliza Leslie, and Catharine Beecher.

The extraordinarily polished appearance of Martha Stewart food belies a class-specific aura that transcends ethnicity and becomes accessible by cultivation rather than by heritage. Martha Stewart food is enveloped in a high-Protestant, New England Yankee gloss. Stewart's upper-middle-class taste culture provides those who aspire to it a kind of cultural capital that has helped shape ideals of modern American food. Not only is the preparation of Martha Stewart food a sign of one's status, but Stewart's food itself is prescriptive, class conscious, and authoritarian, as if she has taken upon herself the task of being a strict arbiter of proper American taste. Appearance is more important than taste, to which the carefully constructed and controlled food photography in Martha Stewart publications attests.

Martha Stewart food lends itself to elaborate, conspicuous consumption and is based upon an invented artisan ethos fully realized only by those who have the luxury to perform the work—whipping cream by hand, for example, or making crackers from scratch. Though many criticize Stewart as an elitist perfectionist with a notorious reputation for her demanding and rude treatment of her staff and household help, many home cooks are fiercely loyal, seeing her as transforming their lives for the better. Many (women in particular) find the intricate world of Martha Stewart food most gratifying for infusing a sense of pleasure into the daily, often mundane activities of procuring and preparing food, and these home cooks derive a sense of accomplishment and pleasure from cooking à la Martha Stewart, to whatever limited extent. While Stewart's handcrafted approach evokes such positive notions as conservation and recycling, in actuality many of these projects (and recipes) are quite complex, require a fair amount of money, and can be wasteful of resources.

The Martha Stewart empire is not all cast in this mold, however. Stewart has produced a range of household goods, including an expanding panoply of "everyday" kitchen and dining implements, for Kmart, a middle- to lower-middle-class shopping venue (although research suggests that people of all economic levels shop at Kmart at least occasionally). Martha Stewart Kmart products, however, are never featured and are infrequently advertised in the magazine *Martha Stewart Living* or on the television program *From Martha's Kitchen*. This disjuncture may be poised to change, however, given that in 2003 Martha Stewart Living Omnimedia launched a monthly periodical of recipes, *Everyday Food*, designed for a much broader audience than *Martha Stewart Living*. *Everyday Food*, which does not feature Stewart's photograph or even her name prominently, is designed to be sold at the grocery store checkout counter. Given her conviction and prison sentence, Martha Stewart's title as preeminent domestic advice giver, as well as the fate of her company, remains to be decided.

BIBLIOGRAPHY

Bentley, Amy. "Martha's Food: Whiteness of a Certain Kind." *American Studies* 42, no. 2 (2001), 89–100.
Leavitt, Sarah Abigail. *From Catharine Beecher to Martha Stewart: A Cultural History of Domestic Advice.* Chapel Hill: University of North Carolina Press, 2002.

AMY BENTLEY

Stills

Two types of stills are used for making alcoholic beverages. The pot still appeared approximately five thousand years ago in India. The column still is less than two hundred years old. Stills were originally tools in two basic human desires: to get rich and to live forever. Just as alchemists tried to transmute base metals into gold, they also tried to transmute plant materials into cure-alls. Scented oils for medicinal use and perfumes made by distillation were the results.

The most basic still consists of three parts: a vessel in which to boil a liquid; a lid that has a tube, or "beak," that runs from the top of the vessel slanting downward to channel vapor away from the boiler and help the vapor to condense; and a vessel for catching the condensing vapor as it drips. (The word "distill" comes from the Latin *destillare*, meaning "to drip.") American colonists made distilled spirits with small pot stills. They bartered their whiskeys freely until a tax on whiskey was imposed in 1791. The tax triggered the Whiskey Rebellion of 1794, which was quelled by President Washington.

Farm produce is perishable. Surplus corn could not be held after it was picked, and it was too bulky to be transported economically. Fermenting, distilling, and bottling surplus corn solved both problems. Bourbon shipped from Bourbon County, Kentucky, around 1780 emerged as the unique American whiskey. Bourbon was distilled from corn to eighty proof and aged in new charred-oak barrels. For another half century or so, the pot still reigned supreme. The inherent disadvantage of the pot still, however, is that it is a single-run processor. The liquid to be distilled, called the "wash," is put into the pot and boiled. The distillate is captured, and the pot must then be emptied and cleaned. The still can then be recharged to repeat the process. The newly distilled wash, called "low wine," often has to be distilled again to result in a substance with a more concentrated alcohol level, called "high wine."

The column still was a nineteenth-century design that allowed uninterrupted feeding of the wash and provided a continuous output of distillate that could complete distillation in one process, directly from wash to high wine. Until the advent of the column still, distilling was done in small quantities, and the start-up cost was small. Column stills, on the other hand, were expensive to build and complex to operate, and they needed considerably larger amounts of raw materials to justify their operation. The result was a new kind of distiller who produced high volumes of marketable spirits at low cost.

Early in the twentieth century Prohibition was enacted, and distilling by commercial producers ceased almost entirely. New categories of distillers were born: bootleggers and their country cousins, moonshiners. After Prohibition ended, the spirits industry rebounded through the last third of the twentieth century, when a downward trend in consumption began. Americans are consuming less distilled spirits than in the past, replacing them with beer and wine. In the early twenty-first century most American commercial spirits are made with column stills. A small movement of artisanal distillers uses the old methods, much as in baking, cheese making, and other culinary arts.

[See also Alcohol and Teetotalism; Alcoholism; Bourbon; Brewing; Corn; Distillation; Gin; Prohibition; Rum; Temperance; Vodka; Whiskey.]

BIBLIOGRAPHY

Agrawal, D. P. *Indian Chemistry through the Ages*. http://www.infinityfoundation.com/mandala/t_es/t_es_agraw_chemistry.htm.

Léauté, Robert. "Distillation in Alambic." *American Journal of Enology and Viticulture* 41, no. 1 (1990). Reprinted (edited) online at http://www.essentialspirits.com/history.asp. Good drawings and photos of the different kinds of stills.

McGee, Harold. *On Food and Cooking: The Science and Lore of the Kitchen*. New York: Scribners, 1984. Good source of historical information and science.

BOB PASTORIO

Stoners, Fruit, *see Cherry Pitters or Stoners; Peach Parers and Stoners*

Stores, *see Grocery Stores*

Stout

The style of beer called stout is a variation of a unique style of malt beverage called porter. The style was developed as a result of the need to manufacture a brew that would meet the demand for a particular mixture popular in England in the early 1700s that consisted of beer, ale, and two penny (a pale small beer). When a customer ordered this popular libation, the publican had to draw from three different casks. Ralph Harwood, of the Bell Brewhouse in Shoreditch, East London, England, in 1722 conceived of a brew in which the three elements were already mixed. It was first called Mr. Harwood's Entire Butt or Entire Butt, and was first dispensed at a pub called the Blue Last, on Great Eastern Street in Shoreditch. The publican began calling the brew porter, after the occupation of most of the Blue Last customers.

The popularity of the brew extended into London market, where demand soon made the product popular with other brewers. Irish laborers, a large percentage of them porters, began demanding the brew when they returned to their native land, and the style of brew slowly spread in popularity to Ireland. In Dublin in 1778 Arthur Guinness began brewing a stronger version of the drink, calling it stout porter. Both the Irish and English versions of stout porter were imported into the American colonies almost as soon as regular trade was established.

A number of stouts are produced, all varying only slightly from the original. The most common product is called dry classic Irish stout (3.8–5.4 percent alcohol by volume) and is represented by the Guinness brand. In the United States, stout is one of the most popular styles of beer made by small breweries. It is a style that is easy to identify, and its unique flavor profile can be forgiving in the hands of small-batch brewers. Examples of stout brewed in the United States are Alaskan Stout, made by Alaskan Brewing Company; Anniversary Stout, Ithaca Brewing Company; Black Hawk Stout, Mendocino Brewing Company; Brooklyn Dry Stout, Brooklyn Brewing Company; Cadillac Mountain Stout, Bar Harbor Brewing Company; Dominion Oak Barrel Stout, Old Dominion Brewing Company; Heart of Darkness, Magic Hat Brewing Company; Shakespeare Stout, Rogue Ales; Sierra Nevada Stout, Sierra Nevada Brewing Company; Ipswich Oatmeal Stout, Mercury Brewing Company; and more than one hundred other stouts brewed by as many breweries.

[See also Beer; Brewing; Microbreweries.]

BIBLIOGRAPHY

Baron, Stanley. *Brewed in America*. Boston: Little Brown, 1962.

Foster, Terry. *Porter*. Boulder, CO: Brewers, 1992

LaFrance, Peter. *Beer Basics*. New York: Wiley, 1995.

Rhodes, Christine P., ed. *The Encyclopedia of Beer*. New York: Holt, 1995.

Van Wieren, Dale E. *American Breweries*. West Point, PA: East Coast Breweriana Association, 1995.

PETER LaFRANCE

Stoves and Ovens

This entry includes two subentries:

Wood and Coal

Gas and Electric

Wood and Coal

American cast-iron cookstoves had their earliest origins in the kitchens of the wealthy in Europe after the Middle Ages. These early ranges were large boxes that held a fire. Flat-bottomed pots placed on the range absorbed sufficient heat for cooking. In some kitchens a sheet-iron oven with hinged doors was set flush in the wall above its own "fireplace" alongside the main hearth. The heat from the fire below circulated around the oven before entering the flue leading to the main chimney. These adjuncts to hearth cooking heated more quickly than large brick ovens but were apparently limited to more affluent homes. It was from such precedents that the American cookstove evolved. The rapid rise in popularity and use of cookstoves coincided with the beginnings of the nineteenth-century American Industrial Revolution. Embraced by middle- and upper-class householders in growing cities, cookstoves played a role in changing American home life and American cuisine.

The development of the capacious multiple-oven cookstove owed much to the experiments and inventions of the American-born physicist Benjamin Thompson (1753–1814), later Count Rumford. While living in Germany, Thompson designed a massive though rudimentary range for cooking meals on a large scale at a Munich workhouse. The large metal structure was built around a fireplace. The heat of the fire was conducted into an oven and into a series of "wells" that held deep cooking pots. Thompson also designed a small, portable iron stove that held a single large pot placed in a well over a fire. Thompson's investigations into the physics of heat conduction and convection were the basis of subsequent cookstove development.

Philo Penfield Stewart (1798–1868), who helped found Oberlin College in Ohio in 1833, was one of the men responsible for bringing Rumford's ideas to fruition in America. One of his most important contributions was slanting the sides of the firebox to concentrate the fuel as it burned down. Sales of the "Oberlin" stove, which was patented in 1834, profited the college.

Early American cookstoves were small and low (the cooking surface was usually about two feet off the floor). Only small amounts of food could be cooked at one time, and the cook had to bend to use either the oven or the stovetop. As larger stoves were made, they were raised on legs, and the oven was elevated, often in a stepped or "horseblock" configuration in relation to the cooking surface. As the stove continued to evolve, the waist-high cooktop became the norm, and cooks could stand upright as they worked.

Internationally renowned for their inventive spirit, Americans secured nearly eight hundred patents for cookstoves and attachments between 1840 and 1864. There seemed to be a mania for improving the stove, whether the innovations changed the efficiency and convenience of stoves or merely their appearance. Patents were issued for ongoing improvement in the design of grates, flues, warming ovens, hot-water reservoirs, and ventilating apparatus. Stoves also became more decorative. Scrollwork, flowers, and other patterns were molded into the black iron, and contrasting shiny nickel or steel was used for trim. Some stoves were made so that they could be taken apart annually for cleaning and for removal to and reassembly in a summer kitchen. However, over time some iron stoves

In the Kitchen. Cooking in the 1870s. *Culinary Archives & Museum at Johnson & Wales University, Providence, R.I.*

were constructed in such monstrous proportions that, once in place, they were not moved.

The closed stove, although it changed the American cooking style, turned out not to be such a labor-saving device. Someone had to cut wood to short lengths to fit the firebox, stack it, and carry it into the house and had to keep on hand a supply of finely split tinder and kindling. However, the quantity of wood used was far less than that consumed by an open hearth or brick oven. When coal became a common fuel, the wood-supply chores diminished, but the burned-out coal clinkers—heavier than wood ash and not as useful—had to be carried out.

To fire the stove, the user laid wood on the grate inside the firebox (a small chamber at one side of the stove) and then lit it enough in advance of cooking time to let the stove heat up. Cookstoves were equipped with a system of dampers that controlled the flow of air into the fire and of smoke up the chimney. At first a damper was opened in the smokestack, producing a strong draft that encouraged the fire to grow. Once a good blaze was in progress, that damper was closed, and the heated air and smoke were redirected through passages between the inner and outer walls of the oven, thus heating the oven, and then up through the stack to the chimney. Other vents controlled airflow into the firebox, supplying more oxygen for a stronger fire or limiting the air supply to slow the fire.

Because even a small fire concentrated its heat efficiently, preheating was accomplished with less fuel and time than had been necessary in a hearth or brick oven. Within twenty minutes, an experienced cook might be setting up coffee water for breakfast and within forty minutes have a pan of rolls or biscuits baking. Keeping the temperature steady long enough to bake a cake was a matter of experience. To determine the heat level, cooks held a hand in the oven for as long as tolerable and judged the temperature by time. (Some authorities recommended thirty-five to forty-five seconds as the time indicative of a "moderate" oven.) This system was highly individual, because it depended on the peculiarities of the oven itself and the heat tolerance of the cook. Another method was to put a piece of writing paper or a cube of bread in the oven to see how long it took to brown. Once the initial temperature was established, the drafts and dampers had to be skillfully manipulated to keep the fire at a steady heat. If the oven overheated, the cook opened the door a bit and then closed it when the heat was judged right. Trial and error, aided by sensory memory, were the cook's learning tools. After the day's cooking, ashes and cinders were

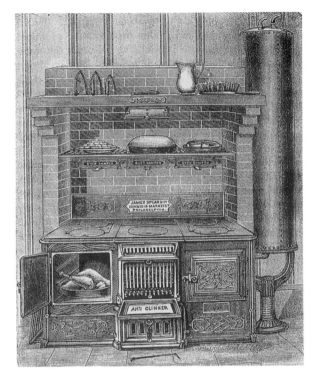

Coal Stove. Illustration from *The Housewife's Library* (Philadelphia, 1883), p. 257.

swept out. From time to time the stove was taken apart so the flues and drafts could be cleaned of soot, the iron surfaces blacked, and the bright trim polished.

As the price of wood continued to increase, anthracite coal, which burned more steadily and less smokily than wood, became less expensive and more widely available and thus more popular as a fuel. Because coal burns hotter than wood, cooks had to adjust their tried-and-true skills in regulating stovetop and oven heat. To accommodate variations in the availability of fuel, some manufacturers began to supply stoves built to burn either wood or coal.

For those who grew up cooking at the hearth, the cookstove represented great progress. Cooking required less time, because the heating was accomplished more quickly. The range top and the oven allowed the development of a more complex cuisine: Cooks prepared more dishes for each meal, because they had the time and technology. They followed the changing cuisine through magazines and newspapers as literacy and communication media grew. Women enjoyed special meals—teas and luncheons—focused on entertaining other women, and homemakers specialized in growing numbers and kinds of baked desserts. Home canning became prodigious, and reputations were made on the quantity and quality of homemade pickles and preserves. Although it was not the only factor in these changes, the cookstove played a substantial role in enablement.

Despite their many advantages, iron cookstoves were far from an ideal solution to all cooking problems. The stoves were notoriously unpredictable and difficult to control. Each stove had its idiosyncrasies, and the cook had to be sensitive to its needs and knowledgeable in responding to them. The fire, hidden from sight in the firebox, could flare up or die down quickly, requiring the cook to check it every few minutes and make appropriate adjustments. Ovens were drafty, especially because the heat was controlled by opening the oven door. Delicate dishes such as angel food cake and soufflés, which require steady and draft-free conditions, were so challenging as to be almost impossible. Roasted meats were not nearly as good as those cooked on a hearth over fire, and breads baked in the cookstove oven were inferior to those from a brick oven. The great back saver of the waist-high cooking surface was countered by arduous weekly cleaning and blacking necessary to prevent rust.

By the 1920s gas ranges had largely replaced solid-fuel cookstoves in cities and towns, but wood- and coal-burning stoves were still used in many rural and remote areas. In the 1970s wood stoves enjoyed a small renaissance, because of fuel shortages, a growing interest in family food traditions, the attraction of simple, basic living, and romanticism regarding country kitchen decor. In the early twenty-first century air-quality regulations and standards of convenience and household efficiency limit the use of wood as fuel.

[See also Kitchens, subentry 1800 to the Present.]

BIBLIOGRAPHY

Brewer, Priscilla. *From Fireplace to Cookstove: Technology and the Domestic Ideal in America.* Syracuse, NY: Syracuse University Press, 2000.

Cowan, Ruth Schwartz. *More Work for Mother: The Ironies of Household Technology from the Open Hearth to the Microwave.* New York: Basic Books, 1983.

Smallzreid, Kathleen Ann. *The Everlasting Pleasure*: *Influences on America's Kitchens, Cooks and Cookery, from 1565 to the Year 2000.* New York: Appleton-Century-Crofts, 1956.

BONNIE J. SLOTNICK

Gas and Electric

For almost three centuries, most Americans cooked before an open fireplace or hearth. In the nineteenth century, Americans shifted to wood- or coal-burning ovens, ranges, and stoves. An oven was simply a metal box used for baking, whereas a range was a flat surface with two or more holes into which pots could be fitted and used for boiling or frying. The word "stove" frequently meant a combination of oven and range.

Coal- and wood-burning stoves had definite advantages over an open fireplace, but they also had disadvantages. Wood did not furnish sustained heat, which made baking difficult. Coal filled the kitchen with dust and ashes. Both coal and wood stoves generated considerable external heat, which was desirable during the winter, but in hot weather the extreme heat made the kitchen almost unbearable. For these reasons alternative fuels, such as gas and electricity, were explored as possible substitutes for coal and wood.

Gas Ranges

Natural gas (methane) was used in many places in the world, but until the mid-nineteenth century, it was difficult to recover and store the gas. In the late eighteenth century, William Murdoch, a Scottish engineer, pioneered a technique for manufacturing gas from coal. After further experimentation, he developed a system that could fuel street lights. Beginning in 1800 Murdoch and others designed and built gasworks for mills and factories. In the United States in 1816, Baltimore chartered the first gas-manufacturing plant, and other American cities followed soon thereafter. Until the late nineteenth century, gas was used almost exclusively for street illumination.

The first known use of gas for cooking is credited to a Moravian chemical manufacturer who in 1802 prepared a meal on a gas cooker, the British term for a small gas range. The gas cooker was not commercialized until James Sharp of Northampton, England, developed the first experimental gas stove in 1826. Ten years later he opened a factory to manufacture gas stoves.

By the 1850s gas ranges were available in the United States. Many early ranges were simply burners placed on tabletops for cooking. One of the first models to appear on the market was Morrill's Evaporator Cooking Stove, which was advertised in Boston in 1858. The allure of gas stoves was obvious. Gas burned cleaner than either wood or coal and required less preparation (wood chopping, coal carrying) and cleanup (ash removal). Compared with gas stoves, wood and coal stoves took a long time to heat up, and they required constant attention to maintain a specific temperature. Gas stoves required a simple turn of a knob for instant heat. Coal and wood ranges required constant replenishment and a large storage area for fuel. Gas was supplied through a pipe or in a "reservoir," a tank filled with gas. Gas stoves produced much less external heat and were therefore more pleasant to use in hot weather.

Despite all these advantages, the adoption of gas cookery occurred slowly in the United States. Early gas stoves were plagued with problems: Gas from municipal systems produced a low-temperature flame useful for gas lighting but too low for heating food. In addition, the gas supply experienced a considerable loss of pressure during times of heavy use, making it impossible to heat ovens when they were most needed. Although reservoirs were used, they frequently ran out of gas before cooking was finished. In winter gas lines occasionally froze. In addition, gas stoves were more expensive than coal and wood stoves, and natural gas was generally more expensive than wood or coal. Early gas stoves constantly needed repair, and maintenance costs added to their expense. Many Americans were frightened by the possibility of gas leaks, which could cause gradual asphyxiation or a sudden explosion.

As gas companies struggled along, some began to manufacture their own stoves and other appliances. Trade associations subsidized firms interested in developing improved models. As the gas delivery system improved, the advantages of the gas stove increased, and the price of natural gas decreased. As improvements were made in design, gas stoves gained wider acceptance. The 1895 Montgomery Ward catalog offered gas ranges with reservoirs, which increased sales in rural areas. In 1915 the American Stove Company sold the first models with oven thermostats, ushering in the era of steady, reliable baking temperatures. Gas stoves with top burners and ovens were found in most households by the 1920s.

Early gas ranges, like their coal- and wood-burning forebears, were black. In 1923 Hotpoint introduced a white enamel range, and within four years, color in the kitchen was becoming fashionable. By 1930 twice as many U.S. households cooked with gas as did with wood or coal.

Electric Stoves

Thomas Edison invented the incandescent lightbulb in 1879. More important, he invented the system that supplied electricity to homes and businesses. Edison opened the first central electricity generating plant in 1882. Like natural gas, electricity was initially used for lighting streets and homes. Beginning in the early 1890s experiments with electric cooking appliances attracted considerable attention. The first electric stove is credited to the Carpenter Electric Heating Manufacturing Company. The organizers of the 1893 Columbian Exposition in Chicago constructed an electrified home equipped with an electrified marble slab intended to heat food. On June 30, 1896, William Hadaway was issued the first patent for an electric stove.

Despite auspicious beginnings, the electric stove remained a novelty well into the twentieth century, in part because few American houses were wired for electricity. By 1907 only 8 percent of American homes were on the power grid, and the price of electricity was high compared with that of coal, wood, and gas. Even homes supplied with electricity had serious problems with electric stoves. The incoming current was weak, and it took an hour to heat an oven for baking. There often was not sufficient amperage to power the stove burners while the oven was heating.

Gas Stove. Illustration from *The Housewife's Library* (Philadelphia, 1883), p. 266

Experimentation with prototype electric stoves continued, and three models, including stoves developed by General Electric and Westinghouse, appeared on the market in 1908. However, these stoves were beset with problems because the heating elements frequently burned out, and the stoves were in constant need of service. In 1920 cooking by electricity was still a novelty.

In the 1920s important changes were made to electric stoves. The first changes were technological improvements. New heating elements, first installed by Hotpoint, decreased problems related to burning out of heating elements. The introduction of the electromechanical thermostat kept the temperature constant in ovens. The second set of changes related to fashion. Electric ranges available in the early 1920s were constructed on tall legs, and the boxlike oven compartment rose above the burners. In new stoves the oven was below the burners. This configuration made possible level countertops and work surfaces throughout the kitchen. Then Westinghouse and other manufacturers dazzled consumers by offering electric ranges in a variety of colors. Despite these improvements, only 875,000 American households had switched to electric stoves by 1930.

In the 1930s electric stoves began to effectively compete with gas ranges. The cost of electricity dropped, particularly after the construction of major hydroelectric projects, such as the Tennessee Valley Authority and Hoover Dam. By 1941, 80 percent of all houses were wired for electricity, and the shift to electric ranges had begun. By the 1950s electric ovens were outselling gas models. By the end of the twentieth century, twice as many American homes cooked with electricity as did with gas.

Gas and electric stoves equipped with thermostats made accurate, standardized temperature control possible, and cookbooks began to include exact cooking times and temperatures in recipes. The introduction of gas and electric stoves meant that new cooking techniques were required. To help educate American consumers, utility companies offered cooking demonstrations, and many stove companies produced cookery booklets to promote their products.

Later in the twentieth century, accessories and improvements were added to kitchen ranges, including timers, storage drawers under the oven, windows in the oven door, interior lights in the oven, self-cleaning functions, preheating signals, and an automatic shutoff function for turning off the oven at a programmed time. Broilers have been added for radiant-heat cooking, and gas stoves have electronic ignitions, which obviate pilot lights. In the late twentieth century, a new competitor arose—the microwave oven. The microwave oven initially had problems with image and function similar to those exhibited by primitive gas and electric ovens.

[*See also* Microwave Ovens.]

BIBLIOGRAPHY

Brewer, Priscilla. *From Fireplace to Cookstove: Technology and the Domestic Ideal in America.* Syracuse, NY: Syracuse University Press, 2000.

Cowan, Ruth Schwartz. *More Work for Mother: The Ironies of Household Technology from the Open Hearth to the Microwave.* New York: Basic Books, 1983.

Franklin, Linda Campbell. *300 Years of Kitchen Collectibles.* 5th ed. Iola, WI: Krause, 2002.

Giedion, Siegfried. *Mechanization Takes Command: A Contribution to Anonymous History.* New York: Norton, 1969.

Plante, Ellen M. *The American Kitchen: 1700 to the Present.* New York: Facts on File, 1995.

Smallzried, Kathleen Ann. *The Everlasting Pleasure: Influences on America's Kitchens, Cooks, and Cookery, from 1565 to the Year 2000.* New York: Appleton-Century-Crofts, 1956.

ANDREW F. SMITH

Strawberries

The modern strawberry (*Fragaria X ananassa*) originated in the early eighteenth century in a garden near Brest, France, as a chance cross of two American species. One, the Chilean strawberry (*F. chiloensis*), is native to the Pacific beaches of North and South America; the other, the Virginia strawberry (*F. virginiana*), is native to eastern North America. Deliberate improvement began in 1817 with the work of Thomas Knight, in England. The ensuing two centuries have given rise to numerous strawberry cultivars differing not only in fruit characteristics but also in disease resistance and adaptability to various soil types and climatic conditions.

The twentieth century saw the development of everbearing varieties of strawberries. The first types of everbearing plants, developed early in the twentieth century, bore two crops each season, one in spring and one in fall. True ever-bearing strawberries—varieties that fruit continuously through the growing season—have been available since approximately 1980.

The strawberry is a woody plant with a much foreshortened stem, from which arises a whorl of leaves. Plants send out runners at the tips of which new plants develop, and these plants can give rise to more runners and daughter plants. The plants' habit of strewing may

Hilton Gem Strawberries. From the 1894 catalog of Peter Henderson & Co., New York.

have led to the name "strewberry," which became "strawberry." An alternative explanation is that the name arose from the straw traditionally used for mulching the plants. Although strawberry plantings can remain productive for a few years before disease and weeds make inroads, the trend has been toward planting and cropping the plants for one season and then removing them. Strawberries are an intensively grown, high-value crop.

Commercial strawberries are extensively grown in warm winter areas, such as California and Florida. Although strawberries were once a springtime treat, varieties bred to withstand the rigors of shipping are available year-round, at some sacrifice to texture and flavor.

Not to be overlooked are two old-fashioned species of strawberry. Alpine strawberries (*F. vesca*) are ever-bearing wood strawberries that do not produce runners. This species also is known by the French name *fraise de bois* and is native to North and South America, Europe, northern Asia, and Africa. Alpine strawberry fruits are tiny but highly colored (except for white-fruited sorts) and are intensely flavored. Cultivated forms of musk strawberry (*F. moschata*), which is native to northern Europe and Siberia, date to the sixteenth century. These strawberries also have been called "hautbois strawberries." Although the fruit is borne only in spring and is very soft and only dull red, the flavor of musk strawberries is intense and delectable, a commingling of the flavor of strawberry with those of raspberry and pineapple.

Botanically, the fruit of the strawberry is what most people consider its seeds. These achenes, as such hard, dry fruits are called, stimulate growth of associated receptacles, which swell together to become the juicy, red "fruits." Strawberries are rich in vitamin C. Although they usually are used fresh, strawberries can be frozen and are frequently processed into preserves, jelly, extracts and flavorings, and pie filling.

[*See also* Fruit; Preserves; Transportation of Food.]

BIBLIOGRAPHY

Darrow, George M. *The Strawberry: History, Breeding and Physiology*. New York: Holt, Rinehart, and Winston, 1966.
Wilhelm, Stephen, and James E. Sagen. *A History of the Strawberry: From Ancient Gardens to Modern Markets*. Berkeley: University of California Division of Agricultural Sciences, 1974.

LEE REICH

Street Vendors

Street vending has been a vital part of meeting physical and emotional needs throughout America's history. Street vending is a poor family's way of supplementing meager income, keeps cultural traditions alive, and supplies customers' needs for variety, sustenance, and sociability. Opposition to this informal practice, however, has consistently produced restrictive regulations as well as complaints from businesses and the public. Street vending traditions reflect the vendors' countries of origin but also have responded to the variety of climates and resources in the United States.

Historical Background

Because customers who want quick food and vendors who supply that need have always existed, traditions of peddling food in the streets and markets have been known worldwide throughout the ages. In a former exhibit at the Field Museum in Chicago, panels of drawings in the reconstructed tomb of an Egyptian ruler who lived more than four thousand years ago reveal colorful evidence of a market. The drawings show vendors selling fruits, vegetables, fish, and other foodstuffs. One panel shows an official with a baboon, apparently keeping order.

Evidence from biblical times indicates that peddlers carried produce from the countryside to towns and returned with wares and crafts needed by the rural people. Despite their role in satisfying needs, these traders were often viewed with suspicion. Throughout the ages all over Europe, market squares surviving from Roman times have been used for the purchase and bartering of food.

By the Middle Ages, Jews, forbidden land of their own, were the main link between East and West—where they traded rice and other grains, spices, dates, and nuts. In the early nineteenth century, when anti-Semitism and antipeddling sentiments barred Jews from vending in cities, thousands of poorer Jews were driven to seek a livelihood in America and to escape persecution in eastern Europe. Economic betterment and escape from oppression have motivated successive waves of immigrants who came to the United States not as slaves but of their own volition from South and Central America, Africa, and Asia.

Immigrants to America brought with them the food culture of their native lands and adapted it to the resources and conditions they found in their new home. For example, street cries of the British Isles were distinctive and commonplace and would call attention to the peddlers' presence and wares, so these cries became a feature of colonial America. Vendors, new arrivals themselves, communicated in immigrants' languages and supplied a variety of familiar foods directly to the doors of their homes. During most of the history of the United States, refrigeration was unavailable, and immigrant populations were accustomed to fresh food daily. Elderly persons in the early twenty-first century recall the "delicious" fresh fish, "lovely" crisp fruit, and hot roasted potatoes sold in winter from mobile, charcoal-burning metal carts.

The unique aspect of street vending in America was the goal of upward mobility. With little proficiency in English and small capital resources, a new peddler could see vendors who had moved from carrying their wares on their backs to using a cart, a stand, a small shop, a horse and wagon, and finally a truck. Beginning vendors expected to follow this pattern and along the way become their own bosses and have their own businesses, despite long hours and physical hardship. Future businesses followed familiar trajectories. For example, many Greek peddlers went into the restaurant business, whereas Italian food vendors progressed to the wholesale trade of fruit, vegetables, and nuts. An Italian boy, who later became a produce wholesaler, boarded a streetcar after school every day and traveled to the south side of Chicago. There he helped his father peddle produce until dark. From this beginning, the boy eventually became an independent businessman.

Street Vendors. Peddlers offering iced drinks and snacks, 1908. *Prints and Photographs Division, Library of Congress*

Because of varying religious and cultural traditions, the role of women who sell food on the streets of America can be ambiguous. Women hawking food are a familiar sight in Africa, South and Central America, and many areas of Asia, so immigrants from these areas continue the practice. If cultural restrictions on engaging in street trade exist, women and children participate in the family food-selling business by performing preparation chores such as cleaning, peeling, and slicing and dicing of raw materials. They may even grow the products used rather than buying them from wholesale houses or farms.

America's multiethnic background is reflected in the sporadic ways vendors have organized. Many vendors come from countries where forming unions is a familiar solution to problems. In the United States, however, meetings can be a babble of tongues, and communication problems arise. In addition, vendors tend to possess an independent, enterprising spirit, so they often prefer to solve their problems independently from one another.

Restrictions

A characteristic of street vending in America is the quantity, variety, and antagonistic quality of municipal regulations. Restrictions on street vendors are in effect worldwide, but in third world countries regulations have been tempered by the sheer numbers of people who depend on vending for their livelihood. Officials in America have been heavily influenced by health and hygiene reforms and by the power of fixed-location business owners who influence city government.

Restrictions on food selling may take the form of stringent and unrealistic requirements for storage, hot and cold running water on a cart, tent or cover over the food, health permit, long lists of forbidden foods, and attendance at food preparation classes. Chicago is widely known as one of the most restrictive cities in America, whereas New York is celebrated for the variety and quantity of food available from street vendors (with restrictions waxing and waning according to the current mayor). Mid-size cities often appreciate food vendors for ambiance but carefully restrict the activity and appearance of food carts.

Many city regulations target arbitrary locations for prohibition. Food vendors often are cited as being threats to "public safety" when the actual issue is that they are considered threats to the profits of fixed-location food businesses. In many locations, however, vendors have been found to increase general customer traffic and safety in the area. Licensing regulations vary, some cities adding to the complexity by issuing distinctive licenses for residential streets, for markets, for parks, and for certain main, designated streets.

Food vendors sometimes are forced from main selling streets to isolated, newly appointed markets, and they usually are barred from selling to schoolchildren, a steady source of sales in their native lands. Street vendors outside the United States commonly sell to factory and downtown business workers, but in America this practice is frequently restricted. Other restrictions limit hours of selling so that selling is prohibited during times that will generate the greatest customer volume. Similarly, city councils have argued heatedly about street cries, some officials citing noise nuisance and others pointing out that this is the only way food vendors can make their presence known in neighborhoods.

Customers

Buyers appreciate street food for reasons of ethnic taste, nostalgia, and the opportunity to eat quickly obtained, reasonably priced, and flavorful food in a sociable setting. Vendors respond to these needs by offering stools and small tables next to their carts and by presenting food that is ethnic but also satisfies American tastes for the new. Vendors barred from central business districts make up for the loss of business there by selling their wares in neighborhoods and market streets. Peddlers sell sweetened, shaved ice cones across the street from schools or tamales and steamed corn on the cob after Spanish-language mass. Every neighborhood has its own version of the hot dog, and in

Fruit Truck Andy Russo and Tony Maldonado sell fruit in the Park Slope neighborhood of Brooklyn. *Photograph by Joe Zarba*

many cities customers can take their pick, or a mix, of Middle Eastern foods.

A trend that reflects these tendencies is the popularity of food festivals all over the United States as cities and towns strive to promote their unique ethnic and regional heritages and capture tourist interest. At a food fair in Washington State, Asian ethnic food is offered by the Buddhist Association, Vietnamese food by the Vietnamese community, and tandoori chicken by Indians. One midwestern town may offer rhubarb tasting and another a strawberry festival. Saint Petersburg, Florida, has become a center for Russian Jewish immigrants who remember street food as an institution that included pastries stuffed with meat, carrots, and potatoes and all kinds of small cakes and pancakes. Some street fairs, such as the Feast of San Gennaro, in Little Italy in New York, feature traditional Italian street food—and anyone who enjoys the food is drawn to them. A relatively new street festival in Illinois, Juneteenth, which celebrates the announcement of the Emancipation Proclamation, features street vendors serving traditional southern style and African food.

[*See also* Farmers' Markets; Food Festivals.]

BIBLIOGRAPHY

Balkin, Steven. *Self-Employment for Low Income People.* New York: Praeger, 1989. An overview of self-employment as a strategy for immigrants and minority groups.

Cross, John. "Introduction to Special Issue on Street Vending in the Modern World." *International Journal of Sociology and Social Policy* 21 (2000): 1–4. Issues of assumptions about street vending, niche markets, and vending as offering a choice to unemployed immigrants.

Eastwood, Carolyn. *Chicago's Jewish Street Peddlers.* Chicago: Chicago Jewish Historical Society, 1991. Long-term history of Jewish vendors and their role when they migrated to urban America.

Eastwood, Carolyn. "A Study of the Regulation of Chicago's Street Vendors" Ph.D. diss., University of Illinois at Chicago, 1988. Material on Jewish, Greek, and Italian immigrant vendors. Regulations in New York, Washington, D.C., and Columbus, Ohio, are compared with those in Chicago.

Light, Ivan, and Carolyn Rothenstein. *Race, Ethnicity, and Entrepreneurship in Urban America.* New York: Aldine de Gruyter, 1995. Adaptation to urban conditions in America through self-employment is examined.

Tinker, Irene. *Street Foods: Urban Food and Employment in Developing Countries.* New York: Oxford University Press, 1997. A description of food and food vending in third world countries. Women's issues and sources of immigrant food customs and tastes are discussed.

Whyte, William H. *City: Rediscovering the Center.* New York: Doubleday, 1988. Results of a number of observational studies on qualities that make a city center lively and viable.

CAROLYN EASTWOOD

Stuckey's

Stuckey's, a multimillion dollar chain known for selling pecan candy, was founded by Williamson Sylvester Stuckey, an entrepreneur and self-taught marketing expert who was a pioneer in the convenience store and fast food concept. Born in Dodge County, Georgia, on March 26, 1909, Stuckey dropped out of the University of Georgia in 1929 because of a lack of funds and went home to plow a mule (the very lowest form of farm employment in the South during the Great Depression). In the early 1930s, after his grandmother lent him thirty-five dollars, Stuckey began buying and selling Georgia pecans. In 1936 Stuckey built a roadside stand on a two-lane highway near Eastman, Georgia. There he sold pecans and later added pralines made at home by his wife, Ethel Mullis Stuckey. The first Stuckey's Pecan Shoppe opened in Eastman, Georgia, in 1937, selling pecan log rolls, pralines, divinity, and pecans. The store later added souvenirs and food and beverage service. Gasoline pumps were installed as other stores opened.

Much of Stuckey's success is attributed to the founder's uncanny business and marketing sense. He offered one-stop shopping years before convenience stores appeared, adopted a universally recognizable store design, and used franchisees to manage his stores. Long before integration in the south, blacks were welcome in Stuckey's stores. A framed copy of Stuckey's customer service philosophy, "The Friendship of a Traveler Means a Great Deal to Us," hung in every store. A parrot or mynah bird greeted customers in many stores. The locations for stores and billboards were carefully selected on the basis of results of traffic studies. Stuckey lived the American dream and saw his name become a household word.

There were 160 Stuckey's stores by 1964, when Stuckey's merged with Pet Inc., the consumer food giant that also owned Whitman's chocolates. Stuckey became a vice president and member of the board of Pet Inc. and remained president of the Stuckey's division until his early retirement in 1970. During the time he managed the division (1964–1970), the number of Stuckey's stores increased from 160 to approximately 350 coast to coast.

After Stuckey's death in Eastman, Georgia, on January 6, 1977, Pet Inc. was bought by Illinois Central Industries, a Chicago conglomerate, after Pet fought the merger and lost. Williamson Sylvester Stuckey Jr. had worked with his father in Stuckey's before he became congressman for the Eighth District of Georgia in the

U.S. House of Representatives, where he served from 1966 to 1976. On May 1, 1985, Stuckey Jr. and his partners, Charles "Chip" Rosencrans and Gregory Griffith, repurchased Stuckey's from Illinois Central Industries, ending seventeen years during which the company had not been under Stuckey family ownership. When co-branding became popular, the Stuckey's Express franchise, a store-within-a-store concept, was established.

In late 2002 Stuckey's had two hundred franchises in nineteen states from Pennsylvania to Florida and as far west as Arizona along interstate highways in convenience stores and travel plazas. Stuckey's capitalizes on its nostalgic appeal to travelers who remember the familiar stores from the 1950s through 1970s. Stuckey's pecan candies, nuts, and souvenirs inside stores along America's highways continue the Stuckey's legend.

[*See also* Nuts; Pecans; Restaurants; Roadside Food.]

BIBLIOGRAPHY

Drinnon, Elizabeth McCants. *Stuckey: The Biography of Williamson Sylvester Stuckey, 1909–1977.* Macon, GA: Mercer University Press, 1997.

ELIZABETH MCCANTS DRINNON

Stuffed Ham

Stuffed ham is a corned or smoked ham that has been stuffed with vegetables and spices. Slits or holes are cut into the ham and the ingredients are packed in. Traditionally, the stuffing consisted of differing amounts of cabbage, kale, and onions. Variations may include celery, watercress, turnip, mustard seed, and spinach. Spicy elements are celery seed, mustard seed, ground red pepper, black pepper, and salt.

Stuffed ham is thought to have originated in southern Maryland, specifically in Saint Marys County where it is a specialty dish. Saint Marys, dating from 1634, was Maryland's first settlement and is located southeast of Washington, D.C., off the Potomac River. Hogs were available to Maryland settlers in the mid-seventeenth century. There are no references to stuffed ham in the seventeenth or eighteenth centuries in Maryland nor are there written references in the nineteenth. However, there are references to vegetable- and parsley-stuffed hams in Maine in 1786 and in Virginia and Kentucky in the early eighteenth century.

Twentieth-century cookbooks contain various recipes and serving the ham, especially at Christmas and Easter, is a tradition at both African American and white church suppers in Saint Marys. Before the twentieth century, oral traditions of Saint Marys County residents can trace stuffed ham to the post–Civil War period. Legends include those that say it originated in England or was brought from Africa by slaves. Some say the slaves used the lower jaw, or the jowl, of the pig as the base, stuffing it with vegetables, such as kale, cabbage, "greasy greens" (wild watercress), or turnip tops.

BIBLIOGRAPHY

Oliver, Sandra L. "Maryland Stuffed Ham for the Holiday." *Food History News* 6, no. 2 (Winter 1999): 1, 10–11.
Randolph, Mary. *The Virginia Housewife.* Baltimore: J. Plaskitt, 1836.
300 Years of Black Cooking in St. Mary's County, Maryland. Pp. 23–25. Citizens for Progress Handbook. Saint Marys County, MD: Saint Marys County Bicentennial Commission, 1975.
Tilp, Frederick. "Potomac Stuffed Ham—A Culinary Art." *Chronicles of St. Mary's* 22, no. 4 (April 1974).

FRED CZARRA

Stuffing, *see Dressings and Stuffings*

Submarine, *see Hoagie*

Suet, *see Fats and Oils*

Sugar

Sugar has long played a complex role in American history, affecting economics, politics, and diet. Supporting early colonial empires of the Dutch, French, and English, sugar was the most important commodity coming from the tropics, emerging as the dominant plantation crop of Barbados by the 1640s and Jamaica by the early 1700s. Throughout the eighteenth century sugar was Britain's most important colonial import, surpassing the value of all other imports combined. With sugar as its anchoring crop, the Caribbean formed the center of a growing Atlantic commerce involving three continents: Africa supplied the vast number of bodies, through human bondage, needed to cultivate the labor-intensive crop; North America provided raw materials, including the timber used to build the increasing number of ships for transporting the commodity; and Europe generated goods and luxuries for its own and export markets.

The success of Britain's Caribbean colonies during the seventeenth and eighteenth centuries helped fuel economic growth and influence in the American colonies. Methods used in the processing of sugarcane, particularly the use of slave labor, provided a template for the cultivation of similarly labor-intensive crops, such as cotton and tobacco, in the South. Moreover, although the American sweet tooth developed nearly a century after Britain's, infiltration of sugar into the diet radically changed the substance and flavor of what people ate.

Molasses and rum, the by-products of sugar refining, have also figured in American history. Molasses, the syrup resulting from the sugar purification process, has functioned primarily as a liquid sweetener in baked goods. Rum (fermented molasses) emerged as an important colonial American trade good by the early eighteenth century and tied remote West Indian plantation owners to interior American commerce. Realizing profits as high as 400 percent, traders exchanged their rum, distilled primarily in New England, for Native American furs, skins, and horses. Rum mediated social interactions between Indians and colonists, who readily presented the drink as a gesture of goodwill. Indians' nearly insatiable appetite for the intoxicating drink caused the social and economic ruin of many native tribes.

Sugar Box. Box of Ben Franklin granulated sugar, c. 1890. *Collection of Kit Barry*

Sugar Production

Even after the introduction of machinery, sugar production, once requiring the effort of thousands of slaves, remained a highly labor-intensive process. A grass ranging from one-half inch to three inches in diameter and reaching up to twenty feet in height, sugarcane grows best in tropical climates and needs plenty of natural rainfall or irrigation. The growing season lasts eight to thirty months, depending on weather conditions. The longer the season, the more sucrose-laden the crop becomes. Rather than using seeds, growers replant cane using cut pieces of stalk, which when buried in soil sprout new growth.

Three key processes transform cane into refined sugar: extraction, purification, and crystallization. At the beginning of extraction stalks of hewn sugarcane are milled to separate sucrose (the sugar, which also is extracted from sugar beets) from bagasse (the leftover vegetable material often used to power the mill itself). Because the plant is extremely fragile, this step is performed on site. Cane mills, which squeeze the stalks, originally consisted of vertically oriented rollers made of stone. Later mills, oriented horizontally, were powered by steam. Early mills could not efficiently extract all sucrose from the plant, but modern mills are able to capture almost all the sucrose.

The extracted sucrose is purified to remove waste products. Before mechanization this process was accomplished by the open kettle method. Water was added to the sucrose in a large copper kettle and heated; the rising foam, containing impurities, was skimmed off the top. Added ox blood, lime, and egg whites effectuated the process, as did straining the liquid through a blanket.

Revolutionizing purification, the steam-powered centrifugal machine, common to most factories by the 1860s, spun the liquid, casting out any molasses still clinging to the sugar crystals. These machines cut purification time by 80 percent and were less taxing on sugar processors.

Once purified, the liquid is crystallized to give sugar its characteristic granularity. This step, too, was originally accomplished by boiling the sugar in gradually smaller pots over ever-hotter fires until the water became so saturated with sucrose as to bring about granulation. The vacuum steam pan, introduced in America in 1855, boiled the liquid at lower temperatures, speeding up the refining process. Once refined, sugar is cooled and dried. In the eighteenth and nineteenth centuries refined sugar—still slightly moist and containing impurities—was packed tightly in conical clay molds to "cure." A hole in the top allowed additional molasses to drain from the inverted cone, resulting in an even whiter, more refined sugar. The many variables involved in refining processes produced sugars of various grades, from dark brown to white and from syrupy to completely dry in texture. When "clayed" sugar, highly refined, reached American kitchens in the eighteenth and early nineteenth centuries, it had to be separated into chunks with special tools, called "sugar snips," and grated to achieve a coarse granularity that could be integrated with other edible and drinkable substances.

After more than fifty years of failed experiments America established viable beet sugar production in the 1880s. The introduction of beet sugar substantially increased the rate of production of sugar and decreased the price, turning the former luxury into an affordable necessity. In the 1850s, for example, beet sugar accounted for only 16.6 percent of the world's supply. By early 1900, beets provided 60.6 percent of the world's sugar. Sugar beets are processed in much the same way as sugarcane. Beets, however, offer a great advantage because they have a shorter growing season and can be grown in temperate climates. Thus a greater portion of U.S. land can be devoted to sugar cultivation. Whereas domestic sugarcane areas have been limited to parts of Hawaii, Louisiana, Florida, and Texas, the geographic range of sugar beets encompasses a swath two thousand miles wide. Key beet sugar regions include the Dakotas, the upper Midwest, the Great Plains, and the Far West.

Other plant sources yield sugar and have been the subjects of occasional experimentation. Entrepreneurs in New York and Pennsylvania championed the cultivation of maple sugar as early as the 1790s, and sugar shortages caused by the War of 1812 furthered the experiments. In 1832 a New Hampshire works was erected to manufacture sugar and molasses from potatoes, and in 1836 people tried to make sugar from Indian corn, an early foray into corn syrup. Sorghum, a grain similar to Indian corn and one of the most common sugar substitutes, was introduced into the United States around 1854 but did not gain popular currency until sugar scarcities during the Civil War. Other experiments with sugar substitutes have included sugar from sweet potatoes, corn stalks, pine trees, acorns, and licorice root. Only sugar beet and sugarcane plants yield enough concentrated sucrose to be profitable.

Sugar and the Economy

Monopolizing the early sugar trade, Britain profited immensely from the taxes it collected from its American colonies. Later, America's own government similarly profited. Since 1789 some form of tariff has been placed on sugar to protect domestic refining industries and generate revenue. From 1842 on, policies became protectionist. Because a higher tariff was placed on imported refined sugar than on raw sugar, tariffs bolstered domestic refineries and raw sugar producers. Although the high 30 percent ad valorem tariff lasted from 1846 to 1857 and increased the price of sugar, rates of consumption continued to rise as Americans became more enamored with and needful of the commodity.

The Panic of 1873 put some domestic refining companies out of business but did not slow individual sugar consumption. The McKinley Tariff Act of 1890 changed the tariff schedule for imported sugar, ultimately decreasing the price and boosting consumption even more. Responding to economic shifts, the Sugar Trust (organized under the name the Sugar Refineries Company) formed in 1887. Forced to reorganize in 1891 because of the Sherman Antitrust Law, the group, consisting of the country's principal sugar refiners, renamed itself the American Sugar Refining Company. Because technological and agricultural advances vastly increased sugar production rates and resulting supplies (thus narrowing profit margins), domestic refiners, like other businesses, consolidated their operations and limited their output. The American Sugar Refining Company originally consisted of eight companies owning twenty refineries. By streamlining production, members of the group were able to reduce by half the number of operating plants while increasing sugar output, having a near monopoly on sugar refining and selling by 1892.

Other than tariffs on imports, the sugar industry remained unregulated by the government until well into the twentieth century. In the wake of the Great Depression, the Sugar Act of 1934 established price controls, set production quotas, and determined equitable distribution of profits among larger beet and cane processors and individual farmers. Throughout the twentieth century this price-support system was adjusted by the government to control supplies and prices of sugar. In the 1980s the U.S. Department of Agriculture became directly involved in this process, giving price supports to domestic growers and establishing import quotas from sugar sources such as the Dominican Republic, Brazil, and the Philippines. In 2000, six companies constituted the American refining industry, operating ten refineries in seven states. These companies marketed their products nationally, with approximately 60 percent of raw sugar supplies coming from domestic sources.

Sugar in the Diet

People have embraced sugar for both psychological and physiological reasons. So hard to come by, sugar was initially considered a spice—not a central ingredient but rather one flavoring agent among many in the larder—to be used sparingly. Women who managed the home kept this precious substance under lock and key along with their saffron, cinnamon, and cumin. Physicians considered sugar a powerful medicine, and early medical textbooks recommended its use for everything from curing palsy to aiding digestion. Hard candies in the early nineteenth century were taken for similar reasons and first appeared in apothecaries as medicated lozenges whose hard, sweet coatings concealed often bitter drugs inside. Without the medicinal centers, lozenges became hard candies marketed directly to children by candy makers in the mid-nineteenth century.

Because it represented refinement and status, those who could afford sugar enjoyed being part of an exclusive group. Even after sugar became more accessible in the nineteenth century, people continued to think of it as a status symbol. Its material versatility—it can be spun, pulled, boiled, molded, creamed, and sprinkled—was another reason American consumers embraced refined sugar. In addition refined sugar could be integrated with many other substances. The ability to sweeten foods inconspicuously also made cane and beet sugar more attractive than maple sugar and honey, which impart distinct flavors to the foods they enhance. Whiteness, fine granularity, and versatility were considered appealing attributes.

Sugar plays an integral part in many small- and large-scale food manufactures. Individual consumers buy it in five-pound bags at grocery stores and use it in their homes for baking, for sweetening beverages, for enhancing the taste of fresh fruits and cereals, and for making confections. People also commonly use brown sugar, which is moister and less refined than white sugar, in baked goods and to add a more robust sweetness to various foods. Professional bakers and confectioners use sugar for both the substance and the icing of decorated cakes, for pastries, and for doughnuts. Candy manufacturers use a combination of sugar and other sweeteners (mostly glucose, dextrose, and high-fructose corn syrup) for making candy bars, lollipops, hard candies, licorice, and other confectionery. Ice cream manufacturers similarly use a combination of sweeteners mixed with cream, eggs, and flavorings to make frozen treats. In the early twenty-first century soft-drink makers, who once used only refined sugar, do not use it at all in manufacturing carbonated beverages. Even foods not consciously considered sweet—condiments, bread, and prepackaged entrees—contain large amounts of refined sugar and other forms of sweeteners. The use of sugar as a preservative in home canning once was common, and extra sugar rations for this purpose were allowed by the government during World War II.

Because it began its cultural life in America as a sought-after substance produced in faraway lands, refined sugar served as a potent status symbol in the eighteenth and early nineteenth centuries. Available only to the rich—its value was once almost equal to that of gold—sugar became a mainstay in elite diets and social rituals. Sugar tempered the bitter taste of other luxurious imported substances such as coffee, chocolate, and tea, becoming essential to their enjoyment. Sweetened imported dainties, such as candied nuts and preserved fruits, constituted the bulk of a confectioner's stock. The accessories of sweetness—sugar bowls, tongs, spoons, and graters—were often fashioned of elaborate materials such as gilt porcelain or pure silver to reinforce the vaunted place of sugar at the tea or dinner table. Sugar has also been used as an artistic medium: nonedible sculptures, often neoclassical in appearance, were the most decadent end to which this luxury good was put.

As sugar became more affordable, its integration into popular rituals became more common. Earlier sugar uses were adapted to meet new American needs and preferences. The massive sugar sculptures created by skilled sugar bakers in the eighteenth century became banquet centerpieces adorning tables at special events and in urban hotels. Beginning in the 1870s wedding cakes, which borrowed from the tradition of sugar monuments and were festooned with sugar frosting flowers and decorative piping, became popular. By the turn of the century wedding cakes had become a central part of the marriage ceremony. People could commission customized versions or purchase more affordable versions already made. Having ready access to recipe books and magazines, women also could make the cakes themselves.

Pyramids of preserved fruits and towering molded gelatins, once available only to the elite, became the inspiration for middle-class desserts in the late nineteenth century. Instant dessert preparations such as Jell-O gelatin democratized upper-class desserts, which before the development of new food technologies and the availability of inexpensive sugar required hours of preparation and costly ingredients. The proliferation of other products, such as mass-produced tin molds and mass-distributed recipes, helped sugar reach new households in new ways. Mass-marketed cookbooks and advertising leaflets helped promote sugar-centered domestic pastimes such as taffy pulls and fudge-making parties.

On a larger scale sugar came to play an important role in American holidays. Imported sweetmeats were treats often enjoyed during Christmas celebrations in upper-class homes. In the nineteenth century the range of holidays incorporating confections expanded. By the late 1860s suitors began giving boxes of fancy bonbons and chocolates on Valentine's Day. Influenced by the folk traditions of the Pennsylvania Dutch, companies began mass producing chocolate Easter eggs and rabbits. In the twentieth century, candy was central to the ritual of trick-or-treating on Halloween.

Sugar became so elemental in the America diet that its absence represented hard times. Scarcity of sugar was an issue during the Civil War, especially in the South. There was some sugar rationing during World War I, and supplies of candy for the soldiers became a priority (because it was a quick and portable energy source and did not spoil). During World War II sugar was the first commodity to be put on the ration list and the last to be taken off, in 1947.

Although Americans embraced sugar from the time it entered the marketplace, it is important to note that consumption of sugar has also aroused controversy for political, social, and dietary reasons. Beginning in the 1790s

Sugar in Wartime. Poster by Ernest Fuhr urging conservation of sugar, 1917. *Prints and Photographs Division, Library of Congress*

abolitionists called for boycotts on commodities produced with slave labor and suggested the use of maple sugar as a substitute for cane sugar. In the early nineteenth century they urged people to shop at "free grocery" stores, which sold only products made with non-slave labor. Sugar from China was a staple in these stores. Because it has no nutritional value and is something that brings pleasure, many nineteenth-century Americans identified sugar as a source of various societal maladies. Forgetting the original use of sugar as a therapeutic agent, nineteenth-century physicians concerned themselves with what they saw as overconsumption of the substance. Victorian medical advisers and reformers alike, preoccupied with personal respectability and good conduct, believed that sugar could arouse one's sexual passions and urged women to control their consumption of sweets and cakes. Religious reformers have viewed eating sugar, which is slightly addictive, as an immoral practice that can easily lead to other deviant forms of short-term gratification, such as gambling and drinking. These and related concerns dogged sugar throughout the twentieth century and became especially acute toward the end of the century, when hyperactivity, obesity, attention deficit disorder, diabetes, and other debilities, especially among children, were thought to be caused by sugar consumption.

Despite the controversies, sugar has remained popular. Consumption rates increased steadily from the eighteenth through the twentieth centuries, the nineteenth century witnessing its true democratization—transformation from a precious luxury into a popular necessity. Average annual per capita consumption for the 1790s was approximately 8 pounds. This figure increased to almost 30 pounds in the 1850s, nearly 80 pounds by 1900, and more than 120 pounds in the 1970s. Although sugar consumption peaked in the late twentieth century, total intake for sweeteners continues to increase, with a greater proportion of liquid and chemical sugar substitutes being integrated into the diet.

By the beginning of the twenty-first century, Americans' consumption of refined sugar flattened out, but this phenomenon did not indicate a growing preference for a diet less sweet. The legacies of more than two centuries of sugar consumption have habituated Americans to sweetness. The addition of both natural and chemical sweeteners has made the entire American diet much sweeter, changing the flavor of foods not ordinarily considered sweet, such as pizza dough, gravy mixes, ketchup, cereal, salad dressing, and soy sauce. Although refined sugar is being consumed in smaller quantities per capita, Americans are taking in more sweeteners altogether (including high-fructose corn syrup, glucose, and dextrose). According to the U.S. Department of Agriculture, in 2001 the intake of caloric sweeteners alone totaled more than 150 pounds per capita. This figure did not include noncaloric chemical sweeteners such as aspartame and saccharin. In the 1950s few people consumed saccharin (the only artificial sweetener on the market at the time). Twenty years later each American was ingesting an average of 7.1 pounds of it annually, and by 1984 annual per capita saccharin consumption reached a high of 10 pounds. In the same year, aspartame (trademarked as NutraSweet) accounted for 5.8 pounds of sweetener per person for the year.

Colonial Americans enjoyed the inconspicuous nature of their refined sugar, watching it disappear into their tea cups. By the same token, Americans of the twenty-first century enjoy the inconspicuous and noncaloric nature of their chemical sweeteners, which they consume mostly through diet soft drinks. Cyclamates, aspartame, and saccharin are not only sweeter than sugar—thirty, two hundred, and three hundred times, respectively—but are also less expensive to produce. Identified as cancer-causing, cyclamates were permanently banned by the U.S. Food and Drug Administration in 1969, and saccharin was temporarily banned in 1977. Because it is so inexpensive to produce and can be made from domestic crops, high-fructose corn syrup (entering commercial production in 1972) has been substituted for sugar in soft drinks and other foods. Candies, ice cream, cookies, and other confections contain not only refined sugar but also high-fructose corn syrup and dextrose.

Sugar Symbolism

When it first appeared on the market, refined sugar represented a modern sweetener to Americans. White, highly processed, and purely sweet, refined sugar differed in both flavor and substance from more traditional sweeteners such as honey and maple sugar. Imported from faraway places and produced by strangers, sugar was material evidence of both human triumph over nature and the civilizing forces of colonialism over what were perceived to be savage people. Sugar was a status symbol representing refinement, luxury, and gentility. By the end of the twentieth century, noncaloric chemical sweeteners had taken the place of refined sugar, which by that time seemed an old-fashioned substance. At the same time less refined sugars, such as Sugar in the Raw, the equivalent of early muscovado (unrefined) sugar, assumed a cultural cachet representing something more earthy and natural. Foods that incorporated "old-fashioned" sweeteners such as maple sugar, honey, and molasses also experienced a culinary resurgence.

Abstract concepts connected to sugar, such as refinement and sweetness, have become important in American culture. Qualities of sweetness have filtered into the vocabulary. "Home sweet home" was a familiar Victorian phrase linking to sweetness the tranquility and sentimentality of a feminized domestic sphere. Girls were said to be made of "sugar and spice," and women continued to assume appellations, such as "eye candy," that referenced sugar and candies. Male athletes known for particular feats of agility and grace have also been nicknamed "Sugar" and "Sweet." Because sucrose is one of the purest forms of food, the vocabulary of sugar and sweetness lends itself to drug references, including "candy" for cocaine and "sugar" for heroin.

Unlike colonial Americans, people living in the early twenty-first century take sugar for granted. It has shifted from being a prized, rare, expensive luxury to being a necessity (and from some perspectives, a nuisance). Sugar has influenced economic policy and has been an important source of governmental revenue. It has also been the basis for many small businesses, such as confectioners, and larger enterprises, such as sugar refineries. The addition of sugar to the American diet has radically altered what people eat and has made them accustomed to a sweeter diet. Sugar and its attendant associations, such as refinement and sweetness, have bred forms of vernacular expression that rely on a common understanding of and familiarity with its qualities that did not exist in early America.

[*See also* Candy Bars and Candy; Corn Syrup; Homemade Remedies; Sorghum Syrup; Sugar Beets; Sweeteners.]

BIBLIOGRAPHY

Abbott, George C. *Sugar*. London: Routledge, 1990.

Deerr, Noël. *History of Sugar*. London: Chapman and Hall, 1949.

Galloway, J. H. *The Sugar Cane Industry: An Historical Geography from Its Origins to 1914*. Cambridge, U.K.: Cambridge University Press, 1989.

Mancall, Peter. *Deadly Medicine: Indians and Alcohol in Early America*. Ithaca, NY: Cornell University Press, 1995.

Mintz, Sidney W. *Sweetness and Power: The Place of Sugar in Modern History*. New York: Viking Penguin, 1985.

Polopolus, Leo C., and José Alvaraz. *Marketing Sugar and Other Sweeteners*. Amsterdam: Elsevier, 1991.

Vogt, Paul L. *The Sugar Refining Industry in the United States*. Philadelphia: Published for the University of Pennsylvania, 1908.

Woloson, Wendy. *Refined Tastes: Sugar, Consumers, and Confectionery in Nineteenth-Century America*. Baltimore: Johns Hopkins University Press, 2002.

WENDY A. WOLOSON

Sugar Beets

American botanists categorize the sugar beet as a modern cultivar of the ancient group *Beta vulgaris* var. *crassa*, native to western Europe and the Mediterranean. In Europe, where the original research and experimentation with sugar beets took place, horticulturalists distinguish members of the species *B. vulgaris* by the significantly different uses to which the plants are put: *B. vulgaris* var. *esculenta* denotes the common red, golden, or white table beet; *B. vulgaris* var. *rapa* indicates the fodder beet; and *B. vulgaris* var. *altissima* identifies the light beige–colored root resembling a parsnip, which for the past two hundred years has been harvested primarily for processing into sugar.

The demand for luxurious, expensive sugar exploded in the seventeenth century, when Europe fell in love with the hot beverage troika of chocolate, tea, and coffee. Dependence on tropical cane for table sugar left Europe and America subject to the vagaries of trade, transportation, and war. By contrast, the beet thrives in the temperate climates found in much of continental Europe and America. In 1747 the German chemist Andres Marggraf discovered that beets contain small amounts of sucrose, the chemical component of table sugar, which can be extracted in crystalline form. Fifty years later Marggraf's student Franz Karl Achard successfully cultivated *altissima* Silesian beets with a higher sugar content than *esculenta* beets, making extraction potentially feasible. From these sugar-rich beets, he refined the first loaf of beet sugar. The process was improved in France in the early nineteenth century under pressure from the British blockade of French ports during the Napoleonic Wars, although beet sugar remained expensive. During the 1820s French manufacturers further improved the process, bringing down the cost of beet sugar.

The technology quickly spread to the United States, brought by Americans who had seen the process first-hand in France. In the 1830s the Beet Sugar Society of Philadelphia was organized to promote practical knowledge for cultivating and processing sugar beets. Early industry crusaders saw beet sugar as a weapon in the fight to abolish slavery. Didactic literature linked the consumption of cane sugar with support for slavery and urged consumers to purchase beet sugar instead, thereby undermining the cane sugar plantations.

But early efforts to manufacture beet sugar in the United States, in Pennsylvania, Michigan, New York, and Utah, ended poorly. Most notably, Brigham Young's Church of Jesus Christ of Latter-day Saints (the Mormons) toiled for five years to establish a beet sugar industry in Utah, but never produced palatable sugar because of technical gaffes and poor growing conditions around Great Salt Lake.

California was home to the first successful U.S. sugar beet industry in the 1870s, with factories in Alvarado and Watsonville. Throughout the country others followed suit, buoyed by the Tariff Act of 1890, which paid a bounty to domestic beet sugar producers. In 1891 a plant financed and operated largely by the Mormons opened in Lehi, Utah. This time, with improved technology, they were successful and soon built additional factories in Utah. They attracted the attention of New York's cane sugar magnate Henry Havemeyer, who purchased a controlling interest in 1902. He financed additional factories, which matured into the Utah-Idaho Sugar Company. After Havemeyer was bloodied in battles involving the new antitrust laws, the Mormons repurchased Havemeyer's interest, just in time to enjoy the escalating sugar prices brought about by World War I.

The boom was short-lived. The market collapsed in 1921, the insatiable beet leafhopper devoured crops, and the Great Depression continued the industry's economic woes. By World War II increasing mechanization became

Sugar Beet Workers. Mexican sugar beet workers near Fisher, Minnesota, 1937. *Prints and Photographs Division, Library of Congress*

the only solution to efficient beet cultivation. Cooperative postwar ventures through the United States Sugar Beet Association, West Coast Beet Seed Company, Western Seed Production Corporation, and Beet Sugar Development Foundation all continue to assist modern growers and refiners, who rank second to cane growers in supplying sugar both in America and worldwide. Federal subsidies and price supports intervened throughout the twentieth century to protect the industry.

Sugar beets are grown primarily in western and midwestern states, with a crop valued in excess of $1 billion annually. Significantly, Utah has had no sugar beet industry since the 1980s, although in 2002 its state legislature named the sugar beet Utah's historic state vegetable. The concentrated sweetness of the sugar beet (a good harvest can reach up to 20 percent sugar) prevented its acceptance as a table vegetable in the eighteenth and nineteenth centuries. Amelia Simmons's *American Cookery* (1796) critiques the "white" beet that "has a sickish sweetness, which is disliked by many." More recently, it has been grown as a specialty vegetable by gardeners whose sweet tooth extends throughout the meal.

[*See also* Sugar.]

BIBLIOGRAPHY

Arrington, Leonard J. *Beet Sugar in the West: A History of the Utah-Idaho Sugar Company, 1891–1966.* Seattle: University of Washington Press, 1966.

Arrington, Leonard J. *Great Basin Kingdom: An Economic History of the Latter-day Saints, 1830–1900.* Salt Lake City: University of Utah Press, 1993. First published 1958.

Church, Edward. *Notice on the Beet Sugar, Containing First, a Description of the Culture and Preservation of the Plant. Second, an Explanation of the Process of Extracting Its Sugar. Preceded by a Few Remarks on the Origin and Present State of the Indigenous Sugar Manufactories of France. Translated from the Works of Dubrunfaut, De Domballe, and Others.* 2d ed. Northampton, MA: J. H. Butler, 1837.

Clauson, Annette L., and Frederic L. Hoff. *Structural and Financial Characteristics of U.S. Sugar Beet Farms.* Washington, DC: U.S. Department of Agriculture, Economic Research Service, 1988.

Myrick, Herbert. *The American Sugar Industry.* New York: Orange Judd Company, 1899.

Schmalz, Charles L. "The Failure of Utah's First Sugar Factory." *Utah Historical Quarterly* 56, no. 1 (Winter 1988): 36–53.

CATHY K. KAUFMAN

Sunflowers

Agricultural historians cannot agree on where the sunflower, *Helianthus annuus*, originated: Peru, Central America, and what is now the southwestern United States are all candidates. Everyone agrees, however, that the sunflower spread through the New World in pre-Columbian times, reaching what is now the eastern United States before the Spanish landed. It was one of two food plants (the other being its botanical cousin, the Jerusalem artichoke) domesticated by Native Americans in central North America between 3000 and 900 B.C.E.

Indigenes extracted oil by crushing the seeds, boiling them, and skimming off the separated oil; the leftover seed mash formed a high protein cake. Native Americans chewed the stems like gum and cooked the petioles, the immature seed receptacles. Seeds made purple and black dyestuffs, and the brilliant golden petals were (and still are) salad fodder. Thomas Hariot's *A Brief and True Report of the New Found Land of Virginia* (1588) described broths and "breads" made from seeds, as well as careful interplanting techniques with maize, beans, and squashes, that resulted in enormous yields.

Spanish conquistadores had exported sunflowers to Europe as an ornamental by 1510; the plant eventually reached its greatest prominence as the major source of food oil in Russia and Eastern Europe. Post-Columbian Americans made comparatively little use of the sunflower, although the 1881 *Household Cyclopedia of General Information* encouraged copying the Native American interplanting techniques to stimulate other crops; the sunflowers themselves were demoted to use as animal fodder and suggested for home-based oil extraction as a substitute for olive oil.

The sunflower's nutritional profile, high in protein, mono- and polyunsaturated fats, fiber, and certain vitamins and minerals, made it a darling of health food enthusiasts in the later twentieth century. At the same time, a relatively small domestic oil industry had started, and sunflower seeds were marketed as a healthy snack and ground into "sunbutter," competing with peanut butter. The brightly named "sunchoke," originally a cross of the sunflower and the Jerusalem artichoke, was commercially unsuccessful; the name has cheerily marketed the Jerusalem artichoke since the late twentieth century.

[*See also* Artichokes; Fats and Oils; Flowers, Edible; Health Food.]

BIBLIOGRAPHY

Couplan, François. *The Encyclopedia of Edible Plants of North America: Nature's Great Feast.* New Canaan, CT: Keats, 1998.
Facciola, Stephen. *Cornucopia II: A Source Book of Edible Plants.* Vista, CA: Kampong, 1998.
Hedrick, Ulysses Prentiss. *A History of Horticulture in America to 1860.* New York: Oxford University Press, 1950.
Heiser, Charles B., Jr. *Seeds to Civilization: The Story of Food.* New ed. Cambridge, MA: Harvard University Press, 1990.
National Sunflower Association. http://www.sunflowernsa.com.

CATHY K. KAUFMAN

Supawn

Supawn was a Native American porridge made of cornmeal and water and introduced to European colonists very early. Transliterated by different Europeans in an age when spelling was inconsistent, the name of the dish appeared variably in print as "suppawn," "sepawn," "sipawn," "sepan," "supon," "sepon," "suppaen," "supporne," and "soupaan." Settlers adopted supawn almost universally as a staple, because corn agriculture and milling were particularly reliable, and culinary preparation was simple. Among newcomers and those on the frontier, supawn often represented survival.

Europeans varied New World versions of the dish by boiling cornmeal in milk and adding butter, cream, or molasses (depending on economic station) and serving it either hot or cold. There were a few ethnic variations. The English ate cornmeal in the tradition of mush and hasty pudding. The Dutch, who were partial to sour flavors, drowned cornmeal in buttermilk. Supawn was prepared for any meal of the day but was a common supper dish. The eighteenth-century Old Albany Dutch Church customarily rang what was called the "suppawn bell," a signal for supper and bed.

Supawn maintained its central place in changing American cuisine but gradually gave way to new fashions.

Patriotic centennial celebrations remembered its original names and role in American history. The dish continues to appear on Native American tables and at powwows.

[*See also* Corn; Dutch Influences on American Food; Native American Foods.]

BIBLIOGRAPHY

Craigie, William A., and James R. Hulbert, eds. *A Dictonary of American English on Historical Principles Compiled at the University of Chicago,* 4 vols. Chicago, 1938–1944.
Lossing, Benson J. *The Hudson from the Wilderness to the Sea.* New York, 1866.
Oxford English Dictionary, Compact Edition, 2 vols. New York: Oxford University Press, 1971.
Parker, A. C. *Iroquois Uses of Maize and Other Food Plants.* Albany: University of the State of New York, 1910. Reprint, Ohsweken, Ontario: Iroqrafts, 1983.

JOHN REES

Supermarkets, *see Grocery Stores*

Supper, *see Meal Patterns*

Swanson

Swanson, the company whose name is synonymous with TV dinners, began as Jerpe Commission Company, a wholesale grocery firm, in 1899 in Omaha, Nebraska. The founders, Carl A. Swanson, Frank D. Ellison, and John P. Jerpe, specialized in the sale of poultry, eggs, and butter. In 1945 the company, which since 1928 had been owned solely by Swanson, changed its name to Swanson and Sons and began producing a line of canned and frozen chicken and turkey products.

When they took over the business in the early 1950s, Swanson's sons realized that postwar America had changed. The most important difference was that record numbers of women were working outside the home. The brothers, seeing an opportunity, in 1951 began selling easy-to-prepare frozen beef, chicken, and turkey potpies. Their efforts met with instant success.

By 1952, television sets, with their eight-inch, black-and-white screens, were becoming the preferred type of home entertainment, and the Swanson brothers were determined to capitalize on this phenomenon. Inspiration came the next year in the form of 520,000 pounds of surplus post-Thanksgiving turkey, which the company had no room to warehouse. Gerald Thomas, a Swanson executive, had the idea for a frozen prepared meal. He presented the idea, along with an initial sketch of an aluminum tray with three compartments, to the Swanson brothers. In December 1953, Swanson introduced on television the first TV dinner, which had been created by Betty Cronin, director of product development. The ninety-eight-cent dinner, which featured turkey with cornbread stuffing and gravy, sweet potatoes, and peas, created a new food category. The decision to call the meals "TV dinners" was the result of research showing that people were already eating Swanson potpies in front of the television. Fried chicken dinners were introduced in 1955 and were followed soon after by Salisbury steak. Almost as soon as the products were launched, the company was blamed for ruining the family dinner, because the variety allowed each member to reach for a different meal.

Campbell Soup Company acquired Swanson in 1955. Under the Campbell auspices, Swanson grew rapidly. Dessert was added to meals in 1960; a breakfast line was launched in 1969; Hungry-Man dinners debuted in 1973 in a television commercial featuring the athlete Mean Joe Green; the entire line was reworked to accommodate microwave cooking in 1986; Fun Feast dinners intended for children were introduced in 1991; and potato-topped potpies entered the market in 1999.

By the end of the 1990s, Campbell had shifted its focus away from frozen foods and moved the Swanson brand to the newly formed Vlasic Foods International, which eventually went bankrupt. In 2001 Pinnacle Foods Corporation bought the Vlasic and Swanson brands out of bankruptcy.

Regardless of ownership, the Swanson TV dinner is such a beloved icon of American food that its aluminum tray was inducted into the Smithsonian Institution—placed alongside the leather jacket worn by Henry Winkler as Fonzie in the popular situation comedy *Happy Days*. Swanson even received a star on the Hollywood Walk of Fame.

[*See also* Campbell Soup Company; Frozen Food; Turkey.]

BIBLIOGRAPHY

Swanson. http://www.swansonmeals.com. The company website outlines the history of Swanson and its products as well as the company's impact on the American food industry.

Trager, James. *The Food Chronology: A Food Lover's Compendium of Events and Anecdotes, From Prehistory to the Present*. New York: Henry Holt, 1995.

DAVID LEITE

Sweeteners

Sweeteners are plant-derived materials used through the ages to mask bitterness in foods, as well as to preserve, lend texture to, develop the flavor and color of, and decorate them. Sweeteners—pivotal to the economy and cultural histories of various civilizations—have evolved from being a precious luxury to a commodity of ubiquitous necessity. Initially used sparingly to enhance the palatability of foods, sweeteners have significantly influenced food manufacture and the way people select and consume foods in the twenty-first century. Urbanization and income growth has further contributed to the pronounced shift in the human diet toward increased consumption of sweeteners and processed foods and away from naturally occurring fruits and vegetables and high-fiber foods.

Most sweeteners owe their sweet taste to simple carbohydrates called sugars. Sugars, produced in plants during photosynthesis, serve as the standard currency of chemically stored energy for all living animals and plants. Of the different kinds existing in nature sucrose, fructose, and glucose are those principally used to sweeten foods. Sucrose, also known as common sugar or table sugar, is found in sugarcane and sugar beets and is composed of a molecule each of glucose and fructose. Glucose and fructose occur naturally in fruits and vegetables and are the major components of honey.

Sweeteners may be classified as caloric, noncaloric, natural, and artificial. Sugar, corn syrups, honey, molasses, and maple syrup are caloric sweeteners, which upon digestion yield four calories per gram. In addition to sweetening, they contribute or enhance various qualities and attributes of foods: They help preserve jams and jellies. They enhance flavor in various processed foods, such as meats and juices. They provide the basis for fermentation and flavor in the production of breads, wines, liquors, and pickles. They depress the freezing point of frozen foods, such as ice creams. And they contribute to the viscosity of beverages. Although caloric sweeteners occur in nature, a majority of them are consumed in forms derived from processing starch and sugar compounds.

Noncaloric sweeteners include substances—such as saccharin, cyclamate (not on the market since 1970), acesulphame-K, aspartame, sorbitol, mannitol, and xylitol—which gained importance as economical and healthy alternatives to sugar in processed foods because they provide sweet taste without contributing any calories. These are generally chemically processed materials and are therefore known as artificial sweeteners.

Sweeteners in History

Early human beings were familiar with the concept of sweetness from fruits and honey. The description of sugarcane, syrup, and foods sweetened with sugarcane in the Sanskrit epic of the *Ramayana* (ca. 1200 B.C.E.) is one of the earliest documented references to sweeteners. The technology of making sugar by squeezing sugarcane and boiling the juice down into crystals for later use was developed in India around 500 B.C.E. Consequently, sugar came to be known as Indian salt.

Sugarcane and the technique for extracting sweeteners were carried westward from India to Persia, where the Persians established sugarcane cultivation and sugar production in the Euphrates-Tigris valley around the sixth century C.E. The Arabs who conquered Persia around 640 C.E. introduced the crop to northern Africa, Syria, and Spain. Sugar was introduced to Christian Europe during the twelfth-century Crusades to the Holy Land. Europeans used sugar and honey in the same manner as pepper, ginger, and other exotic imports, both as flavoring and as medicine. Apothecaries composed "confections" (Latin *conficere*, to put together) with sugar as the predominant ingredient or as an additive to mask the taste of other ingredients in the preparation.

Christopher Columbus may have introduced sugarcane to the West Indies in 1493. The sweetener industry became a major force behind the expansion of slavery and was also responsible for its introduction into the colonies. In the late eighteenth century, increased awareness of the horrors of slavery spawned abolition movements, and many abolitionists and the merchants who served them boycotted everything but East Indian sugar.

The native peoples of North America had used honey and maple tree sap to sweeten their foods. The immigrants taught them to concentrate sap into syrup and introduced a kind of molasses. The early immigrants used these and sugar-based molasses for baked goods, baked beans, meats, such as pork and ham, and even for the production of rum. Molasses remained an important

sweetener until sugar prices plummeted after World War I making sugar more economical to use.

One of the greatest innovations in the food industry was the development of the various types of corn syrups, or maltodextrins, and high-fructose corn syrup derived from cornstarch. The result was a new category of major commercial products that significantly influenced food manufacturing practices and Americans' food consumption pattern. It all began in 1747 with the Prussian chemist Andreas Marggraf's demonstration of sugar production from the juice of sugar beets (*Beta vulgaris*) and the Frenchman Benjamin Delessert's commercialization of the technology into sugar-beet factories. In 1811, Konstantin Kirchhof laid the foundations of sweetener production using acids, enzymes, and potato starch.

Later, enzyme technologies advanced in ways that made corn syrup production economical. Maltodextrin and dextrose syrups became popular. The next significant development involved enzymes, which enabled the production of fructose from dextrose syrups. Fructose-based syrups of varying fructose levels became increasingly popular because corn crops, the raw material source, were more predictable than sugarcane or sugar beets. These syrups were significantly cheaper, since fructose is sweeter than sucrose and maltose. By the late 1960s, HFCS or high fructose corn syrup, was produced commercially and economically, making it the sweetener of choice for the food industry in the United States. Advances in sweetener technology to tailor the sweetness and physical properties of corn syrups economically have made them even more popular in the confectionery, baking, and beverage industries.

Sweeteners and Health

When it became clear that consuming large amounts of sugar was associated with various health issues, such as dental caries, diabetes, and obesity, science provided a solution in the form of nonsugar and noncaloric sweeteners. Saccharin, discovered accidentally in 1879, was the first noncaloric sweetener. The German chemist Constantin Fahlberg happened to taste material being synthesized as a new food preservative and discovered its intense sweetness. He named the compound "saccharin" (*saccharum*, Latin for sugar) and developed a process for manufacturing the compound in bulk.

Saccharin consumption increased dramatically during the two world wars when sugar became scarce. Saccharin was provided to the troops in Europe in little pink packets, which continued to be its characteristic packaging

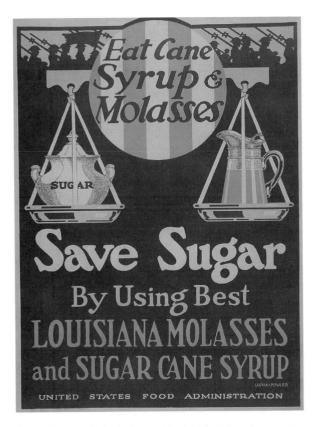

Save Sugar. United States Food Administration poster, 1918. *Prints and Photographs Division, Library of Congress*

into the early 2000s. Research studies in 1960 suggested that saccharin caused cancer in rats and compelled the Food and Drug Administration (FDA) to ban it. However, Congress placed a moratorium on the ban in order to allow for more research on saccharin's safety. The moratorium was extended seven times because of continued consumer demand. While numerous studies clearly show that saccharin, in the dosages consumed, does not cause cancer in humans, labels on products with saccharin must carry a statement saying that saccharin has caused cancer in laboratory animals.

In 1937 Ludwig Audrieth and Michael Sveda, chemists at the University of Illinois, discovered another noncaloric sweetener and called it cyclamate. For many years, cyclamate was subjected to scientific investigations. But even when declared safe in the mid-1950s, it never gained popularity in the United States.

Aspartame, discovered in 1965 by the scientist James Schlatter at G. D. Searle and Company, was the next major artificial sweetener to be developed. The intensely sweet compound was serendipitously found during research on drugs to treat ulcers. Once the safety of aspartame was established, the FDA approved its use in foods and beverages that do not undergo heating. Acesulfame potassium (acesulfame-K), another noncaloric sweetener, although discovered at the same time as aspartame, was approved for use in the United States by the FDA about twenty years later.

A commercial class of sweeteners called polyols, or sugar alcohols, emerged in the early 2000s. Polyols, such as erythritol, sorbitol, maltitol, isomalt, lactitol, and xylitol, have gained popularity because they contribute fewer calories than sugars, are diabetic-friendly, and do not contribute to dental caries. Polyols are present in pears, melons, grapes, and other fruits, as well as in mushrooms and fermentation-derived foods like wine, soy sauce, and cheese, and have been part of the human diet for thousands of years.

Several other new commercial sweeteners are emerging, including plant-derived materials such as stevia, stevioside, agave syrup, Lo Han, mogroside, glycyrrhizin, dihydrochalcones, and thaumatin. These range in sweetness from thirty to three thousand times that of sucrose and have been known to humans since prehistoric times. They are being explored for commercial viability in the early 2000s. Sucralose, an artificial noncaloric sweetener developed in 1976 from sucrose, has rapidly gained acceptance as the noncaloric sweetener of choice in the United States.

Although noncaloric sweeteners were introduced only in the twentieth century, they have gained importance because of their value for those attempting to decrease caloric intake and mitigate other health-related issues, such as diabetes and obesity. But each of the major artificial and noncaloric sweeteners has at least one problem. Saccharin and acesulfame might be carcinogens. Aspartame breaks down at high temperatures and cannot be used by individuals with phenylketonuria (inability to digest phenylketones). Some polyols have laxative side effects limiting the threshold of consumption. So the quest continues for a noncaloric, diabetic-friendly, noncarcinogenic, thermally stable, and easily produced, inexpensive sweetener.

[*See also* Honey; Karo Syrup; Maple Syrup; Molasses; Sorghum Syrup; Sugar; Sugar Beets.]

BIBLIOGRAPHY

Mintz, Sidney W. *Sweetness and Power: The Place of Sugar in Modern History.* New York: Viking Penguin, 1985.

Sokolov, Raymond. *Why We Eat What We Eat.* New York: Summit, 1991.

Toussant-Samat, Maguelonne. *History of Food.* Translated by Anthea Bell, 552–563. New York: Barnes and Noble, 1998.

Trager, James. *The Food Chronology.* New York: Holt, 1995.

KANTHA SHELKE

Sweet Potatoes

The sweet potato (*Ipomoea batatas*) is a root that comes in a variety of shapes, sizes, and colors. Its flavor is largely based on starch and sugar. The plant originated in the tropical areas of Central America and northwestern South America. The earliest archaeological evidence of the sweet potato, however, was found in Peru and dates to 2000 B.C.E. Domestication may have occurred as early as 8000 B.C.E.

In pre-Columbian times sweet potatoes were disseminated throughout much of South America, Central America, and the Caribbean. Spanish explorers in the Caribbean ran across them and called them by the Taino name, *batatas*. The Spanish shipped sweet potatoes back to Europe, where they became a sensation. Sweet potatoes were among the earliest New World foods adopted in Europe. At approximately the same time as the Spanish exploration, Portuguese explorers encountered sweet potatoes in Brazil and transported them to Africa, where they were grown to provision Portuguese ships headed to and from Asia and slave ships headed to the New World. A linguistic imbroglio arose when the Spanish encountered the white potato (*Solanum tuberosa*) in South America in 1529. They called the white potato "batata" and later "patata," which led to confusion between white potato and sweet potato. The shipping activity between South America and Africa and Europe led to confusion between the sweet potato and the yam (*Dioscorea*), another large tuberous root of which many varieties were native to tropical regions of the Old World. Varieties of sweet potatoes and yams are similar in appearance, and sweet potatoes in the United States are frequently misidentified as yams.

Although sweet potatoes were not cultivated in England as a commercial crop, the British esteemed them in the sixteenth and seventeenth centuries. Sweet potatoes were imported from Spain and Portugal, and they became popular, in large part owing to their purported aphrodisiacal qualities, as noted by Shakespeare in *The Merry Wives of Windsor*. In America, sweet potatoes were grown extensively in Virginia, Georgia, and the Carolinas, but they were a luxury in the North before 1830.

From a culinary standpoint, sweet potatoes are extremely versatile. They can be boiled, broiled, baked, roasted, fried, stewed, and mashed. The orange and yellow varieties can be eaten raw, for example by being grated into a salad. Sweet potatoes have been used as an ingredient in pie, bread, and pudding. They can be juiced and made into a drink and can be fermented for use as an alcoholic beverage. In the United States, sweet potatoes are served with a variety of foods, and they are favorites at Thanksgiving.

Sweet potatoes are highly nutritious, containing protein, fiber, vitamins A and C, calcium, folic acid, magnesium, and potassium. They are one of the most important root tubers in the world, and they are the sixth principal food crop worldwide. Approximately 85 percent of the world's sweet potato crop is grown in China. In the United States, North Carolina, Louisiana, and California produce three-fourths of the nation's sweet potato crop.

[*See also* Caribbean Influences on American Food; Potatoes; Thanksgiving.]

BIBLIOGRAPHY

Martin, Franklin W., Ruth M. Ruberte, and Jose L. Herrera. *The Sweet Potato Cookbook*. North Fort Myers, FL: Educational Concerns for Hunger Organization, 1989.

Talmadge, Lyniece North. *The Sweet Potato Cookbook*. Nashville, TN: Cumberland House, 1998.

Woolfe, Jennifer A. *Sweet Potato: An Untapped Food Resource*. Cambridge, U.K: Cambridge University Press, 1992.

ANDREW F. SMITH

Sweet Potatoes. Harvesting sweet potatoes at Claflin University, Orangeburg, South Carolina, ca. 1899. *Prints and Photographs Division, Library of Congress*

Swift, Gustavus Franklin

Gustavus Franklin Swift (1839–1903) was the eponymous founder of one of America's largest and best-known

Swift Plant. Swift packing plant, Chicago. *Culinary Archives & Museum at Johnson & Wales University, Providence, R.I.*

meat-processing companies. He is credited with introducing refrigeration to food transportation networks, but his greater importance lay in the organizational concepts and methods he created: Swift was a father of America's modern food-processing and distribution systems.

Born and reared on hardscrabble Cape Cod, Massachusetts, and with little formal education, Swift went to work as a butcher's apprentice at age fourteen. Not long after, he began his own business, buying cattle, butchering them, and selling the meat door to door. Over the next twenty years, he built a successful wholesale business with James A. Hathaway, and operated a modern market in Clinton, Massachusetts. The lessons of frugality and resource management that he learned in these years were the foundations for his future role as America's "dressed beef king."

Swift's main obsession was expansion of business opportunities. Seeing that Chicago had become the meat-processing center of the nation, he moved to the city in 1875. There he hit upon the formula that would change the production of fresh meats. Companies such as Armour and Morris canned and preserved meats, but the nation was hungry for steaks and roasts. At the time, fresh beef was shipped on the hoof via rail to the great eastern markets. Swift reasoned that since only 60 percent of the animal would become food, he would slaughter and process meat in Chicago and ship only the high-profit carcasses. The extra animal parts became a profit center for the company, hence his phrase, "now we used all of the hog except his grunt."

To use his facilities economically, Swift had to ship meat year-round and keep it at a stable temperature. During the previous decade, refrigeration systems had been introduced to market facilities and experimentally used on a railcar by Chicago packer G. H. Hammond in 1874. After tinkering with several devices, Swift had his engineer friend Andrew J. Chase build the first successful refrigerated car using ice blocks (mechanical refrigeration came later). Swift and company undersold all the eastern competition, made huge profits, and became the country's leading beef producer by the later 1880s. He then set up processing facilities in Kansas City and Saint Joseph, Missouri, to be even closer to his raw ingredients. Later he turned to mutton and then pork, outstripping all his competition.

G. F. Swift's innovations appeared at exactly the same time that new machines were making mass production of meat, and other foods, possible. Perhaps anticipating Frederick W. Taylor's time and motion studies, Swift developed an efficient "disassembly" line for food animals, with each station along it devoted to one task, such as debristling hogs. Hooked to an overhead traveling belt, the carcasses were processed and fed directly into the waiting boxcars for transportation. Swift also established separate plants for each element of the company—from lard and oleomargarine manufacture to marketing. Each division reported to a central office whose watchword was "efficiency." Swift's organization was the model of the modern factory system. It was this system that Henry Ford observed when visiting Chicago's meat plants and then applied to the manufacture of automobiles.

[*See also* Armour, Philip Danforth; Butchering; Ice; Iceboxes; Meat; Sinclair, Upton; Transportation of Food.]

BIBLIOGRAPHY

Swift, Louis F., in collaboration with Arthur Van Vlissingen Jr. *The Yankee of the Yards; the Biography of Gustavus Franklin Swift.* Chicago: A. W. Shaw, 1927.

Wade, Louise Carroll. *Chicago's Pride: The Stockyards, Packingtown, and Environs in the Nineteenth Century.* Urbana: University of Illinois Press, 1987.

BRUCE KRAIG

Switchel

Switchel (also called *haymaker's switchel*, *harvest drink*, *haymaker's drink*, and *ginger water*) is a beverage usually made with molasses, water, vinegar, and spices (most often ginger) and occasionally with rum. Switchel, thought to be of New England origin, was drunk by field workers to quench their thirst during harvest time and is frequently mentioned in nineteenth-century accounts of whaling expeditions and merchant ship voyages.

Although few recipes for switchel appear in nine-teenth-century cookbooks, L. G. Abell included the following recipe in *The Skilful Housewife's Book* (1852):

Harvest Drink—Mix with five gallons of good water, half a gallon of molasses, one quart of vinegar, and two ounces of powdered ginger. This will make not only a very pleasant beverage, but one highly invigorating and healthful.

The addition of ginger was thought to have prevented stomach cramps. Recipes for similar refreshing beverages may appear in cookbooks under the name of raspberry (or other fruit) vinegar or raspberry "shrub." The following modern adaptation of the period recipe calls for similar ingredients:

One tablespoon of vinegar (either cider vinegar or raspberry wine vinegar but not distilled white vinegar); one tablespoon of one of the following sweeteners: honey, molasses, maple syrup, or brown or white sugar; and one cup of cool water. Mix thoroughly. Add one-eighth teaspoon of powdered ginger to taste if raspberry vinegar is not used. Do not use a metal container to mix or store the switchel.

[*See also* Cider; Ginger Ale; Kvass; Punch; Ratafia; Syllabub.]

BIBLIOGRAPHY

Abell, Mrs. L. G. *The Skillful Housewife's Book*. New York: C. M. Saxon, 1852.
Lanzerotti, B. *Parting Glass: An American Book of Drink*. Wheaton, IL: Twin Willows Publishers, 1998.

VIRGINIA MESCHER

Syllabub

Syllabub was a popular drink in England from the sixteenth until the mid-nineteenth century. In America, the popularity peaked in the eighteenth century, when syllabub was a fashionable evening beverage or dessert served at card parties, ball suppers, and public entertainments. Syllabub was prepared by beating warm milk with sweetened, spiced wine, cider, or ale. The froth that formed was set aside to drain. The resulting clear liquid was poured into glasses, and the froth was placed on top. For dramatic effect, a cow might have been milked into the bowl of sweetened alcohol so that the mixture would froth. When the concoction was left to sit for several hours, a honeycombed curd formed on top. Sometimes a layer of thick fresh cream was poured over the curd, providing a rich drink for country parties and festivals. A solid dessert syllabub was made by reducing the ratio of alcohol and sugar to cream and adding beaten egg white or gelatin. The dessert was flavored with citrus or ginger and eaten with a spoon. The first cookbook to be printed in America (*The Compleat Housewife*, 1727) contained a recipe for everlasting syllabubs that would remain in perfect condition for nine or ten days, although they were at their best after three or four. Syllabub has retained seasonal popularity as an alternative to eggnog, especially in parts of the South, where bourbon, rum, or brandy is substituted for wine or ale. Colonial Williamsburg sells packaged syllabub mix.

[*See also* Cider; Desserts; Eggnog; Kvass; Punch; Ratafia; Switchel.]

BIBLIOGRAPHY

Carson, Jane. *Colonial Virginia Cookery: Procedures, Equipment and Ingredients in Colonial Cooking*. Williamsburg, VA: Colonial Williamsburg Foundation, 1985.
David, Elizabeth. *An Omelette and a Glass of Wine*. New York: Lyons and Burford, 1997. The original edition was published in 1984. Includes a chapter on syllabubs and fruit fools.

VIRGINIA SCOTT JENKINS

Szathmary, Louis

Louis Szathmary (1919–1996) was once referred to as "a man for all seasonings" (Johnson & Wales). This Hungarian-born chef brought much flavor and color to America's culinary legacy. A pioneer in frozen food technology, Szathmary helped elevate the official status of all U.S. chefs; influenced American fine-dining standards; became one of the first U.S. "celebrity chefs"; and established one of the premier culinary archives in the United States.

Born on a cattle car en route from Transylvania to Budapest as his parents fled the onslaught of World War I, Szathmary never stopped moving, at least not when it came to accomplishments. He earned a master's degree in journalism and a doctorate in psychology from the University of Budapest and then was drafted into the Hungarian Army during World War II and became an officer. Szathmary immigrated to the United States in 1951.

At the time he spoke no English and had only $1.10 in his pocket.

Szathmary took a job as a short-order cook, learned, and kept moving up, soon catering to the rich and famous on the East Coast. Through his catering company, Szathmary began developing numerous dishes for companies pioneering the field of frozen prepared entrees. In 1959 Szathmary moved to Chicago to work for Armour and Company, where he developed a number of frozen food lines for Armour and for many other companies, including Stouffer. The frozen spinach souffle Szathmary created for Stouffer became a classic. Szathmary also became increasingly involved in the tremendous changes taking place in food-service technology in the 1950s, such as freeze-drying and boil-in bags. Some of the food the astronauts took into space had Szathmary's stamp on it through his work with the U.S. National Aeronautics and Space Administration (NASA).

Szathmary began to see his real niche as a restaurateur. In 1963 with his wife and partner, Sadako Tanino, Szathmary opened The Bakery on the near north side of Chicago. In the first year, more than two hundred articles were written about The Bakery. Many restaurant critics across the nation gave rave reviews. Of those who did not, Szathmary observed, "They don't know shiitake from shinola." (Warner, "Remembering Chef Louis"). Guests came from Tokyo, Sydney, New York, and Montreal. Szathmary hosted almost every celebrity who visited Chicago. The chef Charlie Trotter celebrated his high school prom night at The Bakery. Trotter was so overcome by the sight of Szathmary's grand entrance that he knew at that moment, he, too, would be a chef one day. "It was a decisive moment for me," Trotter recalled (Warner, "Remembering Chef Louis").

When Szathmary opened The Bakery, the standard for fine dining in Chicago was typically a meal of shrimp cocktail, iceberg lettuce with thousand island dressing, prime rib of beef, asparagus with hollandaise sauce, and baked Alaska. Szathmary, however, served such "exotic" fare as grated celery root salad, *paprikás csirke* (also called chicken *paprikash*) drizzled with sour cream, and his signature dish, beef Wellington with Cumberland sauce. Desserts included mocha pecan torte laced with rum and filled with apricot preserves and enrobed in butter-rich icing and eclairs puffed with banana and whipped cream filling and anointed with bourbon-scented chocolate sauce. Szathmary called his cuisine Continental with American undertones and soon had diners waiting weeks for reservations.

It mattered little to the public that the 117-seat restaurant was in an old and rickety building in a then-seedy neighborhood, that Szathmary had filled his three dining rooms with secondhand silverware and furniture he described as "early restaurant and late Salvation Army" (Warner, "Remembering Chef Louis"), or that some of the food was being prepared in full view on a table in one of the dining rooms because the kitchen was not large enough. All diners saw were the cheery red-and-white candy-striped awning outside, the clean white tablecloths, the spotless wooden floors, and Szathmary's family greeting them and seating them.

The show-stopper at The Bakery was the entrance of Chef Louis. All eyes turned to the very large mustachioed figure who would suddenly stride through the swinging kitchen door. Looking like Santa Claus with a towering chef's toque, Szathmary would visit each table, becoming one of the first chefs in America to "work" the dining room of his restaurant and interact with customers. "I treat everyone like a king I know," he said (Warner, "Remembering Chef Louis"). Szathmary was one of the first chef food personalities, "long before Alice Waters and Wolfgang Puck," wrote former *Chicago Sun-Times* food editor Bev Bennett in her obituary of Chef Louis. "His real contribution was in developing the chef as a cult figure," Bennett continued.

Szathmary wrote seven cookbooks. His first one, *The Chef's Secret* (1972), made the *Time* magazine best seller list for nonfiction. Szathmary made guest appearances on more than 150 network and local television shows across the United States and made more than one thousand appearances on radio shows. Szathmary also appeared in television commercials and magazine advertisements for Sears, Lipton Tea, Christian Dior, and Jim Beam. For more than ten years he wrote a food column for the *Chicago Sun-Times*. The "Chef Louis" column he wrote for a wire service appeared in more than one hundred newspapers. Szathmary wrote more than five hundred articles on food service for scientific and educational journals. He kept three secretaries busy full time answering fans' cooking questions and coordinating his touring schedule. Szathmary lectured at hotel schools throughout the United States. Although he downplayed his involvement in the evolution of the profession of chef, Szathmary was one of several industry figures who in the late 1970s successfully petitioned the U.S. Department of Labor to elevate "executive chef" in the *Dictionary of Occupational Titles* from the services category to the professional, technical, and managerial occupations category. No longer would executive chefs be listed with maids and butlers.

Szathmary kept thirty-one apartment rooms upstairs from The Bakery filled with his historical and eclectic collection of food books. When he retired in 1989, Szathmary donated thirty thousand of the books to establish the Culinary Archives and Museum at Johnson and Wales University in Providence, Rhode Island. The collection also included 400,000 culinary items, including a baker's ring found on a skeleton in the ruins of Pompeii and presidential papers about entertaining in the White House. Szathmary was named chef laureate at the university and commuted there regularly until his death at age seventy-seven. The museum is referred to as the "Smithsonian" of food archives.

[*See also* Celebrity Chefs; Freeze-Drying; Frozen Food; Johnson and Wales; Restaurant Critics and Food Columnists; Restaurants; Space Food; Trotter, Charlie.]

BIBLIOGRAPHY

Clarke, Paul. "Third Millennium Chefs: A Conversation with Chef Louis Szathmary." *Chef*, January 1996.
Warner, Scott. "Remembering Chef Louis." *Chicago Sun-Times*, October 11, 1997.

SCOTT WARNER

Taco Bell

During the early 1950s, few Americans outside California and the Southwest knew what a taco was. In the early twenty-first century Mexican American food is one of America's fastest-growing cuisines. Although there are many reasons for this change, one was the Taco Bell fast food chain launched by Glenn Bell.

Bell operated a one-man hamburger and hot dog stand in San Bernardino, California, but he liked eating Mexican take-out food. Taco stands dotted the southern California landscape, but none offered fast food. Bell developed ways to improve the efficiency of preparing Mexican food. At the time, taco shells were made by frying soft tortillas for a few minutes. Bell invented a prefabricated hard taco shell, which did not have to be fried, thus saving time on each order. Bell also developed procedures for accelerating service.

Bell decided to test his new ideas. Bell opened a Taco Tia restaurant in 1954 in San Bernardino, California, the same year and the same city in which Richard and Maurice McDonald opened their revolutionary fast food establishment. Like the McDonald brothers, Bell quickly opened more restaurants in the surrounding area. Bell sold his interest in Taco Tia, and with new partners launched another chain, El Taco. The first outlet was opened in 1958 in Long Beach, California.

In 1962 Bell sold his share in El Taco to his partners and opened the first Taco Bell, in Downey, California. The menu consisted mainly of tacos and burritos plus beverages. This small outlet was quickly followed by eight stores in the Long Beach, Paramount, and Los Angeles areas. These establishments generated fifty thousand dollars per year, and Bell decided to franchise the operation. The resulting Taco Bell chain used the symbol of a sleeping Mexican sitting under a sombrero, and the buildings had a California mission style.

By 1978 Taco Bell had 868 restaurants, which specialized in selling tacos, burritos, and a few other food items. Glen Bell sold the company to PepsiCo, and management was placed in the hands of John Martin, who had worked for several fast food companies. Martin made Taco Bell's Mexican-style dishes popular throughout the United States by means of heavy discounting and value meals, which combined foods and drinks for cost savings. By 1980, Taco Bell had 1,333 outlets and was rapidly expanding. One reason for the expansion was the continuing introduction of new products, such as fajitas, wraps, gorditas, and chalupas.

Taco Bell has had both success and failure in its promotional efforts. The original symbol was a sleepy Mexican. This symbol was thought to be a negative stereotype, and it was immediately replaced by a mission bell when PepsiCo took over. On the success side were commercials that starred a talking Chihuahua, who squealed "*Yo quiero* Taco Bell!"

Taco Bell is the leading Mexican-style quick-service restaurant chain in the United States, with more than $4.9 billion in system-wide sales. Taco Bell serves more than 55 million consumers each week in 6,400 restaurants in the United States. In 1997, Taco Bell was spun off from PepsiCo and became a division of Yum! Brands Inc., which also owns KFC, Pizza Hut, Long John Silver's, and A&W restaurants.

[*See also* Advertising; Fast Food; Mexican American Food; Take-Out Foods.]

BIBLIOGRAPHY

Baldwin, Debra Lee. *Taco Titan: The Glen Bell Story*. Arlington, TX: Summit, 1999.
Smith, Andrew F. "Tacos, Enchiladas and Refried Beans: The Invention of Mexican-American Cookery." In *Cultural and Historical Aspects of Foods*, edited by Mary Wallace Kelsey and ZoeAnn Holmes. Corvallis: Oregon State University Press, 1999.
Taco Bell. http://www.tacobell.com.

ANDREW F. SMITH

Taffy, Saltwater, *see Saltwater Taffy*

Tailgate Picnics

Tailgate picnics are meals served out of doors close to an automobile. A car's tailgate—or rear door—need not be used to assemble a tailgate picnic. The term refers to a form of dining that has followed the evolution of the automotive industry.

Tailgate picnics became popular in the United Kingdom around 1919 as a result of the rise of "woodies," wood-paneled cars and small trucks designed and manufactured to conserve steel, a valuable commodity for the production of war materials. Many of the earliest woodies came equipped with a small trailer, commonly referred to as a "teardrop" because of its elliptical shape. These lightweight wooden trailers contained all of the equipment necessary to create thrifty and savory meals along the roadside: a gas or charcoal stove, cold-storage containers, a folding table, and sometimes chairs.

In the United States, woodies were used primarily as service vehicles for lodges, clubs, and inns. Before World War II these vehicles were status symbols among the wealthy. By the 1930s, with the improvement of roads and a surge in automobile travel, Americans embraced woodies and teardrops as a means of affordable travel. By the late 1940s and early 1950s, tailgate picnics enjoyed even greater popularity as parents creating a postwar baby boom searched for affordable family entertainment and leisure activities. With the advent of motel chains during the 1960s, tailgating began to decline. A new generation of enthusiasts and nostalgic baby boomers, however, has revived this form of dining and entertainment.

The cultural, ethnic, and regional culinary palate of America can be found in tailgate picnics throughout the United States: in the parking lots of large sports arenas before sporting events or rock concerts, along beachfronts, in national parks, at highway rest stops, and at antiques fairs where old woodies are showcased. Tailgate picnics may have reached their culinary apex with the development of state-of-the-art portable gas stoves and cooling facilities that make it possible to prepare dishes that represent the diversity of the American palate, such as sausage and peppers, chili, barbecued spare ribs, and sauerbraten.

[See also Historical Overview, subentry From World War II to the Early 1960s; Picnics.]

JANE OTTO

Take-Out Foods

The term "take-out" describes both a style of eating and a growing list of prepared foods that consumers purchase from a restaurant or food stand and eat in another location. Delivery format, packaging, and types of food vary greatly, ranging from hamburgers to expensive gourmet fare, but all may be categorized as takeout because of this off-premise consumption. In the United States, take-out food is often viewed as synonymous with fast food. Fast food, however, is not always eaten on a take-out basis; fast food restaurants often provide an on-site dining area for their patrons. Other terms for take-out food include "carryout" and "take-home" food. This take-out style of eating, marketed by American restaurant chains, had become popular throughout the world by the late twentieth century.

The concept of take-out food and the practice of buying prepared foods for consumption elsewhere date to early civilization. Roadside stands and food stalls in busy urban markets were commonplace in ancient Greece and Rome, providing hungry travelers and workers with quick and inexpensive food items. Almost every culture in every era has had its version of take-out foods, which were often popular yet mundane types of foods. Notable among these foods was the famed British fish and chips, deep-fried then wrapped in old newsprint for takeout.

Urban industrial workers in nineteenth-century America further popularized take-out foods. Food vendors sold various sausages and stews from carts outside factory gates, catering to workers with little time or money. Many of these food vendors grew their businesses into neighborhood diners, serving workers on the premises or with take-out items. Fast food hamburger restaurants became a specialized variation of these urban diners. Beginning with the White Castle system, founded in Wichita, Kansas, in 1921, hamburger restaurants usually offered a few stools for on-premises seating but sold most of their food on a take-out basis. White Castle even adopted the slogan, "Buy 'em by the sack," encouraging the purchase of a take-out bag of ten hamburgers. White Castle devised insulated paper bags for keeping the food warm. The competing chains White Tower and Steak n Shake followed the White Castle approach, advertising to "Buy 'em by the bag" and "TakeHomaSak." Serving take-out food proved successful for restaurateurs, who could provide greater convenience to customers and sell a larger volume of food than their dining areas could accommodate.

In many urban areas, ethnic Italian and Chinese restaurants competed with early hamburger outlets for take-out customers. Small storefront pizzerias and "chow chow houses" sold inexpensive pizzas and Americanized Chinese foods on a primarily take-out basis. Using broad, flat white cardboard boxes for pizzas and small waxy paper cartons for chow mein and chop suey, these ethnic restaurants standardized distinctive take-out packaging that became synonymous with their foods. Although popular in city neighborhoods, ethnic restaurants long composed only a small share of the take-out food market.

Automobiles revolutionized the take-out food industry, requiring larger-volume production and specialized delivery systems. Drive-in restaurants made early accommodations for patrons by offering carhop service, servers bringing meals directly to the cars of diners. Although they served car patrons foods often associated with take-out restaurants, drive-ins encouraged on-premise consumption, albeit in their parking areas. Closer to true take-out format was the walk-up window featured by the burgeoning franchised hamburger chains of the late 1950s and early 1960s. Built at the crossroads of busy suburban thoroughfares, McDonald's and Burger King first sold their hamburgers, milk shakes, and french fries to walk-up customers. Because dining areas were not provided, the explicit message from fast food purveyors was that the sale of the food would be the only service given. Burger King stores were emblazoned with the words "Self Service." Customers drove to the restaurants, walked up to the front service window, bought their food, and then drove away. This format of walk-up window service of strictly take-out hamburgers was the norm for the fast food industry for much of the 1960s.

By the end of the 1960s fast food restaurants began offering dining areas to customers. Although these dining areas were an alternative to eating the food off premises, fast food companies also began selling food from convenient drive-through windows. Fast food restaurants had experimented with drive-up service off and on since the 1920s, constantly searching for better and faster ways to serve customers. The drive-up format did not become a fast food industry standard until the late 1960s, when most of the major chains adopted it. In 1969, Wendy's built its first restaurants complete with car-service windows and special lanes for motoring customers.

The late 1960s also brought advances in take-out food packaging. Earlier take-out fast food was usually wrapped in waxed paper or light foil and then placed in a paper bag. When the technology became available, restaurants began packaging take-out foods in plastic foam cartons. Plastic foam packaging retained heat well and protected items from being crushed when stacked in bags. Plastic foam continued to be the favored type of take-out packaging for more than two decades, until environmental activists successfully pressured restaurant chains first to recycle the plastic and then to use more environmentally friendly paper wrappings.

Take-out foods became considerably more diverse during the 1960s and 1970s. Tacos, roast beef sandwiches, gyros, chicken, and fish joined hamburgers, pizza, and Chinese carryout food as favorite American take-out offerings. Modern take-out foods extend even further beyond the fast food hamburger industry, encompassing a variety of ethnic, heartland, and gourmet fare. Pizzerias and Chinese restaurants became mainstream and suburban while selling much of their food for off-premise consumption. In the 1980s and 1990s national chains such as Boston Market appeared that featured complete "home-cooked" entrées, side dishes, and desserts on a take-out basis. Many large specialty markets and grocery stores sell hot, prepared meats and complete meals on a take-out basis.

[See also Burger King; Chinese American Food; Diners; Drive-ins; Ethnic Foods; Fast Food; McDonald's; Packaging; Pizza; Pizza Hut; Pizzerias; Street Vendors; Wendy's; White Castle.]

BIBLIOGRAPHY

Belasco, Warren, and Philip Scranton, eds. *Food Nations: Selling Taste in Consumer Societies.* New York: Routledge, 2001.
Levenstein, Harvey. *Paradox of Plenty: A Social History of Eating in Modern America.* New York and Oxford: Oxford University Press, 1993.
Mariani, John F. *America Eats Out.* New York: Morrow, 1991.

DAVID GERARD HOGAN

Tang

Tang, made by General Foods, is a sweetened drink powder artificially colored and flavored orange. It is one of America's most celebrated chemically created foods. Tang is almost synonymous with space travel. Tang went to space on the Gemini and Apollo missions. The mix was delivered to the astronauts in silver pouches. When water was added, the pouches yielded a sweet, slightly tangy, orange-flavored drink that provided an entire day's worth of vitamin C. By the first Gemini flight in 1965, Tang had been languishing on supermarket shelves for six years. Then General Foods dubbed it "the drink of the astronauts," and the new Tang, with a prominent picture of a launch pad on the outside of the canister, soon was rocketing upward in sales and consumption. General Foods also marketed the newly popular Tang as an instant, nutritious, and drinkable breakfast. Children influenced by television demanded the sugary drink, and parents, believing it was healthful, bought it. At the peak of popularity of Tang in the 1960s and 1970s, American households consumed the "instant breakfast" on a regular basis. Sales of Tang declined after the novelty of human travel in space subsided. In 1998 Tang received a much-needed boost in popularity when John Glenn, the first person to orbit the earth and the first human to eat in space, insisted on taking the powder with him on his return to space on the shuttle *Discovery*.

[*See also* Breakfast Drinks; Breakfast Foods; General Foods; Space Food.]

JEAN TANG

Taverns

Taverns were an integral and favored part of British and Dutch culture. Samuel Johnson, the eighteenth-century English author and lexicographer, declared, "There is nothing which has yet been contrived by man, by which so much happiness is produced, as by a good tavern or inn." In the seventeenth century, places that sold intoxicating liquors were called "ordinaries," "taverns," "inns," or "public houses." In 1656 the General Court of Massachusetts made towns liable to a fine for not operating an ordinary. Taverns were frequently located close to the meetinghouse so the congregation could warm and refresh themselves after long services. The terms "tavern," "inn," and "ordinary" did not mean the same thing throughout the colonies. In New England and New York, "tavern" was usually used; in Pennsylvania, "inn" was more common; and "ordinary" was the general term in the South. Small establishments that did not offer lodging, stable, or other services but sold only alcohol were called tippling-houses or petty ordinaries.

In 1714 Boston had a population of ten thousand and supported thirty-four taverns. As the population grew during the eighteenth century and people moved west, there was an enormous increase in turnpikes and stagecoach routes. This growth resulted in an increase in the number of inns and taverns along every major road. By 1809 there were 265 taverns in Albany, New York, alone.

Taverns not only served travelers as places for eating and sleeping and for pasturing horses but also served communities as central meeting places. The tavern was the town's post office—a center for receiving and passing on news. Before and during the Revolution it was in taverns that the political future of the colonies was debated. In the absence of a courthouse, a tavern was where the court met and town selectmen came together to regulate the community. Taverns were the first stop for traveling musicians, actors, animal acts, and magicians. If a tavern had a hall or large room, it was used for balls, assemblies, and dancing. During the Revolution, taverns were used for military trials, prisons, hospitals, and officers' quarters. Numerous existing taverns from Washington, D.C., to Maine justly claim that "Washington slept here!"

During the Revolutionary War, many tavern keepers in Manhattan were Tories, who controlled this strategic location. The signs hanging in front of taverns declared the keepers' allegiance: The Sign of Lord Cornwallis, The King's Arms, and The Prince of Wales. In Boston the names of the taverns were less political: The Punch Bowl, The Green Dragon, and The Golden Ball.

Taverns were everywhere in colonial America because they filled the needs that hotels, motels, bars, lounges, restaurants, and clubs filled later. Taverns were an integral part of the social fabric of both cities and towns, and they dotted the rural landscape wherever a change of stagecoach horses was necessary, such as at highway junctions or ferry landings. Many seventeenth- and eighteenth-century taverns have been converted into private homes and bed and breakfast inns or have been relocated to historical sites such as Old Sturbridge Village in Massachusetts. The taverns at Williamsburg, Virginia, Fraunces Tavern Museum in New York City, and the City Tavern in Philadelphia are open to the public. The 1640 Hart House Restaurant in Ipswich, Massachusetts, may be the oldest structure in America that has a tavern on the premises.

[*See also* Bars; Beer Halls; Boardinghouses; Roadhouses; Saloons.]

BIBLIOGRAPHY

Batterberry, Michael, and Ariane Batterberry. *On the Town in New York*. New York: Routledge, 1999.

Dolan, J. R. *The Yankee Peddlers of Early America*. New York: Bramhall House, 1964.

Larkin, Jack. *The New England Country Tavern*. Sturbridge, MA: Old Sturbridge, 2000.

Rice, Kym S. *Early American Taverns: For the Entertainment of Friends and Strangers*. Chicago: Regnery Gateway, 1983.

JOSEPH M. CARLIN

Tea

Tea is both a beverage and a social occasion, a dual significance it has held since its first use in the American colonies. Although it was an expensive commodity until the late nineteenth century, it remained the most popular hot beverage until about the 1820s, when coffee drinking began to increase dramatically.

Tea in America

Dutch colonists in New Amsterdam introduced tea drinking to America in the 1650s, about thirty years after they brought it to Europe. By the late seventeenth century, tea was being sold in the Massachusetts Bay Colony, but its use was restricted by its very high cost. Ale and wine remained more affordable to the colonists and were more likely to be served to guests than tea. By the 1750s, however, tea drinking was an established social custom among the wealthy. Gradually, tea drinking spread throughout society and was taken up by households of modest means in rural and urban areas.

After the British imposed duties on tea in the 1760s and 1770s, many colonists joined boycotts against it, leading to dramatic raids—"tea parties"—in which tea from British ships was dumped into harbors in 1773 and 1774. It is not known just how widespread the boycotts were and to what extent tea consumption dropped, as tea continued to be brought into the colonies by smugglers to evade taxation. After the Revolution in 1776, tea continued in popularity, and Americans soon began to enter the tea importing business. In the 1780s, tea traders amassed vast fortunes by exchanging furs from the Northwest for tea in China. Duties enacted by Congress in the 1790s encouraged direct importation of tea by American ships but kept prices high nonetheless. Prized green teas had the highest taxes levied on them.

All tea is grown from the same tree, an evergreen of the camellia family (*Camellia sinensis*), which is pruned to

---

THE BOSTON TEA PARTY

Tea, introduced in New York in the early 1600s by the Dutch, was even more popular in colonial America than in England. When Parliament wanted to punish the Americans for rebelling against taxes imposed under the Townshend Act, it enacted a heavy tea tax in 1767. The result was smuggling, and a brisk illicit trade developed between the Americans and the Dutch. The East India Company, which controlled the legal tea trade, saw its profits slide and pressured the British government to take action. In 1773 Parliament enacted the Tea Act, mandating that all tea going to America must pass through English ports. The British hoped that the American desire for tea, coupled with the fact that tea was less expensive in the colonies than in Britain, would minimize anger over trade restrictions. Instead, American resentment flared.

On the evening of December 16, 1773 fifty to sixty men, including Samuel Adams and John Hancock, dressed up as Indians and stole onto the tea ships in Boston Harbor. They hacked open the tea chests, threw the tea overboard, and then melted away into the night. Instead of arresting the lawbreakers, Massachusetts authorities condoned their actions, which infuriated the British. Immediately, Parliament passed four bills designed to punish Massachusetts' insubordination, part of the "Intolerable Acts" which lead to the formation of the Continental Congress and thence to the Declaration of Independence. It can easily be argued that the Boston Tea Party was the first overt act of the American Revolution.

BIBLIOGRAPHY

Chitwood, Oliver Perry. *A History of Colonial America*. 2nd ed. New York: Harper, 1948.

A History of Tea. http://www.atimeremembered.net/teahistory.htm. A useful website on America history with especially good information on the entire history of tea.

A History of Tea. http://www.stashtea.com.

Taylor, Dale. *The Writer's Guide to Everyday Life in Colonial America*. Cincinnati, OH: Writer's Digest Books, 1997.

SYLVIA LOVEGREN

---

remain in shrub form. The three basic kinds of tea—green, oolong, and black—result from the degree of fermentation that the leaves undergo after picking. Green is unfermented, oolong is partially fermented, and black is fully fermented. Historically, China and Japan produced mostly green tea; Formosa (now Taiwan) produced mostly oolong; and India, Ceylon (now Sri Lanka), Java, Sumatra, and a few other countries produced mostly black tea. Most of the black tea imported into America, however, comes from Argentina.

Green tea from China dominated American tea consumption until the twentieth century, although black tea from China, early known as Bohea, was also available during the colonial period. The two teas were also consumed mixed. Green tea from Japan entered the American market during the Civil War, and Formosa oolong came into the country shortly thereafter, becoming an instant hit. America formed the principal world market for Japanese green teas and Formosa oolong until shipment was cut off during World War II.

Black teas grown by the British on large estates in India and Ceylon were introduced to millions of Americans at the World's Columbian Exposition in Chicago in 1893. Lower prices, heavy promotional campaigns, and a belief that black tea was more hygienically manufactured caused black tea eventually to displace green tea in popularity. In the 1880s, Americans became concerned about the addition of coloring agents to green tea, and legislation that was enacted in 1883, 1897, and 1911 drastically decreased the amount of green tea that was brought into the country from China. By 1930, green tea from China had fallen to 8 percent of tea importations.

Japan was better able to meet the new standards for importation. Green and oolong teas from Japan and Formosa remained popular for a time as Chinese imports dropped. Japan green tea use remained high in the northern states along the Canadian border until World War II while oolong retained its popularity in the Northeast until the same time. The war eliminated both from the market, and black tea became dominant. Although in the 1990s health concerns spurred a renewed interest in green teas, black tea holds about 95 percent of the market.

Until the 1890s, teas sold by wholesalers and retailers were marketed unblended, just as they came from tea gardens in Asia. As packaged brand-name black teas sold by large concerns in the later nineteenth century became the norm, the blending of teas became a common practice. Blending teas of varying quality and flavor resulted in a distinctive, uniform, and profitable product. Green teas and oolong teas, however, were less likely to be blended. As black tea consumption rose, Americans became accustomed to purchasing teas with predictable tastes sold under brand names. At the same time, the widely advertised name "orange pekoe," found on packaged black teas in America, took on an aura of high quality. In the tea trade, orange pekoe denotes only the size and shape of tea leaves, and teas graded this way can run the gamut of cup quality.

The appreciation of fine estate teas developed in the twentieth century. Like wine, tea is influenced by such factors as soil, climate, and the elevation at which it is grown, and its quality can vary from one picking to another. Tea connoisseurship is confined to a small percentage of the population who buy loose teas from specialty dealers.

Despite the lowered prices of mass-marketed black teas by the early twentieth century, tea consumption remained limited. By the time tea prices declined, coffee had become established as the nation's customary breakfast drink. According to federal statistics, tea consumption (by gallon volume) in 1999 ranked seventh among all purchased beverages, after carbonated soft drinks, beer, coffee, milk, bottled water, and fruit juice.

Were it not for the popularity of iced tea, which accounts for about 80 percent of all tea consumed, tea consumption in the United States would be considerably lower. Exactly when the custom of drinking iced tea began is unknown, but it dates back at least to the 1860s, if not long before. A hot drink in vogue in the 1870s, tea à la Russe, made with sugar and sliced lemons, was also enjoyed cold. Iced tea was also available in the 1870s in hotels and on railroads. Its consumption increased as more and more American homes were electrified in the 1920s and acquired electric refrigerators. Iced tea has long been especially popular in hotter parts of the country, particularly the South, but it has become a year-round beverage, often consumed ready to drink in cans and bottles.

Tea Accompaniments

From colonial days, sugar has been the most important addition to tea, whether the beverage is drunk hot or cold. Visitors to early America commented on this practice in 1795, and as sugar became cheaper late in the following century, its use soared. Two teaspoons or three lumps to each cup was considered a restaurant industry standard in the 1890s, a decade in which granulated white sugar became affordable. Before the mid-nineteenth century, cone sugar was part of the tea service ritual involving women carefully cutting the cones into cubes with specially designed sugar nippers. By the 1940s, over two-thirds of all tea consumed was drunk with sugar in it. Most canned and bottled tea is sweetened.

Milk and cream have been consumed in hot tea throughout the centuries, but in the eighteenth century cream was preferred. Lemon was not used until later in the nineteenth century, becoming more popular when transcontinental railroads made citrus fruit affordable to the midwestern and eastern portions of the country. In the 1940s, fewer than one-fifth of tea drinkers used lemon in hot tea, although its use in iced tea was, and is, more widespread.

Food served with tea on social occasions is always lighter than food provided at mealtimes. During the eighteenth century, food selections could include cold meats, nuts, preserved fruits, candies, and cakes. In the succeeding century, salads and dainty sandwiches might also be found on the tea table. In the regions of the country where "tea" was another word for supper, mainly in New England, the meal so called was a small one, with fewer items and less meat than would be encountered at midday dinner, approximating what would later be called lunch. Well into the twentieth century, over half of all tea was consumed with the evening meal, and fewer than one cup in ten was drunk for breakfast.

Even though tea consumption was bolstered by the nineteenth-century temperance movement, it would not have been unusual for alcoholic beverages to be served at many elite afternoon or evening tea parties. Green tea was used as an ingredient in punches made with sugar, lemon or other fruit juices, and champagne, brandy, or rum.

Social Aspects of Tea Consumption

A great deal of ceremony has always been attached to tea parties, much of it involving the presentation and handling of elaborate and delicate tea wares. The Dutch in New Amsterdam in the mid-1600s used teapots, silver spoons, and strainers, as well as "bite and stir boxes," which contained partitions for lump and powdered sugar, the former held between the mouth while sipping tea, the latter stirred into the cup.

Tea drinkers in the colonies used porcelain tea wares from China, often blue and white but sometimes red and white or plain white. Chinese export teacups were smaller than coffee cups and had no handles. A full tea set around 1790 contained a teapot, twelve cups, twelve saucers, a milk or cream jug, a sugar bowl, and a slop bowl for pouring out the dregs before refilling a cup. Tea strainers, to catch the tea leaves while pouring, were made, but larger punch strainers were often used instead. By the mid-1900s, straining was made unnecessary with the use of perforated metal tea balls suspended on chains. In the twentieth century, tea bags made of gauze or cheesecloth first came into use in restaurants, later gaining domestic acceptance. By the beginning of the twenty-first century, almost all hot tea was brewed from tea bags. Until prices fell and tea was stored in tin canisters, precious tea was kept fresh in airtight caddies made of fine wood, china, or silver. Silver tea sets were not common until the nineteenth century, and their use became more widespread after the Civil War, following the discovery of new silver mines in the West and the development of a cheaper silver-plating process.

Other equipment devoted to tea in the eighteenth century included wooden tea boards and trays and small tables. The tables were round or square, on four legs or on tripod stands. Often they were collapsible or had leaves that could be extended. Their height was that of a dining table, but their tops were smaller, and they could be moved or set up anywhere with ease.

Evening and afternoon tea parties in private homes or public halls were fashionable social affairs during the late eighteenth century and throughout the following century. Often women organized tea parties to raise funds for restoration of patriotic properties, such as Mount Vernon, or for events, such as the Centennial Exposition in Philadelphia in 1876. Veneration of George Washington after the Civil War stimulated Martha Washington tea parties, where guests dressed in period costumes and recreated an imagined courtly society. More modest tea parties were held in Protestant churches in the nineteenth century, closely resembling the church suppers of later times.

Despite the aura of refinement and propriety surrounding some tea parties, they have historically been social occasions in which participants relaxed, shared light gossip, and departed from the formalities of regular meals or dinner parties. Often they represented a

Tearoom Training. Publicity booklet for the Tea Room Institute of the Lewis Hotel Training Schools, Washington, D.C., early 1920s. *Collection of Alice Ross*

break in the ordinary routines of daily life and conventions, in terms of the foods consumed as well as the time of day and varied locations—outdoors, on porches, or in living rooms—in which tea was served. To a great extent, afternoon tea has shared much of its ambience with that other characteristically informal and portable meal, the picnic.

In the early twentieth century, the afternoon tea custom moved out of the private house into public spaces in hotels, department stores, and small tea rooms often run by women. Greenwich Village in New York City was filled with artistically decorated tea rooms, where informality and a whimsical sense of fun prevailed. Tea rooms peaked in popularity in the 1920s, a decade in which the national outlawing of alcoholic beverages stimulated both tea and

coffee drinking in public eating places; the establishment of tea rooms also eased women's entry into the restaurant business. Most successful tea rooms built their trade around lunch and dinner service since afternoon tea was not in itself sufficiently profitable. In the 1990s, afternoon tea experienced a revival and is served in small tea rooms as well as in hotels and restaurants.

Herbal Teas

Herbal teas can be made from herbs and spices deriving from all parts of a plant, whether leaf, flower, fruit, or root. They are also made of the bark of woody plants.

Although herbal drinks have long been regarded as medicinal, enjoyment of herbal teas mainly as beverages received considerable impetus during the natural food movement of the 1960s. In the later twentieth century, herbal teas became popular with consumers who wished to avoid caffeine. In earlier centuries, herbal teas were drunk as beverages during wartime, when other tea was not available, or as protest beverages—"liberty teas"—during the Revolutionary period. During this time, teas made of chamomile, loosestrife, ribwort, currant leaves, and sage were known.

Teas were also made of sassafras, spicewood, and mint. In the South during the Civil War, people drank the dried bark of the sassafras tree; the leaves of blackberry, raspberry, huckleberry, or currant bushes; and the leaves of the willow tree. In coastal North Carolina, the boiled leaves and twigs of the yaupon shrub made a popular tea substitute. Yaupon, made from holly leaves, was also known as a black drink and was consumed ceremonially by Native Americans in the South. Its use had nearly died out by the twentieth century.

Tea Production in America

Tea growing and processing in America has been tried repeatedly, but even the most promising efforts have resulted in limited commercial success. Congress encouraged experiments in tea growing in the South as early as 1848, but the most serious attempt was made in Summerville, South Carolina, from around 1889 to 1915. With assistance from the U.S. Department of Agriculture, the Pinehurst Tea Plantation, run by Dr. Charles U. Shepard, produced green, oolong, and black teas, which were sold commercially. However, when Shepard died, the effort ceased until the 1960s and following decades, when a series of owners worked to revive the plantation.

The tea tree will grow in any nonarid climate, but it flourishes best in very warm and wet parts of the world. Shepard's cultivation methods made up for the inadequate rainfall and cold winter temperatures of South Carolina, but he faced a bigger problem—finding a workforce that could compete with the exceedingly low wages earned by laborers in Asia. He employed African American children to pick the tea, but even the wages of these workers cost many times more than the wages of Asian tea pickers. Later owners solved the labor problem with mechanical picking, but the commercial viability of American-grown tea is still unproven.

[*See also* Chinese American Food; Coffee; Herbs and Spices; Japanese American Food; Prohibition.]

BIBLIOGRAPHY

Harland, Marion. *Breakfast, Luncheon, and Tea.* New York: Scribner, Armstrong, 1875.

Hooker, Richard J. *Food and Drink in America: A History.* Indianapolis: Bobbs-Merrill, 1981. Detailed account of what Americans ate and drank in all parts of the country from 1800 until the mid-twentieth century.

Roth, Rodris. "Tea-Drinking in Eighteenth-Century America: Its Etiquette and Equipage." In *Bulletin 225, Contributions from the Museum of History and Technology.* Washington, DC: Smithsonian Institution Press, 1961. Separately printed booklet. Reconstruction of tea drinking habits and material culture of tea based on historical documents, travelers' accounts, and contemporary paintings.

Saunders, William. "An Experiment in Tea Culture: A Report on the Tea Gardens of Dr. C. U. Shepard, Pinehurst, S.C." Washington, DC: U.S. Department of Agriculture, 1897. Ten-page booklet reporting on the attempt to grow tea in the United States.

Schapira, Joel, David Schapira, and Karl Schapira. *The Book of Coffee and Tea.* 2nd rev. ed. New York: St. Martin's Press, 1996. Contains information on tea history and on herbal teas.

Tea Bureau. *The Cup That Cheers, A Handbook on Tea.* New York: Tea Bureau, n.d. Forty-page booklet, published about 1948, giving a brief history of tea and information on postwar American consumption habits.

Ukers, William H. *All about Tea.* New York: Tea and Coffee Trade Journal Company, 1935. The major source for information on tea in American and world history. Two volumes. Second volume contains an extensive bibliography on the history of tea production, marketing, and consumption.

Ukers, William H. *The Romance of Tea: An Outline History of Tea, and Tea-Drinking through Sixteen Hundred Years.* New York: Knopf, 1936. A condensed version of his two-volume work.

Waugh, Alec. *The Lipton Story.* Garden City, NY: Doubleday, 1950.

Whitaker, Jan. *Tea at the Blue Lantern Inn: A Social History of the Tea Room Craze in America.* New York: St. Martin's Press, 2002. Describes the development and varieties of tea rooms in the early twentieth century.

Williams, Susan. *Savory Suppers and Fashionable Feasts: Dining in Victorian America.* New York: Pantheon Books, 1985. Contains sample tea menus and information on tea etiquette and wares.

JAN WHITAKER

Temperance

Temperance was a movement combining social, religious, and political efforts to ban the consumption of alcohol in the United States. Convinced that alcohol abuse was the cause of most social problems, anti-alcohol crusaders lobbied and protested throughout much of the nineteenth century and into the early twentieth century, their efforts culminating in 1920 with the federal government's prohibition against the manufacture, importation, and sale of beer, wine, and liquor. Although temperance advocates succeeded in winning Prohibition, overwhelming popular sentiment restored America's right to drink in 1933.

The Origins of Temperance

The origins of temperance are difficult to ascertain. Many Protestant denominations long prohibited the use of alcohol. Colonial ministers railed against "strong drink" from their New England pulpits while many people in their congregations continued to imbibe. Colonists commonly brewed their own beer and drank rum, port, and corn whiskey. Because of the copious production of grain, distilled spirits were abundant and inexpensive. Much of the planning for the American Revolution took place in taverns throughout the colonies. Benjamin Franklin was infamous for his fondness of alcohol, and George Washington won his first election to the Virginia House of Burgesses in 1758 by generously distributing "brandy, rum, cyder, strong beer, and wine" to voters at the polls. Although long opposed by Protestant clergy, the drinking of alcohol remained an important, if discreet, part of mainstream British American culture.

Alcohol consumption became a more contentious public issue in the first half of the nineteenth century as non-Anglo immigrants flocked to East Coast cities. The population of the United States tripled between 1790 and 1830, threatening the balance of political power and the conventions of society. Collective violence erupted as the size of immigrant populations began to rival the numbers of "native born" Americans, whose xenophobic activists became known as "nativists." Centuries-old hatred between English Protestants and Irish Catholics rekindled in America, further deepening the rift between established Anglo residents and Irish newcomers. British Americans viewed the Irish as an inferior people who would undermine American culture, believing their primary loyalty would always be to the pope instead of to the

United States. Exacerbating these biases was the Irish love for alcohol. Long a center of Irish ethnic culture, the drinking of ale and whiskey became a popular pastime for urban Irish workingmen and Irish street gangs. Alcohol was readily available, costing only twenty-five cents per gallon throughout the 1820s. Native-born Americans condemned this frequent drinking by the Irish as proof of their immorality, laziness, and violent tendencies. Protestants fought to contain what they viewed as rampant alcohol consumption, hoping either to reform the corrupt traits of the Irish or at least to contain potential harm. The Second Great Awakening, a wave of religious revivals between 1797 and 1840, strengthened the temperance sentiment when Evangelical Christian organizations, such as the American Temperance Society (1826), crusaded for the prohibition of alcohol. The Washingtonian Movement, founded in 1840, attracted more than 200,000 members, all taking a pledge of abstinence from alcohol, or teetotalism. In addition, temperance became part of both the early women's movement and abolitionism, often tied together as the pressing moral issues of the day. Notable feminist leaders, including Susan B. Anthony and Frances Willard, were outspoken critics of alcohol abuse.

In cities still controlled by native-born Protestant elites, such as Philadelphia in the 1830s, city councils enacted ordinances limiting saloons and grog shops. On a much broader scale, Massachusetts briefly had a law from 1838 to 1840 forbidding the sale of alcohol by the glass. Many New York State towns voted themselves dry. The state of Maine in 1851 banned the manufacture of all alcoholic drinks and their sale by wholesalers and retailers. Consumption of drink in Maine was still permitted, but users had to prove that the beverages were legally imported into the state. A topic of severe political conflict, the Maine Law movement swept across other northern states, and twelve states adopted prohibition laws between 1852 and 1854. Southern states rejected this trend, viewing it as a further cultural difference between North and South. In 1854 the nativist Know-Nothing Party pushed to make prohibition federal policy but ran into opposition, especially from immigrant groups. In 1855 a Know-Nothing mayor of Chicago attempted to close saloons on Sundays, causing a violent backlash, known as the Lager Beer Riot, by German immigrants. That same year, a Maine Law crusader, Mayor Neal Dow of Portland, ordered the state militia to fire on a crowd of Irish workers protesting strict laws. In 1860, when leaders of the newly formed Republican Party de-emphasized temperance and courts struck down state prohibition laws, anti-alcohol crusades were stalled. With the start of the Civil War, Americans moved on to more pressing issues. The government tacitly encouraged drinking during the war, because a tax on distilled spirits helped finance the war effort. Military life also restored drinking as a central part of male culture for millions of conscripted soldiers. Temperance organizations regularly distributed anti-alcohol literature in army camps but had little success in stemming consumption.

After the Civil War

Temperance efforts blossomed at the end of the war. The weakened American Temperance Union re-formed into the National Temperance Society and called for northern states to revitalize their prohibition laws. Massachusetts restored prohibition in 1865, hiring war veterans as state constables whose sole responsibility was enforcement of

Encouragement to Temperance. "The Bar of Destruction," a drawing by Thomas Nast, appeared in *Harper's Weekly*, March 21, 1874. *Prints and Photographs Division, Library of Congress*

alcohol laws. Maine founded its state police force that same year to combat prohibition violators. Many other states banned Sunday sales of beer, wine, and liquor, mandating enforcement by local officials. In 1867 Massachusetts voters temporarily repealed the alcohol prohibition law, and the national Republican Party retreated from the issue, courting working-class urban voters. German and Irish immigrants again formed opposition groups that actively protested against Sunday prohibitions and other restrictions on drinking. In essence, the temperance issue remained the ideological centerpiece in the political and economic power struggle between old-line Anglo Protestant groups and immigrant interests, disguising other concerns. In the context of late-nineteenth-century America, demographic changes threatened the status quo, which favored those holding social and political power. Although many temperance advocates held sincere moral beliefs, historians questioned the extent to which prohibition crusades were a means of preserving control over a changing society.

In 1872, lacking major party support, the newly formed Prohibition Party spearheaded a renewed nationwide campaign for temperance. Although they earned few votes in their first presidential bid, Prohibitionists gained momentum in each subsequent national election. Although consistently a distant third behind the Democrats and Republicans, the Prohibition Party kept temperance alive as a political issue until the close of the nineteenth century. Augmenting the power of party politics, temperance organizations continued to spread across the United States and to grow in membership during the 1880s and 1890s.

Although the leaders usually were men, most of the members of temperance organizations were middle-class women. Temperance eventually became known as a "women's issue" greatly focused on protecting the family and reforming male deviance. Women believed that drinking was a major detriment to healthy family life and the chief reason for working-class poverty, because male breadwinners were squandering their money on drink. Crusaders targeted both alcohol itself and saloons, which they indicted as the center of other vices, such as prostitution, gambling, and fighting. Temperance advocates believed that if they closed the saloons, many of society's ills would be eradicated. An early leader against saloons was the Woman's Christian Temperance Union (WCTU), founded in Fredonia, New York, in 1873. This group quickly spread across the United States, becoming known

Holy War. "Woman's Holy War," lithograph published by Currier and Ives, 1874. *Prints and Photographs Division, Library of Congress*

for both symbolic and direct action. Activists in the WCTU erected elaborate water fountains in saloon districts and urged workingmen and farmers to drink cold water rather than alcohol. Other WCTU crusaders adopted a more aggressive approach, entering saloons and kneeling in prayer until patrons departed. Experiencing success in temperance, the WCTU, under the leadership of the reformer Frances Willard, expanded its political activism to education, prison reform, and women's rights. The WCTU continues to crusade for temperance and other social justice issues.

The campaign against saloons varied in militancy, ranging from large prayer meetings to political activism to physical assaults on drinking establishments. The most infamous anti-saloon crusader was Carrie Nation. A woman of imposing size and demeanor, Nation became notorious for invading scores of saloons, smashing bottles and furniture with a hatchet, and calling patrons "rum-soaked, whiskey-swilled, saturn-faced rummies." Arrested more than thirty times, Nation became the personification of radical temperance.

The Anti-Saloon League was founded in Oberlin, Ohio, in 1893, and changed its name to the National Anti-Saloon League in 1895. Adopting the simple motto, "The saloon must go," this group vowed to solve the "liquor problem" by closing every saloon in the United States. The league's strategy was to endorse and support any political candidate or legislative bill advocating temperance. League leaders began lobbying officeholders, developing a nationwide network of local churches, and publishing temperance periodicals. Founding the American Issue Publishing Company in 1896, with Ernest H. Cherrington as its general manager, the National Anti-Saloon League printed forty tons of paper each month to spread its message. Within a few years, the league established ties with the millionaires John D. Rockefeller and Sebastian Kresge, who provided generous financial support for the temperance cause. Politically and financially empowered by 1913, the National Anti-Saloon League sponsored a protest march on Washington, D.C., in which four thousand participants walked down Pennsylvania Avenue. At the Capitol, league members presented lawmakers with their draft of a constitutional amendment banning alcohol. In 1914 this draft became the Hobson-Sheppard Bill, which called for the prohibition amendment, and was defeated in the Senate. The National Anti-Saloon League increased its efforts, electing additional Republican candidates in 1916.

National Prohibition

Temperance activists gained increased public support in 1917 with the outbreak of World War I. They used anti-German sentiment to fight the major brewing companies, which were largely owned by German American families. Combining anger against German interests with a demand that grain supplies be directed at the war effort rather than the manufacture of alcohol, the temperance movement linked its cause to American patriotism. Congress responded in late 1917 by passing legislation that called for national prohibition. Thirty-six states ratified the Eighteenth Amendment, which mandated the prohibition of alcohol in the United States. In 1919 the National Prohibition Act, popularly called the Volstead Act, specified enforcement measures. When the law went into effect, on January 29, 1920, the United States entered the dry thirteen-year period known as Prohibition.

The temperance movement remained viable throughout Prohibition, constantly advocating stricter enforcement of the Volstead Act. Groups such the National Anti-Saloon League continued their political crusades, although some of their members became less interested after achieving their goal. Despite often ineffective enforcement efforts and an ongoing national political debate between "wets" and "drys," Prohibition remained solidly in effect throughout the 1920s. The economic crisis of the Great Depression, however, quickly shifted power to the Democratic Party, which had made the repeal of Prohibition a plank of its political platform. Alcohol became legal again in 1933, soon after Franklin D. Roosevelt and a huge wave of legislators reclaimed Washington, D.C. The repeal of Prohibition marginalized temperance as a national issue, but temperance remained a controversy in several states.

[*See also* Alcohol and Teetotalism; Alcoholism; Beer Halls; Prohibition; Saloons; Taverns.]

BIBLIOGRAPHY

Blocker, Jack S. *Retreat from Reform: The Prohibition Movement in America, 1890–1913*. Westport, CT: Greenwood, 1976.
Pegram, Thomas D. *Battling Demon Rum: The Struggle for a Dry America*. Chicago: Ivan R. Dee, 1998.

DAVID GERARD HOGAN

Tequila

Tequila, the spirit of Mexico, is made nowhere else in the world, and its origins date to pre-Columbian times. Before the Spanish conquered Mexico, the indigenous people made a naturally fermented beverage called *pulque* from maguey plants. The Spanish transformed the fermented drink into a distilled one and created mescal (also spelled "mezcal"), the general category that includes tequila.

For years tequila was not widely known outside Mexico and adjacent areas of the United States. That situation changed after the Mexican government established the *Norma Oficial Mexicana* (called the *Normas*) in 1978 to regulate tequila quality and consistency. According to the *Normas*, tequila must be made from the blue agave plant, a variety of the maguey plant called *Agave tequilana Weber* (for the German botanist who first classified it). The plants must be grown on the volcanic soil of Jalisco province, which includes the town of

MESCAL

All distilled maguey juices are mescals, a word derived from *mexcalmetl*, the Nauhuatl word for the agave plant. Tequila is mescal from the state of Jalisco. Oaxaca, in southern Mexico, is the production center for the liquor called "mescal" (also spelled "mezcal"). Much mescal is produced locally in the old-fashioned way. Maguey piñas are placed in pits, covered with heated rocks and layers of fiber matting, and then allowed to cook for several days. The process gives mescal its distinctive smoky, earthy flavor. Once cooked, the maguey is placed in wooden barrels and allowed to ferment for up to a month. The resultant mixture of fiber and liquid is distilled twice, sometimes with a chicken breast, in small stills. Like tequila, mescal is classified as aged or not. Three types are unique, among them the 96 proof *tobala*, a rare maguey distilled in black ceramic containers and often sold in ceramic bottles, and *minero*, named for miners who wanted strong triple-distilled liquor. Probably the best known outside Mexico is mescal *con gusano*, sold with a "worm" in the bottle. The "worm" is really the larva of a moth that lives in the base of the maguey plant. Highly prized for their flavor and texture, *gusanos* are sold in markets and eaten out of hand. When dried and ground together with salt and chilies, *sal de gusano* is used with mixed drinks and as a condiment. *Gusanos* are not traditional additions to mescal bottles but are a marketing ploy dating to the 1950s, along with invented folklore stories about macho qualities imparted to those who dare to eat them.

Tequila, and designated nearby areas. Tequila must contain at least 51 percent blue agave juice. The other 49 percent can be cane or corn syrup or juices from other varieties of agave. Tequila made from 100 percent blue agave is so labeled.

Blue agave plants can take ten years to mature and at maturity weigh as much as 150 pounds. The heart, or *piña*, is harvested, cooked, and crushed so that the juice can be extracted. The juice, called *aguamiel*, or honey water, is fermented and then distilled twice. After distillation, tequila may or may not be blended, and it may or may not be aged. Tequila is bottled in Mexico or is shipped in tanker trucks for bottling in the United States.

There are three styles of tequila. Silver, also known as white or *blanco*, is bottled less than sixty days after distillation. *Reposado* ("rested") has been aged for up to one year. *Añejo* ("aged") tequila is aged in barrels for at least one year and up to four. Both the *reposado* and *añejo* styles take on a golden hue as a result of aging. So-called "gold" tequila is simply silver tequila with caramel coloring added. Although often described as fiery, tequila is generally bottled at eighty proof, making it no more potent than gin or vodka.

First exported to the United States in 1873, tequila enjoyed a brief popularity surge during World War II owing to the scarcity of whiskey and other liquors. In the 1970s several factors, including the *Normas*, the industry's marketing efforts, and the growing popularity of Mexican and Tex-Mex cuisines accompanied by margaritas, spurred the growth of tequila. In 1975 the United States consumed 2.5 million cases of tequila; by 2000 consumption had increased to 7.3 million cases. Tequila's share of the spirits market has gone from less than 2 percent to nearly 5 percent, making it one of the few spirits showing growth.

There are many ways to drink tequila. Some people bolt down shots in a ritual consisting of licking their hands between the thumb and forefinger, sprinkling the wet spot with salt, licking it off, downing a shot of tequila, and then biting a lime wedge. Gourmetship in tequila has increased dramatically, some versions costing three hundred dollars and more a bottle. Aficionados sip good 100 percent blue agave *añejo* tequilas in elegant brandy snifters. The most popular tequila drink is the margarita, one of most popular mixed drinks in the United States.

[*See also* Cocktails; Margarita; Mexican American Food; Tequila Sunrise.]

BIBLIOGRAPHY

Adams Liquor Handbook. Norwalk, CT: Adams Business Research, 2001.

Blue, Anthony Dias. "Tequila at the Top." *Bon Appetit*, October 1995.

Cutler, Lance. *The Tequila Lover's Guide to Mexico and Mezcal*. Vineburg, CA: Wine Patrol, 2000.

Grimes, William. *Straight Up or On the Rocks*. New York: North Point, 2001.

Kretchmer, Laurence. *Mesa Grill Guide to Tequila*. New York: Black Dog and Leventhal, 1998.

Quinzio, Jeri. "Vino de Tequila." *Massachusetts Beverage Price Journal*, April 1996.

Walker, Ann and Larry. *Tequila: The Book*. San Francisco: Chronicle, 1994.

JERI QUINZIO

Tequila Sunrise

During the 1970s the tequila sunrise was a trend-setting new drink. It was so popular that a Hollywood film, several restaurants, a hit song, a quilt pattern, and at least three yellow and red flowers—a rose, a snapdragon, and a coreopsis—came to be named after it. The tequila sunrise was one of the emblematic drinks in Cyra McFadden's 1976 novel *The Serial*, a parody of the California lifestyle. No one knows for sure who invented the tequila sunrise, but it is thought to have originated in California. The tequila sunrise was considered the perfect "morning-after" drink, a cure for hangovers brought on by tequila shots or margaritas drunk the night before.

The first published recipes for tequila sunrises, in bartenders' guides of the 1960s and early 1970s, had little resemblance to the sunny orange juice drink bartenders later came to serve. The tequila sunrise originally was made with tequila, lime juice, grenadine, crème de cassis, and club soda and served in a tall glass. The popularity of the cocktail inspired imitation. In Oaxaca, Mexico, restaurateurs who catered to tourists created the Donaji cocktail and used the local mescal rather than tequila. The Donaji is named after a mythical indigenous princess who sacrificed her life for her people. Except for the addition of *sal de gusano*—a mixture of dried agave "worms," chilies, and salt—the Donaji is a sunrise. The Berta, a drink that most likely predates the Donaji, was originally served at Berta's, a bar founded around 1930 in Taxco, Mexico. The Berta is made with tequila, limes, soda water, and honey rather than grenadine.

[*See also* Cocktails; Margarita; Tequila.]

BIBLIOGRAPHY

Blue, Anthony Dias. *The Complete Book of Mixed Drinks*. New York: HarperCollins, 1993.

Duffy, Patrick Gavin. *The Official Mixer's Manual*. Garden City: NY: Doubleday, 1975 edition. Revised and enlarged by Robert Jay Misch. The original edition was published in 1934.

Gaige, Crosby. *Crosby Gaige's Cocktail Guide and Ladies' Companion*. New York: Fireside, 1941.

Saucier, Ted. *Bottoms Up*. New York: Greystone, 1962.

JERI QUINZIO

Thanksgiving

On the last Thursday in November, Americans celebrate Thanksgiving Day. The holiday centers on a family dinner featuring turkey with stuffing or dressing, sweet potatoes, cranberry sauce, and pumpkin pie. Many Americans associate Thanksgiving with the Pilgrims, and many believe that the day celebrates the beginnings of the United States.

Thanksgiving was observed in many communities during the seventeenth century. Thanksgiving proclamations have survived, most of which were issued by ministers and governors in various colonies, particularly in New England. These observances were usually selected in response to specific events, such as a military victory, a good harvest, or a providential rainfall, but no specific thanksgiving day was observed on an annual basis. A Puritan thanksgiving was a solemn religious day celebrated with attendance at church and prayer to God.

Not much is known about early Thanksgiving dinners, or even if there were any. Of all the hundreds of thanksgiving days observed in New England in the seventeenth century, only one church record in 1636 suggests the possibility of a feast. This account reports that after church services came "makeing merry." Unfortunately no description has survived, but the presumption is that a feast of some sort took place. No further references to thanksgiving feasting over the next 150 years have been located.

From the eighteenth century only two descriptions of Thanksgiving dinners have survived. During the Revolutionary War, the Continental Congress declared December 18, 1777, a day of thanksgiving in honor of the American military victory at Saratoga. A soldier, Joseph Plumb Martin, noted in his journal that each man was given rice and a tablespoonful of vinegar. A more sumptuous feast dates to 1784, but the description is not precise. It mentions drinking and eating in general and implies that pigs, geese, turkeys, or sheep were served.

In contrast to eighteenth-century records, a large number of descriptions of Thanksgiving dinners date to the nineteenth century. Two-course Thanksgiving meals were common. The first course consisted of roast turkey, chicken pie, ham, beef, sausage, and duck supplemented with sweet potatoes, yams, succotash, pickles, sweetbreads, turnips, and squash. The second course consisted of pies, tarts, puddings, creams, custards, jellies, floating islands, nuts, and dried fruit. Wine, rum, brandy, eggnog, punch, coffee, and tea were served with the meal.

Perhaps because of the significance of Thanksgiving, many Americans used the day to promote particular causes. In 1835 William Alcott, a physician, wrote that he was opposed to the feast on moral grounds as well as for medical

Thanksgiving Imagery. Thanksgiving greeting. *Culinary Archives & Museum at Johnson & Wales University, Providence, R.I.*

reasons. He called the Thanksgiving holiday a carnival loaded with luxuries. Alcott was particularly concerned because New Englanders were also beginning to celebrate Christmas, and he claimed that the two feasts had already merged into one long period of overindulgence that caused serious health problems. Alcott had another reason for opposing the Thanksgiving dinner—he had become a vegetarian in 1830 and later was one of the founders of the American Vegetarian Society. Although few Americans paid attention to Alcott or other vegetarians at the time, vegetarian concerns reemerged at the end of the century.

Reformers used Thanksgiving to highlight poverty in America. While many Americans were enjoying a sumptuous Thanksgiving feast, others were unable to partake in the festivities. Since before the Civil War, ministers, politicians, and social reformers have used the Thanksgiving holiday to point out economic disparity in America. In the early twenty-first century, this theme continues as newspapers and news broadcasts feature dinners for the homeless or poor on Thanksgiving Day.

Forefathers' Day, the Pilgrims, and the "First Thanksgiving"

Many influences contributed to transforming Thanksgiving from a mainly New England celebration into a national holiday. One major influence was migration. New Englanders migrated to other parts of the country in search of better farmland. The central valley of New York, for example, was largely settled by New Englanders, as was much of the Midwest. Transplanted New Englanders kept the Thanksgiving holiday alive in their new homes and urged their newly adopted communities to celebrate it as well.

By the early nineteenth century Thanksgiving had become part of popular culture. Musical compositions were performed, and Thanksgiving poems were published. Perhaps the most famous Thanksgiving poem was written by Lydia Maria Child, whose "The Boy's Thanksgiving Song" is better known to most Americans by its first line, "Over the river and thro' the wood."

None of the previously mentioned Thanksgiving proclamations, poems, or descriptions of feasts mentioned the first Thanksgiving or the Pilgrims. These were later additions to the rapidly evolving legend, and they sprang from a different tradition. On December 22, 1769, Plymouth luminaries celebrated the day on which the Separatists had arrived in the New World. This event was later commemorated as Forefathers' Day. It gained enough support in Boston that in 1799 the Boston Sons of the Pilgrims sent out an invitation to its Forefathers' Day dinner. This invitation contained the first located use of the word "Pilgrim" applied to the Separatists and Puritans.

One problem with Forefathers' Day was its proximity to Christmas, which was not generally celebrated in New England until the mid-nineteenth century. As Christmas became more important, the celebration of Forefathers' Day declined and Thanksgiving became a substitute. The first association between the Pilgrims and Thanksgiving appeared in print in 1841, when Alexander Young published a copy of a letter dated December 11, 1621, from Edward Winslow to a friend in England. The letter described a three-day event, the dates of which were not given. The letter was published the following year in England. It was not rediscovered until the 1820s. In his letter Winslow reported that after the crops were harvested, William Bradford sent four men to hunt fowl. Native Americans brought deer, and for three days they feasted.

In a footnote to the letter Young claimed that this was "the first Thanksgiving." Young also cited Governor William Bradford's 1650 manuscript *Of Plimoth Plantation*, which had been lost for decades and was not published in its entirety until 1856. In this document Bradford told the story of Plymouth Plantation from 1620 to 1647. Bradford made no mention of the event described by Winslow, but he did report that in the fall of 1621 the settlers had accumulated wild turkeys, venison, cod, bass, waterfowl, and corn.

Whatever happened in 1621, the Puritans did not have special memories of it. They made no subsequent mention of the event and did not observe it in later years. The feast described by Winslow included no prayer, and it had many secular elements. The Puritans would not have considered it a day of Thanksgiving. Yet Young's allegation that the 1621 event was the first Thanksgiving was accepted by others writing histories of the Pilgrims.

Hale's Tale

The first president to issue a Thanksgiving proclamation was George Washington, who did so at the direction of Congress on October 3, 1789. The few presidents who subsequently issued Thanksgiving proclamations commemorated particular events, such as President James Madison's proclamation of celebration at the end of the War of 1812. Few presidents issued Thanksgiving proclamations thereafter.

The driving force behind making Thanksgiving a national holiday was Sarah Josepha Hale, who was born in 1788 in Newport, New Hampshire. She married David Hale, a lawyer, who died in 1822, leaving her with five children. Hale turned to writing to generate money,

publishing her first book of verse in 1823. It is for her verse that Hale is remembered by many Americans. One of her poems was "Mary Had a Little Lamb." Hale was among the first American women to have a novel published, and she was one of the first authors—male or female—to write a novel that addressed the problem of slavery. *Northwood; a Tale of New England*, which appeared in two volumes in 1827, compared life in New England with life in the South. An entire chapter of *Northwood* is devoted to a Thanksgiving dinner that includes roasted turkey with a savory stuffing, beef, pork, mutton, gravy, vegetables, goose, duck, chicken pie, pumpkin pie, pickles, preserves, cakes, sweetmeats, and fruits along with currant wine, cider, and ginger beer.

The publication of *Northwood* brought Hale fame, and she was asked to serve as the editor of *American Ladies' Magazine*, a small magazine published in Boston. Louis A. Godey, who had launched *Godey's Book* in 1830, purchased *American Ladies' Magazine* in 1836 and asked Hale to edit the combined magazine, named *Godey's Lady's Book*. Under Hale's management the magazine went from selling ten thousand copies in 1837 to selling 150,000 copies by 1860. *Godey's Lady's Book* had strict rules against publishing articles on political topics, a practice that was followed even during the Civil War. But this restriction did not prevent Hale in 1846 from launching a campaign in support of creating a national holiday for Thanksgiving.

For seventeen years Hale wrote annually to presidents, members of Congress, and every governor of every state and territory, requesting each to proclaim the last Thursday in November Thanksgiving Day. In an age before word processors and typewriters, this was a daunting task. Hale also wrote editorials in *Godey's Lady's Book* promoting Thanksgiving. Every year, she noted how many states had agreed to celebrate Thanksgiving on the last Thursday of November. Hale encouraged other magazines to join the quest of making Thanksgiving a national holiday, and many published Thanksgiving-related stories, poems, and illustrations.

Hale believed that Thanksgiving Day could pull the United States together while sectional differences, economic self-interest, and slavery were pulling the nation apart. During the 1850s the nation was particularly concerned with the slavery question. In 1852 *Uncle Tom's Cabin*, the novel by Harriet Beecher Stowe, inflamed the public in both North and South. Six months after the publication of *Uncle Tom's Cabin*, Hale revised and republished

Northwood with a new subtitle: *Life North and South; Showing the True Character of Both*. Hale concluded that the way to end slavery was for every church in America to take up a collection on Thanksgiving Day for the purpose of purchasing slaves, educating them, and repatriating them to Africa. Whether or not churches purchased slaves on Thanksgiving Day, Hale hoped the day would serve as a national symbol that would bind people together and perhaps prevent dissolution of the country.

Hale was close to success in 1860, when she announced that Americans were celebrating Thanksgiving Day in thirty states and three territories. Despite Hale's hopes, Americans' sitting down to dinner on the same day was not enough to prevent dissolution of the nation. During the Civil War Hale redoubled her efforts to make Thanksgiving a national holiday. A few months after the North's military victories at Gettysburg and Vicksburg in the summer of 1863, Lincoln declared the last Thursday in November a national day of Thanksgiving. Every president since has proclaimed Thanksgiving Day a national holiday.

Hale's pre-1865 letters and editorials promoting Thanksgiving Day made no mention of the Pilgrims or the first Thanksgiving feast. Neither did the hundreds of previously published local and state Thanksgiving Day proclamations. Neither did George Washington's, Abraham Lincoln's, or other presidential proclamations. And neither did newspaper or magazine articles. There were several good reasons for this. Jamestown had been settled before Plymouth, and colonists in Jamestown had observed days of Thanksgiving before Plymouth was settled. Indeed, Jamestown has a plaque proclaiming the site of the first Thanksgiving celebration. Several other locations make claims of being the place where the "first Thanksgiving" was celebrated in what would become the United States.

Hale made the connection between the Pilgrims and the first Thanksgiving holiday in an 1865 editorial in *Godey's Lady's Book*. This editorial was picked up by newspapers and by other magazines. By 1870 school textbooks contained the story of the "first Thanksgiving." The

---

PRESIDENT'S THANKSGIVING PROCLAMATION, 2003

Each year on Thanksgiving, we gather with family and friends to thank God for the many blessings He has given us, and we ask God to continue to guide and watch over our country.

Almost 400 years ago, after surviving their first winter at Plymouth, the Pilgrims celebrated a harvest feast to give thanks. George Washington proclaimed the first National Day of Thanksgiving in 1789, and Abraham Lincoln revived the tradition during the Civil War. Since that time, our citizens have paused to express thanks for the bounty of blessings we enjoy and to spend time with family and friends. In want or in plenty, in times of challenge or times of calm, we always have reasons to be thankful.

America is a land of abundance, prosperity, and hope. We must never take for granted the things that make our country great: a firm foundation of freedom, justice, and equality; a belief in democracy and the rule of law; and our fundamental rights to gather, speak, and worship freely.

These liberties do not come without cost. Throughout history, many have sacrificed to preserve our freedoms and to defend peace around the world. Today, the brave men and women of our military continue this noble tradition. These heroes and their loved ones have the gratitude of our Nation.

On this day, we also remember those less fortunate among us. They are our neighbors and our fellow citizens, and we are committed to reaching out to them and to all of those in need in our communities.

This Thanksgiving, we again give thanks for all of our blessings and for the freedoms we enjoy every day. Our Founders thanked the Almighty and humbly sought His wisdom and blessing. May we always live by that same trust, and may God continue to watch over and bless the United States of America.

NOW, THEREFORE, I, GEORGE W. BUSH, President of the United States of America, by virtue of the authority vested in me by the Constitution and laws of the United States, do hereby proclaim Thursday, November 27, 2003, as a National Day of Thanksgiving. I encourage Americans to gather in their homes, places of worship, and community centers to share the spirit of understanding and prayer and to reinforce ties of family and community.

IN WITNESS WHEREOF, I have hereunto set my hand this twenty-first day of November, in the year of our Lord two thousand three, and of the Independence of the United States of America the two hundred and twenty-eighth.

GEORGE W. BUSH

---

linkage was salient enough by 1879 for the Reverend I. N. Tarbox to write a history of Thanksgiving in which he traced its origins to the Pilgrims. Tarbox was followed by others, the most important of whom was the Reverend W. DeLoss Love. Love systematically traced the Thanksgiving celebration from its origins as a religious observance and collected proclamations, many of which he published in his *The Fast and Thanksgiving Days of New England*. Love's massive compilation proved that there was no "first Thanksgiving." But the other works had clearly traced the Thanksgiving holiday to the Pilgrims, and the popular press was not far behind in making the connection.

By the late 1880s the concept of the Pilgrim-centered first Thanksgiving had blossomed in popular books. One version appeared in Jane Goodwin Austin's *Standish of Standish: A Story of the Pilgrims*, which contained a full chapter on the "first Thanksgiving." The drama of Austin's account appealed to others; many writers repeated her tale as fact, and it was adopted by many elementary and secondary school teachers. Thanksgiving plays were produced annually, and many schools offered special dinners based on Austin's fictional vision of life in Plymouth in 1621. This curriculum spawned a large body of children's literature focused on the Pilgrims and the "first Thanksgiving." These myths were enshrined in books, magazines, and artworks during the twentieth century.

The rapid adoption of the Pilgrim-Thanksgiving myth had less to do with historical fact and more to do with the arrival of hundreds of thousands of immigrants to the United States. Most of the previous immigrants had come from the United Kingdom and Ireland, and smaller numbers from other western and northern European nations. In the 1880s this immigration pattern changed as peoples from southern and eastern Europe flooded into the United States. The pace of immigration exploded; in 1900, 9 million persons arrived in American cities. Because the immigrants came from many lands, the American public education system attempted to create a common American heritage. One curricular need was to create an easily understood history of America. The Pilgrims were an ideal symbol for America's beginning, so they became embedded in the nation's schools, as did the Thanksgiving feast.

The Thanksgiving Dinner

Although Thanksgiving Day church services continued to be observed, the religious character of the observance gave way to the family dinner. By the late nineteenth century the traditional Thanksgiving dinner had been generally enshrined. At its core were foods considered to have originated in America. The central main course was turkey. Wild turkeys had been an important food for the colonists, so much so that wild turkeys disappeared from New England menus owing to near extinction. Soon after the establishment of Jamestown and Plymouth, however, domesticated turkeys were imported from England, but because of high cost, turkey was a feast dish in early America. By the late nineteenth century the price of turkeys had dropped, making the dish more affordable than other meats.

Other traditional components of the Thanksgiving meal are stuffing, cranberry sauce, potatoes, and pumpkin pie. From the earliest European recipes, turkeys have been stuffed with truffles, chestnuts, sausage, pork back, mushrooms, oysters, breadcrumbs, and butter, to name a

Thanksgiving Monarch. Postcard, early twentieth century. *Collection of Alice Ross*

few variations. Cranberries also have been part of the Thanksgiving meal. Cranberries were gathered by early American colonists, particularly in New England and New Jersey. They became a part of Thanksgiving feasts by the early nineteenth century. White potatoes did not become important in New England until almost the end of the eighteenth century, and sweet potatoes did not become a fixture at the Thanksgiving dinner until late in the following century. Sweet pies were a British culinary legacy. Although pumpkins are of New World origin, the first recipes for pumpkin pie appeared in British cookbooks. From the earliest records pumpkin and other sweet pies were part of Thanksgiving festivities.

Challenges to Thanksgiving

Not everyone has been happy with the turkey as the central focus of the Thanksgiving dinner. Perhaps the most prominent vegetarian during the late nineteenth and early twentieth centuries was John Harvey Kellogg, a Seventh-Day Adventist who managed a sanatarium in Battle Creek, Michigan. Kellogg was a dominant force in culinary Americana at the beginning of the twentieth century. In 1894 his wife, Ella Kellogg, published a totally vegetarian menu for Thanksgiving. It featured "mock turkey," made from nonmeat ingredients but shaped in the form of a turkey. More recently groups such as People for the Ethical Treatment of Animals (PETA) have used Thanksgiving to gain visibility for their beliefs. PETA has sponsored petitions and published leaflets encouraging a turkey-free Thanksgiving under the slogan "Give turkeys something to be thankful for!" To counteract the Butterball Thanksgiving talk line for answering questions about proper techniques of cooking turkey, PETA has encouraged its members to call the hotline and tell operators there is no proper way to kill and cook turkeys. Many vegetarians continue to celebrate Thanksgiving, substituting tofu-based products, such as "Tofurkey," for the traditional meat dishes. This practice has been met with derision by some vegetarians, who believe that not even turkey substitutes should be used.

Historians have debunked the myths surrounding the Pilgrims and the "first Thanksgiving." Businesses have commercialized Thanksgiving Day as the launch date for the Christmas season. Illustrators, filmmakers, and television producers have generated new Thanksgiving images. Immigrant groups have added new ingredients to the Thanksgiving culinary stew. Native Americans have proclaimed Thanksgiving Day the National Day of Mourning as a reminder of spiritual connection and in protest of oppression experienced. Vegetarians have campaigned against the consumption of turkey and other meat products. And those concerned with poor and homeless people have served special dinners for the needy. But the significance of Thanksgiving dinner has not faded.

[*See also* Cranberries; Pies and Tarts; Potatoes; Sweet Potatoes; Turkey; Vegetarianism.]

BIBLIOGRAPHY

Appelbaum, Diana Karter. *Thanksgiving: An American Holiday, an American History*. New York: Facts on File, 1984.

Austin, Jane. *Standish of Standish: A Story of the Pilgrims*. Boston: Houghton, Mifflin, 1889.

Hale, S. J. *Northwood; a Tale of New England*. Boston: Bowles and Dearborn, 1827.

Linton, Ralph, and Adelin Linton. *We Gather Together: The Story of Thanksgiving*. New York: Schuman, 1949.

Love, W. DeLoss, Jr. *The Fast and Thanksgiving Days of New England*. Boston: Houghton, Mifflin, 1895.

Pleck, Elizabeth. "The Making of the Domestic Occasion: The History of Thanksgiving in the United States." *Journal of Social History* 32 (1999): 780–781.

Plimoth Plantation. http://www.plimoth.org/learn/history/thanksgiving/thanksgiving.asp.

Siskind, Janet. "The Invention of Thanksgiving: A Ritual of American Nationality." *Critique of Anthropology* 12 (1992): 182–183, 186.

Smith, Andrew F. "The First Thanksgiving." *Gastronomica* (Fall 2003): 79–85.

Winslow, Edward. *Letter, a Relation or Iournall of the Beginning and Proceeding of the English Plantation Setled at Plimoth in New England*. London: Iohn Bellamie, 1622.

Young, Alexander. *Chronicles of the Pilgrim Fathers of the Colony of Plymouth, from 1602–1625*. Boston: Little and Brown, 1841

ANDREW F. SMITH

Thomas, David, *see Wendy's*

Timers, Hourglasses, Egg Timers

Measuring how long it takes for sand (or other fine granular substances, including ground eggshells) to flow from one blown glass bulb through a narrow neck to another glass bulb has been used for centuries as an accurate way of determining the passage of time. Most famously, hourglasses measure an hour. Short times, especially for cooking eggs, have been measured with similar, smaller hourglass-shaped timers since the 1800s, maybe earlier. Three minutes is a standard. A "three-minute egg" has a cooked white and soft yolk. These glass timers typically are set in a decorative wooden cylinder with windows or are protected by dowels connecting flat bottom and top, so the device can be flipped to double the time or start over. Other timers revolved within a decorative frame. One such device struck a bell after sufficient sand tipped the glass. Around 1910 one kitchen supply company, Silver's, sold a wall-mounted timer. Marked on a plaque behind the rotatable timer were levels denoting "hard boiled," "well done," "medium cooked," and "soft boiled."

Clockwork bell timers were introduced in the early twentieth century. Dials could be set for one to sixty minutes, even 120 on some models. By the 1990s, many clockwork timers came in whimsical shapes, including various kitchen utensils. Electric timers that could be wired to ovens were introduced around 1930, electronic ones sixty years later.

[*See also* Egg-Preparation Tools; Eggs.]

BIBLIOGRAPHY

Franklin, Linda Campbell. *300 Years of Kitchen Collectibles*. 5th ed. Iola, WI: Krause, 2003.

LINDA CAMPBELL FRANKLIN

Toasters

The complexity of colonial hearth toasters reflected the culinary importance of toast, particularly among colonists from Great Britain. Set before the fire, the most elaborate toaster held several pieces of bread in an open, four-legged, wrought iron rack. Kick toasters were used for browning both sides of bread. The cook used a toe to nudge the device around on a central swivel. Long-handled drop toasters were lifted and turned manually. Simpler models required the cook to pick up and turn slices by hand. Cooks of modest means speared a slice of bread on a large, forged-iron fork and held it to the fire.

In the 1890s stovetop toasters were made of perforated sheet iron and had wire supports for bread on four pyramidal sides. The chimney-like effect of these toasters caused rising heat to toast bread one side at a time. Electric heating elements similar to those used in twenty-first century toasters were known in the 1890s, but a functioning electric toaster did not come about until approximately 1910. This toaster was essentially a heavy wire rack on which two slices of bread were positioned near a central mica-insulated heating element. Refinements of many kinds followed, including enclosures for toasting both sides simultaneously; automatic, adjustable timing; warming racks; and pop-up mechanisms. Since the 1940s, styling has been largely cosmetic; the essential heating elements have changed little.

[*See also* Bread; Bread, Sliced; Breakfast Foods; Hearth Cookery.]

BIBLIOGRAPHY

Artman, E. Townsend. *Toasters, 1909-1960: A Look at the Ingenuity and Design of Toaster Makers*. Atglen, PA: Schiffer Publishing Co., 1996.

Franklin, Linda Campbell. *300 Years of Kitchen Collectibles*. 5th ed. Iola, WI: Krause, 2003.

Greguire, Helen. *Collector's Guide to Toasters and Accessories: Identification and Values*. Paducah, KY: Collector Books, 1997.

LINDA CAMPBELL FRANKLIN AND ALICE ROSS

Toasts

Toasting was well established elsewhere when the United States became a country, but America gave its own twist to the custom of saying something clever when glasses were raised. During the American War of Independence, toasts tended in the direction of curses, such as "To the enemies of our country! May they have cobweb breeches, a porcupine saddle, a hard-trotting horse, and an eternal journey." After the war, no official dinner or celebration was complete without thirteen toasts, one for each state. The thirteen-toasts tradition appears to date from the series of banquets held in honor of George Washington on his retirement. For many years, the thirteen toasts were obligatory at local Fourth of July celebrations. At such times each toast was followed by an artillery salute, three cheers from the crowd, and a song. Although they differed somewhat from locale to locale, the thirteen toasts were generally patriotic, proud, and nonpartisan. Those honored ranged from the holiday itself—"May it ever be held in grateful remembrance by the American people"—to the nation's former presidents—"In the evenings of well-spent lives pleased with the fruits of their labors, they cheerfully await the summons that shall waft them to brighter abodes." Invariably there was a toast to the signers of the Declaration of Independence.

Toasting not only transferred easily to North America but also was enhanced by the skill of various practitioners, including some of America's early leaders. If not the best,

Benjamin Franklin certainly ranked with them. A number of Franklin's toasts have been recalled but none more often than one he delivered at Versailles while American emissary to France. On this occasion the toasting was led by the British ambassador, who said, "George the Third, who, like the sun in its meridian, spreads a luster throughout and enlightens the world." The next toast came from the French minister, who said, "The illustrious Louis the Sixteenth, who, like the moon, sheds his mild and benevolent rays on and influences the globe." Franklin finished the round, "George Washington, commander of the American armies, who, like Joshua of old, commanded the sun and the moon to stand still, and both obeyed."

Although quite popular through the colonial period and beyond, toasting fell out of "polite society" by the mid-nineteenth century, when etiquette writers considered toasts not gentlemanly and deemed them appropriate only in taverns. This proscription probably was related to the increase in formal, mixed-sex dining in the nineteenth century. Ladies eschewed what they considered the vulgar custom of "drinking healths." Toasting never disappeared entirely, however. Americans tended away from Old World floweriness to give toasting its own utilitarian spin by getting right down to business. The following are a few examples:

> A drop of whiskey
> Ain't a bad thing right here.
> > *Bret Harte*

> Here's to Prohibition,
> The devil take it!
> They've stolen our wine,
> So now we make it.
> > *Toast to the Volstead Act*

> Here's to today!
> For tomorrow we may be radioactive.
> > *Cold War toast, ca. 1955*

> Here's to Hollywood—
> A place where people from Iowa
> Mistake each other for movie stars.
> > *Fred Allen*

[*See also* Drinking Songs.]

BIBLIOGRAPHY

Dickson, Paul, ed. *Toasts: Over 1,500 of the Best Toasts, Sentiments, Blessings, and Graces.* New York: Crown, 1991.

PAUL DICKSON

Tomatoes

The tomato plant (*Lycopersicon esculentum*) originated in South America but was domesticated in Central America in pre-Columbian times. When Europeans arrived, tomatoes were being consumed only in Central America. The lack of widespread diffusion suggests that tomatoes were a late addition to the culinary repertoire of Mesoamerica. The Spanish first encountered tomatoes after their conquest of Mexico began in 1519. They disseminated tomato plants to the Caribbean and then into Europe, where the fruit was consumed in southern Italy and Spain by the mid-sixteenth century.

The first published record of tomatoes appeared in an Italian herbal in 1544. By the late seventeenth century, tomatoes were being eaten in the eastern Mediterranean region and North Africa. Tomato cookery flourished in southern France late in the eighteenth century, and tomato recipes appeared in French cookbooks by the early nineteenth century. Tomatoes were cultivated in England by 1597; however, there is little evidence of British consumption before the mid-eighteenth century.

Who introduced the tomato into America is unknown. Spanish colonists introduced tomatoes in their settlements in what became the states of Florida, New Mexico, Texas, and California. As they visited and occupied territories previously controlled or influenced by Spain and Mexico, English and American settlers were exposed to tomato cookery. Other Americans were exposed to tomato cookery while living in or visiting the Caribbean region. Whatever the source, American colonists in South and North Carolina were using tomatoes by the mid-eighteenth century.

From the South, tomato culture slowly spread up the Atlantic coast and the Mississippi River system. By the early nineteenth century, tomatoes were consumed in all regions of the United States, and tomato recipes frequently appeared in American cookery manuscripts and cookbooks. Popular myth to the contrary, few Americans ever considered the tomato poisonous. Despite widespread diffusion of tomatoes in the early nineteenth century, there were several reasons why many Americans did not eat them. Many colonists of English, Scottish, and Irish heritage had immigrated to America before the tomato became a common food in Britain and Ireland. The physical isolation of America during the late eighteenth and early nineteenth centuries contributed to the lack of familiarity with the growing popularity of tomatoes in Europe. Other reasons for the lack of early success were that some

Americans did not like the smell, taste, or appearance of tomatoes. Others were concerned about nutritional value.

During the early nineteenth century, refugees and settlers, some of whom had already eaten tomatoes, entered America through cities. Likewise, those engaged in trade with regions of the world that had already adopted tomatoes, such as the islands of the Caribbean, operated through these cities. The popularity of tomatoes spread outward from the urban areas of the United States.

The introduction of tomatoes into a community did not necessarily signal immediate adoption as a culinary ingredient. Tomatoes were grown for years in northern gardens as ornaments or curiosities before they were timidly tasted. Likewise, culinary use by some segments of a community did not mean that everyone ate the fruits. French and Creole refugees ate tomatoes in Philadelphia long before other Philadelphians did. Many northerners were aware that the French, Italians, and Spanish ate tomatoes, but this knowledge was not sufficient to persuade them.

These social and cultural components of diffusion and adoption were mediated by climatic conditions, local soil composition, knowledge of cultivation techniques, and the availability of seeds. In parts of the southern states, tomatoes grew almost spontaneously. In northern and midwestern states, the plants could be grown easily only if the farmer was schooled in their cultivation.

Tomato Cookery

In pre-Columbian times tomatoes were used by the Aztecs and other indigenous peoples of Central America for making sauces, particularly in combination with chilies and ground squash seeds. After the Spanish conquest, vinegar was added to the tomato and chilies to produce what came to be called salsa. Numerous other uses of the tomato were developed in Mexico and Central America. The first located American tomato recipe appeared in Harriott Pinckney Horry's cookery manuscript dated 1770. Tomato recipes appeared in published American cookbooks by 1792.

Although several tomato recipes had been published in America before 1824, most were previously published in Great Britain. The second edition of Mary Randolph's *Virginia House-wife* (1825) featured seventeen tomato recipes, including one for ketchup, two for marmalade, three for soup, and four for Spanish dishes. Randolph's contribution was not only in the quantity of tomato recipes but also in their quality. She set the standard for tomato cookery for the next three decades, and subse-

Tomatoes. Hoop training of tomatoes, from Reeves & Simonson's *Descriptive Catalogue of Choice Selected Seeds,* 1874, p. 27.

quent cookbook authors borrowed extensively from her work, as did newspapers, magazines, and agricultural publications.

The Frugal Housewife by Lydia Maria Child of Massachusetts, published in 1829, summarized the lessons Child had learned as a thrifty New England housekeeper. Child's book included recipes for stewed tomatoes and tomato ketchup. She averred that "the best sort of catsup is made from tomatoes" and that a cup of ketchup added to chowder made the dish "very excellent." This was the first known inclusion of tomatoes in chowder. Although Child's recipe was first published in Boston, a variation of this recipe became known as Manhattan clam chowder. Later editions of the cookbook included the first known recipe for tomato pie, which was similar to "rich squash pie" with the addition of an extra egg or two.

Since the 1820s, American cookbooks have regularly published recipes for tomatoes. In these recipes tomatoes were stuffed, fried, hashed, pickled, baked, scalloped, broiled, chopped, or preserved. Tomatoes were added to soups and gumbos and cooked with poultry, veal, ham, pork, beef, calves feet, or sweetbreads. Tomatoes also were used in sweets, including marmalade and jellies, as well as in and on macaroni, fish, and shrimp. Tomatoes were used to make beverages. The earliest of these were alcoholic drinks: beer, whiskey, champagne, and wine, none of which was particularly successful.

Tomato cookery in America was wildly popular throughout the late nineteenth and early twentieth centuries. The creativity reflected in early tomato recipes then began to wane as attempts to breed tomatoes that were easy to transport and had a long shelf life led to development of the unpalatable tomato varieties whose progeny is stocked in supermarkets. Although these trends made tomatoes accessible in an America that was rapidly moving from rural to urban areas, taste and variety were sacrificed. But there were and continue to be recurrences of inspiration. Southern Italian immigration during the late nineteenth and early twentieth centuries brought new ways of using tomatoes to America. Hispanic immigration from the Caribbean, Mexico, and Central and South America had a similar influence on tomato cookery in the late twentieth century. Because of these influences, tomato cookery has had renewed vigor.

Tomato Processing

In the early twenty-first century, 80 percent of the tomato crop is used in processed foods. Tomatoes were first canned in New Jersey during the 1840s, and the tomato canning industry accelerated during and after the Civil War. Cans were fashioned by hand, and the seams and bottoms were soldered on. The cans were then boiled in water. The cans were hand filled, and the cappers soldered on the lids one at a time.

The effects of the Civil War on tomato-related industries in the North were particularly dramatic. To feed the northern army, contracts were let to canning factories, which employed mostly women. These contracts greatly stimulated the growth of tomato canneries. Confederate soldiers, who often endured meager rations, fought not only for the southern cause but also to acquire a square meal from a defeated Union Army's supplies, which often included canned tomatoes. By the end of the war, empty tomato cans were found everywhere.

Tomato. Beefsteak tomato, from Anderson Canning Co. label. *Warshaw Collection of Business Americana, Archives Center, National Museum of American History, Behring Center, Smithsonian Institution*

These wartime effects were small, however, compared with the dramatic expansion in tomato consumption after the war. Many northern soldiers ate canned vegetables for the first time while they were in the army. After the war, the demand for canned products soared. By 1870 tomatoes were among the three main canned vegetables, along with peas and corn. By 1879 more than 19 million cans of tomatoes were being manufactured annually.

To meet the expanded need, farmers grew tomatoes in hothouses and used other techniques of forwarding them. With the completion of the transcontinental railroad, fresh tomatoes were shipped from California to New York. Commercial production of tomatoes began in northern Florida in 1872, and within ten years, Florida tomatoes were sold on the Chicago market.

To protect American tomato growers against foreign competition, Congress passed the Tariff Act of 1883, levying a 10 percent duty on imported vegetables. In the spring of 1886 John Nix imported tomatoes into New York from the West Indies. Maintaining that they were a fruit rather than a vegetable, Nix paid the duty under protest. In February 1887 he brought suit in New York against the collector, Edward L. Hedden, to recover the duties. After six years of winding through courts and appeals courts, the case of *Nix v. Hedden* was argued before the U.S. Supreme Court. The opinion of the Supreme Court was delivered by Justice Horace Gray, who reported that the single question in this case was whether tomatoes, considered as provisions, were classed as vegetables or as fruit within the meaning of the Tariff Act of 1883.

The tomato canning and bottling processes were automated during the second half of the nineteenth century, when devices for capping, filling, scalding, topping, wrapping, and boxing came into use. This equipment was integrated and interconnected by the 1920s, and tomato canning was fully automated.

Another automation revolution occurred in the harvesting of tomatoes. Before World War II California produced 20 percent of the nation's tomatoes. The mechanical harvester caught on in California during the late 1940s. By 1953 California growers cultivated 83,000 acres and produced 50 percent of all tomatoes in the United States. The acreage had reached 130,000 by 1960. The harvester reduced by two-thirds the cost of processing tomatoes. At the same time, yields have increased greatly. In 1967 California growers harvested between seventeen and twenty tons of tomatoes per acre. By the 1990s they averaged thirty-four tons per acre. Hence, total production of tomatoes for processing increased from 2,250,000 tons in 1960 to more than 9 million tons in 1990. At the beginning of the twenty-first century, 90 percent of all American processed tomatoes were grown in California.

Nutritional Information

The healthful qualities of tomatoes were not established until the mid-twentieth century. Tomatoes have considerable vitamin C and some vitamin A. Tomatoes rank

Tomato Paste. Madonna tomato paste advertising pieces, one in English, the other in Italian. *Collection of Andrew F. Smith*

thirteenth among other commonly consumed fruits and vegetables as a source of vitamin C and sixteenth as a source of vitamin A. Overall, tomatoes rank sixteenth nutritionally behind other vegetables. Despite this comparatively low ranking, tomatoes contribute more vitamin A and C and other nutrients to the American diet than do other fruits and vegetables because so many more tomatoes are consumed. In addition, medical researchers believe that tomatoes may be an anticancer weapon. Tomatoes contain lycopene, the plant pigment that makes fruits red. Research has demonstrated that people with more lycopene in their blood have lower rates of certain forms of cancer.

In the United States, tomatoes are second only to potatoes in annual vegetable consumption. Annual per capita use of tomatoes and tomato products in the United States reached an annual total fresh-weight equivalent of ninety-one pounds per person by 1999. The United States is one of the world's largest tomato producers.

[*See also* Canning and Bottling; Child, Lydia Maria; Ketchup; Mexican American Food; Randolph, Mary; Salsa; Transportation of Food.]

BIBLIOGRAPHY

Collins, Douglas. *America's Favorite Food: The Story of Campbell Soup Company.* New York: Harry N. Abrams, 1994.

Smith, Andrew F. *Pure Ketchup: The History of America's National Condiment.* Columbia: The University of South Carolina Press, 1996.

Smith, Andrew F. *Souper Tomatoes: The Story of America's Favorite Food.* New Brunswick, NJ: Rutgers University Press, 2000.

Smith, Andrew F. *The Tomato in America: Early History, Culture, and Cookery.* Columbia: University of South Carolina Press, 1994.

ANDREW F. SMITH

Tom Collins, *see Cocktails; Collins*

Toothpicks

The humble toothpick likely has been around since the about the time of the discovery of the wheel. Christy G. Turner, an anthropologist at Arizona State University, was quoted as follows in *Smithsonian* magazine in 1997: "As far as can be empirically documented, the oldest demonstrable human habit is picking one's teeth." In America the toothpick is mentioned in the rules that have become known as "George Washington's Rules of Civility" (adopted from Francis Hawkins's *Youth's Behaviour, or Decencie in Conversation amongst Men*, which appeared

in 1664): "Cleanse not your teeth with the Table Cloth Napkin Fork or Knife, but if Others do it let it be done w/t Pick Tooth." Washington's preference was a toothpick made from goose quill. Until 1870 toothpicks were made of bone, quill, ivory, gold, or silver. They were often displayed as signs of personal wealth but were considered an American vulgarity when used in public, as Charles Dickens observed in the 1840s.

America gave the world the throwaway mass-produced wooden toothpick. Working as an exporter's agent in Brazil in the late 1860s, Charles Forster saw young boys selling "wooden slivers" carved from Spanish willow. He sent some home to his wife in the United States, and she gave them away to friends, who found them a pleasure to use. Forster returned to the United States determined to get into the business. He developed a machine for manufacturing toothpicks out of white birch, "a wood that was easily carved and left no aftertaste." In January 1870 in Boston Forster opened his first factory and began to produce toothpicks in huge numbers: One birch tree produced millions of toothpicks. Within weeks Forster realized that he had to establish a demand for his product and hit on a bit of inspired marketing. He recruited Harvard students to work for him in return for free meals. A student would go to one of the best restaurants in Boston, purchase a meal, and then loudly demand a wooden toothpick. When none was forthcoming, the diner would inform the restaurant management that toothpicks could be obtained from Charles Forster. The scheme worked, and soon almost every restaurant and many dining rooms featured toothpicks in holders designed for the purpose. Forster moved his operation to Maine to be close to a ready supply of birch.

Toothpicks became elements of dental hygiene and were sold door to door by children working for prizes. In the mid-1920s every youngster selling one hundred boxes of Velvet toothpicks received a baseball and bat. Advertisements for Velvet toothpicks proclaimed, "Tooth picks should be used as regularly as a tooth brush. They save the teeth and preserve the health." The advent of widespread flossing and the decline in the custom of public tooth picking led the *Wall Street Journal* to proclaim in a 1985 headline, "End of an Era: Toothpicks Fall Out of Favor." The versatility of toothpicks, however, has provided their salvation. Toothpicks are used for purposes ranging from dental hygiene to structural integrity for club sandwiches. In the early twenty-first century the Forster plant in Strong, Maine, which had been purchased by Diamond and then the Jarden Corporation, was supplying the United States with

85–90 percent of its toothpicks. According to one estimate, toothpicks are present in more than 90 percent all American households.

[*See also* Dining Rooms, Table Settings, and Table Manners.]

PAUL DICKSON

Train Food, *see Dining Car*

Transportation of Food

The transportation of food marked the beginning of the colonization of North America. Legend has it that cattle and hogs were transported to Florida by a Spaniard in 1521. A century later, the first groups of English settlers brought seeds with them to Massachusetts and Virginia to plant parsnips, cabbages, wheat, and apples. Potatoes arrived in the 1620s, taking a long and winding route from Peru through Europe. In the middle to late 1700s, new foods—vines, broccoli, chives, and strawberries—arrived with Thomas Jefferson, who planted them in his garden at Monticello.

By the middle of the eighteenth century agriculture was thriving, and America began to develop as an international trading force. Hundreds of thousands of Atlantic codfish were shipped to the world market. Hams and apples went from Virginia to England. Grain and other foodstuffs were exported as the European wars boosted demand. Food continued to be imported into the colonies. From the West Indies came molasses, used widely as a sweetener, and rum, another sugar by-product. Back to the West Indies went codfish from the northern shores. Such trade helped strengthen the system of slavery: The sugar was produced by slaves; the codfish fed them.

A veritable feast crisscrossed the ocean, an exchange that in part formed the historical basis of what is eaten in the early twenty-first century. Combined with native crops, seeds and breeds originally transported from afar became the basis of a unique American diet. But once the foods had taken root, they did not travel far. With the exception of tradable commodities such as sugar, people lived close to where their food was produced. On North American soil, the degree of food transportation was relatively small. Roads were bad or nonexistent, the cost of transportation was astronomical, and the spoilage rate was high.

Steamboats, Canals, and Railroads

In the nineteenth century the urban population was growing rapidly and needed food transported from the countryside. Time was ripe for a transportation revolution, a revolution that was eventually to see trains, planes, and automobiles transporting food all around America.

Before trains came steamboats. The first successful trial of the steamboat was on the Delaware River in 1787, and thirty years later the boats were running on the Mississippi. Faster, less expensive, and safer than the flatboats that had been the chief means of river transportation and able to ship both upstream and downstream, steamboats greatly enhanced the ability to transport perishable agricultural goods. At immense cost to the environment—consumption of firewood by steamboats is said to have been the primary cause of riparian deforestation in the first half of the nineteenth century—market production and commodity flows spread west. Political support for building food transportation networks was gaining. The era of canal building had begun.

The Erie Canal was a major development in food transportation. Funded by New York State, construction began in 1817 with the ambitious aim of linking the Great Lakes and New York City—and therefore the Atlantic Ocean—via the Hudson River. Opening in a piecemeal manner, the 363-mile long canal was completed in 1825. Critical to New York City's development, the canal also encouraged rapid westward migration and became the principal transportation route for midwestern agricultural commodities to the burgeoning eastern markets. Farmers set up all along the course of the canal, and the Midwest became—at the expense of New England—America's breadbasket, shipping corn and oats to feed eastern livestock and wheat and flour for human food. The presence of a terminal at Buffalo, New York, briefly made Buffalo the meatpacking center of the United States. Part of the attraction of transporting food on canals was the lower freight costs—approximately five to ten dollars per ton compared with one hundred dollars by land. This advantage affected food prices. Flour, which had cost approximately sixteen dollars per barrel in eastern cities, cost as little as four dollars after the canal opened. Wheat in the port of Savannah, Georgia, cost less when shipped from central New York via the Erie Canal than when grown in Georgia itself.

The economic attractions of the Erie Canal started a frenzy of further building. In 1824 the U.S. Corps of Engineers embarked on a national project to build harbors, channel rivers, and develop canals. In 1827 the Erie Canal system was connected to Cincinnati and from there via the Ohio River to the Mississippi River. By connecting the Great Lakes with the Mississippi, Cincinnati became a great food center, shipping grain and packing meat. Hogs could be salted and packed in the city—known as "Porkopolis"—and shipped to southern markets. By 1850 U.S. canals covered 3,600 miles, and freight rates were as low as one cent per ton per mile. The result was that more farmers and ranchers could transport more food to more places over more miles.

Canals had achieved great things for food transportation but at considerable cost. Vast swaths of forests had been cut, stream flows diverted, and wilderness forever tamed. With better transport encouraging more white settlement, the building of canals reinforced the displacement of native peoples. Furthermore, the canals had been built on the backs of a labor force—35,000 at its peak and composed mostly of Irish immigrants—who had toiled in notoriously rough and unhealthy conditions. Many died on the job. Although many had been built, canals remained an imperfect method of transporting food. In winter, canals could freeze for long periods. And despite the efficiencies, it still took almost three weeks to transport salt pork from Cincinnati to New York. Food shippers needed something faster, a system that would operate year-round. For that they turned to what would eventually supplant the canals—the railroads.

Railroads appeared in America in 1826 and subsequently developed alongside the steam engine. In 1830 the Baltimore and Ohio Railroad began carrying goods on the first American-built steam engine. From then on, railroads were built at a remarkable rate. The three thousand miles of track laid by 1840 had tripled to nine thousand a decade later. In 1851 the Erie Railroad line was completed. In 1852 the first train from the eastern seaboard reached Chicago by way of the Michigan Southern Railway. The tracks reached Mississippi two years later. Fueled by federal land grants that attracted private investment, transcontinental railroads started to spread. In 1869 the Union Pacific Railroad connected the east and west coasts. The Southern Pacific, linking Los Angeles and New Orleans, was added in 1883. By 1890 there were 125,000 miles of track (a figure that peaked at 254,000 miles in 1916). Freight rates declined precipitously, allowing relatively inexpensive shipment of food to almost every community in the United States.

Transporting Pigs. Driving pigs into a railway car. From George Augustus Sala, *America Revisited*, 3rd edition (London, 1883), vol. 2, p. 322.

The railroads changed meat distribution in the United States. Regional railroad networks focused on Chicago, leading to its development as the nation's meatpacking center. Not only hogs but also cattle shipped eastward from the Great Plains arrived to be slaughtered. Live animals were transported on the hoof to the railroad terminal in Abilene, Kansas, and shipped to the Union Stockyard in Chicago to be slaughtered and then shipped to eastern markets. Railroad expansion ended cattle drives for good. In 1885 the Missouri, Kansas, and Texas Railroads reached the heart of cow country, allowing slaughterhouses and packing plants to be located near the large ranches of the South and Southwest. One result was that the cows produced more meat because they walked shorter distances and thus lost less weight.

In the mid-nineteenth century the development of the refrigerated railroad car allowed the shipping of fresh meat. The first documented refrigerated cars were simply packed with ice. Starting in 1842 these cars were used on the Erie Railroad to ship milk to New York and fresh butter from New York to Boston. Seafood was shipped in

Grain Elevator. Grain elevator of the New York Central and Hudson River Railroad. Drawing by W. P. Snyder, *Harper's Weekly*, 22 December 1877. *Collection of Alice Ross*

the opposite direction, from the coast inland. In 1867 the first patented refrigerator car, an insulated car with ice bunkers at each end, transported strawberries on the Illinois Central Railroad. It was not until a decade later that a meatpacker, Gustavus Swift, applied mechanical refrigeration to railroad cars, enabling their widespread use. At last it was possible to transport—on a large scale—perishable foods such as meat, vegetables, and dairy products over long distances without spoilage.

The refrigerated car revolutionized the American fruit and vegetable industry. The extension of the Illinois Central Railroad to New Orleans opened the booming market of Chicago and the north-central Midwest to fresh southern vegetables, shipped back on trains that carried Midwestern wheat, corn, and salted pork to the south. Arkansas became one of the largest centers of apple production in the United States, and farmers along the rail lines of southern Illinois, Arkansas, and Mississippi were soon specializing in strawberries and other fragile crops for rail shipment to Chicago. Railroads though Maryland, Delaware, and Virginia also encouraged fruit and vegetable production for northeastern markets along their pathways, extending the season and lowering the prices of fresh produce. The Georgia peach industry was saved by expansion of the northern railroad network, which allowed a new breed of longer-lasting peaches to reach northern cities. Refrigerated cars on the Union Pacific railroad allowed transport of fruits from the West to the East Coast. In 1886 the first shipment of oranges left Los Angeles for the east, and the southwestern citrus and vegetable industries developed to feed the ever-growing eastern markets. Expansion of the South Florida Railroad through central Florida also facilitated the development of the citrus industry, allowing perishable produce to be transported to northern markets and to shipping carriers at ports.

The railroad and refrigerated car changed the way Americans ate. No longer did people have to rely largely on food that was locally available. They could eat what was produced anywhere in the United States. Not only was the diet of the nation enlarged, but also the quality of foods changed. Beef was more tender because the cattle no longer walked but rode to market, preventing the development of tough muscles. Fruits and vegetables were no longer partially rotten on arrival, dairy products no longer half-rancid. The cost of food decreased. In 1887 the Interstate Commerce Act ordered U.S. railroads to keep their rates fair and reasonable: Freight costs fell to seventy-five cents per ton per mile by 1900, from

$1.22 in 1883. In 1898, compared with 1872, one dollar could buy 62 percent more fresh mutton, 25 percent more fresh pork, 60 percent more lard and butter, and 42 percent more milk. At the same time, railroads changed the way America looked. As described by environmental historian Carolyn Merchant: "Railroads cut deep scars through the landscape and made heavy demand on forests and mines for firewood, timber, coal and iron. They contaminated their routes with noise, smoke, ashes, and threats of fire" (p. 67). This process of environmental change continued with the next great transportation revolution—the highways.

Highways and the Global Cool Chain

Railroads, steamships, and canals were marvels of food transportation in the nineteenth century. In the twentieth century, that honor belonged to the highways. Construction of a national highway system in the United States began in 1883. By 1910 one thousand miles of concrete road had been constructed. Twenty years later 694,000 miles of surfaced roadway and well over a million trucks crisscrossed the country. In 1932 U.S. Route 66, a 2,200-mile highway linking Chicago with Los Angeles, opened.

After World War II fundamental changes were made in food transportation by road. The Federal-Aid Highway Act of 1956 authorized the construction of a 41,000-mile interstate highway system. By 1976 approximately 38,000 miles of the Interstate Highway System were open, enabling trucks to carry foodstuff shipments once reserved for railroads. Gasoline prices fell, decreasing the cost of transporting food by road. Accompanying the rise of food transportation were technologies that enabled long-term storage. Major innovations in refrigeration after World War II gave birth to the frozen food industry. Scientists developed controlled-atmosphere techniques for controlling the ripening of—and thus extending the shelf life of—fruits, vegetables, and other perishables. With the new techniques, iceberg lettuce, developed to be almost indestructible in any form of transportation, could be vacuum cooled in transit. Ethylene was introduced so that tomatoes could ripen during transport rather than on the plant.

Like the canals and railroads before them, roads changed the functioning of the food economy. An example is milk in New York State. Even with the railroads, dairies had to be located close enough to a railhead to be able to function. That was to change with the advent of the tank truck. First used in 1914 to transport milk, truck

Transporting Milk. New Orleans milk cart, c. 1903. *Prints and Photographs Division, Library of Congress*

transport rapidly expanded during the 1930s. Accounting for only 10 percent of milk transport in 1931, trucks moved more than half of New York City's milk by 1938. The extension of milk trucks into areas previously without access to rail lines encouraged more intensive milk production in the state. It also broke down the division between cheese and butter producers (who previously had less rail access) and fluid-milk producers and led to realignment away from either side of the railway tracks to ring-shaped milk sheds around cities. Roads—and the automobiles that traveled them—were a catalyst for another change in the food economy: the decline in the numbers of people producing America's food. In 1930 the farm population (30.5 million) was approximately one-fourth of all persons living in the United States. By 1980 less than 3 percent (6.1 million) of the population were farmers. The roads had encouraged migration to the cities, the spread of the suburbs onto farmland, and the enlargement of farms.

The advent of road transport—along with development of large-scale supermarkets—later contributed to the changing organization of fresh produce retailing. Before World War II farmers generally delivered their crops to a shipping point such as a produce auction, where buyers paid for the food and then graded, packed, and transported it to wholesalers in terminal markets. The system of transportation has become a great deal more complex. Fruits and vegetables can be graded and packed at or close to the site of production or driven directly to food processors. Brokers for wholesalers or supermarkets tour the country, buying produce and trucking it across the

country to a supermarket distribution center or terminal market. Terminal markets have become less important than supermarkets, handling only 30 percent of U.S. produce, and supermarkets tend to source directly through large-volume centralized buying operations. For example, in the Mid-Atlantic states regional buyers for Safeway procure produce from all over the United States and contract with independent transportation companies to truck the products to the Safeway distribution facility in Maryland. Refrigerated Safeway tractor-trailers then deliver the produce to individual stores in the Mid-Atlantic region. Before they reach a store in Maryland, grapes have traveled approximately 3,370 miles; broccoli, 2,786 miles; and tomatoes, 1,097 miles before the consumer has driven to the supermarket. In some cases use of this system means that food is transported to Maryland from a producer in another state and then shipped back to that state for sale in a local supermarket.

The rise of processed foods has created new transportation patterns. The components of these foods must be transported from all over the United States to be manufactured and then shipped elsewhere. Ben and Jerry's Vanilla Heath Bar Crunch ice cream is manufactured in Waterbury, Vermont, but the eggs are shipped in from Iowa, the Heath Bar candy from Illinois, the milk and cream from Vermont, the cane sugar from Latin America, and the vanilla extract from Costa Rica. Dannon yogurt is manufactured in Ohio, but the company trucks sugar from Michigan, milk from Pennsylvania, corn from Illinois, fruit from California. Juice is flown in from Latin America and the Middle East.

The foregoing examples point to another trend in food transportation: imports. Fruits and vegetables are a notable example. In large part to feed the American demand for counter-seasonal and tropical products, produce is imported from all over the world. Although pineapples and bananas have been arriving in the United States since the nineteenth century, transportation of more tender foods, such as grapes and tomatoes, took the development of more sophisticated technology. By way of what has been termed the "global cool chain," products are transported in an integrated system of refrigeration that chills a product within hours of harvest and maintains controlled cool temperatures from the original place of chilling to consumers, who store the product in a refrigerator. Driving the system is research on the optimal transit conditions for each product, capital investment to build the vehicles necessary for such conditions, packaging and breeding innovations for reducing deterioration, and precision planning on the timing of harvest and transit. Inaugurating this technology on an international scale was the arrival of grapes from Chile in the late 1970s, a step that enabled American consumers to continue eating grapes after the U.S. season ended in winter. Grape consumption has since increased from two and one-half pounds to more than eight pounds per capita per year. Numerous perishables are transported this way—melons and limes from Mexico, tomatoes and bell peppers from Holland, and apples from New Zealand and China.

Transporting fruits and vegetables into the United States is part of a global trend of increasing food trade. Between 1961 and 2001 the value of international food trade tripled, the tonnage of food shipped between nations grew fourfold, and transportation costs declined—it costs 70 percent less to ship cargo by sea and 50 percent less to ship by air than it did in the 1980s. Most international food trade is by ship. But the perishable produce trade is growing rapidly, because fruits and vegetables are increasingly transported by airplane. These changes mean that more than 13 percent of the fruits eaten in the United States are imported. They also mean that more and more people are eating U.S. food. The United States is the largest food exporter in the world.

Food Miles

Food transportation is faster, less expensive, and farther than could have been imagined at the turn of the eighteenth century. Long-distance food travel has become the norm. By way of what has been termed "food miles," food in the United States typically travels between 1,550 and 2,480 miles from field to fork, 25 percent farther than in 1980. Many consumers, however, question the sense of eating globe-trotting food. Apart from the environmental effects of transportation, such as deforestation, environmentalists point out that long-distance travel requires more packaging, refrigeration, and fuel and generates waste and pollution. The shipment of raw and processed foods and agricultural inputs (products used to grow and to produce food) accounts for one-third of all freight transport in the United States, making the agricultural sector the largest user of freight transportation services in the country. More than 90 percent of fresh produce transported between cities in the United States moves by truck. The environmental costs of fuel—including the release of carbon dioxide—have received particular criticism. Analysis indicates that the semitrailers used to transport food are large fuel consumers relative to other

vehicles. Viewed as particularly culpable are high-value food items with relatively low caloric value and a high water content. An example is lettuce grown in the Salinas valley of California and shipped more than 3,100 miles east. The lettuce requires approximately thirty-six times as much fossil fuel energy in transport as it provides in food energy when it arrives. Such products are also criticized for having qualities related more to enduring long-distance transport and long-term storage than to flavor.

The answer to the food miles problem is, according to some experts, to eat more local food. In Iowa, for example, it has been estimated that food from the state—bought at farmers' markets and the like—uses four to seventeen times less fuel than food transported by the conventional system. By eating a chuck roast produced and consumed in Iowa, a diner is eating through ninety food miles compared with 5,375 miles for a roast made with out-of-state ingredients. Local food also travels: it can sometimes take more than two hundred miles to drive produce from farm to farmers' market. But those concerned with the preservation of traditional agriculture point out that buying locally has another benefit: supporting small farmers. Such farmers have struggled to keep up with the development of modern food transportation systems, losing out to large farmers more able to grow the quantities of food needed to make large-scale transportation economical.

A result of the food transportation revolution in the United States is that Americans can eat food from practically anywhere. Although American tastes remain regional, food transportation means that the U.S. food economy is more national and international than it used to be. However, in the face of the long distance between food and consumer, there is a movement in favor of transporting food less. This change would be a progressive one but ironically would take Americans a little closer to the old way of obtaining food—before the rise of trains, planes, and automobiles.

[See also California; Dairy Industry; Farmers' Markets; Fruit; Ice; Lettuce; Meat; Milk; Swift, Gustavus Franklin; Vegetables.]

BIBLIOGRAPHY

DuPuis, E. M. *Nature's Perfect Food: How Milk Became America's Drink*. New York: New York University Press, 2002.

Friedland, W. H. "The New Globalization: The Case of Fresh Produce." In *From Columbus to ConAgra: The Globalization of Agriculture and Food*, edited by A. Bonanno. Lawrence: University Press of Kansas, 1994.

Halweil, B. *Home Grown: The Case for Local Food in a Global Market*. Washington DC: Worldwatch, 2002.

Hora, M., and J. Tick. *From Farm to Table: Making the Connection in the Mid-Atlantic Food System*. Washington DC: Capital Area Food Bank, 2001.

Levenstein, H. *Revolution at the Table: The Transformation of the American Diet*. Berkeley: University of California Press, 2003.

Merchant, C. *The Columbia Guide to American Environmental History*. New York: Columbia University Press, 2002.

Pillsbury, R. *No Foreign Food: The American Diet in Time and Place*. Boulder, CO: Westview, 1998.

Pirog, R., T. Van Pelt, K. Enshayan, and E. Cook. *Food, Fuel and Freeways: An Iowa Perspective of How Far Food Travels, Fuel Usage, and Greenhouse Gas Emissions*. Ames, IA: Leopold Center for Sustainable Agriculture, 2001.

Root, W., and R. De Rochemont. "Transportation." In *Eating in America: A History*. New York: Morrow, 1976.

CORINNA HAWKES

Trotter, Charlie

The chef and restaurateur Charlie Trotter has been quoted as saying, "If it isn't broken, then break it." Trotter made his reputation on a cuisine in which, according to Molly O'Neill (*New York Times*), "the complexity of his recipes pushes the outer limits of culinary sanity." The cuisine, however, has won Trotter international acclaim and almost every major culinary award for his namesake restaurant, his books, and his television series.

Trotter was born in 1959 and reared in the northern Chicago suburb of Wilmette. His family was not food oriented, and Trotter never had ambitions of becoming a chef. However, on his prom night in 1976, while dining at The Bakery restaurant in Chicago, Trotter had an epiphany. Seeing the dramatic persona of the impeccably toqued chef Louis Szathmary, Trotter declared that one day he, too, would be a chef.

In college at the University of Wisconsin, Madison, where he majored in political science, Trotter began his quest by cooking for friends. After graduation he pursued a culinary career full time. With no formal experience, Trotter was given his first break at Sinclair's, a restaurant owned by Gordon Sinclair and Marshall Field IV in Lake Forest, Illinois, a northern suburb of Chicago. After several months at Sinclair's, training under the chef Norman Van Aken, Trotter began a self-styled apprenticeship, working in restaurants in Florida and San Francisco and reading every cookbook he could get his hands on. Trotter moved to France and ate out frequently at Michelin-rated three-star restaurants.

When he returned to the United States, Trotter catered elaborate dinner parties for prominent business and social leaders to hone his skills. In 1987 with his father's financial backing, Trotter purchased a 1908 Victorian house on the north side of Chicago. Trotter remodeled the building into the elegant, wood-paneled fine-dining establishment that bears his name. Trotter's cuisine, superbly paired with wines, quickly earned stellar reviews.

Likening his food to improvisational jazz, Trotter changes menus daily and never repeats a dish. The cuisine is based on classical French techniques, but Trotter freely uses Asian influences, as have other innovative American chefs, including Wolfgang Puck and Jeremiah Tower. Trotter incorporates other international touches in his tasting menu of, typically, fifteen courses. The chef relies on natural vegetable juices and stocks, purees, and infused oils instead of cream and butter-rich sauces, which Trotter believes neutralize flavors. Trotter emphasizes freshness, using organically grown grains and vegetables, meats from free-range animals, and line-caught fish.

To communicate his legacy of cuisine and service, Trotter has published ten books and teaches cooking on his award-winning PBS TV show. He regularly invites inner-city schoolchildren to experience fine dining at his restaurant and awards culinary scholarships through his philanthropic foundation. He has won numerous awards, among them the James Beard Foundation's Outstanding Chef in the United States (1999). *Wine Spectator* magazine cited Charlie Trotter's as the best restaurant in the world for wine and food. Trotter also received the dubious distinction of being named one of the meanest bosses in Chicago by a local magazine. He was cited for overseeing every dish that leaves the kitchen "and often bringing cooks and servers to tears." Trotter has said, "You basically give up your life to the pursuit of perfection."

[*See also* Celebrity Chefs; Puck, Wolfgang; Szathmary, Louis.]

BIBLIOGRAPHY

Austin, Michael. "Charlie in Charge." *North Shore*, October 1999.

Brown, Rochelle. *The Chef, the Story, and the Dish*. New York: Stewart, Tabori, and Chang, 2002.

Eig, Jonathan, and Cynthia Hanson. "The Golden Meanies." *Chicago Magazine*, November 1996.

Lawler, Edmund. *Charlie Trotter's*. New York: Lebhard Friedman, 2000.

O'Neill, Molly. "The Courage of His Confections." *New York Times Magazine*, Jan. 15, 1995.

SCOTT WARNER

Tschirky, Oscar

Oscar Tschirky (1866–1950), better known as Oscar of the Waldorf, was maître d'hôtel of the Waldorf-Astoria Hotel in New York City from 1893 to 1943. Tschirky emigrated from Switzerland in 1883, and with the help of his elder brother, Brutus, who was a chef in New York, Oscar landed a job as busboy at the Hoffman House, the best hotel in the city, the same day he landed in the United States.

From the moment of his arrival, Tschirky worked only at the finest places. In 1887 he was hired by Delmonico's, the most prestigious restaurant in New York City at the time. There Tschirky advanced to become headwaiter for the private dining rooms. Ever ambitious, when he heard about the $10 million Waldorf Hotel (the Astoria came later, with the addition of the Astoria wing in 1897) being built at Thirty-third Street and Fifth Avenue, Tschirky applied for a position. He wrote himself a letter of recommendation on Delmonico's stationery and encouraged the restaurant's well-known patrons to sign it. Four days after he mailed his impressive ten-page list, which resembled a who's who of New York, Tschirky was hired as the hotel's first employee.

Tschirky's management skills, attention to detail—he made a point of remembering what important guests liked to eat and drink—tact, class, good nature, and plain old hard work were some of the qualities that helped him thrive at the Waldorf and become the most influential American maître d'hôtel in his day. Tschirky established standards of service and grace that contributed to making the Waldorf the home away from home of celebrities, society, royalty, and presidents. Although Tschirky married and had three children, the hotel was his home away from home, too.

Guests always assumed that Oscar prepared and supervised all meals at the Waldorf. He was besieged by requests for recipes, especially after 1896, when he wrote *The Cook Book by "Oscar" of the Waldorf*, a hefty nine-hundred-page tome that included recipes from the most famous chefs of the day. But Tschirky admitted that he never cooked anything more difficult to prepare than scrambled eggs. Waldorf chronicler James Remington McCarthy wrote in his book *Peacock Alley*, "His fame . . . has rested upon the condition that the public—erroneously . . .—regards him—as an artist who has composed sonatas in soups, symphonies in salads, minuets in sauces, lyrics in entrees." Tschirky's art, however, was orchestrating the score to create a harmonious meal. In 1902 Tschirky shared his art in a booklet titled "Serving a Course Dinner by Oscar of the Waldorf-Astoria," In the booklet Tschirky explained in simple terms the intricacies of serving a modern course dinner to legions of eager hostesses who wanted to re-create at home the elegance of a meal served under Oscar's guidance.

Oscar is perhaps best remembered for the Waldorf salad, which he did create, but only with apples, celery, and mayonnaise. The salad has become a classic American dish, and there are as many versions of it as there are chefs. It is ironic that Oscar hated the walnuts that somehow became standard in the salad.

Legend around the Waldorf had it that, as a joke, Oscar's wife phoned the hotel one day and asked for Mr. Tschirky, who was paged throughout the hotel but did not answer the call. It seems Tschirky had forgotten his last name. The surname may be forgettable, but the legend of Oscar of the Waldorf lives on.

[*See also* Cookbooks and Manuscripts, *subentry* From the Civil War to World War I; Hotel Dining Rooms; New York Food.]

BIBLIOGRAPHY

McCarthy, James Remington. *Peacock Alley*. New York: Harper Brothers, 1931.
Schriftgiesser, Karl. *Oscar of the Waldorf*. New York: Dutton, 1943.

SHARON KAPNICK

Tuna

At the beginning of the twentieth century, few Americans ate tuna. Within a few decades, tuna rose from obscurity to become America's most consumed fish. At the century's end, high-priced tuna was ranked among America's finest culinary delicacies. Tuna is an oceanic fish in the Scombridae family related to mackerel and bonito. Historically, tuna has been consumed for hundreds of years in the Mediterranean, Latin America, Asia, and Polynesia. Although tuna, particularly albacore, skipjack, yellowfin, and bluefin, was abundant off North American shores, it was rarely consumed. In *The Fisheries and Fishery Industries of the United States* (1884), G. Brown Goode proclaimed that tuna was hardly ever eaten in America, although it was occasionally fed to animals or used as a bait fish. This lack of interest in tuna was most likely due to America's culinary history: British cookery dominated American cookery until the twentieth century, and tuna was not an important fish in British cookery. Beginning in the 1870s, sports fishermen were enthralled with catching tuna. Goode cited one report that fishing for it was "quite exciting, although tiresome and requiring a good deal of skill, as in the efforts of these fish to escape they pull with such violence as to endanger the lives of the fishermen by dragging them overboard." By 1898 tuna fishing was so popular that the Avalon Tuna Club was organized on Santa Catalina Island off mainland California.

Although not consumed by most Americans, tuna was eaten in California by immigrants from Japan and the Mediterranean. Until the twentieth century, the common English word for the fish was "tunny." The precise derivation of the word "tuna" is unknown. The 1881 *Proceedings of the United States Natural History Museum* reported that tuna was caught off California's Santa Cruz Island. Because this is the first located use of the word in English and because similar-sounding words were used in several places in the Mediterranean, the word "tuna" may have derived from these immigrants.

Canned Tuna

Tuna was canned in France and Italy by the late nineteenth century. Small quantities of *thoun* or *tonno* were imported into the United States by the early 1880s. The first American tuna cannery was established by Albert P. Halfhill, a grocer who had moved to Los Angeles in the 1880s. Halfhill joined the California Fish Company, which canned sardines and other fish. In 1903 the sardine catch was extremely limited, so Halfhill looked for another fish to pack. Because albacore was abundant in California waters, Halfhill experimented with canning tuna. In 1908 he successfully packed 250 cases of albacore, labeling them "Tuna," but few were sold. This lack of success changed in subsequent years owing to the promotional wizardry of H. Jevne, the pioneer Los Angeles grocer. Because of Jevne's efforts, Americans began to discover that the white meat of tuna was excellent tasting, especially after the tuna oil had been removed. The depletion of other traditionally consumed fish stocks, coupled with Halfhill's modest success, encouraged more tuna canners.

When albacore were found off the Oregon coast in 1910, salmon fishermen, who supplied the Columbia River Packers Association, began tuna fishing. The association later adopted the brand name Bumble Bee. Another packer was the California Tunny Canning Company, which was purchased by Gilbert Van Camp and his father, Frank Van Camp. They renamed their operation Van Camp Seafood and contracted with Japanese-owned fishing boats to buy albacore. Roy P. Harper, the Van Camp Seafood sales manager, introduced the brand names Chicken of the Sea and White Star. The promotional campaign, which likened tuna to chicken, greatly increased sales of tuna in America. By 1920 thirty-six tuna canneries dotted the West Coast landscape. One new packer was the French Sardine Company, launched by Martin Bogdanovich, from the Dalmatian isle of Vis. Bogdanovich had immigrated to San Pedro in 1908 and bought his first boat two years later. In 1917 he created StarKist Seafood. Decades later, Bumble Bee, Van Camp Seafood, and StarKist became America's, and for a time the world's, largest tuna canners.

The main early challenge facing the tuna canning industry was the migration patterns of tuna stocks off the Pacific coast. By 1925 the albacore had largely disappeared from California waters, and the tuna packing industry almost collapsed. By this time, tuna had become wildly popular in mainstream America. To meet the demand, Halfhill imported frozen tuna from Japan. By 1928 frozen albacore amounted to 7 percent of the California supply. The Japanese continued to sell canned tuna in the United States until the trade came to a halt during the Depression, when Congress levied a duty on imported tuna.

When the albacore departed California waters, the tuna industry shifted to yellowfin, which had a higher percentage of dark meat. Because Americans expected white albacore meat, the shift to yellowfin tuna required careful marketing. Only the white meat was selected from yellowfin, and it was marketed as "light meat tuna." Van Camp Seafood used the term "fancy tuna." Americans made the shift to yellowfin and demanded even more tuna. As tuna fishermen increased in number and expanded their catch to meet demand, yellowfin stocks disappeared along the California coast. Baja California, Mexico, then became the center of tuna fishing. When tuna catches declined off Baja California, tuna fishermen traveled farther south. This movement required a change in the vessels used to catch tuna. Small fishing boats gave way to the tuna clipper, which was equipped to carry live bait and was fitted with an ice system that allowed retention of the catch for long periods. By 1937 these large vessels fished off Central and South America, and in subsequent years fished for tuna in the South Pacific.

Tuna Cookery

Tuna recipes were first published in the United States in the mid-nineteenth century. These appeared in translated French cookery books or in cookbooks written by immigrant chefs and had little influence on American consumption of tuna. Tuna recipes were not published regularly in cookery magazines and American cookbooks until the early twentieth century. The first located tuna advertising cook booklet was published by a canner in 1913, Avalon Tuna, and other companies follow suit. The first noncommercial cookbook devoted exclusively to tuna, *The Tuna Cookbook* by Sheila Metcalf, was not published until 1972.

Early tuna recipes were surprisingly diverse. Recipes were published for canapés, fish cakes, salads, soufflés, loafs, rolls, fish balls, tuna melts, savory pies, cream tuna, croquettes, omelets, puddings, and sandwiches. Tuna was combined with a great variety of foods, including tomatoes, peppers, squash, rice, macaroni, celery, corn, peas, curry, spaghetti, and apples. Two major uses of tuna emerged from this diversity: tuna salad, which was considered healthful and dietetic, and tuna sandwiches, which became a mainstay in children's lunch boxes. The third major use, tuna noodle casserole, made its debut during the 1930s but became emblematic of American foodways in the 1950s. The first located tuna noodle casserole—the classic version with potato chips on top—was published in an advertising cook booklet in 1952.

There were many reasons for the rapid expansion of tuna cookery during the first half of the twentieth century. Once Americans concluded that tuna was palatable, the abundance of tuna off America's east and west coasts assured easy access to the fish. As demand for tuna increased, technological improvements in catching and processing meant that supply expanded faster than demand. The result was a decline in the price of tuna. To improve sales, tuna packers aggressively promoted tuna through advertisements. When the Depression hit during the 1930s, low-cost, healthful tuna became America's most highly consumed fish.

Tuna Challenges

Despite tuna's rapid rise to stardom, several major challenges confronted the American tuna industry. The first was related to health. Tuna was considered a healthful food and was mentioned as a diet food by the 1920s. Indeed, tuna is an excellent low-fat source of protein, contains B vitamins and omega-3 fatty acids, and has half the fat and cholesterol of an equal portion of chicken. However, problems emerged related to mercury, an industrial by-product dumped into America's rivers. Coastal fish ingested the mercury, and when they fed on

these fish, tuna became contaminated with mercury, which is toxic. In 1970 the U.S. Food and Drug Administration recalled canned tuna and found that 200,000 cases contained mercury levels above 0.5 parts per million. Testing procedures have been improved, greatly decreasing the possibility of mercury contamination in processed tuna.

Another challenge was related to the capture of dolphins by tuna boats. In the 1950s, the purse seine had been improved to the point at which other types of tuna fishing were uneconomical. To effectively use the purse seine, larger, faster, and more productive tuna boats were launched. By the early 1970s there were more than two thousand tuna boats in the United States, and 75 percent used purse seines. As the competition increased, fishers sought tuna in new locations. For unknown reasons, the yellowfin tuna in the mid-Pacific swim underneath dolphins. In this area, the nets caught both the yellowfin and dolphins. Entangled in the nets, hundreds of thousands of dolphins died every year. During the 1960s the movie and television series *Flipper* gave visibility to dolphins and caused public indignation with the tuna industry. The outcry led to the Marine Mammal Protection Act of 1972, which called for "insignificant dolphin kill levels approaching zero." The act was later amended to include imported tuna from countries that did not adhere to similar standards. Loopholes in the law led to passage of the International Dolphin Conservation Act in 1992. These laws have decreased the number of dolphin deaths due to tuna fishing, but loopholes remain, and the tuna industry continues to be blamed for killing dolphins.

Beginning in the 1950s, increased foreign competition with lower labor costs and fewer environmental controls led to the most serious challenge to confront the American tuna industry. Tuna companies began to migrate outside the continental United States, and many tuna boats were reflagged or sold to companies in other countries. This practice accelerated during the 1960s, 1970s, and 1980s. By 1989 there was only one surviving tuna cannery in the continental United States, and the tuna fleet, once the world's largest, had declined to only sixty-three boats. These shifts led to shifts in the American tuna industry. In 1950 Bumble Bee was acquired by Castle and Cook, a prominent seafood company based in Hawaii. Ten years later, Bumble Bee Seafoods was launched as a wholly owned subsidiary. In 1977 Bumble Bee acquired a tuna cannery in Puerto Rico and a fishing operation in Ecuador. Beginning in the 1980s Bumble Bee Seafoods went through a series of ownership changes. In 1989 Pillsbury, which had purchased Bumble Bee, sold it to Unicord, which is based in Bangkok, Thailand. In 2000 Bumble Bee Seafoods was acquired by ConAgra. Van Camp (Chicken of the Sea and White Star brands) opened a tuna cannery in American Samoa in 1954 and later started one in Puerto Rico. Ralston Purina purchased Van Camp Seafood in 1963 but sold it to Mantrust, one of Indonesia's largest food companies, in 1988. In 1997 Van Camp was purchased by Tri-Union Seafoods, the second largest tuna canner in the world.

The Pittsburgh-based H. J. Heinz Company bought StarKist and in 1963 launched an advertising campaign starring Charlie the Tuna, created by the Chicago advertising agency of Leo Burnett. In 1992 Charlie's Lunch Kit was introduced by StarKist as a do-it-yourself tuna salad package that includes tuna and packets of mayonnaise and relish. StarKist sells approximately 1 billion cans annually and is America's largest selling brand of tuna. Despite this success, Heinz sold StarKist to Del Monte in December 2002.

The bases of the American tuna industry became American Samoa and Puerto Rico. Both had access to a lower-paid labor pool than did operations on the U.S. mainland, and both had tax laws supportive of the tuna industry. Despite these changes, the American tuna industry has declined since 1989. Correlated with this decline have been the rise of imported tuna and the establishment of foreign tuna operations in the United States. More than 60 percent of the tuna eaten in America is imported.

Whatever the source of the catch, tuna remains America's most important fish. In 2001 Americans consumed 859 million pounds of tuna. In addition to its sale in the inexpensive canned form, tuna has emerged as a gourmet food. Beginning in the 1980s the sale of fresh tuna expanded. It is served in restaurants as grilled or sautéed steaks. Simultaneously, Japanese restaurants serving sushi and sashimi have become popular, and these two raw fish dishes are sold regularly in fish markets and supermarkets. Tuna is estimated as being only 5 percent of the total fish catch worldwide, but economically it is one of the most important fishes in the world.

[*See also* Advertising; Canning and Bottling; ConAgra; Del Monte; Fish, *subentry on* Saltwater Fish; Heinz Foods; Japanese American Food.]

BIBLIOGRAPHY

Bitting, A. W. *Appertizing, or the Art of Canning.* San Francisco: Trade Pressroom, 1937.

Black, Andy. *A Can of Tuna: The Complete Guide to Cooking with Tuna.* Santa Rosa, CA: Prism, 1995.

Block, Barbara A., and E. Donald Stevens, eds. *Tuna: Physiology, Ecology, and Evolution.* San Diego, CA: Academic Press, 2001.

Bonanno, Alessandro, and Douglas Constance. *Caught in the Net: The Global Tuna Industry, Environmentalism, and the State.* Lawrence: University Press of Kansas, 1996.

Doulman, David J., ed. *The Development of the Tuna Industry in the Pacific Islands Region.* Honolulu, HI: East-West Center, 1987.

Goode, G. Brown, and staff. *The Fisheries and Fishery Industries of the United States: Section I, The Natural History of Useful Aquatic Animals.* Washington, DC: U.S. Government Printing Office, 1884.

Grey, Zane. *Tales of Swordfish and Tuna.* New York: Grosset and Dunlap, 1927.

Joseph, James, Witold Klawe, and Pat Murphy. *Tuna and Billfish: Fish without a Country.* La Jolla, CA: Inter-American Tropical Tuna Commission, 1988.

May, Earl Chapin. *The Canning Clan: A Pageant of Pioneering Americans.* New York: Macmillan, 1937.

Metcalf, Sheila. *The Tuna Cookbook.* Garden City, NY: Doubleday, 1972.

National Marine Fisheries Service. *Fisheries of the United States 2001.* Washington, DC: U.S. Department of Commerce; National Oceanic and Atmospheric Administration, National Marine Fisheries Service, 2002.

Smith, Bill. *Tuna.* Short Hills, NJ: Burford, 2000.

ANDREW F. SMITH

Tupperware

Tupperware is the registered trademarked name for all products of the Tupperware corporation. Most famous are the lightweight, odorless, reusable plastic containers with patented airtight lids that epitomize American postwar suburban culture. Tupperware embodies the era of convenience foods and home refrigeration, the age of plastic and industrial production. Perhaps most important, its home-selling plan, the Tupperware Party, promulgated the distinctively American form of entertaining at which hostesses sell consumer products.

Earl Silas Tupper (1907–1983), a twentieth-century Benjamin Franklin, established Tupper Plastics Company in 1939 and developed the first Tupperware prototype around 1942. A home inventor who was raised on a New England farm, Tupper held traditional Yankee values of thrift and self-improvement and believed that industrial innovation could improve everyday life. Tupper's breakthrough came with a milky white, injection-molded plastic "bell tumbler," which launched the Tupperware line. The product reached stores in 1946.

Three years later Tupper published his first mail-order catalog, introduced the brand name "Tupperware," and proclaimed his dream for the "Tupperization" of every home in America. That same year Tupper received the patent for his airtight Tupper seal, which he issued "standard" with all containers beginning in 1948.

Almost indestructible, Tupper's containers were made from a refined polyethylene plastic, which he trademarked as Poly-T: Material of the Future. Tupperware's domestication of an avant-garde material previously used by industry and aviation was revolutionary. Although others sold functional kitchen plastics, Tupperware had no direct competition.

The industrial design movement quickly embraced Tupperware's clean lines and intrinsic utility. To the avant-garde, Tupperware married form and function on an industrial scale, the ideal set forth by the Bauhaus school of design and architecture that arose in Germany in the 1930s. *House Beautiful* magazine described Tupperware as "fine art for 39 cents." In 1947 the Detroit Institute of Arts displayed stacks of Tupperware in its Exhibition for Modern Living. In 1956 the Museum of Modern Art in New York featured the Wonderlier bowl in its exhibition on outstanding twentieth-century design. The museum later singled out Tupperware for its "ingenious hinges, handles and stopper." The curator wrote that "the carefully considered shapes are marvelously free of that vulgarity which characterizes so much household equipment" (quoted in Drexler and Daniel, p. 75).

Tupperware used a Fifth Avenue showroom to foster the image of its containers as sleek, modern conveniences, but the products failed to sell. Brownie Wise, a divorced mother from the suburbs of Detroit, among other top distributors, reported to Tupper that his wares lent themselves perfectly to home demonstration. Wise had sold Stanley Home Products through home parties, a practice introduced by Wearever Aluminum Cooking Products in the 1920s and promoted by Stanley during the 1930s as an alternative to door-to-door selling. Starting in 1948 Wise organized a team of saleswomen to hold "patio parties" at which Tupperware was sold along with other branded housewares and cosmetics. Gift incentives and a weekly sales bulletin motivated her band of dealers. In 1951 Tupper appointed Wise vice president of Tupperware Home Parties. The product was withdrawn from all stores and sold exclusively through home party distribution.

Tupperware and its selling method ideally suited the burgeoning culture of suburbia. The critical demonstration technique became known as the Tupperware burp. "Tupperware ladies" demonstrated the product's indispensability within the comfort of a friend's home while household tips and gossip were exchanged over coffee and cake. Elsie Mortland, billed by the company as an "ordinary housewife" turned "expert hostess," provided dealers with recipes and entertaining ideas that incorporated the product. The 1958 catalog included recipes for Tropicana salad, made of drained pineapple bits, maraschino cherries, and cottage cheese, and sandwich spreads of canned deviled ham spread and mayonnaise. Fruity colors of orange, lemon, raspberry, and lime and an expanding range of forms fueled consumer demand. The Party Susan, a sectioned hors d'oeuvres server, appealed to the taste for casual postwar entertaining. In 1955 Tupperware introduced TV Tumblers, which the catalog promised were "the perfect answer to beverage serving when watching your favorite TV program." From its inception, the Tupperware corporation actively sought co-branding alliances with food producers, such as Red Rooster cheese and Betty Crocker. Tupperware products such as the Giant Canister, which could hold ten-pound bags of flour, a large milk container, or eight king-size Coca-Cola bottles, were designed to fit commercial food packaging.

By 1952 party plan sales had become so indispensable that Tupperware purchased a one-thousand-acre site on the Orange Blossom Trail in Orlando, Florida. Top dealers attended conferences that approximated evangelical revivals, praising the glory of Tupperware and the capitalist economy that saw it thrive. By 1954 tourist buses were arriving in droves to visit the headquarters, where they toured the "Magic Kitchen" to watch product testing and demonstrations. Corporate songs and rituals reinforced the mystique of "Tupper Magic" while select participants were "baptized" at Poly Pond. In 1954 the annual jubilee bringing thousands of managers and distributors together included a "Big Dig" at which six hundred members of the Tupperware sales force vied to unearth more than $48,000 worth of buried prizes—including toasters and radios, diamond rings and mink stoles, and even a toy car, which was traded in for a full-size Ford.

Feminists have accused the Tupperware company of reinforcing the stereotype of the happy housewife and of contributing to the homogenization of American suburban culture. Nevertheless, the Tupperware corporation provided career opportunities for women after those epitomized by Rosie the Riveter relinquished factory jobs to war veterans. Other companies soon imitated the hostess party model that Tupperware made famous. By the end of the 1950s it was estimated that more than three-quarters of a million women were involved in direct selling.

Although in 1954 *Business Week* magazine featured her as the first woman ever on its cover, Brownie Wise was fired by Tupper in 1958, purportedly because of her extravagant spending. That same year Tupper sold the company and its subsidiaries, believing the company's peak of success had passed.

A 1960 marketing report concluded that the Tupperware party plan could not be successfully exported to England, where guests would be offended at the pressure to buy. Similar complaints circulated in parts of the United States, where some also thought the product distastefully lower-middle-class. Yet Tupperware and its home-selling method flourished, extending through Europe, South America, Africa, and Japan. Despite a mixed reception by the press, England adored the shiny wares emblematic of modern American culture. By 1965 Japanese housewives were buying twice as many pieces as their American counterparts. By the late 1970s catalogs transformed the image of the Tupperware hostess from a housewife into a career woman, who might hold parties at the office instead of at home.

In 1998 Tupperware expanded its sales strategy to include mall kiosks, abandoning the exclusivity of the home party plan for the first time since 1951. In the early twenty-first century the company offers products online, on home-shopping television networks, and in selected retail stores. Nevertheless, home parties continue to account for 90 percent of company sales. Tupperware has become a billion-dollar multinational company with a range of products from special containers for cooking in microwave ovens to children's toys to seasoning mixes. The bowls and lids that first made the company famous, however, continue to define Tupperware.

[*See also* Containers; Gender Roles; Historical Overview, *subentry* From World War II to the Early 1960s; Jell-O Molds; Recipes.]

BIBLIOGRAPHY

Clarke, Alison J. *Tupperware: The Promise of Plastic in 1950s America.* Washington, DC: Smithsonian Institution Press, 1999.

Drexler, Arthur, and Greta Daniel. *Introduction to Twentieth-Century Design from the Collection of the Museum of Modern Art, New York.* Garden City, NY: Doubleday, 1959.

Foderaro, Lisa. "If June Cleaver Joined 'Sex and the City': Tupperware Parties for the Cosmo Set." *New York Times,* February 1, 2003.

CAROLIN C. YOUNG

Turkey

In 1784 Benjamin Franklin complained about selection of the bald eagle as America's national symbol, believing that the turkey was "a much more respectable bird, and withal a true original native of America." Although it is difficult to imagine images of turkeys replacing those of bald eagles on top of flag poles and in other national displays, Franklin was right. The turkey is an American icon.

Turkeys in Pre-Columbian America

The turkey (*Meleagris gallopavo*) likely originated north of Rio Balsas, Mexico. In pre-Columbian times, wild turkeys were plentiful from Honduras to the eastern coast of North America, but Native American groups were widely divergent in their approach to wild turkeys. The Tonkawa of Texas, for example, caught turkeys for food and had a special turkey dance. The Cheyenne, however, refused to eat turkey because they believed that the bird was cowardly. Chiricahua and Mescalero Apaches did not consume them because turkeys ate insects. Other Native American groups, such as the Kiowa, Comanche, and Papago, refused to eat them but did use turkey feathers for decoration and specific ceremonies. Many Native American groups refused to eat turkey well into the twentieth century.

Wild Turkeys. *Culinary Archives & Museum at Johnson & Wales University, Providence, R.I.*

European Turkeys

When the Spanish arrived in Mexico in 1519, they found an abundance of domesticated turkeys. They later found domesticated turkeys in what became the southwestern United States. The Spanish had introduced domesticated turkeys into the Caribbean by 1520 and into Spain soon thereafter. From Spain turkeys spread rapidly throughout western Europe and the Mediterranean, making turkey among the first New World food products adopted in the Old World. The reason for this rapid success was the physical similarity between New World turkeys and the highly prestigious Old World pheasants and peacocks. In addition, turkeys had much more meat than did commonly eaten chickens.

Turkeys reached England before 1550. The English called them "turkie cocks," a phrase that had been used in England before the discovery of the New World to refer to the guinea fowl (*Numida meleagris*), which had been imported from West Africa by the Portuguese beginning in the late fifteenth century. Turkey resembled guinea fowl, and both species of birds were called turkeys for a time. As New World turkey became a major success in England, the bird retained the name "turkey," and the less important guinea fowl acquired other names.

American Turkeys

Turkey was an extremely important food for European colonists in North America. Because domesticated turkeys were plentiful in England by 1550, British colonists were familiar with turkey well before their ships landed in North America. In 1621 William Bradford reported that there "was a great store of wild turkeys, of which they took many." Turkeys were also an important food source on the western frontier. Domesticated turkeys were imported from England into British North America soon after the establishment of English colonies.

Along river valleys, turkeys wandered in flocks of five thousand or more birds. The historian Remington Kellogg believed that, had it not been for the supply of meat from deer and turkeys, the westward expansion of America would have been long delayed. Success was accompanied by problems, however. Wild turkeys were depleted in many areas during Colonial times. They became extinct in Massachusetts by 1878 and soon thereafter disappeared from New England. However, wild turkeys were among the first wild animals to be successfully reintroduced, and they abound in New England in the early twenty-first century.

Turkey Cookery

The Aztecs ate turkey with chili sauce. Native Americans roasted turkey on spits. English colonists brought their own ways of preparing turkey with them. The first American to publish a cookbook, Amelia Simmons, had five turkey recipes in her *American Cookery* (1796). Most subsequent cookbooks published additional recipes. In general, cookbook instructions fell into five categories: how to select turkeys; how to roast, boil, fry, steam, or bake them; how to stuff them; foods to accompany them; and what to do with turkey leftovers.

Turkey Talk

Turkey was more than just another food. By the mid-sixteenth century the English had adopted turkey as a substitute for Christmas goose. Episcopalians who settled in the southern colonies of America celebrated Christmas, and the turkey became the centerpiece of the Christmas dinner. Puritans who settled in Massachusetts did not celebrate Christmas, but they did observe days of thanksgiving. In New England, a thanksgiving feast was regularly observed during the seventeenth and eighteenth centuries, but little evidence of foods served at the dinners has survived. By the early nineteenth century, however, turkey was a common feature at thanksgiving meals. The phrase "Turkey Day" did not become a synonym for Thanksgiving until the late nineteenth century.

In the nineteenth century, turkey became integrated into the American social fabric. When Americans wanted to have a serious discussion, they "talked turkey." When Americans sang, it was occasionally about the "Turkey in the Straw." When Americans danced, it was occasionally the "turkey trot," in imitation of turkeys' comically awkward strut. It was not until the twentieth century that the word "turkey" became a metaphor for a failed event, activity, or individual.

Turkey Breeding

Soon after the introduction of domesticated turkeys into the British North American colonies, domesticated birds bred with wild turkeys, and new turkey varieties emerged. During the mid-nineteenth century, poulterers deliberately bred turkeys to produce specific traits. Several turkey varieties were elevated to breeding status, including Bronze, Narragansett, White Holland, and Black. Breed clubs developed to foster interest in turkey varieties, and turkey shows were held in the Midwest and the South. The two most important commercial varieties were the medium-sized White Holland, which could be raised close to population centers and sold directly to nearby customers, and the large Bronze, which could be raised at great distances from population centers and then frozen for transportation.

In 1927, Jesse Throessel, an Englishman, bred very large birds that had exceptionally wide breasts but lacked other important qualities. This variety, later named the Broad Breasted Bronze, revolutionized turkey breeding. Other breeds faded out, and turkeys came to be identified by strain rather than variety. As the breasts of the new turkeys became larger and the legs shorter, it became difficult for turkeys to mate, so artificial insemination became standard practice.

Turkey Production

Until the early twentieth century, turkeys were raised on family farms and were marketed locally. After World War II growers began to expand the size of their operations. In 1961 the turkey market crashed, and many growers lost their businesses. Those who remained had to lower their costs to survive. One way of lowering costs was vertical integration, in which all aspects of turkey farming were combined into one operation to eliminate middlemen. This system tended to concentrate the turkey industry in fewer hands, and most small farmers dropped out of the turkey business.

Centralization of the turkey industry has continued since the 1960s. Among the larger American turkey businesses are Jennie-O Turkey Store, Cargill Turkey Products, and the Butterball Turkey Company. All are controlled by major food conglomerates. Jennie-O was launched in Minnesota by Earl B. Olson. During the 1940s Olson operated a small creamery and raised turkeys on the side. In 1953 the company named its major product "Jennie-O" in honor of Olson's daughter Jennifer. In 1986 the company was acquired by Hormel Foods. When Hormel acquired the Turkey Store Company in 2001, it was merged with Jennie-O Foods Inc., thus creating the world's largest turkey processor.

Cargill, a Minnesota-based multinational food company, began acquiring turkey companies during the 1950s. Their products are marketed under a variety of names, such as Honeysuckle White, Plantation Fiesta, and Black Forest Turkey Ham, but all are managed by Cargill Turkey Products, which was the world's second largest turkey processor by 2000. In 1954 Butterball turkeys were introduced by Swift-Eckrich Co., which had developed a device called a "bar strap" to eliminate the need for skewers and trussing of turkeys. In 1986 Eckrich became a wholly owned subsidiary of Beatrice Foods Company in Chicago. Beatrice merged with Swift and Company and Peter Eckrich and Sons, creating Swift-Eckrich, which was subsequently acquired by ConAgra. Butterball Turkey is America's third largest turkey producer.

Healthful vs. Unhealthful Turkey

Starting in the early twentieth century, turkey meat has consistently been presented as a nutritious, low-calorie alternative to beef and pork. Turkey has the smallest amount of saturated and unsaturated fat of any commercial meat and the highest percentage of protein. Turkey is low in cholesterol and is a source of iron, zinc, phosphorus, potassium, and B vitamins. Yet health concerns related to turkey have regularly been reported.

Turkey producers have confronted problems similar to those faced by the rest of the poultry industry. Reduction in the cost of producing turkey has occasionally meant lowering of health standards. The U.S. Centers for Disease Control and Prevention (CDC) has regularly reported that at least 13 percent of raw U.S. turkey carries salmonella, a bacterium that can cause serious health problems if the meat is not properly handled and thoroughly cooked. A more serious problem is *Listeria monocytogenes* contamination, which can cause death. Several recalls have been issued by the CDC. Critics have called for greater monitoring of the industry to avoid serious problems in the future.

Turkey in the Early Twenty-First Century

In addition to health concerns, the turkey industry faced another major problem: the high concentration of sales before Thanksgiving and Christmas and almost nonexistent sales throughout the rest of the year. To attract year-round buyers, new products were created, such as turkey roll, which many consumers claimed did not taste like turkey, and ground dark turkey meat, which required considerable research. The industry launched a promotional campaign encouraging consumers to substitute turkey meat in traditional chicken and beef dishes. This campaign included circulation of recipe booklets, posters, print advertisements, and other consumer education materials. Turkey consumption has increased throughout the year, but the major reasons for this change have been the consumption of turkey sandwiches and the increase in the sale of frozen dinners that contain turkey.

During 2001 turkeys raised in the United States weighed an estimated total of 7.2 billion pounds valued at $2.8 billion. North Carolina and Minnesota were the two main turkey-producing states followed by Arkansas, Missouri, Virginia, California, Indiana, and South Carolina. In the United States, annual consumption of turkey increased from 8.1 pounds in the early 1980s to more than 13.8 pounds per person in 2001. Regardless of how much is consumed, the turkey is a powerful culinary and social symbol in the United States.

[*See also* Christmas; Club Sandwich; Dressings and Stuffings; Sandwiches; Simmons, Amelia; Swanson; Thanksgiving.]

BIBLIOGRAPHY

Davis, Karen. *More than a Meal: The Turkey in History, Myth, Ritual and Reality*. New York: Lantern, 2001.
Dohner, Janet Vorwald. *The Encyclopedia and Endangered Livestock and Poultry Breeds*. New Haven, CT, and London: Yale University Press, 2001.
Schorger, A. W. *The Wild Turkey: Its History and Domestication*. Norman: University of Oklahoma Press, 1966.
Small, M. C. "Turkeys, Once Only a Holiday Festivities Dish a Great Industry Has Been Developed," In *American Poultry History 1823–1973*, edited by John L. Skinner. Madison, WI: American Poultry History Society, 1974.

ANDREW F. SMITH

Turnip. Advertising card, nineteenth century.

Turnips

The turnip (*Brassica rapa*, *Brassica campestris*) is a root vegetable in the Cruciferae, or mustard, family and is closely related to the rutabaga (*Brassica napobrassica*). Turnips were brought to the North American colonies in the seventeenth century but were not widespread until the eighteenth. By the nineteenth century turnips were well established for two purposes—culinary use and farm animal fodder. The latter was popularized by the English politician and land improver, Charles Townshend, called "Turnip Townshend," who in approximately 1730 developed a system of rotating grain crops with turnips. Because they are a cool weather crop and have a high protein content, turnips are perfect for fattening cattle during the autumn and winter. Forage turnips appear in early farmer's manuals along with the traditional advisory jingle to sow the seeds "Before the Twenty-Fifth of July, whether it be wet or dry."

Until the twentieth century, most culinary turnips were garden crops. Early recipes in America appear in cookery books such as *The Art of Cookery* by Hannah Glasse (1748) and *The Virginia Housewife* by Mary Randolph (1828). Glasse recommended treating turnips like potatoes, boiling and mashing them. She also suggested making wine from turnips. Randolph called for the same treatment but also gave a classic southern recipe, boiled turnip greens with bacon "in the Virginia style." The amount of turnips eaten by humans remains regional. Turnip greens, often cooked with diced turnip root, are a part of the standard southern menu and often are considered "soul food." Turnip roots, cooked in the Glasse style, are more appreciated in the northeast than elsewhere. The bland-tasting and low-fiber turnip, however, remains a barely tolerated visitor to most traditional American tables. Turnips usually are boiled and served with fat or corned meats and are used in vegetable soups.

[*See also* African American Food, *subentry* Since Emancipation; Vegetables.]

BIBLIOGRAPHY

Vaughan, J. G., and C. Geissler. *The New Oxford Book of Food Plants.* Revised and updated edition of *The Oxford Book of Food Plants* (1969). Oxford and New York: Oxford University Press, 1997.

BRUCE KRAIG

Turnspit Dogs

Spits for roasting large joints of meat at the hearth had to be turned constantly. Small servant boys were used in European kitchens, slaves in America. In the eighteenth century, and probably long before, a specially bred short-legged, large-chested dog called a "turnspit dog" was placed into a caged wheel that was mounted to a wall or suspended from joists. The dog then was made to run, sometimes for hours, like a hamster in its wheel. A long leather belt encircled the wheel and turned the smaller wheel of the spit. The English writer Thomas Hone in 1850 wrote that "[in England] the turnspit-dog and apparatus for cooking are now nearly out of use." It is believed that these dogs were used in the United States well into the 1870s. The breed has died out, at least in name, but certain stocky mixed terriers resemble the short-eared, curly-tailed dog seen in old prints.

[*See also* Hearth Cookery; Kitchens, *subentry on* Early Kitchens; Meat.]

BIBLIOGRAPHY

Franklin, Linda Campbell. *300 Years of Kitchen Collectibles.* 5th ed. Iola, WI: Krause, 2003.

LINDA CAMPBELL FRANKLIN

Twinkies

Twinkies, oblong sponge cakes with a cream filling, were created in 1930, during the Depression. James A. Dewar, manager of the Continental Baking Company, in Schiller Park, Illinois, was looking for a way to use the pans used to bake shortbread fingers, which were used only during the summer strawberry season. The original sponge cakes were sold without cream filling for use in strawberry shortcakes. Dewar injected the cakes with a banana filling, creating a year-round item that sold two for a nickel. A banana shortage during World War II prompted Continental to substitute vanilla cream for the original banana-cream filling. The vanilla filling continues to be used in Twinkies. According

to Hostess, the division of Continental that produces Twinkies, the name for the cakes came from a billboard advertising "Twinkle Toe" shoes that Dewar saw on a business trip to St. Louis. Continental was purchased by Interstate Bakeries Corporation, headquartered in Kansas City, Missouri, in 1995.

Twinkies have added to the American lexicon. In the late 1970s, the attorney for Dan White, a San Francisco city councilman, said his client's overindulgence in sugary food rendered him momentarily insane and was to blame for the killing of the city's mayor and another councilman. The jury convicted White of manslaughter rather than murder, and the phrase "Twinkie defense" was coined. Another coinage was "Twinkie tax," after a proposal in 1997 for placing a tax on high-fat foods and soft drinks. The intention was to curb Americans' consumption of "junk" food and to combat obesity.

[*See also* Bakeries; Bananas; Cakes; Desserts.]

BIBLIOGRAPHY

Jackson, Susan. "How about a Big, Fat Tax on Junk Food?" *BusinessWeek*, June 26, 1997.

KARA NEWMAN

DEEP-FRIED TWINKIES

Deep-fried Twinkies are a relatively recent addition to the Twinkie canon. Restaurateur Christopher Sell is credited with concocting this delicacy in early 2001. The native of Rugby, England, is the proprietor of the fish-and-chips restaurant Chipshop, in Brooklyn, New York. The shop was selling fried candy bars such as Mars Bars and Snickers, a longtime treat in Scotland. To pass the time one evening, Sell and his coworkers began tossing random junk food items into the shop's industrial deep fryer and found that the Twinkie worked well as a fried treat.

The result, which can resemble a beignet or a soufflé, is crispy outside and has a soft, pudding-like inside. The deep-fried Twinkie has become a regular on the fair food circuit, alongside other fried snacks such as funnel cake and curly fries. Interstate Bakeries, which makes Hostess Twinkies, is active in promoting the concept of fried Twinkies to vendors at state and county fairs.

KARA NEWMAN

U–V

Uncle Ben

Uncle Ben was a poor African American rice farmer who produced top-quality, high-yield rice near Beaumont, Texas, in the early 1940s. Legend has it that his crops were held in high regard and that local farmers tried to produce rice "as good as Uncle Ben's." Little else is known about him; even his last name is lost to history. He died never knowing that his name would be associated with rice and a line of food products.

During World War II, a Texas produce broker named Gordon Harwell and an English food chemist, Eric Huzenlaub, developed a process for pressure boiling long-grain rice before it was milled. Traditional milling lost all but 5 percent of the nutritional value of rice. The new process retained 80 percent of the vitamins and minerals, representing the first change to rice in more than five thousand years. Pressure boiling also dramatically increased the storage life of rice, making it a practical staple for the U.S. military to ship to troops fighting overseas. The product was sold exclusively to the armed forces under the name "Converted rice" until the war ended.

After the war, Harwell and his business partner, Forrest E. Mars, introduced the product to the American public. They renamed it "Uncle Ben's" after the Texas farmer. The model for the product trademark was a Chicago maître d'hôtel named Frank C. Brown. His likeness continues to be used. In response to complaints that the name "Uncle Ben" and Brown's picture depicted slavery stereotypes, the logo with Brown's likeness was withdrawn in the 1980s. Sales plummeted, and the logo returned two years later. The size of the logo and its placement on packaging have changed over the years, but the picture has remained the same since 1947.

Uncle Ben's Converted rice was one of the first convenience foods introduced in America. It also marked the acceptance of rice as an alternative to potatoes. An advertising theme of "perfect every time," and "each grain salutes you" expanded steadily for more than fifty years. Over time, various grain products, including wild rice, brown rice, and a quick-cook product known as "instant rice," were added to consumers' tables. Basmati, arborio, and jasmine rice have been joined by a no-cook brand of Converted rice for commercial kitchens. Consumers are targeted with more than sixty products associated with rice and pasta plus a line of stir-fry and skillet sauces. Uncle Ben's products are sold in more than twenty countries in North America, Europe, and Asia.

Uncle Ben's Converted rice is the world's top-selling Converted brand. Uncle Ben's Inc., which is owned by the privately held Mars Inc., has expanded to include food for every meal. Brand extensions moved to the freezer aisle with the introduction of a bowl category. Uncle Ben's sales strategy has broadened from selling side dishes to one-dish meals while markedly increasing frozen food sales in supermarkets. Uncle Ben's soups and rice puddings are other additions to grocery aisles. Trademark applications indicate that snack products and more desserts will be added, all bearing the familiar Uncle Ben's logo.

[*See also* Combat Food; Mars; Rice.]

BIBLIOGRAPHY

Kern-Foxworth, Marilyn. *Aunt Jemima, Uncle Ben, and Rastus: Blacks in Advertising, Yesterday, Today, and Tomorrow.* Westport, CT: Greenwood, 1994. Chronicles the history of blacks in advertising and public relations.

MARYANNE NASIATKA

USDA, *see Department of Agriculture, United States*

Utensils, Table, *see Silverware*

Valentine's Day

The feast of Saint Valentine is observed on February 14—a day set aside by the Roman Catholic Church to honor two martyred saints: Valentine of Rome and Valentine of Termi. Some saints' days have long-standing connections with food, such as Saint Patrick's Day with corned beef and cabbage. There are, however, no historic or modern food associations with Saint Valentine. Over time "Saint" was dropped from Saint Valentine's Day, and the feast evolved into a day on which gifts are given to demonstrate love and affection.

Initially, lovers merely sent decorated cards to their "valentines." Later, flowers became appropriate as well as desired gifts. Food, especially candy, joined the Valentine's Day gift trilogy after the Civil War. This phenomenon was apparently due to a decrease in the price of sugar and the rise of America's commercial confectionery. Candy manufacturers created heart-shaped

Valentine Card. Published by Raphael Tuck and Sons, 1907. *Collection of Alice Ross*

boxes of chocolates decorated in the style of hand-decorated Victorian Valentine's Day cards.

Valentine's Day food occupies a seasonal promotional food niche from January 2 to mid-February, when stores are overstocked with chocolates and sweets. The quintessential Valentine's Day candy gift is a small box of assorted Sweethearts Conversation Hearts candy. These small, heart-shaped pastel wafers—printed with such Valentine's Day messages as "Be Mine," "Kiss Me," and "Sweet Talk"—have been made by the New England Confectionery Company since 1902.

Most other Valentine's Day food is also heart shaped or heart related. Popular Valentine's Day salads include artichoke hearts, hearts of palm, or hearts of romaine as essential ingredients. Cookies, cakes, and tarts are heart shaped and usually are filled with red raspberry jam. Some adult Valentine's Day dinner menus feature foods that are popularly believed to be aphrodisiacs, such as oysters, champagne, and chocolate.

[*See also* Candy Bars and Candy; Chocolate.]

BIBLIOGRAPHY

Cohen, Henning, and Tristam Potter Coffin, eds. *The Folklore of American Holidays: A Compilation of More Than 400 Beliefs, Legends, Superstitions, Proverbs, Riddles, Poems, Songs, Dances, Games, Plays, Pageants, Fairs, Foods, and Processions Associated with over 100 American Calendar Customs and Festivals.* 3rd ed. Detroit, MI: Gale, 1999.

Woloson, Wendy A. *Refined Tastes. Sugar, Confectionery, and Consumers in Nineteenth-Century America.* Baltimore, MD: Johns Hopkins University Press, 2002.

ROBERT W. BROWER

Vanilla

The genus *Vanilla*, a member of the enormous orchid family, includes about one hundred species, all of which are tropical vines with trailing stems that attach themselves to nearby trees. All species of vanilla produce elongated pods filled with tiny seeds, but only two species of vanilla (*planifolia* and *tahitensis*) are used for commercial purposes.

Vanilla is native to southern Mexico, Central America, and the West Indies. The source of its distinctive flavor is the "bean"—the long, flat, slender seedpod, which is odorless when picked. The distinctive vanilla aroma develops only when the pod is properly cured. In pre-Columbian times, the Totonac people discovered that

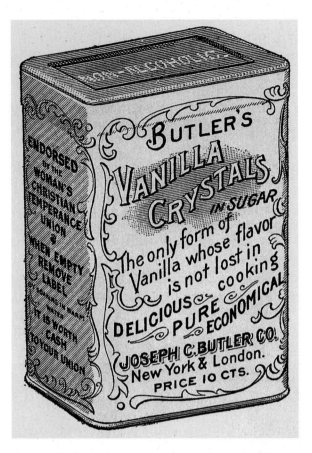

Vanilla Advertisement. Advertisment for Butler's Vanilla Crystals, 1898.

beans left in the sun became fragrant, and they sold great quantities of the beans to the Aztecs, who called them *tlilxochitl*, or black flower.

The first European to make mention of vanilla was Bernal Díaz, a soldier in the army of the explorer Hernán Cortés, who conquered Mexico in the early sixteenth century. Díaz noted that vanilla beans were added to ground cocoa beans to make a frothy and fragrant (though bitter) drink that was the delight of the Aztec nobility. The Spanish called the newly discovered product *vania*, which means a sheath or pod.

Cortés sent vanilla and cocoa beans to Spain, where they were among the first New World foods to be adopted in the Old World. Large quantities of vanilla beans were shipped to Europe, where people readily took up the habit of drinking chocolate beverages flavored with vanilla. Vanilla was in such demand that repeated unsuccessful attempts were made to grow the plants in greenhouses in Europe. The reason for the failure, which was not understood until the nineteenth century, is that vanilla's natural pollinators are the *Melipona* bees and other insects native to Mexico. These insects did not thrive outside of southern Mexico, which was the only supplier of vanilla beans until the nineteenth century.

Charles Morren of Liège, Belgium, succeeded in artificially fertilizing vanilla in 1836. The French grew vanilla on their islands in the Indian Ocean. Five years after Morren's discovery, Edmond Albius, a former slave on the island of Réunion, discovered a better way of pollinating the flowers that greatly increased productivity. Vanilla growing expanded to other tropical French islands, including Madagascar and Tahiti.

Although vanilla was used extensively in French cookery, it was not an important flavoring in colonial America, although small quantities of vanilla beans were imported into the United States prior to 1800. Thomas Jefferson imported vanilla beans and used them in making ice cream, but vanilla remained a rare flavoring in America until the mid-nineteenth century, when the vast increase in world production greatly decreased its cost.

Joseph Burnett, a Boston chemist, figured out how to make extract from vanilla beans, and he began bottling and selling the product in 1847. The extract was easier to ship and store than the whole beans, and the extract was pale brown, making it useful for flavoring white or light-colored sauces. In 1874, German chemists synthesized vanillin, the dominant flavor component of vanilla beans. While synthetic vanillin does not have the full flavor of natural vanilla, its production did greatly lower the cost of vanilla-like flavoring for home and commercial use.

By the late nineteenth century, vanilla was an important ingredient in American recipes for sauces, ice cream, baked goods, and beverages. Aside from the Joseph Burnett Company, vanilla extract was produced by many other firms, including the C. F. Sauer Company of Richmond, Virginia, and the J. R. Watkins Company of Winona, Minnesota.

As the prices of vanilla and vanillin declined, the flavoring was used in a much wider range of foods and dishes, including custards, puddings, cakes, candies, cookies, meringues, macaroons, and pies. In the 1870s, soda fountain proprietors began using vanilla as a flavoring, and the cream soda was invented. In addition to cookery, vanilla also became an important ingredient in making perfume and other scent-based commercial products.

Vanilla manufacturers produced cookbooklets filled with recipes to encourage the use of their products. The first noncommercial vanilla cookbook was published in

1986 by Patricia Rain. She has subsequently promoted vanilla cookery throughout the United States and has been referred to as the "Vanilla Queen."

The largest culinary use of vanilla is in the making of ice cream. Until the mid-twentieth century, vanilla was America's favorite ice cream flavor, followed by chocolate. Although no longer America's favorite flavor of ice cream, vanilla remains an important ice cream flavor. The largest American manufacturer of vanilla extract and vanillin is McCormick and Company, which was founded in Baltimore in 1889.

BIBLIOGRAPHY

Coe, Sophie D. *America's First Cuisines*. Austin: University of Texas Press, 1994.
Rain, Patricia. *Vanilla Cookbook*. Berkeley, CA: Celestial Arts, 1986.
Vanilla: The Watkins Kitchen Collection. Winona, MN: Watkins, 1994.

ANDREW F. SMITH

Vegetables

A vegetable is defined as any herbaceous crop grown for parts that can be eaten fresh or processed. The origins of the word are instructive. In Old French the word *vegetable* meant "living or fit to live," in medieval Latin *vegetabilis* meant "growing or flourishing," and in the Latin of ancient Rome *vegetare* meant "to enliven."

The first American settlers arrived with seeds sewn into their hems and cuttings in their pockets. They were looking for arable land—and they found it. Throughout its history the United States has produced fresh vegetables, in small kitchen gardens and bare urban lots primped and tended by hand and in vast fields tilled and prodded by machine and sometimes ravaged by chemicals. In the context of wars, technological advances, and the American zeal for convenience, vegetables have known ups and down, but their strongest patrons and protectors often have been the smallest. Owing largely to the diligence of home gardeners and small farmers and growers throughout American history, vegetables and their reputation continued to thrive in the United States in the first decade of the twenty-first century.

Early History to 1850

The original settlers initially had little time for vegetable gardening. Instead, they subsisted mostly on grains, meat,

Vegetables. From *Aaron Low's Illustrated Retail Seed Catalogue and Garden Manual*, 1887, p. 46.

fish, and game—and the occasional leaf of spinach to keep scurvy at bay. Native Americans already produced beans, squash, and flint corn (not the sweet corn we know today), and settlers adopted these "three sisters" early and avidly, bringing them into their kitchen gardens to grow among the English and European transplants. Onions might have been the first vegetable planted in the colonies—they enlivened the drab monotony of a daily porridge. Other sturdy specimens, such as cabbages, and roots—from skirrets (a relative of the carrot) and swedes (or rutabagas, so called by virtue of their popularity in Scandinavia) to turnips, beets, parsnips, and carrots—took residence in the root cellar without withering to death. Cucumbers and radishes also counted among the first of the Old World crops cultivated in the colonies, and both culinary and medicinal herbs were planted in vegetable gardens.

With the arrival of potatoes, circuitously returned to the New World by eighteenth-century Scottish and Irish immigrants after this South American native was introduced into Europe, vegetables here largely mirrored the vegetables found on English and European tables. The first American cookbook—*American Cookery*, published in 1796 by Amelia Simmons—mentions all of these vegetables, as well as asparagus, peas, lettuce, and herbs (any of which could be found in an English cookbook of the same period); she also mentions American crops such as corn, Jerusalem artichokes, pumpkins, and several varieties of string beans. While most of these vegetables had been or would be accepted by other culinary cultures, fresh corn remains largely an American culinary fetish, with few Old World cultures (Turkey is a notable exception) embracing corn on the cob.

If many of the crops were familiar, the North American climate was not; it required growing adjustments on the part of farmers. Summers were hotter and the winters, in New England at least, considerably colder than in England and much of the Continent. Among the roster of staple crops, those that flourished in warm weather did better in the southern colonies, while those that liked a hard frost or cold storage fared better in New England. Both climate and luxury of space account for the fact that colonial Americans used open fields to grow vegetables that the English grew only in walled kitchen gardens, among them, beans, peas, squash, and pumpkins.

Annual vegetable varieties of the late seventeenth and eighteenth centuries, handed down from year to year as seeds, almost certainly no longer exist, whereas perennial vegetables, such as artichokes and asparagus, and perennial herbs, as well as self-pollinating annuals like beans, have suffered fewer changes. The latter have, in some cases, survived unchanged. Actual plant breeding for specific qualities, and with it the creation of new varieties, did not begin until the early nineteenth century, but it quickly took off. By the mid-nineteenth century companies produced, sold, and marketed seeds in the United States: new varieties were available for purchase, able to move from place to place, and many old varieties were, as a result, simply forgotten.

By the mid-nineteenth century, American interest in horticulture had grown dramatically, its most notable amateur enthusiast certainly being Thomas Jefferson. Jefferson's garden journal spans sixty years and records seventy species and numerous varieties of vegetables—many of which he grew as curiosities. Resplendent gardens of the time were located for the most part in southern colonies, where the growing season was long and slave labor plentiful. Abundant and varied produce was not strictly the province of the wealthy. Early American cookbooks contain vegetable recipes of stunning variety—often

with cultivar-specific information and preparation tips. Cookbooks such as Lettice Bryan's *The Kentucky Housewife*, published in 1839, were thoughtfully recorded and savvy in ingredients and techniques. For tomatoes Bryan offered recipes for stewing, baking, broiling, frying, dressing raw, and making condiments with now unfamiliar names—like tomato jumbles and tomato soy.

From 1850 to World War II

In the nineteenth century, with the rise of market gardens and truck farms, commercial vegetable growing advanced to the level of a skilled profession. (In 1850 farmers made up 64 percent of the labor force nationwide.) Market gardeners, occupying high-rent acreage on the outskirts of major cities, used interplanting, cold frames, and other production practices to grow a broad variety of vegetables—including valuable perishable specimens—in relatively small spaces. Horse manure, collected from city liveries, was the preferred fertilizer, and newly arrived immigrants provided the labor. Truck farmers, on the other hand, grew less-perishable vegetables, often only one or two kinds, on land several miles from market and transported them to market or to nearby canneries or pickle packers by truck. Refrigerated railcars, developed in the late nineteenth century, made even longer shipping distances possible. Around this time southern farmers began taking advantage of their early spring to ship vegetables up north, and southern Florida became a major center for vegetable production. (The wholesale flight of Americans to the suburbs after World War II shortened the distance, and ultimately blurred the boundaries, between market and truck farms.)

Vegetable Market. Engraving, nineteenth century. *Culinary Archives & Museum at Johnson & Wales University, Providence, R.I.*

With the California gold rush, the American frontier pushed beyond the Great Plains and Rocky Mountains and onward to the Pacific Coast, and agricultural settlements began to form heavily on the prairies. The gold rush hastened California's drive toward statehood, and the completion in 1869 of the transcontinental railroad linked the new state with the rest of the nation, poising the Central Valley—a four-hundred-mile-long fertile pocket between the coastal and the Sierra Nevada mountains—to become the most dynamic agricultural region in the world.

The pace of change quickened in the first half of the twentieth century, driven in no small measure by the needs and requirements of two great wars. Vegetables went from glass jars into cans and then into thick, dried wafers for soldiers on the front lines. During World War I vegetable producers were mobilized to counteract food shortages at home and abroad. A grassroots movement of community gardens, including both private gardens and those planted on urban lots to supply vegetables to poor neighborhoods, experienced renewed vitality as individ-uals "planted for freedom." At the end of World War I, Clarence Birdseye, a field naturalist working for the U.S. government in the Arctic, discovered that quick-frozen fish, when thawed, retained characteristics of freshness. The same would prove true for vegetables.

Although community gardening was largely unsustained in the period between the wars, it made a comeback during World War II as part of the national "victory garden" program. In an effort to reduce demand for commercial produce, as well as the demand for the metal in commercial cans, and to leave the railroads free for munitions transport, Americans were asked to plant gardens and preserve their own vegetables. Nearly 20 million Americans planted victory gardens during World War II; not to do so was considered unpatriotic.

Postwar Period

In the years immediately after World War II, Americans grew in numbers and affluence, while the proportion of farmers in the labor force declined to about 15 percent. Farming became big business; as farming grew, the bulk of vegetable production shifted to just a few states, and regional vegetable selection and variety fell dramatically. Agriculturally, this period was characterized by a rise in the use of pesticides and the development of hearty vegetable hybrids that could travel long distances.

By the 1960s the contentment and prosperity of postwar America were giving way to a mass movement that came to be called the counterculture. Among the ecologic and environmental concerns of this movement was the charge that manufacturers had lost contact with the process and had forfeited responsibility for how food made its way to the consumer. In 1962 the *New Yorker* magazine published several chapters of a book manuscript by a former U.S. Fish and Wildlife employee named Rachel Carson. Carson charged that synthetic chemicals used to control insect populations—in particular, DDT—crept into the soil, water, and air, and, thus, the food chain, poisoning humans and animals and disrupting a fragile ecosystem. Although they were repudiated by the chemical industry, Rachel Carson's premises—painstakingly documented in fifty-five pages of footnotes and ultimately published as a book, *Silent Spring*—were upheld by many in the scientific community and led to investigations that brought about the banning of DDT. Just as significantly, *Silent Spring* made people aware, for the first time, of the earth's vulnerability to man-made interference. *Silent Spring*'s cautionary tale had a profound effect on the consciousness of a generation.

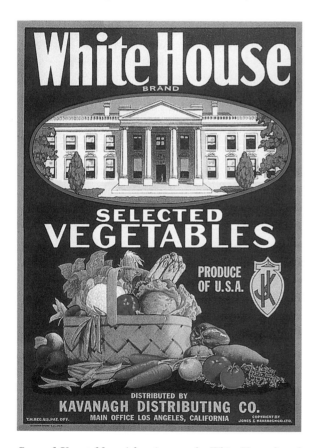

Canned Vegetables. Advertisement for White House brand vegetables. *Culinary Archives & Museum at Johnson & Wales University, Providence, R.I.*

J. I. Rodale, in many ways, can be considered the father of this counterculture movement. Rodale was a New York researcher and publisher who bought a farm in the late 1930s and moved to rural Pennsylvania to practice organic gardening based on the principles of the English horticulturist Sir Albert Howell. Howell's belief that the fertility of the soil must be maintained for any permanent system of agriculture to succeed, led Rodale to theorize that human health could be protected and preserved only by food grown in healthy, naturally fertilized soil. Rodale became a vigorous proponent of protecting and enriching the soil, keeping it free from contaminants, and growing healthy and nutritious food. As early as 1942 he published a magazine called *Organic Farming*; in the 1950s he began publishing a magazine called *Prevention*, which emphasized health maintenance and illness prevention through diet, rather than treatment. Today Rodale is credited with being the father of the natural foods movement in the United States and is considered to have been instrumental in bringing environmental awareness to the late twentieth century. The organic gardening movement in the United States owes its inception as much to the hope inspired by J. I. Rodale as to the fear stimulated by Rachel Carson.

Over the next several decades, increased foreign travel, a new health consciousness, and shifting demographics created demands for different vegetables, segmenting and diversifying the American market. Mainstream Americans were no longer wholly satisfied with the convenience of frozen vegetables—they wanted fresh vegetables at their service year-round. Technology had the ways, and the economy had the means to deliver. The vegetables that used to wind up in cans or freezers now found themselves on trucks—spared from processing.

Although the development of new products occurred at a record rate after 1980 and fresh vegetable consumption rose, the vegetables themselves often left much to be desired. New varieties, developed to extend the vegetables' seasons, left many worthy cultivars behind, and the traveling schedule of even generic vegetables made proper ripening impossible—even undesirable.

At about this time, in California, a state blessed with an extended growing season and adventurous residents, another countermovement was taking root in kitchen and community gardens. One such garden in Berkeley, California, was attached to the kitchen of the restaurant Chez Panisse. Its creator, Alice Waters, eager to provide herself and her friends a place to eat good-quality French country fare, began growing vegetables for her restaurant, often heirloom varieties rescued from oblivion by seed collectors and breeders. These vegetables were harvested at the moment of perfect ripeness and cooked and served simply.

The central precept to emerge from Alice Waters's approach to food—that a dish is only as good as its ingredients—was not in itself remarkable or untested. But it was a dramatic departure from the classical French fare served in many upscale American restaurants. The trend, which swept the country, became known as new American cuisine. As a result, the 1990s saw a striking upsurge in local and community organic and heirloom gardening in the United States and in the small, vibrant restaurants that supported them.

Eating Habits Today

Americans on the whole are eating only about 17 percent more vegetables—fresh and processed—than they were in the 1980s. This stems, in part, from the fact that food consumption in countries with low population growth and generally high incomes, like the United States, remains relatively stable. Because the demand for produce is considered inelastic, growth in one area of consumption tends to predict decline in another. Processed vegetables continue to outsell fresh, though by a narrow margin. According to the United States Department of Agriculture (USDA), head lettuce tops the list of most-consumed vegetables, followed by frozen potatoes, fresh potatoes, canned tomatoes, potatoes for chips, and dried beans. Dark yellow and green vegetable consumption comes in at around 5 percent.

California is the dominant producer of vegetables in the United States, followed by Florida. The balance of vegetable production is dispersed among other states, among them Arizona, Oregon, Washington, and New York. Despite a new awareness of the health benefits associated with eating them, fresh vegetables do not hold as prominent a place in the mainstream American diet as they do among U.S. Asian and Hispanic populations. Americans frequently dine out, where studies indicate they eat even fewer vegetables than at home, and when they dine in, it is likely that components of their evening meals were purchased outside the home, already prepared.

Americans who *are* serious in their efforts to eat well have little time to cook (and many Americans do not know *how* to cook). Increasingly, however, working women and men demand quality produce for their families even if their kitchen time is brief. The industry has responded with fresh convenience products developed initially for the food service industry—clean mixed bagged greens, prewashed bagged spinach, shredded cabbage, broccoli and cauliflower florets, baby carrots, peeled garlic, shucked corn, sliced mushrooms, and so on—to lighten the load. The increasing numbers of households with a single person, and their relatively high income levels, contribute dramatically to the brisk sales of bagged fresh and precut vegetables. Single-person households eat proportionately more vegetables than a family of six. Older Americans eat more vegetables than younger Americans.

Vegetable sales show significant gains, however, in the so-called niche markets. First, greater numbers of Americans in various ethnic groups in the United States and Americans who travel abroad have heightened awareness of ethnic or exotic vegetables and have created a demand for them in supermarkets. The examples are numerous. Italian cooking, for instance, has added dark, leafy greens to the American repertoire in the form of escarole and *lacinato* kale. Americans eat salads brightened with radicchio, arugula, and shaved fennel.

Southeast Asian cuisine has brought the stir-fry and its many vegetables to the American table. Americans frequently cook bok choy, or Chinese cabbage, and broccoli, snow peas, and bean sprouts. Even pea shoots are becoming more and more available in supermarkets. Mexican cuisine has opened a world of incendiary sauces made with chilies. Jalapeño and serrano peppers are used fresh, and many others (chipotle, ancho, pastillo, and serrano) are used dried. Avocados, jicama, and tomatillos find their way into cooling salsas, chayote into stews, and yucca into the deep fryer. Cooking with these vegetables used to require a trip into ethnic neighborhoods. Today they have become common in large urban supermarkets. Mainstream Americans buy 75 percent of all ethnic vegetables sold in the United States.

The second major area of growth is in organic produce. The organic movement may have found its footing in health food stores and greenmarkets, but it has worked its way slowly into supermarkets. Beginning on October 21, 2002, producers and handlers were required to have USDA accreditation for all organic products. The national standards replace what was a tangle of certification systems run by individual states. Vegetables may carry the USDA organic label if they are 95 to 100 percent organic based on current regulations, which dictate that organic food be produced without the use of conventional pesticides, petroleum- or sewage sludge–based fertilizers, bioengineering, or ionizing radiation. Research suggests that average consumers show growing interest in organic produce but are more likely to purchase organic produce when it is comparably priced to conventional produce and when it is available in supermarkets or mainstream stores. At present, 9 to 19 percent of Americans report that they buy organic produce at least once a week.

Vegetable Classification

There are a number of ways in which vegetables can be classified. Botanists and horticulturists use a taxonomic system founded by the eighteenth-century Swedish botanist Carolus Linnaeus to describe the genetic relationship between vegetables. In plant taxonomy, as in animal taxonomy, the basic unit is the species. The species defines those plants that breed only with each other. One level above the species is the genus (plural: genera), which comprises numerous related species. Genera, in turn, fit within a family that possesses similar broad characteristics. The common potato, *Solanum tuberosum*, for instance, belongs to the Solanaceae, or nightshade, family, which counts tobacco, potato, and petunia among its members. (All these plants have simple alternate leaves and five flower petals fused into a tube.) The first part of the scientific name for potato, *Solanum*, refers to the genus. The second, *tuberosum*, refers to the species.

Ranking below the species is the subspecies, a group that may interbreed with other populations within the species, although it often is geographically distant and occasionally distinct in morphologic characteristics. A cultivar is a variety of species that humans have produced using horticultural techniques and cultivated for specific characteristics. Although it is more complicated than common-name designation, this system of botanical classification has the advantage of universal transparency. An understanding of vegetable taxonomy allows for a common and universal recognition of plants using the same vocabulary.

Another way to classify vegetables is through their dazzling array of edible parts. Underground are two parts of a plant harvested for their edible portions, the roots—which absorb nutrients and anchor the plant to the soil—such as carrots, turnips, jicama, and sweet potatoes, and tubers—fat underground stems that store food and from which a plant grows—such as potatoes and Jerusalem artichokes. Kohlrabi, leeks, and fennel are the stems of plants that

Kohlrabi. From *Aaron Low's Illustrated Retail Seed Catalogue and Garden Manual*, 1887, p. 33.

support buds and leaves and carry water, minerals, and food upward through the plant. Hearts of palm, brussels sprouts, and alfalfa sprouts are shoots or young stems with leaves. Enlarged buds—that is, undeveloped shoots from which leaves or flower parts grow—include broccoli, cabbage, artichokes, and head lettuce. Celery and rhubarb are petioles, or stalks that hold leaves away from stems. Kale, collards, watercress, and romaine are leaves whose job it is to catch and store the sun's energy to perform photosynthesis. Peas, corn, and lima beans are the seeds of a plant.

Temperature is a major factor in plant growth. Although each vegetable has its own special temperature requirements for ideal growth, vegetables are often classified as cool- and warm-season crops. Cool-season crops, among them peas, lettuce, cabbage, kohlrabi, and carrots, thrive in temperatures between 50°F and 65°F. They can grow in both the spring and the fall. Higher temperatures will cause spinach and leaf lettuce to bolt—that is, to flower and go to seed before the vegetable reaches full production—and become bitter. Hot-weather crops, such as tomatoes, peppers, cucumbers, sweet corn, okra, eggplant, and beans, on the other hand, germinate, grow, and ripen properly only in temperatures

between 65°F and 85°F and should be planted after the danger of a killing frost is past. The phenomenon makes sense when one considers that cool-weather vegetables are technically vegetables, whereas most warm-weather vegetables are actually fruits. Fruits contain seeds surrounded by water, which makes them susceptible to chilling injury. (Peas are a notable exception.)

Most vegetables are annual plants, meaning that they come up each year from seed and return to seed in the fall. A few vegetables, however, are considered perennials and are put into the ground as bare-root crowns (clumps of roots and dormant buds); root divisions; or, in the case of Jerusalem artichokes, tubers. Vegetables such as artichokes, asparagus, and rhubarb may be planted in late winter or early spring (depending on the hardiness zone), and Jerusalem artichokes in the spring. Artichokes are considered perennials in temperate coastal areas; in chillier parts of the country they are planted in the spring from root divisions. Once established, however, asparagus, which takes two to three years to reach full production, and rhubarb, which can take three or four years, offer several seasons of dependable growth.

Post-Harvest Factors

Vegetables have specific requirements after harvesting as well. Vegetables are living, breathing plants, which take in carbon dioxide and release oxygen. Moisture and nutrient losses that vegetables sustain immediately upon harvesting increase their rate of respiration. When a vegetable is bruised or sliced—and, to a lesser degree, when it is harvested—it responds by using stored food reserves to repair the damage or by attempting to grow new cells. The loss of stored food reserves through respiration means a corresponding loss in nutrient value, flavor, moisture, and weight, and this precipitates the vegetable's overall deterioration. Temperature is the principal component in maintaining the quality of a vegetable after harvest.

Because freshly harvested vegetables hold heat from the sun and the soil, those with inherently high respiration rates must undergo rapid precooling to slow their respiration before they are shipped, processed, or stored. Vegetables with high respiration rates include artichokes, brussels sprouts, green onions, fresh beans (those eaten in the pod), asparagus, broccoli, mushrooms, peas, and sweet corn. Those with low respiration rates include garlic, onions, mature potatoes, and sweet potatoes.

Precooling methods also vary with the type of vegetable. Artichokes, asparagus, beets, broccoli, carrots, cauliflower, endive, green onions, leafy greens, radishes, spinach, and sweet corn all benefit from rapid cooling with ice. Tomatoes, squash, green beans, cucumbers, garlic, okra, bulb onions, and most lettuces sustain damage by direct contact with ice and generally are chilled with forced air or cold water. Many vegetables are susceptible to chilling injury and store best at temperatures between 45°F and 55°F—cucumbers, eggplants, summer squash, okra, and sweet potatoes are particularly sensitive. Other vegetables are stored best at temperatures just above freezing. The relative humidity at which a vegetable is stored is also instrumental in slowing its rate of moisture loss and deterioration. Most vegetables prefer humidity levels around 80 percent, but humidity encourages bacterial growth as well. Lettuces and leafy greens typically are washed in mild chlorine solutions to disinfect them.

Storage crops must be cared for with particular attention if they are to remain salable or stable in a root cellar after their harvest. Beets, carrots, rutabagas, and leeks like temperatures just at the freezing mark in conjunction with very high humidity. Potatoes store best in high humidity as well but prefer more moderate temperatures—between 40°F and 60°F. Onions and garlic appreciate temperatures at the freezing mark, but with only moderate humidity, and winter squash stores best at moderate temperatures and low humidity.

Nutritional Properties

Even before their vitamin and micronutrient properties were fully understood, vegetables were considered healthful. Today, however, Americans are more likely to look to vegetables for their antioxidant properties.

In addition to their role as the precursors of important vitamins, the chemical compounds found in plants, called phytonutrients, appear to repair and prevent cellular damage. When we breathe, a small number of oxygen molecules are converted in our bodies to free radicals, unstable oxygen atoms that, in seeking their missing electrons, attack healthy cells. Although the impact of free radicals (estimated at ten thousand hits a day) is normally held in check by defenses within our bodies, exposure to air pollution, chemicals, or foods high in fat and sugar can overwhelm these defenses. The resulting damage is known as oxidation. Free-radical damage can greatly diminish the body's ability to combat aging and disease.

Antioxidants, among them enzymes, coenzymes, vitamins, and sulfur-containing compounds that are contained in many vegetables work to prevent or slow damage done by free radicals in the body. Often called "free radical scavengers," phytonutrients fall into two main classes, carotenoids and flavonoids. The most prevalent are the carotenoids, a family of pigments that exist within plant cells. Beta-, or orange, carotenes are found in carrots, corn, and squash. Alpha-, or yellow-orange, carotenes are present in carrots, pumpkin, and red and yellow peppers. The carotene lutein is found in spinach, kale, and collard greens and the red-pigmented lycopene in tomatoes. Carotenoids are fat soluble, meaning that they are stored in the liver and fatty tissues and remain in foods after those foods are cooked. They are sensitive to oxidation, however, and lose color and nutrients after they are cut.

Flavonoids, another protective group of plant pigments, help prevent inflammation and improve the absorbability of vitamin C. Red flavonoids, called "anthocyanins," are present in red cabbage and eggplant. Yellow flavonoids, or "anthoxanthins," are present in onions, potatoes, and cauliflower. Flavonoids are water soluble (necessitating their regular replacement in the body), which means that the pigments leach easily from vegetables when they are cooked or processed. In terms of their antioxidant properties, the most protective vegetables are, in descending order, spinach, garlic, broccoli, brussels sprouts, carrots, sweet potato, red pepper, winter squash, and frozen peas. Garlic, which contains more than one hundred active compounds, including some flavonoids, has more antioxidant power per gram than any vegetable.

The vitamin and mineral content of vegetables, though secondary to their antioxidant properties, is not inconsiderable. Most vegetables provide a healthy dose of vitamin A (in the form of beta-carotene) and a supporting dose of minerals (particularly calcium). Vegetables also are good sources of vitamin C and folate. Folate, a B vitamin that is important for the production and maintenance of new cells, is contained in leafy greens, such as spinach and watercress, and in Belgian endive. Its levels are best maintained in raw vegetables and those that have not spent a great deal of time in the refrigerator. In addition to other important B vitamins, vegetables contain a serviceable amount of vitamin E.

The debate over the relative nutritional value of fresh versus frozen or canned vegetables has ended in a draw. Processed vegetables do not appear to have substantially fewer vitamins, and their antioxidant properties do not seem to decline. (Some vegetables, such as canned tomatoes, lose vitamin C but experience an increase in the carotene lycopene.) Whether the vegetable is destined for can, freezer, or saucepan, post-harvest variables of any kind make these calculations difficult. In general, the farther a vegetable travels from the field, the greater the likelihood that its overall quality will be compromised. Nevertheless, most nutritionists agree that the critical component in vegetable nutrition is how many vegetables one eats, not whether they are fresh or processed. Quantity may be more important than quality.

Cooking Techniques

How a fresh vegetable is prepared influences its appearance, palatability, and, to some degree, its nutritional value. Raw-food proponents claim that the enzymes present in unheated food lend it superior digestibility and bioavailability (the extent to which a nutrient can be used by the body after it is eaten). Lightly dressed salad vegetables are superb eaten raw. But many vegetables, such as winter squash, are simply more palatable cooked; others, like potatoes, are more easily digested. Cooked carrots have more available beta-carotene than raw carrots.

In most early American recipes, vegetables were seasoned simply, often sent to the table with a pitcher of melted butter but not much else. Garlic, Amelia Simmons warns us, is "better adapted to the uses of medicine than cookery." In *The Kentucky Housewife*, mint makes its way into a pot of peas and vinegar and butter into a saucepan of beets. By the mid-nineteenth century, vegetables, whatever their form of preparation, were cooked much longer than is typical today. Boiling was the standard treatment for green vegetables; according to Mrs. Lincoln in *The Boston Cookbook*, an hour in the pot was not uncommon. Any vegetable that was not fully cooked was considered "unwholesome." Lettice Bryan recommends cooking asparagus until the stalk mashes easily. Miss Leslie, in her *Directions for Cookery*, cooks green beans an hour and a half and a head of cauliflower two full hours. Potatoes, cucumbers, and eggplant might be fried, but boiling eggplant was not uncommon either. Many vegetables were stewed in a bit of water, butter, or cream, but only potatoes were roasted. Colonial housewives pickled far more vegetables than we do, and salad vegetables, which were "likely to ferment in the stomach," according to Mrs. Lincoln, were dressed with "oil, vinegar, salt and pepper." Rice, pasta, and salads, today considered separate categories, are all included in the vegetable chapters of nineteenth-century recipe books.

Vegetable Costumes. Advertising card, nineteenth century. *Culinary Archives & Museum at Johnson & Wales University, Providence, R.I.*

The current trend is to consider vegetables individually and to cook each one just enough to bring out its best, and not a moment longer. We like many of our vegetables with a bit more bite than colonial Americans did. Green beans or brussels sprouts are often blanched in boiling water to set their color and cook them until almost done; then they are finished in a sauté pan with butter. Tender vegetables, like peppers and summer squash, frequently are simply sautéed. Leafy greens with the few drops of water still clinging to their leaves might be steamed briefly in a covered sauté pan. When a vegetable is cooked through in liquid, the medium is often a flavorful broth. We are, however, just as likely to remove liquid from vegetables by roasting them in a hot oven or grilling them over a flame. The influence of other cultures is apparent in the variety of vegetable recipes we might make: soy sauce, coconut milk, toasted nuts and garlic, curry, fresh ginger, and olive oil are part of our standard inventory of seasonings.

[*See also* Birdseye, Clarence; California; Canning and Bottling; Community-Supported Agriculture; Cookbooks and Manuscripts, *subentry* From the Beginnings to 1860; Counterculture, Food; Department of Agriculture, United States; Health Food; Italian American Food; Jefferson, Thomas; Mexican American Food; Native American Foods; Nouvelle Cuisine; Organic Food; Organic Gardening; Southeast Asian American Food; Vitamins; Waters, Alice; *and entries for individual vegetables.*]

BIBLIOGRAPHY

Anderson, Luke. *Genetic Engineering, Food, and Our Environment.* White River Junction, VT: Chelsea Green, 1999.

Bachmann, Janet, and Richard Earles. *Post Harvest Handling of Fruits and Vegetables.* 2000. http://attra.ncat.org/attra-pub/PDF/postharvest.pdf.

Becker, Robert F. "Vegetable Gardening in the United States: A History, 1565–1900." *Horticultural Science* 19, no. 5 (October 1984): 624–629.

Bellasco, Warren J. *Appetite for Change.* New York: Pantheon, 1989. Reflections on the counterculture and the food industry.

Bryan, Lettice. *The Kentucky Housewife.* Bedford, MA: Applewood, 2000. Facsimile edition of the 1839 text.

Carson, Rachel. *Silent Spring.* Repr. New York: Mariner, 1994.

Cook, Roberta L. *The U.S. Fresh Produce Industry: An Industry in Transition.* Davis: Department of Agricultural and Resource Economics, University of California at Davis, 2001. http://www.agecon.ucdavis.edu/facultypages/cook/articles.htm. *The History of Kitchen Gardens in America.* http://www.mannlib.cornell.edu/about/exhibit/KitchenGardens/intro.htm.

Dauthy, Mircea. *Fruit and Vegetable Processing.* Rome: Food and Agriculture Organization of the United Nations, 1995. The second chapter contains information on the chemical composition of vegetables.

Diver, Steve. *Biodynamic Farming and Compost Preparation.* http://attra.ncat.org/attra-pub/biodynamic.html.

Doyle, Jack. *Altered Harvest: Agriculture, Genetics, and the Fate of the World's Food Supply.* New York: Penguin, 1986.

Hawkes, J. G. *The Diversity of Crop Plants.* Cambridge, MA: Harvard University Press, 1983.

Leighton, Ann. *American Gardens in the Eighteenth Century.* Boston: Houghton Mifflin, 1976.

Leslie, Eliza. *Miss Leslie's Directions for Cookery.* New York: Dover, 1999. Facsimile edition.

Lincoln, Mrs. D. A. *Boston Cooking School Cookbook.* New York: Dover, 1996. Facsimile edition.

Peavy, William, and Warren Peary. *Super Nutrition Gardening.* Garden City Park, NY: Avery, 1992. Why organic gardening produces vegetables with higher nutrition.

Robertson, Gordon L. *Food Packaging: Principles and Practice.* New York: Marcel Dekker, 1993. The author discusses vegetable respiration and shelf life.

Schoneweis, Susan D., and Durward A. Smith. *Storing Fresh Fruits and Vegetables.* University of Nebraska, Institute of Agriculture and Natural Resources, 1996. http://ianrpubs.unl.edu/Horticulture/g1264. htm.

Simmons, Amelia. *The First American Cookbook.* New York: Dover, 1984. Facsimile edition.

United States Department of Agriculture. *A History of American Agriculture, 1776–1990.* 2002. http://www.usda.gov/history2.

United States Department of Agriculture, Agricultural Research Service. Food and Nutrition Research Briefs. http://www.ars.usda.gov/is/np/fnrb. Antioxidant capacity of vegetables.

United States Department of Agriculture, National Organic Program. http://www.ams.usda.gov/nop/indexIE.htm.

United States Department of Agriculture, Agricultural Research Service, Nutrient Data Laboratory 2002. USDA Nutrient Database for Standard Reference. http://www.nal.usda.gov/fnic/cgi-bin/nut_search.pl. Statistics on the nutritive value of foods.

Weaver, William Woys. *Heirloom Vegetable Gardening.* New York: Holt, 1997.

Weaver, William Woys. *100 Vegetables and Where They Came From.* Chapel Hill, NC: Algonquin, 2000.

Wiersema, John H., and Blanca León. *World Economic Plants: A Standard Reference.* Boca Raton, FL: CRC, 1999. Taxonomic descriptions and photographs.

KAY RENTSCHLER

Vegetarianism

Before the coining of the terms "vegetarian" and "vegan" in the nineteenth and twentieth centuries, respectively, Americans and Europeans who ate a fleshless diet were widely known as Pythagoreans, after the founder of the first vegetarian society of the West—Pythagoras, the Greek mathematician and philosopher who flourished in the sixth century B.C.E.

Ancient Period

In Croton, a town in Magna Graecia (a grouping of ancient Greek colonies in the southern Italian peninsula), Pythagoras founded his society for the study of philosophy and mathematics, which served as the prototype for the Platonic Academy and the modern university. As a condition of membership in the order, members were required to take a vow pledging that they would abstain from the eating of animal flesh. The fleshless diet that Pythagoras recommended was based primarily on compassion for animals and opposition to animal sacrifice in Greek civic religion, with health being a secondary consideration.

The Pythagoreans' commitment to vegetarianism was reinforced by their belief in the doctrine of metempsychosis, which held that after death the soul has the potential to transmigrate into the bodies of other animals. Many of the greatest thinkers of antiquity counted themselves as disciples of Pythagoras; they include Socrates, Empedocles, Plato, Epicurus, Plutarch, Plotinus, and other Neoplatonists of the late Roman Empire. (One of

Pythagoras. The ancient Greek sage and religious teacher was the namesake of nineteenth-century American vegetarians. Portrait by Glory Brightfield from *Famous Vegetarians and Their Favorite Recipes*, by Rynn Berry (New York and Los Angeles, 2003), p. 2. *Collection of Rynn Berry*

them, Porphyry, wrote the first history of Pythagoreanism, called *De Abstinentia*.) So closely was Pythagoras identified in the Western world with abstinence from animal flesh that "Pythagorean" became an adjective for describing a fleshless diet. In antiquity, a Pythagorean diet consisted exclusively of fruits, vegetables, nuts, and grains. Eggs and dairy products were little consumed in ancient Greece and would have been avoided by Pythagoreans on ethical grounds.

Early American Vegetarianism

The writings of the German mystic Jakob Böhme were instrumental in converting a young English rustic with a literary bent to a Pythagorean diet. His name was Thomas Tryon. In numerous works, Tryon advocated a Pythagorean diet on practical and moral grounds. One of his books, *Wisdom's Dictates* (1691), which was a digest of Tryon's voluminous *The Way to Health, Long Life, and Happiness* (1683), found its way into the hands of the young Benjamin Franklin in the 1720s. For three years, during his late adolescence, the young printer's apprentice embraced the Pythagorean system. In his *Autobiography* (1791), Franklin acknowledges his debt to Tryon and, in the same

passage, makes it plain that his reasons for adopting a fleshless diet were chiefly pecuniary. By not eating flesh, he found that he could cut his food expenses in half, enabling him to acquire more books for his library.

Two of Franklin's contemporaries, both Quakers in Philadelphia, were more high-minded. One of them, Benjamin Lay, combined vegetarianism with abolitionism. He claimed that witnessing the horrors of slavery on the Caribbean island of Barbados had fired him with the desire to adopt a Pythagorean diet and become an abolitionist. He was the author of a scathing anti-slavery book entitled *All Slave Keepers That Keep the Innocents in Bondage Apostates*, which was published by Benjamin Franklin in 1737. As few of his contemporaries did, Lay was able to see the connection between human servitude and animal enslavement.

The other vegetarian abolitionist of Franklin's acquaintance was John Woolman, an itinerant Quaker preacher whose two-part work *Some Considerations on the Keeping of Negroes* (1754) is credited with having turned the Quakers against the slave trade. (Franklin, to his credit, printed the second part of Woolman's work.) Unlike Franklin, Woolman was an ethical vegetarian who energetically campaigned against the mistreatment of animals, particularly horses and oxen.

A former British army officer named William Dorrell founded the first Pythagorean commune in the United States, on the Vermont-Massachusetts border in the late 1790s. Members of the commune followed a fleshless regimen and wore no clothing that had been made from animal skin, though they did wear woolen shoes. Dorrell's was a religious sect that had strong millennial propensities; followers believed that the Second Advent (the Second Coming of Christ) was at hand, and they were preparing for the new millennium by recreating a utopian paradise in which no animals could be harmed or exploited, which had been the state of nature in the prelapsarian world of Adam and Eve in the Garden of Eden.

The Dorrellites came to grief when Dorrell bragged that his beliefs had made him impervious to pain. One day a skeptical onlooker at one of his lectures, one Captain Ezekiel Foster, decided to put Dorrell's claim to the test. He mounted the podium and delivered a well-aimed blow at Dorrell's chin, which floored him. When Dorrell struggled to his feet, Foster repeated the fisticuffs until Dorrell cried out that he did feel pain and that he had had quite enough. Disillusioned with their leader's braggadocio (to say nothing of his glass jaw), the

Dorrellites disbanded. It would be another fifty years or so before another millennial group took up the cudgels for a spiritually based fleshless diet—the Seventh-Day Adventists, who built their new sect on the remnants of the failed prophecies (of a Second Coming of Christ in 1843) of the American sectarian leader William Miller and the Millerites.

Pythagoreanism arrived in America as a fledgling social movement only in 1817. This was the year in which William Metcalfe and forty-one other members of the Bible Christian Church set sail from England, bound for Philadelphia. The Bible Christian Church had been founded by a Swedenborgian minister with the improbable name of William Cowherd. Cowherd had became a vegetarian after immersing himself in the mystical writings of the Swedish philosopher Emanuel Swedenborg, who asserted that eating flesh was an evil that had brought about the fallen state of humanity. From his Swedenborgian pulpit, Cowherd preached vegetarianism and kindness to animals. He also averred that Jesus had been a vegetarian. When the Swedenborgian establishment frowned upon the ethical vegetarian tenor of his sermons, he quit the Swedenborgian Church and in 1809 started his own church, the Bible Christian Church, in the town of Salford.

Much to the consternation of the other churches, the little Bible Christian Church thrived and prospered, so much so that Cowherd conceived the plan of sending a group of Cowherdites, headed by William Metcalfe to convert the heathen American flesh eaters of European descent. On March 29, 1817, they set sail from Liverpool in the ship *Philadelphia Packet*, and eighty days later they arrived in Philadelphia. Not all of the Cowherdites survived the rigors of the voyage as vegetarians. Half, in fact, had succumbed to the lure of the meat rations. But Metcalfe and his wife, Susanna, came through the hardships unscathed and untainted to found the North American branch of the Bible Christian Church—the first vegetarian church to be planted on American soil. Despite its detractors' prophecies of a speedy demise, America's first vegetarian church survived into the early twentieth century.

Although his reception in Philadelphia by the orthodox Swedenborgian Church and other denominations was decidedly chilly, the Reverend Metcalfe was undaunted. The first public vegetarian advocate in the United States, Metcalfe continued to preach vegetarianism from the pulpit and to write essays on moral dietetics in the newspapers. In 1821, Metcalfe penned a pamphlet called *On Abstinence from the Flesh of Animals* (echoing Porphyry)

that won to the cause two converts who would play an indispensable role in launching the vegetarian movement in America.

His first convert was America's first vegetarian physician, Dr. William A. Alcott, cousin to the transcendentalist philosopher and teacher Bronson Alcott; William, in turn, converted Bronson. Not long after hearing Metcalfe's sermons, William gave up eating flesh. In the course of his long career, he wrote numerous works advocating a vegetarian diet, including his best-known book, *Vegetable Diet* (1838). Bronson Alcott, father of the novelist Louisa May Alcott, founded the first ethical vegetarian commune in America: Fruitlands, near Harvard, Massachusetts, which was financed by Alcott's neighbor, Ralph Waldo Emerson, another transcendentalist.

Not since the time of Pythagoras had there been a more ethical vegetarian commune. No draft animals were used to help plant the crops, because that would have meant enslaving them. None of the communards wore wool, because clothes made from wool were exploitative of sheep. Dairy products and eggs were shunned, since they were taken from animals without their consent. Out of respect for bees, the use of honey was forbidden. A strict Pythagorean diet was observed at all times. Unfortunately, the communards had waxed conversational and contemplative when they should have been planting crops. Come autumn, there was scant food to be harvested. So the commune disbanded, and in the end the Fruitlands experiment proved to be as fruitless as it was short-lived.

Although Fruitlands failed egregiously, one vegetarian commune that was notable for its financial success was the Oneida Community in upstate New York. Founded by John Humphrey Noyes, a Dartmouth graduate and Yale Divinity School dropout, the community effectively started in 1847, thirteen years after the momentous day on February 20, 1834, when—in an event called the "High Tide of the Spirits" by his followers—Noyes declared himself to be free of all sins. If Fruitlands was an ethical vegetarian community, Oneida was just the opposite. The vegetarian communards supported themselves by manufacturing fur traps. By the 1850s, they were turning out more than 100,000 traps a year.

Metcalfe's other illustrious convert was himself a Protestant minister and an impressive pulpit orator—the Reverend Sylvester Graham. Although people tend to think of vegetarianism as a secular movement, the fact that Graham, a Presbyterian minister, launched the health food reform movement in America and that his

Bronson Alcott. Portrait by Glory Brightfield from *Famous Vegetarians and Their Favorite Recipes*, by Rynn Berry (New York and Los Angeles, 2003), p. 130. *Collection of Rynn Berry*

mentor, Metcalfe, started the first religious vegetarian society in America are suggestive of an underlying connection between diet and religion.

Outraged that commercial bakers were removing the vital nutrients from the bread and using stretchers such as plaster of Paris, slaked lime, and alum, Graham called for bakers to put back the bran and other nutrients. Invoking Genesis 1:13, he also denounced the butchers as fiends and the doctors as vampires. Despairing of being able to reform the milling industry in his lifetime, he marketed his own flour and breadstuffs. Graham flour, Graham bread, Graham crackers, and Graham gems found a ready market among his followers, who were legion. To enable Grahamites to eat a vegetarian meal in public without being gawked at, Graham founded a network of vegetarian boardinghouses throughout the country.

Although his nutritional theories, as set forth in his books *A Treatise on Bread, and Bread-making* (1837) and *Lectures on the Science of Human Life* (1839), were derided by the medical establishment of his time, his theory that dietary fiber is a vital force in human health has been vindicated by such pathbreaking medical researchers of the twentieth century as Dr. Peter Cleave. Cleave's theory of the saccharine disease, propounded in the 1960s, holds that all modern degenerative diseases, such as diabetes, heart disease, and diverticulitis, stem from a lack of suf-

ficient dietary fiber. With any justice, Graham would be remembered for far more than the Graham crackers or the breakfast cereal that bear his name—both of which have been adulterated beyond recognition.

Graham also spawned numerous vegetarian converts of his own, notably, Asenath Nicholson, an accomplished vegetarian cook. Her cookbook *Nature's Own Book* (1833) is replete with vegetarian recipes and tributes to Graham. In 1844, she set sail for Ireland, where she chronicled the Great Hunger in her book *Annals of the Famine in Ireland in 1847, 1848, and 1849* (1851). For almost a decade, she ministered to the famine-stricken poor by cooking them vegetarian meals that she had first learned to prepare as a chef in the Grahamite boardinghouse that she had run with her husband in New York.

Sometime in the early 1840s in England, the term "vegetarian" was coined. No one knows exactly when or by whom. The story that it was first coined by a vegetarian classical scholar from the Latin word *vegetus* is apparently apocryphal. What is historically attested is that on September 29, 1847, at a hydropathic clinic in Ramsgate, the first Vegetarian Soceity was formed. The outmoded term "Pythagorean" was officially replaced by the neologism "vegetarian." Implicit in the word "Pythagorean" had been the notion of abstaining from animal flesh and animal products for ethical reasons. The coining of the word "vegetarian" seemed to legitimize the adoption of a fleshless diet for other than moral reasons. Consequently, a chasm opened between ethical and health vegetarians that has only widened and deepened. According to certain surveys, 37 percent of animal rights activists are not vegetarians, and 85 percent of vegetarians are not primarily impelled by animal rights concerns. Perhaps it was not coincidental that the same year in which the term "vegetarian" was first officially adopted saw the founding of the Oneida commune, in which the vegetarian communards supported themselves by manufacturing fur traps.

In 1850, three years after the vegetarian society in England had begun to call their diet "vegetarian," Graham, Metcalfe, William Alcott, and Dr. Russell Trall founded America's first secular vegetarian society, the American Vegetarian Society, at Clinton Hall in New York City. Now defunct, the society continued to hold meetings until 1922.

Another influential figure during this period was Dr. James Caleb Jackson. Employing the latest techniques of hydropathy, which he had imported from Germany, he founded America's first successful health spa, Our Home on the Hillside, in Dansville, New York, in 1858. His patients would proffer their ailing anatomical parts to be healed, and Jackson or his partner, Dr. Harriet Austin, would slosh the offending organ with water, swathe the patients in wet sheets, and put them on a diet of fresh fruit, vegetables, and Graham mush. Like many prominent figures in the vegetarian movement in the early nineteenth century, Jackson was a fervent abolitionist. He was also a feminist. Many leading feminists of the period were frequent guests at the spa; some of them, such as Amelia Bloomer, Elizabeth Cady Stanton, Susan B. Anthony, and Clara Barton, were vegetarians or were sympathetic to the cause.

Although his health spa was a highly lucrative enterprise, Jackson made his fortune from selling Grahamite food products along with a few food inventions of his own, such as Somo, a "coffee" made from cereal, and Granula, America's first ready-to-eat breakfast cereal (which was made from crumbled Graham bread). Both products were later pirated by a visitor at Our Home—none other than the noted Seventh-Day Adventist physician Dr. John Harvey Kellogg.

Cornflake Crusaders

Through Ellen White, founder of the Seventh-Day Adventists and a former patient of James Caleb Jackson's at Our Home, the early Adventists became acquainted with the latest in health-care procedures. Sister White, as she was affectionately dubbed by her followers, absorbed her immense health knowledge partly through divine revelation and partly through a close reading of the works of food reformers like Graham and Jackson. She was an avid reader of Jackson's *Water-Cure Journal*. She also saw, in one of her visions, that God had fashioned the human body as his temple, so that any abuse of the body was a violation of God himself. Alcohol, tobacco, and meat were detrimental to the body, so she roundly denounced them and declared them to be proscribed foods. Eventually, through her prophecies and teachings, the Seventh-Day Adventists became strong advocates of a vegetarian diet.

As sedulously as Ellen White had studied Jackson's methods, so did her protégé, the young John Harvey Kellogg. In one of her visions, White saw that Kellogg was destined for great things as an Adventist physician. (Despite her prescience, she did not foresee that one day Kellogg would grow so agnostic in his views that he would question White's infallibility and be expelled

from the Adventist Church.) White and her husband, James, financed Kellogg's education through medical school. In 1876, her husband prevailed upon the young doctor to become head of the Western Health Reform Institute—renamed the Battle Creek Sanitarium—which became a sort of laboratory for Kellogg's food inventions. At the sanitarium, Kellogg developed into the most successful abdominal surgeon of his time. He attributed his success, in large measure, to putting patients on a vegetarian diet before surgery, which often obviated the need for surgery.

In the kitchen of his wife, Ella, Kellogg and his brother, Will, discovered the cereal-flaking process that yielded Granose Flakes, the precursor of cornflakes—those golden flakes that gave rise to the modern breakfast cereal industry and the uniquely American practice of eating cold cereal for breakfast. Kellogg was a Promethean inventor of an array of other food products that helped many Americans effect a smooth transition to a vegetarian diet. Among these foods was America's first meat analogue, Nuttose, which was made from flour, water, and steamed peanuts. Kellogg's other popular ersatz meats, such as Protose, Battle Creek Skallops, and Battle Creek Steaks, were made from varying combinations of peanuts and wheat gluten. Kellogg, in fact, claimed to be the inventor of peanut butter. Whether or not he actually concocted this goober paté is still a matter for conjecture, but there is no doubt that he was instrumental in its adoption as a vegetarian food all over the country.

Although Kellogg's primary emphasis was on the health aspects of a vegetarian diet, he was not unmindful of the ethical arguments. In perhaps his best-known book, *The Natural Diet of Man* (1923), he marshals compelling arguments in favor of adopting a meatless diet out of compassion for animals.

In an ironic turnabout, just as Kellogg had pirated the cereal-based coffee Somo and the ready-to-eat breakfast cereal Granula from James Caleb Jackson, a malingering patient at Kellogg's sanitarium, Charles W. Post was accused by Kellogg of having pirated several of the sanitarium's foods. It is thought that Post took three recipes with him: Caramel Cereal Coffee, which he turned into Postum; Kellogg's Cornflakes, which became Post Toasties; and Kellogg's Malted Nuts, the basis for Grape-Nuts. Whether Post was guilty of this theft remains unconfirmed, but he parlayed these foods into a personal fortune so vast that it enticed unscrupulous cereal makers to imitate his methods. The result was that America was soon being deluged with copycat krispies, krumblies, toasties, and flakies with quaint-sounding names like Vim Wheat Flakes, Rippled Wheat, Sugar Smiles, Malti-Vita, Maple-Vita, Norka ("Akron" spelled backward) Oats, and Trya-bita. The first of the cereal kings to spend lavishly on advertising that made extravagant health claims for his products, Post was also innovative in being the first to put a premium inside each cereal box to boost sales. In each box of Grape-Nuts, for instance, Post inserted a copy of his inspirational leaflet, *The Road to Wellville*.

Unfortunately, Charles Post—who like Kellogg was an Adventist but unlike Kellogg was not a vegetarian—took a permanent detour on the road to "Wellville." At the comparatively young age of sixty, plagued by a stomach ailment, he ended his life with a hunting rifle. His rival, Kellogg, died in his sleep at the ripe age of ninety-one.

Since 1939, Worthington Foods, an Adventist-run company, has been supplying vegetarian Adventists with meat alternatives that are based on the pioneering work of John Harvey Kellogg. From its humble beginnings, Worthington Foods has grown into the world's largest manufacturer of meat substitutes and other health products. In an ironic turn of events, in 1999 Worthington Foods was acquired by the Kellogg Company, a publicly traded company that no longer has any affiliation with Dr. Kellogg's family or with the Seventh-Day Adventists.

Modern American Vegetarianism

Although Dr. Kellogg carried his vegetarian crusade into the 1940s, during the early decades of the twentieth century a triumvirate of self-appointed food authorities were helping to change the way Americans viewed the meat on their plates. The first of these was Upton Sinclair. A novelist and social reformer, Sinclair became a food reformer quite by accident. His novel *The Jungle* (1906), which he had intended to be a diatribe against capitalism, was so vivid in its portrayal of the horrors of the meatpacking industry that it gave the country a case of national dyspepsia. It was influential in the passage of the Pure Food and Drug Act (1906), and one year after its publication, the U.S. Food and Drug Administration was formed (1907). Sinclair himself became a vegetarian, albeit for only three years; however, there is no doubt that many Americans were stirred by his book to swear off meat eating altogether.

The next was Horace Fletcher. A corpulent American businessman, Fletcher lost weight by developing a system called Fletcherism, whereby each morsel of food was to be chewed from fifty to sixty times. When he found that meat offered the greatest resistance to being liquefied through chewing, Horace stopped eating meat and recommended that earnest followers of his regimen do likewise. When Americans found that they could lose weight simply through vigorous mastication, Fletcherism swept the country. Dr. Kellogg even posted a big sign in the dining room of his sanitarium that urged his patients to "Fletcherize!" Americans continued to masticate their food well into the 1940s.

The third reformer, Bernarr Macfadden, was a rags-to-riches physical culturist, turned publishing magnate and charismatic public health figure. Macfadden published a plethora of popular magazines, among them *Physical Culture, True Romance, True Confessions, True Story*, and a sleazy but successful tabloid, the *New York Evening Graphic*. Amid the lurid articles on sensational murders and scandalous divorces, he would run pensive essays promoting a vegetarian lifestyle. As one of America's richest young tycoons, he could have indulged his appetite on a Lucullan scale, but he lived chiefly on raw vegetables and fruit. (Later in life, he became a bit of a backslider and included some meat in his diet, but in his heyday, he lived mainly on raw vegetarian food.) On rare occasions when he fell ill, he cured himself through fasting. In 1902, he opened one of New York's first vegetarian restaurants, Physical Culture (named after his fitness magazine), where for a nickel one could dine on an entree like "Hamburger Steak," which was made from nuts and vegetables. By 1911, twenty vegetarian Physical Culture restaurants had sprung up in Philadelphia, Chicago, and sundry other locations.

In 1936, Bernarr Macfadden ran for the presidency of the United States as a Republican candidate, and even as an octogenarian continued to attract publicity (into the mid-1950s) with stunts like parachuting onto the grounds of his health hotel, the Macfadden–Deauville in Miami Beach, in order to exhibit his undiminished physical vigor.

In 1927, America's longest continuously running vegetarian society was founded in Washington, D.C., by Milton Trenham, with strong Seventh-Day Adventist backing. The Vegetarian Society of the District of Columbia is the oldest vegetarian organization in either North America or South America.

Out of the social and cultural ferment of the late 1960s arose America's largest and most durable vegetarian intentional community. Established in 1971 and located in Summertown, Tennessee, it is called The Farm and is still flourishing three decades after its founding. One of its many cottage industries is the generically named Book Publishing Company—the largest and most successful publisher of vegetarian and vegan books in the world.

One of America's most effective vegetarian organizations is EarthSave. Founded in 1988 by Baskin & Robbins ice cream heir, John Robbins, it advocates a plant-based diet and promotes awareness of the ecological destruction that results from the rearing of animals for food. There are forty EarthSave chapters throughout the United States.

In 1971, the landmark book *Diet for a Small Planet* helped put vegetarianism on the American map, as did the founding of the North American Vegetarian Society (1974), the monthly journal *Vegetarian Times* (1974), and the Vegetarian Resource Group (1981). Other books like *The Vegetarian Resource Book* (1983), *Diet for a New America* (1987), *Judaism and Vegetarianism* (1988), *Famous Vegetarians and Their Favorite Recipes* (1994), *Prisoned Chickens, Poisoned Eggs* (1996), *Vegan: The New Ethics of Eating* (1998), *Food for the Gods: Vegetarianism and the World's Religions* (1998), and *Deep*

Frances Moore Lappé. Portrait by Glory Brightfield from *Famous Vegetarians and Their Favorite Recipes*, by Rynn Berry (New York and Los Angeles, 2003), p. 192. *Collection of Rynn Berry*

Vegetarianism (1999) have also helped popularize vegetarianism in America.

Veganism

In 1944 in Leicester, England, Donald Watson and his wife, Dorothy, coined the word "vegan," which they formed from the first three and the last two letters of "vegetarian." With this new term, the Watsons wanted to encompass the meaning of "vegetarian" imparted by the Pythagoreans and Buddhists: one who, for reasons of compassion, abstains from consuming all foods and other products of animal origin. It took time for the word to catch on in the United States, but now it has become almost a competing term with "vegetarian." To help win recognition for the vegan concept in America, H. Jay Dinshah started the American Vegan Society in 1960. Dinshah's wife, Freya, published the first ethical vegetarian or vegan cookbook in the United States, *The Vegan Kitchen* (1966), which remains a steady seller.

Impact of Asian Religions

From the late 1960s to the present, the influence of Asian religions has played a key role in orienting many Americans toward a vegetarian lifestyle. One of the earliest manifestations of this trend was macrobiotics, a quasi-religious food-reform movement with dietary principles based on a yin-yang dichotomy derived from Taoism.

Indian religions, with their time-honored taboos against harming animals, have been especially active in persuading Americans to forswear meat eating. Notable for their culinary prowess have been the Hare Krishnas from the Vaishnava sect of Hinduism. There are Hare Krishna restaurants and vegetarian food carts in every major city in the United States. The Krishnas also have produced the definitive book on Indian vegetarian cookery, *Lord Krishna's Cuisine* (1987), written by Yamuna Devi (née Joan Campanella), the American secretary to Swami Prabhupada, the founder of the Krishna movement in America.

Yoga has also fomented the spread of vegetarianism in America. The first precept of the classical yoga systems is *ahimsa*—the same ethical imperative that has guided the eating practices of Jains and Buddhists for thousands of years. Serious students of yoga are taught, according to this principle, that in order to make spiritual progress they must refrain from eating animal flesh. Buddhism, one of the fastest-growing religious denominations in America, also has stimulated the growth of vegetarianism. Buddhist monks hold the first precept, *ahimsa*, in the highest veneration and are vegetarians on ethical grounds.

The Zen Buddhist *roshi* (enlightened master) Philip Kapleau founded America's first vegetarian Zen center in Rochester, New York, in 1966. Buddhist temple cuisine from China and Japan has furnished American Buddhists with a wide array of mock meats made from wheat gluten and soy that have found their way into such popular American meat analogues as Smart Dogs (simulated hot dogs made from tofu) and Barbecued Seitan Slices (simulated cold cuts made from wheat gluten). William Shurtleff, a Stanford-educated physicist who became a Zen monk, and his wife, Akiko, wrote a series of bestselling books—among them, *The Book of Tofu, The Book of Tempeh*, and *The Book of Miso*—that helped introduce soy foods such as tofu, tempeh, okara, and miso to Americans in the 1970s and 1980s.

Influence of Animal Rights

Another significant force for dietary change in North America has been the animal rights movement. Individual activists, such as John Woolman; Henry Bergh, founder of the Society for the Prevention of Cruelty to Animals (1866); J. Howard Moore, author of *The Universal Kinship* (1908); Curtis and Emarel Freshel, founders of the Millennium Guild, a vegetarian group; and Henry Spira have distinguished themselves in this fight.

Animal Rights did not start to crystallize as a social movement, however, until the 1980s, with the founding of PETA (People for the Ethical Treatment of Animals) and FARM (Farm Animal Reform Movement), both in 1981. In 1984, FARM started an annual spring event, the Great American Meatout, which is modeled after the Great American Smokeout (an attempt to rid Americans of their smoking habit). PETA, FARM, and other animal rights organizations, along with such books as *Animal Liberation* (1975), *The Case for Animal Rights* (1983), *An Unnatural Order* (1993), *Judaism and Animal Rights: Classical and Contemporary Responses* (1993), *Slaughterhouse* (1997), *Rattling the Cages* (2000), and *Dominion* (2002), have given enormous impetus to the spread of ethical vegetarianism in the United States.

Raw Food Movement

Within recent years a new vegetarian dietary trend has burst upon the scene. The raw food movement eschews enzyme-depleted cooked foods in favor of high-enzyme raw vegetables and fruits. It would be more accurate to say that the trend started back in the 1840s with Sylvester Graham, who recommended living on unfired vegetables and fruits as the optimum diet. The raw food movement was given its greatest public exposure in the modern era by Bernarr Macfadden, who for the first four decades of the twentieth century ran a successful publishing empire while living ostentatiously on a raw vegetarian diet.

Systematized by Herbert Shelton as Natural Hygiene in the 1920s and 1930s, the raw food movement suddenly blossomed into a full-blown social movement. Although America's first raw foods restaurant, the Eutropheon, opened in San Francisco in 1917, until the last years of the twentieth century, raw food restaurants had been rather sparse on the ground. Numerous raw food restaurants opened to critical acclaim in the early 2000s in America's culinary capitals of New York, Chicago, Los Angeles, and San Francisco. By 2004, there were forty raw food restaurants in the country, and their numbers were growing.

The only foodstuffs to be identified closely with the raw food movement are sprouted grains, beans, seed and nut cheeses, and wheatgrass juice—all the legacy of Anne Wigmore. Drawing on the knowledge passed on to her by her grandmother, a village healer in her native Lithuania, Wigmore concocted wheatgrass juices and sprouted foods to feed her ailing patients at the Hippocrates Institutes, holistic raw food health centers that she opened throughout the United States.

Another immigrant to whom the raw foods movement owes much is Aris La Tham. A native of Panama, he is considered to be the father of gourmet ethical vegetarian raw food cuisine in America. He debuted his raw food creations in 1979, when he started Sunfired Foods, a live-foods company in New York City. In the years since, he has trained thousands of raw food chefs and added innumerable gourmet raw food recipes to his repertoire.

A Paradigm Shift

Famous vegetarians, such as the Nobel laureate writer Isaac Bashevis Singer; the entertainer Dick Gregory; the founder and chief executive officer of Apple Computer, Steve Jobs; the self-help guru Anthony Robbins; the techno-music star Moby (née Richard Melville, a descendant of the writer Herman Melville); and Paul McCartney and his late wife, Linda, have thrown their considerable support behind the vegetarian cause over the years. In fact, in the late 1990s Paul and Linda McCartney launched a successful line of frozen vegetarian entrees.

In freezer cases across America, one can find a vast array of vegetarian entrees, from the sophisticated to the ordinary. Supermarkets are stocking more and more vegetarian food products, including soy milk and cheese; rice milk; a line of frankfurters, cutlets, and patties made from fungus; fake bacon, and soy hotdogs and burgers. One can even purchase complete meals in a box: breakfast burritos, vegan pizzas, vegan enchiladas, "chili non carne," mock-chicken potpie, "un-turkey" with giblet gravy, and even mock-spareribs. Nondairy soy ice creams, like Chunky Nut Madness and Mint Marble Fudge, and rice milk ice creams, like Neapolitan, Cappuccino, and Cocoa Marble Fudge, also abound. Vegetarian restaurants in such cities as New York, Seattle, and San Francisco continue to proliferate. All of this suggests that the popular image of vegetarianism as an eccentric, cranky, fringe movement has undergone a paradigm shift. Among younger generations of Americans, it is very much in vogue to be vegetarian, if not vegan.

[*See also* Advertising; Boardinghouses; Cereal, Cold; Counterculture, Food; Food and Drug Administration; Graham, Sylvester; Health Food; Kellogg, John Harvey; Nuts; Organic Food; Peanut Butter; Pure Food and Drug Act; Sinclair, Upton; Soybeans; Vegetables.]

BIBLIOGRAPHY

Belasco, Warren J. *Appetite for Change: How the Counterculture Took On the Food Industry, 1966–1988.* New York: Pantheon, 1989.
Berry, Rynn. *Famous Vegetarians and Their Favorite Recipes.* New York: Pythagorean Publishers, 1994.
Berry, Rynn. *Food for the Gods: Vegetarianism and the World's Religions.* New York: Pythagorean Publishers, 1998.
Carson, Gerald. *Cornflake Crusade.* New York: Rinehart, 1957.
Green, Harvey. *Fit for America: Health, Fitness, Sport and American Society.* New York: Pantheon, 1986.

RYNN BERRY

Velveeta

In *The Joy of Cooking*, the editor Irma S. Rombauer sniffs, "We can only echo Clifton Fadiman when he declares that processed cheese represents the triumph of technology over conscience."

The chemist Elmer E. Eldredge, employed by Phenix Cheese Company in Lowville, New York, invented Phenett in 1915—a processed cheese containing whey protein, cheese (american, swiss, or camembert), and sodium citrate, an antioxidant. Meanwhile scientists for J. L. Kraft

Brothers were formulating NuKraft, a similar product. Kraft patented its tinned cheese in 1916, and it was included in the rations of soldiers going overseas during World War I.

Phenix and Kraft agreed to share patent rights to their processed cheeses, and in 1928 Velveeta was born. Kraft's brand name reflects the velvety texture of the product when melted.

By law Velveeta must contain at least 51 percent cheese; Velveeta blends colby, swiss, and cheddar. The ingredients are heated to incorporate more moisture, rendering the product easier to spread and melt. Pasteurization prevents ripening, so Velveeta has a remarkable shelf life. Velveeta was originally packaged in a wooden box with a tinfoil lining; it does not require refrigeration.

In 1937 a Kraft salesman suggested combining Velveeta with a box of macaroni noodles; the product became Kraft Macaroni & Cheese Dinner. Over a million boxes were sold each day in 2002.

[*See also* Cheese; Combat Food; Kraft Foods.]

BIBLIOGRAPHY

Harte, Tom. "The Power of (Pasteurized and Prepared) Cheese." *Southeast Missourian,* January 22, 2003.
Rombauer, Irma S. *The Joy of Cooking.* Indianapolis, IN: Bobbs-Merrill, 1967.

SARA RATH

Vending Machines

The first American vending machine appeared in 1888, when the Thomas Adams Gum Company (American Chicle, Pfizer) placed a machine selling Tutti-Frutti chewing gum on a platform of the elevated train in New York City. The following year, a penny vending machine was developed that could dispense handfuls of candy and peanuts. Round, bubble-topped penny gumball machines were introduced in 1907. Because vending machines were still quite unreliable, most sold only penny items until the 1920s. One exception was the Horn and Hardart Baking Company, which opened the first coin-operated Automat restaurant in Philadelphia in 1902, where diners selected their menu choices for prepared food displayed behind a wall of small glass windows.

In 1908 the Public Cup Vendor Company (Dixie Cup Company), devised a machine that served cooled water in a paper cup for a penny; later machines sold just the cup (the

Vending Machines. *Photograph by Joe Zarba*

water was free). "Sodamats," forerunners of the modern soda machine, were installed in amusement parks in 1926; grouped together to use the same compressors and pumps, the machines had attendants to keep them running.

In the 1930s vending machines began to offer a variety of candy bars. Movie theaters, popular sites for candy machines, displayed large, ornately designed versions. In 1935 the first cup-type soft-drink vending machine, made by Vendrink Corporation, appeared in Chicago, and Coca-Cola introduced the first standardized coin-operated bottled soda machines selling nickel Cokes. By 1950, 25 percent of all Cokes were sold through vending machines. There were approximately 1.2 million soft-drink machines in 1964, and soda cans, introduced in 1961, made up a large percentage of the sales. Using dry ice for cooling, ice cream vendors became available in 1933, followed by milk machines in 1938. Refrigerated machines were perfected in the early 1950s.

The War Production Board stopped the production of vending machines in 1942 because of the need for metal to support the war effort. Still, vending machines sustained the war effort, feeding factory workers during their long shifts, which led to the later acceptance of vending machines in the workplace.

By 1960 some companies and schools and colleges abandoned their cafeterias and replaced them with banks of the less-expensive vending machines. Sandwiches, desserts, hot coffee, and soup created a growing market in factories and plants, today one of the largest categories for

vending-machine sales. This period also saw the introduction of machines that exchanged coins for dollar bills and the arrival of vending machines onto college campuses and public schools. Hot coffee machines were invented in 1945 and remained unchanged until the 1980s, when new innovations allowed coffee beans to be ground within the machine, as needed. This innovation produced the 1990s explosion of gourmet coffee and espresso machines.

Advances in payment systems during the 1990s included the use of debit or credit cards and cell phones, helping allay the problem of slugs, the fake coins that have plagued the industry from its infancy. In 2002 a supersized sidewalk "convenience store," an idea that had been tried unsuccessfully in past decades, was opened in Washington, D.C. The wall of two hundred vended products, ranging from motor oil to roast beef sandwiches, has raised hopes for a new era in vending.

[*See also* Automats; Cafeterias; Candy Bars and Candy, *sidebar on* Penny Candy; Soda Drinks.]

BIBLIOGRAPHY

National Automatic Merchandising Association. http://www.vending.org. Posts a time line of highlights and a short history of the vending industry.
Segrave, Kerry. *Vending Machines: An American Social History.* Jefferson, NC, and London: McFarland & Co., 2002.

JOY SANTLOFER

Venison, *see Game*

Vermouth

Originating in the late eighteenth century in Italy and served in France and Italy as an aperitif or digestif, vermouth is better known in America as the mixer that makes Manhattans, Rob Roys, French kisses, and martinis. Vermouth can be dry, bitter or sweet, and white or red. A wine fortified with brandy, vermouth gets its name from the German word for the bitter root wormwood, *Vermut*. Some vermouth is still made with wormwood (now known to be hallucinogenic), but it is more often made with other herbs and botanicals, giving it a distinctive aromatic taste.

American production is centered in California, where several brands make this complex wine. Grape varietals used to make the wine include Orange Muscat,

Colombard, Picpoul, and Valdepenas. The wine from these grapes is made and then fortified with brandy and infused with dried herbs or essential oils, depending on the producer. The mixture of botanicals creates a distinctive type of vermouth, and each maker's vermouth is proprietary. The selection of botanicals used can range widely, including angelica, coriander seed, sage, quinine, linden, cloves, juniper, rosemary, mace, marjoram, citrus rinds, and other pungent spices.

The origins of vermouth are as murky as the recipes for making it. Undisputed is that it was first produced in the Piedmont region of northern Italy—Turin is the greatest producer. Although the truth is yet to be discovered, three beliefs predominate as to its creation: first, to balance the taste of astringent wines; second, as a medicinal tincture (the botanicals were considered healing); and third, as a replacement for polluted water. According to *The Dictionary of American Food and Drink*, the word "vermouth" was first printed in 1806. The alcohol content hovered around 15 percent, somewhat higher than wine and about the same as port.

As a mixer, vermouth adds complexity to drinks—the aromatics create layers of flavor, while the wine and brandy add fruitiness. This complexity was particularly effective during the era of Prohibition, when most of the alcohol being drunk in America was gin, easily and quickly distilled and comparatively crude by present-day standards. The martini was created many years earlier, but its popularity bounded when vermouth was added to the crude gin.

Although the origins of the first martini are obscured, there is consensus among cocktail connoisseurs that both the vermouth and the gin were sweeter then than is popular today. Consequently, the term "dry" martini may not mean that there is less vermouth but that dry vermouth, rather than sweet vermouth, is used. American vermouth production has divided into two camps: those vintners who use lesser-quality grapes and wine for large vermouth production, to be used as mixers and for cooking, and smaller and boutique producers who make vermouth to be tasted on its own or as a complex mixer.

[*See also* Brandy; Cocktails; Gin; Herbs and Spices; Martini.]

BIBLIOGRAPHY

Grimes, William. *Straight Up or On the Rocks: The Story of the American Cocktail*. New York: North Point Press, 2001.

Mariani, John F. *The Dictionary of American Food and Drink*. New York: Ticknor and Fields, 1983.

McGee, Harold. *On Food and Cooking: The Science and Lore of the Kitchen*. New York: Collier, 1984.

Vya. http://www.vya.com. Vermouth contents and production.

LISA DELANGE

Vienna Sausage

The Vienna sausage is one of those foods brought to America by immigrants and then naturalized into an iconic item. Hailing from German-speaking Europe, it has several incarnations. One is the wiener, from *Wienerwurst*, or "Vienna sausage" (from Wien, the German spelling of Vienna), originally made mainly from pork and appearing in bundles of links. In late-nineteenth- and early-twentieth-century America, the name "wiener" came to be used interchangeably with "hot dog" and sometimes "frankfurter," a different formulation of beef and pork. Properly speaking, the Vienna or Vienna-style sausage is a linked sausage, often with a frankfurter-style mixture of meats. It was sold in braided links, but in America it transformed into something else: canned sausage. In this form it became an early example of convenience food.

Home sausage canning is a preservation technique associated with the winter slaughter of hogs on farms across America. Commercial canning of sausage had appeared by the mid-nineteenth century and became more popular with the introduction of mechanized meat processing and canning production in the 1860s. The term "Vienna" or "Vienna-style" seems to have appeared around 1903. The term meant a sausage (skinless after the 1950s) cut into two-inch lengths and then canned. Small, one- or two-inch "cocktail sausages" at times have been touted as the origin of the canned variety, but they are different products.

By the end of the century, such Chicago-based companies as Armour, Swift, and Libby (Libby, McNeill and Libby) as well as Hormel in Minnesota dominated the market for canned sausages. Armour, with its pop-top aluminum can, remains the industry sales leader. In the South, where canned meats appeared in the 1890s, one company became synonymous with canned sausages, the first commercial meat canner in Mississippi, Bryan Packing Company of West Point. Beginning in 1938 Bryan packed Vienna sausages in oil, unlike most northern products, and the product achieved such renown that it was identified with southern regional food. Canned bologna, produced in the United States only at the

Plumrose plant in Booneville, Missouri, is a variation on the Vienna canned sausage.

Although the product is still widely sold, famously to hikers and fishermen, Vienna sausage consumption has declined since its heyday from the 1940s to the 1970s. At its height the sausage seeped into international cuisines through U.S. military bases. The sausages are used in Filipino *pancits*, and there is even a popular Cuban dish consisting of Viennas cooked with rice and flavored with Cuban spices, no doubt courtesy of Guantánamo Bay.

[*See also* Sausage.]

BIBLIOGRAPHY

Loebel, Leon, and Stanley Loebel. *All about Meat.* New York: Harcourt, 1975.

BRUCE KRAIG

Vitamins

Vitamins are a group of organic substances that are essential for human growth and normal metabolism. They occur naturally in small amounts in most foods and beverages and can be produced synthetically. The lack of certain vitamins in the diet can bring about specific diseases. Although research into the link between diet and some of these diseases had been going on for well over a century, vitamins did not gain widespread public attention until the period between World Wars I and II.

History of Vitamins

By the mid-eighteenth century, the problem of scurvy on shipboard had led some doctors to suspect that a mysterious "element" in fresh fruits, vegetables, wine, and malted barley was necessary for life, even though most scientists still believed that only fats, carbohydrates, proteins, and salts were essential for adequate nutrition. Early advances in the search for this unknown element came from unexpected field trials associated with tragic circumstances. In 1747 James Lind was caring for sailors on the British ship *Salisbury* during a scurvy epidemic and selected twelve subjects for an experiment. He administered six different "anti-scorbutic" diets to pairs of the sick men, and the two who received citrus fruits recovered dramatically. The study, which Lind reported in *A Treatise of the Scurvy* (1753), led his pupil, Sir

Gilbert Blane, to introduce citrus fruits to the required rations on British sailing ships.

In 1871, J. B. A. Dumas wrote of the German siege of Paris, during which nutritionists created artificial milk from pure fat and sugar syrups for the children. The mixture did not sustain the children, and Dumas concluded that, though the liquid was pure, something was lacking that exists in natural milk. Laboratory studies in the late nineteenth and early twentieth centuries began to shed light on the existence of these organic compounds.

In 1890 the Dutch physician Christiaan Eijkman, working in Java, discovered and extracted a "protective factor" in the germ and pericarp of rice that kept domestic fowl from exhibiting symptoms resembling those of beriberi (which occurred when they were fed polished rice). This factor was eventually named "thiamine."

In 1905 animal studies at the University of Utrecht, conducted by C. A. Pekelharing, proved that a diet of pure fats, carbohydrates, proteins, and salts was not adequate for survival. When he added small amounts of milk to the diet, the animal's health was restored. Sir Frederick Gowland Hopkins, of Cambridge University, reported briefly in 1906 and fully in 1912 on experiments that showed that there must exist in certain foods "accessory food factors" not previously known but essential.

The year 1912 became a turning point in the search for these essential factors. Casimir Funk, at London's Lister Institute, wrote in *Die Vitaminen* that beriberi, rickets, pellagra, and sprue might be caused by the lack of special substances in the diet. Believing that the unknown substances must be coenzymes that provide the transfer site for biochemical changes catalyzed by the recently discovered enzymes, and therefore would be amines, he combined the prefix "vita," meaning life, and "amine" (at the time it was thought that all coenzymes were amines, or derivations of ammonia) to name these unknowns "vitamines." In 1913 two groups of Americans, T. B. Osborne and L. B. Mendel and E. V. McCollum and M. Davis extracted from butter and cod liver oil the missing growth factors that the latter workers called "fat-soluble A." It later came to be called simply vitamin A. McCollum wrote that there might be important differences between adequate and optimal quantities of vitamins in nutrition and that just a small amount of milk or of certain fruits and vegetables made the diet adequate.

As soon as the existence of vitamins was confirmed, biochemists started work to isolate them, trying to find out how much of each of these compounds exists in different foods and ascertain whether there is an optimal intake of each in human nutrition. In 1920 the name "vitamine" was changed to "vitamin" through the efforts of J. C. Drummond, who suggested that not all coenzymes had to be amines. In addition to the fat-soluble vitamin A, a water-soluble vitamin B (the antiberiberi substance) and the antiscorbutic vitamin C had been identified by that time. Vitamins are still distinguished as water soluble or fat soluble; the vitamin B complex and vitamin C are water soluble, and the rest are fat soluble. Although by 1938 all thirteen vitamins considered essential had been isolated and some had been synthesized, research on the importance of vitamins in human and animal health continued at many American university and government research centers.

Vitamin Properties

Vitamin A was the first vitamin to be isolated. It is obtained from carotene and occurs in green and yellow vegetables, egg yolk, butter, and cod liver oil and other seafood products. It is essential to growth, protects the skin, and prevents night blindness. Because it is fat soluble, it can build up in the body and be toxic if taken in excess.

Vitamin B at first was thought to be just one coenzyme. The isolation of what became known as thiamin, or B_1, in 1926 showed that vitamin B had to have more than one factor, because the antiberiberi factor was heat sensitive and other factors were thought to be heat stable. The second factor to be discovered, riboflavin or vitamin B_2, promotes healthy skin and good vision. As more related substances were identified, the group was renamed the "vitamin B complex." Vitamin B_3, also known as niacin or nicotinic acid, functions in the prevention of pellagra, a disease marked by gastrointestinal disorders and dermatitis. Vitamin B_6, or pyridoxine, aids in nutrient metabolism. Folic acid, or folacin, once known as vitamin B_9, has a role in human reproduction and promotes the production of red blood cells. Vitamin B_{12}, or cobalamin, has been found to prevent pernicious anemia and certain nervous system disorders. Pantothenic acid and biotin, also factors of the B complex, function in the metabolism of nutrients.

Vitamin C got its name in 1920, although as the "antiscorbutic substance" it already had the longest history of research. In 1928 ascorbic acid was isolated but not recognized; in 1932 it was isolated and identified and, within months of that discovery, was synthesized. In 1937

researchers thought that it should be renamed "ascorbic acid," and both names are now used.

Vitamin D includes any of several fat-soluble compounds that can be produced in the skin by the action of the sun or supplied by fortified foods. A deficiency of this compound causes rickets, a disease in which insufficient calcium and phosphate is deposited in the bones. In 1918 Sir Edward Mellanby showed that rickets was a nutritional disease that could be remedied by a substance present in cod liver oil. In 1922 scientists at Johns Hopkins distinguished the "anti-ricketic factor" from vitamin A. This fourth discovered nutrient was named vitamin D. In 1923 it was discovered that irradiating foods stimulated the provitamins (substances that are converted to vitamins) in them, so that the body could turn them into vitamin D more easily. Although the natural concentration of vitamin D in milk varies considerably, milk is the only product that the government has allowed to be fortified with vitamin D. The first vitamin D–fortified milk was sold in 1933.

Vitamin E, or alpha-tocopherol, is a fat-soluble vitamin abundant in vegetable oils, whole-grain cereal, butter, and eggs. It is important as an antioxidant in the deactivation of free radicals and in the maintenance of the body's cell membranes. Although natural deficiency is rare, when deficiency is produced in a laboratory, it causes reproductive failure. Vitamin E sometimes is used as a food supplement and, because it is not eliminated by the body, can cause toxicity if taken in doses larger than recommended.

Vitamins K_1 and K_2 are fat-soluble vitamins found in leafy vegetables, brown rice, bran, and pork liver. They increase the content of the plasma protein, prothrombin, in the blood, thereby promoting blood clotting. The Danish biochemist Henrik Dam described the condition caused by a deficiency of this factor and suggested calling the factor vitamin K, from the German word *Koagulation*.

[*See also* Barley; Butter; Citrus; Eggs; Fats and Oils; Fruit; Irradiation; Milk; Rice; Vegetables.]

BIBLIOGRAPHY

Davidson, Sir Stanley, A. P. Meiklejohn, and R. Passmore. *Human Nutrition and Dietetics*. Baltimore: Williams and Wilkins, 1959.

McCollum, Elmer Verner. *A History of Nutrition*. Boston: Houghton Mifflin, 1957.

Sherman, Henry C., and Caroline Sherman Lanford. *Essentials of Nutrition*. New York: Macmillan, 1951.

Wardlaw, Gordon. *Contemporary Nutrition: Issues and Insights*. New York: McGraw-Hill, 2002.

JOANNE LAMB HAYES

Vodka

Scholars debate the beginnings of vodka. Most agree that vodka has been made for one thousand years or so. Some believe it was distilled first in the area that became Russia. The word "vodka" comes from the Russian *zhizenennia voda* (water of life). Others think that vodka was born a little west of Russia, in present-day Poland. Still other scholars stake claims for other European nations and even the British Isles.

The great difficulty in identifying the origins of vodka comes from its ill-defined nature. The U.S. Bureau of Alcohol, Tobacco, and Firearms (BATF) defines vodka as a colorless, odorless, tasteless spirit. But vodka does have flavor and aroma—few are likely to mistake it for water. The way to make sense of this apparent contradiction is by understanding that vodka (except those types that are labeled "flavored") is not made flavorful by being aged in barrels (like whiskey) or infused with herbs (like gin) or syrups (like liqueurs). It is distilled, filtered, and then bottled.

Unlike other spirits, vodka is not classified by the materials from which it is distilled. (Bourbon, for instance, is mostly corn.) Vodka is made from grains, like wheat and rye, and nongrains, such as potatoes, sugar beets, and even mare's milk (the Mongolian *kumiss*). Whereas many spirits are defined in part by where they are made (for example, Scotch whisky can be made only in Scotland), vodka can be made anywhere. Thus, vodka is produced in England, France, Italy, and many other nations, including, of course, America.

It is entirely possible that vodka existed in America in the nineteenth century. Anyone who distilled moonshine and softened it through filtration would have been making vodka. However, vodka did not appear as vodka until 1934. In 1933 Rudolph Kunett, a Russian émigré to the United States, visited France. There he met Vladimir Smirnoff. The Smirnoff family's fortunes had been hurt when the Bolsheviks took over Russia and seized their factories in 1917. The Smirnoffs had looked around Europe for new places to distill their family spirit. Smirnoff licensed Kunett to make an American version. The next year Kunett began producing Smirnoff vodka in Connecticut. Kunett struggled in the distilling business and sold out to the Heublein Company in 1939.

By 1946 Americans bought thirty thousand cases of Smirnoff a year. In 1955 Smirnoff sales in America topped one million cases per year. Vodka's immediate popularity was largely a function of its near absence of flavor. This made it inoffensive and easy to mix into cocktails (among them, the Moscow mule, screwdriver, and Bloody Mary). Heublein's advertisements, which reminded consumers that vodka is odorless on the breath ("Smirnoff—It will leave you breathless!"), also helped.

The booming American economy of the late twentieth century invited an enormous influx of vodka brands. Many of them are made in the United States, and even more are imported, especially from nations where state-subsidized distilleries have been privatized. Clever marketing of vodka in print periodicals and as chic cocktails (such as the vodka martini and cosmopolitan) helped draw many consumers to vodka. The result has been soaring quality and wide-ranging product diversification. Numerous "boutique" brands have appeared, fetching twenty-five dollars or more per one 750-milliliter bottle. There also are more flavors of vodka than ever: apple, peach, lemon, ginseng, vanilla, and chocolate, to name just a few.

[*See also* Cocktails; Distillation.]

BIBLIOGRAPHY

Emmons, Bob. *The Book of Gins and Vodkas*. Peru, IL: Open Court, 2000.

KEVIN R. KOSAR

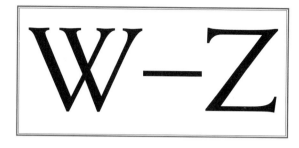

W–Z

Waffle, Wafer, and Pizelle Irons

Waffles and wafers were festive delicacies baked on the hearth on flat, hinged, wrought, and cast-iron plates worked with long, scissor-action handles. Originally communion wafers, they were sometimes incised with pictorial references to saints or holidays; they were later secularized. Brought to the American colonies, the waffle and wafer irons produced thin, crisp, and meltingly tender Dutch *hard waffels*, English wafers, Swedish *krumkaga*, Italian *pizzele*, and French *gaufrettes*.

Waffle irons that originated in the Netherlands and Belgium were similar but had deeper waffle patterns. Fifteenth-century offshoots of wafer irons, they were used in the American colonies in the same way—propped or held over fires or embers, one at a time.

Handles were shortened to adapt cast-iron waffle irons to the nineteenth-century cookstove. The hinged irons now rested in supporting frames and required less work

to swivel and turn. In 1854 the plates of a large, round "waffle furnace" were scored to break the waffle into four wedges; others were rectangular with demarcated lines for cutting. By 1900 most were of cast iron and a few were of aluminum, some having decorative waffling patterns that included hearts, diamonds, squares, Xs, or crosses. By 1917 or 1918 electric waffle irons were popular for use right at the breakfast table.

[*See also* Breakfast Foods.]

BIBLIOGRAPHY

Franklin, Linda Campbell. *300 Years of Kitchen Collectibles.* 5th ed. Iola, WI: Krause, 2003.
Smith, David G., and Chuck Wafford. *The Book of Griswold and Wagner: Favorite Piqua, Sidney Hollow Ware, Wapak: With Price Guide.* Atglen, PA: Schiffer, 1995.
Smith, David G., and Chuck Wafford. *The Book of Griswold and Wagner: Favorite Pique, Sidney Hollow Ware, Wapak: With Revised Price Guide.* rev. 2nd ed. Atglen, PA: Schiffer, 2000.

ALICE ROSS AND LINDA CAMPBELL FRANKLIN

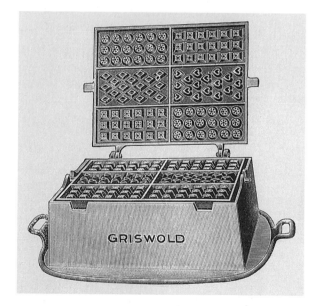

Waffle Iron. From the Duparquet, Huot, & Moneuse Co. catalog (Boston, 1915), p. 168.

Walnuts

Walnuts are common to both the New World and the Old World. The black walnut (*Juglans nigra*) is native to eastern North America. Black walnuts were consumed by Native Americans, but as the nuts are small, the yield is low, and black walnuts never became a major commercial crop. The black walnut is highly sought after as a hardwood and has become scarce. Old-world walnuts (*J. regia*) were domesticated at a very early date, probably in central Asia. Walnuts have been found in many archaeological sites in Europe, Persia, and China. The Greeks and the Romans were fond of them. European (also called English) walnuts were brought to New England by early settlers. Franciscan missionaries from Spain also introduced walnuts to California in the eighteenth century. Walnuts have been made into ketchup and preserves, pressed for their oil, and made into candies, cakes, and cookies, including American favorites like fudge, penuche, Toll House cookies, and brownies. Green walnuts are made into vinegar, and the leaves of the tree have been used to make tea. California produces the vast majority of commercial walnuts, and the United States is the leading world producer of these popular nuts.

[*See also* California; Nuts.]

ANDREW F. SMITH

Washington's Birthday

George Washington was born on February 12, 1732. In 1752, Britain adopted the Gregorian calendar, recalculating February 12 to February 22 and setting the stage for a great deal of confusion. This ambiguity was finally settled by an act of Congress in 1968, which moved the official celebration of Washington's Birthday to the third Monday of February.

The first recorded celebration of Washington's Birthday took place during the Revolutionary War; the occasion was marked by a military band at Valley Forge in 1778. Food first entered into the festivities three years later, at a dinner hosted by America's French allies in honor of Washington and his officers. By 1782, Americans were celebrating the occasion with similar public and private parties. These patriotic dinners grew into the "birth-night balls" of the new republic, where the eating of "American" foods like turkey and turtle were accompanied by round upon round of toasts from glasses filled with "domestic" spirits.

Washington's death in 1799 furthered his iconic status in a young nation in search of its identity on the world stage. Parson Mason Locke Weems capitalized on the hunger for American heroes by writing a spurious biography of Washington, *A History of the Life and Death, Virtues and Exploits of General George Washington* (1800). The most enduring "tall tale" invented by Weems is the confession of the young Washington that he "chopped down" a cherry tree because he could not "tell a lie." In the spirit of the allegorical age, cherries were immediately featured on the menu for Washington's Birthday celebrations.

Perhaps because fresh cherries were rare and difficult to procure in February, pie made from sweet cherry preserves quickly became the featured dish of holiday

Washington and the Cherries. Embossed postcard, early twentieth century. *Collection of Alice Ross*

celebrations. Menus from modern-day magazines and popular cooking shows use the featured cherries in various forms, from fresh to frozen to canned, in every course, including the traditional pie.

[*See also* Cherries.]

BIBLIOGRAPHY

Douglas, George William. *The American Book of Days: A Compendium of Information about Holidays, Festivals, Notable Anniversaries and Christian and Jewish Holy Days with Notes on other American Anniversaries Worthy of Remembrance.* 8th ed. Revised by Helen Douglas Compton. New York: H.W. Wilson Company, 1970. Well written, informative and comprehensive, this volume includes excellent information on the history and celebrations of the birthdays of Washington and Lincoln.

Imbornoni, Ann Marie. *Presidents' Day or Washington's Birthday?* http://www.factmonster.com/spot/washington1.html. An excellent site, cross-referenced to other topics of interest.

ESTHER REESE

Water

Bountiful supplies of potable water were touted as wonders of the New World in a Renaissance Europe troubled by large-scale pollution and water scarcity. But within one hundred years of the establishment of colonies in America, contamination and excessive exploitation of water resources led to disease and crises. Modern public water systems evolved from a need to make the nation's abundant resources safe and accessible. The experience in New York is emblematic of the chain of events leading to creation of regulated municipal water systems in all major cities across the United States.

Early Systems of Water Supply

In the original Dutch colony of New Amsterdam (now New York), poor sanitation resulted in the pollution of the available freshwater and in disease. In 1639, when there were only a few hundred settlers, water was drawn from local streams, ponds, and springs. While plans for a public well were drawn up in 1658, they were never carried out, and residents began to dig wells in their yards. The English captured New Amsterdam in 1664 largely because the Dutch leader, Peter Stuyvesant, surrendered after determining that there was not a sufficient water supply in the fort to maintain a lengthy defense. The English later dug a well in the fort, which provided sufficient potable water, much to the astonishment of the Dutch.

Wells, hand pumps, and springs provided inconsistent but adequate supplies of water for the next hundred years, though it is known to have been of poor quality. Travelers to New York City remarked that even horses balked at the quality of water offered them. By the dawn of the American Revolution, plans were being made for construction of a storage reservoir in lower Manhattan. A large well was dug, and water was pumped by a steam engine to the reservoir in the settled lower part of the island through a system of wooden pipes made of pine logs. The system was abandoned during occupation by the British army in September 1776.

The years after the Revolutionary War saw the rise of private water supply companies, many of them disreputable. One such venture, the Manhattan Company, started by Aaron Burr (soon to become vice president of the United States) and his friends in April 1799, constructed a system much like the one scuttled by the Revolution, using hollow logs to transmit water from a well to a reservoir and then to customers' houses. The firm used its ostensible mission—establishment of a supply of wholesome drinking water—as a ruse to cement unlimited banking privileges. The company survives today as the Chase Manhattan Bank.

By 1830 the city's population had reached 200,000, and supplies of water were poor and clearly inadequate. An epidemic of yellow fever underscored the need for new sources, and the growing city reached north to Westchester County's Croton River for an infusion of 80 million gallons of water per day. A diverting dam was built, and water was piped thirty-four miles via aqueducts to the nearby city of Yonkers, from where it was piped through the Bronx to distributing reservoirs. One reservoir was between Seventy-ninth and Eighty-sixth Streets, in the area that is now Central Park, and the other at Forty-second Street and Fifth Avenue, the site of the present-day New York Public Library. The Croton supplies were quickly outgrown, and as the population swelled with waves of immigrants in the late 1800s, stopgap measures were added to harness more water from Croton tributaries.

Severe droughts in the 1880s highlighted the need for additional works; a ten-year water-tunnel construction project resulted in a thirty-one-mile underground aqueduct to a terminus at 135th Street. A series of forty-eight-inch pipes conveyed a daily supply of 336 million gallons into a new distribution reservoir in Central Park. The reservoir still exists, though it was dropped from the city's water supply system in the mid-1990s. The separate municipalities of the Bronx and Brooklyn sourced their water separately, with the Bronx also tapping the Croton supplies and Brooklyn piping in from underground aquifers beneath Long Island. Most American cities followed a similar pattern of exploiting local supplies to the point of extinction and then reaching out to outlying areas for more.

Interstate treaties were enacted in the West, such as one in the 1870s diverting plentiful California river water to newly founded cities in Arizona. No one at the time could have predicted that, a century later, cities like Phoenix would be battling Golden State farmers for the precious resource that had once seemed inexhaustible. Eastern regions early on had established systems of water-usage trading, whereby some amount of water must be returned to the source after use (runoff, for example). Western states allowed a more first-come, first-served usage system, which has fueled agriculture and aquaculture development but led to more contentious water disputes in those areas.

Solutions of the Twentieth Century and Beyond

In New York, the turn of the twentieth century brought the greatest immigration surge in American history, taxing the water supply to its limit. The city undertook the most massive urban public water project in history, to create a secondary series of reservoirs in the Catskill Mountains northwest of the city. By 1917, 571 square miles of mountainous land was designated a "watershed" region, protected as a system of collection basins for New York's water supply. The construction of dams along the Esopus Creek and aqueducts forming the Ashokan Reservoir guaranteed a supply of at least 500 to 600 million gallons per day, even in times of drought.

The system is based on gravity. The water flows on its three-day journey to the city, without pumping, through aqueducts constructed of various materials (some of which consist of tunnels blasted through mountains, while other sections are massive underground channels made of poured concrete). The 1940s saw even greater water demand, and the city then expanded its watershed system to include sources from the headwaters of the Delaware River and other Catskill tributaries. The Delaware system was placed in service in stages: The Delaware Aqueduct was completed in 1944, Rondout Reservoir in 1950, Neversink Reservoir in 1954, Pepacton Reservoir in 1955, and Cannonsville Reservoir in 1964.

Per capita water consumption in the city, which was approximately one hundred gallons per day in 1900, reached a peak of more than two hundred gallons a day in the late 1980s and has settled down, in the early 2000s, thanks to conservation, migration of businesses, and improved technology, to 155 gallons a day. The city consumes 1.184 billion gallons per day. By the early 2000s two major water tunnels supplied all of New York's water from the Croton and Catskill watersheds. A third water tunnel, conceived in 1960, has been under construction since the 1970s and will provide the city with flexibility in maintenance and supply.

In the years immediately preceding World War II, science became aware of the hygienic benefits of a naturally occurring element in groundwater, fluoride. Dental experts determined that it strengthens tooth enamel and is the most effective defense against tooth decay, and in 1945 the city of Grand Rapids, Michigan, became the first water system to add fluoride to drinking water. Once the beneficial results of the Grand Rapids experiment became known, other cities and smaller municipalities proposed that solutions of fluoride be added to water supplies to promote general dental health. By the late 1950s the vast majority of municipal water supplies incorporated some degree of fluoride treatment, added at treatment plants along the route from source to consumer. Another element, chlorine, is also added to inhibit the growth of harmful microbes. No national standard exists for water treatment, and the U.S. Centers for Disease Control and Prevention is examining levels and setting parameters, which may be instituted nationally in the future.

While America is still blessed with an abundance of naturally occurring freshwater, the country has followed the European pattern of overexploitation and pollution, limiting possibilities for future contingency usage. Contamination by industry and agriculture has led to "dead" rivers, streams, and lakes, which ultimately must be cleaned up at great public expense. Two of the most notable (and successful) waterway cleanups were those of Lake Erie and the Hudson River, both in the 1970s and 1980s.

[See also Food and Drug Administration; Ice; Seltzer; Water, Bottled; Water, Imported.]

BIBLIOGRAPHY

Steuding, Bob. *The Last of the Handmade Dams: The Story of the Ashokan Reservoir*. Fleischmanns, NY: Purple House Press, 1989.

JAY WEINSTEIN

Water, Bottled

Bottled water is defined as water that is sealed in food-grade bottles and intended for human consumption. Thus, bottled water is classified as food and regulated by the Food and Drug Administration. In the late 1970s the bottled-water industry began to make an unprecedented climb toward its top position as purveyor of the world's fastest-growing bottled-beverage choice. Two main factors explain this growth: awareness of the real problems with the quality of public drinking water supplies and the growing preference among Americans for bottled water over sugar-laden soft drinks as a thirst quencher (with no fat and no preservatives). The demand for clean, fresh water is everywhere, and quite apart from the question of taste, more Americans are now drinking bottled waters because they think they have true therapeutic value.

There are several types of bottled water. Sparkling water is carbonated, and water without carbonation is called still water. Bottled still water is the type of water most frequently used to substitute tap water. Bottled water can come from a large variety of sources; it can be groundwater from a well, water from a protected spring, or water from a public supply.

The bottled water industry saw significant mergers and acquisitions in the last years of the twentieth century. Among the major U.S. companies are Nestlé Waters North America Inc. (Poland Spring, Perrier, Arrowhead, Deer Park, Zephyrhills, Ozarka, Ice Mountain, Calistoga, and Great Bear brands), Danone Waters of North America (Evian, Dannon, AquaPenn, Volvic, and McKesson brands), PepsiCo (Aquafina), Coca-Cola (Dasani), Suntory Water Group (Crystal Springs, Sierra Springs, Hinckley Springs, Kentwood Springs, and Belmont Springs brands), Crystal Geyser (Alpine Spring), and U.S. Filter (Cullingan). In 2001 consumers spent about $6.4 billion on bottled water, making it the fastest-growing beverage category for the tenth year in a row. Although U.S. bottled water consumption more than doubled from about 1993 to 2003, when compared with other countries (for example, European countries), it is still low. This implies that there is significant potential for expansion and that the industry will continue to grow into the twenty-first century.

[*See also* Food and Drug Administration; Water; Water, Imported.]

BIBLIOGRAPHY

International Bottled Water Association. http://www.bottledwater. org/. The IBWA website discusses bottled water regulation, safety, and industry standards.

ALFREDO MANUEL DE JESUS OLIVEIRA COELHO

Water, Imported

Until the late 1970s bottled water was imported for health concerns and in response to a fashionable trend. With the growing globalization of firms and consumption patterns, more and more foreign companies started to export their own brands. As a result, the volume of bottled water tripled in the last decade of the twentieth century, from 55.6 million gallons in 1989 to 151.1 million gallons in 1999. The prestige of imported waters seems to justify the considerable transport costs. The leading imported bottled water brands are Evian, Aberfoyle Springs, Naya, Perrier, San Pellegrino, Avalon, Fiji, Apollinaris, Volvic, and Vittel. Perrier is the foremost imported spa water in the growing U.S. market.

Bottled water imported into the United States is regulated at three levels, through federal and state agencies and trade associations. In addition, all bottled waters imported from countries outside the United States must meet the regulatory requirements established by their own countries as well as comply with all U.S. regulations.

[*See also* Food and Drug Administration; Water; Water, Bottled.]

BIBLIOGRAPHY

International Bottled Water Association. http://www.bottledwater. org/. The IBWA website discusses bottled water regulation, safety, and industry standards.

ALFREDO MANUEL DE JESUS OLIVEIRA COELHO

Watermelon

Watermelon (*Citrullus lanatus*) is a member of the gourd family (Cucurbitaceae) and is native to central Africa. Watermelons were disseminated to Asia in prehistoric times and were widely distributed throughout the Old World by the time the Americas were colonized. The Spanish introduced watermelons into the Caribbean and Florida and later into the American Southwest. Early French explorers and trappers planted watermelon seeds in Canada and subsequently in the Midwest and along the Mississippi River system. The first known references to watermelons in the English colonies are from Massachusetts, dated 1629. John Josselyn, in *New-England's Rarities Discovered* (1672), reports that these melons grew well in Massachusetts. Watermelons also grew easily in other colonies; they were a field crop in many places and were commonly consumed throughout colonial America.

WATERMELON CAKE

A popular nineteenth-century conceit was the watermelon cake, which imitates the appearance of the fruit without including it as an ingredient: Baked in a round or oval pan, the cake had an outer layer made from white batter; the batter for the center was tinted a bright pink and studded with raisins. With the outside sprinkled with green sugar after baking, it resembled a ripe watermelon.

Amelia Simmons published a watermelon recipe in her *American Cookery* (1796), and most nineteenth-century cookbooks included directions for serving them cold and recipes with watermelons as ingredients. With its refreshing juiciness and sherbet-like texture, chilled watermelon was a favorite picnic food; the fruit was eaten as a snack and incorporated into salads, desserts, and preserves (marmalade, jelly, and spicy pickled rind served as a condiment with meats). Watermelons also were used to flavor ice cream and other frozen desserts. As watermelons contain considerable amounts of sugar, their juice has been used as a sweetener in cooking. It also has been fermented to make wine and other alcoholic beverages, which became a specialty in the South. Watermelon juice is sold as a specialty item in natural food stores, and it is served occasionally in restaurants, blended with lemonade.

Beginning in the 1830s medical professionals proclaimed that watermelons were deleterious to health, a view that survived for decades. The cookbook writer Pierre Blot pronounced in his *Hand-Book of Practical Cookery, for Ladies and Professional Cooks* (1867) that watermelons were "considered very unwholesome by the great majority of doctors, chemists, and physiologists." Most Americans continued eating watermelons despite the warnings.

The wide availability of commercial frozen desserts has pushed watermelon out of the summer-dessert spotlight. "Ice-cold" is no longer a novelty. In 2002, however, Americans still consumed about fourteen pounds of watermelon per capita, and the United States ranked fourth in production worldwide. The states with the largest production are Florida, Texas, California, and Georgia. There are more than twelve hundred varieties of watermelon, but only about fifty are popular in the United States. Most varieties are grown regionally. Breeders have developed "baby" varieties, designed to fit in a modest-sized refrigerator, and seedless varieties, which are taking over the market from seeded kinds.

[*See also* Condiments; Desserts; Fruit Juices; Fruit Wines; Ice Cream and Ices; Preserves.]

BIBLIOGRAPHY

Maynard, Donald N., ed. *Watermelons: Characteristics, Production, and Marketing.* Alexandria, VA: ASHS Press, 2001.
Turner, Patricia A. "Watermelons." In *Rooted in America: Foodlore of Popular Fruits and Vegetables,* edited by David Scofield Wilson and Angus Kress Gillespie. Nashville: University of Tennessee Press, 1999.

ANDREW F. SMITH

AFRICAN AMERICANS AND WATERMELONS

The stereotypical association between African Americans and watermelons is a post–Civil War phenomenon. Slaves grew and ate watermelons in the South, as did most other Americans. After the Civil War, Negro minstrels sang songs such as "The Watermelon Song" and "Oh, Dat Watermelon" in their shows. These songs were first published in the 1870s and were mainstream America's first printed evidence of an association between African Americans and watermelons. When film came along in the 1890s, African Americans' association with watermelons moved into mainstream culture. During the early twentieth century and up to about 1940, the association between African Americans and watermelons was cemented through print caricatures (postcards, posters, and advertisements) and as a decorative theme for household goods, especially kitchen accessories. The most common caricature depicts a man with a wide, open-mouthed smile, the deep red interior of his mouth paralleling the color of the watermelon. Many African Americans deeply resented the caricature. When the 1893 Columbian Exhibition tried to attract African Americans to the world's fair, a special "Colored People's Day" was planned, which included African American entertainers and the distribution of free watermelons. The African American community in Chicago boycotted the day as did many of the scheduled performers. In 1939 the actress Butterfly McQueen, playing Scarlett O'Hara's slave, refused to eat watermelon in the film *Gone with the Wind*.

Waters, Alice

Alice Waters (1944–) is the owner and executive chef of the landmark restaurant Chez Panisse in Berkeley, California. Waters's commitment to using local, seasonal products has defined Chez Panisse's daily menu since it opened in 1971. Nationwide attention on the restaurant publicized her efforts to link the farm to the table. It helped launch a movement for sustainable agriculture, which stimulated a rebirth of independent, small-scale food producers across the country. A role model of the restaurateur-activist,

Waters has become a leading advocate for making fresh, high-quality foods commonly available, from public schools to the White House. She is credited with fostering the widespread accessibility of organic foods and the resurgence of community farmers' markets.

Born in Chatham, New Jersey, Waters graduated from the University of California at Berkeley in 1967 and trained as a Montessori teacher. Her food philosophy was shaped in part by her travels and eating experiences in France during college, and she was strongly influenced by Elizabeth David and Richard Olney, the authors of cookbooks on provincial French food.

Waters's insistence on using only the finest California ingredients made Chez Panisse an exemplar of American regional cooking. The restaurant has been a training ground for many prominent chefs, including Jeremiah Tower, Mark Miller, and Deborah Madison. Eight cookbooks have been published in its name. The first, *The Chez Panisse Menu Cookbook* (1982), authored by Waters, begins with a chapter entitled, "What I Believe about Cooking." Her Jeffersonian ideals of using the best from the garden have inspired a generation of chefs and influenced the eating preferences of the American public.

[*See also* Celebrity Chefs; Farmers' Markets.]

BIBLIOGRAPHY

Reardon, Joan. *M. F. K Fisher, Julia Child, and Alice Waters: Celebrating the Pleasures of the Table*. New York: Harmony Books, 1994.
Waters, Alice. *The Chez Panisse Menu Cookbook*. New York: Random House, 1982.

LYNNE SAMPSON

Waxed Paper

For much of the twentieth century waxed paper was found in nearly every kitchen. At the beginning of the twenty-first century, it could be found in one of every two American homes, particularly in the homes of people who grew up with the product and knew how useful it can be in the kitchen.

Waxed paper is also called "glassine" because of its clarity. Glassine is made by passing paper through a device called a supercalender (alternating chilled cast iron and paper or cotton rolls). The result is a paper that is translucent and very smooth and glossy on both sides. When coated with paraffin, a petroleum-based wax, it is resistant to oils, grease, and odors.

In 1926 Laura Scudder reportedly invented the first potato chip bag. She took sheets of waxed paper, cut them to size, and ironed them into bags. After they were filled by hand, the tops were sealed with a warm iron. Prior to this innovation, potato chips were sold fresh or packed into five-gallon metal cans with removable lids. Once the cans were empty, they were returned to the store to be refilled. In 1933 the Dixie Wax Paper Company of Dallas, Texas, introduced the first preprinted waxed glassine bags, using inks that did not fade or bleed. Some potato chip companies did not switch from glassine to foil bags until the 1970s.

In the home, waxed paper has many kitchen uses, such as wrapping sandwiches, lining baking pans, rolling out piecrust, wrapping cheese, and catching crumbs. In 1932 Nicholas Marcalus, a self-taught engineer and a mechanical designer, received a patent for a continuous roll of waxed paper packaged in a dispenser box with a serrated cutter. He called his new invention Cut-Rite waxed paper. Marcalus reportedly got the idea after watching his wife prepare for a Sunday picnic. She had a hard time separating the waxed paper sheets because of the summer heat. At that time waxed paper was precut, folded, and placed in envelopes.

Glassine paper was used by the Hershey Chocolate Company as an inner wrap for its milk chocolate bars as far back as the 1940s.

Besides the hundreds of uses of waxed paper in the kitchen, it is reported that in 1938 Chester Floyd Carlson made the first xerographic copy in Queens, New York, when he pressed waxed paper against an electrostatically charged plate covered in dark powder. Generations of children have used a piece of waxed paper and a comb to make an improvised kazoo. Waxed paper is an essential element for hundreds of craft projects constructed at the kitchen table.

[*See also* Packaging.]

BIBLIOGRAPHY

Stohs, Nancy. "Waxing on about Rolls of Paper, Foil, and Plastic." *Milwaukee Journal Sentinel*, March 12, 2002.

JOSEPH M. CARLIN

Weddings

It is difficult to overestimate the role of food in weddings and associated events. Celebratory eating and drinking is central to the engagement party, bridal shower, bachelor party, rehearsal dinner, and wedding reception. The marriage ceremony may include consecration with wine or sacramental Communion. Despite such significance, there are surprisingly few food rites specific to American weddings.

In precolonial times weddings were linked more to food security than to romance. For many Native Americans marriage was a way to extend families and solidify clan relationships, providing a safety net during times of scarcity. Furthermore, a potential spouse might be evaluated on his ability to hunt or her skill at grinding corn. Elder tribal women arranged Cherokee marriages, though approval of the couples was sought. The girl demonstrated acceptance by preparing a bowl of hominy, and the boy indicated agreement by eating it. In some Hopi villages a girl took

---

WEDDING CAKES

The modern American wedding cake emerged from various religious and cultural traditions dating back centuries. The Romans crumbled cakes made of barley or wheat over a bride's head to symbolize fertility and abundance. Displaying their economic power and social status, the extremely wealthy of the Middle Ages arranged lavish banquets featuring highly decorative food made of exotic ingredients, including towering sculptures formed of almond paste. French chefs employed by King Charles II, during his seventeenth-century reign, took to coating pyramids of English spice cakes with sugar icing, a practice adopted on a smaller scale at weddings of the general populace.

The elite of England and its colonies in the eighteenth century celebrated marriages with one-tiered cakes incorporating prized ingredients of the time, such as sugar, imported spices, fresh butter and eggs, nuts, and dried fruits. The surfaces of the dense cakes often were brushed with thin layers of sugar glaze or sprinkled with rose water. In the 1830s recipes for cakes covered in layers of almond paste began appearing in American cookbooks. Later in the century fancy confectioners added sculpted marzipan and sugar piping to their repertoires of cake decoration.

Well into the nineteenth century these special cakes, like the ceremonies they accompanied, remained accessible only to the very rich, emphasizing the economic and social status of the bride and groom as much as symbolizing communal sanction of the marriage. The extremely wealthy commissioned skilled bakers (often immigrant German "sugar bakers") to create custom cakes and often had two—a lighter "bride's" cake and a darker, fruitcake like "groom's" cake. Both were festooned with personalized ornaments of molded sugar and marzipan. Others had their own cooks create the ceremonial cakes. Still others, who could afford the ingredients but not the labor, made their own cakes.

By the end of the nineteenth century, technological improvements helped democratize the wedding cake. Cheaper and more accessible ingredients, including refined flour and sugar, more reliable ovens, and mass-produced cake ornaments, helped bring the wedding cake's basic ingredients to more people of the middle classes. Bakers themselves were able to profit from selling prebaked, pre-ornamented cakes and offered different sizes and models. At the same time, the groom's cake fell out of fashion, leaving the bride's cake as the ceremony's culinary focal point. The improved quality of baking powder, baking soda, refined sugar, and flour allowed the most fashionable cakes to grow ever lighter, whiter, and taller by the end of the nineteenth century.

By the early twentieth century the highly decorated white cake had become the norm for most American weddings of all but the lowest classes. Those who could afford it added more tiers and embellishments, and after the advent of domestic freezers, it became common for couples to save the top tier and eat it on their first anniversary. Cutting the cake, a practice that first appeared in the mid-nineteenth century, had by the 1930s become a significant part of the ritual, involving both the bride and the groom and witnessed by all the guests. These practices remained fairly unchanged until the end of the twentieth century, when more couples opted for personalized wedding cakes in idiosyncratic shapes and incorporating exotic combinations of ingredients. What had not changed, however, was the necessity of a ceremonial cake to mark the occasion, serve as a personal expression of the bride and groom, and foster community solidarity through its collective consumption.

BIBLIOGRAPHY

Charsley, Simon. *Wedding Cakes and Cultural History*. London: Routledge, 1992.

Woloson, Wendy. *Refined Tastes: Sugar, Confectionery, and Consumers in Nineteenth-Century America*. Baltimore: Johns Hopkins University Press, 2002.

WENDY A. WOLOSON

---

the initiative by bringing a *piki* (thin blue cornmeal cake) to her intended. If he took a bite, they were engaged. In Navajo marriages the bride's mother would prepare cornmeal porridge and place it in a basket woven with designs symbolizing the union of Sky Father and Earth Mother. Corn pollen, representing fertility and the cardinal directions, was sprinkled across the top. The couple concluded the ceremony by eating small amounts of the mush, sharing the rest with guests. In the early twenty-first century Native American weddings are frequently Christian based; however, traditions such as the basket of cornmeal porridge might be incorporated into the service.

The colonists brought marriage customs from their countries of origin and various faiths to the United States. The food traditions most associated with American weddings are of European, Christian derivation, including celebration of the Eucharist (in some denominations), tossing of rice at the couple as they leave the church, and a reception meal with an elaborate cake and a champagne toast. Both the rice and cake originated from the ancient practice of tossing wheat to ensure fertility. The Romans modified the concept, throwing small wheat cakes at the couple or crumbling cakes over the bride's head. Over time the wedding cake was served rather than thrown, and rice was substituted for tossing. The cake usually included fruit (another symbol of fecundity), and it was this type that was introduced by British settlers. With the development of white cakes in the nineteenth century, the fruitcake was relegated to duty as a smaller groom's cake. The champagne toast also has a long history, dating to a time when the bell-like chime of clinking glasses was believed to frighten away evil spirits and bring good luck. While champagne is the customary drink, owing to its association with celebration, other beverages sometimes are used.

Beyond the standard cake and champagne (rice is losing favor at modern weddings and often is prohibited by churches and other venues), numerous variations on American wedding food practices exist. In the Jewish tradition the betrothal benediction is read over a glass of wine, which the couple then drinks. At the end of the ceremony the glass is shattered by the groom with his foot. The meaning of this custom is obscure: It may commemorate the destruction of the Temple in Jerusalem (70 C.E.), or it may represent the marriage relationship, in which only the couple can partake. In Eastern Orthodox weddings the bride and groom take three sips of wine from a common cup, symbolic of a shared life.

Muslim marriage is considered a religious duty but a civil contract. Thus, Muslim American traditions are more dependent on nationality than faith; for example, molded sugar cones traditionally are grated over the heads of Iranian American couples as an expression of best wishes, and Jordan almonds are served to symbolize sweetness in marriage at Pakistani American weddings. Hindu wedding ceremonies are also diverse. Hindu American couples may make a fire offering of rice or ghee (clarified butter) to ask for blessings, or they may feed each other five mouthfuls of sweets, signifying the bride's duty to care for her husband and the groom's obligation to provide for his wife.

African Americans may add pan-African elements to their ceremony or offer African, Brazilian, Caribbean, or soul food dishes at the reception. In Latino weddings the reception may feature traditional items, such as a Mexican heart-shaped piñata, a Jamaican rum–soaked fruitcake, or a Peruvian wedding cake with ribbons inserted between layers. In the latter tradition unmarried women each pull an end of ribbon, and the one who finds a ring attached will be the next to marry. Japanese Americans may incorporate the *san san kudo* ritual, bonding the couple and their families through the ceremonial sipping of sake (rice wine). Traditional elements are common in Chinese American weddings, such as drinking wine from two cups tied together with red string during the vows or serving auspicious foods at the reception, including whole fish (for abundance) and lotus seed desserts (for fertility). Korean Americans may add the *pyebaek* ritual to their ceremony, in which the bride formally greets her parents-in-law, who, in turn, pelt her with chestnuts and jujubes (a datelike fruit) to ensure wealth and the birth of sons.

Wedding Banquet. Wedding of Rabbi David Matt and Lena Friedman, Minnesota, 1913. *Minnesota Historical Society*

[*See also* Cakes; Champagne.]

BIBLIOGRAPHY

Fuller, Robert C. *Religion and Wine: A Cultural History of Wine Drinking in the United States*. Knoxville: University of Tennessee Press, 1996.

Gourse, Leslie. *Native American Courtship and Marriage Traditions*. New York: Hippocrene Books, 2000.

Mordecai, Carolyn. *Weddings: Dating and Love Customs of Cultures Worldwide*. Phoenix, AZ: Nittany, 1999.

PAMELA GOYAN KITTLER

Wendy's

The restaurant chain Wendy's was significant in changing the public's perception of fast food, challenging conventional wisdom by successfully offering upscale menu items to consumers at prices far higher than its major competitors. Under the direction of the founder, R. Dave Thomas, Wendy's became the third-largest fast-food chain in the United States within a decade of its inception, behind only McDonald's and Burger King, and a leading innovator in the American restaurant industry.

Thomas learned the restaurant trade early in life, having escaped an unhappy home at the age of twelve by working the night shift at a local diner. He was living on his own by age fifteen. Thomas worked in several restaurants, gaining experience and honing his ideas about product quality and customer service. At age seventeen he enlisted in the army as a cook, soon gaining a reputation for crafty resourcefulness, which led to positions of quickly increasing responsibility. Recognized for his competence, Thomas, just two years later, was hired to manage an enlisted men's club in Germany, where he improved the menu offerings and increased food sales from forty dollars each day to more than seven hundred dollars.

After his army service, Thomas returned to his home state of Indiana to manage a Hobby Ranch House restaurant in Fort Wayne. There he met "Colonel" Harlan Sanders, an elderly restaurateur from Kentucky who was traveling from state to state trying to sell franchises for restaurants to sell his fried chicken recipe. Colonel Sanders convinced Thomas and his employer that his "Kentucky Fried Chicken" would be a popular item. Chicken soon became the mainstay of their business, and Thomas's career thrived. He started by selling Sanders's franchises and managing the restaurants and eventually became a senior executive with Kentucky Fried Chicken. When Thomas finally left the company in 1968, he was thirty-seven years old and a millionaire. He soon became restless, however, and began supervising the national operations of the Arthur Treacher's Fish and Chips chain.

The late 1960s was a bleak time for the fast food industry: a saturation of hamburger restaurants was causing many major chains to fail. Entering this industry at that time defied all conventional wisdom and logic. Acting against the advice of friends and restaurant-industry analysts, Thomas left Arthur Treacher's in 1969 to open a fast-food hamburger restaurant in downtown Columbus, Ohio, featuring large, made-to-order burgers, each selling at more than twice the price of those at the major chains. Borrowing his youngest daughter's nickname, he called his restaurant Wendy's Old Fashioned Hamburgers. To differentiate his restaurant from other hamburger chains, he chose an upscale motif, with hanging Tiffany lamps, carpeting, and bentwood chairs. Workers wore aprons, bow ties, and males wore chef's hats. Although Thomas offered a streamlined menu similar to those of the major chains, he stressed an "old-fashioned" approach, grilling each burger to order and serving it with the precise condiments selected by the customer. Accompanying these fresh-made burgers, he offered customers french fries; a thick, milkshake-like "Frosty"; and chili. His premise in founding Wendy's was that customers would happily pay more for higher-quality food and service, and he proved to be correct.

Thomas saw a net profit in less than six weeks, and his business boomed. Success in downtown Columbus spawned additional locations within a year, all featuring automobile pickup windows to enhance sales volume. For the next two years Thomas expanded his company throughout Ohio, before opening his first out-of-state restaurant in Indianapolis, Indiana, in 1972. Selling franchises to eager investors for $200,000 each, he had blanketed the United States with more than one thousand Wendy's by 1976.

Responding to enthusiasm from Wall Street, that same year Thomas took Wendy's public, offering one million shares of stock, each at an initial price of twenty-eight dollars. Remaining as majority stockholder and company chairman, he oversaw further fast food industry innovations, such as the introduction of a salad bar; an assortment of chicken sandwiches; and, eventually, such diverse items as baked potatoes, stuffed pitas, and caesar salads. Primarily marketing to a middle-class customer base, Wendy's captured and retained a consistent third-place position in the fast-food industry, and by 1990 had opened more than five thousand units worldwide.

By the late 1980s Thomas had relinquished control of the company while still remaining active as Wendy's highly recognizable television pitchman. In his quasi-retirement, he volunteered in philanthropic causes, focusing on adoption issues and medical research. Dave Thomas died on January, 8, 2002, but the company that he founded continues to be a major force in the American restaurant industry.

[*See also* Burger King; Drive-Ins; Fast Food; Kentucky Fried Chicken; McDonald's; Roadside Food; Sanders, Colonel.]

BIBLIOGRAPHY

Thomas, R. David. *Dave's Way: A New Approach to Old Fashioned Success.* New York: G. P. Putnam's Sons, 1991.
Jakle, John A. *Fast Food: Roadside Restaurants in the Automobile Age.* Baltimore: Johns Hopkins University Press, 1999).

DAVID GERARD HOGAN

Wheat

Wheat, a member of the grass family that includes barley and rye, evolved from wild einkorn (*Triticum monococcum*), which likely originated in Armenia, Georgia, and Turkey. Prior to the Neolithic revolution, women gathered, ground, and cooked the heads of this and other grains. Wild einkorn crossed spontaneously with goat weed (*Aegilops speltoides*) to produce wild emmer (*T. dococcoides*), which grows wild in the region stretching from northern Israel and Lebanon to western Iran.

Most wild wheat types have fourteen chromosomes; the exception is wild emmer, which has twenty-eight chromosomes. Domesticated emmer (*T. dicoccum*), the oldest cultivated wheat, has been found in Turkey dating to 8700 B.C.E. Wheat was widely cultivated in prehistoric times, reaching North Africa and the Indus valley in northern India by 4000 B.C.E. northern China by 3000 B.C.E., and western Europe by 2000 B.C.E. Most likely, wheat was initially consumed in porridges, which, if left to dry, could be baked on a flat rock near a fire. The descendants of this early use of wheat include flatbreads, such as pita from the Mediterranean and chapati from India. In China, wheat was mainly used to make noodles. These foods have been introduced into the United States by immigrant groups and became popular during the second half of the twentieth century.

Spelt wheat (*T. spelta*) emerged during the Bronze Age (about 2000 B.C.E.). It had a low yield: even after being threshed, it consisted mainly of husk. Along with emmer wheat, spelt was grown extensively in Europe during ancient Roman times. Spelt is used for making specialty breads and breakfast cereals. Durum (*T. durum*), also called semolina, is the main commercially cultivated wheat that has twenty-eight chromosomes; it is one of the hardest of wheat varieties and has a yellow endosperm. Due to its density, it is used mainly for making pasta and couscous.

In the ancient world, wheat was used to make both foods and drinks, including porridges, noodles, breads, and ales. The Egyptians are thought to have been the first makers of raised bread, possibly as a result of the connection between brewing and baking.

Wheat used for making raised bread generally has forty-two chromosomes and contains higher quantities of protein than wheat with fewer chromosomes. Bread wheats have a higher level of glutenin and gliadin, two proteins that, when moistened and stirred or kneaded, combine to create gluten. Gluten, while possessed by other grains, is found in high enough concentrations to make raised bread only in wheat. Gluten provides a bubble that traps carbon dioxide and steam, thus creating small pockets when baked, resulting in a light, porous loaf.

Wheat was introduced into the New World by the Spanish. It thrived in Mexico and subsequently in Spanish California. English settlers also introduced wheat into their North American colonies. Wheat never flourished in Massachusetts, but it did thrive in Virginia. By 1621, the English colonists at Jamestown had enough wheat to require the construction of a gristmill to grind the wheat into flour. The wheat was ground between two

Winnowing Wheat. Tewa Indians winnowing wheat near San Juan, New Mexico. *Prints and Photographs Division, Library of Congress/Edward S. Curtis*

flat millstones, which removed the outer husks but ground the remaining portions of the grain so finely that they could not be separated. Dozens of small mills were constructed during the following decades. The first mills were human and animal powered; subsequently water and wind were harnessed to turn the grindstones. Mills operated on a toll system in which the miller took a portion of the flour in payment. The miller could then barter with or sell the flour. As the seventeenth century progressed, Virginia farmers found that they could make more money growing tobacco, so wheat acreage declined, but by that time wheat was being grown extensively in the middle colonies from New York to Delaware. These colonies met their own needs for grain and had extensive surpluses to export. Some of the wheat was shipped to New England and the West Indies, and the rest was sent to England. Because of their prodigious wheat production, New York, New Jersey, Pennsylvania, Delaware, and Maryland became known as the "bread colonies."

Oliver Evans

Small mills had been constructed in most communities in the colonies by 1700. The wheat was usually not bolted (sifted), so the bran remained in the flour. By the late eighteenth century, finer flour was being produced, but mills were much more labor intensive: millers carried sacks of grain up ladders to the top floor and dumped the grain into a "rolling screen" that removed the dirt and chaff. The resulting meal was then ground between millstones on the first floor, where it was shoveled into buckets, which were then hoisted by hand to the mill's third floor; there the meal was spread out on the floor to cool and dry. It was then pushed to the center of the floor and down a chute to the bolting cylinder, which separated the flour from the lower-grade "middlings" flour, which generally consists of bran, germ, and coarse flour remnants. Middlings flour was sold at a lower price or used for animal feed. The flour was then shoveled into barrels, which were sealed for shipment. Even with these improvements, the flour varied in quality from one season, batch, or barrel to the next.

In 1782, the wheelwright Oliver Evans was contracted to build a mill near Wilmington, Delaware. He studied existing mills and improved the traditional design, connecting the different machines through the use of bucket elevators, conveying devices, and a "hopper boy," a mechanical device that cooled and dried the meal before feeding it into the bolting cylinder. Wheat could be taken directly from a wagon or boat, cleaned, ground, dried, cooled, sifted, and packed without the intervention of a human operator, except as adjustments to the machinery became necessary. Evans's Delaware mill, which began operation in 1785, ground grain more finely and consistently than did earlier mills. To promote his ideas, Evans wrote *The Young Mill-Wright and Miller's Guide* (1795); it revolutionized mills in Europe a decade after the changes had occurred in the United States.

The Erie Canal, which was to connect Lake Erie with Albany, was begun in 1817, and even before it was completed eight years later, its beneficial effect on transportation had already begun to affect the price of flour. New mills using Evans's technologies were constructed along the route of the Erie Canal. Wheat growing and flour milling greatly expanded around Lake Erie. This trade was enhanced by the rapid construction of railways from 1835 to 1860. By the 1830s, wheat grown in western New York and Ohio was much less expensive than wheat grown in New England, even after transportation was calculated, due to better growing conditions in the Midwest. Consequently, many eastern farmers, particularly New Englanders, moved to the Midwest and established new farms on more productive land.

Inventions

Three important inventions greatly increased wheat production in the Midwest. The first was the reaper. Until the nineteenth century, wheat was cut by hand with sickles and scythes. In 1834, Cyrus McCormick, an American inventor, patented a reaping machine. A threshing machine was also invented in 1834 by two brothers from Maine. The development of these machines allowed farmers to do in only a few hours the work that once took several days. The second invention was the steel plow, which replaced the iron plow. In 1837, John Deere developed a steel plow with a highly polished moldboard, which scoured itself as it turned furrows. This development made plowing easier and faster. Deere perfected his invention and in 1846 opened a factory to produce steel plows. Two years later he moved the factory to Moline, Illinois. This invention made it easier to turn over the sod, and wheat began to be cultivated throughout the Midwest. The third invention was the thresher, initially developed by A. H. Pitt of Winthrop, Maine, in the 1830s. Within ten years threshers could process twenty to twenty-five bushels of wheat per hour.

Harvesting Wheat. Engraving, nineteenth century. *Culinary Archives & Museum at Johnson & Wales University, Providence, R.I.*

Wheat and the Civil War

During the two decades before the Civil War, America's major agricultural crops doubled, with the largest growth occurring in five states—Ohio, Indiana, Illinois, Wisconsin and Iowa—thanks to the canals and the railroads constructed before the war. In 1839, these states produced 25 percent of the nation's wheat and corn. Twenty years later, the production of these states had increased to 50 percent of the national total.

Because of the abundance of grain during the war, northern soldiers and sailors were comparatively well fed, as were northern civilians. Just as important, England and France had poor grain harvests just before the war and needed increased imports. Grain exports from the North increased during the war, and the need for these exports was one reason that England and France did not recognize the Confederacy.

Southerners belatedly recognized the importance of food—particularly wheat—to their war effort. Confederate leaders encouraged southern farmers to grow food crops rather than cotton and tobacco, but the farmers were unsuccessful in making the shift. In 1862, flour cost $25 a barrel in Richmond, Virginia. In September 1863, wheat flour cost $35 a barrel, in October $45, in November $70, and in December $110. In January 1864, wheat flour could not be purchased at any price, and Southerners turned to rice flour and cornmeal as substitutes.

After the war, mechanization continued on the farm. The stationary baler or hay press was invented in the 1850s. Mechanical mowers, crushers, windrowers, and other machines came into widespread use during the twentieth century. The combine, which performed virtually all these functions, revolutionized the speed at which wheat was harvested. As the combine was expensive and worked better on flat land, wheat farms on the Great Plains became the center of American grain growing. By the beginning of the twentieth century, wheat production and milling had become a mechanized, standardized, large-scale industry. American farmers and millers worked for quantity and sought the qualities that customers wanted: a bright white color and a low price.

American Roller Mills

During the late nineteenth century, entrepreneurs in Minnesota began constructing new mills, using technology developed in Switzerland and Hungary. Minnesota farmers had been growing grain and milling flour since 1823, and by the 1870s Minneapolis was home to some of the nation's finest mills, thanks to St. Anthony's Falls, which provided an abundant power source. The first

American mill using steel rollers as opposed to millstones was built in Minneapolis in 1879.

The leaders in Minneapolis milling were Cadwallader C. Washburn, John Sargent Pillsbury, and Pillsbury's nephew, Charles Alfred Pillsbury. Washburn had founded the Minneapolis Mill Company in 1856 but did not acquire his own mill until 1866. He built another mill in 1871 and by 1874 had the capital to construct yet another, larger mill. Within ten years, Washburn's flour was winning awards. Washburn went into partnership with John Crosby in 1877 to form the Washburn, Crosby Company. In 1899, the company concentrated on promoting its Gold Medal flour, named for the award it had won at the 1880 Cincinnati Milling Exposition in Ohio.

The Pillsburys, encouraged by Washburn's success and the extension of railroads to Minneapolis, created the Pillsbury Company, which included flour mills. In 1872, Charles Pillsbury began using the XXXX trademark for the company's flour. Medieval millers had branded their best products with three Xs; Pillsbury added an additional X to make his product unique.

Roller mills were costly to build, and most millers did not have the capital or the right conditions to apply these technologies. As the flour produced by roller mills was much cheaper than flour ground by millstones, most small mills closed because they could not compete. The milling industry became increasingly centralized. In the mid-1800s, there were an estimated 25,000 mills in America; by 1900, there were only 13,000 mills; by 2000, there were a mere 100 flour milling companies. In 2001, the Pillsbury Company was acquired by General Mills, and a handful of companies, including General Mills and Nabisco, controlled the vast majority of American flour milling.

Hard and Soft Wheat

Most American wheats can be divided into four categories: winter and spring, and hard and soft. Winter wheat is planted in the fall and harvested in early summer while spring wheat is planted in the spring and harvested in late summer. Winter wheat ripens earlier in the early summer than wheats planted in the spring, but it suffers from an especially harsh winter.

Soft wheats differ from hard wheats in that their starchy endosperm is less flinty. Hard wheat develops strong gluten, suitable for bread baking, while soft wheat develops weak gluten, making it preferable for delicate baked goods. Since colonial times, most American wheat has been of the soft variety; gristmills did not do a good job of grinding hard wheats, and the flour was discolored by specks of bran. With the advent of roller mills, hard wheat could be milled with complete removal of the bran. Virtually all American bread is made from hard wheat while soft wheat is used for making cakes, pastries, crackers, and similar products, which require less gluten.

Wheat-Based Commercial Products

Wheat flour is the major ingredient in tens of thousands of commercial products. One of the first branded wheat products was the Aunt Jemima Pancake Mix, which was first manufactured in 1889 by Chris L. Rutt and Charles G. Underwood of St. Louis, Missouri. It became the model for a vast array of premixed food products, many of which contained flour. Cake mixes were first sold by Duncan Hines in 1929, followed by Jiffy and Bisquick in 1930 and General Mills and Pillsbury in the late 1940s.

Commercial crackers and cookies had been manufactured by many companies during the nineteenth century, but their popularity soared about 1900. When the National Biscuit Company, the forerunner of Nabisco, was formed, its first signature product was Uneeda Biscuit, a wheat cracker that was promoted by one of America's first national food advertising campaigns in 1898. In that same year, the company also introduced another wheat product, called the Graham Cracker in honor of Sylvester Graham. The product actually had little in common with what Sylvester Graham had originally advocated. In 1902, the company relaunched yet another cracker, Animal Biscuits, by changing the product's name to Barnum's Animals. Subsequently, thousands of other wheat-based cookies and crackers have been manufactured in the United States.

Yet another use of wheat was made by Henry D. Perky of Denver, Colorado, who invented a machine to make biscuits in 1892. He launched a company called the Cereal Machine Company, but he had few sales. In 1893, he opened bakeries in Boston and Worcester, Massachusetts, selling biscuits, which became popular. He made the decision to manufacture biscuits, and in 1901 he moved his company to Niagara Falls, New York. The following year he expanded his operation to include the production of a small wheat cracker he named Triscuits. While the company had several names, Perky eventually settled on the Shredded Wheat Company. In December 1928, the Shredded Wheat Company was sold to Nabisco.

Many other companies manufactured wheat-based cereals. In 1902, Ralston Purina, for instance, introduced Ralston Wheat Cereal. In 1937, the company introduced Wheat Chex. In 1928, the Washburn Mills Company, soon to be renamed General Mills, introduced Washburn's Gold Medal Whole Wheat Flakes; the name was soon changed to Wheaties. The cereal's first connection with sports was not until 1933, and the slogan "Wheaties— The Breakfast of Champions" soon emerged. During the 1950s, cereal manufacturers concluded that their major target was children, and sugarcoated wheat cereals became the norm.

Modern Wheat

Wheat has many uses in America, and it is found in more foods than any other cereal grain. There are thousands of varieties of bread on the market and tens of thousands of different types of rolls, buns, crackers, cookies, biscuits, and other baked goods. Wheat flour is also used in pasta, noodles, packaged goods, sauces, canned goods, frozen foods, and many other products.

Wheat is one of the most widely produced and consumed cereal grains in the world. The United States has been consistently the largest exporter of wheat for decades. About 60 million acres of wheat are harvested each year in the United States. In 2001, America produced 2.6 billion bushels of wheat, of which 1.1 billion bushels were exported. America's wheat belt extends north from Texas through Oklahoma and Kansas, which is the largest producer, and from eastern Washington to central Montana.

[*See also* Aunt Jemima; Bread; Cereal, Cold; General Mills; Nabisco; Pillsbury.]

BIBLIOGRAPHY

Ferguson, Eugene S. *Oliver Evans: Inventive Genius of the Industrial Revolution.* Greenville, DE: Hagley Museum, 1980.

Ham, George E., and Robin Higham, eds. *The Rise of the Wheat State: A History of Kansas Agriculture, 1861–1986.* Manhattan, KS: Sunflower University Press, 1987.

Jaradat, A. A. *Triticeae III.* Enfield, NH: Science Publishers, 1998.

Miner, H. Craig. *Harvesting the High Plains: John Kriss and the Business of Wheat Farming, 1920–1950.* Lawrence: University Press of Kansas, 1998.

Morgan, Dan. *Merchants of Grain.* New York: Penguin Books, 1980.

Storck, John, and Walter Dorwin Teague. *A History of Milling Flour for Man's Bread.* Minneapolis: University of Minnesota Press, 1952.

ANDREW F. SMITH

Whiskey

American whiskey is a group of distinct alcoholic products made only in the United States, produced by fermenting then distilling a mixture, or mash, of barley, rye, wheat or corn, water, and yeast. While whiskey is made in other countries, there are several types made only in America: rye, corn, blended whiskey, Tennessee whiskey, and bourbon.

The word "whiskey" comes from the ancient Gaelic word *uisqebeatha* or *uisebaugh*, pronounced OOS-kee-baa or whis-kee-BAW (water of life). When the word refers to the product made in Scotland, Scotch whisky, it is spelled without the "e." The U.S. Bureau of Alcohol, Tobacco, and Firearms has approved "whisky" as the standard spelling, but American producers continue to spell the word with the "e."

History

Missionary monks probably brought the process of distillation to Ireland during the Middle Ages from the Continent. These holy men distilled herbs, roots, and other botanicals for medicine and soon distilled grains for the same purposes. The ancient Celts in Ireland and then Scotland were quickly converted to Christianity and whiskey making. Distilling excess grain after the harvest became an important skill on the farm and an important part of local commerce as a means of barter.

Rum was the most readily available and cheapest distilled spirit in the American colonies until the Revolutionary War. When the Scots, the Irish, and later the Germans immigrated to America in the 1730s, they brought their stills with them. The grains they knew, such as barley, wheat, and rye, did not grow well in the soils and conditions of New England, and they began to move west to western Virginia and Pennsylvania. Corn, or Indian maize, was abundant, but it took some time to perfect its distillation.

Only when neither molasses (rum's raw material) nor rum could be imported from the British West Indies during the Revolutionary War did distilling rye and other grains become economically viable. George Washington and Thomas Jefferson both had distilleries on their estates in the 1780s.

Politics and Taxes

When the fledgling American government needed to raise revenue in 1791 to retire the debt incurred during the Revolution, it turned to taxing liquor production.

Angry farmers in the western portion of the new country revolted and refused to pay the tax. Finally, President Washington called for the mustering of fifteen thousand federal troops for the first time in U.S. history. By 1794 the Whiskey Rebellion had been quelled, and the new federal government had withstood its first test of centralized power.

Many farmers, still angry over the taxing of their hard labor, began to push ever farther westward and settled in the western part of Virginia, Pennsylvania, Kentucky (then a western county of Virginia), Tennessee, Illinois, and Indiana. There, grains like rye and wheat were easier to grow, but the hills, poor roads, and long distances made it economically unfeasible for farmers to ship their grain in bulk. Instead, they could distill twelve bushels of grain into one keg of whiskey, which was much easier to load on a wagon and move to market.

The development of bourbon whiskey in the late 1780s in Kentucky is a story full of folklore and colorful characters. Bourbon and whiskey also played a large part in the lore of the Wild West. Modern research shows the error of Western movie depictions of the seedy saloon serving only whiskey. Historical reality is that the saloon on the frontier was a rather refined place of heavy, carved furniture and ornate back bars that offered many whiskies, beers, liquors and liqueurs, iced drinks, and fancy cocktails.

The production and consumption of American whiskey continued to rise until Prohibition in 1919. Not only did this federal law decrease consumption dramatically, but also it irrevocably changed the consumer's taste. Those who imbibed illegal spirits were able to obtain "bathtub" gin and other lighter-tasting alcoholic beverages. When Prohibition was repealed in 1933, consumers did not return to their former high levels of whiskey consumption.

Excise taxes and fees continue to be one of the leading industry issues. In 2002 the Distilled Spirits Council of the United States reported that when indirect federal, state, and local taxes along with federal and state excise taxes are added up, they account for 55 percent of the purchase price of a bottle of distilled spirits.

Whiskey-Making Process

The taste and quality of whiskey depend on the type of grain used, how the grain is processed, whether the wort is distilled in a pot or a column still, in what container and under what conditions the product is stored, and how

long the whiskey is aged. The final variable is if and how the whiskey will be blended. Experts disagree as to whether the water used makes any difference in the taste of the final product.

It is the master distiller who controls the whiskey-making process from beginning to end, to create just the qualities desired in the finished product. All along the process, but especially during distillation, the distiller is looking for a finished product with just the right combination of substances in the whiskey called "congeners." These substances contribute the distinct aroma, taste, and color associated with whiskey.

In step one, grain (corn, rye, wheat, or barley—the exact mix is part of the proprietary recipe of each distiller) is ground to break the tough outer coating of the grain kernel. This process allows the starches within the kernel to be converted more easily into fermentable sugars in step three.

In step two the mash is created by mixing crushed grain and malted grain. Malting involves wetting grain kernels and allowing the kernels to sprout. The sprouted grain releases enzymes that help the natural starches convert into fermentable sugars.

In step three the mix of malted and unmalted grain is soaked in warm water and is now called "wort."

In step four yeast is added to the wort and goes into vats to ferment. A sour mash whiskey is made from the sour residues of the spent yeast from the last batch of wort made and then is added to the new wort of the next batch. A sweet mash whiskey is made with new yeast in every new batch. Alcohol, heat, and carbon dioxide are naturally produced by the wort during fermentation, creating the illusion that the wort is "boiling" in the vats.

In step five the fermented mix, now called beer, is then distilled, either in copper pot stills or in column stills also known as continuous patent stills. The latter can produce far more product as they are in use continuously. Copper pot stills must be cleaned after each distillation. The distilled product is clear and is now called whiskey.

Step six involves aging. Most whiskey is aged, an exception being corn whiskey, which is bottled at this point in the process. During the aging process, the whiskey is pumped from the still into wooden barrels that are then placed in rows in warehouses. The insides of these barrels have been charred. The charring or toasting is done by putting an open flame into the barrel and burning the wood evenly on all sides of the barrel for a light, medium, or heavy toast. Some, but not all, makers char the top and bottom of the cask as well. A light toast could char only the top layer of the wood; a heavy toast might char one-fourth to one-half of an inch into the wood. Charring gives the whiskey its color and additional caramel, toasty flavors from the natural sugars in the oak. As the temperature and humidity change in the warehouse where the barrels are aging, the whiskey passes in and out of the walls of the oak barrel. How quickly this process takes place depends on the climate of the area and the placement of the barrel in the warehouse. For instance, barrels at the top of the warehouse, where the environment is warmest, age faster.

In step seven, blending or bottling takes place. If the whiskey is to be bottled as a "single barrel," or "straight," the barrel is opened, distilled water is added to reduce the proof (expressed in degrees and double the amount of beverage alcohol in the spirit) to no lower than eighty degrees, and the product is then bottled. If the whiskey is to be blended, the master distiller tastes samples of many barrels, then combines the whiskey to attain a consistent taste for the brand, and ends by adding distilled water to lower the proof of the final product. Thus the taste of an American blended whiskey, such as Seagram's 7 Crown, will be consistent over time.

Types of American Whiskey

Corn whiskey was probably the first American whiskey. Made of maize, the wild corn abundantly available in the New World, this unaged product was probably a very rough drink on the palate with a very harsh taste. Illegally produced whiskey, called moonshine or white lightening because of its colorlessness, is made of corn because of its ready availability and ease in fermenting. America's only producer of premium corn whiskey is Heaven Hill of Bardstown, Kentucky.

Bourbon is the most famous corn whiskey and is a true American innovation. To be labeled as such legally, bourbon must contain at least 51 percent corn, be distilled at less than 160 proof, and age for a minimum of two years in new white oak charred barrels. All bourbon distillers in Kentucky use continuous "column" stills to produce their products. The exception is the Labrot and Graham Distillery, which uses copper pot stills.

Rye, a grain similar to wheat, makes a full-bodied, pungent whiskey. Very little rye whiskey is bottled. Most of its production is incorporated into blended whiskey. Even Canadians often refer to Canadian whiskey as "rye";

however, almost all Canadian whiskey is made from corn. Makers of rye whiskey include Jim Beam, Wild Turkey, and Heaven Hill in Kentucky as well as the Anchor Distillery, a maker of Old Potrero (100 percent rye), in California. The great rye whiskey cocktail is the sazerac.

Straight whiskey is American whiskey with a minimum proof of 160, aged at least two years in new white charred oak barrels. The addition of water brings the alcohol down to no lower than 80 proof, with a minimum of 51 percent of the volume being the grain. Most straight whiskey is drunk neat, with ice or a small amount of water added.

Blended whiskey is a product of at least 20 percent straight whiskey mixed with neutral spirits. This category generally has a lighter flavor and body than a straight whiskey. Blended whiskey has been made since about 1860. It uses the highly rectified spirit that is produced by column or "patent" stills. If the final product does not have the rich brown tones of straight whiskey, coloring from natural caramel can be used to darken the product. Blended whiskey can be drunk alone or mixed in a cocktail.

Tennessee whiskey is made using the same process that is used in making bourbon, with the addition of a final step of filtering the whiskey through thick beds of sugar maple charcoal before bottling. This filtration removes some of the congeners and creates a smooth, mellow taste. Jack Daniel's is the most famous example. George Dickel is the only other Tennesse whiskey made.

Contemporary Consumption

Blended American whiskey had a great sales boost during and after World War II, extending into the late 1960s. Since the 1960s lighter goods, such as vodka, have become the largest sellers in distilled beverages.

To fight their decreasing market share, whiskey distillers have introduced single barrel and small batch bottlings as line extensions. "Single barrel" refers to a limited bottling, usually three hundred bottles, all from one barrel of whiskey. "Small batch" is a limited, slightly larger bottling. A master distiller specially chooses both for their richer, distinctive taste. Both are often in elaborate packaging.

Beverage Industry reports that distilled spirits sales in stores totaled more than $2.356 billion in 2002. Of this figure, bourbon made up only $155 million in sales (up 3.1 percent from 2001), and Tennessee whiskey accounted for $84 million in sales (up 6 percent from 2001).

[*See also* Bottling; Bourbon; Cocktails; Distillation; Fermentation; Rum; Sazerac.]

BIBLIOGRAPHY

Dikty, Alan S., ed. *The Beverage Testing Institute's Buying Guide to Spirits.* New York: Sterling, 1999. A unique work that contains concise histories of spirit categories and detailed tasting notes of individual spirit brands. Classic cocktail recipes are included.

Grimes, William. *Straight Up or On the Rocks: The Story of the American Cocktail.* New York: North Point Press, 2001. A history of the distilled beverage in the United States and social history of entertaining and cocktail making.

Jackson, Michael. *The World Guide to Whiskey.* Topsfield, MA: 1988. An unparalleled overall look at this topic from a well-known and respected authority. The photos and maps are second to none.

Johnson, Byron A., and Sharon Peregrine Johnson. *Wild West Bartenders' Bible.* Austin, TX: Texas Monthly Press, 1986. A remarkable study of a relatively unresearched topic. Over five hundred classic drink recipes.

Lichine, Alexis. *Alexis Lichine's New Encyclopedia of Wines and Spirits.* 4th ed. rev. New York: Knopf, 1985. A concise and remarkably well-organized volume from a pioneering author in the spirit and wine field.

Murray, Jim. *Classic Bourbon, Tennessee and Rye Whiskey.* London: Prion Books, 1998. An exhaustive look at these topics with an especially fine focus on rye and corn whiskey.

"Spirits Remain High." *Beverage Industry*, June 2002.

MARK C. GRUBER

Whiskey Sour

The making of a whiskey sour and sour drinks in general is an art form that distinguishes amateur bartenders, who like to toss an occasional cocktail party in the den, from professionally trained bartenders. For that reason, the whiskey companies that wanted to promote this popular classic cocktail had to come up with a ready-mix product that would aid the home bartender in preparing sour drinks. The whiskey sour traditionally calls for fresh lemon juice and a sweetener, and the balance between sweet and sour is critical and difficult to achieve. Fresh lemon juice is so concentrated that adding too much produces an overly sour, undrinkable cocktail. The downside of the premade sour mixes is flavor; unfortunately, the flavor of fresh fruit cannot be re-created with modern chemistry.

The whiskey sour has just three main ingredients: whiskey, usually blended American but sometimes a straight whiskey (like Bourbon or rye); fresh lemon juice; and some form of sugar. Over the years bartenders have played with the ingredients to achieve certain effects, for example, adding a small amount of egg white to give the drink a handsome layer of foam on top. Somewhere along the line a bartender added a splash of orange juice to the mix and called it a California, or stone, sour. In the nineteenth century, when the technology to inject gas into water was perfected, sours were doused with sparkling water; the results were Collins-style drinks.

The tradition of combining lemon juice with spirits and other alcoholic beverages probably dates back to ancient times, when wine was flavored with flowers and other additives to make it more palatable. The Italians, who were pioneers in infusing spirits with fruit and herbal and spicy ingredients, were making a *limoncello*-style infusion five hundred years ago by combining spirits with lemon juice and lemon oil from the rind. But the custom that led to the modern use of lemon in cocktails was probably the punch craze that Americans went through in colonial times. English tea traders brought back the punch recipe from trips to India, along with the mnemonic for remembering the five ingredients: strong, sweet, sour, spicy, and weak. In order, the ingredients were rum; sugar; lemon juice; a mixture composed of nutmeg, cinnamon, mace, and other spices; and tea, juice, or water.

The modern sour evolved between 1862 and 1880. The early cocktail book *How to Mix Drinks* (1862), by Jerry Thomas, does not have a sour recipe under that name. But just after the short cocktail section, Thomas lists the Whiskey Crusta, a drink made with lemon juice, whiskey, and gum syrup that was shaken and served in a glass with a sugared rim and a large peel of lemon. To make a simple sour cocktail, start with 1½ to 2 ounces of the base liquor. Add ¾ ounce of the sour ingredient (for example, fresh lemon juice) and 1 ounce of one or more sweet ingredients (a simple syrup). Shake very hard while slowly counting to ten. Dale DeGroff tells us, in *The Craft of the Cocktail*, that adding egg white to a sour can leave behind an offensive flavor. Foam also can be produced simply by shaking the drink harder.

[*See also* Cocktails; Flavorings; Whiskey.]

DALE DEGROFF

White Castle

White Castle, through its founder, Edgar "Billy" Ingram, successfully popularized the hamburger sandwich; created a uniform company standard of architecture, menu, and quality among its many outlets; and introduced consumers to a carryout style of eating. Many of White Castle's culinary and corporate innovations would later become fundamental to both the American diet and modern business operations.

Partnering with Walter Anderson, a fry cook, in Wichita, Kansas, in 1921, Ingram founded the White Castle System of Eating Houses. The premise of Ingram's White Castle operation was simply to sell inexpensive hamburger sandwiches in large volume. To accomplish this goal, however, he had to convince hungry consumers that ground beef was a safe and healthy food, that his restaurants were clean and hygienic establishments, and that his products were a good value. The buying public distrusted the meat industry in the early twentieth century and held ground meat in particularly low regard. The popular perception during this era was that butchers routinely ground up meat when it began to spoil, giving them a few additional days to sell it. Compounding this public disregard for ground meat, small sandwich shops customarily carried a stigma of being both transient and unsanitary.

The White Castle System

In creating his White Castle restaurants, Ingram countered these negative stereotypes by grinding choice cuts of fresh beef directly in front of his customers, constructing his buildings out of gleaming stainless steel and white enamel, and adopting a crenellated roof design that resembled a castle. Even his choice of name was a marketing tactic, stressing that "white" would symbolize purity and cleanliness and that the "castle" image would signify strength and permanence. His message to consumers was that White Castles were clean, healthy, and here to stay. Ingram's marketing strategies, combined with an affordable price of five cents for a hamburger, made his White Castle restaurants an overnight success in Wichita.

White Castle saturated the Wichita market in less than two years, and Ingram expanded to other cities in the region. He spread his chain to Omaha in 1923, to Kansas City the following year, and to St. Louis in 1925. Similar success in these cities led to even further expansion, with new White Castles opening in Chicago, Minneapolis, Louisville, Indianapolis, Columbus, Cincinnati, and New York City by the end of the decade. Ingram stressed consistency in standards and menu throughout his growing chain and purchased company biplanes to allow senior managers greater access to their expanding territory. Friends suggested to Ingram that he sell franchises of his business, rather than fund the expansion with his own capital. He opposed this approach, however, believing that franchising would lead to his losing control over standards and practices, undermining uniformity of quality.

As Ingram opened restaurants in new cities, he placed advertisements in local papers with coupons that offered customers their initial ten hamburgers at the half price of only twenty-five cents. These discount coupons led to huge lines of hungry coupon-holders and to an almost instant customer base. As White Castle spread from city to city, popular enthusiasm for its hamburger sandwich continued to grow.

Soon the White Castle name and crenellated architecture became synonymous with the product itself. Hundreds of enterprising restaurateurs in the 1920s capitalized on White Castle's success by selling White Castle–style hamburgers in small, white buildings, often featuring a confusingly similar name, such as White Tower, Red Castle, or White Palace. One leading competitor even borrowed White Castle's "Buy 'em by the Sack" slogan, changing it only slightly to "Buy 'em by the *Bag*." For the next two decades, until after the end of World War II, the vast majority of restaurants featuring hamburgers remained very close to Ingram's system in architectural style, image, and food products. In fact, the fast food king Richard McDonald later publicly credited White Castle as being the original model for his successful chain. If imitation is truly the highest compliment, restaurant entrepreneurs in the 1920s and 1930s accorded Billy Ingram great respect. White buildings and catchy slogans however were relatively insignificant in comparison to Ingram's real success. In 1929, the president of the American Restaurant Association declared hamburger and apple pie to be "America's favorite foods." The cumulative effect of White Castle's success, and the successes of its competitors and imitators, elevated the hamburger sandwich from disgrace and obscurity in 1921 to a position of respect and prominence by the close of the decade.

Changes and Challenges

The 1930s brought changes to White Castle. In 1934, Billy Ingram moved his corporate headquarters to Columbus, Ohio, in order to be more centrally located in the middle of his Kansas to New York territory. This was also a decade of extreme economic hardship. White Castle survived the Depression, while most of its competitors went bankrupt. Realizing that his predominantly working-class customer base had fewer nickels to spend on hamburgers, Ingram redirected his marketing emphasis to attract more of a middle-class clientele. After studying the success of Betty Crocker and other fictional "corporate hostesses," Ingram hired a real woman to serve as White Castle's company spokeswoman. Operating under the pseudonym Julia Joyce, Ingram's spokeswoman visited garden clubs and women's groups in order to convince middle-class women that White Castle hamburgers were good, healthy family fare. Supported by the findings of company-sponsored scientific studies—one such study fed a student only water and White Castle hamburgers for sixty days—Julia Joyce taught these women how a sack of hamburgers could be a proper family entrée, served side-by-side with potatoes and vegetables. Her marketing efforts, in conjunction with an intensive ad campaign depicting middle-class families dining on hamburgers, succeeded in attracting the middle class to White Castle. This additional customer base helped the company weather the economic downturn of the 1930s. It ended the decade even larger and more profitable than it had been before the Depression began.

White Castle's continued prosperity, however, came to an abrupt halt with the beginning of World War II. Civilian workers quickly became soldiers, draining the domestic labor force and driving up wages. Available workers flocked to higher paying factory jobs, leaving White Castle's counters unmanned. Unable to fully staff his restaurants and often unable to purchase rationed food supplies, such as meat, sugar, and coffee, Ingram curtailed hours of operation and ultimately had to shut down half of his White Castles. Ravaged by the wartime shortages, he struggled to keep his company afloat throughout the rest of the 1940s. Exacerbating this already bleak situation, burgeoning postwar suburbs lured away a large segment of young adults, leaving Ingram's remaining restaurants to sell hamburgers in less-populated and deteriorating urban neighborhoods.

Still profitable in its reduced form, White Castle remained in these city locations while the giant franchised fast food hamburger chains appearing in the 1950s and 1960s focused their building and marketing efforts on the developing suburbs. Without the capital to build new locations and still averse to the concept of franchising, Ingram could not afford to compete in suburbia. In many ways, Ingram's White Castle System was left behind for several decades, stagnating while its franchised competitors dominated the new markets. Later, in the late 1960s and 1970s, the company rebounded under the direction of Ingram's son, Edgar, and grandson, Bill Ingram, eventually opening successful outlets in the suburbs, while also retaining some of its traditional locations and customers in city neighborhoods.

Still small in size in the early 2000s, compared to the multinational fast food giants, the White Castle chain operated restaurants in fourteen American cities and enjoyed a very loyal customer following. Often serving hamburgers to the great- and great-great-grandchildren of its original customers, White Castle's popularity and success are perhaps based more on its longevity and mystique than its burgers.

[See also Drive-Ins; Fast Food; Hamburger; McDonald's; Take-Out Foods.]

BIBLIOGRAPHY

Hogan, David. Selling 'Em by the Sack: White Castle and the Creation of American Food. New York: New York University Press, 1997.
Langdon, Philip. Orange Roofs and Golden Arches: The Architecture of American Chain Restaurants. New York: Knopf, 1986.

DAVID GERARD HOGAN

White House

Food carries powerful symbolism, and nowhere is this more clearly seen than at the White House dinner table, which marries American culinary culture and politics. Even humble chocolate chip cookies are analyzed when they involve the presidency: the 1992 campaign produced dueling recipes between Barbara Bush and Hillary Clinton in a competition to qualify them as "First Mom."

From the Founding Fathers' continental tables through the gargantuan meals of the larger-than-life Ulysses S. Grant and William H. Taft to Dwight Eisenhower's common man TV tray dinners and Richard Nixon's spartan cottage cheese and ketchup, the First Table reflects both presidential personality and political exigencies. All occupants of 1600 Pennsylvania Avenue grapple with setting a table appropriate to the office. Some presidents, most notably Thomas Jefferson, were avid gastronomes, sparing no expense in the pursuit of epicurean delights that also needed to impress visitors to the new country. Others, like Calvin Coolidge and Jimmy Carter, elected in uncertain economic times, were frugal by nature and merely ate to live. Coolidge scrutinized White House food bills and claimed that the greatest disappointment of his presidency was the White House hams: after carving slices from a large joint to serve the president and Mrs. Coolidge, the butler whisked the ham away. Coolidge could never learn what happened to the leftovers.

Public Table and Private Table

George Washington understood the need to balance the formality and dignity suitable to a head of state on the international stage with the competing demands of serving as national host to a young democracy's constituents. He established the custom of holding open houses at which any respectable citizen—that is, one who had a proper letter of introduction and who was suitably dressed—could be admitted to enjoy light refreshments such as tea, coffee, cakes, and ice cream. These levees were the basic model for public entertaining until the Civil War. Andrew Jackson's were notorious for the "curious mix of democracy and aristocracy" that clamored in the White House. Scandalized reports of overturned punch bowls and uncouth youths cramming sticky candied oranges into their pockets were pitted against abolitionists' critiques that the entertainments were racially exclusionary. Jackson's successor, Martin Van Buren, was complimented for restoring decorum by preventing "the mobocracy from intruding themselves at his levees," although the image of Van Buren's elitist table would dog his unsuccessful reelection campaign.

Refined French cooking was the language of culinary diplomacy used at state and political receptions. Starting with the Adams and Jefferson administrations, many of the White House chefs and stewards (the steward is in charge of the dining room and, until the twentieth century, often supervised the kitchen) have been French or French trained. (George Washington had hired Samuel Fraunces, of Fraunces' Tavern of New York City, as steward.) Nineteenth-century chroniclers judged the White House table by whether it imitated French style. Dolley Madison was known for her brilliant, unpretentious parties, described as "always abundant and sumptuous, more, however, in the Virginian style than in the European." The homespun Jackson loved French food, contrary to his corncob-pipe image. One newspaper reported that Jackson's table was so rarified that two senators opposing Jackson's policies would eat little of the fancy fare. Those more sympathetic to Jackson smiled upon his "gorgeous supper table shaped like a horse-shoe, covered with every good and glittering thing French skill could devise, and at either end a monster salmon in waves of meat jelly."

By the latter half of the nineteenth century, much of the cooking for official functions was delegated to outside caterers, many of whom were French cooks. The private table, however, tried to suit the preferences of each president. Although James K. Polk's official table was set in the height of French style, he begged for a little cornbread and boiled ham as he left office. Similarly, while Grover Cleveland maintained Chester A. Arthur's French chef, M. Fortin, for political dinners, he longed for "a pickled

---

MARTIN VAN BUREN AND THE "GOLD SPOON" SPEECH (1840)

Martin Van Buren's enjoyment of French food and fine tableware may have cost him a second term. Representative William Ogle's famous "Gold Spoon" speech on the floor of Congress grossly misrepresented Van Buren's expenditures on White House furnishings, falsely accusing him of profligate spending on gold and silverware that had been purchased by his predecessors, especially James Monroe. Coming on the heels of the populist Andrew Jackson and running against William Henry Harrison, whose log cabin homestead (itself a myth) was depicted on souvenir glass and ceramics, the patrician Van Buren was painted as hopelessly effete and out of touch:

> How delightful it must be . . . to eat his *pâté de foie gras*, *dinde desosse* and *salade à la volaille* from a silver plate with a golden knife and fork. And how exquisite to sip with a golden spoon his *soupe à la Reine* from a silver tureen.

> What will honest Loco Focos [a political group] say to Mr. Van Buren for spending the People's cash in foreign Fanny Kemble green finger cups, in which to wash his pretty, tapering, soft, white lily fingers after dining on *fricandeau de veau* and *omelette soufflé*? How will the friends of temperance relish the foreign "cut wine coolers" . . .?

The smear was successful. Van Buren took the bait, grousing that Harrison was content with a barrel of hard cider. Harrison won, and his brief tenure was marked by dinner parties at which the liquor was reported to flow freely.

CATHY K. KAUFMAN

DINNER AT THE WHITE HOUSE, 5 P.M., DECEMBER 19, 1845, UNDER THE POLK ADMINISTRATION

Sit! I guess we did sit—for four mortal hours, I judge one hundred fifty courses for everything was in the French style and each dish a separate course. Soup, fish, green peas, spinach, canvas back duck, turkey, birds, oyster pies, cotolettes di mouton [sic], ham deliciously garnished, potatoes like snowballs, croquettes poulet in various forms, duck and olives, pate de foie gras, jellies, orange and lemon charlotte Russe, ices and "pink mud" oranges, prunes, sweetmeats, mottos and everything one can imagine, all served in silver dishes with silver tureens and wine coolers and the famous gold forks, knives and spoons for dessert. The china was white and gold and blue with a crest, the eagle of course, and the dessert plates were marine blue and gold, with a painting in the center of fruits and flowers. . . . The glass ware was very handsome, blue and white, finely cut, and pink champagne, gold sherry, green hock, Madeira, ruby port and sauterne formed a rainbow round each plate with the finger glasses and water decanters. . . . Coffee was served and liquors and we adieu and reach home at 10 o'clock.

The diary of Mrs. J. E. Dixon, held at the Connecticut Historical Society, quoted in Jane Shadel Spillman, *White House Glassware: Two Centuries of Presidential Entertaining* (Washington, DC: White House Historical Association, 1989).

---

herring, Swiss cheese and a chop . . . instead of the French stuff I shall find." For his personal table, Cleveland imported his female cook from his days as the governor of New York. William McKinley similarly hired a "plain cook" at forty dollars per month for family meals while bringing in a French chef from New York for formal entertaining. Elizabeth Jaffray, the White House housekeeper from the Taft through Coolidge administrations, wrote with pride of the miserly salaries paid to the women cooks hired for the president's table and also of new cost-cutting measures, introduced by the Tafts, of having the private staff prepare official receptions, aided by caterers only in extreme cases.

Part of this economy had to do with the expense of living in the White House: until the Coolidge administration, all food costs, including staff meals, were paid for personally by the president, leaving virtually every president poorer for his tenure. Starting in the mid-1920s, the president was given an entertainment budget for official functions. The president is still expected to pay for the costs of private dinners for family and personal guests out of his salary. Rosalynn Carter was stunned by a food bill in excess of six hundred dollars for Jimmy Carter's first ten days as president. A career staffer commiserated, "It's not cheap to live in the White House."

Personally selected cooks did not guarantee delicious food. Franklin Roosevelt's table was reportedly atrocious, even at state events. Some have blamed Eleanor's alleged indifference to cuisine (notwithstanding that she regular-

ly scrambled eggs for Sunday night suppers in a chafing dish brought into the family quarters) and her hiring as housekeeper the inexperienced but politically loyal Henrietta Nesbitt, who supervised all meals. The job may simply have been impossible, for Nesbitt had to contend with Roosevelt's poor health, Depression-era mores, and World War II rationing. Setting a succulent table while others sacrificed could have been political suicide.

No one doubted the gourmet dining during the Camelot years, when Jacqueline Kennedy chose the Frenchman René Verdon as the White House chef for both the public and the private table. This choice flaunted the tradition of having a "plain" private cook; because of a potential political storm over hiring a foreigner for the president's personal table, Verdon's naturalization papers were expedited so that an American could be praised for bringing haute cuisine to the White House. The Clintons went even further, bringing an American-trained chef, Walter Scheib, to run the White House kitchen. The menus for Clinton's state dinners were the first to be written exclusively in English and emphasized low-fat, American cuisine.

White House Table as Bully Pulpit and Culinary Inspiration

The White House table sometimes functioned as a strong moral exemplar. Many mid- to late-nineteenth-century presidents banned hard liquor, either from personal conviction or as a nod to the growing temperance movement.

Most extreme was Rutherford B. Hayes, influenced by his wife, "Lemonade Lucy," who banned wine from all dinners except those entertaining foreign dignitaries. While Hayes himself liked wine, his diary shows the astute political calculation that underlay his decision: in addition to being "wise and useful as an example," Hayes wanted to reward his temperance supporters and to keep them voting Republican. Although menus from the Hayes administration include frozen punches normally spiked with alcohol, Hayes's diary and the White House purchase receipts suggest that nonalcoholic flavorings were used in the kitchen.

Other presidents rejoiced in the gifts of Bacchus. Chester A. Arthur ignored vigorous temperance lobbying. His dinners epitomized the Gilded Age ideal: fourteen courses supported by eight different wines, capped by brandy and cigars. Prohibition meant little to Warren G. Harding. His official dinners were dry, but "Duchess" Lillian Harding freely poured the "medicinal" liquor in the family quarters. Accompanying the booze were knockwurst, sauerkraut, and little containers of toothpicks, specifically requested by Harding for his late-night poker games. Even the butlers felt that these activities made Harding "too much a man of the people."

The most controversial meal ever served at the White House was Theodore Roosevelt's October 1901 impromptu invitation to Booker T. Washington to join a family dinner to discuss southern politics. Some sources claim that Roosevelt had misgivings about being the first president to invite a black man to an intimate meal in the White House, while others claim that he felt the invitation was perfectly natural. Whatever Roosevelt's inner thoughts, the dinner ignited a firestorm. Conservative newspapers labeled the dinner "the most damnable outrage" while liberal voices called the meal "splendid in its recognition of the essential character of the presidential office." The dinner is believed to have sparked race riots in Louisiana a few weeks later, in which eleven people died. Washington recounts in his memoirs a conversation with a white southerner who claimed that Washington was the greatest man in America. When asked why not Roosevelt, the man replied, "I used to think Roosevelt was a great man until he ate dinner with you. That settled him for me."

White House cachet has also fed a voracious public. The former White House chefs François Rysavy and René Verdon, as well as the housekeeper Henrietta Nesbitt, all wrote cookbooks purporting to disclose recipes served to the First Family. But the earliest and most influential of these works was *The White House Cookbook*, first published in 1887 by Hugo Ziemann, Grover Cleveland's White House steward, and Frances Gillette. Revealing the White House kitchen to be very much like its private, middle-American counterparts, the book was more a didactic cookery manual, complete with home remedies and housekeeping tips, than a repository of elite dining. The instructions for serving a state dinner were its one concession to rank. It went through many

BUY AMERICAN, OR AT LEAST DECORATE AMERICAN

An 1826 federal law required that "all furniture purchased for the use of the President's House [the name "White House" was adopted only during Theodore Roosevelt's presidency] shall be as far as practicable of American or domestic manufacture." This legislation helped to promote the fledgling domestic glass industry: virtually all glassware since then has been purchased from American manufacturers. Not so with porcelain. American porcelain manufacturers were judged inferior to their European competition. Thus artists created designs, most commonly incorporating the Seal of State, for European manufacturers to place on high-quality blanks. A striking exception to this motif was Rutherford B. Hayes' state china. Designed and signed by the artist Theodore R. Davis, each piece depicted American flora and fauna; executed by the French company Haviland, the service is unparalleled. First Lady Caroline (Mrs. Benjamin) Harrison was accomplished at china painting, a genteel hobby in the nineteenth century; she designed dishes incorporating the indigenous goldenrod and maize in the border, executed by the French company Tressemannes and Vogt in 1892. It was not until 1918 that a complete set of American porcelain (termed "fine china" by its producer, the Lenox China Company) was purchased as the official state dinner service.

CATHY K. KAUFMAN

editions, although the 1996 edition, by two registered dieticians, bears little firsthand connection to the White House. Closer to the First Table are the carefully planned newspaper and magazine features that appear at holiday times, highlighting the meals that the First Family will enjoy. These recipes emphasize the regional background, family traditions, and preferences of the president or First Lady, creating a vogue for clam chowder and *poulet à l'estragon* during the Kennedy years and endless variations on barbeque for much of the past forty.

[*See also* French Influences on American Food; Temperance.]

BIBLIOGRAPHY

Ellet, Elizabeth Fries, Mrs. *The Court Circles of the Republic; or, The Beauties and Celebrities of the Nation.* Hartford, CT: Hartford Publishing, 1869. A detailed description of the social scene through Andrew Johnson. Should be approached cautiously, but it has information otherwise buried in obscure sources.

Furman, Bess. *White House Profile: A Social History of the White House, Its Occupants, and Its Festivities.* Indianapolis: Bobbs-Merrill, 1951. A good compilation of information with bibliography.

Haber, Barbara. *From Hardtack to Home Fries: An Uncommon History of American Cooks and Meals.* New York: Free Press, 2002. Contains a fascinating chapter on Franklin D. Roosevelt's table, with short bibliography.

Jaffray, Elizabeth. *Secrets of the White House, by Elizabeth Jaffray, Housekeeper from the Days of Taft to Coolidge.* New York: Cosmopolitan Book Corporation, 1927. A firsthand account of life in the Taft, Wilson, Harding, and Coolidge administrations, with very detailed information on managing the household.

Klapthor, Margaret Brown. *Official White House China: 1789 to the Present.* 2nd ed. New York: Abrams, 1999. A more scholarly account of entertaining at the White House, with a very heavy emphasis, as the title suggests, on dishes. Lavishly illustrated. No recipes, but detailed notes on sources.

Klapthor, Margaret Brown, and Helen Duprey Bullock. *The First Ladies Cook Book: Favorite Recipes of All the Presidents of the United States.* Rev. ed. New York: Parents Magazine Enterprises, 1982. A chatty, popular account with some primary source documentation, but no bibliography. Some adapted recipes.

Morris, Edmund. *Theodore Rex.* New York: Random House, 2001. Useful introduction to the Booker T. Washington incident; good bibliography for further research.

Spillman, Jane Shadel. *White House Glassware: 200 Years of Presidential Entertaining.* Washington, DC: White House Historical Association, 1989. Similar to *The White House China,* with excerpts from journals and newspaper accounts.

Whitcomb, John, and Claire Whitcomb. *Real Life at the White House: 200 Years of Daily Life at America's Most Famous Residence.* New York: Routledge, 2000. A readable popular history of private life through the Clinton administration, with some mention of food for virtually every president. No bibliography, though citations are provided for quotes.

CATHY K. KAUFMAN

Wieners, *see Hot Dog*

Wild Rice, *see Rice*

Wiley, Harvey

Harvey Washington Wiley is generally considered to be the father of pure food and drug legislation and the U.S. Food and Drug Administration. He was a central figure during the passage of the Pure Food and Drug Act of 1906, called by some the Wiley Act, and its successor, the 1938 Federal Food, Drug, and Cosmetic Act.

Wiley was born in 1844 in Indiana, served as a corporal in the Civil War, received his medical degree from Indiana Medical College, and later completed a bachelor's degree at Harvard. In 1874, Wiley joined the faculty of Purdue University as its first professor of chemistry. There he turned his attention to the study of sugar. In 1883, he left Purdue to become head of the Division of Chemistry at the U.S. Department of Agriculture (USDA), a position he held until 1912.

From an early date Wiley identified himself with the pure food movement in the United States and used it as a springboard to expand his department. One of the more controversial things Wiley did was to set up the infamous human feeding study on the safety of food preservatives. Twelve young, able-bodied men, all employees of the USDA, volunteered to let the government lace all of their meals with borax, salicylic acid, sulfuric acid, sodium benzoate, and formaldehyde. They consumed their meals in the basement of the Department of Agriculture for at least six months. George Rothwell Brown of the *Washington Post* dubbed the volunteers the "Poison Squad" and they became a national sensation. The study ended because the chemicals made some of the volunteers so sick from nausea, vomiting, and stomachaches that they could not do productive work.

The study was seriously flawed scientifically since there was no control group and no norms with which to compare the findings. In addition, the experiment as conceived by Wiley reflected his bizarre and unusual notions about digestion. He believed in the archaic idea that digestion and spoilage were the same thing. He reasoned that if preservatives prevent foods from spoiling, they must also interfere with digestion. While the government never followed up with the men on the long-term effects of the chemicals they consumed, anecdotal evidence suggests that no one was harmed. William O. Robinson, one of the original human guinea pigs, lived to the age of ninety-four.

Because of Wiley's many dealings with business interests (for a time he worked for and accepted gifts from Arbuckle, the coffee company) and his commercial favoritisms, he was frequently in conflict with other government officials, especially the secretary of agriculture. After leaving the USDA, he became director of the Bureau of Foods, Sanitation, and Health at *Good Housekeeping* magazine, where he wrote a monthly column and established the Good Housekeeping Seal of Approval.

He died in 1930 and is buried at Arlington National Cemetery.

[*See also* Department of Agriculture, United States; Food and Drug Administration; Good Housekeeping Institute.]

BIBLIOGRAPHY

Coppin, Clayton A., and Jack High. *The Politics of Purity: Harvey Washington Wiley and the Origins of Federal Food Policy.* Ann Arbor: University of Michigan Press, 1999.

Lewis, Carol. "The 'Poison Squad' and the Advent of Food and Drug Regulation." *FDA Consumer Magazine*, November–December 2002.

Wiley, Harvey Washington. *1001 Tests of Foods, Beverages and Toilet Accessories Good and Otherwise: Why They Are So.* New York: Hearst's International Library, 1914.

JOSEPH M. CARLIN

Wilson, Mary Tolford

Mary Tolford Wilson (*b.* 1899 in Wisconsin; *d.* 1998 in Connecticut) is known for her scholarly work in culinary history. Her admirable essay "The First American Cookbook" served as the introduction to a 1958 facsimile edition of *American Cookery* (1796) by Amelia Simmons; the essay stands as a model study of culinary Americana. Later, Wilson wrote a scholarly account concerning *The Pocumtuc Housewife* (1897), which was falsely claimed by the publisher to have originally been published in 1805, giving rise to numerous phantom citings of a spurious work in certain august lexicons.

[*See also* Cookbooks and Manuscripts, *subentry* From the Beginnings to 1860; Simmons, Amelia.]

BIBLIOGRAPHY

Simmons, Amelia. *American Cookery.* 1796. A facsimile of the first edition with an essay by Mary Tolford Wilson. New York: Oxford University Press, 1958.

Wilson, Mary Tolford. "To Lay a Ghost." *Harvard Library Bulletin* 28, no. 1 (January 1980).

KAREN HESS

Wine

This entry includes four subentries:

Historical Survey
Later Developments
Eastern U.S. Wines
California Wines

Historical Survey

The history of the United States is often written as a quest for economic opportunity or for freedom of conscience, but it might also be written, with considerable truth, as a quest for wine. North America first appeared to European consciousness as the land that Leif Eriksson called "Vinland"—Wineland. No one now knows what it was that Leif Eriksson found growing on the Newfoundland shores—was it grapes? meadow grass? cranberries?—but the name at least was truly prophetic, for North America is home to more species of grape than any other part of the world. This fact was immediately apparent to the first explorers and to the earliest colonists: Wild grapes rioted in profusion all over the woodlands of the eastern seaboard, as they continue to do. How could this New World not also be a New World of wine?

Failure of Vinifera

The earliest English settlement, at Jamestown in 1607, was intended from the beginning to be a source of wine. But wine from native grapes proved to be too low in alcohol to be stable, too high in acid and too full of strange flavors to be drinkable. The European vine—*Vitis vinifera*—was then tried but could not be made to grow; over and over again the experiment was made, and over and over again the imported vines soon sickened and died. French experts were brought in but also failed; laws were passed to compel the settlers to plant vines, to no avail; King James sent a book on wine making to every householder in Virginia, without result.

Why did every effort fail? The answer, which was not clearly grasped for the next two centuries, was a paradox: the New World would not yield wine just because it abounded in grapes. The native American vines were accompanied by a formidable array of native American vine diseases and pests: black rot, powdery mildew, downy mildew, phylloxera, Pierce's disease. All of these were unknown to the tender European vine, *Vitis vinifera*, which inevitably succumbed to one or another of them, or to a combination. The experience in North America was very different from what it was in other sites of European colonization. In South Africa, in Argentina and Chile, in Australia, one had merely to put *Vitis vinifera* into the ground and stand back to watch it flourish. The only obstacles to wine production in those countries were economic; nature was wholly willing. But in North America it was entirely different. To the devastating effect of pests and diseases one had also to add the American climate, more extreme than that of Europe, and, in the East, more humid as well. Vines that were injured by freezing or steamed in humidity were all the more susceptible to the onslaught of the potent native diseases.

The early experience of repeated failure in Virginia was the model for all the other settlements in colonial America, from Maine to Florida. Uncounted numbers of private individuals vainly tried to grow vinifera in every new region without exception. Well-organized and extensive efforts fared no better. The first German settlement in America, at Germantown, Pennsylvania, in 1683, was typical. The German pietists, from the wine-growing regions of the river Main, took for granted that they would carry on their wine making in Pennsylvania. They soon learned otherwise. There were wine-growing colonies founded in Florida, in Georgia, South Carolina, North Carolina, Virginia, and New York—to name a few—but they all came to the same defeated conclusion.

Just before the Revolution there was a fresh outburst of effort. In 1769 a Frenchman was subsidized by the Virginia House of Burgesses to make wine from a vineyard at Williamsburg; a Virginia gentleman named Robert Bolling having planted a vineyard on his estate, wrote a manuscript titled "Sketch of Vine Culture for Pennsylvania, Maryland, Virginia and the Carolinas"; an Italian named Mazzei was sponsored by Thomas Jefferson in an ambitious wine-growing venture near Monticello. Nothing came of all these attempts, but it showed that the determination to produce wine in Virginia persisted after a century and a half of frustra-

tion. George Washington, James Madison, James Monroe, and Jefferson were all would-be wine growers, as was virtually every other Virginia gentleman. At the same time, Edward Antill, of New Jersey, inspired by a prize offered by the Royal Society of Arts in London for colonial wine, had planted a vineyard and had, as well, written a book on the subject. *Essay on the Cultivation of the Vine* (1771) is the first American publication on wines and vines. Antill died before the treatise was published, and his vineyard did not survive him.

As settlement moved west after the Revolution, the same thing persisted. There were efforts to establish wine growing in Alabama—where exiled Napoleonic officers founded a colony on land granted by the federal government—and in Ohio, Kentucky, and points west. The same experience was repeated with monotonous regularity because there was no way to put together the lessons of these many isolated failures; along the frontier, hopeful ignorance was always ready to make a new trial.

Discovery of Native Hybrids

After the Revolution yet another Frenchman, one Peter Legaux, promoted his "Pennsylvania Vine Company," near Philadelphia; he had vinifera vines from the finest sources, including Chateau Margaux and Chateau Lafite, and he had the support of Philadelphia's leading citizens, who persisted in hoping that vinifera could, somehow, be made to grow. Only one among Legaux's many vines survived; it was, he said, a vinifera from the Cape of Good Hope, and he called it the "Cape grape." In fact, though he did not know it, what he had was the result of a chance combination of an unknown vinifera with a native grape, probably originating near the vineyard that William Penn himself had planted on the Schuylkill River years earlier. The grape had been found by James Alexander in 1740 and later came to be called the Alexander. It is the first recognized native hybrid, showing the resistance to disease of its American parent and something of the superior fruit quality of its European. From Legaux the grape passed to John James Dufour, a Swiss who took it first to Kentucky and then to Indiana, where, from around 1806, on the banks of the Ohio River, he and his associates produced the first wine in commercial quantity in what is now the United States.

Other native hybrids began to attract attention, the most valuable of which was the Catawba, introduced by Major John Adlum at his vineyard in Washington, D.C., in 1823. The Catawba was then taken up by Nicholas

Longworth, a wealthy Cincinnatian, who made still and sparkling wines from the Catawba that gained a national reputation. By the time of the Civil War, diseases, particularly black rot, put an end to wine growing around Cincinnati, briefly regarded as the "American Rhineland." However, what Longworth had started survived elsewhere. Wine growing based on the Catawba spread to the Lake Erie shore in Ohio, to the Finger Lakes region in New York, and to the German settlement of Hermann in Missouri. The Germans also favored a native grape called the "Norton," a black grape first found in Virginia. With the establishment of the Catawba it could at last be said that there was an American wine.

After the Civil War the wine-growing industry in the eastern states was consolidated in the regions where it had already been begun: New York led, with vineyards on the Hudson and the Lake Erie shore as well as in the major region of the Finger Lakes, which excelled in sparkling wines; Ohio came next, with vineyards along the shore and on the islands of Lake Erie, followed by Missouri, where the industry developed along the Missouri River, upstream from St. Louis. There was a small industry in New Jersey, and a sprinkling in other states. Though it had been active in experiments before the Civil War, the South of Reconstruction days was essentially wineless, except for the wines produced by Paul Garrett in North Carolina from the native *rotundifolia* grape called the "scuppernong."

The most successful wines of the East were primarily dry white table wines, still or sparkling, from such native hybrids as the Catawba, Dutchess, and Delaware; red wines were made from Clinton, Ives, and Eumelan, or, especially in Missouri and New Jersey, the Norton. The wines from such grapes did not closely resemble the European wines that they sought to imitate; they might be delicate and attractive (Delaware) or merely coarse and acid (Clinton), but they all, to a greater or lesser degree, had the flavor and aroma called "foxy" (derived from methyl anthranilate) that was characteristic of most native grapes, a flavor that seems strange and disagreeable to anyone accustomed to vinifera wines.

It is important to note that throughout this history there had been close cooperation between the public authorities and the people who persisted in trying to grow wine. Since the Prohibition years (1920–1933) the official position toward American wine has been largely hostile, expressed as obstructive regulation, heavy taxation, or both. Before that things were far different. Among the

colonial authorities, wine making was one of the economic activities most eagerly encouraged, whether by land grants, subsidies, tax credits, premiums, or other inducements. After the Revolution the federal government kept up the tradition; Congress made several large grants of land to entrepreneurs in the hope that a supply of native wine might follow; the Patent Office, forerunner of the Department of Agriculture, undertook to gather and disseminate information on wine growing from all over the country; an experimental vineyard was established in Washington, D.C., as a part of the U.S. Propagating Garden, and wine was not taxed.

California

The annexation of California after the Mexican War in 1847 put American wine growing on a new basis, though it would be a generation before the eastern industry felt much competition from the western region. In the arid American West, where phylloxera and a variety of fungal diseases were unknown, the European grape will readily grow. Vinifera had been brought to California not long after the founding of the missions in 1769; a date around 1782 is now accepted as that of the first vintage in California. The wine makers were the Franciscan priests, and the place was probably the mission at San Juan Capistrano. Vineyards were soon established at most of the twenty-one missions that stretched from San Diego, on the Mexican border, to Sonoma, north of San Francisco Bay. The wine they made sufficed for celebrating the mass and for the tables of the Franciscans, but there is no evidence that mission wine ever had any commercial significance. Gradually, the vines spread to secular California from the missions. The first such vin yards were in Los Angeles, beginning in the 1820s; commercial production was established there by the 1830s. The modern California industry is directly descended from the Los Angeles vineyards and hence from the missions. The only grape known until the middle of the nineteenth century was called the "Mission," a true vinifera but unknown in Europe and therefore probably a genuine creole plant, born in the New World of Old World parentage and brought to California from Mexico by the Franciscans. The Mission yielded mediocre wine at best, but it produced it reliably and abundantly.

The gold rush transformed wine growing as it did everything else in California. Among the thousands who poured into California (made a state in 1850) were many who took up land and planted grapes; they were of varied

European origins—French, German, Swiss, English, Italian—and gave to California wine growing its cosmopolitan character. By the 1860s grapes had spread into most of the regions cultivated in the early twenty-first century. Led by such merchants as Kohler and Frohling, Californians began to build up a national trade after the opening of the transcontinental railroad in 1869. The Los Angeles region, augmented by the successful development of the German wine-making community of Anaheim, continued to lead the state's wine production, but the region around San Francisco Bay was growing rapidly and would overtake the south before the end of the nineteenth century.

Beginning in the 1850s many new varieties of European grapes were brought into California, notably by nurserymen in Santa Clara County. Within a decade almost every variety of any subsequent importance in the state had been introduced, and, although there was much to learn about cultivation practices and wine-making procedures, the basis for a mature industry was well laid. For many years the legend persisted that the Hungarian émigré Agoston Haraszthy de Mokcsa (1812–1869) had brought the new varieties, including the Zinfandel, to California, but that has been shown to be false. Haraszthy de Mokcsa did, however, do much to publicize California wine, especially through his *Grape Culture, Wines, and Wine-Making* (1862), one of the first books to be devoted to the subject.

By the end of the century California wineries, scattered the length of the state from San Diego to Mendocino County, were producing 30 million gallons of wine of all kinds. Wine growing not only had become an important economic activity but also had attracted many wealthy and prominent people who gave it a certain glamour: Senator Hearst, Leland Stanford, James Fair, Julius Smith. The coastal valleys were the main locus of wine growing, but from the 1870s there were also large-scale wineries in the great central valley that produced large volumes of fortified wines. The industry then suffered two heavy blows. The first was economic. The Panic of 1893 produced conditions so depressed that it did not pay to harvest the grapes from the vines. To meet the situation the California Wine Association (CWA) was formed, an amalgamation of the leading San Francisco wine merchants and producers. Their combination proved powerful enough to dominate the trade and thus to control production and prices. The California wine trade from 1893 until Prohibition in 1920 is essentially the

story of the CWA. There were producers outside the system, but even they operated under conditions largely determined by the CWA.

The second blow was the devastation of the vineyards by phylloxera. A minute aphid that kills vines by attacking their roots, phylloxera is native to the American East. In the 1860s it had arrived in Europe with such catastrophic effect that for a time it was feared that European wine growing would come to an end. Largely through the efforts of French scientists and growers a method was devised to control phylloxera by grafting European vines on to the phylloxera-resistant rootstocks of native American species. When phylloxera made its appearance in California vineyards around 1873, this practice was already established in Europe, but Californians were slow to accept that their vineyards were doomed unless they took such measures as the French had. The consequence was that some regions were almost wiped out: Napa County slumped from twenty thousand acres of vines to three thousand in the 1890s.

Prohibition and Repeal

Recovery had taken place and, despite the earlier setbacks, there was a vigorous American wine trade, both east and west, when it was shut down by national Prohibition after World War I. Prohibition, which had long been in preparation, came at last with seeming suddenness: The Eighteenth Amendment to the Constitution, prohibiting the manufacture and sale of intoxicating drink, was submitted to the states in 1917 and ratified in January 1919. One year later, under the terms of the Volstead Act, it went into force. What it meant to American wine was not clear; the Volstead Act prohibited the sale of all drink containing more than one-half of 1 percent of alcohol, but a special proviso allowed the domestic production of "nonintoxicating fruit juices." This was interpreted to mean that home wine making was permitted, and, despite repeated challenges, that interpretation was upheld. The immediate effect was that the vineyards of California doubled in the next five years in order to feed the demand for wine grapes; there was a comparable growth in vineyards outside of California as millions of Americans made wine at home. America, someone said, might become a wine-drinking nation if Prohibition lasted long enough.

The effect on the wineries, however, was destructive. Some wineries kept going by producing wine for the permitted uses: as a sacrament, as a medicine, as a food flavoring, and as a source of vinegar. They could also produce fresh juice and concentrate. Many wineries continued to make wine and store it, even though they could not sell it. Many more went out of business.

The growing conviction that Prohibition did not work was strengthened by the effects of the Great Depression. When Franklin Roosevelt was nominated in 1932, the Democrats accepted Repeal as a part of their platform, and their victory made Repeal virtually certain. It came with the ratification of the Twenty-first Amendment, repealing the Eighteenth, on December 5, 1933: Prohibition had thus lasted within a month of fourteen years. Repeal, when it came, was seriously incomplete and has remained so. The Twenty-first Amendment, while repealing Prohibition, at the same time gave unlimited power to each state to create its own regulations for the sale of alcoholic drink, or to impose any scheme of prohibition. The result has been fifty different sets of regulations. The Twenty-first Amendment has thus been both an enabling and a crippling work of policy.

The restoration of the wine business—and of a body of educated wine drinkers—had now to be begun. A clearly marked pattern soon emerged. Though many small growers who hoped to cash in on the renewed wine trade set up in business, few of them survived. Instead, the big wineries dominated. Some of them were cooperatives, a familiar arrangement in the 1930s; others were private corporations. Both specialized in bulk wine, that is, wine sold in large quantities—shipment by eight thousand–gallon rail tank car was the norm—to bottlers around the country, who would put their own labels on the bottles. Such wines were sold under generic names—Chablis, Burgundy, port, sherry—as had often been the practice before Prohibition. And, overwhelmingly, the wine that was sold was fortified wine. Thus the American public grew accustomed to wine without any indication of its origin (apart from "California" or "New York") or composition or anything reliably descriptive; and on the whole the public was taught that wine was fortified and mostly sweet. All this was inimical to the cause of authentically labeled table wine. Wine sales grew slowly through the 1930s, but without any visible changes of an encouraging kind, if what one hoped for was a discriminating market that asked for well-made table wine.

There were counterforces at work, however, both in the field and in the classroom. The few wineries upholding the standards of fine wine—Beaulieu, Inglenook, and Wente were among the unquestioned leaders—combined with the research and instructional work carried out at the University of California were to have a powerful impact, although it would take time.

Wartime

The war helped to produce two positive changes. The wine importer and merchant Frank Schoonmaker, who was also in his time the best writer about wine in the United States, turned to domestic sources when World War II put his European supplies at risk. Schoonmaker had long argued that American wines should be sold under their own names, with clear indication of their origins. He contracted with producers all across the country to supply him with wines labeled in accordance with his own principles: New York State Delaware produced by Widmer, or Sonoma Pinot Noir produced by Fountaingrove, for example. The main part of the trade was deeply hostile to this change—why trouble a market that was comfortable with established bad practices?—but it was ultimately to become the standard American rule.

The second change came about because of wartime price controls. Thanks to the peculiar character of the rules, it was much more profitable for a winery to bottle its own wine and ship it than it was to send it in bulk to bottlers across the country, as had been the custom. By the end of the war a wine that was "bottled at the winery," which had been an unusual and exotic practice, had become standard and has remained so into the twenty-first century. A few bottlers still survive, but they are from a different era of the American wine trade.

Postwar

The American wine makers confidently expected boom times after the war. They had not been able to make enough wine to meet the demand under wartime restrictions. In 1946 they eagerly competed for the supply of grapes, bidding prices up to unprecedented heights and producing a large quantity of wine. They then found that there was no market for it. People had returned to their whiskey-drinking habits, and wine, which was pretty much what it had been ever since Repeal, piled up in the warehouses. Wartime prosperity was followed by peacetime difficulties and uncertainties.

The counterforces mentioned above continued their work. A handful of small California wineries devoted to producing estate wines of the highest quality began to have their effect—Souverain, Stony Hill, Mayacamas, Hallcrest, and Martin Ray were among the leading names. Technical advances began to have their effect as well: Temperature-controlled fermentation in stainless steel, cold fermentation of white wines, and control of malo-lactic fermentation all contributed to fresher, sounder, more reliable wines, as did new methods in filtration. Aging in small oak cooperage revealed new possibilities. Superior varieties, such as Cabernet Sauvignon and Chardonnay, began to be planted in significant quantity, a first step in the essential work of improving the grape supply. Effective promotion of varietally labeled wines on a national scale was carried out by Frank Schoonmaker at Almadén Vineyards. By the 1960s there were signs that the American idea of wine was changing from port, sherry, and muscatel to dry table wines, still mostly mislabeled as Chablis or Burgundy but now increasingly identified as Cabernet Sauvignon, Zinfandel, or Chardonnay. In 1967 the shift was confirmed beyond question when the sale of table wine in the United States passed that of fortified wine. That reversal is so complete in the early 2000s that only a small fraction of American wine production is fortified.

Comparable changes were taking place in the eastern industry, first through the increasing commercial interest in French hybrid grapes. These grapes, largely developed by French experimenters, aimed to combine the disease resistance of native American varieties with the fruit quality of European vinifera vines. They were first effectively promoted in this country by Philip Wagner at his Boordy Vineyard in Maryland, beginning in the late 1930s. Wagner's earliest customers were almost entirely amateurs who wished to make their own wine, but by the 1950s some eastern wineries began to show an interest. In the years since, the French hybrids have spread to every state east of the Rockies, providing a reliable source of palatable wines in regions where vinifera is at risk or impossible. The old native grapes—Catawba, Concord, Niagara, Delaware—still survive, but in rapidly diminishing numbers.

A second change came about largely through the work of a Russian immigrant named Konstantin Frank, who believed that vinifera could be made to grow despite the eastern winter. By grafting vinifera to cold-resistant native rootstocks he succeeded to his own satisfaction. Frank was an active propagandist for his work and inspired many others to make renewed trials of vinifera. In the first decade of the twenty-first century there were significant plantings of vinifera vines in southern New England, New York, Pennsylvania, Maryland, Virginia, Ohio, and points west; the quality of the wines they yield is increasingly recognized.

Wine Revolution

From 1967, when the sales of table wine passed those of fortified wine, one could speak of a "wine revolution" in America: New wineries began to proliferate; new people were attracted to wine growing from every direction; the vineyard acreage in the established regions grew rapidly, and new regions were opened up; the common, productive varieties that had dominated the vineyards were now rejected in favor of superior but less productive varieties; and the American public, aided by the proliferation of wine publications, wine tastings, wine competitions, wine festivals, and wine classes, began to take an interest in wine such as it had never shown before. The statistics are impressive. In 1967 there were 424 bonded wineries in the United States, 227 in California, 197 in other states; thirty years later, in 1997, there were 1,988 bonded wineries, 1,011 in California, 977 in other states. In 1967 the United States produced 170 million gallons of wine; in 1997, 533 million. By the turn of the twenty-first century the United States had become the fourth-largest producer of wine in the world, preceded only by Italy, France, and Spain.

How had this come about? Some said foreign travel in the jet age had given Americans a new awareness of wine; some said that greater affluence had allowed people to take up wine; some said that the new interest in good food and improved cooking had done the trick. But one should not forget the steady work that had been in process since Repeal—efforts by university scientists and the wine makers who listened to them to improve American wine, supported by the sustained promotional efforts of such agencies as the Wine Institute and the Wine Advisory Board. The change was sudden when it came, but it had long been in preparation.

The going was not always smooth; there were several episodes of oversupply, of declining sales, of falling prices, but growth has continued. One particularly challenging difficulty became clear in the middle of the 1980s, when a number of forces hostile to alcoholic drink, including wine, seemed to take on a new power. The appeal now was not to prohibition on moral grounds but to prohibition on grounds of health and safety: Campaigns to raise alcohol taxes, campaigns against drunken driving, campaigns for ingredient labeling, campaigns for health warnings on all bottles of wine were more or less successfully waged. The policy of all relevant federal agencies was against the consumption of alcoholic drink. The wine makers, brewers, and distillers were lumped together as they had been in the years before the passage of national Prohibition. "Alcohol and other drugs" was a familiar phrase; "just say no" was the approved response. In vain did the wine makers protest that wine was different: One did not drink wine to get drunk but to promote good digestion and good fellowship; wine was the drink of moderation, of civilized enjoyment. But to the neo-prohibitionists, as they were called, such protests were only self-serving deceptions.

A right about-face came in 1991 when the CBS television program *Sixty Minutes* presented the views of some experts as to why the French, who ate more fats than the Americans, had a lower incidence of heart disease. The solution to this "French Paradox," it was suggested, might be that the French drank red wine. This was all that the American public seemed to need. The demand for red wine immediately soared. Supermarket sales went up by 44 percent in the month following the program, and the effect continued through the next year and after. For the rest of the decade the wine industry was not only prosperous but also relatively untroubled by assaults upon wine as a detriment to health. Although the federal authorities would not allow the wine makers to make claims for the therapeutic value of wine, the press had much to say on the matter.

At the turn of the twenty-first century wine making was flourishing and was more widespread than ever before. There were 145 American Viticultural Areas (AVA), a scheme introduced by the federal government in 1980; these AVAs were to be found in twenty-seven states. All fifty states (North Dakota's first bonded winery appeared in 2002) had a wine-making enterprise of one sort or another, and substantial new developments had been firmly established. New York, long the number two wine-making state, still led in the East, but it had been surpassed nationally by Washington. Oregon, Texas, Missouri, Michigan, Ohio, Virginia, and Pennsylvania were also sites of considerable and varied production of all sorts of wine: red and white, sweet and dry, still and sparkling. Varieties previously unknown in the United States—Viognier, Sangiovese, Lemberger—were introduced by wine makers looking for new ways to appeal to the market, and varieties previously not well regarded—Syrah, Zinfandel, Semillon—were treated with a new interest in their possibilities for fine wine. The spectrum of available wines ran from simple reds and whites sold

in jugs or in bag-in-box containers to so-called cult wines offered in minute quantities at impossible prices to the eager few who could afford them. In theory, the choice was immense: sparkling wine from New Mexico, Vidal from Michigan, Norton from Missouri, Cabernet from Ohio, Chambourcin from Pennsylvania. In practice, access to wine was limited by what the distributors in each individual state made available. The Twenty-First Amendment still impeded the flow of wine across state lines, and the possibilities of Internet wine sales had generated a defensive flurry of legislation from states seeking to guard their rights to control the traffic in alcoholic drink. Several states made such sales a felony for the seller. The consumer's "right of access" was an issue for the courts in the early 2000s.

Given such conditions, it cannot be said that the United States is yet a wine-drinking country, although it is certainly a major wine-producing country. The national adult per capita consumption of wine in 1999 was 2.44 gallons; most of that wine was drunk by a small segment of the population, and that small segment tended to be older, not younger, and to live in cities (not the country), on the coasts (not the interior), and in the North (not the South). Such has long been the pattern. How it is to be altered and whether it is to be altered remain questions.

[*See also* Alcohol and Teetotalism; Alcoholism; California; Champagne; Fermentation; French Influences on American Food; Fruit Wines; Gallo, Ernest and Julio; Grapes; Jefferson, Thomas; Mondavi, Robert; Mondavi Wineries; Prohibition; Sangria; Sherry; Temperance; Vermouth; Wineries.]

BIBLIOGRAPHY

Adams, Leon. *The Wines of America*. 4th ed. New York: McGraw-Hill, 1990.

Adlum, John. *A Memoir on Cultivation of the Vine in America, and the Best Mode of Making Wine*. Washington, DC: Davis and Force, 1823.

Amerine, Maynard, and A. J. Winkler. "Composition and Quality of Musts and Wines of California Grapes." *Hilgardia* 15 (February 1944): 493–676.

Antill, Edward. "An Essay on the Cultivation of the Vine, and the Making and Preserving of Wine, Suited to the Different Climates of North-America." *Transactions of the American Philosophical Society*. Vol. 1., 180–262. 2nd ed. Philadelphia, 1789.

Dufour, John James. *The American Vine-Dresser's Guide*. Cincinnati, OH: S. J. Brown, 1826.

Gohdes, Clarence. *Scuppernong: North Carolina's Grape and Its Wines*. Durham, NC: Duke University Press, 1982.

Haraszthy, Agoston. *Grape Culture, Wines, and Wine-Making*. New York: Harper and Brothers, 1862.

Hedrick, U. P. *The Grapes of New York*. Albany, NY: J. B. Lyon, 1908.

Husmann, George. *American Grape Growing and Wine Making.* 4th. ed. New York: Orange Judd, 1896.

Lapsley, James. *Bottled Poetry: Napa Winemaking from Prohibition to the Modern Era.* Berkeley: University of California Press, 1996.

Muscatine, Doris, Maynard A. Amerine, and Bob Thompson, eds. *The University of California/Sotheby Book of California Wine.* Berkeley: University of California Press; London, Sotheby, 1984.

Peninou, Ernest P., and Gail Unzelman. *The California Wine Association and Its Member Wineries, 1894–1920.* Santa Rosa, CA: Nomis, 2000.

Pinney, Thomas. *A History of Wine in America: From the Beginnings to Prohibition.* Berkeley: University of California Press, 1989.

Schoonmaker, Frank, and Tom Marvel. *American Wines.* New York: Duell, Sloan and Pearce, 1941.

Sullivan, Charles. *A Companion to California Wine.* Berkeley: University of California Press, 1998.

Wagner, Philip. *A Wine-Grower's Guide.* New York: Knopf, 1955.

Wait, Frona Eunice. *Wines and Vines of California.* San Francisco: Bancroft, 1889.

Winkler, A. J., J. A. Cook, W. M. Kliewer, and L. A. Lider. *General Viniculture.* Rev. ed. Berkeley: University of California Press, 1974.

THOMAS PINNEY

Later Developments

For the American wine industry, the 1990s were a period of consolidation, marketing innovation, technological advances, hype, and speculation. There is little doubt that by the beginning of the twenty-first century, the American wine industry was providing a better quality product at a lower cost than ever before, but America's largely unregulated production has limited the global success of its wines.

In 1997 the United States had approximately 778,000 acres designated as vineyard area, whereas France, Italy, and Spain had a combined total of more than 7 million acres. Per capita wine consumption in America, although rising, is still miniscule when compared with Europe. In 1996 the annual per capita wine consumption in France and Italy was more than 15 gallons; in the United States consumption was 2.03 gallons, a modest increase from 1.88 gallons in 1991. Australia, whose wines have taken the world by storm, has approximately 222,000 vineyard acres and, at 4.78 gallons, a per capita consumption more than twice that of the United States.

The potential market for increased wine consumption in the United States, with its relatively affluent population, is perhaps the single most important factor related to the majority of later developments. It is little wonder that major corporations from around the world are investing in American land and production facilities to take advantage of this attractive situation. Another attraction could be the relative lack of production regulation. To produce an appellation wine in France or in most European Union (EU) countries, a wine maker must adhere to numerous regulations, including limitations on additives. The American system, which establishes approved viticultural areas (AVA, American Viticultural Area), requires only that 85 percent of the grapes come from the district of the AVA (75 percent of the variety if the wine is a varietel) and imposes no regulatory structure on the wine maker for providing this information. This laissez-faire style of production has drawbacks and is one of the major reasons why even premium wines from the United States have not penetrated the European market to any great extent. The substantial decline in the U.S. dollar in late 2003 relative to the euro may change that, but it will certainly increase domestic wine sales and provide a further incentive for the acquisition of vineyards by international corporations.

Wine consumers in the United States have been gratified by a number of court rulings allowing vineyards to sell directly to consumers across state lines. The removal of these sales restrictions, remnants of Prohibition, is important for the survival of the small vineyard owner in a market increasingly dominated by a few distributors. Vineyard owners of all sizes face questions about ground pollution and water usage, issues that could result in major consequences and costs to producers throughout the country. New techniques and technologies will continue to be developed to meet these and other challenges.

One important resource to the industry is the University of California, Davis (UC Davis), one of the premier training schools in the scientific aspects of wine making. The ascendancy of wine making as a science has allowed graduates of such schools as UC Davis to become important executives at some of the largest producers in the United States, much in the way that technocrats have replaced entrepreneurial operators in other evolving industries.

One of the least desirable later developments is the establishment of many small AVA vineyards that produce inferior products. These wines take on a local cachet (Martha's Vineyard has AVA status) that becomes more important than the wine itself. In many cases these small vineyards would seem to exist to take advantage of the tax credits available, giving prestige to their owners, who may be speculating that urban sprawl will increase land value. Another unfortunate trend is the purchase of brands for market share by large conglomerates that do little to improve the product. The exception is the Gallo family, with their investment in premium wines and dedication to producing a better product at a fair price. Gallo, which already has America's largest market share of table wine, has proven that big is not always bad.

It is the consumer who will decide the future of the American wine industry. The interest in wine is growing. Wine educators conduct classes and wine tastings in almost every major city; wine tours are often sold out, be they on Long Island, New York, or in Napa Valley, California; and books on wine meet with a substantial readership. Wine auctions have expanded into a multi-million-dollar business, and there are buyers who are investing in wine based on the knowledge that even a slight change in the demographics of drinkers will catapult the demand for high-quality wine from great vineyards. Research suggesting that wine, when taken in moderation, may be healthful has helped create a new group of health-conscious consumers. The transition of America to a wine-drinking nation may be slow to develop, but an increasingly knowledgeable public bodes well for the future of an industry that barely survived Prohibition.

[*See also* Gallo, Ernest and Julio; Mondavi, Robert; Mondavi Wineries; Wineries.]

BIBLIOGRAPHY

Adams, Leon. *The Commonsense Book of Wine*. New York: McGraw-Hill, 1986.

Gallo, Ernest, and Julio Gallo, with Bruce B. Henderson. *Ernest and Julio: Our Story*. New York: Times Books, 1994.

Meltzer, Peter D. "Tough Times for California Wines at Auction." *The Wine Spectator*, October 15, 1995.

Mondavi, Robert, with Paul Chutkow. *Harvests of Joy: My Passion for Excellence*. New York: Harcourt Brace, 1998.

The Oxford Companion to Wine. 2nd ed. Edited by Jancis Robinson. New York: Oxford University Press, 1999.

STEVEN M. CRAIG

Eastern U.S. Wines

The broad expanse of the North American continent east of the Rocky Mountains forms a unique wine region marked by difficult and challenging conditions for growing grapes. As opposed to the Mediterranean climate in California, the continental mass east of the Rockies has extreme weather conditions, with winter temperatures plunging below zero in many areas, damaging late spring and early autumn frosts, high humidity that provides ideal conditions for fungus diseases, hurricanes that can bring heavy rains during harvest, extended droughts, hail, and in some areas intense bird pressure.

Along with extremes of weather, another unifying factor across this huge region, with its diverse soils and climates, is the similarity of the grape varieties grown, some of which are not found anywhere else in the world. Winter hardiness and the ability to resist diseases and insect pests have been determinants in the choice of varieties to grow.

There are three broad categories of grapes grown in the East, two main species and a mixture of species commonly referred to as the hybrids. The native American

HYBRIDIZATION

Hybridization is an important tool in agriculture used to create new or different varieties of plants, flowers, vegetables, or fruits with a desired quality or set of characteristics. For grapes, particularly those to be grown in the East, the goal is to create varieties that will be disease resistant and cold tolerant while at the same time bearing fruit that will make a European-style table wine.

Seeds are nature's way of reproducing grapevines. Grape growers, however, prefer to propagate vines by planting cuttings, pieces of the canes of one-year-old shoots cut into six- to eighteen-inch lengths. This assures that the new vines will be identical to the vines from which the cuttings were taken.

Creating new varieties, or hybridizing, requires the use of seeds. The hybridizer pollinates the flowers of one variety with pollen from another so that the resulting berries will have the characteristics of both parents. These seeds are planted and the seedlings allowed to bear fruit. Over a period of years, wine is made from the strongest and healthiest of these new vines. The vines with the best wine-making potential are kept and the remainder discarded. Eventually the new grape variety will be given a name if it is to be used commercially.

HUDSON CATTELL

varieties, such as Concord and Niagara, are primarily members of the species *Vitis labrusca*; the varieties originating in Europe, such as Chardonnay and Cabernet Sauvignon, belong to the species *Vitis vinifera*; and the hybrids for the most part are crosses between these two species.

It was not possible to grow the classic vinifera varieties in the East until after World War II because they were not cold tolerant and had no natural immunity to diseases and insects prevalent in the East. In contrast to the familiar and relatively subtle European-style table wines, the wines made from the American varieties were stronger and often had a grapey flavor that some wine drinkers found objectionable. These varieties were lower in sugar, higher in acid, and, with considerable sweetening needed, were better suited for making fortified wines and champagnes than dry table wines. For more than three hundred years, one common thread in the history of wine in the East was the desire to make dry table wines, and part of that search involved the hybrids.

Early History

Wild grapevines were growing along the Atlantic seaboard long before Leif Eriksson and the Vikings found them there in the year 1000. Most of the early colonists, starting with the first English settlers in Jamestown, Virginia, in 1607, made wine from the grapes they found growing in the woods. The wines from these wild vines were coarse and strong and very different from the wines made in Europe. In 1622, wines from these vines were sent to England, and the Virginia Company to which the colony had to answer commented that they were "rather of scandal than credit to us."

As early as 1619, vinifera vines were brought from England, and in Virginia and Georgia the colonists were required to plant mulberry trees and grapevines for the benefit of the mother country. None of these imported vines survived long enough to produce a crop sufficient for making wine, but some of them did cross with vines growing in the wild, producing "chance hybrids" or "wilding" varieties.

The Pilgrims landed in Plymouth in 1620, and Edward Winslow, one of the founders of the Plymouth Colony, described what historians later referred to as the first Thanksgiving, in 1621. He makes no mention of wine, although he refers to the red and white grapes growing there as "very sweete and strong." It would be pleasant to think that wine complemented food at that initial Thanksgiving.

The first commercial vineyard in the United States was founded in 1793 by Pierre Legaux in Spring Mill, along the banks of the Schuylkill River in Pennsylvania, just north of Philadelphia. None of the vinifera vines planted there succeeded, but a variety known as the Alexander grape, discovered around 1740 by James Alexander, a gardener working for one of William Penn's sons, did survive and bear fruit. The Alexander, a chance hybrid between one of Penn's vinifera vines and a vine in the wild, was hardy, produced a good crop, and made a wine praised by many, including Thomas Jefferson, who had been trying to grow vines brought from France for more than thirty years at Monticello. In 1808, he wrote that "we can produce in the United States as many varieties of wines as Europe does; not the same ones, but undoubtedly of the same quality."

Eastern Wines. Advertisement for Germania Wine Cellars that appeared in *Harper's Monthly*, August 1894. *Collection of Georgia Maas*

Among those buying vines from Legaux was a native of Switzerland, Jean Jacques Dufour, who bought ten thousand vines in 1799 and planted them in Kentucky, where he set up the Kentucky Vineyard Society. There, and in Vevay, Indiana, the Alexander was the leading grape planted in vineyards. It was soon replaced by the Catawba, the first commercially significant American variety, which was discovered growing in the wild near Asheville, North Carolina, about 1802. The Catawba was a far superior grape for wine-making purposes than the Alexander, and by 1840 the Alexander grape had disappeared.

The first important commercial wine-making center in the United States was in Cincinnati, Ohio. Nicholas Longworth, who moved from New Jersey to Cincinnati in 1804, made his fortune in real estate. He planted his first vineyards in 1813, but it was not until 1825, when he first received cuttings of Catawba, that the industry began to grow. By 1859, there were more than two thousand acres of Catawba in the Cincinnati area and more

than a dozen wineries. Longworth's Sparkling Catawba, the first sparkling wine to be produced in the United States, won critical acclaim in Europe.

Other important grape varieties were beginning to make their appearance about this time. Isabella, thought to have come originally from South Carolina, was introduced into New York in 1816 and along with Catawba became one of the most widely planted grapes in the East. In 1850, Delaware was discovered growing in a garden in New Jersey. Both Isabella and Delaware had been growing in the wild before being transplanted into vineyards. Since their parentage includes *Vitis vinifera,* they are chance hybrids.

Starting about 1830, a number of American hybridizers began introducing new varieties in an attempt to solve the dual dilemmas of delicately flavored vinifera that could not be grown successfully in the East and sturdy native American grapes that could be grown easily but whose strongly flavored wines were not to their liking.

"CHAMPAGNE" OR "SPARKLING WINE"?

In the wake of Prohibition, the Federal Alcohol Administration (later to become part of the Bureau of Alcohol, Tobacco, and Firearms) was set up in the U.S. Treasury Department to create licensing and permit requirements and to establish regulations. Charles Fournier of Gold Seal Vineyards in Hammondsport, New York, became involved in the promulgation of federal regulations to legalize use of the term "champagne" in the United States. The regulations state that an American champagne must be "a type of sparkling light wine which derives its effervescence solely from the secondary fermentation of the wine within glass containers of not greater than one gallon capacity, and which possesses the taste, aroma, and other characteristics attributed to champagne as made in the Champagne district of France." A sparkling wine not having these characteristics can only be called a sparkling wine.

France and the European Union (EU) have long claimed that the producers in the Champagne district of France should have the exclusive rights to the term "champagne," and they also claim exclusive rights to the term *méthode champenoise,* the French term for the secondary fermentation in the bottle. Other countries in the EU have been required to use other terms; the Spanish, for example, use the term *cava.* Some pro-

ducers in the United States respect the French position and have voluntarily chosen to use the term "sparkling wine" instead of "champagne." There is no requirement that they do so unless they plan to export their wines into EU countries.

Fournier, who had been the wine maker at Veuve Cliquot Ponsardin in France, felt strongly that the champagnes he made in New York State were worthy of the great French name "champagne" and proudly used the term on the label. His sparkling wines that did not meet that standard were called simply "sparkling wine." Throughout his career, Fournier stated his strong opposition to those who used the term "champagne" on the label of inferior foaming wine.

In the early 2000s, Dr. Konstantin Frank's son Willy, president of Chateau Frank Champagne Cellars in Hammondsport, New York, adamantly insisted on using the term "champagne" on his Finger Lakes champagnes for exactly the same reasons that Charles Fournier did. He makes them by the *méthode champenoise,* keeps them for at least four years, and uses all three classic grape varieties, Pinot Noir, Chardonnay, and Pinot Meunier. Only when he is emulating the French does he place the word "champagne" on the label.

HUDSON CATTELL

PHYLLOXERA

All the grapes grown in Europe were of the species *Vitis vinifera*, and until the nineteenth century they were not exposed to diseases and insects that could threaten their existence. Beginning in the 1860s, vine cuttings from the United States introduced powdery mildew into the French vineyards. Shortly afterward *Phylloxera vastatrix*, a plant louse that could attack the roots of the vinifera, was accidentally imported from America and was responsible for devastating hundreds of thousands of acres of grapes throughout Europe. This was followed by yet another fungal disease, downy mildew.

There were two responses to the phylloxera crisis in France. One was to find phylloxera-resistant rootstocks on which the classic vinifera varieties could be grafted, and it was discovered that the rootstocks of American varieties could be used successfully because they were strongly resistant to phylloxera. A second response came from private French hybridizers, such as Albert Seibel, who made hundreds of thousands of crosses. Some of these with the potential for making dry table wines eventually found their way into the United States. Among those that found a permanent place in the East were Seyval Blanc, Vidal, Maréchal Foch, and Chambourcin.

HUDSON CATTELL

Among the leading hybridizers were E. S. Rogers in Massachusetts, J. H. Ricketts and Jacob Moore in New York, Hermann Jaeger and Jacob Rommel in Missouri, and Thomas Volney Munson in Texas.

No grape variety won instant popularity faster than Concord. The originator of Concord was Ephraim Wales Bull, who was born in Concord, Massachusetts. In 1843, Bull planted seeds from wild grapes on his property, and in 1849 one of the seedlings yielded fruit of such quality that he gave it a name. Concord was first shown at the Massachusetts Horticultural Society in 1852 and was offered for sale two years later. Within a few years Concord grape acreage accounted for 75 percent of the grape acreage in the East and an estimated 90 percent of its profits. Concord was sought after as a juice grape and for use in making jams and jellies, but a large percentage was used for wine. Concord was also crossed with Cassady, and the resulting offspring was Niagara. In the early 2000s, Niagara, Concord, Catawba, and Delaware are the primary native American varieties used in wine making.

Many of the large wineries of the mid-twentieth century also got their start during this period: Brotherhood Winery in 1839, Pleasant Valley Wine Company in 1860, the Taylor Wine Company in 1860, the Urbana Wine Company (later renamed Gold Seal Vineyards) in 1865, Widmer's Wine Cellars in 1865, and Renault Wine Company in Egg Harbor City, New Jersey, in 1868. Another large winery, the Canandaigua Wine Company in Canandaigua, New York, began as a bulk wine plant in 1945 and consequently acquired Taylor, Gold Seal, and Widmer's. By the mid-1990s, Canandaigua would become the second-largest winery in the United States.

Ohio's wine production of 570,000 gallons in 1859 made it the largest wine-producing state in the nation. This was more than one-third of the national total and more than twice the amount produced in California. From 1871 to about 1874, the Golden Eagle Winery on Middle Bass Island in Lake Erie was the largest winery in the United States, making more than 500,000 gallons a year.

Wines from Ohio, New York, and Missouri dominated the eastern wine scene in the years before 1900. They competed directly in the best restaurants with wines from Europe and they won international recognition. At the Vienna Exposition in 1873 a Great Western champagne from New York State became the first American champagne to win a gold medal in Europe. In the first head-on competition between American and French sparkling wines at the Paris Exposition in 1879, two Gold Seal champagnes from New York won medals. Between 1873 and 1904, Stone Hill Winery in Hermann, Missouri, won eight gold medals at world's fairs. At the Paris Exposition in 1900, wines from Florida, New Jersey, North Carolina, Virginia, and the District of Columbia were among the thirty-six American medal-winners.

The supremacy of eastern wines began to fade in the late 1800s, when many vineyards started to succumb to diseases for which sprays had not yet been invented. Another factor was the boom period in California, which began in the 1880s and led to California becoming the leading wine-producing state by the end of the century. National Prohibition in 1920 was the final blow.

Starting Over after Prohibition

The commercial wine industry in the United States came to an end when Prohibition became effective on January 17, 1920. Most wineries closed, and the few that remained open made sacramental wines or medicinal tonics. When repeal came on December 5, 1933, the industry was slow to revive. The larger wineries that had remained open began making the same wines they had been making before Prohibition: the ports, sherries, and sparkling wines for which they had had an established market.

The Twenty-first Amendment, repealing Prohibition, gave each state the right to regulate its own alcoholic beverage industry. In some states wine was tightly controlled as if it were a distilled spirit; in others the wine industry was given relative freedom. Quite often pressure had to be brought on state legislatures to pass laws permitting the existence of small wineries.

The years following Prohibition marked a turning point in the search in the East for grapes that would make dry table wines. One of the early pioneers of the modern grape and wine industry was Philip Wagner, a career journalist with the *Sun* papers of Baltimore. Wagner's interest in grape growing and wine making had led him to start growing grapes and making wine in the early 1930s, while Prohibition was still in effect. In 1936, he left Baltimore to spend a year in England as the London correspondent for the Baltimore *Sun*. During his year abroad he became aware of the French hybrids that had been developed as one response to the phylloxera crisis in France in the nineteenth century, and on his return to the United States he began searching for French hybrid varieties to plant in his vineyard in Riderwood, Maryland. In 1940, he and his wife, Jocelyn, decided to start a wine grape nursery, which they called Boordy Nursery, and by 1944 they were selling and shipping vines to half the states in the country. In the fall of 1941, Wagner made eleven wines that convinced him that the French hybrids were the most promising path to take. In August 1945, the Wagners opened a small commercial winery, Boordy Vineyard, which during the 1940s had a production of only a few hundred gallons a year. Their 1945 Baco noir was the first commercial varietal French hybrid wine to be produced in the East.

A key tasting took place in Fredonia, New York, on September 21, 1945. A group of researchers from the New York State Agricultural Experiment Station at Geneva and wine makers from western New York and Canada got together for a tasting following a morning of inspecting vineyards at the Geneva Station, in Fredonia.

PHILIP WAGNER

Philip Marshall Wagner (1904–1996) moved to Baltimore, Maryland, to begin what was to be a thirty-four-year career, becoming editor of the *Evening Sun* in 1938 and the *Sun* in 1943. He began making wine in 1931, and in 1933 bought property in Riderwood, Maryland, where he began planting vines. In May of that year he finished writing his first book, *American Wines and How to Make Them*, which at that time was the only book in English on wine making.

After his book was published, he began experimenting with an increasing number of grape varieties in his search for the right ones for making European-style table wines. In 1939, he imported twenty-five vines of Baco No. 1 from France, the first shipment of French hybrid vines into American viticulture for wine production. He and his wife, Jocelyn, started their grapevine nursery in 1940 and opened their winery, Boordy Vineyard, in 1945. In that same year he published *A Wine-Grower's Guide*, a book on grape growing that included information on growing the French hybrids.

Wagner met other needs as well. In those days it was difficult to obtain grape-growing and wine-making equipment suitable for small operations, and in 1950 Boordy Vineyard began selling hardware. Satisfactory inexpensive wine glasses were also hard to find. What was needed were good size glasses of clear glass or crystal with a simple shape that were sturdy enough to put into a dishwasher. In 1950, Jocelyn Wagner located an eight-ounce glass of the classical tulip shape in New York made by Morgantown Glassware Guild in West Virginia. Boordy Vineyard had Morgantown adapt the glass to its specifications, and for many years Boordy was a major supplier of wine glasses in the East and California.

Throughout the 1950s, Boordy was the only commercial nursery selling French hybrid vines, and the combination of Wagner's knowledge and the services he could provide made him a major influence throughout this period.

HUDSON CATTELL

CHARLES FOURNIER

Charles Fournier (1902–1983) was born in Reims, France, and in 1926 became the wine maker at the French champagne house of Veuve Cliquot Ponsardin, as his uncle had been before him. In 1933, he was offered the job of wine maker and production manager at Gold Seal Vineyards, then called the Urbana Wine Company, in Hammondsport, New York. When he arrived at Gold Seal in 1934, he found that the Finger Lakes region could produce traditional champagne flavors by using the right combination of soil and grapes. Catawba was particularly useful when it was made sparkling and aged in the bottle, on the sediment. His

Charles Fournier Champagne won a gold medal at the California State Fair in 1950, when the competition was opened for the first time to wines from outside California. Gold Seal's champagnes and sparkling wines were sales triumphs, along with Catawba pink, a fruity rosé.

Fournier is best remembered for his decision in 1953 to hire Konstantin Frank to develop a vinifera program at Gold Seal. Commercial plantings began at Gold Seal in 1957, and 60 acres of vinifera were planted by 1966 and 150, by 1977.

HUDSON CATTELL

Unknown to anyone, Wagner had brought along some samples of wines made from the French hybrid vines in his vineyard. Not many people knew about the French hybrids at that time. As he described it later, there was stunned silence on the part of some as they realized for the first time that hybrids could make good wine. One of those attending was Adhemar de Chaunac, the winemaker at Brights Wines in Niagara Falls, Ontario. He was so impressed with the tasting that the winery that same fall ordered twenty French hybrid varieties and three vinifera varieties from France, which arrived and were planted in 1946. A similar order was placed by the Horticultural Research Institute of Ontario at Vineland a year later, and these two shipments to Canada were the first large plantings of the French hybrids in the East. Prunings from these vines would eventually be shipped down to the Finger Lakes in New York.

When the shipment of vines arrived at Brights, the person in charge of viticultural research, George Hostetter, was given the job of supervising their care. Hostetter had a theory that applying sprays before disease symptoms became evident could be a key to controlling diseases. He put his theory to work, and it was successful not only for the hybrids but for the vinifera as well. The vinifera vines planted by Brights in 1946 became the start of the first successful vinifera vineyard in the East, and grapes from this vineyard led to the first commercial vinifera wines to be produced in the East, Brights Pinot Champagne in 1955 and Pinot Chardonnay in 1956.

Another successful pioneer in the search for dry table wines was Charles Fournier at Gold Seal Vineyards in Hammondsport, New York. Fournier left the champagne

house of Veuve Clicquot Ponsardin in France in 1933 to become the winemaker at Gold Seal. In the mid-1950s, he established a successful vinifera program and hired Dr. Konstantin Frank to run it. Frank was a Russian-born viticulturist who had settled in Geneva, New York, after immigrating to the United States in 1951. He had had long experience growing the vinifera in Russia and after arriving in America had tried in vain to persuade people to give him the opportunity to grow it in New York State. That opportunity came when he was recruited by Fournier. The key to growing the vinifera, Frank believed, involved finding the proper rootstocks. It took five years of experimentation before the right combination of rootstocks and viticultural approaches led to the winery's decision to begin commercial plantings in 1957. Large-scale plantings followed, and Gold Seal's 1960 Pinot noir and 1960 Pinot Chardonnay were the first commercial vinifera wines to be released in New York State.

The Industry Grows

High Tor Vineyards in Rockland County, New York, about thirty-two miles north of New York City, was one of the first small wineries to open after Philip Wagner's Boordy Vineyard. Everett and Alma Crosby bought the seventy-eight-acre High Tor property in 1950. The following year they purchased 3,500 French hybrid vines and sought advice on winery design from Wagner, and in 1954 they began selling their wine. The almost unbelievable difficulties in opening a winery at that early date, ranging from dealing with bureaucracies to being able to buy bottles, is recounted by Everett Crosby in *The Vintage Years: The Story of High Tor Vineyards* (1973).

Wineries opened with increasing rapidity in the 1960s and 1970s against the backdrop of what was known as the vinifera-hybrid controversy. More than a third of the wineries were started as a result of the influence of Wagner or Frank, and that influence determined whether the varieties they planted were primarily French hybrids or vinifera. Frank was a tireless and often outspoken advocate of growing the vinifera and insisted repeatedly that "Americans have everything excellent and they deserve to have excellent grapes and excellent wines." Frank's cultivation of the highly desirable classic varieties of Europe in spite of the long history of not being able to grow them in the East was enough to bring interested growers to see him. His vineyard at Vinifera Wine Cellars was a showplace, and he was constantly called on for advice or to graft vines. By temperament he was a born crusader; he "sold" people on growing vinifera with the same fervor that he attacked the French hybrids, which he considered to be inferior, and he passed on the European myth that hybrid grapes were toxic and could cause birth defects.

Wagner, on the other hand, was quick to cite the risks involved in growing the vinifera. Repeatedly he would say that while it was true that the classic varieties of grapes grown on a few very special vineyard sites in France made the world's best wine, he could not in good conscience recommend that retirees or new growers on a limited budget take the financial risk of growing them in the East. Practical growers, he said, owed it to themselves to discover which grapes would be the most reliable and profitable producers in their location.

One person who did much to further Frank's crusade on behalf of the vinifera was Robert de Treville Lawrence Sr., who had served in France as a press attaché for the State Department. When he retired, he decided to try growing grapes and making wine at his home in The Plains, Virginia. He met Frank, was impressed with what he had to say, and in 1972 organized an annual seminar in The Plains on growing vinifera. In 1973, he founded the Vinifera Wine Growers Association and established its quarterly journal. The journal and the annual meetings were influential in persuading Virginians and others to try growing the vinifera.

Among the pioneering vineyards and wineries in the late 1960s and early 1970s were the Stone Hill Winery in Missouri; Markko Vineyard in Ohio; Oliver Wine Company in Indiana; White Mountain Vineyards in New Hampshire; Presque Isle Wine Cellars in Pennsylvania; Frederick S. Johnson Vineyards, Bully Hill Vineyards, Benmarl Wine Company, and Hargrave Vineyard in New York; Chicama Vineyards in Massachusetts; Tabor Hill Vineyard in Michigan; Wollersheim Winery in Wisconsin;

KONSTANTIN FRANK

Konstantin Frank (1899–1985) was born in a German enclave in the Ukraine not far from Odessa, and he always considered himself German rather than Russian. He grew up working in his father's vineyard and making wine. At the time of the Russian Revolution, in 1917, he was studying viticulture, and after the civil war in 1924 he was appointed an assistant professor of viticulture at the agricultural college level. In 1926, he was put in charge of restoring a vineyard nine miles long and four miles wide, near the Dnieper River, that had been ravaged by phylloxera. He restored the vineyard using phylloxera-resistant rootstocks and invented a number of machines for use in the vineyard. In the Ukraine, where winter temperatures could reach -40°F, vines had to be buried in the winter, and Frank invented a grape plow to cover and uncover the vines. He received his doctorate from the Odessa Polytechnic Institute in 1930. The title of his dissertation was "Protection of Grapes from Freezing Damage."

When the German armies invaded Russia in 1941, Frank and his family managed to escape to Austria. At the end of the war, when Soviet troops were occupying Austria, the Franks moved to Bavaria, where he was put in charge of a large estate confiscated from the Nazis. In 1951, at the age of fifty-two, he came to the United States.

The Franks settled in Geneva, in the Finger Lakes, but it was not until 1953 that he was able to get a job growing the vinifera, for Charles Fournier at Gold Seal Vineyards. His experience in the Ukraine served him well, but it took five years and hundreds of thousands of grafts to establish a successful vinifera vineyard. In 1962, he left Gold Seal to start his own winery, Vinifera Wine Cellars.

HUDSON CATTELL

and Meredyth Vineyards in Virginia. In 1976, there were approximately 140 wineries in twenty-two states east of the Rockies. By this time, the vinifera-hybrid controversy gradually had faded out, when it was generally realized that there were locations where growing the vinifera was not practical or even possible and that the French hybrids had a very real place in eastern viticulture.

One of the major reasons for the increase in the number of small wineries was the passage of farm winery legislation in many eastern states. This legislation, although it varied in detail from state to state, permitted grape growers to make and sell wine on the premises where the grapes were grown. From the 1960s through 1980s, virtually all legislation benefiting wine was tied to agriculture, and the impetus for passage was to help local agriculture.

In 1968, Pennsylvania was the first state to enact a farm winery law, called the Limited Winery Act, the term "limited" referring to the cap on the amount of wine a winery could make each year. This amount was initially set at fifty thousand gallons and was soon doubled. Most of the early farm winery legislation in other states set similar maximum limits. A common provision was a requirement that the wineries use only grapes grown in their own state for making wine. Pennsylvania was a liquor monopoly state, and wine could only be sold through the state store system. The Limited Winery Act was the first crack in the monopoly system, because a winery could now for the first time sell its wine at the winery and to hotel, restaurant, club, and public service licensees of the Pennsylvania Liquor Control Board.

Indiana was the second state to pass a farm winery bill, and it was modeled on the Pennsylvania legislation. Other states followed. In New Jersey, the bill included a reduction in the state's excise tax from 30 cents to 10 cents a gallon, and in New York State the annual license fee was lowered from $1,500 a year to $125. Each time a farm winery law was enacted, it was followed by an increase in the number of wineries in that state. The passage of the farm winery bills made it easier to pass other legislation, such as permitting Sunday sales or opening sales outlets away from the winery.

Most of the small wineries started during the 1950s, 1960s, and 1970s were begun by one or two individuals, often a husband and wife. They grew the grapes, made the wine, and marketed it. The feeling of accomplishment that came from making a good wine was frequently the major motivation for opening a winery. Profit was seldom a consideration because the winery and its owners were usually supported by a full-time job or family money. Running a winery for profit or as an investment did not start to become a primary consideration until the 1980s. Investments by California and European interests in eastern vineyards and wineries were a rarity. However, in the late 1970s, the Zonin family in Italy invested in the Barboursville Winery in Barboursville, Virginia, and Dr. Gerhard Guth of Hamburg, Germany, planted vines for what was to become Rapidan River Vineyards in Culpeper, Virginia.

Many factors entered into the growth of the industry. The demand for information on how to grow grapes and make wine led to an increase in the amount of assistance available from state extension services. New research projects at universities included field trials to determine which varieties of grapes were best suited for various areas, disease control methods, types of yeasts to use in wine making, and vineyard and winery economics. Grower workshops and conferences were established, one of the first being the Pennsylvania Wine Conference, which attracted attendees throughout the East from the time it was first held in 1968.

Various organizations came into being that brought people together to learn, share experiences, and simply get to know one another. The American Wine Society, founded on Dr. Frank's front porch in 1967, was one of the first and quickly attracted a membership of more than one thousand. The Eastern Section of the American Society for Enology and Viticulture (then called the American Society of Enologists) was formed in 1976, and the start of the Society of Wine Educators included a group of people who first met at the American Wine Society conferences.

Trade conferences also helped bring people together. One of the oldest in the East—Wineries Unlimited, held for the first time in Lancaster, Pennsylvania, in 1976—featured seminars and a large trade show of vineyard and winery equipment and supplies. Newsletters and magazines were established in the 1970s, three of the most important being *The Vinifera Wine Growers Journal*, *The Pennsylvania Grape Letter* (later changed to *Wine East*), and *Eastern Grape Grower* (later changed to *Vineyard and Winery Management*).

Grower and winery organizations were formed in many states, sometimes statewide and sometimes for part of a state. In addition to providing services and programs for their members, they played a significant role in providing a voice for their industry in state government. In Maryland, Virginia, and Ohio, state organizations organized festivals for their states' wineries that attracted as many as 35,000 visitors in a single weekend. Many state organizations began to sponsor competitions in which their wineries could enter wines and win awards. One of the largest organizations, the New York Wine and Grape Foundation, was established in 1985 with first-year funding of $2 million from the state. Activities sponsored by the foundation have included research grants, highway signage, promotional programs, and a long-term export program designed to open new markets for New York wines.

Increasingly wineries from the East have entered wines in national and international competitions and have been rewarded with top medals, not only for vinifera wines but also for wines made from both hybrid and American varieties. These awards have helped the wineries sell their wines and have given the entire eastern wine industry credibility.

A major threat to the industry in the 1980s and early 1990s was an accelerating campaign by anti-alcohol groups to limit the consumption of alcohol. Often referred to as "neo-Prohibitionists," these groups used the same tactics against alcohol, including wine, that had been used so successfully by the anti-tobacco forces to limit smoking. In November 1991, CBS News devoted part of its televised *60 Minutes* program to "The French Paradox." The French Paradox referred to a 40 percent lower incidence of coronary disease in France than in the United States even though the French had a higher fat diet, exercised less, and smoked more. The French and American researchers interviewed pointed to moderate alcohol consumption, particularly of red wine, as an explanation for the paradox. The effect of the *60 Minutes* program on the wine industry was dramatic. Red wine sales increased by 44 percent during the weeks following the telecast. The subsequent publicity remained at a high level and included a revisiting of the French Paradox on a second *60 Minutes* program. Because of the health aspect of the publicity, the attacks on alcohol lost their momentum, and the industry escaped a major threat.

Eastern Wines in the Twenty-first Century

In 2001, two wineries were licensed in North Dakota, and for the first time all fifty states had wineries in operation. Sometime in the early 2000s, the number of wineries east of the Rockies was expected to pass the one thousand mark. On both Long Island and the Niagara peninsula of Ontario, multimillion dollar investments were being made in winery properties.

In several important ways the industry reflects its past. Wines are made from a wider variety of grapes and fruits than elsewhere in the world. Thanks to advances in viticulture and technology, the classic vinifera varieties can be grown in areas where it would not have been possible a few decades ago. The French hybrids and hybrids more recently developed at the New York State Agricultural Experiment Station and elsewhere are grown not only because of limitations of climate but also out of choice. Chambourcin, Vidal, Seyval Blanc, Vignoles, Cayuga White, and the newer Traminette are all being grown because there is a substantial market for wines made from them. Niagara, Concord, and other American varieties remain popular, particularly in the older grape-growing areas of the East, where generations of people have enjoyed those wines. One wine that was making a strong comeback in the early 2000s was Norton, a red American variety first introduced in 1830 by Dr. D. N. Norton of Richmond, Virginia, who had planted seeds from a native grape near a vinifera vine and later selected one of the promising seedlings, which became known as Norton.

In the South, where it has not been possible to grow the vinifera and French hybrids except at higher altitudes because of Pierce's disease, Muscadine wines have a wide following. Hybridizers at the Florida Agricultural Experiment Station have developed hybrid varieties, such as Stover and Blanc du Bois, that are resistant to Pierce's disease and do not have the grapey flavor of the Muscadines. In Minnesota, Wisconsin, and South Dakota, hybridizers have developed grape varieties that can withstand low winter temperatures while making wines that consumers enjoy.

Fruit wines have become popular in many parts of the East, and not just in Maine and other states where grapes either cannot be grown or grow only with the greatest difficulty. Blueberry wines, for example, have been made as nouveaus using carbonic maceration, as both dry and sweet wines and aged in various kinds of oak. Cherry and pear wines lightly aged in oak have a following, as do cranberry wines. More wineries make apple wines than wines from any other fruit. One Vermont winery in the early 1990s produced as many as twenty different varietal apple wines.

While there are many different climates in the continental mass east of the Rockies, they are all unlike the Mediterranean climate found in California. Growing conditions in the East more closely resemble those of France and Germany, and the Rieslings, Chardonnays, Cabernets, and many other varietals grown in the East have a closer resemblance to the wines of Europe than to the wines of California. There are of course subtle differences in varieties that are grown in different regions. Chardonnay, for example, can be made into a lower alcohol wine in the East than in California and is often considered a better match with seafood. Other wines unique to the East are blends of wines made from both vinifera and hybrid varieties.

If the eastern wine industry reflects its past, the past has also built a solid base for the future. It is because of its past that the East has become an important and unique wine region of the world.

[See also Alcohol and Teetotalism; Champagne; French Influences on American Food; Fruit Wines; Grapes; Prohibition; Temperance; Wine Barrels; Wine Books; Wine Bottles; Wine Casks; Wine Cellars; Wine Coolers; Wine Glasses; Wineries; Wine-Tasting Rooms.]

BIBLIOGRAPHY

Adams, Leon D. *The Wines of America.* 3rd ed. New York: McGraw-Hill, 1985. Chapters on eastern states include some history and brief winery references.
Cattell, Hudson, and Lee Miller. *Wine East of the Rockies.* Lancaster, PA: L and H Photojournalism, 1982. An overview of the industry in the early 1980s with many photographs.
Cattell, Hudson, and Linda Jones McKee. *Eastern Wines since Prohibition.* Forthcoming. The first book-length study of the modern wine industry in the East, utilizing thousands of pages of diaries and letters heretofore unavailable. The first comprehensive bibliography is also included.
Crosby, Everett. *The Vintage Years: The Story of High Tor Vineyards.* New York: Harper and Row, 1973. A good account of the difficulties and successes in establishing an early vineyard and winery in the wake of Prohibition.
Miller, Mark. *Wine—A Gentleman's Game: The Adventures of an Amateur Winemaker Turned Professional.* New York: Harper and Row, 1984. Memoirs of the founder in the 1960s of Benmarl Vineyards.
Morton, Lucie T. *Winegrowing in Eastern America: An Illustrated Guide to Viniculture East of the Rockies.* Ithaca, NY: Cornell University Press, 1985.
Pinney, Thomas. *A History of Wine in America from the Beginnings to Prohibition.* Berkeley: University of California Press, 1989. An excellent history with extensive bibliography.

HUDSON CATTELL

California Wines

For more than a century, California has been America's great wine-growing vineyard. Since World War II, between 80 percent and 90 percent of American wine production has come from the vineyards of the Golden State. Much of California, its deserts and high mountains, is not hospitable to viticulture. But the state's coastal valleys, from San Diego to Mendocino County, having an almost classic Mediterranean climate, are a natural home for wine grapes. So too are some of the western foothill areas of the Sierra Nevada mountain range. The great Central Valley, covering about 25,000 square miles, is one of the most important agricultural regions in the world. In this hot land, wine grapes also thrive under irrigation, but they rarely exhibit the fine quality found in those grown in the coastal valleys.

Mission and Rancho Wine

Viticulture arrived in Alta California, the region that is the state of California today, with the Franciscan fathers, who established a string of missions, beginning with San Diego in 1769. But the first grapes were not planted until 1778, just north of San Diego at Mission San Juan Capistrano. The first wine vintage was probably 1782. By 1823, there were twenty-one missions in the province, the most northerly at Sonoma.

Vineyards were established at all of the missions except for Mission Dolores at San Francisco. Their main purpose was to supply wine for the mass. The variety of grape that was ubiquitous in the Franciscan vineyards has become known as the Mission, an Old World variety whose origins have never been satisfactorily identified. It did well in the warm climate and gave prodigious yields, but its dry wines were poor, indeed. However, Angelica, which was more of a cordial than a wine, received high marks from foreign visitors to California when it had been well aged.

After Mexican independence from Spain in 1822, the flow of settlers from the south increased greatly. The pueblos at San Jose, Los Angeles, and Monterey grew, and ranchos, whose main products were cattle and hides, sprang up near the missions. Most settlers with land planted small vineyards. Wine and its distilled brandy, *aguardiente*, could be had throughout the province by the 1830s.

In 1834, the Mexican government began secularizing mission lands, a process that brought more settlers, who in turn planted more vineyards. Most of the mission vineyards declined in these years, but they also acted as a source for viticultural expansion. In the south, some mission vineyards became commercially important, especially at San Gabriel and San Fernando, both near Los Angeles. By the 1840s, a fairly profitable local wine industry had grown up around Los Angeles. The leader there was the French immigrant Jean-Louis Vignes, who transformed wine growing in the area into a commercial enterprise. In the mid-1840s, his El Aliso winery was producing up to forty thousand gallons of wine annually. He depended on the Mission grape, from which he was able to coax better wine than had been common at the missions.

Americans began trickling into Alta California in the 1840s, and many of them planted vineyards and made wine. Chief among these were William Wolfskill at Los Angeles and Jacob Leese at Sonoma. In 1846, Alta California was conquered almost bloodlessly by American forces and in 1848 was acquired by treaty from Mexico. Almost at the same moment gold was discovered in the Sierra Nevada foothills and the world rushed in. Mostly these newcomers were young men who collectively had a powerful thirst. Statistics for importation of alcoholic beverages at the port of San Francisco after 1849 suggest that this thirst ran from Champagne to Cognac. By the early 1850s, more than ten thousand barrels of foreign wine were passing through customs annually. In 1855, there were about twenty thousand "baskets" of Champagne imported.

Many newcomers saw fortunes to be made from supplying locally the needs of the prospectors and adventurers that would otherwise be filled by imports. Such was the case with wine, but it was clear to many that to compete with the foreign imports, better foreign wine grapes must be grown. Several historic importations were made in the 1850s, mostly by French and German nurserymen. Fine varieties were brought in to San Jose by A. Delmas, C. Lefranc, and P. Pellier, and to Sonoma by E. Dresel. These imports included Riesling, "Cabrunet," "Merlau," and many others. Nursery stock of all sorts was brought in from the East Coast, including vines for table grapes. The Zinfandel, which had come to Long Island from Austria as a table grape in 1829, was included in several such loads. However, most growers were content to plant more Mission vines.

By the early 1860s, a tiny wine industry was operating in California. Production centered in the Los Angeles area, but the wine was then shipped to San Francisco. The pioneer in this commerce was Charles Kohler, who had arrived in California from Germany in 1853. His partner, John Frohling, made their first vintage in 1854, and Kohler sold their wines in the north. The firm of Kohler and Frohling has been correctly identified as California's "pioneer wine house."

Although production began in Los Angeles, it was northern California that was destined to be the center of the state's wine industry within a few years. The market was there, as were the best soils and climate. The new centers were the Santa Clara Valley (Silicon Valley today) and the northern San Francisco Bay counties of Sonoma and Napa. The leader in Sonoma was Agoston Haraszthy, whose Buena Vista estate was the largest wine operation in California in the 1860s. Near San Jose, Charles Lefranc's Almaden Vineyard was the leader. And in the Napa Valley, the most important pioneers were Charles Krug and George Belden Crane. There were also many vineyards and small wineries in the Sierra foothills, but they were isolated and had to wait long for their glory days.

Hard Times in the 1870s

By the early 1870s, it was clear that northern California had surpassed the south in wine quality and total production. In 1874, Kohler shifted his main operation to the Sonoma Valley. Most wine was still made from the Mission grape and brought few plaudits to the state's producers. But gradually more and more producers saw the value in planting better European wine grape varieties. The good reputation of California wine, tiny as it was, came from a few white wines, the best produced in the German style from Riesling and Sylvaner grapes. For red wine production, it was understood by the mid-1870s that the Zinfandel was the most profitable, both for its high yield and good quality. Its wines were able to compete successfully with the inexpensive red Bordeaux that were commonly imported. However, it was almost never sold as Zinfandel. In fact, before the 1950s it was rare for California wine to be sold under varietal names. Generic terms were the order of the day, Claret, Burgundy, Chianti, Sauterne, and Chablis being the most common.

Attempts to compete with European sparkling wine, particularly Champagne, were not as successful. It was not until the 1870s that Agoston Haraszthy's son, Arpad, and Isador Landsberger were able to produce any real competition. Their Eclipse "Champagne" was a complex blend of wines, mostly white Zinfandel, Colombard, and Malvasia bianca. Later, Korbel (Sonoma), Paul Masson (San Jose), and Italian Swiss Colony (Sonoma) produced even better sparklers.

In the 1870s, large-scale wine growing began in the lower Central Valley, particularly in Fresno County. Francis Eisen was the pioneer there. Several large operations attempted to produce table wines, but their quality was not high. Gradually it became clear that fortified wines, mostly sherry and port, were to be the main products in this hot land. To the north, near Stockton, in the Lodi area, the beginnings of successful table wine production in the great valley took place at George West's El Pinal winery. This was possible because of the cooling air that moves east from the San Francisco Bay Area through the great water gap of the Sacramento River.

From 1873 to 1877, California wine producers suffered from the effects of the great depression that hurt all of the United States. Many producers were forced out of business. But those who managed to survive had the skills and the intelligence to take advantage of the good times that lay ahead in America's Gilded Age.

The Great Wine Boom

By the end of the 1870s, the general contours of the young wine industry were clear. Almost all table wine producers sold their products to merchants with large blending cellars in San Francisco. These businessmen blended the purchased wines and shipped them in bulk throughout the country. Some large merchants had their own bottling plants and retail outlets in larger eastern and midwestern cities. But lots more wine was sold to independent bottlers. However, there were a few wineries that had their own brands and developed this trade in the 1880s and 1890s. It was unheard of for producers to bottle their wines at the winery, the standard practice since the 1950s. Napa's Inglenook was the first, in the 1890s. And there were almost no followers.

The wine boom lasted from the late 1870s to the late 1880s. A combination of factors was involved in this growth and prosperity. European, and particularly French, wine imports to the East Coast were cut sharply by the phylloxera vine pest plague on the Continent. Good economic times in the United States helped to attract a huge flow of emigrants from southern and eastern Europe. These were people for whom wine with meals was a matter of everyday habit. Finally, after years of critical disdain, some California wines, at first Rieslings, had begun to catch the eye and palate of several influential eastern wine merchants. There was an explosion of wine-grape acreage in the valleys around the San Francisco Bay Area: Napa, Sonoma, Livermore, and Santa Clara were the leaders. During the boom years Napa and Sonoma wine-grape plantings grew by more than 30,000 acres.

The new plantings were more focused on good wine varieties than in earlier years. There was heavy emphasis on red wine production, for that finally had become the emphasis in the eastern markets. Zinfandel was by far the leader of this expansion. Lagging behind were Mataro (Mourvèdre), Grenache, and Cinsaut. There was some Cabernet Sauvignon planted, particularly in the Napa and Sonoma valleys and the Santa Cruz Mountains. Less emphasis was placed on white wines, but whites in the style of dry and sweet Bordeaux were somewhat fashionable. These were usually made with Sauvignon vert, Semillon, and Sauvignon blanc, often stretched with the bland Palomino. German whites from Riesling and Sylvaner were also popular in midwestern markets, such as St. Louis and Milwaukee. These were often stretched with the high-yielding but bland Gutedel and Burger.

Although much of this expansion resulted from massive corporate investment, a large number of enthusiastic entrepreneurs, who had usually made their fortunes in other fields, were attracted to the world of wine growing. This was most obvious in Napa, Livermore, and along the East Bay around the town of Mission San Jose, south of Oakland. More than the industrial producers, these men were attracted to the lighter-yielding wine varieties associated with world-class wines, particularly those of Bordeaux. A few experimented with Pinot Noir, Chardonnay, and Syrah, but with little success. There was also a strong ethnic character to these enthusiasts. Germans owned 49 percent of Napa's wineries in 1890. In Santa Clara County, 52 percent of the owners were foreign born, mostly French. There was also a very powerful Italian influence in Sonoma County. But before 1880, any Italian name associated with wine growing usually indicated an Italian Swiss from Ticino.

Two important institutions supported the wine boom of the late 1870s to the late 1880s. In 1880, the California legislature appropriated money for the Agriculture Department at the University of California at Berkeley earmarked for viticulture and wine-making research. Under Professor Eugene Hilgard, the university began a series of programs to promote better wine making. Hilgard was also a leader in the fight against the phylloxera, the plant louse that had devastated European vineyards, which had been spotted in Sonoma in 1873 and was slowly spreading.

Another state institution of importance was the Viticultural Commission, established and funded by the legislature, also in 1880. Here the emphasis was on the threat from phylloxera, but the commission also did much to spread useful information on viticultural techniques and sound wine-making principles. Later it became a leading voice proclaiming the excellence of California wine. In 1895, hard times and conflicts with the university brought an end to the commission.

By the 1890s, urban consumers in virtually all parts of the United States were able to buy California wine, which was almost always bottled locally. For the most part, they drank table wine generically labeled Claret, Burgundy, or Chianti. These were almost always blends put together by the West Coast wine merchants. If a wine was made from Cabernet Sauvignon or other red Bordeaux varieties, it was usually labeled Medoc, or sometimes merely Cabernet. Zinfandel, probably blended into 85 percent of all California red table wine, was almost never seen on a label except occasionally in California, where the strange name, unknown in Europe, was well known by wine drinkers. There was also a growing market for fortified California wines, usually sweet and mostly produced in the Central Valley. It should be noted that by far the greatest market for California wines was the Golden State itself, whose population in the 1890s barely exceeded 1 million, less than that of Silicon Valley in the early 2000s. California still held the position of being its own greatest market in the early twenty-first century.

Hard Times in the 1890s

By 1888, it was clear that far too many acres of grapes had been planted in California during the boom. A huge oversupply of wine was the result, followed by steeply falling prices. When the nation was hit in 1893 by its most devastating economic depression to that time, the California wine industry was beaten to its knees. Meanwhile, the phylloxera root louse had become a deadly infestation throughout the northern California coastal valleys. By 1897, there were barely 4,000 acres of wine grapes alive in Napa, down from more than 20,000 in 1890.

The oversupply and falling prices led to cutthroat competition among the California wine merchants. Wine producers and vineyardists could hardly cover their expenses. Good Zinfandel, which before 1890 averaged about $35 per ton, was soon bringing a grower less than $10 per ton. A result of this chaos was the creation in 1894 of the California Wine Association (CWA), dubbed the "wine trust" by its opponents. The CWA was made up of most of the large wine merchants of San Francisco, many of whom also owned large wineries and vast acreages of vineyards. Wine producers, who had to sell to the merchants, fought back by forming the California

Wine Corporation (CWC) in an attempt to sidestep the CWA monopoly. But the merchants had the upper hand, and after 1897, with the end of the depression, the CWC gave up. Thereafter most wine produced and sold in California was controlled by the CWA. Nevertheless, individual producers and merchants were able to keep their own brand identity, so the consumer rarely had a glimpse of the "trust" at work. It controlled prices and allocated markets, but within a few years most producers and vineyardists agreed that the CWA had brought relative stability to the California wine industry.

Prosperity Again

The good times after 1898 led to rapid replanting of most areas devastated by the phylloxera. By 1910, Napa growers had replanted about 12,000 acres of their blackened vineyards with phylloxera-resistant rootstock. There was significant expansion into new areas, the most important of which were the southern Santa Clara Valley, Mendocino County, the Lodi area, and the Cucamonga region of southern California.

Before the 1890s, a few California wineries had participated in the great international expositions of the late nineteenth century. The most significant of these was the Paris Expo in 1889, where a Livermore and two Napa wines won gold medals. Californians went all out at Chicago's Columbia Exposition in 1893 and won numerous awards. But the greatest accolades came in 1900, when two wineries won gold medals for Cabernet Sauvignon. One was located on Napa's Howell Mountain, the other on Monte Bello Ridge, above the Santa Clara Valley. Both areas are noted for their Cabernets in the twenty-first century.

Prohibition

With the prosperity and stability of the period before World War I, the wine industry faced its greatest threat ever, that of national prohibition of the production of alcoholic beverages. Several states already had their own prohibition laws, but a national policy would cripple the wine industry. The Eighteenth Amendment, which banned the production and sale but not necessarily the consumption of alcoholic beverages, was submitted to the states in 1917 and rode to victory on a wave of patriotic rhetoric in 1919.

Most California wineries went out of business, unless they had vineyards that kept them alive. Because sacramental and medicinal wines were not legally considered beverages, a few wineries maintained some production. Beaulieu Vineyards (Napa) and Wente Brothers (Livermore) were the leading examples.

Although the California wine industry had to all but close shop during the dry years, California vineyardists struck gold by selling their grapes all over the country to home wine makers. The Volstead Act, enforcing the amendment, drew the line on a legal beverage at 0.5 percent alcohol, but it allowed "fruit juices" to be made by the heads of households. If these happened to ferment, the 0.5 percent rule did not apply, unless the government could prove before a jury that the resulting beverage was in fact intoxicating. In no case was such a finding ever made during the thirteen years of Prohibition, and government at all levels rarely challenged the home wine maker.

Most Americans had never drunk wine, but they were not inclined to imprison their neighbors for allowing a barrel of crushed fruit to ferment. And a family could legally make two hundred gallons, or about four barrels, of homemade wine per year. Between 1920 and 1930, Americans consumed approximately 5 billion bottles of homemade wine, most of it red. The favorite varieties were Alicante Bouschet, Zinfandel, Petite Sirah (Durif), and Mataro (Mourvèdre).

So great were the profits from the "fresh grape deal," as it was called, in the early 1920s that California's vineyards grew in size to an acreage that was not surpassed until the boom years of the 1970s. The best grapes for shipping were the thick-skinned varieties, which meant that there was little demand for Cabernet Sauvignon or Sauvignon blanc. Such shy-yielding world-class varieties as these all but disappeared from California vineyards. (There had not been many anyway—less than 3 percent of the wine grape total.)

The trade in fresh grapes turned less profitable when the stock market crashed in 1929. Agricultural prices, which had been turning down since 1926, plummeted. By this time it was clear that Americans were fed up with Prohibition. The "noble experiment" had bred crime and an unhealthy attitude toward the consumption of alcoholic beverages. Now the "kick" of the alcohol content was what counted for almost all consumers. What interest there had been in drinking a good glass of wine with a meal did not disappear, but most who still had such tastes lived in homes where they had been making their own wine. Repeal in 1933 did not bring an end to the "fresh grape deal." In fact, in 1936 more homemade table wine was being consumed by Americans than that produced by California wineries.

Repeal and the Doldrums

Repeal came to the nation in the depths of the Great Depression. The wine that raced onto the market in 1934 was mostly of poor quality, produced with rundown equipment from the most ordinary of grapes by wine makers who, for the most part, did not know how to make good wine. The only wines that sold well in the years to come were fortified sweet wines, ports, sherries, and muscatels. And these were attractive mostly for their high alcohol content and their low price. A quart of port could be had in New York or Los Angeles for 29 cents.

From the 1930s through the 1950s, cheap fortified wines manufactured in huge wine factories in the Central Valley and southern California were overwhelmingly the chief product of California wineries. As late as 1950, more than 70 percent of California production consisted of fortified rather than table wines.

But a semblance of quality remained in the wines from the coastal valleys of northern California. A few producers of premium table wines had survived Prohibition and maintained their standards: Inglenook, Beringer, Larkmead, and Beaulieu in Napa; Fountaingrove and Korbel in Sonoma; Wente, Concannon, and Cresta Blanca in Livermore; and Almaden and Paul Masson in the Santa Clara Valley. And there were a few more scattered around these areas. They all still made good table wine for the small American market, mostly located in California, that wanted that style. Nevertheless, most of the production from these beautiful valleys left the area in tank cars to be bottled elsewhere and marketed under generic terms, such as Burgundy, Claret, Sauterne, and Chablis.

In the late 1930s, there was a small movement to produce fine wine that could be identified by the grape variety in California. Such varietal production would do away with the use of generic labels, which told the consumer little about what went into the bottle. The new idea was to sell Cabernet Sauvignon rather than Claret, Chardonnay rather than Chablis. By 1940, this idea was catching on, particularly as producers saw war in the offing, war that would surely cut the flow of wine from Germany and Italy, and probably from France. By 1943, one could find such varietal California wines in hotels and restaurants all over the United States, although generic wines were still popular and cheaper.

One unforeseen wartime situation changed the California wine industry forever. Few tank cars could be spared from the war effort to haul wine. This forced the wineries to bottle their own wines on site. Happily, this led to better control of quality and a more uniform and dependable product.

Another plus for California wine during these years came from the work of the Viticulture and Enology Department of the University of California at Davis, whose professors went out into the field to bring practical assistance to the state's wine makers. They worked to get growers to plant better wine varieties that were more suited to the soils and climate situations. In addition, Davis students were soon employed in the industry, practicing what they had learned. Good work was also done at Fresno State College, which established a viticulture program in 1948. Enology was added in 1956.

The Second Wine Boom

As had been the case in the 1880s, the growing interest in fine table wines brought enthusiastic entrepreneurs into small-scale production of such wines from world-class varietals. Cabernet Sauvignon, Pinot Noir, Chardonnay, Sauvignon blanc, and Chenin Blanc were the most popular varieties of French origin. Riesling and Sylvaner led the field of fine German grapes.

Between 1936 and 1955, several such producers began attracting attention, particularly from consumers in northern California, Los Angeles, New York, and Washington, D.C. In Napa there were Mayacamas, Souverain, Stony Hill, and Freemark Abbey; in Sonoma, Buena Vista and Hanzell; in the Santa Cruz Mountains, Martin Ray and Hallcrest. And there was a pair of larger-scale newcomers in the Napa Valley with similar ideas. Louis Martini's varietal wines came on the market in 1940, and the Mondavi family took over the old Charles Krug winery in 1943.

By the late 1950s, California table wines were clearly on the rise. By the mid-1960s, they had passed fortified wines in total gallons produced, and there were scores of wineries, large and small, in a race to attract those consumers whose tastes were now focused on fine continental cuisine and the proper wines to accompany it. It is no coincidence that Julia Child's hugely popular *Mastering the Art of French Cooking* appeared in 1961.

By the early 1970s, it was clear that California, and America as a whole, was experiencing a second wine boom. Foreign imports soared as fast as did California production. There were wine-tasting clubs, consumer wine publications, and wine columns in leading newspapers. There was even a rush of interest in home wine making using top varieties. Wine-grape acreage in

California rose 120 percent between 1969 and 1975. Most of the expansion was in table wine varieties, but a large number of these new acres were in the Central Valley, where inexpensive jug wines were produced. These also had an escalated popularity.

The question of whether California was capable of producing truly world-class wines was answered in Paris in 1976. A blind tasting was put together there by the wine merchant Steven Spurrier. He matched fine California Chardonnays with five top white Burgundies, and fine California Cabernet Sauvignons with five *grand cru* red Bordeaux. The tasters represented the height of the French wine establishment. When the results were announced, they were shocked to learn that they had picked a 1973 Chateau Montelena Chardonnay and a 1973 Stag's Leap Wine Cellars Cabernet Sauvignon, both of Napa, as winners. This world-famous tasting did not prove that California wines were better than French wines, but it certainly placed the Golden State's best on a level with the best of France. The American wine-drinking public was made well aware of the outcome by the press and often reminded of it thereafter.

In the 1970s and 1980s, new regions were opened to premium California wine growing. Most significant was the Central Coast, from Santa Barbara to Monterey. At first the most important area was Monterey County, where the explosion raised the acreage from 2,000 to 30,000 in the span of six years. The growth in San Luis Obispo County, to the south, emphasized red wine around the town of Paso Robles. Chardonnay was dominant in and around the Edna Valley. Between 1970 and 1977, the county acreage grew from 600 to 4,400; by 2001, it stood at 22,000.

Just to the south, vineyard land in Santa Barbara County also expanded. Here the emphasis was on varieties that enjoyed the cool maritime climate of the coastal valleys, particularly Pinot Noir and Chardonnay. From 170 acres of wine grapes in 1970, the total grew to 6,000 in 1977 and to more than 17,000 in 2001.

Sparkling wines had been economically successful in California since the 1880s. But after 1970, statistics soared, partly as the result of large-scale California investment in bottle-fermented sparklers by major French Champagne producers. Production of bulk-process sparkling wine from Central Valley grapes also grew in these years.

This second California wine boom began leveling off in the mid-1980s, with American per capita consumption of wine peaking in 1986, having more than doubled since 1969. This number drifted down about 4 percent per year and began heading back up again in 1994. The greatest decline was in the most inexpensive segment of California wine production, but in the premium sector of the market, sales continued to rise. It was said that Americans were perhaps drinking less, but drinking better, California wine.

The 1990s and After

The general rise in national prosperity after 1991 was reflected in nearly all aspects of the California wine industry. Sales of table wine led the way, with an almost complete domination of varietal labels over all but the most inexpensive jug wines. Cabernet Sauvignon led the reds, with Merlot as a varietal taking over second place from Zinfandel in 2000. All red Bordeaux varieties were on the rise in the 1990s.

For whites, no wine variety in California could approach Chardonnay in acreage. Its closest premium rival, Sauvignon blanc, had but one-eighth as many vines in 2001. German-style whites were one of the casualties of this period. Riesling and Gewürztraminer acreage fell from 14,000 to 3,500 between 1980 and 2000.

California wine producers have searched for additional varieties to attract customers and expand their product lines. Of the reds, Merlot has been the most successful, followed by the French Syrah of the Rhône and the Italian Sangiovese. Among the whites there has been no success story. In the late 1980s, some thought white Rhône varieties had a chance, but by the early 2000s only the Viognier had had even a small success.

The great comeback story was the Zinfandel. After a blossoming of its premium image in the 1970s, it fell from favor in the 1980s, but its pink cousin, white Zinfandel, from the same grape, proved a great success. Thought a fad at first, this light, slightly sweet wine continued it sales in the millions of cases as the twenty-first century opened. And in the late 1980s, the rich and extracted Zinfandel that was possible in the cooler valleys and foothills roared back to popularity. One could find numerous Zinfandels selling for $30 and up. In 2001, Sonoma Zinfandel growers were paid more per ton than Napa growers had received three years earlier for their Cabernet Sauvignon.

Consolidation and growth have typified the California wine industry since 1990. In the early 2000s, big corporations controlled a large percentage of the most popular and, in some cases, the most prestigious brands. And it is often impossible to tell from reading the label who actually owns the winery, where the wine was produced, or where the grapes were grown. Since the 1980s, the U.S. government has administered through the Bureau of Alcohol, Tobacco, and Firearms (BATF) an appellations-of-origin system that might tell the consumer if the wine came from grapes of the Napa Valley or the Sierra Foothills. But the commonplace "California" designation is found on most bottles of California wine. Still, most of the best and most expensive California wines do bear an authentic appellation designation on their front labels.

The rising prestige of California wines can be seen partly in export figures. In the early 1980s, California wine exports were barely 10 million gallons. By the mid-1990s, this number had climbed to 30 million. In 2001, it stood at more than 75 million. The top five direct markets were the United Kingdom, Canada, Japan, Germany, and Ireland. Belgium and the Netherlands were important transshipment destinations.

The California wine industry's accelerated expansion in the 1990s, like most such booms, went too far. Much of the acreage growth came from the planting of world-class wine varieties in the Central Valley to produce what the industry has come to call "fighting varietals." Technical advances have made much better, yet inexpensive, varietal wines possible in hot climates. Between 1990, and 2000, Central Valley acreage of Cabernet Sauvignon and Merlot grew from 8,000 to 47,000. Chardonnay grew from 8,000 to 27,000. When the new vines came into production after 1999, grape prices in the valley fell below cost of production.

But the image of California as the home of world-class wines has not been tarnished by such events. As the twenty-first century opened, prices for many Napa Valley Cabernets exceeded those of the *grand cru* wines of Bordeaux. Pinot Noirs from selected locations rivaled *premier cru* Burgundies. It is a strange fact that more than 80 percent of California wine production was consumed by about 12 percent of the adult U.S. population. But, as of the early 2000s, sales had continued to rise every year since 1992. And in that period the retail value of these sales had climbed 74 percent, to almost $20 billion annually. The greatest part of this growth was in the wines from the world-class varieties that in the 1950s had rarely been a part of California's vineyard land.

[*See also* Alcohol and Teetotalism; California; Champagne; Child, Julia; French Influences on American Food; Gallo, Ernest and Julio; Grapes; Mondavi, Robert; Prohibition; Mondavi; Temperance; Wine Barrels; Wine Books; Wine Bottles; Wine Casks; Wine Cellars; Wine Coolers; Wine Glasses; Wineries; Wine-Tasting Rooms.]

BIBLIOGRAPHY

Adams, Leon A. *The Wines of America*. Boston: Houghton-Mifflin, 1973. 2nd ed., New York: McGraw-Hill, 1978; 3rd ed., New York: McGraw-Hill, 1985; 4th ed., New York: McGraw-Hill, 1990. Excellent on developments through the 1980s. Earlier editions have the most complete historical coverage.

Amerine, M. A., and V. L. Singleton. *Wine: An Introduction*. Berkeley: University of California Press, 1976. Technical, but a perfect reference for the serious amateur.

Baldy, Marian W. *The University Wine Course*. San Francisco: Wine Appreciation Guild, 1993. A basic text on wine and its appreciation. Technical, but a good read.

Conaway, James. *The Far Side of Eden*. Boston: Houghton-Mifflin, 2002.

Conaway, James. *Napa: The Story of an American Eden*. Boston: Houghton-Mifflin, 1990. Both Conaway books are controversial for their observations of the private lives of Napa celebrities. But both give excellent insight to Napa society and environmental issues.

Gallo, Ernest, and Julio Gallo. *Ernest and Julio: Our Story*. New York: Random House, 1994. Useful inside information on the world's largest wine operation. Many controversial issues sidestepped.

Lapsley, James T. *Bottled Poetry: Napa Winemaking from Prohibition to the Modern Era*. Berkeley: University of California Press, 1996. A scholarly and well-written history. Well-documented. Gives a good picture of the California wine industry in these years, as well as Napa's.

Lukacs, Paul. *American Vintage: The Rise of American Wine*. Boston: Houghton-Mifflin, 2000. A general history.

Mondavi, Robert. *Harvest of Joy: How the Good Life Became Great Business*. New York: Harcourt Brace, 1998. Recollections by one of the key movers of the modern wine revolution in America.

Peninou, Ernest P. *History of the Sonoma Viticultural District*. Santa Rosa, CA: Nomis Press, 1998. A huge compendium of useful North Coast wine history.

Peninou, Ernest P., and Gail G. Unzelman. *The California Wine Association and Its Member Wineries: 1894–1920*. Santa Rosa, CA: Nomis Press, 2000. Loaded with information on many of California's most important wine operations.

Pinney, Thomas. *A History of Wine in America: From the Beginnings to Prohibition*. Berkeley: University of California Press, 1989. By far the best and most comprehensive work on the subject. Very good on early California.

Robinson, Jancis. *The Oxford Companion to Wine*. Oxford and New York: Oxford University Press, 1994. Numerous entries on all aspects of California wine and its history.

Stuller, Jay, and Glen Martin. *Through the Grapevine: The Business of Wine in America*. New York: Wynwood Press, 1989. Emphasis is on California since the 1960s.

Sullivan, Charles L. *A Companion to California Wine: An Encyclopedia of Wine and Winemaking from the Mission Period to the Present*. Berkeley: University of California Press, 1998.

Sullivan, Charles L. *Like Modern Edens: Winegrowing in the Santa Clara Valley and Santa Cruz Mountains, 1798–1981*. Cupertino, CA: California History Center, 1982.

Sullivan, Charles L. *Napa Wine: A History from Mission Days to the Present*. San Francisco: Wine Appreciation Guild, 1994.

Sullivan, Charles L. *Zinfandel: A History of a Grape and Its Wine*. Berkeley: University of California Press, 2003.

Teiser, Ruth, and Catherine Harroun. *Winemaking in California*. New York: McGraw-Hill, 1983. Good for its regional emphasis and for the period from 1933 to 1960. Much of the material is based on oral history interviews. Wonderful illustrations.

Thompson, Bob. *The Wine Atlas of California and the Pacific Northwest*. New York: Simon and Schuster, 1993. The maps are excellent, as is the discussion of the federal government's system of American Viticultural Areas.

CHARLES L. SULLIVAN

Wine, Fruit, *see Fruit Wines*

Wine, Hot Spiced

Hot spiced wine, often called "mulled wine," is typically made by simmering red, and occasionally white, wine with a mixture of citrus (juice, slices, or zest from lemons or oranges) and virtually any combination of spices, including cinnamon, clove, allspice, ginger, cardamom, nutmeg, or mace. Wines ranging from dry table wines to sweet ports or fortified wines (strengthened with additional alcohol) are used. Brandy, liqueurs, or other spirits and water are sometimes added.

This beverage has an ancient history, stemming from early civilizations of 5000 B.C.E. (Mesopotamia and Egypt) and subsequently Greece and Rome. Wines were sometimes infused with herbs and spices for a range of gastronomic, hallucinogenic, medicinal, religious, and preservation purposes. In medieval Europe wine was customarily consumed as a safer, healthier alternative to often-contaminated water. In colder climates, wine and other fermented beverages were sometimes heated to create longed-for and much-needed warmth. At the same time, local substances such as tree bark, resin, leaves, flowers, roots, and seeds were often added for preservation, to mask bad tastes in deteriorating wine, or for their perceived healing properties. For those who could grow or buy them, it was also possible to use European bay leaf, caraway and coriander seed, saffron, myrtle, wormwood, and such sweeteners as raisins and honey.

The introduction of tropical spices to medieval Europe opened the door to a wide range of flavors. Wildly expensive and exotic at the time, they were available only to the wealthy and were used to enrich the libation hippocras, the descendant of an ancient Roman drink. Hippocras was made from wine heated with honey, pepper, and many other spices, such as galingale (similar to ginger), and it was often consumed as an elixir at the end of a large feast. Although it occasionally appeared later in seventeenth-century cookbooks, it had lost most of its high status and popularity by then.

By the latter part of the seventeenth century, European trade with India and the Indonesian Spice Islands had begun to flourish. The trade brought in substantial quantities of spice at somewhat lower prices, but products were still not available economically to all. These tropical spices (such as cinnamon and nutmeg) began to replace earlier European flavorings in heated wines and dramatically changed the taste and character of the wines. In addition, the British in India encountered a local spiced "paunch" (later called "punch"), a warmed beverage consisting of a fermented drink, sugar, water, citrus, and spices. Taken back to England, it became a favorite drink; the elite substituted their own wine or spirits and served it hot or cold at large social gatherings. Other European nations involved in the spice trade (France, Germany, the Netherlands, Norway, and Sweden) enjoyed their own versions. These appeared in the American colonies as mulled wine, sometimes made with thickening raw eggs or yolks, which would be cooked by the hot wine. The resultant curdling was reminiscent of such other period concoctions as possets, caudles, and syllabub.

Many English, German, Dutch, and Scandinavian emigrants who came to America brought these long-held traditions and prepared heated and spiced libations for winter festivals, in particular Christmas. Somewhat varied, they were served under such names as Swedish glogg, German *Glühwein*, and English wassail or mulled wine. Successive waves of European immigration brought others. By the late 1800s these warmed spiced wines had become an integral part of the American Christmas menu, largely because of the strong influence of the mid-nineteenth-century novel *A Christmas Carol* by Charles Dickens. Hot spiced wine was frequently served alongside or in lieu of eggnog enjoyed at middle-class tables, sometimes with appropriate temperance substitutions of fruit juice. At this time tropical citrus fruits were becoming more common in local shops, and packaged ground spices were more affordable and available.

Like many foods resulting from the American amalgam of heritages, adult Americans of diverse backgrounds and cultures consume hot spiced wines during the winter months. Still centered on the Christmas season at holiday parties, caroling, and family gatherings, it has also become integral to the hospitality at many American ski resorts. Recipes for hot spiced wine and its many namesakes are usually included in special holiday issues of contemporary American food and wine publications, as well as in popular cookbooks. With increasing focus on good quality and tradition, they sometimes highlight early techniques that include manual grinding and the individualistic creation of spice and fruit blends. For those with less time, premixed mulling sachets and spice blend packets dissolve instantly in warmed wine. Some modern American recipes call for the substitution or addition of fruit juices, such as cranberry or apple, making the drinks more appropriate for youngsters.

[*See also* Christmas; Fruit Wines.]

BIBLIOGRAPHY

Brown, John Hull. *Early American Beverages*. Rutland, VT: Tuttle, 1966.
McGovern, Patrick E. *Ancient Wine: The Search for the Origins of Viniculture*. Princeton, NJ: Princeton University Press, 2003.
Oliver, Sandra L. "Joy of Historical Cooking: Possets, Caudles, Syllabubs, and Various Mulled Items." *Food History News*, Fall 1997.

TONYA HOPKINS

Wine Barrels

Wine barrels have a long history and are essential to the making of many wines. The American wine industry is the largest user of imported French oak barrels, employing them as well as domestic oak barrels. The importance of these wooden barrels lies in the flavors the wood imparts during wine's maturation process. The woods used come from various sources, but the most important is oak. American oak, *Quercus alba*, or European oak, *Q. rubur* and *Q. sesslis*, are the most sought after; they are, however, processed in entirely different ways and impart very distinct flavors. Most American oak is kiln-dried from sawn wood, which lends very strong flavors to wine. European oak is split wood and, for the most part, air-dried, ideally for three years, which gives wine a softer flavor that changes with the age of the wood used. This processing method also imparts a higher tannin level to the wine. It is essential that wine makers know the source and age of the woods they are using. For example, tannins are more evident in wood that is harvested in summer than in spring, and each wooded area may have a *goût de terroir* ("taste of the earth") that makes its flavor unique; thus, a mistake in the selection of wood can lead to difficulties as the wine matures.

In the United States, many wooden barrels still come from whiskey industry cooperages, which produce about 800,000 barrels; of this total, a scant fifty thousand are for the wine trade. The standard American barrel, which holds fifty gallons, is made from domestic oak, accounting for about 3 percent of the annual oak harvest. Unlike the European trade, there does not seem to be the demand for specificity in wood by American wine makers, perhaps because of the stronger initial flavors American oak imparts. Several prominent French coopers are experimenting in the United States with specific wood sources and plan to produce barrels in the European manner.

[*See also* Wine Casks.]

STEVEN M. CRAIG

Wine Books

The earliest books on wine in America were either practical (John Adlum, *A Memoir on the Cultivation of the Vine in America*, 1823) or promotional (Agoston Haraszthy, *Grape Culture, Wines, and Wine-Making*, 1862). Such encyclopedic books of European origin as André Jullien's *The Topography of All the Known Vineyards* (1824) and Cyrus Redding's *A History and Description of Modern Wines* (1833) were influential authorities. Their tradition continues in the present day through such works as Frank Schoonmaker's *Encyclopedia of Wine* (1964) and Alexis Lichine's *Encyclopedia of Wines and Spirits* (1967). The discussion and appreciation of wine for the general reader rather than for the wine maker or merchant was begun by the Englishman George Saintsbury, in his *Notes on a Cellar-Book* (1920). What he started was carried on by other English writers such as Warner Allen and Maurice Healy and by the Anglo-French André Simon, who wrote more than a hundred books on food and wine between 1905 and 1973. Saintsbury himself enjoyed all sorts of wines, but his followers took a narrower view: for them, wine meant the *grands vins* of Bordeaux, Burgundy, and Champagne, and that view powerfully influenced American ideas about wine for many years.

They were succeeded by other generations of English writers, of more catholic tastes, who continue to have a large American readership: Cyril Ray, Hugh Johnson, Gerald Asher, Jancis Robinson, and Oz Clarke are the best known. Johnson's *World Atlas of Wine* (1971) gave a new detail to the study of wine, and Jancis Robinson's *Oxford Companion to Wine* (1994) comes first among the works of general reference.

American writers in this English mode appear rather late and irregularly, beginning with Frank Schoonmaker and Tom Marvel, whose *Complete Wine Book* (1934) is still a readable and instructive book. They collaborated again on *American Wines* (1941), a book that had no predecessor and is still important. Rather different, but widely influential, were the books of Philip Wagner. His *American Wines and How to Make Them* (1933) was meant to instruct the home wine maker under Prohibition but managed to convey much general information; a later version is called *Grapes into Wine* (1976). Wagner belongs to the tradition of practical literature, but he was read for general interest as well. *Wine: An Introduction for Americans* (1965), by the University of California scientists Maynard Amerine and Vernon Singleton, was published when the American boom in wine was beginning, and it profited from that coincidence: it is now seriously out of date. The first coffee-table book about California wine is by M. F. K. Fisher and Max Yavno: *The Story of Wine in California* (1962). It has had many imitators.

Many, if not most, living American writers on this topic are journalists turning out immediate copy or compiling guides that tell readers what to buy. But substantial and original books, reflecting the new status of American wines, have been written, among them, Leon Adams's *The Wines of America* (1973), Ruth Teiser and Katherine Harroun's *Winemaking in California* (1983), and Charles Sullivan's *A Companion to California Wine* (1998).

[*See also* Wine, *subentry* Historical Survey.]

THOMAS PINNEY

Wine Bottles

The modern wine bottle, a bottle capable of being laid on its side, probably dates to the early 1700s in Europe. Prior to this, wine bottles were often flask shaped and stood upright. Some, because of their rounded appearance, are referred to as "onions" or "bladders." In ancient times, wine was stored in standing containers; the Romans were known to have transferred the liquid into smaller glass containers when it was served.

The development of the modern bottle came about with the desire to age and store wine effectively while using as much of the storage area's space as possible. This resulted in the development of a bottle that could be laid horizontally in row upon row, a system called "binning." Laying bottles horizontally would not have been possible without a change in their stoppers from glass and attached string to cork. Although cork had been used in ancient times, it was not widely used again until its attributes were rediscovered in the 1700s. Cork was ideal for complementing the new bottle design. It was economical, provided a tight seal, and its ability to breathe allowed for an aging process that enhanced the wine. The capacity of cork to maintain the stability of the wine's condition while the bottle rested on its side altered the storage and aging process.

The standard modern wine bottle is 750 milliliters, although bottles are made in a variety of sizes, the largest being the Nebuchadnezzar, which is the equal of sixteen bottles and usually is used only by sparkling-wine producers. More common large-format bottles are the magnum, 1.5 milliliters, or the equivalent of two bottles; the double magnum, 3 liters; and the Imperiale, 6 liters. There is a cachet to the large bottle. Some argue that because of the large size the wine will mature more slowly and age with finer attributes. There is by no means unanimous agreement on this, but the theory has done much to enhance the collectibility and price of these limited edition behemoths when they are released by prestige producers.

Since the early 1990s, some subtle changes in bottle shape have occurred that allow for the elimination of the capsule covering the stopper. And a variety of synthetic stoppers have also been developed. American wine producers, such as Robert Mondavi, have been involved in the research and creation of these innovations but have been slow to adopt the changes for their premium wine brands.

[See also Bottling; Corks; Mondavi, Robert; Mondavi Wineries; Wine Barrels; Wine Casks; Wine Cellars.]

STEVEN M. CRAIG

Wine Casks. Cask of aging wine, Sonoma County, California, January 1942. *Prints and Photographs Division, Library of Congress/Russell Lee*

the wine making process, such as an open vat. Wooden casks have been used to ferment, store, and ship wine for well over two thousand years. A major change in modern wine making techniques with respect to wooden casks centers on the use of stainless-steel tanks during the initial fermentation process and then transfer of the wine into wooden casks.

The wooden cask still has a very important part to play in the wine making process: if wine were made entirely in stainless steel, it would display strong elements of the fruit and have a less tannic quality, making the aging process difficult and long-term aging almost impossible. The character of the wine would also be completely different, as wood is an essential part not merely of aging but also of adding flavor. Robert Mondavi, one of America's premier vintners, conducted extensive experiments with different wooden casks and the same base wine, confirming the major effect of wood and, specifically, of aging in casks in the creation of desired flavors in wine. The wooden cask may not be as important as the grape, but great red wines cannot be created without it, and knowledge of wood is essential for a competent wine maker.

[See also Mondavi, Robert; Wine Barrels.]

STEVEN M. CRAIG

Wine Casks

"Wine cask" is a term for a cylindrical wooden container; it is often used in the same context as "wine barrel" but can indicate any form of wooden container used in

Wine Cellars

The wine cellar is where wine is often stored by the producer, the merchant, or the consumer. In all cases the desire is the same: to allow the wine to mature and to protect it from deterioration. Cellars, or wine storage areas, can be traced to the ancient world, where it became known that the aging of some wines would bring about positive changes. Cellars were often just that, below-ground areas, but since the twentieth century they may be any area where it is possible to control temperature, humidity, light, and vibration.

Wine does not thrive in extreme or changing temperatures. A constant 45° to 60° F is often recommended, along with a relatively high humidity of 70 percent or more, to ensure the cork's stability as the wine rests on its side, a position that allows the liquid to keep the cork damp. Light also changes the aging process, so the environment should be dark as well as free from vibration. This is, of course, the ideal and is rarely achieved in most private cellars. Consequently, many wine drinkers are increasingly relying on commercial storage cellars for their fine wines.

The condition of the wine when it is cellared is of critical importance. Unless purchased by the consumer at the estate or winery, it is impossible to ascertain every step of a wine's shipping and storage process. A wine may be subject to any number and manner of abuses before it is even received by the local distributor, at which point it still may have several steps to go before it reaches its initial buyer, who may then in turn sell it at auction. Although it is possible to discover certain characteristics—the fill, clarity, and cork integrity among others—of a poorly stored wine by looking at the bottle, the only real test is to taste it. A cellar, no matter how ideal its conditions, will not reclaim a poorly handled wine. It is therefore strongly recommended that a wine be sampled before putting it in long-term storage.

There have been numerous experiments in the storage of wine, including changing the stopper material from natural cork to man-made material and even storing the wine under water (which seems to delay the aging process). However, be it a closet adapted to create a controlled environment in a city apartment or a historic cellar at a fine estate, the purpose is the same—to age, preserve, and store wine.

[See also Wine Bottles; Wine, subentry Historical Survey; Wine, subentry on Later Developments.]

STEVEN M. CRAIG

Wine Coolers

Wine coolers, low-alcohol (5 percent) beverages made with wine, sweetened fruit juices, and carbonation, are similar to the wine-based cocktails and "coolers" historically prepared in saloons, taverns, and bars across America. These prepackaged drinks successfully entered the retail market on a small scale in 1981, when two entrepreneurs from Santa Cruz, California, created the California Cooler. Concurrent with an escalating American fondness for convenience and portability, the coolers were sold chilled in colorful four-packs of single-serving bottles through widespread distribution channels. Positioned as a beer alternative, they appealed primarily to young social drinkers and to female consumers.

Many manufacturers followed with similar brands, such as E. and J. Gallo's Bartles & Jaymes and Seagram's Coolers. Sizable advertising expenditures of these larger companies elevated consumer awareness and fueled significant growth in this new alcoholic beverages category. Wine coolers reached peak popularity in the mid-1980s with flavors like strawberry, peach, and tropical fruit, which proved enjoyably refreshing to a generation weaned on soft drinks. This welcome spike for then-declining alcohol sales was seen as promising; it was thought to offer the possibility to cultivate future wine consumers.

Changing market dynamics, consumer preferences, and plummeting sales rendered wine coolers a fad by the early 1990s. The term is still used in reference to a category now comprising mostly fruit-flavored, malt liquor–based brews more appropriately called "malternatives" or "hard beverages."

[See also Cocktails; Fruit Wines.]

BIBLIOGRAPHY

"Prepared Cocktails." In *Adams Liquor Handbook*, 195–206. Norwalk, CT: Adams Business Media, 2002.

Houston, Kerri. "Liquor Manufacturers Court Young Buyers with Alcopop." *Investor's Business Daily*, 24 Oct. 2002.

Lender, Mark Edward, and James Kirby Martin. *Drinking in America: A History*. Rev. ed. New York: Free Press, 1987.

"Wine Coolers." In *Adams Wine Handbook*, 49–61. Norwalk, CT: Adams Business Media, 2002.

TONYA HOPKINS

Wine Glasses

Wine through the ages has been consumed from every kind of vessel imaginable: pottery bowls, bejeweled gold goblets, fine Venetian glass, and ordinary glass containers.

It is known that the ancient Romans drank and served from glass containers and that the Venetians in the sixteenth century perfected a specialized form of glass-making, but it was in the seventeenth century that the British developed a lead and flint glass that revolutionized the industry. This new glass was further adapted by designs and shapes for different wines and spirits into the eighteenth century.

Although no one can say with certainty what the ideal glass form is from which to drink wine, certain standards are universal. The glass should be clear with an unobstructed view of the contents, and the bowl should be large enough to allow the release of the aroma when the wine interacts with the air. It should have a stem long enough that it is possible to hold the glass without warming the liquid in it. The International Standards Organization (ISO) set the basic standard for a tasting glass at a total capacity of 215 milliliters for a tasting of 50 milliliters. The tasting glass should be tulip shaped with the bowl at its widest diameter being 65 millimeters and with a top diameter of 46 millimeters, giving it a modest chimney effect. The height of the glass should be 155 millimeters with a bowl height of 100 millimeters. This glass would serve for the drinking of almost any kind of wine including sparklers.

The preferred style for sparkling wines is the flute, which gives maximum opportunity to view the bubbles while affording them a longer life as the wine is consumed. The coup glass, which according to legend was modeled from the breast of Marie Antoinette, is not desirable because it does not show the bubbles rising, and it dissipates the bouquet over too wide an area. Variations to the classic tasting glass include a larger bowl for Pinot noir, a more enhanced chimney for Cabernet Sauvignon and Merlot, and a less enhanced chimney for Chardonnay and other white wines.

Georg Riedel, an Austrian manufacturer, has designed glasses for dozens of different varietals, including a tasting glass of just 26 milliliters, or five-eighths of an ounce, that allows for thirty-five portions from the standard 750 milliliter bottle. They range in price from several hundred dollars for the finest crystal glass in its own leather carrying case to less than ten dollars for an everyday potash-based glass. Riedel has even designed glasses for specific appellations and ages of wine. The basics are the same, however, and no one needs a dozen different glass styles to appreciate wine.

[See also Dining Rooms, Table Settings, and Table
   Manners; Glassware; Wine, subentry Historical Survey;
   Wine-Tasting Rooms.]

STEVEN M. CRAIG

Wineries

Wineries are the physical establishments where wine and brandies are made from grapes as well as other fruits (such as berries and peaches). The wine-making process involves many stages, from grape growing, harvesting, and crushing to fermentation, filtering, blending, aging, bottling, and storing. This process places wineries at the heart of production and manufacturing for the U.S. wine industry. Many American wineries grow and harvest grapes from vineyards on their own estates, and a large number purchase grapes from independent growers, later applying their wine-making techniques. A more elastic and virtual definition of the term is frequently used to refer to wine producers without traditional facilities who may rent space or produce wines at various locations.

Wineries range in types and sizes from smaller boutiques utilizing artisanal methods to larger industrial enterprises producing more mass-market products. While the majority of American wineries are small, family-owned operations, the four largest U.S. wineries account for nearly 50 percent of the nation's entire wine storage capacity. California is home to more than half of the wineries in America, but there is at least one winery in all fifty states (wineries in Alaska and North Dakota are the most recent additions). Nearly all wineries are in rural areas, close to their grape or fruit crops.

Wine making has long been part of American history and has connections to early settlers, colonists, and subsequent waves of European immigrants who brought long-held traditions of making and drinking wine. Spanish missionaries are considered to be the first to have brought the art of wine making to the Americas to parts of Texas and California. By the last quarter of the eighteenth century the missionaries had successfully planted vineyards to make sacramental wines at the twenty-one California missions they founded, stretching from as far south as San Diego to as far north as Sonoma. Some of the nation's earliest wine-making experiments took place in the oldest states along the eastern seaboard (Virginia is among the best-known early but failed attempts of the French wine enthusiast Thomas Jefferson). In the early to mid-1800s, states such as Indiana, Kansas, Missouri, Ohio, North Carolina, New Jersey, and New York were all successful grape-growing and wine-making regions. In the 1840s Nicholas Longworth, regarded as the founding father of American wine, produced the country's first successful commercial wines using the native American Catawba grape, grown near Cincinnati, Ohio.

Aside from the phylloxera that led to the closing of several California wineries that had successfully grown European vines (*Vitis vinifera*), by the late nineteenth century there was a vibrant, thriving American wine industry. But it would soon all come to an end. The temperance movement and, later, Prohibition, a massive disruption for American wineries and the industry as a whole, was firmly in place in many states by 1912 and full scale by 1919 via the Eighteenth Amendment to the Constitution, which outlawed the production and sale of all alcoholic beverages throughout the nation. Thousands of acres of vineyards were uprooted, and many winemaking facilities were demolished or converted to other commercial use. Some California wineries remained legal to make sacramental wines, and home winemaking flourished in large part due to a loophole in federal law allowing families to make up to two hundred gallons of fruit juice a year for personal use. The repeal of Prohibition in 1933 led to new laws granting individual states (and counties within states) legislative power over the distribution and sale of wine and spirits.

The subsequent road to rebuilding the wineries and the industry overall was paved by a number of visionaries and pioneering scientists, both homegrown and from abroad. After World War II many American wineries were in the habit of producing cheap, sweet, fortified wines that were popular at the time. Eventually, as American tastes in food changed with growing interest in more sophisticated fare, so did the desire for better-quality table wines. On course with this trend, the first completely new facility since Prohibition was built in the mid-1960s in Napa, California, by the Mondavi family, followed shortly thereafter by the opening of the largest winery in the United States (Ernest and Julio Gallo). In 1975 there were approximately six hundred federally bonded, licensed wineries in the United States. Since then, the numbers have grown substantially each decade, amounting to more than three thousand by the early twenty-first century. The most significant growth (more than a third) took place after 1990. New wineries continue to open nationwide along with an expanding American interest in and consumption of wine.

Scientific advancement, technology, academic (enological) knowledge, innovation, and shared international techniques have ushered in an era of modern winemaking, dramatically changing the way most wineries have traditionally operated. The resulting increases in quality control, sterile environs, automation, and the ability to offset seasonal weather uncertainties have also led to greater volume increases and product consistency.

Wine grapes are now among the fastest-growing agricultural crops in the country and the highest-valued American fruit crop. This phenomenon, along with the increasing number of trade groups dedicated to supporting and growing the business, signals the increasing importance of regional U.S. wineries to the overall American economy. Some wineries are now becoming part of big businesses, being purchased by large brewing and liquor companies that in turn invest in agricultural and winemaking technology as well as in growing marketing budgets to assist with the increasingly competitive global wine market.

American wineries are a key part of state and county tourism, offering increasingly popular packages of "agritourism" for those seeking agrarian landscape getaways. Promoting destination wineries, many convention and visitors bureaus link prospective visitors to wineries and local attractions like harvest festivals and jazz concerts. Many American vintners compete to open the most lavish hospitality centers, complete with high-profile draws like celebrity chef appearances, cooking classes, picnic areas, and fine restaurants—in addition to traditional cellar tours. Winery gift shops offer accessories, gift baskets, gourmet foods (with cheeses and other products often made with the facility's wines), and on-premise wine. The winery tasting room, virtually nonexistent in earlier times, has emerged as an important marketing tool representing a multimillion-dollar industry and often exists in urban centers far from the related winery. In quintessential American fashion, Robert Mondavi and Disney together opened the Golden Vine Winery in February 2001 as a major attraction at the Disneyland theme park in Anaheim, California.

[*See also* Gallo, Ernest and Julio; Mondavi Wineries; Wine, *subentry on* California Wines.]

BIBLIOGRAPHY

Folwell, Raymond J. "The Changing Market Structure of the USA Wine Industry." *Journal of Wine Research* 14, no. 1 (April 2003): 25–30.

Lukacs, Paul. *American Vintage: The Rise of American Wine.* Boston: Houghton Mifflin, 2000.

Peters, Gary L. *American Winescapes: The Cultural Landscapes of America's Wine Country.* Boulder, CO: Westview Press, 1997.

Pinney, Thomas. *A History of Wine in America: From the Beginnings to Prohibition*. Berkeley: University of California Press, 1989.

U.S. Department of Commerce. U.S. Census Bureau. *Wineries: 1997 Economic Census*. Manufacturing Industry Series. 2nd ed. Washington, DC: Government Printing Office, 2002.

TONYA HOPKINS

Wine-Tasting Rooms

The first tasting rooms were probably established by the Greeks and Phoenicians in their trading settlements along the Mediterranean during the period from 1500 to 500 BC and quite possibly even earlier, by wine sellers in the ancient world. Tasting rooms, whether they are attached to a winery, an estate vineyard, or a merchant's business, are simply showrooms to display, taste, and sell wine.

The physical plant of a tasting room can be as simple as a few folding chairs and a card table in a wine cellar or as elaborate as antique furnishings and old master paintings at a wine merchant. Many tasting rooms are an integral part of modern wineries, which use them not only as sales points but also to establish brand loyalty. Some have restaurants (the laws permitting) and sales areas for a variety of items, from locally produced foodstuffs to souvenirs. In California many wineries have extensive tasting areas, and some sell their wine across the country directly to the consumer. While this sales method is traditional in Europe, it can run afoul of some states' laws. If this situation, which is yet to be resolved, is decided in favor of the wine makers, it could have a dramatic effect on the way small-production wines are sold. Many distributors and retailers fear that luxury wineries will take their tasting rooms on tour, leaving them with only the large commercial wines to sell. Such retailers have lobbied against any out-of-state liquor sales, citing grievances ranging from the loss of tax revenue to the illegal purchase of spirits by children. Whatever the resolution of this issue, the tasting room experience enhances the understanding of the product as much today as it did in ancient times.

[*See also* Wine, *subentry* Historical Survey; Wineries.]

STEVEN M. CRAIG

Wonder Bread, *see Bread; Bread, Sliced*

World's Fairs

World's fairs are expositions in which nations and corporations feature their foods, cultures, consumer goods, and technological advancements. Beginning in the 1850s, these expositions became the forum for introducing new inventions, such as the telephone, medical X-rays, and television, and new, often futuristic architectural designs. While being part entertainment fair, part international diplomacy, and part marketplace, world's fairs have always stressed innovation and the diversity of world cultures while allowing fairgoers to sample new foods from around the globe and visit exhibits featuring scientific and mechanical innovations. Cities competed to host fairs to enhance their civic reputation and boost local economies. World's fairs were extremely popular during the nineteenth and twentieth centuries but had declined in attendance and commercial importance by the end of the twentieth century.

Early History

Fairs and events that celebrate national pride and commercial success began in medieval times. Large-scale markets developed at the intersection of major trade routes, especially in the European cities of Lyon, Frankfurt, and Leipzig. Larger trade, art, and commercial fairs became increasingly popular and frequent in France and England during the 1700s. The first recorded "universal and international" exhibition was held in London in 1851, widely known as the Crystal Palace Exhibition, but formally titled the Great Exhibition of the Works of Industry of All Nations. Nicknamed for the event's immense, nineteen-acre iron and glass pavilion, the Crystal Palace Exhibition purported to represent the entire world, while primarily honoring British global hegemony and American and British industrial advancements. Attracting 6 million visitors in less than five months made the Crystal Palace Exhibition both a political and financial success, encouraging over sixty similar fairs in different cities around the world before 1915.

Fairs in the United States

Notable among the early imitators was the New York Crystal Palace Exhibition, held in Manhattan between 1853 and 1854, which introduced George Crum's "potato chip" as a new snack food. New York promoters closely modeled their fair on the London success, complete with a restyled, yet leaky, Crystal Palace, but poor planning and an increasingly divided pre–Civil War nation resulted in financial failure for this exhibition.

Civil War production stimulated America's industrial economy. To display America's industrial might and to commemorate the signing of the Declaration of Independence, the United States Centennial Commission, funded by Philadelphia's wealthy elite, held the Centennial International Exhibition in Philadelphia in 1876. New and exotic foods became a focus of this fair, with an assortment of food pavilions offering German, French, and regional American fare. Soda water stands were popular, as was Goff, Fleischmann and Company's Vienna Model Bakery, which sold cakes and confections baked with that company's compressed yeast products. The Centennial International Exhibition succeeded beyond the hopes of its promoters, with 10 million of the nation's 47 million people attending.

Witnessing Philadelphia's successful Centennial Exhibition, other major cities sought recognition by holding fairs. Chicago led the way with the World's Columbian Exposition in 1893, belatedly celebrating the four-hundredth anniversary of Christopher Columbus's voyage. Planners built magnificent-looking, imitation marble buildings on the south side of the city, many of which were constructed out of cheap plaster applied over wood and wire frames. Attempting to exceed the grandeur of the Eiffel Tower, built for Paris's Universal Exposition in 1889, Columbian fair promoters commissioned the engineer George Ferris to erect an enormous wheel, 264 feet high and holding thirty-six gondolas, on the midway of the fairgrounds.

Chocolate Pavilion. Exhibit of the Maillard chocolate company, World's Columbian Exhibition, Chicago, 1893.

Visited by 27 million fairgoers in six months, the Columbian Exposition once again spotlighted new technological advancements and introduced consumer goods, including a wide range of new food products. Canada advertised its cheese industry by displaying an eleven-ton block of "Monster Cheese." Schlitz and Pabst, the competing American breweries, served beer from their popular booths, while Heinz made a map of the United States from its various pickle products. Ethnic restaurants introduced Americans to a wide range of unfamiliar foods, while an ongoing New England clambake fed visitors clam chowder, baked beans, and pumpkin pie. A new combination of caramelized popcorn and peanuts, branded as Cracker Jack, was the popular snack among patrons strolling around the fairgrounds.

The Twentieth Century

Despite some setbacks and a disastrous fire in 1894 that destroyed many of the buildings, the Chicago fair earned over $1.4 million, proving the potential value of hosting a major exposition. Encouraged by Chicago's success, Buffalo opened its Pan-American Exposition in 1901. Though 8 million people attended the Pan-American Exposition, its promoters lost $3 million. Even worse than the financial loss, however, was the real tragedy that came on September 6, 1901, when anarchist Leon Czolgosz assassinated President William McKinley, who was shaking hands in an exposition receiving line.

Undaunted by the tragedy and losses of the Buffalo exhibition, Saint Louis mounted its own world's fair in 1904. Christened the Louisiana Purchase Exposition, after Thomas Jefferson's famed 1804 land acquisition, the Saint Louis fair rivaled Chicago's in size and influence. Visitors ate more conventional foods than at other fairs but were first introduced to iced tea, Eskay's healthy baby foods, sliced bread, and, purportedly, hot dogs and hamburgers. Most noteworthy among the new foods that were verifiably introduced at this fair was the ice cream cone. Legend holds that ice cream cones began when the midway ice cream vendor Charles Menches ran out of bowls. In the next booth, Ernest Hamwi was selling *zalabia*, a Middle Eastern waferlike pastry. Rather than closing down his stand, Menches had Hamwi wrap his *zalabia* into makeshift dishes for the ice cream. Customers loved this consumable "bowl," and the popular ice cream cone was born. The Louisiana Purchase Exposition proved to be equally popular, effectively showcasing Saint Louis and earning huge profits for its promoters.

Saint Louis's success encouraged Norfolk (1907) and San Francisco (1915) to hold smaller world's fairs. Because of World War I and its aftermath, no significant world's fairs were held again until the late 1920s. To regulate future fairs and to prevent counterproductive scheduling conflicts, fair host countries convened the International Convention of 1928 in Paris. As a result of this convention, the Bureau of International Expositions was created to regulate the frequency of world's fairs and to outline the rights and obligations of exhibitors and organizers. Based in Paris, it became the sole authority over world exhibitions.

Despite being in the midst of the Great Depression, Chicago held its Century of Progress World's Fair in 1933. Commemorating Chicago's centennial and designed in colorful art deco style, this fair had extraordinary scientific and industrial exhibits, in addition to elaborate entertainment for visitors. Fairgoers could also choose from a vast array of foods, sampling Moroccan, Asian, and Middle Eastern dishes. For the less daring patrons, the 3,500-seat Old Heidelberg Inn offered a menu of sausages and other German foods, and American brewers served countless pitchers of beer. Food companies introduced relatively few products at the Chicago fair, but Kraft unveiled its new Miracle Whip salad dressing, which eventually became an American staple. Even though the United States was on the brink of financial disaster in 1933 and 1934, Chicago's Century of Progress World's Fair attracted 48 million visitors and made a modest profit.

Chicago World's Fair. The Wonder Bakery pavilion at the Century of Progress Exposition, Chicago, 1933–1934. Back cover of "The Wonder Book of Good Meals," distributed by the Continental Baking Company at the exposition. *Collection of Andrew F. Smith*

Not to be outdone by Chicago, New York promoters planned to hold an even more spectacular fair later in the decade. They built their expansive fairgrounds on 1,216 swampy acres in Queens. Food became a central theme of the 1939 New York World's Fair, featuring a massive mural painted by Witold Gordon that depicted 150 years of advancements and improvements in food production and quality. Fairgoers met Borden's "spokescow" Elsie, sampled varieties of new doughnuts, and could choose from Polish, Chinese, Norwegian, French, Indian, and Swedish restaurants. Despite huge commercial and governmental investments, the New York World's Fair suffered from the growing turmoil in Europe and bad weather, ultimately losing $18.7 million.

Because of the devastation brought by World War II, no major expositions would be held in the world for almost two decades. Seattle's Century 21 Exposition in 1962 renewed American interest in world's fairs. Fairgoers ate at either the Food Circus, which offered a wide assortment of meals, or from innovative vending machines offering such items as hot hamburgers or salmon dinners. Rather than constructing ornate, but temporary buildings, most of the fair consisted of permanent structures that remained in use after the fair's close. Notable among these structures was the Space Needle, which dominates Seattle's skyline.

The New York World's Fair of 1964–1965 was one of the most celebrated, yet least successful, of the twentieth-century expositions. Held on the same Flushing Meadows site in Queens as its 1939 predecessor, this fair suffered a $20 million deficit in its first year, with attendance numbers only half of those expected. Coca-Cola and Pepsi openly competed for soft drink consumers, staging the first round of the famed "Cola Wars." While the fair's exhibits were largely unspectacular, its foods came from every corner of the world, including Korean kimchi, tandoori chicken, hummus, and Turkish coffee. Though less exotic, the most popular food vendors were Van Dam's Belgium waffles, the Chungking Inn offering ninety-nine cent "Chinese American" meals, and Mastro's Pizza, which featured pizza bakers stretching dough and tossing it into the air. This wonderful array of food could not compensate for the fair's many problems. Some exhibitors departed before its second season began, and 1965 attendance remained slow. Ultimately, the financial failure of the 1964–1965 New York World's Fair ended the era of the grand expositions in America.

The End of an Era

Popular enthusiasm for world's fairs waned toward the end of the twentieth century. Small fairs such as Montreal's Expo '67, Fairbanks's Alaska '67, San Antonio's Hemisfair '68, Spokane's Expo '74, and the Knoxville International Energy Exposition of 1982 all achieved modest success, but New Orleans's 1984 Louisiana World Exposition filed for bankruptcy even before its close, citing losses of $121 million. Seeing New Orleans's failure, Chicago promoters scrapped plans for a 1992 world's fair. Media observers branded expositions as "cultural dinosaurs."

Fairs had once been the only way for most Americans to experience the people, food, and cultures of the broader world, but by the 1980s inexpensive air travel, a wide variety of ethnic restaurants, and television provided more accessible and attractive alternatives. Private enterprise also intentionally usurped the paying audience for world's fairs. Disneylands in general and Disney's Epcot Center in particular had become permanent world's fairs, providing millions of visitors each year with exposure to other cultures and exotic entertainment. Though fairs continue around the world, they no longer possess the influence or mystique of their predecessors in the nineteenth and twentieth centuries.

[*See also* Amusement Parks; Cola Wars; Cracker Jack; Borden, *sidebar on* Elsie the Cow; Myths and Folkore, *sidebar on* The Ice Cream Cone and the Saint Louis World's Fair.]

BIBLIOGRAPHY

Allwood, John. *The Great Exhibitions*. London: Cassell and Collier Macmillan, 1977.
Benedict, Burton, ed. *The Anthropology of World's Fairs*. London: Scolar Press, 1983.
Rydell, Robert W. *All the World's a Fair: Visions of Empire at American International Exhibitions, 1876–1916*. Chicago: University of Chicago Press, 1984.
Rydell, Robert W. *Fair America: World's Fairs in the United States*. Washington, DC: Smithsonian, 2000.

DAVID GERARD HOGAN

Wraps

During the 1990s, wraps became a popular new form of sandwich in the United States. Flour tortillas, plain or flavored, or various flat breads are used as a base on which imaginative pairings of ingredients, often reflecting international cuisines, such as Asian, Latin American, or Mediterranean, are layered. Fillings typically include very thinly sliced meats and cheese, and greens like spinach, basil, or cilantro. Onion, roasted red pepper, avocado, or hot peppers, along with a variety of flavored dressings, provide additional taste. The tortilla or flat bread is then folded in at one or both ends and rolled up from one edge. Wraps originated in Northern California, based on the concept of the burrito, which utilizes a flour tortilla in the same fashion to hold various combinations of Tex-Mex food.

Breakfast burritos have become one of the most popular forms of wraps in the United States. They are made from a variety of American breakfast favorites like sausage, eggs, potatoes, and cheese folded into flour tortillas and accompanied by salsa. Fusion cooking often incorporates the wrap concept in such dishes as duck breast, hoisin sauce, and scallion in Mandarin pancakes or flour tortillas. International cousins of the American wrap include Mexican tacos, Italian calzone, and Asian specialties like spring rolls and moo shu pork or Peking duck wrapped in thin pancakes called "bao bing." Wraps are popular menu items in restaurants and as take-out food from sandwich shops throughout the United States.

[*See also* Fusion Food; Mexican American Food; Sandwiches; Take-Out Foods.]

BIBLIOGRAPHY

Mercuri, Becky. *Sandwiches That You Will Like*. Pittsburgh, PA: WQED Multimedia, 2002.

BECKY MERCURI

Yeast

Yeast is the great transformer, the catalyzing agent that converts boiled grains into beer, fruit juice into wine, and dense, sticky dough into light and airy bread and cake. Yeast is a single-celled fungus. It is found everywhere—in the air we breathe, on the surfaces of fruits and grains, and in the soil. Yeasts of interest to cooks are those that digest sugars to produce alcohol, carbon dioxide, and a number of other compounds that affect the flavor and character of the finished beverage or food.

Five thousand years ago, Egyptian bakers are known to have leavened bread with yeast. In the early Middle Ages, around 1000, the word "yeast" was introduced

NO USE TALKING! I AM ALWAYS SUCCESSFUL WITH MY-BAKING WHEN I USE
FLEISCHMANN'S YEAST !!!

Yeast. Advertisement for Fleischman's yeast.

Markham's *The English Hus-wife* (1615). Colonial bakers knew how to balance conditions and ingredients to make recipes work. They understood that temperature extremes, and an excess of salt or sugar, retarded the growth of yeasts. Most colonial bakers preferred leavening bread and some cakes with the yeasty sediments left behind by the brewing process. When brewer's yeast was not available, home bakers used either previously dried brewer's yeast, fermented dough held back from the previous baking, or wild yeasts in a spontaneously fermented starter.

The nineteenth-century American cookbook literature reveals a vibrant tradition of leavening breads with yeast starters, many of which included a tea made of dried hops flowers (*Humulus lupulus*), an herb added to discourage souring but that also contributed its own distinctive flavor. *The Home Cook* (1882) includes a rich array of recipes for these starters.

Until the late nineteenth century, American bread bakers often multiplied their yeast by adding it to a batter of flour and water. When this "sponge" had risen, which took some hours, they added the remaining ingredients, which then fermented for several more hours. Bread dough sometimes was started the afternoon or evening before the actual baking day. Long rising contributes to the texture and flavor of the loaf.

Commercially produced yeast first appeared in the United States in the 1860s. Charles and Maximillian Fleischmann, immigrants from Austria-Hungary, with the financial backing of James Gaff, patented and sold standardized cakes of compressed yeast (*S. cerevisiae*) produced in their factory in Cincinnati. By the early twentieth century, factory-produced yeast was widely available. Cookbook recipes began specifying that commercial yeast be added directly to bread dough in sufficient quantities to leaven it in less than two hours. Bread changed in texture, becoming lighter and softer, and its flavor turned blander. (Bread leavened quickly has a lighter texture than does bread leavened slowly.)

In the early nineteenth century, American cooks began widely substituting chemical leavening agents—initially pearl ash—for the yeast called for in English cake recipes. By the early twentieth century, chemical leavening, such as baking soda and baking powder, was widely available to home cooks. The English tradition of yeasted dessert cakes had passed completely out of favor. Cookbooks, such as *The Boston Cooking-School Cook Book* (1896), specified

into English. By the time European settlers arrived in North America in the early seventeenth century, they had wide experience working with yeasted beverages, breads, and cakes. The yeast they preferred, although at the time unnamed by science, was the robust yeast *Saccharomyces cerevisiae*, called "baker's" or "brewer's" yeast in cookbooks.

Colonists usually fermented beer and herbal wines with yeast reserved from a previous brewing. For fruit wines they relied on spontaneous fermentation—the action of wild yeasts, already present on the fruit, revived by contact with nutrients in a moist and warm environment. Early American baking practices were the same as those described in seventeenth- and eighteenth-century English cookbooks, such as Gervase chemical agents, sometimes supplementing them with eggs, as the primary leaven. This remains the customary practice. These chemical leavenings contributed to changes of texture and flavor.

Ginger ale, root beer, and other refreshing and so-called medicinal beverages had been fermented with brewer's yeast. However, with the growing influence of the temperance movement in the nineteenth century, increasingly chemicals like baking soda were used to produce the fizz. These temperance beverages became the basis of the huge American soft drink industry in the twentieth century.

The last third of the twentieth century saw a revolution in American food culture, which included a revival in the arts of wine making, brewing, and baking. Winemakers and brewers transformed their industries by taking a scientific approach to managing selected strains of *S. cerevisiae*. Artisanal bakers looked to European breadmaking methods to improve their breads' flavor, texture, and character. They slowed the fermentation process, employed the older sponge system, often used spontaneous ferments, and frequently dispensed with baking tins.

Historically, aside from some German rye breads and San Francisco sourdough, American sourdough breads were made in a way that minimized or eliminated sourness. In the late twentieth century, for the first time, Americans as a whole began to appreciate sourness in their bread, a flavor that is common in many artisanal and homemade loaves. At same time, "fast the rising" yeast strains were developed for home cooks who felt they did not have time to let bread rise slowly. By the end of the twentieth century, cookbooks, such as *Joy of Cooking* (1997), reflected these changes in the American artisanal bread-baking style.

[*See also* Bread; Brewing; Fruit Wines.]

BIBLIOGRAPHY

David, Elizabeth. *English Bread and Yeast Cookery*. New York: Viking, 1977.

Farmer, Fannie Merritt. *The Boston Cooking-School Cook Book*. Boston: Little, Brown, 1924.

Home for the Friendless, Chicago. *The Home Cook*. Chicago: J. Fred. Waggoner, 1882.

Markham, Gervase. *The English Housewife*. Edited by Michael R. Best. Kingston, Canada: McGill-Queen's University Press, 1986.

Rombauer, Irma S., Marion Rombauer Becker, and Ethan Becker. *Joy of Cooking*. New York: Scribners, 1997.

WILLIAM RUBEL

Zombie

The zombie was the brainchild of the talented bartender Ernest Raymond Beaumont-Gantt, nicknamed "Donn Beach." He and his business-savvy wife, Cora Irene Sund, a former schoolteacher turned cocktail waitress, opened Don the Beachcomber in 1937 in Hollywood, California. Their timing was flawless. The country was a few short years past Prohibition, and many of the Hollywood stars had spent that dry time in the playground of Havana, Cuba, where rum drinks were the order of the day. The famous Trader Vic, Victor Bergeron, was inspired by the success of the Beachcomber to reinvent Hinky Dinks, his saloon in Oakland, California, as Trader Vic's. Tiki was definitely the order of the day.

The recipe for the zombie takes advantage of the unique quality that rum possesses. Unlike other spirits, rum is best when combined with other kinds of rum. When different rums are mixed together, the individual rums synergistically produce spectacular results. Gantt and Bergeron both mastered this blending technique in their recipes. They created a library of rum recipes that is still consulted. The original zombie recipe like all Donn Beach's recipes was a closely guarded professional secret throughout his lifetime. Twenty-three years after his death in 1978 his widow Phoebe Beach and her second husband Arnold Bitner decided to tell the Donn Beach story in their book *Hawai'i Tropical Rum Drinks & Cuisine by Don the Beachcomber*. The original zombie recipe illustrated Beach's genius for blending five different rums to make the base for the zombie.

ZOMBIE

¾ ounce lime juice

½ ounce grapefruit juice

½ ounce Falernum

½ ounce simple syrup

1¼ ounce Ramirez Royal Superior rum (substitute Captain Morgan rum)

1 ounce Lemon Hart Demerara rum 151°

1 ounce Palau 30-year-old Cuban rum (substitute 30-year-old Ron Zacapa Centenario rum)

1 ounce Myers's dark rum

1 ounce Treasure Cove 32-year-old Jamaican (substitute Appleton Estate Rum)

2 dashes each Angostura bitters and Pernod

3 dashes grenadine

¾ ounce maraschino liqueur

Pour ingredients into a blender. Add a handful of small cracked ice. Blend at medium speed. Pour into a fourteen-ounce glass with three or four cubes of ice.

Decorate with a spear of fresh pineapple, orange slice, cherry, and sprig of mint. Serve with a straw. Sip with eyes half closed.

[*See also* Cocktails; Rum.]

BIBLIOGRAPHY

Bitner, Arnold, and Phoebe Beach. *Hawai'i Tropical Rum Drinks & Cuisine by Don the Beachcomber*. Honolulu, HI: Mutual Publishing, 2001.

DALE DEGROFF

FOOD BIBLIOGRAPHY

General Histories

Bower, Anne L., ed. *Recipes for Reading: Community Cookbooks, Stories, Histories*. Amherst: University of Massachusetts Press, 1997.

Carson, Barbara G. *Ambitious Appetites: Dining, Behavior, and Patterns of Consumption in Federal Washington*. Washington, DC: American Institute of Architects Press, 1990.

Cummings, Richard Osborn. *The American and His Food: A History of Food Habits in the United States*. Chicago: University of Chicago Press, 1940.

Conlin, Joseph R. *Bacon, Beans, and Galatines: Food and Foodways on the Western Mining Frontier*. Reno: University of Nevada Press, 1986.

Haber, Barbara. *From Hardtack to Home Fries: An Uncommon History of American Cooks and Meals*. New York: Free Press, 2002.

Holland, Leandra Zim. *Feasting and Fasting with Lewis and Clark: A Food and Social History*. Emigrant, MT: Old Yellowstone, 2003.

Hooker, Richard J. *A History of Food and Drink in America*. Indianapolis: Bobbs-Merrill, 1981.

Levenstein, Harvey A. *Paradox of Plenty: A Social History of Eating in Modern America*. New York: Oxford University Press, 1993.

Levenstein, Harvey A. *Revolution at the Table: The Transformation of the American Diet*. New York: Oxford University Press, 1988.

Shapiro, Laura. *Perfection Salad: Women and Cooking at the Turn of the Century*. New York: Holt, 1987.

Williams, Susan. *Savory Suppers and Fashionable Feasts: Dining in Victorian America*. Knoxville: University of Tennessee Press, 1996.

Bibliographies

Bitting, Katherine. *Gastronomic Bibliography*. San Francisco: Halle-Cordis Composing Room/Trade Freeroom, 1939.

Brown, Eleanor, and Bob Brown. *Culinary Americana: Cookbooks Published in the Cities and Towns of the United States of America during the Years from 1860 through 1960*. New York: Roving Eye, 1961.

Cagle, William R., and Lisa Killion Stafford. *American Books on Food and Drink*. New Castle, DE: Oak Knoll, 1998.

Cook, Margaret. *America's Charitable Cooks: A Bibliography of Fund-Raising Cook Books Published in the United States (1861–1915)*. Kent, OH: n.p., 1971.

Longone, Janice B., and Daniel T. Longone. *American Cookbooks and Wine Books, 1797–1950*. Ann Arbor, MI: Clements Library/Wine and Food Library, 1984.

Lowenstein, Eleanor. *Bibliography of American Cookery Books, 1742–1860*. Worcester, MA: American Antiquarian Society, 1972.

Wheaton, Barbara Ketcham, and Patricia Kelly. *Bibliography of Culinary History: Food Resources in Eastern Massachusetts*. Boston: Hall, 1987.

Cookbooks: Reprints and Facsimiles

Benson, Abraham Benson, ed. *Penn Family Recipes: Cooking Recipes of William Penn's Wife Gulielma*. York, PA: Shumway, 1966.

Blot, Pierre. *Hand-Book of Practical Cookery*. New York: Appleton, 1869. Facsimile, New York: Arno, 1973.

Bryan, Lettuce. *Kentucky Housewife*. Cincinnati, OH: Shepard and Stearns, 1839. Reprint, Columbia: University of South Carolina Press, 1991.

Capital City Cookbook. 3rd ed. Madison, WI: Grace Church Guild, 1906. Published with *Midwestern Home Cookery*. Originally titled *Presbyterian Cookbook*. Dayton, OH: Thomas, 1875. Facsimile, New York: Arno, 1973

The Capitol Cookbook: A Facsimile of the Austin 1899 Edition. Austin, TX: State House Press, 1995.

Cushing, C. H., and B. Gray, comps. *The Kansas Home Cook-Book*. 5th ed. Leavenworth, KS: Crew, 1886. Reprinted with introduction and suggested recipes by Louis Szathmáry. New York: Arno, 1973.

Davidis, Henriette. *Pickled Herring and Pumpkin Pie: A Nineteenth-Century Cookbook for German Immigrants to America*. Edited by Louis A. Pitschmann. Madison: University of Wisconsin Press, 2002.

Estes, Rufus. *Good Things to Eat as Suggested by Rufus*. Chicago: Published by the author, 1911. Reprinted as edited by D. J. Frienz. Jenks, OK: Howling at the Moon Press, 1999.

Eustis, Celestine. *Cooking in Old Creole Days*. New York: Russell, 1904. Reprint, New York: Arno, 1973.

Farmer, Fannie Merritt. *Boston Cooking-School Cook Book*. Boston: Little, Brown, 1896. Facsimile, New York: Weathervane, 1986.

Fisher, Mrs. Abby. *What Mrs. Fisher Knows about Old Southern Cooking*. San Francisco: Women's Co-operative Printing Office, 1881.

Reprinted with historical notes by Karen Hess. Bedford, MA: Applewood, 1995.

Glasse, Hannah. *Art of Cookery Made Plain and Easy*. London. First edition published by the author in London, 1796. Facsimile, Schenectady, NY: United States Historical Research Service, 1994.

Graham, Sylvester. *Treatise on Bread and Bread-Making*. Boston: Light and Stearns, 1837. Reprint, Milwaukee, WI: Lee Foundation for Nutritional Research, n.d.

Hearn, Lafcadio. *La Cuisine Creole: A Collection of Culinary Recipes from Leading Chefs and Noted Creole Housewives, Who Have Made New Orleans Famous for Its Cuisine*. New York: Coleman, 1885. Reprint, Baton Rouge, LA: Pelican/Moran, 1967.

Hill, Mrs. A. P. *Mrs. Hill's New Cook Book*. New York: Carleton, 1872. Reprinted with *The Confederate Receipt Book*. Birmingham, AL: Oxmoor, 1985.

Hooker, Richard J., ed. *A Colonial Plantation Cookbook: The Receipt Book of Harriott Pinckney Horry, 1770*. Columbia: University of South Carolina Press, 1984.

Josselyn, John. *New-England Rarities Discovered*. London: Widdowes, 1672. Reprint, Boston: Massachusetts Historical Society, 1972.

Kander, Mrs. Simon, and Mrs. Henry Schoenfeld, comps. *The "Settlement Cookbook": The Way to a Man's Heart*. Milwaukee, WI, 1903. Facsimile, New York: Grammercy Publishing Co., 1987.

Kinsley, H[erbert] M. *One Hundred Recipes for the Chafing Dish*. New York: Gorham Manufacturing Company and Silversmiths, 1894. Facsimile, New York: Arno, 1973.

[Kirtland, Elizabeth Stansbury]. *Six Little Cooks*. Chicago: Jansen, McClurg, 1879. Facsimile, New York: Arno, 1973.

Lea, Elizabeth Ellicott. *A Quaker Woman's Cookbook: The Domestic Cookery of Elizabeth Ellicott Lea*. Edited with an introduction by William Woys Weaver. Philadelphia: University of Pennsylvania, 1982.

Lee, N. K. M. *The Cook's Own Book*. Boston: Munroe and Francis, 1832. Reprint, New York: Arno, 1972.

Leslie, Eliza. *Directions for Cookery: Being a System of the Art, in Its Various Branches*. 10th ed. Philadelphia: Carey and Hart, 1848. Reprint, New York: Arno, 1973.

Leslie, Eliza. *Indian Meal Book*. Reprinted under title *Corn Meal Cookery: A Collection of Heirloom Corn Meal Recipes Dating from 1848*. Hamilton, OH: Burns, 1998.

Levy, Esther. *Mrs. Esther Levy's Jewish Cookery Book*. Philadelphia, 1871. Reprint, Cambridge, MA: Applewood, 1988.

Lincoln, Mrs. D. A. *Boston Cooking School Cook Book*. Boston: Roberts, 1884. Reprinted with an introduction by Janice (Jan) Bluestein Longone. Mineola, NY: Dover, 1996.

McLaren, L. L., comp. *High Living: Recipes from Southern Climes*. San Francisco: Elder, 1904. Reprinted with an introduction and suggested recipes by Louis Szathmáry. New York: Arno, 1973.

Midwestern Home Cookery. Facsimile of three cookbooks. New York: Arno, 1973.

[Moss, Maria J.] *A Poetical Cook-Book*. Philadelphia: Caxton Press of C. Sherman, 1864. Reprint, New York: Arno / New York Times, 1972.

The New Family Book, or Ladies' Indispensable Companion. Originally published with Mrs. Chadwick. *Home Cookery*. Boston: Crosby, Nichols, 1853. Reprint, Birmingham, AL: Oxmoor, 1984.

Pennell, Elizabeth Robins. *The Delights of Delicate Eating*. Introduction by Jacqueline Block Williams. Urbana: University of Illinois Press, 2000.

Pinckney, Eliza Lucas. *Recipe Book*. Charleston: Committee on Historic Activities of the South Carolina Society of the Colonial Dames of America, 1969.

Porter, M. E. *Mrs. Porter's New Southern Cookery Book*. Philadelphia: Potter, 1871. Reprinted with an introduction and suggested recipes by Louis Szathmáry. New York: Arno, 1973.

Presbyterian Cook Book, Compiled by the Ladies of the First Presbyterian Church. Dayton, OH: Thomas, 1875. Reprinted with an introduction and suggested recipes by Louis Szathmáry. New York: Arno, 1973.

Randolph, Mary. *The Virginia House-wife*. Washington, DC: Davis and Force, 1824. Facsimile edited by Karen Hess. Columbia: University of South Carolina Press, 1984.

Ranhofer, Charles. *The Epicurean*. New York: Ranhofer, 1893. Reprint, New York: Dover, 1971.

Rombauer, Irma S. *Joy of Cooking*. 1931. A facsimile of the first edition. New York: Scribners, 1998.

Rose, Peter G., trans. and ed. *The Sensible Cook: Dutch Foodways in the Old and the New World*. Syracuse, NY: Syracuse University Press, 1989.

Seely, Mrs. L. *Mrs. Seely's Cook Book*. Edited by Shirley Abbot. New York: Macmillan, 1902. Reprint, Birmingham, AL: Oxmoor, 1984.

Simmons, Amelia. *American Cookery*. A facsimile of the first edition with an essay by Mary Tolford Wilson. New York: Oxford University Press, 1958.

Simmons, Amelia. *American Cookery*. 2nd ed. Albany, NY: Webster, 1796. A facsimile with an introduction by Karen Hess. Bedford, MA: Applewood, 1996.

Szathmáry, Louis, comp. *Along the Northern Border: Cookery in Idaho, Minnesota and North Dakota*. Introduction and suggested recipes by Louis Szathmáry. New York: Arno, 1973.

Szathmáry, Louis, comp. *Cool, Chill, and Freeze: A New Approach to Cookery*. Introduction and suggested recipes by Louis Szathmáry. New York: Arno, 1973.

Szathmáry, Louis, comp. *Fifty Years of Prairie Cooking*. Introduction and suggested recipes by Louis Szathmáry. New York: Arno, 1973.

Szathmáry, Louis, comp. *Southwestern Cookery: Indian and Spanish Influences*. Introduction and suggested recipes by Louis Szathmáry. New York: Arno, 1973.

Thornton, P. *The Southern Gardener and Receipt Book.* Newark, NJ: Denis, 1845. Reprint, Birmingham, AL: Oxmoor, 1984.

Ude, Louis Eustache. *The French Cook.* Philadelphia, 1828. Reprint, New York: Arco, 1978.

[Washington, Martha] *Martha Washington's Booke of Cookery.* Edited by Karen Hess. New York: Columbia University Press, 1981.

Weaver, William Woys. *Sauerkraut Yankees: Pennsylvania German Foods and Foodways.* Philadelphia: University of Pennsylvania Press, 1983.

[Webster, Mrs. A. L.] *The Improved Housewife.* 6th ed., revised. Hartford, CT: Hobbs, 1845. Facsimile, New York: Arno, 1973.

Wilcox, Estelle Woods, comp. *Centennial Buckeye Cook Book.* Reprinted with an introduction and appendices by Andrew F. Smith. Columbus: Ohio State University Press, 2000.

Ziemann, Hugo, and Mrs. F. L. Gillette. *The White House Cookbook.* New York: Saalfield, 1903. Reprint, Old Greenwich, CT: Devin Adair, 1983.

Encyclopedias

Katz, Solomon, ed. *Encyclopedia of Food and Culture.* 3 vols. New York: Scribners, 2003.

Kiple, Kenneth F., and Kriemhild Coneè Ornelas, eds. *The Cambridge World History of Food.* 2 vols. New York: Cambridge University Press, 2000.

Ethnic Food

Gabaccia, Donna R. *We Are What We Eat: Ethnic Food and the Making of Americans.* Cambridge, MA: Harvard University Press, 1998.

Zanger, Mark H. *The American Ethnic Cookbook for Students.* Phoenix, AZ: Oryx, 2001.

Regional Histories

Luchetti, Cathy. *Home on the Range: A Culinary History of the American West.* New York: Villard, 1993.

Williams, Jacqueline B. *The Way We Ate: Pacific Northwest Cooking, 1843–1900.* Pullman: Washington State University Press, 1996.

Restaurants

Thomas, Lately. *Delmonico's: A Century of Splendor.* Boston: Houghton Mifflin, 1967.

Specific Foods and Food Products

Brenner, Joël Glenn. *The Emperors of Chocolate: Inside the Secret World of Hershey and Mars.* New York: Broadway, 2000.

Carson, Gerald. *Cornflake Crusade.* New York: Rinehart, 1957.

Jenkins, Virginia Scott. *Bananas: An American History.* Washington: Smithsonian, 2000.

Smith, Andrew F. *Peanuts: The Illustrious History of the Goober Pea.* Urbana: University of Illinois Press, 2002.

Smith, Andrew F. *Popped Culture: A Social History of Popcorn in America.* Columbia: University of South Carolina Press, 1999.

Smith, Andrew F. *Pure Ketchup: A History of America's National Condiment.* Columbia: University of South Carolina Press, 1996.

Smith, Andrew F. *The Tomato in America: Early History, Culture and Cookery.* Columbia: University of South Carolina Press, 1994.

Wilson, David Scofield, and Angus Kress Gillespie, eds. *Rooted in America: Foodlore of Popular Fruits and Vegetables.* Nashville: University of Tennessee Press, 1999.

Woloson, Wendy A. *Refined Tastes: Sugar, Confectionery and Consumption in Nineteenth-Century America.* Baltimore: Johns Hopkins University Press, 2002.

Wyman, Carolyn. *Spam, A Biography: The Amazing True Story of America's "Miracle Meat"!* New York: Harcourt Brace, 1999.

Wyman, Carolyn. *Jell-O, A Biography: The History and Mystery of "America's Most Famous Dessert."* San Diego: Harcourt, 2001.

Special Topics: Reform and Counterculture

Belasco, Warren J. *Appetite for Change: How the Counterculture Took on the Food Industry 1966–1988.* New York: Pantheon, 1989.

Crump, Nancy Carter. *Hearthside Cooking: An Introduction to Virginia Plantation Cuisine, Including Bills of Fare, Tools and Techniques, and Original Recipes with Adaptations for Modern Fireplaces and Kitchens.* McLean, VA: EPM, 1986.

Davis, Adelle. *Let's Eat Right to Keep Fit.* New York: Harcourt, Brace, 1954.

Hess, John, and Karen Hess. *The Taste of America.* New York: Grossman, 1977.

Lappé, Frances Moore. *Diet for a Small Planet.* New York: Friends of the Earth/Ballantine, 1977.

Sack, Daniel. *Whitebread Protestants: Food and Religion in American Culture.* New York: St. Martin's, 2000.

Schlosser, Eric. *Fast Food Nation: The Dark Side of the All-American Meal.* Boston: Houghton Mifflin, 2001.

Other Food Books

Franklin, Linda Campbell. *300 Years of Kitchen Collectibles.* 5th ed. Iola, WI: Krause, 2002.

Funderburg, Anne Cooper. *Sundae Best: A History of Soda Fountains.* Bowling Green, KY: Bowling Green State University Popular Press, 2002.

Gutman, Richard J. S. *American Diner, Then and Now.* Baltimore: Johns Hopkins University Press, 2000.

Inness, Sherrie A., ed. *Kitchen Culture in America: Popular Representations of Food, Gender and Race.* Philadelphia: University of Pennsylvania Press, 2001.

ANDREW F. SMITH

FOOD PERIODICALS

American Cookery. 1897–1946. Originally *The Boston Cooking-School Magazine.*

American Kitchen. 1895–1903. Originally *New England Kitchen.*

Art of Eating, The. 1986–. http://www.ArtofEating.com.

Berney's Mysterious Magazine. 1868.

Best Recipes. 1900–1946.

Bon Appetit. 1956–. http://www.bonappetit.com.

Boston Cooking-School Magazine. 1896–1897. Name changed to *American Cookery,* 1897.

Caterer and Households Magazine. 1900s.

Chile Pepper. 1987–. http://www.chilepepper.com.

Chocolatier. 1984–. http://www.bakingshop.com/magazine/chocolatierhtm.

Cook, The: A Weekly Handbook of Domestic Culinary Art for All Housekeepers. 1885–1886, 1895–1917.

Cooking Club. 1895–1917.

Cooking Light. 1986–. http://www.cookinglight.com.

Cook's Illustrated. 1993–. http://www.cooksillustrated.com.

Cook's Magazine. Exact date unknown–1985.

Cuisine. Exact date unknown–1984.

Cuisine. 2000. Name changed to Cuisine at Home, 2001.

Cuisine at Home. 2001–. http://www.cuisine.com.

Culinary Thymes. 2000 (Exact date unknown) –. http://www.culinarythymes.com. Also titled *Texas Culinary Thymes.*

Eating Well. 1980–. http://www.eatingwell.com.

Epicure. 1887– Exact date unknown

Epicure. 1972 (Exact date unknown)

Everyday Food. 2003–. http://www.everydayfood.com.

Fiery Foods and Barbecue Magazine. 1997–. http://www.fieryfoods.com.

Fine Cooking. 1994–. http://www.taunton.com/finecooking.

Food and Wine. 1983–. http://www.foodandwine.com.

Food History News (newsletter). 1989–. http://www.foodhistorynews.com.

Gastronomica. 2001–. http://www.gastronomica.com.

Gourmet. 1941–. http://www.gourmet.com.

Healthy Exchange Food (newsletter). 1992–. http://www.healthyexchanges.com.

Herb Quarterly. 1979–. http://www.herbquarterly.com.

Home Cooking. 1970 (Exact date unknown)–. http://www.homecookingmagazine.com.

Hometown Cooking. 1999–2002.

Light n' Tasty. 2001–. http://www.lightntasty.com.

Louisiana Cookin'. 1997–. http://www.louisianacookin.com.

National Food Magazine. 1908–1920.

New England Kitchen. 1894–1895. Name changed to *American Kitchen,* 1895; changed to *Home Science Magazine,* 1903; changed to *Modern Housekeeping,* 1905; changed to *Everyday Housekeeping,* 1906–1908.

Pasta. 2000–. http://www.inlandempiremagazine.com/pastafallo1.html.

Quick Cooking. 1998–. http://www.quickcooking.com. Also titled *Taste of Home's Quick Cooking'.*

Saveur. 1994–. http://www.saveur.com.

Simple Cooking. Newsletter. 1980–. http://www.outlawcook.com.

Simply Seafood. 1990–1992.

Table. 1873.

Table Talk. 1886–1916.

Taste of Home. 1993–. http://www.tasteofhome.com.

Today's Magazine. 1909 (Exact date unknown)

Vegetarian Times. 1978–. http://www.vegetariantimes.com.

Veggie Life. 1993–. http://www.veggielife.com.

What to Eat. 1896–1908. Name changed to *National Food Magazine,* 1908.

Service Magazines

American Analyst. 1885–1894. Pure-food information.

American Home. 1887–1898.

American Home. 1928–1978.

Backwoods Home. 1989–. http://www.backwoodshome.com.

Better Homes and Gardens. 1924–. http://www.bhg.com.

Changing Woman, The. 1971–1974.

Coastal Living. 1997–. http://www.coastalliving.com.

Cottage Hearth, The. 1880s.

Country Home. 1929–1939.

Country Living. 1980–. http://www.magazines.ivillage.com/countryliving.

Delineator. 1873–1937.

Demorest's Monthly Magazine. 1860–1899.

Essence. 1970–. http://www.essence.com.

Everyday Housekeeping. 1906–1908. Name changed from *Modern Housekeeping,* 1905–1906; *Home Science,* 1903–1905; *American Kitchen Magazine,* 1895–1903; *New England Kitchen Magazine,* 1894–1895.

Family Circle. 1932–. http://www.familycircle.com.

Farmer's Wife, The. 1857–1929.

FDA Consumer. 1972–. http://www.fda.org.

Frank Leslie's Monthly Magazine. 1854–1882.

Godey's Lady's Book. 1830–1898.

Good Housekeeping. 1885–. http://www.goodhousekeeping.com.

Health. 1900–1904.

Health. 1981–. http://www.health.com.

Healthy Exchanges Food Newsletter. 1992–.

Home-Maker, The. 1888–1893.

Home Science. 1903–1905

House and Garden. 1901–1988.

House Beautiful. 1896–. http://www.housebeautiful.com.

Household. 1860–1861; 1867–1874?; 1900–1958.

Household Companion. 1879–1919.

Household News. 1893–1896.

Illustrated Home Guest. 1890s.

Ladies Annual Register. 1832.

Ladies' Home Journal. 1883–. http://www.lhj.com.

Larkin Family Magazine. 1909 (Exact date unknown)

McCalls. 1873–2001.

Martha Stewart Living. 2000–. http://www.marthastewart.com.

Midwest Living. 1987–. http://www.midwestliving.com.

Miss Leslie's Magazine. 1843.

Modern Housekeeping: A Monthly Companion for the Fair Sex. 1905–1906.

Modern Priscilla. 1920s.

New Lady's Magazine. 1860.

New Mexico Magazine. 1974–. http://www.nmmagazine.com.

Northwest Palate. 1998–. http://www.nwpalate.com.

People's Home Journal. 1894–1911.

Peterson's. 1842–1894.

Pictorial Review. 1899–1939.

Prevention. 1950–. http://www.prevention.com.

Real Simple. 2000–. http://www.realsimple.com.

St. Louis Magazine. 1871–1896. Began as *St. Louis Ladies' Magazine.*

Science News. 1966–. http://www.sciencenews.com.

Self. 1979–. http://www.self.com.

Southern Living. 1966–. http://www.southernliving.com.

Southern Woman's Magazine. 1913–1918.

Sunset. 1898–. http://www.sunset.com.

Table and Home. 1901–1918.

Texas Monthly. 1973–. http://www.texasmonthly.com.

Tufts University Health and Nutrition Newsletter. 1997–. http://www.healthletter.tufts.edu.

Weight Watchers. 1988–.
http://www.weightwatchers.com/shop/h_sh_mag.asp.

Wine Country Living. 2002–. http://www.winecountryliving.com.

Woman's Day. 1937–. http://www.womansday.com.

Woman's Home Companion. 1873–1957.

Working Woman. 1970–. http://www.workingwoman.com.

Yankee Magazine. 1935–. http://www.YankeeMagazine.com.

VIRGINIA K. BARTLETT

DRINK BIBLIOGRAPHY

General Histories

Barr, Andrew. *Drink: A Social History of America*. New York: Carroll and Graf, 1999.

Brown, John Hull. *Early American Beverages*. Rutland, VT: Tuttle, 1966.

Conroy, David. *In Public Houses: Drink and the Revolution of Authority in Colonial Massachusetts*. Chapel Hill: University of North Carolina Press, 1995.

Firth, Grace. *Secrets of the Still: A Zesty History of How-to for Making Spirits, Fragrances, Curables, Gasohol and Other Products of the Stillroom*. McClean, VA: EPM, 1983.

Hooker, Richard J. *A History of Food and Drink in America*. Indianapolis: Bobbs-Merrill, 1981.

Lender, Mark Edward, and James Kirby Martin. *Drinking in America: A History, The Revised and Expanded Edition*. New York: Free Press, 1987.

Salinger, Sharon V. *Taverns and Drinking in Early America*. Baltimore: Johns Hopkins University Press, 2002.

Thompson, Peter. *Rum Punch and Revolution: Taverngoing and Public Life in Eighteenth-Century Philadelphia*. Philadelphia: University of Pennsylvania Press, 1999.

Bibliographies

Amerine, Maynard A. *Vermouth: An Annotated Bibliography*. Richmond, CA: Division of Agricultural Sciences, University of California, 1974.

Amerine, Maynard A., and Axel E. Borg. *A Bibliography on Grapes, Wines, Other Alcoholic Beverages, and Temperance: Works Published in the United States before 1901*. Berkeley: University of California Press, 1996.

Amerine, Maynard A., and Louise B. Wheeler. *A Checklist of Books and Pamphlets on Grapes and Wine and Related Subjects, 1938–1948*. Berkeley: University of California Press, 1951.

Amerine, Maynard A., and Herman Phaff, comps. *Bibliography of Publications by the Faculty, Staff, and Students, of the University of California, 1876–1980, on Grapes, Wines, and Related Subjects*. Berkeley: University of California Press, 1986.

Gabler, James M. *Wine into Words: A History and Bibliography of Wine Books in the English Language*. Baltimore: Bacchus, 1985.

Noling, A. W., comp. *Beverage Literature: A Bibliography*. Metuchen, NJ: Scarecrow, 1971.

Beer

Baron, Stanley. *Brewed in America: A History of Beer and Ale in the United States*. New York: Arno, 1972.

Cochran, Thomas C. *The Pabst Brewing Company: The History of an American Business*. New York: New York University Press, 1948.

Krebs, Roland. *Making Friends Is Our Business: 100 Years of Anheuser-Busch*. St. Louis, MO: n.p., 1953.

LaFrance, Peter. *Beer Basics: A Quick and Easy Guide*. New York: Wiley, 1995.

Cider

Orton, Vrest. *The American Cider Book: The Story of America's Natural Beverage*. New York: Farrar, Straus, and Giroux, 1973.

Cocktails

Bullock, Tom. *173 Pre-Prohibition Cocktails*. Jenks, OK: Howling at the Moon Press, 2001.

Regan, Mardee Haidin. *The Bartender's Best Friend: A Complete Guide to Cocktails, Martinis, and Mixed Drinks*. New York: Wiley, 2003.

Coffee

Pendergrast, Mark. *Uncommon Grounds: The History of Coffee and How It Transformed Our World*. New York: Basic Books, 1999.

Ukers, William H. *All about Coffee*. 2nd ed. New York: Tea and Coffee Trade Journal Company, 1935.

Mint Julep

Harwell, Richard Barksdale. *The Mint Julep*. Charlottesville: University Press of Virginia, 1975.

Milk

Dillon, John J. *Seven Decades of Milk: A History of New York's Dairy Industry*. New York: Orange Judd, 1941.

Soda

Louis, J. C., and Harvey Yazijian. *The Cola Wars: The Story of the Global Corporate Battle between the Coca-Cola Company and PepsiCo*. New York: Everest House, 1980.

Martin, Milward W. *Twelve Full Ounces.* 2nd ed. New York: Holt, Rinehart, and Winston, 1969.

Pendergrast, Mark. For *God, Country and Coca-Cola.* New York: Scribners, 1993.

Riley, John J. A *History of the American Soft Drink Industry: Bottled Carbonated Beverages 1807–1957.* Washington, DC: American Bottlers of Carbonated Beverages, 1958.

Prohibition and Temperance

Asbury, Herbert. *The Great Illusion: An Informal History of Prohibition.* Garden City, NY: Doubleday, 1950.

Chidsey, Donald Barr. *On and Off the Wagon: A Sober Analysis of the Temperance Movement from the Pilgrims through Prohibition.* New York: Cowles, 1969.

Tyrrell, Ian. *Woman's World/Woman's Empire: The Woman's Christian Temperance Union in International Perspective, 1880–1930.* Chapel Hill: University of North Carolina Press, 1991.

Spirits

Brander, Michael. *The Original Scotch: A History of Scotch Whisky from the Earliest Days.* New York : Potter/Crown, 1975.

Carson, Gerald. *The Social History of Bourbon: An Unhurried Account of Our Star Spangled American Drink.* New York: Dodd, Mead, 1963.

Furnas, J. C. *The Life and Times of the Late Demon Rum.* London: Allen, 1965.

Tea

Roth, Rodris. *Tea Drinking in 18th-Century America: Its Etiquette and Equipage.* Paper 14. Contributions from the Museum of History and Technology, 1961.

Ukers, William H. *All about Tea.* New York: Tea and Coffee Trade Journal Company, 1935.

Water

Cummings, Richard O. *The American Ice Harvests: A Historical Study in Technology, 1800–1918.* Berkeley: University of California Press, 1949.

Wine

Fuller, Robert C. *Religion and Wine: A Cultural History of Wine Drinking in the United States.* Knoxville: University of Tennessee Press, 1996.

Gabler, James M. *Passions: The Wines and Travels of Thomas Jefferson.* Baltimore: Bacchus, 1995.

Haraszthy, Arpad. *Wine-Making in California.* Introduction by Ruth Teiser and Catherine Harroun. San Francisco: Book Club of California, 1978.

Pinney, Thomas. *A History of Wine in America from the Beginnings to Prohibition.* Berkeley: University of California Press, 1989.

Sullivan, Charles L. *Napa Wine: A History.* San Francisco: Wine Appreciation Guild, 1994.

Other

Chazanof, William. *Welch's Grape Juice: From Corporation to Co-operative.* Syracuse, NY: Syracuse University Press, 1977.

Lathrop, Elise. *Early American Inns and Taverns.* New York: Tudor, 1937.

Rice, Kym S. *Early American Taverns: For the Entertainment of Friends and Strangers.* Chicago: Regnery Gateway/Fraunces Tavern Museum, 1983.

Weiss, Harry B. *The History of Applejack or Apple Brandy in New Jersey from Colonial Times to the Present.* Trenton: New Jersey Agricultural Society, 1954.

ANDREW F. SMITH

FOOD WEBSITES

Long before there was a World Wide Web, the Internet was already a major gathering place for food information. Listservs, Usenet, telnet, gopher sites, and bulletin boards were filled with recipes, and dozens of databases of food information were available by subscription. The Web has become the dominant form of Internet publishing, and thousands upon thousands of websites are dedicated to food—and not just recipe and commercial sites, either.

This small, and by no means comprehensive, appendix deals only with American food, but with an even narrower focus. Most of these sites are at least partially historical in nature, although some manage to convey their historical information in a casual fashion.

The Web is, however, a very fluid and changeable place, and many of the sites listed may already have moved or morphed into something else by the time this book goes to press. There is little that can be done to avoid that, but sometimes a little judicious searching, through whatever search engine is most effective at the time, can discover the new location of these peripatetic sites:

Alternative-Hawaii: Ethnic Food Glossary
http://www.alternative-hawaii.com/gloss.htm#c

American Brewery History Page
http://www.beerhistory.com

American Culinary Federation (ACF)
www.acfchefs.org

American Diner Museum
http://www.dinermuseum.org

An American Feast
http://www.lib.udel.edu/ud/spec/exhibits/american.html

American Indian Ethnobotany Database
http://www.umd.umich.edu

The Appetite Network (restaurant database)
http://www.appetitenet.com

Apple of Your Pie (antique apples, history, varieties, orchards, pies, and baking)
http://www.appleofyourpie.com/index.html

Apple Varieties
http://www.applejournal.com/var001.htm

Back of the Box Recipes
http://backofthebox.com

The Boston Cooking-School Cook Book (text of Fannie Farmer's 1918 edition)
http://www.bartleby.com/87

The Boston Cooking-School Magazine: The First Seven Volumes, 1896–1902
http://students.washington.edu/bparris/bcsm.html

A Bowl of Red News (chili)
http://www.abowlofred.com/news.shtml

Brooklyn Brewery (history of brewing in New York)
http://www.brooklynbrewery.com

The Burgoo Page
http://www.angelfire.com/ky/burgoo

California Figs
http://www.californiafigs.com/index.html

Candy USA
http://www.candyusa.org

Cape Cod Cranberry Growers Association
http://www.cranberries.org

A Chocolate Timeline
http://www.cuisinenet.com/digest/ingred/chocolate/timeline.shtml

Coca-Cola Advertisements
http://memory.loc.gov/ammem/ccmphtml/colahome.html

Common Sense in the Household: A Manual of Practical Housewifery (Marion Harland's 1872 book)
http://www.hti.umich.edu/cgi/t/text/text-idx?c=moa;idno=AEL7637

A Complete Guide to Cooking in the Civil War Era
http://www.civilwarinteractive.com/cookbook.htm

Cookbook Collectors' Exchange
http://ccexonline.com

A Cookbook Lover's Guide
http://www.friktech.com/cai/cai.htm

Cookery Collection
http://www.lib.msu.edu//coll/main/spec_col/cookery

The Cook's Decameron (text of Mrs. W. G. Water's 1901 book)
http://www.worldwideschool.org/library/books/tech/cooking/TheCooks
Decameron/Chap1.html

The Core Historical Literature of Agriculture (CHLA)
http://chla.library.cornell.edu

Creole and Cajun Recipe Pages
http://www.gumbopages.com/recipe-page.html

Crisco: A Short History of America's Shortening
http://www.epicurus.com/food/crisco.html

The Culinary Collection
http://www.tulane.edu/~wc/text/culinary.html

Culinary History: A Research Guide
http://www.nypl.org/research/chss/grd/resguides/culinary

The CWi Civil War Cookbook
http://www.civilwarinteractive.com

Diner City
http://www.dinercity.com

Emergence of Advertising in America: 1850–1920
http://scriptorium.lib.duke.edu/eaa

Ethnic America Links
http://users.telerama.com/~cass/EthnicAm.html

Etiquette in Society, in Business, in Politics and at Home (Emily Post's 1922 edition)
http://www.bartleby.com/95/

Family Indigestion, The Illustrated Folio of Food (dishes from the 1950s, 1960s, and 1970s)
http://www.drokk.com/familyindigestion/index.html

FAQ of the Internet BBQ List
http://www.eaglequest.com/~bbq/faq/toc.html

Farmer's Market Online
http://www.farmersmarketonline.com

Feeding America: The Historic American Cookbook Project
http://digital.lib.msu.edu/cookbooks

Final Meal Requests (273 last requests from death row)
http://www.tdcj.state.tx.us/stat/finalmeals.htm

Flavors of the South
http://myweb.cableone.net/howle

Floridata: Fruits, Nuts, and Edible Plants
http://www.floridata.com/main_fr.cfm?state=ref_master&viewsrc=lists
/featlist.cfm?request=Edible

Food and Culture
http://www.utexas.edu/courses/stross/bibliographies/foodbib.htm

Food and Drink Marketing Trends Reports
http://pursglove.com

Food and Drug Administration (FDA) Center for Food Safety and Applied Nutrition
http://www.foodsafety.gov/list.html

Food and Nutrition Information Center (FNIC)
http://www.nal.usda.gov/fnic

Food and Nutrition Publications
http://extension.usu.edu/cooperative/publications

Food Dictionaries
http://www.1000dictionaries.com/food_dictionaries_1.html

Food History News
http://foodhistorynews.com

Food History Yellow Pages
http://foodhistorynews.com/linkmain.html

The Food Museum
http://www.foodmuseum.com

Food Network
http://www.foodtv.com

The Food Reference Website
http://www.foodreference.com

Food Review
http://www.ers.usda.gov/publications/foodreview/archives

Food Timeline
http://www.gti.net/mocolib1/kid/food.html
http://extension.usu.edu/cooperative/publications/
History Notes
http://www.gti.net/mocolib1/kid/foodfaq3.html

Foodnavigator (food technology and science)
http://www.foodnavigator.com

Foodstuff
http://goodstuff.prodigy.com/Mailing_Lists/foodstuff.html

The Fruit Pages
http://www.thefruitpages.com

Gallery of Regrettable Food (food advertisements from the 1950s and 1960s)
http://www.lileks.com/institute/gallery

Garlicana
http://www.garlicfestival.com

The Great Pop vs. Soda Controversy
http://www.ugcs.caltech.edu/~almccon/pop_soda

A Guide to Pillsbury Cookbooks and Premiums 1869–1969
http://www.friktech.com/pills/pills1.htm

Hardtack
http://www.kenanderson.net/hardtack/index.html

Healthy School Meals
http://schoolmeals.nal.usda.gov

Historic Texas Recipes
http://car.utsa.edu/historicrecipes.htm

Historical Culinary and Brewing Documents Online
http://www.thousandeggs.com/cookbooks.html

Historical Facts (Jewish cookery)
http://www.pbs.org/mpt/jewishcooking/history.html

History and Legends of Favorite Foods
http://www.whatscookingamerica.net/History/HistoryIndex.htm

The History of Cheese Making in Monroe
http://www.monroecheesefestival.com/history.html

History of Household Technology
http://www.loc.gov/rr/scitech/tracer-bullets/householdtb.html

The History of Rations
http://www.qmfound.com/history_of_rations.htm

The History of the American Barbecue
http://www.oscaruk.fsnet.co.uk/main_page_history.html

The Illinois Cooperative Extension Service
http://www.ag.uiuc.edu

Index of Ethnobotanical Leaflets
http://www.siu.edu/~ebl/leaflets

The Inglenook Cook Book
http://www.foodreference.com/html/recipesinglenookcookbook.html

Institute of Food Science and Technology (IFST)
http://www.easynet.co.uk/ifst

International Chili Society
http://www.chilicookoff.com

The International Dutch Oven Society's Homepage
http://www.idos.com

The International Federation of Competitive Eaters (IFOCE)
http://www.ifoce.com

It's Spam
http://www.SPAM.com

Jell-O Museum Web Site
http://www.jellomuseum.com

Just for Openers (virtual museum of bottle and can openers)
http://www.just-for-openers.org

Key Ingredients—America by Food
www.keyingredients.org

The Kitchen—History of Kitchen Appliances
http://inventors.about.com/library/inventors/blkitchen.htm

Kitchens Have Seen Great Changes, yet Trends of Past Recur
http://www.dispatch.com/news/newsfea99/century/food/100food.html

Kwakiutl Recipes
http://www.hallman.org/indian/recipe.html

Louisiana Stuff (or, Eat, hear music, eat, dance, eat, sweat, and eat)
http://www.gumbopages.com/index.html#louisiana

The Magic of Fire (hearth cookery)
http://www.williamrubel.com

Making of America
http://moa.umdl.umich.edu

Manufacturing of Foods in the Tenements
http://www2.arts.gla.ac.uk/www/ctich/eastside/foods12.html

Manuscript Collections—Agricultural Technology to Viticulture and Enology
http://www.lib.ucdavis.edu/specol/html/manu_idx.html

Maryland Blue Crab
http://skipjack.net/le_shore/crab/crab.html

Mint
http://cafecreosote.com/Reference/MintPage.php3

Moonpie.com
http://moonpie.com

The Moxie Collectors Page
http://www.xensei.com/users/iraseski

The Museum of Beverage Containers and Advertising
http://gono.com/vir-mus/museum.htm

The National Association Breweriana Advertising (NABA)
http://www.nababrew.org

Native Herbal, Plant Knowledge
http://indy4.fdl.cc.mn.us/~isk/food/plants.html

Native Way Cookbook: The Cookbook of the Grandmothers
http://www.wisdomkeepers.org/nativeway

The New Crop Resource Online Program
http://www.hort.purdue.edu/newcrop

Newspaper Food Columns Online
http://www.recipelink.com/newspapers.html

Not by Bread Alone
http://rmc.library.cornell.edu/food/default.htm

Nutrition and Food Science Links
http://www.science.wayne.edu/~nfs/nfslinks.htm

NYFood Museum
http://www.nyfoodmuseum.org

Old Cook Books
http://www.wmol.com/whalive/cook.htm

The Onion that Came to Texas but Never Left the Same
http://aggie-horticulture.tamu.edu/plantanswers/publications/onions/onionhis.html

Open Air Markets on the Web—North America and U.S.A.
http://www.openair.org/opair/namusa.html

Overrated and Underrated: Food Fads
http://www.americanheritage.com/AMHER/2002/05/over-under9.shtml

Pennsylvania Dutch Life, Tales, and Cooking
http://midatlantic.rootsweb.com/padutch/life.html

Peppers: History and Exploitation of a Serendipitous New Crop Discovery
http://www.hort.purdue.edu/newcrop/proceedings1993/v2-132.html

Pioneer Cookin'
http://www.texfiles.com/pioneercooking/index.htm

Po' Boys Rich in Taste and History
http://www.freep.com/fun/food/qpoor14.htm

Produce guide
http://1webblvd.com/coosemans/guide.php

Producers Rice Mill
http://producersrice.com/rice/index.html

Professional Cooking Schools
http://www.sallys-place.com/food/chefs-corner/schools_pro_usa.htm

Professional Food Organizations
http://www.sallys-place.com/food/chefs-corner/organizations.htm

Pumpkin Links
http://www.backyardgardener.com/pumplink.html

Records of the Food and Consumer Services
http://www.archives.gov/research_room/federal_records_guide/food_and_consumer_services_rg462.html

Records of the Food and Drug Administration
http://www.archives.gov/research_room/federal_records_guide/food_and_drug_administration_rg088.html

References, Resources, Information
http://osu.orst.edu/food-resource/ref.html

Resources for the Anthropological Study of Food Habits
http://lilt.ilstu.edu/rtdirks

The Rhubarb Compendium
http://www.rhubarbinfo.com

Rick's BBQ Page
http://www.azstarnet.com/~thead/bbq

RoadFood
http://www.roadfood.com

Salt Institute
http://www.saltinstitute.org

Salt: MRBLOCH Archive
http://salt.org.il/frame_palc.html

Savory Fare (eighteenth-century American foods)
http://www.monmouth.com/~cssmith/savory.html

Select Committee to Investigate the Use of Chemicals in Food and Cosmetics
http://www.archives.gov/records_of_congress/house_guide/chapter_22_select_food_and_cosmetics.html

Shelby and Chili
http://www.carrollshelby.com/chili.htm

A Short History of Spice Trading
http://www.spiceadvice.com/history/history.html

Sinclair Jerseyana Cookbooks
http://www.libraries.rutgers.edu/rul/libs/scua/sinclair/sinclair_cook_books_main.shtml

Soulfood Searching
http://www.uwf.edu/tprewitt/sofood/soulfood.htm

Sourdough FAQs
http://www.nyx.net/~dgreenw/sourdoughfaqs.html

A Southern Cultural Icon (barbecue)
http://xroads.virginia.edu/~MA95/dove/bbq.html

Southern Foodways Alliance (SFA)
http://www.southernfoodways.com

Southwest Foodie
http://SWfoodie.com

Special Collections in the Library of Congress: Joseph and Elizabeth Robins Pennell Collection
http://lcweb.loc.gov/spcoll/183.html

Still Cookin' by the Fireside (African Americans in food service)
http://www.si.edu/anacostia/food/index.htm

The Story Behind a Loaf of Bread
http://www.botham.co.uk/bread/index.htm

Subsistence and Army Cooks History Page
http://www.qmfound.com/army_subsistence_history.htm

Taquitos.net: The Crunchiest Site on the Interweb
http://www.taquitos.net/

Taste of Wisconsin: Food and Culture in the Heartland
http://www.globaldialog.com/~tallen

Texas Cooking Online
http://www.texascooking.com

The Toaster Museum
http://www.toaster.org

Traditional Food, Health and Nutrition (Native American food and foodways)
http://www.kstrom.net/isk/food/foodmenu.html

Twentieth Century Timeline Edibles and Quaffables
http://www.geocities.com/Athens/Rhodes/4190/timeline.htm

University of Florida, Institute of Food and Agricultural Science
http://gnv.ifas.ufl.edu

USDA Food Composition Data
http://www.nal.usda.gov/fnic/foodcomp/Data

The Vidalia Onion Story
http://www.vidaliaga.com/history.htm

Welcome to One Mans Junk (virtual museum of old soda cans and beer bottles)
http://www.one-mans-junk.com

Wheat People: Celebrating Kansas Harvest
http://www.kshs.org/exhibits/wheat/wheat.htm

Your Food in History Bibliography
http://vi.uh.edu/pages/lprtomat/bib~1.htm

One of the joys of the Web is its free-spirited exchange of information, which is also one of its most dispiriting shortcomings. Since most of the information found there has not been scrutinized by an editor—let alone peer-reviewed by competent scholars—a healthy skepticism must be maintained about its veracity. The following sites may help in separating the wheat from the chaff:

Evaluation of Information Sources
http://www.vuw.ac.nz/staff/alastair—smith/evaln/evaln.htm

How to Be a Skeptic
http://www.uiowa.edu/~anthro/webcourse/lost/shermer.htm

Thinking Critically about World Wide Web Resources
http://www.library.ucla.edu/libraries/college/help/critical/index.htm

BIBLIOGRAPHY

Allen, Gary. *The Resource Guide for Food Writers.* New York: Routledge, 1999.z

GARY ALLEN

MAJOR LIBRARY COLLECTIONS

This survey of American library culinary collections highlights those libraries with at least 2,500 volumes related to American food, foodways, and cookery. In a few instances, smaller collections with significantly rich or unique holdings are included.

Alabama

Alabama Public Library, Montgomery, AL
http://www.apls.state.al.us/, 334-213-3900
2,000 volumes
Collection includes general food and cookery volumes as well as a core of volumes related to Alabama cuisine and foodways.

Samford University Libraries, Birmingham, AL
http://davisweb.samford.edu, 205-726-2748
2,000 volumes
In addition to general food holdings, the Samford Special Collections Library holds the Gottlieb Cookbook Collection and English and American books dating from late nineteenth century to the 1930s.

Arizona

Phoenix Public Library–Burton Barr Central Library, Phoenix, AZ
http://www.phoenixpubliclibrary.org/, 602-262-4636
12,000 volumes
Holdings are primarily general and contemporary food and cookery books.

Arkansas

Arkansas State Library, Little Rock, AR
http://www.asl.lib.ar.us/, 501-682-2053
4,000 volumes
Holdings include general circulating collection as well as government documents, such as hearings and reports from the United States Department of Agriculture, Food and Drug Administration, and the House Committee on Agriculture.

California

California State University at Fresno–Henry Madden Library, Fresno, CA
http://www.lib.csufresno.edu, 559-278-4051
1,700 volumes
Relevant holdings are part of the library's Viticulture and Oenology Collection.

City College of San Francisco–Alice Statler Library, San Francisco, CA
http://www.ccsf.org/Library/alice/statler.html, 415-239-3460
6,000 book volumes, 3,000 pamphlets, 1,000 periodicals, 600 menus
This collection supports the curricula of the City College of San Francisco's hotel and restaurant program. Resources include books, periodicals, videos, CDs, and software related to the hospitality and restaurant industries.

The Huntington Library, San Marino, CA
http://www.huntington.org/LibraryDiv/LibraryHome.html, 626-415-2100
1,300 volumes
Collection is composed primarily of British and American books published before 1900.

Los Angeles Public Library–Science, Technology and Patents Department, Los Angeles, CA
http://www.lapl.org/central/science.html, 213-228-7201
4,500 volumes, 1,000 menus
Library holds one thousand Southern California menus and the Fritzch Collection of five hundred early cookbooks. Collection strengths include California cookery, food technology, and institutional cookery.

San Diego Public Library, San Diego, CA
http://www.sannet.gov/public-library/, 619-236-5800
7,300 volumes, 6,000 pamphlets, 1,500 menus
Collection strengths include hospitality and restaurant management magazines dating from the nineteenth century to present.

Stanford University–Cecil H. Green Library, Stanford, CA
http://www-sul.stanford.edu/, 650-725-1064
13,000 volumes
Much of collection focuses on agriculture, food security, and sustainability. Many volumes are in East Asian languages.

The University of California at Berkeley Libraries, Berkeley, CA
http://www.lib.berkeley.edu/, 510-642-6481
18,000 volumes
Collection includes the Bransten Coffee and Tea Collection, an oral history series on California winemakers, and the records of Chez Panisse.

The University of California at Davis Library, Davis, CA
http://www.lib.ucdavis.edu/, 530-752-6561
27,000 volumes
The collection supports the university's wine technology and agriculture programs. In addition, Davis's Special Collections Library holds eight hundred Chinese cookery volumes.

The University of California at San Diego–Mandeville Special Collections Library, La Jolla, CA

http://libraries.ucsd.edu/, 858-534-3336
3,000 volumes
Collection includes the Simon–Eleanor Lowenstein Collection of seventeenth- to nineteenth-century European cookery books. More recent acquisitions focus on the foodways of Asia, Mexico, Latin America, California, and the American West.

Wine Institute Library, San Francisco, CA
http://www.wineinstitute.org/wilib/, 415-512-0151
3,000 volumes
Collected volumes focus on wine appreciation and the California wine industry.

Colorado

The University of Denver–Penrose Library, Denver, CO
http://www.penlib.du.edu/, 303-871-3428
7,000 volumes
The nucleus of this library is the Husted Culinary Collection. Holdings have an American focus and date from 1600 to the present.

Connecticut

Connecticut Historical Society, Hartford, CT
http://www.chs.org/, 860-236-5621
250 volumes
Library holds important collection of Amelia Simmons's early works and nineteenth- to twentieth-century Connecticut cookbooks.

Yale University–The Sterling Memorial Library and The Beinecke Rare Book and Manuscript Library, New Haven, CT
http://www.library.yale.edu, 203-432-1775
5,000 volumes
Collection includes over one hundred rare and old volumes.

Delaware

The University of Delaware–Hugh M. Morris Library, Newark, DE
http://www.lib.udel.edu/, 302-831-2965
4,000 volumes
Holdings include general food and cookery books.

Georgia

Atlanta History Center–James G. Kenan Research Center, Atlanta, GA
http://www.atlhist.org/archives/html/archives.htm, 404-814-4000
Holdings include British cookbooks from the seventeenth century, southern foodways books, and the Shillinglaw Cookbook Collection.

Hawaii

University of Hawaii at Manoa Libraries, Honolulu, HI
http://libweb.hawaii.edu/uhmlib/index.htm, 808-956-7321
3,000 volumes
Holdings include general food and cookery volumes as well as books highlighting Hawaiian foodways.

Illinois

Chicago Public Library–Harold Washington Library Center, Chicago, IL
http://www.chipublib.org/cpl.html, 312-747-4300
2,500 volumes
Library holds large general circulating collection of cookbooks.

Glenview Public Library, Glenview, IL
http://www.glenview.lib.il.us/, 847-729-7500
4,100 volumes
Collection includes filmstrips, audiotapes, and cookbooks maintained as part of the health and domestic science subject center.

The University of Chicago Libraries, Chicago, IL
http://www.lib.uchicago.edu/, 773-702-7409
3,500 volumes
The nucleus of the university's rare and important food collection is held at the John Crerar Library. This collection of primarily English, French, and German titles is strong from the fifteenth century to the twentieth century. The library also holds the Levis Collection of approximately five hundred volumes.

Indiana

Indianapolis–Marion County Public Library, Indianapolis, IN
http://www.imcpl.lib.in.us/, 317-269-1700
6,000 volumes, 100 menus
Collection includes circulating cookbooks as well as the Wright Marble Collection of Cookbooks and the Arthur Stumpf Collection of menus.

Indiana University–The Lilly Library, Bloomington, IN
http://www.indiana.edu/~liblilly/, 812-885-2452
14,000 volumes
The Mrs. John T. Gernon Collection of more than four hundred American cookbooks forms the heart of the Lilly Library's cookery collection. This collection consists of essential cookbooks from early American history including British cookbooks, such as *The Frugal Housewife*, and the first cookbooks published in America, such as *American Cookery*.

Purdue University Libraries, West Lafayette, IN
http://thorplus.lib.purdue.edu/, 317-494-2914
2,500 volumes
Collection emphases include food science, professional cooking, and international cuisines.

Iowa

Iowa State University–Parks Library, Ames, IA
http://www.lib.iastate.edu/, 515-294-0447
2,200 volumes
Holdings include general collection of cookery and food science materials.

University of Iowa Libraries, Iowa City, IA
http://www.lib.uiowa.edu/, 319-335-5867
15,000 volumes, 3,500 pamphlets
The Szathmary Culinary Archives forms the nucleus of this collection focusing on food preparation and service from the fifteenth century to the present. The collection is multinational and in addition to cookbooks also includes materials related to nutrition, cannibalism, food erotica, food literature, and food practices.

Kansas

Kansas State University Libraries, Manhattan, KS
http://www.lib.ksu.edu/, 785-532-3014
4,500 volumes
The nucleus of this collection is the Abby Lillian Marlatt Collection. It is augmented by the Clementine Paddleford Collection, which

includes the papers of Clementine Paddleford and six hundred volumes of rare cookbooks.

Kentucky
Louisville Free Public Library, Louisville, KY
http://www.lfpl.org/, 502-574-1611
3,000 volumes
Collection includes general cookery and food books.

Maryland
National Agricultural Library, Beltsville, MD
http://www.nal.usda.gov/, 301-504-5755
1,500 volumes
Volumes focus primarily on agriculture, food safety, and nutrition.

National Library of Medicine, Bethesda, MD
http://www.nlm.nih.gov/, 1-888-346-3656
2,000 volumes
Collection includes materials on gastronomy, seventeenth- and eighteenth-century English household texts, and the early books on food and drink from the Army Medical Library.

Massachusetts
American Antiquarian Society, Worchester, MA
http://www.americanantiquarian.org/, 508-775-5221
1,100 volumes
Holdings focus on texts published in the United States prior to 1876.

Harvard University Libraries, Cambridge, MA
http://hcl.harvard.edu/houghton, 617-495-2441
3,000 volumes
Although the majority of Harvard's cookery collection was transferred to the Schlesinger Library, the Houghton Rare Books Library holds a few old and rare volumes and the Widener library holds a basic collection of general food volumes.

Harvard University, Radcliffe Institute for Advanced Study–The Arthur and Elizabeth Schlesinger Library on the History of Women in America, Cambridge, MA
http://www.radcliffe.edu/schles/, 617-495-8647
16,000 volumes
Collection includes cookery and domestic science books dating from the sixteenth century to the present as well as the papers of several culinary luminaries including Julia Child, M. F. K. Fisher, Irma Rombauer, and Marion Rombauer.

University of Massachusetts Library, Amherst, MA
http://www.library.umass.edu/, 413-545-2780
1,500 volumes
Library holds the Carolyn Maddox Beard collection of approximately one hundred titles of primarily late-nineteenth- and early-twentieth-century texts as well as the Regional Community Cookbooks Collection of four hundred titles dating from 1886 to the present.

Michigan
Detroit Public Library, Detroit, MI
http://www.detroit.lib.mi.us/, 313-833-1000
2,500 volumes
Collection emphasizes early English and American cookery texts and includes the Fred Sanders Collection.

Michigan State University Libraries, East Lansing, MI
http://www.lib.msu.edu/, 517-355-3770
4,500 volumes
Collection includes four hundred volumes published before 1900, the collections of Mary Ross Reynolds and Beatrice V. Grant, and materials supporting the curricula of the School of Hotel, Restaurant, and Institutional Management.

University of Michigan–University Library, Ann Arbor, MI
http://www.lib.umich.edu/, 734-764-9356
8,000 volumes
Holdings include food and food science books as well as some first edition and rare materials.

Minnesota
University of Minnesota–Meredith Wilson Library, Minneapolis, MN
http://www.lib.umn.edu/, 612-624-0303
5,500 volumes
In addition to general food and cookery holdings, collection emphasizes the foodways of Swedes in the United States.

New Jersey
Rutgers University Libraries,
http://www.libraries.rutgers.edu/, 732-932-7505
9,000 volumes
Holdings include general circulating collection as well as the Sinclair Jerseyana Cookbook Collection housed in the University's Special Collections.

New York
Columbia University–Butler Library, New York, NY
http://www.columbia.edu/cu/lweb, 212-854-2271
15,000 volumes
The majority of this collection is housed at the Butler Library, which includes approximately forty titles prior to 1800. Additionally, the Teacher's College Russel Library holds approximately one thousand titles written by women who operated or taught at domestic science and cookery schools.

Cornell University Libraries, Ithaca, NY
http://campusgw.library.cornell.edu/, 607-255-3673
18,000 volumes
The nucleus of Cornell's food and cookery materials are held at the Nestle Library and supports the Cornell School of Hotel and Business Administration. The library includes the J. B. Herndon collection of mostly late nineteenth- and early twentieth-century materials and the Joseph D. Vehling collection of approximately five hundred titles from the fifteenth to early twentieth century.

The Culinary Institute of America–Conrad N. Hilton Library, Hyde Park, NY
http://www.ciachef.edu/hilton, 845-452-9600
23,000 volumes, 20,000 menus
This collection of primarily twentieth-century texts supports academic and professional courses at the Culinary Institute of America. The library's collection of rare materials consists mainly of French classics dating from the sixteenth century through the nineteenth century. Collected menus date generally from 1950 to 1990 and include menus from every state, over seventy-five countries, and airline, cruise ship, and railroad menus.

The James Beard Foundation, New York, NY
http://www.jamesbeard.org/, 212-675-4984
2,500 volumes
Collection consists of James Beard's books; James Beard Award–winning books; and complete sets of *Petits propos culinaires, Journal of Gastronomy, Cuisine,* and *Gourmet.*

New York Academy of Medicine Library, New York, NY
http://www.nyam.org/library/historical/collection.shtml, 212-822-7310
5,000 volumes, 5,000 pamphlets
Holdings date from the ninth century to the present and include the Dr. Margaret Barclay Wilson Collection. Contemporary materials focus primarily on health and diets.

The New York Public Library–Humanities and Social Sciences Division, New York, NY
http://www.nypl.org, 212-930-0800
17,000 volumes, 25,000 menus
The library holds a large variety of cookery and food materials with an emphasis on the seventeenth and eighteenth centuries. The library also holds the Helen Hayes Whitney Collection of over two hundred cookbooks from the fifteenth to the twentieth century and the Buttoloph Menu Collection.

New York State Library and Archives, Albany, NY
http://www.nysl.nysed.gov/, 518-474-5355
6,500 volumes
Collection includes American cookery books published primarily between the late nineteenth century and the twentieth century.

New York University–Elmer Holmes Bobst Library, New York, NY
http://www.nyu.edu/library/bobst.genlinfo.htm, 212-998-2500
16,000 volumes, 5,000 pamphlets
Collection supports curricula of the food studies and food management programs and includes materials on food preferences and habits, cookery, food science, and management. These holdings include the Cecily Brownstone Collection of primarily twentieth-century cookery and food books.

North Carolina

Duke University Libraries, Durham, NC
http://www.lib.duke.edu/, 919-660-5816
11,000 volumes
Collection is of general food, food science, and food preference materials.

The University of North Carolina, Greensboro, NC
http://www.lib.unc.edu/, 919-962-1335
11,000 volumes
Holdings include general food and food preference books as well as North Carolina cookbooks and volumes from the nineteenth century.

Ohio

Cleveland Public Library–Main Library, Cleveland, OH
http://www.cpl.org, 216-623-2800
4,500 volumes
Holdings include primarily twentieth-century American cookbooks.

Ohio State University Libraries, Columbus, OH
http://www.lib.ohio-state.edu/, 614-292-6154
4,500 volumes

Holdings are primarily current and support the university's home economics curricula.

Pennsylvania

Carnegie Free Library of Pittsburgh, Pittsburgh, PA
http://www.carnegielibrary.org, 412-622-3114
2,700 volumes
Holdings include primarily contemporary cookbooks.

Pennsylvania State University Libraries, University Park, PA
http://www.libraries.psu.edu, 814-865-0401
12,000 volumes
Collection includes books related to the food industry, food safety, food choices, and professional cooking.

University of Pennsylvania Libraries, Philadelphia, PA
http://www.library.upenn.edu, 215-573-9079
2,500 volumes
University holds a basic collection of food and cookery materials as well as the Esther B. Aresty Collection of Rare Books on the Culinary Arts housed in the Walter H. and Leonore Annenberg Rare Book and Manuscript Library.

Rhode Island

Johnson and Wales University, Harborside Culinary Library, Providence, RI
http://library.jwu.edu/prov/ab_cul.htm, 401-598-1466
10,000 volumes
The library's collection supports Johnson and Wales's culinary arts, culinary nutrition, baking, and pastry arts programs. In addition to books and periodicals, the library also holds a unique collection of videos and menus.

Johnson and Wales University, Culinary Archives and Museum, Providence, RI
http://www.culinary.org/, 401-598-2805
500,000 pieces of ephemera, 100,000 volumes, 4,000 volumes
The archives and museum holdings includes the personal collections of Louis Szathmary, Paul Fritzsche, Heinz Bender, and Rose Levy Beranbaum, as well as the institutional records of the Honorable Order of the Golden Toque, Les Dames d'Escoffier, and the International and International Food and Beverage Forum. The museum's collections include approximately 100,000 volumes and over 4,000 menus, but the institution's primary strength is its collection of ephemera. The museum's 500,000 items represent over five thousand years of culinary and food service history.

Texas

Texas Women's University–Blagg-Huey Library, Denton, TX
http://www.twu.edu/library/collections.htm, 940-898-2665
15,000 volumes
Holdings include twentieth-century cookbooks, the Marion Somerville Church Collection, the Julie Benell Collection, the Margaret Scruggs Collection of regional cookbooks, and seventeenth-century collections of recipes and related medical information.

Washington, DC

Library of Congress, Washington, DC
http://www.loc.gov/, 202-707-5000
50,000 volumes
In addition to the Library of Congress's general repository collection,

the library also holds the Joseph and Elizabeth Robins Pennell Collection and the Katherine G. Bitting Collection.

BIBLIOGRAPHY

Ash, Lee, ed. *Subject Collections*. New Providence, NJ: Bowker, 1993. This source lists, by subject, self-reported subject specialties of U.S. libraries.

Feret, Barbara L. *Gastronomical and Culinary Literature: A Survey and Analysis of Historically-Oriented Collections in the U.S.A.* Metuchen, NJ: Scarecrow Press, 1979. This source provides in depth descriptions of selected U.S. libraries as well as an introduction to historically oriented culinary literature.

Griswold, Madge. *A Selective Guide to Culinary Library Collections in the United States*. http://www.cs.arizona.edu/people/madge/LibraryReport.pdf. This document provides contact information and overviews of U.S. libraries with culinary holdings.

MIMI MARTIN

FOOD-RELATED MUSEUMS

These food and beverage museums or collections are only a small number of the total existing throughout the United States. They are listed in the following order: A. food and drink in general (alphabetized by state); B. specific foods; C. nonalcoholic beverages, brewed beverages, fermented products, and distilled spirits; and D. food containers.

A. Food and Drink in General

1. Desert Botanical Garden, Phoenix, AZ
   480-941-1225;
   www.dbg.org

   A living museum of arid-land plants, especially succulents and those native to the Southwest. It occupies 145 acres and includes a very large number of food plants, including agave, amaranth, lima and tepary beans, black mission fig, and purslane—for purposes of exhibition, conservation, and study, in both outdoor and greenhouse settings. Objects for traditional food processing: grinding, pounding, roasting, and drying are on view; demonstrations and special events are scheduled. Founded in 1939; privately funded and nonprofit.

2. Copia, the American Center for Wine, Food, and the Arts, Napa Valley, CA
   707-257-3603
   www.theamericancenter.org

   An education center rather than a museum but with a curator of food; three half-acre outdoor gardens of organic edibles; and frequent exhibits on food and wine in its exhibit galleries. Galleries, classrooms, a rare book library, a theater for films and lectures, and a demonstration kitchen total eighty thousand square feet. Opened in November 2001; nonprofit with the American Institute of Wine and Food, the University of California at Davis, and Cornell University School of Restaurant and Hotel Administration as partners in its efforts.

3. Smithsonian Institution's National Museum of American History, Washington, DC
   202-357-2700
   www.americanhistory.si.edu

   Food-related objects are on view in almost every exhibition: agricultural implements from the eighteenth through the twentieth centuries; fishing industry objects; tableware of silver, ceramics, plastic, aluminum, earthenware, and glass belonging to presidents, ordinary citizens, and the Santa Fe Rail Road; small electrical appliances and large kitchen equipment; food containers from canning jars to rice-harvesting baskets and a grape crate; sections of the Stohlmann Confectionery, a 1902 Automat, and the Greensboro, North Carolina, lunch counter where the first civil rights sit-in took place; Julia Child's entire kitchen; mess kits for soldiers from George Washington to World War II fighters; the role of Americans in the battle for pure food and water; and the role of chemistry in developing saccharin and genetically engineered tomatoes. Not currently on exhibit, but available to see by appointment, are the museum's vast holdings in the collections of the Division of Cultural History, the Division of Social History, the Division of the History of Technology, and the Archives Center, with its collections of papers, photos, and other materials related to the production, packaging, and marketing of many foodstuffs, as well as the collections of the Wine History Project.

4. National Agricultural Center and Hall of Fame, Bonner Springs, KS
   913-721-1075
   www.AgHallof Fame.com

   Focused on the history and importance of agriculture, with a growing collection of poultry-raising objects, farm trucks, steam engines, threshing machines, and ice-harvesting tools, among many other collections. The complex covers 172 acres.

5. New Jersey Museum of Agriculture (Cook Campus of Rutgers University), New Brunswick, NJ
   732-249-2077
   www.agriculturemuseum.org

   Exhibits devoted to the evolution of agriculture from before European settlement to the present and the history of New Jersey's contributions to worldwide food production. The Krueger Collection of Agricultural, Scientific, and Household Artifacts (over 3,700 pieces of farm equipment, scientific instruments, and household appliances) and the George H. Cook Collection of Agricultural and Scientific Photographs are important parts of the museum's objects. Opened in 1990.

6. Farmers' Museum Inc., Cooperstown, NY
   888-547-1450
   www.farmersmuseum.org

   This living history museum's emphasis, with its heritage plants and breeds of livestock and more than 23,000 objects, is on mid-nineteenth-century upstate New York. The land has been farmed since 1813 when James Fenimore Cooper was its owner. The museum, with close links to the New York State Historical Association, is privately funded and nonprofit.

7. Culinary Archives and Museum at Johnson and Wales University, Providence, RI
401-598-2805
www.culinary.org

Exhibits of the late chef Louis Szathmary's collection of food-related items from many parts of the world and from 3000 B.C.E. to the present, plus objects from other donors. Its more than 300,000 objects include cooking utensils and equipment, large and small appliances, menus, cookbooks, and a myriad of other culinary materials.

B. Specific Foods

1. Candy Americana Museum (Chocolate), Lititz, PA
888-294-5287

History, manufacturing, and advertising of candy; re-created 1900s candy kitchen, antique implements, molds, containers, and chocolate pot collection. Modern working candy kitchen.

2. Cranberry Expo Limited, Warrens, WI
608-378-4878
cranberryexpo@tomah.com

Exhibits on cranberry industry history, bog maintenance, specially devised harvesting machinery and implements, plus a close-up view of growing cranberry plants.

3. Hershey Museum, Hershey, PA
717-534-8940
www.hersheymuseum.org

A variety of exhibits, original working machinery, and unique artifacts relate the story of Milton Hershey, the candy empire he created, and the model town he founded. Old-time candy kitchen.

4. National Apple Museum, Biglerville, PA
717-677-4556
www.nationalapplemuseum.com

The focus is on apple production, processing, and utilization; historical farm equipment; peelers, cider presses, and vinegar generator; early orchard. Exhibit space of 9,500 square feet in restored Civil War barn.

5. Southwest Dairy Center, Sulphur Springs, TX
903-439-MILK
swdairycenter@geocities.com

Exhibits on past and current production of milk products, from barn to home, including 1930s-kitchen production of cream and butter. Sited in leading dairy county in the United States.

6. Mystic Seaport, Mystic, CT
860-572-0711
mysticseaport.org

Oystering, lobstering, and salmon-fishing exhibits; fishing industry vessels and equipment.

7. Chesapeake Bay Maritime Museum, St. Michaels, MD
410-745-2916
www.cbmm.org

Exhibits on oystering, crabbing, and extensive collection of seafood industry objects.

8. Mount Vernon Gristmill, Mount Vernon, VA
703-780-2000
www.mountvernon.org

George Washington's 1771 gristmill: rebuilt stone mill with a working waterwheel.

9. Honey Acres (Honey Museum), Ashipppun, WI
800-558-7745

Presents the story of beekeeping with exhibits on pollination, beeswax, and a bee tree, plus a view of a functioning hive, and a twenty-minute multimedia show, "Honey of a Story."

10. Jell-O Gallery, LeRoy, NY
585-768-7433
www.jellomuseum.com

History and technology of Jell-O in town where the product was invented in 1897. Permanent exhibition: "There's Always Room for Jell-O." Part of LeRoy Historical Society site.

11. New England Maple Museum, Pittsford, VT
802-775-1650

Contemporary and antique sugaring tools and equipment. Demonstrations: candy making to construction of wood buckets. Sugaring history depicted by murals.

12. Mount Horeb Mustard Museum, Mt. Horeb, WI
800-438-6878
www.mustardmuseum.com

Thousands of kinds of mustards and antique mustard pots from all over the world, housed in a 7,700 square foot building; video show.

13. First Peanut Museum, Waverly, VA
804-834-3327/2151

Collection of peanut-growing and -harvesting equipment, photos, peanut memorabilia.

14. Wyandot Popcorn Museum, Marion, OH
740-387-4255
www.wyandotpopcornmus.com

Large collection of restored antique poppers, popcorn vending trucks, wagons, and carts.

15. Idaho's World Potato Exposition, Blackfoot, ID
208-785-2517

History of potato growing and potato lore in about fourteen hundred square feet of a former railroad depot.

16. Rice Museum, Georgetown, SC
   843-546-7423
   www.ricemuseum.com

   Rice culture in early South Carolina, a society based on one crop; dioramas, tools, equipment, maps, and graphics. In 1842 Old Market Building. Opened in 1970.

17. Spam Museum, Austin, MN
   800-LUV-SPAM
   www.Spam.com

   Sponsored by Hormel, the museum tells how Spam is produced and distributed and the role it played in World War II. Spam ads and memorabilia; interactive exhibits.

18. International Vinegar Museum, Roslyn, SD
   877-486-0075
   museum@vinegarman.com

   How vinegars are made from many plants worldwide, used and enjoyed; research kitchen; 2,500 square feet.

C. Beverages

1. World of Coca-Cola Atlanta, Atlanta, GA
   404-676-5151
   www.woccatlanta.com

   Coca-Cola's history from its 1886 beginnings, through exhibits featuring advertising, promotional, and packaging materials, especially from the 1950s onward; re-created 1930s soda fountain, ten-minute film, and self-guided tours.

2. Dr Pepper Free Museum and Free Enterprise Institute, Waco, TX
   817-757-1024
   www.drpeppermuseum.com

   Collection of objects in renovated original bottling plant of Dr Pepper; focused on the story of the entire soft drink industry; includes a functioning 1930s soda fountain. Opened 1991.

3. Terre Haute Brewing Company and Museum, Terre Haute, IN
   812-232-2466
   www.terrehautebrewery. com

Brewing artifacts and advertising materials from the early history of Terre Haute's first brewery, in operation since the mid-1800s. Former underground cold storage area was being excavated in the early 2000s.

4. Greyton H. Taylor Wine Museum, Hammondsport, NY
   607-868-3610
   www.bullyhill.com

   Wide assortment of wine-related objects tracing development of wine making in New York State's Finger Lakes region from the late nineteenth to the mid-twentieth century. Wine-barrel coopering tools, a collection of wine bottles, and other items. At Bully Hill Vineyards.

5. Oscar Getz Museum of Whiskey History, Bardstown, KY
   502-348-2999
   http://www.ohwy.com/ky/o/osgemuwh.htm

   History of the American whiskey industry over more than two centuries. Distilling equipment, advertising posters, pre-Prohibition whiskey bottles and other containers, historical documents and distillery records. Getz was an American whiskey historian, writer, and lecturer.

D. Food Containers

1. Tupperware Museum of Historic Food Containers, Kissimmee, FL
   407-826-5050
   www.Tupperware. com

   Large collection of food containers, varying in size, shape, function, materials, and age, from a six thousand-year-old Egyptian jar to today's American plastics. At Tupperware headquarters.

2. Lunch Box and Pop Art Museum, Columbus, GA
   706-322-0516
   www.roadsideattraction.com

   More than 3,500 metal lunch boxes, decorated with images of entertainment figures and marketed for schoolchildren since 1951, amassed by two avid collectors. Allen M. Woodall Jr., founder.

SHIRLEY E. CHERKASKY

FOOD-RELATED ORGANIZATIONS

The first food-related society established in America was the Massachusetts Society for Promoting Agriculture. It was founded in Boston, Massachusetts, in 1792 with a charter membership of twenty-eight people. By 1820 membership had grown to over six hundred individuals, some from as far away as China. The organization's logo was "The Source of Wealth" set into a seal emblazoned with a yoke of oxen working a furrowed field. Ever since, professional dietitians, chefs, food technologists, and flavor chemists have formed professional societies to develop their skills, share information among their membership, and monitor high ethical standards within their profession.

Besides professional societies, a slew of marketing associations, focused on one particular food or product, developed during the twentieth century to promote the industry. Whether they go by the name of association, board, commission, or institute, their primary mission is to promote increased consumption of their particular agricultural product (such as potatoes, raisins, or walnuts) or processed food (such as biscuits or candy). Many of these trade associations are located close to where their product is harvested or manufactured. For example, the American Mushroom Institute is located in Pennsylvania, and the Cranberry Institute is in Massachusetts, places long associated with the production and marketing of these products. In recent years, trade associations have opened offices in or around Washington, DC, in order to lobby their interests before Congress and to interact with government agencies that monitor, evaluate, or regulate their industries.

This list of associations will serve as a valuable resource for students researching a particular product or industry. For writers, newspaper food editors, and journalists, these associations can open the door to experts in every facet of the food and culinary industry.

This list is divided into two sections: associations for professionals and trade associations.

Professional Associations

American Association of Candy Technologists
175 Rock Rd.
Glen Rock, NJ 07452
201-652-2655
F: 201-652-3419
http://www.aactcandy.org
Professional group of technologists, educators, and students dedicated to the advancement of the confectionery industry.

American Association of Cereal Chemists
3340 Pilot Knob Rd.
St. Paul, MN 55121-2097
651-454-7250
F: 651-454-0766
http://www.aaccnet.org

American Correctional Food Service Association
4248 Park Glen Rd.
Minneapolis, MN 55416
952-928-4658
F: 952-929-1318
http://www.acfsa.org
The international association of correctional food service professionals.

American Dietetic Association
120 S. Riverside Plaza, Ste. 2000
Chicago, IL 60606-6995
800-877-1600
http://www.eatright.org
In the early twenty-first century, the world's largest organization of food and nutrition specialists with nearly seventy thousand members.

American Institute of Wine and Food
304 W. Liberty St., Ste. 201
Louisville, KY 40202
502-992-1022
800-274-2493
F: 502-589-3602
http://www.aiwf.com
Educational organization devoted to improving the appreciation and understanding of food and drink.

American Meat Science Association
1111 N. Dunlap Ave.
Savoy, IL 61874
217-356-5368
F: 217-398-4119

http://www.meatscience.org
Professional society of meat scientists.

American School Food Service Association
700 S. Washington St., Suite 300
Alexandria, VA 22314
703-739-3900
F: 703-739-3915
http://www.asfsa.org

American Society of Brewing Chemists
3340 Pilot Knob Rd.
St. Paul, MN 55121-2097
http://www.asbcnet.org

American Society of Sugar Beet Technologists
(*See* Beet Sugar Development Foundation.)

Association of Food Journalists
38309 Genesee Lake Rd.
Oconomowoc, WI 53066
http://www.afjonline.com
Networking organization for journalists who devote most of their
working time to planning and writing food copy for news media.

Institute of Food Technologists
525 W. Van Buren, Ste. 1000
Chicago, IL 60607
312-782-8424
F: 312-782-8348
http://www.ift.org
Membership includes researchers, academicians, regulators,
scientists, and technologists in the food industry.

International Association for Food Protection
6200 Aurora Ave., Ste. 200 W
Des Moines, IA 50322-2864
800-369-6337
F: 515-276-8655
http://www.foodprotection.org
Founded in 1911 to serve the needs of food safety professionals.

International Association of Culinary Professionals
304 W. Liberty St., Ste. 201
Louisville, KY 40202-3011
502-581-9786
F: 502-589-3602
http://www.iacp.com
Provides continuing education and development for members who are
engaged in the areas of culinary education, communication, or
preparation of food and drink.

Poultry Science Association
1111 N. Dunlap Ave.
Savoy, IL 61874
217-356-5285
F: 217-398-4119
http://www.poultryscience.org
Represents professionals from academia, industry, and government.

Research Chefs Association
5775 Peachtree-Dunwoody Rd.
Bldg. G, Ste. 500

Atlanta, GA 30342
404-252-3663
F: 404-252-0774
http://www.culinology.com

Society for Foodservice Management
304 W. Liberty St., Ste. 201
Louisville, KY 40202
502-583-3783
F: 502-589-3602
http://www.sfm-online.org

Trade Associations

Almond Board of California
1150 Ninth St., Ste. 1500
Modesto, CA 95354
209-549-8262
F: 209-549-8267
http://www.almondboard.com

American Association of Meat Processors
P.O. Box 269
Elizabethtown, PA 17022
717-367-1168
F: 717-367-9096
http://www.aamp.com
North America's largest meat and poultry trade organization.

American Cheese Society
304 W. Liberty St., Ste. 201
Louisville, KY 40202
502-583-3783
F: 502-589-3602
http://www.cheesesociety.org
Upholds the traditions and preserves the history of American
cheesemaking.

American Dairy Products Institute
116 N. York St.
Elmhurst, IL 60126
630-530-8700
F: 630-530-8707
http://www.americandairyproducts.com
http://www.adpi.org
Membership organization of manufacturers of evaporated and dry
milks, cheese, and whey products.

American Dry Bean Board
8233 Old Courthouse Rd., Ste. 210
Vienna, VA 22182
703-556-9300
F: 703-556-9301
http://www.americanbean.org

American Egg Board
1460 Renaissance Dr.
Park Ridge, IL 60068
847-296-7043
F: 847-296-7007
http://www.aeb.org
Organization of egg producers to increase markets for eggs through
promotion, research, and education.

American Emu Association
P.O. Box 224
Sixes, OR 97476
541-332-0675
F: 928-962-9430
http://www.aea-emu.org
Represents emu producers, processors, and marketers.

American Frozen Food Institute
2000 Corporate Ridge, Ste. 1000
McLean, VA 22102
703-821-0770
F: 703-821-1350
http://www.affi.com
Represents all aspects of the frozen food industry supply chain,
including manufacturers, distributors, suppliers, and packagers.

American Lamb Board
7900 E. Union Ave., Ste. 1003
Denver, CO 80237
303-217-7598
http://www.americanlambboard.org

American Meat Institute
1700 N. Moore St., Ste. 1600
Arlington, VA 22209
703-841-2400
F: 703-527-0938
http://www.meatami.com
Represents the interests of packers and processors of beef, pork,
lamb, veal, and turkey products and their suppliers.

American Mushroom Institute
1284 Gap Newport Pike, Ste. 2
Avondale, PA 19311
610-268-7483
http://www.americanmushroom.org
National trade association representing the growers, processors, and
marketers of cultivated mushrooms.

American Ostrich Association
P.O. Box 163
Ranger, TX 76470
254-647-1645
F: 254-647-1645
http://www.ostriches.org

American Peanut Council
1500 King St., Ste. 301
Alexandria, VA 22314
http://www.peanutsusa.com
Forum for all segments of the peanut industry to discuss issues
impacting the production, utilization, and marketing of peanuts.

American Pie Council
P.O. Box 368
Lake Forest, IL 60045
847-371-0170
F: 847-371-0199
http://www.piecouncil.org
Committed to preserving America's pie heritage.

American Sheep Industry Association
9785 Maroon Circle, Ste. 360

Centennial, CO 80112
303-771-3500
F: 303-771-8200
http://www.sheepusa.org
Federation of individual sheep and goat producers.

American Society of Baking
27 E. Napa St., Ste. G
Sonoma, CA 95476
707-935-0103
866-920-9885
F: 707-935-0174
http://www.asbe.org
Promotes the professional development and knowledge of its
members.

American Soybean Association
12125 Woodcrest Executive Dr., Ste. 100
St. Louis, MO 63141-5009
314-576-1770
800-688-7692
F: 314-576-2786
http://www.amsoy.org
Membership-driven, grassroots policy organization that represents
U.S. soybean farmers.

American Spice Trade Association
2025 M St. NW, Ste. 800
Washington, DC 20036
202-367-1127
202-367-2127
http://www.astaspice.org
Founded in 1907 to serve members in over thirty-four spice-
producing nations around the world.

Association of Food and Drug Officials
2550 Kingston Rd., Ste. 311
York, PA 17402
717-757-2888
F: 717-755-8089
http://www.afdo.org
Devoted to promoting uniformity on public health and consumer
protection issues related to foods, drugs, and consumer products
since 1896.

Association of Food Industries
3301 Rt. 66, Ste. 205, Bldg. C
Neptune, NJ 07753
732-922-3008
F: 732-922-3590
http://www.afius.org

Beet Sugar Development Foundation and
American Society of Sugar Beet Technologists
800 Grant St., #300
Denver, CO 80203
303-832-4460
http://www.bsdf-assbt.org
Organizations supplying research and development as well as
education programs to the beet sugar industry.

Biscuit and Cracker Manufacturers' Association
8484 Georgia Ave., Ste. 700

Silver Spring, MD 20910
301-608-1552
F: 301-608-1557
http://www.thebcma.org
Founded in 1901, during the true "cracker barrel" era, to serve the interests of biscuit and cracker makers.

California Avocado Commission
38 Discovery, Ste. 150
Irving, CA 92618
949-341-1955
F: 949-341-1970
http://www.avocado.org
Established to promote the avocado to consumers, the media, and the foodservice industry by providing information and merchandising ideas.

California Dried Plum Board
3841 N. Freeway Blvd., Ste. 120
P.O. Box 348180
Sacramento, CA 95834
916-565-6232
F: 916-565-6237
http://www.californiadriedplums.org

California Fig Advisory Board
7395 N. Palm Bluffs, Ste. 106
Fresno, CA 93711
559-440-5400
F: 559-438-5405
http://www.californiafigs.com
State trade association to promote the health benefits of California figs.

California Olive Industry
P.O. Box 7796
Fresno, CA 93747
800-452-4993
http://www.calolive.org

California Pistachio Commission
1318 E. Shaw Ave., Ste. 420
Fresno, CA 93710-7912
559-221-8294
F: 559-221-8044
http://www.pistachios.org
Established to provide information on pistachios to the industry, students, and consumers.

California Strawberry Commission
180 Westridge Dr., Ste. 101
P.O. Box 269
Watsonville, CA 95077
831-724-1301
F: 831-724-5973
http://www.calstrawberry.com
State-chartered marketing organization founded in 1955.

California Table Grape Commission
392 W. Fallbrook, Ste. 101
Fresno, CA 93711-6150
559-447-8350
F: 559-447-9184

http://www.freshcaliforniagrapes.com
http://www.tablegrape.com
Trade association to promote the consumption of fresh grapes from California.

Center for Science in the Public Interest
1875 Connecticut Ave. NW, Suite 300
Washington, DC 20009
202-332-9110
F: 202-265-4954
http://www.cspinet.org
Nutrition and food safety policy advocacy group.

Cherry Marketing Institute
P.O. Box 30285
Lansing, MI 48909-7785
http://www.usacherries.com
National nonprofit promotion organization for tart cherries.

Chocolate Manufacturers Association
(*See* National Confectioners Association.)

Cranberry Institute
3203-B Cranberry Hwy.
East Wareham, MA 02538
800-295-4132
F: 508-759-6294
http://www.cranberryinstitute.org

Distilled Spirits Council of the United States
1250 Eye St. NW, Ste. 400
Washington, DC 20005-3998
202-682-3544
F: 202-682-8856
http://www.distilledspirits.org
Trade association representing producers and marketers of distilled spirits sold in the United States.

Florida Tomato Committee
P.O. Box 140635
Orlando, FL 32814-0635
407-894-3071
F: 407-898-4296
http://www.floridatomatoes.org

Food and Drug Law Institute
1000 Vermont Ave. NW, Ste. 200
Washington, DC 20005
202-371-1420
800-956-6293
F: 202-371-0649
http://www.fdli.org
Forum for government agencies and business, academic, and consumer communities to engage in the exchange of information on public policy, law, and regulations subject to Food and Drug Administration (FDA) oversight.

Foodservice and Packaging Institute
150 S. Washington St., Ste. 204
Falls Church, VA 22046
703-538-2800
F: 703-538-2187
http://www.fpi.org

Georgia Pecan Commission
328 Agricultural Bldg.
Capitol Square
Atlanta, GA 30334
404-656-3678
F: 404-656-9380
http://www.georgiapecans.org
Founded in 1995 to raise consumer awareness and promote the year-round consumption of Georgia pecans.

Grocery Manufacturers of America
2401 Pennsylvania Ave. NW, 2nd Floor
Washington, DC 20037
202-337-9400
F: 202-337-4508
http://gmabrands.com
World's largest association of food, beverage, and consumer product companies.

Hazelnut Marketing Board
21595-A Dolores Way NE
Aurora, OR 97002-9738
503-678-6823
F: 503-678-6825
http://oregonhazelnuts.org
Also represents the Oregon Hazelnut Commission, the Nut Growers Society, and the Oregon Association of Hazelnut Industries.

Herb Research Foundation
4140 Fifteenth St.
Boulder, CO 80304
303-449-2265
F: 303-449-7849
http://www.herbs.org
Source of scientific information on medicinal plants.

Idaho Potato Commission
P.O. Box 1068
Boise, ID 83701
208-334-2350
F: 208-334-2274
http://www.famouspotatoes.org
State agency responsible for promoting potatoes from Idaho.

Independent Bakers Association
1223 Potomac St. NW
Washington, DC 20007
202-333-8190
F: 202-337-3809
http://www.independentbaker.org
Association of over four hundred mostly family-owned wholesale bakeries and allied industry trades.

Institute of Shortening and Edible Oils
1750 New York Ave. NW, Ste. 120
Washington, DC 20006
202-783-7960
F: 202-393-1367
http://www.iseo.org
Information on edible fats and oils, their nutrition, processing methods, and industry contacts.

International Bottled Water Association
1700 Diagonal Rd., Ste. 650
Alexandria, VA 22314
703-683-5213
F: 703-683-4074
http://www.bottledwater.org
Founded in 1958 to represent the bottled water industry.

International Dairy-Deli-Bakery Association
313 Price Pl., Ste. 202
P.O. Box 5528
Madison, WI 53705-0528
608-238-7908
F: 608-238-6330
http://www.iddba.org

International Dairy Foods Association
1250 H Street NW, Ste. 900
Washington, DC 20005
202-737-4332
F: 202-331-7820
http://www.idfa.org

International Food Information Council
1100 Connecticut Ave. NW, Ste. 430
Washington, DC 20036
202-296-6540
F: 202-296-6547
http://www.ific.org
Mission is to communicate science-based information on food safety and nutrition to health and nutrition professionals, educators, journalists, and others who provide information to consumers.

International Natural Sausage Casing Association
1200 Sunset Hills Rd., Ste. 130
Reston, VA 20190
703-234-4112
F: 703-435-4390
http://www.insca.org
Producers, suppliers, and brokers of natural casing products.

Juice Products Association
1156 Fifteenth St. NW
Washington, DC 20005
202-785-3232
F: 202-223-9741
http://www.njpa.com

Maine Potato Board
744 Main St.
Presque Isle, ME 04769
207-769-5061
F: 207-764-4148
http://www.mainepotatoes.com

Master Brewers Association of the Americas
3340 Pilot Knob Rd.
St. Paul, MN 55121-2097
651-454-7250
F: 651-454-0766
http://www.mbaa.com

Michigan Asparagus Advisory Board
12800 Escanaba Dr., Ste. A
P.O. Box 550
DeWitt, MI 48820
517-669-4250
F: 517-669-4251
http://www.asparagus.org

Mushroom Council
11501 Dublin Blvd., Ste. 200
Dublin, CA 94568
925-558-2749
F: 925-558-2740
http://www.mushroomcouncil.org

National Aquaculture Association
111 W. Washington St.
Charles Town, WV 25414-1529
304-728-2167
F: 304-876-2196
http://aqua.ucdavis.edu/organizations/organizations.NAA.html
Works with aquaculture community to create a U.S. infrastructure
capable of supporting a profitable, competitive, and environmentally
responsible industry.

National Association for the Specialty Food Trade
120 Wall St., 27th Floor
New York, NY 10005
212-482-6440
F: 212-482-6459
http://www.specialtyfood.com
Founded in 1952 to foster trade and interest in the specialty food
industry. Publishes *Specialty Food* magazine.

National Association of Flavors and Food-Ingredient Systems
3301 Rte. 66, Ste. 205, Bldg. C
Neptune, NJ 07753
732-922-3218
F: 732-922-3590
http://www.naffs.org

National Association of Margarine Manufacturers
1101 Fifteenth St. NW, Ste. 202
Washington, DC 20005
202-785-3232
F: 202-223-9741
http://www.margarine.org
Trade association formed in 1936 to serve health-conscious
consumers and the margarine industry.

National Beer Wholesalers Association
1101 King St., Ste. 600
Alexandria, VA 22314-2944
800-300-6417
703-683-4300
F: 703-683-8965
http://www.nbwa.org
Represents over 1,850 family-owned small businesses.

National Bison Association
1400 W. 122nd Ave., Ste. 106
Westminster, CO 80234
303-292-2833

F: 303-292-2564
http://www.bisoncentral.com

National Cattlemen's Beef Association
9110 E. Nichols Ave., #300
Centennial, CO 80112
http://www.beef.org

National Chicken Council
1015 Fifteenth St. NW, Ste. 930
Washington, DC 20005-2622
202-296-2622
F: 202-293-4005
http://www.nationalchickencouncil.com
Represents companies that produce, process, and market 95 percent
of the chickens and chicken products sold in the United States.

National Coffee Association of U.S.A.
15 Maiden Ln., Ste. 1405
New York, NY 10038
212-766-4007
F: 212-766-5815
http://www.ncausa.org
Founded in 1911 as the first trade association for the U.S. coffee
industry.

National Confectioners Association
8320 Old Courthouse Rd., Ste. 300
Vienna, VA 22182
703-790-5750
F: 703-790-5752
http://www.candyusa.org

National Corn Growers Association
632 Cepi Dr.
Chesterfield, MO 63005
636-733-9004
F: 636-733-9005
http://www.ncga.com
National organization founded in 1957. Represents over 32,000
growers from forty-eight states.

National Country Ham Association
P.O. Box 948
Conover, NC 28616
828-466-2760
800-820-4426
F: 828-466-2770
http://www.countryham.org
Organized in 1992 to represent interests and concerns of the country
ham industry.

National Fisheries Institute
1901 N. Fort Myer Dr., Ste. 700
Arlington, VA 22209
703-524-8880
F: 703-524-4619
http://www.nfi.org

National Food Processors Association
1350 I Street NW, Ste. 300
Washington, DC 20005
202-639-5900

F: 202-639-5932
http://www.nfpa-food.org
Voice of the $500 billion food industry on scientific and public policy issues.

National Frozen and Refrigerated Foods Association
4755 Linglestown Rd., Ste. 300
Harrisburg, PA 17112
717-657-8601
F: 717-657-9862
http://www.nffa.org

National Grocers Association
1005 N. Glebe Rd., Ste. 250
Arlington, VA 22201-5758
703-516-0700
F: 703-516-0115
http://www.nationalgrocers.org

National Hot Dog and Sausage Council
1700 N. Moore St., Ste. 1600
Arlington, VA 22209-1995
703-841-2400
F: 703-527-0938
http://www.hot-dog.org
Established in 1994 as a source of information to consumers and media on questions related to quality, safety, nutrition, and preparation of hot dogs and sausages.

National Honey Board
390 Lashley St.
Longmont, CO 80501-6045
303-776-2337
F: 303-776-1177
http://www.honey.com
http://www.nhb.org
Serves as a liaison between the honey industry and food manufacturers to expand domestic and foreign markets for honey.

National Meat Association
1970 Broadway, Ste. 825
Oakland, CA 94612
510-763-1533
F: 510-763-6186
1400 16th St. NW, Ste. 400
Washington, DC 20036
202-667-2108
http://www.nmaonline.org
Association represents meatpackers and processors.

National Meat Canners Association
1700 N. Moore St., Ste. 1600
Arlington, VA 22209
703-841-3680
F: 703-841-9656
http://www.meatami.com
Represents suppliers and canners of meat products.

National Milk Producers Federation
2101 Wilson Blvd., Ste. 400
Arlington, VA 22201
703-243-6111

F: 703-841-9328
http://www.nmpf.org

National Oilseed Processors Association
1300 L St. NW, Ste. 1020
Washington, DC 20005-4168
http://www.nopa.org

National Onion Association
822 Seventh St., Ste. 510
Greeley, CO 80631
970-353-5895
F: 970-353-5897
http://www.onions-usa.org

National Pasta Association
1156 Fifteenth St. NW, Ste. 900
Washington, DC 20005
202-637-5888
F: 202-223-9741
http://www.ilovepasta.org

National Pork Producers Council
122 C St. NW, Ste. 875
Washington, DC 20001
202-347-3600
F: 202-347-5265
http://www.nppc.org

National Restaurant Association
1200 Seventeenth St. NW
Washington, DC 20036-3097
202-331-5900
800-424-5156
F: 202-331-2429
http://www.restaurant.org
Represents and promotes the restaurant and hospitality industry.

National Soft Drink Association
1101 Sixteenth St. NW
Washington, DC 20036
202-463-6732
F: 202-463-8277
http://www.nsda.org
Founded in 1919 as the American Bottlers of Carbonated Beverages. Represents beverage manufacturers, distributors, and support industries.

National Sunflower Association
4023 State St.
Bismarck, ND 58503-0690
701-328-5100
http://www.sunflowernsa.com

National Turkey Federation
1225 New York Ave. NW, Ste. 400
Washington, DC 20005
202-898-0100
F: 202-898-0203
http://www.eatturkey.com
Advocate for all segments of the turkey industry with the goal of increasing demand for high-quality, nutritious turkey products.

National Watermelon Promotion Board
P.O. Box 140065
Orlando, FL 32814-0065
407-657-0261
F: 407-657-2213
http://www.watermelon.org

National Yogurt Association
2000 Corporate Ridge, Ste. 1000
McLean, VA 22102
http://www.aboutyogurt.com

North American Meat Processors Association
1910 Association Dr.
Reston, VA 20191
703-758-1900
F: 703-758-8001
http://www.namp.com
Nonprofit trade association serving the meat industry.

North Carolina Muscadine Grape Growers Association
23548 Dan Smith Rd.
Wagram, NC 28396
910-369-4575
F: 910-369-2620
http://www.ncwine.org/grgrassn.htm
Founded in 1973 to promote methods of production, processing, and marketing muscadine grapes and grape products.

Nut Growers Society
(*See* Hazelnut Marketing Board.)

Oregon Association of Hazelnut Industries
(*See* Hazelnut Marketing Board.)

Oregon Hazelnut Commission
(*See* Hazelnut Marketing Board.)

Organic Trade Association
P.O. Box 547
Greenfield, MA 01302
413-774-7511
F: 413-774-6432
http://www.ota.com
Founded in 1985 to cultivate a strong organic industry.

Pacific Northwest Canned Pears
105 S. Eighteenth St.
Yakima, WA 98901-2145
509-453-4837
F: 509-453-4880
http://www.eatcannedpears.com

Peanut Advisory Board
1025 Sugar Pike Way
Canton, GA 30115
http://www.peanutbutterlovers.com
Nonprofit trade association of peanut farmers in Georgia, Alabama, and Florida, who grow 60 percent of the U.S. crop.

Peanut Institute
P.O. Box 70157
Albany, GA 31708-0157

229-888-0216
F: 229-888-5150
http://www.peanut-institute.org
Supports nutrition research and develops educational programs to encourage healthful lifestyles.

Pickle Packers International
P.O. Box 606
One Pickle and Pepper Plaza
St. Charles, IL 60174
http://www.ilovepickles.org

Produce for Better Health Foundation
5241 Limestone Rd.
Wilmington, DE 19808
302-235-2329
F: 302-235-5555
http://www.5aday.org
Promotes consumption of fruits and vegetables for improved public health.

Produce Marketing Association
1500 Casho Mill Rd.
P.O. Box 6036
Newark, DE 19714-6036
302-738-7100
F: 302-731-2409
http://www.pma.com
Founded in 1949 to serve members who market fresh fruits and vegetables.

Refrigerated Foods Association
2971 Flowers Rd. S, Ste. 266
Atlanta, GA 30341-9717
770-452-0660
F: 770-455-3879
http://www.refrigeratedfoods.org
Association of manufacturers and suppliers of refrigerated foods, such as wet salads, home meal replacement options, refrigerated entrées, desserts, ethnic foods, and side dishes.

Salt Institute
700 N. Fairfax St., Ste. 600
Fairfax Plaza
Alexandria, VA 22314-2040
703-549-4648
F: 703-548-2194
http://www.saltinstitute.org
Source of authoritative information about salt (sodium chloride) and its more than fourteen thousand known uses.

Seafood Choices Alliance
1731 Connecticut Ave. NW, Ste. 450
Washington, DC 20009
866-732-6673
http://www.seafoodchoices.com
Promotes sustainable seafood on the international level.

Snack Food Association
1711 King St., Ste. One
Alexandria, VA 22314
703-836-4500
F: 703-836-8262
http://www.sfa.org

Sugar Association
1101 Fifteenth St. NW, Ste. 600
Washington, DC 20005
202-785-1122
F: 202-785-5019
http://www.sugar.org

Tortilla Industry Association
Preston Commons West
8117 Preston Rd., Ste. 300
Dallas, TX 75225
214-706-9193
F: 214-706-9194
http://www.tortilla-info.com

U.S. Poultry and Egg Association
1530 Cooledge Rd.
Tucker, GA 30084-7303
770-493-9401
F: 770-493-9257
http://www.poultryegg.org
Formerly the Southeastern Poultry and Egg Association. Dedicated to the growth, progress, and welfare of the poultry industry.

Walnut Marketing Board
1540 River Park Dr., Ste. 203
Sacramento, CA 95815-4609
916-922-5888
F: 916-923-2548
http://www.walnut.org

Wheat Foods Council
10841 S. Crossroads Dr., Ste. 105
Parker, CO 80138
303-840-8787
F: 303-840-6877
http://www.wheatfoods.org

Whey Protein Institute
11000 W. Seventy-eighth St., Ste. 25

Eden Prairie, MN 55344
952-833-0969
F: 952-914-0887
http://www.wheyoflife.org
Promotes the use of whey proteins from cow's milk as an ingredient in manufacturing processed foods.

Wild Blueberry Association of North America
59 Cottage St.
P.O. Box 180
Bar Harbor, ME 04609-0180
207-288-2655
F: 207-288-2655
http://www.wildblueberries.com
Wild blueberries from Maine, Atlantic Canada, and Quebec are found in a wide variety of supermarket foods from jams and jellies to cereals and muffin mixes, as well as juice, yogurt, pie fillings, and fruit bars.

Wine Institute
425 Market St., Ste. 1000
San Francisco, CA 94105
415-512-0151
F: 415-442-0742
http://www.wineinstitute.org

Wisconsin Cheese Makers Association
8030 Excelsior Dr., Ste. 305
Madison, WI 53717-1950
608-828-4550
F: 608-828-4551
http://www.wischeesemakersassn.org

Wisconsin Milk Marketing Board
8418 Excelsior Dr.
Madison, WI 53717
608-836-8820
F: 608-836-5822
http://www.producer.wisdairy.com

JOSEPH M. CARLIN

FOOD FESTIVALS

American Royal Barbecue, Kansas City, MO. First weekend in October. Invitational and open barbecue competition for pork, ribs, chicken, and brisket; other competitions include side dishes, sausage, dessert, and the International Sauce, Baste, and Rub Contest for professionals.
Contact: American Royal Association, 1701 American Royal Court, Kansas City, MO 64102
816-221-9800
http://www.americanroyalbbq.com

Apple Butter Festival, Berkeley Springs, WV. Columbus Day weekend. A celebration of old-fashioned mountain cooking with cider making, fresh apple butter, an apple-baking contest, apple butter contest, and country ham and chicken.
Contact: Berkeley Springs–Morgan County Chamber of Commerce, 304 Fairfax Street, Berkeley Springs, WV 25411
800-447-8797
http://www.berkeleysprings.com/apple

Asian Moon Festival, Milwaukee, WI. Father's Day weekend. The diverse traditions of more than a dozen Asian cultures are celebrated with music, dance, sports, handicrafts, and foods presented by Asian restaurants.
Contact: Wisconsin Organization for Asian Americans, P.O. Box 11754, Shorewood, WI 53211
http://www.asianmoonfestival.org

Bagelfest, Mattoon, IL. Last full weekend in July. Promotes the local bagel industry with a bagel breakfast, games, a parade, and bagel-related food. Contact: Mattoon Chamber of Commerce, 1701 Wabash Avenue, Mattoon, IL 61938
217-235-5661
www.mattoonillinois.com

Beef Empire Days, Garden City, KS. First two weeks in June. Promotes Kansas's beef industry with rodeos, sports events, cowboy poetry, and a variety of food events featuring beef.
Contact: Beef Empire Days, P.O. Box 1197, Garden City, KS
620-275-6807
http://www.beefempiredays.com

Bratwurst Days, Sheboygan, WI. First weekend in August. The Bratwurst Capital of the World promotes its local sausage industry with entertainment, a bratwurst-eating contest, and an eclectic variety of bratwurst dishes.
Contact: Sheboygan County Chamber of Commerce, 712 Riverfront Drive, Sheboygan, WI 53081
800-457-9497
http://www.sheboygan.org

Breaux Bridge Crawfish Festival, Breaux Bridge, LA. First full weekend in May. The Crawfish Capital of the World celebrates Cajun cooking and heritage with music, traditional crafts, a crawfish-eating contest, and crawfish étouffée cook-off.
Contact: Breaux Bridge Crawfish Festival, P.O. Box 25, Breaux Bridge, LA 70517
337-332-6655
http://www.bbcrawfest.com

Burgerfest, Hamburg, NY. Third Saturday in July. Honors the all-American hamburger, reportedly introduced at the Hamburg Fair in 1885, with a burger contest and a variety of entertainment.
Contact: Hamburg Chamber of Commerce, 8 South Buffalo Street, Hamburg, NY 14075
716-649-7917
http://www.hamburg-chamber.org

California Strawberry Festival, Oxnard, CA. Third weekend in May. Promotes California's strawberry industry with entertainment, arts and crafts, strawberry-shortcake-eating contest, strawberry foods, and a recipe contest.
Contact: California Strawberry Festival, 1661 Pacific Avenue, # 15, Oxnard, CA 93033
805-385-4739
http://www.strawberry-fest.org

Castroville Artichoke Festival, Castroville, CA. A weekend in September. The Artichoke Capital of the World promotes the local artichoke crop with exhibits, music, arts and crafts, a parade, cooking demonstrations, and artichoke cuisine.
Contact: Castroville Festivals Inc., P.O. Box 1041, Castroville, CA 95012
831-633-2465
http://www.artichoke-festival.org

Central Maine Egg Festival, Pittsfield, ME. Fourth Saturday in July. Promotes Maine's major export with a traditional ham and egg breakfast, a cheesecake contest, cheesecake dessert luncheon, and a chicken barbecue.
Contact: Central Maine Egg Festival, P.O. Box 82, Pittsfield, ME 04967
207-368-4698
http://www.pittsfieldmaine.com/eggfestival

Chocolate Fest, Burlington, WI. Weekend following Mother's Day. Promotes Burlington's chocolate industry with exhibits, a chocolate-tasting tent, music, parade, carnival, exhibits, and a chocolate cook-off.
Contact: Chocolate Fest, P.O. Box 411, Burlington, WI 53105
262-763-6044
http://www.chocolatefest.com

Deutsch Country Days, Marthasville, MO. Third Weekend in October. Historic Luxenhaus Farm preserves and celebrates

nineteenth-century German American heritage with exhibits, crafts demonstrations, and food preparation.
Contact: Deutsch Country Days, 5437 Highway O, Marthasville, MO 63357
636-433-5669
http://www.deutschcountrydays.org

Eastport Salmon Festival, Eastport, ME. First Sunday after Labor Day. Promotes Maine's salmon-farming industry with music, educational displays, farmers market, crafts, and barbecued salmon dinners.
Contact: Eastport Area Chamber of Commerce, P.O. Box 254, Eastport, ME 04631
207-853-4644
http://www.eastportme.net

Feast of San Gennaro, New York, NY. Eleven days including September 19. Vendors and restaurants in Little Italy celebrate this religious holiday and fair with multicultural foods, a cannoli-eating contest, music, and processions featuring the statue of San Gennaro, Patron Saint of Naples.
Contact: Figli di San Gennaro Inc., Most Precious Blood Church, 109 Mulberry Street, New York, NY 10002
212-226-6427
www.sangennaro.org

Feast of the Hunter's Moon, West Lafayette, IN. A weekend in October. Re-creation of an eighteenth-century French and Native American trade gathering along the Wabash River featuring eight thousand costumed participants, traditional craft demonstrations, and over sixty French and Native American foods prepared on open fires.
Contact: Tippecanoe County Historical Association, 909 South Street, Lafayette, IN 47901
765-476-8411
http://www.tcha.mus.in.us/feast.htm

Festival of American Folklife, Washington, DC. Last week of June and first week of July. Smithsonian Institution annually focuses on folkways, music, dancing, and arts and crafts of specific American cultural groups, regions, or states with emphasis on ethnic makeup and foodways, including cooking demonstrations and samples.
Contact: Smithsonian Institution Center for Folklife and Cultural Studies, 750 Ninth Street NW, Suite 4100, Washington, DC 20560
202-275-1150
http://www.folklife.si.edu

Fiesta Day, Tampa, FL. Second Saturday in February. Historic Ybor City celebrates Cuban and Latin heritage with music, a parade, arts and crafts, and food specialties, including the world's largest Cuban sandwich.
Contact: Ybor City Chamber of Commerce, 1600 Eighth Avenue East, Tampa, FL
813-248-3712
http://www.ybor.org

Fillmore Orange Festival, Fillmore, CA. First weekend in May. Honors citrus farming and orange production with a carnival, parade, train rides through the orange groves, and orange-flavored foods.
Contact: Fillmore Chamber of Commerce, 354 Central Avenue, Fillmore, CA 93015
805-524-0351
http://www.fillmorechamber.com

Finger Lakes Wine Festival, Watkins Glen, NY. A weekend in July. Tasting of five hundred wines from sixty Finger Lakes wineries.

Contact: Watkins Glen International, 2790 County Route 16, Watkins Glen, NY 14891
607-535-2481
http://www.flwinefest.com

Georgia Peanut Festival, Sylvester, GA. Third weekend in October. The Peanut Capital of the World promotes peanut farming and peanut butter manufacturing with parades, arts and crafts, street dances, and peanut-related foods.
Contact: Sylvester-Worth County Chamber of Commerce, P.O. Box 768, Sylvester, GA 31791
912-776-6657
http://www.worthcounty.com/html/sylvester.html.

Gilroy Garlic Festival, Gilroy, CA. Last full weekend of July. Growers promote garlic with children's entertainment, dancing, garlic products and food, and a cook-off.
Contact: Gilroy Garlic Festival, P.O. Box 2311, Gilroy, CA 95021
408-842-1625
http://www.gilroygarlicfestival.com

Goleta Lemon Festival, Goleta, CA. Third weekend in October. Promotes local lemon and citrus crops with a farmers' market, musical entertainment, arts and crafts, a lemon pie–eating contest, a pie-baking contest, and lemon-flavored food and drink.
Contact: Goleta Valley Chamber of Commerce, P.O. Box 781, Goleta, CA 93116
800-646-5382
http://www.goletavalley.com/lemonfestival

Great American Beer Festival, Denver, CO. Last weekend in September. A public tasting of twelve hundred beers from three hundred American breweries.
Contact: Association of Brewers, P.O. Box 1679, Boulder, CO 80306
303-447-0816
http://www.gabf.org

Great Taste of the Midwest, Madison, WI. Second Saturday in August. A public tasting of four hundred beers from one hundred breweries and brewpubs.
Contact: Madison Home Brewers and Tasters Guild, P.O. Box 1365, Madison, WI 53701
http://mhtg.org

Great Wisconsin Cheese Festival, Little Chute, WI. First full weekend in June. Promotes Wisconsin's cheese industry with a parade, sporting events, contests, cheese-carving demonstrations, a cheese omelet breakfast, and cheesecake contest.
Contact: Great Wisconsin Cheese Festival, 200 West McKinley Avenue, Little Chute, WI 54140
920-788-7390
http://www.vil.little-chute.wi.us/calendar_events/cheesefest.html

Gumbo Festival, Bridge City, LA. Second weekend in October. The Gumbo Capital of the World celebrates Louisiana's famous Cajun gumbo with a champion gumbo-cooking contest and regional specialty foods.
Contact: Gumbo Festival, P.O. Box 9069, Bridge City, LA 70094
504-436-4712
http://www.hgaparish.org/gumbofestival.htm

Hatch Chile Festival, Hatch, NM. Labor Day weekend. The Chile Capital of the World promotes chiles and celebrates New Mexico culture with music, crafts, dancing, a chile cook-off, jalapeno-eating contest, and southwestern cuisine.

Contact: Hatch Chamber of Commerce, P.O. Box 38, 112 West Hall Street, Hatch, NM 87937
505-267-5050
http://www.lascruces.org

Hellenic Festival, Buffalo, NY. Second-to-last Friday and Saturday in May. Greek life and heritage is celebrated with music, dancing, shopping in a Greek market, and traditional foods.
Contact: Hellenic Orthodox Church of the Annunciation, 146 West Utica Street, Buffalo, NY 14222
716-882-9485
http://www.buffalocvb.org

Holland Dutch Winterfest, Holland, MI. Day after Thanksgiving through third Sunday in December. Dutch Christmas traditions are celebrated with historic home tours and holiday teas, shopping in an open-air market, theater productions, and special Christmas foods.
Contact: Holland Convention and Visitors Bureau, 100 East Eighth Street, Suite 120, Holland, MI 48423
800-506-1299
http://www.holland.org

Hood River's Pear and Wine Festival, Hood River, OR. A Saturday in October. Tasting of Oregon wines, pear sherry, and pear hard cider, plus cooking demonstrations.
Contact: 888-771-7327
http://pearandwine.com

Hot Dog Festival, Frankfort, IN. Last weekend in July. Celebrates the all-American hot dog with a flea market, farmers' market, parade, sports tournaments, music, and arts and crafts.
Contact: Frankfort Main Street, 301 East Clinton Street, Frankfort, IN 46041
765-654-4081
http://www.accs.net/mainstreet/festival.htm

Hungarian Festival, New Brunswick, NJ. First Saturday in June. Celebrates Hungarian culture with music, dancing, crafts, and traditional foods.
Contact: Hungarian Civic Association; P.O. Box 1144, New Brunswick, NJ 08903
732-846-5777
http://www.ahfoundation.org/festival.htm

Idaho Spud Day, Shelly, ID. Third Saturday in September. Promotes Idaho's potato industry with musical entertainment, sports events, baked potatoes, and a Dutch Oven Cook-Off.
Contact: Shelley Chamber of Commerce, Box 301, Shelley, ID 83274
208-357-7661

Indio International Tamale Festival, Indio, CA. First weekend in December. Celebrates Hispanic culture and cuisine with sporting events, a parade, sports competitions, music, dancing, and a tamale-tasting contest.
Contact: City of Indio, 100 Civic Center Mall, Indio, CA 92201
760-342-6532
http://www.tamalefestival.org

International Chili Society World's Championship Chili Cookoff, Reno, NV. First weekend in October. Winners of ICS sanctioned cook-offs compete in four contests: Last Chance Red Chili, World's Championship Salsa, World's Championship Chili Verde, and World's Championship Traditional Red Chili.
Contact: International Chili Society, P.O. Box 1027, San Juan Capistrano, CA 92693

877-777-4427
http://www.chilicookoff.com

International Dutch Oven Championship Cookoff, Sandy, UT. Annually in March. Ten qualifying teams compete for the world championship by cooking a main dish, bread, and dessert.
Contact: International Dutch Oven Society, 4558 Midland Drive, Roy, UT 84067
http://www.idos.com

International Horseradish Festival, Collinsville, IL. First weekend in June. The Horseradish Capital of the World promotes horseradish with sports events, a horseradish-eating contest, and a horseradish recipe contest.
Contact: International Horseradish Festival, P.O. Box 766, Collinsville, IL 62234
http://www.discovercollinsville.com

International Pancake Day Race, Liberal, KS. Shrove Tuesday. Traditional competition with Olney, England, in which married women race while flipping pancakes in skillets; includes pancake breakfast, parade, and eating contest.
Contact: International Pancake Day Inc., P.O. Box 665, Liberal, KS 67905
620-624-6423
http://www.pancakeday.com

International Ramp Cook-Off and Festival, Elkins, WV. Last weekend in April. Spring ramp harvest is celebrated with a traditional ramp dinner, a ramp cook-off, and public tasting.
Contact: Randolph County Convention and Visitors Bureau, 200 Executive Plaza, Elkins, WV 26241
800-422-3304
http://www.randolphcountywv.com

Jack Daniel's World Championship Invitational Barbeque, Lynchburg, TN. Fourth weekend in October. An invitational event involving fifty competition teams that have won a major contest the previous year.
Contact: Lynchburg Chamber of Commerce, P.O. Box 421, Lynchburg, TN 37352
931-759-4111
http://jackdaniels.com

Jambalaya Festival, Gonzales, LA. Memorial Day weekend. The Jambalaya Capital of the World holds its championship jambalaya cooking contest accompanied by music, dancing, and regional Louisiana foods.
Contact: Jambalaya Festival Association, P.O. Box 1243, Gonzales, LA 70707
225-647-9566
http://www.ascensionparish.com/festival.

J. Millard Tawes Crab and Clam Bake, Crisfield, MD. Third Wednesday in July. The Soft-shell Crab Capital of the World celebrates the harvest with an all-you-can-eat feast.
Contact: Crisfield Area Chamber of Commerce, P.O. Box 292, Crisfield, MD 21817
800-782-3913
http://www.crisfield.org/clambake.cfm

Kentucky Bourbon Festival, Bardstown, KY. A weekend in September. Promotes American bourbon including a food court, seminars, and cooking demonstrations.
Contact: Bardstown Tourist and Convention Commission, P.O. Box

867B, Bardstown, KY 40004
800-638-4877
http://www.kybourbonfestival.com

Kona Coffee Cultural Festival, Kailua-Kona, HI. First week in November. Promotes Hawaii's cultural heritage and coffee industry with tours, exhibits, parades, a farmers' market, cooking demonstrations, and coffee recipe contests.
Contact: Kona Coffee Cultural Festival, P.O. Box 1112, Kailua-Kona, HI 96745
808-326-7820
http://www.konacoffeefest.com

Kutztown Pennsylvania German Festival, Kutztown, PA. Fourth of July week. Celebrates Pennsylvania Dutch life with traditional crafts demonstrations, pageants, a quilt sale, farmers market, and foods.
Contact: Kutztown Pennsylvania German Festival, P.O. Box 306, Kutztown, PA 19530
888-674-6136
http://www.kutztownfestival.com

Ligonier Marshmallow Festival, Ligonier, IN. Labor Day weekend. The Marshmallow Capital of the World promotes local marshmallow production with parades, arts and crafts, sports events, marshmallow cuisine, and marshmallow cooking contest.
Contact: Ligonier Visitors Center and Radio Museum, 800 Lincolnway South, Ligonier, IN 46767
219-894-9000
http://www.marshmallowfestival.com

Louisiana Sugar Cane Festival and Fair. Last weekend in September. Promotes the state's sugar industry with concerts, art shows, the blessing of the crop, a street fair, boat parade, and sugar cookery contest.
Contact: Louisiana Sugar Cane Festival and Fair Association, P.O. Box 9768, New Iberia, LA 70562
337-369-9323
http://www.hisugar.org

Louisiana Yambilee, Opelousas, LA. Last weekend in October. Promotes Louisiana yam industry with arts and crafts, a parade, sweet potato auction, and yam cooking contest.
Contact: Louisiana Yambilee, P.O. Box 44, Opelousas, LA 70570
337-948-8848
http://members.tripod.com/yambilee/festival.htm

Maine Lobster Festival, Rockland, ME. First weekend in August. Promotes Maine's lobster industry with boat rides, marine exhibits, Maine crafts and products, a carnival, and lobster culinary competition.
Contact: Maine Lobster Festival, P.O. Box 552, Rockland, ME 04841
800-562-2529
http://www.mainelobsterfestival.com

Marion Popcorn Festival, Marion, OH. Weekend after Labor Day. Largest popcorn festival in the world celebrates Ohio popcorn manufacturing with a parade, sports events, musical entertainment, midway, beer gardens, and popcorn treats.
Contact: Marion Popcorn Festival, P.O. Box 1101, Marion, OH 43301
740-387-3378
http://www.popcornfestival.com

Monterey Wine Festival, Monterey, CA. A weekend in April. America's oldest wine festival; wine tasting, seminars, cooking

demonstrations.
Contact: 800-765-2122
http://www.montereywine.com

Morton Pumpkin Festival, Morton, IL. Second week in September. Promotes the Pumpkin Capital of the World with a carnival, parade, entertainment, sports events, arts and crafts, the Punkin' Chuckin' Contest, a pumpkin cooking contest, and pumpkin foods.
Contact: Morton Chamber of Commerce, 415 West Jefferson Street, Morton, IL
888-765-6588
http://www.pumpkincapital.com

Morro Bay Harbor Festival, Morro Bay, CA. First weekend in October. Promotes California's seafood industry with maritime heritage exhibits, an oyster-eating contest, entertainment, seafood cuisine, and albacore barbecue.
Contact: Morro Bay Harbor Festival, P.O. Box 1869, Morro Bay, CA 93443
800-366-6043
http://www.morro-bay.com

Mushroom Festival, Kennett Square, PA. Second weekend in September. Honors the birthplace of the American mushroom industry with exhibits, mushroom sampling, a parade, mushroom auction, arts and crafts, mushroom farm tours, mushroom cooking demonstrations, and cook-off.
Contact: Mushroom Festival, P.O. Box 1000, Kennett Square, PA 19348
888-440-9920
http://www.mushroomfest.com

Napa Valley Mustard Festival, Napa Valley, CA. February to April. Promotes the agriculture, food, and wines of the region with entertainment, an array of casual and black-tie events, and cooking demonstrations by renowned chefs.
Contact: Napa Valley Mustard Festival, P.O. Box 1385, Sonoma, CA 95476
707-938-1133
http://www.mustardfestival.org

National Apple Harvest Festival, Arendtsville, PA. First two weekends in October. The Apple Capital of the U.S.A. promotes apple production with apple products, heritage demonstrations, apple pancake breakfast, apple pie–eating contest, and baking contest.
Contact: Upper Adams Jaycees, P.O. Box 38, Biglerville, PA 17307
717-677-9413
http://www.appleharvest.com

National Asparagus Festival, Hart and Shelby, MI. Second weekend in June. Celebrates the asparagus harvest with a parade, food show, sports events, asparagus lunch and bake sale, fish boil dinner, and asparagus and roast beef smorgasbord.
Contact: National Asparagus Festival, P.O. Box 117, Shelby, MI 49455
231-861-8110
http://oceana.net/naf

National Basque Festival, Elko, NV. First weekend in July. Celebrates Basque heritage with dancing, contests, a sheepherder's bread-baking championship, and the festival meal on Sunday.
Contact: Elko Basque Club, P.O. Box 1321, Elko, NV 89803
800-428-7143
http://www.elkonevada.com

National Buffalo Wing Festival, Buffalo, NY. Labor Day weekend. Celebrates chicken wings, created at the Anchor Bar in Buffalo, with a wing-eating contest, a wing sauce contest, and entertainment.
Contact: RMI Promotions Group, 9060 Main Street, Clarence, NY 14031
716-565-4141
http://buffalowing.com

National Cherry Festival, Traverse City, MI. Eight days beginning the first Saturday after July 4. The Cherry Capital of the World promotes cherries with parades, sporting events, arts and crafts, a midway, air shows, concerts, cherry orchard tours, cherry products, and a cherry pie–eating contest.
Contact: National Cherry Festival, 108 West Grandview Parkway, Traverse City, MI 49684
231-947-4230
http://www.cherryfestival.org

National Cornbread Festival, South Pittsburg, TN. Last weekend in April or first weekend in May. Celebrates southern cornbread with music, a car show, arts and crafts, a working gristmill, southern barbecue, and a cornbread-baking contest.
Contact: National Cornbread Festival, P.O. Box 247, South Pittsburg, TN 37380
423-837-0022
http://www.nationalcornbread.com

National Date Festival, Indio, CA. Third weekend in June. Promotes local date production with entertainment based on an Arabian theme, exhibits, cooking demonstrations, and recipe contest.
Contact: Riverside County Fair and National Date Festival, Fairgrounds Administration Office, 46-350 Arabia Street, Indio, CA 92201
800-811-3247
http://www.datefest.org

National Shrimp Festival, Gulf Shores, AL. Second full weekend in October. Promotes local shrimp industry with music, a boat show, sailboat regatta, arts and crafts, and shrimp culinary specialties.
Contact: Alabama Gulf Coast Area Chamber of Commerce, P.O. Drawer 3869, Gulf Shores, AL 36547
334-968-6901
http://www.nationalshrimpfestival.com

Nebraska Czech Festival, Wilber, NE. First weekend in August. The Czech Capital of the United States honors its heritage with a kolache-eating contest and traditional Czech dinners.
Contact: Wilber Chamber of Commerce, P.O. Box 1164, Wilber, NE 68465
888-494-5287
http://www.ci.wilber.ne.us/festival.htm

Ninth Avenue International Food Festival, New York, NY. Third weekend in May. Celebrates the cuisine and culture of multiple ethnic groups in the Ninth Avenue neighborhood with food sold by local businesses and street vendors plus music and entertainment.
Contact: Arthur Metz Public Relations, 122 West Twenty-sixth Street, NY, NY 10001
212-333-7222
http://9th-ave.com/9thAveFestival.htm

North Beach Festival, San Francisco, CA. Third weekend in June. California's Little Italy honors Italian heritage with a street fair, including a book sale, arts and crafts, music, dancing, blessing of neighborhood pets, and food from local restaurants and vendors.
Contact: North Beach Chamber of Commerce, 556 Columbus Avenue, San Francisco, CA 94133
415-989-2220
http://www.sfnorthbeach.com

North Carolina Seafood Festival, Morehead City, NC. First weekend in October. Promotes the state's seafood industry with the blessing of the fleet, exhibits, demonstrations, entertainment, ship tours, arts and crafts, sporting events, dances, and seafood sampling.
Contact: North Carolina Seafood Festival, P.O. Box 1812, Morehead City, NC 28557
252-726-6273
http://www.ncseafoodfestival.org

North Carolina Turkey Festival, Raeford, NC. Third weekend in September. Promotes North Carolina's turkey industry with musical entertainment, children's activities, car show, arts and crafts show, sports events, dog show, Stompin' Turkey Dinner and Dance, Turkey Hoagie Brunch, and turkey cooking contest.
Contact: North Carolina Turkey Festival, 101 North Main Street, Raeford, NC 28376
910-875-5929
http://www.hoke-raeford.com/nctf.htm

Oktoberfest-Zinzinnati, Cincinnati, OH. Third weekend in September. The world's second-largest, authentic Oktoberfest, modeled on that in Munich, celebrates German heritage with German food, beer, games, a parade, and music.
Contact: Greater Cincinnati Chamber of Commerce, 441 Vine Street, Cincinnati, OH 45202
513-579-3100
http://www.oktoberfest-zinzinnati.com

Oregon Brewers Festival, Portland, OR. Last weekend in July. A public tasting of handcrafted beers from seventy top American craft breweries.
Contact: Oregon Brewers Festival, 5019 SW Lowell, Portland, OR 97221
503-778-5917
http://www.oregonbrewfest.com

Original Terlingua International Frank X. Tolbert–Wick Fowler Memorial Championship Chili Cookoff, Behind the Store, Terlingua, TX. First weekend in November. Competitions include the Terlingua International Chili Cookoff Championship, World's Championship Margarita Mixoff, and Brisket BBQ, Bean, and Black-eyed Pea Cookoffs.
Contact: The Cook Off, 1400 Mockingbird Drive, Grapevine, TX 76051
930-874-5601
www.abowlofred.com

Parke County Maple Syrup Festival, Rockville, IN. Last weekend in February and first weekend in March. Promotes maple syrup production with tours of sugar camps and covered bridges, pancake feeds, and maple products.
Contact: Parke County Maple Syrup Festival, P.O. Box 165, Rockville, IN 47872
765-569-5226
http://www.southernin.com

Peach Days, Brigham City, UT. Weekend after Labor Day. Promotes the local peach crop with sports tournaments, an antique car show, a

carnival, parade, and Dutch Oven Cook-Off that includes an event requiring peaches.
Contact: Brigham City Chamber of Commerce, P.O. Box 458. Brigham City, UT 84302
435-723-3931
http://www.boxelder.org

Peanut Butter Festival, Brundidge, AL. A Saturday in October. Promotes area peanut production with a street dance, arts and crafts, a parade, contests, the South's largest peanut butter and jelly sandwich, and peanut butter cuisine.
Contact: Brundidge Historical Society, 128 South Main Street, Brundidge, AL 36010
334-735-3608
http://www.brundidge.com

Persimmon Festival, Mitchell, IN. Last weekend in September. Celebrates the American persimmon and Hoosier cooking with sports events, a parade, carnival, dinners, and a persimmon pudding contest.
Contact: Greater Mitchell Chamber of Commerce, 602 West Main Street, Mitchell, IN 47446
812-849-4441
http://www.mitchell-indiana.org/persimmon.htm

Phelps Sauerkraut Festival, Phelps, NY. First weekend in August. Promotes the local cabbage industry with arts and crafts, bands, a parade, and sauerkraut cuisine.
Contact: Canandaigua Chamber of Commerce, 113 South Main Street, Canandaigua, NY 14424
585-394-4400
http://www.canandaigua.com

Pie Town Festival, Pie Town, NM. Second Saturday in September. Pie-eating and pie-baking contests, pie sale, breakfast, pit barbecue, fiddling contest, and hot air balloons.
Contact: Pie Town Community Council, Pie Town, NM 87827
505-772-2667
http://www.pietown.org

Polish Fest, Milwaukee, WI. Third weekend in June. The largest Polish festival in the country features folk dancing, polka bands, a cultural village with crafts, and traditional foods.
Contact: Polish Fest, 6941 South Sixty-eighth Street, Franklin, WI 53132
414-529-2140
http://www.polishfest.org

Reynoldsburg Tomato Festival, Reynoldsburg, OH. Weekend after Labor Day. Celebrates Reynoldsburg as the birthplace of the tomato, developed commercially by resident Alexander W. Livingston, with a parade, car show, rides, exhibits, and tomato cookery.
Contact: Reynoldsburg Tomato Festival, P.O. Box 599, Reynoldsburg, OH 43068
614-866-2861
http://www.reynoldsburgtomatofestival.org

Rhode Island May Breakfasts, RI. Throughout the month of May. Traditional May fund-raising breakfasts featuring johnnycakes at various venues throughout Rhode Island.
Contact: Rhode Island Economic Development Corporation Tourism Division, 1 West Exchange Street, Providence, RI 02903

401-277-2601
http://www.riedc.com

St. Mary's County Oyster Festival, Leonardtown, MD. Third weekend in October. Celebrates the opening of the Chesapeake's fall oyster season with oysters, entertainment, a carnival, arts and crafts, exhibits, the National Oyster Shucking Championship, and the National Oyster Cook-Off.
Contact: St. Mary's County Oyster Festival, P.O. Box 653, Lewistown, MD
301-863-5015
http://www.usoysterfest.com

Selma Raisin Festival, Selma, CA. First weekend in May. The Raisin Capital of the World promotes local production with a carnival, photography exhibits, craft vendors, entertainment, and a raisin-baking contest.
Contact: Selma District Chamber of Commerce, 1710 Tucker Street, Selma, CA 93662
831-423-5590

Staunton's Annual African-American Heritage Festival, Staunton, VA. Third weekend in September. African American heritage is honored with music, dance, arts and crafts, exhibits, children's activities, and traditional foods.
Contact: Staunton Convention and Visitors Bureau, P.O. Box 58, Staunton, VA 24402
800-332-5219
http://www.staunton.va.us.com

Summer Loaf: A Celebration of Bread, Portland, OR. First Saturday in August. The Bread Capital of America honors Oregon's wheat industry with artisan breads, milling and baking demonstrations and classes, a bread-baking contest, and a farmers' market with local foods and produce.
Contact: Portland Farmers Market, P.O. Box 215, Portland, OR 97207
503-241-0032
http://www.portlandfarmersmarket.org

Swedish Festival, Stromsburg, NE. Third weekend in June. The Swede Capital of Nebraska celebrates its heritage with sporting events, parades, dancing, a band concert, smorgasbord, and Swedish pancake breakfast.
Contact: Swedish Festival, P.O. Box 715, Stromsburg, NE 68666
402-764-2226
http://www.stromsburgnebraska.com

Terlingua International Chili Championship, Chili Appreciation Society International, Rancho CASI de los Chisos, Terlingua, TX. First weekend in November. Winners of CASI sanctioned cook-offs compete in the TICC International Chili Championship Cookoff; other competitions include wings, beans, and salsa.
Contact: Chili Appreciation Society International, 493 Stonegate Drive, Johnson City, TX 78636
http://www.chili.org

Texas Folklife Festival, San Antonio, TX. Second weekend in June. Celebrates the heritage of over forty Texas ethnic groups with pioneer crafts demonstrations, entertainment, and Texas ethnic and regional foods.
Contact: The University of Texas Institute of Texas Cultures, 801

South Bowie, San Antonio, TX 78205
210-458-2249
http://www.texancultures.utsa.edu/public/index.htm

Texas Rice Festival, Winnie, TX. Last weekend in September. Promotes Texas rice with livestock shows, farm equipment displays, competitions, music and dancing, exhibits, a parade, BBQ and fajita cook-offs, and rice cooking contest.
Contact: Texas Rice Festival, P.O. Box 147, Winnie, TX 77665
409-296-2231
http://www.texasricefestival.org

Trigg County Ham Festival, Cadiz, KY. A weekend in October. Promotes Kentucky country hams with a ham judging and giveaway, a horse and mule pull, parade, the world's largest ham and biscuit sandwich, canning contest, and baking exhibit.
Contact: Cadiz-Trigg County Tourist Commission, P.O. Box 735, Cadiz, KY 42211
888-446-6402
http://www.hamfestival.com

United Tribes International Powwow, Bismarck, ND. Weekend after Labor Day. A celebration of Native American culture with drumming, singing, and dancing competitions, traditional foods, and Sunday dinner, Native American–style.
Contact: United Tribes Technical College, 3315 University Avenue, Bismarck, ND 58504
701-255-3285
http://www.unitedtribespowwow.com

Vidalia Onion Festival, Vidalia, GA. Last weekend in April. Promotes Georgia's sweet Vidalia onion industry with entertainment, an onion-eating contest, cooking demonstrations, and cooking contest.
Contact: Vidalia Onion Festival, P.O. Box 2285, Vidalia, GA 30475
912-538-8687
http://www.vidaliaga.com

Virginia Wineries Festival, The Plains, VA. A weekend in June. Virginia's oldest and largest wine festival features 45 wineries pouring 350 selections, seminars, and cooking demonstrations.
Contact: The Virginia Wineries Association, P.O. Box 31342, Alexandria, VA 22301
800-277-2675
http://showsinc.com/vvwine/body.html

Warrens Cranberry Festival, Warrens, WI. Third weekend in September. The Cranberry Capital of Wisconsin promotes its crop with antique vendors, a flea market, farmers market, cranberry marsh tours, cranberry pie sales, cranberry foods, and cranberry recipe contest.
Contact: Warrens Cranberry Festival, P.O. Box 146, Warrens, WI 54666
608-378-4200
http://www.cranfest.com

West Virginia Black Walnut Festival, Spencer, WV. Second weekend in October. Promotes Spencer's black walnut crop with a parade, carnival, flea market, sports events, Civil War encampment, and the Black Walnut Bake-Off.
Contact: West Virginia Black Walnut Festival, P.O. Box 1, Spencer, WV 25276

304-927-1780
http://www.wvblackwalnutfestival.org

The Whole Enchilada Festival, Las Cruces, NM. First weekend in October. Honors New Mexico's culinary heritage with enchiladas and other southwestern foods, a parade, games, street dances, historical exhibits, and the world's largest enchilada.
Contact: Las Cruces Convention and Visitors Bureau, 211 North Water, Las Cruces, NM 88001
800-343-7818
http://www.lascruces.org

Wild Blueberry Festival, Machias, ME. Third weekend in August. Promotes Maine wild blueberries with sports events, quilts, a pie-eating contest, blueberry pancake breakfast, and blueberry dessert bar.
Contact: Machias Wild Blueberry Festival, Centre Street Congregational Church, P.O. Box 265, Machias, ME 04654
207-255-6665
http://www.machiasblueberry.com

World Catfish Festival, Belzoni, MS. First or second Saturday in April. Promotes Humphreys County as the Catfish Capital of the World with music, arts and crafts, the South's Largest Catfish Fry, a catfish-eating contest, and celebrity chef's cook-off.
Contact: World Catfish Festival, P.O. Box 385, Belzoni, MS 39038
800-408-4838
http://www.catfishcapitalonline.com

World Championship Barbecue Cooking Contest, Memphis, TN. Third weekend in May. Part of Memphis in May, this contest is billed as the "Superbowl of Swine" because the emphasis is on pork barbecue.
Contact: Memphis in May, 245 Wagner Place, Memphis, TN 38103
901-525-4611
http://www.memphisinmay.org

World Chicken Festival, London, KY. Last weekend in September. Honors Colonel Sanders and Kentucky-style fried chicken with parades, magic shows, rides, musical entertainment, a chicken wing–eating contest, and fried chicken dinners.
Contact: London-Laurel County Tourist Commission, 140 West Daniel Boone Parkway, London, KY 40741
606-878-6900
http://www.chickenfestival.com

World Grits Festival, St. George, SC. A weekend in April. Celebrates grits as southern heritage food with dancing, music, a parade and carnival, and contests, including a grits cooking competition.
Contact: World Grits Festival, P.O. Box 756, St. George, SC 29477
843-563-4366

BIBLIOGRAPHY

Carlson, Barbara. *Food Festivals: Eating Your Way from Coast to Coast.* Detroit, MI: Visible Ink Press, 1997.
Mercuri, Becky. *Food Festival U.S.A.: 250 Red, White and Blue Ribbon Recipes from All 50 States.* San Diego, CA: Laurel Glen Publishing, 2002.

BECKY MERCURI

TOPICAL OUTLINE OF ENTRIES

This topical outline offers an overview of the Encyclopedia, with entries listed in the following subject categories:

The History of American Food
The Geography of American Food
Ethnic and Cultural Cuisines
Types of Food Staples
Cooked and Processed Foods
Drinks and Beverages
Preparing, Serving, and Distributing Food
Meals and Eating
Food and Culture
Holidays
Education and Food Writing
Cookbooks and Manuscripts
Food and Society
Food Corporations
Politics, Policy, and Issues
Science and Health
Biographies

Some entries may appear in more than one category.

THE HISTORY OF AMERICAN FOOD

Culinary History vs. Food History
Historical Overview
  The Colonial Period
  The Revolutionary War
  From the Revolutionary War to the Civil War
  The Civil War and Reconstruction
  From Victorian America to World War I
  World War I
  From World War I to World War II
  World War II
  From World War II to the Early 1960s
  From the 1960s to the Present
Historic Dining Reenactment
Historiography
    FOOD-HISTORY ORGANIZATIONS (sidebar)
Myths and Folklore
    JOHNNY APPLESEED (sidebar)
    ROBERT GIBBON JOHNSON AND THE TOMATO (sidebar)
    THE ICE CREAM CONE AND THE SAINT LOUIS WORLD'S FAIR (sidebar)

Periodicals
    GASTRONOMICA (sidebar)
    FOOD HISTORY NEWS (sidebar)
Pioneers and Survival Food
Prohibition
Tea
    BOSTON TEA PARTY (sidebar)
Temperance

THE GEOGRAPHY OF AMERICAN FOOD

Alaska
Appalachian Food
California
Chesapeake Bay
Frontier Cooking of the Far West
Hawaiian Food
Mid-Atlantic Region
Midwestern Regional Cookery
New England Regional Cookery
New York Food
Pacific Northwestern Regional Cookery

Sprouts
Squash
Strawberries
Sugar Beets
Sunflowers
Sweet Potatoes
Tomatoes
Turnips
Vegetables
Watermelon

Fruits, Vegetables, and Grains: Grains

Barley
Corn
Oats
Rice
Sorghum Flour
Supawn
Wheat

Fruits, Vegetables, and Grains: Nuts and Peanuts

Almonds
Brazil Nuts
Cashews
Chestnuts
Filberts
Macadamia Nuts
Nuts
Peanuts
Pecans
Pine Nuts
Pistachios
Walnuts

Dairy

Buttermilk
Cheese
   Historical Overview
   Later Developments
Cheese, Moldy
Dairy
Milk
Milk, Powdered
Velveeta

Fats and Oils

Butter
Crisco
Fats and Oils
Margarine

Fish and Seafood

Clams
Fish
   Freshwater Fish
   Saltwater Fish
   Saltwater Shellfish
Oysters
Seafood
Tuna

Meat and Poultry

Buffalo
Butchering
Chicken
Chicken Cookery
Chili
Duck
Eggs
Game
Goose
Insects
Lamb and Mutton
Meat
Partridge
Passenger Pigeon
Pig
Poultry and Fowl
Turkey

COOKED AND PROCESSED FOODS

Breads

Anadama Bread
Bagels
Bialy
Bread
     TOAST (sidebar)
Bread, Sliced
Chemical Leavening
Hardtack
Matzo
Sally Lunn
Scandinavian and Finnish American Food
     FINNISH PULLA (sidebar)

Processed Meats

American Chop Suey
Bully Beef
Chipped Beef
Chorizo
Cincinnati Chili
Corned Beef

Fudge
German American Food
    SHOOFLY PIE (sidebar)
Jelly Rolls
Ladyfingers
New England Regional Cookery
    COFFEE GELATIN (sidebar)
Pies and Tarts
    CHESS PIE (sidebar)
Puddings
    HASTY PUDDING (sidebar)
Southern Regional Cookery
    MOON PIE (sidebar)
Twinkies
    DEEP-FRIED TWINKIES (sidebar)
Weddings
    WEDDING CAKES (sidebar)

Sweets

Candy Bars and Candy
    PENNY CANDY (sidebar)
    JELLY BEANS (sidebar)
Chocolate
  Historical Overview
  Later Developments
Cookies
Cracker Jack
Crullers
Doughnuts
Fudge
Ice Cream and Ices
Jelly Rolls
Krispy Kreme
Ladyfingers
Marshmallow Fluff
Pastries
Saltwater Taffy
Twinkies

Salty Snacks

Crackers
Dips
French Fries
  Historical Overview
  The Twentieth Century
Popcorn
Snack Food

DRINKS AND BEVERAGES

Non-Alcoholic Beverages

Birch Beer
Breakfast Drinks

Bubble Tea
Buttermilk
Chocolate Drinks
Cider
Coffee
Coffee, Decaffeinated
Coffee, Instant
Coffee Substitutes
Cream Soda
Dr. Brown's
Dr. Pepper
Egg Cream
Frappes
Fruit Juices
Ginger Ale
Hot Toddies
Ice
Ice Cream Sodas
Kool-Aid
Lemonade
Milk
Milk, Powdered
Milkshakes, Malts, and Floats
Moxie
Nestlé
    NESTLÉ COFFEE PRODUCTS (sidebar)
Orange Flower Water
Orange Juice
    CONCENTRATED ORANGE JUICE (sidebar)
Orange Julius
Phosphates
Root Beer
Rose Water
Sarsaparilla
Sassafrasses
Seltzer
7-UP
Snapple
Soda Drinks
Switchel
Tang
Tea
Water
Water, Bottled
Water, Imported

Wine

Champagne
Fruit Wines
Sangria
Wine
  Historical Survey
  Later Developments
  Eastern U.S. Wines
  California Wines

Food Processing and Preserving

Food Distribution

MEALS AND EATING

Campbell Soup Kids
Jolly Green Giant
Mr. Peanut
Pillsbury Doughboy
Popeyes Chicken and Biscuits
Quaker Oats Man
Rastus
Ronald McDonald
Uncle Ben

POLITICS, POLICY, AND ISSUES

Advertising
Department of Agriculture, United States
Farm Labor and Unions
Farm Subsidies, Duties, Quotas, and Tariffs
Food and Drug Administration
Food Marketing
Food Stamps
Hunger Programs
International Aid
Law
Meals on Wheels
North American Free Trade Agreement
Politics of Food
Pure Food and Drug Act
Radio and Television
School Food
Settlement Houses
Soup Kitchens

SCIENCE AND HEALTH

Alcoholism
Aseptic Packaging
Baby Food
Biotechnology
Chemical Additives
Community-Supported Agriculture
Diets, Fad
Eating Disorders
Food and Nutrition Systems
Health Food
Heirloom Vegetables
Homemade Remedies
Irradiation
Nutrition
Obesity
Organic Food
Politics of Food
Vegetarianism
Vitamins

BIOGRAPHIES

Armour, Philip Danforth
Bayless, Rick
Beard, James
Beecher, Catharine
Birdseye, Clarence
Bitting, Katherine
Brady, Diamond Jim
Brown, Helen Evans
Campbell, Tunis G.
Carver, George Washington
Child, Julia
Child, Lydia Maria
Claiborne, Craig
Farmer, Fannie
Fisher, M. F. K.
Gibbons, Euell
Graham, Sylvester
Harvey, Fred
Hearn, Lafcadio
Hines, Duncan
Jefferson, Thomas
Jennie June
Johnson, Howard
Kellogg, John Harvey
Lagasse, Emeril
Leslie, Eliza
Lincoln, Mrs.
Lowenstein, Eleanor
Mondavi, Robert
Parloa, Maria
Pennell, Elizabeth
Pinedo, Encarnación
Prudhomme, Paul
Puck, Wolfgang
Pullman, George
Randolph, Mary
Ranhofer, Charles
Redenbacher, Orville
Richards, Ellen Swallow
Rombauer, Irma
Rorer, Sarah Tyson
Sanders, Colonel
Simmons, Amelia
Sinclair, Upton
Stewart, Martha
Swift, Gustavus Franklin
Szathmary, Louis
Trotter, Charlie
Tschirky, Oscar
Waters, Alice
Wiley, Harvey
Wilson, Mary Tolford

DIRECTORY OF CONTRIBUTORS

Gary Allen
Food Writer, Kingston, New York
Armour, Philip Danforth; Crab Boils; Food Websites; Herbs and Spices; Saint Patrick's Day; Sinclair, Upton

Jean Anderson
Cookbook Author and Journalist, Chapel Hill, North Carolina
Food Processors

Hea-Ran L. Ashraf
Department of Food and Nutrition, Southern Illinois University
Diets, Fad

Josephine Bacon
Writer, Editor, and Translator, London
Chickpeas; Jennie June; Olives; Partridge; Passover; Pastrami; Salsify; Squash

Virginia K. Bartlett
Independent Scholar, Hingham, Massachusetts
Cooking Manuscripts; Food Periodicals; Leslie, Eliza; Periodicals; Radio and Television

Linda Bassett
Department of Culinary Arts, North Shore Community College, Massachusetts
Howard Johnson; Johnson, Howard

Amy Bentley
Department of Nutrition and Food Studies, New York University
Historical Overview, subentry World War II; Stewart, Martha

Jennifer Schiff Berg
Department of Nutrition and Food Studies, New York University
Egg Cream

Rynn Berry
Author of *Food for the Gods: Vegetarianism and the World's Religions*
Vegetarianism

Linda Murray Berzok
Independent Scholar, Tucson, Arizona, and Stephentown, New York
Dairy; Fusion Food; Jell-O Molds; Obesity; Southeast Asian American Food

Marian Betancourt
Food Writer, Brooklyn, New York
Cheese, Moldy; Cuba Libre; Hearts of Palm; Moxie; Scandinavian and Finnish American Food, sidebar on Finnish Pulla; Snapple

Charlotte Biltekoff
Ph.D. Candidate, American Civilization, Brown University
Quaker Oats Man

Daniel R. Block
Department of Geography, Sociology, Economics, and Anthropology, Chicago State University
Butter; Buttermilk; Dairy Industry; Milk

Anne L. Bower
Department of English, Ohio State University
Cookbooks and Manuscripts, subentry Community Cookbooks

Barrett P. Brenton
Department of Sociology and Anthropology, St. John's University, Jamaica, New York
Food Stamps; Health Food; Hunger Programs; International Aid; Organic Food

Robert W. Brower
Chef and Attorney, El Sobrante, California
Adulterations; Food and Drug Administration; Good Housekeeping Institute; Kellogg Company; Law; Molasses; North American Free Trade Agreement; Pasties; Pizza; Pizzerias; Saltwater Taffy; Valentine's Day

Thomas Burford
Orchard and Nursery Consultant, Monroe, Virginia
Apples; Cider; Myths and Folklore, sidebar on Johnny Appleseed

Joseph M. Carlin
Founder and Owner, Food Heritage Press, Ipswich, Massachusetts
Aseptic Packaging; Automats; Bars; Beatrice; Birdseye, Clarence; Birds Eye Foods; Borden; Clams; ConAgra; Culinary Historians of Boston; Food-Related Organizations; General Foods; General Mills; Historiography, sidebar on Food-History Organizations; Kraft Foods; Krispy Kreme; Meals on Wheels; Milk Packaging; Nestlé; Nutrition; Orange Juice, sidebar on Concentrated Orange Juice; Puddings; Punch; Saloons; Taverns; Waxed Paper; Wiley, Harvey

John F. Cassens
President, Cassens Consulting Company, Fort Lee, New Jersey
Flavorings

Hudson Cattell
Editor, *Wine East*, Lancaster, Pennsylvania
Wine, subentry *Eastern U.S. Wines*

Ann Chandonnet
Independent Scholar, Juneau, Alaska
Alaska; Honey

Shirley Cherkasky
Founder, Culinary Historians of Washington, D.C.
Food-Related Museums

Andrew Coe
Food Writer, Brooklyn, New York
Lamb and Mutton; Phosphates; Seltzer; Soda Drinks

Alfredo Manuel de Jesus Oliveira Coelho
Agro-Montpellier, University of Montpellier, France
Water, Bottled; Water, Imported

Steven M. Craig
New York Epicurean
Gallo, Ernest and Julio; Mondavi, Robert; Mondavi Wineries; Wine, subentry *Later Developments; Wine Barrels; Wine Bottles; Wine Casks; Wine Cellars; Wine Glasses; Wine-Tasting Rooms*

James Crawford
Curator, Canajoharie Library and Art Gallery, Canajoharie, New York
Beech-Nut

Fred Czarra
Food Writer, Saint Mary's City, Maryland
Pepper, Black; Stuffed Ham

Tom Dalzell
Independent Scholar, Berkeley, California
Slang, Food

Charles Daniel
Department of Biology, University of California, Santa Cruz
Chicken

Mitchell Davis
James Beard Foundation, New York City
Restaurant Awards and Guides; Restaurant Critics and Food Columnists; Restaurants

Sally DeFauw
Independent Scholar, DeKalb, Illinois
Corn Syrup

Dale DeGroff
Master Mixologist, Institute for Culinary Education, New York
Cocktails; Collins; Mai Tai; Sazerac; Screwdriver; Singapore Sling; Whiskey Sour; Zombie

Lisa DeLange
Researcher and Writer, New York City
Sherry; Vermouth

Jonathan Deutsch
Department of Tourism and Hospitality, Kingsborough Community College, City University of New York
Chuck Wagons; Firehouse Cooking

Paul Dickson
Writer, Garrett Park, Maryland
Combat Food; Space Food; Toasts; Toothpicks

Susan Feakes Dorschutz
Technical Editor and Writer, Rodale Institute, Kutztown, Pennsylvania
Organic Gardening

Elizabeth McCants Drinnon
Writer, Macon, Georgia
Stuckey's

Carolyn Eastwood
Author of *Near West Side Stories: Struggles for Community in Chicago's Maxwell Street Neighborhood*
Street Vendors

Rebecca L. Epstein
Department of Film, Television, and Digital Media, UCLA
Film, Food in

Astrid Ferszt
Writer, London and Albuquerque, New Mexico
Biotechnology; Drying; Fermentation

Hope-Marie Flamm
Writer, New York City
Mimosa

Cheryl Foote
Author of *Women of the New Mexico Frontier, 1846–1912*
Pinole; Southwestern Regional Cookery

Cheryl Forberg
Author of *Stop the Clock! Cooking: Defy Aging with Natural Healing Comfort Foods*
Sorghum Flour; Sorghum Syrup

Linda Campbell Franklin
Artist, Writer, and Collector, Baltimore
Apple-Preparation Tools; Biscuit Cutters; Bread-Making Tools; Butter-Making Tools and Churns; Cabbage Cutters and Planes; Can Openers; Cheese-Making Tools; Cherry Pitters or Stoners; Chopping Knives and Food Choppers; Cookie Cutters; Corn-Preparation Tools; Coffee Makers, Roasters, and Mills; Containers; Cornbread Baking Pans; Cupboards and Food Safes; Dishwashing and Cleaning Up; Doughnut-Making Tools; Egg-Preparation Tools; Flytraps and Fly Screens; Frying Baskets; Graters; Juicers; Kettles; Lunch Boxes, Dinner Pails, and Picnic Kits; Mortar and Pestle; Nutcrackers and

Grinders; Nutmeg Graters; Peach Parers and Stoners; Pie-Making Tools; Pot Holders; Potato-Cooking Tools; Pressure Cookers; Sieves, Sifters, and Colanders; Timers, Hour-glasses, and Egg Timers; Toasters; Turnspit Dogs; Waffle, Wafer, and Pizelle Irons

Rebecca Freedman
Writer, White Plains, New York
Freeze-Drying

Elyse Friedman
Author of *Dial-Out, Dine-In: Chicago Restaurants That Deliver*
Cooperatives; Kitchen Gardening

Rachelle E. Friedman
Independent Scholar, New York City
Historical Overview, subentry *From the Revolutionary War to the Civil War*

James Futrell
Author of *Amusement Parks of New Jersey*
Amusement Parks

Fran Gage
Food Writer and Cookbook Author, San Francisco
Eggs

Randy Garbin
Roadside Magazine, Jenkintown, Pennsylvania
Diners; Roadside Food

Judy Gerjuoy
Independent Scholar, Helsinki, Finland
Apple Pie

Carolyn M. Goldstein
Industrial Historian, Somerville, Massachusetts
Home Economics

Darra Goldstein
Department of Russian, Williams College
Periodicals, sidebar on *Gastronomica; Russian American Food*

Alexandra Greeley
Author of *Asian Soups, Stews, and Curries*
Bread Machines; Coconuts; Slow Food Movement

Carol A. Greenberg
Proprietor of Cornucopia, Brattleboro, Vermont
Etiquette Books

Fred Griffith
Coauthor of *Nuts! Recipes from around the World That Feature Nature's Perfect Ingredient*
Chestnuts; Garlic; Onions

Linda Griffith
Coauthor of *Nuts! Recipes from around the World That Feature Nature's Perfect Ingredient*
Chestnuts; Garlic; Onions

Madge Griswold
Editor, The peripatetic epicure, Tucson, Arizona
Library Collections

Mark C. Gruber
Wine and Spirits Instructor, Northwestern University
Whiskey

Barbara Haber
Food Historian, Winchester, Massachusetts
Child, Lydia Maria; Culinary History vs. Food History

Carol Mighton Haddix
Food Editor, *Chicago Tribune*
Cookbooks and Manuscripts, subentry *From the 1970s to the Present*

Annie S. Hauck-Lawson
Department of Health and Nutrition Services, Brooklyn College
Polish American Food

Corinna Hawkes
Consultant, International Food Policy Research Institute
Farm Subsidies, Duties, Quotas, and Tariffs; Sanders, Colonel; Transportation of Food

Joanne Lamb Hayes
Food Writer and Historian, New York City
Lincoln, Mrs.; Richards, Ellen Swallow; Vitamins

Karen Hess
Independent Scholar, New York City
French Fries, subentry *Historical Overview; Jefferson, Thomas; Lowenstein, Eleanor; Randolph, Mary; Simmons, Amelia; Wilson, Mary Tolford*

Lynn Hoffman
Independent Scholar, Philadelphia
Brewing

David Gerard Hogan
Department of History, Heidelberg College
Alcoholism; Budweiser; Fast Food; Hamburger; Kentucky Fried Chicken; Pizza Hut; Prohibition; Take-Out Foods; Temperance; Wendy's; White Castle; World's Fairs

Peggy Holmes
Writer and Farmer, Chillicothe, Illinois
Soybeans

Tonya Hopkins
Food Writer and Wine Consultant, Brooklyn, New York
Fruit Wines; Kwanzaa; Rum; Wine, Hot Spiced; Wine Coolers; Wineries

Roger Horowitz
Center for the History of Business, Technology, and Society, Hagley Museum and Library, Wilmington, Delaware
Meat

Lynn Marie Houston
Independent Scholar, Covington, Louisiana
Airplane Food; Kitchens, subentry *1800 to the Present*

Sharon Hudgins
Author of *The Other Side of Russia: A Slice of Life in Siberia and the Russian Far East*
Chili; Salsa

Phyllis Isaacson
James Beard Foundation, New York
Beard, James

Janet Jarvits
Independent Scholar, Pasadena, California
Brown, Helen Evans

Virginia Scott Jenkins
Author of *Bananas: An American History*
Bananas; Chesapeake Bay; Eggnog; Halloween; Ice; Sally Lunn; Syllabub

Richard J. Jensen
Senior Adviser to the President, University of Nevada, Las Vegas
Farm Labor and Unions

Liza Jernow
Cookbook Author and Food Stylist, New York City
Birthdays; Gibbons, Euell; Heirloom Vegetables; Highball

Eve Jochnowitz
Ph.D. Candidate, Department of Performance Studies, New York University
Borden, sidebar on *Elsie the Cow; Community-Supported Agriculture; Jewish Dietary Laws; Matzo*

Sharon Kapnick
Food Writer and Sommelier, New York City
Jolly Green Giant; Pillsbury Doughboy; Tschirky, Oscar

David Karp
Food Writer, Venice, California
Cactus; Citrus; Dates; Fruit; Kiwis; Persimmons; Plums; Pomegranates

Karen Karp
Director, Karp Resources, New York City
Settlement Houses; Soup Kitchens

Robert Kaufelt
Proprietor of Murray's Cheese, New York City
Cheese, subentry *Later Developments*

Cathy K. Kaufman
Institute of Culinary Education, New York City
Appetizers; Bakeries; Carrots; Chicken Cookery; Christmas; Cooking Schools, subentry *Twentieth Century; Cooking Techniques; Cordials, Historical; Creams, Dessert; Cucumbers; Custards; Dining Rooms, Table Settings, and Table Manners;*

Easter; Glassware; Flowers, Edible; Historic Dining Reenactment; Hotel Dining Rooms; Ladyfingers; Leeks; Mushrooms; New Year's Celebrations; Nouvelle Cuisine; Pastries; Plates; Restaurants, sidebar on *The Rise of Restaurants; Sauces and Gravies; Sprouts; Sugar Beets; Sunflowers; White House*

Patricia M. Kelly
Editor, Culinary Historians of Boston newsletter, Dorchester, Massachusetts
Ice Cream Sodas; Milkshakes, Malts, and Floats; Soda Fountains

C. T. Kennedy
Fruit Grower and Attorney, San Francisco
Blackberries; Figs; Grapes; Mulberries; Pears; Quince

Pamela Goyan Kittler
Food, Culture, and Nutrition Consultant, Sunnyvale, California
Broccoli; Insects; Kvass; Weddings

Steven Kolpan
Wine Studies and Gastronomy, Culinary Institute of America
Champagne

Kevin R. Kosar
Editor, AlcoholReviews.com
Cider, Hard; Vodka

Bruce Kraig
Roosevelt University, Chicago (Emeritus), and President, Culinary Historians of Chicago
Archer Daniels Midland; Brady, Diamond Jim; Hearn, Lafcadio; Hines, Duncan; Hot Dogs; Luncheonettes; Myths and Folklore, sidebar on *The Ice Cream Cone and the Saint Louis World's Fair; Pig; Sara Lee Corporation; Swift, Gustavus Franklin; Turnips; Vienna Sausage*

Kris Kranenburg
School of Journalism, Southern Illinois University
Popeyes Chicken and Biscuits

Michael Krondl
Independent Scholar, New York City
Advertising; Crisco; Fats and Oils; Margarine; Post Foods

Peter LaFrance
Publisher, BeerBasics.com, Brooklyn, New York
Beer; Beer Cans; Coors Brewing Company; Microbreweries; Miller Brewing Company; Stout

Desmond R. Layne
Department of Horticulture, Clemson University
Pawpaw

Hyon Jung Lee
M.A. Candidate, Gallatin Program, New York University
Korean American Food; Salt and Salting

James C. Lee
Independent Scholar, Lookout Mountain, Georgia
Poke Salad

David Leite
Food Writer and Editor, New York City
Burger King; Chorizo; Kale; Swanson

Walter Levy
Independent Scholar, Accord, New York
Picnics

William Lockwood
Department of Anthropology, Michigan State University
Midwestern Regional Cookery

Yvonne Lockwood
Michigan State University Museum
Midwestern Regional Cookery

Lucy M. Long
Department of Popular Culture, Bowling Green State
University
Myths and Folklore

Janice Bluestein (Jan) Longone
Curator of American Culinary History, Clements Library,
University of Michigan
Cookbooks and Manuscripts, subentries *From the Beginnings
to 1860* and *From the Civil War to World War I*

Sylvia Lovegren
Independent Scholar, Midland Park, New Jersey
*Barbecue; Breakfast Foods; Bridge Luncheon Food; Bubble Tea;
Bully Beef; Chafing Dish; Chipped Beef; Cream Soda;
Department of Agriculture, United States; Fondue Pot; Historical
Overview*, subentries *From World War II to the Early 1960s* and
*From the 1960s to the Present; Irish Coffee; Muslim Dietary
Laws; Passenger Pigeon; Pure Food and Drug Act; Refrigerators;
Root Beer; Slow Cookers; Tea*, sidebar on *Boston Tea Party*

Cathy Lee Luchetti
Independent Scholar, Oakland, California
Frontier Cooking of the Far West

Robynne L. Maii
Food Writer and Chef, New York City
Hawaiian Food

M. M. Manring
Independent Scholar, Columbia, Missouri
Aunt Jemima

Andrew Mariani
Independent Scholar, Morgan Hill, California
Apricots; Cherries; Peaches and Nectarines

Lisa B. Markowitz
Department of Anthropology, University of Louisville
Farmers' Markets

Mimi Martin
Department of Nutrition, Food Studies, and Public Health,
New York University
Major Library Collections; Prison Food

Marty Martindale
Host of FoodSiteoftheDay.com, Largo, Florida
Barley; Bread, Sliced; Sassafrasses

Kevin McIntyre
Department of Southeast Asian Studies, University of
California, Berkeley
*Food Stamps; Health Food; Hunger Programs; International
Aid; Organic Food*

Matt McMillen
Writer, Washington, D.C.
Frozen Food

Anne Mendelson
Author of *Stand Facing the Stove: The Story of the Women
Who Gave America the* Joy of Cooking
Cookbooks and Manuscripts, subentry *From World War I to
World War II; Historical Overview*, subentry *From World War I
to World War II; New York Food; Rombauer, Irma*

Becky Mercuri
Food Writer, Rushford, New York
Club Sandwich; Cookbooks and Manuscripts, subentry *From
World War II to the 1960s; Cookies; Cooking Contests;
Culinary Institute of America; Dagwood Sandwich; Denver
Sandwich; Dr Pepper; Food Festivals; French Dip; Gyro;
Hoagie; Hot Brown Sandwich; Italian Sausage Sandwich with
Peppers and Onions; Monte Cristo Sandwich; Muffaletta
Sandwich; Oyster Loaf Sandwich; Panini; Philadelphia
Cheesesteak Sandwich; Pimiento Cheese Sandwich; Po'boy
Sandwich; Reuben Sandwich; 7-Up; Sloppy Joe; Wraps*

Virginia Mescher
Independent Scholar, Burke, Virginia
Candy Bars and Candy, sidebar on *Jelly Beans; Switchel*

Ellen Messer
Departments of Anthropology and International Studies, The
George Washington University, and School of Nutrition
Science and Policy, Tufts University
Potatoes

Jackie Mills
Independent Scholar, Jackson Heights, New York
Southern Regional Cookery, sidebar on *Moon Pie*

Jennifer Minnick
Independent Scholar, New York City
Batidos; Beer Mugs; New Orleans Syrup

Mary Mooney-Getoff
Independent Scholar, Northampton, Massachusetts
Boston Cooking School; Fireless Cookers; Parloa, Maria

Robin M. Mower
Independent Scholar, New York City
Cherry Bounce; Coffee Substitutes; Johnson and Wales; Lemonade; Maple Syrup; Orange Flower Water; Ratafia; Rose Water; Spinach

Maryanne Nasiatka
Researcher and Writer, Plymouth, Michigan
Uncle Ben

Joan Nathan
Author of *Jewish Cooking in America*
Bagels; Jewish American Food

Marion Nestle
Department of Nutrition, Food Studies, and Public Health, New York University
Politics of Food

Jacqueline M. Newman
Queens College (Emerita), and Editor, *Flavor and Fortune*
Chinese American Food

Kara Newman
Independent Scholar, New York City
Historical Overview, subentry *World War I; Twinkies*

Lucy Norris
Cookbook Author and Independent Scholar, Portland, Oregon
Pickles; Pickling

Maura Carlin Officer
Independent Scholar, Gloucester, Massachusetts
Eggplants

Beatrice Ojakangas
Independent Scholar, Duluth, Minnesota
Scandinavian and Finnish American Food

Sandra L. Oliver
Food Historian and Founding Editor of *Food History News*
Chemical Leavening; Fish, subentries on *Freshwater Fish, Saltwater Fish,* and *Saltwater Shellfish; New England Regional Cookery; Periodicals,* sidebar on *Food History News; Seafood; Ship Food*

Lynne Olver
Editor, The Food Timeline, Morris County Library, Whippany, New Jersey
Mock Foods

Jane Otto
Food Consultant, Culinary Adviser, and Pastry Chef, Brooklyn, New York
Liquor Cabinets; Tailgate Picnics

Howard Paige
Author of *Aspects of African American Foodways*
African American Food, subentry *To the Civil War*

Russ Parsons
Food Columnist, *Los Angeles Times*
Ranhofer, Charles

Bob Pastorio
Independent Scholar and Food Writer, Swoope, Virginia
Bistros; Chemical Additives; Distillation; Fourth of July; Humor, Food; Poetry, Food; Songs, Food; Stills

Mark Pendergrast
Independent Scholar, Essex Junction, Vermont
Coca-Cola; Coffee; Coffee, Decaffeinated; Coffee, Instant; Coffeehouses; Cola Wars; Folgers; Maxwell House; Nestlé, sidebar on *Nestlé Coffee Products; Starbucks*

Charles Perry
Staff Writer, Food Section, *Los Angeles Times*
Middle Eastern Influences on American Food

Marge Perry
Food Writer and Journalist, Tenafly, New Jersey
Irradiation; Packaging

Ross Petras
Independent Scholar, Midland Park, New Jersey
Department of Agriculture, United States

Jeffrey Pilcher
History Department, The Citadel, Charleston, South Carolina
Mexican American Food

Thomas Pinney
Author of *A History of Wine in America from the Beginnings to Prohibition*
Wine, subentry *Historical Survey; Wine Books*

Susan McLellan Plaisted
Proprietor, Heart to Hearth Cookery, and Director of Foodways, Pennsbury Manor, Morrisville, Pennsylvania
Corn; Mid-Atlantic Region

Kirk W. Pomper
Principal Investigator of Horticulture, Kentucky State University
Pawpaw

Colleen Joyce Pontes
Writer, Bronx, New York
Gas Grill; Sandwich Trucks

Barry Popik
Independent Scholar, New York City
Chicken Cookery, sidebar on *Chicken à la King; Pies and Tarts,* sidebar on *Chess Pie*

James D. Porterfield
Independent Scholar, State College, Pennsylvania
Dining Car; Harvey, Fred; Pullman, George

Maricel Presilla
President, Gran Cacao Company, and Chef-owner of Zafra, Hoboken, New Jersey
Chocolate, subentry *Later Developments; Cuban American Food*

Kathleen Purvis
Food Editor, *Charlotte Observer*
Funeral Food

Jeri Quinzio
Writer, Boston, Massachusetts
Iceboxes; Ice Cream and Ices; Ice Cream Makers; Ice Cream Molds; Tequila; Tequila Sunrise

Jean Railla
Writer, New York City
Frito-Lay, sidebar on *Frito Pie; Navajo Tacos*

Nancy Ralph
Director, New York Food Museum
School Food

Jessy Randall
Curator of Special Collections, Colorado College
Boilermaker; Brandy Alexander; Drinking Songs; Grasshopper; Lime Rickey; Moonshine

Sara Rath
Author of *The Complete Cow*
Asparagus; Casseroles; Cream; Dumplings; Piggly Wiggly; Rhubarb; Velveeta

Krishnendu Ray
Professor in Liberal Arts and Management, Culinary Institute of America
Indian American Food

Joan Reardon
Author of *Poet of the Appetites: The Lives and Loves of M. F. K. Fisher*
Fisher, M. F. K.; Oyster Bars; Oysters

John U. Rees
Independent Scholar, New Hope, Pennsylvania
Hardtack; Historical Overview, subentries on *The Revolutionary War* and *The Civil War and Reconstruction; Supawn*

Esther Della Reese
Independent Scholar, Whitewright, Texas
Beer, Corn and Maple; Beer Barrels; Chocolate Drinks; Clambake; Milk, Powdered; Spruce; Washington's Birthday

Gary Regan
Publisher, ArdentSpirits.com
Bourbon; Cordials; Gin; Manhattan; Martini

Mardee Haidin Regan
Publisher, ArdentSpirits.com
Bourbon; Cordials; Gin; Manhattan; Martini

Lee Reich
Author of *Uncommon Fruits for Every Garden*
Blueberries; Cranberries; Currants; Raspberries; Strawberries

Kay Rentschler
Food Writer, Boston, Massachusetts
Endive; Radishes; Ramps; Sorrel; Vegetables

Oswald Rivera
Author of *Puerto Rican Cuisine in America: Nuyorican and Bodega Recipes*
Puerto Rican Food

Richard W. Robinson
Department of Horticultural Sciences (Emeritus), New York Agricultural Experiment Station, Geneva
Melons

Anthony Rodale
Chairman, Rodale Institute, Kutztown, Pennsylvania
Organic Gardening

Edgar Rose
Independent Scholar, Glencoe, Illinois
Pecans

Peter G. Rose
Food Historian, South Salem, New York
Dutch Influences on American Food

Meryl S. Rosofsky
Department of Nutrition, Food Studies, and Public Health, New York University
Blenders; Corks

Alice Ross
Director, Alice Ross Hearth Studios, Consultant, Author, Teacher, Smithtown, New York
Beecher, Catharine; Boardinghouses; Canning and Bottling, sidebar on *Home Canning; Cookbooks*, subentry *Children's Cookbooks; Doughnuts; Dutch Ovens; Frying Pans, Skillets, and Spiders; Fund-Raisers; Gender Roles; Grinders; Hearth Cookery; Kitchens*, subentry *Early Kitchens; Material Culture and Technology*, subentry *Social Aspects of Material Culture; Measurement; Native American Foods*, subentries *Before and After Contact, Spiritual and Social Connections* and *Technology and Sources; Pancake Pans; Parsnips; Pioneers and Survival Food; Preserves; Puddings*, sidebar on *Hasty Pudding; Rastus*

Peter Ross
Master Blacksmith, Colonial Williamsburg
Material Culture and Technology, subentry *The Technology of Cooking Containers*

William Rubel
Author of The *Magic of Fire*
Yeast

Paul Ruschmann
Writer and Editor, Ann Arbor, Michigan
Beer Gardens; Beer Halls

Lynne Sampson
Food Writer, Joseph, Oregon
Celebrity Chefs; Child, Julia; Lagasse, Emeril; Prudhomme, Paul; Waters, Alice

Mary Sanker
Writer and Librarian, Cincinnati, Ohio
Cincinnati Chili; Desserts; Goetta

Joy Santlofer
Food Historian, New York City
Cereal, Cold; Mars; Pillsbury; Vending Machines

Stephen Schmidt
Independent Scholar, New York City
Cakes

Amanda Watson Schnetzer
Writer and Editor, Dallas, Texas
Cajun and Creole Food

Mary Anne Schofield
Core Humanities Program, Villanova University
Literature and Food

Laura Shapiro
Food Writer, New York City
Farmer, Fannie

Kantha Shelke
Independent Scholar, Chicago
Butchering; Pepperoni; Salami; Sausage; Smoking; Sweeteners

Clara Silverstein
Associate Food Editor, Boston Herald
Birch Beer; Frappes; Marshmallow Fluff; New England Regional Cookery, sidebar on *Coffee Gelatin*

Robert Simmons
Food Writer and Cookbook Author, Foster City, California
Ale Slipper; Breakfast Foods, sidebar on *Avena*

Bonnie J. Slotnick
Owner of Bonnie Slotnick Cookbooks, New York City
Betty Crocker; Delmonico's; Graham, Sylvester; Lüchow's; Pillsbury Bake-Off; Rorer, Sarah Tyson; Stoves and Ovens, subentry *Wood and Coal*

Andrew F. Smith
Food Historian, Brooklyn, New York
Advertising Cookbooklets and Recipes; Almonds; Applejack; Artichokes; Avocados; Bitting, Katherine; Bloody Mary and Virgin Mary; Brazil Nuts; Bread; Cabbage; California; Campbell Soup Company; Campbell Soup Kids; Canning and Bottling; Carver, George Washington; Cashews; Cauliflower; Cheesecake; Chocolate, subentry *Historical Overview; Celery; Condiments; Cooking Schools,* subentry *Nineteenth Century; Counterculture, Food; Cracker Jack; Crackers; Cranberries,* sidebar on *Cranberries in History; Delicatessens; Dips; Drink Bibliography; Duck; Filberts; Food Bibliography; Freezers and Freezing; French Fries,* subentry *The Twentieth Century; French Influences on American Food; Frito-Lay; Fruit Juices; Game; Goose; Grocery Stores; Grog; Heinz Foods; Historical Overview,* subentry *The Colonial Period; Historiography; Kellogg, John Harvey; Ketchup; Kool-Aid; Lettuce; Macadamia Nuts; Margarita; Mason Jars; Mayonnaise; McDonald's; Meal Patterns; Microwave Ovens; Mr. Peanut; Mustard; Myths and Folklore,* sidebar on *Robert Gibbon Johnson and the Tomato; Nuts; Oats; Okra; Orange Juice; Peanut Butter; Peanuts; Pine Nuts; Pancakes; Pineapple; Pistachios; Popcorn; Poultry and Fowl; Pumpkins; Redenbacher, Orville; Rice; Ronald McDonald; Salads and Salad Dressings; Sandwiches; Sangria; Snack Food; Soups and Stews; Soy Sauce; Stoves and Ovens,* subentry *Gas and Electric; Sweet Potatoes; Taco Bell; Thanksgiving; Tomatoes; Tuna; Turkey; Vanilla; Watermelon; Wheat*

Jeffery Sobal
Division of Nutritional Sciences, Cornell University
Food and Nutrition Systems

Mark F. Sohn
Culinary Analyst, Pikeville, Kentucky
Appalachian Food

Gerd Stern
Cheese Importer and Consultant and Media Producer
Cheese, subentry *Historical Overview*

Bob Stoddard
Independent Scholar, Claremont, California
Pepsi-Cola

Dan Strehl
Author of *Encarnación's Kitchen: Mexican Recipes from Nineteenth-Century California*
Pinedo, Encarnación

Helen H. Studley
Cookbook Author and Food and Travel Writer, New York City
Buffalo; Claiborne, Craig

Charles L. Sullivan
Author of *A Companion to California Wine: An Encyclopedia of Wine and Winemaking from the Mission Period to the Present Wine,* subentry *California Wines*

Jean Tang
Independent Scholar, New York City
Tang

John Martin Taylor
Cookbook Author and Owner of HoppinJohns.com,
Charleston, South Carolina
Southern Regional Cookery

Gerry Thomas
Writer, Paradise Valley, Arizona
Frozen Foods, sidebar *TV Dinners: A Firsthand Account*

Ruth Tobias
Food Writer, Boston
Beans; Brandy; Bread, sidebar on *Toast; Cafeterias; Corned
Beef; Crullers; Dressings and Stuffings; Eating Disorders;
Ginger Ale; Hot Toddies; Old Fashioned; Pickles, Sweet;
Roadhouses; Sarsaparilla*

Elisabeth Townsend
Freelance Writer and Photographer, Concord, Massachusetts
Breakfast Drinks; Juice Bars; Low-Calorie Syrup

Alison Tozzi
Independent Scholar, Brooklyn, New York
Historical Overview, subentry *From Victorian America to World
War I*

Alexa Van de Walle
Marketing Consultant and Writer, New York City
Clarifying

Brian Wansink
Departments of Marketing and Nutritional Science, University
of Illinois
Food Marketing

Scott Warner
Food Writer, Chicago
*Bayless, Rick; Puck, Wolfgang; Szathmary, Louis; Trotter,
Charlie*

Nach Waxman
Proprietor, Kitchen Arts & Letters, New York City
Recipes

Lynn Weiner
College of Arts and Sciences, Roosevelt University, Chicago
Baby Food

Jay Weinstein
Author of *The Everything Vegetarian Cookbook*
*Bottling; Jelly Rolls; Karo Syrup; Plastic Bags; Rice Cookers;
Water*

Jan Whitaker
Independent Scholar, Northampton, Massachusetts
Tea

Merry White
Department of Anthropology, Boston University
Japanese American Food

Pat Willard
Writer, Brooklyn, New York
Communal Gatherings; Homemade Remedies; Pies and Tarts

Jacqueline Block Williams
Author of *The Way We Ate: Pacific Northwest Cooking
1843–1900*
*Arbuckles; Camas Root; Mint Julep; Pacific Northwestern
Regional Cookery; Pennell, Elizabeth*

Michael Karl Witzel
Author of *The American Drive-In*
Drive-Ins

Izabela Wojcik
James Beard Foundation, New York City
Bialy

Wendy A. Woloson
Program in Early American Economy and Society, The
Library Company of Philadelphia
*Candy Bars and Candy; Hershey Foods Corporation; Sugar;
Weddings*, sidebar on *Wedding Cakes*

Carolyn Wyman
Independent Scholar, Philadelphia
Jell-O; Spam

Sandra Yin
Associate Editor, *American Demographics*
Dr. Brown's; Nabisco; Plastic Covering; Slang, Food, sidebar
on *Military Slang*

Carolin C. Young
Author of *Apples of Gold in Settings of Silver: Stories of Dinner
as a Work of Art*
Anadama Bread; Silverware; Tupperware

Russell Zanca
Department of Anthropology, Northeastern Illinois University
Central Asian Food

Mark H. Zanger
Independent Scholar, Boston
African American Food, subentry *Since Emancipation; Alcohol
and Teetotalism; American Chop Suey; Brownies; Campbell,
Tunis G.; Caribbean Influences on American Food; Cassava;
Cowpeas; Ethnic Foods; Fudge; German American Food;
Iberian and South American Food; Italian American Food;
Scrapple*

INDEX

Page numbers in boldface refer to the main entry on the subject. Page numbers in italics refer to illustrations, figures, and tables.

Bryan, Lettice, **1:**288, 441, 628, 688. *See also*
    Kentucky Housewife, The
  on mushrooms, **2:**128
  on vegetables, **2:**571, 577
Bryan Brothers Packing, **2:**402, 588
Bryant, Charlie, **2:**105
Bt *(Bacillus thuringiensis)*, **1:**91
Buarnaschelli, Maria, **2:**371
bubble tea, **1:138**
buckler-shaped sorrel. *See* sorrel
Buckley, T. H., **1:**389
Buck's fizz, **2:**117
buckwheat
  in colonial America, **1:**618
  kasha, **1:**414; **2:**377
  kasha varnishkes, **1:**743
Buddhism, vegetarianism and, **2:**584–585
Budweiser, **1:138–139**
  frogs ads, **1:**15
buffalo, **1:139–140**, 517, 547, 549
  colonial America, **1:**616
  hunting strategies for, **2:**175–176
  milk cheese, **1:**368
  Native Americans and, **2:**150, 175–176
buffalo berries, **2:**161
Buffalo Trace, **1:**113
Buffalo wings, **2:**97
Bugialli, Giuliano, **1:**308
Bugialli on Pasta, **1:**308
bulb fennel, **1:**645
bulge pots, **2:**315
bulgogi (fire beef), **2:**19
bulgur, **2:**99–100
bulimia, **1:**422
Bulkin, Rena, **1:**379
bulk pork, **2:**73
Bull, Ephraim Wales, **2:**628
Bull, Ole, **2:**456
Bullock, Tom, **1:**298
bully beef, **1:140**
Bully Hill Vineyards, **2:**631
Bumble Bee, **2:**558, 559–560
  purchase by ConAgra, **1:**281
bumbo-zab. *See* filé
Buonopane, Marguerite Dimino, **1:**719
Burbank, Luther, **1:**530; **2:**294
  rhubarb, **2:**361
Bureau of Alcohol, Tobacco, and Firearms
    (BATF), **2:**591
Bureau of Chemistry (USDA), **1:**383, 493; **2:**334
  and additives, **1:**215
  Wiley head of, **2:**616
Bureau of Home Economics (USDA), **1:**383, 680
Bureau of Indian Affairs, **2:**150
Bureau of International Expositions, **2:**650
Bureau of Plant Industry, **1:**645
burek, **1:**743
Burger Chef, **1:**457
Burger King, **1:140–141**, 457, 458, 653
  advertising, **2:**304–305
  automats and, **1:**55
  breakfast, **1:**133
  purchase by Pillsbury, **1:**140; **2:**280
burgoo, **1:**548; **2:**207, 467, 474
Burnet, William, **2:**432
Burnett, Joseph, **2:**569
Burnett, Leo, **1:**750; **2:**281, 560
Burnham and Morrill (B&M), **1:**71, 259
Burns, Jabez, **1:**267

Burns, Robert, **1:**409–410
Burns Club, **2:***355*
Burpee seed mail-order operation, **1:***636*
Burr, Aaron, **2:**595
burritos, **1:**171
  breakfast burrito, **1:**132; **2:**485, 651
  steak, **2:**85
Burton, Richard, **1:**128
Busch, Adolphus, **1:**138, 139
Busch, August A., Sr., **1:**139
Business Week (magazine), **2:**562
butchering, **1:141–142**
  kosher, **1:**737, *737*, 739; *1:739*; **1:**747–748
  men and, in colonial period, **1:**555
  Muslim, **2:**129, 130
  pigs, **2:***278*
  refrigeration and, **1:**509
  turkeys, **1:***141*
butcher shops
  beef in, **2:**74
  delicatessens and, **1:**378
  German American, **1:**561, 565
  Polish, **2:**298
  regulation of, **2:**72
Butler, Abraham, **1:**741
butter, **1:142–144**, 459
  adulteration with other animal fats, **1:**459
  butter-making tools and churns, **1:144**
  butter molds, **1:***144*
  cooperative plants, **1:**459
  in English diet, **2:**182
  exports, **1:**373
  knives, **2:***436*
  New York State, **1:**372, 459
  pasteurization and, **1:**384
  soybean, **2:**487
  substitutes, **1:**370
Butterball Turkey Company, **1:**281; **2:**564
butter cakes, **1:**161
butter cracker, **1:**353
Butterflies in My Stomach (Taylor), **1:**712–713
buttermilk, **1:144–145**, 521
  Dutch use of, **1:**416
butternuts *(Juglans cinerea)*, **2:**158
  Native Americans and, **2:**204
butter tarts, **2:**101
Buttolph Menu Collection of the New York
    Public Library, **2:**313
butylated hydroxyanisole (BHA), **1:**216
butylated hydroxytoluene (BHT), **1:**216
buying clubs, **1:**337
Byce, Lyman, **1:**426
Bynum, Caroline Walker, **1:**421
Byrd, William, **1:**64
Byrd, William, II, **1:**247

cabbage *(Brassica oleracea capitata)*, **1:***147*,
    147–148. *See also* coleslaw
  in African American food, **1:**20
  cutters and planes, **1:**148
  kale, **2:**1
  in kimchi, **2:**19–20
  in kitchen gardens, **2:**8
  stuffed, **2:**99, 377
Cabernet Sauvignon, **2:**640
Cabeza de Vaca, Álvar Núñez, **2:**252
Cabinet-Maker's and Upholsterer's Guide, The
    (Hepplewhite), **1:**393

cable television, **1:**15
cacao tree *(Theobroma cacao)*, **1:**240
cachaca, **2:**375
cachupa, **1:**700
cactus, **1:148**
  harvesting, **2:***481*
  Native Americans and, **2:***158*, 161–162, 172
cactus pears, **1:**148
Cadbury Schweppes, **1:**407; **2:**428
  purchase of Snapple, **2:**450
Cadillac, Antoine Laumet de La Mothe, Sieur de,
    1:470
Caesar Cardini Foods, **2:**385
Caesar salad, **1:**169; **2:**385
Café du Monde (New Orleans), **2:**357
café frappé, **1:**507
Café Martin (New York), **2:**356
Café Moutarde (Brooklyn, N.Y.), **1:***515*; **2:***357*
cafeterias, **1:148–150**
  eating houses, **2:**356
  in New York, **2:**194–195
  vending machines, **2:**587
Cagney, James, **1:**464, *465*
cajeta, **1:**156
Cajun and Creole food, **1:150–157**, 440, 441, 663
  African Americans and, **1:**25–26
  folk foods, **2:**134
  as Iberian/South American, **1:**699
  Kwanzaa and, **2:**23
  Lagasse and, **2:**25
  New Orleans syrup, **2:189**
  ratafia, **2:**346
  restaurants, **2:**357
Cajun Kitchen, **2:**310
Cajuns, **1:154–155**
  crayfish prime identity marker of, **1:**472
cake
  watermelon, **2:**597
Cake Bible, The (Beranbaum), **1:**164, 310
cake mixer, **1:***644*
cakes, **1:157–165**. *See also* birthday cakes
  antebellum, **1:**625
  babka, **1:**742
  decoration, **1:**491
  dried-apple stack, **1:**38, 40
  German-Jewish, **1:**738
  jelly rolls, **1:**735
  in Korean American food, **2:**19
  Kwanzaa, **2:**23
  ladyfingers, **2:**25
  lekakh, **1:**745
  mixes, **1:**100, 387; **2:**606
    Airy Fairy, **1:**48
    Betty Crocker, **1:**560
  as New Year's food, **2:**190
  pecan-bourbon, **2:**479
  wedding, **2:**512, 600
calamari. *See* squid
calas, **1:**415
Calavo
  Calavo Book of Popular Avocado Recipes, **1:**55,
    56
  cookbooklets, **1:**18–19
  guacamole, **1:**405
calcium, **1:**645
  added to white flour, **1:**123
  barley, **1:**67
  broccoli, **1:**135
  in dairy, **1:**367, 371

deer, **1:**547, 549
  colonial America, **1:**616
Deere, John, **2:**604
Deetz, James, **1:**667
Deglet Noor dates, **1:**377
De Gouy, Louis, **1:**549–550
DeGroff, Dale, **2:**610
De Gustibus teaching kitchen, **1:**329
De honesta voluptate (Concerning honest
    pleasure), **1:**670
dehydrated foods. *See also* drying
  Birdseye and, **1:**97
  in military rations, **1:**277
  onions, **2:**214
  parched corn, **1:**343
Dekafa, **1:**269
De Knight, Freda, **1:**302, 303
Delaplane, Stanton, **1:**715
Delaware, **2:**97
  wheat production, **2:**604
Delaware, The (Wildes), **2:**135
Deleboe, Franz (Dr. Sylvius), **1:**568
Delessert, Benjamin, **2:**518
delftware, **2:**291, 292
*Deli: 101 New York–Style Deli Dishes, from
    Chopped Liver to Cheesecake* (Kreitzman),
    1:379
delicatessens, **1:378–380**
  Japanese, **1:**727
  Jewish, **1:**432, 743–744
  and kosher pickles, **2:**266
  New York, **2:**193
  Russian food in, **2:**377
Delicious Fireless Cooked Dishes (Toledo Cooker
    Co.), **1:**469
Déliée, Felix, **1:**413, 514; **2:**462
  and bouillabaisse, **2:**465
Delights of Delicate Eating, The (Pennell), **2:**253
Delineator (magazine), **2:**258, 259
Delmarva Chicken Festival, **1:**222
Delmarva Peninsula
  figs, **1:**462
  peaches, **1:**529
  poultry, **1:**222
Delmas, A., **2:**635
Delmonico, John, **1:**380, 514
Delmonico, Lorenzo, **1:**380, 514
  Ranhofer and, **2:**344
Delmonico, Peter, **1:**514
Delmonico potatoes, **2:**313
Delmonico's, **1:380–381**, 514; **2:**192, *192*
  artichokes at, **1:**50
  French food at, **1:**718
  Hamburg Steak, **1:**587
  lamb and mutton at, **2:**26
  Prohibition and, **1:**646; **2:**357–358
  Ranhofer and, **2:**343–344, 356–357
  salads at, **2:**383
Del Monte, **1:**168, **381–382**, 602
  advertising, **1:**381, 601
  baby food, **1:**59
  cookbook by Neil, **1:**381, *381*
  ketchup, **2:**6
  purchase of StarKist, **2:**560
De Loup, Maximilian, **2:**384
Del Taco, **2:**84
Demorest's, **1:**735; **2:**257
dendê oil, **1:**604
Denny's, **1:**391; **2:**368

Denver, University of, culinary collections, **2:**34
Denver omelet, **1:**132, 698
Denver sandwich, **1:382**, 698
De Palma, Al, **1:**677
Department of Agriculture, United States
    (USDA), **1:382–385**. *See also* Bureau of
    Chemistry; Bureau of Home Economics
  Aunt Sammy, **2:**337
  on dairy, **1:**371
  dates and, **1:**377
  farmers' bulletin on fireless cookers, **1:**468
  Food and Drug Administration part of, **1:**494
  food education by, **1:**13
  Foreign Seed and Plant Introduction Section,
    1:530
  international aid and, **1:**713–714
  on irradiation, **1:**716
  meals on wheels, **2:**67–68
  Muslim dietary laws and, **2:**129–130
  NAFTA and, **2:**198–199
  on nutrition, **2:**203
  organic accreditation by, **2:**574
  "Poison Squad" experiment, **2:**616–617
  Pure Food Act and, **1:**2–3
  recommended daily calorie counts, **2:**208
  regulation of biotechnology, **1:**91
  on rice, **2:**364
  Standard of Identity for pepperoni, **2:**254
  on vegetable consumption, **2:**573
Department of Health and Human Services,
    United States, **2:**203
  Food and Drug Administration part of, **1:**493,
    494
Department of Labor, United States, **2:**358
De re coquinaria (Apicius). *See* Apicius, Marcus
    Gavius
De re culinaria Libri I–XI (Apicius), **2:**33
Derrydale Cook Book of Fish and Game, The
    (De Gouy), **1:**549–550
Description of the New Netherlands, A (van der
    Donck), **1:**415
designated driver programs, **1:**33
De Soto, Hernando, **2:**142–143
  Native Americans and, **2:**148
Dessert Bible, The (Kimball), **1:**310
desserts, **1:***385*, **385–387**
  African American, **1:**25
  apple pie, **1:43–44**
  Chesapeake Bay, **1:**223
  in colonial America, **1:**619
  Columbian exchange of, **2:**147
  cream in, **1:**355
  dairy in, **1:**369
  dumplings, **1:**414–415
  in French service, **1:**399
  grasshopper, **1:**577
  ice cream and ices, **1:**703–707
  Indian, **1:**710
  Italian, **1:**718, 723
  Jell-O, **1:732–734**
  jelly rolls, **1:**735
  Karo Syrup, **2:**1
  Korean American, **2:**19
  ladyfingers, **2:**25
  Mid-Atlantic region, **2:**93
  mock, **2:**121
  molasses in, **2:**123
  Native Americans and, **2:**161
  in New England cookery, **2:**184–185

New Orleans syrup, **2:188**
  in the 1980s, **1:**663
  orange flower water in, **2:**215
  Philadelphia and, **2:**93–94
  in southern cookery, **2:**478–479
  strawberries Romanoff, **2:**378
  sugar in, **2:**512
  syrup soppin', **2:**189
  vanilla in, **2:**569
Desserts for Dummies (Miller and Yosses), **1:**310
Detroit Institute of Arts, Tupperware and, **2:**561
developing countries, international aid to,
    1:713–714
Devereaux, Elizabeth, **1:**326
Devi, Yamuna, **1:**310
  on vegetarianism, **2:**584
De Voe, Thomas F., **1:**297, 549
DeVoto, Bernard, **2:**49
Dewar, James A., **2:**566
dewberries, **1:**103; **2:**157–158, 161
Dewey, Thomas E., **2:**83
dextrose, **1:**346; **2:**518
diabetics
  low-calorie syrups and, **2:**38–39
  Native Americans and, **2:**152
Diageo PLC, **1:**141; **2:**280
Dias, Isaac, **1:**426
Diat, Louis, **1:**300, 435–436
Díaz, Bernal, **2:**569
Dickens, Charles, **1:**50, 380
  on evening parties, **1:**158
  on toothpicks, **2:**549
Dickinson, R. S., **1:**281
Dickson, Paul, **2:**441–442, 443
Dickson's Word Treasury (Dickson), **2:**443
Dictionary of American Food and Drink, The,
    1:132
  on vermouth, **2:**588
Dictionary of Occupational Titles, **2:**523
Dictionary of the English Language (Johnson),
    1:264; **2:**207
diet
  American daily consumption of processed
    foods, **1:**683
  English, **2:**182
  food magazines and, **2:**262–263
  Native American, **2:**150–151, 157–158
  as a political issue, **2:**306
  sugar in, **2:**511–513
Diet, Louis, **2:**261
Dietary and Supplement Health and Education
    Act (1994), **2:**203
dietary fat, **2:**210
Dietary Guidelines for Americans, **2:**203
  on dairy, **1:**371
  sugar trade pressures on, **2:**302
dietary recommendations, politics of, **74–77**
Dietary Reference Intakes (DRIs), **2:**203
Dietary Supplement Health and Education Act
    (1994), **1:**13
Diet Coke, **1:**261
Diet for a New America, **2:**584
Diet for a Small Planet (Lappé), **1:**305, 349, *349*
  vegetarianism and, **2:**584
dietitians, **2:**202
Diet Pepsi, **2:**452
diets
  fad, **1:387–389**; **2:**209
  failure of low-fat diets, **2:**210

cookies and, **1:**319
Native Americans and, **2:**151
as preservative and additive, **1:**214
production, **2:**509–510
rationing during World War II, **1:**648
sculptures, **2:**511–512
tea and, **2:**530–531
trade, **1:**188–189
U.S. dietary guideline, **2:**302
World War I rationing, **2:***519*
Sugar Act (1764), **2:**123, 376
Sugar Act (1934), **2:**511
Sugar and Slaves: The Rise of the Planter Class in the English West Indies (Dunn), **1:**672
Sugar an' Spice and All Things Nice (Kiene), **1:**316
sugar beets *(Beta vulgaris* var. *altissima),* **1:**687; **2:504–505,** 518
sugar beet workers, **2:***515*
sugarcane, **1:**687
molasses and, **2:**122–123
rum and, **2:**375–376
Texas, **2:**483
Sugar Refineries Company, **2:**510
Sugar Trust, **2:**510
sulforaphane in broccoli, **1:**135
Sullivan, Charles, **2:**643
sumac berries, **2:**173
Sumerians
beer, **1:**77–78
recorded recipes, **1:**669
summer boardinghouses, **1:**107
summer kitchens, **2:**14
summer meal programs for children, **2:**413, 425, 426
Summer Food Service Program, **1:**695; **2:**460
summer purslane. *See* purslane
summer sausages, **2:**408
summer savory *(Satureja hortensis),* **1:**610
Sun Also Rises, The (Hemingway), **2:**38
Sund, Cora Irene, **2:**653
sundaes, **1:**709
Sunday American Cook Book (Tetrazzini), **1:***719*
Sundblom, Haddon, **1:**261; **2:**335, 346
sun-drying of grapes, **1:**576
Sunfired Foods, **2:**585
sunfish, **1:**474
bluegill, **1:**471
read ear, **1:**471
sunflowers *(Helianthus annuus),* **2:515–516**
Native Americans and, **2:**175
sunflower seeds
in colonial America, **1:**616
use by Native Americans, **1:**458
Sunfresh, **1:**382
Sunkist, **1:**531
advertising, **1:**7
and fruit juices, **1:**534–535
Sun-Maid raisin recipe booklet, **1:***167*
Sunset (magazine), **1:**136, 656
on freezing meals, **1:**657
recipes in, **1:**307
Sunset All-Western Cook Book (Callahan), **1:**259
sunshine cake, **1:**161
Sunshine Salad, **1:**733
Sunsweet, **1:**132, 168
Suntory Water Group, **2:**597
Suomalais-Amerikalainen Keittokirga (Walli), **1:**294
supawn, **2:516**

Supermarket Handbook, The: Access to Whole Foods (Goldbeck and Goldbeck), **1:**306
supermarkets, **1:**579–580, 644. *See also* grocery stores
air-conditioning in, **1:**581
carbonated water sold at, **2:**424
in Corpus Christi, Texas, **1:***581*
delicatessens in, **1:**379–380
hot dogs, **1:**689
ice cream, **1:**705–706
more important than terminal markets, **2:**554
supper in colonial America, **1:**620; **2:**66
Supplemental Food Program for Women, Infants, and Children (WIC), **1:**695
Supreme Court cases
Commack Self-Service Kosher Meats, Inc. v. Weiss, **2:**29–30
Grocery Manufacturers of America, Inc. v. Gerace, **2:**29
Nix v. Hedden, **2:**547
on Pure Food Act, **2:**28
Strauss, United States v., **2:**28
Varela-Cruz, United States v., **2:**27–28
Weigle v. Curtice Bros. Co., **2:**29
sushi, **1:**439, 661
in Japanese American food, **1:**726
rice cookers and, **2:**366
Sustacal, **1:**126
sustainable agriculture, **1:**311
Alice Waters and, **1:**172; **2:**598
and chocolate, **1:**243
and farmers' markets, **1:**452
Sutherland, Daniel E., **1:**403
Sutherland, J. B., **1:**701
Sveda, Michael, **2:**519
Svensk Amerikansk Kokbok, **1:**294
swamp cabbage. *See* hearts of palm
Swan, Donald, **1:**410
swans, **1:**548
Swans Down, **1:**559
Swanson, **1:**9, 510, 523, 524–525, 527, 657; **2:516–517**
owned by Campbell, **1:**175
Swanson, Carl A., **1:**524–525; **2:**516
Swanson, Clarke, **1:**524–525
Swanson, Gilbert, **1:**524–525
Swedenborg, Emanuel
Johnny Appleseed and, **2:**133
vegetarianism and, **2:**580
Sweeco, **2:**48
Sweeney, Joanna, **1:**109
Lincoln and, **2:**35
sweet adas. *See* dill
sweet bay. *See* bay leaf
sweet bay leaf. *See* bay leaf
sweet cumin. *See* fennel
sweeteners, **2:517–520.** *See also* corn syrup; honey; maple syrup; molasses; sugar; syrups
artificial
low-calorie syrups, **2:**38–39
chemical, **2:**513
in colonial America, **1:**619
Karo Syrup, **2:**1–2
in Kellogg's cereals, **2:**4
Native American, **2:**167–168
in New England cookery, **2:**184–185, 186
New Orleans syrup, **2:189**
sweet fennel. *See* fennel

Sweethearts Conversation Hearts, **2:**568
sweetkraut, **2:**266
sweet laurel. *See* bay leaf
sweetmeats, **1:**385
Philadelphia and, **2:**93–94
Sweetness and Power: The Place of Sugar in Modern History (Mintz), **1:**361, 672
sweet orange *(C. sinensis),* **1:**254–255
sweet pigweed. *See* epazote
sweet potatoes *(Ipomoea batatas),* **2:**520
in African American food, **1:**20, 27
in colonial America, **1:**616, 618
Columbian exchange of, **2:**146
harvesting at Claflin University (S.C.), **2:***520*
in Hawaiian food, **1:**591
in kitchen gardens, **2:**9
pie, **1:**386; **2:**327, 479
as South American, **1:**697
and Thanksgiving, **2:**538, 543
sweets. *See also* candy bars and candy; desserts; fried sweets
antebellum, **1:**625
and Christmas, **1:**629
Sweet Success, **1:**126, 389
Swendson, Patsy, **1:**310
Swett, Lucia Gray, **1:**297
swienconka, **2:**299
Swift, **1:**632
butchering, **1:**142
hot dogs, **1:**689
packing plant, **2:***521*
Vienna sausage, **2:**588
Swift, Gustavus Franklin, **1:**635; **2:520–521**
refrigerated railroad cars, **1:**701–702; **2:**553
Swift-Eckrich Co., **2:**564
swill dairies, **2:**109
swill farms, **1:**372–373
Swingle, Walter, **1:**531
Swiss cheese, **2:**125
Swiss rolls, **1:**735
Swiss steak, **1:**653
switchel, **1:**569, 687; **2:521–522**
swordfish, **1:**477, 484
syllabub, **1:**619; **2:**477, **522**
Sylvia's (New York), **1:**26
symbolism
of eggs, **1:**427
fry bread, **1:**433–434
of hamburger as American culture, **1:**588
horseradish, **1:**419
of martini glass for bar, **1:**68
of olive, **2:**213
of pies, **2:**274
of pumpkin, **2:**332
of sugar, **2:**513–514
Symonds, Elizabeth, **2:**133
Sympsium for Professional Food Writers, **2:**354
synthetic aroma chemicals, **1:**490
synthetic fat, **1:**460–461
Syrah, **2:**640
syrups, **2:**319. *See* corn syrup; maple syrup
Aunt Jemima, **1:**54
cassava syrup *(cassareep),* **1:**194
in ice cream sodas, **1:**708–709
Karo, **2:**1–2
low-calorie, **2:**38–39
spruce-tip, **2:**494
syrup soppin', **2:**189